John Dryden and His World

Portrait of Dryden "painted from the life for Mr. Jacob Tonson" by James Maubert, ca. 1695.

John Dryden and His World

James Anderson Winn

Yale University Press   New Haven and London

Designed by James J. Johnson
and set in Ehrhardt Roman type by
The Composing Room of Michigan, Inc.
Printed in the United States by Vail-Ballou Press, Binghamton, New York.

Library of Congress Cataloging-in-Publication Data

Winn, James Anderson, 1947–
John Dryden and his world.

Bibliography: p.
Includes index.
1. Dryden, John, 1631–1700—Biography.   2. Dryden,
John, 1631–1700—Contemporary England.   3. Authors,
English—Early modern, 1500–1700—Biography.
4. England—Civilization—17th century.   I. Title.
PR3423.W5 1987   821'.4 [B]   87-2193
ISBN 0-300-02994-2 (cloth)
0-300-04591-3 (pbk.)

3   5   7   9   10   8   6   4   2

For Ellen and Philip

Contents

Illustrations

Preface

"To judge rightly of an author," wrote Dr. Johnson, "we must transport ourselves to his time, and examine what were the wants of his contemporaries, and what were his means of supplying them."[1] Yet all Dryden's biographers, including Johnson, have inevitably judged him by the standards of their own times, and our recognition of their biases has not made it much easier for us to "transport ourselves" to the seventeenth century, since we live in a world even more distant from Dryden's, dominated by political and literary values quite unlike those he struggled with and celebrated. Social and political historians have shown us how little we know about the causes of such major events as the English Civil War and the Glorious Revolution, but literary and cultural historians still tend to reduce the period to a set of comfortable stereotypes: the iconoclastic Roundhead, the flamboyant Cavalier, the Restoration rake, the Williamite merchant. Like most stereotypes, these reflect but distort reality, not least in the supposedly sharp distinctions that start to blur as soon as we examine individual lives and poems.

This book is a fresh attempt to transport its reader to Dryden's time, to examine the wants of his contemporaries by considering the subtle relations linking their religious beliefs, their political alliances, and the artistic styles they practiced or favored. It is thus, inevitably, a book with several purposes. Thanks to recent research, by no means entirely my own, I can provide a more accurate factual biography than those already in print, though I have profited greatly from the labors of my distinguished predecessors.[2] But I have also tried to cast my nets more broadly than previous biographers, to reach beyond the facts toward a fuller sense of the man and his times. Any biographical narrative, even one written on far stricter principles than mine, is inevitably interpretive, and in the case of Dryden, inference and speculation are particularly necessary, since the kinds of primary material usually available for later writers are almost entirely absent in his case: we have only one early poetic manuscript and a handful of letters, mainly late; our "information" about his personality consists largely of unreliable gossip. Yet even if more hard facts were available, I should still have wished to present Dryden in the context of his culture. His patterns of thought and expression were shaped by the chaotic events of his boyhood; his published works and critical judgments shaped in turn the emerging culture of the Restoration, and thus ultimately the culture of the eighteenth century. He is not only a fascinating individual talent, but a man whose associations illuminate the crucial ideas and events of his time. He encountered Puritanism, for example, not as a hardened ideology but as a living movement embraced by his family and expounded by his village preacher; later experiences brought him into similarly intimate contact with Royalists, scientists, courtiers, actresses, and Roman Catholic recusants. By studying these people and Dryden's responses to them, we may replace inadequate stereotypes with human faces, and gain some fresh insights into Dryden's own elusive character.

His literary works, many of them analyzed in some detail here, must also be understood as products of Dryden's particular historical situation; they were, to borrow Johnson's helpful economic metaphor, means of supplying the wants of his contemporaries. Of course, like all great literature, they are something more: at their best, Dryden's poems, plays, translations, and essays have a largeness and resonance to which readers can strongly respond; poets as different as Pope, Byron, Keats, Eliot, and Auden have honored his memory and profited from his example. Still, any candid teacher of English literature must admit that many students find little pleasure or stimulation in those few selections from Dryden we now ask them to read. This book is grounded in the belief that such deafness to Dryden may be partially cured by removing the prejudices and simplifications about his culture that keep our ears from hearing his mighty music.

When we examine the wants of Dryden's contemporaries, we discover that different kinds of readers wanted quite different things, a situation Dryden dramatized by writing his *Essay of Dramatick Poesie* as a dialogue. If the aesthetic "wants" of playgoers and readers were often intimately connected to political and religious ideas, they were not simply dictated by those beliefs. Bernini's flamboyant bust of Thomas Baker, carved while Baker was in Rome arranging for Bernini's bust of Charles I, looks like the quintessential Royalist work of art, but Baker fought for Parliament in the Civil War. The Puritan lawyer William Prynne lost his ears for attacking the Queen's participation in the extravagant masques of the Caroline court, yet later supported the return of Charles II. Jeremy Collier, whose attack on the stage at the end of the century echoes many of Prynne's essentially Calvinist objections, was a high-church Tory clergyman, so convinced of the Divine Right of Kings that he supported the Roman Catholic James II.[3] These apparent but typical contradictions should establish the principle that each of the already reductive dichotomies we use to divide Dryden's contemporaries—Cavalier and Roundhead, Court and Country, high-church and low-church, Tory and Whig— is a *separate* division. Attempts to lump together political, economic, and religious groups, such as the notion that Puritanism was simply "the ideology of the bourgeoisie,"[4] will inevitably distort the far more complex relations between these forces and the expression they found in the arts. Discovering that Dryden's contemporaries did not necessarily like the kinds of poetry or painting we might expect them to like from some political, economic, or religious graph need not reduce the importance of politics,

Bust of Thomas Baker by Giovanni Bernini, 1636.

economics, or religion for the study of the arts; it should remind us that individual responses to these powerful forces display considerable subtlety and nuance, especially in the case of a major writer.

Poet, dramatist, critic, propagandist, translator, adapter, and consummate professional, Dryden dominated English literature for forty years; his public discussion of his changing political and religious beliefs, his collaboration with composers and painters, and his manipulation of the patronage system make him an ideal subject for an attempt to "judge rightly of an author" by engaging wider issues of cultural history. A concentration on such cultural contexts may seem to point away from a deeper understanding of Dryden the man, but exploring the people he knew and the environments through which he passed can yield surprising dividends in this area as well, including the discovery of private dimensions in apparently public poems. Dryden's favorite poetic pronoun, "we," is ambiguous about the size of the group included; rhetorically, it often refers to the nation as a whole, but as I have learned more about the particular groups of which Dryden was a part, I have noticed that "we" sometimes refers to a specific smaller group: to the boys of Westminster School, the employees of the Protectorate, the professional writers of the restored theatre, the loyalists of the Tory party, or the persecuted adherents of the Roman Catholic Church. There are even moments when "we" simply means "I." So, too, with the plays: the information about casting, direction, and production amassed by recent scholarship helps us understand how Dryden's characters dramatize his own concerns as well as those of his society. Dedications and critical works, in which Dryden does use the first-person singular, require similar attention to context. To point out that he was "insincere" in his flattering addresses to the great, or "inconsistent" in his various positions on the critical issues he faced in his long career is not to make a very precise or challenging statement; only when we understand the particular circumstances in which he chose to flatter people whose weaknesses he evidently perceived, or the practical necessities of stage and publishing house that led him to alter his critical opinions, can we become attuned to the wit, intelligence, and charm of his prose.

To say "we" as Dryden habitually does is to make a gesture of inclusion. If the group included by the "we" varies from the nation as a whole to some smaller particular group to the poet himself in his role as the monarch of one of his literary kingdoms, it is virtually never the intimate couple of Donne's love poems, shutting out the world to revel in each other. Nor is it normally an exclusive club of those who already agree; Dryden's inclusive "we" invites us to join him in his consideration of religious truth, political propriety, and literary excellence. To be sure, he hopes to persuade us, but his rhetorical tools include "an intensely social outlook and a startling intimacy of public address."[5] The intimacy that Dryden achieves even while addressing public matters will become more and more apparent to the student of his world. Because he is not merely a "public" or "rhetorical" writer, but also a great writer, that intimacy can reach into our world as well; my fondest hope for this biography is that it may allow others to know and enjoy Dryden as I have during the years of its making.

In an attempt to make this book available to as many as possible, I have not assumed that the reader has a detailed background in seventeenth-century history or literature. Important figures and ideas are briefly identified on their first appearance, plots of plays are summarized when necessary, and quotations are sufficiently generous to give some impression of works few but specialists have read. My references to the massive secondary literature on Dryden have been suppressed to the notes, so that readers primarily interested in an account of Dryden's life and works may read the main text without being distracted by my citations and corrections of other scholars. All dates are Old Style, but the year is treated as beginning on 1 January.

Acknowledgments

This book began in 1981–82, with a year of research in England, where I immediately began to depend on the knowledge and friendship of British scholars concerned with my subject: the late Helen Belgion, historian of Titchmarsh, was my guide to Dryden's first small world; John Field, archivist of Westminster School, acted as a medium through whom I could communicate with the ghost of Dr. Busby; Paul Hammond, Reader of English at Leeds and Junior Fellow of Trinity College, Cambridge, generously shared with me his then unpublished research on Dryden's university career; Mrs. Marjory Clifford of Banbury became my secret agent among the historians of English Catholicism. Then Robert D. Hume, that astonishing American polymath of the theatre, appeared as if by magic in the British Library, insisting that the smaller book I thought I was writing must become a biography, and offering his crucial assistance on theatrical matters. Other American colleagues who have aided my research during their own trips to England include Judith Milhous, William Ingram, Linda Merians, and Julie Stone Peters. Many of these people have read and commented on the manuscript at various stages, as have Maynard Mack, Conrad Russell, James Gindin, Russell Fraser, Joseph Blotner, James Garrison, Kenneth Fox, Robert Sullivan, David Vieth, Dustin Griffin, Steven Zwicker, Donna Landry, Cedric Reverand II, Alan Roper, Robert Parker, Ira Konigsberg, Howard Weinbrot, Moti Feingold, Claudia Thomas, Debora Shuger, John Shawcross, Herbert Tucker, Earl Miner, and the late C. A. Patrides. Let me also thank librarians on both sides of the Atlantic, particularly those of the Public Record Office, the British Library, the London Library, and the University of Michigan Library. Thanks to the interest of George Rousseau, the Clark Library in Los Angeles granted me a fellowship for research there; a typescript chronology of Dryden's career, prepared by Nancy Shea of the Clark staff, has been an invaluable tool. My students in Ann Arbor, particularly those in courses on Dryden and his period, have constantly stimulated my thinking; Doris Gurke, Todd Farrington, Robert Ewing, and Elizabeth Thomas were my tireless research assistants. Two grants from the National Endowment for the Humanities, supplemented by Yale University and the University of Michigan, made the first and last years of this project possible. A supplementary grant from the Michigan Faculty Research Fund helped defray the cost of the illustrations.

Three small portions of this book have already appeared in print. A preliminary version of the Pickering genealogy in Appendix A appeared in *Notes and Queries* 227 (1982):506–10; a less complete chronology of the career of Anne Reeves appeared in *Restoration* 10 (1986):1–13; a longer version of my reading of Dryden's first poem, the elegy for Lord Hastings, appeared in *Modern Language Review* 79 (1984):21–31. My thanks to the editors of these journals, and to those scholars whose responses to all three articles helped make the versions that appear here more accurate.

My family has cheerfully endured two full-scale moves and numerous smaller dislocations during the years taken up by this work. Without the constant stimulation provided by my late mother-in-law, Diana Fox, I might well have read nothing during these years except material on Dryden; her demands for relevance made this a better book, and I grieve that she did not live to see it. Without the love and support of my wife, Kathe Fox, I might never have finished; her faith in my ability to bring the work to completion has kept me going. To my children, those endless sources of joy and wonder, this book is fondly dedicated.

24 September 1986

John Dryden and His World

CHAPTER ONE

The Milk of the Word
1631–1643

John Dryden's reticence about his childhood will immediately disappoint anyone expecting his works to explore an inner self. He left no epistolary or poetic portrait of mother or father, no fond reminiscence of a lazy afternoon in a green Northamptonshire meadow, no charming anecdote of a boyish truancy from a village school—only a few brief references, in prose, to books read as a boy. His taciturn nature may partly explain this silence: "of all the Men that ever I knew," wrote Congreve, Dryden was "one of the most modest."[1] But the fact that no contemporary sought to discover details of Dryden's upbringing, that no Boswell appeared, notebook in hand, to record his table talk, reminds us that poetry in his culture was a public act: the attention paid to a new poem was far more likely to focus on its success as an argument and its quality as an artifact than on its overt or covert revelation of its author's soul; the fascination with childhood we find in Wordsworth and his contemporaries reflects a radically changed view of creativity.[2] When Dryden's opponents in the party controversy of the 1680s mentioned his Puritan ancestors, they were resorting to a cheap smear, not seeking to explain his poetry by examining his childhood.

   Yet one of my aims in the early chapters of this book will be to recover and explore some aspects of Dryden's upbringing not mentioned in his works, to consider how he was affected by growing up among the Puritan country gentry, attending school in a kingless London under the tutelage of a fiercely Royalist master, and going up to a university shaken by the ferments and fears of the Interregnum. Politics and personality are not entirely separable: Dryden's violent prejudice against the Dissenters, one of the strongest and most consistent features of his adult work, involved an emotional rejection of the Calvinist ideology in which he had been reared, an equally emotional endorsement of the hierarchical ideology he first encountered in his schoolmaster, and a deeply felt determination to fend off any return of the civil strife that had darkened his childhood.

Puritans by Tenure

Dryden's ancestors in sixteenth-century Northamptonshire offer striking instances of the "rise of the gentry."[3] Gilbert Pickering, the poet's maternal great-great-grand-father, described in the Titchmarsh Lay Subsidy of 1525 as a "husbandman" and assessed at the modest rate of £14, was no peasant; his uncle, Sir James Pickering, was a knight. But as the younger son of a younger son, Gilbert needed to make a profitable marriage to secure gentry status, so he married Elizabeth Staynbancke, daughter of James Staynbancke, the only "yeoman" in the village, who was assessed at £40.[4] By 1553, Pickering had acquired sufficient capital to purchase the manor of Titchmarsh from the grandson of Charles Somerset, Earl of Worcester and Lord Chamberlain to Henry VIII. About the same time, the first John Dryden, the poet's paternal great-grandfather, was acquiring hundreds of acres in and around Adston, a process climaxed by his building a splendid new manor house at Canons Ashby. Although this Dryden evidently had considerable capital of his own, he too made a profitable marriage, in 1551, to Elizabeth Cope, daughter of Sir John Cope, who had purchased the old priory at Canons Ashby and its surrounding land in 1538, just one year after they had been seized as part of Henry VIII's dissolution of the monasteries.[5]

Dryden's ancestors profited directly from the policies of Henry VIII, whose re-distribution of the abbey lands dramatically increased the number of large landowners in England. They may also have been helped by such developments in Tudor econom-ics as enclosure and the improvement of the wool trade, though there is no direct evidence.[6] So it should come as no surprise that when people with opinions start to emerge out of the dust of the ancient records, both Drydens and Pickerings are evi-dently Puritans or "Precisians," members of the group defined by a local clergyman as "the hotter sort of Protestants."[7] Without necessarily impugning the heat of their faith, we may suspect that the way these families acquired their land was also relevant; years later, a high-church loyalist attacking the poet's uncle Sir John Dryden noted that he was "a *Puritan* by Tenure; his House being an ancient College [an abbey], and his Lands the Revenues of that College."[8] Like most propaganda, this claim is an unsound basis for generalization; the Roman Catholic Petre family, for example, gained huge tracts of land from the dissolution of the monasteries, yet remained recusants for centuries. The Drydens and Pickerings, however, who had become members of the gentry through hard work and shrewd marriages, clung to their Puritan values, even when that meant defying the authorities.

No member of either family is recorded as a martyr or exile under Queen Mary, whose persecutions left Northamptonshire virtually untouched,[9] but the memory of the Marian persecutions, strongly encouraged by an edict placing a copy of John Foxe's *Actes and Monuments* in every parish church, doubtless fed a suspicion of Roman Catholics further reinforced by the rumored and actual Spanish invasions of the 1580s. The Pickering squires helped muster the local militia of Titchmarsh when such trouble seemed imminent,[10] and their suspicions must have seemed justified by the Catholic Gunpowder Plot of 1605, which touched the family directly: Dryden's great-aunt Margaret Pickering was married to Robert Keyes, one of the thirteen conspirators.

Map of eighteenth-century Northamptonshire from *The Gentleman's Magazine*.

According to the church historian Thomas Fuller, who was born in nearby Aldwincle and might therefore have based his account on local reminiscences, Keyes was in Titchmarsh a few days before the Plot was attempted; at the home of his brother-in-law, Gilbert Pickering (II), he "suddenly whipped out his sword, and in merriment made many offers therewith, at the heads, necks, and sides, of many Gentlemen then in his company."[11] Given this strange behavior, it is hardly surprising that Gilbert (II), Dryden's great-uncle, believed that he himself was among the intended victims of the Plot. According to a later and less reliable source, Gilbert (II) owned a swift horse, which Keyes borrowed and took to London, where he gave it to Guy Fawkes. The plan was that Pickering, a noted Puritan, would be "murdered in his bed, and secretly conveyed away; and also that Fawkes . . . should be murdered, and so mangled, that he could not be known." Fawkes's mangled corpse, lying next to Pickering's horse, would then appear to be Pickering's, and people would therefore conclude that the Puritans were to blame for the explosion. Outrageous as this tale is, Gilbert (II) apparently believed it. Not only did he help to apprehend his own brother-in-law, but he carried out a raid on the Catholic Vaux family at Harrowden Hall in 1611 with memorable fury, seizing religious objects that his son John (II) was later forced to return.[12]

These violent family stories were surely a part of the Pickering lore in which John Dryden was reared two decades later; he probably also knew that another Gilbert Pickering, first cousin to the squire, had been married to the sister of Robert Browne, founder of the radically Congregationalist Brownists.[13] These Pickering marriages to religious extremists at both ends of the spectrum confirm the findings of a recent statistical study of Puritans in Tudor Northamptonshire, which describes the county as "a region . . . in which catholic and puritan were in close contact with each other, . . . [where] a vigorous gentry of strong views and relatively recent origin provided a ready audience for puritan preaching, and indeed for catholic missionary activity."[14] A product of that vigorous gentry, Dryden enacted in his career the close contact between Puritan and Catholic that had once marked his native county: he was reared by Puritans, became an apologist for the Restoration Anglican settlement, and finally converted to Catholicism.

Across the county at Canons Ashby, the Copes and Drydens, closely allied by the marriage of John Dryden and Elizabeth Cope and the proximity of their houses, were active supporters of Puritan clergymen. In 1587, Bishop Howland reported that Edward Cope, the grandson and heir of Sir John Cope, was "an honest gentleman, but that he doth over greatly countenance such preachers as do impugn all orders established."[15] The poet's grandfather, Sir Erasmus Dryden, did more than "countenance" Puritan preachers; he circulated a petition on their behalf and found himself imprisoned by the crown in 1604. Released in 1605 and evidently unrepentant, Erasmus took into his home the celebrated preacher John Dod, who had been suspended from his living at Hanwell by Bishop Bridges. In the church at Canons Ashby, privately owned and thus not subject to the control of a bishop, Dod preached his way through the prophecies of Daniel, but when Edward Cope invited Dod to preach at the parish church in nearby Moreton Pinkney, where he had control of the rectory, the church authorities protested.[16] Even after King James ordered Archbishop Abbot to "silence"

Dod officially in 1611, Dryden and Cope continued to support and protect him. Dod had already acknowledged this friendship in print: among the many "expositions" of Scripture he wrote with his collaborator Robert Cleaver was one published in 1609, dedicated "To the Right Worshipful our approued good friend Erasmus Driden *Esquire*, beseeching Almightie God . . . to multiplie his gratious mercies upon your selfe, your godlie wife, and hopefull familie."[17]

By this time, the "hopefull familie" included Dryden's father, another Erasmus, probably born about 1602.[18] Much younger than his older brothers, young Erasmus grew up in a house combining splendor with moral instruction. The Winter Parlor, where the family normally dined, had panelled walls decorated with scores of brightly painted coats of arms; the stern moral injunctions in Latin above those arms were designed to remind the Dryden heirs that the wealth and prominence attested to by heraldry were gifts from God, accompanied by obligations and responsibilities. In one of the upstairs bedrooms, a vigorously painted mural depicted the events of I Kings 13, an episode chosen by the Drydens for its appropriate and obvious parallels to Puritan beliefs about kingship, prophecy, and the dangers of false clergymen.[19] In the story, a young prophet confronts King Jeroboam, who has been sacrificing to false gods. The king's hand is withered as a sign from God, and the prophet heals it, but when invited to dine with the king, he explains that God has commanded him not to eat or drink until he returns home. On his way home, however, he is misled into disobeying that command by an older prophet, who falsely claims that an angel has told him that the young man may dine with him. Riding home on his ass, the young prophet is slain by a lion, who leaves his corpse undevoured on the ground; the old prophet buries the young one in his own tomb. A Puritan preacher like John Dod would have read this story as an allegory warning the Stuart kings against idolatry and the reformed clergy against Papists in disguise. Dryden, who saw the mural depicting these strange events when he visited Canons Ashby as a boy, would spend his life struggling with the issues of religious authority at the heart of that legend and would draw a similar parallel between Old Testament narrative and contemporary politics in his most famous poem.

Since Dod was a member of the household, Dryden's father was deeply immersed in the beliefs expressed in these decorations; his childhood probably followed the pattern recommended by Dod and Cleaver in their most popular work, *A Godlie Forme of Household Gouernment*, a detailed Puritan guide to child-rearing.[20] When Susannah Dryden, Erasmus's older sister, married Sir John Pickering (II) in 1609, a copy of *A Godlie Forme* probably came with her to Titchmarsh, if the Pickerings did not already own one themselves, for this first Dryden-Pickering marriage was an alliance of like-minded Puritan families. The "country" politics shared by the families were soon and sorely tested by the accession of Charles I. When Charles, hoping to raise money without calling a Parliament, levied a forced loan on his subjects in September 1626, both Sir Erasmus Dryden and his son-in-law Sir John Pickering (II) refused to pay. They made known their opposition at a meeting in Northampton on 12 January 1627; a week later they were required to appear before the Privy Council, which clapped them into the Gatehouse. After seventeen days there, the imprisoned Northamptonshire gentry, including Dryden and Pickering, petitioned for their release, claiming to have been "much prejudiced both in our health and estates by this restraint." Not until summer were they moved out of London, and even then they remained in custody: Pickering went to Middlesex, and Dryden went to Oxfordshire, where the sheriff, Sir Cope Doyley, was his second cousin. Finally, on 2 January 1628, they were released, but John Pickering's claim to have been "prejudiced . . . in [his] health" proved all too true: he made his will on 1 October 1627, still a prisoner, and died on 20 January 1628, less than a month after finally coming home. The Pickerings had ample reason to regard him as a martyr, and his nephew John Dryden specifically mentioned the episode in a poem written to a Dryden cousin in the last year of his life.[21]

The marriage of Dryden's own parents was among the consequences of the early death of John Pickering (II). Since John had no brothers, his widow Susannah faced many responsibilities alone. Her oldest child, Gilbert (III), an undergraduate at Emmanuel College, Cambridge, was only sixteen; when he received his B.A. in 1629, he began law studies at Gray's Inn in London. John's will appointed a committee of trustees to oversee the estate until Gilbert's majority, predictably including Sir Erasmus

(*Above and opposite*) Brookside Farm in Titchmarsh, possibly the boyhood home of Dryden.

Dryden, and gave his wife "the use and occupation of my chiefe Mansion House at Titchmersh . . . during the minoritie of my heire," enjoining her to keep it "in good repair"—no small task, since the house had over forty rooms. At least three younger children were still at home; the sons, John and Edward, attended the school in nearby Oundle.[22] Both as Susannah's father and as a trustee of the estate, Sir Erasmus must have been concerned; he apparently decided that Susannah should have a trustworthy man nearby. His younger son Erasmus, now in his late twenties, who had also studied at Emmanuel and Gray's Inn, was an obvious candidate; the most logical way to place him in Titchmarsh was to arrange a marriage with a Pickering; and there was a suitable maiden available: Mary Pickering, daughter of the late squire's uncle Henry, rector of Aldwincle All Saints, the spire of which was visible from the Titchmarsh manor house. Married in 1630, Erasmus and Mary settled in Titchmarsh, probably in a strong stone house now called Brookside Farm, a short walk from Susannah at the manor. Mary was soon pregnant, and when her time came, she traveled the mile or so to the Aldwincle rectory, where her mother Isabella could assist her, a normal ritual for a woman having

her first child. The baby was a son named John, possibly in memory of his martyred uncle, born 9 August 1631 and christened five days later by his grandfather Henry Pickering.[23]

Dryden's other grandmother, Frances Wilkes Dryden, died six months before he was born, and old Erasmus died before he was a year old, but their deaths did not materially alter the situation at Titchmarsh. Young Erasmus had been granted his portion of land, in Blakesley near Canons Ashby, in 1623, and had already been receiving its modest rents for nine years. His much older brother, Sir John (1580–1658), another possible namesake for the baby, became the squire at Canons Ashby, but Erasmus was still much needed at Titchmarsh, where he would remain until his own death. He probably helped his sister Susannah oversee the many acres of Pickering land surrounding Titchmarsh, and his son John grew up knowing that the visible features of his world—the fields, the rambling manor house, and the splendid church with its fifteenth-century tower—belonged to his mother's family. One episode in 1633, which had important results for Dryden's early life, will suggest the influence Erasmus Dryden had acquired among the Pickerings. In that year the well-endowed pulpit of St. Mary Virgin Titchmarsh became vacant. The advowson, or right to appoint the rector, normally belonged to the squire of the manor, but shortly before his death, John Pickering (II) had sold the next presentation to his father-in-law Erasmus Dryden, his brother-in-law Robert Horsman, and the prominent Puritan aristocrat Lord Saye and Sele.[24] By 1633, old Erasmus was also dead, but Saye and Sele and Horsman presented a candidate of whom he would surely have approved, a committed young Presbyterian named Thomas Hill who had just received his B.D. from Emmanuel College. In the absence of old Erasmus, the presenters must have consulted with his son, since both Thomas Hill and young Erasmus were at Emmanuel from 1618 until 1622, when Hill received his B.A. and Erasmus left without a degree.[25] Hill's preaching, described by an admiring eulogist as "plain, powerful, spiritual, frequent, and laborious," was John Dryden's first experience with the formal spoken word, and presumably the beginning of his lifelong distrust of the clergy. For Hill was to haunt Dryden for the next twenty years, serving as a regular morning preacher at Westminster Abbey while Dryden was at Westminster School, and as Master of Trinity College, Cambridge while Dryden was an undergraduate there.[26] Perhaps the old poet still remembered the "laborious" length of Hill's sermons when he wrote the lighthearted song in *King Arthur* (1691), in which the country people curse the parson "For Prating so long like a Book-learn'd Sot, / Till Pudding and Dumplin burn to Pot" (V, p. 47).[27]

The Naughty Nurse and the Private Pew

No pulpit, however "laborious," could be as formative as a home; the very title of Dod and Cleaver's handbook, *A Godlie Forme of Household Gouernment*, typifies the Puritan emphasis on the family unit. "An Household," according to the authors, "is as it were a little Commonwealth, by the good gouernment whereof, Gods glorie may be aduanced" (sig. A7r), and we may be quite certain that Dryden's parents, their own attitudes formed and shaped by Puritan preaching and country politics, were deter-

St. Mary Virgin Titchmarsh.

mined to advance God's glory in their growing family. Popular history describes Puritan child-rearing methods as stern and brutal, but Dod and Cleaver do not fit that stereotype. They strongly advocate breast-feeding by the mother, despite the widespread use of wet-nurses, and their exegesis of the commandment to "Honour thy father and mother" discusses not only the duties of children to their parents, but those of parents to their children, including "the speciall dutie of the mother, which is, to nurse vp her own childe, if God hath giuen her abilitie there-vnto."[28] In *A Godlie Forme*, the two preachers argue that such children will "suck in godlinesse together with their mothers milke" (sig. Q3r), and warn against the bad effects of vicious nurses in a passage embracing physical determinism: "And if that be true which the learned do say, that the temperature of the minde followes the constitution of the body, needs must it be, that if the nurse be of a naughty nature, the child must take thereafter" (sig. P4v). In a rare moment of wit, they even satirize wealthy mothers who excuse themselves by claiming to have insufficient milk: "this perpetuall drought," they argue, "is like the gowt, no beggars may haue it, but Citizens or Gentlewomen" (sig. P5r).

While these passages hardly constitute unequivocal evidence that Mary Dryden nursed her son, I strongly suspect she did. He was, after all, the firstborn son of a marriage between two families devoted to the beliefs enunciated in Dod's treatises, a marriage that was itself a consequence of the stubbornness with which both Pickerings and Drydens clung to those beliefs. At a more fundamental level, these passages on breast-feeding also illustrate some of the inherent contradictions in Puritan thought, and considering those larger issues may allow us to detect in Dryden's adult opinions the consequences of his boyhood among the conservative Puritans of Titchmarsh. The satirical account of "Citizens or Gentlewomen," for example, which correctly implies that they use wet-nurses because they can afford them, not because they are physically unable to suckle their children, is a comic development of an orthodox idea stated quite simply in the treatise on the *Ten Commaundements*: "outward ease is no sure signe of Gods fauour" (p. 23). That principle would ultimately be used to argue for the idea of levelling, which burst out strongly in Cromwell's New Model Army, but while "Whig" historians have always stressed such democratic or "progressive" elements in Puritan thought, Dod and Cleaver were Puritans of an earlier, less apocalyptic generation. They were certainly not Levellers and would surely have been surprised to see their work used to justify the overturning of established hierarchies. Explaining the passage in Romans 13 in which Paul advises Christians to submit to worldly magistrates, they argue that "He commands not only a bodily subiection, . . . but an inwarde submission of the soule." Nor do they endorse political disobedience, though John Knox, for one, had argued that there were circumstances in which Christians should defy unjust monarchs. According to Dod and Cleaver, "if the King be vniust and wicked, then we must pray to God to conuert him, as Paul commands" (*Ten Commaundements*, pp. 235–36).

The radicals who executed Charles in 1649 had moved quite far from these ideas, but they were always a minority, and many within the Parliamentary movement were deeply conservative, most of all the country gentry from whom Dryden sprang.[29] The conservatism of the gentry included a desire to maintain their property and position, and a sense of themselves, however recent their wealth, as "above" the common people. In a graphic case of this attitude, the Pickering family built an elevated pew for themselves over the south porch of St. Mary Virgin, which they reached by a private, exterior staircase and had warmed by their own fireplace. Despite the orthodoxy of the idea that wealth was not synonymous with election, Dod and Cleaver's other argument for maternal breast-feeding, with its emphasis on the dangerous effects of a "nurse of a naughty nature," doubtless had a distinct appeal to such class snobbery. Even though their preachers regarded Original Sin as a universal condition, people like the Pickerings were most likely to picture a naughty nurse as an unclean wench from the lower classes.

This contradiction between a potentially democratizing theology and a conservative clinging to rank, which was to produce a devastating struggle among various Puritan factions during the later stages of the Civil War, can sometimes be found in embryonic form in a single passage from an earlier period. Here, for example, is part of Dod and Cleaver's advice on education in *A Godlie Forme*:

> So, the greater the childe is (both by birth, and by inheritance) so much the more need is it for him to be brought vp in learning, and in good literature. For learning, knowledge, and understanding, is profitable both for rich and poore: so that (as the Grecians say) he that is ignorant and vnlearned, seeth nothing, although he haue eyes. [sig. X3v]

In the first sentence, a wealthy child is said to have a greater need for good literature than a peasant, but in the next sentence, with a typical recourse to economic language, learning is called "profitable both for rich and poore," and the authors demonstrate their own learning by alluding to a Greek proverb. Dod and Cleaver fail to anticipate a more disruptive effect of more widespread education: the questioning of hereditary "greatness" as defined by financial "inheritance." But the radicals who raised such questions did not include Dryden, a relatively "great" child by birth and inheritance, who was evidently "brought vp in learning, and in good literature," and whose work embraces the idea that order depends upon hierarchy. To be sure, both Dryden's celebration of the Stuart monarchy and his ultimate conversion to Rome would have appalled his Puritan ancestors. But from what we can discover about Dryden's ancestors, their sort of Puritanism had little to do with levelling. Dryden's nasty dismissal of popular preachers as "*Rabble*" whose "horney Fists . . . gaul'd . . . the tender Page" of Scripture (*Religio Laici*, ll. 403–04) is not directed against the Puritan divines of his own boyhood, well-educated men like Thomas Hill, whose hands were certainly not calloused with labor, but against those "mechanick" evangelists who, to the surprise and discomfort of the Puritan gentry, succeeded briefly in extending the political radicalism latent in some aspects of Puritan theology.

Trying to infer what people in a culture unlike our own were thinking is difficult, and assuming that their ideas, or even their emotions, were the principal reasons for their actions is even riskier. As an illustration, we may glance briefly ahead to consider the career of Dryden's most famous Pickering relative. His first cousin Sir Gilbert Pickering (III), who was only twenty years older than the poet, was reared in a comparable climate of ideas, since he too was the eldest son of a Dryden-Pickering marriage, grew up in Titchmarsh, and took a Cambridge B.A. But while Dryden ultimately became a supporter of the Stuart monarchy, Sir Gilbert became, and apparently remained, a thorough Parliamentarian. A member of the Short and Long Parliaments, he sided with the army in the crisis of the late 1640s and was among the judges at the trial of Charles I (though he prudently did not sign the death warrant); during the 1650s, he served on the Protector's Privy Council and as Cromwell's Lord Chamberlain, employing his young cousin John Dryden as a clerk and translator.

Shortly after Cromwell's funeral, Pickering retired to Titchmarsh. His brother-in-law Edward Montagu, later Earl of Sandwich, was an important defector to Charles II at the time of Booth's premature Royalist uprising in August of 1659; his younger brother Edward Pickering and his son John Pickering (III) actually went to Breda to pay court to the King as he set sail for England in May of 1660. While Sir Gilbert himself made no such gesture of obeisance to the new regime, he did submit a "humble petition" to the House of Commons, read on 9 June 1660, which resulted only in his being promised that he would not be executed; other "Pains, Penalties, and Forfeitures" were a definite possibility. Lady Pickering was evidently worried about her husband's possible fate: on 19 June, she bribed her brother's secretary, the diarist Samuel Pepys, in order to secure Montagu's protection for her husband. Thanks to a motion introduced by the new Earl, Pickering was pardoned in August; an absolute prohibition against holding office was his only punishment, and scholars have long assumed that he was only too happy with this fate—especially since the official regicides, those who had signed Charles I's death warrant, were being hunted down, exhumed, hanged, drawn, and quartered. But when the new rector, Henry Deane, arrived to take possession of his living in Titchmarsh in October, he actually encountered violent opposition from Sir Gilbert and his wife. They refused to hand over the keys to the church or the parsonage, and Lady Pickering organized a riot in opposition to Deane, "exhort[ing] her male and female Myrmidons to force into the house."[30]

A historian of ideas might account for Sir Gilbert's intransigence by praising his stubborn theological or political consistency. A psychological historian might legitimately discuss the powerful effect on a teenage boy of seeing his young father die shortly after a term in prison brought on by stubborn opposition to Charles I; he might even consider the possible effect of a phrase in Sir Gilbert's grandmother's will, made in 1620, when he was nine: "To my hopefull grandchilde Gilbert Pickering I gyve fyve pounds . . . beseeching God to gyve him his blessing and make him like his worthie grandfather my deare husband." That grandfather was Gilbert (II), the man who fancied himself a target of the Gunpowder Plot and pursued recusants with savage violence; if contemporary accounts of the implacable fury of Sir Gilbert (III) are to be credited, his grandmother's prayers were answered.[31] Yet without wishing to invalidate either of these approaches, I might point to a physical fact that also had a bearing on Sir Gilbert's opposition to a new rector in 1660: he had been keeping the tithes for himself during the later years of the Interregnum and thus stood to lose the grain stored in the tithe-barns if Deane was allowed to take office.

When Dryden took up the issue of human inconsistency, he gave full credit to such

physical causes. In the dedication to *Aureng-Zebe* (1676), he announced his abandonment of rhymed drama, a form he had championed vigorously for thirteen years, and
defended his right to change his mind with an account of changeability derived from
Montaigne:

> As I am a Man, I must be changeable: and sometimes the gravest of us all are so, even
> upon ridiculous accidents. Our minds are perpetually wrought on by the temperament
> of our Bodies: which makes me suspect, they are nearer alli'd, than either our Philoso-
> phers or School-Divines will allow them to be. . . . An ill Dream, or a Cloudy day, has
> the power to change this wretched Creature, who is so proud of a reasonable Soul, and
> make him think what he thought not yesterday. [sig. a1r–v]

The physical determinism of that passage brings us all the way back to Dod and
Cleaver, who advocate breast-feeding in strikingly similar language, arguing that "the
temperature of the minde followes the constitution of the body." Unlike Dryden and his
Puritan forebears, however, modern science normally looks at psychosomatic phenomena in the opposite way, stressing the capacity of ideas and emotions to produce physical
symptoms, and modern scholarship in the humanities, naturally focused on ideas and
their development, has assumed too easily that people are primarily motivated by their
beliefs. But Dryden, speaking here with the voice of common sense, reminds us that the
body can influence the mind, that hunger, cold, or sexual arousal can alter our thoughts,
a perception that may improve our understanding of the complex relations between
ideas and actions in his career and those of his contemporaries. Dryden lived to see one
monarch executed, another restored, and a third deposed; in a period with such volatile
changes in politics, there were few prominent men who were *not* accused of "changing
sides" at one time or another. To be sure, such powerful ideas as Calvinism, Divine
Right, and the "new science" sometimes affected their decisions, but family loyalties,
greed, and survival were at least as important.

Dryden's political conservatism, for example, which entailed a rejection of the
radical views of some of the Puritans in his cousin's generation, may have owed something to the conservatism of his other Puritan ancestors. In his partisan writings during
the Exclusion Crisis of the early 1680s, which include bitter attacks on Calvinists as
"Fanaticks," he defended the rights of James, Duke of York, the Catholic successor, by
referring to the same biblical passages about subjection to monarchs that Dod and
Cleaver had cited.[32] But we should also remember that as a poet, Dryden had everything to gain from the Restoration and continuation of the Stuart monarchy. When he
argued in 1678 that those "who endeavour the Subversion of Governments" would
always "discourage Poets and Historians" (XIII, 3), he was speaking not merely from
ideology, but from his practical knowledge of the Interregnum, when the courtly and
aristocratic patronage on which all the arts depended had been interrupted. Though he
cannot have anticipated all of this in 1660, the return of the monarchy reopened the
theatres, refueled the patronage system, and ultimately made him the Laureate. The
prospect of a climate more favorable to the arts surely helped to motivate Dryden's
poetic celebration of the Restoration, in poems highly critical of the Puritans, just as the

barns full of grain helped to motivate his cousin's opposition to a new rector appointed by the King. The baby at the breast may possibly "suck in godlinesse"; he certainly learns to expect to be fed when hungry.

Art and Nature: Theology, Politics, or Aesthetics?

The problem of assessing the impact of Dryden's upbringing on his later career is no less severe when we turn from such overtly political and religious issues to more nebulous questions of taste and aesthetics. Accounts of the Puritan suspicion of the arts generally describe it as a logical consequence of their Augustinian and Calvinist theology, and there are powerful passages in both Augustine and Calvin that may be construed as pretexts for iconoclasm and asceticism.[33] But iconoclasm was always a political act, and an asceticism that defined itself in opposition to courtly magnificence was often a political statement. Even aesthetic positions that seem quite abstract may have political dimensions; one of the anecdotes preserved in *The Worthy Sayings of Old Mr. Dod* may serve as an example: "Being at Holmby-House, and invited by an Honourable Personage to see that stately Building, erected by Sir Christopher Hatton, he desired to be excused, and to sit still looking on a Flower in his Hand, giving this Reason: I see more of God in this Flower, than in all the beautiful Edifices in the World."[34] Dod's choice of the flower over the building looks like an abstract preference for Nature over Art—until we enquire into the identity of Sir Christopher Hatton (1540–91), an elegant dancer and participant in early court masques who was Elizabeth's Lord Chancellor, may have been her paramour, and certainly was a staunch ally of the bishops in their opposition to the Puritanism of the other lay members of the Queen's Privy Council. Once we know these facts, Dod's distaste for a showy building erected by a powerful courtier opposed to his kind of preaching begins to look more than a little political, as do many later Puritan positions on aesthetic issues.

When Charles I's close advisor William Laud became Archbishop of Canterbury in 1633, he ordered the use of altars instead of simple communion tables, a position immediately decried as an innovation and greeted with stubborn resistance in the country. Laud's Calvinist opponents thought his liturgical practices too much like those of Roman Catholicism, which was irrationally feared by men brought up on Foxe's lurid tales of martyrdom and the popular demonology of the Spanish Armada and the Gunpowder Plot; they also knew that he accepted the theology of Jacob Arminius, a softening of Calvinism firmly rejected by the Synod of Dort in 1619. But their opposition to Laud's altars was doubtless also increased by the purely political abuses of the Star Chamber, a summary court that the King and the Archbishop used to stifle dissent. Other aesthetic positions with similar political overtones included the widespread Puritan distaste for contrapuntal choir music and the claim, most vigorously argued by William Prynne, that Charles I's growing collection of great paintings and statues at Whitehall was the result of a Papist plot "to seduce the King himself with Pictures, Antiquities, Images & other vanities brought from *Rome*."[35]

When confronted with the arts of the Caroline court—the expensive, visually seductive masque; the ostensibly religious but patently sensuous Italian painting; or the

Laudian liturgy, filled with incense and counterpoint—Puritans like Dod and Prynne talked of preferring Nature. Dryden, by contrast, embraced the baroque and courtly arts that had offended some of his Puritan forebears. His first published poem, the extravagant and histrionic elegy for the young Lord Hastings (1649), shows a thorough familiarity with the traditional iconography of the Caroline masque; his poems of 1660, "To Sir Robert Howard" and *Astraea Redux*, invoke technical analogies with painting and music; the genre of the rhymed heroic play, to which he devoted so much creative and critical energy, is highly "artificial," though Dryden often treats that adjective as a term of praise. Even his mature poetry involves an attention to proportional architecture and a rich encrustation of allusive ornament that has made it seem quite alien to such later proponents of Nature as the Romantics and their followers, who might be surprised to discover their own affinities to John Dod. Given Dod's choice, Dryden chose the building over the flower, but his choice was at least as highly influenced by politics, since the court he came to serve was defining itself by promoting those arts suppressed by the Commonwealth.

Of course, I have simplified these issues in a way that distorts both Dryden and the Puritans. Given a stark choice between a Nature defined as God's creation and an Art defined as seductive graven imagery, most Puritans would surely have opted for Nature. But few real choices are so stark or abstract, and only the extremists and simplifiers within that complex and various movement we call Puritanism ever advocated a dogmatic rejection of all forms of art. Some of the finest lyric poetry of the seventeenth century draws upon a "Protestant poetics" in which the emotions of the soul as charted by Calvin are described in language drawn from the kind of close reading of the Bible that lay at the heart of Reformation thought.[36] The century's greatest poet, John Milton, whose pamphlets place him among the more radical Puritan thinkers, reserves some of his finest language for his lines in praise of music. Even Puritan sermons often reveal considerable devotion to rhetorical architecture. If the caricature Roundhead of Cavalier propaganda (and of much later history) had no aesthetic sense at all, many actual Puritans drew upon their faith to make impressive aesthetic judgments. During the Interregnum, when men believing in some version of Calvinist ideas held power, artists working in many media attempted to restrain their fancy and submit to a more sober aesthetic, which may remind us of the rigorous self-discipline of such Jansenist French artists as Racine. The modern poet Donald Davie has even argued that the "*simplicity*, *sobriety*, and *measure* . . . that Calvinist aesthetics demands of the art object" are qualities necessary in all art: "Art *is* measure, *is* exclusion; is therefore simplicity (hardearned), is sobriety, tense with all the extravagances that it has been tempted by and has denied itself."[37] Dryden's criticism is frequently alert to these issues, and if his plays and much of his poetry display a baroque and courtly exuberance of imagery, I believe we may also identify, particularly in his later poetry, some attention to "measure" and "exclusion." That Dryden should have written his most "Calvinist" poems while a Roman Catholic may seem paradoxical, but here as elsewhere, there is a complexity in Dryden's vision that makes his work richer than that of poets with a more consistent or monistic aesthetic philosophy.

Nor was Nature a monistic concept, even for the Puritans. God had created

Nature, but thanks to Original Sin all Nature was fallen, and if Dod and Cleaver were willing to argue that suckling one's own child was "so naturall a thing, that euen the beasts will not omit it," other passages make harsher comparisons to animals, such as this exposition of Proverbs 12.1: "*He that loueth correction, loueth knowledge: but he that hateth correction*, is brutish . . . a beast in a mans shape."[38] Here, "correction" is recommended as a way to reform natural brutishness, a point reiterated in *A Godlie Forme* with a metaphor from the world of skill and craft: "We find this old Prouerb true: *Vse ouercommeth Nature*: as the Wheelwright doth by strength bow his timber" (sig. Q6r). Now Nature takes the form of a piece of raw material to be "overcome" by "use," "bowed" or bent by "strength," "corrected" as a poet corrects a poem. This view of Nature comes much closer to that embraced by the mature Dryden in theory and practice. In the *Essay of Dramatick Poesie*, for example, he employs the metaphor of a musician turning the peg in the neck of a string instrument, which is simply a more refined version of the metaphor of the wheelwright bending his timber: "a serious Play is indeed the representation of Nature, but 'tis Nature wrought up to an higher pitch" (XVII, 74). As the Puritan preference for Nature over Art involved the recognition that Nature was fallen, in need of correction, so Dryden's preference for Art over raw, undigested Nature involved the recognition that Art might disastrously overwhelm Nature. He worried about over-correcting his later poems, and was willing to argue that Nature at its best could surpass Art. To take only one example from his poetry, ignoring for the moment the rich discussions of this idea in the prose criticism and its frequent dramatization in the plays, we might consider these lines from his poem in memory of the amateur poet and painter Anne Killigrew:

> Art she had none, yet wanted none:
> For Nature did that Want supply,
> So rich in Treasures of her Own,
> She might our boasted Stores defy:
> Such Noble vigour did her Verse adorn,
> That it seem'd borrow'd, where 'twas only born.
>
> [ll. 71–76]

No man can entirely shed his upbringing, and the ambiguity that enriches these lines is a part of Dryden's heritage from the Puritans. Anne Killigrew's Nature compensates for the Art she lacks; her innate "Noble vigour" suffices as ornament. "Our boasted Stores," the accumulated reserves of allusion, mythology, tradition, and technique on which a professional poet ordinarily depends, are defied by a woman "rich in Treasures of her Own." These lines from a complimentary elegy need not be taken too seriously, but even in a more private context, Dryden returns to the idea of natural talent: in a letter written in the last year of his life, he refers to Charles Hopkins as "a poet who writes good verses without knowing how, or why; I mean he writes naturally well, without art or learning, or good sence."[39] Again, there is a whiff of irony, but such phrases nonetheless suggest that Dryden's confidence in his own professionalism was far from smug, that there was room for the "natural" or "Puritan" or "Calvinist" virtues of simplicity and directness in his conception of Art.

As we try to estimate the psychological consequences of Dryden's Puritan child-hood, we may usefully ponder Dod and Cleaver's metaphor of the wheelwright. Most modern accounts of Puritan child-rearing describe it as a process intent on breaking the will of the child,[40] but in Dod and Cleaver, the more frequent metaphor is bending, not breaking. To be sure, they caution parents against immoderate affection and "cocker-ing" of children, but on the whole, they advise a milder sort of correction than one might expect:

> Some there be, that will not haue their children taught vntill they be ten or twelue yeares old, because (as they say) at that age they haue but an apish imitation.
>
> To whom we answer, that although they cannot then deeply discerne, nor pro-foundly conceiue things: yet how many things before these years will they both receiue and remember?
>
> And we demand, . . . may they not much better doe apishly good whiles they are young, which they may carefully doe when they are old? Besides, let them goe vn-taught, and they will grow so head-strong, that they will sooner be broken than bended: sure it is, that one stripe, or two words will doe more good to a child in time than an hundred stripes afterward. . . .
>
> Neither do we purpose to take away naturall affection, and a Christian kind of compassion in all our censures: for it is our great complaint of the brutish vnmer-cifulnesse of many parents here. [*Godlie Forme*, sig. T5v–T6r]

Now "affection" picks up the loaded adjective "naturall," while "apish imitation" is defended as a necessary stage in education, and the adjective "brutish" is reserved for parents who punish their children excessively, who should instead "consider how noble a thing a child is, whom God himself both shaped and formed in his mothers wombe" (sig. Q2v). The tough Calvinist doctrine of Total Depravity apparently did not preclude this surprising acknowledgment of Original Nobility, and we may detect "a Christian kind of compassion," in some way a result of his own Puritan childhood, in John Dryden's later affection and concern for his three Roman Catholic sons.

Puritan Attitudes toward the Arts

I believe the young Dryden was reared with considerable affection and concern, not only because of the "affective individualism" incipient in Dod and Cleaver,[41] but also because some more traditional values made him an object of attention, hope, and educational rigor. He was the firstborn son of a prominent family, and for seven years the only son, since Mary's next five children were girls. His father, conscious of the Puritan emphasis on education and well-educated himself, was surely eager to see the boy learn, as was his bachelor uncle John Pickering, M.D., an amateur poet who lived in Aldwincle and may claim some credit for the extraordinary survival rate of Dryden's siblings.[42] The local clergy had excellent reasons to take an interest in the boy's education: Henry Pickering, rector of Aldwincle All Saints, was his grandfather; Thomas Hill, rector of St. Mary Virgin Titchmarsh, was his father's college friend and owed his substantial living to the Dryden and Pickering families. Hill was resident and active in his pastoral duties from 1633 until 1643, when he went to London to take part

in the Westminster Assembly, and when Henry Pickering died in 1637, he was succeeded by a Puritan named Thomas Ford, who had already quarreled with Bishop
Laud; like his new neighbor Hill, Ford would later preach before the Long Parliament.[43] Such men often sponsored free grammar schools, but if there was a school in
Titchmarsh, it has left no record. There had been a school in Aldwincle as early as 1615,
however,[44] and since the Pickering cousins rode daily to Oundle for schooling as small
boys, I suppose the Drydens would have been willing to see their firstborn travel the
much shorter distance to that village school, where he probably took his first steps
toward the mastery of English and Latin on which his later fame depended.

Although we cannot know exactly what parts of Dryden's education came from
these early local sources, and what parts from his later formal tutelage at Westminster
School and Trinity College, we may be certain that his first Puritan teachers in Northamptonshire, like his later Royalist master at Westminster, held the Word in high
esteem. Interest in literacy was a Puritan tradition. Elizabethan and Jacobean Puritans,
who thought of themselves as the learned party in the church, frequently criticized
those parsons content to read the liturgy without giving a sermon for ignorance and
laziness; the program of Sunday afternoon lectures by "combinations" of such Puritan
preachers was designed to improve the biblical knowledge and preaching ability of the
clergy. As the heirs of the previous century's costly battle for a vernacular Bible and
liturgy, these early Puritans were also enthusiastic promoters of literacy among the laity.
By encouraging more widespread reading of the Bible, they hoped to escape the
ignorance and superstition they associated with the Roman Catholic Middle Ages,
which Dryden later described as a time "When want of Learning kept the *Laymen*
low, / And none but *Priests* were *Authoriz'd* to *know*" (*Religio Laici*, ll. 372–73). Of
course, there were other motives for learning to read, as Dod and Cleaver acknowledge
in a somewhat inept endorsement of more widespread education:

> It is also the duty of parents to prouide that their children may learne, at the least to
> write and reade: for it may bee vnto them a great helpe in the course of this life, and a
> treasure of much greater account than mony. . . . Neuerthelesse, the principall end
> thereof, should not haue respect to such commoditie, as the children may reape
> thereby towards the vse of this present life: but rather that they may reade the word of
> God to their comfort, and instruction to saluation. [*Godlie Forme*, sig. Q4v]

The "principall end" of teaching a child to read may be his "comfort, and instruction to
saluation," but the words that leap out from the page, despite the protests of the
authors, are "treasure," "mony," and "commoditie." For some staunch supporters of
Puritan values, such as the City merchants in London, the rewards of literacy were not
merely spiritual.

In the next generation, however, there was disagreement among Puritan leaders
on this issue, as on many others. Well-educated "Presbyterian" clergymen like Thomas
Hill remained concerned to increase literacy for the traditional reasons. In a sermon
preached before the House of Commons in 1642, with the marvelously Puritan title *The
Trade of Truth Advanced*, Hill attacks "*Popery*" and "*Arminianism*" for "compound[ing]
unwritten *Traditions* most presumptuously with *Holy Scripture*," and offers this striking

paraphrase of 1 Peter 2.2: "*All* new borne babes will desire . . . *Word-milke, Sermon-milke* without guile, *without adulterating Sophistication* of it."[45] Hill would probably have regarded the ornate rhetoric of a high-church preacher like Launcelot Andrewes as "*adulterating Sophistication*," but his metaphor of the Word, preached or written, as nourishing milk for infants indicates his continuity with the Reformation ideal of an educated clergy and a literate laity. Among the more radical "Independents," however, this tradition was swept aside by millenarian enthusiasm: the wild-eyed Parliamentary soldier who preached in a churchyard in Surrey in 1648, advocating the abolition of the Sabbath, tithes, the clergy, and magistrates, was thinking of the same passage when he climaxed his performance by igniting the Bible with a candle and describing it as "beggarly rudiments, milk for Babes. But now Christ is in his glory among us, and imparts a fuller measure of his Spirit to his Saints, than this can afford."[46] For such utopian visionaries, who rejected the mercantile interests of some of their Puritan predecessors, the possible impurity of some motives for literacy was bothersome: a child taught to read in order to study the Bible might apply his skill to gaining earthly riches; worse yet, he might become corrupted by Papist propaganda or secular poetry.[47] Some antinomian preachers were therefore ready to argue that books were devilish, and that sermons were the only legitimate form of the Word.

The presence of such ideas on the radical fringes of Puritanism during the 1640s made it possible for the high-church party to denigrate all Puritan preachers as ignorant "mechanick" fanatics and to identify themselves as the educated party, a claim for which the later ejections of Laudian scholars from the universities looked like powerful proof. Similarly, Laud's emphasis on the liturgy made it possible for the Puritans to denigrate his followers as superstitious crypto-Papists, mystifying the laity with incomprehensible ceremonies and neglecting their duty to preach the Word with the power of the Spirit. If we discount these accusations as the propaganda they are, we can recognize that the majority of clergymen on both sides remained committed to an education fundamentally centered on the written word, though they differed about its emphases. The commitment and the controversy were both important factors in Dryden's education.

For conservative Puritans like Thomas Hill, the search for a coherent middle ground led to some tension about the proper preaching of the Word. In a sermon preached in 1648, Hill explicitly rejected the heterodox ideas being circulated by preachers like the soldier in Surrey: "Many of us run so far from *Popery and Prelacy*, that we run into other *Extremities*, very dangerous and unhappy." Describing with horror the savaging of Scripture by such extremists, he begged "the Lord [to] deliver us from this opinion."[48] But while Hill would never have ignited a Bible, he shared with the soldier an emphasis on inspiration: in a letter to the Senior Fellows of Trinity College, Cambridge, written just two years before Dryden arrived there as an undergraduate, Hill urged them to preach "in the demonstration of the Spirit, and of power, not with the enticing words of man's wisdom."[49] According to most Puritans, such preaching ought to be plain, and Hill's introductory epistle to *The Trade of Truth Advanced* actually calls it "this plaine Discourse," but neither the rhetorical patterning of the language that follows nor its confidence in its own power authenticates that disclaimer:

This sermon, such an one as it is, I humbly tender to your Gracious Acceptance, who have adopted it; I put it into your Honourable Protection, who have lifted it; I commend it to your Practicall Observation, for whom I intended it; heartily desiring Gods Blessing upon your spirits in the perusal of it; that you may read and act it, turning *words into works*, which is the best repetition of Sermons. [sig. A3r]

While hardly Ciceronian, this passage includes textbook examples of such figures as isocolon, homoeoteleuton, and paranomasia. Hill's diction, here and elsewhere, is relatively simple, and he avoids elaborate suspensions in his syntax, but this sermon is not the work of an inspired improviser; it is the work of a well-read university man with a bad conscience about formal language, trying to find some middle ground between "the enticing words of man's wisdom" and the radical prizing of incoherence that Swift was to satirize so memorably as Aeolism.

Such Puritan uncertainties about the preached Word were bound to color Puritan attitudes toward poetry. There was indeed a "war against poetry" in Elizabethan and Jacobean England; men devoted to the preaching and reading of God's Word sometimes exploded into virulent protests against the secular art of words, most obviously in the battles between the Privy Council and the Corporation of London about the theatres. But this argument was not exclusively theological: there were powerful economic motives behind the attack on the theatre launched by the City merchants, and Puritan criticism of secular poetry often masked a political attack on the aristocracy that had traditionally fostered such poetry.[50] Moreover, the Puritans were not as consistent in waging war against poetry as they were in attacking the other arts; indeed, their attacks on the visual arts, the court masque, and polyphonic music may be explained in part as expressions of a fundamental preference for the word over these more sensuous forms of communication. While this valuing of the word is a typical feature of Renaissance humanism,[51] it occurs with particular poignancy in English Puritanism, and I believe Dryden's fundamental faith in the primacy of language began with his Puritan training in Titchmarsh and Aldwincle.

As Puritan attitudes toward poetry were affected by their opinions about preaching, their attitudes toward the other secular arts were strongly affected by the debate about the liturgy. Believing as they did that "the Word preached is the meanes to beget men to a new life" (*Godlie Forme*, sig. B2v), Puritans naturally regarded Archbishop Laud's program to increase liturgical spectacle as a dangerous innovation. Laud himself described the altar as "the greatest place of God's residence upon earth, . . . greater than the pulpit; for there 'tis *Hoc est corpus meum*, 'This is my body'; but in the pulpit 'tis at most but *Hoc est verbum meum*, 'This is my word'."[52] For his Puritan opponents, however, the priority of the Word over the body had been established by Calvin, who used the example of God's speaking from the burning bush; Moses, he pointed out, "heard a voice, [he] did not see a body."[53] Dod and Cleaver, in their *Exposition of the Eleuenth and Twelfth Chapters of . . . Prouerbes*, even minimize Christ's physicality:

It was an indulgence of Christ to *Thomas*, to help his faith in his resurrection, by the senses of sight and feeling: but for matters of punishment, and damnation, it is good to go from them, and not to come at them: to heare Gods testimonie, and not to see it fulfilled vpon themselues: to beleeue the trueth of that which is spoken, and not to feele it by their own experience. [p. 134]

Decades of struggle in the Church may be described as a battle between these positions, and there were secular manifestations of the conflict as well. For a particularly revealing example of the liturgical struggle, we may sample the "Articles against the Durham *Innovators*" filed on 3 August 1630 by Peter Smart, a Puritanical member of the cathedral clergy, who watched in horror the "popish and superstitious rites" brought in as a result of Laud's "haereticall Arminianisme":

> Peter Smart . . . perceiv[ed] the simple people inveigled and begiled, by your popish baits and allurements of glorious pictures, and Babylonish vesturs . . . and especially the horrible profanation of both the sacraments with all manner of musick, both instrumentall, and vocall, so lowde that the Ministers could not be heard, what they said, as if *Bacchanalia*, . . . and not the Death and Passion of our Saviour Christ were celebrated. . . . You have not only banished the singing of psalmes, in the vulgar tunes . . . but you have so changed the whole liturgie, that though it be not in Latin, yet by reason of the confusedness of voices of so many singers, with a multitude of melodius instruments . . . the greatest part of the service is no better understood, then if it weare in Hebrue or Irish. Nay the Sacrament itself is turned wel neere into a theatricall stage play. . . . representing to us Apolloe's solemnities at Delos, which the poett describeth in the 4th of his Æneidos:
>
> > Instauratque choros, mistique altaria circum
> > Cretesque Dryopesque fremunt, pictique Agathyrsi.[54]

These angry sputterings, which provide in compact form arguments made in hundreds of Puritan sermons and tracts, reveal a hierarchy of hostility: Smart treats the visual arts with unqualified contempt; he opposes contrapuntal and instrumental music, but does not propose to ban music entirely; and he unwittingly reveals an ambiguous attitude toward poetry in the pride and accuracy with which he quotes Virgil as part of the claim that the new rites are pagan. Dryden's aesthetic judgments were neither so extreme nor so passionate; he knew and collaborated with the leading painters and composers of his time, and was often generous in praise of their work. But he never doubted the priority of the art of words, and his witty assertions of poetry's precedence over the other arts betray curious similarities to Puritan polemic.

Theologically, the Puritan opposition to the visual arts, here expressed not as argument but as mere name-calling ("popish baits and allurements of glorious pictures"), rested on a greatly expanded interpretation of the commandment forbidding graven images. Historically and politically, it involved angry opposition to the Roman Catholic claim that pictures, especially church icons, were "the books of the uneducated," a claim forcefully rejected by Calvin, who blamed the ignorance of the laity on the failure of the Church to make them literate. According to Calvin, "those in authority in the church turned over to idols the office of teaching for no other reason than that they themselves were mute," ignoring the example of St. Paul, who "testifies that by the true preaching of the gospel 'Christ is depicted before our eyes as crucified.'"[55] Preferring such mental pictures generated by the Word preached to the all-too-physi-

cal images of painting or statuary, the English Puritans were not only heirs to a reduced
and ascetic version of Platonic idealism, but necessarily promoters of spirited preaching. For all their protestations that their sermons were plain and modest, they were
trusting such sermons to rouse their hearers to a vigorous pursuit of Christ's kingdom;
they believed, in Hill's phrase, that they could turn *words into works.*" Ironically and
sadly, the most rabid Puritans sometimes responded to such words by destroying those
works of art, in sculpture and stained glass, that their fathers had made to adorn their
churches.

Dryden's relatives, however, were not extremists on this issue. Sir John Cope, his
great-great-grandfather, demolished those parts of the priory church at Canons Ashby
that had once housed the high altar, using the materials to build his own house, but
some ancestor in the next generation commissioned a decoration depicting the Dryden
and Cope families at prayer, which survives in the house at Canons Ashby.[56] The
biblical mural painted for old Erasmus Dryden proves that he too was an active patron
of religious art. In Dryden's own generation, his first cousin Gilbert Pickering was
considered a qualified judge of art: the Puritan Council of State appointed him to the
committee charged with identifying items to be "reserved" when Charles I's art collection was sold off at auction in 1649, and in 1651, he was made director of the Mortlake
tapestry factory.[57]

While Puritan attitudes toward visual and verbal art in secular contexts were
naturally more complex than their attitudes toward the liturgy, there were connections:
some of the hostility toward the visual that produced iconoclasm spilled over onto the
secular visual arts, and some of the prestige of the preached Word spilled over onto the
secular art of words. Xenophobia may have been a factor as well: although the medieval
glass and statuary smashed by the Puritans had often been comparable in quality to
corresponding work in continental cathedrals, English artists of the Renaissance had
not kept pace with continental developments; since the native tradition in painting and
secular statuary was far weaker than the native tradition in poetry, it was more vulnerable to attack from Puritan polemicists. The magnificent art objects Charles I was
purchasing, largely from Catholic Italy, were much more advanced work than anything
done by a native Englishman, as Charles recognized by seeking to hire Rubens and
successfully hiring his chief assistant, Van Dyck; but to William Prynne and others, the
royal collection was Papist, foreign, and obscene. When country Puritan gentry had
their portraits painted, they chose conservative painters like Marcus Gheeraedts or
Cornelius Janssen, men whose sober "neo-Elizabethan" style ignored the dazzling
innovations of Van Dyck. Two of Dryden's Pickering relatives, for example, had their
portraits made by Janssen, who was "closely involved with the families of artists and
craftsmen who belonged to the Dutch Reformed Church in Austin Friars."[58] In practice, then, Dutch Protestant painters employing a recognizably English style were not
regarded as foreign—at least not to the extent that Italian Catholic painters were.

In the Elizabethan years, there had been voices ready to make similarly xenophobic
judgments about literature, such as Roger Ascham's description of chivalric romances
as "the inchantments of *Circes*, brought out of *Italie*, to marre mens maners in England."
Although Ascham believed that "Mo[re] Papistes [were] made, by your mery bookes of

Portraits of Christopher Pickering (ca. 1630?) and Elizabeth Pickering (ca. 1640?)
by Cornelius Janssen.

Italie, than by your earnest bookes of *Louain*,"[59] his remarks reveal greater hostility to
Italy than to literature; they reflect the same prejudice expressed in the famous advice
that William Cecil, Lord Burleigh, gave to his son Robert: "Suffer not thy sonnes to
pass the Alpes. For they shall learne nothing there, but pride, blasphemy, & atheism."[60]
Dryden's Pickering ancestors were clients of the Cecils, but someone called "John
Pickering of Northamptonshire," probably one of the younger sons of John (I), went to
Italy in 1581;[61] evidently neither his religious sentiments nor his political alliances
dissuaded him from making the journey. The successful adaptation to English of Italian
poetic forms and styles made it more difficult to use xenophobia as a weapon against
poetry than as a weapon against painting or music. Even Ascham's diatribe comes from
a textbook of instruction in elementary Latin and makes an allusion to Homer; the
implicit distinction between ancient and Renaissance Italy could not withstand the
Italian claim to continuity with the classic line, a claim accepted by most English poets
under Elizabeth and James. Spenser's *Faerie Queene*, thoroughly Protestant and aggressively English, was sufficient disproof of the fear that Italianate chivalric epic would
lead to Papism and sin; Dryden read it as a boy, presumably with the approval of his
Puritan family.[62]

　　If poetry was less suspect than painting in the country, at the court the leading poet
had to defend his art, not against Puritan scruples, but against the increasing dominance of the visual; in doing so, he drew on the imagery employed in the liturgical
debate. Six months after Peter Smart's protest against the Laudian innovations at
Durham cathedral, and six months before John Dryden's birth, the "inventors" who
had been collaborating for years on the spectacular court masques, Ben Jonson and
Inigo Jones, quarreled and parted over the issue of whose name should appear first on
the title page of *Love's Triumph through Callipolis*.[63] Jonson was no Puritan; his comedies
include memorable caricatures of Puritan merchants as greedy hypocrites, and he told
his friend William Drummond a scurrilous story designed to discredit the Dryden
family preacher, John Dod, and his followers. In this implausible tale, "a Gentlewoman
fell jn such a Phantasie or Phrensie w^t one Mr Dod a Puritan preacher yt she requeested
her husband that for the procreation of ane Angel or Saint he might lye wt her, which
having obtained it was bot ane ordinarie birth."[64]

　　Despite these prejudices, when Jonson needed an argument for the priority of the
text in the masque, he stressed the capacity of poetry to exert lasting moral force while
complimenting and entertaining the court, and sought to deny that Jones's brilliant
"inventions" had any permanent effect; moreover, he began with a distinction between
words and pictures, souls and bodies, that will remind us of Calvin. Long before the
quarrel with Jones, in the preface to the Jacobean masque *Hymenai* (1606), he had set up
that distinction in general, philosophical terms:

> It is a noble and iust aduantage, that the things subiected to *understanding* have of those
> which are obiected to *sense*, that the one sort are but momentarie, and meerely taking;
> the other impressing, and lasting: Else the glorie of all these *solemnities* had perish'd
> like a blaze, and gone out, in the *beholders* eyes. So short-liu'd are the *bodies* of all
> things, in comparison of their *soules*. [VII, 209]

And in the angry, polemical "Expostulation with Inigo Jones" (1632), the language comes surprisingly close to that employed by Peter Smart; Jonson implies that Jones's work is superstitious, fraudulent, and (by extension) Papist:

> But wisest Inigo! who can reflect
> On yᵉ new priming of thy old Signe postes,
> Reuiuing wᵗʰ fresh coulors yᵉ pale Ghosts
> Of thy dead Standards: or (wᵗʰ miracle) see
> Thy twice conceyud, thrice payd for Imagery?
> And not fall downe before it? and confess
> Allmighty Architecture?
>
> [VIII, 405–06]

Fighting a secular and aesthetic battle for prominence in the court, Jonson presents the architect as a dealer in bogus miracles, like Spenser's Archimago. By 1636, however, a much more sweeping political, theological, and economic battle between court and country had become unavoidable—a battle in which the country party would make in all seriousness the equation Jonson makes as a sally of wit. For country Puritans like Dryden's family, the court masque and the high-church liturgy were equally vain shows; one of the first acts of the Long Parliament after Charles left London in January 1642 was to halt work on the renovation of St. Paul's, for which Laud had hired Jones as his architect. Three years later, in January 1645, Laud was executed; later in the same year, Jones, gleefully described as the "Contriver of *Scenes* for the Queens *Dancing-Barne*,"[65] was captured, stripped, and carried away in a blanket by Parliamentary troops at Basing House. The causes of the Civil War in which these events were episodes were many and complex, but not least among them was Charles I's faith in his own propaganda, his belief in a myth of kingship that most often found visual rather than verbal expression. As his subjects sought redress through petitions and remonstrances, and expressed their growing dissatisfaction with his personal rule through sermons and tracts, Charles allowed himself to believe, at least during the "short bravery of the night," that "the complexities of contemporary issues [might be] resolved through idealisations and allegories, visions of Platonic realities."[66]

Thomas Carew's *Coelum Brittanicum*, for example, one of the masques produced after Jones's break with Jonson, presents the problem of poverty as an antimasque of gypsies. Speaking for the idealized celestial court, Mercury offers this answer to the plight of the poor:

> we advance
> Such vertues only as admit excesse,
> Brave bounteous Acts, Regall Magnificence.[67]

But Charles's "Regall Magnificence," while it included a more informed, generous, and tasteful patronage of all the arts than England would ever see again, was no answer to the pressing economic problems of his realm. The people of Titchmarsh, whose late squire, Dryden's uncle, had been a victim of the forced loan, were unlikely to place much store in Charles's "Brave bounteous Acts"; from their point of view, the "excesses" committed in "the Queens *Dancing-Barne*" were keeping their own barns empty of grain and violating the Lord's commandment against idolatry. Nor could the royalist allegory embodied in the masques function effectively as propaganda, since the performances were restricted to a tiny audience, incomprehensible even to some of those privileged to see them, and cast in a visual form regarded with immediate hostility by people like Dryden's family.[68]

Dryden's propaganda in support of the Stuart monarchs is more effective than that of his predecessors because his tough, argumentative prose draws some of its oral techniques from Puritan preaching; the language of abuse in his satirical verse, though often directed against the Dissenters, nonetheless owes something to Puritan pamphlets. Yet his poetry also draws upon the visual imagery associated with the Caroline court. Modern authorities on that court and its masques have emphasized Inigo Jones's fascination with lighting,[69] and such imagery plays a central role in some of Dryden's finest poems; the virtuoso treatment of the fire in *Annus Mirabilis* (1667) and the moonlit opening of *Religio Laici* (1682) are obvious examples. Well-informed references to the techniques of the painter are common in Dryden's prose and poetry, and many of his plays were elaborately mounted; his opera *Albion and Albanius* (1685), which bankrupted a theatrical company, was the last attempt to write a masque. Yet for all his apparent sympathy with and interest in the visual arts, Dryden ultimately shared with Jonson a faith in the priority and superiority of words. In his late verse epistle to the court painter Godfrey Kneller, this preference finds comic expression:

> Our Arts are Sisters; though not Twins in Birth:
> For Hymns were sung in Edens happy Earth,
> By the first Pair; while Eve was yet a Saint;
> Before she fell with Pride, and learned to paint.

[ll. 89–92]

Like many satirical lines by Dryden, these verses are playful, but not merely playful. The immediate joke turns on the verb "paint," which refers to applying cosmetics as well as to portraiture, so that we have a lovely picture of Eve painting her face with white lead and rouge as soon as she has girded her loins with fig leaves. But lurking behind this version of the Fall as a comedy of manners is the Puritan insistence that the making of visual images was a sin; the reference to Eve as "a Saint," picking up a term widely applied to themselves by the Puritans, signals that part of the joke. The aged Roman Catholic Dryden who wrote the poem to Kneller obviously did not believe that painting was sinful, but he did believe, like Jonson quarreling with Jones, that poetry was the standard by which the other arts must be judged and would be found wanting. After all, one might describe these lines as a comic dramatization of the opening of John's Gospel: "In the beginning was the Word."

Significantly, Dryden's example of prelapsarian poetry is the singing of "Hymns," an activity involving music as well as words. Like earlier Christians, the English Puritans were concerned about the relative importance of the two components of vocal music: Peter Smart's complaint that complex music makes the service "no better understood, then if it weare in Hebrue or Irish" is not only typical of English Puritan thought, but typical of a strain in Christian thought that reaches back at least as far as the early patristic polemic against musical instruments and includes similar statements by Augustine, Erasmus, and Calvin.[70] In England, this kind of thinking eventually produced the wanton destruction of irreplaceable organs. As Smart's sneering anti-Semitic and anti-Catholic jibe about "Hebrue or Irish" suggests, this prejudice also involved a version of the xenophobia we noticed in Puritan strictures on the visual arts; many of the royal musicians were Italian Catholics. But Smart's complaint also embodies a simple truth: innovations in musical style that attract attention for their own sake, including complex counterpoint, do reduce the audibility of the sung text.[71]

Dryden's career took him from a country church where the traditional Psalter was sung to the "vulgar tunes" to a court and theatre where his own poems were set, in various styles, by Louis Grabu, Giovanni Baptista Draghi, and Henry Purcell; when he took up the subject of the relations between words and music, he too insisted on the priority of words, as any poet in the Renaissance tradition would have. But the terms in which he makes that common distinction are revealing. In the preface to *Albion and Albanius*, he explains that "the recitative part of the *Opera* requires a more masculine Beauty of expression and sound" than "*The Songish Part*," which "must abound in the softness and variety of Numbers: its principal Intention, being to please the Hearing, rather than to gratify the understanding. . . . 'Tis my part to Invent, and the Musicians to Humour that Invention" (XV, 3–4, 10). This distinction between arias, belittled as merely appealing to the hearing, and recitatives, praised as "masculine," rational, and verbal, will remind us of Jonson's distinction between things "subjected to the understanding" and those "objected to the sense." But it also resembles Puritan attacks on music, such as this passage from a dedicatory epistle by Thomas Hill, written to the Parliamentary committee supervising Westminster School in 1648, when Dryden was in the fifth form there; Hill rejoices that since the Puritan victory, the services at Westminster Abbey no longer involve "*Pompous Altars* only to humour the *Eyes*, and taking *Musick* to please their *Eares*. All such *tedious Chauntings* with *Musick and multiplied repetitions* did little *Edifie* the mind of *Hearers*."[72] Again, I do not mean to equate Dryden's mature opinions about the relations of the arts with the Puritan dogma in which he was reared; my point is that Puritan polemic provided a vocabulary on which he could draw when necessary, just as he also drew on the vocabulary and imagery of the Caroline masque.

For all their intense resistance to instrumental music and other Laudian innovations, the Puritans' attitude toward music was substantially different from their horror of the visual; even Peter Smart's criticisms bespeak a desire to control music, not a need to eliminate it altogether. Again, there were radicals offering extreme solutions: the early Quakers, like their descendants, had no music at all. But for most Puritan preachers, including those who educated Dryden, the power of hymns to bind a congregation together made a sufficient case for church music; "the singing of Psalms in the vulgar tunes" had helped maintain the morale of embattled Protestants in Switzerland and Scotland, and would serve that function again in the New Model Army. As Charles I discovered when he tried to promulgate the marginally better version of the Psalter written by his father, the clumsy traditional verses of Sternhold and Hopkins were much loved.[73] Another comic passage from the mature Dryden suggests the ultimate effect of his boyhood experience with the sung Psalter; at the conclusion of *Religio Laici*, the poet explains the relative lack of ornament and "music" in that argumentative poem:

> And this unpolish'd rugged Verse I chose;
> As fittest for Discourse, and nearest Prose:
> For while from *Sacred Truth* I do not swerve,
> *Tom Sternhold*'s or *Tom Shadwell*'s *Rhimes* will serve.

[ll. 453–56]

The equation of Sternhold and Shadwell, grounded on the accident that both are named Thomas and the fact that both are poor poets, ultimately serves a political purpose: here, as so often in the 1680s, Dryden seeks to identify the Whigs, and their "true-blue Protestant poet" Shadwell, with the rebellious excesses of Puritanism. But Dryden's suggestion that his own "unpolish'd rugged Verse" resembles "*Tom Sternhold*'s . . . *Rhimes*" is more puzzling. Rhetorically, it has a disarming effect, reminding us that the poem we have just finished reading is more polished and sophisticated than anything dreamt of in Sternhold's theology or poetry. Psychologically, it may reveal the continuing appeal to Dryden of a principle held dear by the very Calvinists he was now rejecting: the idea that "*Sacred Truth*" was best expressed in simple language.

Especially if contrasted with his more ornate style in *The Hind and the Panther* (1676), Dryden's style in *Religio Laici* suggests the "simplicity, sobriety, and measure" by which Davie defines the "Calvinist style," but a critic hostile to poetry might still ask why he did not simply write in prose, especially since he describes the form he has chosen as "fittest for Discourse, and *nearest* Prose." Presumably, the same critic might appear as the Quaker opponent of church music, questioning even the singing of Psalms as obscuring naked truth, or as the antinomian opponent of literacy, fearful lest the newly literate miss the millenarian moment while reading books. Such a consistent advocate of the Word as pure essence or Platonic idea would not be susceptible to the temptation that appears to have overcome Peter Smart, who proudly parades his own knowledge of the pagan poet Virgil as part of an attack on the "heathen" excesses of the Laudian liturgy. But Smart, inconsistent as he may seem, was a real person, while the consistent Puritan Platonist I have been describing is a composite fiction, made up from extreme opinions. In real life, the men who first taught Dryden were shaped by their university education as well as their adherence to the Puritan cause. The local preachers probably shared Smart's hostility to the visual arts: someone systematically stripped Titchmarsh church of its glass, its painting of the Virgin, its roodloft, and its exterior statues.[74] They certainly shared his preference for congregational Psalms over other forms of church music: Thomas Ford, who went from Aldwincle to the Westminster Assembly to a post as cathedral preacher at Exeter, published a series of sermons on psalm-singing amplifying Hill's opposition to the "*tedious Chauntings*" of "Cathedral Musick."[75] An analogous hostility to poetry also sometimes appears in their works: Hill compares the "bewitching pompe in the outside of popery" to the "many wanton Metaphors" of "Ancient Writers" (*Trade of Truth*, p. 26). Both men, however, quote

Greek and Latin in their published sermons; Hill's marginal notes include citations of such ancient prose writers as Aristotle and Livy. An education that produced such learning could hardly fail to include Homer and Virgil, and I believe that Hill and Ford would have been as quick and accurate with a quotation from the *Aeneid* as Peter Smart. Indeed, I should not be surprised to learn that one of them gave Dryden the first volume of poetry we know he read, Joshua Sylvester's translation of Du Bartas's *Divine Weeks*.[76]

"A World of Words"

A Puritan translation of a Huguenot poem, *The Divine Weeks* was doctrinally unimpeachable. In the opening of the second day of the first week, the speaker is at pains to distinguish his work from that of secular love-poets:

> For, under th' hony of their learned Works
> A hatefull draught of deadly poyson lurks;
> Whereof (alas) Young spirits quaffe so deep,
> That, drunk with Love, their Reason fals asleep;
> . . . .
>   Therefore, for my part, I have vow'd to Heav'n
> Such wit and learning as my God hath giv'n;
> To write, to th' honour of my Maker dread,
> Verse that a Virgin without blush may read.
>
>   [I, ii, 30–33; 44–47]

His account of the seventh day includes a thoroughly Puritan description of proper activities for the Sabbath:

>   God would, that men should in a certain place
> *This-Day* assemble as before his face,
> Lending an humble and attentive ear
> To learn his great Name's dear-drad Loving Fear:
> He would, that there the faithfull Pastor should
> The Scripture's marrow from the bones unfould,
> That we might touch with fingers (as it were)
> The sacred secrets that are hidden there.
> For, though the *reading* of those holy lines
> In private Houses som-what move our minds;
> Doubtless, the Doctrin *preacht* doth deeper pierce,
> Proves more effectuall, and more weight it bears.
> He would, that there in holy Psalmes, we sing
> Shrill praise and thanks to our immortall King.
>
>   [I, vii, 422–35]

Some of the translator's additions to his French original would also have been attractive to the Titchmarsh Puritans; they include an execration against the Gunpowder conspirators (II, iii, 1230–1304) and a warning to England, characterizing the unreformed clergy as

> *Thy blind, dumb,* Idol-shepheards, *choak'd with steeples,*
> *That fleece thy Flocks, and do not feed thy Peoples.*

[I, ii, 941–42]

But for all the purity of Sylvester's Calvinist doctrine, his style does not display the "simplicity, sobriety, and measure" of "Calvinist aesthetics." The last couplet quoted makes use of a standard polemical image of the corrupt clergy as careless shepherds (developed more impressively in Milton's *Lycidas*), adds a pun on "idle" and "idol" that also appears frequently in Puritan pamphlets, and includes a grotesque and preposterous visual image of the clergy "choak'd with steeples." Such conflation of insufficiently related images is the fault Dryden discusses in the dedication to *The Spanish Fryar* (1681), where he admits his boyish fondness for Sylvester:

> An injudicious Poet who aims at Loftiness runs easily into the swelling puffie style, because it looks like Greatness. I remember, when I was a Boy, I thought inimitable *Spencer* a mean Poet in comparison of *Sylvester*'s Dubartas: and was rapt into an ecstasie when I read these lines:
> > Now, when the Winter's keener breath began
> > To Chrystallize the Baltick Ocean;
> > To glaze the Lakes, to bridle up the Floods,
> > And periwig with snow the bald-pate Woods.
> I am much deceiv'd if this be not abominable fustian, that is, thoughts and words ill sorted, and without the least relation to each other. [sig. a3r][77]

Fair enough. But with his usual disarming candor, Dryden concedes in the same preface that this kind of "fustian" often secures applause when spoken on the stage, and admits having indulged in it himself in some of his own early dramas. He may not have remembered that Sylvester had pictured a priest eating a steeple, but that image recurs in this very play: complaining about the corruption of Friar, Gomez asks, "Was ever man thus Priest-ridden? wou'd the Steeple of his Church were in his Belly: I am sure there's room for it" (II, pp. 25–26). If the Dryden of 1681, moving away from excess toward a more chastened and "natural" language, could cite Sylvester as an example of "thoughts and words ill sorted," he knew how to use such grotesquerie for comic effect, and he could also admit that the Dryden of 1641, curled up in a corner with Sylvester's poem, was "rapt into an ecstasie." We may be certain that ecstasy of this sort, a delight in language for its own sake, was not the response desired by the relative or clergyman who gave the boy the book.

Sylvester's style has been called "baroque" with considerable justice.[78] We may associate that label with the arts of Catholic Europe, but both the poet and the translator of the *Divine Weeks* were Protestants, and their faith did not prevent them from indulging in a fullness of scope, an exuberance of imagery, and a habit of amplification. The mature Dryden associated this kind of writing with the theatre, and recent scholars have concurred, locating the essence of the baroque style, for all the arts, in its "obsession with the underlying theatricality of life."[79] Predictably, the influence of Sylvester on Dryden is most apparent in the early poetry: in the multiplication of metaphors in the highly theatrical elegy for Lord Hastings, or in the straining after exotic language in

Astraea Redux or even *Annus Mirabilis*. The lasting impact on Dryden of the "ecstasie" he felt on first reading Sylvester is more apparent in attitudes than in verbal echoes. The linking of God's Creation and the human creative arts, which was habitual in Dryden's work throughout his career and common in the work of other poets from midcentury on, is already explicit in Sylvester's poem, published complete in 1605. Despite Puritan scruples about the arts, Sylvester's God is a *"great Architect of wonders,"* by whom the confusion of primal Time has been "confin'd" into an "ordred Dance." His Creation is compared to "a school," "a Stage," and "a Book in Folio,"[80] the last image particularly suggesting the folio editions in which Sylvester's poem appeared, which feature elaborate woodcuts, diagrams of the Trinity, and an exuberance of typography compatible with the poem's extravagant imagery. When the Creation is complete, Sylvester's God steps back to admire it like an artist stepping back from his canvas:

> The cunning *Painter*, that with curious care,
> Limning a Land-scape, various, rich, and rare,
> Hath set a-work, in all and every part,
> Invention, Judgement, Nature, Use and Art:
> And hath at length (t'immortalize his name)
> With weary Pencill perfected the same;
> Forgets his pains; and inly filled with glee,
> Still on his Picture gazeth greedily.
>
> [I, vii, 11–18]

Such passages doubtless provided a powerful antidote to the Puritan suspicion of the arts to which the boy Dryden had been exposed. Sylvester validates the arts in the most powerful possible way by using human creation as an analogue to divine Creation; he also acknowledges such secular motives as the "glee" that can fill the successful artist and the possibility that he may "immortalize his name," motives Dryden would acknowledge in his own candid prefaces. As a consequence of his unceasing amplification of his subject, Sylvester even has space to explore the technique of the arts, as in this revealing passage on the elements, which make up all creation by being endlessly shuffled and recombined, as a composer rearranges a few notes, or a poet the letters of the alphabet:

> They frame the various Forms, wherewith the face
> Of this faire World is so imbellishèd,
> As six sweet Notes, curiously varièd
> In skilfull Music, make an hundred kindes
> Of Heav'nly sounds, that ravish hardest mindes;
> And with Division (of a choice device)
> The Hearers' soules out at their ears intice:
> Or, as of twice-twelve *Letters, thus transpos'd,*
> *This world of Words is variously compos'd;*
> *And, of these Words, in divers order sow'n,*
> *This sacred Volume* that you read, is grow'n.
>
> [I, ii, 272–81]

Frontispiece of Joshua Sylvester's translation of the *Divine Weeks* of Du Bartas, folio edition of 1641.

In its sheer size alone, Sylvester's volume is a "world of Words," providing at many levels examples of the reordering of the materials described here. The front matter, for example, includes a poem to the King based on an anagram made from his name ("James Stuart" becomes "a just master"); a *corona* of connected sonnets to James, each enclosing the name of a muse, each employing as its first line the last line of the preceding sonnet; and a triangular shape-poem in which Sylvester declares his unworthiness to attempt a translation once begun by Sidney. The mature Dryden would jest at such techniques in *Mac Flecknoe*, where Flecknoe recommends that Shadwell "Leave writing Plays, and chuse for [his] command / Some peacefull Province in Acrostick Land" (ll. 205–06)," but one of the real distinctions of Dryden's poetry is its framing, its architectural sense of proportion, its ordering of material on a large scale. Dryden's verse-paragraphs, from the very beginning of his poetic career onward, are not only units of thought and rhetoric but units of form, balanced and ordered with a mathematical attention to symmetry. Yet this symmetry rarely calls attention to itself; its aim is coherence, not display. Dryden's achievement in framing his "various Forms" was to prove far more subtle than Sylvester's geometry, but it was probably Sylvester's work that first made him aware of ingenious ordering as an aspect of poetic craft. Looking at the clever, if artificial devices of Sylvester's courtly dedications, the boy in Titchmarsh was reaching back past the Platonizing, Puritan, broadly Renaissance view of the Word as idea to make contact with the Pythagorean, Catholic, broadly medieval view of the word as an ordering of letters, itself susceptible to mosaic, mathematical, and mysterious arrangement. Whoever gave Dryden Sylvester's book, hoping to reinforce with pious poetry the doctrine the boy was learning in his catechism, his family prayers, and the Sunday sermon, delivered him a Trojan horse.

If the idea of poetry as a legitimate and fascinating profession was powerfully implicit in Sylvester, it was entirely explicit in the works of the Puritan divine who succeeded Thomas Ford at Aldwincle, Nathaniel Whiting. By the time he published his own first poem, the elegy for Hastings (1649), Dryden had certainly read Whiting's *Le hore di recreatione, Or The Pleasant Historie of Albino and Bellama* (1637). Attempting to extract poetry from Hastings's death from smallpox, the schoolboy poet composed a particularly dreadful line: "So many Spots, like *naeves*, our *Venus* soil" (l. 55). Though borrowing such a line is no less a failure of taste than making it up, Dryden must have remembered Whiting's prefatory verses "To the Reader," which use similar language to apologize for the defects of the ensuing poem:

> The purest-boulted floure that is, has bran.
> *Venus* her *Naeue*, *Helen* her staine, nor can,
> I think these lines are censure-free.
>
> [sig. A4r][81]

Since Whiting's book also includes prefatory verses to the author by Dryden's uncle John Pickering, I suspect Dryden had seen the poem well before he went off to Westminster. Whiting's whereabouts between 1638 and 1645 are unknown, but since Pickering's undistinguished lines are addressed "to his friend" and speak of "how much I owe / To you," I should think it likely that Whiting spent time in Aldwincle before taking over as rector in 1653, by which time Dryden was at Cambridge.[82] But even if Dryden never met Whiting, his uncle surely owned a copy of *Albino and Bellama*, and a boy who was reading the Roman historian Polybius at ten could surely have managed Whiting's attractively risqué poem at twelve.[83]

Perhaps the initial attraction was the racy story, in which the smooth-faced monk Albino, searching for his beloved Bellama, gains entry to a nunnery disguised as a woman and systematically impregnates its entire population. Yet the author of this naughty trifle was ejected from Aldwincle in 1662 for refusing to conform to the Established Church, and licensed in 1672 as a nonconformist preacher. Whiting's career as a poetic Puritan provides another example of the danger of stereotypes, and the arguments for poetry in his "Vindication of Poesie," a dream vision that follows the narrative poem, echo those used by Sir Philip Sidney and anticipate those used by John Dryden.

Despite Plato's banishing of the poets, Whiting invokes the authority of ancient philosophy:

> The first Philosophie that Fame ere knew,
> Was honourd with the name of Poetrie.

In his own philosophical and theological poems, Dryden would demonstrate his belief that poetry was the highest mode of argument, once alleging that "Religion was first taught in Verse (which the laziness or dulness of succeeding Priesthood, turned afterward into Prose)" (X, 109). Like Sylvester, Whiting links the human creative arts with God's creation:

> The Greek [language] . . .
> . . . calles all that which takes not essence by
> A matter pre-existent, Poesie.
> So makes the world a Poem, and by this
> The great creator a great Poet is.

Though clumsily stated here, this principle informs the opening of Dryden's "Song for St. Cecilia's Day, 1687," in which the "tuneful voice" organizes primal chaos into harmonious order; in the hands of a great poet, that standard idea could sing. Whiting also invokes Old Testament authority for poetry, using the obvious example of King David the Psalmist:

> The Regall Prophet was a true born Poet
> As to the life his well-tun'd meeters show it,
> Compos'd to musicke by that holy man,
> Ere *Hopkins* and *Sternhold* knew how to scan.

Dryden's use of the story of David, like his reference to "*Tom Sternhold's . . . Rhimes*," would prove far more memorable than anything in Whiting's work, but we may imagine his interest in both topics beginning with his reading of Whiting's book. The claim for the precedence of poetry over painting, which we have detected elsewhere in Puritan polemic, and which Dryden would express in those marvelously comic lines to Kneller, appears as well in Whiting:

> I might be infinite, should I but show
> For what grave Arts the world to Poets owe.
> *Apelles* had not been without *Parnasse*.

[sig. H5v]

None of these ideas is original, striking, or well expressed, but finding such ideas in the work of a Puritan divine is significant. As we imagine Dryden responding not only to *Albino and Bellama* but to the spirited defense of poetry that frames it, encountering for the first time ideas about eloquence that he would fulfill in his own career, we should also revise our sense of the Puritan movement as monolithic and unbending in its opposition to the arts. Like other political and religious movements, then and now, Puritanism was a loose alliance of people sharing certain class interests, aims, and prejudices. If Thomas Hill represents a kind of center, there was room at the extremes for the antinomian Bible-burner and the witty author of Italianate romance. The emergence of a poet like Dryden, with his sensitivity to art in all forms and his exquisite taste, from a Puritan boyhood in a tiny Northamptonshire village need not be considered a victorious Oedipal struggle against the bigotry of his parents. Far from it. His village and family nurtured his verbal talents, feeding him with many kinds of "word-milke." If he squirmed while sitting through Hill's stern sermons, he could look forward to reading Polybius's exciting account of the Punic wars, with its elephants and sea-battles; Sylvester's all-inclusive "world of words," with its promise of poetic fame; and even Whiting's romantic narrative, with its appeal to boyish curiosity about sex. And when his teachers and relatives recognized that his abilities were extraordinary, they sent him to the finest available school, Westminster, to sit at the feet of the most famous schoolmaster in the country, Richard Busby, even though they knew full well that Busby was an Arminian Royalist.

❯❯❯ CHAPTER TWO ❮❮❮

Westminster School
1644–1650

Learning and Loyalty: Westminster under Busby

For a lad of perhaps thirteen,[1] accustomed to the tiny confines of a Northamptonshire village, London must have been overwhelming, though Dryden would certainly have heard accounts of the wonders of the city from his many relatives who had spent time at the Inns of Court, including his father and several of his Pickering cousins. Country gentry like the Drydens and Pickerings often maintained rented establishments in London, and though Charles I's decision to rule without a Parliament for more than a decade took away one incentive for seasonal residence in London, the rapid events of the 1640s drew people connected with Dryden to the capital for long periods of time. When the Short Parliament began its momentous proceedings in 1640, the two members for Northamptonshire were Dryden's uncle Sir John Dryden and his cousin Sir Gilbert Pickering (III); both men returned for the Long Parliament and took an active part in its work for the next thirteen years. The Reverend Thomas Hill, his local parson, came to London in 1641 as a member of a committee investigating liturgical innovations; in 1643, he took his seat as one of the original members of the Westminster Assembly and began preaching regularly at Westminster Abbey and St. Martin's in the Fields.[2] Any one of these men would have been aware of the excellence of the King's School at Westminster and its extraordinary Headmaster, Richard Busby; any one of them might have encouraged Dryden's parents to send him to Westminster, offered to look after the boy, or provided lodging for him. Even with such family support, however, the young Dryden had to adjust to surroundings much more stimulating and challenging than any he had ever known, in a city that would be his home during his entire adult career.

Perhaps his family decided to send him to Westminster for his own safety. In the "Epistle Dedicatory" to a sermon preached in 1648, Thomas Hill thanks Richard Foxton of Cambridge for his aid and comfort "in 1643, when Providence cast mee for some time amongst you, *the sons of violence* having forced mee from the place I then had in *North-Hampton*-shire."[3] Since the summer of 1643 saw some notable Royalist victories, I take it that Hill was unable to make his way back to Titchmarsh from London. The capital, however, remained firmly in the hands of Parliament from the day Charles left it in 1642; for the Dryden family, uncertain about what the wars might bring to Northamptonshire, the relative stability of a school in London for their eldest son would have been attractive. In November 1645, the family connection with the school became stronger: Sir John Dryden was named to the Parliamentary committee appointed to supervise the school and elect the King's Scholars, a small group of special boys who had the privilege of living in the school and received stipends for two or three years before standing for election to either Christ Church, Oxford or Trinity College, Cambridge. Dryden held one of these prized scholarships, but we need not conclude that his uncle's influence was decisive. Although there is evidence that the "major elections," in which King's Scholars were chosen for the universities, were subject to political interest, the "minor elections," known as "challenges," were the most genuinely competitive admissions process among English schools of the period. A boy had to have been at school for at least a year, normally boarding outside, in order to challenge for a place as a King's Scholar; John Locke, who came to the school in 1647, did not succeed in the challenge until 1650. Dryden's success in the challenge and his eventual admission to Trinity as "Captain of his election," ranking at the head of that year's group from Westminster, suggest what we would expect from his later career: a talent for academic work, and serious application to it.[4]

The importance of Westminster School in the intellectual life of the seventeenth century can scarcely be exaggerated. James I enjoyed cracking jokes and capping Latin verses with his Scholars, who were traditionally allowed to hear speeches in the House of Commons and the law courts. Archbishop Laud, who installed Busby as Master, took the trouble to copy out in his own hand an account of the Westminster curriculum by a man who had been in the sixth and seventh forms in the 1620s; Anthony Ashley Cooper, first Earl of Shaftesbury and Dryden's bitter foe, copied out in his own hand an extremely detailed account of the readings and exercises performed by the second form in the 1670s, when he was making inquiries about a school for his grandson. Not only are these documents important sources for reconstructing the Westminster curriculum in the 1640s, when Dryden was a student, but their very existence confirms the interest taken in the school by powerful men of all shades of political opinion. Laud and Shaftesbury may stand as polar opposites in the political debates of the seventeenth century, and they clearly had different ideas about education, but both acknowledged the leading position of Westminster, as did Thomas Hill, who described the school, in the "Epistle Dedicatory" to the sermon he preached before the Parliamentary committee in 1648, as "a most *famous Nursery* . . . where many *Parliament men, Nobles*, and *Gentry* in their tender yeares, may be either seasoned with *good*, or desperately leavened with *evill*" (sig. A2r).

Richard Busby, who taught Christopher Wren, John Locke, Robert South, Robert Hooke, Matthew Prior, and a host of judges and bishops, was Headmaster of Westminster from 1638 until his death in 1695; his unbroken tenure bears testimony to the

Portrait of Richard Busby by John Riley, ca. 1690.

high value placed on education by the various groups who ruled England in those years. Although Busby initially gained his position because his politics and theological beliefs were in keeping with those of Archbishop Laud, the Parliamentary committee retained him, despite those beliefs, because of his sheer excellence. Under Charles II and James II, he was an honored and important man, carrying the eagle holding the oil for Charles's coronation and the orb for James's; unlike his pupil Dryden, he did not lose his post in the Glorious Revolution, presumably because the victorious supporters of William III in 1688, like the supporters of Cromwell in 1649, valued his pedagogy sufficiently to overlook his politics.

Busby's initial appointment in 1638, however, was the result of a Star Chamber proceeding of just the kind that outraged those opposed to Charles I's personal rule. Lambert Osbaldeston, then Headmaster, wrote a letter referring to someone as a "little medling *Hocus-Pocus*," and Archbishop Laud, who had the letter intercepted, read those words as a reference to himself. He brought Osbaldeston up on charges before the Star Chamber, where he was sentenced to "stand in the Pillory in the *Dean's Yard*, before his own school, and his Ears to be only nailed to the Pillory." Osbaldeston escaped the execution of this grotesque sentence by slipping away in the crowd and remaining in hiding until the Long Parliament arrested Laud.[5] His replacement was Busby, who had come to the attention of Charles and Laud in 1636, when he played the leading role of Cratander in William Cartwright's *The Royal Slave*, presented before the King and Queen at Oxford. Contemporary reports give high praise to Busby's performance in this stern, high-minded part,[6] but he was to make a more lasting impression in his real-life role as Headmaster of Westminster. Even after Osbaldeston came out of hiding, even after Laud was executed, even after Parliament appointed its supervisory committee, even after Busby lost his ecclesiastical sinecure as a Prebendary of the cathedral at Wells, no one seems to have considered removing him as Headmaster.

Even Thomas Hill, who evidently knew of Busby's Arminian and Royalist sentiments, praised the Master while criticizing the school. His "Epistle" makes a number of predictably Puritan suggestions: he advocates releasing the boys from classes to attend daily morning services (at which he had been one of the regular preachers), proposes that the school appoint a catechist to instill correct doctrine, derides the traditional Latin grace in the dining hall as "Popish," and complains obscurely about "some corner in the Schoole full of Leaven which spreads most unhappily: Your inquisition after, purgation of it, likewise the removing of it utterly . . . would be of singular use. . . . Much of this Leaven lurks amongst youths in the seventh Forme" (sig. A3r). From the larger context, we may infer that "Leaven" is a metaphor for the kind of sexual sophistication an eighteen-year-old seventh-former might easily acquire in London and spread to younger youths, but it may also stand for the Royalist attitudes most likely to be found in boys who had come to Westminster before the appointment of the committee, attitudes encouraged (as Hill well knew) by a Royalist Headmaster. Nonetheless, Hill praises Busby in the same "Epistle" as "both very able and industrious," apparently believing that his pedagogical excellence could be separated from his political and theological influence: "were the *Moralls*, and *Spiritualls* in *Westminster-Schoole* answerable to the *Intellectuals*," he declares, "it would be inferiour . . . to none in England" (sig. A2v). In deciding to send Dryden to Westminster, Hill and Dryden's family in Titchmarsh reckoned that the quality of education to be had there outweighed the danger that the boy would be exposed to theological and political ideas unlike those in which they had reared him; by leaving Busby in office, the Parliamentary committee made a similar judgment on a larger scale. Both calculations were wrong: Dryden's elegy for Hastings, written one year after Hill's sermon, shows how thoroughly his education had been leavened with Royalism, and the surprising resurgence of high-church Anglicanism after the Restoration was led by men schooled under Busby.

Even during the Interregnum, Busby was capable of fierce determination in pursuit of his own beliefs. In 1656, the Puritan Master of Christ Church, Dr. John Owen, attempted to place a different kind of influence in the school by arranging the appointment of Edward Bagshawe as Second Master. Bagshawe, who had been at school with Dryden, retained the Puritan opinions of their shared Northamptonshire gentry background. Busby found fault with his keeping his hat on in church, manipulated the school regulations to force him to teach only the very young boys, and finally resorted to the extreme tactic of sending some older boys to dismantle the stairs leading to his chamber. After a series of frantic appeals to the Parliamentary committee, Bagshawe finally resigned, defeated by Busby's persistence, and by the unwillingness of the committee to interfere with the Headmaster's control of his school, even for the sake of an earnest young Puritan.[7]

After the Restoration, many of Busby's former pupils found occasion to praise his loyalty. One of the leaders of the Anglican resurgence, Robert South, who had been just one year behind Dryden at school, took up this topic in a sermon written to be preached to a gathering of Old Westminsters, describing "an able, well-principled schoolmaster" as "one of the most meritorious subjects in any prince's dominions" and his school as "a seminary of loyalty and a nursery of allegiance." South then recalls his own troubled school days, when Westminster was

> so untaintedly loyal, that I can truly and knowingly aver, that in the very worst of times (in which it was my lot to be a member of it) we really were King's scholars as well as called so. Nay, upon the very day, that black and eternally infamous day of the king's murder, I myself heard, and am now a witness, that the king was publicly prayed for in this school but an hour or two (at most) before his sacred head was struck off.

Even after that execution, says South, Busby counteracted the strong Puritan sermons then being preached at Westminster Abbey by teaching "other doctrines in the school," which "proved an effectual antidote against the poison."[8] Another distinguished churchman, Bishop Edward Wetenhall, wrote a dedication to Busby explaining how the "prejudices" against church music he had brought to school had been altered by the example of his schoolmaster: "If a man of such real Devotion, as I knew You to be of, would keep an Organ for sacred Use, even when it was interdicted and of dangerous consequence, there was certainly more reason for it, and serviceableness in it, than I apprehended."[9] And Dryden himself, in a passage praising John Dolben, Dean of Westminster after the Restoration, links the school with intellectual learning, political loyalty, and support for the arts:

> The Prophets Sons by such example led,
> To Learning and to Loyalty were bred:
> For *Colleges* on bounteous Kings depend,
> And never Rebell was to Arts a friend.
>
> [*Absalom and Achitophel*, ll. 870–73]

Just as Wetenhall, seeing the pious Busby at the organ, could no longer dismiss
that instrument as immoral, so Dryden, hearing from the enormously learned and
personally magnetic Busby ideas about politics, religion, poetry, and music that contradicted the verities of Puritan Titchmarsh, could hardly remain impervious. For the
bookish lad from Northamptonshire, Busby's wide-ranging erudition may have been
even more impressive than the threat of his notorious birch. He was a man who owned
more books than Dryden had ever seen; a man who knew what could be known about
languages, sciences, mathematics, and the arts; a man with a commanding presence,
who had acted before the King and could quiet a room with his penetrating stare; a man
with courage enough to defy the edicts of Parliament a few hundred yards from their
chambers; a man committed to excellence, whose demanding personality also had a
softer side. In 1656, a poor Puritan undergraduate came down from Oxford to speak
with Busby about a place at Westminster for his younger brother. After the interview, he
wrote to his father:

> When I was wth Mr Busby he did speake soe loveinly unto me and wth soe much feileing
> of my necessity as if he had knowne our condicon, truely he spooke unto me as kindely
> as an Indulgent father could speake to a Dutifull sonne y^t had escaped many dangers
> and had arrived safely then unto his deare father, this did soe much amase me, that I
> was in a greate wonder as I came home, and truely I could scarce containe my selfe as I
> came home from weepeing to consider how god had dealt wth me.[10]

The compassion Busby showed to this anonymous writer, attested to in other
anecdotes as well, served as a counterpoise to his better-known propensity for flogging.
The brutality of the flogging, however, was no myth; even South, in the sermon that
praises Westminster and Busby, includes some pointed cautions against "excesses of
the lash." The psychologically potent combination of strictness and indulgence might
help account for the deference shown to Busby in later years by the scientist Robert
Hooke, who completed two architectural projects for his old Master; by the preacher
Philip Henry, who maintained close relations even after becoming a nonconformist;
and by the poet Dryden, who sent two of his sons to Westminster and wrote respectful
letters to Busby about them.[11] In a late letter to Charles Montagu, who had experienced
Busby's instruction in a much later era, Dryden uses flogging as a metaphor for the
correction of poetry: "These verses [the poem "To my Honour'd Kinsman"] had
waited on you with the former, but they then wanted that Correction, which I have since
given them. . . . I am now in feare that I have purgd them out of their Spirit; as our
Master Busby, usd to whip a Boy so long, till he made him a confirmd Blockhead"
(*Letters*, p. 120).

The metaphor is as significant as the testimony; Dryden evidently believed in both
kinds of "Correction" but recognized that both could be carried to unreasonable
excess. His adult attitude was not merely a memory of his boyish awe for a man who had
the power to punish or forgive, nor even the recognition that Busby's opinions lay
behind political and artistic positions he later made his own. Dryden also believed that
the intellectual "correction" provided by the literary curriculum at Westminster, far

from purging him out of his spirit, had helped him develop his poetic facility. He said as much in a recently discovered poem to the grammarian Lewis Maidwell, who had also studied under Busby:

> Let then our Reverend Master be ador'd
> And all our gratefull Penns his praise Record;
> I dare not name my selfe, yet what I am
> From his examples and his precepts came.
> Our Noblest witts from his instructive care
> Have grac'd the Senate and have judg'd the Bar;
> But, above all, the Muses sacred Band
> Have been transplanted from his Eden Land.[12]

The metaphor of Busby's Westminster as a paradise for poets may seem extravagant, but even writers who had not studied under Busby recognized his unique abilities. Richard Steele, himself a Charterhouse boy, spoke with envy of those fortunate enough to have attended Westminster under Busby, emphasizing their unusual imaginative capacity: "Those of great Parts, who have passed through his Instruction, have such a peculiar Readiness of Fancy and Delicacy of Taste, as is seldom found in Men educated elsewhere."[13] Dryden's "Readiness of Fancy," apparent in the ease with which he crowded his poems with metaphors, and his "Delicacy of Taste," apparent in the confidence with which he passed judgments on drama, poetry, music, and painting, were surely consequences of his "great Parts," his natural talents; but they also owed something to the instruction of Busby, which honed and refined those talents, preparing Dryden for a life of writing.

The Education of a Poet

In the absence of a document describing the Westminster curriculum at exactly the time Dryden passed through it, we must reconstruct the regimen by comparing the earlier and later sources we do have. The document in Laud's handwriting is well known, and accounts of Dryden's education have often simply paraphrased it, but the daily routine it describes is that followed under Osbaldeston or his predecessor Wilson;[14] from what we know of Busby's personality, we may safely assume that he imposed important changes. The document in Shaftesbury's hand dates from the late 1670s, and describes only the routine of the second form, but it has the great advantage of describing readings and exercises prescribed by Busby himself, and its accuracy is confirmed by a briefer outline of the entire curriculum dictated to the founders of Dulwich College in 1684 by "Mr ffrowick, that had been Usher under Dr Busby for severall yeares."[15] Of course, we cannot assume that the later sources represent the curriculum of Dryden's day either; Frowick's outline, for example, refers to "ye greek liturgy by Dr Duport" as a set text for the fourth form, and that book was not published until 1665. But two other pieces of evidence, closer in time to Dryden's school days than any of the others, suggest that there was motion toward something like the curriculum of the Frowick and Shaftesbury documents by the early 1640s. Four small notebooks were recently discovered under the flooring of a room in Trinity College, Cambridge; they belonged to Francis Gregory, elected to Trinity from Westminster in 1642, and include extensive notes on Ovid and Terence, two authors assigned in the Shaftesbury and Frowick documents, but not mentioned in the Laud document. Harvard holds an early seventeenth-century printed text of the *Anthologia Graeca*, the flyleaf of which has a number of signatures by John Dryden; no Greek lyric poetry is mentioned in the Laud document, but Frowick speaks of "ye Anthologia made for the use of Westminster school," which was a later edition of the Greek anthology.[16]

Besides establishing the fact that Busby had made changes in the prescribed authors by the time Dryden came to school, the Gregory notebooks also show that he had made changes in the method of instruction. The education described in the Laud document is primarily oral:

> We made *verses ex tempore* lat: and gr: upon 2 or 3 sev: theames. . . .
> We had the practise of *Dictamina*. one of the 5.th forme being call^d out to translate some sentences of an unexpect^d Author (ex tempore) *into good Latin*. . . .
> That *Lesson . . . appointed for that day . . . was to be exactlie gone thorough*, by *construing* & other grammatical waies, *examining all the Rhetoricall figures*, . . . Then were they enjoyned to committe that to memorie against the next morning.

Not surprisingly, Busby's teaching retained versions of all these exercises. Hill's "Epistle," published while Dryden was in the sixth form, records Busby's desire that members of the Parliamentary committee visit the school and set themes for extemporaneous versification, doubtless in Latin and Greek. The Frowick document lists "a dictamen, which is a translation of some English Authour into Lattin," among the exercises of the second form. And the Shaftesbury document establishes the continued practice of memorization: "In the afternoone they repeate all they learn'd in Esope, Ovid, Terence & Martiall." But the later documents also describe many more written exercises than the Laud document; the sentence just quoted, for example, continues by describing the preparation for Saturday: "they transcribe in a fayre book all the corrections, w:^ch they writ the day before; and all the Latine words w:^ch they looked in their dictionaryes that week and all the phrases yt were observed to them, in any of their Lessons or makeing their Latines." Surely each of the Gregory notebooks began as such a "fayre book." They contain careful lists of vocabulary in Latin and Greek, rules of rhetoric, and renderings of English phrases into ornate Ciceronian Latin—doubtless useful when composing the formal orations delivered at Election time, a custom described in the Laud document and verified by several complete speeches in the Gregory notebooks.

The mature Dryden retained many kinds of mental discipline encouraged by this regimen. As Congreve testifies, "his Reading had been very extensive," and he was "very happy in a Memory tenacious of everything that he had read."[17] The tenacity of that "happy" memory, apparent to anyone who has ever attempted to track Dryden's borrowings, was unquestionably improved by the relentless oral repetition that had been a continuous feature of education at Westminster from its medieval beginnings, the kind of repetition that Pope attacks in *Dunciad* IV, where the ghost of Busby, a "dreadful wand" of birch in his hand, expounds the virtues of memorization:

> Plac'd at the door of Learning, youth to guide,
> We never suffer it to stand too wide.
> To ask, to guess, to know, as they commence,
> As Fancy opens the quick springs of Sense,
> We ply the Memory, we load the brain,
> Bind rebel Wit, and double chain on chain,
> Confine the thought, to exercise the breath;
> And keep them in the pale of Words till death.
>
> [ll. 153–60]

Brilliant as they are, these lines are not entirely fair to Busby, who evidently valued creativity. The real Busby told Hill that he liked to have his students asked to versify because that exercise would "incredibly *whet* up and *raise* their *Phansies*" (sig. A3r), and it was "a peculiar Readiness of Fancy" that Steele identified as the distinguishing feature of old Westminsters.

Busby also helped his students develop their invention by modifying the oral and extemporaneous nature of the old curriculum, laying a greater stress on preparation and written work. As the Shaftesbury document puts it, "he tells them some tyme before the lines he would have construed that they may have some tyme to look in the Dictionary the words they know not which they are to write downe in a paper." The purpose of such exercises, more likely to be realized in the case of a genius like Dryden than in the case of a "Confirmed Blockhead," was to encourage eloquence, not merely by "load[ing] the brain" with memorized material, but also by teaching the student how to collect useful written material on which to draw in his compositions. By encouraging his students to keep notebooks listing striking words and apt phrases, Busby helped men like Dryden establish the habit of note-taking, surely essential to a writer producing the quantities of verse, drama, and prose that Dryden was to publish. Even Dryden's enemies bear testimony to that habit: Mr. Bayes in Buckingham's *The Rehearsal*, who is meant as a caricature of Dryden, explains that he uses a commonplace book filled with useful quotations from ancient and modern authors to speed the "business" of invention;[18] though intended satirically, this description of Dryden's working methods is surely closer to the truth than Pope's caricature of Busby. For those less well endowed than Dryden, the continued emphasis on rote learning and the quick recourse to the birch may have made Busby's Westminster a frightening and stultifying place, but for Dryden and others of "great Parts," the schooling there involved more than discipline and the acquisition of inert facts; the success of Busby's best students in all the professions suggests that he had a special ability to stimulate talented minds, to teach them how to think.

Like most great teaching, Busby's looks fairly ordinary when reduced to a series of exercises and assignments. The practice of translation, for example, which was to support Dryden in his old age, was central to the Westminster routine. We know from

Dryden's own testimony that his school exercises included translating Persius and other Latin authors into English verse,[19] and the various documents on the curriculum describe exercises in translating English into Latin, Greek into Latin, and Latin into Greek. Even within a single language, exercises often involved recasting a given text in a new form: "sometimes," says the Frowick document, "any oration in any Historian is turned into verse," and "sometimes they turn Horace his Odes into different sort of verses."[20] Perhaps Dryden's mature facility in a wide range of forms, which sets him apart from so many other writers, owed something to this early practice: "he was," according to Congreve and most later critics, "equally excellent in Verse, and in Prose";[21] he wrote with impressive ease in a variety of poetic meters; and he was not only one of the finest translators among English poets, but an important theorist of translation.[22] Even when composing in English, he imposed upon that language the rigorous syntax of an inflected tongue, as he himself confessed:

> I am often put to a stand, in considering whether what I write be the Idiom of the Tongue, or false Grammar, and nonsence couch'd beneath that specious name of *Anglicisme*; and have no other way to clear my doubts, but by translating my *English* into *Latine*, and thereby trying what sence the words will bear in a more stable language. ["Epistle Dedicatory" to *Troilus and Cressida*; XIII, 222]

Dryden's interest in the English language is apparent in this passage, in his frequent attempts to organize a British Academy on the French model,[23] and in his description of himself, late in life, as "a Man, who have done my best to improve the Language & Especially the Poetry" (*Letters*, p. 123). Although Busby was a famous classicist, he may also have encouraged this interest in native eloquence. As the Shaftesbury document shows, he took the trouble to compose an English grammar for his younger pupils; that kind of emphasis on the vernacular had not been a normal feature of English schools before, though there is some evidence that Osbaldeston had also encouraged serious study of English composition.[24] Certainly Westminster had a long tradition of producing poets; three of the poets whose influence is detectable in Dryden's early verse were old Westminsters: Ben Jonson, whose schooling at Westminster under William Camden constituted his entire formal education; Abraham Cowley, who published his first volume of poetry while still at school and dedicated it to Osbaldeston; and William Cartwright, another Osbaldeston student, whose Oxford play brought Busby into prominence.[25] A modern historian of the school has gone so far as to claim that "the bent of poetical feeling, which [Samuel] Johnson oddly called metaphysical, had its home in Westminster, and found a fostering spirit in Osbaldeston."[26] If this claim is a trifle extravagant, given the absence of Donne and others from the list of old Westminsters, there is nonetheless a discernible line of poetic development stretching from Ben Jonson through Cowley (whom Dryden called "the Darling of my youth") and Cartwright (whom Jonson called "my son") to the young Dryden, especially the schoolboy Dryden of the Hastings elegy. In allowing Dryden to write that poem in English, while the other Westminster boys who published elegies in the same volume wrote theirs in Latin, Busby was announcing in print the continuation of the line of Westminster poets; by drawing on the seasonal and astronomical imagery of the Jonsonian masque, emulating the fanciful multiplication of metaphor so typical of Cowley, and associating virtue with nobility and learning in the manner of Cartwright, Dryden was self-consciously taking his place in that succession.

Not all the lessons to be learned at Westminster were poetic, or even intellectual. With such formidable schoolmates as John Locke, Robert South, and the notorious Bagshawe, Dryden surely learned much about competition. The Laud document records the custom of rewarding those who made the best verses with money, and there is no reason to believe that this practice had ceased under Busby. Indeed, a good deal of money seems to have changed hands in the other direction: every boy was expected to give the Master at least a guinea at Christmas, and Locke's account books include entries recording his purchase of "A paire of gloves for Mr Busby" (eight shillings) and "A New Yr's gift for Mr Busby" (one pound).[27] Money also passed between students; according to Thomas Hill, some seventh-formers abused their status as Monitors by forcing their juniors "to *sell* their *Books* sometimes to serve their *Lusts*" (sig. A3r). If all these cash payments strike us as odd, they were a suitable preparation for the world in which Dryden would have to live, the thoroughly venal regime of Charles II, in which votes, offices, fine ladies, and poetic talents were distinctly for sale. If the floggings that unquestionably took place seem brutal, they too had analogues in the adult world: torture, branding, hanging, disembowelling, and the kind of privately sponsored violence of which Dryden was later a victim in Rose Alley. If Dryden was absorbing some classical and Christian ideals from his schoolwork, he was doing so in an environment where such ideals were tempered by the need to compete and survive.

In the world outside the school, ideals were proving costly for men on both sides. By the time Dryden arrived at Westminster, Cartwright was dead of camp fever in Oxford, and Cowley had followed the Queen into exile in France. In 1645, Busby's patron, Archbishop Laud, was executed, and Dryden's cousin, Colonel John Pickering, who had fought for Parliament in several major battles, also died of camp fever. We cannot know how Dryden responded to either of these deaths—one the public and dramatic beheading of a man bitterly opposed by his family but strongly supported by his Headmaster, the other the loss of a cousin whom he might have admired as a boy, but who had become so consumed by his religious fury that even his own troops regarded him as a fanatic.[28] Nor can we know how he responded to the stirring events surrounding him in London, whether he attended the often heated debates of the Long Parliament, witnessed Laud's execution, or saw one of the illegal theatrical performances at the Red Bull, which stubbornly defied the order of 1642 banning public plays, despite raids and assaults by Parliamentary soldiers.[29] On any Thursday afternoon, if he chose to walk east toward the City, rather than west or south into what was then open country, Dryden could have purchased newspapers, sermons, and pamphlets reporting on and responding to the progress of the wars. These included the Royalist *Mercurius Aulicus*, published in Oxford by the brilliant propagandist John Berkenhead, later Dryden's friend, and the Parliamentary *Mercurius Britanicus*, devoted to the task of discrediting *Aulicus*.[30]

While Dryden apparently had some knowledge of these ephemeral publications, since his mature satires draw on conventions developed in Royalist propaganda, the

Execution of Charles I in 1649 as shown in a contemporary Dutch print.

impact of such journalism on his early work is not so immediately apparent as that of the classical and English poetry he had evidently read before composing his elegy for Hastings. Even an omnivorous reader might have found it difficult to keep up with contemporary pamphleteering while satisfying the strenuous requirements of Busby's curriculum and preparing to stand for election to the university. But some of the major events of the late 1640s were too close to ignore: when Colonel Pride stationed himself outside Parliament in December 1648, and purged those members still opposed to the will of the Army, he was standing within sight of Westminster School; the next month, Charles was on trial for his life, with Dryden's cousin Gilbert Pickering serving as one of the judges; and on 30 January 1649, to the horror of the Royalists and the amazement of all, the King stepped onto the scaffold in front of Inigo Jones's splendid Banqueting House in Whitehall, ten minutes' walk from the school where his Scholars, including John Dryden, were saying their usual prayers for his life and health.

The Promise of the Elegy for Hastings

Five months later, a promising young Royalist named Henry Hastings, who was probably Dryden's Westminster schoolmate,[31] died of the smallpox on his wedding eve. Dryden's poem "Upon the Death of the Lord Hastings," his contribution to a memorial volume called *Lachrymae Musarum*, allows us to glimpse his response to recent public events as well as his assimilation of his literary education. The poem has some obvious juvenile weaknesses: much of the imagery is conceited in the manner of Cowley, especially in the notorious passage on the smallpox, and many of the lines are metrically clogged with awkward contractions.[32] But it also provides, in its organization and rhetoric, some tentative indications of the poetic skill that would be apparent in Dryden's later work. If the schoolboy poet was far too susceptible to the temptations of cleverness, he had the good sense to organize his poem around the most universal themes suggested by the particular death of young Hastings, and to forge connections between that death, the public events of the 1640s, and the Renaissance cultural traditions of which his schooling had made him aware.

The opening lines illustrate Dryden's skill and betray his uncertainty:

> Must Noble *Hastings* Immaturely die,
> (The Honour of his ancient Family?)
> Beauty and Learning thus together meet,
> To bring a *Winding* for a *Wedding-sheet?*
>
> [ll. 1–4]

Dominating the first line in length and accent, the word "Immaturely" announces the poem's most telling theme, the irony that death should fall upon the young while the old survive. The secondary themes, "Beauty and Learning," appear as personified figures holding a winding sheet, like statues on a baroque funerary monument. But those three universal themes, to which Dryden will wisely devote most of his attention, share space here with his polite if parenthetical acknowledgment of the importance of Hastings's family, and with the particular irony of Hastings's death on his wedding eve, expressed in the puerile play on "*Winding*" and "*Wedding.*"

The opening question leads into a series of increasingly insistent rhetorical questions, an appropriate if obvious way to develop the theme of learning. By breathlessly questioning the worth of acquiring "*Vertue,*" "*Grace,*" and "*Art*" through "*Merit,*" "*Discipline,*" "*Labour,*" and "*Study,*" Dryden indirectly credits Hastings with all those attributes; he also dramatizes an inadequate and immature response to a classmate's death: "shall Art / Make us more Learned, onely to depart?" (ll. 7–8). The implication that Hastings's death was a warning *against* study might have been comforting for adolescents in the process of having Greek grammar flogged into them by Busby, but Dryden, despite his own adolescence, does not draw that conclusion. In the last couplet of this section, the shrill complainer yields to a wiser speaker, who describes "Our *Noble Youth*" in the third person, as if he were older, and invalidates the boyish questions with a stern *reductio ad absurdum*:

> Our *Noble Youth* now have pretence to be
> Dunces securely, Ign'rant healthfully.
>
> [ll. 13–14][33]

After that cadence comes a shift in tone; direct praise of Hastings's linguistic skills leads, through allusions to Alexander the Great and the gift of tongues at Pentecost, to a compressed statement of the theme of youth and age:

> Nature gave him, a Childe, what Men in vain
> Oft strive, by Art though further'd, to obtain.
>
> [ll. 25–26]

The most successful sections of this poem develop the oppositions between the four chiastically ordered nouns in this couplet—oppositions relevant to both Hastings and Dryden. Hastings, a child, has died as men do, on the eve of taking on the adult role of husband. He cannot naturally father children of his own, though the ending will comfort his "*Virgin-Widow*" by claiming that his soul can still father arts and virtues. Dryden, a child now taking on the adult role of poet, is writing a Royalist poem in opposition to the political beliefs of his natural father, though calculated to please his surrogate artistic father, Busby. His poem draws life from tensions that would continue to engage his mind throughout his career: the tension between generations, central to *Absalom and Achitophel* and virtually all the plays; and the tension between Art and Nature, a leading problem of the criticism, richly reflected in such mature works as the poem to Godfrey Kneller and the elegy for Anne Killigrew.

Dryden develops the theme of physical beauty with abstract imagery drawn from astronomy, an interest that remained with Dryden all his life, and a clear instance of the influence of Busby, who taught Aratus to fourth-formers, and whose library contained works by Theodosius, Ptolemy, Tycho Brahe, and Kepler.[34] The student poet's desire to display his learning makes the lines developing a comparison between Hastings's body and the "Sphear" of Archimedes coldly intellectual, but the tone soon shifts again: having made Hastings into a heavenly body, Dryden challenges "learned *Ptolomy*," by 1649 a somewhat discredited astronomer, to measure "this Hero's Altitude" (ll. 39–40). I suspect this is a bad joke for the boys of Westminster; Dryden will later refer to Hastings as "one so young, so small" (l. 74), and he may mean to undermine the already light-hearted picture of a Ptolemy unable to find the altitude of the star Hastings by reminding his classmates of the ease with which a real tailor could measure the height of the real Hastings. He would learn to manage such comic moments within a serious poem more deftly by the Killigrew ode, and there can be little doubt that such jokes weaken the Hastings elegy; but the habits of mind they reveal, a restlessness about maintaining decorum and a temptation to undercut his own seriousness, have been frequently detected in Dryden's adult poems and plays by modern critics.[35]

In the ensuing lines on the disease, Hastings becomes an analogue for Charles I, an identification prepared by restating the theme of youth and age in terms of light; now Hastings is a "Ray, (which shone / More bright i' th' Morn, then others beam at Noon)" (ll. 43–44). Not only is the opposition between generations here collapsed into a contrast between "Morn" and "Noon," but the imagery of stars, beams, and rays had long been established as the imagery of monarchy—not least by the Jacobean and Caroline masques, where that imagery could become spectacle through lighting and machinery. Charles I, himself only five feet four inches tall, was magnified at his masques by being placed in the highest and best seat, and magnified verbally by sun imagery, not only in the poetry of the masques, but in the prose of *Eikon Basilike*, the tract claiming to record his meditations while awaiting his execution, which ran through sixty editions in the year preceding this poem. Moving closer to the political situation, Dryden presents "The Nations Sin" as the veiling or shrouding of the sun, producing an unwholesome atmosphere in which Hastings's "Foul Disease" can appear.[36] So badly damaged is the covenant between heaven and earth, itself analogous to the broken covenant between King and people, that "Heaven would no longer trust its Pledge; but thus / Recall'd it; rapt its *Ganymede* from us" (ll. 51–52).

This extravagant turn of wit begins the process by which the poem runs off the rails. The pun on the word "Pledge" (security deposit and toast) deflects our attention from the carefully prepared sun imagery of the preceding lines, as do the ensuing allusions to Pandora's box, Venus's *naeves*, jewels and foils, and weeping pimples. Presumably the young poet hoped to produce a climactic effect by crowding in every invention he could manage, offering plenitude as a version of intensity. Or perhaps his uncertainty about how his family might respond to the Royalism of this section led him to obscure matters with these extraneous images. Still, the copiousness that weakens these lines is very much in the tradition of Westminster poetry and oratory; when Busby and his predecessors sought to "*whet* up and *raise* [the] *Phansies*" of their students, they encouraged such multiplication of metaphors,[37] and a greatly chastened version of such copiousness remains one of the strengths of Dryden's adult poetry. In any case, the last metaphor is the most important; it describes the pox, "Who, Rebel-like, with their own Lord at strife, / Thus made an Insurrection 'gainst his Life" (ll. 61–62). This person-ification of the pox as rebels is the vehicle for a larger comparison of two deadly phenomena: the disease that ravaged Hastings's body and the war that ravaged En-gland. Usually explained as a "Metaphysical conceit," the metaphor owes much to the Royalist propaganda of the Civil War, which frequently portrayed the Parliamentary forces as infections in the body politic. The grotesquerie, while fatal to the decorum of the elegy, is surely intentional. Outrage often provoked this kind of response from Dryden; the boy who could picture Cromwell and the Roundheads as pimples became the man who could picture Shaftesbury as a counterfeit coin, a squeaking bagpipe, and a painful cure for venereal disease:

> thy *Mercury*
> Has pass'd through every Sect, or theirs through Thee.
> But what thou giv'st, that Venom still remains;
> And the pox'd Nation feels Thee in their Brains.[38]

The similarity with the later satire suggests the anger behind these lines and points the problem as well. Funeral elegies of the seventeenth century have a wider range of tone and diction than those of later eras, but even in 1649, grief usually sings in softer notes. The noisiness of Dryden's climax, produced not only by the sheer number of meta-phors but by the violence of some of them, negates the abstraction he had earlier sought. After the ugly physical picture of the disease here, even astronomical imagery, lofty and detached in the earlier parts of the poem, comes crashing to earth:

> No Comet need foretel his Change drew on,
> Whose Corps might seem a *Constellation*.

> [ll. 65–66]

Dryden regains some composure and detachment by restating the theme of youth
and age in seasonal imagery:

> But hasty Winter, with one blast, hath brought
> The hopes of Autumn, Summer, Spring to nought.
> Thus fades the Oak i' th' sprig, i' th' blade the Corn;
> Thus, without Young, this *Phoenix* dies, new born.
>
> [ll. 77–80]

Even here there are political overtones: Hastings died on 24 June 1649, and could thus
hardly be termed a victim of "hasty Winter," but Charles I stepped onto the scaffold on
a cold day in January, and the poem has already connected the two deaths. The
disordering of the seasons, the blighting of fertility, and the final death of the phoenix
reverse positive images associated with monarchy in Ben Jonson's masques. In *The
Vision of Delight* (1617), for example, a spring scene elicits these questions from a
character named *Wonder*:

> What better change appeares?
> Whence is it that the ayre so sudden cleares,
> And all things in a moment turn so milde?
> . . . .
> How comes it Winter is so quite forc't hence,
> And lockt up under ground?

Another character, *Fant'sy*, doubtless pointing toward King James's chair, replies:

> Behold a King
> Whose presence maketh this perpetuall *Spring*,
> The glories of which Spring grow in that Bower,
> And are the marks and beauties of his power.
>
> [VIII, 469]

The appearance of spring in the dead of winter is a royal miracle, made visible by the
artifice of Inigo Jones and the magical poetry of Jonson. But in a nation without a king, a
winter blast can kill a promising youth in June.

The shrill, questioning voice of the angry youth returns, asking why "old three-
legg'd gray-beards with their Gout, / Catarrhs, Rheums, Aches, live three Ages out?"
(ll. 81–82). Again, Dryden is expressing more than one eighteen-year-old's frustration
at the death of another. According to statistical studies, the average Royalist was about
ten years younger than the average Parliamentarian,[39] and Royalist propaganda could
therefore picture the Civil War as a generational struggle in which gray-haired Puritan
generals left gay young blades dead on the battlefield. Having been exposed to such
propaganda, and having learned from Busby to regret the loss of a court whose rich and
varied culture he was just too young to have seen, Dryden questions a world where
"none live but such as should die," a category presumably including old men, regicides,
and a Rump Parliament including members of his own family. Eleven years later,
celebrating the return of Charles II, he would return to the same theme:

> Youth that with Joys had unacquainted been
> Envy'd gray hairs that once good days had seen:
> We thought our Sires, not with their own content,
> Had ere we came to age our Portion spent.
>
> [*Astraea Redux*, ll. 25–28]

But these later lines, the work of a greatly improved poet, do not yield to shrillness as does the attack on "Ghostly Fathers" in the Hastings poem, where even Dryden seems to recognize and apologize for his bitter excess:

> Grief makes me rail; Sorrow will force its way;
> And, Show'rs of Tears, Tempestuous Sighs best lay.
> The Tongue may fail; but over-flowing Eyes
> Will weep out lasting streams of *Elegies*.
>
> [ll. 89–92]

The final image is as flat and conventional as anything in the poem, but two briefer phrases, linked by internal rhyme and including the only first-person singular in the poem, are more revealing. "Grief makes me rail," while evidently an apology for the excesses we have noticed, suggests the similar impulses behind elegy and satire; "The Tongue may fail," undercutting the earlier praise of Hastings's talented tongue, acknowledges not only the inadequacy of words as expressions of grief, but the poet's recognition that his control is not yet that of a mature artist. Even after achieving artistic maturity, Dryden often ended his poems with similar gestures of self-criticism; the closing lines of *Religio Laici*, with their modest talk of "unpolish'd, rugged Verse," are an obvious example.

By adding the envoi to Elizabeth Mayerne, Dryden gains one more shift in perspective. Instead of offering Elizabeth sentimental religious anodynes, as had several other poets, he urges her to consummate her thwarted marriage intellectually:

> With greater then *Platonick* love, O wed
> His Soul, though not his Body, to thy Bed:
> Let that make thee a Mother; bring thou forth
> Th' *Idea's* of his Vertue, Knowledge, Worth.
>
> [ll. 97–100]

But bringing forth ideas, however apt the maternal metaphor, is what poets do, and if we suspect that Dryden is speaking to himself as much as to Elizabeth, the next line confirms our suspicions, asking her to "Transcribe the Original in new Copies" (l. 101). Dryden is telling Elizabeth to do what he has done, to make Hastings into a work of art. Transformed into an idea by Dryden's poem and Elizabeth's memory, Hastings will cast his "Irradiations" in an England darkened by civil war; he will become the exemplary "great Grandsire . . . Of an Heroick Divine Progenie," so that Dryden need no longer rail at "gray-beards."

Elegy and Satire: The Royalist Style

In the absence of any other primary document from Dryden's Westminster years, we must base our conclusions about his reading, opinions, and poetic development on this interesting, but hardly imposing poem. Reading too much into such a conventional and occasional poem is an obvious danger, and the Royalist sentiments overtly expressed here, which are certainly less polemical than those expressed in several of the companion poems, are hardly an adequate basis for any sweeping conclusions about the political allegiances of the eighteen-year-old Dryden. The poem's Royalism may simply be a consequence of its occasion, the death of the Earl of Huntingdon's eldest son, whose fiancée was the daughter of Sir Theodore Mayerne, physician to the late King; Dryden may have been simply writing to order, as on numerous later occasions, hoping to please Busby, the Hastings and Mayerne families, and the other Royalist contributors to *Lachrymae Musarum.* But the Royalism of the poem's *style* suggests that Dryden had indeed been profoundly affected by Busby, whose interest in classical imagery and theatrical effects was of a piece with his Laudian faith in liturgy and monarchy; and some of the poem's more vigorous moments suggest that he had also been affected by reading Royalist satire. Both influences were important for Dryden's future development: the visual and mythological imagery drawn from the masque tradition would reappear, in chastened form, in his official court poetry; the histrionic raillery and violent imagery that sometimes weaken this poem would find a more appropriate place in the great satires of his maturity.

When Dryden personifies "Beauty and Learning," presents Hastings as a glass model of the universe, and describes death as a disordering of the seasons, he comes quite close to some of the visual effects and Platonizing tendencies of the Caroline masque. A modern analysis of the set for *Albion's Triumph* (1632), a masque presented by Inigo Jones and Aurelian Townshend after Jones's break with Jonson, will suggest Dryden's debt to such "almighty architecture":

> The *meaning* of what the court is witnessing depends on its ability to make certain assumptions about the truth of images. Two symbolic figures, of Theory looking toward heaven, and Practice gazing downward, adorn Jones's proscenium, 'showing that by these two all works of architecture and ingining have their perfection.' . . . If we recall Ficino's observation that Archimedean models of the spheres reveal the essential divinity of man's mind, we shall see that the architect's aims are quite as serious as the poet's had been. Through 'architecture and ingining'—the word retains its implications of wit and understanding—we create the universe, and comprehend and control its workings.[40]

Much of what is said here is directly applicable to Dryden's poem, which asks us to share its assumptions about the truth of its images, to participate willingly in the fiction that Hastings is an exemplar of all the art, beauty, learning, and virtue that have perished with the court. His poem also has "two symbolic figures" perched on its proscenium, "Beauty and Learning" with their winding-sheet, and he explicitly presents Hastings as an "Archimedean model of the spheres." His Cowleian excesses of fancy and invention are, to use Jones's word, "ingining," effects designed to ravish our understanding by wit and surprise; if they fail, as Jones's machines sometimes failed for those not seated at optimal angles, the contrast with the Puritan emphasis on naked truth, direct language, and the rational ordering of the sermon remains marked.

In their use of mythology, *Albion's Triumph* and the other masques were attempts, however unrealistic, to present Charles as an ideal ruler, a new Roman emperor, a version of Jove, a sacramental hero. Available only to the court, they failed as propaganda. But after the execution of the King, the standard imagery of the Caroline masque took on a more tragic and nostalgic force; *Eikon Basilike*, hawked on the streets within hours of the beheading, began this process, and many of the poems in *Lachrymae Musarum*, not least Dryden's, draw on the image-complex of Charles as martyr developed in that tract. Objecting to the popularity of *Eikon Basilike* in his own *Ikonoklastes*, Milton complains that "quaint emblems and devices begged from the old pageantry of some Twelfthnight's entertainment for Whitehall, will do but ill to make a saint or martyr."[41] However self-evident this objection may have seemed to Milton, in practice the "quaint emblems and devices" of the masque tradition worked *better* as ways to create and perpetuate a cult of Charles as martyr than they had as ways to praise a live Charles on the throne. As Dryden would discover when he attempted to employ some of this imagery for his poems in praise of Charles II, the suspension of disbelief required to accept a living, palpably flawed monarch as a "sacred Majesty," a divinely ordained avatar of Hercules, Christ, and sundry other heroes, is different in kind from that required when the same imagery is used of a dead man; panegyric can be invalidated by the actions of its subject, as elegy cannot. Dead at eighteen, and thus eternally promising, Hastings was a perfect subject on which to lavish the idealization, abstraction, and iconography of the Royalist style; like the unknown sitter for a great portrait, he lives only as a work of art, a virtually self-contained universe created by "architecture and ingining."

Nostalgia and mythopoesis were not the only Royalist responses to defeat and disaster, however. The anger, self-dramatization, and physical shock we have noticed in Dryden's poem also have Royalist analogues, for example in the bitter satires of the poet John Cleveland or the mordant prose of the journalist John Berkenhead, later Dryden's friend. The similarities extend to matters of form. Cleveland's outrage at the reversal of traditional values by the Parliamentary victors sometimes finds a tight, compressed expression:

> *Faces about*, saies the *Remonstrant* Spirit;
> Allegeance is Malignant, Treason Merit.[42]

And some of Dryden's tightest lines in the Hastings poem use similar techniques to point similar ironies:

> If Merit be Disease, if Vertue Death;
> . . . .
> Our *Noble Youth* now have pretence to be
> Dunces securely, Ign'rant healthfully.
>
> [ll. 9; 13–14]

Both examples depend heavily on trochaic inversion ("*Faces about*"; "Dunces secure-ly"), zeugma ("Treason Merit"; "Vertue Death"), alliteration ("Malignant . . . Merit"; "Disease . . . Death"), and emphatic caesurae. These devices, which we associate with the satiric couplets of the mature Dryden, seem out of place in an elegy, but in the Royalist writings on which Dryden was drawing, satiric and elegiac impulses quite naturally occurred together, as they did for the Puritan Milton of *Lycidas*, who used the occasion of the death of Edward King to "foretell the ruin of our corrupted clergy." After the execution of King Charles, Royalist writers often expressed their frustration by assuming the pose of Prince Hamlet, mourning for a simpler, nobler past, but expressing their sorrow with a paradoxical wit, a fondness for images of disease, and a hostility toward the previous generation; Dryden's attack on "old three-legged gray-beards" is a strong example. As the Royalists saw it, the King had been murdered, the rightful heir dispossessed, the throne usurped; something was rotten in England; the time was out of joint.[43] Dryden himself experienced that wrenching change from a monarchial past to a Parliamentary present as the impressionable teenaged student of a man who pointedly emphasized the values that were being lost in the collapse of the Caroline court. The anger he expresses in parts of the Hastings poem, in which we may detect the first faint stirrings of the more sustained savagery of *The Medall*, arises from the same impulses as the sorrow.

"Upon the Death of the Lord Hastings" naturally has more in common with the elegies of Dryden's maturity—the Killigrew ode, *Eleonora*, or *Threnodia Augustalis*—than with his mature satires: those later elegies also magnify the dead by invoking the classical and Christian imagery of the Renaissance; they too exhibit an old-fashioned rhetorical structure. Superficially, Dryden's official panegyrics appear to employ the same techniques of amplification, but there is an important difference between elegy and panegyric. Dryden's Restoration panegyrics, concerned as they were to exorcise the Civil Wars and Interregnum, could not recover the mythological and hierarchical illusions of the masque, which were already unrealistic in their own time. His gestures toward that past world are always hedged in by conscious or unconscious irony, by a profound sense of the fragility of human institutions, successions, hierarchies. As the chief architect of the chastened Royalist style of the Restoration, Dryden was acknowl-edging changed literary circumstances as well as partisan necessities by developing, to the immeasurable benefit of his eighteenth-century heirs, the satiric consequences of a literary strategy that measured the present against the classical or biblical past and found it ludicrously wanting. By every standard, including that of propaganda, his satiric masterpiece, *Absalom and Achitophel* (1681), is a more successful poem than his poem on the birth of the Pretender, *Britannia Rediviva* (1688). But the energy that fuels the great satires has a common source with the nostalgia apparent in the baroque court panegyrics, a source already detectable in the Hastings elegy: Dryden's sense of having been born too late, his longing for an irrecoverable past. While the panegyrics normally invoke that past by alluding to myth or ancient history, the emotional source for the nostalgia they express lies in the complicated feelings Dryden and his readers had about their own times, particularly the passing of the court of Charles I, where ceremony and the arts had been prized as they would never be again. The satires are even more explicit about their Cavalier roots; Dryden frequently denigrates the Whigs of the 1680s by identifying them with the self-righteously iconoclastic Roundheads of the 1640s.

During the war years, Royalist writers routinely denied any kind of stature to the enemy. Here, for example, is Dudley Diggs, in a volume lamenting the death of a Cavalier hero:

> We've oft lost
> Powder; to kill such Rogues doth not quit cost.
> . . . What honour is't to tell
> That here a Sergeant-Major-Cobler fell,
> There a mechanick-Colonell dropt down,
> Not fit to serve in any honest Town.
> Our Conquest is unpleasant; we must grieve
> And wish the punisht Rebells did still live,
> Reserv'd for more ignoble fall.[44]

Dryden often used this kind of attack: as early as *Astraea Redux*, he was referring to the Parliamentarians as "Rabble," and in later prefaces, pamphlets, and satires, he subjected his enemies to withering class scorn; when those enemies were aristocrats, he resorted to metaphors implying that they were acting like tradesmen, ironically reversing the procedure of writers like Diggs, who complained that a "mechanick" could not legitimately be a "Colonell." Still, there is one important strength in Dryden's greatest satires that separates them significantly from their ancestors in Royalist polemic. Although he could use class prejudice with brilliant rhetorical effect, he knew that it was a simplification, a caricature; his own dead cousin, who had actually been a Parliamentary Colonel and a religious "Fanatick," was nonetheless a baronet's son and a solicitor, hardly a "mechanick." In Dryden's mature satires, especially in *Absalom and Achitophel*, those on the other side are not mere caricatures, but formidable adversaries, capable of presence and grandeur. Berkenhead's biographer, analyzing his limitations as a satirist, points out that he "could never have imagined an Achitophel or an Absalom . . . because he was unwilling even to countenance, as Dryden could, the existence of potential human greatness in the enemy."[45]

Perhaps Dryden had this capacity to understand his partisan enemies because he had been reared as a Puritan, then converted to Royalism as a world-view and literary style by Busby. Andrew Marvell, writing for the other side, sometimes achieved a similar complexity of vision, hence the impossibility of an "organic" or consistent reading of his "Horatian Ode," which praises Cromwell but acknowledges the dignity of Charles at his execution. Perhaps the reason was the same: Marvell wrote Latin poems in praise of Charles at college and contributed a poem to *Lachrymae Musarum* containing a Royalist conceit in which the "democratic stars," jealous of Hastings's accomplishments, rise in rebellion and "ostracize" him. He seems to have been converted to the Parliamentary ideology in the 1650s, quite possibly by Milton.[46] The zeal of the convert is a familiar phenomenon; both Marvell and Dryden exhibit it at times. Less familiar, but more important for the development of literary irony, complexity, and depth, is the ability of the convert to comprehend fully the motives of his antagonists, having once been of their number himself. For Dryden, this process was continuous. Not only did his schooling at Westminster and Trinity include training in arguing both sides of any question, a skill his plays gave him ample opportunity to display, but his early career, roughly divisible by decades, involved a series of alternating experiences with conflicting systems of belief and their attendant styles. The ideas instilled in him by his Puritan upbringing in the 1630s were "leavened" by the powerful influence of Busby's Royalism in the 1640s, but his experiences in the 1650s involved renewed contact with the values and personalities of his Puritan boyhood: he went up to a Cambridge college presided over by Thomas Hill, and took employment from a Commonwealth government in which Gilbert Pickering was a powerful official. We know very little about how Dryden responded to those experiences at the time he was passing through them, but the doubleness of his mature writing, its richness of implication and irony, is surely in part a consequence of the doubleness of his early life.

CHAPTER THREE

Trinity College
1650–1655

Purging and Pruning: Cambridge under the Puritans

On 21 July 1643, Thomas Hill preached a sermon to the Long Parliament entitled *The militant Church triumphant over the Dragon and his Angels*. The Civil War was at its height; the outcome was far from certain; military concerns, as Hill's apocalyptic title suggests, were the order of the day. Nevertheless, Hill's exhortations included a plea for educational reform:

> *Forget not*, I beseech you, forget not the *purging* and *pruning* of the *Universities, the nurseries of piety and learning*. If *Satan* have a *seate* there; if there bee such that hold the doctrine of *Balaam*, who taught *Balak to cast a stumbling block before the children of Israel, to eate things sacrificed to Idols, and to commit fornication*, what Papists such *Tutors* are like to send abroad, we have found by too much unhappy experience. [p. 23]

Hill and his allies had good reason to regard the universities as nurseries in need of pruning. Earlier in the same month, Oxford had become the headquarters of the Royalist camp, its academic functions virtually abandoned and its energies devoted to housing the King and Queen in appropriate splendor, entertaining the displaced court with drama and music, raising money and troops for the royal cause, and printing barbed propaganda. Cambridge, despite the presence of such Puritan centers as Emmanuel, and despite its location in a thoroughly Parliamentarian town for which Cromwell himself was the Member of Parliament, could number many Royalists among its Fellows: in the summer of 1642, several Cambridge colleges forwarded their silver plate to the King, and Cromwell had to act quickly to intercept part of a large shipment of arms designed to help the colleges defend themselves against the citizens of the town.[1]

Such overtly political and military actions were not Hill's only concern, however. Confidently looking ahead to the rule of the saints, he was reminding the Parliament that the thorough reformation for which they were praying could only be brought about by reforming the universities. Emmanuel College, founded by Sir Walter Mildmay in

1584 for the purpose of training Puritan clergymen, had shown on a small scale the power of godly education; its graduates, including Hill, were taking a leading role in the Westminster Assembly, and many of them hoped for a time when all the colleges of both universities would more closely resemble Emmanuel. Some parts of the reform program were strictly religious; Hill's allusions to idolatry and papism reflect typically Puritan disapproval of the liturgical and theological innovations introduced while Laud was Chancellor of Oxford. But the more political notion of advancement by merit, soon to be validated by the success of the New Model Army, was an equally important part of Hill's plan; in a sermon preached on 24 April 1644, he explicitly opposed admissions to the university based on wealth and special favors, and proposed to base them upon "the pregnancy of parts and capacity in Children."[2]

Within a year of this second sermon, Hill and his allies were given the opportunity to put their proposals into practice: twelve heads of Cambridge houses and hundreds of Fellows were ejected from their places for refusing to subscribe to the Solemn League and Covenant; of the twelve new heads, nine were members of the Westminster Assembly, and seven were graduates of Emmanuel.[3] Hill himself, first nominated for the mastership of Emmanuel, became Master of Trinity, the largest college, in April 1645. Three years later, in his "Letter to the Seniors," he recalled "the many *difficulties* I met with in the managing of that great *Trust committed* unto me in *purging, setling, and governing* that *Royal foundation.*" The most obvious of the difficulties, of course, resulted from the purge, as Hill reveals in remembering "in what a condition wee found the Colledge, an *exhausted Treasurie, few Scholars* in it, and divers of *those opposite* to the intended *Reformation*, divers *fellowships made void by ejectment*, which wee could not supply" (sig. A1v). Each of these problems was serious. Contributions to the royal cause by Thomas Comber, the ejected Master, were not the only reason why the treasury was exhausted; Parliamentary agents had illegally sequestered some of the college lands in 1643, and Trinity had to file petitions to recover the lost income.[4] There were indeed few scholars, and those who remained, since they had been admitted under a system favoring wealth and privilege, were frequently "*opposite* to the intended *Reformation*"; forty-nine fellows, including Cowley, had been ejected, and as Hill's remarks suggest, finding similarly qualified men to fill their places was difficult. With characteristic energy and optimism, Hill set about rebuilding the foundation: by November 1645, he had secured the appointments of four new seniors, including Robert Metcalfe, who had formerly been the Regius Professor of Hebrew,[5] and by 1648, when he wrote his letter to a full complement of eight seniors, Hill could rejoice that the junior places were being filled as well. He thanked God for "bless[ing] us with a store of *able and conscientious* Tutors (which will bee much increased by the ten Batchelor-Fellows you chose last Michaelmas, of singular worth according *to their degree* and of *speciall hopes* for Piety)" (sig. A3v).

These pious young tutors included John Templer, the man who would become Dryden's tutor two years later. While Hill hoped that such appointments would eventually lead to "a learned, *as well as a religious Reformation*," he must have realized that most of these new fellows were at present considerably less learned than the men ejected to make way for them. Like the committee supervising Westminster, who left

Busby in his place because they considered his excellence more important than his politics, the new Puritan leadership of Cambridge had to make some compromises in order to retain some educational strengths. James Duport, for example, a Senior Fellow of Trinity who was the Regius Professor of Greek, was considered exempt from taking the Covenant; as his biographer points out, there was a pragmatic reason for this lenient treatment: "there probably would have been considerable difficulty in supplying Duport's place with a Presbyterian Greek Professor."[6] Hill's fondness for Isaac Barrow, who made no secret of his Royalism, and who would himself become Master of Trinity after the Restoration, suggests that he was susceptible to the idea that academic excellence might atone for political intransigence; Barrow's earliest biographer provides two relevant anecdotes:

> One day Dr. Hill, master of the college, laying his hand on his head, said, *Thou art a good lad; 'tis pity thou art a cavalier*: and when in an Oration on the Gunpowder-Treason he had so celebrated the former times, as to reflect much on the present, some Fellows were provoked to move for his expulsion; but the master silenced them with this; *Barrow is a better man than any of us*.[7]

This second incident took place in November 1651, when Dryden was already in his second year as an undergraduate; whether or not he heard Barrow's Latin oration in the College Hall, he was surely aware of the ensuing controversy, which may serve us as an example of the way the growing quarrels among various Puritan factions affected the universities. As his attitudes toward the arts suggest, Hill was no antinomian extremist; like most of the new Cambridge masters, he was a "Presbyterian," if we use that word in the way historians generally have, to designate the relatively conservative members of Parliament and the Westminster Assembly, men who hoped to bring about change within an orderly framework, who were impressed by hard work and intellectual achievement, and hence tolerant of a Busby or a Barrow or a Duport.[8] But the coalition that defeated the crown also contained more radical elements; after the failure of the Westminster Assembly and the purging of Parliament by Colonel Pride, men like Hill were subject not only to subtle pressures from the Royalists and crypto-Royalists in their midst, but to impatient cries for radical reform from the segments of opinion loosely described as "Independent," which ranged from Cromwell himself to the utopian Diggers and Levellers. "Independent" opinion was too various to admit of easy summary, and Cromwell remained a staunch supporter of learning, but some of the enthusiasts who had supported him in the war were so convinced that knowledge could only come from inspiration that they opposed any kind of systematic instruction; others resented the obvious class bias of the universities, or the impractical nature of the scholastic curriculum, or the absence of universities in provincial centers.

By 1649, the year before Dryden came up, Cambridge had begun to experience the unsettling consequences of this controversy. In April of that year, William Dell, an opinionated Independent who had been an Army chaplain, was elected Master of Caius College; he would soon use his prominence to advocate sweeping changes in the organization and curriculum of the universities, opposing the granting of degrees in divinity on the grounds that authority in preaching came from the Spirit, not from scholarship.[9] Yet in July, the Committee for Regulating the Universities, possibly under Milton's influence, passed a resolution requiring the use of Latin and Greek in conversations between students, an action unlikely to please those Cambridge townspeople and Parliamentary soldiers who had forcibly prevented the preaching of a Latin sermon in the heady days of 1643.[10] One year after that resolution, John Dryden, already accustomed to speaking Latin from his years at Westminster, arrived at Trinity. During his years there, the Presbyterian leadership of the college and university remained under pressure from both sides. The Royalist nostalgia of many students and some Fellows found means of expression, and the Independent impatience at the slow pace of change reached its high-water mark in 1653 and 1654, with the publication of sweeping attacks on the universities by John Webster and William Dell. Some even feared that the Barebones Parliament might actually move to disendow the universities, for the reasons satirically expressed in this passage from *Rump Songs*:

> Wee'l down with all the Versities
>   Where Learning is professt
> Because they practice and maintain
>   The language of the Beast;
> Wee'l drive the doctors out of doors
>   And parts what ere they be;
> Wee'l cry all Arts and Learning down
>   And hey then up go we.[11]

Important and disconcerting as all this political ferment doubtless was, it did not prevent the continuation of most normal functions of the university. In an oration delivered in 1654, the year Dryden received his B.A., Isaac Barrow boasted about the flourishing state of studies in ancient and modern languages, philosophy, mathematics, optics, anatomy, botany, and chemistry.[12] Even if we allow for some rhetorical exaggeration, we may conclude that significant teaching and learning took place in Trinity College during Dryden's years in residence there. If political and religious disagreements within the Fellowship and the undergraduate body bred continual controversy, the daily life of the college remained the life of learning; years later, in his life of Plutarch, Dryden recalled reading the Greek historian "in the Library of *Trinity College* in *Cambridge*, (to which foundation I gratefully acknowledge a great part of my education)" (XVII, 269).[13]

A "Learned, Godly, Grave, and Prudent Tutor"

Early in May of 1650, Thomas Hill and his Junior Bursar, Nathaniel Rowles, traveled to London to conduct the annual election of Trinity Scholars from Westminster School. They chose five young men: John Dryden, Walter Needham, Alexander Rokeby, Thomas Greenwood, and Charles Ireton. Only King's Scholars could stand for such elections, and since the studentships at Christ Church, Oxford were significantly more lucrative, the traditional preference had been for Christ Church.[14] In 1650, however, there were a number of reasons why any King's Scholar might have preferred Trinity;

in Dryden's case, there were powerful family reasons as well. Although neither university was entirely stable in 1650, the aftermath of the Civil War had been even more severe at Oxford, where enrollments were just beginning to recover. The current Dean of Christ Church was Dr. John Owen, a fierce controversialist for the Independent side and a sworn enemy to Busby, even though Busby was a graduate of Christ Church. The Master of Trinity, by contrast, was not only a more tolerant Presbyterian, but an old friend of Dryden's father from their college days at Emmanuel. Surely the family had long intended Trinity as the next step in the education of their firstborn, and if they recognized in their son's behavior or his first published poem the taint of Busby's Royalism, they could have taken comfort in the hope that Hill, who had been preaching to Dryden from his earliest days, would take special care in supervising his university career.

Hill's "Epistle" to the Westminster Committee, at which we have glanced before, places particular stress on the importance of choosing godly tutors for new university students:

> Unlesse there be much circumspection in the choice of their *Tutors*, especially in these times when they come to the Universitys, all your former care may be lost. . . . Many very hopefull youths are miserably undone for want of *learned*, *godly*, *grave* and *prudent Tutors, and such as are hearty friends to a thorough Reformation*, which makes many tender-hearted Parents bleed with perpetuall sorrow. [*Strength of the Saints*, sig. A3v]

From the point of view of Hill and Dryden's parents, John Templer, under whose care Dryden was placed when he signed the Trinity College admission book on 13 May 1650, was an ideal choice.[15] Just five years older than Dryden, he was a native of Northamptonshire and a graduate of Emmanuel College; shortly after taking his B.A., he had been appointed to one of the Trinity fellowships vacated by ejection. He was clearly eager to take on pupils; four of the five Westminster Scholars in Dryden's year were assigned to his care. At the same time, he was continuing his own studies; Cambridge granted him an M.A. in 1648, a B.D. in 1655, and a D.D. in 1666. Unfortunately, our knowledge of Templer's methods and opinions during the years in which he taught Dryden does not extend much further than these bare facts. The two contemporary documents that provide guidelines for undergraduates—Duport's *Rules* and Holdsworth's *Directions for a Student*—describe a routine in which each undergraduate meets with his tutor daily for several kinds of exercises, ending the day with prayers in his tutor's chambers,[16] but college and university statutes also mandated attendance at lectures, and our fragmentary knowledge of seventeenth-century Cambridge makes it difficult to assess the balance between lectures and tutorials in any particular student's case. Dryden probably attended the lectures of Duport, who was famous for managing to bring his own Royalist politics into play while elucidating the Greek classics,[17] but he must also have worked closely with Templer.

Templer's later writings are those of a man well versed in classical philosophy and literature; he probably took Dryden through the normal routine of Aristotelian studies in the mornings and classical literature in the afternoons, and he clearly did his job well. Although Dryden was not one of the two Trinity men in his year to make the Honours

List for the University as a whole, he stood at the top of the *Ordo Senioritatis* for Trinity, thus standing third in his college; one of the two men to outrank him, his Westminster classmate Walter Needham, also had Templer for a tutor.[18] The only contemporary testimony about Dryden's intellectual reputation comes from Dr. Robert Creighton, who was several years behind him: "Dryden he said . . . was reckoned a man of good parts & Learning while in Coll: he had to his knowledge read over & very well understood all yᵉ Greek & Latin Poets."[19] Fragmentary and inconclusive as it is, this evidence suggests that Dryden's education at Trinity had considerable continuity with the training he had received at Westminster, and that his principal interest was in literature. Since Barrow's oration of 1654 claims that studies in modern languages were flourishing, we may suppose that Dryden did some reading in French and Italian as well as Latin and Greek, though we cannot know whether Templer would have encouraged such work.

The evidence for other subjects is even less clear. Dryden attacked Aristotle in his poem "To Dr. Charleton" (1663; quoted below, p. 133), but we cannot know whether his opposition to the "Tyranny" of "the *Stagirite*" was a consequence of his experience with the scholastic part of the college curriculum or a later response to reading Hobbes. Charleton and his colleagues in the Royal Society opposed scholasticism and advocated experimental science; that intellectual revolution, already apparent in Bacon's works on education, was brewing during the 1650s, when Hill successfully sought funds to endow a chair of mathematics. Many of the undergraduates who were at Trinity with Dryden, including Needham, were strongly interested in experiments during their college years; the frequent scientific metaphors in John Templer's later writings establish his competent knowledge of the sciences.[20] While this evidence suggests that Dryden was at least exposed to scientific ideas, it cannot tell us whether the "new philosophy" piqued his interest. Similarly, we cannot know whether the Cambridge Platonists, mainly at Emmanuel and St. John's, had much impact on students in Trinity, though some biographers of Dryden have speculated at length about their supposed influence on him.[21] Most frustrating of all, we cannot know whether Templer encouraged Dryden's poetic talents, since the only poetic remains of Dryden's Trinity years are his congratulatory verses to his friend John Hoddesdon, who published a collection of biblical epigrams in 1650, shortly after Dryden came up, and some conventionally gallant lines in a letter to his cousin Honor, written in either 1653 or 1655.[22] With or without tutorial encouragement, he must have worked on his writing; the poems he published in 1659 and 1660 represent such a marked advance over the Hastings elegy that the only plausible explanation is a great deal of poetic practice, with the results presumably destroyed by a Dryden whose capacity for self-criticism had also grown stronger.

We have more evidence about Templer's theological opinions, but our sources—a sermon preached in London in 1659, a refutation of Hobbes's theology in Latin (1673), a sermon defending the rights of bishops to make visitations of the university (1676), and a posthumously published *Treatise Relating to the Worship of God* (1694)—were all written well after his years as Dryden's tutor. The young Puritan appointed to help set Trinity on a godly path eventually became a defender of the Restoration Anglican establishment, but we cannot know whether this change had begun to occur by the early 1650s. Still, Templer had a basic inclination toward scholarship, evident in the classical and patristic lore he packed into the text and margins of all these writings, and I suspect that his fear of Independent anti-intellectualism made him susceptible to the influence of men like Barrow and Duport, intellectually formidable Fellows of Trinity who were known to be Royalists, and who became leaders of the university after the Restoration.

When Thomas Hill died in 1653, his friend Anthony Tuckney, who preached his funeral sermon, mentioned Templer as one who would perform "a Panegyrick of his deserved praises" in the College Hall;[23] at this point, Templer was evidently above suspicion in Presbyterian circles. In 1654, he was appointed a Visitor of the University, and in 1656, Senior Dean of Trinity, presumably with the approval of the new Master, John Arrowsmith, a stern Calvinist who vigorously defended university education from the attacks of Dell and his Independent allies. By the time of his London sermon, *The Saints Duty in Contending for the Faith Delivered to Them* (1659), Templer had left Trinity to devote himself to his living at Balsham.[24] Despite its militant title, the sermon is a cautious document. Templer was preaching before John Ireton, Lord Mayor of London in 1658, whose late brother Henry, the Parliamentary general, had been married to Cromwell's daughter; he was preaching on 17 July 1659, two months after the fall of Richard Cromwell and two weeks before Booth's premature Royalist uprising. The resulting sermon is contradictory, even in its use of metaphor. Templer begins with what sounds like an exhortation to recover the old Puritan fervor:

> How many have lost their former heat and vigour, and are ready to dispute that Faith in defence of which they were once ready to die. . . . When they were in a night of Persecution, their hearts were hot; when the day of deliverance approached, their heat abated; and now at noon-time, when the Sun is come to his Zenith, they are grown stark cold. [p. 2]

But the chaotic summer of 1659 was hardly the zenith of any form of faith, and Templer later cautions against sectarian controversy; the "heat" he had used as a metaphor for faith a few pages earlier now becomes a metaphor for dangerous intemperance:

> A mutual love in our strivings for the faith . . . would more prevail against Errour, then exasperation and bitterness. . . . When intemperate heats prevail amongst parties, there is reason to suspect, whether it be Truth they contend for. [pp. 32–33]

In this plea for reconciliation, Templer sounds much like Hill, who preached several sermons calling for a cessation of hostilities between Presbyterians and Independents.[25] But like Hill, Templer seems to have desired a reconciliation that would exclude those who claimed to be able to interpret the Bible by virtue of "a light within them":

> Their understandings being coloured with a false light, they look through it upon the scripture, and so make the scripture appear to them of the same colour; just as to men, that put green or blew glass before their eyes, all the objects round about will appear blew or green. [p. 15]

Fifteen years later, Dryden would attack the young poet Elkanah Settle with a similarly dismissive reference to the inner light:

> He is a kind of Phanatick in Poetry, and has a light within him; and writes by an inspiration which (like that of the Heathen Prophets) a man must have no sense of his own when he receives. [XVII, 182]26

Like his tutor, Dryden is skeptical about claims to inspiration; believing instead that knowledge comes from study, he blames Settle's weakness as a writer on his "never haveing studied any sort of Learning but Poetry, and that but slenderly." For Templer, even in 1659, scriptural interpretation had to be grounded in scholarship:

> If we desire this Spirit may be a Guide to go before us through the dark passages of Scripture, 'tis good to apply our selves to the use of such means which may help to possess us of it. . . . When the Apostle [Paul] had received the Spirit it self, he doth not lay aside his former study and industry, he was solicitous about his books, 2. *Tim*. 4.13. [pp. 38–39]

Seven years and a Restoration later, in the sermon defending the rights of bishops, Templer's disapproval of the Independent (now Dissenting) emphasis on inspiration had become even stronger:

> There is much more reason to presume, that the Spirit of God may rather fall upon men in a Library, then in a Shop: upon those, who are studious and industrious, then upon such as are idle, and stand gazing about them.27

I doubt that the young John Templer who instructed John Dryden and prayed with him nightly in the early 1650s foresaw that his fondness for libraries would lead him to endorse the return of episcopacy in the 1660s, but I do believe that the distaste for enthusiasm expressed in these later writings, including the class bias against those claiming inspiration "in a Shop," was always present in Templer's mind, as it was in the mind of his most talented student, whose own attack on the same enemy surpasses Templer in vehemence as in eloquence:

> The tender Page with horney Fists was gaul'd;
> And he was gifted most that loudest baul'd:
> The *Spirit* gave the *Doctoral Degree*:
> And every member of a *Company*
> Was of *his Trade*, and of the *Bible free*.
> Plain *truths* enough for needful *use* they found;
> But men wou'd still be itching to *expound*:
> Each was ambitious of th' obscurest place,
> No measure ta'n from *Knowledge*, all from *GRACE*.
> *Study* and *Pains* were now no more their Care;
> *Texts* were explain'd by *Fasting*, and by *Prayer*:
> This was the Fruit the *private Spirit* brought;
> Occasion'd by *great Zeal*, and *little Thought*.
> While Crouds unlearn'd, with rude Devotion warm,

About the Sacred Viands buz and swarm,
The *Fly-blown Text* creates a crawling Brood;
And turns to *Maggots* what was meant for *Food*.

[*Religio Laici*, ll. 404–20]

Controversy and Contumacy

As those powerful lines demonstrate, Dryden the adult poet, playwright, and critic was a master of controversy. The memorable ugliness of the imagery here suggests a passionate memory of the threat to learning posed by such men as William Dell, but Dryden could muster nearly equivalent rhetorical power when expressing opinions with which he disagreed, a talent he was able to display to particular advantage in his plays. The Trinity College of the Interregnum was a fine place for sharpening such skills. The ancient scholastic curriculum through which Dryden and his contemporaries passed proceeded by argumentation, with disputants attacking and defending propositions ultimately derived from Aristotle. The increasingly obvious irrelevance of that curriculum was itself a topic of controversy, especially after the publication of Hobbes's *Leviathan* (1651), with its devastating attack on the "schoolmen." Theological controversy was rampant. Benjamin Whichcote, founder of the Cambridge Platonists, was delivering his popular lectures in Trinity Church; in 1651, his former tutor, Anthony Tuckney, exchanged a series of letters with him debating the questions of reason and revelation that would later occupy Dryden. William Dell, John Hall, and John Webster attacked the university at its very foundations, provoking responses by Seth Ward and John Arrowsmith. Even funerals were occasions for controversy: the funeral of Thomas Comber, the ejected Master of Trinity, on 29 March 1653, saw a sermon in his defense by Robert Boreman; Hill's funeral on 22 December of the same year produced not only an official panegyric from Tuckney but a crack-brained pamphlet by a Fifth-Monarchy Man, proclaiming itself *Dr. Hill's Funeral Sermon* and crowing over his death as a judgment of God against the Presbyterians for their slow pace of reform.[28] National politics continued their unsettling ways: in 1653 alone, Cromwell dissolved the Rump of the Long Parliament (April), summoned the appointed Barebones Parliament (July), and took the reins of power entirely into his own hands as Lord Protector (December).

Unfortunately, there is not one shred of evidence to tell us what side Dryden took in any of these ongoing controversies. But there is evidence that his behavior was combative, first in the record of his being discommonsed and gated on 19 July 1652:

Agreed then that Dreyden be put out of com̃ons for
   a forthnight at least, & that he goe not out of
   the Colledg during the time aforesaid, excepting
   to sermons wthout express leave frō the Master
   or Vicemaster & that at the end of the forthnight he
                          confession of his crime
   read a [recantation *deleted*] ∧ in the hall at
   Dinner time; at the three fellowes table.

His crime [alledged *deleted*] was his disobedience to
        his contumacy in
the vicemaster & [∧] taking of his punishment
inflicted by him.[29]

Officially, the Vice-Master was Robert Metcalfe, the former Professor of Hebrew, a quiet and innocuous man by all accounts, but Metcalfe made his will on 9 October 1652, less than three months after this action, and may already have been too ill to function in his office. At least one document states that the man acting as Vice-Master was actually Alexander Akehurst, a far more likely candidate for a squabble with Dryden than Metcalfe.[30] Recommended to Oliver Heywood by Hill as "the most pious and laborious [tutor] in all the college" in 1647, Akehurst later "degenerated, or, as Mr. Heywood says, 'grievously apostasized, becoming a common Quaker.' But he retraced his steps and became at last 'a sober physician in Surrey.'"[31] Other evidence suggests that Akehurst's "apostasy" was more Royalist than Quaker: Heywood thought his "pride . . . was too visible in his apparel, gestures, and other outward tokens"; he allowed one of his students, Nicholas Hookes, to dedicate to him an openly Royalist volume of poems, the *Miscellanea Poetica* (1653); and in 1654, he was accused of using "atheistical and blasphemous expressions" in a complaint directed to Cromwell himself.[32] Whatever his shifting theological and political positions, Akehurst seems to have been combative, and we may easily imagine a witty undergraduate named Dryden disobeying him and eventually paying the penalty. But we shall never know the whole story, and the incident may have been a simple academic infraction involving Metcalfe, with no political overtones at all.

We are even less certain of the other piece of evidence suggesting that Dryden was a satirical undergraduate, since it comes from Shadwell's *The Medal of John Bayes* (1682), a wide-ranging attack on Dryden in retaliation for Dryden's own attacks on Shaftesbury and Shadwell:

> At *Cambridge* first your scurrilous Vein began
> When sawcily you traduc'd a *Nobleman*,
> Who for that Crime rebuk'd you on the head,
> And you had been Expell'd had you not fled.

[p. 8]

This may be pure fabrication, since there is little to link it with the real record of Dryden's being punished, and since no other document, not even another attack, provides any kind of confirmation. An expulsion, or an "admonition" threatening expulsion, would certainly have been recorded; although we cannot precisely date Dryden's departure from Cambridge, nothing among the facts we know suggests that he fled to escape punishment. He received his B.A. in early 1654; his father died in June of that year; he probably returned to Trinity after his father's funeral, but seems to have departed by 23 April 1655, when the Master and Seniors resolved that a scholar be elected in his place—unless he chose to return to claim it.[33] Creighton's memory sounds plausible: "He stayed to take his Batchelors degree; but his head was too roving and active, or what else you'll call it, to confine himself to a College Life; & so he left it &

went to London into gayer company, & set up for a Poet; wch he was as well qualified for as any man."[34]

Taken together, these puzzling scraps of evidence suggest a young man whose "roving and active" head sometimes got him into trouble, but who had the good sense to keep such scrapes from interfering seriously with the completion of his academic career. The punishment inflicted on him by the Master and Seniors was appropriate to a fairly minor offense, and did not carry with it the threat of expulsion.[35] The "confession of his crime" that Dryden presumably read in the College Hall was not to be his last palinode, and if he actually did absent himself briefly from Cambridge in order to keep a quarrel with a nobleman's son from escalating into physical violence, as Shadwell implies, he was acting with characteristic prudence. Violence was still commonplace: Dryden's cousin Gilbert Pickering narrowly escaped being run through from behind in a London alley when a loyal servant boy interposed his own body;[36] the Parliamentary Acts forbidding duelling were notably ineffective. Dryden would be accused of cowardice again in his adult career; one lampoon calls him "a Coward so^e Stupid, as never was fought wth."[37] But a man with his capacity for satirical verse and polemical prose had sufficient outlet for his aggressive feelings—and sufficient regard for his own survival to leave duelling to the young sparks of the town. He was not by nature an ideologue, and his capacity to argue both sides of many questions, doubtless sharpened by his Cambridge years, must have convinced him that no mere opinion was worth dying for—indeed, that few opinions were worth maintaining at the cost of one's career. The Cambridge dons, many of whom maintained their own careers by compromise and evasion when faced with the Covenant and Engagement, provided examples of such pragmatism; Templer's reasons for embracing episcopacy surely included survival.

Poetic Alternatives: *Amanda* and *Gondibert*

Perhaps a similar prudence dissuaded Dryden from publishing poetry during his undergraduate years, since the very act of publishing a poem implied some kind of participation in the ongoing national controversy. Poetry was employed less frequently by apologists for the Commonwealth than it had been by those celebrating the monarchy. Even Milton, who had published a remarkable collection of poems in 1645, devoted most of his efforts during the 1650s to writing prose pamphlets in defense of the regime. His sonnet to Cromwell (1652), arising as it does out of religious controversy, is as muscular and argumentative as those prose defenses, far removed from the luxuriant imagery and lyrical music of the early poetry:

> peace hath her victories
> No less renown'd than war, new foes arise
> Threat'ning to bind our souls with secular chains:
> Help us to save free Conscience from the paw
> Of hireling wolves whose Gospel is their maw.

[ll. 10–14]

The crowding of some of these lines with extra syllables suggests the impetuosity of the argument; "yet much remains / To conquer still," and this is no time for smooth or courtly praise.

Three years later, a poet who had been a master of courtly praise, Edmund Waller, made his peace with the new regime after a period of exile in France; his burnt offering, *A Panegyrick to My Lord Protector* (1655), moves deliberately away from the smoothly entertaining Cavalier style he had perfected in the two previous decades, seeking instead a terse, laconic style with affinities to Scripture and Puritan sermonizing:

> To pardon, willing; and to punish, loath;
> You strike with one Hand, but you heal with both.
> Lifting up all that prostrate lye, you grieve
> You cannot make the dead again to live.[38]

Of course, this quatrain is an extreme example. Other, wittier lines show that Waller could not entirely abandon his earlier voice, any more than Dryden, whose poems of 1659 and 1660 betray careful study of Waller, could entirely break free from the conceited "Westminster" style in which he had been trained. From the point of view of someone like Busby, whose definition of poetry stressed elaborate wit and formal diction, poems like Waller's *Panegyrick* must have seemed a sad and prosaic consequence of the replacement of an art-loving monarch by a soldier not known to be particularly sensitive to poetry, whose own speech and writing were blunt and plain. With the advantage of hindsight, we may recognize that the motion away from earlier poetic styles detectable in such poems was not merely a temporary consequence of the Interregnum; the poets of the Restoration, including Waller and Dryden, would discover in 1660 that they could not simply pick up where Jonson, Carew, Townshend and the other court poets of Charles I had left off. The tougher poetry that Milton and Waller were writing in the 1650s (in their quite different ways, and for quite different motives) may have begun as an attempt to address plain verses to that self-styled plain man Oliver Cromwell, but it did not vanish with the return of Charles II. Indeed, some of Dryden's most effective poetic arguments for Charles and for the idea of monarchy would employ rhetorical devices that came to prominence in poems written for Cromwell.

For disgruntled Royalists, however, especially for youthful Royalists longing for a world they had never actually known, poetry in the older styles was an ideal expression: by the simple act of writing in verse, one could offend the most narrow elements within the Puritan establishment; by writing to one's mistress in the Cavalier style, one could further offend Puritan scruples by employing sexual innuendo; and if one wished to be explicitly political, poetry had the advantage over prose of continually reminding its audience of the courtly arts swept away by the wars, arts that its authors hoped might one day be restored. When Nicholas Hookes, who was one year ahead of Dryden at both Westminster and Trinity, published his *Amanda* (1653), a collection of Cavalier poems to an imaginary mistress in an overtly Royalist format, one of the poets congratulating him, a certain "M.P." of the Middle Temple, touched on all these points:

> Courage, (my friend,) boldly assay the stage,
> Maugre the uncouth humors of the age,
> *T*hough wit th' unsavoury thing be out of date,
> And judgement triumph in the fancies fate,
> *Poetry's* heresie, and schisme pure,
> (As is *free-will* or humane literature.)
> Yet shall thy Mistresse thaw the Stoicks breast.[39]

In 1653, of course, there was no more chance that a poet could "boldly assay the stage" than there was that the defeated Royalists could stage a successful coup, yet in *Amanda* we can find Hookes making just such a suggestion in a poem "To his most Noble Friend Sir T[homas] L[eventhorp] B[aronet] of *Shingle-hall*":

> And yet some hope to see our *Noblemen*
> Some such as *you* confute the *times* agen;
> Though in their *wisdomes* now they dormant ly,
> Hush't in their private mansions quietly,
> Had they such Martial *souls*, such *fighting hands*,
> Redemption of their *rights*, *three* [crowns][40] *and lands*
> Were easie work.
>
> [p. 54]

The fact that lines like these were published at all suggests that the Puritan censorship created by the Printing Ordinance of 1643 was no longer effective.[41] In a period when such Royalist conspirators as the Sealed Knot group sporadically attempted armed resistance, the government's inability or unwillingness to prevent the publication of poems advocating rebellion is remarkable. At least as remarkable is the dedication of Hookes's companion volume, *Miscellanea Poetica*, to Alexander Akehurst, the acting Vice-Master of Trinity, in a florid Latin essay that gives the tutor credit for inspiring and correcting the poems. Evidently the ejections and loyalty oaths had not produced the "thorough Reformation" for which Hill hoped in 1648; indeed, the examples of Akehurst and Templer suggest that the Fellowship was becoming more Royalist during Dryden's years at Trinity, as the positive examples of Barrow and Duport and the threat posed by Dell and other Independents pushed former Presbyterians toward the belief that scholarship might be better protected by the monarchy.

Hookes's collection mentions so many people closely connected to Dryden that the absence of any mention of Dryden himself is puzzling. The poems in *Miscellanea Poetica* name many of the teachers and students they both knew at Westminster and Cambridge;[42] *Amanda* is dedicated to one such student, Edward Montagu of Boughton, who was among the Westminster contributors to *Lachrymae Musarum*. Montagu's grandfather had been a political ally of Dryden's grandfather, and he was also related to the wife of Gilbert Pickering (III), Dryden's powerful cousin, but his current opinions, like those of Hookes, were decidedly Royalist.[43] In its style, Hookes's effusive prose dedication to Montagu resembles Dryden's letter to his pretty cousin, Honor Dryden, written at about the same time. Here is Hookes, addressing the young nobleman with extravagant and sexually ambiguous flattery:

> It is *Amanda* my *Dear Mistris*, that bright lamp of *beauty* and goodnesse, which views perfections with the best constellated *goddesse*, that ever was deified by the most amorous *Enthusiast*, and beyond all, with the admirable *Idea* of your person. She it is, in whom I love and worship your picture, in whose likenesse I adore you. And in truth, I think my *Religion* in this transcendently reasonable to that of the common *Catholique*, whose best devotions have not more zeal, but lesse sense, and not half so lively a resemblance of a *Seraphical* being. [p. xi]

And here is Dryden, trying out his conceits on Honor:

> I am sure the poore paper smarts for my Idolatry, which by wearing it continually neere my brest will at last bee burnt and Martyrd in those flames of adoration it hath kindled in mee. But I forgette Madame, what rarityes your letter came fraught with besides words; You are such a Deity that commands worship by provideing the Sacrifice. [*Letters*, p. 4]

Both young writers treat religious controversy lightly by transmuting it into playful metaphor. While the jocular tone suggests an assumption that Roman Catholic rites are idolatrous and foolish, both young men find such rites a convenient metaphor for more earthly kinds of adolescent devotion. The Dryden who wrote this letter seems unlikely to have been recaptured by the forces of Puritan thought while at Trinity.

The congratulatory verses in the front of Hookes's volume, in addition to those by "M.P.," are by R. Moyle, a Fellow of Trinity; Charles Ireton, who came up with Dryden from Westminster and had Templer as his tutor; Thomas Adams, a Westminster scholar who had contributed to *Lachrymae Musarum*; and one "J.A. Gent.," whose closing lines closely resemble the closing lines of Dryden's poem to his friend Hoddesdon, published some three years earlier. Here is the ending of the poem to Hoddesdon:

> Reader, I've done, nor longer will withhold
> Thy greedy eyes; looking on this pure gold
> Thou'lt know adult'rate copper, which, like this,
> Will onely serve to be a foil to his.
>
> [ll. 23–26]

And here is the ending of the poem to Hookes by "J.A.":

> I've done, for none can reach thy Poems worth,
> *Amanda* wants no foiles to set her forth.
>
> [p. xxv]

While the resemblance is striking, the image is so commonplace that we cannot attach much importance to the parallelism. Dryden could conceivably have decided to masquerade as "J.A.," especially if his family's response to the Hastings elegy had made him cautious about being associated in print with explicit Royalist propaganda, but the poem by "J.A." is even weaker than the silly lines for Hoddesdon. I prefer to believe that Dryden declined to write a poem for Hookes's volume, and avoided publishing his own undergraduate efforts, because he had some inkling of the literary futility of poems like those Hookes was writing. He sensed, I suspect, that Hookes and the many lesser

Royalist poets like him were mechanically repeating the outdated and irrecoverable devices of the Cavalier style, not from any real sense that that style suited their needs for self-expression, but out of the foolish and nostalgic notion that they could conjure up the dead world of the Caroline court by performing incantations in its characteristic idiom. A symptom of the futility of this procedure is the fact that collections by dead poets served the same function at least as well; the posthumous publication of Cartwright's works in 1651, eight years after his death, with numerous prefatory verses expressing Royalist frustrations, is one example.[44]

Dryden had no difficulty writing in the Cavalier style. His poetic lines in the letter to Honor closely resemble Hookes's poems to Amanda. Here is Dryden, apologizing for blotting the paper sent to him by his cousin:

> For since t'was mine the white hath lost its hiew
> To show t'was n'ere it selfe but whilst in you;
> The Virgin Waxe hath blusht it selfe to red
> Since it with mee hath lost its Maydenhead.

And here is Hookes, "To *Amanda* putting flowers in her bosome":

> Tis not the *pinck* I gaze upon,
> Nor th' pleasant *Cowslip* I look on
> . . . .
> Not the white *lilie* now and than,
> For envie looking pale and wan:
> Nor th' ruddie scarlet *damask rose*,
> Like thy *lips* where *Coral* growes;
> . . . .
> No nor the primrose, though it be
> Modest, and simper too like thee:
> Which gladly spoiled of its balme,
> Mingled its moisture with thy palme,
> Ravish't this morning in its bed,
> Bequeath'd thy hand of its *maiden-head*.

[pp. 17–18]

But Dryden did not print his college poems, and when he next appeared as a public poet, with his stanzas on the death of Cromwell (1659), he had broken free from the closed conventions of the Cavalier style, though he would remember and exploit the lyricism of that style when writing songs for his plays. The liberating influence was a Royalist poet who used his exile and imprisonment to literary advantage, developing a diction and imagery more suited to depicting great men than the played-out Petrarchan flowers of poets like Hookes, forging a stanza Dryden would employ in the Cromwell poem and in *Annus Mirabilis*, and announcing a theory of heroic poetry upon which Dryden's whole career would build: Sir William Davenant, author of *Gondibert*.

Despite its incompleteness, unevenness, and obscurity, *Gondibert* is a formidable piece of work, arguably the most significant attempt at epic between *The Faerie Queene* and *Paradise Lost*, certainly the most important long poem of the 1650s in its influence on Dryden. In contrast to the smooth emptiness of *Amanda*, *Gondibert* is dense with matter: its plot has great range and variety without the wildly episodic fecundity of Italian Renaissance epic; its characters, arranged in contrasting pairs like those in Dryden's heroic plays, have considerable complexity and excellent opportunities for heroic speech; and its quatrain form (four pentameter lines rhyming ABAB) encourages a muscular compression. When the lovely Birtha appears, for example:

> The sooty *Chymist* (who his sight does waste,
> Attending lesser Fires) she passing by,
> Broke his lov'd Lymbick, through enamour'd haste,
> And let, like common Dew, th'Elixer fly.[45]

"Attending lesser Fires" accomplishes in three words a conceit Hookes might have stretched into half a page, and something about the sounds of this stanza caught Dryden's ear; six years later he began his "Heroique Stanza's" on Cromwell with a quatrain using two of the same rhyming words ("haste" and "fly") and the same verb construction in its final line:

> And now 'tis time; for their Officious haste,
> Who would before have born him to the sky,
> Like *eager Romans* ere all Rites were past
> Did let too soon the *sacred Eagle* fly.
>
> [ll. 1–4]

The resemblance is distant, since Dryden is more careful than Davenant about medial caesurae, not only in this stanza but in his general practice. While he too sought to achieve compression by such strategies as zeugma, he was never guilty of a line so clumsy as Astragon's declaration to Birtha: "Degree is monarch's Art, Love, Nature's Law" (III, v, 28). Still, any reader of Dryden's poem in 1659 would have recognized his stanza as that used in *Gondibert*, and when Dryden discusses his choice of that stanza in the preface to *Annus Mirabilis*, he concludes that "it is much better defended in the Preface to *Gondibert*" (I, 51).[46]

Davenant's preface, cast as a letter to Hobbes and answered more briefly by its addressee, shows us a poet seeking to respond to changed circumstances by moving deliberately away from the kind of verse that had made him a successful writer of late Caroline masques. Its prose is much closer to the natural critical idiom Dryden would perfect in the next half-century than to the elaborate cadences of a Thomas Browne, and its principal concerns—how properly to learn from the epic poetry of the past, how to be at once elevated and realistic, and how to define true wit—would be Dryden's concerns and those of the poets of the early eighteenth century. In its toughness and urbanity, Davenant's preface looks ahead to the idea of poetry as civilized argument that Dryden would work out after the Restoration, not backward to the notion of poetry as "Fancy" in which Dryden and Hookes had been trained at Westminster. One of Davenant's paragraphs on wit may stand as an adequate critique of *Amanda* and similar youthful effusions:

> Yong men (as if they were not quite deliver'd from Childhood whose first exercise is Language) imagine [wit] consists in the Musick of words, and believe they are made wise by refining their speech, above the vulgar Dialect: which is a mistake almost as great, as that of the people, who think Orators . . . the ablest men. . . . From the esteem of speaking they proceed to the admiration of what are commonly call'd *Conceits*, things that sound like the knacks or toyes of ordinary *Epigrammatists*: and from thence, after more conversations and variety of objects, grow up to some force of *Fancy*. [p. 19]

If Dryden read this preface while at college, as I believe he did, that passage alone would have given him sufficient pause about printing his verses, if not a twinge of regret at having printed the Hastings elegy. When his turn came to discuss the proper wit of heroic poetry, in the preface to *Annus Mirabilis*, he too would reject "the jerk or sting of an Epigram, . . . the seeming contradiction of a poor Antithesis, . . . [and] the gingle of a more poor *Paranomasia*" (I, 52).

Although Davenant's preface, like some of Dryden's later criticism, is feeling its way toward genuinely new principles for poetic composition, its tone is never pompous. Davenant has a genial way of tossing out some of his most important precepts and definitions in parenthetical phrases; here are a few examples:

> Poets (whose businesse should represent the Worlds true image often to our view) . . .
>
> Language (which is the only Creature of Man's Creation) . . .
>
> Learning (which is not Knowledge, but a continu'd Sayling by fantastick and uncertaine windes toward it) . . .
>
> Poets (who with wise diligence study the People, and have in all ages, by an insensible influence govern'd their manners) . . .
>
> Religion (which is our Art towards God) . . . [pp. 4, 7, 8, 12, 42]

Rhetorically, the parentheses imply that Davenant is merely reminding his reader of principles everyone accepts, but in fact these are challenging assertions. They point away from the Caroline definitions of poetry as hazy mythic propaganda or brain-teasing intellectual conceit, reject the underground Royalist limitation of poetry to effete Cavalier nostalgia, and anticipate the emergence of poetry in the Restoration as a manly, urbane, public, persuasive, and potentially heroic activity, drawing principally upon the real world and aiming to affect moral and political decisions in that world.

For Dryden, these principles were perhaps more decisive than Davenant's actual poetic practice. Despite arguing that poets "should represent the Worlds true image often to our view," Davenant sets *Gondibert* in medieval Lombardy; Dryden's mature heroic poetry deals far more explicitly with contemporary England. So, too, with language: Dryden's innovations in diction build upon but surpass Davenant's. His first exercises in Davenant's stanza reveal a superior ear, and his prose essays developing points made by Davenant do so with more balance and certainty. Still, *Gondibert* opened the way that led to *Annus Mirabilis*, and we may imagine the undergraduate Dryden reading both the preface and the poem as a bracing challenge to the definitions of poetry he had learned from Busby.

Of course, Davenant's parenthetical definition of the proper "businesse" of poets is not a narrow plea for flat realism. In developing this idea, Davenant draws on the usual distinction between historians and poets, and allows poets to use fiction in order to make truth more "operative":

> Truth narrative, and past, is the Idoll of Historians, (who worship a dead thing) and truth operative, and by effects continually alive, is the Mistresse of Poets, who hath not her existence in matter, but in reason.
>
> . . . [T]o make great actions credible is the principall Art of Poets; who though they avouch the utility of Fictions, should not (by altering and subliming Story) make use of their Priviledge to the detriment of the Reader: whose incredulity (when things are not represented in proportion) doth much allay the rellish of his pitty, hope, joy, and other Passions. [p. 11]

Dryden would make a similar argument in the preface to *Annus Mirabilis*, defining "the proper wit of an Heroick or Historical Poem" as "some lively and apt description, dress'd in such colours of speech, that it sets before your eyes the absent object, as perfectly and more delightfully then nature" (I, 53). To modern minds, the theory of "realism" set forth in these passages may seem hopelessly contradictory: the poet is supposed to describe things "*as* perfectly [yet] *more* delightfully" than nature, "to make great actions credible" by using fiction, but *not* by "altering and subliming Story." But there is no such thing as objective literary realism, even in Robbe-Grillet, and Davenant and Dryden are both discussing the *degree* of embellishment necessary to make truth "operative" without rendering the reader so incredulous that his feelings are detached. A rough comparison along these lines might contrast Davenant's masque *Salmacida Spolia* (1640), in which Charles I danced the part of Philogenes, Lover of his People, with Dryden's heroic poem *Annus Mirabilis* (1667), in which Charles II offers up a dramatic prayer for his people during the Great Fire of London. Both are propaganda. But *Salmacida Spolia*, staged just three months before the opening of the Short Parliament, is an example of "altering and subliming Story," an absolute denial of political realities outside the Banqueting House, while *Annus Mirabilis* makes Charles's actions during the Fire, which were in fact commendable, more "credible" by giving them a rhetorical and poetic form. Such a distinction may seem like casuistry, but the larger distinction between baroque and neoclassical art, of which this smaller shift is symptomatic, may also be described as an alteration in the *degree* of embellishment.

If Davenant's preface provided explicit and implicit criticism of the kind of poetry Dryden saw being written at Trinity and probably wrote himself, it did not discourage the young wit in his desire to "set up for a Poet." Davenant's definition of learning as "not Knowledge, but a continu'd Sayling by fantastick and uncertaine windes toward it" might be read as positive encouragement to leave the university and seek other kinds of knowledge in the "gayer company" of London; his proud definition of language as "the only Creature of Man's Creation" suggested that a poet might continue that Adamic exercise by improving the language, as the old Dryden believed he had done; his surprising definition of religion as "our Art towards God" was not only a challenge to Puritan scruples about art, but an assertion that men might seek God through an art worthy of His notice, as Dryden would later do in his major poems on religion and (more lyrically) in his translated hymns. Most important of all, however, was Davenant's confidence that Poets "in all ages" had "govern'd the manners" of the people "by an insensible influence." Unlike some of the other assertions in the preface, this one is memorably developed in the poem, when Gondibert takes refuge in the house of Astragon, a kind of academy of the arts. Gazing at Astragon's collection of books, Gondibert's soldiers imagine that they see "the bury'd writers rise." Egyptian mythologists, Persian magi, biblical authors, theologians, philosophers, moralists, historians, and physicians parade before their eyes. Last come the poets, for whom Davenant reserves a powerful peroration:

> Now they refresh, after this long survay,
> With pleasant *Poets*, who the Soule sublime;
> Fame's *Heraulds*, in whose Triumphs they make way;
> And place all those whom Honor helps to climbe.
>
> And he who seem'd to lead this ravish'd Race,
> Was Heav'n's lov'd *Laureat*, that in *Jewry* writ;
> Whose Harp approach'd Gods Ear, though none his Face
> Durst see, and first made inspiration, wit.
>
> And his Attendants, such blest Poets are,
> As make unblemish'd Love, Courts best delight;
> And sing the prosp'rous Batails of just warre;
> By these the loving, Love, and valiant, fight.
>
> O hyreless Science! and of all alone
> The Liberal! Meanly the rest each State
> In pension treats, but this depends on none;
> Whose worth they rev'rendly forbear to rate.
>
> [II, v, st. 65–68]

The Davenant who wrote these lines in exile in Paris was planning to start a colony in America and finish his poem there, but the actual course of his later career made this talk of pensions and dependencies ironic. Although he had called poetry a "hyreless Science," he was so far in debt by the time he secured his release from prison that he hit upon the expedient of persuading those in power to let him present private theatrical performances, so long as they were called representations or operas rather than plays; on the Restoration of Charles, he was quick to secure his patent as Poet Laureate, though his salary, like Dryden's, was often in arrears.[47] What the two poets had in common, not entirely compromised by their need to pay their debts and their consequent willingness to hire out their skills, was a vision of the poet as the herald of fame, the man who would ultimately determine which of his contemporaries deserved heroic treatment; as the laureate of heaven, whose "Art toward God" would place him in the line of sacred poets descended from King David; as the singer of love and war, who would celebrate the heroic unions and sacrifices of those truly deserving to be thought royal or aristocratic; as the practitioner of the most liberal of the arts and sciences, whose skill could not be "rated" at a set price—even if he himself accepted a salary. We think of the Romantics as the originators of the idea of the poet as hero, but Davenant's is surely a baroque version of that theme, and when Dryden, in one of his greatest poems, presented Charles II as King David, he was not only thinking of polygamy and troublesome sons, the obvious political analogues; he was doing Charles the special honor of likening him to an heroic poet.

If Creighton's reminiscences are to be believed, Dryden had discovered his own poetic vocation by the time he left Cambridge for London in the middle 1650s. There were no poet-kings or courtly lovers to celebrate, so Dryden went to work as a clerk and translator, waiting several more years before publishing his "Heroique Stanza's" on Cromwell's death, a poem that shows how fully he had assimilated and surpassed the example of Davenant. There is little evidence that his curricular work at Cambridge had helped him discover his talents; even under the stresses and strains of the Interregnum, the university was seeking to train scholars, and Dryden's mind, as Creighton points out, was "too roving and active" for mere scholarship. Dr. Johnson, extrapolating from his published works alone, reached the same conclusion:

> As, having distinguished himself at Westminster under the tuition of Busby, who advanced his scholars to a height of knowledge very rarely attained in grammar-schools, he resided afterwards at Cambridge, it is not to be supposed that his skill in the ancient languages was deficient, compared with that of common students; but his scholastick acquisitions seem not proportionate to his opportunities and abilities. He could not, like Milton or Cowley, have made his name illustrious merely by his learning. . . .
>
> Yet it cannot be said that his genius is ever unprovided of matter, or that his fancy languishes in penury of ideas. His works abound with knowledge, and sparkle with illustrations. There is scarcely any science or faculty that does not supply him with occasional images and lucky similitudes; every page discovers a mind very widely acquainted both with art and nature, and in full possession of great stores of intellectual wealth.[48]

The years at Trinity made their contribution to those "great stores"; in formal and informal ways, Dryden was exposed to many kinds of intellectual ferment and controversy. But he also reached the conclusion that the life of a gowned scholar was not for him. Although the traditional requirement that Fellows of a college be ordained had been cast into doubt by the abolition of bishops, the expectation was still that Fellows would be clergymen, and Dryden, who had spent most of the Sundays of his life listening to the "laborious" sermons of Thomas Hill, was apparently reluctant to take the cloth. His lifelong suspicion of "Priests of all Religions" surely owed something to his observation of the bitter struggles of the ever-partisan Fellows, and while his enemies later claimed that he had been denied ordination, there is no evidence to support that charge. I am inclined to believe the poet's declaration in the preface to the *Fables*, written in the last year of his life: "tak[ing] to the Church . . . was never in my Thoughts" (*Poems*, IV, 1461). Dryden could no more have become a Duport, responding to the deaths of his colleagues in studied Latin epigrams, than he could remain content with the limited definition of poetry implicit in *Amanda*; his "roving and active" mind was more likely to be impressed by *Gondibert*, with its invigorating claims for the power of poetry. His life was to be lived in London; his works were to reach a wide audience; he could not "study the People, and . . . govern their manners" from an academic cloister. The poetry of the past was of enormous interest to him, but principally for what he could learn from it as he sought to write the poetry of the present. The stage, the coffeehouse, and the restored court were to be his arenas, though his success there made use of skills acquired in the library and the common room.

CHAPTER FOUR

From Protectorate to Restoration
1655–1661

A Place at Cromwell's Court

The story of Dryden's employment by Cromwell's government begins with the dissolution of the Barebones Parliament and the establishment of the Protectorate. Born out of the fear that radical elements in the appointed Parliament might succeed in distributing property and the franchise more equally, this constitutional change was a victory for the kind of Puritan conservatism in which Dryden had been reared; predictably, his relatives profited by it. Sir Gilbert Pickering and his brother-in-law Edward Montagu became members of the new Council of State; in the ensuing redistribution of offices, they had an opportunity to help their kinsman Erasmus Dryden. During the early 1650s, a wealthy Baptist merchant named Samuel Moyer had held the office of Check Inwards in the London Customs, which paid £300 a year and did not require his actual presence. In January 1654, thanks to his opposition to the Protectorate, he lost that sinecure, and the Council appointed Erasmus Dryden to take his place.[1] Unfortunately, Dryden's father had less than six months to enjoy his new post; he was buried in Titchmarsh on June 18. Erasmus's will suggests that the additional income from the government appointment would have been helpful. Although he made cash bequests to his children totalling some £1280, the only piece of real estate he owned was the 330 acres in Blakesley left him by his own father. In his quiet career at Titchmarsh, during which he had served as a Justice of the Peace but had not been otherwise active in a political or military way, Erasmus had not acquired additional land. He left the Blakesley farm to his son John, with the stipulation that his widow receive one-third of the quarterly rent during her lifetime.[2] The annual rent was less than £100 before taxes,[3] considerably less than Erasmus stood to receive as Check Inwards of the Customs; Dryden's two-thirds share, while doubtless welcome to a young man intending to "set up for a Poet," was hardly a sufficient income for life as a gentleman in the city.

Having tried to help the father, Sir Gilbert Pickering apparently felt an obligation to help the son, for on 19 October 1657 we find John Dryden signing a receipt for fifty pounds paid him by John Thurloe, Secretary of State to Cromwell, master spy, and one of the most able of all Commonwealth bureaucrats.[4] From other evidence, namely two documents that record Dryden's participation in Cromwell's state funeral, where he marched with Milton and Marvell as "Secretarys of yᵉ ffrench and Latin Toungs,"[5] we may infer that this payment from Thurloe was a salary for work as a clerk and translator. Shadwell, in *The Medal of John Bayes*, is quite specific:

> The next step of Advancement you began,
> Was being Clerk to *Nolls* Lord *Chamberlain,*
> A Sequestrator and Committee-man.

[p. 8]

Pickering, who had been close to the center of power from the beginning of Cromwell's ascendancy, had indeed been active in sequestering the estates of Royalists, and had served on the Northamptonshire Committee for the ejection of "scandalous" ministers; he was appointed Lord Chamberlain under the Protectorate.[6] In the days of the monarchy, that post had normally been filled by an earl, under whom several vice-chamberlains and an enormous staff saw to such functions as the maintenance and expansion of royal dwellings, the appropriate entertainment of foreign dignitaries, and the mustering of the various royal guards. The revival of the position under the Protectorate was but one of many signals that the government was taking on the appearance of a monarchy; a left-wing pamphlet attacking this development suggested that Pickering had been appointed because he was "so finical, spruce, and like an old courtier."[7] But Cromwell's court, even in its most glorious days, operated on a much smaller budget and with a much smaller staff than the Stuart courts, and Pickering, who continued to sit on what was now called the Protector's Privy Council, and in 1658 took his seat in the newly created Other House, never seems to have devoted his full time to the post as Lord Chamberlain—except on the occasion of Oliver's splendid funeral.

The fragmentary evidence about Dryden's duties is open to several interpretations: he may have worked directly for Pickering, whose dealings with foreign dignitaries would have required the services of a competent translator; he may have been employed, as Milton and Marvell were, in the office of the Latin Secretary, where diplomatic correspondence was prepared; he may have performed either or both of these functions on a part-time or piece-work basis, as the receipt from Thurloe, which occurs in a collection of miscellaneous disbursements, suggests. No record survives appointing Dryden to a post with a stated annual salary, though such records do exist for Milton and Marvell.[8] Since he had a small income of his own, Dryden may not have wanted to work as a full-time clerk; the possibility that he wrote some prefaces for books published as early as 1657 supports the hypothesis that his work for the government was part-time.[9]

When he left London for Cambridge in 1650, Dryden was a schoolboy; now he was technically a gentleman, though the actual income from the land he owned was modest at best. In his first play, *The Wild Gallant*, the impecunious Loveby begs his landlord to "stay thy fury till my Rents come up," and this comic scene may reflect the eagerness with which the young Dryden awaited the quarterly payment of his own rents. Begging the landlord not to banish him to a tiny garret room, Loveby protests that "a penny Looking-glass cannot stand upright in the Window"; and Tom Brown, in a pamphlet published in 1688, makes Dryden say that his first lodging in London "had a Window no bigger than a Pocket Looking-glass."[10] The phrase is common enough, and might even have been borrowed by Brown from Dryden's play, but it does sound like the sort of detail the older poet might have remembered from his impecunious youth. Still, even if he did find himself on a tight budget, the young Dryden was unlikely to get into any real difficulties, since his Pickering relatives were in positions of power and influence; his aunt Susannah, for example, had a house in London throughout the 1650s and probably gave her nephew an occasional dinner.[11]

Although Dryden had added greatly to his intellectual assets during his Cambridge years, he may not have added so much to his social sophistication; another story attributed to the poet himself by an enemy illustrates this point:

> You may know he is no concealer of himself, by a story which he tells of himself, *viz.* That (when he came first to Town) being a young raw fellow of seven and Twenty, as he call'd himself when he told the story, he frequenting but one Coffee-house, the Woman (it seems finding him out) put Coffee upon him for Chocolate, and made him pay three pence a dish for two years together: till at length, by what providence I know not, he discovered the Cheat.[12]

If Dryden was indeed so naive, he soon had opportunities to become better accustomed to the ways of London. His first cousin Edward Salwey, called to the bar in 1658, was a knowledgeable companion, having been at the Inner Temple during Dryden's Cambridge years, and there were surely other young men willing and able to introduce him to the customs of the town.

His official duties, whatever they were, brought Dryden into contact with the other secretaries with whom he marched in Cromwell's funeral procession; since these included two other important poets, our lack of knowledge about their relations with Dryden at this time is particularly frustrating. All three men were graduates of Cambridge with literary interests, but in the case of Milton, intimate relations seem unlikely. The Latin Secretary was totally blind by 1652 and stayed at home most of the time, relying on his assistants to handle the work at the office. Nonetheless, Milton did write a number of important state letters in 1657 and 1658[13] and marched in the Protector's *cortège* on 23 November 1658. Dryden, who marched with him, had presumably met the celebrated poet and controversialist in the office, but I should imagine their relations at this time were rather distant and formal. Milton was fifty and famous; Dryden was twenty-seven and unknown. His later career as Poet Laureate would involve the celebration of political and religious beliefs quite unlike Milton's, but he never attacked his former supervisor, as some gloating Royalists did in 1660; his references to Milton throughout his career are respectful. When Charles Sackville, Lord Buckhurst, sent him a copy of *Paradise Lost* in 1669, Dryden's reported acknowledgment of Milton's greatness was candidly accurate: "that Poet has cutt us all out."[14] Grounded in such an acknowledgment of Milton's poetic skill, the deference with which Dryden treated

Milton in the 1670s also owed something to the fact that he had worked under Milton as a young man.

For Marvell, with whom he later engaged in controversy, he had no such respect, although their backgrounds were quite similar: both had grandfathers who had been imprisoned for refusing the Forced Loan of 1626; both had fathers who had attended Emmanuel; both were graduates of Trinity and contributors to *Lachrymae Musarum*.[15] But Marvell was ten years older than Dryden, a significant gap in age and experience, particularly in the troubled 1650s. Milton had recommended him for a position in the office of the Latin Secretary as early as 1653, when Dryden was still an undergraduate, and when Marvell failed to secure that appointment, he made an extensive tour of Europe, an experience Dryden never enjoyed. Eventually, there was another opening, and Marvell was formally appointed Latin Secretary in September 1657, one month before Dryden signed the receipt for Thurloe. Marvell's close association with the Parliamentary general Thomas Fairfax, who had opposed the execution of Charles and the ascendancy of Cromwell, may have prevented him from securing a place on his first attempt, but he could now point to a number of poetic performances likely to please those in power: he had written poems extolling Cromwell's victories in Ireland (1650), attacking the Dutch at the time of the First Dutch Naval War (1652–54), and celebrating the first anniversary of the Protectorate (1655). In view of the later hostility between Marvell and Dryden, anything we might discover about their relations during the Protectorate would be fascinating, but neither has left behind a comment or a personal line that will allow us to speculate.[16]

If the Whitehall and Hampton Court of these years were not the centers of high culture they had been under Charles I, and certainly not the arenas of sexual and political intrigue they would become under Charles II, they cannot be painted entirely in shades of gray. Wine flowed freely; musicians performed on secular occasions; paintings and tapestries still adorned the walls. Later satirists would taunt Dryden with having served in Cromwell's court, but he learned lessons there that proved applicable to the restored Stuart court. By the time he came to London, the millenarian fervor for revolutionary reform had been contained; after the end of the brief and disastrous rule of the Major Generals (August 1655-September 1656), power seemed to be returning to the hands of the "natural rulers," the nobility and gentry, who were forging a working alliance with Cromwell by the traditional means: marriage and money. When Cromwell's daughters married into aristocratic families, the celebrations were reminiscent of royal splendor. On 11 November 1657, Frances Cromwell married Robert Rich, grandson of the Earl of Warwick, at Whitehall, where forty-eight violins accompanied "mixt dancing (a thing heretofore accounted profane) till 5 of the clock"; the Earl of Newport danced with the Protector's wife.[17] Eight days later, Frances's sister Mary married Lord Fauconberg (or Falconbridge) at Hampton Court, where the guests heard two songs with pastoral texts by Marvell. In the same month, the Royalist Sir Robert Howard, Dryden's future collaborator and brother-in-law, concluded his negotiations with the Privy Council for a renewal of the lease of the Post Fines, which his father had held under Charles I; as Howard's biographer concludes, "what we should call bribery was certainly involved."[18] John Dryden was hardly important enough to have attended the weddings, though his cousin and employer Gilbert Pickering was certainly there, but he might well have met Howard in the course of the bargaining over the Post Fines. Merely by being present at court, he was absorbing at first hand a kind of knowledge that would prove as important to his later career as the languages and facts he had acquired at Westminster and Trinity; he was learning about power, traditions, family wealth, and the capacity of the establishment to resist or adapt to change.

The Protectorate, the Arts, and the "Heroique Stanza's"

Even after Oliver refused the crown, many in the court believed that the Cromwells would become a new dynasty; once the succession to the office of Lord Protector was made hereditary, the refusal of the title of king looked merely semantic. When Oliver died, those unable to make him a king in life attempted to make him one in death: his effigy, clothed in robes of state, wore an imperial crown and held an orb. Like monarchial Lord Chamberlains in previous reigns, Sir Gilbert Pickering marched directly in front of the bier, wearing close mourning, with servants bearing his train; he was directly responsible for issuing mourning to those marching and arranging their order according to protocol.[19] The "Heroique Stanza's" composed on this occasion by the Lord Chamberlain's cousin and clerk reflect the official rhetoric of Cromwell's quasi-royal funeral: according to the *Mercurius Politicus* of 6 September 1658, Sir Oliver Fleming, the Master of Ceremonies, was ordered to notify foreign ambassadors "that it hath pleased God to take out of this world the most serene and renowned Oliver, late Protector of the Commonwealth,"[20] and Dryden's poem is "Consecrated to the Glorious Memory of his most Serene and Renowned Highnesse OLIVER Late *LORD PROTECTOR* of this Common-Wealth." If Cromwell's court was far more royal than his republican followers in the New Model Army would have expected, the refusal of actual kingship was still central to the style of that court, and the restraint of Dryden's poem suggests a literary version of this style. The imagery drawn from astronomy, the classics, and the arts resembles the imagery of the Caroline masque or the Hastings elegy, but it is carefully controlled by rhetorical qualification and occasional irony; traditional royal topoi are altered and adjusted for the purpose of praising a leader whose "Vertue" was *not* "poyson'd . . . With the too early thoughts of being King" (ll. 27–28). By making such alterations and adjustments, Dryden was responding shrewdly to the special circumstances that affected all forms of artistic expression under the Protectorate.

The eighteen years from the start of the Civil Wars to the Restoration saw a profound disruption in the course of the arts in England. Royal patronage vanished. Laws disbanding cathedral choirs and outlawing theatrical presentations took effect. Many foreign artists returned to the Continent. Some English artists, such as the composer William Lawes, were killed in action; many others spent some of these years in exile or in prison. The extent of the disruption varied from art to art, but for all the arts, the increased tolerance of the Protectorate marked a welcome change from the conditions that had prevailed under the Barebones Parliament. The diarist John Evelyn saw women appearing with painted faces in May 1654, and the Lord Mayor's Show was revived in 1655 after a hiatus of fourteen years; "the times," as one former bishop remarked, were "now more open."[21] Artistic responses to the years of disruption included defiance, nostalgia, and adaptation. Those who learned to adapt, particularly during the more "open" times of the Protectorate, began to determine the course English culture would take after the Restoration, although their very willingness to adapt often indicated their doubt that a Restoration would ever occur.

In the theatre, the only art to be legally outlawed, defiance seemed the only proper strategy at first. The Red Bull and the Fortune were open intermittently during the Interregnum, despite periodic violent raids by Parliamentary soldiers. Without the court support that even popular theatre had enjoyed under the monarchy, however, these illegal performances could not hope to be serious or innovative; most were clumsy versions of old plays.[22] Yet in 1656, the Royalist Davenant, freshly released from the Tower but still adept at wooing Cromwell's courtiers, succeeded in legally presenting *The first dayes entertainment at Rutland House, by declamations and music, after the manner of the ancients*, a deliberately undramatic piece that prepared the way for later productions. This "entertainment" begins with a debate between Diogenes the cynic and Aristophanes the poet, the first attacking and the second defending poetry, music, and drama; a song awards the victory to Aristophanes. Then comes a similar debate between a Parisian and a Londoner on the respective merits of their cities, followed by a song defending London. The simple symmetry of the whole thus connects drama with English patriotism, despite the fact that plays were actually flourishing in Paris and outlawed in London. Having identified the opponents of drama directly with cynicism and indirectly with France, Davenant could safely move on to present *The Siege of Rhodes*, an "opera" written entirely in rhyme. Unlike the vulgar farces at the illegal theatres, which were exercises in survival, *The Siege of Rhodes* involved significant innovation; as Dryden himself would later acknowledge, it provided a precedent for the rhymed heroic plays of the Restoration. Just as many politicians who had accepted employment from the Protectorate, such as Dryden's kinsman Edward Montagu, found themselves ideally placed to help effect the Restoration, so Davenant, having adapted to the circumstances of the Protectorate, was ideally placed to profit from the return of courtly patronage: Charles II renewed his patent as Poet Laureate and awarded him one of two patents issued for theatrical companies—a highly desirable prize sought by several contestants.[23] Moreover, Davenant's observation of French theatrical practices during his exile proved invaluable: he used such continental innovations as wing-and-drop scenery to make his fledgling Duke's Company a worthy rival to the more experienced King's Company.

The situation for musicians was different. Many lost their annual salaries as cathedral choristers or gentlemen of the King's Music, though Cromwell did maintain a small musical establishment. Some found employment as teachers, taking private pupils or posts at schools and universities; a "Mr. Lilly, Musick Master in Cambridge," for example, is praised in Hookes's *Amanda*. Others may have gained some income by publishing their pieces: Henry Lawes, an unreconstructed Royalist who was perhaps the best known English composer at this time, published several collections of his works during the 1650s, and John Playford, the first English publisher to deal mainly in music, brought out numerous miscellaneous collections and instruction books. Patronage for music cut across the political spectrum: Lawes was associated with the circle of Royalist poets around Katharine Philips, "the matchless Orinda," but there was also music at the homes of Commonwealth grandees, and even humble Puritans were not always averse to secular music as recreation.[24] In 1657, the Protector's Privy Council actually appointed a "Committee for the Advancement of Musicke" whose members included Sir Gilbert Pickering and General (i.e., Admiral) Montagu; a petition addressed to them by John Hingston, Davis Mell, and three of their colleagues in Cromwell's small orchestra proposed "That there bee a Corporacion or Colledge of Musitians erected in London, with reasonable powers to read and practise publiquely all sorts of Musick, and to suppress the singing of obscene scandalous and defamatory Songs and Ballads."[25] Despite the shrewd appeal to Puritan sensibilities in the promise to suppress improper ballads, the petition, which went on to propose endowing the college with the lands and rents formerly used to support cathedral choirs, was not approved. Still, it was an attempt to adjust to changed times, not unlike Davenant's more successful plan for producing "entertainments."

But there were crucial differences. Davenant made a profit from his theatrical ventures after the Restoration and saw the stylistic innovations of the poetry and drama he had written during the Interregnum bear fruit in the work of Dryden and others. Hingston and Mell were restored to their places in the royal orchestra, but found their salaries virtually impossible to collect.[26] Worse yet, before Charles had even arrived in London, when Lawes and other English composers were joyously preparing music to greet him, six French musicians arrived with the news that they had been commissioned to compose the festive music, and the royal preference for French dance tunes continued.[27] Despite a good deal of musical activity during the Interregnum, there had been no substantive development in style; indeed, many of Playford's publications were reprints of the works of Elizabethan composers.

In at least one case, an important composer moved backwards self-consciously. Thomas Tomkins, cathedral organist at Worcester and heir to the great English tradition of contrapuntal keyboard composition, saw his organ dismantled in 1646; in 1649 he composed *A Sad Pavan: for these distracted times* on the occasion of the execution of Charles I. Thereafter, the old man filled his commonplace book with pieces that retreat from modern devices, coming to resemble ever more closely the compositions of his own teacher William Byrd.[28] Here was Royalist nostalgia with a vengeance, a denial of the future and the present in a retreat to the past. Even before the Interregnum, English music had been conservative: the flowering of the English madrigal, for example, came some twenty years after the high point of the Italian madrigal school. But the enforced insularity of English music during the Interregnum put composers even further behind, and if Tomkins's retreat into the past produced some of his finest pieces, those pieces were no more a basis for future development in music than the nostalgic verse of underground Cavaliers was a basis for future development in poetry. As Dryden was painfully aware, there was no native composer capable of collaborating with him on an opera even twenty-five years after the Restoration, when he wrote *Albion and Albanius* with Louis Grabu; the emergence of the Englishman Henry Purcell, with whom he collaborated on *King Arthur* (1691), was a cause for rejoicing, but Purcell's premature death five years later, mourned by Dryden in a lovely ode, left English musical culture vulnerable to another foreign takeover.

Despite the Puritan hostility to the visual arts, painters fared better than actors and musicians during the Interregnum. To be sure, there was no official court painter, and the Commonwealth government sold off much of Charles I's incomparable collection. But one of the major buyers at those auctions was the Dutch painter Peter Lely, who kept his appointment book filled throughout the Interregnum. Wealthy people of all shades of opinion continued to patronize portrait painters, and Lely became principal painter to Charles II, despite having painted Cromwell's portrait. The miniaturist Samuel Cooper, who became Charles II's limner, painted a famous head of Cromwell "warts and all" that established the public image of the Protector; Lely's full-size portrait is based on that miniature. Yet Cooper was no Puritan; he was a Roman Catholic, a skilled lutenist, and the uncle by marriage of Alexander Pope; his employment by the Protectorate suggests that in painting at least, skill was more important than politics or religion. Nonetheless, the preferences of the Puritan leadership had some long-lasting effects: a proposal by Lely and two partners to decorate Whitehall with murals depicting the victories of the Parliamentary armies was not approved,[29] and even after the Restoration, there were fewer opportunities for history painting on a large scale than before. When Dryden complains, in his poem to Kneller, that Kneller lacks "just Incouragement" for history painting and must drudge along with portraits, he blames the taste of "this Age," and compares his own inability to find support for epic poetry.[30] Accurate as a judgment of the artistic and poetic taste of the 1690s, Dryden's poem reflects trends in both arts that began in the 1650s.

His poem on Cromwell refers repeatedly to the art of the painter. Glancing at the traditional notion of the perfection of the circular or *tondo* form, and perhaps mindful of the fact that both Cooper and Lely had painted the Protector in circular compositions, the poet asks,

> How shall I then begin, or where conclude
> To draw a *Fame* so truly *Circular*?
> For in a round what order can be shew'd,
> Where all the parts so *equall perfect* are?

[ll. 17–20]

In this metaphor, the poet becomes a visual artist; he wonders how to "draw" Cromwell's fame. Later, in claiming for Cromwell the naval victories won by Admiral Blake, Dryden describes the Protector as a master-painter like Lely, supervising a studio of assistants:

> When absent, yet we conquer'd in his right;
> For though some meaner Artist's skill were shown
> In mingling colours, or in placing light,
> Yet still the *faire Designment* was his own.

[ll. 93–96]

Again, the central concern is "*Designment*," which Dryden's poem displays by strictly following the form of a classical oration.[31] Not entirely consistent with these passages is the metaphor in which God becomes the artist who has drawn Cromwell:

> Heav'n in his Portraict shew'd a Workman's hand
> And drew it perfect yet without a shade.
>
> [ll. 59–60]

Since dramatic effects employing light and shade were not only important for Inigo Jones's masques, but central to the technique of royal portrait painters from Rubens to Van Dyck to Lely, Cromwell's famous request to be drawn "warts and all" was a refusal of the traditional flattery made possible by clever shading. The portrait of the Protector by the Puritan painter Robert Walker uses flat lighting, avoiding the shading so typical of earlier royal portraits, and even Lely paints Cromwell in armor, eschewing his usual bravura effects with drapery. Evidently aware of these aesthetic concerns, Dryden emphasizes Cromwell's honest or "natural" greatness by describing God as a realistic painter, a "Workman" more like a Walker than a Van Dyck.[32]

Ironically, Dryden's literary portrait of Cromwell is highly shaded: he glosses

Miniature of Oliver Cromwell by Samuel Cooper, signed and dated 1656.

Portrait of Cromwell by Peter Lely, ca. 1657.

quickly over the English Civil War and concentrates on the Protector's popular foreign victories; he relies heavily on metaphor; he omits the personal references to Cromwell's daughters that make Marvell's poem on the same occasion almost maudlin;[33] he makes no mention of Richard, Oliver's ineffective successor. A realistic or "unshaded" poem on Cromwell would have had to mention his inconsistencies and alterations of policy, the "warts" upon his political and military career; though Dryden might seem to endorse such artistic "naturalness" in a metaphor, he knew in practice that the special circumstances of the Protector's funeral required all the delicacy and shading of which he was capable. The published poem is "Consecrated to the Glorious Memory" of Cromwell, but in the manuscript, Dryden had first written "Glorious and Happy Memory."[34] Perhaps he struck out the word "Happy" to avoid giving offense to those many Englishmen who might concede the glory of the Protector's foreign conquests,

Portrait of Cromwell by Robert Walker, ca. 1649.

but who could not consider his domestic reign a happy one; whatever his reasons, this late cancellation may serve as an example of Dryden's rhetorical care in this poem, which charts a course between conflicting principles of style.

The conventional metaphorical vocabulary for glory was royal, and many of Dryden's images come from that stock of commonplaces, but he qualifies the traditional language in revealing ways. In the Hastings elegy, he had drawn upon the idea of the monarch as the sun, common in all strands of European poetry and memorably developed in Shakespeare's histories and Jonson's masques, to equate Lord Hastings's disease and the national chaos of the 1640s:

> The Nations Sin hath drawn that Veil, which shrouds
> Our Day-spring in so sad benighting Clouds.
>
> [ll. 49–50]

A similar image in the Cromwell poem has quite different force:

> His *Grandeur* he deriv'd from Heav'n alone,
> For he was great e're Fortune made him so;
> And Warr's like mists that rise against the Sunne
> Made him but greater seem, not greater grow.
>
> [ll. 21–24]

The wars are still clouds or mists, but instead of shrouding Hastings (or Charles I), they create an optical illusion that magnifies Cromwell, who *seemed* greater because of his military prowess, but did not *grow* greater. Predestined to greatness by Heaven, Cromwell is praised because he did not take advantage of his success as a war leader to insist upon the crown; a standard royal metaphor thus serves the purpose of praising the Protector's refusal to "grow greater" by taking the crown. Among the many icons pictured in the frontispiece to *Eikon Basilike*, was a palm tree with heavy weights tied to its branches, with a Latin motto insisting that the monarch's virtue had grown despite adversity. For Cromwell, toward whom Fortune had been more kind, this image needed only a little retooling:

> His *Palmes* though under weights they did not stand,
> Still thriv'd; no *Winter* could his *Laurells* fade;
>
> [ll. 57–58]

The implication is that Cromwell's good fortune gave him a freedom for expansive growth, including the opportunity for kingship, which might have proved just as dangerous as being weighed down by adversity.

Not only did Dryden carefully adjust such traditional metaphors; he also avoided that part of traditional royal language typified by Carew's lines on the Stuart court:

> we advance
> Such vertues only as admit excesse,
> Brave bounteous acts, Regall Magnificence.[35]

If Dryden emphasizes Cromwell's "Magnificence," he avoids the "excesse" he would let loose in his panegyrics on the Restoration; the "Heroique Stanza's" come close to Davie's definition of Calvinist art as "sobriety, tense with all the extravagances that it has been tempted by and has denied itself."[36] Although such courtiers as Sir Gilbert Pickering were giving the Protector a royal funeral, they had fought a war against "excesse." The budget of Cromwell's establishment was tightly controlled, as is the language of praise in Dryden's poem.

Dryden's awareness of these matters is particularly apparent in the first four stanzas of the poem. He begins by contrasting his own patience in waiting to publish his poem until after the official funeral with the "Officious haste" of those who had rushed into print earlier. There was a long delay: Oliver died on 3 September 1658, but Pickering's preparations for the funeral were so complex that it did not take place until 23 November; the corpse, despite having been embalmed, had to be buried on 10 November.[37] By congratulating himself on waiting, Dryden may be obliquely defending his cousin's deliberate proceeding; he also gains a sonorous monosyllabic opening, "And now 'tis time," and an early statement of the theme of propriety.

Stanzas 2–4 elaborate that theme:

> Though our best notes are treason to his fame
> Joyn'd with the loud applause of publique voice;
> Since Heav'n, what praise we offer to his name
> Hath render'd too authentick by its choice:
>
> Though in his praise no Arts can liberall be,
> Since they whose muses have the highest flown
> Add not to his immortal Memorie,
> But do an act of friendship to their own:
>
> Yet 'tis our duty and our interest too
> Such monuments as we can build to raise;
> Lest all the World prevent what we should do
> And claime a Title *in him by their praise.*
>
> [ll. 5–16]

Grammatically, these twelve lines constitute one sentence; the main clause, long delayed and elaborately qualified, comes at the beginning of the fourth stanza. If we take the first-person plurals as collective references to the nation as a whole, these lines argue that it is a national duty to honor Cromwell's memory, and that is surely their public sense. But if we focus more narrowly on Dryden himself, for whom writing this poem was a *duty* connected with his official employment, a task distinctly in his *interest*, a more private and complex meaning emerges. "Such monuments as we can build" looks like conventional humility ("the best poem I can write, young and inexperienced as I am"), but the phrase also engages the political and aesthetic problems we have been exploring: Dryden is acknowledging that he cannot write for Cromwell the kind of poem earlier poets had written for monarchs, just as the actual monument raised to Cromwell in Westminster Abbey was deliberately unlike royal tombs. The earlier qualifications of this ambiguous main statement involve similar ironies. "Though our best notes are treason to his fame" again suggests conventional humility, but if we remember the sad case of Thomas Tomkins, whose "best notes" on the cathedral organ were regarded as "treason" by the Parliamentary soldiers who tore it down, the phrase yields another sense: if we think of a poet's "best notes" as the unqualified royal language of praise, such praise would be "treason to [the] fame" of a man who had deliberately refused the crown. "Though in his praise no Arts can liberall be," beyond the pun on the "liberal arts," reminds us that liberality, in the sense of Carew's lines praising royal "excesse," was strenuously avoided by Cromwell's court. The poets

Frontispiece to *Eikon Basilike* (1649).

"whose muses have the highest flown" are therefore not only self-serving, as Dryden explicitly states, but guilty of a failure of decorum; they have dressed Cromwell in borrowed robes. "What praise we offer" must be qualified by a knowledge of what praise Cromwell would have found acceptable; "Such monuments as we can build" must be restrained and dignified.

In practice, Dryden's attention to decorum necessitated not only the qualification of royal imagery, but the denial of emotional language. In the Hastings elegy, he had dramatized anger and grief, and in his Restoration panegyrics, he would find verbal equivalents for the euphoria that swept much of the nation. But the Cromwell poem maintains a porcelain calm, as we can see by contrasting it with Marvell's. Here is Marvell, in his last lines before turning to the praise of Richard Cromwell, directly addressing the dead chief:

> For we, since thou art gone, with heavy doom,
> Wander like ghosts about thy loved tomb;
> And lost in tears, have neither sight nor mind
> To guide us upward through this region blind.
> Since thou art gone, who best that way couldst teach,
> Only our sighs, perhaps, may thither reach.[38]

Here is Dryden's conclusion:

> His Ashes in a peacefull Urne shall rest,
> His Name a great example stands to show
> How strangely high endeavors may be blest,
> Where *Piety* and *valour* joyntly goe.

[ll. 145–48]

For Marvell, Cromwell is a spirit to be addressed in the second person by a nation "lost in tears"; for Dryden, he is an urn filled with ashes, a "great example," and finally a combination of two abstract virtues, "*Piety* and *valour*."

Despite the fact that his political opponents later reprinted this poem, taunting the Laureate with having praised the "Usurper," Dryden's poem is so cautious as to suggest that he sought to avoid offending the Royalists, many of whom, in 1659, would have been ready to agree that Cromwell was a genuinely heroic figure whose conquests had been glorious for England.[39] Marvell concludes his poem with sixteen lines on Richard Cromwell, alleging that "A Cromwell in an hour a prince will grow" (l. 312), but Dryden does not mention the new ruler, an omission suggesting that he may have guessed at the shortness of the second Protector's reign. Since Sir Gilbert Pickering went on serving the new Protector as Lord Chamberlain, Dryden probably had some chance to observe the inadequacies of "Tumble-down Dick." By the time he wrote this poem, he had also probably met Sir Robert Howard, who was corresponding with Charles Stuart in France,[40] and whom he would praise, in June of 1660, for anticipating the Restoration:

> Ere our weak eyes discern'd the doubtfull streak
> Of light, you saw great *Charls* his morning break.
> ["To my Honored Friend, Sr Robert Howard," ll. 89–90]

Again, the first-person plural includes the first-person singular; if Dryden's eyes were strong enough to see a short reign for Richard Cromwell, they were too weak to see that the future would be royal. Had he been so prescient, he would surely not have published

"Heroique Stanza's," which, for all its caution and qualification, is nonetheless a poem in praise of Cromwell.

Years later, when the poem was reprinted, one of his metaphors gave Dryden particular cause for regret. In his truncated account of the Civil War, he contrasts Cromwell with "Our former Chiefs"—presumably the less effective Parliamentary generals Fairfax, Manchester, and William Waller—and portrays those men as greedy, ineffective doctors, while making Cromwell a successful physician:

> Warre our consumption was their gainfull trade,
> We inward bled whilst they prolong'd our pain:
> He fought to end our fighting and assaid
> To stanch the blood by breathing of the vein.

[ll. 45–48]

His political opponents in the 1680s pounced upon the last image, claiming that it was an approving reference to the execution of Charles I,[41] but the image was frequent in Puritan polemic during the early days of the Civil War, long before that execution was contemplated. Dryden might first have heard it in a sermon preached by Thomas Hill in 1643, where the reference is clearly to the war: "There are now many *veines opened in England*, it is in the body *Politick*, as in the *Naturall*, much *bad bloud* cannot be let out, but we shall lose some *good*."[42] I am not insisting that Dryden picked up the image of bloodletting from Hill; the metaphor was common enough, and his use of it is far more precise—medically and poetically—than Hill's. Still, the fact remains that the very image for which Dryden would later be accused of Puritan sentiments had actually been employed by the Puritan pastor of his Titchmarsh boyhood.

Finally, this use of a standard Puritan image to describe a Puritan victory can best be understood as another example of Dryden's habitual care in matching his style to his subject. His potentially conflicting aims in this poem—dignified praise of Cromwell's heroic qualities, subtle qualification of that praise to reflect the Protector's refusal of the crown, and cautious detachment in the face of the unsettled political situation—produce a more disciplined poem than the Restoration panegyrics he wrote in the next several years, in which the indulgence of Royal excess in the style produces some passages nearly as incoherent as the weaker parts of the Hastings elegy. In the Cromwell poem, the oratorical organization and the elegant *Gondibert* stanza prevent the praise from sliding into enthusiasm or grandiloquence, while in *Astraea Redux, To his Sacred Majesty*, and *To My Lord Chancellor*, couplet poems in celebration of the Restoration, the Coronation, and the ascendancy of Clarendon, smaller ironies and implications are the only forces restraining fervent praise. The resulting imbalance accurately reflects the national euphoria of the early 1660s; the more cautious artistry of the Cromwell poem reflects the constraining circumstances of the Protector's funeral. As his later works would show, Dryden was at his best in poems balancing equally poised elements, poems arguing both sides of a question or treating one topic in terms of another. The elements brought into such a temporary equilibrium in "Heroique Stanza's"—royal grandeur and Calvinist restraint—were particularly important ones for him, since they were the stylistic equivalents of the conflicting forces that had shaped his early life.

Herringman and Howard

Our knowledge of Dryden's activities in the years following Cromwell's death brings two figures into focus: the literary publisher Henry Herringman and the politician and amateur poet Sir Robert Howard. Both men would assume considerable importance in Dryden's future: Herringman was his publisher until 1678, and Howard became his brother-in-law, literary collaborator, and opponent in literary and political controversy. Beyond their individual interest, they may stand as examples of the two ways a writer could hope to support himself: commercial publication, still in its infancy and not yet the viable system it would become in the later eighteenth century; and noble patronage, the traditional system of support, itself undergoing important changes in the altered circumstances of the Restoration.

According to *The Medal of John Bayes*, Dryden lodged with Herringman until Howard provided better accommodations:

> But he being dead, who should the slave prefer [Cromwell],
> He [Dryden] turn'd a Journey-man t'a †Bookseller;
> Writ Prefaces to Books for Meat and Drink,
> And as he paid, he would both write and think.
> Then by th' assistance of a *Noble *Knight*,
> Th'hadst plenty, ease, and liberty to write.
> First like a *Gentleman* he made thee live;
> And on his bounty thou didst amply thrive.
> †Mr. Herringman, *who kept him in his House for that purpose.*
> *Sir R. H. *who kept him generously at his own House.*
>
> [pp. 8–9; original notes]

The claim that Dryden lodged with Herringman cannot be verified, though several prefaces to books issued by Herringman during this period may conceivably be by Dryden.[43] In the case of Howard, however, there are two confirming scraps of evidence: on 6 September 1661, when Howard signed an indenture for the Post Fines, having once again secured that privilege from yet another government, Dryden witnessed his signature; and in October 1663, when Howard was arranging to purchase from Sir Andrew Henley a house in Lincoln's Inn Fields in which he was already living as a tenant, he received a letter from Henley naming some pieces of furniture the seller wished to retain, including "the serge bed Mr Dreiden useth."[44]

Dryden's associations with both men probably began before the death of Cromwell: some of the prefaces that may be his date as early as 1657, and Howard had been in and out of Whitehall in the same year.[45] With the collapse of the Protectorate, Dryden needed some form of employment to supplement his Blakesley income, and he had the literary tools to be useful to someone like Herringman, whose publications included poems, religious tracts, scientific treatises, and translated romances. Lest we imagine that Herringman's business operated on the scale of later publishers, however, we should recall that literacy remained appallingly low; books were a luxury, and Herringman's customers, virtually without exception, were "gentlemen." Without hope for a sustaining public, young writers like Dryden had to hope for patronage, and Howard's friendship with Dryden in these years looked like a promising pattern for the renewal of noble patronage that seemed likely in the happy days of the early Restoration. Howard's aristocratic credentials were impeccable: sixth son of the Earl of Berkshire, born some five years before Dryden, he had danced before the King in a masque as a young boy; when the Civil War broke out, he became a teenage Cavalier, and was knighted on the

The Honble Sr Robert Howard.

Engraving of Sir Robert Howard after a portrait by Sir Godfrey Kneller, frontispiece to
Five New Plays (1695).

field for his valor in 1644; married in 1645, he already had several children by his first wife, Anne Kingsmill, who died in 1657 or 1658.[46] When Dryden first knew him, he was a dashing young widower in London, negotiating with the Protectorate, intriguing for the return of the King, and trying his hand at verses, translations, and plays. The fact that Howard was a writer, as were many other aristocrats of the period, is of vital importance. Poets depended for their support upon gentlemen who amused themselves by writing verses, just as musicians depended upon such gentleman amateurs as Pepys,

Portrait of Samuel Pepys by John Hayls, 1666.

who enjoyed taking part in sacred and secular music, and was painted holding one of his compositions, as if he were a professional composer. Booksellers like Herringman, recognizing that literary amateurs would be even better customers if they, too, had books in print, were quite ready to print collections like Howard's *Poems* of 1660, just as the restored theatres were more than willing to produce plays by the prominent court- iers on whose support they depended.

In the court of Charles II, who valued spoken and written wit, professional writers often competed with their courtier patrons. Dryden thus later came into conflict with Howard, Buckingham, and Rochester,[47] but when his literary association with Howard began, it looked quite advantageous for both men. On 16 April 1660, a month after the

Self-portrait by Nicholas Lanier.

dissolution of the old Parliament but two weeks before the new one formally invited Charles to return, Herringman entered Howard's *Poems* in the Stationers' Register; the book was advertised for sale on 21 June, less than a month after the King's triumphal entry into London. In his preface "To the Reader," Sir Robert acknowledged having "prevail'd with a worthy Friend to take so much view of my blotted Copies, as to free me from grosse Errors," and Dryden seems the likeliest person to have performed such editorial services;[48] certainly he served Howard by writing an elegant prefatory poem for the volume. Lacking Dryden's university education and literary experience (not to mention talent), Howard doubtless appreciated these favors, but Dryden had much to gain as well: his association with a prominent Royalist helped remove the taint of his Puritan upbringing and recent service to the Protectorate, and his prefatory poem for Howard's collection gave him an opportunity to declare his own loyalty to the new regime.

"To my Honored Friend, Sr Robert Howard, On his Excellent Poems" is a giant step forward from the weak prefatory verses Dryden had composed for Hoddesdon's epigrams a decade earlier. Howard's poems were far from excellent, as Dryden obviously knew and may ironically suggest,[49] but praise for his patron's verses was not Dryden's only purpose, as a glance at the structure of the poem will indicate. "To Howard" has three main sections. The first forty lines praise Howard's natural talent as a poet, touching on painting and music and developing a general theory of creativity that anticipates much of Dryden's later criticism. The central section (lines 41–86) describes and praises the main contents of the volume: Howard's lyric poems, translations from Virgil and Statius, and learned notes; a play, *The Blind Lady*, goes unmentioned. The last twenty lines congratulate Howard on his prophetic skill in including poems in praise of Charles II and General Monck, his most prominent restorer; taking up Howard's "Mantle," Dryden prophesies that the new book will share the good fortune of the new monarch. Even within the middle section, the poem reaches out to embrace the larger concerns of its framing sections: Howard's "easier Odes" are praised by means of a complex political metaphor that anticipates the conclusion, and the "Numbers" of his translation of Statius call forth a comparison to painting that recalls the imagery of the opening section. If Howard was fortunate in having such a deftly turned introduction to his book, Dryden was at least as fortunate in having such an opportunity to develop his own ideas about creativity, "Morall Knowledge," and the Restoration. "To Howard" is an early example of his skill at turning a specific occasion to a larger use; it is the first action in his campaign to achieve recognition from the restored court, and it is unmistakably a "Restoration" poem. In its best lines, we hear a new voice— urbane, confident, and polished. It is the voice we have learned to call "Dryden," in a larger sense the style we have learned to call "Restoration," but we should remind ourselves that Dryden developed that voice in response to a new set of cultural circumstances. Adjusting to a world in which "Poesie" had a renewed opportunity to be the "Queen . . . of Morall Knowledge," he abandoned the tortured elaboration of the Hastings elegy and the cautious dignity of the Cromwell poem; he began to articulate ideas about art and politics that would engage his attention, and that of other poets, for the next forty years; and he wrote in a style that actually displays the qualities he generously attributes to Howard's verse: metrical sweetness, intellectual strength, and a controlling wit.

The poem begins with the first of Dryden's many passages on Art and Nature, and the clearest early example of his borrowing from Milton:

> As there is Musick uninform'd by Art
> In those wild Notes, which with a merry heart
> The Birds in unfrequented shades expresse,
> Who better taught at home, yet please us lesse:
> So in your Verse, a native sweetnesse dwells,
> Which shames Composure, and its Art excells.
>
> [ll. 1–6]

Of course, the main literary precedent here is "L'Allegro" (1633), where the list of pleasures includes the stage

> If *Jonson's* learned Sock be on,
> Or sweetest *Shakespeare*, fancy's child,
> Warble his native Wood-notes wild.
>
> [ll. 133–35][50]

Howard was no Shakespeare, and Dryden has therefore been criticized for this borrowing,[51] but he borrows only the vehicle of Milton's metaphor, expanding it to contrast the songs of wild birds with the more artful, though less pleasing songs of caged birds taught to sing by copying tunes played on a flageolet. He would return frequently to the contrast between Jonson and Shakespeare implicit in Milton's lines, most prominently in the *Essay of Dramatick Poesie* and the later "Defence" of that essay, both involving controversy with Howard, but here the metaphor is friendly: the paradoxical fact that the "better taught" bird, like the "learned" professional poet, may give less pleasure than the naive or "native" singer provides a gracious way for Dryden to compliment Howard without overtly devaluing his own status as a professional poet.

Most of the other compliments Dryden pays to Howard's verse in the opening section are reflections of his own stylistic concerns. He credits Howard's lyrics with self-sufficiency, for example:

> Singing, no more can your soft numbers grace
> Then paint adds charms unto a beauteous face.
>
> [ll. 7–8]

But Howard's conventional Cavalier songs actually gain much by being sung; one of them had already been set by Henry Lawes, and Sir Robert would go on writing words for music throughout his career.[52] Dryden, by contrast, would complain about having to cramp his verses to suit Grabu, and would ultimately preempt the composers who set his St. Cecilia poems by packing so much musical content and metrical virtuosity into the texts themselves as to make a musical setting seem redundant.[53] Similarly, Dryden praises Howard for eschewing Metaphysical conceits at the very moment when he himself was beginning to escape their seductive appeal:

> Such is your Muse: no Metaphor swell'd high
> With dangerous boldnesse lifts her to the sky;
> Those mounting Fancies when they fall again,
> Shew sand and dirt at bottom do remain.

[ll. 11–14]

Yet Howard, lacking both Dryden's imagination and his Westminster training, had an earthbound muse by nature; Dryden, always inventive and fertile, was learning to bridle his fancy. The most fully developed of the compliments, the claim that Howard's verses combine strength and sweetness, cannot be taken seriously at all as a description of Howard's poems, which are thin in content and wooden in sound; perhaps for that reason, Dryden directs our attention away from the inaccuracy of the compliment by employing an interesting allusion:

> So firm a strength, and yet withall so sweet,
> Did never but in *Sampson*'s riddle meet.

[ll. 15–16]

The answer to Sampson's riddle, a honeycomb in the body of a lion, was a particularly appropriate compliment to the Royalist Howard at a moment when the royal arms, with their prominent lion, were coming out of hiding all over London.[54] But the literary goal of combining strength and sweetness evaded Howard; as his sympathetic biographer has pointed out in a discussion of his "Panegyrick to Generall Monck," when Howard "does succeed . . . in stating an interesting theme . . . , he is quite unable to develop it."[55] Dryden, by contrast, was engaged in wedding the intellectual toughness of the Metaphysicals to the metrical smoothness of the Cavaliers; he would ultimately make the heroic couplet into an instrument capable of a *Religio Laici* or an *Absalom and Achitophel*.

The second part of the opening section considers possible reasons for the combined strength and sweetness the first part has claimed for Howard. Perhaps his "Art hides Art," as Dryden's was learning to do; perhaps a certain "happinesse," or luck, follows his muse; perhaps "Fortune" has placed a miraculous "Net" in his head that filters out trivial thoughts and catches "rich Idea's." But Dryden rejects those hypotheses:

> Sure that's not all; this is a piece too fair
> To be the child of Chance, and not of Care.
> No Atoms casually together hurl'd
> Could e're produce so beautifull a world.
> Nor dare I such a doctrine here admit,
> As would destroy the providence of wit.

[ll. 29–34]

These lines draw on imagery and vocabulary conventionally associated with accounts of the Creation, a topic to which Dryden would return, with memorable results, in *Religio Laici*, *The Hind and the Panther*, and "A Song for St. Cecilia's Day, 1687."[56] As in those later poems, Dryden dismisses the Epicurean notion of Creation as a random collision of atoms, and makes God's ordered Creation a metaphor for poetic creation. His insistence that "Care" is more important than "Chance" in the making of poems, however, involves a polite retreat from the apparent preference for "Nature" over "Art" in the opening lines. Attractive as an aesthetic based upon "wild Notes," "happinesse," and "Fortune" might be, "such a doctrine . . . would destroy the providence of wit," and Dryden, himself engaged in a witty, careful, shrewdly structured poem, dares not destroy that providential principle. He concludes that Howard's "strong Genius" is responsible for his poetic excellence, and ends the section with an allusion to Hercules that neatly balances the earlier allusion to Sampson; the Greek hero wears a lion's skin. But strong as they were, both Hercules and Sampson were frequently outwitted; neither was distinguished for wit or genius. By associating Howard with these two club-wielding heroes, Dryden directs our attention away from Howard's limited ability to wield a pen. If the effect is not quite overt enough to be called irony, since Dryden is not really attacking Howard, his allusions do undermine his assertions. By emphasizing Howard's heroic strength in lines ostensibly concerned with his poetic genius, Dryden deftly maintains the distinction between poet and hero, professional and amateur.

This process continues in the central section, where we might expect a more detailed account of Howard's works. After a forced "Panegyrick to the King," the volume offers fifteen "Songs and Sonnets," highly conventional Cavalier lyrics for which Dryden makes the equally conventional but altogether dubious claim that they simultaneously delight and instruct us. Instead of validating that claim with reference to the poems, however, he uses it as a springboard for a private joke and a public allegory:

> Your easier Odes, which for delight were penn'd,
> Yet our instruction make their second end,
> We're both enrich'd and pleas'd, like them that woo
> At once a Beauty and a Fortune too.

[ll. 41–44]

Again, the first-person plural includes the first-person singular. Dryden, whose twenty-ninth birthday was approaching, was hoping to augment his inadequate income by making an advantageous marriage; three years later, he would marry Lady Elizabeth Howard, Sir Robert's sister. Sir Robert himself, recently widowed and busily trying to repair his fortunes and those of his family, was also in the market for a wife.[57] Even for readers who could not have known the specific ways in which this couplet was an in-joke, the metaphor has sufficient sparkle to prevent a close examination of the claim that Howard's thin lyrics contain enriching instruction. The political allegory that follows engages far larger issues than the quality of Howard's lyrics:

> Of Morall Knowledge Poesie was Queen,
> And still she might, had wanton wits not been;
> Who like ill Guardians liv'd themselves at large,
> And not content with that, debauch'd their charge:
> Like some brave Captain, your successful Pen
> Restores the Exil'd to her Crown again;
> And gives us hope, that having seen the days

When nothing flourish'd but Fanatique Bays,
All will at length in this opinion rest,
"A sober Prince's Government is best."

[ll. 45–54]

As would have been immediately apparent to any reader in 1660, this allegory is a version of recent British political and cultural history; its portrayal of both sides in the Civil War as extremes is surprisingly balanced and nonpartisan, given the poem's occasion and date. Abuses of the Court of Wards were among the many complaints lodged against the personal government of Charles I, a fact that sharpens the edge of Dryden's narrative, in which "Poesie" loses her status as the "Queen . . . of Morall Knowledge" when her "ill Guardians" spend her wealth and debauch her person. Because these licentious Cavalier poets failed to guard "Poesie" responsibly, the nation has had to endure the corrective rhetoric of the millenarian Independent preachers; in their different ways, both "wanton wits" and "Fanatique Bays" are traducers of language. Howard's "successful Pen" will restore poetry to her rightful role, just as Monck and Montagu have restored Charles. In fact, the poems in question, while neither licentious nor fanatical, are free from any obvious concern with "Morall Knowledge"; as so often in this poem, Dryden is really talking about his own poetry, which would not only concern itself with political and ethical questions, but find a new voice, neither Cavalier nor Calvinist, in which to address those questions. His claim that Howard's "successful Pen . . . gives us hope" for national unity is not so much an endorsement of the quality of Howard's poems as a reflection of Dryden's hope for support—moral as well as financial—from Howard and other noble amateurs of poetry. We may search in vain for an unequivocal example of instruction in the midst of delight in Howard's "Songs and Sonnets," but Dryden's poem, ostensibly structured by the contents of Howard's volume, manages to express hope for an end to political conflict and support for stable government under "A sober Prince" at its precise midpoint.

Howard's translations of Virgil and Statius did not offer Dryden equivalent opportunities, and the ensuing lines are therefore less interesting than the poem's first half. Even the conclusion, with its compliment to Howard's prophetic skill and its direct praise of Charles and General Monck, is weaker than the allegorical lines on the Restoration at the poem's center. Dryden would often write most effectively when coming at a topic obliquely, when describing contemporary politics by retelling the book of Samuel, or defending a conversion by inventing a beast fable. Within this poem, the allegory of the Restoration of "Poesie" by Howard provides a witty occasion for Dryden's own endorsement of the Restoration of Charles, and this indirect, slightly contrived endorsement is more memorable than the direct praise of the conclusion.

Restoration Panegyrics

There is plenty of direct praise, however, in *Astraea Redux*, Dryden's contribution to the flood of poems on the Restoration. Advertised for sale at the same time as Howard's collection, this poem is a full-blown panegyric, with the most heavily perfumed lines coming in the peroration, where Dryden addresses the King directly:

How shall I speak of that triumphant Day
When you renew'd the expiring Pomp of *May*!
(A Month that owns an Intrest in your Name:
You and the Flow'rs are its peculiar Claim.)
That Star that at your Birth shone out so bright
It stain'd the duller Suns Meridian light,
Did once again its potent Fires renew
Guiding our eyes to find and worship you.

[ll. 284–91]

Such association of the monarch with springtime, flowers, propitious stars, dazzling light, and Christian mystery was central to the masque tradition, and the numerous poems celebrating the Restoration predictably picked up those traditional images; there were also close precedents for much of Dryden's language in Malherbe's poems in praise of Henri IV, which he had probably encountered by this time.[58] Still, the presence of models, English or French, cannot entirely explain the emotional force of the poem. The Dryden who had exercised and celebrated restraint in the Cromwell poem was now betraying something like euphoria; one need not share Dr. Johnson's outrage at the sacrilegious excess of the final image in this passage to recognize that it indicates a loss of control. 1660 was not 1640, and the conditions under which Charles was returning to England would make him a far less powerful monarch than his predecessors, one for whom such exalted imagery would prove even more inappropriate than it had been for his father. Yet Dryden, like many of his countrymen, appears to have believed, at least for a moment, that the Restoration could miraculously negate or exorcise the events of the previous twenty years.

The sense of miracle that Dryden's poem records was widespread during the first days of the Restoration, which came about more swiftly and less violently than anyone might have predicted after the chaos of the previous months. Despite fervent Royalist hopes, neither Cromwell's death nor the fall of his son had immediately produced a return of the Stuart monarchy. A loose coalition of quite disparate religious and political factions, held together for twenty years by the necessities of war and the force of Cromwell's leadership, was obviously coming apart, but nobody knew what the outcome might be. The chaotic events of 1659, including Booth's Royalist uprising and Lambert's attempted republican coup, reflected the lack of a national consensus or an effective central government; Sir Gilbert Pickering, sensing the danger, retired to Titchmarsh in the winter of that year. For his younger cousin, who presumably remained in London, the ensuing months must have been exciting. Quakers and other Independents predicted an imminent apocalypse, while more conservative churchmen attacked those radical groups with renewed vigor. Some Presbyterians thought that bringing back the King might solidify their hold on church and state, failing to anticipate the readiness of the displaced bishops to return to power, or the effectiveness with which the Anglicans would enforce uniformity. A few diehard Rumpers, notably Milton, held out hope for a continuing Commonwealth. But for the many who were not deeply committed to any partisan position, probably including Dryden, the most common desire was for stability. The early pages of Pepys's *Diary* record some of the

Portrait of Charles II from the studio of John Michael Wright, ca. 1661.

wonder with which Londoners greeted the events of early 1660: General Monck's arrival with his army, the return to Parliament of the members purged in 1648, the eventual decision to bring Charles Stuart home from the Continent. As rumps of beef roasted over fires in the streets, the jubilant crowds celebrated their hope that the King would at least restore order; the poets added justice, religion, and liberty to that list. After twenty years of surprising, even unprecedented events, the nation had come round to a desire for the old order.

In 1649, just after the execution of Charles I, Dryden had described the death of Hastings as God's reclaiming his pledge after the breaking of a covenant by "the Nations sin":

> Heaven would no longer Trust its Pledge; but thus
> Recall'd it; rapt its *Ganymede* from us.

[ll. 51–52]

In 1660, repeating some of that language and imagery, he pictured God as freely restoring Charles to a nation unable to pay its debts:

> Heav'n would no bargain for its blessings drive
> But what we could not pay for, freely give.
> The Prince of Peace would like himself confer
> A gift unhop'd without the price of war.
> Yet as he knew his blessings worth, took care
> That we should know it by repeated pray'r;
> Which storm'd the skies and ravish'd *Charles* from thence
> As Heav'n itself is took by violence.

[ll. 137–44]

The idea that "repeated pray'r" has "ravish'd *Charles* from . . . the skies" reverses the Ganymede myth, in which Jupiter reaches down from the skies to snatch up Ganymede; the implication, reinforced by the title and the Virgilian epigraph, is that the Restoration will bring back a Golden Age, undoing the evils of the Civil Wars and the Interregnum. So pivotal was this event for Dryden that he invoked the words "Restoration" and "restore," and their attendant mythology, again and again—even long after the explicit political hopes of the particular Restoration of 1660 had proven false. The final couplet of *Absalom and Achitophel* (1681) rhymes "Restor'd" with "Lord,"[59] and in *Britannia Rediviva* (1688), written when Charles was dead and James was clinging to a shaky throne, Dryden was still attempting to rally his countrymen to support of the monarch by recycling the imagery of Restoration. He addresses the newborn Prince:

> Hail Son of Pray'rs! by holy Violence
> Drawn down from Heav'n; but long be banish'd thence,
> And late to thy Paternal Skyes retire:
> To mend our Crimes whole Ages wou'd require.

[ll. 35–38]

In this late poem as in its model, the princely blessings are not deserved; equal emphasis falls upon the nation's crimes. When developing that theme in *Astraea Redux*, Dryden seems more subtle in his appraisal of the new political situation than when rejoicing at the miraculous return of Charles. Indeed, his understanding of the relationship between the nation's guilt and its joy anticipates the moral complexity of *Absalom and Achitophel*, in which he would again consider the tension between justice and mercy, and sets his poem apart from others written on this occasion. Cowley, who had written a preface in 1656 urging submission to the Protectorate, makes no mention of his own complicity in his long Pindaric ode on the Restoration, which shares with Dryden's such images as stars, storms, and the likening of Charles to Aeneas. Far from acknowledging any connection between himself and Cromwell, Cowley crows over the Protector's death and his son's downfall:

> Wher's now that *Ignis Fatuus* which e're-while
>   Miss-led our *wandring Isle?*
> Where's the *Impostor Cromwell* gon?
> Where's now that *Falling-star*, his *Son?*[60]

Dryden, by contrast, avoids naming names, criticizing the Puritan clergy and the Rump Parliament by comparing them to those "devouter *Turks*" who disobey the Moslem commandment against drinking, or those "zealous Missions" (presumably Spanish) who pretend to seek converts while accumulating gold. Generalizing the nation's guilt by frequent first-person plurals, Dryden stresses unity and healing; Cowley's tone is victorious but divisive. Waller, who had even more reason than Cowley to feel some guilt, having written a panegyric to Cromwell in 1654 and a poem on his death in 1658, mentions the nation's guilt as a counterbalance to its joy:

> if Your Grace incline that we should live,
> You must not (SIR) too hastily forgive.
> Our guilt preserves us from th'excess of joy,
> Which scatters spirits, and would life destroy.

But the notion that Charles "must not . . . too hastily forgive" merely to prevent his subjects from excessive joy trivializes those acts requiring his forgiveness. Waller's next lines seem more forthright:

> All are obnoxious, and this faulty Land
> Like fainting *Hester* doth before you stand,
> Watching your Scepter, the revolted Sea
> Trembles to think she did Your Foes obey.[61]

But both images are misleading: Esther, the innocent queen of the Old Testament, awaits the motion of her husband's scepter without any sense of her own wrongdoing; the sea will obey (or disobey) one master as readily as another. Neither is a sufficiently serious or complex metaphor.

Mindful of his own association with the Protectorate, Dryden develops the theme of guilt and forgiveness in greater depth. Aware that Charles will need the support and talents of many who participated in or cooperated with the governments of the Interregnum, he recommends a policy of toleration to the King, employing the time-honored panegyric technique that Erasmus had described as "exhorting to virtue under the pretext of praise":[62]

> Not ty'd to rules of Policy, you find
> Revenge less sweet than a forgiving mind.
>
> [ll. 260–61]

There was already some evidence to support this hopeful compliment: the Declaration of Breda had offered a broad amnesty, and on 9 June 1660, less than two weeks before Dryden's poem was advertised, Sir Gilbert Pickering had learned that his punishments would not include execution.[63] Dryden's claim that "tears of joy for your returning spilt / Work out and expiate our former guilt" (ll. 274–75) is thus another case of his use of the first-person plural to make public and private statements simultaneously. At a time when many were eager to "Work out and expiate [their] former guilt," Dryden's poem captures the national mood; it also reflects his knowledge of specific cases. His cousins Edward and John Pickering, for example, Sir Gilbert's younger brother and eldest son, were among those motivated by "the joy that hurried o're / Such swarmes of *English* to the Neighb'ring shore" (ll. 215–16). Pepys, who had sailed over to bring back the King with General Edward Montagu, uncle by marriage to young John Pickering, was contemptuous of John's attempt to play the part of a Royalist courtier:

> This evening came Mr. John Pickering on board like an asse, with his feathers and new suit that he had made at The Hague. My Lord [Montagu] very angry for his staying on shore, bidding me a little before to send for him, telling me that he was afeared that, for his father's sake, he might have some mischief done him—unless he used the Generalls name.[64]

But Dryden, himself now sporting the full literary plumage of the Royalist style, was defending such convenient changes of heart and costume as appropriate responses to Charles's forgiving spirit.

Since Charles had exempted all but the actual regicides from capital punishment, the men thus spared might serve as a warning to others, like the slaves the Spartans used to make drunk as a warning to their children:

> Suffer'd to live, they are like *Helots* set
> A vertuous shame within us to beget.
>
> [ll. 205–06]

Dryden could hardly have written that couplet without thinking of Sir Gilbert Pickering, who was among those "Suffer'd to live" though he might easily have been condemned. Nor could he have written the next couplet without thinking of his own employment under Sir Gilbert:

> For by example most we sinn'd before,
> And glass-like, clearness mixt with frailty bore.
>
> [ll. 207–08]

Although many Englishmen in 1660 could have applied these lines to themselves, Dryden was surely thinking of the way his own poem on Cromwell had reflected the views of his then-powerful cousin: what he had then regarded as "our duty and our interest too," he now regretted as a case of "glass-like . . . frailty."

As the passage continues, the ambiguity of the first-person plurals increases:

> But since reform'd by what we did amiss,
> We by our suff'rings learn to prize our bliss:
> Like early Lovers whose unpractic'd hearts
> Were long the May-game of malicious arts,
> When once they find their Jealousies were vain
> With double heat renew their fires again.
>
> [ll. 209–14]

At its most public, the "we" is national; having wrongly revolted against Charles I, the English have learned by their sufferings under the Interregnum to prize the blissful return of Charles II. Of course, this "we" again includes the poet, who now regards his

own employment under Cromwell as something done "amiss," but who has learned
from the constraints of the Interregnum to prize the better conditions for poetry he
hopes will obtain under Charles. But through the simile of the "early Lovers," the "we"
expands again to embrace Charles himself, who has already been described, early in the
poem, as the sexual lover of his people:

> Our cross Stars deny'd us *Charles* his Bed
> Whom Our first Flames and Virgin Love did wed.
>
> [ll. 19–20]

The idea of the *felix culpa*, compactly expressed in the claim that "We by our suff'rings
learn to prize our bliss," forms a moral and thematic link between the King and his
people, including his future Laureate. That idea is the central theme of the account of
the King's years in exile (ll. 49–104), during which, Dryden argues, Charles has been
"forc'd to suffer for Himself and us" (l. 50). The poet must "both regret and bless
[the King's] suff'rings" (l. 72), since Charles has learned from them to govern wisely
and to appreciate his Restoration:

> Inur'd to suffer ere he came to raigne
> No rash procedure will his actions stain.
>
> [ll. 87–88]

Dryden even manages to acknowledge that Charles has had his own share of things
done "amiss"; despite the allusions that make him a type of Christ, the King, like his
subjects, is touched by Original Sin:

> Such is not *Charles* his too too active age,
> Which govern'd by the wild distemper'd rage
> Of some black Star infecting all the Skies,
> Made him at his own cost like *Adam* wise.
>
> [ll. 111–14]

Like the poet who would celebrate him as a hero, then, Charles has sinned and
suffered; *Astraea Redux* offers the hope that both men, and the entire nation, will be
"reform'd by what [they] did amiss."

The exuberance of Dryden's gestures of praise, in this poem and elsewhere, has
been more frequently noticed than the subtlety with which he indicates the fallibility of
those he praises. In later poems on Charles, such admissions of human frailty in the
sacred monarch become more overt and serve more obvious rhetorical purposes: the
prayer of the King in *Annus Mirabilis*, in which Dryden has Charles acknowledge his
"heedless Youth" (l. 1057), is a sufficient example. In *Astraea Redux*, however, the poet's
claim to a special relationship with the monarch is muted, implicit: both are men, both
suffer under Adam's curse, both have reason to regret particular actions of the previous
decade. Still, as a close reader of Davenant's *Gondibert*, Dryden was keenly conscious of
the reciprocal needs of poets and heroes; as an ambitious and talented writer, he was
hopeful that Charles would recognize his potential to serve the court. These are surely
the motives for the classical allusion of the grand conclusion:

> Oh Happy Age! Oh times like those alone
> By Fate reserv'd for Great *Augustus* Throne!
> When the joint growth of Armes and Arts foreshew
> The World a Monarch, and that Monarch *You.*

[ll. 320–23]

As these lines suggest, many hoped that Charles would perform great feats of arms, a hope Dryden acknowledges in the proud boast that "Our Lyon now will forraign Foes assail" (l. 118), and a hope destined to go largely unfulfilled. In his role as the new Augustus, however, Charles will preside over "the *joint* growth of Armes *and Arts*," and Dryden, even in 1660, hopes to serve as his Virgil; he adopts both the role and the manner of the Roman poet, who was to prove the most lasting of many influences absorbed during his long career. At the simplest level, he treats Charles as a type of Aeneas, as Virgil had treated Augustus, most obviously when he refers to the King as "toss'd by Fate" (l. 51), an appropriation of a phrase in the *Aeneid*'s second line ("fato profugus"). At a larger level, he employs a more generally Virgilian tone to give grandeur to the poem's final verse-paragraph, the most sonorous passage he had yet written. Even more important for his development as a poet are the structural and thematic lessons Dryden had learned from Virgil: he had learned how to use recurring patterns of imagery as an allusive "counterplot" to bind together a longer poem (and *Astraea Redux* was more than twice the length of anything he had previously attempted); he had learned how to bring a complex moral perspective to bear upon political events, a perspective including an insistence on the civilizing power of the arts. "Armes and Arts," a phrase he would employ several more times during his career, is a revealing departure from Virgil's "Arms and the man."

We may begin to examine these more complex uses of Virgil by considering the lines describing the Interregnum:

> For when by their designing Leaders taught
> To strike at Pow'r which for themselves they sought,
> The Vulgar gull'd into Rebellion, arm'd,
> Their blood to action by the Prize was warm'd.
> . . . .
> The Rabble now such Freedom did enjoy,
> As Winds at Sea that use it to destroy.
> Blind as the *Cyclops*, and as wild as he,
> They own'd a lawless salvage Libertie,
> Like that our painted Ancestours so priz'd
> Ere Empires Arts their Breasts had Civiliz'd.

[ll. 31–34; 43–48]

Dryden has reversed the tenor and vehicle of the first simile in the *Aeneid*, in which Neptune, calming the winds that Juno has persuaded Aeolus to release, is compared to an upright citizen calming an angry mob; here the mob is real, the winds imaginary. The "designing Leaders" by whom "The Vulgar" have been "gull'd into Rebellion" present a striking contrast to Virgil's "grave and Pious man," who calms the "ignoble crowd," and "soothes with sober Words their angry Mood."[65] For Virgil, both the storm and the mob are examples of the *furor* that threatens civilization, the madness exemplified by such monsters as the Cyclops, but capable of infecting people as well; Dido and Turnus are among the victims of *furor*, and Aeneas must learn to control his own *furor* in order to realize his destiny and found a city that will harbor civilized values ("Empires Arts"). For Dryden, concerned with the same contrast, the "lawless salvage Libertie" of mob rule is a regression to the barbaric state of nature that Hobbes had recently described in memorable language. As so often in Dryden, wit helps to make a serious point: by using "our painted Ancestours" as an example of barbarous "Libertie," Dryden stresses the political similarity linking the blue war-painted Britons Caesar found ranged against his troops and the more recent Puritan ancestors whose painted portraits hung in many a civilized home, including the Pickering and Dryden manors.

"Empires Arts," according to this poetic account of history, have "Civiliz'd" the British, as the pious citizen of the Virgilian simile calms the potentially barbaric mob. While they create an atmosphere in which the creative arts can flourish, "Empires Arts" are essentially political; they are the "Imperial Arts" that Virgil claims for Rome in Anchises's prophecy to his son:

> Let others better mold the running Mass
> Of Mettals, and inform the breathing Brass;
> And soften into Flesh a Marble Face;
> Plead better at the Bar; describe the Skies,
> And when the Stars descend, and when they rise.
> But, *Rome*, 'tis thine alone, with awful sway,
> To rule Mankind; and make the World obey:
> Disposing Peace, and War, thy own Majestick Way.
> To tame the Proud, the fetter'd Slave to free;
> These are Imperial Arts, and worthy thee.[66]

Virgil's lines graciously acknowledge the preeminence of Greek culture in sculpture, rhetoric, and astronomy, distinguishing those arts from the "Imperial Arts" claimed for Rome: conquest, diplomacy, administration. *Astraea Redux*, however, describes these political arts by using metaphors from the visual arts. Charles, who has spent his exile "viewing Monarchs secret Arts of sway" (l. 77), will govern wisely because he understands the theory of governance, like an artist who has studied proportion:

> To bus'ness ripened by digestive thought
> His future rule is into Method brought:
> As they who first Proportion understand
> With easie Practice reach a Masters hand.

[ll. 89–92]

The English, accustomed to violent changes in government, are so amazed by the Restoration that they cannot explain it, just as viewers of skillful paintings, though amazed by their technique, cannot tell where one color leaves off and another begins:

> Yet as wise Artists mix their colours so
> That by degrees they from each other go,

> Black steals unheeded from the neighb'ring white
> Without offending the well cous'ned sight:
> So on us stole our blessed change; while we
> Th'effect did feel but scarce the manner see.
>
> [ll. 125–30]

General Monck, who has effected this change, is credited with an artist's or a rhetorician's sense of the power of order:

> The blessed Saints that watch'd this turning Scene
> Did from their Stars with joyful wonder leane,
> To see small clues draw vastest weights along,
> Not in their bulk but in their order strong.
> Thus Pencils can by one slight touch restore
> Smiles to that changed face that wept before.
>
> [ll. 153–58]

But just at this point, Dryden rejects his own metaphor, and by extension, calls into question the whole equation of politics and the arts he has been developing:

> With ease such fond *Chymaera's* we pursue
> As fancy frames for fancy to subdue,
> But when ourselves to action we betake
> It shuns the Mint like gold that Chymists make:
> How hard was then his task . . .
>
> [ll. 159–63]

The "fond *Chymaera's*" here are the conceits and inventions of poets, the illusions of painters, the tricks of rhetoricians, framed by "fancy" as exercises for the imagination. At their worst, as in Dryden's poem on Hastings, such devices resemble the gold that alchemists claim to have made, gold that will not pass the test of the mint. Real political action, as the success of Monck had shown, requires real armies and real coins with which to pay them. In this highly self-conscious passage, placed at the mathematical center of the poem, Dryden dismisses the chimerical conceits of Cowleian wit as inadequate to the task of political persuasion. He recognizes that comparing the active Monck to an artist with a pencil risks belittling the hard task that the general has just successfully brought to completion. By retreating from the apparent earlier equation of the "Arts of sway" with the arts of pencil, brush, and pen, he makes at a personal level a distinction like the one Virgil had made between Greek and Roman arts. Yet it was from Virgil's seriousness, elevation, and moral complexity that Dryden would learn to develop a poetic voice that could have a real effect on politics. He was not a man of action; his future lay with "Arts," not "Armes." But if the "fond *Chymaera's*" of the poetry he had read as a boy were counterfeit, inadequate to the new political realities of the Restoration, Dryden perceived that the best response to this situation was not to abandon poetry for a military career, but to develop a new and more muscular kind of political poetry. Seven years later, in the preface to *Annus Mirabilis*, he would declare that "The former part of this Poem, relating to the War, is but a due expiation for my not serving my King and Country in it" (I, 50). That highly Virgilian poem was more than a mere "expiation"; it was a triumph of propaganda, a service so signal that Charles soon afterwards made Dryden his Poet Laureate, doubtless delighted that his service had been performed at his desk, not on board ship.

Astraea Redux was surely conceived as a step toward securing such royal attention; poetically, it takes some important, if uncertain steps toward the public voice Dryden was to achieve in the 1680s. There are still some puerile conceits, unresolved clashes between adjacent images, metrically flat lines, and moments of euphoric excess. But there are great strengths of structure: the opening sequence, moving from the international situation (ll. 1–20) to the national situation (ll. 21–48) to the sufferings of Charles (ll. 49–105), gains power from its narrowing focus; the shift into direct address to Charles at line 250 is similarly effective. Dryden's organizational skill, which we noticed in embryo in the Hastings poem, is at work here on a much larger scale; the verse rarely threatens to break apart into separate couplets. Among the forces unifying the poem is the use of recurring imagery in Virgilian fashion: the comparison of the vulgar to destructive winds at sea, for example, picks up the description of the international situation in the opening lines as a calm before a storm, "An horrid Stillness" (l. 7); after several other metaphors involving tempests, the actual winds of the Channel, "that never Moderation knew," blow "too faintly" as they waft Charles gently home to Dover (ll. 242–49). Rhetorically, the poet's acute sense of audience is everywhere apparent; such effects as the manipulation of first-person plurals show how much he had learned about the persuasive aspects of his craft. Thematically, *Astraea Redux* is by far the most serious poem on the Restoration; while other poets were content with mere praise, Dryden tempered his compliments by addressing such issues as learning through suffering, the King's unity with his people (and his poet), and the proper relation between "Armes and Arts." If Charles bothered to read this poem, he should have recognized the potential of its poet.

By the time of the coronation (23 April 1661), those who had hoped for glorious naval conquests, courtly grandeur, and a settled state had ample reason for doubt. The King had displayed no imperial ambition; Pepys despaired of even getting the Navy paid. He was notoriously informal, toying with his mistresses at the theatre in a way that suggested indifference to reputation. His financial situation limited his architectural improvements; so far the most he had managed was a new canal in St. James's Park for his ducks, which Waller immediately praised as a model for the improvements the King would make in the nation. But even the ducks were gifts from Louis XIV and the Russian ambassador, and Charles simply did not have the funds to make Whitehall rival the Louvre, or Hampton Court Versailles. He could not even provide regular salaries for the royal musicians and artists who had returned so joyfully to their places at court. His amnesty irritated some of his most loyal supporters, who had expected greater rewards for themselves and sterner punishments for their enemies. The question of religious toleration also remained unsettled. These and other controversies were already beginning to produce the factionalism in Parliament that would eventually lead to the full-blown party controversy of the 1680s; the hope for national unity implicit in *Astraea Redux* was not to be realized. There had even been one episode of urban terrorism, the revolt of Venner and the Fifth-Monarchy Men in January, which raised fears of renewed civil strife.

In Dryden's poem on the Coronation, *To His Sacred Majesty*, we may detect an awareness of these problems that weakens the poet's capacity for praise.[67] The traditional imagery of royal panegyric appears once more: Charles's "kind beams . . . [have] warm'd the ground" (ll. 13–14); he is "Not King of us alone but of the year" (l. 32); he can attune discord, since "His Name [*Carolus*] is Musick of it self alone" (l. 58). But these standard metaphors now seem distinctly hollow, and others must be qualified in ways that fatally weaken their force. With no military victory to celebrate, Dryden must displace martial imagery onto the ladies watching the Coronation parade from the rooftops:

> Your Cavalcade the fair Spectators view
> From their high standings, yet look up to you.
> From your brave train each singles out a prey,
> And longs to date a Conquest from your day.
>
> [ll. 37–40]

But for many readers, these lines would serve as a reminder that James, Duke of York, who might have made a foreign marriage to cement an alliance, had weakly fallen "prey" to Anne Hyde, daughter of the Lord Chancellor, and that the King himself, as yet unmarried, had proved dangerously susceptible to the weapons of "the fair," notably those of Barbara Palmer, later Countess of Castlemaine and Duchess of Cleveland, who seemed unlikely to let any queen displace her.

When Dryden seeks to picture Charles planning future naval campaigns, he encounters similar difficulties:

> In stately Frigats most delight you find,
> Where well-drawn Battels fire your martial mind.
>
> [ll. 107–08]

The word "mind," brought into unfortunate prominence by the rhyme, points the problem: these battles are merely imaginary, thoughts attributed to a king who actually spends his time sailing for pleasure on his royal yacht and feeding his royal ducks on their new canal in St. James's Park. Dryden is reduced to the dubious claim that the King's pleasure sailing is preparing him for warfare and the ludicrous assertion that his protection of the ducks certifies his paternal care for all his subjects:

> What to your cares we owe is learnt from hence,
> When ev'n your pleasures serve for our defence.
> Beyond your Court flows in th' admitted tide,
> Where in new depths the wondring fishes glide:
> Here in a Royal bed the waters sleep,
> When tir'd at Sea within this bay they creep.
> Here the mistrustfull foul no harm suspects,
> So safe are all things which our King protects.
>
> [ll. 109–16]

For a merchant worried about the safety of his ships in seas patrolled by the Dutch, the analogy to the ducks could not have carried much weight, nor does it seem to carry much conviction from Dryden.

Even more unconvincing are the lines alluding to religious unrest:

> You have already quench'd seditions brand;
> And zeal (which burnt it) only warms the Land.
> The jealous Sects that dare not trust their cause
> So farre from their own will as to the Laws,
> You for their Umpire and their Synod take,
> And their appeal alone to *Caesar* make.
> Kind Heav'n so rare a temper did provide
> That guilt repenting might in it confide.
> Among our crimes oblivion may be set,
> But 'tis our Kings perfection to forget.
>
> [ll. 79–88]

Dryden hardly believed that the execution of Venner's rebels constituted a final quenching of "seditions brand"; the conceit claiming that "zeal . . . only warms the Land" is a "fond *Chymaera*" of just the kind that he had apparently disavowed in *Astraea Redux*, as weak in its way as the lines about the waterfowl, the yacht, and the "fair Spectators," trivializing a serious problem as Waller had trivialized the nation's guilt. The claim that the "jealous Sects" will make their appeal to Charles reflects the fact that the King was less vindictive toward Dissenters than the Cavalier Parliament, but Parliament's view prevailed, producing the Act of Uniformity of 1662 and the consequent ejection of many quite moderate Presbyterian clergymen. The hopes for religious unity or toleration were also proving vain.

The couplet on "oblivion," another witty evasion of a serious issue, may serve to illustrate how the disappointments of the year between the Restoration and the Coronation affected Dryden's style. When treating the theme of forgiveness in *Astraea Redux*, he had acknowledged the Royalist belief that Charles I's failure to deal sternly with the opposition had led to the Civil War, but had argued that a similar willingness to forgive and compromise was nonetheless the best policy for the restored Charles II:

> But you, whose goodness your discent doth show,
> Your Heav'nly Parentage and earthly too;
> By that same mildness which your Fathers Crown
> Before did ravish, shall secure your own.
>
> [ll. 256–59]

Behind this paradox lies a shrewd assessment of the political realities of 1660: a vindictive absolutism would have been a foolish policy for a monarch seeking to regain his throne and unite his people. Less than a year later, however, with the restored bishops robed for the Coronation and poised to take revenge on the Presbyterians, Charles was being maneuvered into a more vindictive posture than he personally favored. Himself a similarly tolerant man, Dryden now had to rely on a less convincing paradox:

> Among our crimes oblivion may be set,
> But 'tis our Kings perfection to forget.

Here the later poem seems more old-fashioned than the earlier one; Dryden is drawing on an outmoded, almost Metaphysical wit, abandoning his own distinction between chimerical fancies and the true coin of action. That failure to heed his own advice is not surprising: even those like Dryden who point in the direction of new styles are likely to retain vestiges of the old, particularly when they lack confidence. Throughout his career, Dryden would resort to paradox and allegory when he lacked a strong logical argument, when he could not claim for Charles actions that the King had not performed. *Threnodia Augustalis*, his poem on Charles's death, written after such brilliantly argumentative works as *Absalom and Achitophel* and *Religio Laici*, is as dependent on Renaissance wit and traditional hierarchy as *To His Sacred Majesty*, and even contains a passage comparing the poets to the royal ducks. In 1685 as in 1661, Dryden fell back upon "fond *Chymaera's*" when seeking to defend a King whose actions had disappointed many, including (in both cases) the poet himself.

If the year between the Restoration and the Coronation was a disillusioning one for Dryden, it was doubtless also a stimulating one. Sir Robert Howard had already written a play and would soon become a stockholder in the Bridges Street Theatre; we may imagine Dryden attending the newly reopened theatres with Howard, and he may have tried to make his own mark on the drama. Years later, in the *Vindication of the Duke of Guise*, he claimed that he had written a version of that play in 1660, but had suppressed it because "It was Damn'd in Private, by the Advice of some Friends to whom I shew'd it; who freely told me, that it was an Excellent Subject; but not so Artificially wrought, as they could have wish'd" (p. 1). In 1683, this was a convenient defense against accurate Whig claims that Dryden and his collaborator, Nat Lee, had used the story of the Duke of Guise to attack the Duke of Monmouth, and Dryden's claim to have written the play in 1660 cannot be proved.[68] Still, the parallel between the Catholic League of the 1580s in France and the English Solemn League and Covenant was being urged in many pamphlets during 1660, and Dryden's own *Astraea Redux*, in lines comparing Charles II's sufferings to those of his grandfather Henri IV, makes that comparison explicit:

> The name of *Great his famous Grandsire gain'd:*
> *Who yet a King alone in Name and Right,*
> *With hunger, cold and angry Jove* did fight;
> Shock'd by a covenanting Leagues vast Powr's
> As holy and as Catholique as ours.

[ll. 98–102]

Dryden's claim that he withdrew the play upon the advice of friends (presumably including Howard) also tallies well with our earlier suspicion that he kept his Cambridge poems unpublished; his capacity for self-criticism, which is one of the most striking characteristics of his later prefaces, seems to have operated strongly from the very outset of his career.

Thanks to Howard, Dryden's circle of friends and acquaintances widened during this year; he probably met some of Sir Robert's brothers—at least Henry, James, and

Edward, who had ambitions as playwrights—and their sister Elizabeth, whom he married in 1663. His own family had a continuing claim on his attention. Sometime after his father's death in 1654, his mother packed up her children and went to live with her brother Henry Pickering, a former Parliamentary colonel. With the proceeds of his advantageous marriage to the daughter of the goldsmith Thomas Vyner, Lord Mayor of London in 1653, Henry purchased the manor of Whaddon in Cambridgeshire; he served in the Parliaments of 1654, 1656, and 1658–59; Cromwell knighted him in 1658. As a widow still caring for most of her children, the youngest of whom was less than a year old when Erasmus died, Mary Dryden needed the support of her successful brother, especially since her sister-in-law Susannah, her cousin Gilbert, and her eldest son John were all in London during the later 1650s. Although physically separated from his family, Dryden was surely kept informed about their lives; the year between the Restoration and the Coronation saw a number of major family events. In September of

Anonymous portrait of Dryden, dated 1657 but probably ca. 1662.

1660, his sister Agnes, closest to him in age of all the siblings, died in childbirth. In October came his cousin Gilbert's intransigent resistance to the new rector of Titch-marsh, an embarrassing episode for the author of *Astraea Redux*, but one he could hardly ignore.[69] In January 1661, his uncle Henry, evidently more successful than Gilbert at adapting to the new political climate, was created a baronet by Charles II. Later that year, Dryden's sister Lucy left her uncle's home to marry Stephen Wombwell, a London distiller. Just one week before the Coronation, his aunt Susannah, whose early widowing had brought his own parents together, was buried at Titchmarsh.[70]

While Dryden can hardly have been indifferent to these events and perhaps attended some of the weddings and funerals, such family concerns have left no mark on his poetry. We may imagine him grieving for his sister or rejoicing in his uncle's success at winning the King's favor, but all we know for certain is that his sense of poetic vocation remained unaltered. His belief that the Restoration would increase oppor-tunities for a professional man of letters was confirmed by the reopening of the theatres, and by the reprinting of his poem on the Coronation with a French translation.[71] His life in Sir Robert's house in Lincoln's Inn Fields was the life of a writer: he was reading widely in many languages, probably still producing some translations and prefaces for Herringman, evidently circulating drafts of plays and poems among his literary friends. The "young raw fellow of seven and Twenty" who had come to London to work for his cousin was now a gentleman poet of nearly thirty, the author of impressive verses on the Restoration and the Coronation, closely associated with an aristocratic promoter of the drama, beginning to move in the cultured circles forming around the restored court. If the King was not yet aware of Dryden's talents, some of the courtiers were. Dryden's pride at his literary success comes across in the earliest portrait we have of him, dated 1655 on the canvas but evidently painted after the Restoration.[72] His short, squat figure later led his enemies to call him "Poet Squab," and the plump, birdlike face in this picture justifies the nickname. The anonymous painter has also captured that confi-dence in his own wit that Dryden exhibited throughout his career. Although the next decade would bring him even wider recognition, the Dryden painted here had already achieved what he aimed for when he left Cambridge: he had "set up for a Poet."

CHAPTER FIVE

"Draydon the Poet and all the Wits of the Town"
1661–1665

Friends and Relations

Dryden's poem on the Coronation is so circumstantial in its details of the procession and ceremony that we may be confident he watched the celebrations, as did his Cambridge friend Samuel Pepys, who rose even earlier than usual to secure a good vantage point. The mounted cavalcade from Tower Hill to Whitehall on 22 April 1661 was larger and more colorful than the funeral cortège for Cromwell, in which Dryden himself had marched: barons, dukes, and earls wore their richest robes; the new knights created for the occasion were all in crimson; the helmets and weapons of the guards glistened in the sunlight of the first bright day after weeks of rain; and the tall young King was dazzling in a dark suit embroidered with precious metals, with a bareheaded General Monck, now Duke of Albemarle and Master of the Horse, leading a spare mount beside him. Among the powerful men passing by, Dryden could identify several he knew, most of them Howards. Colonel Philip Howard, younger brother to Sir Robert, rode at the head of the General's Horse Guard; Sir Robert himself, now Clerk of the Patents of Chancery, appeared with the other Chancery officials; their elder brother Charles, as Lord Howard of Charlton and Viscount Andover, moved past in the group of "Barons Two by Two According to their Antiquity," side by side with Edward Montagu, second Baron of Boughton, father of Dryden's Westminster and Cambridge friend of the same name. The more prominent Edward Montagu whose sister had married Sir Gilbert Pickering was now numbered among the Earls, having been created Earl of Sandwich by a King grateful for his help in 1660; his suit, made in France at a cost of £200, impressed his employee Pepys as "very rich," though it can hardly have compared with the clothing of George Villiers, second Duke of Buckingham, who was said to have spent £30,000 on his suit. We have no contemporary testimony about the attire of the other Earl Dryden would have recognized: Thomas Howard, Earl of Berkshire, father of Charles, Robert, and Philip Howard—and of Lady Elizabeth

Thomas Howard 1ˢᵗ Earl of Berkshire

From a miniature at Apethorpe.

Portrait of Thomas Howard, first Earl of Berkshire, Dryden's father-in-law. An eighteenth-century watercolor by Athow, after a lost miniature at Apthorpe.

Howard, soon to be John Dryden's bride, who was surely among the "fair Spectators" gallantly noticed in his poem.[1]

While Berkshire's clothing was doubtless as fine as his straitened circumstances would permit, it may have been somewhat threadbare; despite his steadfast loyalty, the old Earl was far worse off financially than the new Duke of Albemarle and the new Earl of Sandwich, both of whom had fought against Charles I, served in the governments of Cromwell, and embraced the cause of Charles II for motives including opportunism. As he watched the new Duke of Albemarle going through the motions of his lucrative new role as Master of the Horse, Berkshire may have wondered whether anyone now remembered his own appointment as Master of the Horse to Charles I in 1614, when Charles was still Prince of Wales. He accompanied Charles to Spain when the Prince went to court the Infanta in 1623, and was rewarded with an earldom in 1626 and a place on the Privy Council in 1639, but his loyalty cost him dearly when the Long Parliament imprisoned him and sequestered his lands; in 1645, he wrote cynically to the Earl of Bath, declaring his opinion that "the soldiers on both sides [were] resolved to make their fortunes out of the Nobles' Estates." Confused and disappointed, he had reached the conclusion that "No body can tell what we have been fighting about all this while, or where the quarrel lies."[2] Nonetheless, he took his post as Governor to the Prince of Wales seriously, sailing for the Continent with his young charge in 1646 when the war was lost. On 18 August of that year, his wife petitioned the Parliamentary victors to allow her husband, who was waiting in Holland, to compound for his estates, but when Berkshire returned, there was little left of his once substantial holdings; his finances never recovered.[3] By the time the King was restored, Berkshire was over seventy and failing; he lived on for nine more disappointing years, in which his hopes to see his loyalty recompensed went largely unfulfilled. A post as one of the twelve Gentlemen of the Bedchamber, with an official salary of £1,000, probably not often paid, was the only office Charles provided for his old tutor.

Dryden's friendship with Sir Robert Howard thus brought him into contact with old Cavaliers who had suffered in the Royalist cause, men whose view of the Civil War was quite unlike that prevailing in Titchmarsh. The Howard connection also included some Roman Catholics. Berkshire's beautiful wife, Elizabeth Cecil Howard, was the daughter of William Cecil, second Earl of Exeter, who had become a Roman Catholic by 1586. Mixed marriages were common, and many aristocratic Catholics attended the services of the Established Church while secretly maintaining priests to say Mass. English Catholics also differed from their Protestant neighbors in adhering to the old seasonal cycle of fasts and feasts, and women, who took charge of the preparation of food and could thus control adherence to these customs, were a powerful force in maintaining a Catholic community in the face of harassment. The understandable caution of "church-Papists" about keeping records and the frequent changes of faith from generation to generation in noble families make it notoriously difficult to establish the religion of individuals, but there is no evidence that Elizabeth Cecil Howard ever abandoned her father's faith. Her eldest son, Charles Howard, was unquestionably a Catholic. In 1637, he married Dorothy Savage, daughter of a prominent Catholic family. Summoned to the House of Lords as Viscount Andover, he spoke vigorously on the King's behalf in the Short Parliament, but was prevented by the Civil War from taking up the position as Ambassador to Venice with which Charles I rewarded him in 1641. After the war, he became a part of the court in exile, appointed Gentleman of the Bedchamber to Charles II in 1658. His second cousin Philip Howard, a Dominican priest who later became a Cardinal, was active in that court, a circumstance that may also be relevant to Andover's Catholicism. Even after Andover became second Earl of

Anonymous portrait of Elizabeth Cecil Howard, Dryden's mother-in-law, ca. 1625.

Berkshire in 1669, he made no effort to conceal his religion: he appears on many lists of recusant aristocrats, and finally fled England at the height of the Popish Plot scare in 1678.[4]

The first Earl's religion is less certain. He was sufficiently Protestant to appeal to the Puritan faction at Cambridge in 1626, when they supported him as a rival candidate for Chancellor against the first Duke of Buckingham, who was favored by the court and Archbishop Laud.[5] Nonetheless, he may also have become a Roman Catholic around the time of the Restoration, though the evidence in his case is limited to one anecdote, which may actually refer to his son. After the ejection of the Presbyterians in August 1662, a prominent preacher named Thomas Manton, who had been the vicar of St. Paul's Covent Garden, began preaching illegally; his congregation eventually moved to the home of Lord Wharton in St. Giles's. According to Manton's first biographer, "the good-natur'd Earl of BERKSHIRE lived next Door, who was himself a Jansenist Papist; and offered [Manton] the liberty, when he was in Trouble, to come to his House; which it was easy to do, by only passing over a low Wall, which parted the Gardens."[6] The implication is that the Earl of Berkshire (either Dryden's father-in-law or his brother-in-law) correctly perceived that Roman Catholics and Dissenters had a common need for toleration.

Despite the bigoted strictures of the Cavalier Parliament, toleration was an idea much in vogue in the intellectual circles in which the young Dryden was now moving, in the company of Sir Robert Howard, Berkshire's Protestant younger son. As early as 16 December 1661, Dryden knew Thomas Sprat, later the historian of the Royal Society and a notable advocate of toleration; he accompanied Sprat on a visit to Cowley after a performance of Cowley's play *Cutter of Coleman Street*.[7] Both Sprat and Cowley were closely associated with the second Duke of Buckingham, later Dryden's adversary; like their patron, they were early members of the Royal Society, which Dryden joined in 1662. As Sprat points out in his *History*, the Society prided itself on accepting men of all faiths. Among the prominent Catholics active in its deliberations were Henry Howard, Earl of Norwich, and Charles Howard of Greystoke, brothers of the priest and second cousins to Lady Elizabeth. Henry, who became Earl of Norfolk and head of the senior Howard line in 1677, was part of an influential group of Catholics based at the court of the Queen Mother; the leader of that group, another active member of the Royal Society, was Colonel Samuel Tuke, soldier, diplomat, and playwright.[8]

Although Sir Robert Howard remained a staunch Protestant and eventually became a Whig, I suspect that his younger sister Elizabeth was at least sympathetic toward Catholicism when Dryden began courting her. I have already suggested that the Countess was a Catholic, and the daughters of mixed marriages were often reared in the religion of their mothers. The most striking evidence is the testimony of the Earl's Dominican cousin, Philip Howard. When Catharine of Braganza came to England in 1662, Howard was among her priests. The Queen's chapel provided Masses with sermons in English beginning in September of 1662; Howard became her Grand Almoner in 1665. Years later the same man, now Cardinal Howard, wrote a letter of recommendation for Dryden's sons, referring to the poet as "a Convert," but calling Elizabeth "a Cath^c. Sister to y^e. Lord Berkshire,"[9] as if he had always known her as a fellow Catholic. Perhaps he remembered seeing her at the Queen's Chapel in the early 1660s when he was preaching there. After Elizabeth's recusant brother succeeded to the earldom in 1669, there was probably a priest at the family estate at Charlton in Wiltshire, and there may have been one there earlier: her first son Charles Dryden, born at Charlton on 27 August 1666, was probably named for that Catholic elder brother, and no Anglican baptismal document for that child has ever come to light.[10] Since recusants had every reason to conceal themselves, firmer evidence about Elizabeth's faith seems unlikely to surface, but even if she was not yet a Roman Catholic

Portrait of Philip, Cardinal Howard, signed by Andrea Casali, ca. 1685.

when Dryden married her, his deepening connection with her family brought him into contact with some people who were certainly recusants. His own eventual conversion to Rome and his lifelong advocacy of religious toleration take on a new light when we recognize that they were not positions taken in the abstract, but responses to human realities.

Elizabeth's religion was not the only factor that might have given Dryden pause, however. As his enemies in the 1680s often reminded him, she had been linked in some way to Philip Stanhope, the womanizing Earl of Chesterfield, whose letter-book contains a note Elizabeth apparently wrote to him in 1658, which could certainly be interpreted as implying a compromising relationship:

> My Lord
>
> I received yours though not without great trouble, but am not guilty of any thing you lay to my charge, nor will I ever alter from the expressions I have formerly made, therefore I hope you will not be so unjust as to beleive all the world sayes of mee, but rather credit my protestation of never having named you to my freinds, being allwayes carefull of that for my own sake as well as yours, and therefore let it be not in the power of any, nor of your own inclinations to make mee less
>
> Your very humble servant
>
> If you will meet mee
> in the Old Exchange about
> six a clock I will justify
> my selfe.[11]

Elizabeth says she has been "allwayes carefull," and this letter is certainly not sufficient evidence upon which to conclude that she was Chesterfield's mistress.[12] Perhaps twenty years old when she wrote this note, she had excellent reason not to name Chesterfield to her "freinds," meaning her family, who might be chary indeed of allowing her to be seen with a man about five years her senior who already had a rakish reputation. It may help to place this puzzling letter in context to compare another note in the same letter-book, this one sent to Chesterfield in 1657 by two women with whom he certainly had sexual relations—Ann Hamilton and Barbara Villiers, both later notorious in the court of Charles II, both now mere teenagers:

> My Lord,
>
> My freind and I are just now abed together a contriving how to have your company this afternoune, If you deserve this favour, you will come and seek us at Ludgate Hill, about three a clock, at Butlers shop, where wee will expect you, but least wee should give you too much satisfaction at once, wee will say no more, Expect the rest when you see
>
> Yours &c.[13]

The contrast between this brazen epistolary seduction and the cautious phrasing of Elizabeth's letter is instructive, and my guess is that Elizabeth was too "carefull" to become deeply entangled in Chesterfield's snares. *Azaria and Hushai* (1682), a vicious attack on her husband, would claim that she was "a teeming Matron ere she was a Wife" (p. 29),[14] but there is no confirming evidence for this dubious charge; we may compare again the case of Barbara Villiers, one of whose many bastards was known to be by Chesterfield. Still, the odor of an intrigue with Chesterfield probably clung to Elizabeth's reputation, whether justly or not, and may help explain why she was unmarried at twenty-five. The sexual activities of the aristocracy were a subject of universal fascination, and such gossip touched others in Elizabeth's family: in 1668, when Charles II began his affair with the actress Moll Davis, Pepys reported the rumor that Moll was "a bastard of Collonell Howard, my Lord Barkshire, and that he doth pimp to her for the King, and hath got her for him." He probably meant to write "Collonell

Howard, [son of] my Lord Barkshire," since at least three of Elizabeth's brothers were colonels; our uncertainty about whom he meant, or about whether the story had any basis in fact, may provide a useful warning about all sexual rumor-mongering during this period, including that later directed against Dryden and his wife.[15]

Speculation about why the Earl of Berkshire allowed his daughter to marry an impecunious poet from a Puritan background has often made much of Elizabeth's supposedly tarnished reputation; some have even supposed that Elizabeth's brothers forced Dryden to marry her. Unnoticed in all this fiction-making is the fact that both of Elizabeth's parents were distantly related to Dryden. Her mother's uncle, Richard Cecil, had married Elizabeth Cope, daughter of Dryden's well-known Puritan kinsman Sir Anthony Cope of Banbury.[16] Her father was the son of Catharine Knyvett, whose grandmother, Anne Pickering, was descended from the Northamptonshire Pickerings.[17] In a period when family ties, even distant ones, were an important factor in the making of marriages, these links were probably more important than Elizabeth's religion and reputation—or those of others in her family.

Had Dryden been wealthy as well as acceptably descended, his marriage into such an aristocratic family would not look at all unusual—especially since Berkshire's embarrassing poverty was his most pressing concern in the 1660s. Lacking significant monetary wealth, the young writer shrewdly directed his chief asset, his poetic talent, toward relieving Berkshire's poverty and securing his Elizabeth a dowry. On New Year's Day of 1662, he addressed an elegant poem to Edward Hyde, Earl of Clarendon and Lord Chancellor, the most powerful man in the government. Carefully tailored for its recipient, the poem seems deliberately old-fashioned, complimenting the Chancellor and the King in language and imagery drawn from the world before the Civil War, and repeating the emphasis on forgiveness so prominent in the poems on the Restoration and Coronation. If such style and matter were attractive to the Chancellor, the King's preference ran to lighter fare: Samuel Butler's *Hudibras*, a rollicking satire against the Puritans published in the same year, was his favorite book.[18]

Aware that Clarendon had lodged with Davenant as a young man, and had even tried his hand at poetry, Dryden mentions the Chancellor's "early courtship" of "the Muses," then shifts his rhetoric so that "the Muses" represent not only the idea of poetry but the actual poets of the nation, who are elated by Clarendon's rise to power, just as members of particular Roman Catholic orders (Dominicans or Franciscans, for example) are elated when one of their number rises to become Pope:

> For still they [the Muses] look on you with such kind eyes
> As those that see the Churches Soveraign rise
> From their own Order chose, in whose high State
> They think themselves the second choice of Fate.

[ll. 13–16]

To be sure, this is only a simile, one of many crammed into a self-consciously learned poem, but the unqualified use of a simile in which Clarendon plays the Pope and the poets play priests suggests that Dryden's attitudes had shifted away from those apparent in the witty jibes at Catholicism in his letter to his cousin Honor a few years earlier (quoted above, p. 71). Moreover, the similes that make the poets into Muses, priests, and "Druyds" are leading to an appeal for support:

> The Nations soul (our Monarch) does dispence
> Through you to us his vital influence;
> You are the Channel where those spirits flow,
> And work them higher as to us they go.
>
> [ll. 27–30]

Among the meanings of this passage is surely Dryden's hope that Clarendon, as the "Channel" through which "spirits" and money flow, will see to it that poets get sufficient royal support.

Later in the same month, during a meeting of the Privy Council, Clarendon scribbled this note to the King: "Indeede you are to blame, that you have not yett giuen your warrant to my Ld Barkeshyre, I pray do not deferr it." Charles replied, mentioning £11,000 as the promised sum, and on 27 February, he issued warrants promising to pay £3,000 to Elizabeth over the next three years, and £8,000 to the old Earl, beginning in 1665. Although Elizabeth did not finally receive her £3,000 until the last years of the decade, the plan to give her grant precedence over her father's strongly suggests that it was intended as a dowry.[19] Clarendon had other reminders of the poverty of the loyal and long-suffering Berkshire, who filed frequent petitions asking for places and patents, and whose wife, according to the King, considered the Chancellor her "great favourite,"[20] but the closeness in date of Dryden's poem and Clarendon's note is persuasive; it suggests that the Chancellor wished to support poets, including a promising young poet named Dryden, that he knew about Dryden's interest in Lady Elizabeth Howard (perhaps through her mother), and that he responded to Dryden's poem by taking the next opportunity to "dispence" some of Charles's "vital influence" in the direction of Elizabeth, correctly anticipating that the money would enable Dryden to go on writing poems in praise of the regime. Dryden's unflagging loyalty to Clarendon, later transferred to his son Lawrence Hyde, may well reflect the poet's recognition that Clarendon's intercession with the King had made his marriage possible.[21]

Beyond its usefulness in securing the loyalty of a talented writer, the marriage between John Dryden and Lady Elizabeth Howard was just the kind of match between the offspring of families on opposite sides in the Civil War that Clarendon and the King perceived as a way to achieve national reconciliation. Cromwell, who had also sought such peacemaking marriages, complained in 1655 that the Royalists had "very much confined their marriages and alliances within their own party, as if they meant to entail their quarrel and prevent the means to reconcile posterity."[22] Similarly concerned to heal the dissensions that were still erupting in periodic violence, the King and his Chancellor in 1662 were similarly alert to the usefulness of marriages in reconciling old enemies. Though we cannot know whether members of both families attended the wedding, on 1 December 1663 at St. Swithins in London, I strongly suspect that they did.

Dryden clearly got along with both families. When his cousin Edward Salwey fell seriously ill in June of 1664, the poet rushed to his bedside; very much the concerned kinsman, he wrote at once to Edward's uncle, the old Parliamentary soldier Richard Salwey, informing him of the condition of his barrister nephew, attempting to patch up a recent quarrel between them, and offering his own servant as a messenger to help in the necessary process of rounding up attorneys to help make adjustments in Edward's will. Like Gilbert Pickering, Richard Salwey had been regarded as sufficiently "fanatic" to be excepted from the Act of Oblivion in 1660; in the terms Dryden had used in *Astraea Redux*, he was one of the "Helots" whose function was to beget a "vertuous shame" in their former associates. Yet Dryden's letter shows no such shame: he addresses the old soldier as "ye much honour^d, Rich: Salwey Esqr" and protests his own "sincere desires to serve . . . your selfe and y^r worthy relations" (*Letters*, p. 6).[23] Evidently Dryden did not regard his new alliance with the Howards as altering in any way his obligations to the Drydens and Pickerings.

When the plague struck a year later, the young couple decamped to the Howard estate at Charlton, where they remained for more than a year. Although the religious and political opinions entertained at Charlton were quite unlike those in which Dryden had been reared, he clearly found it possible to work productively there. Another incident in 1664 suggests that he may even have been able to broker a business deal between connections from both families. In August of that year, Sir Robert Howard sold the office of Clerk of the Patents in Chancery, a lucrative post granted to him by Clarendon at the Restoration, from which he had accrued considerable income while leaving the actual work to an experienced silent partner. The purchaser was Sir Thomas Vyner, the former Lord Mayor, whose daughter had married Dryden's uncle Henry Pickering, now a baronet at Whaddon and the protector of Dryden's mother.[24] With his family connections to both men, Dryden might easily have brought Vyner and Howard together at a moment when Howard needed cash and Vyner needed a secure place for his son. If, as I have suggested, Clarendon helped bring about Dryden's marriage in the hope that it might contribute to the process of reconciliation, Dryden's apparent ability to get along with both families must have seemed a fulfillment of that hope. Ironically, this same business deal began to strain the relations between Dryden's two benefactors: Clarendon later expressed surprise that Sir Robert did not immediately cut him in for a share of the profits.[25]

Arts and Sciences

Another of the offices Howard acquired in 1660 was the post of Serjeant Painter to the King. Although he sold that post in February 1663, it necessarily brought him into contact with professional painters, and we may imagine Howard's friend and lodger Dryden making similar contacts; his poetry had already made expert reference to artistic technique.[26] Howard was also a Colonel of Infantry, a Member of Parliament, and the holder of several other appointive posts, but he coveted literary fame; his financial involvement in the Bridges Street Theatre and his ambitions as an amateur playwright were important factors in Dryden's early dramatic career. Both men also remained in contact with the publisher Herringman, through whom they probably met the scientist and antiquary Walter Charleton. Dryden may even have known Dr. Charleton before the Restoration; the prefaces to two of the doctor's treatises, published in 1657 and 1659 and signed by Herringman, look suspiciously like Dryden's work.[27]

For Charleton's *Chorea Gigantum*, published in the fall of 1662 with an imprint date of 1663, both Dryden and Howard provided signed prefatory poems. The book expounds the theory that Stonehenge was a site for the coronation of Danish kings, refuting Inigo Jones's notion that it was a Roman temple; both poets consequently gave their poems a political dimension. Dryden's longer and more complex effort conflates royal and intellectual politics: he concludes with a witty compliment to the King, but his central lines praise the Royal Society, of which Charleton was an active member, frequently presenting papers and bringing in specimens.[28] Doubtless motivated by the poem, Charleton proposed Dryden as a Fellow on 12 November 1662; in accordance with the Society's usual procedures, the young poet was elected on 19 November and admitted on 26 November.[29] Although two of his Catholic cousins were quite active Fellows, Sir Robert never joined the Society.[30]

We have no hard evidence that Dryden ever attended another meeting after being admitted. In 1664 he was appointed, along with Berkenhead, Evelyn, Tuke, Sprat, Waller, and several other luminaries, to a "committee for improving the English language," a project in which he often expressed interest, but that committee's meetings were interrupted by the Plague of 1665 and eventually came to nothing.[31] Dryden is never recorded as having spoken at a meeting of the Society, and he never paid any dues except his entrance fee; in 1666, when the Society decided to purge its rolls of those whose dues were seriously in arrears, he was among the first to be expelled.[32] Yet *Annus Mirabilis*, published after his expulsion, contains a friendly "*Apostrophe to the Royal Society*," and in 1668, defending his *Essay of Dramatick Poesie* against objections raised by Sir Robert Howard, he compared his "Sceptical" method in that discourse to "the modest Inquisitions of the Royal Society" (IX, 15).[33]

Much in Dryden's background might have disposed him toward support of the Society's aims. As a boy in Titchmarsh, he had been friendly with his physician uncle John Pickering; physicians, including Dr. Charleton, made up a significant and vocal percentage of the membership of the Royal Society.[34] At Westminster, he had learned astronomy from Busby (with unfortunate results in his poem for Hastings); Robert Hooke, author of *Micrographia* and a leading member of the Society, was now among Busby's closest associates. At Trinity College, where the study of "natural philosophy" afforded a degree of freedom from the theological controversies of the Interregnum, many of Dryden's contemporaries had engaged in scientific study; some of them were now participating in the Society. Even under the Puritans, Trinity gloried in having been the home of Bacon, the inspirer of the Royal Society's methods: Thomas Hill, who secured the endowment of a chair in mathematics while Master of the College, pointedly quoted Bacon in the "Epistle Dedicatory" of a sermon preached before Sir John Wollaston, who endowed that chair.[35] Since coming to London, Dryden had met in other connections several men who were now among the Society's leaders: certainly Sprat and Charleton, possibly Samuel Tuke and Charles Howard of Greystoke. Such other poets as Denham, Waller, and Cowley were already members, though none of them proved to be much more active than Dryden.[36] If we consider his social and professional aspirations in 1662, Dryden's becoming a Fellow of the Royal Society was a predictable event.

Intellectually, there were some parts of the Society's program to which Dryden could respond quite positively. The Baconian insistence on open-mindedness was a welcome contrast to the Aristotelian dogmatism of the university curriculum and the religious and political dogmatism of the Civil War and Interregnum. Here was a "scientific" idea with welcome social consequences for a poet who had been exposed to all these versions of dogmatism, but who was now associated with men and women from every part of the religious and political spectrum. Although some conservative university men, threatened by the modest success of the Society, would attempt to smear the "virtuosi" with charges of "atheism" and "Jesuitism," the leadership of the Royal Society was largely "Latitudinarian," aiming at a broadly comprehensive church and tolerant of those nonconformists and Roman Catholics who could not be comprehended within it.[37] The Society itself contained prominent Roman Catholics, some of them known to Dryden; it also included some outspoken Dissenters, and the range of political opinion was wide.[38] Even in scientific matters, the Society's members often held beliefs we would consider contradictory: physicians accepting Harvey's theory of the circulation of the blood nonetheless prescribed such Galenic remedies as bleeding and purging;[39] proponents of empirical experiment nonetheless pursued interests in witchcraft and alchemy. For Dryden, whose poetry employs either Ptolemaic or Copernican cosmology, depending upon which suits the metaphor at hand, this tolerance of theoretical contradictions was evidently attractive. In the *Essay of Dramatick Poesie*, for example, his spokesman Neander defends the "variety and copiousness" of English stage plots by recourse to an apparently contradictory piece of "scientific" lore:

> Our Playes, besides the main design, have under plots or by-concernments, of less considerable Persons, and Intrigues, which are carried on with the motion of the main Plot: as they say the Orb of the fix'd Stars, and those of the Planets, though they have motions of their own, are whirled about by the motion of the *primum mobile*, in which they are contain'd: that similitude expresses much of the *English* Stage: for if contrary motions may be found in Nature to agree; if a Planet can go East and West at the same time; one way by virtue of his own motion, the other by force of the first mover; it will not be difficult to imagine how the under Plot, which is onely different, not contrary to the great design, may naturally be conducted along with it. [XVII, 47]

French "rules" for drama, including the insistence on a single plot, are as dogmatic and imprisoning as the ancient scientific orthodoxies of an Aristotle or a Ptolemy; in both cases, English freedom leads to an acceptance of "variety and copiousness."

If Dryden's joining the Royal Society in 1662 tallies well with our sense of his mind and ambitions at that time, his losing interest and allowing himself to be expelled by 1666 is equally plausible. Having married, written several plays, and achieved a growing reputation in the literary world, Dryden no longer needed the Society as a place to make connections that might aid his career. On 3 February 1664, Pepys "stopped at the great Coffee-house" in Covent Garden, later known as Will's, where he saw "Draydon the poet (I knew at Cambrige), and all the wits of the town," engaged in "very witty and pleasant discourse."[40] With the opportunity to participate in that kind of literary talk, Dryden was less likely to find the scientific discussions at the Royal Society attractive. If he had read the first part of Sprat's *History of the Royal Society*, which was certainly extant in manuscript and probably printed before the Plague,[41] he also had reasons to regard parts of the Society's reform program as inimical to poetry. In the most famous passage of that *History*, Sprat expresses a deep hostility to metaphor, rhetoric, and the other skills of tongue and pen that Dryden had spent his life acquiring:

> Of all the Studies of Men, nothing may be sooner obtain'd, than this vicious Abundance of *Phrase*, this Trick of *Metaphor*, this Volubility of *Tongue*, which makes so great a Noise in the World. . . .
>
> They [the Royal Society] have therefore been more rigorous in putting in Execution the only Remedy, that can be found for this *Extravagance*; and that has been a constant Resolution, to reject all the Amplifications, Digressions, and Swellings of Style; to return back to the primitive purity and Shortness, when Men deliver'd so many *Things*, almost in an equal number of *Words*. They have exacted from all their Members, a close, naked, natural way of Speaking; positive Expressions, clear Senses; a native Easiness; bringing all Things as near the mathematical Plainness as they can; and preferring the Language of Artizans, Country-Men, and Merchants, before that of Wits, or Scholars.[42]

Of course, Sprat's *History* is "as much a confession of faith as a factual record"; despite the ideals announced here, there were few merchants and virtually no artisans among the members of the Royal Society,[43] and Sprat's own language, as this passage shows, is no more free from metaphor, no more successful in attaining "primitive Purity and Shortness," than the language of Thomas Hill, who had sought simplicity in the cause of Puritanism. Like Dryden, many of those interested in linguistic reform had been reared as Puritans; Bishop John Wilkins, whose remarkable *Essay towards a Real Character, and a Philosophical Language* (1668) represents an end point in the process, was the grandson of John Dod. The contradictory impulses toward primitive simplicity and spiritual power that we noticed in Puritan prose recurred in this more secular arena; Sprat's proposal to express "so many *Things*, almost in an equal Number of *Words*" proved as elusive a goal as the alchemical solutions on which many Fellows were hard at work. Even as a theoretical ideal, however, his dismissal of metaphor and rhetoric laid down a challenge to poets.

In the ode "To the Royal Society" printed in the front matter of Sprat's *History*, Cowley seems oblivious to the threat: he writes in his extravagant Pindaric vein, but in a stanza praising Bacon, he appears to accept the valuing of things over words:

> From Words, which are but Pictures of the Thought,
> (Though we our Thoughts from them perversly drew)
> To Things, the Mind's right Object, he it brought:
> Like foolish Birds to painted Grapes we flew;
> He sought and gather'd for our Use the true;
> And when on Heaps the chosen Bunches lay,
> He press'd them wisely the mechanic Way,
> Till all their Juice did in one Vessel join,

Ferment into a Nourishment Divine,
  The thirsty Soul's refreshing Wine.
Who to the Life an exact Piece would make,
Must not from others Work a Copy take;
  No, not from *Rubens* or *Vandike*;
  Much less content himself to make it like
Th' Ideas and the Images which lye
In his own Fancy, or his Memory,
  No, he before his Sight must place,
  The natural and living Face;
  The real Object must command,
Each Judgement of his Eye, and Motion of his Hand.

[sig. B2r]

Previous art, even such superbly successful art as the grapes of the Greek painter Apelles or the portraits of Rubens and Van Dyck, is not the model for creation; careful attention to "The real Object" is preferable to drawing on "Th' Ideas and the Images which lye" in a poet's "Fancy, or his Memory." Yet this apparent endorsement of a hardheaded, empirical theory of artistic or poetic representation comes in a poem whose principal techniques are allusion ("Memory") and conceited wit ("Fancy").

Dead by the time this poem was published, Cowley never worked his way clear of the fanciful "Westminster" style; the manner of his poem in praise of Baconian clarity entirely contradicts its matter. Dryden, by contrast, was already struggling to free himself from Cowleian conceits before the founding of the Royal Society. At the center of *Astraea Redux*, he had punningly equated the false conceits of poets ("fond *Chymaera's*") with the false products of science ("gold that Chymists make"), arguing that "action," in this case Monck's military action, lay in a different sphere from either poetry or science. Remarkably enough, despite the hopes of many in the Royal Society that their work would have practical utility, despite projects concerning agriculture and shipping, modern historians have concluded that the Society actually had little real impact on England's economy, and have traced the process by which most of the Fellows withdrew from studies of what we now call technology in favor of a theoretical science as separate from "action" as poetry.[44] Even Sir Isaac Newton, who left his academic post at Cambridge for a seemingly practical position as Master of the Mint, spent much of his later career in such hermetic studies as alchemy and biblical chronology.

If Dryden would later identify skepticism as an attitude he shared with the members of the Royal Society, he did not hesitate to apply a certain skepticism to the Society's own claims. In this respect, the poem "*To my Honour'd Friend*, Dr Charleton, *on his learned and useful Works; and more particularly this of* STONE-HENG, *by him Restored to the true Founders*" closely resembles the earlier poem "*To my Honored Friend*, Sr ROBERT HOWARD, On his Excellent Poems." In both cases, there is no reason to doubt the friendship, and in both cases, Dryden does what he can to praise the book to which the poem is prefaced. But just as the metaphors of the poem to Howard ultimately blur the opening distinction between the "native sweetnesse" of amateur poets and the "Composure" of professionals, so the subtle rhetoric of the poem to Charleton suggests that Dryden's respect for the accomplishments of the new science had not altered his faith in the powers of poetry.

In the first eight lines, Dryden shrinks Aristotle from a universal tyrant to a coat of arms on the paper wrapped around a container of patent medicine:

> The longest Tyranny that ever sway'd,
> Was that wherein our Ancestors betray'd
> Their free-born *Reason* to the Stagirite,
> *And made his Torch their universal Light.*
>
> [ll. 1–4]

The political terms ("Tyranny," "sway'd," "betray'd," "free-born"), the orotund reference to Aristotle as "the *Stagirite*" (as if he were "the Turk"), and the vaguely theological implication of "universal Light" all contribute to a sense of overinflated grandeur. The next four lines deflate that grandeur by their political and commercial particularity:

> So *Truth*, while onely one suppli'd the State,
> Grew scarce, and dear, and yet sophisticate,
> Until 'twas bought, like Emp'rique Wares or Charms,
> Hard words seal'd up with *Aristotle's* Armes.
>
> [ll. 5–8]

The idea of one man "suppl[ying] the State" was sure to suggest the Cromwell era, and the word "Emp'rique," here properly applied to quack remedies, had already served Dryden in its most common metaphorical sense, as a term for "politicians [who] use deceipt, / Hide what they give and cure but by a cheat" ("To My Lord Chancellor," ll. 67–68). The wording of the last line, we have recently learned, actually comes from an advertisement in one of Herringman's books puffing "Buckworth's famous Lozanges or Pectorals": "for more convenience to those that live remote," reads the notice, "quantities of [Lozanges] *sealed up with* their Coat of *Armes* are left constantly at the house of Mr. H. Herringman at the Anchor in the New Exchange."[45] After the earlier indirection of "the *Stagirite*," even the naming of Aristotle cuts him down to size; in this context, Dryden implies, his name might as well be "Buckworth."

Thus reduced by Dryden's verbal wit, Aristotle no longer seems so formidable a tyrant, and the poem goes on to explain how Columbus, by discovering a temperate region where Aristotle had declared the climate would be torrid, "was the first that shook his Throne" (l. 9). In that surprisingly temperate Caribbean paradise, Columbus found "guiltless *Men*, who danc'd away their time, / *Fresh* as their *Groves*, and *Happy* as their *Clime*" (ll. 13–14). As their "*Happy . . . Clime*" disproves the assertions of Aristotle, the "guiltless *Men*" themselves disprove the assertions of Dr. Charleton's friend Hobbes, who had insisted on the savagery of primitive men. Dryden had used that Hobbesian version of "lawless salvage liberty" in *Astraea Redux*, but his rhetorical aims here are quite different, so he cheerfully adopts a more optimistic and pastoral picture of the primitive. His reasons for choosing that alternative soon become apparent:

> Had we still paid that homage to a *Name*,
> Which onely *God* and *Nature* justly claim;
> The *Western* Seas had been our utmost bound,
> Where *Poets* still might dream the *Sun* was drown'd:
> And all the *Starrs* that shine in *Southern* Skies,
> Had been admir'd by none but *Salvage* Eyes.

[ll. 15–20]

Had Europeans retained their awe for Aristotle (now finally reduced to "a *Name*"), no Columbus would have sailed, no Western eyes would have admired the constellations of the Southern hemisphere, and "*Poets* still might dream the *Sun* was drown'd." Dropped neatly into this context, poets, with their charming but scientifically inaccurate dreams, become analogous to those "guiltless *Men*," as ignorant of Copernicus as of Aristotle, who surely also dream the sun is drowned, albeit several thousand miles further west. Dryden thus dissociates poetry from both the old and the new science, and associates it with the pleasures of a prelapsarian dream, perhaps remembering that Hobbes, whose attack on rhetoric and metaphor anticipates Sprat's, had listed among the acceptable uses of speech, "playing with our words, for pleasure or ornament, innocently."[46]

Narrowing his perspective, Dryden now discusses English science, Charleton's place in that movement, and the particular book at hand:

> Among th' *Assertors* of free Reason's claim,
> Th' *English* are not the least in Worth, or Fame.

[ll. 21–22]

Since he has called the Italian Columbus the first to shake Aristotle's throne, Dryden's claim for the English must be somewhat qualified, but the double negative ("not the least") recurs three more times in this section. A catalogue of English scientists, including Bacon, Gilbert, Harvey, and Ent, centers upon "noble *Boyle*, not less in *Nature* seen, / Than his great *Brother* read in *States* and *Men*" (ll. 27–28). Robert Boyle the chemist may be "not less" well informed than his brother Roger, Earl of Orrery, author of rhymed heroic plays, kinsman by marriage to the Howards, and prominent courtier, but he is surely of less interest to Dryden, whose first published play, *The Rival Ladies* (1664), would be dedicated to Orrery.

Even Charleton, who comes at the end of the catalogue, is introduced with a double negative: "Nor are *You*, Learned Friend, the least renown'd" (l. 33). The ensuing series of compliments to Charleton on his ability to bring together the truths of other authors (not in itself a particularly strong piece of praise) leads to yet another double negative, this one introducing the book on Stonehenge:

> Nor is This Work the least: You well may give
> To *Men* new vigour, who make *Stones* to live.

[ll. 43–44]

The tone is neither ironic nor disrespectful; Dryden was proud to be Charleton's friend and appropriately impressed with his scholarship. Yet these lines are gently, even affectionately comic: a doctor who could make the "*Stones*" or testicles of men more lively would indeed be giving them "new vigour."[47] Dryden does not imply that he disagrees with Charleton's theory about Stonehenge (though many antiquaries did immediately and scornfully reject it); he does, I believe, imply that the really difficult task is making those ancient stones and their origin lively enough to tempt anyone to read the book.

Dr. Charleton, who was among the officially appointed physicians to both Charles I and Charles II, dedicated his book to the King, mindful of the monarch's fondness for retelling the story of his adventures after the Battle of Worcester, which included hiding at Stonehenge. Dryden's conclusion also plays on that connection:

> These Ruines sheltred once *His* Sacred Head,
> Then when from *Wor'sters* fatal Field *He fled;*
> *Watch'd by the Genius of this Royal place,*
> *And mighty Visions of the Danish* Race.
> His *Refuge* then was for a *Temple* shown:
> But, *He* Restor'd, 'tis now become a *Throne.*
>
> [ll. 53–58]

These lines are not only a compliment to the King, like that with which Dryden had concluded the poem to Howard two years earlier, but another instance of Dryden's humorous detachment from the controversy Charleton had entered into with *Chorea Gigantum.* According to the title, Charleton has "*Restored*" Stonehenge "*to the true Founders,*" the Danes, by his argument that the mysterious ring is a coronation site, not (as Jones had argued) a temple. So it is when science turns dogmatic, implies Dryden: one theory or the other must be incorrect. But poetry, with its capacity for irony, metaphor, and wit, can easily accommodate both theories at once, as Dryden demonstrates by explaining that Stonehenge was a temple or sanctuary when it sheltered the fugitive Charles, but has now become a throne—not because Charleton has restored it intellectually, but because Charles has been restored politically. By picturing the King seeing "mighty Visions of the *Danish* Race," Dryden makes him a dreamer, like those "*Poets* [who] might dream the *Sun* was drown'd," poets among whom, despite his interest in and sympathy for the new science, he would always number himself.

While Dryden's early association with Charleton and the other "virtuosi" did not shake his sense of the validity of his poetic vocation, it may ultimately have persuaded him that even poets needed some scientific knowledge. In 1674, attacking Elkanah Settle's *Empress of Morocco,* he wrote a remarkable passage contrasting poets lacking such scientific knowledge with those whose education controls their fancy:

> Fancyfull Poetry, and Musick, us'd with moderation are good, but men who are wholy given over to either of them, are commonly as full of whimsyes as diseas'd and Splenatick men can be: Their heads are continually hot, and they have the same elevation of Fancy sober, which men of Sense have when they drink. So Wine used moderately does not take away the Judgement, but used continually debauches mens understandings; and turns 'em into Sots, making their heads continually hot by accident, as the others heads are by nature; so meer Poets and meer Musicians, are as

sottish as meer Drunkards are, who live in a continuall mist without seeing, or judgeing any thing clearly.

A man should be learn'd in severall Sciences, and should have a reasonable *Philosophicall*, and in some measure a *Mathematicall* head; to be a compleat and excellent Poet: And besides this should have experience in all sorts of humours and manners of men: should be thoroughly skil'd in conversation, and should have a great Knowledge of mankind in generall. [XVII, 181–82][48]

The denigration of "meer Poets" by associating them with musicians and drunkards may remind us that those groups were among the favorite targets of Puritan polemic, but in light of Dryden's interest in music and his frequent recourse to a Longinian literary aesthetic that made much of inspiration (if not of the simpler forms of intoxication), these comments seem surprisingly strong. However fleeting, Dryden's association with the Royal Society left its mark, not least in his inclusion of reason, science, and mathematics among the criteria for poetry.

A "First Attempt in *Dramatique Poetry*"

In the original version of *The Wild Gallant*, Dryden's first play to be acted, the actor playing the Prologue visits two astrologers, who give some ambiguous and discouraging advice about the play's chance for success. That bit of stage business, couched in comically technical terms, may remind us of the schoolboy Dryden's immature display of astrological learning in the elegy for Hastings; "learned Ptolomy" figures in both works. But the lines that follow, in which the Prologue asks the audience to receive the play kindly despite the absence of "any thing that's new," sound a theme with more important implications for Dryden's sense of his task as a playwright in early 1663:

> Nature is old, which Poets imitate,
> And for Wit, those that boast their own estate,
> Forget *Fletcher* and *Ben* before them went,
> Their Elder Brothers, and that vastly spent:
> So much 'twill hardly be repair'd again.

> [ll. 42–46]

Inexperienced and uncertain about writing for the theatre, as were virtually all the men who attempted plays during the 1660s, Dryden saw himself and his fellow playwrights as the younger sons of a family in which the "Elder Brothers" had spent all the wit.[49] He envied "*Fletcher* and *Ben*" not only their wit and their capacity to dramatize nature, but their long daily contact with a living theatre, and his sense of the War and Interregnum as a deluge interrupting the continuity of the English theatre was still lively in the 1690s, when he referred to Fletcher, Jonson, and the other playwrights before the Civil War as "the Gyant Race, before the Flood" ("To Congreve," l. 5).

At the time this first play was acted, Dryden probably knew as much about the theatre as any Englishman his age, though his knowledge was scant compared to that available to Jonson, who lived in a London where the Globe, the Swan, and the other Elizabethan playhouses offered daily performances. By the 1640s, when Dryden came up to Westminster, the few plays to be seen in London were illegal and crude, and even the annual school plays had been suspended, though the former Oxford actor Busby surely saw to it that his scholars had access to plays in books; his library included the folio edition of Jonson and *The Royal Slave* of Cartwright, from which the schoolboy Dryden may have borrowed some imagery for the Hastings poem.[50] We may imagine the undergraduate Dryden continuing to read drama in English and French at Cambridge, and I should think it likely that he managed to see Davenant's operatic productions during the last years of the Protectorate. Sir Robert Howard's *Poems* of 1660, for which Dryden wrote the prefatory poem, included a comedy, *The Blind Lady*, and if Dryden's later assertions about *The Duke of Guise* may be credited, he wrote an unproduced drama himself in 1660.[51] Like Howard, however, Dryden lacked practical theatrical experience; for both men, the productions newly available on stage after the Restoration, virtually all of which were revivals of Jacobean and Caroline plays, were a first opportunity to see drama performed.[52] Even for older men who remembered the "last Age," these first productions were strikingly new: boys had played women's roles in the theatre before the Civil War, but the new theatres employed actresses.

Thanks to Howard, Dryden was probably well informed about the power struggle in which Sir William Davenant, whose poetry he had already imitated, and Thomas Killigrew, who had acted as a kind of court jester to the exiled Charles II, seized control of the three quasi-legal troupes operating in London at the time of the Restoration. Killigrew secured the services of most of the experienced actors, the rights to hundreds of old plays, and the use of Gibbons's Tennis Court at Vere Street, where his players, known as the King's Company, were still performing at the time of the premiere of *The Wild Gallant*.[53] Davenant had to make do with younger actors and fewer scripts, though he did have one rising star in Thomas Betterton; his troupe, now known as the Duke's Company, acted at Salisbury Court until June 1661, when they opened their splendid new theatre at Lincoln's Inn Fields with an elaborate operatic production of *The Siege of Rhodes*.[54] The competition between the theatres was keen; in the prologue to *The Wild Gallant*, for example, the astrological talk of ascendants and houses leads to some broad allusions to recent successes by the rival theatre. When the First Astrologer advises the Prologue that the play "should have been but one continued Song, / Or at the least a Dance of 3 hours long" (ll. 34–35), Dryden is glancing at the popularity of Davenant's opera, which so captured the audience that it left the Vere Street theatre practically empty.[55] When the Second Astrologer "conclude[s] it is your Authors lot, / To be indanger'd by a *Spanish* Plot" (ll. 38–39), Dryden is deliberately using the exact rhymes of a couplet from the prologue to *The Adventures of Five Hours*, adapted by Sir Samuel Tuke from a Spanish source suggested by Charles II, which had just enjoyed a long run at Lincoln's Inn Fields.[56] By working together to secure their royal patents, however, Killigrew and Davenant established a monopoly limiting such competition to their two companies; that monopoly would prove a fact of considerable importance to Dryden's dramatic career.

Howard was involved with Killigrew both financially and artistically, and that involvement probably accounts for Dryden's dealings with the King's Company. Passions ran high during the early seasons, and relations between Howard and Killigrew were apparently strained; a bizarre episode in August of 1661 actually saw Sir Robert and two of his younger brothers imprisoned along with several members of the Killigrew family.[57] Whatever the cause of this quarrel, it was soon patched up: all the combatants were released within a week, and when the agreement to build the Bridges Street Theatre, designed as a more permanent home for the King's Company, was signed on 20 December 1661, Howard purchased nine shares, one quarter of the total; two of his plays, *The Surprisal* and *The Committee*, were acted by the King's Company at Vere Street during 1662.[58]

As the intensity of the struggle for power suggests, there was money to be made in the new theatres, and Dryden, whose marriage came in the same year as his first play, needed money, a concern perhaps betrayed by his recourse to the economic metaphor about the "Elder Brothers, . . . that vastly spent." He was at this point considerably more adept at poetry than at drama; the witty, polished lines to Charleton are the work of a highly skilled poet, while this first play is clumsy apprentice work at best. But poetry had no commercial viability; Milton's profits from *Paradise Lost*, published later in the same decade, were less than a farthing a line. The theatre, with its set expenses for actors and scenery, involved financial risk; indeed, old plays dominated the boards because they were less risky. But there was a paying audience, and a successful new play could bring its author the profits of the third day's performance, though that was all he could normally expect, even if there were a long run or a revival. Still, the King's keen interest and frequent attendance insured that success in the drama—as an actor, manager, or playwright—would not escape the notice of the court.

Dryden's decision to write plays is thus far less surprising than the fact that he became "the only professional playwright of the 1660s."[59] Most of the other men who wrote new plays during the first years of the restored theatres, men like the Howard brothers, Sir Samuel Tuke, and the Earl of Orrery, were "gentleman amateurs." Older professional writers who might have turned to the theatre, such as Waller, Denham, and Cowley, remained relatively uninvolved.[60] But Dryden was prescient about the possibilities of the restored theatre, recognizing the stage as a platform from which a rhetorically astute writer might address and persuade a select and powerful audience. He grasped the central importance of the theatre in that larger process to which he would devote much of his career: the reinvention of English culture, the selective recovery of imperfectly remembered English traditions and the necessary appropriation of more recent materials from the Continent.

Convinced of the importance of the drama, Dryden methodically set about acquiring the experience he lacked. His theatrical knowledge in 1663 may have been mere book-learning, but by 1667, when the theatres reopened after being closed by the Plague for over a year, Dryden had become an experienced professional. The characterization in his early plays is often flat, betraying his lack of those very qualities he would later hold to be so important for the making of "a compleat and excellent Poet": "experience in all sorts of humours and manners of men, . . . skil[l] in conversation, and . . . a great Knowledge of mankind in generall" (XVII, 182). Yet in these very years, his conversations with the literary set at Will's coffeehouse, the scientific virtuosi from the Royal Society, and the recusant aristocracy among whom his wife had grown up were greatly increasing his knowledge and experience. The *Essay of Dramatick Poesie* betrays his voracious reading of plays and dramatic theory during this period, and the steady improvement of his own plays suggests that he knew how to use that reading. If the early plays themselves are unimpressive, Dryden's determination to become a playwright, even after the failure of *The Wild Gallant*, is impressive. By the time Shadwell and Settle began to write plays, Dryden's apprentice work was already behind him.

In the case of *The Wild Gallant*, Dryden's disarming admission that his play lacks "any thing that's new" reflects not only his general respect for the "Elder Brothers" of earlier drama but the particular circumstances of this play's composition. Tuke's prologue to *The Adventures of Five Hours* had made a point of its novelty:

> I dare boldly say,
> The *English* Stage ne'er had so New a Play;
> The Dress, the Authour, and the Scenes are New.[61]

The Duke's Company, now in their new theatre, did have splendid costumes and modern painted scenery, far outdoing the drab productions at Vere Street, and Tuke was a "New . . . Authour" in the sense that he had never before written a play. But the emphasis on scenes, dress, and the author's inexperience was evidently meant to deflect attention from the fact that Tuke's plot and characters were *not* new; he had translated and adapted a Spanish play. In his prologue, Dryden casts doubt on the whole concept of novelty, emphasizing the "Spanish plot" as a way of implying that Tuke's play is new only because imported, and appealing to the audience's patriotism:

> This Play is *English*, and the growth your own;
> As such it yields to *English* Plays alone.

> [ll. 48–49]

There is more at stake in these lines than Dryden's belief, more elaborately developed in the *Essay of Dramatick Poesie*, that the English dramatic tradition could prove as viable a source for the new theatre as the French or Spanish. In the preface to the revised version of *The Wild Gallant*, published by Herringman in 1669, he acknowledges having taken his play from an older original, evidently English: "The Plot was not Originally my own: but so alter'd, by me (whether for the better or worse, I know not) that, whoever the Author was, he could not have challeng'd a Scene of it" (VIII, 3).

Although Dryden seems not to have known the name of the original author, internal and external evidence points strongly to Richard Brome, once Ben Jonson's manservant, who became a professional playwright in the 1630s and served (curiously enough) as the editor for *Lachrymae Musarum*, the volume in which Dryden's first poem appeared. When Brome died in 1652, some of his plays apparently fell into the hands of the publisher Humphrey Mosely, who patiently saved a large collection of dramatic manuscripts during the Interregnum. With the Restoration, Mosely had an opportunity to peddle his wares; the actor Charles Hart, one of the shareholders in the King's Company, appears to have purchased some of his manuscripts and distributed them to several writers (including Howard and Dryden) for revision. That much of the story we may reconstruct with some confidence.[62] But since the only text of *The Wild Gallant* we have is that of the revised version, clearly somewhat altered by Dryden from the 1663 version, and since the old manuscript from which he worked has long since disappeared, we have no firm basis on which to assign its authorship, assess the accuracy of Dryden's claim to have made massive revisions, or reconstruct even Dryden's first version, let alone the lost play behind it. Nonetheless, the theory that Brome wrote the original version rests on some impressive similarities in plot and dialogue between this play and several of his surviving works. By reworking a play by an "Elder Brother" from the time "before the Flood," Dryden was undertaking a kind of work appropriate to an apprentice playwright, though Brome was hardly a "Gyant Wit." He was also testing an idea to which he would often return in his criticism, the belief that certain fundamental realities transcend particular cultures and times. If "Nature is old, which Poets imitate," little that a playwright presents is likely to be truly "new."

As Dryden's preface suggests, the plot of *The Wild Gallant* is thoroughly old-fashioned, hinging on such farcical contrivances as a pregnancy feigned with a pillow. In this respect, Dryden's insistence on the Englishness of his play is legitimate; the relatively loose, episodic construction he presumably found in his source was one of the more obvious differences between the English dramatic tradition and the continental insistence on the unities. Most of the characters display Jonsonian humours; the lowlife scoundrels Failer and Burr, for example, are distant relatives of Subtle and Face in *The Alchemist*.[63] Whether or not he changed the plot as extensively as he later claimed, Dryden must have made hundreds of verbal changes for the version performed in 1663; a few contemporary jokes, for example, are surely attempts on his part to bring the play up to date. Waiting in a dark alley for a mysterious benefactor he fears may be the devil, Loveby muses thus:

> he told me he was a Scholar, and had been a Parson in the Fanatick times; a shrewd suspicion it was the Devil; or at least a limb of him. If the Devil can send Churchmen on his Errands, Lord have mercy on the Layety! [II, ii, 4–8]

Here we may detect not only an instance of Dryden's lifelong anticlerical feeling, but an attempt to garner a laugh at the expense of the "Fanatick times" of recent memory.[64] Presumably this passage reflects the particular circumstances of 1663, as does Constance's suspicion that Loveby may be "as poor as a decimated Cavalier" (II, i, 151). If a later jest alleging that "an *Hollander* with Butter will fry rarely in Hell" (V, ii, 18–19) appeared in the version of 1663, it shows Dryden's awareness of the hostility toward the Dutch that would soon lead to another naval war, but I rather suspect that he added these lines for the revival of 1667, produced *after* that war.[65]

Trivial as these alterations are, there is little else in *The Wild Gallant* that we may confidently ascribe to Dryden. The witty "proviso scene" in which Isabelle agrees to marry Sir Timerous if he will allow her such minor concessions as complete control of his money (III, i, 210–73) may suggest similar scenes in familiar comedies of the 1670s, but there were precedents for it in Massinger, Shirley, Fletcher, and Brome.[66] The repartee of Jack Loveby and Lady Constance probably represents an attempt by Dryden to satisfy the contemporary fondness for sparkling wit, but the "Cavalier drama" of the later 1630s was hardly devoid of wit, so that we cannot easily ascertain which lines Dryden added and which he found in his source.

Dryden's hope that his amalgam of old and new material might succeed was quickly disappointed: *The Wild Gallant* failed, both at Vere Street and at court. Not terribly different from the older plays that made up the bulk of the repertory, since it was in fact a revision of such a play, Dryden's piece was nonetheless billed as a "new play" and therefore inevitably compared to Tuke's popular sensation, which was no "newer" chronologically, but seemed fresher to an audience unfamiliar with its conventions. Pepys's response to the premiere of Tuke's play will serve as an example: "the play, in one word, is the best, for the variety and the most excellent continuance of the plot to the very end, that ever I saw."[67] A few weeks later, he saw *The Wild Gallant* at court, "performed by the King's house; but it was ill acted, and the play so poor a thing as I never saw in my life almost, and so little answering the name, that from beginning to end I could not, nor can at this time, tell certainly which was the wild gallant."[68] Since he knew Spanish and was generally well read in continental drama, Dryden was surely aware that Tuke's work was no more original than his own, but he did not dwell on the unfairness of his play's fate: accepting the popular verdict, he wrote an unabashed imitation of Tuke, *The Rival Ladies*, as his next play; it may have been on stage as early as the fall of 1663.[69] This practical response did not mean that Dryden had abandoned the idea of drawing on the English tradition in writing for the theatre; his *Essay of Dramatick Poesie* would soon argue that case. But in this instance as in many later ones, Dryden's practice was not the slave of his own critical theory; he was willing to try his hand at the sort of "Spanish plot" that had worked for Tuke.

Among Tuke's advantages in the competition was the fact that the King himself had put the Spanish original into his hands, while Dryden had presumably received the Brome manuscript, directly or indirectly, from the handsome actor Charles Hart. Curiously enough, the one prominent person who approved and promoted Dryden's play was a woman who had both Hart and the King among her lovers: Barbara Villiers Palmer, now Countess of Castlemaine. We do not know what pleased her in *The Wild Gallant*; perhaps she liked the tough minds and ready tongues of Isabelle and Constance. Nor do we know just how she "encouraged" Dryden; one plausible theory is that she saw the play at Vere Street during its brief run and urged Charles to request it for a court performance.[70] In any case, her stunning appearance on the evening of the unsuccessful performance at court did not escape the ravenous eyes of Pepys, who found her more worth watching than the play. Scanning the faces of the great for different reasons, Dryden can hardly have failed to notice, as did Pepys, that "the King did not seem pleased at all, all the whole play." In these circumstances, the smiles of the King's most beautiful mistress were welcome indeed.

Eager to celebrate those smiles, and to repair whatever damage the play's failure had done him at court, Dryden wrote a charming verse epistle "TO THE Lady *CASTLEMAIN*, UPON *Her incouraging his first Play*," a poem designed not only to flatter its recipient, but to be shown about by her as evidence of the author's skill in the courtly art of praise. In this "paper of verses," perhaps the result of a morning's labor,

Portrait of Barbara Villiers Palmer, Countess of Castlemaine and Duchess of Cleveland, after Peter Lely, ca. 1665–75.

we may observe Dryden recycling imagery and language from earlier poems, often in ways that reveal some of his deeper concerns. He begins with an image that recalls the use of Columbus in the poem to Charleton:

> As Sea-men shipwrackt on some happy shore,
> Discover Wealth in Lands unknown before;
> And what their Art had labour'd long in vain,
> By their misfortunes happily obtain:
> So my much-envy'd Muse by Storms long tost,
> Is thrown upon your Hospitable Coast.

[ll. 1–6]

As in the prologue, with its talk of "Elder Brothers, . . . that vastly spent," economic success is clearly on Dryden's mind. Unlike some of his Puritan forebears, however, he recognizes that hard work is not the only path to wealth or fame: a lucky "misfortune" may help a man obtain the wealth for which his "Art had labour'd long in vain." The rhymes in that second couplet are those he had used as a teenager to praise Lord Hastings's facility with languages:

> Nature gave him, a Childe, what Men in vain
> Oft strive, by Art though further'd, to obtain.

But in this poem Lady Castlemaine, as the "Hospitable Coast" on which Dryden's Muse has been shipwrecked, plays the role of a bountiful Nature, dispensing her miraculous favors to a poet who had pictured himself, in the conclusion of the epilogue to this very play, as a Leander swimming the dangerous Hellespont of theatrical opinion.[71]

At some level of consciousness, this image of a female patron as a "Hospitable Coast," which Dryden would employ again in dedicating *The Indian Emperour* to Anne, Duchess of Monmouth,[72] is a sexual one: during the next winter, Dryden's friend Charles Sackville, Lord Buckhurst, would use it that way in a scabrous verse epistle to the playwright George Etherege:

> Some do compare a man t'a bark—
> A pretty metaphor, pray mark—
> And with a long and tedious story
> Will all the tackling lay before ye:
> The sails are hope, the masts desire,
> Till they the gentlest reader tire.
> But howsoe'er they keep a pudder,
> I'm sure the pintle is the rudder:
> The powerful rudder which of force
> To Town will shortly steer my course;
> And if you do not there provide
> A port where I may safely ride,
> Landing in haste, in some foul creek,
> 'Tis ten to one I spring a leak.[73]

Such sexual comparisons of men to ships and women to ports, as Buckhurst evidently knew, are as old as literature, occurring in *Oedipus Rex*, for example. Yet Dryden, who never overtly signals a sexual meaning for that imagery in this poem, had used it for quite different purposes in *Astraea Redux*, where a Virgilian Charles is "toss'd by Fate," and the Restoration is a fortunate shipwreck: "those loud stormes that did against him rore / Have cast his shipwrack'd Vessel on the shore" (ll. 123–24). By appropriating such imagery to his own literary career ("So my much-envy'd Muse by Storms long tost"), Dryden insinuates an analogy between himself and the King. As in *Astraea Redux*, where the more serious idea of learning from one's sufferings to prize one's bliss similarly connects the poet and the monarch, the analogy operates by implication; Dryden is far too skilled to risk an overt equation. Yet when he praises Lady Castlemaine's efforts on his behalf as surpassing those of Cato for Pompey, the language again strongly suggests the King's recent Restoration: "you have done what *Cato* could not do, / To chuse the Vanquish'd, and restore him too" (ll. 11–12). Lady Castlemaine, after all, had chosen Charles for her lover after he had been vanquished at Worcester; for anyone who caught the implication, Dryden was wittily giving her credit for the Restoration of the King, not merely credit for the restoration of his own literary reputation. If pleasant thoughts about Lady Castlemaine were a part of that analogy between poet and monarch, Dryden was not the only man to cherish such fantasies: Pepys once wrote rapturously of "my last night's dream, . . . which was, that I had my Lady Castlemayne in my armes and was admitted to use all the dalliance I desired with her."[74]

Dryden also praises Castlemaine's father, "Noble *Grandison*," who had died in the Royalist cause, and lavishes upon her the astronomical imagery he had employed in all his works, which serves here to prepare the idea that the royal mistress, like a star or a goddess, is "above" ordinary morality:

> You, like the Stars, not by reflexion bright,
> Are born to your own Heav'n, and your own Light:
> Like them are good, but from a Nobler Cause,
> From your own Knowledg, not from Natures Laws.
>
> [ll. 25–28]

Now, at the very center of the poem, Dryden delicately addresses Castlemaine's powerful position as the King's favorite, in lines that make the courtly wars of reputation and influence analogous to heroic warfare:

> Your pow'r you never use, but for defence,
> To guard your own, or others Innocence.
> Your Foes are such as they, not you, have made;
> And Virtue may repel, though not invade.
> Such courage did the Ancient *Hero's* show,
> Who, when they might prevent, would wait the blow;
> With such assurance, as they meant to say,
> We will o'recome, but scorn the safest way.
>
> [ll. 29–36]

These are risky lines, since many people would have found any reference to the "Innocence" of a prominent adulteress ludicrous: Dryden's cousin Edward Pickering, who frequently complained about the lewdness of the court, is an obvious example, and even Pepys, who often attended the theatre for the purpose of ogling Castlemaine and the other court ladies, worried about the damage done the King's reputation by his open immorality.[75] But Dryden did not write these verses for publication, and the Ned Pickerings of the world were not the audience at whom he was aiming.[76] By describing Lady Castlemaine as a goddess or a star, he was setting her above ordinary morality; by praising her judicious use of her power, and by referring to her "Innocence," "Virtue," "courage," and "assurance," he was not only endorsing the legitimacy of her place at court, but quietly urging her to make good use of it.[77]

Having skillfully dealt with these serious issues in a way certain to please Castle-maine and impress those at court to whom she chose to show his poem, Dryden works back toward his own reasons for praising her, and toward the more playful tone with which the poem began. Thanks to her "great Fate," which can only mean her powerful position, he may "rest secure"; her "Beauty, which captives all things," has paradox-ically set him free;[78] she has played the role of a deus ex machina, and made him as fortunate as a Greek poet: "Some God descended and preserv'd the Play" (l. 44). The conclusion, another of Dryden's many passages on inheritances, is an amusing eco-nomic allegory in which Beauty incurs a debt by engaging Poesie "For sums of praises, till she came to age" (l. 50). Castlemaine, by encouraging Dryden, has discharged this entire debt, and the poem ends with a receipt:

> Receiv'd in full this present day and year,
> One soveraign smile from Beauties general Heir.
>
> [ll. 57–58]

The word "soveraign" (as the name of a coin) continues the economic metaphor; it also betrays Dryden's hope that "Beauties general Heir" will serve as his advocate with her lover, the sovereign of England.

Heroic Drama in Practice and Theory

Two days after the ill-fated court performance of *The Wild Gallant*, that sovereign wrote a letter, in his own hand, to the author of a very different kind of play, Roger Boyle, Earl of Orrery, who was at work on his second rhymed heroic drama. "I will now tell you," wrote the King, "that I have read your first play, which I like very well, and doe intend to bring it upon the Stage, as Soone as my Company have their new Stage in order, that the Seanes may bee worthy the words they are to sett forth."[79] Like Killigrew, Howard, Dryden, and the actors, Charles was eagerly anticipating the opening of the Bridges Street Theatre, which finally took place on 7 May 1663, but the King's Company did not actually produce a play by Orrery until they mounted *The Generall* in September 1664, goaded by the success of Orrery's *Henry V*, which Davenant and the Duke's Company had produced in August. Killigrew may have felt little urgency about mount-ing a play by Orrery because his company had produced successful rhyming plays of its own: *The Indian Queen*, a rhymed heroic play by Dryden and Howard, opened in January 1664, and Dryden's *The Rival Ladies*, a "Spanish" tragicomedy with some sections in rhyme, was still being performed in August 1664.

In *The Indian Queen*, Dryden and Howard catered to the public taste for spectacle, which the new theatre was finally able to satisfy, and which was evidently among the monarch's theatrical interests; they also conformed, surely not by accident, to the King's well-known preference for rhyme, and to the ideal of an "heroic" drama that was emerging in the King's instructions to Orrery. From his Restoration on, Charles had taken a keen interest in shaping the drama. We have noticed his furnishing Tuke with the plot for *The Adventures of Five Hours*, and the "commands" he gave to Orrery in 1660 were even more decisive for the development of Dryden's career. Our source is a letter from Orrery to James Butler, Duke of Ormonde, written from Ireland on 23 January 1662:

> When I had the Honnor, & unhappyness the Last Time to Kiss his majts hande, he Commanded me, to write a Play for Him; . . . And therfore, som months [later] I Presumed to lay at his majts Feete, a Trage-Comedi, All in Ten Feet verse, & Ryme. I writt it, in that manner upon two accounts; First, because I thought it was not fit, a Command soe Extraordinary, should have bin obeyd in a way that was Common; Secondly, because I found his majty Relish'd rather, the French Fassion of Playes, then the English.[80]

Several of Orrery's implicit assumptions here would loom large in the ensuing history of heroic drama and the critical controversy about the place of rhyme in the drama. He assumes that rhyme is an appropriate form for a play commanded by so "Extraordinary" a person as the King, and that prose is "Common," ignoring (or not knowing) the fact that many quite vulgar old plays employed rhyme. He also associates rhyme, correctly, with "the French Fassion of Playes," but his corollary assumption that the English fashion was restricted to prose is false, as a glance at the heavily rhymed *Romeo and Juliet* might have reminded him. Dryden's discussions of rhyme in the dedication to *The Rival Ladies* (1664) and the *Essay of Dramatick Poesie* (1668) involve similar distortions of the actual formal range of Elizabethan and Jacobean drama and a similar claim that rhyme ennobles or elevates the drama.

Nor should we interpret Orrery's implicit claim to have satisfied the King's taste for "the French Fassion of Playes" as evidence of mere translation or slavish imitation of French dramatic practice. Several other courtiers would soon join forces to translate Corneille's *Pompey*, and Orrery had evidently read some Corneille, but his plays show more dependence on English drama of the Jacobean and Caroline eras than on any specific French plays.[81] Prose romance, with its elevated language and obsessive concern for love and honor, was another important source: in the letter to Ormonde, Orrery acknowledges borrowing Hylas, a character for his new play, from the *Astrée* of Honoré D'Urfé, an enormously influential prose romance published in France between 1607 and 1626.

In the essay "Of Heroique Plays," which served him as a preface when he published *The Conquest of Granada* in 1672, Dryden downplays these three sources, all of which he also followed, in order to argue that heroic poetry, especially Renaissance epic, is the most important model for heroic drama. He acknowledges the importance of Corneille only by noting his influence on Davenant, misrepresents Fletcher and Shakespeare by implying an almost complete contrast between their poetic practice and his own, and minimizes his debt to romance by declaring himself "more in love with *Achilles* and *Rinaldo*, than with *Cyrus* and *Oroondates*" (XI, 16). As so often in his criticism, however, Dryden is constructing a theory after the fact, trying to make his heroic plays, which had been pilloried as bombast in *The Rehearsal* (1671), appear as serious as possible by emphasizing their affinities with epic and disregarding the real debts they also owe to French drama, English "Cavalier" plays, and prose romance. His description of the beginnings of the heroic play after the Restoration, which purports to describe his own creative process at the moment in his career we are now considering, must therefore be treated as a partial fiction, though it is revealing enough to be worth quoting:

> For Heroick Plays, (in which only I have us'd it without the mixture of Prose), the first light we had of them on the *English* Theatre was from the late Sir *William D'Avenant* [in the "entertainments" at Rutland House under the Protectorate]. The Original of this musick and of the Scenes which adorn'd his work, he had from the *Italian* Opera's; but he heighten'd his Characters (as I may probably imagine) from the example of *Corneille* and some *French* poets. In this Condition did this part of Poetry remain at his Majesties return: When growing bolder, as being now own'd by a publick Authority, he review'd his *Siege of Rhodes*, and caus'd it be acted as a just Drama; but as few men have the happiness to begin and finish any new project, so neither did he live to make his design perfect: There wanted the fulness of a plot, and the variety of Characters to form it as it ought: and, perhaps, something might have been added to the beauty of the   stile. [XI, 9]

Dryden is about to explain how he added fullness of plot, variety of characters, and beauty of style to Davenant's model by drawing on Ariosto, but we may interrupt him here to notice that those were among the strengths most often praised in prose romance. When the English translation of *Astrée* was issued from Herringman's shop in three volumes in 1657 and 1658, each volume had a preface signed "J. D."; these puffs are quite possibly the work of the young Dryden, who was in any case at least as familiar as Orrery with French romance. In the first preface, "J. D." praises D'Urfé's "cleare *representation* of the Noblest and most generous *images of life*," his "extraordinary sententiousnesse," and the emotions of his characters:

> Here thou hast a jealous and distrustfull ASTREA; a despairing, yet faithfull CELA-DON; a fickle and unconstant HYLAS; and such intricate scenes of *Courtship, Love, Jealousie,* and the other *passions,* as cannot but raise in thee a consideration of humane Affairs, sutable to the severall emergencies.[82]

With the names of the characters altered, this passage would serve admirably as a description of the intent of *The Indian Queen*. The second preface even refers to the writers of romance as "those who spend their endeavours and Estates," perhaps an early instance of one of Dryden's favorite metaphors, but we need not rely on identifying this "J. D." as Dryden in order to establish the importance of romance for the origins of the heroic play: *The Indian Queen* is demonstrably dependent for its plot and characters on three separate prose romances: *Polexandre, Cléopâtre,* and *Cassandre.*[83]

When Dryden and Howard sat down together in their rooms in Lincoln's Inn Fields to sketch *The Indian Queen,* they were doubtless aware of the King's instructions to Orrery; indeed, they too had probably read Orrery's work in draft, since the Earl was married to Sir Robert's first cousin, and since Dryden's letter dedicating *The Rival Ladies* to Orrery speaks of an ongoing literary correspondence across the Irish Sea. The romances from which they assembled the plot were surely on the table, along with the new quarto edition of *The Siege of Rhodes,* which included a dedication on the subject of "*heroique Plays*" explicitly praising Corneille, with whose plays Dryden was also familiar by this time. In his own later essay "Of Heroique Plays," however, Dryden insists on the presence of another book:

> I observ'd then, as I said, what was wanting to the perfection of [Davenant's] *Siege of Rhodes*: which was design, and variety of Characters. And in the midst of this consideration, by meer accident, I open'd the next Book that lay by me, which was an *Ariosto* in *Italian*; and the very first two lines of that Poem gave me light to all I could desire.
>
> > Le Donne, I Cavalier, L'arme, gli amori,
> > Le Cortesie, l'audaci imprese jo canto, &c.
>
> [XI, 10][84]

We cannot know whether this charming story is an accurate recollection of what happened in 1663 or a convenient fiction suiting the circumstances of 1672, but what finally matters is the larger truth the story shadows forth: Dryden was concerned, from the very outset of his dramatic career, to make the drama *poetic* in all the senses of that word. Not only would his heroic plays rhyme, but their fiction, their *poesis*, their making would reach for the heights of plotting, characterization, and language previously associated with epic and its close prose relative, romance.[85] There were practical considerations in Dryden's embracing this theory, to be sure. Grand heroic drama was well suited to exploit the sensational effects made possible by the new wing-and-drop scenery at Bridges Street, which Sir Robert Howard had helped to design.[86] The King, who had not been pleased with *The Wild Gallant*, was on record as favoring rhymed heroic plays. The success of *The Siege of Rhodes* and the continuing popularity of prose romance suggested that a play like *The Indian Queen* might capture an enthusiastic audience. But the essay also reveals a creative impulse that we need not doubt; still speaking of Davenant, Dryden explains that

> The Laws of an Heroick Poem did not dispence with those of . . .the common drama, but rais'd them to a greater height: and indulg'd him a farther liberty of Fancy, and of drawing all things as far above the ordinary proportion of the Stage, as that is beyond the common words and actions of humane life. [XI, 10]

Not only does the author of heroic plays have an opportunity to raise his actions above common life by two degrees, but he has, in Dryden's telling phrase, "liberty of Fancy." Gaining such freedom for his imagination was surely Dryden's major aim in embracing and developing the idea of the heroic play.

Yet in practical terms, Dryden's imagination in *The Indian Queen* was far from free. He was collaborating with his friend and patron Howard, a part owner in the theatre whose power would guarantee a performance and whose own plays, especially *The Committee*, had been far more successful than *The Wild Gallant*. Whatever his private opinion of Howard's talents as a poet, Dryden had to reckon with those facts. He had done some editing for Howard before, probably cleaning up the proof sheets for the *Poems* of 1660, but this time he clearly did some of the actual writing, though we cannot know how much. Howard published the play as his own in 1665, and Dryden referred to it, probably in the same year, as "the *Indian Queen*, (part of which Poem was writ by me)." There is no other contemporary evidence, and modern attempts to sort out the particular contributions of the collaborators are contradictory and inconclusive.[87] My own guess is that Dryden and Howard worked together closely, each overlooking and revising what the other had written. They were living together during 1663, when this play was being written, and they became brothers-in-law a month before its premiere. Although Dryden would necessarily have been cautious in his criticism of his noble partner's work, any collaboration was sure to limit his "liberty of Fancy," and this joint effort brought together strong-willed men who would be quarreling openly a few years later.

Among the topics in those later quarrels was the effect of rhyme in the drama; from the very beginning, Dryden found rhyming a more congenial procedure than did Howard. Even in the first blush of his enthusiasm for rhyme, however, he never pretended that it added to the poet's "liberty of Fancy." In the revealing dedication to *The Rival Ladies*, the earliest of the many essays in which Dryden opens the door to his poetic workshop, he praises rhyme for controlling and limiting the poet's imagination:

> Rhyme so Knits up [Memory] by the Affinity of Sounds, that by remembring the last Word in one Line, we often call to Mind both the Verses. Then in the quickness of Reparties, (which in Discoursive Scenes fall very often) it has so particular a Grace, and is so aptly Suited to them, that the suddain Smartness of the Answer, and the Sweetness of the Rhyme, set off the Beauty of each other. But that benefit which I consider most in it, because I have not seldome found it, is, that it Bounds and Circumscribes the Fancy. For Imagination in a Poet is a faculty so Wild and Lawless, that, like an High-ranging Spaniel it must have Cloggs tied to it, least it out-run the Judgment. [VIII, 100–01]

The imagery of binding and clogging suggests *The Indian Queen*, where the major characters frequently wear the real manacles of captivity and struggle within the psychological manacles of love and honor. Like one of those characters, Acacis, whose nice sense of honor repeatedly prevents him from escaping captivity, Dryden embraced the idea of rhymed drama as a welcome discipline, and clung to it punctiliously through thirteen years, thousands of lines of rhymed drama, and hundreds of pages of combative prose defending that drama. When he did finally change sides, like his other character Montezuma, he remembered the metaphor of chains. In the prologue to *Aureng-Zebe* (1675), which at last announces the poet's weariness of "his long-lov'd Mistris, Rhyme," Dryden argues, as Howard had much earlier, that "Passion's too fierce to be in Fetters bound."

The vigorous passions of the characters in *The Indian Queen* do often seem bound in heavy verbal fetters, and not merely to modern ears. Pepys called the play "a most pleasant show, and beyond my expectation; . . . but spoiled with the Ryme, which breaks the sense."[88] If the last phrase is his way of observing the disastrous effect of the rhyming on the syntax, he was an acute critic indeed on this occasion. The Dryden of 1663, who had recently composed the deft poems to Charleton and Castlemaine, knew how to drape a sinuous and ironic syntax across the frame of the heroic couplet, but in *The Indian Queen*, the emphasis on "quickness of Reparties" and "suddain Smartness of . . . Answer[s]" too often produces a simple, heavy, crudely aphoristic syntax. The play is hardly three minutes old when the victorious warrior Montezuma, having demanded the hand of the princess Orazia from her father (the Ynca of Peru), rankles at being refused and resolves to pursue the Ynca with his sword, only to be prevented by the prince Acacis, a brave prisoner of war. This dialogue then ensues:

> *Mont.* Can a Revenge that is so just, be ill?
> *Aca.* It is *Orazia*'s Father you wou'd kill.
> *Mont. Orazia*! how that name has charm'd my Sword!
> *Aca.* Compose these wilde distempers in your breast;
>   Anger like madness is appeas'd by rest.
> *Mont.* Bid children sleep, my spirits boil too high;
>   But since *Orazia*'s Father must not dye,
>   A nobler vengeance shall my actions guide,
>   I'le bear the conquest to the conquered side,
>   Until this *Ynca* for my friendship sues,
>   And proffers that his pride does now refuse.
>
> [I, i, 63–73]

Tempting as it might be, we cannot necessarily blame these wretched lines on Howard, since the rhyming passages in Dryden's own *Rival Ladies*, produced during the same season, are equally stiff. In attempting to simplify the responses of their characters, perhaps in the mistaken belief that such stylized speech would seem nobly plain, Dryden and Howard produced a heavily end-stopped verse whose obvious, leaden rhymes made it immediately susceptible to parody. If we strain to hear in *The Indian Queen* the melodious voice we know from Dryden's poems, we shall find it in less overtly "dramatic" places: in the lyrical prologue, in the magical scene in which the prophet Ismeron conjures up the God of Dreams (III, ii), or in speeches by messengers describing events offstage, such as this account of Montezuma's arrival in the Mexican camp:

> *Messenger.* The Troops gaze on him, as if some bright Star
>   Shot to their Aids; call him the God of War:
>   Whilst he, as if all Conquest did of right
>   Belong to him, bids them prepare to fight;
>   Which if they shou'd delay one hour, he swears
>   He'l leave them to their Dangers or their Fears,
>   And Shame (which is th' ignoble Cowards choice.)
>   At this the Army seem'd to have one voice,
>   United in a shout, and call'd upon
>   The God-like Stranger, *Lead us, lead us on.*
>
> [I, ii, 67–76]

Here the impetuous excitement of the narrative produces frequent enjambment, variety in the placement of caesurae, and a syntax far less clogged by the couplets than the syntax in most of the dialogue. Had Dryden and Howard actually dramatized this scene, writing for Montezuma the speech the messenger summarizes, they would probably have written less effective poetry.

Perhaps Dryden had some inkling of the tendency of couplets to compress and simplify psychology, for at one of the more complicated psychological moments in the play, the dialogue falls into quatrains, the form Dryden had used for the Cromwell poem and would soon use again in *Annus Mirabilis*. Davenant, whose *Gondibert* served Dryden as a formal model for those poems, had already experimented with dramatic quatrains in *The Siege of Rhodes*. In *The Indian Queen*, the quatrains begin when Montezuma, having successfully led the Mexicans against the Ynca, confronts his former master and feels shame rather than joy:

> *Mont.* 'Twere vain to own repentance, since I know
> Thy scorn, which did my passions once despise,
> Once more would make my swelling anger flow;
> Which now ebbs lower then your miseries:
> The Gods that in my fortunes were unkinde,
> Gave me not Scepters, nor such gilded things;
> But whilst I wanted Crowns, inlarg'd my minde
> To despise Scepters, and dispose of Kings.
>
> [II, i, 21–28]

While hardly at the poetic level of the Cromwell poem, these lines have sufficient complexity to show Montezuma contemplating how he would feel if he were to acknowledge his regret at having conquered the Ynca. Not angry now, he realizes that he would be freshly angered by the Ynca's predictable scorn. The spreading out of the rhyming greatly facilitates the expression of a state of mind involving more than one stylized passion, yet Dryden pursued this promising experiment with quatrains in the drama only occasionally: one of the soliloquies in *The Rival Ladies* ends with a pair of quatrains, and a tender moment of courtship in *The Indian Emperour* also employs the form, but most of Montezuma's dramatic descendants, such as Almanzor in *The Conquest of Granada*, confine their rant to couplets.

The experiment of mixing blank verse, rhyme, and occasional prose, which Dryden first attempted in *The Rival Ladies*, proved more fruitful: such later plays as *Secret Love* and *Marriage A-la-Mode* employ varying mixtures of the three forms, using the stylistic contrast to delineate character and class. As drama, however, *The Rival Ladies* is simply a competent exercise in the mode of Tuke's "Spanish" success, its cardboard characters mouthing appropriately high-minded sentiments in smooth but uninspired verse. Perhaps Dryden took some pleasure in its modest success, which helped heal the wounds caused by the failure of *The Wild Gallant*, but he must also have recognized that all of his plays thus far were apprentice work. All three had consequences: *The Wild Gallant* led to such later prose comedies as *Sir Martin Mar-All* and *The Kind Keeper*; *The Rival Ladies* became the prototype for the later tragicomedies; and *The Indian Queen*, whatever Dryden's share in it was, led to his important and successful series of rhymed heroic plays, which were central to his reputation for the rest of his career.

The first of these, a play in which Dryden began to find his voice as a playwright, was *The Indian Emperour*, which opened at Bridges Street early in 1665, in direct competition with Orrery's *Mustapha* at Lincoln's Inn Fields.[89] Nominally a sequel to *The Indian Queen*, the new play allowed the King's Company to use again the expensive sets and costumes designed for the first play, an economy humorously noted in the prologue. Of the original characters, however, only Montezuma appeared again, and Dryden guaranteed himself a thematically richer plot by choosing to dramatize the conquest of Mexico by the Spaniard Cortez. Davenant had explored a similar episode in *The Cruelty of the Spaniards in Peru*, a piece of Interregnum propaganda designed to foment anti-Catholic feeling, and some of Dryden's scenes involve similar caricatures of priests and soldiers, but his hero Cortez, a man of consummate honor, opposes the greed and cruelty of the other Spaniards. The Indian warrior Montezuma, now a dignified emperor, has similar stature, so that the clash between cultures is not morally skewed toward either side. In that clash, Dryden saw rich literary possibilities, including the opportunity to dramatize themes he had been working out in his poetry.

The play begins with a speech conflating material from the poem to Charleton, in which Columbus discovers "guiltless *Men*, who danc'd away their time, / Fresh as their *Groves*, and *Happy* as their *Clime*" (ll. 13–14), with similar material from the verses to Castlemaine, in which the Muse "Is thrown upon your Hospitable Coast" (l. 6). But what had been mere metaphor and wit in those occasional poems is now presented as the response of a real explorer on a real coast (represented by an actor on an elaborately painted stage). Gazing in wonder at the "pleasant Indian *Country*," Cortez asks:

> On what new happy Climate are we thrown,
> So long kept secret, and so lately known;
> As if our old world modestly withdrew,
> And here, in private, had brought forth a new!
>
> [I, i, 1–4]

This optimistic description of the new world as the child of the old suggests that the relations between the cultures will be like the relations between parents and children, but those relations are not always warm and nurturing, as we learn in the second scene, which presents a struggle between the generations in the Indian camp. Montezuma chooses as his new bride Almeria, the daughter of the usurping queen he had scorned as a young warrior; citing his cruelty to her mother, she rejects him, and an attempt to intervene by Montezuma's son Odmar only makes matters worse. By the time the Spaniards enter, later in the scene, Odmar and his younger brother Guyomar have revealed their rival passions for Almeria's sister Alibech; one couplet in their exchange reminds us that these family struggles resemble those about to ensue between the old and new worlds:

> *Odmar.* My claim to her by Eldership I prove.
> *Guyomar.* Age is a plea in Empire, not in Love.
>
> [I, ii, 139–40]

The age of their empire is precisely the basis on which the Spaniards stake their paternalistic claim to Mexico. In the Hastings elegy and *Astraea Redux*, Dryden had treated the English Civil War as a generational conflict, revealing considerable personal hostility toward his elders. In a play, as he was now discovering, such equations between familial and political struggle could be made explicit; such hostilities could be dram-atized.

Another of Dryden's favorite oppositions, that between Nature and Art, finds fresh dramatic expression here. In the first scene, Vasquez, taking up the metaphor established by Cortez, describes the infant world as "Naked and bare . . . all untaught and salvage"; Cortez responds with a speech declaring his preference for Nature:

> Wild and untaught are Terms which we alone
> Invent, for fashions differing from our own:
> For all their Customs are by Nature wrought,
> But we, by Art, unteach what Nature taught.
>
> [I, i, 11–14]

While virtually all Dryden's poems had touched on this topic, the opening lines of the poem "To Sir Robert Howard" (quoted above, p. 100) are particularly relevant. In *The Indian Emperour*, written as Dryden broke free from his dependence on Howard, the literary and aesthetic contrast between the wild birds, whose pleasing "Musick" is "uninform'd by Art" and the caged birds, "Who better taught at home, yet please us less," gains a political dimension. When the "natural" Indians look at the products of European "art," they first attempt to understand them in terms of Nature, as in Guyo-mar's description of the Spanish galleons:

> The object I could first distinctly view
> Was tall straight trees which on the waters flew,
> Wings on their sides instead of leaves did grow,
> Which gather'd all the breath the winds could blow.
> And at their roots grew floating Palaces,
> Whose out-bow'd bellies cut the yielding Seas.
>
> [I, ii, 107–12]

Yet when the Spanish leaders demand that Montezuma yield to Charles V of Spain, hand over his gold, and consent to have his people converted to Christianity, explaining that the Pope has granted Mexico to Spain, the Indian emperor "naturally" remarks that the Pope "gives another what is not his own" (I, ii, 288). The simple truth of this response neatly validates the preference for Nature over Art first stated by Cortez.

But as the two worlds become entangled, this opposition becomes less schematic. Like many later writers, Dryden recognizes the opportunity for satire presented by the naive response of primitive men to customs Europeans take for granted. In this scene, that satire is directed against clergymen, always a favorite target for Dryden:

> *Odmar.* What numbers of these Holy Men must come?
> *Pizarro.* You shall not want, each Village shall have some;
>   Who, though the Royal Dignity they own,
>   Are equal to it, and depend on none.
> *Guyomar.* Depend on none! you treat them sure in state,
>   For 'tis their plenty does their pride create.

Montezuma. Those ghostly Kings would parcel out my pow'r,
    And all the fatness of my Land devour;
    That Monarch sits not safely on his Throne,
    Who suffers any pow'r, to shock his own.
    They teach obedience to Imperial sway,
    But think it sin if they themselves obey.

[I, ii, 309–20]

Here what starts as standard anti-Catholic satire expands into a general attack on the clergy, then leads to a strikingly advanced statement of monarchial philosophy from Montezuma, a conclusion sure to remind Dryden's audience of the difficulties Charles I had faced from his clerical opponents. Now the naive or "natural" Indian seems artfully prescient, since his suspicions about the relations between clergymen and kings had recently been validated in England.

    While this amusing exchange is taking place, Cortez is courting Cydaria, the beautiful daughter of Montezuma, in dumb show; the romantic passions already seething among the Indians touch the Spaniards as well, with complicated consequences for the plot. The sexual imagery Dryden had used to link Charles II and his people in *Astraea Redux* takes dramatic form here: Cortez lays political claim to the land and sexual claim to Cydaria as its representative. He rejoices to find his love returned, but Almeria, who has rejected Montezuma, also discovers a passion for Cortez, and her desire proves destructive. At a crucial juncture in the war, Vasquez and Pizarro are seduced by the apparently artless music of an Indian woman, who sings a song that celebrates birds and Nature in language recycled from the poem to Howard:

    See how on every bough the Birds express
      In their sweet notes their happiness.
    They all enjoy, and nothing spare;
    But on their Mother Nature lay their care.

[IV, iii, 6–9]

Enjoying this song, the Spaniards lie "carelessly un-arm'd," and are captured by a band of Indians. The Indian woman's "natural" song turns out to have been part of an artful military plot. At this point, the "natural" Emperor Montezuma proves quite adept at modern political philosophy: explaining why he intends to sacrifice his newly captured enemies, he sounds as if he has been reading Hobbes:

    Posterity be juster to my Fame;
      Nor call it Murder when each private Man
    In his defence may justly do the same:
      But private persons more then Monarchs can:
    All weigh our Acts, and what e're seems unjust,
    Impute not to Necessity, but Lust.

[IV, iii, 45–50]

    At the time of the premiere of this play, many "private persons" were imputing Charles II's political acts to lust, fearful of the ascendancy Lady Castlemaine seemed to have gained over him. Yet in Dryden's play, Cortez and Montezuma seem more powerfully motivated by necessity—military orders from the Spanish crown in one case, the suffering and starvation of the people in the other—than by lust. Dryden treats the sexual feelings of the high heroic figures, male and female, as grand compulsions, but he treats the economic greed of the minor characters as a kind of sexual perversion. The first reference to this greed in the play mixes fantasy with excremental imagery; Vasquez exclaims at the fecundity of the land:

> Methinks we walk in dreams on fairy Land,
> Where golden Ore lies mixt with common sand;
> Each downfal of a flood the Mountains pour,
> From their rich bowels rolls a silver shower.
>
> [I, i, 27–30][90]

That natural mineral wealth, even though associated with "rich bowels," proves more attractive to some of the Spaniards than does the sexuality of the Indian women. When the fortunes of war turn to favor the Spaniards, the unnatural lust for gold tempts Pizarro to desert his post as a guard for Cydaria. Together with an equally greedy priest, Pizarro tortures Montezuma on the rack, but the Emperor grandly refuses to divulge his secrets in a scene much admired by such later writers as Voltaire.[91]

If the dramatizing of the oppositions between Nature and Art, rival lovers, and generations in this play extends work Dryden had already begun, the torture scene looks forward to the political and theological concerns of his great poems of the 1680s. As the Christian priest urges the Emperor to convert, an Indian High Priest, also on the rack, exhorts him to remain faithful to his own religion. Montezuma's response antici-pates the issues addressed in *Religio Laici* and *The Hind and the Panther*:

> In seeking happiness you both agree,
> But in the search, the paths so different be,
> That all Religions with each other Fight,
> While only one can lead us in the Right.
> But till that one hath some more certain mark,
> Poor humane kind must wander in the dark;
> And suffer pains, eternally, below,
> For that, which here, we cannot come to know.
>
> [V, ii, 53–60]

In answer to this speech, the Christian priest alleges that both religions come "From Natures common hand," but that Christianity is superior because of Revelation; he then makes the rhetorical error of employing martyrdom as an argument for Christian-ity, which gives Montezuma an opportunity for a dramatic retort:

> *Chr. Pr.* But we by Martyrdom our Faith avow.
> *Mont.* You do no more then I for ours do now.
>   To prove Religion true——
>   If either Wit or Suff'rings would suffice,
>   All Faiths afford the Constant and the Wise:
>   And yet ev'n they, by Education sway'd,
>   In Age defend what Infancy obey'd.
>
> [V, ii, 81–87]

Coming as they do from a Dryden who had himself rejected the Puritan religion of his "Infancy," and who knew from the examples of his Howard relatives that Roman Catholics could have wit and suffer bravely for their outlawed faith, these are fascinating lines indeed. He echoed them twenty-two years later in *The Hind and the Panther*, the poem announcing his conversion to Catholicism, where the Catholic Hind explains her "slow encrease" by pointing to the power of education:

> By education most have been misled,
> So they believe, because they so were bred.
> The *Priest* continues what the nurse began,
> And thus the child imposes on the man.

                                                              [III, 389–92]

In the play, Montezuma's speech begins the poetic process by which all the leading themes return to conclude the drama. The contrast between "Age" and "Infancy" recalls the generational imagery with which the play began; a minute later, when Cortez enters to rescue Montezuma, addressing him as "Father," the Emperor scorns his "Infants Comfort." Cortez rebukes Pizarro and the priest, describing their avarice as a form of parricide:

> Accursed Gold, 'tis thou hast caus'd these crimes;
> Thou turn'st our Steel against thy Parent Climes!

                                                              [V, ii, 135–36]

Montezuma turns his sword against himself, declaring his monarchial authority over death:

> But I'm a King while this is in my Hand,———
> He wants no Subjects who can Death Command.

                                                              [V, ii, 234–35]

Cydaria, stabbed for her beauty by her jealous rival Almeria, recovers to wed Cortez, but Almeria dies a suicide, like her would-be lover Montezuma. Guyomar and Alibech, going into exile, imagine a landscape deliberately unlike that celebrated by Vasquez in the beginning:

> Northward, beyond the Mountains we will go,
> Where Rocks lye cover'd with Eternal Snow;
> Thin Herbage in the Plains, and Fruitless Fields,
> The Sand no Gold, the Mine no Silver yields:
> There Love and Freedom we'l in Peace enjoy;
> No *Spaniards* will that Colony destroy.

                                                              [V, ii, 368–73]

Cortez declares himself "doubly Blest, with Conquest, and with Love," but the contrast between the sterile landscape of Guyomar's speech and the celebration of fertility with which the play began is a telling reminder of the costs of such political and sexual victory; the corpses of Montezuma and Almeria, martyrs to conquest and love, bear mute witness to the hollowness of the Spanish triumph.

In *The Indian Emperour*, as these examples illustrate, Dryden began to bring to the drama the literary, moral, and political complexity he had displayed in his more ambitious poems. Greater complexity of characterization was among the results: Cortez, strongly affected by his love for Cydaria, his loyalty to his King, and his fundamental sense of honor, was a splendid role for Charles Hart, who played him in the premiere; Montezuma, whose political perception deepens with each scene of the play, was a test for the versatile Michael Mohun. The women's parts, while not as fully rounded as some Dryden would later write, afforded fine opportunities for Anne Marshall and Elizabeth Weaver. The poetry, even in scenes of rapid dialogue, is at once more muscular and more flexible than the stiff couplets of *The Indian Queen* and *The Rival Ladies*.

Always his own shrewdest critic, Dryden must have realized that *The Indian Emperour* was a giant step forward. But the pleasure he and the players could take at the play's success was overshadowed by ominous events in the world outside the theatre. On 22 February, England declared war on the Dutch; the widespread belief that such a war would be easy to win and profitable for English trade soon proved false. By the end of April, the entire fleet had set sail, with James, Duke of York, in command as Lord High Admiral, seconded by Dryden's kinsman the Earl of Sandwich; there were high hopes for their success, but professionals like Pepys also recognized the potential for disaster. Not least among the problems facing a Navy perennially short of men was the bubonic plague, which had appeared in London during the cold winter of 1664–65. By spring, the epidemic seemed sufficiently under control for the royal family to return to the capital, but during April, the month in which Pepys saw *The Indian Emperour*, the disease began to spread again, and as the weather grew warmer, the number of reported deaths climbed ominously. On 3 June, the two navies fought at Lowestoft, within earshot of London; an English victory was spoiled by a failure to pursue their advantage properly, though the cause of that failure was covered up for several years.[92] If Dryden based the setting of his *Essay of Dramatick Poesie* on a real experience, he spent that day listening for the cannon in a boat with several distinguished friends interested in literary matters. Two days later, the Lord Chamberlain issued a proclamation closing the theatres because of the plague. Like his more affluent associates, Dryden wisely abandoned the stricken city, traveling with his wife to her family's country estate at Charlton in Wiltshire. Their stay in the country, which lasted more than a year, was a fruitful one, producing a son and a number of important poetic and critical offspring. When Dryden returned to London, he was ready to claim it as his literary kingdom.

⋙ CHAPTER SIX ⋘

"To Delight the Age in which I Live"
1665–1669

The Theatre as an "Absent Mistress"

The London John and Elizabeth Dryden left behind in the summer of 1665 was an increasingly terrifying place. In virtually every neighborhood, crude red crosses chalked across doors and guards posted to keep the inhabitants from escaping marked out those houses afflicted by the plague. Not yet able to purchase a house for themselves, the Drydens were living in lodgings,[1] and could have been shut up indefinitely had anyone in their house shown the dreaded marks of infection. Every morning men and boys, all furiously smoking tobacco in the hope that it would protect them from contracting the disease, drove their dead-carts through the streets, shouting "Bring out your dead!" Procuring food and drink became increasingly difficult as the families of butchers, bakers, and brewers succumbed to the spreading pestilence. The court, the Parliament, and many of the regular clergy fled to the country, and the ejected Presbyterians seized the opportunity to occupy many City pulpits, preaching sermons describing the plague as God's judgment on a sinful nation.[2] The fleet, back at sea in July after its incomplete success of early June, suffered a costly defeat at Bergen on 2 August; Dryden's Westminster and Cambridge schoolmate Edward Montagu of Boughton, the dedicatee of Hookes's *Amanda*, was among those killed.

On 10 August, thanks to a recommendation from the King, Robert Howard married the wealthy widow Honoria O'Brien at Wooton Bassett in Wiltshire. Although the new manor Howard acquired through that marriage was a day's journey from the family estate in Charlton, I should imagine the Drydens were in attendance. Perhaps they traveled out from London for the wedding, then on to Charlton.[3] Whenever they got there, the country house of the Earl of Berkshire must have seemed Edenic, compared to the nightmarish scenes in plague-stricken London. Charlton offered clean air, fresh food, and the opportunity for rural sports. Metaphors from hunting in Dryden's works written during this period have the sharpness of the freshly observed.

In *Annus Mirabilis*, for example, he compares two ships disabled in a sea fight to an exhausted hare and hound:

> So have I seen some fearful Hare maintain
> A Course, till tir'd before the Dog she lay:
> Who, stretch'd behind her, pants upon the plain,
> Past pow'r to kill as she to get away.
>
> With his loll'd tongue he faintly licks his prey,
> His warm breath blows her flix up as she lies:
> She, trembling, creeps upon the ground away,
> And looks back to him with beseeching eyes.

[ll. 521–28]

The detail of the dog's breath raising the fur on the hare is Ovidian, but the "beseeching eyes" are Dryden's invention, and the first-person usage ("So have *I* seen") may be quite literal: the poet probably did ride to hounds with some of Elizabeth's brothers.[4] Fishing, in which Dryden took considerable pleasure during the summers he spent in Northamptonshire as an older man, was also excellent in this part of Wiltshire. Thomas Baskerville, who walked past the Howard estate in 1665, has left an extensive description of the road from Charlton to Malmesbury, which we may imagine Dryden traversing as well; among other details, he mentions "a fine purling river which affords good fish, and many moor-hens sporting and playing in it."[5]

Dryden probably missed the excitement of the theatrical world and the stimulation of the literary conversations at Will's; he later referred to the *Essay of Dramatick Poesie*, composed during this period, as an "incorrect Essay, written in the Country without the help of Books, or advice of Friends" (XVII, 7). Yet despite this disclaimer, he evidently took some books with him to Charlton, including Corneille's prefaces, and the peace of the country setting proved conducive to literary labor: between the summer of 1665 and the late autumn of 1666, Dryden wrote the *Essay*, which established his importance as a theorist of the drama and embroiled him in controversy; a play, *Secret Love*, which the King took under his own protection; and a substantial heroic poem, *Annus Mirabilis*, in which he elevated the astonishing events of the year he spent away from the metropolis to the status of myth.

Before embarking on these larger projects, Dryden composed some "*Verses to her* Highness *the* DUTCHESS, *on the memorable Victory gain'd by the* DUKE *against the* Hollanders, June *the* 3. 1665. *and on Her Journey afterwards into the North.*" Probably written soon after he came to the country, this "paper of verses" responds to a public event in a deliberately private way. In practical terms, Anne Hyde, daughter of the Lord Chancellor and wife of the Duke of York, was a particularly appropriate addressee for a poet still awaiting the first payment on the grant to his own wife arranged by Clarendon in 1662. In literary terms, expressing his praise for the Duke's courage at Lowestoft indirectly, in a poem "address'd to a Lady," allowed Dryden to "affect the softness of expression, and the smoothness of measure, rather then the height of thought," as he put it in defending these verses against the coffeehouse wits who had thought them lacking in "height of fancy" and "dignity of words."[6] Unlike those wits, Dryden sensed

Portrait of Anne Hyde, Duchess of York, after Peter Lely, ca. 1670.

the incompleteness of the naval victory; he shrewdly avoided rushing into print with a large-scale panegyric, and the literary and military events of the next year justified his caution. Waller's poem on Lowestoft, "Instructions to a Painter," praising the Duke in traditional heroic language and imagery much like that Dryden had used in his Coronation poem, was soon and soundly parodied, probably by Marvell, in "Second Advice to a Painter," a satire pointing out the missed opportunities and foolish strategy of the summer's campaign.[7]

If we may believe the *Essay of Dramatick Poesie*, Dryden and his literary friends correctly anticipated that the naval victory would produce a flood of ill-written praise from

> those eternal Rhimers, who watch a Battel with more diligence than the Ravens and birds of Prey; and the worst of them surest to be first in upon the quarry, while the better able, either out of modesty writ not at all or set that due value upon their Poems as to let them be often desired and long expected! [XVII, 9]

If Dryden was not quite modest enough to write not at all, he valued his poems enough to wait another year before producing *Annus Mirabilis*, in which the naval victories and defeats of two years, including Lowestoft, become part of a complex heroic tapestry including the Great Fire of 1666. In that large poem and this smaller one, Dryden takes the "court" view, as opposed to the "country" position vigorously argued in the continuing series of satirical "Painter" poems, but his gestures of praise are rarely open to the charges of emptiness and convention, to which Waller proved so vulnerable. In the years since the Coronation poem, Dryden had gained considerable poetic depth and range. If the verses to the Duchess were a minor holding action in his ongoing campaign to secure the attention and support of the court, they were nonetheless another significant stage in his poetic development, an experiment in mixing elements from several kinds of poetry.

Such standard heroic devices as Old Testament typology, extensively employed in Dryden's Restoration panegyrics, are softened here by a wit closer to that employed in the verses to Castlemaine. James is like Moses, two of whose friends helped him hold his hands outstretched all day during a battle, but here the force that lends "new vigour to his wearied arms" is the prayer of "the fair and pious" ladies, led by his wife. Like Cortez and Almeria in *The Indian Emperour*, the Duke and his lady are susceptible to the powers of heroic love and military honor, but here that dramatic conflict is merely a vehicle for a compliment:

> Ah, what concerns did both your Souls divide!
> Your Honour gave us what your Love deni'd:
> And 'twas for him much easier to subdue
> Those foes he fought with, then to part from you.
>
> [ll. 9–12]

Finally, by moving beyond the battle to celebrate the Duchess's subsequent "progress" through the North, which began on 5 August 1665, Dryden can refer to her "Conquests," wittily describing a ceremonial journey as a military campaign. The journey did have some political significance; Charles was taking advantage of James's popularity, and the reception of the Duke and his consort by such important noblemen as the Duke of Newcastle served an important propaganda purpose.[8]

Lacking firsthand knowledge of the Duchess's "progress," Dryden treats it fancifully, concluding with a playful but revealing image:

> So when the new-born *Phoenix* first is seen,
> Her feather'd Subjects all adore their Queen.
> And, while she makes her progress through the East,
> From every grove her numerous train's increase:
> Each Poet of the air her glory sings,
> And round him the pleas'd Audience clap their wings.
>
> [ll. 52–57]

As in his poem to Anne Hyde's father a few years earlier, in which he had praised Clarendon for channeling support toward "the Muses" in order to request particular support for himself, Dryden's self-reference is cautious. He displaces the whole relationship between poet and patroness into the airy world of the birds,[9] but the masculine singular pronoun of the final line, achieved by the coy reference to "Each Poet of the air," is a personal touch: the applause is not for the phoenix herself, but for a bird who has sung her glory with a skill that separates him from those "eternal Rhimers" who awaited the outcome of Lowestoft like "Ravens and birds of Prey." A poem that has announced its purpose as praise for James, Duke of York, Lord High Admiral of the fleet, thus concludes with a round of applause for John Dryden, poet and playwright, who had now experienced the applause of several pleased audiences.

The verses to the Duchess may reflect not only Dryden's growing sense of his power as a writer, but his particular activities on 3 June 1665. We first see the battle of Lowestoft as an allegorical painting, with Neptune holding his trident before the two navies and the waves parting like the Red Sea at the Exodus, but some later, less grandiose lines, thanks to one of Dryden's characteristic uses of the pronoun "we," hint at a more realistic perspective:

> While, from afar, we heard the Canon play,
> Like distant Thunder on a shiny day,
> For absent friends we were asham'd to fear,
> When we consider'd what you ventur'd there.

[ll. 30–33]

In the *Essay of Dramatick Poesie*, written during the same stay in the country, Dryden used the same setting: a barge on the Thames in which four men, each concerned for "absent friends," listen for the cannon and alleviate the "dreadful suspence of the event" by engaging in a spirited discussion of the theory and practice of drama. The four speakers have usually been identified, on fairly good evidence, as Dryden (Neander), Sir Robert Howard (Crites), Charles Sackville, Lord Buckhurst (Eugenius), and Sir Charles Sedley (Lisideius).[10] Although Dryden may have been conflating an actual boat ride with some of these companions and a series of literary conversations at Will's with others, he certainly knew these three "persons [of] witt and Quality" well by this date: he had mentioned Buckhurst in the dedication to *The Rival Ladies*, published the previous year, and Sedley's marriage to the Catholic beauty Katherine Savage made him a kinsman of both Howard and Dryden.[11] No one will ever know exactly what Dryden and his friends actually did and said on "that memorable day," but his fictional version of their ongoing literary conversation reveals as much about his personal relations with his social superiors as about his developing theories of the drama.

Dryden's use of a dialogue form proves generically appropriate to his subject; by presenting a genial discussion of the arguments for and against ancient drama, French rules, and rhymed dialogue, he also hoped to protect himself from the charge of critical dogmatism. Our sense of an ongoing social drama, necessarily subdued during the longer speeches, is strongest at the beginning and end of the *Essay*, and during important transitions. After the first debate, in which Crites and Eugenius have propounded the merits of ancient and modern drama, Lisideius proposes a related topic:

> *Lisideius* after he had acknowledg'd himself of *Eugenius* his opinion concerning the Ancients; yet told him he had forborn, till his Discourse were ended, to ask him why he prefer'd the *English* Plays above those of other Nations? and whether we ought not to submit our Stage to the exactness of our next Neighbours?
> Though, said *Eugenius*, I am at all times ready to defend the honour of my Countrey against the *French*, and to maintain, we are as well able to vanquish them with

our Pens as our Ancestors have been with their swords; yet, if you please, added he, looking upon *Neander*, I will commit this cause to my friend's management; his opinion of our Plays is the same with mine: and besides, there is no reason, that *Crites* and I, who have now left the Stage, should re-enter so suddenly upon it; which is against the laws of Comedie. [XVII, 33]

Eugenius's clever remark about swords and pens is one of many references meant to remind us of the appropriateness of the battle setting, a connection Dryden establishes at the very beginning by applying to the battle a verb appropriate to the conversation and telling us that the fleets "disputed the command of the greater half of the Globe" (XVII, 8). Eugenius reminds us of national pride here because he is assigning to his friend Neander the patriotic task of defending English literary honor against the French while the Navy defends English military honor against the Dutch. Such concern was no fiction: a travel book by a Frenchman named Samuel Sorbière, which criticized English dramatic conventions, had already drawn fire from Dryden's friend Sprat.[12] But the assignment of that task to Neander has social significance as well: Neander is in a vulnerable position in this company, just as Dryden was in a vulnerable position in writing this essay. He lacked the protective nimbus of title and fortune that surrounded his aristocratic acquaintances, and he bore the stigma of his employment by the Protectorate, a vulnerability dramatized when Lisideius looks pointedly at Neander while remarking, with evident reference to the Interregnum, "we have been so long together bad *Englishmen*, that we had not leisure to be good Poets" (XVII, 33).[13] Yet just as the aristocrats in charge of the Navy soon learned to respect and value the managerial skills of Pepys, a "new man" who had learned his skills under the Interregnum, Eugenius confidently "commit[s] this cause to [his] friend's management." His self-conscious reference to "the laws of Comedie" is a witty excuse; his real reason for deferring to Neander is the value he places upon his friend's professional opinion.

The generosity shown by Eugenius in this instance is entirely in keeping with the reputation Buckhurst (later the Earl of Dorset) gained as a patron; the finicky particularity of Crites and the arrogant superiority of Lisideius are also personality traits in keeping with what we know of Howard and Sedley.[14] We may therefore give some credence to the picture of himself Dryden has left us in Neander: a serious, well-read young man, content to remain silent in the presence of his "betters," but somewhat long-winded when asked to talk; a self-conscious professional whose systematic approach to the issues at hand separates him from the younger wits, and whose largeness of scope separates him from his narrower contemporary Sir Robert. That picture includes some gentle self-mockery, especially at the conclusion, when Neander is so wrapped up in his own discourse that he fails to notice that the barge has landed. Of course, such self-mockery may be Dryden's way of complimenting his companions for their wit by portraying himself as a bit more "wide-eyed"[15] than he really was. Still, Neander's social deference to his companions looks a lot like the deferential gestures in Dryden's poems and prefaces: if Neander is always conscious of his inferior social standing, and therefore quick to compliment the literary talents and judgments of his "betters," he nonetheless values his own talents and judgments.

After Neander has defended the English tradition, Eugenius asks his opinion of Ben Jonson. "I fear, replie[s] *Neander*, That in obeying your commands I shall draw some envy on my self" (XVII, 55). That fear of provoking envy probably contributed to Dryden's delay in publishing the *Essay*, which first appeared in print in late 1667 or early 1668, after *Annus Mirabilis* and several theatrical successes, and which did provoke envious comments from Sir Robert Howard, his brother Ned, and several other writers. Yet despite his powerful motives for caution, at least caution about publication, Dryden's experiences had given him equally powerful motives for working out critical positions on the questions debated in the *Essay*. The anonymous prefaces he probably wrote for Herringman before the Restoration were useful apprentice work in critical prose, and after the Restoration, he had established himself as the leading professional dramatist working in the English theatre. His plays, including that recent success *The Indian Emperour*, were therefore being cited by the wits at Will's as examples for comparing ancient and modern drama, French and English plotting, rhymed and unrhymed dialogue. These are the three issues explicitly debated in the *Essay*, where Dryden's preferences for modern authors, English "mixed" plots, and rhymed dialogue are apparent despite the dialogue form.

Two more general issues, however, lurk just below the surface. Dryden's central concern is to develop an argument for a heightened kind of mimesis, "Nature wrought up to an higher pitch" (XVII, 74), and he cunningly organizes his dialogue to allow that aesthetic position to emerge convincingly from all three discussions. By allowing in the drama a kind of grandeur more normally associated with epic, this theory of heightened imitation not only justified Dryden's procedure in plays he had already written, especially *The Indian Emperour*, but established a basis for his later heroic plays.[16] The debates about the relative merits of ancient and modern or French and English drama also occasionally approach that more touchy comparison between the new plays composed after the Restoration and those of "the last Age," a rivalry that had worried Dryden as early as *The Wild Gallant*, with its talk of "Elder Brothers." Such comparisons were inevitable in a theatre where plays by Jonson, Fletcher, and Shakespeare remained the principal staples of the repertory, and had interested Dryden sufficiently to produce a critical response, not merely a dramatic one. In the dedication to *The Rival Ladies* (1664), his only published play, he had discussed the interactions of imagination and convention, arguing the case for rhymed drama in a letter to Orrery filled with critical judgments of earlier poets and playwrights; this discussion includes many ideas and phrases later reworked in the *Essay*.[17] Sir Robert Howard, despite having written rhymed plays himself, took an opposing view: his *Four New Plays* (including *The Indian Queen*) appeared in March 1665, with a preface "To the Reader" disagreeing with Dryden's arguments in favor of rhyme.[18] In constructing the arguments against rhyme offered by Crites in the *Essay*, Dryden closely followed Howard's preface, just as he drew on Corneille, Sorbière, and Sprat in other parts of the argument.

Such public exploration of the theories upon which he proceeded, first apparent in the dedication to *The Rival Ladies*, was a fundamental habit of Dryden's mind: he later published essays on heroic plays, the art of translation, and the history of satire, explaining his principles for each of those genres, and he apparently collected materials for an essay on English versification.[19] Like the *Essay of Dramatick Poesie*, these later writings left their author open to various kinds of criticism, not least the easy charge that his works did not always conform to his theories; and Dryden, early and late, often devoted his critical efforts to defending his dramatic or poetic practice, though he also learned how to disarm his critics by citing his own earlier works as cautionary examples of various excesses. The complex, subtle, and flexible relations between Dryden's creative and critical writings set him apart from any earlier English poet or playwright, and provided precedents for such later poet-critics as Coleridge and Eliot.

Distinctive as this interest in theory is, its development in Dryden may owe something to his particular circumstances in 1665. He had just produced, in *The Indian Emperour*, a drama in which he was beginning to find his voice as a playwright; because of the plague, however, he was unable to test his developing theories on stage, so he took the opportunity to work them out in a critical dialogue, and the interest provoked by the publication of that dialogue proved as important to the development of his reputation as the success of his plays. As he put it a few years later, when dedicating the published *Essay* to Buckhurst, "Seeing then our Theaters shut up, I was engag'd in these kind of thoughts with the same delight with which men think upon their absent Mistresses" (XVII, 3). At a literal level, this sly metaphor was calculated to please Buckhurst, whose mistresses included the actress Nell Gwyn, but Dryden applied it to his own relations with the muse of drama, acutely aware that one of the emotions felt by a man thinking about his absent mistress is delight at his own remembered and anticipated performance.

In *Secret Love*, the play to which Dryden turned his attentions after the *Essay*, he was anticipating the performance of Nell Gwyn and her partner Charles Hart. In the play's second scene, Celadon (Hart) confronts a masked Florimell (Gwyn), who asks him what kind of beauty he likes; he responds with a precise description of Nell's features: "Ovall face, clear skin, hazle eyes, thick brown Eye-browes" (I, ii, 48–49). Of course, such details could have been added in rehearsal, but the whole construction of the play suggests that Dryden intended it not only as an example of the dramatic principles he had worked out in the *Essay*, but as a vehicle for the particular talents of the King's Company. He had probably seen or read *All Mistaken*, by his brother-in-law James Howard, in which a serious plot drawn from Beaumont and Fletcher was played off against the farcical antics of a "gay couple" played by Hart and Gwyn.[20] Howard's play got its laughs from the slapstick actions of a fat character, Pinguister, who attempts to lose weight in order to court Mirida (Gwyn); he rolls across the floor with his beloved in his arms, and takes a powerful purge that forces him to run about the stage undoing his breeches. Dryden's play was hardly so crude, but he evidently recognized the potential lurking in Howard's device of the double plot. By combining a pair of witty, bantering lovers, not unlike Constance and Loveby in *The Wild Gallant*, with a serious plot involving the stifled passions of a queen and the treasonous plots of some of her subjects, he could make use of the talents of Rebecca Marshall, who excelled in serious parts, and those of Nell Gwyn, who excelled in physical action, and who had the opportunity to come on stage in men's clothing, displaying her excellent legs and her ability to mimic the strutting of a young spark.[21]

Portrait of Nell Gwyn from the studio of Peter Lely, ca. 1675.

He could also draw on his own talents for blank verse and couplets without making the whole play seem weighty (like the two *Indian* plays) or precious (like *The Rival Ladies*). The serious plot, as he confessed in the preface, he took from a well-known romance, *Le Grand Cyrus* of Madeleine de Scudéry,[22] but the playful dialogue and sparkling antics of Celadon and Florimell provided an ironic parallel: even Celadon's name would seem ironic for readers of D'Urfé's *Astrée*, in which Celadon had been a fanatically faithful lover; Dryden's Celadon was a model of unfaithfulness. Although the "gay couple" served as a counterweight to the serious plot, their presence did not prevent Dryden from discovering and adding to the political implications of Scudéry's story. His one major addition is the rebellion led by Lysimantes, whose remarks about monarchs must have seemed all too familiar to Charles II:

> You see, that Princes faults,
> (How e're they think 'em safe from publick view)
> Fly out through the dark crannies of their Closets.

[V, i, 308–10]

Lysimantes is speaking of the Queen's undeclared passion for Philocles, but Dryden was surely thinking about Charles's all-too-declared passion for Castlemaine, a well-known "fault" in the eyes of some of the "publick." The King's brother James might also have smiled wryly at the sentiments expressed by Candiope, sister to the queen:

> The greatest slaves, in Monarchies, are they,
> Whom Birth sets nearest to Imperial sway.

[III, i, 167–68]

Not long before Dryden wrote those lines, the Duke of York had been thanked for his heroism at Lowestoft but relieved from further naval duty because of his proximity to the throne.

Besides being the best practical model for taking advantage of the players available in the King's Company, the double plot allowed Dryden to display his political sophistication in a play that also included the dancing of a jig; he would employ such a structure several more times. On a more theoretical level, the double plot made possible a mixture of styles—prose for comedy, blank verse for more serious dialogue, rhyming couplets for the most highly charged passages—and allowed Dryden to draw on the English comic tradition and the French tragic and romance traditions at the same time. He said as much in the prologue, condensing into poetic triplets the issues of the *Essay:*

> He who writ this, not without pains and thought
> From *French* and *English* Theaters has brought
> Th' exactest Rules by which a Play is wrought:
>
> The Unities of Action, Place, and Time;
> The Scenes unbroken; and a mingled chime
> Of *Johnsons* humour, with *Corneilles* rhyme.

[ll. 1–6]

Dryden's claim to have followed "Th' exactest Rules" is somewhat rhetorical; his writing in all forms was actually far more likely to seek "a mingled chime," to bring together in harmonious relation materials and styles drawn from disparate sources. Interested as he was in structure and rules, he recognized that they were inanimate things, referring to them in the next verse of the prologue as "dead colours," or background painting, and contrasting them with "Wit, or Plot . . . , Which are the living Beauties of a Play." In the most passionately felt section of the *Essay*, his Neander had confessed that Shakespeare's plays were "irregular," but had presented their author as "the man who of all Modern, and perhaps Ancient Poets, had the largest and most comprehensive soul" (XVII, 55). When he came to write the preface to the published version of *Secret Love*, after its stage success and its particular approval by the King, Dryden applied a similar distinction between structure and inspiration to himself:

> I think all Writers, of what kind soever, may infallibly judg of the frame and contexture of their Works. But for the ornament of Writing, which is greater, more various and bizarre in Poesie then in any other kind, as it is properly the Child of Fancy, so it can receive no measure, or at least but a very imperfect one of its own excellencies or failures from the judgment. Self-love (which enters but rarely into the offices of the judgment) here predominates. And Fancy (if I may so speak) judging of it self, can be no more certain or demonstrative of its own effects, then two crooked lines can be the adaequate measure of each other. [IX, 116]

The subjectivity of the "Fancy," which renders its "crooked" productions more difficult to measure than the neat parallel lines of rule-bound writing, is nonetheless its chief attraction, which makes real poetry "greater, more various and bizarre" than less inspired kinds of writing. Moreover, the writer who will achieve that kind of greatness will need some degree of "Self-love." When the works Dryden wrote at Charlton were published, his enemies were quick to point out his self-confidence, and they were correct. Despite the various strategies for self-protection Dryden employed in these works, they reveal his growing faith in his own creative power.

A Year of Wonders

The year 1666, long expected to be a year of portents and disasters because 666 was the number of the beast in Revelation, proved to be eventful indeed, both for the nation and for the Drydens. As the New Year began, Elizabeth realized she was pregnant; her son Charles was born on 27 August. The difficult, week-long journey back to London would hardly have been desirable for an expectant mother, and with the theatres still closed, the Drydens had no immediate incentive to return to the city. Some of Elizabeth's family may have been at Charlton from time to time during this year, but her erratic old father was certainly in London on 28 March, when he was attacked outside his house by three thugs, who temporarily seized possession of the house and forced the old man to take refuge from the cold in his coach.[23] Perhaps the three assailants were sent to collect a debt, since Berkshire was being constantly besieged by his creditors; neither he nor Elizabeth had yet received any of the money promised them by the King in 1662.[24]

The urban violence the old Earl suffered may also reflect the continued chaos and anarchy of a city still recovering from the plague, and there were international worries as well. Louis XIV had declared war against England on 6 January, and there was reason to fear that the French fleet would now enter the naval war on the side of the Dutch. At the beginning of the spring campaign, the English divided their fleet. A group of twenty vessels under the command of Charles's cousin Prince Rupert sailed off in a vain attempt to engage the French, who were actually cruising far away in the Mediterranean, while sixty other vessels under the command of the Duke of Albemarle remained in the Channel. Outnumbered by the Dutch fleet of eighty-four warships, Albemarle bravely decided to engage them; in the resulting Four Days Battle (1–4 June), a severe defeat was averted by the return of Rupert's squadron, though English losses were still heavy. Later in the same summer, after a rapid refitting of the fleet, came the St. James's Day Fight (25 July), a solid victory for the English. Isolated as he was in the country, Dryden learned about these stirring events through pamphlets and gazettes; he recognized in the naval campaigns of both 1665 and 1666 the material for a grand heroic poem on a Virgilian scale, and I believe he began drafting that poem during the summer months, perhaps at the urging of Sir Robert Howard, who was just across the county at Wooton Bassett.[25]

Meanwhile, there was progress on the financial front. On 25 June, prompted by yet another petition from the old Earl, the King finally wrote a letter to the Lord Treasurer reviewing the history of the grants, including the fact that Berkshire had mortgaged his share in a complicated transaction that required him to convey the entire grant, at least on paper, to Elizabeth.[26] He directed the Treasurer to find money for the grants from the revenues of the counties of Somerset and Dorset, since the revenues of York, from which the original grants were to have been paid, had been paid to the Queen instead. Charles displayed his shrewd understanding of the Earl's character by mandating that Elizabeth's money be paid first, and that it be "discharged by her Acquittance, and not by the Acquittance of the said Earle."[27] With the help of Sir Robert Howard, who understood the workings of the Exchequer, the Drydens enlisted the aid of Sir Robert Long, Auditor of the Receipt in the Exchequer, and one of his assistants, Richard Sheppard, who were eventually able to turn these promises into real money, now more urgently needed with a baby on the way.[28]

Berkshire's troubles continued. His financial situation was now so desperate that he found it difficult to appear in clean attire, even when taking his turn as Gentleman of the Bedchamber. On 25 July, Pepys saw him "waiting at table and serving the King drink, in that dirty pickle as I never saw man in my life."[29] As the King anticipated, the Earl did make one more attempt to get hold of Elizabeth's money: when the Drydens finally received their first payment, a few weeks before their son was born, they wrote a letter of thanks to Sir Robert Long, asking him to "keep what money you receive for us in your hands till we come up. As for the unreasonable proposition my Lord Berkshire made, & writ us word that you approv'd it, we well know it was only to be rid of his importunityes" (*Letters*, pp. 6–7). The "unreasonable proposition" was surely some scheme that would have had Berkshire himself receive the money. A week later, the King reaffirmed his desire to aid the old man, "taking into Our Gracious consideracion the great extremity of ye s^d Earles affaires, & of his present necessity & Wants." He asked his Treasurers to draw on any source possible to find some money for Berkshire, but was careful to affirm once again that his orders should "stand good & in force as to ye other three thousand pounds assigned & made payable to ye s^d Lady Elisabeth Dryden."[30]

The news of the English victory in the St. James's Day Fight would have reached Charlton in early August, perhaps suggesting a fitting climax for Dryden's new poem and a happy interpretation of the idea that 1666 would be a year of wonders. The actual receipt of £768 15s. about the same time, however, was a more significant stroke of personal good fortune for the Drydens, who had been waiting for some payment on Elizabeth's dowry since before their marriage. The birth of a healthy son at the end of the month was another happy event, since childbirth was always a dangerous process.

With the plague at last abating, and with money in hand to use toward setting up a house, Dryden could begin to think of returning to London and publishing the results of his fruitful stay in the country. But 1666 held one more surprise: before the baby was two weeks old, news arrived of the Great Fire of London (2–7 September), which destroyed most of the city and was widely interpreted as a punishment from God, though the interpreters disagreed about who was being punished for what sins.[31] Since I believe Dryden had already written much of his poem on the naval campaign, I imagine him considering how an account of the fire would add to the Virgilian grandeur he was attempting to achieve, and deciding that the additional thematic complexity would be worth the inevitable loss of unity. The resulting poem, *Annus Mirabilis*, was much the longest and most ambitious he had yet attempted; on 10 November, he sent it to Sir Robert Howard, who had returned to London to take up his seat in Parliament, asking him to supervise the printing.

Cluttering Dryden's desk as he composed this remarkable poem were journalistic accounts of the war and the fire; someone in London (perhaps the publisher Herringman) must have sent him the *London Gazette* and *Current Intelligence* on a regular basis, along with poems, pamphlets, and even sermons dealing with current events.[32] These accounts, of course, were far from "objective"; the government's official report of the Four Days Battle, *A True Narrative of the Engagement*, which Dryden follows quite closely, seeks to paint a defeat in which the English lost five thousand men as a victory or at worst a standoff. Nor were the papers a substitute for personal experience; Pepys's famous pages on the fire, a private record of one man's observations and emotions, are infinitely more vivid than the official account in the *London Gazette*, Dryden's main source. From our point of view, writing about such events from a distance looks like a crippling disadvantage, but Dryden was not principally concerned with either particular detail or "objective" truth. Like most of those who wrote about the war or the fire, he was a propagandist, and his poem provides a "court" interpretation of the astonishing events of 1666. Although he had probably not seen the best of the satirical poems on these events, "The Third Advice to a Painter" now attributed to Marvell, Dryden was surely aware of the kinds of criticism being levelled at the naval commanders and their superiors by the "country" opposition; he could similarly anticipate that some sectarian prophets would interpret the Great Fire as God's direct punishment of the lewdness of the court.[33] Instead of attempting to rebut such damaging interpretations frontally, as a mere pamphleteer might have done, Dryden drew upon his literary experience and classical reading to present the year of wonders as a series of episodes from an epic poem. His Albemarle, Rupert, Charles, and James are heroes from the grand mold, not the petty squabblers Marvell makes them out to be. The disasters suffered by the fleet and the city become part of the larger patterns of tragic fate to which all men are subject, not simply the results of human mismanagement and cowardice. In a concluding prophecy, the new London rises phoenix-like from its ashes and plays Rome to its own Troy, its widening streets and worldwide commerce making it a shimmering vision, an ideal city.

Several interlocking motives may explain Dryden's decision to paint these events on a broad, mythic canvas. Pragmatically, he knew that his continued success as a writer would depend upon court patronage. He had already written two poems to the King, one to the Lord Chancellor, one to the King's principal mistress, and one to the King's sister-in-law, daughter of the Lord Chancellor and wife to the heir apparent. Moreover, these efforts to attract the attention of the court had been rewarded; the grant Clarendon had engineered for Elizabeth in 1662 was paying off at last. With these incentives to loyalty in mind, and aware, even in Wiltshire, of the anticourt sentiment swirling about the City and the House of Commons, Dryden moved vigorously to defend the court. He can hardly have been unaware of the possibility of future rewards, and *Annus Mirabilis*, written in the quatrains Davenant had used for *Gondibert*, was surely among the factors leading to his appointment as Poet Laureate when Davenant died in 1668.

Without access to the daily ebb and flow of opinion, rumor, and information about current events so meticulously recorded by Pepys, Dryden could not conduct a defense of the court concerned to answer every allegation made by the various groups opposing the conduct of the war, nor had he yet discovered his gifts as a satirist. He neatly avoided the particular controversies about such issues as the payment of seamen and the distribution of spoils by presenting recent history as if it were ancient myth, with epic similes, painterly allegories, and imaginary dramatic speeches. His poem is no less political than the satires from the other side, and presents an equally slanted and selective version of the events of 1666, but his treatment of public events in a high heroic mode, in part constrained by his physical absence from London, allows him to conduct his argument through allusion, typology, and imaginative vision. This choice of style also reflects a renewed engagement with the classics: Dryden's interest in translating the *De Rerum Natura* of Lucretius dates from this period of retirement, and he may have been experimenting with Virgil's *Georgics* as well;[34] Ovid, Petronius, and Lucan were also in his mind, as his own notes to the poem reveal. Perhaps he saw this heroic poem as a study for the larger epic he might someday write; the "account of the ensuing Poem, in a LETTER to the Honorable, Sir ROBERT HOWARD" suggests as much:

> I have call'd my Poem *Historical*, not *Epick*, though both the Actions and Actors are as much Heroick, as any Poem can contain. But since the Action is not properly one, nor that accomplish'd in the last successes, I have judg'd it too bold a Title for a few *Stanza's*, which are little more in number then a single *Iliad*, or the longest of the *Aeneids*. [I, 50]

This clever disclaimer cites some plausible reasons for not calling *Annus Mirabilis* epic: it is short by comparison with the ancient models; its action is "not properly one"; the history it relates (as the disastrous naval events of 1667 would show) is incomplete. But the poem is hardly historical in the sense of reporting fact; like the rhyming plays Neander defends in the *Essay of Dramatick Poesie*, it is "Nature wrought up to an higher pitch" (XVII, 74). Having actually seen none of the events he depicts, Dryden paints in an unabashedly mythic mode, and the rich visual imagery turns the reported details of the war and the fire into stylized pictures. When the fleet narrowly avoids running aground, for example, a deity intervenes:

> It seem'd as there the *British Neptune* stood,
>   With all his host of waters at command,
> Beneath them to submit th' officious floud:
>   And, with his Trident, shov'd them off the sand.
>
> [ll. 733–36]

This scene is "history painting," not journalism. When the fire reaches the Thames, it produces a terrible beauty:

> A Key of fire ran all along the shore,
>   And lighten'd all the River with the blaze:
> The waken'd Tydes began again to roar,
>   And wond'ring Fish in shining waters gaze.
>
> [ll. 921–24]

In both these stanzas, Dryden's notes acknowledge an immediate debt to that painterly poet Virgil, who was also working from imagination, since he had not seen Troy in flames or Aeneas in stormy seas. Pepys, who watched the London fire with his usual eye for detail, records such particulars as the burning of the wings of pigeons who hovered about their houses; Dryden's "wond'ring Fish," by contrast, are wholly imaginary.

But the generic tension implicit in the distinction between the terms "Historical" and "Epick" is also a source of moral complexity for Dryden's poem. Imagery with epic resonance may also acknowledge historical realities, particularly in the passages describing the King, who is both an avatar of the ancient gods and a harried modern monarch. This process begins as Charles considers the mercantile rivalry between the English and the Dutch:

> This saw our King; and long within his breast
>   His pensive counsels ballanc'd too and fro;
> He griev'd the Land he freed should be oppress'd,
>   And he less for it th[a]n Usurpers do.
>
> His gen'rous mind the fair Idea's drew
>   Of Fame and Honour which in dangers lay;
> Where wealth, like fruit on precipices, grew,
>   Not to be gather'd but by Birds of prey.
>
> The loss and gain each fatally were great;
>   And still his Subjects call'd aloud for war:
> But peaceful Kings o'r martial people set,
>   Each others poize and counter-ballance are.
>
> [ll. 37–48]

We first see Charles in the epic pose of the Homeric Zeus or the Virgilian Jupiter, balancing the fate of nations in his scales, but the unmistakable historical reference to "Usurpers" reminds us that part of the background for the Second Dutch War was the victory Blake had won for the Commonwealth in the First. According to the official mythology of the Restoration, Charles had "freed" England, but with the Dutch Navy "oppress[ing]" English merchants, the people, "call[ing] aloud for war," fondly remembered the military successes of the usurping government. Emulation for his pre-decessor, as Dryden suggests, helped persuade Charles to act, but the imagery of scales, used here to describe a king concerned to keep political forces in balance, is actually borrowed from a poem describing Cromwell as a ruler who threw those forces out of balance. In his *Discourse Concerning the Government of Oliver Cromwell* (1661), Cowley had described the Protector's dependence on military force in strikingly similar language:

> Curs'd be the man, . . .
>   Who seeks to overpoise alone
>   The balance of a nation:
>   Against the whole, but naked state,
> Who in his own light scale makes up with arms the weight.[35]

If surveying the international situation and balancing the "pensive counsels" are "Epick" actions, taken from some lofty perch by a Charles who resembles Jupiter, Dryden's description of kings and people as "Each others poize and counter-ballance" is a recognition of the "Historical" realities that now placed limits on kingly power, not least the increased importance of Parliament, itself a result of the Civil War.

    Alert to the derivation of the word "Idea" from the Greek verb for seeing, Dryden also presents the King as an artist drawing the "fair Idea's . . . Of Fame and Honour," perhaps as allegorical damsels in a dangerous landscape. The similar image of wealth as a fruit "to be gather'd . . . by Birds of prey" even looks like a heraldic device, an eagle triumphantly plucking a berry from a precipice. If such visionary imagery takes us far away from the economic realities of the actual decision to go to war with the Dutch, including the fact that many members of Charles's Privy Council had investments in the monopolistic trading companies that stood to profit from a victory,[36] Dryden nonetheless tempers vision with reality, epic with history. The next stanza, in which the decision is finally made, fuses ancient mythology and modern science:

> He, first, survey'd the charge with careful eyes,
>   Which none but mighty Monarchs could maintain;
> Yet judg'd, like vapours that from Limbecks rise,
>   It would in richer showers descend again.
>
> [ll. 49–52]

The image of the "richer showers" of gold descending is delicately, mythologically sexual, recalling Jove's dalliance with Danae disguised as a golden cloud,[37] but the reference to "Limbecks," equipment used in alchemy, connects this vision of heavenly potency more directly to the modern science of the Royal Society, praised in a later stanza repeating several phrases from the passage on the King:

> O truly Royal! who behold the Law,
>   And rule of beings in your Makers mind,
> And thence, like Limbecks, rich Idea's draw,
>   To fit the levell'd use of humane kind.
>
> [ll. 661–64]

The Society is "truly Royal" because its members, like its founding monarch, draw "rich Idea's" and distill useful products from "Limbecks." "Your Makers mind" is richly ambiguous: the members of the Royal Society were engaged in discovering truths about the universe and thus about the mind of God, its Maker, but the political words "Law," "rule," and "levell'd" suggest that they were also engaged in understanding the mind of the ruling monarch who had chartered their Society, seeking practical ways to further his aims by pursuing research into improved sailing vessels and guns.

When Charles "survey[s] the charge" early in the poem, he is simply considering the cost of war, but when he supervises the refitting of the fleet with cannons near the center of the poem, in a stanza rich with sexual imagery,[38] the charges he surveys are explosive:

> Our careful Monarch stands in Person by,
>   His new-cast Canons firmness to explore:
> The strength of big-corn'd powder loves to try,
>   And Ball and Cartrage sorts for every bore.
>
> [ll. 593–96]

Charles's sexual activities, much criticized by various groups in opposition, thus become a necessary part of his identity as a "mighty Monarch"; Dryden would employ this kind of argument more overtly fifteen years later, in the opening lines of *Absalom and Achitophel*, where the identification of the philandering Charles with the polygamous David humorously concedes (and thus defuses) one of the principal charges of those opposed to the King.

The King's human frailties appear even more dramatically in the section on the fire, where his "Sacred Face" is disfigured by "pious tears which down his cheeks did show'r" (ll. 956, 958). In that later passage, Dryden quickly acknowledges the King's dual nature as monarch and man by claiming that "Subjects may grieve, but Monarchs must redress" (l. 966); he has nonetheless shown us a grieving monarch. Odysseus and Aeneas conceal their grief while rallying their men, and Dryden probably has that epic motif in mind when he shows us a Charles who "chears the fearful, and commends the bold" (l. 968), but the King's prayer for his city, a few stanzas later, is spoken by a monarch who "Out-weeps an Hermite" (l. 1042), and whose grand gestures of self-sacrificial heroism do not preclude humble gestures of human inclusion:

> Thou, who has taught me to forgive the ill,
>   And recompense, as friends, the good misled;
> If mercy be a Precept of thy will,
>   Return that mercy on thy Servant's head.
>
> [ll. 1053–56]

As he had in *Astraea Redux*, Dryden emphasizes the King's mercy to those who had served the previous regime, including a poet named Dryden, who had been "misled" during the Protectorate, but had now begun to receive generous "recompense" from the Treasury. The King who can forgive in this godlike manner is nonetheless a "Servant" of God, asking for similar mercy toward himself. In the next stanza, interceding for his people, he takes on the role of a suffering scapegoat:

> Or, if my heedless Youth has stept astray,
>   Too soon forgetful of thy gracious hand:
> On me alone thy just displeasure lay,
>   But take thy judgments from this mourning Land.
>
> [ll. 1057–60]

Dryden's daring rhetoric here blunts the arguments of those who blamed the fire on the King's immorality; the Charles of his poem acknowledges that immorality but beseeches God to punish him alone, sparing the nation. As the prayer continues, the enemies of the court are reminded that sin is a universal human condition:

> We all have sinn'd, and thou hast laid us low,
>   As humble Earth from whence at first we came:
> Like flying shades before the clowds we show,
>   And shrink like Parchment in consuming flame.
>
> [ll. 1061–64]

Not only are we all sinners, but we are weak, ephemeral, shadows of fleeting clouds, parchment crackling in the flame. The theme of human weakness, which Dryden first develops by considering the fate of the Dutch sailors captured after Bergen, expands to include the English and their King. The passage on the Dutch, brilliantly adapted from Petronius, takes off from the irony that the spices and treasures carefully brought back from the East have been captured just off the coast of Holland:

> Go, Mortals, now, and vex your selves in vain
>   For wealth, which so uncertainly must come:
> When what was brought so far, and with such pain,
>   Was onely kept to lose it neerer home.
>
> The Son, who, twice three month's on th' Ocean tost,
>   Prepar'd to tell what he had pass'd before,
> Now sees, in *English* Ships the *Holland* Coast,
>   And Parents arms in vain stretch'd from the shore.
>
> This carefull Husband had been long away,
>   Whom his chast wife and little children mourn;
> Who on their fingers learn'd to tell the day
>   On which their Father promis'd to return.
>
> Such are the proud designs of human kind,
>   And so we suffer Shipwrack every where!
> Alas, what Port can such a Pilot find,
>   Who in the night of Fate must blindly steer!
>
> [ll. 125–40]

Even in this passage, the Dutch are merely one local example of a fate to which all mortals, including kings, are subject. We all "suffer Shipwrack" (an obsessive image with Dryden) "every where." A later glance at the history of the previous century reveals the ironic fact that the Elizabethan English helped the Dutch throw off the domination of Spain, with unexpected results for their descendants:

> In fortunes Empire blindly thus we go,
>   And wander after pathless destiny:
> Whose dark resorts since prudence cannot know
>   In vain it would provide for what shall be.

[ll. 797–800]

Moreover, such reversals can take place suddenly; the fire arrives when the English are "Swell'd with [their] late successes on the Foe"; by their very pride, Dryden implies, they "urge an unseen Fate to lay [them] low" (ll. 837, 839).

At first blush, such general moralizing on fate seems far removed from the immediacies of political propaganda, and may remind us of such later passages as the opening of *Religio Laici*, where men seeking religious truth are pictured as lonely travelers on a dimly lit road, or the dedication to *Aureng-Zebe*, where a man's thoughts are changed by "an ill Dream, or a Cloudy day." Still, this emphasis on our inability to understand, predict, or alter our fate also serves the local purpose of shifting blame for the disasters of 1666 away from the court. In *Astraea Redux*, Dryden had discovered that tempering the traditional imagery emphasizing the King's royal stature with language acknowledging his human frailties was an effective form of rhetoric. In *Annus Mirabilis*, the alternation between "Epick" grandeur and "Historical" reality is a large-scale version of that useful rhetorical device.

In 1666 as in 1681, Dissenters were among the King's most vocal critics, as Dryden could anticipate without even reading their pamphlets and sermons. Thanks to the obviously deranged confession of a man named Robert Hubert, the Great Fire was blamed on those universal scapegoats, the Jesuits, but Dryden, writing his poem from a recusant house, aims his rhetoric instead at the Protestant "Fanatics" whose attitudes he remembered well from his youth. At the beginning of the section on the fire, he seizes on the obscure beginning of the flames in a baker's shop on Pudding Lane to achieve a memorable personification:

> As when some dire Usurper Heav'n provides,
>   To scourge his Country with a lawless sway:
> His birth, perhaps, some petty Village hides,
>   And sets his Cradle out of Fortune's way:
>
> Till fully ripe his swelling fate breaks out,
>   And hurries him to mighty mischiefs on:
> His Prince surpriz'd at first, no ill could doubt,
>   And wants the pow'r to meet it when 'tis known:
>
> Such was the rise of this prodigious fire,
>   Which in mean buildings first obscurely bred,
> From thence did soon to open streets aspire,
>   And straight to Palaces and Temples spread.

[ll. 849–60]

Like Cromwell, the fire is a "Usurper," a "scourge" provided by Heaven, a surprise to an unsuspecting Prince; despite its obscure breeding, it aims at the seats of power; soon it will become an "infant monster, with devouring strong" (l. 871). This epic language is infinitely more effective, as propaganda and poetry, than some dubious attempt to spin a conspiracy theory directly blaming the Dissenters for the fire, and for those who knew Marvell's unpublished "Horatian Ode," there was a further subtle irony: "Palaces and Temples" is a direct echo of Marvell's description of the irresistible Cromwell: "Then burning through the air he went, / And palaces and temples rent" (ll. 21–22).[39] By taking his simile and some of his language from a poem in praise of Cromwell, Dryden complicates the comparison between the fire and the "lawless sway" of the Interregnum, preparing us for a stanza in which Venner and the Fifth-Monarchy Men, whose heads were still impaled on London Bridge, rejoice at the destruction in a nightmarish ritual:

> The Ghosts of Traitors, from the *Bridge* descend,
>   With bold Fanatick Spectres to rejoyce:
> About the fire into a Dance they bend,
>   And sing their Sabbath Notes with feeble voice.
>
> [ll. 889–92]

The Sternhold and Hopkins version of the hundredth Psalm, which Dryden had sung as a boy, employs the same rhyme:

> All people that on Earth do dwell,
>   Sing to the Lord with cheerful voice,
> Him serve with mirth, his praise forth tell,
>   Come ye before him and rejoice.[40]

As Dryden imagined the fire as a Witches' Sabbath, he heard the "feeble voice[s]" of the "bold Fanatick Spectres" singing Puritan Psalms.

Throughout *Annus Mirabilis*, the fecundity of Dryden's imagination may distract us from his argumentative intent. What looks like a fanciful piece of scene-painting here is actually an important part of the process by which the poem intends to refute Dissenting claims about the fire and the other events of 1666; the echoes of Marvell's poem and Sternhold's hymn, even if heard only subliminally, were ways of making that political argument. The subtlety and complexity of Dryden's technique contrast powerfully with the more limited perspective of other poems on these events: Waller's "Instructions to a Painter," for example, is so conventional in its imagery that it virtually invites the satirical attacks of Marvell's "Painter" poems, with their insistence on the human bungling behind supposedly glorious actions.

Using the epic past and his own poetic imagination to illuminate present realities was Dryden's special gift; it sets him apart not only from the smoothly empty Waller and the pungently specific Marvell of the "Painter" poems, but from the greatest poet of his century as well. In Milton's *Paradise Lost*, published later in the same year, there are occasional glancing references to the Westminster Assembly, the invention of the telescope, and other events of the poet's lifetime, but Milton's choice of an epic mode deliberately limits such direct commentary on his own times. Unlike most of his contemporaries, who were ready to dismiss *Paradise Lost* as the crackbrained work of a discredited regicide, Dryden generously acknowledged Milton's success, and his respect for Milton may be among the reasons why *Annus Mirabilis* was his last original poem for over a decade. But when he returned to poetry in the great satires of the 1680s, he continued the process of fusing past and present established in this work. He may have admired the grandeur and purity of Milton's epic; his projected plans for an epic of his own and his grandiose heroic plays suggest as much. But his greatest successes as a poet and a playwright are generically impure, combining aspects of forms more stringently "neoclassical" critics would have kept separate. In *Annus Mirabilis*, he teaches us how to see the events of 1666 as both "Epick" and "Historical"; his poem is both effective propaganda for the court and a moving vision of human suffering and triumph.[41]

Theatrical Politics

With the plague subsiding and the serious fighting over, the players in London were anxious to reopen the theatres. There were some performances at court in October, including a revival of Orrery's *Mustapha*, and by late November, the Bridges Street theatre was operating again. Among the first plays revived was *The English Monsieur* of James Howard, starring Nell Gwyn, which Pepys attended on 8 December; on 15 January 1667, his friend the actress Mary Knepp took part in a revival of *The Indian Emperour*.[42] Although the winter was bitter cold, with the Thames frozen over, Dryden now had a powerful incentive to pack up his wife and infant son for a return to the city: the players would need him to help them prepare *Secret Love*, in which both Gwyn and Knepp had roles, and since that play was probably produced in late January, I should suppose the Drydens had returned to London and found new lodgings by the beginning of the new year.[43] If 1666 had been a year of public wonders, 1667 was to prove a year of literary wonders, including the publication of the original *Paradise Lost* in ten books and Sprat's influential *History of the Royal Society*; in France, the same year saw the publication of Molière's *Tartuffe* and Racine's *Andromaque*. All these works would prove important to Dryden's later work as a poet, prose writer, and playwright, but his own plays were a more immediate concern as the new year began; no fewer than five of them were on stage during 1667.

The London theatre world, which would be Dryden's major arena for the next fourteen years, was a nest of tangled rivalries and intrigues, in which theatrical, sexual, and courtly politics often intertwined, as the example of George Villiers, second Duke of Buckingham may suggest. Before the theatres closed, Buckingham and several collaborators had put together a farce called *The Rehearsal*, poking fun at playwrights and plays; the leading character, a pompous playwright named Bilboa, was apparently modelled upon Sir Robert Howard. Among Buckingham's reasons for choosing Howard as his butt was a violent scuffle that took place on the occasion of the premiere of a play called *The United Kingdoms* by Henry Howard, Sir Robert's brother: Buckingham brought some friends along to scoff at the play from the pit, and found himself engaged in combat by the Howard brothers. Henry, never destined to be an important playwright, died in 1663, and before Buckingham had a chance to pillory Sir Robert on stage, the plague struck.[44] By the time the theatres reopened, the original jokes were

GEORGE VILLERS DUKE OF BUCKINGHAM.

Portrait of George Villiers, second Duke of Buckingham by Peter Lely, ca. 1675.

dated, and political events had brought Buckingham and Sir Robert Howard together as allies opposed to the Lord Chancellor and the Duke of York. In the Parliamentary debates of the winter months, Howard took Buckingham's side on the Irish Cattle Bill, and introduced a famous "Proviso" to the Poll Bill that opened the door for a Parliamentary investigation of the conduct of the naval war.[45] Theatrical collaboration followed immediately: Howard contributed a song to Buckingham's revision of Fletcher's *The Chances*, which was on stage in early February.[46]

Unlike Howard, who had cordial dealings with Clarendon during the first years of the Restoration, Buckingham had opposed both Clarendon and York for most of his life. Reared with the sons of Charles I, he held a low opinion of York's intelligence, and was snubbed by his old foe when he volunteered to go to sea with the Navy in 1665. His struggle against Clarendon for influence over Charles began as early as 1650, in the exiled court, and had continued with little intermission. The most recent cause for offense was Buckingham's violent behavior during the debate over the Cattle Bill: his differences with Lord Ossory, son of Dryden's friend the Duke of Ormonde, nearly led to a duel, and another disagreement with the Marquis of Dorchester led to a hair-pulling fight in the Painted Chamber.[47]

Despite such buffoonery, and despite the evident displeasure of the King, Buckingham now emerged as the leader of a group of courtiers sometimes called anti-Yorkists or anti-Clarendonians, who formed a temporary alliance with those country gentlemen opposed to the heavy taxes levied to support the naval war. He also attempted to gain popular support by friendly gestures toward the religious nonconformists and by opposing the payment of seamen with worthless tickets, although he knew full well that the Treasury had no money. There was already private talk of legitimizing Charles's most attractive bastard, the Duke of Monmouth, in order to alter the succession, but overt Parliamentary opposition to York was not yet possible. The main hostilities of the anti-Yorkists were therefore directed against Lord Chancellor Clarendon, whose old-fashioned attitudes, including his disapproval of the Countess of Castlemaine, separated him from such younger courtiers as Buckingham, who approved and emulated the King's adultery. Such differences about public policy and private morality were among the motives of the anti-Clarendonians, but were finally less important than their own lust for power. Ambitious men like Howard and Buckingham saw in the weakness of the Chancellor an opportunity to gain power for themselves, and when the military disaster of June 1667 made Clarendon vulnerable, they sprang to the attack as committed allies. By this point, both men had far too much to gain to let an old quarrel over a forgotten play by a dead playwright stand between them.

Dryden had no political employment at this time, but he still felt the force of these rivalries. He had written poems to Clarendon and his daughter, and had praised the Duke of York in *Annus Mirabilis*; he had also written a poem to Castlemaine, and had enjoyed the patronage of Anne, Duchess of Monmouth, wife to the darling of the anti-Yorkists.[48] Although he made no overt gesture to alienate either party, his sympathies lay with the Chancellor and the heir apparent, and this preference would soon affect his relations with Sir Robert Howard, who was siding more and more with Buckingham, despite many favors done him by Clarendon. The Howard-Dryden feud of 1668, though fought on literary turf, was motivated, at least in part, by these political differences.[49]

Clarendon's relations with Howard during early 1667, though somewhat strained by Howard's Parliamentary alliance with Buckingham, had not yet reached the point of open enmity. The post of Clerk of the Patents in Chancery, to which Clarendon appointed Howard at the Restoration, proved highly profitable, since many patents had to be issued for those appointed to posts in the new government, and since the actual work was done by a silent partner. Howard sold that post in 1664 for at least £2,600, with the Chancellor's permission, but failed to give his benefactor a share of the proceeds, as would have been normal. When Howard's marriage, a strictly financial alliance in which he had also been aided by the King and the Chancellor, began to break down, Lady Honoria petitioned for redress, and her complaints came to Clarendon. As early as 23 February 1667, the Chancellor wrote a letter about Lady Honoria's complaints of ill-usage to Henry Bennett, Earl of Arlington, in which his irritation with Howard shows clearly. Clarendon suggests that a committee of bishops and aristocrats be appointed to attempt to reconcile the couple: "If the Lady desyres I should be one I shall submitt, though I have no mind to have any thinge to do with the kn[igh]t."[50] In March, the appointed "Referees," including the Archbishop of Canterbury, the Bishop of London, and the Chancellor, held a meeting at Clarendon's house, and Howard had every reason to believe that Clarendon might influence the committee against him. When they concluded that Sir Robert's "behavior [was] much better than hers," Howard acknowledged that Clarendon "had treated him with more Candour than he had reason to expect." In June, the man who had been his mother's "great favourite" intervened again on Howard's behalf, helping him secure a commission as the colonel of a regiment stationed in Portsmouth. Mindful of all these favors, Howard came to Clarendon's house one night and gave him a canvas bag containing £300, describing the money as a delayed payment for the Chancellor's approval of the sale of the Chancery office three years earlier. If the sequence of events Clarendon set down in 1669 was correct, this payment occurred less than a month before Howard began attacking his benefactor publicly in the Commons.[51]

During the same period, Dryden characteristically tried to maintain connections with both groups. He composed his first plays for the Duke's Company in collaboration with two men closely associated with Clarendon. With William Cavendish, Duke of Newcastle, he put together a highly successful comedy, *Sir Martin Mar-All*, and with William Davenant, the patentee of the Company, he turned Shakespeare's *Tempest* into a spectacular entertainment. But during the autumn months, when these plays were on stage, he also turned to Sir Robert Howard for assistance in securing renewed payments on his wife's grant, and wrote a flattering dedicatory epistle to Anne, Duchess of Monmouth, which was printed with the first published edition of *The Indian Emperour*.

While Dryden's motives for preferring the Yorkists doubtless included Clarendon's efforts on Elizabeth's behalf in 1662, his distaste for the opportunism and vindictiveness of such men as Buckingham was also a factor. Something about the sturdy, old-fashioned loyalty of Clarendon and Newcastle attracted Dryden, whose heroic plays frequently celebrate such virtues, and something about the shifty, self-serving pragmatism of a Buckingham repelled him; the Machiavellian villains in those same plays were based on observation, not merely on literary precedent. Self-conscious about his own change of allegiance at the time of the Restoration, Dryden had come to value both loyalty and forgiveness. In *Secret Love*, his Celadon, who has been caught up in a conspiracy against the Queen, demurs when she attempts to reward him:

> I was in hope your Majesty had forgot me; therefore if you please, Madam, I onely beg a pardon for having taken up armes once to day against you; for I have a foolish kind of Conscience, which I wish many of your Subjects had, that will not let me ask a recompence for my loyalty, when I know I have been a Rebel. [V, i, 476–82]

If Buckingham had never taken up arms against a monarch, as many now prominent at court had done, he had deserted the exiled court in 1657, returning to England
and marrying Mary Fairfax, daughter of the Parliamentary general Thomas Fairfax,
who was Marvell's patron. Not at all afflicted with Celadon's "foolish kind of Conscience," he gained a pardon from Charles at the Restoration and steadily increased his
influence at court by a brilliant series of temporary alliances and contrivances. His
ability to seem all things to all men contrasted markedly with the stolid simplicity of
James, whose intellectual limitations were already apparent, and made him the natural
enemy of Clarendon, whose old-fashioned approach to administration and diplomacy
was ill-suited to the court of a king whose style and personality were closer to Buckingham's. If Dryden could appreciate such variety and agility in a literary context, he
sensed its danger in the political arena. His memorable portrait of Buckingham in
Absalom and Achitophel describes the biblical Zimri (transparently Buckingham) as "A
man so various, that he seem'd to be / Not one, but all Mankinds Epitome" (ll. 545–
46). Up to that point it might be praise, and in some sense it is grudging praise of
Buckingham's dazzling mutability. But variety holds dangers; Zimri is also

> Stiff in Opinions, always in the wrong;
> Was every thing by starts, and nothing long:
> But, in the course of one revolving Moon,
> Was Chymist, Fidler, States-Man, and Buffoon:
> Then all for Women, Painting, Rhiming, Drinking;
> Besides ten thousand freaks that dy'd in thinking.
> Blest Madman, who coud every hour employ,
> With something New to wish, or to enjoy!
>
> [ll. 547–54]

The oxymoron "Blest Madman" captures Dryden's own ambivalence about Buckingham's style. He could see the attractiveness of always having "something New," but
he also felt the appeal of the loyalty, justice, and mercy for which he had praised
Clarendon in 1662:

> Justice that sits and frowns where publick Laws
> Exclude soft mercy from a private cause,
> In your Tribunal most her self does please;
> There only smiles because she lives at ease.
>
> ["To My Lord Chancellor," ll. 49–52]

Clarendon's merciful actions toward Howard in 1667 confirm the validity of Dryden's
praise and contrast strikingly with Buckingham's cruel vindictiveness toward the harried Chancellor, an early instance of that stiffness in opinions for which Dryden would
later criticize him.

Perhaps aware of these attitudes, Buckingham was already somewhat hostile to
Dryden when the theatres reopened after the plague: his prologue to *The Chances*,
which was probably on stage about the same time as *Secret Love*, has a sneering reference to "Nel . . . danc[ing] her Jigg,"[52] alluding to a crowd-pleasing feature of Dryden's new play. But before the Duke had an opportunity to pursue his theatrical rivalry

with Dryden, he found himself in serious trouble with the court. Charged with illegally casting the horoscope of the King (a treasonous offense), Buckingham went underground in February 1667, concealing himself at the home of Sir Henry Bellassis.[53] While his rival was in hiding, Dryden's successes continued. *Annus Mirabilis* ran through several editions; Pepys, who read it on 2 February, thought it "a very good poem."[54] *The Indian Emperour*, which had been on stage when the theatres closed, continued to be performed frequently, making a larger impression than had been possible in the few months before the plague. In March, the King attended *Secret Love*, declared it to be "his play," and commanded a court performance, which took place on 9 April. Thanks to these successes, the King's Company even decided to try a revival of *The Wild Gallant*, probably in May, for which Dryden added a new scene and a revealing new prologue and epilogue.

The new prologue, much the bawdiest poem Dryden had yet written, reflects the increasing fascination with sex in the theatre after the plague, a fascination that would ultimately lead to the famous sex comedies of the 1670s. As the prologue makes clear, the double entendres implying that Jack Loveby is bedding his landlord's wife were part of the first version of the play; in the new version, Dryden says he has "played [his hero] at three Wenches more," presumably referring to an added scene with three prostitutes. Calling attention to this deliberately increased bawdry, Dryden uses the prologue to compare himself to a sexual neophyte:

> As some raw Squire, by tender Mother bred,
> Till one and Twenty keeps his Maidenhead,
> (Pleas'd with some Sport which he alone does find,
> And thinks a secret to all Humane kind;)
> Till mightily in love, yet halfe afraid,
> He first attempts the gentle Dairymaid:
> Succeeding there, and led by the renown
> Of *Whetstones Park*, he comes at length to Town,
> Where enter'd, by some School-fellow, or Friend,
> He grows to break Glass-Windows in the end:
> His valour too, which with the Watch began,
> Proceeds to duell, and he kills his Man.
> By such degrees, while knowledge he did want,
> Our unfletch'd Author, writ a *Wild Gallant*.

[ll. 1–14]

Since the old Dryden, recalling his own early days in London, may later have referred to himself as "a young raw fellow of seven and twenty,"[55] it is tempting to see the experiences of the "raw Squire" as a version of Dryden's own initiation into town pleasures, and to imagine "some School-fellow" from Westminster or Cambridge escorting the young clerk to Whetstone Park, notorious for its prostitutes. Some such personal experience may lie behind these lines, but the conventions of the theatrical prologue allow for many levels of irony; the actor refers to "Our unfletch'd Author" in the third person, even though everyone in the theatre knows that the author has written the prologue. If comparing the development of a playwright to a gentleman's "progress" from masturbation to fornication to murder, even in a lighthearted prologue, is astonishingly cynical, the purpose of the rhetoric is not confessional. Dryden is commenting upon changes in social and theatrical style in the years since his first play, and his prologue ultimately reflects upon the attitudes and actions of such courtiers as Buckingham, who had been conducting an adulterous affair with the Duchess of Shrewsbury for several years, and would soon kill her husband in a duel.[56]

A few lines later, the Prologue asks the audience to pardon the author's "lack of wickedness," and that satirical request is certainly directed against an audience now demanding sexual titillation and violent personal satire, an audience whose tastes were shifting away from those apparent in the earlier success of such high-minded plays as *The Adventures of Five Hours*. In the new epilogue, using even more shocking imagery, Dryden calls the same audience

> Salvages:
> Nothing but Humane flesh your taste can please:
> And as their Feasts with slaughter'd slaves began,
> So you, at each new Play, must have a Man.
> Hither you come, as to see Prizes fought;
> If no Blood's drawn, you cry the Prize is naught.
>
> [ll. 13–18]

Like cannibals, the playgoers devour victims of all kinds: actors, playwrights, and the actual persons satirized in comic plays. Like the vulgar crowds at prizefights, which were often held in the theatre buildings on days when no play was presented, they cry out for blood.[57] Dryden's professionalism was taking on a hard edge, and not without reason. Not only had he begun to be attacked by others in the theatre world, but he had seen the theatre used as a weapon in the increasingly vicious political struggles of the court. On 15 April 1667, less than a week after the court performance of *Secret Love*, the King's Company produced Edward Howard's political drama *The Change of Crowns*, in which a country gentleman pointedly named Asinello ("little ass") discovers the corruption of a court in which places of all kinds are openly for sale. Produced just as his brother Robert began to feel some pressure to pay off Clarendon for helping him sell a profitable place, Ned Howard's play expresses the irritation of the "country" party at the venality of all courtiers. It was evidently considered offensive by the court: Charles II personally forbade further performances; the comedian John Lacy, who played Asinello, was briefly imprisoned; and during the recriminations that followed, the actor and the author came to blows.[58] But buying and selling of places was at least as widespread among Clarendon's foes as among his friends: not only did Sir Robert Howard dispose profitably of most of the offices he received at the time of the Restoration, but when Buckingham purchased the lucrative post of Master of the Horse from Albemarle in 1668, he paid an unheard-of £20,000.[59]

Shortly after Ned Howard's play, a national disaster provided the occasion for an all-out attack on Clarendon, who had already been blamed for problems well beyond his control, such as the Queen's failure to produce an heir. Undermanned and underfinanced, the fleet had not gone out to meet the enemy this spring, and Sir William

Coventry had been dispatched to begin negotiating a peace. But on 11 June 1667, surprising an unprepared Navy, the Dutch fleet broke the chain across the river at Chatham, sailed up the Medway, burned many of the British ships, and captured the *Royal Charles*. This national disgrace led to charges and recriminations on all sides; Dr. Robert Creighton, who had been at Westminster and Trinity with Dryden, actually preached a sermon before the King "against the sins of the Court, and particularly against adultery, over and over instancing how for that single sin in David, the whole nation was undone."[60] Yet the prudish Clarendon, not the adulterous King, was made the scapegoat: over the next several months, his enemies, including Buckingham and Howard, succeeded in driving him from his office and moving his impeachment on charges of high treason. Buckingham was able to participate in this sustained attack on Clarendon because of Howard's help in reconciling him to the King. On 28 June, he asked Howard to carry a letter to the King asking for forgiveness, and when Clarendon insisted on a formal surrender, Buckingham managed to turn his own incarceration into a triumph: on his way to the Tower, he dined with a large group of friends, including Buckhurst, at a tavern called the Sun, and a crowd gathered to accompany him to prison. Ineffectual hearings were held on his case, and before the opening of Parliament in late July, he was back in his seat in the House of Lords.[61]

Disgruntled by the naval defeat, the court was painfully aware of the power of the theatre as a political weapon. Hoping to avoid embarrassments worse than that already caused by *The Change of Crowns*, the Lord Chamberlain closed the theatres for late June and most of July, during which time an irritated Parliament bayed for Clarendon's blood and a shaken government negotiated an unsatisfactory treaty with the Dutch. Dryden spent that interval polishing several works for publication and preparing at least one new play. On 7 August, Herringman entered *An Essay of Dramatick Poesie*, *Secret Love*, and *The Wild Gallant* on the Stationers' Register; the first two were published with 1668 on the title page, but may have been available late in 1667. *Sir Martin Mar-All*, which opened on 15 August, was probably being completed and rehearsed during the enforced break, though we have no solid evidence from which to ascertain the extent of Dryden's collaboration with Newcastle in preparing it.[62] Rooted in Italian *commedia dell'arte* and based on two French comedies, this play is an entertaining, loosely plotted romp; the title role was a marvelous vehicle for James Nokes, the comic star of the Duke's Company, who made it a popular success in its first run and in frequent later revivals.[63]

While such farce hardly conforms to the theories of the drama Dryden had expressed in the *Essay of Dramatick Poesie* and more fully exemplified in *Secret Love*, he had also demonstrated, as early as *The Rival Ladies*, that he knew how to give the public what it wanted, even when his own dramatic theories pointed in another direction. Perhaps the decision to write a character farce was motivated by the way Newcastle and Dryden read the public mood; they may simply have decided that a theatrical public rocked by the naval defeat and the Parliamentary squabble over Clarendon wanted entertainment, and the play continued to entertain audiences throughout Dryden's lifetime. Still, the contrast between this morally empty play and *Secret Love* or *The Indian Emperour* is suggestive; neither of those earlier plays hits directly at current politics, as Ned Howard had tried to do with *The Change of Crowns*, but both engage issues of public and private morality that might prove suggestive to a thoughtful theatregoer concerned with public affairs. The occasional tame political allusions in *Sir Martin*, by contrast, seem exceedingly cautious. At the very end of the play, the witty servant Warner, who has just outsmarted his master and married the lively Millisent, is revealed as the kinsman of a lord, who explains that "his Father's sufferings in the late times have ruin'd his Fortunes" (V, ii, 121), but such allusions to the Civil War no longer carried much political bite. If Dryden and Newcastle had wanted to enter into the current political fray, they would surely have chosen more pointed language—or a more pointed plot.

Just after the enforced theatrical holiday, on 28 July, Dryden had a personal experience with the "honorable" violence he had satirized in the new prologue to *The Wild Gallant*. Sir Henry Bellassis, the man who had harboured the fugitive Buckingham, fell into a drunken quarrel with his friend Tom Porter at the home of Sir Robert Carr in Covent Garden. Prevented from fighting Bellassis in the house, Porter departed. As he came outside, he met Dryden, who was walking by with his linkboy, a servant who held a torch. Drunk and belligerent, Porter asked Dryden to lend him his servant, left the boy to see which way Bellassis would drive in his coach, and waited for word at Will's coffeehouse. When the coach came by, Porter stopped it, challenged Bellassis, and ran him through; the wounded man gallantly stayed on his feet and urged his friend and murderer to escape; he died a few days later. Pepys heard this story from John Creed, who married Dryden's cousin Elizabeth Pickering the next year; Dryden himself was probably the original source.[64] Although Pepys does not tell us whether Dryden accompanied Porter to Will's or merely allowed him to use his servant, we may be certain that the experience was an unpleasant reminder of how quickly disagreements between friends could turn into bloody brawls.

Dryden's own relationship with Sir Robert Howard, though doubtless placed under some strain by Howard's alliance with Buckingham, had not yet degenerated into enmity. When the Earl of Southampton, the old Lord Treasurer, died, the Treasury was placed "in commission," and old orders were not honored unless reconfirmed. Once again, the Drydens needed Howard to help them with their financial affairs, and on 21 August 1667, he "move[d] ye Confirmation of a Warrant of the Late Lord Treasurer on behalfe of his sister the Lady Draydon, being £3,000 of which part paid," with the result that Elizabeth received another £500 on 19 September. Despite the intended reform of the Treasury, the nation was deeply in debt for the unsuccessful naval war, and Charles was trying to repair his damaged fortunes by persuading his subjects to lend him money. Howard probably advised Dryden to take the £500 and lend it to the King, who was promising to pay 10 percent; Dryden did so on 16 October.[65] Not repaid until 1673, this loan was nonetheless a useful gesture of loyalty on the part of an ambitious young poet. Dryden, who was now collaborating with Davenant on the new version of *The Tempest*, may have had some reason to suspect that the older man was growing frail; Davenant lived just six more months. Cowley, who might have been a rival for the laureateship on Davenant's death, had died in August; Buckingham gave him a splendid funeral.[66] The possibility of securing a permanent, salaried court position was thus a more than plausible reason for Dryden to lend the

King a sum his own family could surely have used, with one child just a year old and another now expected. His second son John was probably born early in 1668.[67]

National attention was now fixed upon the fall of Clarendon, an event for which Buckingham was working at court and in the House of Lords, while his ally Howard argued passionately in the Commons. Even Howard's Catholic older brother Lord Andover joined with the anti-Clarendonians in the Lords, perhaps hoping to secure some place that might relieve his poverty.[68] On 26 August, Charles sent the Duke of York to ask Clarendon to give up the great seal of office, a mission York can hardly have enjoyed. Although Clarendon refused and sought to plead his case, Charles was adamant, dispatching Orlando Bridgeman to demand the seal on 30 August.[69] Not content with removing and disgracing the Chancellor, his more rabid enemies, including Howard, now began a new campaign to impeach him on charges of high treason, a capital offense. Many Parliamentarians who had supported the Chancellor's removal from office recognized these new charges as fraudulent; Marvell may have been among this group.[70] Nonetheless, thanks to the vigorous efforts of Sir Robert Howard, the House moved the impeachment of Clarendon in October. Fearing for his life, the old man departed for exile in France on 29 November, leaving behind a defiant petition to the Lords, in which he claimed that he would return "when his Majesty's justice may not be obstructed or controlled by the power and malice of those who have sworn my destruction."[71] Until Clarendon died in 1674, those who had accomplished his disgrace were haunted by the fear that he might indeed return and wreak revenge.

The political storms of the autumn months were accompanied by real storms at sea; in September alone, scores of commercial vessels were cast away, with considerable loss of life. The King's Company, perhaps supposing that capitalizing on the weather was less dangerous than alluding to the governmental crisis, responded by staging Fletcher's *Sea Voyage*, retitled *The Storm*, on 25 September.[72] As Dryden would later point out in his preface to *The Tempest*, Fletcher's play was derived from Shakespeare's, and Davenant, who owned the performing rights to Shakespeare's romance, was probably already at work revising it for a production the same fall. Hoping to entertain just the sort of audience Dryden had satirized in the prologue and epilogue to the revived *Wild Gallant*, Davenant hit upon the idea of doubling Miranda, the woman who has never seen a man, by creating Hippolito, a man who has never seen a woman; since Hippolito will ultimately need a mate, this change also suggested the creation of the fair Dorinda, Miranda's younger sister. The supposed innocence of these characters occasions much sexual humor, and Davenant enlisted Dryden to write the necessary dialogue.[73] Shakespeare's Caliban refers to his mother as the witch Sycorax; Dryden and Davenant bring his *sister* Sycorax on stage as a sexual object for the sailors, whose number is also doubled: Shakespeare's Stephano and Trinculo become Stephano, Trincalo, Ventoso, and Mustacho. Someone decided to multiply the sexual confusion on stage by casting a woman as Hippolito; the ending of Dryden's prologue, which turns upon this device, will suggest the flavor of the whole play:

> But, if for *Shakespear* we your grace implore,
> We for our Theatre shall want it more;

Who by our dearth of Youths are forc'd t'employ
One of our Women to present a Boy.
And that's a transformation you will say
Exceeding all the Magick in the Play.
Let none expect in the last Act to find,
Her Sex transform'd from man to Woman-kind.
What e're she was before the Play began,
All you shall see of her is perfect man.
Or if your fancy will be farther led,
To find her Woman, it must be abed.

[ll. 27–38]

This cheapened *Tempest* was a theatrical success, not only in this version, but in a later operatic version revived for the next half-century. Among the plays the King's Company mounted to run against it in November was a revival of *The Indian Emperour*, so that Dryden had the satisfaction of seeing his plays at both houses. He must have taken even more satisfaction in a special court performance of *The Indian Emperour* on 13 January 1668, in which the Duke and Duchess of Monmouth actually took part, though such aristocratic acting was amateurish at best, and though any sensation the performance might have caused was immediately forgotten in the real-life drama of the Buckingham-Shrewsbury duel, which took place just three days later.[74]

If Dryden and Davenant responded to the fate of their friend and patron Clarendon with sorrow or anger, their *Tempest*, on which they were working as he fell, reflects only caution. Their play may be "more explicitly and exclusively political" than Shakespeare's,[75] but it avoids particular reference to the events of 1667. The number and importance of the court party are reduced, and while we might infer that Dryden and Davenant were simply seeking to make room for the low comedy of the new characters, the omissions are suggestive. Sebastian, the plotting brother to King Alonso, disappears, a change that keeps the play focused on romantic comedy by eliminating any serious threat to Prospero; that omission also avoids any possible analogy with the Duke of York, whose cause both dramatists favored. Gonzalo's proposal to govern the island as a commonwealth without magistrates, a politically dangerous speech, also disappears, and only the clownish sailors are allowed to make similar proposals, which have no more immediate relevance to current English politics than the allusions to the Civil War in *Sir Martin Mar-All*. Ariel's accusation of the court party, the most morally imposing speech in Shakespeare's play, is cut altogether from the Dryden-Davenant version, though Dryden may well have felt that Buckingham and Howard were "men of sin" for plotting against Clarendon.[76] When Dryden and Davenant do allude to current events, they look far from home: Alonso, who had been King of Naples in Shakespeare's play, becomes the Duke of Savoy, doubtless because the newspapers had been describing the attempts of the real Duke of Savoy to take over the lands of the Duke of Mantua, a title the collaborators give to Hippolito.[77] Neat as this analogy is, it directs the attention of anyone seeking political meaning in the play away from the current crisis in England. A similar caution may have motivated the most distressing of all the alterations and omissions: the radical shrinking of Prospero, who loses most of his Shakespearean dignity and becomes a mere conjuror; his "revels" speech disappears, along with his final renunciation of revenge. Although such an argument from omission is speculative, this diminishing of Prospero, a particularly surprising decision on the part of the authors of *Gondibert* and *The Indian Emperour*, might possibly have reflected their desire to avoid any potential analogy between the banished Duke of Milan and the recently deposed Chancellor. If keeping the play free from current political relevance was their aim, Dryden and Davenant succeeded; Pepys declared *The Tempest* "the most innocent play that ever I saw."[78]

But if the Yorkist dramatists were self-consciously cautious about alluding to Clarendon, the party of Buckingham and Howard, swelled with victory, was not. On 20 February 1668, the King's Theatre presented *The Great Favourite* or *The Duke of Lerma* by Sir Robert Howard, a revision of an older play (probably by John Ford) that now struck unmistakably at the exiled Chancellor. Lacking the original from which Howard worked, we may only speculate about his alterations and additions; when he published the play a few months later, he told a plausible enough story about its making:

> For the Subject, I came accidentally to write upon it; for a Gentleman brought a Play to the King's Company, call'd *The Duke of* Lerma; and by them I was desir'd to peruse it, and return my opinion, whether I thought it fit for the Stage; after I had read it, I acquainted them, that in my judgement it would not be of much use for such a design, since the contrivance, scarce would merit the name of a plot; and some of that, assisted by a disguise; and it ended abruptly: and on the Person of *Philip* the 3. there was fixt such a mean Character, and on the Daughter of the Duke of *Lerma*, such a vitious one, that I cou'd not but judge it unfit to be presented by any that had a respect, not only to Princes, but indeed to either Man or Woman; and about that time, being to go into the Countrey, I was Perswaded by Mr. *Hart* to make it my diversion there that so great a hint might not be lost, as the Duke of *Lerma* saving himself in his last extremity by his unexpected disguise, which is as well in the true story as the old Play.[79]

If we may believe it, this account makes several inferences possible. The "Gentleman" who proposed the play cannot have been the author, as Ford was long dead by the Restoration. The proposal to the players and Howard's subsequent perusal of the play apparently took place before the plague, since Howard mentions taking the manuscript to the country, where we know he was staying in 1665 and early 1666. The "great hint" that made the play attractive was the stunning scene in which the title character escapes what seems inevitable punishment by suddenly appearing in the habit of a Cardinal and claiming immunity.

Already exciting theatre, this scene became even more attractive to Howard after the events of late 1667, since the Duke could now be perceived as a version of Clarendon, who had escaped possible execution by fleeing to France. Thanks to his daughter's marriage to James, whose Catholic sympathies were already well known, the old Chancellor had been frequently accused of Papism, and was unjustly blamed by the Dissenters for the repression under which they labored; his disgrace and exile never satisfied his enemies, who claimed until his death that the old man was plotting to return to power. In these circumstances, Howard's version of the old play became a timely and riveting drama, especially since Howard inserted a number of details that could only refer to the recent political struggle.[80]

Dryden was furious. Not only had Howard continued to kick the defeated and exiled Chancellor, but he was being credited with a play Dryden knew was not his; Howard's later published admission that he had worked from an earlier source was evidently forced from him by the ensuing controversy. Ford's original play had probably been among the manuscripts purchased by Hart from Humphrey Mosely in the early 1660s, and since Dryden based *The Wild Gallant* on another manuscript in that bundle, he had probably seen the old version of *The Duke of Lerma*; indeed, I should think it possible that Dryden was the "Gentleman" referred to in Howard's preface. Perhaps he had partly revised the play himself in those earlier days, and therefore saw Howard's play as an infuriating double theft, in which Howard was taking credit for the work of both a dead author and a living author, having also altered the play to make it into an attack on the patron of that living author.[81] Lacking hard evidence, I cannot prove that thesis, and several other causes for Dryden's anger are possible,[82] but some sense that he had been personally wronged seems the most plausible explanation for his immediate response. For a revival of an old play called *Albumazar*, staged by the Duke's Company the day after Howard's play, Dryden wrote a prologue attacking literary theft:

> But this our age such Authors does afford,
> As make whole Playes, and yet scarce write one word:
> Who in this Anarchy of witt, rob all,
> And what's their Plunder, their Possession call;
> Who like bold Padders scorn by night to prey,
> But Rob by Sun-shine, in the face of day;
> Nay scarce the common Ceremony use,
> Of stand, Sir, and deliver up your Muse;
> But knock the Poet down; and, with a grace,
> Mount *Pegasus* before the owners Face.
> Faith if you have such Country *Toms*, abroad,
> 'Tis time for all true men to leave that Road.
> Yet it were modest, could it but be sed
> They strip the living, but these rob the dead:
> Dare with the mummyes of the Muses Play,
> And make love to 'em, the *Ægyptian*, way.
> Or as a Rhyming Authour would have sed,
> Joyn the dead living, to the living dead.

[ll. 15–32]

The charge of plagiarism was an ordinary one, and if Howard had done nothing more serious in appropriating Ford's play than Dryden had done in appropriating Brome's for *The Wild Gallant*, there would be little excuse for Dryden's irritation. But if Dryden himself had worked on some earlier draft of *The Duke of Lerma*, he had a stronger reason to be outraged, and I believe the reference to "a Rhyming Authour" was meant to make the general charge of theft specific by alluding to the controversy between Dryden and Howard on the subject of dramatic rhyme. Dryden's *Essay of Dramatick Poesie*, the latest chapter in that controversy, was now in print. Yet even if my hypothesis that Dryden had a hand in some earlier version of *The Duke of Lerma* should prove incorrect, his irritation at the continued hounding of Clarendon by Howard and Buckingham gave him another motive for attacking Howard. Their quarrel, which became genuinely nasty during the next six months, was too bitter on both sides to be the result of wounded pride about the authorship of revised plays (let alone a mere disagreement about dramatic rhyme); if the insults the former collaborators hurled at each other were literary, the anger behind those insults owed much to the political differences that led one man to ally himself with Buckingham while the other mourned for Clarendon.

"A Wrong Measure of his own Proportion"

The confidence with which Dryden now attacked his onetime associate and collaborator was in part a consequence of his increasing poetic, theatrical, and critical success. *Annus Mirabilis* had proved popular enough to be pirated; five of his plays had been produced in 1667 alone, and the three new ones had all been successful; the *Essay of Dramatick Poesie*, to judge from the references to its ideas that now began to bristle forth from the prefaces and prologues of rival playwrights, was a critical sensation. Aware of his success, Dryden seems to have engaged in negotiations with both theatrical companies, doubtless seeking an income more secure than the conventional third day's proceeds. Perhaps there was even a bidding war for his services, in which Davenant thought he had secured Dryden as a house playwright for the Duke's Company, only to find that the King's Company could offer better terms; some such affair may be the truth lurking behind the story Shadwell tells in a footnote to his *Medal of John Bayes*:

> When he had thrice broken his Word, Oath, and Bargain with Sir *William Davenant*, he wrote a Letter to this great Lady [Anne, Duchess of Monmouth] to pass her word for him to Sir *William*, who would not take his own; which she did. In his Letter he wisht God might never prosper him, his Wife or Children, if he did not keep his Oath and Bargain; which yet in two Months he broke, as several of the Dukes Play-house can testifie. [p. 10]

However the bargain was arrived at, Dryden eventually made a formal agreement with the King's Company, promising to write three plays a year in return for a share in the company comparable to that held by a leading actor: one and one-quarter shares out of the twelve and three-quarters available. In a good year, such a share in the profits of the company might prove substantial indeed; according to his fellow-sharers, Dryden often realized a yearly income of over £300 from this contract.[83]

Success in courtly preferment arrived at about the same time. Davenant died on 7 April 1668, and on 13 April, a warrant was issued appointing Dryden as the new Poet Laureate; he was sworn in as a servant of His Majesty's Household before the Lord Chamberlain, the old Earl of Manchester, on 22 April.[84] He was an obvious candidate, as the leading professional playwright, the persuasive author of a number of poems in praise of the King and his court, and the generous recent lender of £500 to the King's depleted Treasury. Charles thought his Poet should hold the degree of Master of Arts, and since Dryden had left Cambridge without taking that degree, the King asked Gilbert Sheldon, Archbishop of Canterbury, to grant Dryden an M.A. under a Lambeth Dispensation; Sheldon did so on 17 June 1668.[85] The Poet Laureate was officially paid £100 a year, along with a butt of canary wine, but the state of the Treasury made the collection of salaries difficult; Dryden received no payments on either salary until 18 February 1671, and his loan to the King remained unpaid until 1673.[86] Nonetheless, his financial situation now improved dramatically. He began to enjoy the proceeds from his contract with the King's Company, and his wife received another large payment on her grant in August 1668. With some money in hand and the prospect of a more regular income, the Drydens purchased a house conveniently close to the Bridges Street Theatre, on the north side of Longacre in the fashionable Westminster parish of St. Martin's in the Fields. According to tax records, they were living there by Easter of 1669; they stayed for the next nineteen years.[87] As the daughter of an Earl, Elizabeth Dryden was of course accustomed to having servants, and the London establishment she now set up in this house probably required several maids; we know from Pepys's account of the Porter-Bellassis duel that Dryden himself maintained a linkboy as well. For the next several years, his income proved sufficient to support the kind of life-style he established in the Longacre house, but later interruptions in his theatrical and court income led to serious financial problems.

We may glimpse a part of Dryden's response to his recent success in the prologue to the first play produced by the King's Company under the new contract: *An Evening's Love* or *The Mock-Astrologer*, a lively adaptation of materials from Thomas Corneille, Madame de Scudéry, Calderón, and others that opened on 12 June 1668.[88] Dryden himself supposedly dismissed this comedy as "a fifth-rate play,"[89] but it was ideally suited to the talents of the King's Company, especially those of the actresses and singers, and its frequent double entendres were doubtless designed to appeal to an audience more and more interested in sex. Always aware of his audience, Dryden evidently realized that the sexually charged dialogue he had written for the characters Davenant added to *The Tempest* was one reason for that play's success. Other recent comedies, including Etherege's *She Wou'd if She Cou'd* (6 February 1668) and Sedley's *The Mulberry Garden* (18 May 1668), used similar language, though they were less openly ribald than the comedies these men and others were to write in the 1670s.[90] Dryden's new prologue, like the one he had written for the revised *Wild Gallant*, applies sexual imagery to the poet himself:

> When first our Poet set himself to write,
> Like a young Bridegroom on his Wedding-night
> He layd about him, and did so bestir him,
> His Muse could never lye in quiet for him:
> But now his Honey-moon is gone and past,
> Yet the ungrateful drudgery must last:
> And he is bound as civil Husbands do,
> To strain himself, in complaisance to you:

> To write in pain, and counterfeit a bliss,
> Like the faint smackings of an after-kiss.
>
> [ll. 1–10]

While we may wonder what Elizabeth Dryden, soon to be pregnant with her third child in three years, thought of these ungrateful lines, Dryden's literary cynicism is even more striking than his personal cynicism. By picturing himself, again in the third person, as a victim of the sexual ennui that seems to have afflicted so many Restoration courtiers, he is affecting the pose of the man about town, falling in with the popular fashion for sexual humor, and suggesting the mode of the ensuing play, but the way his metaphor changes values in these lines reveals his deeper disillusionment with the theatre. The bride whom the honeymooning poet loved so vigorously is first identified as "his Muse," but a few lines later, she has metamorphosed into the fickle audience. The poet who had recently thought fondly of the theatre as his absent mistress is now a bored husband going through the motions of lovemaking, constrained to give the audience what they want, even though his own inclinations lie elsewhere. At this point, Dryden may possibly have been more interested in epic poetry than in drama of any kind; his criticism suggests that he would have preferred writing heroic plays or tragi-comedies to assembling popular comedies from French and Spanish sources. But the timing of this prologue is astonishing: at the very outset of a lucrative contract to write plays, Dryden presents that work as "ungrateful drudgery," and his complaints would continue for the duration of the contract, the terms of which he never satisfied.

Hard as "our poet" has worked to satisfy the audience, they prove unfaithful:

> But you, like Wives ill pleas'd, supply his want;
> Each writing *Monsieur* is a fresh Gallant:
> And though, perhaps, 'twas done as well before,
> Yet still there's something in a new amour.
>
> [ll. 11–14]

The reference to the "writing *Monsieur*" may reflect the success of visiting French troupes, who often seduced fickle audiences away from the patent houses, but competition among English authors was also increasing: not only were such gentlemen amateurs as Howard, Buckingham, Sedley, and Etherege active, but Thomas Shadwell, who would prove a formidable professional rival to Dryden for many years, had just seen his first play, *The Sullen Lovers*, succeed handsomely at the Duke's Playhouse. First performed on 2 May 1668, Shadwell's play featured broad caricatures of Sir Robert Howard and his brother Edward as "Sir Positive At-All" and "Poet Ninny," and came on stage just as Howard's ill-treatment of his wife was being discussed in the House of Commons. The prologue, poking fun at rhymed heroic plays, probably glances at Dryden.[91] Responding to such increased competition with a confidence born of his newfound security as a contract playwright and Poet Laureate, Dryden portrays all his rivals as inadequate lovers:

> Your several Poets work with several tools,
> One gets you wits, another gets you fools:

> This pleases you with some by-stroke of wit,
> This finds some cranny, that was never hit.
> But should these janty Lovers daily come
> To do your work, like your good man at home,
> Their fine small-timber'd wits would soon decay;
> These are Gallants but for a Holiday.
>
> [ll. 15–22]

Part of the satirical power of these lines comes from their indiscriminate lumping together of all Dryden's rivals, but the prologue continues with a passage that takes aim more particularly at Howard:

> Others you had who oftner have appear'd,
> Whom, for meer impotence you have cashier'd:
> Such as at first came on with pomp and glory,
> But, overstraining, soon fell flat before yee.
> Their useless weight with patience long was born,
> But at the last you threw 'em off with scorn.
>
> [ll. 23–28]

Howard's plays had appeared "oftner" than those of most of Dryden's competitors; his serious plays were often guilty of "overstraining"; he was a physically large man whose "useless weight" was not merely stylistic. To be sure, Dryden was cautious enough to couch these lines in the plural, but playgoers alert to personal satire probably recognized Howard as the main target.

Twelve days after this prologue was spoken, Herringman entered Howard's *Duke of Lerma* on the Stationers' Register; this printed version, probably available by late summer, begins with a preface in which Howard confesses that his eagerness to publish the play has been increased by those who have disapproved of it or alleged that it was borrowed. He claims that such critics (obviously including Dryden) have actually been "obliging to me . . . since I most gratefully acknowledge to have received some advantage in the opinion of the sober part of the World, by the loss of theirs" (sig. A2r). After telling the story about the mysterious "Gentleman" and the "great hint," he announces his intention "not to trouble my self nor the World any more in such subjects . . . since that little fancy and liberty I once enjoy'd, is now fetter'd in business of more unpleasant Natures" (sig. A2v). As Buckingham's right-hand man in the Commons, Howard was much occupied with politics; as a shrewd and manipulative businessman, he was also devoting much time to financial matters; and in late April, he had vigorously defended himself in the Commons against another petition from his wife, this one alleging that she had been abandoned, with little or no money to live on, in a house in Lincoln's Inn Fields (perhaps the one Dryden and Howard had shared some five years earlier).[92]

Despite these claims on his time, Howard continued some literary activity for another year: a political poem dedicated to Buckingham, "The Duel of the Stags," was entered on the Stationers' Register four days later, and a political drama, *The Country Gentleman*, on which he collaborated with Buckingham, was forbidden performance in early 1669.[93] After that disappointment, however, Howard did concentrate on politics, publishing only occasional pamphlets until the 1690s. For the rhetorical purposes of this preface, however, his slightly premature gesture toward retirement is effective: it allows Howard to "confess, that the manner of Plays which are now in most esteem, is beyond my pow'r to perform" (sig. A2v–3r), a piece of false humility that leads into a rebuttal of the rules for drama propounded by "the Author of an Essay of Drammatick Poesie" (sig. A3r–v). Howard's essential claim here is that "nature" and "fancy," rather than rules, are the best guides to dramatic composition, and he concludes this section with another gesture of humility, acknowledging Dryden's superior talents as an author of rhyming plays. Anyone comparing *The Indian Emperour* with the clumsy couplets in the concluding scene of *The Duke of Lerma* would make a similar judgment, but Howard's willingness to acknowledge Dryden's talent is impressive. If he recognized the prologues to *Albumazar* and *An Evening's Love* as the attacks on him I believe they were, Howard was relatively restrained. His conclusion makes use of the metaphor of engendering, on which Dryden's bawdy prologue had been based, then modulates into an optical conceit resembling those Dryden had used in many of his poems. Despite his earlier appeals to "fancy," Howard now portrays himself as an advocate of "reason":

> Thus as I am one that am extreamly well pleas'd with most of the *Propositions*, which are ingeniously laid down in that Essay for regulating the Stage; so I am also alwayes Concern'd for the true honour of reason, and would have no spurious issue Father'd upon her[.] Fancy, may be allow'd her wantonness; but reason is always pure and chast: and as it resembles the Sun, in making all things clear, it also resembles it in its several positions, when it shines in full height, and directly ascendant over any Subject, it leaves but little shaddow; But when descended and grown low, its oblique shining renders the shadow larger then the substance, and gives the deceiv'd person a wrong measure of his own proportion. [sig. a1r]

Howard's resentment is easier to understand than his sputtering prose. He remembered the Dryden he had first met a decade earlier, a minor clerk and struggling author of anonymous prefaces, who needed such friends as Howard to help him avoid the taint of having served the Protectorate. Although Howard had helped him gain access to the revived theatre, Dryden was proving ungrateful, presumably because he had surpassed his former collaborator in the eyes of the literary world. The pride in his professional skill that we noticed as an undertone in his deferential verses to Howard in 1660 had become overt, and if Dryden could still make flattering gestures of fealty in prefaces to other aristocrats, he was no longer bowing in Howard's direction. When Howard accuses Dryden of having "a wrong measure of his own proportion," he conflates the claims of class with the claims of literary excellence, as Dryden himself would often do in complimenting aristocrats on their meager talents as versifiers. Dryden was normally alert to the claims of class: his portrait of Howard as Crites in the *Essay*, while far from flattering, takes due notice of Howard's birth. But the two prologues of 1668, metaphorically describing Howard as a highwayman and an impotent lover, vigorously deny their barely anonymous target his status as a nobleman. Dryden's anger at the way Howard had turned on Clarendon in the Commons and in the theatre was doubtless a motive for the first attack; his professional success probably made him brave enough to continue with the second. But even this combination of reasons cannot adequately account for the scathing contempt with which he now replied to Howard's relatively mild preface. For a new edition of *The Indian Emperour*, he wrote "A Defence of an Essay of Dramatique Poesie, being an Answer to the Preface of *The Great Favourite, or the Duke of* Lerma," a sarcastic, bitter, and lengthy attack on his brother-in-law.

Dryden evidently composed his "Defence" with Howard's preface on the table, systematically responding to every sentence. He scores some telling points, particularly when he pretends to praise Howard, but exaggerates his panegyric gestures to make them sarcastic, a technique he would employ again in his poetic satires of the 1680s:

> I cannot but give this testimony of his Style, that it is extream poetical, even in Oratory; his Thought elevated, sometimes above common apprehension; his Notions politick and grave, and tending to the instruction of Princes, and reformation of States; that they are abundantly interlac'd with variety of Fancies, Tropes, and Figures, which the Criticks have enviously branded with the name of obscurity and false Grammar. [IX, 10]

This contemptuous passage comes *after* Dryden himself has devoted several pages to catching Howard in some errors in Latin translation and English grammar. If the most immediately striking aspect of the "Defence" is the passionate anger behind it, that very anger makes Dryden's critical arguments unusually sharp. To Howard's vague appeals to "fancy" and "taste," for example, he offers this two-fisted reply:

> I am of the opinion that they cannot be good Poets who are not accustomed to argue well. False reasonings and colours of Speech, are the certain marks of one who does not understand the Stage: For Moral Truth is the Mistress of the Poet as much as of the Philosopher: Poesie must resemble Natural Truth, but it must *be* Ethical. [IX, 12]

Dryden may have believed, as one astute modern commentator suggests, that "it was necessary for him to dissociate himself in a public way from his brother-in-law's politics,"[94] but the record of the Howard-Dryden feud as we have it, even if supplemented by an understanding of the political dimensions of their quarrel, seems insufficient to account for the emotional intensity of the "Defence." To Howard's remark about being "fetter'd in business," for example, Dryden replies: "The Muses have lost him, but the Commonwealth gains by it; The corruption of a Poet is the Generation of a Statesman" (IX, 10). By calling the state the "Commonwealth," Dryden tars Howard with the brush of republicanism; by employing the metaphor of "corruption" and "Generation," using the still-current belief that vermin were generated by carrion, he deliberately arouses disgust. If that metaphor draws some of its power from Dryden's proud opinions about the relative merits of literature and politics, it also draws on intense personal anger.

We may sample that anger more fully in a paragraph where the continuing argument about rhymed drama shades into a defiant claim to professionalism as a legitimate motive, which leads in turn to a rare moment of personal candor:

> But I perceive I am falling into the danger of another rebuke from my Opponent: for when I plead that the Ancients used Verse, I prove not that they would have admitted Rhyme, had it then been written: all I can say is only this, That it seems to have succeeded Verse by the general consent of Poets in all Modern Languages, for almost all their serious Plays are written in it: which, though it be no demonstration that therefore they ought to be so, yet, at least the practice first, and then the continuation of it, shews that it attain'd the end, which was to please; and if that cannot be compass'd here, I will be the first who shall lay it down. For I confess my chief endeavours are to delight the Age in which I live. If the humour of this, be for low Comedy, small Accidents, and Raillery, I will force my Genius to obey it, though with more reputation I could write in Verse. [IX, 7–8]

After all the scholarly and theoretical arguments about the legitimacy of rhymed drama, Dryden falls back to the simplest of defenses: dramatic rhyme in modern languages has been pleasing to audiences; when it is no longer pleasing, he will abandon it, as indeed he did some eight years later. Writing to please his own age is the task of the professional writer, and Dryden's pride in his professional skill, recently recognized by the crown and the theatre, is the central emotion in this passionate essay.

Although his own preferences run to serious verse drama, Dryden is a professional; he can compose comedies if necessary. So at this point, angry though he is, he takes the trouble to reply to an attack on his comic technique from another quarter. In the preface to the published version of *The Sullen Lovers*, which Dryden had evidently seen, Shadwell contrasts his own Jonsonian "humours" comedy with the comedy of wit written by Dryden in such plays as *Secret Love* and *An Evening's Love*:

> I have known some of late so Insolent to say, that *Ben Johnson* wrote his best *Playes* without Wit; imagining that all the Wit in *Playes* consisted in bringing two persons upon the Stage to break Jests, and to bob one another, which they call Repartie.[95]

To this accusation, based in part on an over-reading of his comments on Jonson in the *Essay of Dramatick Poesie*, Dryden replies in a confessional mode, carefully echoing much of Shadwell's vocabulary:

> I know I am not so fitted by Nature to write Comedy: I want that gayety of humour which is required to it. My Conversation is slow and dull, my humour Saturnine and reserv'd: In short, I am none of those who endeavour to break Jests in Company, or make reparties, so that those who decry my Comedies do me no injury, except it be in point of profit: reputation in them is the last thing to which I shall pretend. [IX, 8]

If Dryden knows that his personality is ill-suited to comedy, he also knows the difference between "profit" and "reputation," and if he hopes to make a reasonable profit, even from a "fifth-rate play" like *An Evening's Love*, he will stake his ultimate reputation on his poetic dramas, including, of course, *The Indian Emperour*, a particular favorite of the aristocracy, acted at court by the Duke and Duchess of Monmouth and now being printed in its second edition.

Even while writing the "Defence," Dryden must have known that such a display of pique was an error. He attempted to soften the force of his blows by concluding with some handsome compliments to Howard's "person and parts," acknowledging his "particular Obligations" to his former friend, and proposing that the debate about rhyme, which had now stretched on for four years, be concluded:

> In my Epistle Dedicatory, before my *Rival Ladies*, I had said somewhat in behalf of Verse, which he was pleased to answer in his Preface to his Plays: that occasioned my Reply in my Essay, and that Reply begot this rejoynder of his in his Preface to the Duke of *Lerma*. But as I was the last who took up Arms, I will be the first to lay them down. For what I have here written, I submit it wholly to him; and if I do not hereafter answer what may be objected against this Paper, I hope the World will not impute it to any other reason, than only the due respect which I have for so noble an Opponent. [IX, 22]

Howard did not reply, and the "Defence" was withdrawn long before all the copies of *The Indian Emperour* in this edition were printed.[96] There are various explanations for Dryden's decision to expunge his preface. One "R. F.," who took it upon himself to reply for Howard later in the same year, alleged in a vituperative pamphlet that Dryden had refused to accept a challenge to a duel, a charge later repeated by other antagonists, who added the inference that Dryden had been terrified into cancelling the "Defence."[97] Howard had apparently been ready to draw his sword in theatrical quarrels on two previous occasions (see above, pp. 138, 178), but I wonder whether he would really have issued a challenge to his sister's husband. Perhaps Dryden acted after some kind of reconciliation, but we have no evidence of renewed friendly contact between the brothers-in-law until 1695; the political differences that had separated them remained strong, and they were on opposite sides in the crises of the 1680s. The simplest explanation for Dryden's decision to withdraw the "Defence" is that he thought better of it. His anger cooled, he recognized that his pedantic preoccupation with pointing out Howard's solecisms left him open to attack, and he moved to cut his losses. Pepys thought the pamphlet by "R. F." was "mighty silly,"[98] and his verdict might be extended to the other papers in this controversy as well.

But if publishing the "Defence" was an error, working his way through the anger that generated it proved therapeutic for Dryden. During the next two years, his professional pride led him away from farces and adaptations; he refused to "force [his] Genius to obey" the popular preference for "low Comedy, small Accidents, and Raillery," concentrating instead upon a grand heroic drama for which he did feel suited: the two parts of *The Conquest of Granada*. His continued professional success also allowed him to maintain a posture of aloofness, though various lesser writers continued to amplify the criticisms made by Howard, Shadwell, and "R. F." Although Dryden seems to have read most of these attacks, and frequently took the trouble to defend himself against their literary charges in his prefaces, he generally avoided public rituals of vituperation: not until the full-blown party controversy of the Exclusion Crisis called forth *The Medall* would he display so nakedly the anger he had indulged in the "Defence."

CHAPTER SEVEN

"Success,
Which Can no More than Beauty Last"
1669–1673

"Bad Enough to Please"

Even before his irritation with Howard prompted the "Defence," Dryden had begun to think about the materials from which he would forge his most ambitious play, a ten-act verse drama undertaken with concern for future "reputation" as well as immediate "profit": *The Conquest of Granada*. *An Evening's Love*, set in modern Spain, provides clear evidence that medieval Spain was on his mind. Like most of the other "gay couple" comedies written for Charles Hart and Nell Gwyn, it uses disguise: the Englishman Wildblood (Hart) pretends to be an astrologer in order to court his Spanish lady, Donna Jacinta (Gwyn); she tests his devotion by pretending to be a Moslem named Fatyma, and a delighted Wildblood, falling for the disguise, declares that he is "got among the *Hamets*, the *Zegrys*, and the *Bencerrages*" (III, i, 459). Those names, referring to various Moorish clans within Granada during the fifteenth century, could only have come from some reading about the wars between the Moors and Spaniards, either in history or romance; all of them reappear in the *Conquest*.[1]

Not only had Dryden been reading about Spain, but he must have believed that at least part of his audience in 1668 knew enough about Spanish history to catch the allusion. From the Restoration on, hostility toward the Dutch and the French had softened the traditional English enmity toward the Spaniards; as early as 1661, when rivalry between the servants of the French and Spanish ambassadors led to bloodshed, Pepys reported that public sentiment favored the Spaniards.[2] Although the King chose a Portuguese princess over a Spanish one as his bride, he maintained good relations with Spain; when news of the death of Philip IV arrived in early 1666, the court went into mourning, and Charles sent the Earl of Sandwich, Pepys's employer and Dryden's kinsman by marriage, to Spain as his new Ambassador.[3] In his account of a dinner conversation with John Creed and Henry Sheeres, both of whom were also employed by Sandwich, Pepys shows a typical fascination with Spanish "ceremoniousness,"

repeating stories about the punctilious code of honor controlling duelling and courtship, and Dryden had probably heard similar stories: Sir Gilbert Pickering's daughter
Elizabeth, his Titchmarsh cousin, married John Creed in October 1668, and Sheeres
was still close to Dryden in the 1690s.[4] The Spanish code of honor was also a central
feature of the many plays with Spanish sources and settings on the early Restoration
stage; Tuke's *Adventures of Five Hours* and Dryden's own *Rival Ladies* are obvious
examples. In the Spanish sources from which he borrowed *The Conquest of Granada*,
Dryden saw an opportunity to return to the theme of honor in love and war, which had
served him well in *The Indian Emperour*, another play with Spanish characters. Since the
historical siege of Granada had pitted Christians against Moors, he could also stage a
clash of cultures like that in the earlier play. Distanced from contemporary England in
time, geography, religion, and culture, medieval Granada was an ideal setting for a play
making use of the grandly heroic gestures of epic and romance.

I believe Dryden had begun to work on the *Conquest* as early as the winter of 1668–
69. If so, he interrupted his labors in the spring to write another rhymed heroic play,
Tyrannick Love, or the Royal Martyr, which pits early Christians against imperial Romans. When he published this play in 1670, Dryden defended his choice of a religious
subject by reminding his readers that "Religion was first taught in Verse (which the
laziness or dulness of succeeding Priesthood, turned afterwards into Prose)." He also
claimed that "Precepts and Examples of Piety" were the proper "business of a Poet" (X,
109). This high-minded argument, made with tongue at least partly in cheek, stands in
ironic contrast with the comic epilogue, where Nell Gwyn calls *Tyrannick Love* a

> godly out-of-fashion Play:
> A Play which if you dare but twice sit out,
> You'l all be slander'd, and be thought devout.
>
> [ll. 22–24]

As the light tone suggests, Dryden's play was not really "out of fashion": the "godly"
subject he chose to treat was politically urgent, the Roman tyrant he created gave
ranting speeches that were "bad enough to please," and the female victims sacrificed by
that tyrant were played by the sexiest actresses in the company. Despite the pious claims
of the preface, Dryden had not entirely abandoned his declared intention to delight the
age in which he lived.

That age, at least its theatre audience, was showing an increased interest in plays
related to contemporary political and social life, and playwrights were using different
methods to satisfy that interest. During the previous theatrical season, Howard had
retooled *Duke of Lerma*, another Spanish play, to emphasize parallels with modern
England, turning Lerma into a version of Clarendon; Shadwell's *Sullen Lovers*, with its
caricatures of the Howard brothers, had delighted such important theatregoers as the
Duke of York, who insisted on the accuracy of its portrayal of the pompous Sir Robert.[5]
Mindful of those successes, actors in both companies angered prominent people by
imitating them during the next season: in January 1669, Katherine Corey of the King's
Company was briefly imprisoned after she impersonated Lady Elizabeth Harvey while
acting as Sempronia in Jonson's *Catiline*; and in early February, Edward Kynaston of

the Duke's Company was soundly beaten by hired thugs after he impersonated Sir Charles Sedley in a performance of *The Heiress*, a play by the Duke of Newcastle in which Dryden himself may also have had a hand.[6] An even more spectacular case of such caricature was forbidden before it came on the stage, yet had a serious impact on politics and diplomacy. Sir Robert Howard and his ally the Duke of Buckingham collaborated on a comedy called *The Country Gentleman*, the central scene in which depicted the office furniture and personal habits of their rival Sir William Coventry, a hardworking bureaucrat loyal to the Duke of York. Before the play's scheduled premiere on 27 February, Coventry got wind of the plot and challenged Buckingham to a duel. The King forbade the play, imprisoned Coventry in the Tower, and in March, dismissed him from his ministerial posts, losing the services of a man with vastly more administrative ability than Buckingham.[7]

Satire and impersonation were not the only ways for plays to make reference to prominent persons in the audience: just two days before the Howard-Buckingham play was scheduled to open at Bridges Street, the King attended a performance of *The Royal Shepherdesse* at Lincoln's Inn Fields. Revised by Shadwell from a manuscript by a dead gentleman named John Fountain,[8] this play is a high-minded pastoral romance like Dryden's *Secret Love*; it ends with the discovery that its disguised heroine is pregnant, an expression of the hopes of the court and the nation for a legitimate heir that must have seemed happily prophetic when the real Queen became pregnant later in the spring. Dryden's play, in which the "Royall Martyr," St. Catharine, overwhelms fifty pagan philosophers with her simple Christian faith, was also designed to compliment the Queen, but in this case, the compliment had a sharper political and religious edge. When his St. Catharine defends Christianity against her pagan torturers, she employs language close to that used by the famous Anglican preacher John Tillotson in several pamphlets; Dryden evidently meant to downplay the denominational issue by dramatizing the more basic conflict between Christian and pagan, thus deflecting attention away from the real Catharine's Catholicism.[9]

The new ministry, like earlier groups, was called a "Cabal," a name now justified by the initials of its members: Clifford, Arlington, Buckingham, Ashley, and Lauderdale. It was a divided and distrustful group, and Dryden's defense of the Queen neatly served the propaganda purposes of its two crypto-Catholic members: Sir Thomas Clifford, to whom he would later dedicate *Amboyna*, and Henry Bennet, Lord Arlington, with whom he would be paired by Buckingham in *The Rehearsal*. Neither Clifford nor Arlington was openly a Roman Catholic at this early date, though Clifford's wife, like Dryden's, came from a recusant family.[10] By the time Dryden began writing his play, however, both ministers already knew that Charles intended to make the agreement with Louis XIV later known as the Secret Treaty of Dover; in a secret meeting on 25 January 1669, the King explained his plan to Arlington, Clifford, the Duke of York, and the Catholic peer Lord Arundell.[11] Finally signed in May of 1670, the Secret Treaty committed Charles to providing better conditions for English Catholics and included the promise that the King would eventually declare his own Catholicism. A treaty omitting those clauses was signed in December 1670; Buckingham and Ashley, who were privy to that bogus treaty, remained ignorant of the real agreement. Both

Portrait of Sir Thomas Clifford after Peter Lely, ca. 1672.

versions committed the two monarchs to an alliance against the Dutch, with the British carrying the major load in a planned naval attack while the French were to invade by land. James expected to regain glory by commanding the fleet; Buckingham was fobbed off with the promise that he would command a large English unit within the French land forces. Though they certainly would not have let the Poet Laureate in on the explosive religious provisions of the secret treaty, either Arlington or Clifford might well have hinted that a play on St. Catharine the martyr would be pleasing to the court, and Dryden's reference to "the Commands of some Persons of Honour" in the published preface is probably an acknowledgment of such courtly desires.

Portrait of Henry Bennet, first Earl of Arlington, after Peter Lely, ca. 1665–70.

On 4 June 1669, a few weeks before the premiere of Dryden's play, Arlington hosted a dinner party at which the guests included his ally Clifford and Dryden's father-in-law, the old Earl of Berkshire.[12] The divisions within the ministry, however, did not entirely determine the guest lists at such social gatherings: the naval hero Sir Robert Holmes, Buckingham's second in the Shrewsbury duel, was also present, as was Sir Robert Howard, well known as Buckingham's friend and agent. Already planning a new naval war, Arlington and Clifford obviously needed the support of Holmes, and Clifford, who was the Treasurer of the King's Household, needed to maintain reasonably civil relations with a financial expert like Howard; inviting Sir Robert to a dinner with his aged father was an obvious gesture.[13] Dryden's decision to dedicate the published play to the King's Protestant bastard Monmouth ought to be seen in the same light. If he was aware that some parts of his play might be gratifying to those courtiers loyal to the Duke of York, that was no reason to ignore his obligations to the Duke and Duchess of Monmouth.[14]

Whatever political or religious motives lay behind the new play, there were pragmatic considerations as well: *The Country Gentleman*, which might have proved scandalous enough to be popular, had been forbidden, so Killigrew hoped to mount a sensational new heroic play for the height of the social season. If they heard the rumors of the Queen's pregnancy, both author and producer had even stronger reasons for haste, and Dryden later admitted writing *Tyrannick Love* in only seven weeks.[15] Preparing the scenery took longer than the actors had anticipated, however, and by the time *Tyrannick Love* reached the stage, the Queen had miscarried: her pet fox leaped onto her bed on 7 June 1669, ending the pregnancy that had probably been among the reasons for Dryden's play, which was finally acted on 24 June.[16] The Drydens were more fortunate: their third son, named Erasmus-Henry for his two great-grandfathers, was born on 2 May and christened on 20 May; the proud parents celebrated his birth by purchasing some silver from the goldsmith Blanchard.[17]

The story of the scenery can be partially reconstructed from a suit filed a year later by the principals of the King's Company against an alcoholic scene-painter named Isaac Fuller, who had already gone to court to force them to pay him £335 10s. for painting the elaborate scenes required by Dryden's play.[18] According to their testimony, the actors Hart and Mohun, acting on Killigrew's behalf, visited Fuller on 14 April 1669 and asked him to paint a "Scaene of Elysium," presumably the background for Act Four, in which the aerial spirits Nakar and Damilcar descend singing from the clouds. The actors claim that Fuller, despite frequent warnings, took too long about his task and produced an inferior product, so that they were unable to present the play during Easter and Trinity terms, when many "Gentry & persons of quality" could be expected to attend the theatre. Fuller, in his effective and scornful reply, counters these charges by explaining that the poet Dryden and a carpenter named Wright visited him in late April or early May to discuss the set, that he painted it in six weeks' time, beginning on 12 May and finishing on 23 June, and that Robert Streeter, another well-known painter, testified in court that his work was of high quality. If we may believe Fuller, and he is a far more detailed and plausible witness than the players, the play ran for fourteen days and made a considerable profit, though the players might well have made even more money had they been able to mount it a month earlier. What really rankled Killigrew, Hart, and Mohun, I suspect, was the success of a somewhat similar play, Betterton's adaptation of John Webster's *Appius and Virginia* as *The Roman Virgin*, at Lincoln's Inn Fields in May. Part of the satisfaction of having a theatrical hit was hearing that the other house was sparsely attended, and *Tyrannick Love*, with its excessive characters, musical masque, and hilarious epilogue, might well have bested *The Roman Virgin* in a head-to-head competition. But by the time the King's Company managed to mount Dryden's play, the Duke's Company, with their profits in their pockets, had gone off to spend July acting in Oxford.

In their document, the actors refer to their adversary as "one Isaack Fuller . . . , being a Painter & one who sometimes did apply himselfe for painting of Scaenes"; stung by this demeaning description, Fuller mockingly refers to the Poet Laureate as "One Mr. Dryden (a Poett as this Defendant hath heard that Sometimes makes Playes [for] the Company of Comedians or Actors)." Despite its scorn, Fuller's reply provides a rare glimpse into the everyday workings of the King's Company. There can be little doubt that Dryden and the carpenter Wright actually came to Fuller's house to discuss the painting of the scenery, and that visit should remind us of a truth sometimes forgotten in merely literary criticism of Dryden's plays: having signed his contract with the King's Company, Dryden was intimately involved in its fortunes. His choice of subjects and genres was not disinterested; Killigrew's sense of what the public wanted was often an important factor in what Dryden set about writing. In this case, for both theatrical and political reasons, the opportunity to compliment the Queen by writing a play about her namesake took precedence over Dryden's greater interest in the materials that would eventually become *The Conquest of Granada*. Setting aside his Spanish romances, he did a little reading in Roman history and rapidly produced an uneven but popular play that provided the pattern for the many "horror tragedies" of the 1670s.[19]

As in all his plays, Dryden's responsibilities did not end with writing out a fair copy of the dialogue; he instructed the players in their parts,[20] helped plan the music, and described his visual requirements to the scene painter. His development of particular characters reflected his knowledge of the capacities and limitations of the available actors. Michael Mohun, for example, had been successful in parts calling for complex villainy: Volpone, Iago, Cassius. Dryden had used him in roles as varied as the emperor Montezuma in *The Indian Emperour* and the gay blade Bellamy in *An Evening's Love*.[21] For this versatile actor, he now conceived the juicy part of Maximin, a ranting villain whose intense emotions are the driving force of this play.

Maximin's cruelty is established early on. He responds to the death of his son Charinus by ordering a decimation of the troops with whom the young man was fighting; when his ally Porphyrius protests that he "will lose by this severity [his] Souldiers hearts," Maximin snaps back, "Why, they take Pay to dye" (I, i, 163–65). But when the captive Christian princess Catharine enters, Maximin feels the stirrings of love, which he expresses in martial and tempestuous metaphors:

> This Love that never could my youth engage,
> Peeps out his coward head to dare my age.
> Where hast thou been thus long, thou sleeping form,
> That wak'st like drowsie Sea-men in a storm?
> A sullen hour thou chusest for thy birth:
> My Love shoots up in tempests, as the Earth
> Is stirr'd and loosen'd in a blust'ring wind,
> Whose blasts to waiting flowers her womb unbind.
>
> [II, i, 1–8]

Catharine, however, is far too interested in her virginity and her glorious crown of martyrdom to yield to Maximin, who threatens her with torture by the wheel in a notoriously grotesque outburst:

> Go, bind her hand and foot beneath that Wheel:
> Four of you turn the dreadful Engine round;
> Four others hold her fast'ned to the ground:
> That by degrees her tender breasts may feel,
> First the rough razings of the pointed steel:
> Her Paps then let the bearded Tenters stake,
> And on each hook a gory Gobbet take;
> Till th'upper flesh by piece-meal torn away,
> Her beating heart shall to the Sun display.

> [V, i, 245–53]

An angel conveniently destroys the wheel, forcing a slightly less lurid martyrdom (offstage) for Catharine, but the play nonetheless ends in a welter of blood. Furious at his inability to turn back time and countermand his own orders, Maximin kills the soldier who comes to report the execution of St. Catharine and her mother; the stage direction specifies a ludicrous action: *"Kills him, then sets his foot on him, and speaks on."* When Porphyrius, who loves Maximin's wife Berenice, attempts unsuccessfully to rescue the empress, Maximin orders them both executed. Valeria, Maximin's virtuous daughter who loves Porphyrius, stabs herself; Placidius, who loves Valeria, stabs Maximin, who wrests away the knife, sits down upon his victim, and stabs him repeatedly in a scene in which tragic rant turns into comedy.[22] Porphyrius and Berenice, who have escaped execution, arrive in time to declaim over three corpses, one of whom, Valeria, comes to life in her real identity as Nell Gwyn to speak an explicitly comic epilogue. Cursing the soldier who means to carry off her body, Nell breaks the frame of the play:

> Hold, are you mad? you damn'd confounded Dog,
> I am to rise, and speak the Epilogue.

> [ll. 1–2]

Addressing the "kind Gentlemen" and "Sweet Ladies" of the audience, she explains that she is the "Ghost of poor departed *Nelly*" (ll. 3–5); "trust[ing] no Poet," she provides her own epitaph:

> Here *Nelly* lies, who, though she liv'd a Slater'n,
> Yet dy'd a Princess, acting in S. *Cathar'n*.

> [ll. 29–30]

Shortly after her performance as Valeria, Nell became mistress to the King. She had previously been the mistress of Charles Hart, who played Porphyrius, and of Charles Sackville, Lord Buckhurst, dedicatee of Dryden's *Essay of Dramatick Poesie*; she wittily called her new lover her Charles the Third. Margaret Hughes, who played St. Catharine, had been Charles Sedley's mistress and now became mistress to Prince Rupert. If Dryden intended a compliment to the Queen by his choice of subject, he also knew that his audience would enjoy seeing those notorious slatterns Gwyn and Hughes cast as punctilious virgins.

Dryden's impatience is everywhere apparent in this play. The exposition of the various tyrannic loves and jealousies that complicate the plot is as absurdly compressed as the conclusion: Porphyrius, Berenice, Valeria, and Placidius establish their inter-locking passions, mainly through asides, in exactly thirty-two lines (I, i, 177–208); within twenty more lines, the corpse of Charinus has been carried in by the soldiers. The theological debate between St. Catharine and the heathen philosopher Apol-lonius, which concludes with his conversion and immediate execution, is boiled down to sixty-three lines (II, i, 180–242). Even the many scenes of unsuccessful courtship seem perfunctory and flat. Perfectly aware of these and other defects, Dryden defends himself in the prologue by emphasizing the virtues of hasty composition:

> Poets, like Lovers, should be bold and dare,
> They spoil their business with an over-care.
> And he who servilely creeps after sence,
> Is safe, but ne're will reach an Excellence.
> Hence 'tis, our Poet in his conjuring,
> Allow'd his Fancy the full scope and swing.
> But when a Tyrant for his Theme he had,
> He loos'd the Reins, and bid his Muse run mad:
> And though he stumbles in a full career;
> Yet rashness is a better fault than fear.
>
> [ll. 12–21]

In the "conjuring" scene, the spirits Nakar and Damilcar "descend in Clouds," singing a rapid anapestic lyric. Matching his language to the scenic and musical extravagance of this scene, Dryden "Allow[s] his Fancy the full scope and swing," combining motifs from the prophecy scenes in the two *Indian* plays with "faery" language conned from Shakespeare's Ariel. Although the songs, lighthearted and fantastic, do nothing to advance the plot, their lyrical lines provide relief from the numbing regularity of the uninspired couplets. The ranting speeches already quoted from Maximin are a suffi-cient sample of what happened when Dryden "bid his Muse run mad." A decade later, in the "Epistle Dedicatory" to *The Spanish Fryar* (1681), he would acknowledge the defects of those lines in a passage that makes an intriguing claim about his state of mind when writing *Tyrannick Love*:

> I remember some Verses of my own *Maximin* and *Almanzor* which cry, Vengeance upon me for their Extravagance, and which I wish heartily in the same fire with *Statius* and *Chapman*: All I can say for those passages, which are I hope not many, is, that I knew they were bad enough to please, even when I writ them: But I repent of them amongst my sins. [sig. A2v]

Sweeping the Stakes

Just after the first run of *Tyrannick Love*, on 16 July 1669, Dryden's father-in-law died, possibly from the effects of a fall; he was buried in Westminster Abbey on 20 July.[23] The old Earl of Berkshire had little to leave to his survivors, and may even have died intestate; his Catholic son Charles, Viscount Andover, succeeded him in the earldom, and his widow quickly petitioned the Treasury, asking for £3,000 "for the benefit of her younger children." Although there is no reason to believe that her mother's petition succeeded, Elizabeth Dryden, who was probably the youngest of the Countess Dowager's children, received the final payment on her dowry on 11 August.[24] Her financial struggles with her father and the Treasury were finally over, and the death of the old Earl may have also been a relief. His behavior had long been erratic, and Elizabeth had three small sons to care for; her oldest, Charles, namesake of the new Earl, was not quite three when his grandfather died.

The theatrical season of 1669–70 was the first for many years without a new play by Dryden. His contract with the King's Company called for three new works each year, but he never fulfilled the letter of that contract, and in this season, the company would hardly have been able to mount a new play of ambitious proportions. The opening of the season was probably delayed by a period of mourning for the death of the Queen Mother, and Nell Gwyn, who had acted in most of Dryden's successful plays, was unavailable; she gave birth to a royal bastard, the Duke of St. Albans, in May of 1670. Several other actresses in both companies had similar problems, and when *The Conquest of Granada* was finally performed, Dryden took notice of those pregnancies, claiming, in the epilogue to Part I, that he had completed his work in time for a much earlier premiere. Speaking of "our sad Poet," Mohun asked the audience to pity both author and players:

> Think him not duller for this years delay;
> He was prepar'd, the women were away;
> And men, without their parts, can hardly play.
> If they, through sickness, seldome did appear,
> Pity the virgins of each Theatre!
> For, at both houses, 'twas a sickly year!
> And pity us, your servants, to whose cost,
> In one such sickness, nine whole Mon'ths are lost.

[ll. 25–32]

Revivals and publications kept Dryden in the public eye: *Secret Love* was performed at the Inner Temple, probably in November 1669, and *The Tempest* was published in early 1670; Dryden's preface, praising Davenant for his invention and taste, is dated 1 December 1669. The publication of two different reprintings of *The Indian Emperour* in 1670, both claiming to be the third edition, may point to a revival of that play. This slack theatrical year, doubtless given over mainly to the writing of *The Conquest of Granada*, also brought Dryden another official post. James Howell, the Historiographer Royal, died in 1669, and Dryden was appointed to succeed him, at a salary of £100.[25] On 18 August 1670, the King's scriveners drew up a formal patent, confirming Dryden in this new appointment and the post of Poet Laureate, and promising to pay him £200 annually in quarterly payments, along with the traditional butt of wine. Although he knew from experience that this promise was unlikely to be kept, Dryden could take considerable pride in the official account of the reasons for his appointment:

> Know yee, that wee, for and in consideration of the many good and acceptable services by John Dryden, Master of Arts, and eldest sonne of Erasmus Dryden, of Tichmarsh in the county of Northampton, Esquire, to us heretofore done and performed, and taking notice of the learning and eminent abilities of him the said John Dryden, and of his great skill and elegant style both in verse and prose, and for diverse other good causes and considerations us thereunto especially moving, have nominated, constituted, declared, and appointed, and by these presents do nominate, constitute, declare and appoint, him the said John Dryden, our POET LAUREAT and HISTORIOGRAPHER ROYAL.[26]

By appointing Dryden to this additional post, the King was officially contracting for the services of a man who had shown himself an able propagandist in *Annus Mirabilis* and a skilled controversialist in his prose prefaces and essays. Arlington and Clifford, who probably advised Charles about the appointment, would have been reminded of Dryden's deft propaganda on behalf of the Queen in *Tyrannick Love* by the Parliamentary debates of the spring session of 1670. A major issue in that session was the Roos divorce bill, which permitted a husband to remarry after divorcing his wife. Hoping to provide a precedent that would allow the King to divorce the barren Catharine and marry a Protestant, Buckingham, Ashley, and Sir Robert Howard vigorously supported the bill; they may even have consulted the old poet Milton, who was an expert on divorce.[27] But the King, who had no intention of divorcing his Queen, had now signed the Secret Treaty, and was planning to issue a Declaration of Indulgence as a first step toward acknowledging his Catholicism; he was surely aware that such controversial policies would eventually require some defense by a writer possessing "great skill and elegant style both in verse and prose."

I should also suppose that the "diverse other good causes and considerations" cited in the patent included Charles's belief that Dryden would be willing to defend his new policies. The recent succession of the Catholic Andover to the earldom of Berkshire would have reminded the King of the recusancy of some members of Dryden's wife's family; like the King, the new Historiographer Royal had excellent family reasons to support a policy of increased religious toleration. In the very month in which the patent was issued, Anne, Duchess of York, to whom Dryden had earlier addressed an elegant poem, quietly converted to the Roman Catholic faith; sixteen years later, as Historiographer Royal to James, Dryden would be called upon to defend the authenticity of the papers describing that conversion. At the time he received this additional appointment, however, he was probably more immediately concerned with polishing *The Conquest of Granada*, the grandest and longest drama he had yet attempted, though that drama also has a political dimension: it ends with the conversion of a Moorish queen and her heroic lover to Roman Catholicism, and was dedicated when published to James, Duke of York.

The first edition of *Tyrannick Love*, listed in the Term Catalogue for November 1670, provides some indications of Dryden's sense of his own literary development as the *Conquest* was nearing its premiere. In his witty dedication to Monmouth, written for that edition, he thanks the Duchess again for her early patronage of *The Indian Em-*

perour. Comically employing imagery drawn from the myth of the Fall, he suggests that "A zealous Fanatick would have . . . called [him] the Serpent, who first presented the fruit of Poetry to the Wife, and so gain'd the opportunity to seduce the Husband" (X, 107). Perhaps Dryden had this myth in mind because he had recently read *Paradise Lost*.[28] To Buckhurst, who had sent him a copy of Milton's poem, he was candid about its excellence; "that Poet," he wrote, "has cutt us all out."[29] But in a public dedication for a play that occasionally shows Milton's influence, he couples a flippant allusion to the Fall with a sneering phrase about "a zealous Fanatick," which might easily be read as a reference to the old Puritan poet who had once been his employer. His appreciation of *Paradise Lost* may have had something to do with Dryden's decision to attempt a play on a religious subject, but the same need to appear fashionable that led him to cast himself as Satan in the dedication had already led him to frame that play with a prologue indicting himself for haste and an epilogue describing the result as "a godly out-of-fashion play." Concerned to appear neither too pious nor too profane, Dryden busily defends himself in the preface: he explains that the character of Maximin, on the basis of which "some ignorant or malicious persons" had charged him with "Prophaneness and Irreligion," was "designed by me to set off the Character of *S. Catharine*" (X, 110), and insists that the impiety of the heathen emperor is properly punished. He appeals to his "due reverence of that Religion which I profess" and to "the witness of my own Conscience," but those pious phrases frame the claim that he is "already justified by the sentence of the best and most discerning Prince in the World" (X, 111). Dryden was doubtless proud of his success in achieving the two posts he held under Charles, but an appeal to a notably immoral monarch was not likely to blunt the criticisms of those who had thought his play profane.

Dryden's interest in heroic poetry, apparent from his earliest poems and his constant interest in Virgil, was probably intensified by reading Milton. In the dedication, he makes the first of his many references to an epic on the Stuarts: "Instead of an Heroick Play," he tells Monmouth, "you might justly expect an Heroick Poem, filled with the past Glories of your Ancestors, & the future certainties of your own" (X, 107). This projected epic was never written, but the play Dryden was watching in rehearsal when he wrote these words, *The Conquest of Granada*, brings epic grandeur and complexity to the stage, and his satiric masterpiece, *Absalom and Achitophel*, draws on Miltonic language and casts the beautiful Monmouth in the role of the tempted Adam. *The Conquest of Granada* is not a sustained political allegory like *Absalom and Achitophel*, even though Dryden's printed dedication insists that the impetuous hero Almanzor is modeled on the Duke of York. Still, the pointed political passages it does contain sound the note of monarchial privilege that would echo again and again in Dryden's controversial writings of the 1680s. Harried by the demands of his besieged people for the return of the military victor Almanzor, the weak king Boabdelin laments his fate, referring to the crowd as "the many-headed Beast":

> See what the many-headed Beast demands.
> Curst is that King whose Honour's in their hands.
> In Senates, either they too slowly grant,

Portrait of James Scott, Duke of Monmouth, after William Wissing, ca. 1683.

> Or sawcily refuse to aid my want:
> And when their Thrift has ruin'd me in Warr,
> They call their Insolence my want of Care.
>
> [Pt. II; I, ii, 29–34]

Boabdelin's people are divided into two feuding factions, the Zegrys and the Abencerrages, but this speech is the only time "Senates" are mentioned, and Dryden was not really thinking of Granada when he wrote these lines. Charles II firmly believed that he had lost the Second Dutch War because of insufficient supply from Parliament, and resented the witch-hunting Parliamentary inquiries after that war, in which those who had been unwilling to vote more money for the Navy sought scapegoats on whom to blame the national disgrace. Abenamar's reply to Boabdelin's complaint would have struck him as a perfect description of such men as Buckingham and Sir Robert Howard, who loudly proclaimed their interest in the "public good" and their desire to save public money, yet rarely missed a chance to secure profitable places for themselves:

> Curst be their Leaders who that Rage foment;
> And vail with publick good their discontent:
> They keep the Peoples Purses in their hands,
> And Hector Kings to grant their wild demands.
> But to each Lure a Court throws out, descend;
> And prey on those, they promis'd to defend.
>
>   [I, ii, 35–40]

The immediate political relevance of this scene seems obvious enough, yet the recorded responses to the opening of the play in December of 1670 do not mention such specific political barbs. *The Conquest of Granada* was a major theatrical event, and the controversy that came to surround it was largely literary. Like the author, the company evidently conceived of the play as one giant drama of ten acts; they staged Part II within a week or two of the premiere of Part I. Nell Gwyn returned to the stage to play Queen Almahide; Charles Hart was her grandly heroic lover Almanzor; Kynaston took the part of her jealous husband Boabdelin. The juiciest part of all, the temptress Lyndaraxa, went to Rebecca Marshall, and there was even a small part, as Almahide's Christian servant Esperanza, for Anne Reeves, a beautiful young actress who was soon rumored to be Dryden's mistress.[30] The "very glorious scenes & perspectives" painted by Robert Streeter impressed the diarist John Evelyn,[31] and the characterization and dialogue impressed his wife, whose famous comment on the play raises issues that have remained lively in criticism ever since:

> I have seene "The siege of Grenada," a play so full of ideas that the most refined romance I ever read is not to compare with it: love is made so pure, and valor so nice, that one would imagine it designed for an Utopia rather then our stage. I do not quarrell with the poet, but admire one borne in the decline of morality should be able to feigne such exact virtue: and as poetick fiction has been instructive in former ages, I wish this the same event in ours.[32]

Mrs. Evelyn, whose husband frequently laments the immorality of the court and the theatre in his diary,[33] captures the apparent incongruity between the high-minded romance conventions of the *Conquest* and the fashionable immorality of its audience. She evidently has no illusions about Dryden's own morality, as her pointed use of the verb "feigne" suggests, and Dryden's casting the notorious Nell Gwyn as a punctilious queen unjustly accused of adultery was indeed a witty piece of "feigning." Moreover, the prologues and epilogues to this play, like those for Dryden's comedies, are aimed at an audience inclined to enjoy being "borne in the decline of morality." The prologue to Part I, spoken by Nell Gwyn in an absurdly large hat, pokes fun at the reliance of the Duke's Company on such sight gags, complaining that the excellent comedians of that troupe

> Must be worn out, with being blocks o' th' Stage.
> Like a young Girl, who better things has known,
> Beneath their Poets Impotence they groan.
>
> [ll. 20–22]

The epilogue, in an extended comparison between "Fame" and "a little Mistriss of the town," taps the same vein. The prologue to Part II compares the as yet "unfinished Play" to a "Vizard Masque" in the pit, an imagined beauty who may prove to be a frightening "Dowdy" when unmasked. Even more striking than these casual references to contemporary sexual conventions are the frankly erotic songs performed in the play itself, especially the song accompanying the "Zambra Dance" in Part I, which may have been sung by Anne Reeves.[34] Yet despite these acknowledgments of the taste of the age for sexual humor, this play presents a heroine who claims a high-minded purity about sex and a hero who talks of obeying her Utopian code. Moreover, in the epilogue to Part II, Dryden himself claims that his contemporaries have an advanced taste for "Love and Honour." In an argument that was to prove controversial, he contrasts the modern drama with Ben Jonson's "Mechanique humour":

> If Love and Honour now are higher rais'd,
> 'Tis not the Poet, but the Age is prais'd.
>
> [ll. 21–22]

The aspect of the new age that makes possible the "raising" of "Love and Honour," the main subjects of the *Conquest*, is not some Utopian sense of virtue, but the prevalence of wit in society:

> Wit's now ariv'd to a more high degree;
> Our native Language more refin'd and free.
> Our Ladies and our men now speak more wit
> In conversation, than those Poets writ.
>
> [ll. 23–26]

Remembering that "wit" meant not only sparkling repartee but also simple intelligence may help us make sense of this odd argument, and of Mrs. Evelyn's praising the play not only for its refined virtues but for its "ideas." As Dryden clearly knew, the *Conquest* was by far his most complex drama: its ideal audience would be capable of responding to the immediate political reference of Boabdelin's complaints, the sexual innuendo of the songs, the epic grandeur of the poetic language, the self-conscious excess by which some of that language shades into amusing bombast, the witty exaggeration and ironic questioning of Hobbist theories of political power, and the psychological strain placed on the characters as their declared devotion to the pure, almost abstract virtues of love and valor is tested by wrenching situations and impossible choices. No one hearer was likely to respond with equal sensitivity to all these aspects of the play; Mrs. Evelyn, for example, missed not only the political references but the disparity between moral declaration and moral action. Yet for those able to modulate their responses as Dryden modulated his many styles, the play was and is richly rewarding.

As far back as *The Indian Queen*, Dryden had been more successful when letting his characters describe offstage action than when actually staging battles or rescues. In *The Conquest of Granada*, he uses such speeches to set up the entrance of Almanzor. Before the hero comes on stage, others describe his prowess in a bullfight:

> Thus, while he stood, the Bull who saw this foe,
> His easier Conquests proudly did forego:
> And, making at him, with a furious bound,
> From his bent forehead aim'd a double wound.
> A rising Murmure, ran through all the field,
> And every Ladies blood with fear was chill'd.
> Some schriek'd, while others, with more helpful care,
> Cry'd out aloud, Beware, brave youth, beware!
> At this he turn'd, and, as the Bull drew near,
> Shun'd, and receiv'd him on his pointed Spear.
> The Lance broke short: the beast then bellow'd lowd,
> And his strong neck to a new onset bow'd
> Th'undaunted youth————
> Then drew; and from his Saddle bending low,
> Just where the neck did to the shoulders grow,
> With his full force discharg'd a deadly blow.
> Not heads of Poppies, (when they reap the grain)
> Fall with more ease before the lab'ring Swayn,
> Then fell this head:————
> It fell so quick, it did even death prevent:
> And made imperfect bellowings as it went.
> Then all the Trumpets Victory did sound:
> And yet their clangors in our shouts were drown'd.
>
> [Pt. I; I, i, 76–98]

Like his epic predecessors, Dryden manages his sounds carefully: the triplet describing the "deadly blow" gives us the crucial action in a kind of slow motion, and we hear the bull's bellowing and the clangor of the trumpets in the frequent open vowels. This passage also appropriates memorable images from Virgil and Homer, though the world of Dryden's play is more chivalric and fantastic than the world of true epic. During the funeral games for Anchises in the *Aeneid*, the old boxer Entellus fells a prize bull with his fist, but neither an epic hero nor a butcher with a meat-axe could sever a bull's head with one stroke. In a Virgilian episode that Dryden later chose to translate in *Sylvae* (1685), the doomed Euryalus is cut down like a flower; that night raid imitates a similar episode in the *Iliad*, in which the head of the spy Dolon falls to earth still speaking when struck clean off by Diomedes. When applied to the bull, these epic motifs seem absurd: Virgil's comparing the drooping, severed head of the beautiful boy Euryalus to a flower is pathetic, but Dryden's comparing a bull's head to a poppy is grotesque.[35]

So, too, with the characters, who have some qualities that suggest epic models, but who also reflect Dryden's reading of romance and his awareness of contemporary realities. In the essay "Of Heroique Plays," prefixed to the published version of the *Conquest*, Dryden specifically mentions Achilles as a model for Almanzor, and the two characters obviously share courage, impetuosity, and military prowess. Homer's hero, for all his grandeur, causes wholesale destruction for his own side, and indulges in barbaric behavior that grossly violates the high code he sometimes appears to support. Dryden's hero is similarly destructive and self-centered, but his romance gestures toward a selfless and Platonic love have nothing to do with the world of the ancient epic, in which women are property, not goddesses. Perhaps because she perceives the play as simply a dramatization of romance, Mrs. Evelyn responds to the speeches in which love is made pure and valor nice; she does not appear to recognize that the behavior of Almanzor and Almahide frequently invalidates their speeches, and it may well be that Hart and Gwyn were unable to communicate that irony.[36] Achilles, by contrast, is sufficiently self-conscious to recognize his contradictions, and thus ultimately gains the stature of a tragic figure.

Dryden cannot consistently sustain an epic manner in a play whose plot is largely drawn from romance, and when the characters speak, especially when they describe their own feelings, he indulges in a kind of excess that goes beyond either epic or romance. In the narrative of the bullfight, the blood of the frightened ladies runs cold, as does that of numerous epic characters; perhaps because we are hearing about their fright after the fact and in a narrative mode, the image does not seem particularly extravagant. Yet when Almanzor describes similarly conventional symptoms in his response to Almahide, the claim to immediacy produces a comic effect:

> I'me pleas'd and pain'd since first her eyes I saw,
> As I were stung with some *Tarantula*:
> Armes, and the dusty field I less admire;
> And soften strangely in some new desire.
> Honour burns in me, not so fiercely bright;
> But pale, as fires when master'd by the light.
> Ev'n while I speak and look, I change yet more;
> And now am nothing that I was before.
> I'm numm'd, and fix'd and scarce my eyeballs move;
> I fear it is the Lethargy of Love!
> 'Tis he; I feel him now in every part:
> Like a new Lord he vaunts about my Heart,
> Surveys in state each corner of my Brest,
> While poor fierce I, that was, am dispossest.
> I'm bound; but I will rowze my rage again:
> And though no hope of Liberty remaine,
> I'll fright my Keeper when I shake my chaine.
>
> [Pt. I; III, i, 328–44]

The writers of the chivalric romances from which some of this language comes could at least describe such sudden psychological changes in the third person and the past tense; by bringing such a moment onto the stage and having the character himself describe his paralysis, Dryden achieves immediacy but sacrifices any hope of seriousness. The audience saw Charles Hart standing on the stage, doing his best to look "numm'd, and fixed" by the sight of his former mistress Nell Gwyn. The temptation to smile must have been considerable, and producing a smile was surely a part of Dryden's intent: the sudden paralysis of a fierce warrior by love *is* ludicrous, and the deliberate excess of Dryden's language, here and elsewhere, emphasizes not only the power of love but the irrational folly that accompanies yielding to that power. In a play in which kings are actually dispossessed and heroes appear in real chains, the conventional Petrarchan equation between the language of love and the language of battle gains dramatic force; the grandest hero of all has been captured by a triumphant Cupid who "vaunts about [his] Heart," "survey[ing]" his new kingdom "in state." Such imagery was sure to remind the audience of their own monarch's notorious sexual intrigues, including his affair with the actress now playing Almahide. To argue that such moments are wholly serious or wholly ironic is to miss the pleasure Dryden and his audience took in the mixture of the two: Almanzor in love is a comic figure—and so was Charles II.

Dryden's awareness of his own milieu shows not only in the casting and the humor, but in figurative passages using the events described in *Annus Mirabilis* as new epic similes: Almanzor is consumed by his love for Almahide as a city is consumed "when some fierce fire lays goodly buildings waste" (Pt. I; V, i, 432–43); Ozmyn describes a chaotic battle as if it were a shipwreck (Pt. II; III, ii, 9–12). Even Almanzor's most excessive metaphors, which do not immediately seem related to the realities of Dryden's England, sometimes bring contemporary theories of political power into the play. If the physical action of the play displays nothing quite so absurd as Maximin sitting on his victim, the imagery of many of Almanzor's speeches comes close: claiming that he has "that Soul which Empires first began," for example, he issues this impossible boast:

> The best and bravest Souls I can select,
> And on their Conquer'd Necks my Throne erect.
>
> [Pt. I; IV, ii, 478–79]

Again, the excess is a part of Dryden's meaning; men in the grip of Almanzor's vaunting pride, he insists, will believe they can erect their thrones on conquered necks. But the politics behind Almanzor's rant are at least as important as the psychology; his claim to force as the only source of political legitimacy is a reductive version of the theory of natural law developed in Hobbes's *Leviathan* (1651).

While there are excellent reasons for believing that Dryden read *Leviathan* with care and skepticism soon after its publication, this play makes a more sustained use of Hobbesian ideas and categories than his earlier works, and since Hobbes was popularly considered a dangerous and atheistical thinker, some of Dryden's contemporaries seized on his use of Hobbesian ideas as another reason to criticize him, failing to recognize that his use of Hobbes was both skeptical and creative.[37] When Almanzor first strides onto the stage, a street brawl between the Zegrys and the Abencerrages is in progress; instinctively taking the weaker side, he disobeys the king's order to desist, kills his man, and is condemned to death. The defiant speech he addresses to Boabdelin at this juncture is a dramatic caricature of Hobbes's ideas about the "state of nature":

> No man has more contempt than I, of breath;
> But whence hast thou the right to give me death?
> Obey'd as Soveraign by thy Subjects be,

> But know, that I alone am King of me.
> I am as free as Nature first made man
> 'Ere the base Laws of Servitude began
> When wild in woods the noble Savage ran.
>
> [Pt. I; I, i, 203–09]

This speech bears the same kind of relation to its source in Hobbes that the speech on the lethargy of love bears to its sources in romance. In neither case is Dryden endorsing the view of life his character announces; in both cases, exaggeration has an ironic effect. Almahide and Almanzor make themselves look foolish by attempting to cast themselves into the Utopian patterns of romance figures, and the many characters who exhibit what Hobbes had called the "generall inclination of all mankind, a perpetuall and restlesse desire of Power after power," especially Abdalla and Lyndaraxa, find that such desire "ceaseth onely in Death" (*Leviathan*, I, ii, p. 161). The ending, in which Almahide is converted to Christianity by Esperanza, and Almanzor learns that his parents were Christians, deliberately integrates both characters into an ethical and political system opposed to the ideological excesses popularly associated with Hobbes; the promise of their eventual marriage after Almahide's "year of Widowhood" integrates them into a sexual relationship unlike the Platonic impossibilities advocated in some romances.

But Dryden knew how to learn from his sources, even those sources with which he had fundamental disagreements, and his frequent use of political and military language to describe the interior strife between passion and reason reveals his complex intellectual engagement with Hobbes, whose challenging theory of politics begins with a theory of psychology. A particularly striking example comes early on, when the king's brother Abdalla, entranced by the temptress Lyndaraxa, decides to attempt a revolt, refusing what he knows to be the good advice of Abdelmelech:

> Your Councels, noble *Abdelmelech*, move
> My reason to accept 'em; not my Love.
> Ah, why did Heav'n leave Man so weak defence
> To trust frail reason with the rule of Sence?
> 'Tis over-pois'd and kick'd up in the Air,
> While sence weighs down the Scale; and keeps it there.
> Or, like a Captive King,'tis born away:
> And forc'd to count'nance its own Rebels sway.
>
> [Pt. I; III, i, 56–63]

Three successive couplets offer three related metaphors. "Frail reason," like a weak king, is unable to rule over "Sence," which Hobbes had already called the "Originall" of all human thoughts (I, i, p. 85). Heavy and physical, "sence" will inevitably "over-pois[e]" the nebulous reason. Outweighed and disarmed by "sence," reason is finally led away like a captive king, an image sure to remind Dryden's audience of Charles I. By employing these metaphors, Dryden is describing three usurpations at once: the usurpation of Abdalla's reason by the force of "sence," in this case the powerful sexuality of Lyndaraxa; the consequent usurpation of the kingdom of Granada, which Abdalla seeks in order to win her hand; and the usurpation of the kingdom of England by

Cromwell, still the chief bugbear of official mythology.[38] Although the character here describing his own yielding to "sence" is eventually killed as a result of his stage Hobbism, the essential metaphor upon which his speech depends, equating civil disorder within the body politic and psychological disorder within one man's mind, comes straight from Hobbes.

If Mrs. Evelyn was responding to this kind of intellectual complexity when she praised Dryden's play for being "full of ideas," that phrase was acute criticism indeed. But what finally sets *The Conquest of Granada* apart from Dryden's earlier plays is his success in integrating materials drawn from political philosophy, prose romance, and epic poetry into a coherent dramatic whole. If we compare the stylized exchanges between St. Catharine and Maximin in *Tyrannick Love* with such powerful scenes as Lyndaraxa's attempted seduction of Almanzor (Pt. II; III, iii, 59–188) or Almanzor's attempted seduction of Almahide (Pt. II, IV, iii, 155–284), we can only conclude that the time Dryden devoted to the *Conquest* was well spent. The play is indeed "full of ideas," but part of its greatness lies in Dryden's dramatization of the limits of ideology. When Almanzor approaches Almahide in the second of those scenes, she appeals to his "Vertue":

> *Almahide.* Remember the great Act you did this day:
>   How did your Love to Vertue then give way?
>   When you gave freedom to my Captive Lord;
>   That Rival, who possest what you ador'd.
>   Of such a deed what price can there be made?
>   Think well: is that an Action to be paid?
>   It was a Myracle of Vertue shown:
>   And wonders are with wonder paid alone.
>   And would you all that secret joy of mind
>   Which great Souls only in great actions find,
>   All that, for one tumultuous Minute loose?
> *Almanzor.* I would that minute before ages choose.
>   Praise is the pay of Heav'n for doing good;
>   But Love's the best return for flesh and blood.
>
> [Pt. II; IV, iii, 251–64]

Almanzor's reply powerfully acknowledges the psychological reality of sexual desire; thanks to his interest in Anne Reeves, Dryden was freshly aware of that reality. By choosing "that minute before ages," Almanzor objects to the absurd ideology of romance, which imposed upon heroes the duty of chivalric behavior without the "return" of fleshly love. But he is willing to lose everything for that "one tumultuous Minute," a passionate and irrational refusal of the cynical pragmatism of Hobbes, who had claimed that "the object of mans desire, is not to enjoy once onely, and for one instant of time; but to assure for ever, the way of his future desire" (*Leviathan*, I, xi, pp. 160–61).

Despite the bravado of the self-deprecating prologues and epilogues, Dryden's sense that this play was his best comes through poignantly. Here are the opening lines of the epilogue to Part I:

> Success, which can no more than beauty last,
> Makes our sad Poet mourn your favours past:
> For, since without desert he got a name,
> He fears to loose it now with greater shame.
>
> [ll. 1–4]

Six months shy of his fortieth birthday, conscious of the fragility of his wife's beauty, and anxious lest a play into which he had poured the accumulated sophistication of his literary life lose him a fame earned by such lesser efforts as *An Evening's Love* or *Tyrannick Love*, Dryden compares Fame to an unfaithful mistress:

> Fame, like a little Mistriss of the town,
> Is gaind with ease; but then she's lost as soon.
> For as those taudry Misses, soon or late
> Jilt such as keep 'em at the highest rate:
> (And oft the Lacquey, or the Brawny Clown,
> Gets what is hid in the loose body'd gown;)
> So, Fame is false to all that keep her long;
> And turns up to the Fop that's brisk and young.
>
> [ll. 5–12]

If Dryden was already "keeping" Anne Reeves, he made himself vulnerable to satire with these lines, and in less than a year, Buckingham would allude to the affair in *The Rehearsal*. While dating the beginning of this liaison is obviously impossible, I should imagine that Dryden had become sexually involved with Anne Reeves by the time this play came on stage. After rapidly producing three sons between August of 1666 and May of 1669, Lady Elizabeth had no further children, a fact that suggests some change in the pattern of her sexual relations with Dryden.

Whether or not Dryden's passion for Anne had been consummated when he wrote this epilogue, his choosing to describe his mixture of motives for writing this play in the language of love is psychologically revealing. Like the related prologue to *An Evening's Love*, this one glances at the poet's rivals: perhaps he had the obese Shadwell in mind when picturing the "Lacquey, or the Brawny Clown" who enjoys the favors of Fame. But this prologue, for all its high spirits, is also a confession, as Dryden goes on to explain his decision to keep on pursuing Fame:

> Some wiser Poet now would leave Fame first:
> But elder wits are like old Lovers curst;
> Who, when the vigor of their youth is spent,
> Still grow more fond as they grow impotent.
> This, some years hence, our Poets case may prove;
> But yet, he hopes, he's young enough to love.
> When forty comes, if 'ere he live to see
> That wretched, fumbling age of poetry;
> 'Twill be high time to bid his Muse adieu:
> Well he may please him self, but never you.
>
> [ll. 13–22]

The audience and the Muse, cynically equated in the prologue to *An Evening's Love*, are now kept more separate, and a new distinction between present Fame and future Fame also begins to emerge. With this play, the man who had recently declared his intention "to delight the Age in which I live" began to be more concerned to "please him self," and in so doing to educate his audience and lay some claim to future reputation.

After acknowledging the extra time given him to polish the play by the pregnancies of the actresses, Dryden admits that he has not used that time to best advantage:

> They thought they gave him leisure to do well:
> But when they forc'd him to attend, he fell!
>
> [ll. 35–36]

The haste he had used to excuse the faults of *Tyrannick Love* is no longer an available excuse. Aware of the remaining weaknesses in *The Conquest of Granada*, he is nonetheless proud that he has aimed at greater complexity and depth:

> Yet though he much has faild, he begs to day
> You will excuse his unperforming Play:
> Weakness sometimes great passion does express;
> He had pleas'd better, had he lov'd you less.
>
> [ll. 37–40]

Like his own Almanzor, who discovers his "great passion" through symptoms of physical weakness, Dryden discovers his love for his audience (present and future) by acknowledging that his straining for psychological, political, and moral complexity has weakened his play as mere theatre; that, I take it, is the self-criticism implicit in the description of the *Conquest* as an "unperforming Play." Perfectly aware that he might have "pleas'd better" with mere rant or even knockabout farce, he now had the financial security and the increased maturity to woo a more lasting fame by attempting something more difficult, something closer to the epic poem that he saw as a poet's highest calling. Mrs. Evelyn's final wish for his play, that its "poetick fiction" would prove "instructive," would surely have pleased him, though he would have understood "instruction" in a more complex way than she did.

The epilogue to Part II, however, attracted much more attention. In that instantly controversial performance, Dryden dared to compare the age of Ben Jonson, when "Fame . . . was cheap," with his own theatrical age, when playgoers spoke in witty repartee and critics stood ready to note every fault. His rivals, who sprang vigorously to Jonson's defense, thought Dryden more critical of Jonson than he intended to be, but they were correct in interpreting his ostensible praise of his age as ill-concealed praise of himself. After explaining that the conversation of his contemporaries is more witty than that of the Elizabethans, Dryden draws a conclusion bound to irritate other playwrights:

> Then, one of these is, consequently, true;
> That what this Poet writes comes short of you,
> And imitates you ill, (which most he fears)
> Or else his writing is not worse than theirs.

> Yet, though you judge, (as sure the Critiques will)
> That some before him writ with greater skill,
> In this one praise he hath their fame surpast,
> To please an Age more Gallant than the last.
>
> [ll. 27–34]

The success of the play in pleasing the gallant world of the court brought tangible rewards. On 11 January 1671, Dryden's friend the Duke of Ormonde signed a warrant for the delivery of the butt of wine "in kind or in money," together with the arrears due on the Laureate's salary. This action apparently set official wheels in motion: on 27 January, the Treasury issued a money warrant for the £500 owed to Dryden for his two official posts, and on 18 February he received the money. At the same time, the Treasury promised to begin repayment of the £500 the poet had lent the King more than three years earlier.[39] The court performance of the *Conquest* that Evelyn records took place on 10 and 11 February, and on 13 February, the published version of *An Evening's Love* appeared, with an elegant dedication to Dryden's former collaborator the Duke of Newcastle and a preface in which we may measure the increase in confidence Dryden had gained from the success of his most highly wrought play. Dismissing those who had correctly charged him with stealing the stories for most of his plays, he loftily declares that

> these little Criticks do not well consider what is the work of a Poet, and what the Graces of a Poem: The Story is the least part of either. . . . [T]he employment of a Poet, is like that of a curious Gunsmith, or Watchmaker: the Iron or Silver is not his own; but they are the least part of that which gives the value: The price lyes wholly in the workmanship. [X, 212]

Though Dryden goes on to refer to "that little reputation I have got, and which I value not" (X, 213), the preface as a whole is a vigorous defense of that reputation and a clear indication of what a high value he placed on his workmanship. During the next two years, his attackers would multiply, and Dryden, ever sensitive to criticism, would bristle more than once in attempting to defend himself against their charges. But his accomplishment in *The Conquest of Granada* was decisive. When he published the play in February of 1672, *after* being publicly attacked by Shadwell, Buckingham, and a host of lesser wits, he described his satisfaction at its success with a metaphor probably even more applicable to his state of mind at the time of the premiere:

> That there are errors in it, I deny not . . . But I have already swept the stakes; and with the common good fortune of prosperous Gamesters, can be content to sit quietly; to hear my fortune curst by some, and my faults arraign'd by others, and to suffer both without reply. [XI, 18]

Mr. Bayes

The success of *The Conquest of Granada* consolidated Dryden's fame. From this date onward, he remained a public figure, vulnerable to attacks from writers jealous of his professional status, politicians opposed to the powerful men with whom he was associated, and university pedants scornful of his verbal innovations. His first public quarrel, the debate with Sir Robert Howard, taught him a valuable lesson about the costs of controversy; Dryden came out of that experience determined to remain aloof from his critics. If he did not always manage to maintain a posture of indifference, his patience was sorely tested; his simple statement in the "Discourse concerning the Original and Progress of Satire," written in 1692—"More Libels have been written against me, than almost any Man now living" (IV, 59)—is no exaggeration.

Although the public controversy with Sir Robert had ended with the "Defence of the Essay" and the anonymous answer from "R. F." in 1668, the addressee of that last pamphlet, Edward Howard, continued to hound Dryden. In *The Women's Conquest*, probably first performed in September of 1670,[40] Howard brought the ghost of Ben Jonson up through a trapdoor to speak a prologue; when he published the play in early 1671, he developed his praise of Jonson and his criticism of rhyming tragedy in a long and pointed preface. Howard's next play, less successful, was *The Six Days Adventure*, staged on 6 March 1671 and published in July; it too had a preface aimed at Dryden. Although Ned Howard had been lampooned as "Poet Ninny" in Shadwell's *The Sullen Lovers*, his attacks on Dryden thus followed the literary line laid down by Shadwell, who had praised Jonson and attacked Dryden in the preface to that play, published in 1668, to which Dryden replied in passing in his "Defence of the Essay."[41] Others joined the fray, following the same lead. Richard Flecknoe, the eccentric Irish priest whose poetry often praised the Catholic members of the Howard family, periodically published collections of pseudo-Jonsonian epigrams, including one in praise of Dryden; for a new edition in 1671, he added a poem called "Former Plays and Poets Vindicated," directly replying to the Epilogue to Part II of the *Conquest*.[42]

Ned Howard was no real threat to Dryden, since his attempts at drama, like his even more wretched poems, were merely the amusements of a gentleman amateur. Flecknoe was also unimportant. But Shadwell, a professional who depended on the theatre for his livelihood, was a more formidable rival. In his new play, *The Humorists*, acted in the same month as *The Conquest of Granada*, Shadwell moved the controversy onto the stage: he introduced a character called Drybob, the first of a number of theatrical versions of Dryden.[43] In contemporary slang, a "dry bob" was a harmless or glancing blow; in sexual contexts, it was also a term for coition without emission. Shadwell's Drybob, whose impotence is literary, is described in the Dramatis Personae as "A Fantastick Coxcomb, that makes it his business to speak fine things and wit as he thinks; and alwayes takes notice, or makes others take notice of any thing he thinks well said" (I, 191). Overly impressed with his own wit, proud of his knowledge of literature, music, and dance, Drybob is not unlike Sir Positive At-All, Shadwell's caricature of Sir Robert Howard in *The Sullen Lovers*, but he bears an even closer family resemblance to such later caricatures of Dryden as Mr. Bayes in Buckingham's *The Rehearsal* and the Tutor in Joseph Arrowsmith's *The Reformation*.

Shadwell creates a spoken idiom for Drybob by repeating two phrases he had first used against Dryden in 1668, when he accused him of "imagining that all the Wit in *Playes* consisted in bringing two persons upon the Stage to break Jests, and to bob one another, which they call Repartie" (I, 11). Dryden had replied, "I am none of those who endeavour to break Jests in Company, or make reparties" (IX, 8), but Shadwell obviously saw that claim as a piece of false humility. His Drybob makes weak efforts at such gestures of humility, but those efforts reveal his inflated pride in his own cleverness. When Bridget, a servant to Lady Loveyouth, calls him "the Chief of all the Wits," Drybob's answer reveals his hypocrisy: "I! no alas, not I; I know they will have me one amongst them, do what I can, but deuce take me, if I care much for the Name on't. Indeed I do value my self upon Reperty a little" (I, 204). A few lines later, he criticizes a rival as "a damn'd dull fellow, he cannot break a jest in an hour" (I, 205); both phrases are frequently repeated.[44] Shadwell's implication that Dryden actually valued himself on his skill at repartee was solidly based: in his first published piece of literary criticism, the dedication to *The Rival Ladies* (1664), Dryden had defended dramatic rhyme by referring to "the quickness of Reparties," in which "the suddain Smartness of the Answer and the Sweetness of the Rhyme, set off the Beauty of each other," and in the same paragraph, he had referred to "Imagination in a Poet" as "a faculty so Wild and Lawless, that, like an High-ranging Spaniel, it must have Cloggs tied to it" (VIII, 100–01). Shadwell makes Dryden's metaphor ludicrously literal: Drybob makes his first entrance carrying a French dog, and when he presents the dog to Theodosia, he sings a ridiculous song in which the word "Clog" is put to another use:

> I hope it is your pleasure
> To accept of this Dog for a Treasure,
> From him that loves you beyond all measure
>   Which may mystically shew
>   What to your Eies I owe.
> That of your affection I have put on the Clog,
> And am your most humble Servant and Dog.
> With a Bow, Wow, Wow, &c.
>
>   [I, 214]

Crazy, Drybob's rival for Theodosia, courts her by declaring, "I feed a Flame within, which so torments me," a line Drybob correctly identifies as "stole out of a Play," namely Dryden's *Secret Love* (IV, ii, 23). Drybob runs away from a duel, as Dryden was accused of having done after the publication of the "Defence" (I, 216), displays a detailed knowledge of astrology (I, 242), and prides himself on his "University Learning" (I, 243). He even complains that "stoppage of Wit [is] as great a pain to me as stoppage of Urine" (I, 224), just possibly our earliest evidence that Dryden suffered from kidney stones.[45]

Dryden can hardly have been unaware of so specific an attack, but he refrained from any immediate reply. Shadwell's play was not notably successful, and Drybob was not at the center of its plot. Shadwell's main targets in the original version were the Countess of Castlemaine and the court gallant Henry Jermyn; even though he made significant alterations before actually staging the play, it "met with the clamorous opposition of a numerous party . . . resolved, as much as they could, to damn it," and had to be salvaged by the addition of dances.[46] The attention of the theatrical world was fixed upon *The Conquest of Granada*, and we have no evidence that anyone noticed

Shadwell's particular references to Dryden, who evidently concluded that silence would be wise. Several years later, in *Mac Flecknoe*, he had an opportunity for an answer in kind, but in the interim, there was apparently some kind of reconciliation. When Shadwell published *The Humorists*, in April of 1671,[47] he attempted to deny that any of his characters had been intended as specific satire:

> I challenge the most clamorous and violent of my Enemies (who would have the Town believe that every thing I write, is too nearly reflecting upon persons) to accuse me, with truth, of representing the real Actions, or using the peculiar, affected phrases, or manner of speech of any one particular Man, or Woman living.
>
> I cannot indeed create a new Language, but the Phantastick Phrases, used in any Play of mine, are not appropriate to any one *Fop*, but applicable to many. [I, 185]

Since he had called Drybob "A Fantastick Coxcomb," I suppose Shadwell had that character particularly in mind in this strained apology. Even more surprising are his direct compliments to Dryden in the same preface. Although Shadwell continues to praise Ben Jonson, as he had in all his previous prefaces, and therefore to disagree with Dryden, he now approaches that controversy with caution:

> And here I must make a little digression, and take liberty to dissent from my particular friend, for whom I have a very great respect, and whose Writings I extreamly admire; and though I will not say his is the best way of Writing, yet, I am sure, his manner of Writing it is much the best that ever was. . . . His Verse is smoother and deeper, his thoughts more quick and surprising, his raptures more mettled and higher; and he has more of that in his writing, which *Plato* calls σώφρονα μάνιαν [sound madness], than any other Heroick Poet. And those who go about to imitate him, will be found to flutter, and make a noise, but never rise. [I, 186–87]

We shall never know how serious Shadwell was in this apparent praise, or what caused his change of heart. Perhaps he was genuinely impressed by *The Conquest of Granada*; perhaps he and Dryden drank a friendly pint of beer together and reconciled their differences. They had a common patron in the Duke of Newcastle and common enemies in the Howard brothers; they would both soon join the young playwright John Crowne in a pamphlet attack on a dramatic newcomer, Elkanah Settle, whose first play, *Cambyses*, was on stage in January 1671, and whom Shadwell may have had in mind here as an imitator of Dryden who could only "flutter, and make a noise." Despite that one instance of temporary alliance, the rivalry between Shadwell and Dryden generated intense literary and political hostility, and Dryden's refusal to rise to the bait provided by Drybob is a remarkable instance of his early resolve to remain aloof from controversy. In "The Defence of the Epilogue," an essay attached to the published version of *The Conquest of Granada* (in print by 7 February 1672), he defends his earlier criticism of Ben Jonson by enumerating some of Jonson's grammatical faults, but carefully refers to those who had attacked him as his friends, responding in kind to Shadwell's conciliatory gestures. Calling Jonson "the most judicious of Poets," Dryden says "he always writ properly; and as the Character requir'd: and I will not contest farther with my Friends who call that Wit: It being very certain, that even folly it self, well represented, is Wit in a larger signification" (XI, 213).

At this point, the rivalry between Dryden and Shadwell did not have a political dimension, but an even more formidable adversary, the Duke of Buckingham, already had political, social, and literary reasons for his hostility to Dryden. Politically, Buckingham knew that Dryden was associated with his old adversaries Clarendon and Ormonde, and with his current rivals Arlington and Clifford. Those enmities, old and new, were not disinterested squabbles about foreign or domestic policy, but consequences of bitter class hostility. As a born aristocrat, Buckingham disliked sons of the gentry who rose in rank through their abilities: he particularly resented the political ascendancy of Arlington, a former secretary, who aggressively played the part of an old Cavalier by wearing a patch on his nose to cover a saber scar, just as he resented the literary ascendancy of Dryden, another mere gentleman, who was now playing the part of a court wit by writing delicately sexy lyrics and witty comic dialogue.

In the spring of 1671, while Arlington and Buckingham were opposing each other as candidates for Chancellor of Cambridge University (Buckingham won), Dryden was at work on an elegant new comedy, *Marriage A-la-Mode*, a much more sophisticated version of the double-plot play he had tried before in *Secret Love*. He was freed from any immediate theatrical duties at the end of March, when the theatres closed for six weeks because of the death of the Duchess of York. Not much later, probably in June, he made a visit to the court at Windsor, where he became intimate with the dashing young Earl of Rochester, who helped correct the manuscript of the new play and showed it to the King.[48] The polished repartee of the courtly characters in this play may thus owe something to Rochester,[49] and if Shadwell may be believed, Dryden himself quickly learned to imitate Rochester's rakish speech, if somewhat crudely. In *The Medal of John Bayes* (1682), Shadwell claims that "At *Windsor* in the company of several persons of Quality, Sir *G*[eorge] *E*[therege] being present," Dryden responded to a question about how to spend the afternoon by saying, "*Let's Bugger one another now, by G—d*" (p. 3). His caricature Dryden also "Commends *Reeve*'s Arse, and says she Buggers well, / And silly Lyes of vitious pranks does tell" (p. 4). Obviously, this kind of hearsay can hardly be verified, but such bisexual braggadocio, expressed in similarly vulgar language, is commonplace in Rochester's verse. Yet when Rochester turned against Dryden a few years later, he also accused the Laureate of clumsy obscenity. Sir Charles Sedley, according to Rochester, was the acknowledged master of "songs and verses mannerly obscene,"

> That can with a resistless charm impart
> The loosest wishes to the chastest heart.
> . . . .
> Dryden in vain tried this nice way of wit,
> For he to be a tearing blade thought fit.
> But when he would be sharp, he still was blunt:
> To frisk his frolic fancy, he'd cry, "Cunt!"[50]

Dryden may have occasionally used such language, though I see no reason to imagine that his casual references to sodomy, if indeed they occurred, were anything more than verbal attempts to play the role of the court wit. But the amorous songs in his new comedy, like the songs in the *Conquest*, are polished exercises in the more "mannerly" idiom of the court. As the curtain goes up, for example, Doralice and her servant Beliza sing a lovely lyric, libertine but hardly obscene:

> Why should a foolish Marriage Vow
>   Which long ago was made,
> Oblige us to each other now
>   When Passion is decay'd?
> We lov'd, and we lov'd, as long as we cou'd,
>   Till our love was lov'd out in us both:
> But our Marriage is dead, when the Pleasure is fled:
>   'Twas Pleasure first made it an Oath.

[I, i, 3–10]

In fact, Rochester's later attempt to denigrate Dryden for obscenity is more likely to be a complex example of the class prejudice his friend Buckingham held for both Arlington and Dryden. Buckingham, Sedley, and Rochester engaged in acts of public violence, drunkenness, and obscenity, and wrote verses that were not merely suggestive but deliberately disgusting. At some level, they evidently believed that they were above the law, which rarely punished them for their excesses, above ordinary morality, above literary criticism. What they may actually have resented in Dryden, then, was not his failure to emulate their literary style but his success. If a plainspoken Northamptonshire squire could write such courtly lyrics as those in *Marriage A-la-Mode*, the claim that the ability to write such lyrics was a matter of aristocratic birth was clearly damaged.

By taking an attractive actress as his mistress, Dryden had also begun to act the part of one of his "betters." Buckhurst, Sedley, Sir Robert Howard, and the King all had actresses among their mistresses, and at least one playwright had recently been rewarded for his theatrical wit by acquiring a famous court beauty as his mistress. The last important play produced before the theatres closed to mourn the Duchess of York was William Wycherley's first comedy, *Love in a Wood*, a success that brought its author to the attention of Barbara Villiers, now Duchess of Cleveland, with whom he began an affair. By this time, Barbara had been replaced in the King's affections, which were divided between Louise de Kéroualle, a French beauty whom he later made Duchess of Portsmouth, and Nell Gwyn, who proudly called herself "the Protestant whore" in order to avoid confusion with the unpopular Catholic Kéroualle. Socially and financially, the successful Laureate presumably felt that he could claim at least a minor actress for himself, and the speed with which Buckingham pounced on the Reeves affair in *The Rehearsal* again suggests resentment of Dryden as a social climber.

A better than average writer of courtly lyrics, Buckingham liked to fancy himself the leader of the court wits. He organized evening parties in which such men as Buckhurst, Rochester, John Lord Vaughan, Sprat, Martin Clifford, Shadwell, and "Hudibras" Butler traded quips and composed impromptu lampoons; three such squibs satirizing Ned Howard's ludicrous attempt at a heroic poem, *The British Princes*, survive.[51] If the professional writers and clergymen in this group were dependent on Buckingham, and could therefore be expected to support him in his opposition to

Dryden, the aristocrats were more independent. Buckhurst had already been Dryden's patron for several years; sometime in 1671, he wrote a note to Joseph Williamson, Lord Arlington's secretary, supporting a piece of lobbying by Dryden on behalf of one Captain Bowen.[52] Vaughan's laudatory verse epistle was printed with the published *Conquest*. Rochester, who had helped Dryden prepare and promote *Marriage A-la-Mode*, would remain his friend for several more years. For Buckingham, a higher-ranking aristocrat who had been brought up with the King and the Duke of York, Dryden's acceptance by such courtiers was probably irritating.

We cannot know when Buckingham first heard about *Marriage A-la-Mode*; he might have seen the manuscript that was circulating at court, or he might have had to wait for the first performance, which probably took place in late November or early December 1671.[53] While the play is not a direct attack on Buckingham or anyone else, there was much in it that might have increased the Duke's hostility to Dryden. The high plot concerns the discovery of two beautiful young peasants, Leonidas and Palmyra, who are the long-lost son of the rightful king and the long-lost daughter of the usurping king. When they appear at court, the people there consider it unlikely "that such a Youth, so sweet, so graceful, / Should be produc'd from Peasants" (I, i, 350–51). Hermogenes, a faithful retainer who has served as foster-father to both children, retorts:

> Why, Nature is the same in Villages,
> And much more fit to form a noble issue
> Where it is least corrupted.
>
> [I, i, 352–54]

Himself the product of a tiny village, Dryden doubtless enjoyed writing these lines, which reflect not only his pride in his origins but his recent experiences with the jealousies and hypocrisies abounding at court. When he published the play in 1673, he mentioned those experiences in his dedication to Rochester: "In my little Experience of a Court (which I confess I desire not to improve) I have found in it much of Interest, and more of Detraction: Few men there have that assurance of a Friend, as not to be made ridiculous by him, when they are absent" (XI, 221–22). Dryden may have been thinking specifically of Buckingham's habit of imitating Arlington by wearing a black nose patch and strutting with a staff.

While the high plot develops the issues of class and power in a way unlikely to please Buckingham, the low plot concerns the taking of mistresses, though the double adultery we are led to expect never quite takes place.[54] Dryden must have had his own marital situation in mind when writing the opening song, and when writing the bit of dialogue in which Melantha, disguised as a boy, twits the similarly disguised Doralice for being so inexperienced as to "make it the height of your ambition to get a Player for your Mistris" (IV, iii, 138–39). Again, Dryden would seem to be inviting satire directed at himself, especially since the player who was now his mistress played the servant Philotis, who extracts money and a jewel from Palamede in an effective comic scene (V, i, 30–76). But literary controversy, like political controversy, was brutal, and the self-mockery we have noticed in the passages about mistresses Dryden wrote about this time may ultimately be a self-protective device. By describing Fame as a "little Mistriss of the town" or joking about a young man who aspires "to get a Player for [his] Mistris," Dryden may have been attempting to forestall similar remarks from his theatrical rivals. Part of the game in the lighthearted and frequently obscene verse-writing of the court wits was to acknowledge that the pursuit of mistresses was a foolish and dangerous business, while making no secret of one's own involvement. The verse letters of Buckhurst and Etherege, with their self-loathing references to venereal complications, are good examples.

But if Dryden knew how to write like a court wit, he was ultimately careful to separate his enterprise from theirs. In the epilogue, Rhodophil explains that "our Poet"

> would not quite the Women's frailty bare,
> But stript 'em to the waste, and left 'em there.
> And the men's faults are less severely shown,
> For he considers that himself is one.

[ll. 13–16]

Dryden implies that he is not only a man, but a man liable to the faults of his male characters, namely the pursuit of mistresses, and takes pains to contrast his gentle treatment of sexual foibles with that of other satirists:

> Some stabbing Wits, to bloudy Satyr bent,
> Would treat both sexes with less complement:
> Would lay the Scene at home, of Husbands tell,
> For Wenches, taking up their Wives i' th' *Mell*,
> And a brisk bout which each of them did want,
> Made by mistake of Mistris and Gallant.
> Our modest Authour, thought it was enough
> To cut you off a Sample of the stuff.

[ll. 17–24]

These lines sound suspiciously like a description of a play called *The Mall*, in which a maid pretending to be her mistress is stripped on stage and hauled into bed by the husband, while another wife appears at what she thinks is an assignation made by her husband, and copulates with another man in the dark.[55] Given that kind of competition, Dryden's comedy was indeed "modest." The line about "Some stabbing Wits, to bloudy Satyr bent" employs the same metaphor that Rochester would turn against Dryden a few years later, accusing him of wishing to be "a tearing blade," but may also glance at Buckingham, who had slain the husband of his mistress in a celebrated duel two years earlier.

By the time *Marriage A-la-Mode* came on stage, Buckingham had been opposed to Dryden for at least four years. Dryden's recent theatrical and courtly successes may have sharpened his enmity, but politics, the original motive for Buckingham's hostility, remained important. He knew that Dryden owed considerable allegiance to York, Arlington, and Clifford, whom he hated passionately, and he was beginning to suspect that he had been tricked by his ministerial colleagues in the negotiations leading to the treaty with France. In October 1671, a month or so before Dryden's new play came on stage, Buckingham learned just how successful his rival Arlington had been in moving against him. The expeditionary force of 6,000 men that he was expecting to command in the coming war was suddenly shrunk to 2,400, and command was given jointly to the Duke of Monmouth and the Earl of Ossory, who was Ormonde's son and Arlington's brother-in-law. By mid-November "soldiers and horses . . . for the French King's service" were massed at Dover, where bad weather detained them until early December.[56] Dryden's prologue refers to "Warriours, in Red Wastecoats," who have already bid the actresses farewell in the "Tireing-room," but Buckingham, despite his courage and ambition, was not among them.

Sensing a chance to settle both literary and political scores, Buckingham revised his old farce *The Rehearsal*, which had lain fallow since before the plague. Drawing on Dryden's heroic plays, especially *The Conquest of Granada*, and on his detailed knowledge of the personal idiosyncrasies of the poet and the minister, Buckingham created Mr. Bayes, a ludicrous figure designed to attack Dryden and Arlington at the same time. Bayes insists on taking two gentlemen, Smith and Johnson, to watch a rehearsal of his new play, a pastiche of scenes illustrating the excesses of heroic drama, with many particular parodies of Dryden's work. As Smith and Johnson watch with increasing disbelief, Bayes obnoxiously praises his own wit and invention, but when he attempts to demonstrate a tricky dance step to the actors, he falls and breaks his nose, making possible a later entrance with a black patch resembling Arlington's. Although such eyewitnesses as Evelyn seem to have taken the play as a merely literary satire, it pretty clearly has a political dimension as well.[57]

Since Buckingham's play was staged by the King's Company, Dryden must have been aware of the preparations, but he made no move to interfere. As a sharer in the company, he actually had reasons to hope for the play's success. On 9 November 1671, the rival Duke's Company had opened its new theatre in Dorset Garden with a performance of *Sir Martin Mar-All*. Well equipped and closer to the City than the Duke's old theatre in Lincoln's Inn Fields, the new playhouse was an important factor in the process by which the Duke's Company gradually gained the upper hand in the theatrical competition.[58] *The Conquest of Granada* had helped the King's Company hold its own in the previous season, and *Marriage A-la-Mode* was probably staged at this time in order to draw patrons away from the new rival house. But Buckingham's farce, which made an entire play out of the frame-breaking Dryden had occasionally practiced in such episodes as the epilogue to *Tyrannick Love*, and which gave the talented John Lacy a wonderful opportunity to practice his skills as an impersonator, promised to be popular indeed, and with the available audience reduced by the military mobilization, popular plays were a matter of survival. One tradition insists that Buckingham and Buckhurst maneuvered Dryden into sitting in their box at the premiere; if he did so, the pain he felt at the play's often acute criticism of his work may have been lessened by the knowledge that he stood to profit from its success.[59]

Years later, Dryden explained his silence in a curious and puzzling passage:

I answer'd not *The Rehearsall*, because I knew the author sate to himself when he drew the Picture, and was the very *Bays* of his own Farce: Because also I knew, that my Betters were more concern'd than I was in that Satire: And lastly, because Mr. *Smith*,

> and Mr. *Johnson*, the main Pillars of it, were two such Languishing Gentlemen in their
> Conversation, that I cou'd liken them to nothing but to their own Relations, those
> Noble Characters of Men of Wit and Pleasure about the Town. [IV, 8–9]

The last of the reasons is the least plausible, since Smith and Johnson are hardly the
"main Pillars" of the play; perhaps the old Dryden, choosing to forget that the play
came on stage at the moment in his career when he was most concerned to act the part
of a man "of Wit and Pleasure about the Town," meant to dissociate himself from the
social milieu of the onlookers. The claim that "my Betters were more concern'd than I"
may indicate Dryden's awareness that some of Buckingham's satire was directed at
Arlington, though why he should have been so obscure about that fact in 1692, when
Arlington and Buckingham were both dead, is puzzling. The first reason, however, is a
piece of interesting literary and social criticism. Mr. Bayes is monstrously proud of his
own inventive talents, praising his most ludicrous lines as full of true poetic fire. Despite
Dryden's gestures of modesty and reticence, Shadwell had already recognized and
pilloried the Laureate's similar creative pride in the figure of Drybob. Still, Dryden
realized that Buckingham was more explicit in claiming originality and praising himself
than he had ever been. "A man so various that he seem'd to be / Not one, but all
Mankinds Epitome," Buckingham was not only a "Chymist, Fidler, States-Man, and
Buffoon," but had a driving need to do all those things well, spending considerable
money on alchemical experiments and practicing his virtuoso technique on the violin
with surprising discipline. As far back as the subtle poem to Sir Robert Howard in 1660,
Dryden had known the difference between professional writers and gentleman amateurs; he had the knack of complimenting gentleman writers for their "native sweetnesse" without debasing his own professionalism. But Buckingham, by aggressively
seeking to compete in the world of the theatre, by taking the trouble to read through
scores of plays in search of lines to parody, was (perhaps unconsciously) becoming a
version of his own Mr. Bayes. *The Rehearsal* is not a whimsical skit tossed off in an
evening, but a carefully crafted, brilliantly effective attack on the theatrical conventions
of heroic drama. If Buckingham thought Dryden was presumptuously climbing above
his station by acting, however briefly and clumsily, the part of a court wit, the old
Dryden thought Buckingham had been descending socially by acting, however successfully, the part of a professional writer.

    In the absence of more objective primary documents describing Dryden's person-
al characteristics, biographers have often used *The Rehearsal*, and some of the details by
which Buckingham characterizes Bayes, such as the taking of snuff and the wearing of
spectacles, are confirmed by other sources.[60] Others, such as the maintaining of a
commonplace book or the jotting down of witty comments heard in a coffeehouse, are
certainly plausible. Less verifiable, though intriguing, is the notion that the poet prepared himself for various kinds of writing by taking different kinds of medicine. Here is
Bayes:

> If I am to write familiar things, as Sonnets to *Armida*, and the like, I make use of Stew'd
> Prunes only; but, when I have a grand design in hand, I ever take Phisic, and let blood:

for, when you would have pure swiftness of thought, and fiery flights of fancy, you must have a care of the pensive part. In fine, you must purge the Belly. [II, i, 114–20]

In a late letter to Tonson, Dryden passes on a message to his wife, asking her to buy him "a sieve full . . . [of] Damsins . . . to preserve whole"; the fondness for "Stew'd Prunes" was evidently real. Moreover, two eighteenth-century commentators on *The Rehearsal* allege that something like the medical regimen proposed here was indeed Dryden's practice, and his letters show us a man much concerned with his health.[61] But Buckingham was also concerned to attack Arlington, and his earlier version of *The Rehearsal*, written before the Plague, had been aimed at Sir Robert Howard and Davenant, aspects of whose characters may remain in Bayes. Although these uncertainties and Buckingham's obvious hostility dictate caution, the picture of Bayes that emerges in *The Rehearsal* fits well with some aspects of the picture of Dryden that emerges from other evidence: he was, on the testimony of his prologues and dedications, proud of his poetic "fancy," impatient with his critics, likely to undervalue his predecessors, eager to invent dramatic devices that would be new and surprising, and not entirely at ease when dealing with those who outranked him.

However accurate or exaggerated the portrait, it cannot have been fun for Dryden to watch. With extraordinary self-restraint, he refrained from striking back, even though Buckingham's secretary, Martin Clifford, was circulating manuscript letters critical of his work at about this time, hoping to rile him into replying.[62] Instead, Dryden actually paid Buckingham a compliment. In the "Defence of the Epilogue," published within two months of the premiere of *The Rehearsal*, he expanded on his contention that the present age was more gallant than the last, and praised the court for "mixing the solidity of our Nation with the air and gayety of our [French] neighbours" (XI, 217). As an example of improved courtly speech on the stage, he cited "*Fletcher's Don John*," a character in *The Chances*, the last two acts of which Buckingham had rewritten several years earlier: "I may affirm, without suspision of flattery, that he now speaks better, and that his Character is maintained with much more vigour in the fourth and fifth Acts than it was by *Fletcher* in the three former" (XI, 215). "Without suspision of flattery" is Dryden's magnificently understated way of pointing out that no one could suspect him of wanting to flatter Buckingham after the rough treatment he had just suffered at the hands of his courtly rival.

Shipwreck

Dryden probably wrote the essays attached to the published *Conquest* in the fall of 1671, when he had good reason to regard himself as having "swept the stakes." All of his plays since the plague had been successful; the members of the King's Company, among whom Anne Reeves was now officially included, had gained much by the bargain that made the poet a sharer in their profits. If the new theatre at Dorset Garden was helping the Duke's Company, they had nonetheless opened that theatre with one of the two plays by Dryden in their repertoire. Thanks to his theatrical successes and his careful dedications, the Laureate enjoyed the patronage of several powerful men, and had risen sufficiently in the eyes of the court to feel safe in dedicating the *Conquest* to the Duke of York, who was preparing to go to sea again with the fleet. As that dedication suggests, Dryden continued to cherish the idea of an epic poem on the Stuarts, and hoped to gain backing for such a project from the court. If Buckingham was a powerful enemy, Dryden could take comfort in the support offered him by his powerful friends Arlington and Clifford. The arrears of his salary had been paid a year earlier, and a document confirming the plan to repay his old loan to the King had been drawn up on 29 November.[63] Secure in his fame and fortune, Dryden could afford to ignore the likes of Richard Flecknoe, Ned Howard, and Martin Clifford; his conciliatory gestures toward Shadwell and even Buckingham in these essays are further evidence of his self-confidence.

But between the writing and publishing of these essays, a series of unhappy events plunged Dryden and his company into disaster. On 20 January 1672, the government took the bold step of closing the Exchequer; by suspending payments for a full year, the Treasury hoped to keep sufficient funds on hand to carry on the war against the Dutch. The Stop of the Exchequer, which was eventually renewed for another full year, necessarily delayed the repayment of Dryden's loan, but his friend Clifford, who had engineered the Stop, took care to limit the damage to the Laureate, whose salary was paid in full in 1672 and 1673, while the pleas of many of the government's other creditors went unheeded.[64] For the Drydens, who were experienced at waiting for payments from the Treasury, the delay in repaying the loan might not have been a serious blow by itself, but it came coupled with another financial reversal. Five days later, on the evening of 25 January, the Theatre Royal at Bridges Street, site of most of Dryden's dramatic triumphs, burned to the ground, destroying all of the company's stage properties, including Fuller's expensive sets for *Tyrannick Love* and Streeter's "glorious perspectives" for *The Conquest of Granada*. Richard Bell, a promising young actor, died in the fire.

The King's Company never fully recovered from the burning of the playhouse. Dryden, who had been enjoying a steady income as a sharer, probably found his contract with the company a financial liability for the next several years.[65] On the literary side, the consequences were also serious: having lost their playhouse and their sets, the King's players were now unable to produce the kind of play in which Dryden was most interested, the grand, heroic spectacle of epic proportions. Needing some-where to act, they took over the old theatre at Lincoln's Inn Fields, which the Duke's Company had abandoned. A month and a day after the fire, they mounted an appropri-ately titled play by Fletcher called *Wit without Money*, for which Dryden, faithfully performing his job as the house playwright, provided a revealing prologue. "The Curtaine being drawne up all the Actors were discover'd on the stage in Melancholick postures, & Moone [Mohun] advancing before the rest speaks as follows, addressing himself chiefly to ye King":

> So shipwrack't Passengers escape to Land,
> So look they, when on the bare Beach they stand,

> Dropping and cold; and their first fear scarce o're,
> Expecting Famine on a Desart Shore;
> From that hard Climate, we must wait for Bread,
> Whence even the Natives forc't by hunger fled.
> Our Stage does humane chance present to view,
> But ne're before was seen so sadly true,
> You are chang'd too, and your pretence to see
> Is but a nobler name for charity.
>
> [ll. 1–10][66]

In Dryden's poem to Lady Castlemaine, written at the beginning of his theatrical career, he had referred to "Sea-men shipwrackt on some happy shore," and in *Annus Mirabilis*, memorably developing the theme of "humane chance," he had argued that "the proud designs of human kind" inevitably lead us to "suffer Shipwrack every where," but the shipwreck of *The Wild Gallant* was a playful metaphor, and the shipwrecks of the Second Dutch War, though real enough, had not touched Dryden. This time, however, the metaphor was "sadly true"; until they could build a new theatre, the King's Company would be playing in an inadequate and unfashionable house, without the sets and costumes that had been such an important part of their previous successes. "Famine" was a real possibility, and the praise to the King for his charity bespeaks the real exigency of the situation. Moreover, some "blind unmanner'd *Zealots*" had been quick to pronounce the fire "a judgement on the Stage"; Dryden answers this argument as he had answered the Dissenting view of the Fire of London:

> But, as our new-built City rises higher,
> So from old *Theaters* may new aspire,
> Since Fate contrives magnificence by fire.
>
> [ll. 20–22]

"Magnificence," however, was over for the King's Company. Not only was Lincoln's Inn Fields ill-suited to grandiose productions, but when Killigrew's men built their new theatre in Drury Lane, they designed it for ordinary plays, not for the expensive and elaborate operatic productions Betterton had in mind for Dorset Garden. When the new theatre finally opened in March of 1674, Dryden's prologue accurately called it a "Plain Built House."[67]

The King, like his players, was also passing through a crisis, in which financial problems were among his most pressing concerns. Thanks to the Secret Treaty of Dover, he was receiving private funds from his cousin Louis, but the presence of many Roman Catholic clergymen in London in the previous spring had so disturbed the Parliament that Charles had only been able to insure an adequate supply of public money by issuing a proclamation ordering "Jesuits and Romish priests" to leave England by 1 May 1671; he also ordered the existing laws against "popish recusants" enforced.[68] Having thus secured funds, the King prorogued Parliament, which did not meet again until February 1673. The announced plan to persecute Catholics, however, was a fraud. On 14 May 1671, well after the deadline, John Evelyn attended a dinner at Lord Clifford's; the guests included Arlington, the Catholic peer Lord Arundell of

Wardour, Philip Howard (cousin to Dryden's wife and Grand Almoner to the Queen), and two French abbots. Even the credulous Evelyn now began to suspect Clifford of "a little warping to *Rome*."[69]

In early 1672, with Parliament safely prorogued and his money secured by the Stop of the Exchequer, Charles reversed himself. On 12 March, just two weeks after the King's attendance at *Wit without Money*, the old pirate Sir Robert Holmes engaged the Dutch Smyrna fleet, providing an excuse to begin the long-planned war, and on 15 March, claiming that he wished to unite the nation, Charles issued a Declaration of Indulgence, suspending all the laws against nonconformists and recusants that he had recently ordered enforced. Dissenting ministers could now hold public services if licensed, and Nathaniel Whiting promptly procured a license to hold services at Lady Pickering's home in Titchmarsh. Lady Elizabeth Pickering, born a Montagu, was the widow of Dryden's early patron Sir Gilbert, and had led the riot in opposition to the conforming rector in 1660; she evidently clung to her Dissenting beliefs. Dryden's aged mother, who had returned to her Titchmarsh home, was probably among those who heard Whiting preach at the manor house; the religious language in her will sounds a distinctly Puritan note, and Lady Pickering was among the witnesses to that will.[70] Roman Catholics were also now free to worship in their homes and private chapels, a decision welcome to the many recusant relatives of Dryden's wife. Her cousin Philip, credited in Catholic circles with having persuaded the King to issue the Declaration, was rewarded with a bishop's mitre on 26 April, though Rome prudently kept his promotion secret.[71] Since he had relatives in both religious groups to whom indulgence was granted, the Poet Laureate could see the Declaration of Indulgence as an advanced and tolerant policy, though the baptism of his son Erasmus-Henry at St. Martin's in the Fields, his regular parish church, is evidence that he continued to conform to the Established Church. The Anglican hierarchy and their Parliamentary allies, however, regarded the Declaration as a serious threat; looking back on these events some years later, Evelyn remembered "Papists & Swarmes of sectaries now boldly shewing themselves in their publique meetings . . . to the extreame weakning the Church of England & its Episcopal Government."[72]

On 17 March, England declared War on Holland. Charles and his ministers, especially Clifford and Arlington, were desperately gambling on victory. If the alliance with France could bring the English control of the trade routes, the resulting economic prosperity might allow the crown to repay the mounting debts incurred by the Stop of the Exchequer; military and economic success might even make the King's subjects willing to swallow his new religious policy. Buoyed up by the short-lived support with which that new policy and the military adventure were greeted, the King promoted several members of his cabinet in April: the Earl of Lauderdale became the Duke of Lauderdale; Arlington, the Earl of Arlington; Ashley, the Earl of Shaftesbury; and Clifford, Baron Clifford. Only Buckingham, already a Duke, failed to profit, and he suffered the further indignity of being refused permission to fit out a ship for the fleet.[73] But the "humane chance" of Dryden's prologue was to prove as unkind to the King's navy as it had to his players. In the first major battle of the war, fought off Sole Bay on 28

May, the Duke of York had to move his command post from disabled ships twice, and the Earl of Sandwich, brother to Lady Pickering, was drowned; their valor was not sufficient to attain a decisive victory, in part because the French ships with whom they were allied failed to obey orders and became separated from the main fleet. Although both sides claimed victory, Sole Bay was another costly draw.[74]

At the time of the last national crisis, brought on by the Dutch victory in the Medway in the summer of 1667, the Duke's Company had satisfied the popular demand for lively entertainment with a comedy starring James Nokes, *Sir Martin Mar-All*; that play, partly written by Dryden, was still in their repertory. During the spring and summer of 1672, while the nation worried over a new set of political, religious, and military uncertainties, the Duke's players were again able to provide lighthearted relief; their new smash hit was another comedy starring Nokes, *The Citizen Turned Gentleman*, adapted from Molière by the theatrical newcomer Edward Ravenscroft. The prologue took a conventional swipe at "Playes of Rhyme and Noyse with wond'rous show," but Dryden was probably less irritated by that reference to the *Conquest* than by the sheer success of Ravenscroft's loosely structured romp, the most popular scenes of which portrayed an elaborately costumed scheme to convince Mr. Jorden (Nokes) to give up his worldly goods in order to become a Turkish "Mamamouchi." According to John Downes, the prompter of the Duke's Company, "Mr. *Nokes* in performing the *Mamamouchi* pleas'd the King and Court, next Sir *Martin*, above all Plays."[75] Yet this play, despite its appeal to courtly and popular audiences, was precisely the kind of comedy Dryden had argued against in the preface to *An Evening's Love* a year earlier:

> Most of those Comedies, which have been lately written, have been ally'd too much to Farce: and this must of necessity fall out till we forbear the translation of *French Plays*: for their Poets wanting judgement to make, or to maintain true characters, strive to cover their defects with ridiculous Figures and Grimaces. [X, 204]

To his credit, Dryden goes on to acknowledge that some of his own plays are guilty of these faults; he specifically mentions *An Evening's Love* and may also have been thinking of *Sir Martin Mar-All*. The play on which he was now at work, *The Assignation*, was a further development of the more courtly or heroic kind of comedy he had attempted in *Secret Love* and perfected in *Marriage A-la-Mode*. Its prologue continues the argument of the earlier preface, twitting the audience for applauding "Th' unnatural strain'd Buffoon" (l. 24), repeating some of the "Turkish" gibberish spoken in Ravenscroft's "Mamamouchi" scenes, and attributing the success of the rival play to "Grimace and habit" (l. 38).

Comic theory notwithstanding, "ridiculous Figures and Grimaces," a vastly superior playhouse, and an increasingly versatile set of players had given the Duke's Company so decisive a competitive edge that there was even talk of merging the companies. Joseph Haines, who had been active in the King's Company from 1668 through *The Rehearsal*, attempted to begin that process on his own, deserting to the Duke's House for Ravenscroft's play, in which he played a French dancing master.[76] In an epilogue Dryden wrote at this time for a special revival of *Secret Love* with an all-female cast, he let Anne Reeves, who had played one of the male roles, acknowledge and defuse current criticisms of his company. Glancing at the increasing age of Hart and Mohun, Reeves asks,

> Why should not then we Women act alone,
> Or whence are men so necessary grown,
> Ours are so old, they are as good as none.

[ll. 9–11]

Pointing to the real reason for the female cast, she boasts that "our Legs are no ill sight, / And they will give you no ill Dreams at night" (ll. 22–23). The conclusion couples a rejection of the plan to join the houses with a swipe at Ravenscroft's success; the setting up of "a female house," says Reeves,

> would prevent the houses joyning too,
> At which we are as much displeas'd as you.
> For all our Women most devoutly swear,
> Each would be rather a poor Actress here,
> Then to be made a *Mamamouchi* there.

[ll. 26–30]

Age was an issue for the playwright as well. Like Elkanah Settle, whose first play, *Cambyses*, had been staged earlier in the season, Ravenscroft was significantly younger than Dryden, and most of Dryden's literary quarrels during the next several years would pit him against younger men: not only did such aspirants to theatrical fame as Settle and Ravenscroft prove irritating at a time when the wretched state of the King's Company limited the scope of Dryden's own theatrical ambitions, but other critics continued their attacks on *The Conquest of Granada*, now in print and therefore open to detailed verbal criticism. Martin Clifford's letters, the last of which is dated 1 July 1672, are exercises of this kind, and some university wits were also beginning to engage in the coffeehouse criticism that would produce a series of anti-Dryden pamphlets and another lampooning drama in 1673. Dryden's impatience with this kind of criticism shows in the second edition of *Tyrannick Love*, published some time in 1672: in a paragraph added to the preface, he defends several lines that had been thought incorrect by pointing to their sources in Horace and Ovid, and goes out of his way to defend a line in *The Indian Emperour*, which had been attacked by "R. F." in the pamphlet of 1668, as "borrow'd from Virgil" (X, 113). Although these additions to the preface make the usual gesture of indifference to the "little Criticks," the fact that Dryden bothered to make changes at all suggests his sensitivity to criticism, particularly at this time.

Dryden hoped to answer the success of Ravenscroft and the cavils of his critics with his new comedy, *The Assignation, or Love in a Nunnery*, which was probably on stage not later than the early autumn of 1672.[77] Although it involves masquerades and mistaken identities, this play turns on a psychologically potent device: a father (the Duke of Mantua, played by Mohun) and his son (Prince Frederick, played by Kynaston) both love the same woman (Lucretia, played by Rebecca Marshall). When the Duke, whose "boyling passion" is occasionally suggestive of Maximin, attempts to banish his son and lay claim to Lucretia in the garden of her convent, the rivalry threatens to develop military and political consequences, which are avoided in a high-minded scene of mutual repentance and forgiveness (V, iv). This intense sequence falls into blank verse, but most of the play is in prose, and Dryden was not so caught up in the avoidance of farce as to forget his audience: he loaded the dialogue of the three other pairs of lovers with double-entendres of the sort that had proved effective in *Marriage A-la-Mode*, wrote a showcase part as the bungling servant Benito for Haines, who had been reclaimed from the rival house, and gave Anne Reeves another chance to display her legs as the page Ascanio.

Despite these concessions to the audience, the play failed. When Dryden published it a year later, he took a philosophical attitude toward this misfortune in the dedication to Sir Charles Sedley:

> It succeeded ill in the representation, against the opinion of many the best Judges of our Age, to whom you know I read it, e're it was presented publickly. Whether the fault was in the Play it self, or in the lameness of the Action, or in the number of its Enemies, who came resolv'd to damn it for the Title, I will not now dispute: that wou'd be too like the little satisfaction which an unlucky Gamester finds in the relation of every cast by which he came to lose his Money. I have had formerly so much success, that the miscarriage of this Play was onely my giving fortune her revenge: I ow'd it her; and she was indulgent that she exacted not the paiment long before. [XI, 319]

The gambling imagery echoes the happier claim to have "swept the stakes" in the preface to *The Conquest of Granada* a year earlier; it also reflects an increasingly urgent reality. The disasters of the first part of 1672—the Stop of the Exchequer, the playhouse fire, and the unsettled international situation—were beyond Dryden's control, but this failure, whatever the deficiencies of the theatre or the cast, was partly his. We cannot know who "the best Judges of our Age" were (I should suppose they included Sedley, Buckhurst, and Rochester), but Dryden was not writing only for them. Their approval of the play when Dryden read it to them was doubtless gratifying to him, but at this point, he also needed to pay his bills. The death of his wife's mother, who was buried beside her husband at Westminster Abbey on 24 August 1672, apparently did not result in a legacy, and repayment of the £500 he had lent to the King remained blocked by the Stop of the Exchequer. His share in the King's Company probably yielded no money this year, when a successful run for his play might have helped both Dryden and his theatrical partners. That left him with his income from Blakesley and his salary as Poet Laureate—clearly not enough to support a house, a wife, three children, servants, and a mistress.

Dryden's reference to "Enemies, who came resolv'd to damn it for the Title" is also intriguing. Plays were cried down by organized groups often enough, and the subtitle might indeed have proved irritating to various parties. In the absence of hard evidence, I might offer the speculation that those who "came resolv'd to damn" Dryden's play were taking one of a very few available opportunities to protest against the Declaration of Indulgence. With Parliament meeting only for a day in order to be formally prorogued again, there was no political outlet for opposition to the policies of the government; a play with a Catholic milieu by a poet closely associated with Clifford, who was promoted to the powerful position of Lord Treasurer in this same autumn, offered a tempting target.

Whatever its causes, the failure of *The Assignation* provided ammunition for Dryden's literary rivals. In the prologue to *The Careless Lovers*, acted by the Duke's Company in March of 1673, Ravenscroft congratulated the audience for disliking Dryden's play:

> Nay, and you Damn'd his Nunns in Masquerade.
> You did his Spanish Sing-Song too abhor,
> . . . .
> In fine, the whole by you so much was blam'd,
> To act their Parts, the Players were asham'd.[78]

Another Duke's Company comedy called *The Reformation*, by a Cambridge wit named Joseph Arrowsmith, was also on stage around this time; it features an English Tutor, a lineal descendant of Drybob and Mr. Bayes, who explains his writing methods to his Italian pupils:

> You must always have two Ladies in Love with one man, or two men in love with one woman; if you make them the Father and the Son, or two Brothers, or two Friends, 'twill do the better. . . . But give me leave and mark it for infallible, in all you write reflect upon religion and the Clergy; you can't imagine how it tickles.[79]

Since *The Assignation* had featured a father and son in love with the same woman and a prologue and epilogue continuing Dryden's usual habit of "reflect[ing] upon religion and the Clergy," I suppose Arrowsmith had that recent failure particularly in mind, though he also shows considerable familiarity with Dryden's earlier plays, prologues, and prefaces. The play was not notably successful, and Dryden ignored it, as he had both earlier theatrical caricatures of himself.

The same spring also saw the publication of four pamphlets originating in university discussions of Dryden's work, largely taken up with close considerations of the impropriety of various passages in *The Conquest of Granada*.[80] The first of these ephemeral productions, *The Censure of the Rota*, originated in Oxford; its author dredges up some of the charges against Dryden made by "R. F." in 1668. A reply from Cambridge, falsely entitled *The Friendly Vindication of Mr. Dryden*, accuses him of depending on his reputation to insure the success of any new play, and sees the failure of *The Assignation* as exposing this tactic:

> A forward Wit of his Party . . . said . . . that Mr. *Dryden* writ as well as any man that could write no better; and was no less himself in his last Play, called *Love in a Nunnery*; the fate whereof had occasioned him to confess, that he sometimes by their help had slurred a Play on the Audience, and that it was his utmost expectation and desire, that they would continue still so kind as to question nothing of his; that it had been likewise acknowledged by him, that he intended the same, for this last Catholick *Intrigue* of his, which he called *pawming of a Play on the Town*. [pp. 15–16]

Dryden had indeed spoken critically of his own work in several prefaces and prologues, and in casual conversation, if Pepys' secondhand report that he called *An Evening's Love* "a fifth-rate play" may be credited. But his implied defense of this play in the dedication to Sedley, in which he portrays himself reading the manuscript for the "best Judges," suggests quite careful preparation; he does not employ the old excuse of haste, which he had used for *Tyrannick Love*, and *The Assignation* does not look like a play quickly slapped together with the intention of palming it off on the town. What made its failure hurt, I suspect, was that Dryden had worked hard on the play and expected it to succeed. The phrase describing the play as a "Catholick *Intrigue*" may remind us that even the university pedants responsible for these pamphlets were not engaged in merely literary criticism; the author clearly meant to associate Dryden with the unpopular Declaration of Indulgence.

The other play by Dryden produced during this theatrical season, *Amboyna, or the Cruelties of the Dutch to the English Merchants*, was a direct response to the political crisis. The naval campaign after Sole Bay had remained indecisive, but in June of 1672, the land army of Louis XIV captured three of the seven United Provinces; Prince William of Orange, installed as chief Stadtholder during this crisis, resisted not only these armed incursions but an attempt by Buckingham and Arlington to force a negotiated peace.[81] The spectacle of Protestant Holland invaded by a Catholic army was unlikely to win popular support in England—especially in view of the Stop of the Exchequer, the failure of the Navy to secure a decisive victory, and the publication, early in the same month, of a pamphlet revealing the true contents of the Secret Treaty of Dover.[82] Mindful of his official duties, and quite possibly prompted by Clifford, Dryden therefore wrote a propaganda play designed to stir up hatred toward the Dutch. A massacre of Englishmen by the Dutch, which took place at Amboyna in the East Indies in 1623, had become part of official anti-Dutch mythology. Working in haste from a pamphlet first published in 1624 but now freshly reprinted,[83] Dryden dramatized this story of Dutch sadism, adding scenes of rape and torture; he may also have been attracted to this subject because the King's Company had inherited the Duke's Company's old scenery, and could use the sets left over from Davenant's *The Cruelty of the Spaniards in Peru* for this drama.[84]

Dryden had no illusions about *Amboyna*; "though it succeeded on the Stage," he wrote to Clifford in the dedication to the published version, it "will scarcely bear a serious perusal, it being contriv'd and written in a Moneth, the Subject barren, the Persons low, and the Writing not heightned with many labored Scenes" (sig. A4r–v). The last phrase refers to Dryden's decision to write most of the play in prose; only a few scenes are in blank verse, and rhyming appears only in two songs and a few exit lines. The play's success, for which Dryden's claim here is the only evidence, was not sufficiently marked to alter the straitened circumstances of the King's Company, and may have been undercut by a similarly titled drama produced in November of 1672 by one Anthony di Voto, who staged puppet shows in a booth at Charing Cross.[85] The date of Dryden's play is uncertain, but I should suppose it was first produced during the noisy meetings of Parliament, which returned from its long prorogation on 4 February 1673. Many of the "country" members, irritated by the Declaration of Indulgence, the Stop of the Exchequer, and the uncertain progress of the war, were far more opposed to the Catholic French, now official allies, than to the Protestant Dutch, now official enemies, and Dryden's prologue specifically refutes the arguments of those reluctant to attack the Dutch on the grounds of a common religion:

> The doteage of some *Englishmen* is such
> To fawn on those who ruine them; the *Dutch*.
> They shall have all rather then make a War
> With those who of the same Religion are.
>
> . . . .
>
> Religion wheedled you to Civil War,
> Drew *English* Blood, and *Dutchmens* now wou'd spare:
> Be gull'd no longer, for you'l find it true,
> They have no more Religion, faith—then you.
>
> [ll. 5–8; 15–18]

Dryden's argument here parallels the speech on behalf of the government's policy delivered at the opening of Parliament by Shaftesbury, who had become Lord Chancellor when Clifford was made Lord Treasurer. Echoing Cato's speech to the Roman Senate on the Punic Wars, Shaftesbury used the phrase "Delenda est Carthago,"[86] and Dryden's epilogue ends with the same allusion:

> As *Cato* did his *Affrique* Fruits display:
> So we before your Eies their *Indies* lay:
> All Loyal *English* will like him conclude,
> Let *Caesar* Live, and *Carthage* be subdu'd.
>
> [ll. 19–22]

Neither Shaftesbury's speech nor Dryden's play could sway the Commons, however; the spring session of 1673 was the worst Parliamentary defeat of a king and his ministers since the Long Parliament. Faced with a clear majority unwilling to vote financial supplies for the war unless the Declaration of Indulgence was withdrawn, Charles surrendered, cancelling the Declaration on 8 March. Opposition to the Declaration was not unanimous: The Catholic playwright Sir Samuel Tuke spoke bravely in favor of toleration,[87] and Sir Robert Howard, later a fierce opponent of Catholicism, supported the King on this occasion, explicitly opposing the removal of Roman Catholics from their military posts. Howard may have been thinking of the recusants in his own family, including his oldest brother, but his position in this debate was also related to patronage: in October 1671, he had gained the valuable position of Secretary to the Treasury, and in March of 1673, he was granted the reversion of the even more lucrative post of Auditor of the Receipt, to which he succeeded the next July. This office entitled its holder to £1 from every £100 disbursed; Howard held it until his death in 1698.[88] For the next fifteen years, during which Dryden was drawing, or attempting to draw, his salary from the crown, he could reflect, doubtless unhappily, on the fact that his brother-in-law would pocket 1 percent of any money he received.

Pressing their advantage, the Parliamentary majority opposed to the King's policies now passed a Test Act requiring all those holding office to declare that transubstantiation did not occur during the eucharist. The debate on this issue exposed the split in the ministry, with Clifford speaking passionately against the Test, only to be disputed by Shaftesbury.[89] On Easter Sunday, the day after Parliament recessed, the Duke of York failed to take Anglican communion, in effect officially declaring his Catholicism; since he remained the heir apparent, the Anglican interests now victorious in the Parliament had to face the prospect that a Papist would eventually inherit the throne. In June, refusing to take the oath required by the Test, York left his post as Lord Admiral of the fleet. In the same month, for the same reason, Lord Treasurer Clifford retired to the country, but before leaving office, he peremptorily ordered the repayment of Dryden's old loan, with interest.[90]

The Laureate's gratitude for this act, undertaken when Clifford might have been preoccupied with his personal crisis, shows powerfully in the dedication to *Amboyna*, written between Clifford's retirement and his death on 18 August 1673. Dryden thanks Clifford for his "*Generosity* and *Goodness*," and gives a glowing description of his friend's performance in his official post:

> If any went ill-satisfy'd from the Treasury, while it was in your Lordship's Manage-ment, it proclaim'd the want of Desert, and not of Friends: You Distributed your Masters Favour with so equal hands, that *Justice* her self could not have held the Scales more even. . . . No man attended to be deny'd: no Man brib'd for Expedition: want, and desert were pleas sufficient. [sig. A3r]

We may hear the voice of a man who had probably spent many a fruitless morning at the Treasury during the past decade, first about his wife's dowry, then about his own loans and pensions, and who knew that his brother-in-law was increasing his already sub-stantial fortune by receiving "brib[es] for Expedition." But Dryden's admiration for Clifford went beyond gratitude. At a time when his own fortunes were in decline, Dryden was genuinely impressed with Clifford's response to the loss of power:

> Fortune may desert the wise and brave; but, true Vertue never will forsake it self. 'Tis the Interest of the World that Vertuous Men should attain to Greatness, because it gives them the power of doing good. But, when by the Iniquity of the Times, they are brought to that extremity, that they must either quit their Vertue or their Fortune, they owe themselves so much, as to retire to the private exercise of their Honour; to be great within, and by the constancy of their Resolutions, to teach the inferior World, how they ought to judge of such Principles, which are asserted with so generous and so uncon-strain'd a Tryal. [sig. A3v]

Fifteen years later, Dryden would face a similar choice; his decision then to remain a Catholic and lose his public posts owed much to the example of Clifford. In a larger sense, the equanimity with which Dryden dealt with many of his future crises and reversals was grounded in lessons he learned during these difficult years in the early 1670s. As he had pointed out in the epilogue to Part I of *The Conquest of Granada*, success, whether theatrical, financial, or political, could last no longer than beauty. The same fortune that had allowed a talented Dryden to "sweep the stakes" or a virtuous Clifford to "attain to Greatness" could just as quickly deal them a playhouse fire or a Test Act. Clifford was unable to sustain the classical ideal of retirement that Dryden praises here as an appropriate response to such reversals; beaten and ill, he hanged himself just two months after his resignation.[91] But Dryden, who wrote some of his finest poetry during the twelve years he lived after his own "disgrace" in 1688, ultimately had stronger personal resources, developed in part during the 1670s, a decade in which he learned to take a larger view of his own personal and literary worth than that suggested by the success or failure of a particular play.

CHAPTER EIGHT

"Another Taste of Wit"
1673–1676

"Protection and Patronage"

Parliament's actions during the spring session of 1673 significantly weakened the King's position, though Charles, ever the survivor, adroitly shifted his policies and weathered the storm. The same Parliamentary actions indirectly weakened Dryden's quasi-regal position in the literary world. Fourteen years earlier, in the troubled period following the death of Cromwell, he had failed to anticipate the Restoration and its consequences, but this time, he was all too aware of his vulnerability. Urgent political, financial, and theatrical problems inevitably affected the choices he made as he wrestled with the literary issues of inspiration, correctness, poetic license, and dramatic form—all of which he considered carefully during the next five years. The same problems also helped him discover his aptitude for satire. The inconsistencies and uncertainties of Dryden's actions during this period begin to make sense when we recognize that he was not only rethinking his aesthetic principles but struggling to survive. As he faced the personal crisis of his forties, a decade in which the style and direction of his writing changed decisively, he could hardly ignore the political and theatrical crises through which the nation and the King's Company were passing.

In the halcyon days of the early Restoration, the succession to the throne was no real cause for worry, but in the 1670s, with everyone aware that the Queen was barren and the Duke of York a Catholic, the succession became a critical issue. Though careful as always to keep lines of communication open to those who might help him financially, Dryden maintained his loyalty to the Duke of York. He had ample reason to know that such political alliances would figure in literary controversies; the author of the *Friendly Vindication*, for example, though primarily concerned to criticize Dryden's literary practice, tried by innuendo to identify him with those policies of toleration toward Catholicism successfully reversed by Parliament in the spring of 1673.[1] York's resignation from the Navy and Clifford's resignation from the Treasury in June of that year probably weakened Dryden's position at court; well before those resignations, indeed, as soon as the Test Act was passed, the Poet Laureate began searching for new patrons. In the dedications of *Marriage A-la-Mode* and *The Assignation*, both published in the spring of 1673,[2] he made a bid for support from Rochester and Sedley, literary courtiers who were not then openly engaged in political or religious controversy.

Aware of the jealousies endemic to the court, Dryden hoped these new patrons would protect him from his various rivals, but simple money was also among the reasons why he sought their aid. A significant part of his income between 1668 and 1672 had come from his position as a sharer in the King's Company, and the interruption of what had once been dependable profits from that source made his financial situation precarious; a year after the fire, there had been no real improvement. The Duke's Company were thriving in their elaborate playhouse: in February 1673, for example, with the town full for the opening of Parliament, they staged a spectacular version of Davenant's old revision of *Macbeth*, with Betterton in the starring role and a dazzling array of visual effects for the scenes of ghostly magic. At the same time, there was additional competition from a group of French comedians, who acted from December 1672 until May 1673, apparently pleasing even those who could not understand what was being said. Dryden glances ruefully at both rivals in a prologue for *Arviragus*, written during the French company's stay:

> With sickly Actors and an old House too,
> We're match'd with Glorious Theatres and New,
> And with our Alehouse Scenes, and Cloaths bare worn,
> Can neither raise Old Plays, nor New adorn.
> If all these ills could not undo us quite,
> A brisk *French* Troop is grown your dear delight.
> . . . .
> Each Lady striving to out-laugh the rest,
> To make it seem they understood the Jest.
>
> [ll. 1–6; 17–18]

The French comedians were followed immediately by an Italian "Scaramouche" and his company, who stayed until September. For Dryden, who had attacked English imitations and translations of continental farce, and whose own inclinations ran to very different kinds of drama, the success of these visitors, which depended upon their skill at "ridiculous Figures and Grimaces," can hardly have been pleasing. It was a sign that the audience would not easily be won back to the King's Company, even when the new playhouse was finished, and a sign that winning them back might require writing exactly the kind of farce he had so strenuously attacked in recent prefaces and prologues.

The failure of *The Assignation*, a play in which he had attempted to combine comedy with serious emotional engagement, also made Dryden's position as the leading playwright shakier than it had looked a few years earlier. He had always had competition in comedy, not only from Shadwell, for whom he had no particular respect, but also from Wycherley and Etherege, who are surely the men he calls "the best Comick Writers of our Age" in the dedication of *Marriage A-la-Mode* to their friend Rochester:

I am sure, if there be any thing in this Play, wherein I have rais'd my self beyond the ordinary lowness of my Comedies, I ought wholly to acknowledge it to the favour, of being admitted into your Lordship's Conversation. And not only I, who pretend not to this way, but the best Comick Writers of our Age, will joyn with me to acknowledge, that they have copy'd the Gallantries of Courts, the Delicacy of Expression, and the Decencies of Behaviour from your Lordship, with more Success, then if they had taken their Models from the Court of *France*. [XI, 221]

Besides combining a compliment to Rochester with a compliment to several of his close friends, this modest disclaimer to skill in comedy repeats a judgment upon himself that Dryden had already made many times, and indirectly strikes a pose of unconcern at the failure of *The Assignation*. By referring to the "ordinary lowness" of his comedies and alleging that he "pretend[s] not to this way," Dryden is staking his primary claim to greatness on heroic drama.

Yet even in that arena, where no professional playwright had challenged him for some time, Dryden was beginning to encounter problems: in March or April 1673, about the time he was writing the dedications to Sedley and Rochester, a cast including noble amateurs gave several court performances of Elkanah Settle's *Empress of Morocco*, a clumsy imitation of Dryden's heroic plays. Settle based his plot on a lurid story of poisonings and stabbings in the Moroccan court, which he had apparently heard from the Catholic peer Henry Howard, Earl of Norwich and effective head of the senior line of the Howard family, who had made an unsuccessful embassy to Morocco in 1669–70. When he published the play, Settle thanked the Earl for arranging the production at court, and there is no reason to doubt his testimony. Dryden thus saw an upstart imitator of his style securing the patronage of one of his wife's most powerful relatives, patronage that brought him not only the prestige of a court performance by the same kind of cast that had once presented *The Indian Emperour*, but even a courtesy appointment as a royal servant.[3] Both this court production and a public production by the Duke's Company, which opened in July, had elaborate scenery and music; Matthew Locke, a talented composer, provided the music for the masque of Orpheus and Eurydice, during which one of the murders takes place.[4] At the court performances, Elizabeth Howard, daughter of the Countess of Suffolk and cousin to Dryden's wife, spoke prologues written by Rochester and John Sheffield, Earl of Mulgrave: neither is a distinguished poem; both allude gently to the King's fondness for women. Within a year, these two young courtiers would be leading distinct factions, with Rochester supporting Buckingham and Mulgrave supporting the Duke of York; Dryden, not surprisingly, would throw in his lot with Mulgrave. At this point, however, the significant fact, potentially distressing to Dryden, was that men who agreed about little else were both willing to contribute verses to Settle's play.

In need of the financial aid and political protection that only aristocratic patrons could provide, Dryden hoped that Rochester and Sedley, to whom he was now turning, would afford him "Protection and Patronage," words he explicitly couples in the dedication to *Marriage A-la-Mode*. Even when flattering Rochester, he reveals how closely he has observed the man to whom he is writing and how carefully he has considered his own situation. By all accounts, Rochester could be as charming as the

Portrait of John Wilmot, second Earl of Rochester, after Jacob Huysmans, ca. 1665–70.

stage characters modelled upon him by such writers as Etherege, but in assessing Dryden's compliments to Rochester on his exemplary "Gallantries," we ought to remember the Erasmian notion of "exhorting to virtue under the pretext of praise." Rochester's poems are not notable for their "Delicacy of Expression," nor were his public actions examples of "the Decencies of Behaviour," so both men were probably aware of the potential for irony in those phrases. In the similar dedication of *The Assignation* to Sedley, Dryden compares the courtly poets of his own age to those who flourished under the emperor Augustus: Lord Treasurer Clifford becomes "a better *Maecenas*"; Sedley himself, "a more Elegant *Tibullus*." The "way of Living" of those classical patrons and poets, according to Dryden, "was to pursue an innocent and inoffensive Pleasure":

We have, like them, our Genial Nights; where our discourse is neither too serious, nor too light; but always pleasant, and, for the most part, instructive: the raillery neither too sharp upon the present, nor too censorious on the absent; and the Cups onely such as will raise the Conversation of the Night, without disturbing the business of the Morrow. . . . I have often Laugh'd at the ignorant and ridiculous Descriptions which some Pedants have given of the Wits; . . . those wretches Paint leudness, Atheism, Folly, ill-Reasoning, and all manner of Extravagances amongst us, for want of under-standing what we are. [XI, 321]

By insistently using the first-person plural, Dryden claims membership in the group; by suggesting that the wits are actually moderate, even in their drinking habits, he seeks to paint an ideal form of social interaction, doubtless aware of the contrary reality. Sedley had twice been arrested for public nudity, and Rochester later told Bishop Gilbert Burnet that "for five years together he was continually Drunk: not all the while under the visible effects of it, but his blood was so inflamed, that he was not in all that time cool enough to be perfectly Master of himself."[5] Still, Dryden had excellent social and rhetorical reasons for his defense of the wits as genial and temperate. Even though he was eight years older than Sedley and sixteen years older than Rochester, he was sufficiently conscious of rank to know that he could only advise them to moderate their behavior under the guise of compliment. By arguing here for a distinction between the true wits (including himself) and the ignorant pedants who attack them, Dryden is also setting up his conclusion, which alludes briefly to the author of *The Censure of the Rota*, whom he calls "my contemptible Pedant," and the author of the *Friendly Vindication*, "who follows the Fashion at a distance, and adores the *Fastidious Brisk* of *Oxford*." Dryden wisely avoids a point-by-point defense, already offered for him by two men he claimed not to know: the lively writer of *A Description of the Academy of the Athenian Virtuosi*, and the teenaged Charles Blount, author of *Mr. Dreyden Vindicated*. Loftily refusing to "gratifie the ambition of two wretched Scriblers, who desire nothing more than to be Answer'd," he contents himself with the general contrast between pedants and wits, concluding with a compliment that sets Sedley up as a shield to protect him from his attackers:

I wish to be hated by them and their Fellows, for the same reason for which I desire to be lov'd by you. And I leave it to the world, whether their judgment of my Poetry ought to be preferr'd to yours; though they are as much prejudic'd by their Malice, as I desire you should be led by your Kindness, to be partial to, sir,
      Your most Humble
      and most Faithful Servant,
            John Dryden. [XI, 323]

Just as he uses Sedley here to help him cast aspersions on his literary attackers, Dryden uses Rochester in the other dedication to help him criticize his enemies at court. Probably thinking most particularly of Baptist May, the Keeper of the King's Privy Purse, he refers to "a midling sort of Courtiers, who become happy by their want of wit," and complains that "there is no such persecution as that of fools." Perhaps May, a rakish friend of Buckingham, had attempted to stand in the way of payments of money

to Dryden; perhaps Rochester also had reasons to dislike May. Some such set of affairs
would help make sense of Dryden's thanking Rochester for taking pity on

> other men, who being of an inferiour Wit and Quality to you, are yet Persecuted, for
> being that in Little, which your Lordship is in Great. For the quarrel of those people
> extends it self to any thing of sense; and if I may be so vain to own it amongst the rest of
> the Poets, has sometimes reach'd to the very borders of it, even to me. [XI, 222]

Dryden's talk of being "Persecuted" for being witty, like his earlier phrase about
the "persecution . . . of fools," anticipates a letter he wrote four years later, which
complains of "Mr. Mayes persecuting me" (*Letters*, p. 12).[6] In the later complaint, the
context is clearly financial, and in this dedication, Dryden explicitly thanks Rochester
for financial help: "you have not onely been careful of my Reputation, but of my
Fortune." Dryden is evidently aiming at May when he speaks of "those people, who
have the liberality of Kings in their disposing; and who, dishonouring the Bounty of
their Master, suffer such to be in necessity, who endeavour at least to please him." His
effusive praise of Rochester for having been "Sollicitous to supply my neglect of my
self" may remind us that if Dryden was not, as he modestly claimed, "on the very
borders" of sense, he was, to his cost, "on the very borders" of the court. His personal
friendship with Clifford was the only reason why he secured regular payment of his
salary during the Stop of the Exchequer and the repayment of his long-standing loan
two months after this dedication. Already aware that Clifford's days as Lord Treasurer
were numbered, he may have been praising Rochester for some small financial favor in
the hope that the Earl would continue to look after his financial interests in the ever-
treacherous court.[7]

The post of Lord Treasurer was by now the most powerful position in the government, and in the spring of 1673, many prominent politicians were angling for that job.
From Dryden's point of view, any change at the Treasury was undesirable, though the
change that occurred did not actually hurt him. Passing over the survivors of the Cabal,
Charles chose a new and tough administrator, Thomas Osborne, later Earl of Danby.
Since Osborne had begun his political career as a protégé of Buckingham during the
attack on Clarendon, and since there is no evidence that he had even met Dryden when
he came to power, the Laureate had every reason to fear interference with his salary.
Yet Osborne, despite inheriting a confused and strained Treasury, managed to pay
Dryden in full, and almost on time, for the years 1673–77.[8] But that salary, even as
supplemented by the Blakesley rents, was not sufficient to support the kind of life
Dryden had enjoyed during the years when he also realized significant income from the
theatre. Unhappy with the state of the King's Company and disillusioned with the
drama in general, Dryden now wanted some source of additional income that would
allow him to work on the epic poem he had proposed several years earlier. His desire to
secure the leisure to write in nondramatic forms was probably also a motive for this
approach to Rochester and Sedley.

But Dryden's attempt to use his acquaintance with Rochester and Sedley to secure
his fortune and reputation was doomed, in part because of their continuing loyalty to
Buckingham and his continuing loyalty to York, and in greater part because class lines

Portrait of Thomas Osborne, Earl of Danby, from the studio of Peter Lely, ca. 1680.

and fundamental differences in personality effectively prevented any true intimacy or candor between these mercurial aristocrats and the more stolid Dryden, regardless of the literary interests they shared. The idealized picture of Rochester that Etherege has left us in the character of Dorimant, hero of *The Man of Mode*, captures the delight in dissembling central to the life of the court wits, just as the negatively exaggerated picture of Dryden that Buckingham has left us in the character of Bayes, butt of *The Rehearsal*, captures the clumsiness of Dryden's attempt to play the part of a sophisticate. As early as 1663, Pepys had realized "that it is a troublesome thing for a man of any condition at Court to carry himself even, and without contracting enemies or envyers; and that much discretion and dissimulacion is necessary to do it."[9] But "discretion and dissimulacion" did not come naturally to Dryden: "Dissembling . . . is not my talent," he wrote to his sons in 1697, acknowledging "the plain openness of my nature" (*Letters*, p. 93).[10] If many of his dedications are exercises in written dissembling, he was evidently less skilled at dissembling in person; he could write like a court wit, but he could not be one. The "Genial Nights" described in the dedication to Sedley were not imaginary, but if the court wits were willing to include Dryden in some of those evenings, they were not finally willing to accept him as one of them, and Dryden recognized the difference between his social skills and theirs. While praising Rochester's courtly graces, he revealingly refers to "my little Experience of a Court (which I desire not to improve). . . . Few men there have that assurance of a Friend, as not to be made ridiculous by him, when they are absent" (XI, 221–22). I have already suggested that he may have been thinking of Buckingham's skill in ridiculing Arlington; he would soon learn that Buckingham's friend Rochester was just as likely to ridicule his absent acquaintances, including a poet named Dryden, whom he effectively criticized in a brilliant imitation of Horace that was circulating in manuscript early in 1676, and cruelly referred to in a later letter as "a rarity which I cannot but be fond of, as one would be of a hog that could fiddle, or a singing owl."[11] This caricature accurately captures the condescending attitude of an aristocrat who liked to believe that the making of poetry required noble birth, and who was thus unable to account for the literary skills of a man like Dryden.

The medium in which relations between needy writers and aristocratic patrons were conducted was flattery, so it should not surprise us that flattery is the mode and the subject of the one private letter we have from Dryden to Rochester. The Earl responded to the published dedication for *Marriage A-la-Mode* in a lost letter, evidently complimentary; Dryden's reply, written in the summer of 1673, begins with an elaborate apology for his delay in answering. The Laureate calls himself "unmannerly and ungratefull," and explains that he has finally been roused from his "Sloath" by his unwillingness "to receive, as if it were my due, the most handsom Compliment, couchd in the best language I have read, and this too from my Lord of Rochester, without showing myself sensible of the favour" (*Letters*, pp. 7–8). Without knowing exactly what the "most handsom Compliment" was, we are at some disadvantage in interpreting this letter, but the problematic nature of the relationship between poet and patron shows clearly enough. Both men knew there was a fine line between the witty and artful exaggeration endemic to the panegyric style and the ironic exaggeration that turned compliment into criticism. Both of them also knew that some of the compliments Dryden had paid Rochester in the published dedication were not his due, and Dryden may well be hinting here that he recognizes a similar potential for irony in the "handsom Compliment" of Rochester's letter.[12] He goes on to explain that

> the Shame of seeing my self overpayd so much for an ill Dedication, has made me almost repent of my Addresse. I find it is not for me to contend any way with your Lordship, who can write better on the meanest Subject than I can on the best. I have onely ingag'd my selfe in a new debt, when I had hop'd to cancell a part of the old one: And shou'd either have chosen some other Patron, whom it was in my power to have

oblig'd by speaking better of him than he deserv'd, or have made your Lordship onely a hearty Dedication of the respect and Honour I had for you, without giveing you the occasion to conquer me, as you have done, at my own Weapon. [p. 8]

Dryden's playful contention that he "shou'd . . . have chosen some other Patron" reveals another reason why his relationship with Rochester could not last. By far the most talented of the court wits, Rochester was beginning to show his considerable powers as a poet, so the competition that had marred Dryden's relations with Sir Robert Howard and assured him the enmity of Buckingham was even more inevitable here. Although Dryden's later works show evidence of Rochester's influence,[13] the courtly patrons with whom he had longer and more satisfactory relationships were less talented writers like Buckhurst and Mulgrave, men who turned to Dryden for help with their own poems, and who were conscious of their obligations toward a poet who praised their work beyond its deserts. The rueful admission that Rochester has conquered Dryden at his own weapon may refer to the high level of literary skill that Rochester had doubtless displayed in his letter; it probably refers even more specifically to the "weapon" of flattery, a weapon Dryden himself wielded with consummate skill, at least on paper, but which he knew to be a two-edged sword.

In the remainder of the letter, trying hard to affect the sparkling style of a court gossip, Dryden offers to entertain Rochester, who was in the country, "with a thousand bagatelles every week," sent down from the city like a regular newsletter. He does not, however, discuss the progress of the war, in which costly naval battles fought off the coast of Holland in May and June had again proved indecisive, except to "hope your Lordship will not omitt the occasion of laughing at the Great Duke of B[uckingham] who is so oneasy to [him]self by pursueing the honor of Lieutenant Generall which flyes him, that he can enjoy nothing he possesses." Buckingham had secured that rank in May, but resigned it in July when he was again passed over for the post of commander of the English land forces.[14] By encouraging Rochester to laugh at Buckingham, whom he goes on to criticize as "unfit to command an Army" and as "lov[ing] idlenesse so well as to destroy his Estate by it," Dryden was probably sending up a trial balloon. Fully aware of the close ties between his enemy Buckingham and his potential patron Rochester, he was trying to see whether Rochester might be sufficiently detached from Buckingham to laugh at him—and thus sufficiently detached to prove a reliable backer of Dryden. These critical remarks on Buckingham, Dryden admits, "would easily run into lampoon, if I had not forsworn that dangerous part of wit." He then illustrates the dangers of satire, the form in which Rochester excelled and the form toward which his own work would soon move, by telling a story about Etherege, who had plugged appropriate English names into a translation of one of Boileau's satires, but "read it so often that it came to their eares who were concernd; and forc'd him to leave off the design e're it was half finish'd." Two versions of a remembered couplet from that lost satire follow; in the second, coyly referred to as the work of "one of [Etherege's] friends" and thus probably by Dryden himself, those held up to ridicule are Viscount Dunbar, Henry Brounckard, and Aubrey Vere, Earl of Oxford. Dryden obviously knew that Rochester had come

close to fighting a duel against Dunbar in March of 1673, as he indicates by calling
Dunbar "a Bully"; in the cases of Brounckard and Oxford, he may again have been
trying to join in the courtly game of ridiculing absent acquaintances.

Sensing that a letter from one court wit to another ought to contain more poetry
than a pair of couplets, Dryden sent Rochester a more substantial enclosure, though his
description of it is curiously apologetic:

> Because I deale not in Satyre, I have sent Your Lordship a prologue and epilogue
> which I made for our players when they went down to Oxford. I heare, since they have
> succeeded; And by the event your Lordship will judge how easy 'tis to passe any thing
> upon an University; and how grosse flattery the learned will endure. [p. 8]

The prologue and epilogue Dryden sent to Rochester had been spoken by Hart at a
performance of Jonson's *The Silent Woman* at Oxford in early July. The epilogue, like
the earlier prologue to *Arviragus*, complains about the French comedians; it also notices
the "*Italian* Merry-Andrews" who "quite Debauch'd the Stage with lewd Grimace"
and the "wicked Engines call'd Machines" that made *Macbeth* "the *Simon Magus* of the
Town." By sending this vigorously satiric poem to Rochester, Dryden was deliberately
demonstrating that he could indeed "deale . . . in Satyre." The epilogue closes with a
small gesture of praise to the university audience: unlike the foolish Londoners who
have been taken in by sight-gags and machines, says Dryden, the academic wits remember the worth of "Staple Authours" like Ben Jonson; their praise will help the
King's players raise the price of such plays when they return to London.

The "grosse flattery" to which the letter refers, however, comes in the prologue,
where Dryden praises the university wits as "*Athenian* Judges." He pictures the poets,
whose task it is to correct the "Follies and Faults" of society, returning to the university
to have their own follies corrected and "beg[ging] they may be better taught." In the
concluding lines, contrasting Oxford and London, Dryden identifies himself with
learning in order to cast aspersions on those "Haughty Dunces whose unlearned
Pen / Could ne'er Spell Grammar":

> Such build their Poems the *Lucretian* way,
> So many Huddled Atoms make a Play,
> And if they hit in Order by some Chance,
> They call that Nature, which is Ignorance.
> To such a Fame let mere Town-Wits aspire,
> And their Gay Nonsense their own Citts admire.
>
> [ll. 32–37]

"Our Poet," by contrast, knows that the gentlemen of the university are better judges
than mere "Citts."

> Not Impudent enough to hope your Praise,
> Low at the Muses feet, his Wreath he lays,
> And where he took it up Resigns his Bays.
> Kings make their Poets whom themselves think fit,
> But 'tis your Suffrage makes Authentique Wit.
>
> [ll. 42–46]

This was the gesture of obeisance that Dryden felt obliged to dismiss as "grosse flattery" when he sent the poem to Rochester, presumably because he had already used the same technique with the court wits. In the dedication to Sedley, he had identified himself with the court wits in order to cast aspersions on his university attackers (the "Athenian Virtuosi," according to one of his defenders). Now he was identifying himself with the "*Athenian* Judges" of the university in order to cast aspersions on "mere Town-Wits." Dismissing such a piece of rhetoric as flattery in a flattering letter is a piece of witty bravado, but it reveals, as do many of Dryden's activities in this period, an almost pathetic vulnerability. With his old patrons disabled by the Test Act, his theatrical company bested by the competition, his plays dissected by pedantic pamphleteers, and his domestic situation strained by his affair with Anne Reeves, Dryden felt the need for "Protection and Patronage." But the sources from which he sought that protection in 1673 were not fruitful: he could not really become a court wit in the Rochester mode, despite his occasional successes at imitating a courtly literary style, any more than he could really become an academic, though he later toyed with the idea of retiring from the literary fray to a post at Oxford.

This letter, probably written at the moment of greatest intimacy between Rochester and Dryden, is uncertain and cautious; the bravado is hollow, revealing Dryden's fear that Rochester would not prove a reliable patron, and in the months that followed, public events conspired to make it impossible for a poet loyal to York and a court wit loyal to Buckingham to maintain even a temporary alliance. In August, Prince Rupert fought another costly and inconclusive naval battle at Texel Bay; the French fleet, despite urgent signals, did not join the fight, and when word of that failure of the alliance reached England, the policy of the court was irreparably damaged. Charles would once again have to come to terms with the Dutch without securing the financial gains for which he had gone to war. Meanwhile, James, Duke of York, barred by the Test Act from such naval engagements, showed his Catholicism ever more clearly by taking a new bride. Acting on the advice of the Catholic priest Philip Howard, he chose Maria Beatrice, the fourteen-year-old daughter of the duchess Laura of Modena; Louis XIV, eager to secure a Catholic succession in England, provided a handsome dowry. Their marriage, which may have been celebrated by an English priest sent to Italy by Howard, took place by proxy on 30 September; the Earl of Peterborough, who had been sent to Modena in July to work out the details, took the vows for James.[15]

Parliament, which met on 20 October, immediately voted an address asking James to marry a Protestant; they were aware of the negotiations in Modena, but not of the proxy ceremony. Prorogued for a week, the legislators returned in an even uglier mood, refused to vote a bill of supply, and expressed their many grievances with the French alliance and the ministry. Charles prorogued them again on 4 November; on 9 November, he dismissed Shaftesbury, who cheerfully buckled on his sword and joined Sir Robert Howard in energetically promoting the old plan to have the King divorce the Queen. The new Duchess arrived, only to be greeted by the public burning of effigies of the Pope; James confirmed his marriage by taking the vows himself on 21 November.

When Parliament met once again on 7 January 1674, Lord Keeper Finch, who had replaced Shaftesbury, gave a speech advocating a fresh start; with Osborne moving

actively behind the scenes, Parliament now attacked Lauderdale, Arlington, and Buckingham, all of whom were constrained to defend their actions in support of the disastrous French alliance, which they did by blaming each other. All three were damaged:
Buckingham, despite efforts on his behalf by Sedley and Rochester, was dismissed
from all his offices in February; Arlington lasted until the next September, when he sold
his office as Secretary of State to his longtime aide Joseph Williamson and bought the
less important office of Lord Chamberlain; Lauderdale survived, though attacked in
several subsequent Parliaments. On 11 February, the King announced that he had
concluded a peace treaty with the Dutch; there was already talk of a marriage between
William of Orange, hero of the Dutch land defense, and Mary, James's daughter by his
first Duchess. On 24 February, in order to kill bills under debate that would have
further limited his power or begun the process of excluding his brother from the
succession, Charles prorogued his noisy Parliament, which did not meet again for over
a year.[16]

About the time Charles concluded his unsuccessful experiment with the French
alliance, Dryden was concluding his unsuccessful experiment with the Rochester-
Sedley alliance. We have no record of the Laureate's immediate response to the Duke's
new marriage, which was crucial to the politics of the next fifteen years; we do know that
the cautious Earl of Berkshire, Dryden's Catholic brother-in-law, suggested to James
that he "retire with his new Dutchess to Audly end, or some such place in the Country
remote from publick business, where he might hunt and pray without offence to any, or
disquiet to himself."[17] The arrogant James scoffed at this advice, and Dryden's later
actions suggest that his support for the Duke was more vigorous than Berkshire's.
Thanks to his relations with his wife's recusant kinsmen, Dryden knew that this new
marriage was not only anathema to the many Parliamentarians concerned to preserve
the Protestant succession, but cause for alarm among those Roman Catholics content to
be left alone; yet he continued to admire those stubborn qualities in James that had
already led him to compare the Duke to Achilles and Almanzor. A dedication he wrote
to James's new Duchess in 1677 is one of his most heavily perfumed pieces of prose, and
the dedication of *Aureng-Zebe* to the Yorkist Earl of Mulgrave, published early in 1676,
leaves no doubt that Dryden's old loyalty to James, itself the result of his early patronage
by Clarendon, remained intact.

Dryden probably made up his mind to ally himself with Mulgrave during the
winter of 1673–74, and Mulgrave's bitter enmity to Rochester, which had nearly
produced a duel on at least one occasion, was probably another factor in the demise of
the once-promising relationship between Dryden and Rochester. In dedicating *Aureng-Zebe* to his new patron, Dryden emphasizes Mulgrave's loyalty to his friends:
"Your kindness, where you have once plac'd it, is inviolable: And 'tis to that onely I
attribute my happiness in your love." Later in the same paragraph, he argues that it is
"the same composition of Mind, the same Resolution and Courage, which makes the
greatest Friendships, and the greatest Enmities" (sig. A3r). This discussion, which is
probably meant to allude to Mulgrave's troubles with Rochester, continues with a
proverb about forgiveness credited to "the Italians," perhaps a sidelong compliment to
James's new Duchess, and offers an explicit compliment to James himself, "A prince,

who is constant to himself, and steady in all his undertakings."[18] Dryden's own constancy to James, which would cost him dearly in the turmoil of the 1680s, owed something to the distaste he developed for the mercurial Rochester. Yet Dryden managed to learn literary lessons even from Rochester; it is surely no accident that his first couplet satire, *Mac Flecknoe*, probably written late in 1676, follows the path marked out by Rochester's "Allusion to Horace," which was circulating earlier in the same year.

The Controversy with Settle

Three days after the Duke's London wedding, the Term Catalogue advertised *The Empress of Morocco*, now printed in an ostentatious and expensive edition adorned with "Sculptures" picturing some of its more spectacular scenes. According to his later testimony, Dryden had not criticized Settle's play at the time of its court or public performances in the previous spring and summer:

> Though I found it then to be a Rapsody of non-sense, I was very well contented to have let it pass. . . . In order to this, I strain'd a point of Conscience to cry up some passages of the Play, which I hop'd would recommend it to the liking of the more favourable *Judges*. But the ill report it had from those that had seen it at *Whitehall*, had already done its Business with Judicious Men. [XVII, 83]

Dryden's claim that he was willing to overlook the faults of a young author and even praise "some passages" may well be true; a performance promoted by his wife's relatives and graced with prologues from the very courtiers whose support he was soliciting was hardly an occasion for public criticism. Nonetheless, Settle had given Dryden a possible reason to dislike him before those first performances: he had contributed an epilogue to Ravenscroft's *Careless Lovers*, a play whose prologue attacked the Laureate.

If Dryden politely "cried up" Settle's work in March or April of 1673, I believe he was already criticizing it in the Oxford prologue spoken in July. Although the criticism of ignorant authors in that prologue could apply to many playwrights, Dryden evidently had Settle in mind; the language of the prologue anticipates the language he later used in the preface and postscript to *Notes and Observations on the Empress of Morocco*, a collaborative attack on Settle published anonymously in early 1674.[19] The Oxford prologue speaks of those who "build their Poems the *Lucretian* way, / So many Huddled Atoms make a Play"; and in the preface to the *Notes and Observations*, Dryden calls *The Empress of Morocco* "a confus'd heap of false Grammar, improper English, strain'd Hyperboles, and downright Bulls" (XVII, 84). Both passages draw on the notion of primal chaos, which Dryden's boyhood favorite Sylvester had called a "confus'd heap" (*Divine Weeks*, I, i, 258), and which Dryden himself would later describe, in "A Song for St. Cecilia's Day," as the time "When Nature underneath a heap / of jarring Atomes lay" (ll. 3–4). In that great poem and many similar passages, Dryden pictured creation as the ordering of chaotic materials; in the first such passage he wrote, the dedication of *The Rival Ladies*, he had described the way a poet's "Fancy" creates "Images," which are then "either chosen or rejected by the Judgment," but he had also confessed to finding "a disorderly kind of Beauty" in his first ideas about that play "When it was only a confus'd Mass of Thoughts, tumbling over one another in the Dark" (VIII, 95). As he attacked Settle, probably in the prologue and certainly in the preface, Dryden may have chosen to forget that he had once placed a higher value on what he now called "the *Lucretian* way" of making plays.

Dryden's participation in the attack on Settle was a departure from the policy of aloofness to his enemies that he had successfully followed since the controversy with Howard in 1668. Even the "Rota" pamphlets, with their grammatical cavils and personal slanders, had only elicited the wise decision not to "gratifie the ambition of two wretched Scriblers, who desire nothing more than to be Answer'd" (XI, 322).[20] Settle thought Dryden was his main attacker in the *Notes and Observations*, but I should think it more likely that the Laureate contributed his anonymous preface and postscript as a favor to John Crowne, a more respectful younger imitator who provided the bulk of the pamphlet, and who presumably recruited his Duke's Company colleague Shadwell to help out. Whether or not Dryden was the instigator of the attack, the vehemence of his remarks requires some explanation, and Dr. Johnson's patronising notion that he was jealous of Settle is hardly adequate. A careful examination of the specific charges Dryden hurls at Settle will support a more interesting psychological theory: that Dryden, now urgently questioning the whole direction of his own literary career, was attacking in Settle ideas and attitudes he had once held himself. Settle's theory of creativity, implicit in the way he defends his metaphors in his lengthy reply to the *Notes and Observations*, was close to the Longinian claims to inspiration Dryden had offered in the dedication to *The Rival Ladies* and the prologue to *Tyrannick Love*, where he claimed that "Poets, like Lovers, should be bold and dare, / They spoil their business with an over-care." Since Dryden was now moving away from that theory toward an aesthetic placing more emphasis on "Judgment,"[21] his attack on Settle's trusting to chance and inspiration was in effect an attack on his own youthful excesses.

In attacking Settle's ignorance of grammar, Dryden may have wished to ignore the similarity between Settle's education and his own: his young imitator had attended Westminster School under Busby and spent one year at Oxford. If Dryden was more fully educated, the early 1670s were nonetheless years of intense study for him, years in which he moved beyond the learning of his school and college days.[22] Not only was he reading Boileau, as the letter to Rochester suggests, but the publication of Thomas Rymer's translation of Rapin's *Reflections* on Aristotle in early 1674 drew his attention to French criticism, especially since Rymer's preface praised the night-scene in *The Indian Emperour* as superior to its models in Latin, Italian, and French.[23] Dryden also made a fresh study of English poetry during these years, rediscovering Spenser, whom he had undervalued as a boy, and escaping at last from his early fondness for the "Westminster style" of Cowley. Since Settle, in his blundering way, was still writing in that style, Dryden's attack on Settle's education may have been a way of expressing a growing sense of the gaps in his own education.

The remarkable passage in which Dryden describes his program of reading during the 1670s and the consequent new direction in his poetic career is worth quoting at length; it comes in the "Discourse concerning the Original and Progress of Satire," written in 1692:

Had I time, I cou'd enlarge on the Beautiful Turns of Words and Thoughts, which are as requisite in this, as in Heroique Poetry it self; of which this Satire is undoubtedly a Species. With these Beautiful Turns I confess my self to have been unacquainted, till about Twenty Years ago, in a Conversation which I had with that Noble Wit of *Scotland*, Sir *George Mackenzy*: He asked me why I did not imitate in my Verses, the turns of Mr. *Waller*, and Sir *John Denham*; of which, he repeated many to me: I had often read with pleasure, and with some profit, those two Fathers of our *English* Poetry; but had not seriously enough consider'd those Beauties which give the last perfection to their Works. Some sprinklings of this kind, I had also formerly in my Plays, but they were casual, and not design'd. But this hint, thus seasonably given me, first made me sensible of my own wants, and brought me afterwards to seek for the supply of them in other *English* Authors. I look'd over the Darling of my youth, the Famous *Cowley*; there I found instead of them, the Points of Wit, and Quirks of Epigram, even in the *Davideis*, a Heroick Poem, which is of an opposite nature to those Puerilities; but no Elegant turns, either on the word, or on the thought. Then I consulted a Greater Genius, (without offence to the *Manes* of that Noble Author) I mean *Milton*. But as he endeavours every where to express *Homer*, whose Age had not arriv'd to that fineness, I found in him a true sublimity, lofty thoughts, which were cloath'd with admirable *Grecisms*, and ancient words, which he had been digging from the Mines of *Chaucer*, and of *Spencer*, and which, with all their rusticity, had somewhat of Venerable in them. But I found not there neither that for which I look'd. At last I had recourse to his Master, *Spencer*, the Author of that immortal Poem, call'd the *Fairy-Queen*; and there I met with that which I had been looking for so long in vain. *Spencer* had studi'd *Virgil* to as much advantage as *Milton* had done *Homer*; and amongst the rest of his Excellencies had Copy'd that. [IV, 84–85]

The process Dryden describes here evidently took several years: his vague dating of the conversation with Mackenzie would place the beginning of his search for "Beautiful Turns of Words and Thoughts" in about 1672; his most serious grappling with Milton took place in 1674; he still had kind words for Cowley in an essay on poetic license first published in early 1677; and the copy of Spenser in which he made extensive markings is an edition published in 1679.[24] The publication of *The Empress of Morocco*, coming at a time when Dryden was seeking a new set of literary models, reminded him all too poignantly of the models that had shaped his early plays, which he now regarded as containing only "sprinklings" of the kind of writing he most admired; even those passages, he now realized, were "casual, and not design'd." By calling Settle an "upstart illiterate Scribler," censuring him for "want of Learning and Elocution," and complaining of his "false allusions, and mistaken points of Wit," Dryden was breaking decisively with the emphasis on "Fancy" in his own early education, and arguing instead for the more subtle and controlled effects possible when Fancy was "cooled and allay'd by the Judgement," effects he was now studying in Milton and Virgil and hoping to emulate in an epic of his own.

But Dryden's attack on Settle was not merely literary. Although he resented the class snobbery aimed at him by such aristocrats as Buckingham and (later) Rochester, his own attack on Settle involves a version of the same scorn. In the Oxford prologue, he refers to the authors of *"Lucretian"* poems as "mere Town-Wits," who will be admired only by "their own Citts," an insult echoed in the preface to the *Notes and Observations*, where he says "it will be no wonder if [Settle] pass for a great Authour amongst Town Fools and City Wits" (XVII, 85). In the postscript, adding religious contempt to class prejudice, Dryden claims that Settle "would perswade us he is a kind of Phanatick in Poetry, and has a light within him; and writes by an inspiration which (like that of the Heathen Prophets) a man must have no sense of his own when he receives" (XVII, 182). This application of religious terminology to literary creation draws on a kind of guilt by association: Settle's Old Testament name, Elkanah, labeled him as a product of the Puritan artisan class whose "mechanick" enthusiasm often drew deadly contempt from Dryden; the young poet's ancestors were barbers.[25] Again, the similarities in background are striking: if Dryden's Puritan ancestors, landholding Northamptonshire gentry, significantly outranked Settle's City barbers, there were plenty of Drydens and Pickerings, including some now very much alive in Titchmarsh, who believed in the "inner light." In attacking Settle along these lines, Dryden was putting more distance between himself and the religious beliefs of his Dissenting relatives.

The pamphlet attack is nastier than the prologue because the publication of the play gave Dryden more specific reasons to be angry with Settle. Settle's boastful title page identifies him as a "Servant to his Majesty," the very phrase Dryden typically used on his own title pages. The epigraph, from one of Dryden's favorite authors, Petronius, advises young men to give their first years to poetry: the young Settle, twenty-five years old at the time, was twitting the Laureate, now forty-two, who had himself once jokingly referred to forty as "That wretched, fumbling age of poetry." The dedicatory epistle, addressed to Henry Howard, complains about "the Impudence of Scriblers in this Age," criticizing those who dedicated failed plays to prominent men; the obvious example was Dryden's dedicating the failed *Assignation* to Sedley. Settle, too, had motives. He had wanted the King's Company to stage *The Empress of Morocco* because Charles Hart was the best available actor of rhymed parts, but the Duke's Company, which had produced his *Cambyses* in 1671, successfully claimed a prior contract, procuring a judgment to that effect from the Duke of York himself.[26] Although a production by the Duke's Company in their superior theatre was a prize many a young playwright would have coveted, Settle probably wanted Hart and the King's Company to act his play in order to force the comparison with Dryden he seems determined to make in the printed edition. The confusion over which company was to have the play made him look foolish, and he had reason to believe that Dryden had opposed the mounting of his play by the King's players. Moreover, it is just possible that Settle had heard about the Oxford prologue and recognized its criticism of "*Lucretian*" playwrights as aimed at him. Neither man's reports about the early stage history of this play can be trusted, since the controversy that followed its publication made them inveterate enemies for the rest of the century.

The Empress of Morocco might fairly be described as a poor imitation of early Dryden: its couplets lack the energy and drive of those in *The Conquest of Granada*, and are usually at least as thudding as those in *The Indian Queen*; the plot is also a throwback to the rhymed dramas of the early Restoration period, with much greed, deceit, and rant, and very little psychological development. One example of Settle's dramatic poetry will suffice to illustrate what Dryden found distressing. Morena, the young queen, has been tricked into stabbing her husband during a masque; Crimalhaz, the arch villain, immediately claims her hand, and she apparently assents, but her plan is to commit suicide. As soon as Crimalhaz exits, she addresses the ghost of her husband:

> I've found the way. Oh my dear Lord, though now
> Death does embrace what to my Arms is due;
> I'le keep———
> My Vow to Him, and Love to Thee Entire.
> No second King shall to this Throne aspire. [*Points to her Breast.*
> To thee my last Debts payment shall be this,
> I'll die—and dead all that I am is His.
> In thy Revenge when I've Triumphant stood,
> On Traytors necks amid'st a Scene of Blood;
> *Morena's* hand shall wash the stain She wears;
> As Condemn'd men turn Executioners.
> To expiate thy blood I'le let out mine,
> And triumph in my fall, who mourn for thine.
> Then with a gentle gale of dying sighs,
> Ile breath my flying Soul into the Skies.
> Wing'd by my Love I will my passage steer,
> Nor can I miss my way when You shine there.
>
> [pp. 55–56]

Almost every line here is a deformation of an idea or image Dryden had already used; the image of standing on the necks of the conquered, for example, appears in *The Conquest of Granada*, where it functions as an extravagant metaphor, not an actual plan. Such borrowings were a reason for embarrassment, as Dryden points out in the preface to *Notes and Observations*:

> He steals notoriously from his Contemporaries; but he so alters the property, by disguising his Theft in ill English, and bad Applications, that he makes the Child his own by deforming it. . . . A Poet when he sees his thoughts in so ill a dress, is asham'd to confess they ever belong'd to him. [XVII, 84]

This is a moment of astonishing candor. Dryden recognized that Settle had stolen his ideas and expressed them in clumsier, far less artful poetry, but this recognition led not only to anger at Settle, but to a questioning of his own work. His next play, *Aureng-Zebe*, produced at the end of 1675, was his last rhymed drama; in dedicating the published text to Mulgrave, Dryden announced an important shift in his goals:

> If I must be condemn'd to Rhyme, I should find some ease in my change of punishment. I desire to be no longer the *Sisyphus* of the stage; to rowl up a Stone with endless labour (which to follow the proverb, gathers no Mosse) and which is perpetually falling down again. I never thought myself very fit for an Employment, where many of my Predecessors have excell'd me in all kinds; and some of my Contemporaries, even in my own partial Judgment, have out-done me in *Comedy*. Some little hopes I have yet remaining, and those too, considering my abilities, may be vain, that I may make the world some part of amends, for many ill plays, by an Heroique Poem. [sig. A4r]

The prologue makes a similar announcement to the public: Dryden confesses that he has grown "weary of his long-lov'd Mistris, Rhyme," announces that he now has "another taste of Wit," and declares himself "betwixt two Ages cast, / The first of this, and hindmost of the last." As usual, Dryden's self-criticism was accurate: he recognized that the age of the rhymed heroic play was over. He did not succeed in his aim to write an epic poem, and that failure doubtless haunted him, but he did begin to produce serious plays in blank verse, couplet satires (including *Mac Flecknoe*), and translations of the classics—the literary forms for which he is primarily famous today. There were surely many factors in the process that led to Dryden's developing "another taste of Wit," but the controversy with Settle should not be underestimated. Contemplating the ludicrousness of Settle's lines helped Dryden see the potential for ludicrousness in his own.[27]

We may see just how close Dryden came to bringing that process to full consciousness by comparing his comments on Settle's characterization with one of his self-criticisms in the dedication to *Aureng-Zebe*. In the first passage, Dryden explains the flatness and similarity of Settle's characters by alleging that they are all versions of their author:

> He has a heavy hand at Fools, and a great felicity in writing Nonsense for them. Fools they will be in spight of him. His King, his two Empresses, his Villain and his Sub-villain, nay his *Heroe* have all a certain natural cast of the Father: one turn of the Countenance goes through all his Children. Their folly was born and bred in 'em; and something of the *Elkanah* will be visible. [XVII, 85]

Less than two years later, he explains to Mulgrave why he is tired of observing others in order to create dramatic characters:

> The truth is, the consideration of so vain a Creature as man, is not worth our pains. I have fool enough at home without looking for it abroad; and am a sufficient Theater to my self of ridiculous actions, without expecting company, either in a Court, a Town, or a Play-house. 'Tis on this account that I am weary with drawing the deformities of Life, and Lazars of the People, where every figure of imperfection more resembles me than it can do others. [sig. A4r]

The passage about being "the *Sisyphus* of the stage" follows immediately. Dryden implies that writing rhymed drama is the act of a fool, and he evidently had other reasons to feel he had been foolish. From the perspective of early 1676, his attempt to court Rochester probably looked like an embarrassing episode; Rochester's "Allusion to Horace," with its trenchant criticism of Dryden, was passing from hand to hand not long after the publication of *Aureng-Zebe*. His affair with Anne Reeves was another potentially "ridiculous action": there are greatly expanded references to that affair in a new edition of *The Rehearsal* published early in 1675, which presumably gives the text used in the performances given in December 1674, and there is some reason to believe that the lovers had parted by the time *Aureng-Zebe* was staged in late 1675 (see below, pp. 281–82). Dryden's willingness to expose himself to the laughter of others by acknowledging that he was "a sufficient Theater to [him] self of ridiculous actions," a remarkably unguarded statement for a printed dedication, probably owes something to these and other personal follies, but as a literary statement, it springs from the same perception about the potential for unintended comedy in rhymed drama that led to the slapstick epilogue to *Tyrannick Love* and the vigorous satiric prose aimed at Settle.

In the "Discourse of Satire" (1692), that great retrospective summary of his career, Dryden hoped that "Posterity" would forget his "Interest and Passion," his "Partiality and Prejudice." Considering the number of attacks he had endured, he was close to the truth in claiming to have been restrained: "I have seldom answer'd any scurrilous Lampoon; When it was in my power to have expos'd my Enemies: And being naturally vindicative, have suffer'd in silence, and posses'd my Soul in quiet" (IV, 59–60). Consequently, those scattered instances when Dryden did give vent to his "naturally vindicative" temper are especially interesting; they mark turning points in his career. The "Defence of the Essay" (1668), the last chapter in his controversy with Howard, was a hotheaded and counterproductive essay, yet it helped Dryden clarify his aims as a playwright; it led to *The Conquest of Granada*. The framing essays for *Notes and Observations*, answered at length and with some success by Settle, were also counterproductive, yet the controversy led to Dryden's abandoning rhymed drama for new and more fruitful forms. *Mac Flecknoe*, which Dryden kept out of print for many years after writing it, was a work of genius prompted by anger, in which Dryden found a way to transmute his animosity toward Shadwell into high art and discovered his true calling as a satirist. *The Medall* (1682), in which he abandoned the pose of restraint and moderation he had used in *Absalom and Achitophel*, was a passionate declaration of partisan feeling. In each case, a failure to "possess [his] Soul in quiet" led Dryden to define that soul more fully and honestly.

Machines and Operas

The Dryden who was rethinking the direction of his literary career in 1674 remained under contract to the King's Company, now finally preparing to open their new playhouse at Drury Lane. He signed a document committing himself to help pay a daily rent to those who had put up the new building once it opened, and probably also had to contribute £200 toward a new scenehouse.[28] As the King's players limped along toward the opening of Drury Lane, they needed plays for Lincoln's Inn Fields, and Dryden may have obliged them by refurbishing an old comedy called *The Mistaken Husband*, which they produced shortly before moving to the new theatre. When the play was published in 1675, the bookseller implied that Dryden had written a new scene, but his phrasing is so cautious that I should think it merely an attempt to advertise an otherwise undistinguished play.[29]

Meanwhile, the interest in "machines" that had made *Macbeth* a hit in the previous season and the interest in music that had helped make *The Empress of Morocco* a success continued unabated. As early as August of 1673, the Duke's Company had planned an opera featuring "dansers out of France"; the result, not performed until early 1675, was *Psyche*, with music by Matthew Locke and a text adapted from a French source by Shadwell, who had not previously attempted a rhyming play.[30] On 5 January 1674,

Evelyn saw some kind of Italian opera at court, doubtless involving some of the Italian musicians brought to London for the chapel of the new Duchess of York. The composer and organist Giovanni Baptista Draghi, who had been in London since the late 1660s, may also have taken part; he would collaborate with Dryden on "A Song for St. Cecilia's Day, 1687." In February, a group of French musicians gave another court opera. Among their leaders was Louis Grabu, a Spanish violinist who had assumed a French name and compositional style; he would collaborate with Dryden on *Albion and Albanius* (1685). By the time Dryden wrote the prologue to be spoken at the opening of Drury Lane on 26 March, the rival Duke's Company had evidently refurbished the old Dryden-Davenant *Tempest*, always a popular spectacle, as an opera; this new version, which ran intermittently throughout the spring, must have particularly rankled Dryden, since the play retained pages of dialogue from his pen.[31] It was not, however, what we would call an opera. The only fully-sung English operas with recitatives presented in London before the eighteenth century were John Blow's *Venus and Adonis* (1682), Dryden and Grabu's *Albion and Albanius* (1685), and Tate and Purcell's *Dido and Aeneas* (1689); of these, only *Albion and Albanius* was commercially produced, and it proved a failure. The Dorset Garden *Tempest*, like Shadwell's *Psyche*, Dryden's later *King Arthur*, and a number of other productions, was a semiopera, combining spoken dialogue with elaborate sung interludes featuring singers who were not the major actors in the play.

Unable to compete with that kind of spectacle, the King's Company opened their "Plain Built House" with a performance of *The Beggar's Bush*, an old play by Fletcher. They were obviously aware that such plays were unlikely to keep the crowds away from Dorset Garden for long; Dryden's prologue articulates the fear "That as a Fire the former House o'rethrew, / Machines and Tempests will destroy the new." Yet the same Dryden who sneered at "Scenes, Machines, and empty *Opera's*" in the Drury Lane prologue had been busily writing an opera himself a few months or even weeks earlier, a rhymed condensation of *Paradise Lost* called *The State of Innocence and the Fall of Man*. Although it remained unpublished until 1677, the text for this opera was clearly in existence by the spring of 1674; it was entered on the Stationers' Register on 17 April, and was surely intended to compete with *The Tempest*, which was keeping the rival house full. When he finally published the unproduced opera, Dryden claimed to have written it in a month; such haste might well have been a response to a request from the players, who probably felt some pressure to stage an opera as soon after opening the new house as possible. But once *The State of Innocence* was written, the leadership of the King's Company decided against staging it, probably for financial reasons; though Dryden's opera was anything but "empty," it certainly would have required prodigious "Scenes" and "Machines." Instead, Hart and Mohun, who were now performing most of Killigrew's managerial functions, hired the French singers and dancers who had already performed at court to help them stage a French opera, *Ariane*, which was performed at Drury Lane on 30 March, just four days after the opening of the new house; they were able to save even more money by borrowing the scenes that had been used at court.[32]

We may imagine how Hart and Mohun, with the memory of Fuller's bill for the sets for *Tyrannick Love* still sharp in their minds, might have responded to Dryden's first stage direction:

The first Scene represents a Chaos, or a confus'd Mass of Matter; the Stage is almost wholly dark: A symphony of Warlike Music is heard for some time; then from the Heavens, (which are opened) fall the rebellious Angels wheeling in the Air, and seeming transfix'd with Thunderbolts: The bottom of the Stage being open'd, receives the Angels, who fall out of sight. Tunes of Victory are play'd, and an Hymn sung; Angels discovered above, brandishing their Swords: The Music ceasing, and the Heavens being closed, the Scene shifts, and on a sudden represents Hell: Part of the Scene is a Lake of Brimstone or rowling Fire; the Earth of a burnt colour: The fall'n Angels appear on the Lake, lying prostrate; a Tune of Horrour and Lamentation is heard. [I, i, p. 1]

Staging such a scene would obviously have required elaborate scene-painting and sophisticated machines of the kind that had made the shows at Dorset Garden attractive; indeed, one of the scenes pictured in the published *Empress of Morocco*, which shows prisoners impaled on spikes in a torture chamber, may have suggested to Dryden the notion of showing the angels "seeming transfix'd with Thunderbolts." Later scenes include "*A Vision, where a Tree rises loaden with Fruit*" (III, i, p. 19), probably imagined as

Torture-scene in Elkanah Settle's *The Empress of Morocco* (1673).

something like the popular scene in *The Tempest* with the disappearing banquet, and even "*A battle at land, and a Naval fight*" (V, i, p. 43).[33] For the opening scene alone, the incompetent house composer, Nicholas Staggins, would have been required to write several different kinds of music; later musical sequences, especially the dream-vision in Act III, called for sensitive setting of rhythmically charged verses. With Matthew Locke under contract to the rival house, and the recently arrived French and Italian composers uncertain of English rhythms, appropriate music may have been impossible to procure. Beyond these practical problems, Hart and Mohun may well have doubted whether the theatre audience was ready for an opera on so serious a theme. Dryden had miscalculated the willingness of playgoers to accept serious content in a comedy with *The Assignation*, a relatively cheap play producible at Lincoln's Inn Fields. *The State of Innocence* was an even stranger departure from the expectations of the audience, for whom "opera" meant entertainment without much content; staging it effectively would have cost thousands of pounds, too big a gamble for a company down on its luck.

By the time he wrote his prologue for the opening of Drury Lane, Dryden presumably knew that his own opera was not going to be staged—at least not in the current theatrical season. Not much earlier, however, and pretty clearly expecting the play to be staged, he had taken the step of visiting the old Milton to ask his permission to make a rhymed dramatic version of *Paradise Lost*; in some versions of this story, Waller is said to have come along with Dryden. If Milton received his visitors graciously, as the sources claim, he nonetheless retained political views firmly opposed to those of the court.[34] Moreover, Dryden's recent antagonist Sir Robert Howard was friendly with Milton, whose defense of his choice of blank verse in the reprinted *Paradise Lost* was probably his way of taking Howard's side in the literary controversy about rhyme.[35] The old poet's reported response to Dryden's request conveys more than a hint of disapproval: he is said to have given his former employee permission to "tag his points," referring to rhyme as if it were fashionable dress.[36] When Marvell wrote his prefatory verses for the revised, twelve-book version of *Paradise Lost*, which was published in July of 1674, he was evidently aware that Dryden had written a rhyming version and probably aware of Milton's remark. Addressing the issue of rhyme, Marvell congratulates Milton on avoiding it:

> Well mightst thou scorn thy Readers to allure
> With tinkling Rime, of thy own sense secure;
> While the *Town-Bayes* writes all the while and spells,
> And like a Pack-horse tires without his Bells:
> Their Fancies like our Bushy-points appear,
> The Poets tag them, we for fashion wear.[37]

We shall probably never know what old and new hostilities lurk behind Marvell's lines. Although he had worked with both "the Poet blind, yet bold" and the future "*Town-Bayes*" in the office of the Latin Secretary in 1657, Marvell retained closer ties to Milton than to Dryden. As a Member of Parliament, he was now actively opposed to Dryden's patron the Duke of York, and thus allied with Sir Robert Howard, whom he had attacked seven years earlier in the anonymous "Painter" poems.

Dryden was acting shrewdly by seeking permission to prepare his opera, but he also had personal and literary motives for this visit to Milton, who would be dead within a year (8 November 1674). When he spoke, years later, of "consult[ing] a greater genius [than Cowley] . . . I mean *Milton*" (IV, 84), he was probably referring to this visit as well as to his careful study of Milton's works; perhaps this was also the occasion on which Milton "acknowledg'd to [Dryden] that *Spencer* was his Original" (preface to *Fables, Poems*, IV, 1445). Despite their political differences, Dryden recognized Milton as an authentic genius; seizing an opportunity to discuss poetry with such a man was a part of that restless process of reconsidering his career through which he was now passing. Ironically enough, questions about the validity of dramatic rhyme were a part of that process; drafts of the attack on Settle, whose "incorrigibly lewd" rhymes helped raise those questions in Dryden's mind, were probably on his desk along with drafts of his rhymed revision of Milton.

Critics and biographers, even those friendly to Dryden, have responded negatively to *The State of Innocence*, though contemporary readers were sufficiently fascinated that "many hundred copies of it [were] dispers'd abroad" before Dryden printed it; in a prefatory poem to the published version, the young playwright Nathaniel Lee even called it "this best POEM, that you ever wrought, / This fairest labor of your teeming brain" (sig. b1r). Despite our modern sense that any reworking of *Paradise Lost* is necessarily travesty, I consider this unstaged opera far more interesting, in literary and biographical terms, than many of Dryden's staged plays. The very idea was bold, not because *Paradise Lost* had achieved the status of a classic in the seven years since its first publication, but because Dryden was claiming such status for it by basing an opera upon it. The plots of Italian and French operas usually came from mythology, drawing on such sources as Ovid and Tasso: the French opera the King's Company presented instead of Dryden's Miltonic fantasy depicted the marriage of Bacchus, and Shadwell's next opera for the Duke's Company, already written and now being set to music, retold the story of Psyche. By choosing Milton's poem as the basis for an opera, Dryden was patriotically claiming epic status for a living English poet, devoutly directing the attention of his audience to the power of Christian myth (as he had once claimed to be doing in *Tyrannick Love*), testing the capacity of opera to accommodate serious content, and studying the differences between heroic drama and heroic poetry. Like any translation or rearrangement, this opera constitutes an interpretation of the text it revises; as one of Dryden's last exercises in rhymed drama, it has great formal interest; and as another document from his period of uncertainty and rethinking, it reveals some of his own preoccupations.

When he published *The State of Innocence*, Dryden called *Paradise Lost* "one of the greatest, most noble, and most sublime POEMS, which either this Age or Nation has produc'd" (sig. B1r). Yet he did not hesitate to compress its more than ten thousand lines into a play that would hardly have lasted two hours, even with extensive music. Except for the opening tableau, the War in Heaven vanishes entirely, as does the Creation; Milton's complex organization, in which the story is deliberately told out of order, yields to a straightforward chronological presentation. The first two books become one compact scene, which nonetheless manages to preserve the main outlines of the debate among the fallen angels. Act II begins with a Cartesian Adam inferring the existence of his Maker from his own capacity to think:

> What am I? or from whence? For that I am,
> I know, because I think; but whence I came,
> Or how this Frame of mine began to be,
> What other Being can disclose to me?
> I move, I see; I speak, discourse, and know,
> Though now I am, I was not always so.
> Then that from which I was, must be before:
> Whom as my Spring of Being, I adore.

[II, i, p. 8]

Raphael appears immediately, confirming the validity of Adam's reasoning and promising him a companion. Within a few more pages, Lucifer has learned the way to Paradise from Uriel, and Eve has admired herself in a fountain and met Adam. The dream in which Lucifer prepares Eve to yield to his daylight temptation provides a perfect opportunity for a musical scene, in which an angel representing the tempter sings to "a Woman, habited like Eve," a neat device for introducing professional singers without requiring the speaking actors to sing. Here Dryden departs from heroic couplets, as he had at similar places in his earlier plays. The angel's lyrical song, like much of Dryden's writing for music, virtually dictates a rhythmic setting to the composer:

> Look up, look up, and see
> What Heav'n prepares for thee;
> Look up, and this fair fruit behold,
> Ruddy it smiles, and rich with streaks of gold.
>
> The loaded branches downward bend,
> Willing they stoop, and thy fair hand attend.
> Fair Mother of Mankind, make haste,
> And bless, and bless thy senses with the taste.

[III, i, p. 19]

Drawing largely on Book IX of Milton's poem, Dryden then dramatizes the central action of temptation and fall; Milton's last two books, in which Michael shows Adam visions of future history, shrink to a few final pages.

Despite its radical compression of Milton's material, Dryden's play manages to preserve not only the shape of the story, but much of its thematic complexity. His Adam and Eve must convey in speeches of a few lines what Milton's characters have pages to develop, yet the capacity of the couplet for compression helps Dryden pack his lines with content, and even when writing in blank verse, as he does in the scene between Lucifer and Uriel, Dryden effectively tightens Milton's luxuriant syntax. He virtually never tags Milton's points in the sense of tacking rhymes onto otherwise unaltered lines; most of the rhyming words are Milton's, and Dryden either plucks them from the middle of Milton's lines or imports them from related contexts. He had studied Milton's poem with sufficient care to be able to lift a phrase from one part of the poem and insert it into a speech taken from another; when the angel in the temptation dream calls

Eve "Fair Mother of Mankind," for example, Dryden takes that phrase from Raphael's address to Eve (V, 389), not from Eve's recounting of her dream to Adam (V, 28–94), his main source for this passage. Illustrating Dryden's technique in brief is thus difficult, since he frequently condenses several longer speeches to one shorter one. One compact example will have to suffice. When Milton's Gabriel confronts Satan in the Garden, he asks him why he has "broke[n] the bounds prescrib'd / To [his] transgressions." Satan's reply is typical of his rhetoric; I quote only the first half:

> *Gabriel*, thou hadst in Heav'n th' esteem of wise,
> And such I held thee; but this question askt
> Puts me in doubt. Lives there who loves his pain?
> Who would not, finding way, break loose from Hell,
> Though thither doom'd? Thou wouldst thyself, no doubt,
> And boldly venture to whatever place
> Farthest from pain, where thou might'st hope to change
> Torment with ease, and soonest recompense
> Dole with delight, which in this place I sought; . . .
>
> [IV, 886–94]

Dryden's Lucifer says the same thing in four lines:

> Lives there who would not seek to force his way
> From pain to ease; from darkness, to the day?
> Should I, who found the means to scape, not dare
> To change my sulphurous smoak, for upper Ayr?
>
> [III, i, p. 22]

From the immediate passage at hand, Dryden takes the Latinate rhetorical question ("Lives there who . . .") and the opposition of "pain" and "ease." He doubles that contrast in the same line by opposing "darkness" and "day," drawing on one of the most persistent patterns of imagery in Milton's poem, and makes both contrasts more pointed and specific by borrowing "sulphurous smoak" and "upper Ayr" from the first two books of the poem.

However quickly he may have accomplished it, the work of thus condensing Milton had a profound effect on Dryden's poetic technique. He was soon borrowing heavily from Milton's large vocabulary of "admirable *Grecisms*, and ancient words": *Aureng-Zebe* lifts whole lines from Milton, especially from *Samson Agonistes*;[38] later poems, especially *Absalom and Achitophel* and *The Hind and the Panther*, make expert use of Miltonic materials. The flexible couplets in *Aureng-Zebe* reflect the influence of Milton's habitual enjambment, as Dryden acknowledges in the epilogue, which speaks of "Words not forc'd, but sliding into Rhime" (l. 6). In both the opera and the tragedy, the couplets also display the density we associate with the couplets of Dryden's great poems of the 1680s; by condensing Milton's 10,565 lines to a mere 1,400, Dryden taught himself a critical lesson about packing meaning into poetry.[39] The opera's one scene in blank verse points in the direction of Dryden's later plays; the major shift in style announced in the prologue to *Aureng-Zebe* and triumphantly carried out in *All for Love* owes as much to the positive example of Milton as to the negative example of

Settle. In terms of genre, *The State of Innocence* reversed what Dryden hoped would be the direction of his career: he was planning to retire from the stage to write an epic poem, yet this opera was an exercise in turning epic into drama. Still, making such a translation in either direction was bound to engage Dryden's mind in the practical problems of both forms.

The State of Innocence provides some fascinating evidence about Dryden's literary preoccupations at this unsettled moment in his career; it also touches upon a number of temporal and personal issues. Dryden's irritation with Settle's "confus'd heap" of language, for example, probably contributed something to the soliloquy in which Lucifer plans to tempt Eve with a dream:

> So, now they lye, secure in love, and steep
> Their sated sences in full draughts of sleep.
> By what sure means can I their bliss invade?
> By violence? No; for they're immortal made.
> Their Reason sleeps; but Mimic fancy wakes.
> Supply's her parts, and wild Idea's takes
> From words and things, ill-sorted, and mis-joyn'd;
> The Anarchie of thought and Chaos of the mind:
> Hence dreams confus'd and various may arise;
> These will I set before the Woman's eyes;
> The weaker she, and made my easier prey;
> Vain shows, and Pomp the softer sex betray.
>
> [III, i, p. 19]

Not only are the key terms here ("Mimic fancy," "wild Idea's," "Anarchy," "Chaos," and the like) precisely those Dryden uses to denigrate Settle, but the notion that women are more susceptible to "Vain shows, and Pomp" also appears in the Postscript to the *Notes and Observations*, where Dryden speaks dismissively of Settle's "admirers who most commonly are Women." He was not alone in such misogyny; the very poem he was adapting includes some exceedingly harsh remarks about women, many of them coming in the passage where Adam curses Eve for leading him astray (X, 867–908). In Dryden's hands, that passage becomes a domestic squabble, with Eve complaining that "Th' unhappiest of creation is a wife, . . . Curst with that reason she must never use," and Adam replying that "she's proud, fantastick, apt to change; / Restless at home; and ever prone to range" (V, i, p. 39). Although the speech given by Dryden's Adam explicitly repeats a number of phrases from Milton's Adam, including the notion that God was wise to "People his Heav'n with Souls all masculine," I believe we may hear in Dryden's version the distant echoes of similar squabbles between John and Elizabeth Dryden, whose relations were undergoing the strain of Dryden's tightened finances and public infidelity.

The futile Third Dutch War, coming to an end as this opera was written, comes into satiric focus when the devils refer to themselves as the "States-General of Hell," but Dryden's decision to add a naval battle to the vision of death shown to Adam at the end suggests a more serious response to that war. Raphael, who replaces Milton's Michael in this scene, describes the battle as folly:

> See those, more mad, who throw their lives away
> In needless wars; the Stakes which Monarchs lay,
> When for each others Provinces they play.
> Then as if earth too narrow were for fate,
> On open Seas their quarrels they debate;
> In hollow wood they floating Armies bear;
> And force imprison'd winds to bring 'em near.
>
> [V, i, p. 42]

This surprising speech replaces Michael's more general condemnation of "those days [when] Might only shall be admir'd" (XI, 689) with language specifically related to the recent attempt by Charles and Louis to defeat the United Provinces on land and sea. *Amboyna*, Dryden's contribution to the propaganda for that war, staged just one year earlier, had included a song celebrating "this so brave, so bloody Sea Fight" as "a noble sight"; *Annus Mirabilis*, his poem on the Second Dutch War, had been offered as "a due expiation for my not serving my King and Country in it." The quite different attitude Dryden now displayed toward military glory probably owed something to the influence of Milton's powerful passages on the general futility of war,[40] but a writer less concerned to shake his audience might have simply adapted those passages, with their references to ancient wars and weapons. Instead, Dryden insisted on offering up the most recent English war as an example of the fallen world; something about that war, perhaps the death of his kinsman Sandwich, must have struck him as particularly wasteful.

Finally, there is the question of what part *The State of Innocence* might have played in the ongoing public debate about religion or the ongoing private development of Dryden's religious thought. The Anglican Dryden was adapting the work of the Puritan Milton, and would dedicate the results to the Catholic princess Maria Beatrice. He surely meant to emphasize Christian unity rather than denominational diversity, just as he had when he rewrote the Anglican sermons of Tillotson as speeches for the Catholic Queen's saintly namesake in *Tyrannick Love*. Even those passages that engage theological issues, such as Adam's puzzling over predestination and free will with Gabriel and Raphael in Act IV, are not designed to persuade the audience of the validity of any narrowly denominational theological position; instead, such passages sharply dramatize the paradoxical nature of those eternal questions for all Christians. Still, the possibility that someone would accuse Dryden of heretical language or take offense at the very idea of a religious opera may have been among the reasons why the King's players preferred the safely pagan *Ariane*, though I should still suppose saving money was their primary motive.

Although Dryden's preface to the published play expresses no bitterness, seeing his serious work passed over in favor of an "empty" French opera can hardly have been pleasant. Nor was there any financial solace. *Ariane* was no competition for the operatic *Tempest*, which proved the hit of the season. The King's Company attempted to compete by reviving *Marriage A-la-Mode* and *The Indian Emperour* and by staging Nathaniel Lee's brutal first tragedy, *Nero*; they ultimately had to resort to a burlesque *Mock-Tempest* by Thomas Duffett, who had already reduced Settle's *Empress of Morocco* to a farce.[41] When the actors made their summer journey to Oxford, Dryden again furnished them with a prologue and epilogue, but this year he began the epilogue by having the actress Rebecca Marshall explain his desire to retire from the stage to a life of study at Oxford:

> Oft has our Poet wisht, this happy Seat
> Might prove his fading Muses last retreat:
> I wonder'd at his wish, but now I find
> He sought for quiet, and content of mind;
> Which noisfull Towns, and Courts can never know,
> And onely in the shades like Laurels grow.
> Youth, e'er it sees the World, here studies rest,
> And Age returning thence concludes it best.
>
> [ll. 1–8]

Like the earlier dedications to Rochester and Sedley, this epilogue is an attempt to secure patronage. Dryden presumably approached Oxford rather than Cambridge because he thought the leadership of Oxford more likely to be sympathetic to his cause: at Cambridge, his enemy Buckingham had just been succeeded as Chancellor by Monmouth, with whom his relations were distant, but at Oxford, his old patron Ormonde was Chancellor. In both universities, the Vice-Chancellor held power over the kind of academic post for which Dryden may have been angling, and this epilogue singles out Ralph Bathurst, the Vice-Chancellor, for particular praise by name.[42] Virtually any appointment as a Fellow or Master of a college, however, would have required Dryden to become a clergyman, and a "Session of the Poets" that was circulating late in 1676 reports a rumor of his "quitting the Muses to wear the black gown."[43] The probable source of that rumor was a prologue spoken at Oxford in the summer of 1676, in which Dryden reiterated his hope for a post there, and even mentioned his love for religion:

> Our Poets hither for Adoption come,
> As Nations su'd to be made Free of *Rome*;
> Not in the suffragating Tribes to stand,
> But in your utmost, last, Provincial Band.
> If his Ambition may those Hopes pursue,
> Who with Religion loves Your Arts and You,
> *Oxford* to Him a dearer Name shall be
> Than His own Mother University.
>
> [ll. 29–36]

If reasonably remunerated, a post at Oxford would have been an ideal way for Dryden to free himself from the ongoing pressures of writing for the theatre and devote himself to the study necessary for writing an epic poem; he might even have been willing to be ordained in order to gain that security. Still, given his steady hostility to the clergy, and the vehemence with which he denied that he ever intended to "take to the Church" in the preface to the *Fables*, I should think it more likely that he hoped some special arrangement might be worked out that would award him a sinecure at Oxford without requiring him to take orders. Although Dryden continued to hint at such desires in later Oxford prologues and epilogues, no such post ever materialized.

When the new theatrical season began in the fall, the Duke's Company continued to perform *The Tempest*, but the King's Company, their finances too shaky to support a rival opera, had only Duffett's burlesque to offer as competition. In December, they staged *The Rehearsal*, using the revised text expanding the jokes about Dryden's affair with Anne Reeves. Those additions probably reflect a growing interest in sex on the part of the audience; having staged a series of increasingly explicit sex comedies in the last several years, the King's players were the logical choice for *The Country Wife*, which had its premiere in January 1675. We may infer from the relatively low income of the Duke's Company during that month that Wycherley's masterpiece drew a welcome audience to the King's Company at Drury Lane; when the actors "violently shared" the coins in the cash-box, an incident about which Killigrew complained, they were probably grabbing the profits from this play. Arlington, now Lord Chamberlain, negotiated a temporary truce, but dissension, age, illness, and poverty continued to plague the King's Company.[44]

Meanwhile, many of the Duke's players were involved in the court production of John Crowne's masque *Calisto*, which was already being rehearsed in September; there were frequent open rehearsals in December and January, leading to several official performances in February. Presented by the ladies of the court, including Princess Mary and Princess Anne (both still children), *Calisto* featured a large orchestra, elaborate sets, and participants bedecked in jewels.[45] The Duke's Company's own long-awaited *Psyche* had its premiere later in the same month, doubtless delayed once more to avoid conflict with the court extravaganza.

Years later, John Dennis reported that Rochester had used his influence to have Crowne selected to write the text of *Calisto*, and alleged that he did so in order to insult Dryden.[46] As the Laureate, Dryden would have been a more normal choice, and Rochester might conceivably have hoped to injure him by promoting Crowne. Still, there is no evidence that Dryden, whose own Miltonic opera still languished unperformed, had any urgent desire to write a court masque, and when Crowne published *Calisto* the next fall, he paid Dryden a handsome compliment in the preface: "had it been written by him, to whom by the double right of place and merit, the honour of the employment belonged, the pleasure had been in all kinds complete" (sig. a2v). This gracious gesture, implying that Dryden chose not to write a masque, presumably reflects good relations between Dryden and Crowne, based in part on their collaboration against Settle, whose sneering answer to *Notes and Observations* became available early in 1675. Far from being irritated, Dryden may even have written an epilogue, apparently not spoken, for the court performance of Crowne's masque.[47] Intended for Lady Henrietta Maria Wentworth, who played Jupiter, the epilogue praises the King for restoring peace:

> These peaceful Triumphs with your cares you bought,
> And from the midst of fighting Nations brought.
> You only hear it thunder from afar,

And sit in peace the Arbiter of War.
Peace, the loath'd Manna, which hot brains despise,
You knew its worth, and made it early prize.

[ll. 21–26]

Although the evidence is inconclusive, I believe Dryden wrote these lines; typical of his panegyric manner, they convey not only the personal distaste for warfare he had expressed in the unperformed *State of Innocence*, but the widely recognized public benefits of England's withdrawal from the Third Dutch War. In the year after Charles made peace, English trade expanded, increasing government revenues; the Treasury, under the tight management of Osborne, was now making many of its old debts good. Crowne's expensive court masque, a "peaceful Triumph," was thus a celebration of solvency and stability.

The King rewarded his Treasurer by creating him Earl of Danby,[48] and Danby, hoping to consolidate his power in preparation for the spring session of Parliament, won the support of the Anglican bishops and old Cavaliers by persuading Charles to withdraw the preaching licenses issued to Dissenters in 1672 and issue severe edicts against Roman Catholics. The Dominican priest Philip Howard, kinsman to Dryden's wife, was among the victims of this purge; his conversion of an Anglican canon of Westminster had aroused resentment, and he found it necessary to flee to Belgium in March of 1675; two months later, he became a cardinal, but he never returned to England.[49] Roman Catholic peers were also worried: Dryden's brother-in-law, the Earl of Berkshire, wrote a letter on 24 March to Edward Coleman, secretary to the Duke of York, asking him to "send me word . . . what Bills are upon the Stocks, and whether there be one in hand to exclude the Catholick Lords from Sitting and Voting in the House of Peers, that I may prepare accordingly."[50] Despite Danby's preparations, the two sessions of Parliament in 1675 (April-June and October-November) were quite acrimonious. In the first session, Danby fought off an attempt to impeach him led by Shaftesbury, but failed in his attempt to force an oath of nonresistance on all officeholders; in the second session, a motion in the Lords to dissolve Parliament, which would have resulted in the first elections since the Restoration, was defeated by only two votes. Charles, who was enjoying his increased revenues, quickly prorogued the Parliament for the next fifteen months, and persuaded his cousin Louis, who had agreed to pay him £100,000 for dissolving Parliament, that a long prorogation amounted to the same thing.[51]

"What Verse Can Do"

As the party of Danby and the party of Shaftesbury, soon to become the Tories and the Whigs, sniped at each other in Parliamentary debates and barely anonymous pamphlets, Dryden was completing a play about a disputed succession to the throne. Like Settle's *Empress of Morocco*, Dryden's new rhymed tragedy concerned recent events in a distant culture: the real Aureng-Zebe, an Indian Moslem prince whose mother lies entombed in the Taj Mahal, was very much alive; his struggle for the throne, in which he outwitted an erratic father and three rival brothers, took place at about the time of Charles II's Restoration; Dryden adapted the story from Bernier's *Voyages* (1671). The desire to best Settle at his own game by setting a plot full of political treachery in an exotic but contemporary Moslem milieu was surely among Dryden's reasons for choosing this story, as was the political urgency of the issue of succession.

According to the dedication, Mulgrave arranged for the King himself to study Dryden's manuscript: "You were likewise pleas'd to recommend it to the King's perusal, before the last hand was added to it, and when I receiv'd the favour from him, to have the most considerable event of it modell'd by his Royal Pleasure" (sig. A4v). Such participation in the making of drama was not new for Charles: years earlier, he had prompted Orrery to undertake rhymed dramas and suggested a Spanish plot for Tuke's first play. In this case, however, the King's concern probably had a political dimension. Although it presents no sustained obvious parallel to the current English situation, *Aureng-Zebe* celebrates loyalty and patience; the historical Aureng-Zebe was a Machiavellian manipulator, but Dryden's character is a perfect exemplar of filial piety, fighting to preserve his father's throne. We cannot know what "considerable event" Charles suggested for the plot; one possibility is the episode in which the loyal courtier Arimant goes into battle wearing the armor of Aureng-Zebe, like Patroclus in the armor of Achilles. Hearing that this warrior has "rush'd on the stroke / Of lifted Weapons" (V, p. 70), the other characters (and the audience) conclude that Aureng-Zebe is dead; his later entrance is thus a miraculous restoration. This effective device implies that those who fight for the legitimate ruler take on his identity and extend his life; it celebrates a self-sacrificing loyalty achieved by strenuous self-discipline, since Arimant undertakes this suicidal mission despite his irrational passion for Aureng-Zebe's betrothed, Indamora, placing the cause of legitimacy and stability before his own desires.[52]

As the play begins, the court of the aging emperor awaits the outcome of battles between four different armies, each led by one of the emperor's sons. A speech in which the frequent sibilants imitate the sound of whispering probably reflects Dryden's observation of the continually shifting alliances in Charles's court and Parliament:

> The Ministers of State, who gave us Law,
> In corners, with selected Friends, withdraw:
> There, in deaf murmurs, solemnly are wise;
> Whisp'ring, like Winds, ere Hurricanes arise.
> The most corrupt are most obsequious grown,
> And those they scorn'd, officiously they own.
>
> [I, pp. 2–3]

The courtiers in this scene agree about the defects of Aureng-Zebe's brothers: Darah is vengeful, Sujah bigoted, Morat "too insolent,"

> But *Aureng-Zebe*, by no strong passion sway'd,
> Except his Love, more temp'rate is, and weigh'd:
> This *Atlas* must our sinking State uphold;
> In Council cool, but in Performance bold:
> He sums their Virtues in himself alone,

And adds the greatest, of a Loyal Son:
His Father's Cause upon his Sword he wears,
And with his Arms, we hope, his Fortune bears.

[I, p. 4]

Unlike such earlier heroes as Almanzor, Aureng-Zebe exhibits considerable self-restraint. Even when his father treats him unfairly, he remains loyal, quickly reconsidering a rash attempt to rescue his fiancée from house arrest and refusing a later opportunity to lead a rebellion. Though courageous in battle and passionately devoted to Indamora, Aureng-Zebe is a more reflective hero than any of his predecessors, and Dryden dramatizes that change by contrasting him with his impetuous half-brother Morat. Almanzor, echoing Hobbes, had declared himself

> free as Nature first made man
> 'Ere the base Laws of Servitude began
> When wild in woods the noble savage ran.
> [*The Conquest of Granada*, Pt. I; I, i, 207–09]

But Aureng-Zebe, scorning the savagery of Morat, turns such language against his villainous brother:

> When thou wert form'd, Heav'n did a Man begin;
> But the brute Soul, by chance, was shuffl'd in.
> In Woods and Wilds thy Monarchy maintain,
> Where valiant Beasts, by force and rapine, reign.

[III, p. 40]

Morat responds by calling Aureng-Zebe a "dreaming Priest," but the play ultimately celebrates the inner fortitude of its hero, a quality he shares with Aeneas, Redcrosse, Samson Agonistes, and the Christ of *Paradise Regained*.

Dryden's thoughtful reading of Virgil, Spenser, and Milton pointed in the direction of a restrained heroism, a grandeur in suffering, as did the change in his attitude toward warfare that we noticed in *The State of Innocence* and the epilogue to *Calisto*. All the military action in *Aureng-Zebe* takes place offstage, and is usually described with horror; Morat's instinctive recourse to his sword, a cruder version of the impulses of Montezuma and Almanzor, contrasts with Aureng-Zebe's defensive action in the cause of peace and stability. But there were also practical reasons why Dryden created a different kind of hero in this play. Buckingham and others had effectively ridiculed the "huffing" heroes of his earlier plays, and Settle's clumsy imitations of the characteristic rant of Almanzor constituted another warning against returning to that idiom. Charles Hart, who had played those earlier heroes and would play this new one, was growing older; although he had evidently made a convincing Horner in *The Country Wife* in the previous season, there was something to be gained by casting him as a more mature hero and giving the part of Morat to the younger Kynaston. Other motives included Dryden's bitter experience with court and Parliamentary intrigue, his growing cynicism about public applause, whether political or literary, and his consequent appreciation of the virtues of retirement, which he had already praised in dedicating *Amboyna* to

Clifford. In dedicating *Aureng-Zebe* to Mulgrave, he claimed that it was his duty as a poet "to give testimony to Virtue," and praised his patron for being "above the wretched affectation of Popularity":

> A popular man is, in truth, no better than a Prostitute to common Fame, and to the People. He lies down to every one he meets for the hire of praise; and his Humility is onely a disguis'd Ambition. . . . How much more great and manly in your Lordship, is your contempt of popular applause, and your retir'd Virtue, which shines onely to a few. [sig. A2v–A3r]

In these severe comments on those seeking popularity, Dryden was surely thinking of Shaftesbury, who was hoping to mobilize "the People" to topple the established order. Siding instead with those like Mulgrave who loyally supported the Duke of York, Dryden offered a play in praise of restraint, with a hero who refuses to capitalize on his own popularity.

In a crucial soliloquy, Aureng-Zebe recognizes the futility of his political morality, but clings to it nonetheless:

> How vain is Virtue which directs our ways
> Through certain danger, to uncertain praise!
> Barren and aery name! thee Fortune flies;
> With thy lean Train, the Pious and the Wise.
> Heav'n takes thee at thy word, without regard;
> And lets thee poorly be thine own reward.
> The World is made for the bold impious man;
> Who stops at nothing, seizes all he can.
> Justice to merit does weak aid afford;
> She trusts her Ballance, and neglects her Sword.
>
> [II, p. 29]

For Dryden, these were not mere aphorisms: as instances of the failure of justice to protect merit, he could remember the unjust impeachment of his early patron Clarendon and the sad end of his later patron Clifford; he now had reason to fear that Mulgrave and other Yorkist loyalists might suffer similarly if the "bold" and "impious" Shaftesbury had his way. The effective personification of "the Pious and the Wise" as the "lean Train" of Virtue expands an idea he expressed more simply in the dedication, where he spoke of Mulgrave's "retir'd Virtue, which shines onely to a few."

In his own literary milieu, Dryden himself had once vigorously defended his own desire for popularity, his intent "to delight the Age in which I live," but retirement now had a distinct appeal for him, as his attempts to secure a post at Oxford or some tangible court support for the writing of an epic poem suggest. In the dedication of this very play, he asks Mulgrave to remind Charles and James of their interest in his epic project, and praises Epicurus and Cowley for

> preferr[ing] the solitude of a Garden, and the conversation of a friend to any consideration, so much as a regard, of those unhappy People, whom in our own wrong, we call the great. True greatness, if it be any where on Earth, is in a private Virtue;

remov'd from the notion of Pomp and Vanity, confin'd to a contemplation of it self, and centring on it self. [sig. A4r]

Late in 1671, in the epilogue to Part I of *The Conquest of Granada*, the successful poet had complained that it was difficult to please the fickle audience: "Well may he please him self, but never you" (l. 22). Late in 1675, having seen *The Assignation* fail on stage and *The State of Innocence* fail to achieve production, he might well have echoed that complaint, but the prologue to *Aureng-Zebe*, one of his most confessional public gestures, begins instead by self-consciously reversing his earlier claim:

> Our Author by experience finds it true,
> 'Tis much more hard to please himself than you.
>
> [ll. 1–2]

Writing "to please himself" was Dryden's literary version of "a private Virtue . . . confin'd to a contemplation of it self." While sufficiently self-critical to "Damn his laborious Trifle of a Play" in the prologue and declare that it would be his last drama in verse, he also thanked the King for "graciously confirm[ing] . . . that it was the best of all my Tragedies; in which he has made Authentick my private opinion of it" (sig. A4v). Like his patron Mulgrave with his few friends or the personified "Virtue" with her "lean Train," Dryden was now content to have his excellence appreciated by a smaller, more discerning group. The epilogue, after listing the reasons why the play might fail to please ("No Song! no Dance! no Show!"), declares that the author is now writing for those few in the audience "Who can discern the Tinsel from the Gold" (ll. 15, 39).

But neither his own satisfaction nor the praise of a few discerning patrons could feed Dryden's family. With some bitterness, the prologue points out that the playwright will not profit financially from his literary efforts:

> A losing Gamester, let him sneak away;
> He bears no ready Money from the Play.
> The Fate which governs Poets, thought it fit,
> He should not raise his Fortunes by his Wit.
> The Clergy thrive, and the litigious Bar;
> Dull Heroes fatten with the spoils of War:
> All Southern Vices, Heav'n be prais'd, are here;
> But Wit's a luxury you think too dear.
>
> [ll. 23–30]

The cynicism of these lines is not difficult to understand. Dryden's rueful admission that "He bears no ready Money from the Play" acknowledges the fact that his contract with the King's Company had now become a liability: as an independent playwright, he would have received the third day's profits, but as a sharer, he had to suffer from the general indebtedness of the company, even though *Aureng-Zebe* proved quite successful.[53] The swipe at the clergy may reflect Dryden's failure to secure a post at Oxford and his envy of the lucrative parish livings enjoyed by men less eloquent and educated than he; his experiences with the Fuller lawsuit and the recent military mobilization gave him similar reasons to criticize lawyers and soldiers. The "Southern Vices" doubtless include the Italian music and French opera that had made theatre audiences unlikely to relish a more simply mounted play; the prologue closes by comparing the theatre companies to "Monarchs, ruin'd with expensive War" (l. 38). More important than these specific complaints, however, is Dryden's distaste for a world that considered "Wit," in the sense of intelligence, a "luxury." Like his hero Aureng-Zebe, who performs his roles as son, lover, and soldier to perfection, only to find himself awaiting execution, Dryden had reason to complain. Although he had continued to mature as an artist, his income had decreased in the years since the playhouse fire, and his requests for support from the court or the university had not produced the tangible results that might have enabled him to begin an epic poem. The great speech he wrote for the imprisoned hero, specifying an accompaniment of "*Soft Music*," surely draws on his own despair:

> When I consider Life, 'tis all a cheat;
> Yet, fool'd with hope, men favour the deceit;
> Trust on, and think to morrow will repay:
> To morrow's falser than the former day;
> Lies worse; and while it says, We shall be blest
> With some new joys, cuts off what we possest.
> Strange couzenage! none would live past years again,
> Yet all hope pleasure in what yet remain;
> And, from the dregs of Life, think to receive,
> What the first sprightly running could not give.
> I'm tir'd with waiting for this Chymic Gold,
> Which fools us young, and beggars us when old.
>
> [IV, p. 49]

In response to this despairing aria, the aging, passionate queen Nourmahal offers the notion that "Each day's a Mistris, unenjoy'd before," and Dryden's major alteration of the story was to make sexual passion, rather than mere greed for power, the primary motivation for all the characters. Another literary adversary, Joseph Arrowsmith, had meant to twit the Laureate by having his Tutor (in *The Reformation*) recommend plots with "two men in love with one woman," preferably "the Father and the Son, or two Brothers," but Dryden, far from repenting in the face of this criticism, now presented a father and two sons, all three in love with the same woman. While Aureng-Zebe is away defending his father's interests on the battlefield, the emperor falls in love with his son's betrothed, the captive queen Indamora. Blinded by his passion, the old man disowns Aureng-Zebe, delivering power to his younger son Morat, who promptly falls in love with Indamora himself, deserting his own bride Melesinda. Meanwhile, Nourmahal, Morat's mother and Aureng-Zebe's stepmother, conceives a fatal passion for Aureng-Zebe. Thus baldly laid out, these interlocking passions suggest those in Dryden's earlier plays, as does the casting: Mohun, who had played Maximin in *Tyrannick Love* and the lecherous Duke in *The Assignation*, appeared as the old emperor; Rebecca Marshall, who had played Lyndaraxa in the *Conquest*, took the part of Nourmahal.

But the surface texture and psychological depth of the new play are so unlike those of the earlier plays that they produce markedly different effects. Newly concerned to temper fancy with judgment, and fresh from his close study of Milton, Dryden gave his characters a flexible verse idiom in which the sexual motivation for their passions becomes plausible and moving. When the old emperor "Wishes each minute, he could unbeget / Those Rebel-Sons, who dare t'usurp his Seat" (I, p. 3), both the imagery and the enjambment recall *Paradise Lost*; the half-rhyme of "beget" and "Seat" is barely audible. Although the majority of Dryden's lines remain end-stopped, his appropriation of Miltonic vocabulary and syntax subtly alters the way his couplets strike the ear. When Indamora asks Arimant to carry a letter to Aureng-Zebe, having already promised his services in the letter itself, he complains of being "preingag'd without my own consent." Her haughty reply is technically a couplet constructed from two end-stopped lines, but we are unlikely to hear the end-rhymes as strongly as we do in Dryden's earlier plays:

> Unknown t'ingage you still augments my score,
> And gives you scope of meriting the more.

> [III, p. 32]

The compressed, Latinate syntax here will remind us of such Miltonic lines as Satan's retort to Zephon: "Not to know mee argues yourselves unknown" (*Paradise Lost*, IV, 830). The complexity of sound-patterns is also Miltonic: the first three syllables fit three different vowels into an alliteration of *n* sounds, and the main verb, "augments," combines two other alliterative patterns ("ingage—augments—gives" and "augments— my—meriting—more"). Such internal effects inevitably draw our attention away from the end-rhymes.[54]

Isolated short lines of two or three feet had occasionally appeared in Dryden's earlier plays, but *Aureng-Zebe* includes at least six passages in which two short lines occur in close proximity to one another, balancing each other as do Milton's short lines in *Samson Agonistes*.[55] In one such case, the old emperor's confession to Arimant that he loves Indamora, the short lines even continue the rhyming of an earlier couplet:

> Thou shouldst have pull'd the secret from my breast,
> Torn out the bearded Steel to give me rest:
> At least thou should'st have ghess'd———
> Yet thou art honest, thou could'st ne[']r have ghess'd.
> Hast thou been never base? did Love ne'r bend
> Thy frailer Virtue, to betray thy Friend?
> Flatter me, make thy Court, and say, It did:
> Kings in a Crowd would have their Vices hid.
> We would be kept in count'nance, sav'd from shame:
> And own'd by others who commit the same.
> Nay, now I have confess'd.———

> [I, p. 8]

The frequent caesurae and insistent repetitions dramatize the emperor's torment; the rhyming sound of the word "ghessd" concludes five of the eleven lines. The resulting disturbance of the regular pattern of couplets, even when Dryden offers more rhyming, not less, helps make the inner turmoil of the character more plausible. We need only compare this speech with Maximin's couplet speech about his similar passion in *Tyran-nick Love* (quoted above, p. 205) to sense the difference. The old Maximin in love with the young St. Catharine is a ludicrous lecher; the old emperor in love with Indamora is a man who knows that his passion is wrong but cannot resist it.

Such flexible verse helps draw us into the inner lives of the characters, but the construction of the plot is also important: the tension between generations in Dryden's play recalls *King Lear*, with Aureng-Zebe playing Edgar to Morat's Edmund.[56] In pushing most of the physical violence offstage, so that the main dramatized actions are emotional confrontations between pairs of characters, Dryden also drew on Racine, and in developing the incestuous passion of Nourmahal, he reached back beyond Racine to his Latin model Seneca.[57] The resulting play held the stage well into the eighteenth century and provided a passionate idiom on which Pope drew heavily for his *Eloisa to Abelard*.[58]

But the power of *Aureng-Zebe* cannot be fully accounted for by explaining Dry-den's metrical sophistication and tracing his many sources. Although I shall have to construct this argument on the merest shreds of evidence, I believe the dramatic jealousies and quarrels of the many couples in the play reflect the tensions in Dryden's own sexual life in the years leading up to this play. A long anecdotal tradition, depen-dent in part on frequent cynical comments about marriage in Dryden's works, has held that his marriage was unhappy. Typical of these anecdotes is a story Malone attributes to the Earl of Orford:

> Lady Elizabeth Dryden, one morning, having come into his study at an unseasonable time, when he was intently employed on some composition, and finding he did not attend to her, exclaimed, 'Lord! Mr. Dryden, you are always poring upon these musty books;—I wish I was a book, and then I should have more of your company.' 'Well, my dear,' replied the poet, 'when you do become a book, pray, let it be an Almanack; for then, at the end of the year, I shall lay you quietly on the shelf, and shall be able to pursue my studies without interruption.' [pp. 408–09]

First written down a century after Dryden's death, this tale cannot carry much au-thority, but it does portray a moment in which a woman asks for more attention from her husband, only to be rebuked with a sneering remark indicating his boredom with her—a situation not unlike the one Dryden dramatized when Melesinda goes in search of her husband Morat, only to find that he is indifferent to her, having fallen in love with Indamora:

> *Mel.* I have been seeking you this hour's long space,
>   And fear'd to find you in another place;
>   But, since you're here, my jealousie grows less:
>   You will be kind to my unworthiness.
>   What shall I say? I love to that degree,
>   Each glance another way is robb'd from me.
>   Absence, and Prisons I could bear again;
>   But sink, and die, beneath your least disdain.
> *Mor.* Why do you give your mind this needless care,
>   And, for your self, and me, new pains prepare?

> I ne'r approv'd this passion in excess:
> If you would show your love, distrust me less.
> I hate to be pursu'd from place to place:
> Meet, at each turn, a stale domestic face.
> Th'approach of jealousie Love cannot bear,
> He's wild, and soon on wing, if watchful eyes come near.
> *Mel.* From your lov'd presence, how can I depart?
> My eyes pursue the object of my heart.
> *Mor.* You talk as if it were our Bridal night:
> Fondness is still th'effect of new delight;
> And Marriage but the pleasure of a day:
> The Metall's base[,] the Gilding worn away.

[IV, pp. 54–55]

The eighteenth-century anecdote, with its all-too-typical misogyny, was offered as an instance of Dryden's wit; whoever invented or retold it had no sympathy for Elizabeth. But the scene from the play puts such scorn for his wife into the mouth of a man we know to be a villain and serves to generate considerable sympathy for Melesinda. If Dryden treated his wife with contempt and boredom in the early 1670s, as he surely did by having his affair with Anne Reeves, he dramatized such attitudes and actions as the behavior of a villain in *Aureng-Zebe*.

As early as the prologue to *An Evening's Love* (1668), Dryden had written about the tendency of marriage to go stale; by 1671, when he sought "new delight" by beginning his affair with Anne Reeves, he evidently considered Elizabeth "a stale domestic face." For Elizabeth, the years of that affair were unquestionably painful: she had to care for her three small sons on a reduced income while suffering the humiliation of having her husband's infidelity dramatized in the expanded revival of *The Rehearsal*. Through it all, however, the Drydens never broke up their London home. Other quarreling couples simply separated: Buckingham sent his wife home to her father when his affair with the Countess of Shrewsbury was at its height; Elizabeth's brother Sir Robert made a financial settlement with his second wife, the former Honoria O'Brien, in which the spouses agreed to live apart. But the Drydens, perhaps because of their devotion to their children, perhaps also because it was more economical, remained together, though Elizabeth did not accompany her husband on his summer journeys to Northampton-shire.[59] I imagine there were quarrels, perhaps not unlike the quarrels that strained Pepys's marriage when his wife found him with his hand under the waiting-woman's shift, and I believe that Dryden drew on the experience of those quarrels in the shrill scene between Nourmahal and the old emperor in Act II of *Aureng-Zebe*.

Aware of her husband's passion for the younger Indamora, Nourmahal enters complaining of "broken Faith, and an abandon'd Bed." Scorning his hypocritical claims of continued ardor, she rejects the "dregs and droppings of enervate Love" and grandly takes pride in her "known virtue" while criticizing his "wild appetites." The emperor's weary reply may well reflect Dryden's feelings during this strained period in his own home:

What can be sweeter than our native home!
Thither for ease, and soft repose, we come:
Home is the sacred refuge of our life:
Secur'd from all approches, but a Wife.
If thence we fly, the cause admits no doubt:
None but an Inmate Foe could force us out.
Clamours, our privacies uneasie make:
Birds leave their Nests disturb'd and Beasts their Haunts forsake.

[II, p. 23]

But as the quarrel grows worse and the emperor threatens force, Aureng-Zebe enters. Kneeling before his father and entreating his clemency, he reminds the old man that

Secrets of Marriage still are Sacred held:
There sweet and bitter by the wise conceal'd.
Errors of Wives reflect on Husbands still:
And, when divulg'd, proclaim you've chosen ill.
And the mysterious pow'r of Bed and Throne,
Should always be maintain'd but rarely shown.

[II, p. 25]

Again misogyny, though powerfully dramatized, is rebuked, and the reason for reconciliation that the hero offers his father, the avoidance of proclaiming publicly that one has "chosen ill," may have been among Dryden's motives for his own reconciliation with Elizabeth. Charles Dryden, aged nine when this play was first staged, was hardly yet ready to play Aureng-Zebe to his father's errant emperor, but it is just possible that he was the cause of the reconciliation between the Drydens that I believe took place in 1675. Another eighteenth-century anecdote about the quarreling Drydens has the poet casting Charles's horoscope at the time of his birth and predicting that he would suffer a dangerous accident on his eighth birthday. According to this tale, for which there is of course no confirmation, Dryden and his eldest son spent August of 1674 visiting the Earl of Berkshire, Charles's uncle and namesake. On the fatal day, the Earl supposedly organized a hunt; Dryden left the boy inside to study his Latin and rode with the hunters, but a servant persuaded the child to come outside and watch the sport, and an old wall fell upon him, "his poor little head being crushed to a perfect mash."[60] Elizabeth Thomas, who told this tale, claimed to have heard it from Elizabeth Dryden; her association with the notorious publisher Edmund Curll, who first printed the story, is an excellent reason to doubt her veracity, but there are authentic letters from Dryden to Mrs. Thomas, and even such wildly embroidered anecdotes often have some basis in truth. If Charles did indeed suffer some kind of accident in 1674, the danger to his life might well have shocked his parents into recognizing the importance of patching up their own relationship.

Whatever the reason, there certainly was a reconciliation. Anne Reeves, who was re-sworn as a member of the King's Company on 14 June 1675, five days before a revival of *Marriage A-la-Mode*, disappears from theatrical records after that date. She did not play the servant Zayda in *Aureng-Zebe*, a role like those she had previously taken, and later attacks on Dryden mentioning their affair usually employ the past tense. By March of 1678, when Dryden's *The Kind Keeper, or Mr. Limberham* had its brief run, he was surely no longer himself the "keeper" of a mistress, and the later evidence we have about his marriage suggests a stable domestic scene. In 1682, both John and Elizabeth wrote notes to Busby about their sons at Westminster; these radiate a shared concern for the boys that was surely a force in keeping the marriage together (*Letters*, pp. 17–20, 150). A late letter from Dryden to his sons in Rome has a long postscript from Elizabeth, full of concern for the health of her husband and her sons; Dryden's part of that letter explains his reasons for taking on the troublesome task of writing a second St. Cecilia ode: "I coud not deny the Stewards of the feast, who came in a body to me, to desire that kindness; one of them being Mr Bridgman, whose parents are your Mothers friends" (*Letters*, p. 93). This epistolary evidence allows us to glimpse a marriage involving at least mutual respect and shared concern for the children; literary evidence, though obviously far less certain, suggests that the reconciliation took place while Dryden was writing *Aureng-Zebe*. In the prologue to that play, he announced that he had "Grow[n] weary of his long-lov'd Mistris, Rhyme," delaying until the last possible moment the revelation that "Mistris" was a metaphor. Spoken with a pregnant pause before its final word, this line was a delicious joke for an audience aware of Dryden's affair, but it may also have been a way of acknowledging that he had indeed grown weary of Anne Reeves. The plot resonates with the issues of faithfulness and jealousy; without crudely identifying Dryden with his literary creations, any more than we would crudely identify those creations with the English political figures whose problems they also dramatize, we may suspect that he drew upon his own emotional life in the many scenes between couples.

In scene after scene, couples rail at one another, but most of those quarrels lead to reconciliations. In their first scene together, Indamora cannot share Aureng-Zebe's dreams of their future paradise, knowing as she does that the old emperor's lust for her will lead to trouble. Aureng-Zebe immediately leaps to the conclusion that she no longer loves him, and scorns her as a "Fair Hypocrite" (I, p. 13); only her revealing the fatal secret, which leads to her being seized by the guards, can reconcile him to her. His jealousy is thus the major evidence of his passion, and this sequence of suspicion and reconciliation is played out twice more in scenes of increasing complexity.

In Act IV, Aureng-Zebe jealously surmises that his execution has been delayed because Indamora has promised her love to Morat; she is entirely innocent, but he upbraids her with misogynistic phrases borrowed from the Dalila scene in *Samson Agonistes*:

> Ah Traitress! Ah Ingrate! Ah faithless mind!
> Ah Sex, invented first to damn Mankind!
> Nature took care to dress you up for sin:
> Adorn'd without; unfinish'd left, within.
> Hence, by no judgment you your loves direct;
> Talk much, ne'r think, and still the wrong affect.
> So much self-Love in your composures mix'd
> That love to others still remains unfix'd:

Greatness, and Noise, and Show, are your delight;
Yet wise men love you, in their own despight:
And, finding in their native Wit no ease,
Are forc'd to put your folly on to please.

[IV, p. 62]

The Miltonic passage Dryden is adapting here is spoken by the Chorus, and celebrates Samson's refusal to forgive Dalila.[61] Though following Milton's language closely, Dryden puts it to an entirely different dramatic use. Milton's play endorses misogyny; our sympathies are meant to lie with Samson. Dryden's play exposes misogyny as the undeserved result of irrational jealousy; our sympathies are meant to lie with Indamora. When she turns away from Aureng-Zebe, crushed by this abusive speech, he finally recognizes his error and her innocence, reclaiming her in a speech filled with physical passion:

Heard you that sigh? from my heav'd heart it past,
And said, If you forgive not, 'tis my last.
Love mounts, and rowls about my stormy mind,
Like Fire, that's born by a tempestuous Wind.
Oh, I could stifle you with eager haste!
Devour your kisses with my hungry taste!
Rush on you! eat you! wander o'r each part,
Raving with pleasure, snatch you to my heart!

[IV, p. 63]

Unfortunately for Indamora, neither of these experiences has a lasting impact on Aureng-Zebe. In the final scene, he enters in time to see the dying Morat, who has manfully acknowledged his errors and begged Melesinda's forgiveness, kissing Indamora's hand. Again, his jealousy flares up, though this time he expresses it with a kind of tragic despair:

Aur. With, or without you, I can have no rest:
    What shall I do? y'are lodg'd within my breast:
    Your Image never will be thence displac'd;
    But there it lies, stabb'd, mangl'd, and defac'd.
Ind. Yet to restore the quiet of your heart,
    There's one way left.
Aur.   ———Oh name it.
Ind.   ———'Tis to part.
    Since perfect bliss with me you cannot prove,
    I scorn to bless by halves the man I love.

[V, p. 82]

This offer leaves Aureng-Zebe "tortur'd on the Rack, / 'Twixt Shame and Pride," emotions Dryden himself surely felt during the crisis in his own marriage, but the old emperor, who has learned from the tragedy to regret his own romantic folly, enters and reconciles the couple; the hero kneels and begs his lady's forgiveness.

Two more deaths, however, cast a shadow across this scene of joy and resolution.

Melesinda, whose faithfulness and suffering exceed even Indamora's, passes across the stage on the way to mounting her undeserving husband's funeral pyre, and Nourmahal, delirious with the poison she has taken, delivers a frantic dying speech. The misogyny that is undeniably an element in this play makes one last appearance in the emperor's cynical farewell to his wife:

> With thy last breath thou hast thy crimes confest:
> Farewel; and take, what thou ne'r gav'st me, rest.

[V, p. 86]

Although the emperor then turns to the happy couple and closes the play by celebrating love, honor, and loyalty, a Freudian might point to the death of Nourmahal as a projection of Dryden's continuing hostility toward his wife, or indeed toward women in general. I might answer or at least qualify that argument by pointing out that each of the three leading male characters—Aureng-Zebe, the emperor, and even Morat—must finally beg the forgiveness of the woman he has wronged. If Aureng-Zebe, with his courage and self-restraint, is the play's model of political morality, Indamora is its model of sexual morality, her excellence repeatedly tested by his failings.

The argument I have spun here is speculative, and I cannot prove that *Aureng-Zebe* was Dryden's farewell to his fleshly mistress. It certainly was his farewell to the rhymed heroic play, his literary mistress, and thus the end of some thirteen years in which verse drama had been his central literary task. We have already considered many of his motives for abandoning rhymed plays: the negative example of Settle, the positive example of Milton, the interest in writing an epic, the changing tastes of the audience. To these we should also add Dryden's own restlessness and his sense that he had exhausted the possibilities of the genre. Ostensibly defending himself against a crit-icism of his female characters by "some of the fair Ladies," he wrote in the dedication that great passage on changeability acknowledging that "Our minds are perpetually wrought on by the temperament of our Bodies" (sig. a1r); the arguments he made there would prove applicable to many of the later changes in his career. In the prologue, while graciously yielding to the arguments against the artificiality of rhyme that Sir Robert Howard had offered eleven years earlier, he insisted that this play might stand as an example of "What Verse can do":

> Passion's too fierce to be in Fetters bound,
> And Nature flies him like Enchanted Ground.
> What Verse can do, he has perform'd in this,
> Which he presumes the most correct of his.

[ll. 9–12]

As usual, his self-judgment was precise. "Correct" in its adherence to the unities, *Aureng-Zebe* is the most flexible of Dryden's rhymed plays, the one in which we are least conscious of the "Fetters" of rhyme. In his early rhymed plays, the passions of the characters had been drawn from the stylized posturing of the romance tradition, but in this more deeply felt drama, those passions partake of nature: Dryden had now experi-enced a wider range of emotions, and had learned how to draw on his own inner life as a source of strength for his poetry.

→→→ CHAPTER NINE ←←←

The "Bowe of *Ulysses*"
1676–1679

"Satyrs on Poets"

The success of *Aureng-Zebe* did nothing to heal the internal strife of the King's Company. On 14 February 1676, three days before the published play was advertised in the *Gazette*, the King, "understanding That His Company of Comoedians have left off actinge upon private differences and disagreements betweene themselues," instructed the Lord Chamberlain to "require and order the said Company forthwith to act and play as formerly."[1] The Duke's Company, undisturbed by any such problems, continued its series of successes: Etherege's *The Man of Mode* in March and Shadwell's *The Virtuoso* in May were superior offerings in two quite different comic modes; Thomas Otway's *Don Carlos*, acted in June, "got more Money than any preceding Modern Tragedy."[2] Dryden, who was all too aware of the superiority of Betterton's troupe, contributed an epilogue to Etherege's play, his first involvement with the Duke's theatre since the prologue for *Albumazar* in 1668. Although his friendship with Etherege was a sufficient motive, we may suspect that he was also signalling his hope for some change in his contractual arrangement with the troubled King's Company. He knew that the playwrights fortunate enough to write for Dorset Garden were receiving substantial profits for their third days, and he hoped to join them.

Despite Dryden's dissatisfaction with the King's Company, his plays continued to be important properties for Hart, Mohun, and their associates; on 29 May, they performed *Aureng-Zebe* at court, and a revival of *Tyrannick Love* earlier in the same month may also have taken place at Whitehall. Although such court performances meant extra income for the actors, the Laureate had publicly complained about "bear[ing] no ready Money" from *Aureng-Zebe* in its prologue, and was privately "complaining to the Company of his want of proffit." His name is notably absent from an agreement between Charles Killigrew and the principal actor-sharers of the King's Company, signed on 1 May, which involved substantial cash payoffs to Hart and Kynaston. Young Charles made this new agreement in the expectation that his father would sign over the valuable patent to him, but old Tom failed to keep that promise. The omission of Dryden's name is puzzling, since the players later claimed that his contract with the King's Company was still in force, but whatever his legal obligations were, the Laureate was evidently eager to reduce his involvement with the troubled company.[3]

Dryden's epilogue for *The Man of Mode* makes the point that Sir Fopling Flutter, the comic butt of the play, is a composite figure, put together by combining the affectations of many different men; it does not mention Dorimant, the hero, who was widely considered a stage version of the Earl of Rochester. We cannot know whether Dryden avoided mentioning Dorimant because he had already seen the criticism aimed at him by the real Rochester in "An Allusion to Horace," which was now circulating in manuscript; we do know that he was wounded by the poem when he saw it. Sometime during this spring, Rochester's friend Henry Savile sent him word that he was "out of favor with a certain poet,"[4] and the poet had good reason. With the exception of Buckingham's *Rehearsal*, the earlier attacks on Dryden had not been impressive pieces of writing: there were valid criticisms buried beneath the pompous prose of Sir Robert Howard's prefaces, the heavy-handed caricature of Shadwell's Drybob, and the sophomoric nit-picking of the "Rota" pamphlets, but in all those attacks, the presentation weakened the criticism. Rochester's poem, however, couples trenchant criticism with an original presentation. His critical remarks about Dryden are more carefully targeted than the generalized abuse of the earlier attacks, and his poem makes a more serious bid to be considered as literature. It is one of the first imitations of Horace in English, establishing a precedent on which Dryden and Pope would later draw, and it shows Rochester's confident mastery of the couplet as a device for compression and irony.

In the Horatian poem Rochester chose to adapt (*Satire* I. 10), the speaker insists on his right to point out both faults and beauties in other authors, and Rochester's opening lines couple a criticism of Dryden's rhymes as "stol'n, unequal, nay dull many times" with an acknowledgment that "his plays, embroidered up and down / With wit and learning, justly pleased the town" (ll. 2, 5–6). By beginning his poem with an attack on Dryden's rhymes, indeed using the very word as his own first rhyme, Rochester signals his larger method: he will attack those areas of vulnerability exposed by the gestures of modesty in Dryden's published criticism. Dryden, who had worked hard to soften the thud of his end-rhyming in *Aureng-Zebe*, knew to his cost just how precise Rochester's first complaint was, but he could hardly begin defending himself, since he had announced his abandonment of rhymed drama in the prologue to that play.

Not content with criticizing Dryden on stylistic grounds, Rochester also attacks his critical principles and his arrogance:

> But does not Dryden find ev'n Jonson dull;
> Fletcher and Beaumont uncorrect, and full
> Of lewd lines, as he calls 'em; Shakespeare's style
> Stiff and affected; to his own the while
> Allowing all the justness that his pride
> So arrogantly had to these denied?

[ll. 81–86]

The claim that Dryden undervalued his Elizabethan predecessors and overvalued himself was an old one, made many times by Shadwell and others. But if Dryden had compared himself quite favorably to his predecessors in such notorious passages as the epilogue to Part II of *The Conquest of Granada*, he had never called Shakespeare "Stiff and affected." Indeed, he had now moved beyond his early praise of Shakespeare's "comprehensive soul" (XVII, 55) to direct praise of his style. In the prologue to *Aureng-Zebe*, "Our Author" acknowledges his pride and yields the palm to Shakespeare:

> But spite of all his pride a secret shame
> Invades his breast at *Shakespear*'s sacred name:
> Aw'd when he hears his Godlike *Romans* rage,
> He, in a just despair, would quit the Stage.
> And to an Age less polish'd, more unskill'd,
> Does, with disdain the foremost Honours yield.
>
> [ll. 13–18]

Dryden's next play, *All for Love*, would be a blank-verse imitation of one of Shakespeare's "Roman" tragedies, and this prologue may indicate that such a project was already in its early stages. Again Rochester's criticism, with its emphasis on Dryden's pride, uses language taken from Dryden's recent criticism of himself, though there is a considerable rhetorical difference between Dryden's confession of his "secret shame" and Rochester's accusation of arrogance.

Rochester, however, argues that Dryden's criticism of earlier authors gives him the right to criticize Dryden:

> And may not I have leave impartially
> To search and censure Dryden's works, and try
> If those gross faults his choice pen does commit
> Proceed from want of judgment, or of wit;
> Or if his lumpish fancy does refuse
> Spirit and grace to his loose, slattern muse?
>
> [ll. 87–92]

The critical terms Rochester juggles here—"judgment," "wit," "fancy," "Spirit," "grace"—had been the touchstones of Dryden's criticism of Settle, and would figure prominently in "The Author's Apology for Heroique Poetry, and Poetique License," an important critical essay prefixed to the published *State of Innocence* in 1677. The metaphor of the muse as a "loose slattern" also comes from Dryden himself, who had used such humor in the prologue to *An Evening's Love*. Rochester's essential complaint is that Dryden's work is uneven, in part because of hurried composition:

> Five hundred verses every morning writ
> Proves you no more a poet than a wit.
> Such scribbling authors have been seen before;
> *Mustapha, The English Princess*, forty more
> Were things perhaps composed in half an hour.
>
> [ll. 93–97]

The implication that Dryden wrote "Five hundred verses every morning" is a comic exaggeration, and even his weakest work is far better than the plays by Orrery and John Caryll that Rochester maliciously cites, but the Laureate had sought to excuse *Tyrannick Love* and *Amboyna* on the grounds of haste, and *Aureng-Zebe* shows more signs of careful revision than any earlier play. Rochester's general advice to authors recommends such care:

> To write what may securely stand the test
> Of being well read over, thrice at least
> Compare each phrase, examine every line,
> Weigh every word and every thought refine.
>   Scorn all applause the vile rout can bestow,
> And be content to please those few who know.
>
>   [ll. 98–103]

The last couplet is quite close to Dryden's declaration that he was now writing for himself and those few who could "discern the Tinsel from the Gold."

When Rochester names "hasty Shadwell and slow Wycherley" as the only modern writers to have "touched upon true comedy" (ll. 41–43), he implies that Dryden has not. Again, the victim had said the same thing of himself: in dedicating *Marriage A-la-Mode* to Rochester, he made a distinction between himself and "the best Comick Writers of our Age," and in dedicating *Aureng-Zebe* to Mulgrave, he again admitted that others had outdone him in comedy. Since he shared Rochester's high regard for Wycherley, Dryden was doubtless referring to Wycherley and Etherege in those passages, and he was probably surprised to find that Rochester, who had once criticized Shadwell, was now willing to pair him with Wycherley. Rochester's praise of Shadwell, like his criticism of Dryden, is qualified: his "unfinished works," according to this poem, "impart / Great proofs of force of nature, none of art" (ll. 44–45). But Shadwell's claim, throughout his intermittent controversy with Dryden, had been that his own "humours" comedy, with its emphasis on comic characters, was more "natural" than the "artificial" "wit" comedy practiced by Dryden and others. Shadwell might thus have read these lines as a welcome endorsement; *The Virtuoso*, his best comedy, made Rochester's praise seem prophetic when it appeared on stage in May.

In a nastier and less verifiable criticism (quoted above, p. 225), Rochester accuses Dryden of clumsy obscenity in his speech. Combining a sexual insult with a demeaning reflection on Dryden's short, plump figure, he says that Dryden "Would give the ladies a dry bawdy bob, / And thus he got the name of Poet Squab" (ll. 75–76). Rochester's literary criticisms reveal his detailed knowledge of Dryden's works and opinions, but this low blow betrays his awareness of Shadwell's old caricature, Drybob. Moving back to literary matters, Rochester immediately qualifies this unpleasant passage by admitting that Dryden's "excellencies more than faults abound" (l. 78) and acknowledging that "he best deserves to wear" the laurel. Still, Dryden might well have concluded from this and other evidence that Rochester was in league with Shadwell.

Aware of both the accuracy of much of Rochester's criticism and the danger of entering into controversy with an aristocrat, Dryden delayed his reply until the preface to *All for Love*, published early in 1678. Neither of those constraints, however, prevented him from replying to an unfair attack by his social inferior Shadwell in the printed edition of *The Virtuoso*, first advertised on 3 July 1676. Like several of Shadwell's earlier plays, this comedy is dedicated to Dryden's former collaborator the Duke of Newcastle. At the conclusion of the dedication, Shadwell boasts that his play "has succeeded beyond [his] expectation," and says that its "Humours . . . have been approved by Men of the best Sense and Learning." Presumably responding to Dryden's real or imagined disapproval, he then repeats the charges he had been making against the Laureate since 1668 and adds new ones:

> Nor do I hear of any profest Enemies to the Play, but some Women, and some Men of Feminine understandings, who like slight Plays onely, that represent a little tattle sort of Conversation, like their own; but true Humour is not liked or understood by them, and therefore even my attempt towards it is condemned by them. But the same people, to my great comfort, damn all Mr. *Johnson's* Plays, who was incomparably the best Dramatick Poet that ever was, or, I believe, ever will be; and I had rather be Authour of one Scene in his best Comedies, than of any Play this Age has produced. That there are a great many faults in the conduct of this Play, I am not ignorant. But I (having no Pension but from the Theatre, which is either unwilling or unable to reward a Man sufficiently for so much pains as correct Comedies require) cannot allot my whole time to the writing of Plays, but am forced to mind some other business of Advantage. (Had I as much Money, and as much time for it) I might, perhaps, write as Correct a Comedy as any of my Contemporaries. [III, 102]

Shadwell had been insisting upon a distinction between comedy of humours and comedy of wit or conversation for eight years now, and he never tired of accusing Dryden of undervaluing Jonson, even though Dryden had now printed several passages in praise of Jonson and had also tried to indicate his respect for humours comedy. If these criticisms were old hat, Shadwell's stubborn repetition of them was surely irritating, as was his appropriating the weapon of misogyny, which Dryden had used against Settle, to call Dryden a "M[a]n of Feminine understanding."

What probably stung Dryden into replying, however, was Shadwell's new and absurd claim that his own imperfections arose from his "having no Pension but from the Theatre." Dryden, the obvious target, had a pension from the government, his annual salary as Poet Laureate and Historiographer Royal, but it was hardly sufficient to give him the great advantage implied here: his £200 for 1675 arrived in two payments of £100, the first on 28 February 1676, the second on 24 March,[5] and his attempt to secure an increase that would free him to write his projected epic had not yet produced a result. His Oxford prologue spoken in the summer of 1676 (quoted above, p. 270) reiterates his desire to retire to the peaceful shades of the university, a polite way of asking for financial support. Worse yet, his share in the King's Company, which had yielded profits in the good times, was now a liability; indeed, Shadwell's third day for *The Virtuoso* probably yielded him more money than Dryden received from the King's Company between 1672 and 1676. Dryden's omission from the list of sharers in the agreement of 1 May 1676 and his successful later demand for a third day for *All for Love* suggest that he no longer considered himself a sharer.[6]

There was an even more personal reason why Shadwell's remarks about money irked Dryden at this time. Dryden's small income from the property in Blakesley had been slightly increased, a few weeks before Shadwell's attack, by the death of his mother, buried at Titchmarsh on 14 June 1676. Although Mary Dryden had been sufficiently wealthy to lend her brother Henry some £1,300 in 1667, that loan remained unpaid; her daughters Elizabeth and Frances, who were appointed executors, spent the rest of the century trying to collect it.[7] Mary's only cash bequests were £20 each to those two daughters; her other children received furniture and mementos. The gifts to her eldest son and his family were strictly sentimental:

> I give and bequeath to my beloved sonne John Dryden a silver tankard marked with I: D: And a Goold Ring which was my wedding Ring. And it is my will that after the decease of my deare sonne John Dryden that his Eldest Sonne Charles should have the Ring given to him as a guift from his Grandmother M: D: I give my Grandsonne Erasmus Dryden a Goold Ring of Tenn Shillings price to weare in Remembrance of me after my death.[8]

If we imagine Dryden returning to London from his mother's funeral, only to encounter Shadwell's dedication, with its false picture of a well-fed Laureate enjoying the leisure of a profitable pension, we may understand why that dedication was probably the immediate occasion for *Mac Flecknoe.*[9]

Dryden's other reasons for composing this remarkable poem included the whole history of his relations with Shadwell, the restless search for new literary forms in which he was engaged, the practice in prose vituperation he had gained from the controversies with Howard and Settle, and the irritation he felt at being attacked by Rochester, whose poem he emulates in his choice of meter and indirectly answers by attacking Shadwell, whom Rochester had praised. Dryden could hardly have answered Rochester's attack on his short stature in kind; not only was Rochester elegantly shaped, but he was an Earl. The obese Shadwell, however, provided a perfect substitute target for his resentment. If Rochester had called him "Poet Squab," Dryden could refer to Shadwell's "mountain belly" (l. 193). But that phrase, like so much else in this poem, is an allusion as well as an insult: Ben Jonson, Shadwell's hero, had referred to his own "mountaine belly" in a poem to his friend Drummond;[10] for those who caught it, Dryden's echo implied that Shadwell's girth was his only resemblance to Jonson. Although no substantial personal cause for Dryden's choice of Flecknoe as Shadwell's literary father has come to light, that choice was another way of denying Shadwell's claim to the mantle of Ben Jonson, model writer of humours comedy. Far from allowing his rival to be a son of Ben, Dryden anoints him as the son and successor to Flecknoe, a self-styled but laughably incompetent imitator of Jonson's epigrammatic style.[11] Rochester's Horatian speaker, qualifying his praise of Shadwell, had given him credit for "proofs of force of nature, none of art." Dryden's answer, proof of his own considerable art, was to have his fictional Flecknoe enthusiastically claim Shadwell as his own, denying him a share in nature, art, or the Jonsonian tradition:

Thou art my blood, where *Johnson* has no part;
What share have we in Nature or in Art?

[ll. 175–76]

In a more subtle and private reference to Shadwell's obesity, Dryden has Flecknoe declare that Shadwell's "goodly Fabrick fills the eye, / And seems design'd for thoughtless Majesty" (ll. 25–26). Not only does the notion of choosing a successor on the basis of his physical appearance mock the plans of Shadwell's political allies, who were willing to argue that the handsome appearance of the Duke of Monmouth qualified him for the throne, but Dryden himself had actually used the words "goodly Fabrick" when dedicating *Tyrannick Love* to Monmouth in 1670 (X, 108). By the magic of irony, a

Anonymous portrait of Thomas Shadwell, ca. 1690.

phrase once used in a fawning panegyric to an elegant aristocrat became an insult when directed against a fat commoner, who may have been, in the unknowable world of Dryden's subconscious emotions, a substitute for another aristocrat.

I have just offered a speculative account of some of Dryden's motives for writing *Mac Flecknoe*, but we can only guess at those motives because the poem transcends the personal irritations that prompted it. Allusions, including borrowings from Virgil, Horace, Spenser, Milton, Cowley, and Waller, are a part of this process; no previous English satire is so relentlessly literary.[12] But while most of Dryden's borrowings serve mock-heroic purposes, making Shadwell look ludicrous by temporarily casting him as the royal Psalmist David or the dolphin-riding Arion or the youthful heir Ascanius, their cumulative force helps move the poem beyond the realm of mere personal spite. Even the allusions to Shadwell's personal characteristics and recent works, which are frequent and precise, become a part of something larger, a mythic picture of "*Sh——*" as the archetype of dullness. When Flecknoe anoints Shadwell, for example, "His Temples last with Poppies were o'erspread" (l. 126). Any reader would recognize the substitution of poppies for the poet's traditional laurel, and conclude that Dryden considered Shadwell's verses soporific. A reader close to the world of the theatre might also know that Shadwell was addicted to opium; he died of an overdose in 1692. In a more typical seventeenth-century poem of vituperation, the attacker would have pointed overtly at his victim's weakness; six years later, after Shadwell had published a series of outrageous personal slanders against him, Dryden fired back an anonymous but direct reference to Shadwell's addiction.[13] This time, however, he was more elliptical because he saw a chance to move the poem of vituperation into the realm of lasting literature. Like other poems growing out of literary controversy, *Mac Flecknoe* yields specific pleasures to the reader aware of the particular quarrels, in this case, the rivalries of London theatre world of the 1670s; unlike most such poems, it also measures its victim's inflated claims to literary excellence against the more permanent standards of the epic tradition, demonstrating its own author's confident command of that tradition in the process; and its marvelous energy and high spirits are so infectious that readers knowing little about Shadwell or Virgil can nonetheless feel its essential force.

In the opening lines, Dryden applies the solemn theme of entropy and the politically urgent theme of succession to Flecknoe's choice of Shadwell as his literary heir:

> All humane things are subject to decay,
> And, when Fate summons, Monarchs must obey:
> This *Fleckno* found, who, like *Augustus*, young
> Was call'd to Empire, and had govern'd long:
> In Prose and Verse, was own'd, without dispute
> Through all the Realms of *Non-sense*, absolute.

[ll. 1–6]

The tone is almost that of a serious poem; Flecknoe's funny name, which sounds incongruous in the same line with Augustus, is the first indication that language we normally associate with grand occasions is going to be invaded by indecorous words. The next dislocation—"*Non-sense*" where we might have expected "England" or

"Learning"—is broader, and when Flecknoe bursts out into prophetic praise of Shadwell every phrase is oxymoronic: the designated heir is "Mature in dullness" and "confirm'd in full stupidity"; he "never deviates into sense" (ll. 16, 18–19). These phrases are insulting, of course, but their effect is quite unlike that of the insults in lesser poems of literary controversy, up to and including Rochester's attack on Dryden. Years later, in his "Discourse concerning the Original and Progress of Satire," Dryden found the perfect metaphor for describing what he had done: "there is . . . a vast difference between the slovenly Butchering of a Man, and the fineness of a stroak that separates the Head from the Body, and leaves it standing in its place" (IV, 71).

Dryden's manipulation of rhetoric helps keep his strokes fine. Like Pope in the next century, Rochester partially protects himself by assuming the mask of Horace; the "I" of his poem cannot be completely identified with the actual rakish Earl, since the literary judgments cast in its sprightly verse are essentially those of Horace. Moving much further in that direction, Dryden avoids the first person altogether, appearing as the disembodied voice of a mock-epic narrator, but devoting over half of his poem to two long speeches in praise of Shadwell by Flecknoe. Since he had himself been praised by the real Flecknoe in an epigram first published in 1670, he knew that even sincere praise from such a dubious source could quickly turn to blame. When Flecknoe declares that "*Sh*——— alone, my perfect image bears" (l. 10), he is comically unaware of how inappropriate the language of kingly and divine succession is for himself or his chosen son. As readers, we laugh at Shadwell, demeaned by a gesture of praise, at Flecknoe, too foolish to realize that "a vile Encomium doubly ridicules," and at the cleverness of Dryden, who has drawn on his experience as a panegyrist, plugging incongruous words into syntactic structures normally used to praise the great and thus reversing the force of those phrases.

Although this brilliant poem evidently circulated in manuscript, Dryden kept it anonymous and unpublished for many years.[14] The first printing, in October 1682, was apparently unauthorized, though by that time Shadwell had published his anonymous and vituperative *Medal of John Bayes*, an attack that more than justified an answer. Not until the *Miscellany Poems* of 1684 did Dryden publish the poem in a collection of pieces largely from his hand, and even there the poem remained anonymous; he first referred to the poem as his own in the "Discourse concerning the Original and Progress of Satire,"published about a month before Shadwell's death in November of 1692. His hesitancy to publish may well have been a result of his experiences with publishing other retorts. He had reason to regret printing both the "Defence of the Essay" and the *Notes and Observations on the Empress of Morocco*, and this year brought further proof of the danger of attacking other writers: a casual remark Dryden made in criticism of Otway's *Don Carlos* prompted Otway to make a belated attack on *The Assignation* when he published his own play.[15] But *Mac Flecknoe* was more than an ephemeral pamphlet or a coffeehouse impromptu; Dryden's self-restraint in keeping it out of print involved not only controlling his anger but delaying the gratification of seeing one of his best poems widely circulated. In the preface to *All for Love*, he blamed the "many Satyrs on Poets, and censures of their Writings, [which] fly abroad" on the fact that "there are many witty men, but few Poets" (XIII, 14). *Mac Flecknoe* proved that its author was not merely a witty man, but a poet of the first rank; although the anger that fueled the composition was surely intense, the resulting poem is cool and controlled.

"Dis-incumber'd from Rhyme"

Not long after making up his mind to keep *Mac Flecknoe* out of print, Dryden decided to print *The State of Innocence*, which had been circulating in manuscript copies since its composition in late 1673 or early 1674. In "The Author's Apology," which served him as a preface to the published version, he explains his decision as an act of self-defense, "many hundred Copies of it being dispers'd abroad without my knowledge or consent: so that every one gathering new faults, it became at length a Libel against me" (sig. b1r). Although many readers were evidently interested, as the number of copies attests, there was now no chance of the opera's being performed, so Dryden probably decided to make what small profit he could from printing it. Milton, generously praised in the preface, was now dead, so that there was no question of offending him or interfering with his profits. Dryden had no new play ready for performance or publication during this theatrical season, and the state of the King's Company gave him no particular incentive to hurry his work on *All for Love*, which was probably in progress. On 3 August 1676, the Lord Chamberlain ordered the King's players not to act until further notice, and on 9 September, in yet another attempt at reorganization, he appointed Mohun, Hart, Kynaston, and Cartwright to act as managers. On 23 January 1677, Charles Killigrew sued his father in Chancery to gain control of the theatre, and on 22 February, ten days after Dryden published his opera, the suit was settled in favor of the younger man.[16] Despite the continuing turmoil, the King's players mounted two outstanding new plays during this season: Wycherley's *The Plain Dealer* (11 December 1676) and Lee's *The Rival Queens* (17 March 1677). Dryden praised Wycherley's comedy in "The Author's Apology" and wrote a poem in praise of Lee's tragedy that appeared with the published play in November of 1677, returning the favor of Lee's enthusiastic poem in praise of *The State of Innocence*.

Setting the record straight by printing a correct text may have been Dryden's principal reason for publishing *The State of Innocence*, but his decision to dedicate the unperformed opera to the Duchess of York suggests a political motive, as does the timing of the publication for 12 February 1677, just three days before Parliament reconvened. The dedication gave the Laureate an excellent opportunity to expand the praises of James he had printed a year earlier in the dedication to *Aureng-Zebe*; leaving no doubt about his loyalties, he told the Duchess that her husband was

> a Prince who only could deserve You: whose Conduct, Courage, and Success in War, whose Fidelity to His Royal Brother, whose Love for His Country, whose Constancy to His Friends, whose Bounty to his Servants, whose Justice to Merit, whose Inviolable Truth, and whose Magnanimity in all His Actions, seem to have been rewarded by Heaven by the gift of You. [sig. A2r]

Like his patron Mulgrave, who was accused of being a Papist because of his loyalty to York,[17] Dryden was evidently willing to risk having his religious orthodoxy impugned;

Portrait of Maria Beatrice of Modena by Simon Verelst, ca. 1680.

this dedication compares the admiration its author feels for Maria to "the rapture which Anchorites find in Prayer, when a Beam of the Divinity shines upon them: . . . they are speechless for the time that it continues, and prostrate and dead when it departs" (sig. A2v). Of course, this passage is humorously exaggerated, like Dryden's earlier passages using Catholic imagery in the verses to his cousin Honor and the birthday poem for Clarendon, but its language is drawn from the mystical writings of St. Teresa,[18] a curious source for even a comic allusion.

Dryden thus makes use of a kind of religious language sure to distress those in Parliament who had opposed James's choice of a Catholic Duchess; with a similar comic flourish, he also appropriates the very phrases in which the Opposition expressed its fears of arbitrary power and Popery as metaphorical praise of Maria's beauty: "You have subverted (may I dare to accuse you of it) even our Fundamental Laws; and Reign absolute over the Hearts of a stubborn and Free-born people tenacious almost to madness of their Liberty" (sig. A2v). Three days after this dedication appeared, some of those "stubborn and Free-born people," notably Shaftesbury and Buckingham, began the new session of Parliament by claiming that the fifteen-month prorogation was a de facto dissolution, since an old statute held that Parliament should meet every year. Danby and the King had anticipated this call for new elections: in his opening speech, Charles asked the legislators to "judge who is most for arbitrary government, they that foment such differences as tend to dissolve all Parliaments; or I, that would preserve this and all Parliaments from being made useless by such dissensions."[19] The treatment of those who had dared to oppose the government, however, was thoroughly arbitrary: Shaftesbury, Buckingham, and two other Whig lords were committed to the Tower, where Shaftesbury remained for over a year; even Buckingham was not released until June. Busy as he was containing this potential revolt, Lord Treasurer Danby noticed Dryden's demonstration of loyalty: on 20 February, the Treasury issued the Laureate a money warrant for his full salary for 1676, £200, "to be brought in notwithstanding any former restriction."[20]

If the dedication was a way for Dryden to show where he stood in the current political controversy, "The Author's Apology for Heroique Poetry, and Poetique Licence" was a way for him to answer the "Illiterate, Censorious, and Detracting People" (sig. b1v) who had criticized *The State of Innocence* while it was circulating from hand to hand. Publishing this work placed Dryden in an awkward position: in the eyes of some of his critics, *The State of Innocence*, with its "sublime" and luxuriant poetry, might seem open to the very criticisms Dryden had levelled at Settle in the *Notes and Observations*, where he had taken a hard line on poetic license:

> Some little friends of his who are Smatterers in Poetry, will be ready for most of his gross Errors to use that much mistaken plea of *Poetica Licentia*, which word Fooles are apt to use for the Palliateing the most absurd non-sense in any Poem. I can not find when Poets had Liberty from any Authority to write non-sense more than any other men, Nor is that Plea of *Poetica Licentia* used as a Subterfuge, by any but weake professors of that Art, who are commonly given over to a mist of Fancy, a buzzing of invention and a sound of something like Sense, and have no use of Judgement. [XVII, 180–81]

Yet even in the attack on Settle, Dryden had not sought to deny poetic license to himself and other writers; he had simply tried to define that license carefully:

> But some will say after this, what Licence is left for Poets? certainly the same that good Poets ever tooke, without being faulty (for surely the best were so sometimes, because they were but men) and that Licence is *Fiction*, which kind of Poetry is like that of Landschap painting; and poems of this nature, though they be not *Vera* [truths] ought to be *Verisimilia* [likenesses]. [XVII, 183]

"The Author's Apology" is essentially that paragraph writ large. Obliquely replying to Rochester's use of Horace against him, Dryden quotes Horace's well-known acknowledgment that even Homer sometimes nods; he also draws upon Longinus, whom he had evidently read in Boileau's influential translation of 1674, to provide authority for "preferr[ing] the sublime Genius that sometimes erres, to the midling or indifferent one which makes few faults, but seldome or never rises to any Excellence" (sig. b1v). As an example of the kind of bold figure allowable to a heroic poet, he quotes a line of his own describing the seraphs and cherubs "dissolv'd in Hallelujahs," repeats a supposedly witty coffeehouse criticism comparing those angels to "Anchove's dissolv'd in Sauce," and neatly defends himself by quoting a line from Virgil, who had described Troy as "somno vinoque sepultam," buried in sleep and wine (sig. c1v). In order to demonstrate "How easie 'tis to turn into ridicule the best descriptions," he quotes a line from Cowley, points out its potential for absurdity, then defends Cowley (and himself) by arguing that "an Image which is strongly and beautifully set before the eyes of the Reader, will still be Poetry when the merry fit is over" (sig. c1v). For those in the know, however, this piece of the argument had a curious underside: the line Dryden chose, "Where their vast Courts the Mother Waters keep," was one he had himself burlesqued in *Mac Flecknoe*.[21]

Like virtually all of Dryden's criticism, "The Author's Apology" is occasional, and many of the examples adduced to support its general arguments reflect current controversies. When discussing the various genres of literature, for example, Dryden praises "the Author of the *Plain Dealer*, whom I am proud to call my friend" (sig. b2v). He thus advertises a successful play first staged by the King's Company just two months earlier, publicly declares his pride in having Wycherley as a friend, and indirectly continues his argument with Shadwell by praising a satirical play he considered superior to Shadwell's comedies.[22] At the same time, however, this subtle and impressive essay transcends the immediate concerns of 1677. When Dryden extends his own earlier definition of poetic license as "Fiction" to include "Tropes" and "Figures" (sig. c2r), he is defending poetry against scientific skepticism about metaphor, continuing the argument he had begun in the poem to Dr. Charleton some fourteen years earlier; when he defines wit as "a propriety of Thoughts and Words; or in other terms, Thoughts and Words elegantly adapted to the Subject," he is moving away from Sprat's attempt to confine words to the inelegant task of describing mere "things." These arguments set up the triumphant concluding declaration that "all reasonable Men will conclude it necessary, that sublime Subjects ought to be adorn'd with the sublimest, and (consequently often) with the most figurative expressions" (sig. c2v). If the controversy with

Settle had prompted Dryden to advocate tempering fancy with judgment, his study of Longinus, Virgil, Milton, and Shakespeare had kept him aware that poetry had to be more than a narrowly defined "imitation of Nature":

> boldness of expression is not to be blam'd; if it be manag'd by the coolness and discretion, which is necessary to a Poet.
>   Yet before I leave this subject, I cannot but take notice how disingenuous our Adversaries appear: All that is dull, insipid, languishing, and without sinews in a Poem, they call an imitation of Nature; . . . lively Images and Elocution, are never to be forgiven. [sig. b4v]

In writing *Mac Flecknoe*, Dryden produced many "lively Images"; in suppressing it, he showed considerable "coolness and discretion." His dramatic work was moving away from some of the extravagances of his youthful plays, but not in the direction of "dull, insipid" weakness; *All for Love*, drafts of which were probably now on his desk, has "sinews" in abundance. The word itself even occurs, in a thematically charged context, in the opening scene. Before Antony appears, Dryden develops a powerful contrast between the eunuch Alexas, a smoothly hypocritical courtier, and the old soldier Ventidius, a stubbornly loyal Roman. These two characters represent the alternate sides of Antony's character: East and West, pleasure and courage, weakness and strength. In an angry speech criticizing Cleopatra, Ventidius tells Alexas what his mistress has done to Antony:

> O, she has deck'd his ruin with her love,
> Led him in golden bands to gaudy slaughter,
> And made perdition pleasing: She has left him
> The blank of what he was;
> I tell thee, Eunuch, she has quite unman'd him:
> Can any *Roman* see, and know him now,
> Thus alter'd from the Lord of half Mankind,
> Unbent, unsinew'd, made a Womans Toy,
> Shrunk from the vast extent of all his honors,
> And crampt within a corner of the World?
> O, *Antony!*
>
> [I, i, 170–80]

Ventidius believes that Antony's dalliance with Cleopatra has "unsinew'd" him, that only by rejecting entirely the hedonistic side of himself can the defeated emperor recover his vigor. Yet Antony wants to have both worlds: he will take Ventidius and his legions into battle, but he will do so wearing the bracelet of Cleopatra, with its rubies shaped into bleeding hearts. The coffeehouse critics who questioned the propriety of Dryden's metaphors were playing Ventidius to his Antony, insisting that his dalliance with "his long-lov'd Mistris, Rhyme," had unmanned him and demanding that he abandon not only rhyme but the "boldness of expression" he quite rightly saw as essential to poetry. "The Authors Apology" is Dryden's theoretical answer to those critics; *All for Love*, which he later described as the only play he had ever written for himself,[23] is his even more powerful practical answer. Blank verse helps him achieve a more natural dialogue than was possible in his rhymed plays, and his dramatic construction is disciplined and tight; but his blank verse is never prosaic, and his metaphors, like those he had praised in Virgil, Horace, Shakespeare, and Cowley, are often bold and striking. He could no more abandon poetic writing than his Antony could abandon Cleopatra.

Writing about the supernatural had often called forth lyric intensity from Dryden; the scenes of conjuring in *The Indian Queen*, *The Indian Emperour*, and *Tyrranick Love* contain some of the strongest poetry in those plays. But the ghost story the priest Serapion tells in the first scene of *All for Love* easily surpasses those passages; freed from the chains of rhyme, Dryden draws on the atmosphere and idiom of *Hamlet* and *Macbeth*, achieving the "Imitation of *Shakespeare*'s Stile" promised on his title page with very little in the way of direct borrowing:

> Last night, between the hours of Twelve and One,
> In a lone Isle o'th'Temple while I walk'd,
> A Whirl-wind rose, that, with a violent blast,
> Shook all the Dome: the Doors around me clapt,
> The Iron Wicket, that defends the Vault,
> Where the long Race of *Ptolemies* is lay'd,
> Burst open, and disclos'd the mighty dead.
> From out each Monument, in order plac'd,
> An Armed Ghost start up: the Boy-King last
> Rear'd his inglorious head. A peal of groans
> Then follow'd, and a lamentable voice
> Cry'd, Ægypt *is no more*. My blood ran back,
> My shaking knees against each other knock'd;
> On the cold pavement down I fell intranc'd,
> And so unfinish'd left the horrid Scene.
>
> [I, i, 17–31]

The "lamentable voice" is like the voice Macbeth hears crying "Sleep no more," and the vision of past Ptolemies resembles the vision of future Banquos that the weird sisters display to the stricken Macbeth, but the power of this passage owes as much to its expert management of sound as to its appropriation of Shakespearean motifs. When the whirlwind shakes the dome, irregularity shakes the meter, and as the vision grows more horrible, the verse becomes more rapid and disturbed until the fainting of the speaker restores a tenuous regularity. Although Dryden describes himself in the prologue as a soldier who "fights this day unarm'd; without his Rhyme" (l. 7), his blank verse throughout this play exhibits intricately repetitive patterns of sound, a technique he had learned from Milton and begun to employ in *Aureng-Zebe*.

Dryden had tried to achieve such matching of sound to feeling in his rhymed plays, but the necessity of rhyming limited the flexibility of his verse. Studying Shakespeare with new care, he recognized the potential for such expressive freedom in blank verse, as he points out in the preface:

> In my Stile I have profess'd to imitate the Divine *Shakespeare*; which that I might perform more freely, I have dis-incumber'd my self from Rhyme. Not that I condemn

my former way, but that this is more proper to my present purpose. I hope I need not to explain my self, that I have not Copy'd my Author servilely . . . Yet I hope I may affirm, and without vanity, that by imitating him, I have excell'd my self throughout the Play; and particularly, that I prefer the Scene betwixt *Antony* and *Ventidius* in the first Act, to any thing which I have written in this kind. [XIV, 18–19]

More cautious here than in the prologue to *Aureng-Zebe*, Dryden no longer "condemn[s his] former way" of rhyme, which had the advantage of acknowledging that speech was being imitated at a distance; instead, he points out that his "present purpose" requires an idiom less distanced from ordinary discourse, exemplified by the scene of rapid dialogue, broken into many short speeches, which he uses as a particular example. In the rhymed plays, stichomythia always had the potential for humor, as if the two characters supposedly parrying each other's ideas were schoolboys capping rhymes. Dividing such speeches in mid-line, as Dryden had frequently done, could reduce but not eliminate that problem; the return of the rhyme was still inevitable. Blank verse, however, could more naturally accommodate rapid exchanges, as even a brief sample from Dryden's favorite scene will indicate:

> *Ant. starting up*. Art thou *Ventidius?*
> *Ven.*   Are you *Antony?*
>   I'm liker what I was, than you to him
>   I left you last.
> *Ant.*   I'm angry.
> *Ven.*   So am I.
> *Ant.* I would be private: leave me.
> *Ven.*   Sir, I love you,
>   And therefore will not leave you.
> *Ant.*   Will not leave me?
>   Where have you learnt that Answer?
>
> [I, i, 246–51]

Dryden adds to the speed and naturalism of the blank verse by the terse plainness of his diction, but his poet's ear for patterns of sound is still operating; the play upon "love you" and "leave you" is only one part of a relentless alliterative pattern: "liker—left—last—leave—love—leave—leave—learnt."

The compression achieved in these lines extends to the construction of the entire play; Dryden completely abandons the panoramic series of short scenes in which Shakespeare had told the story of the ancient lovers. In the preface, he criticizes the French, particularly Racine, for their excessive "nicety of manners" (XIV, 12), but the structure of his play owes much to Racine. Dryden adheres to the unities, bringing Antony's wife Octavia from Rome to the besieged Alexandria in order to do so; he stringently limits the number of characters, shrinking Shakespeare's cast of thirty-four to a mere ten; and he stages no battles, structuring his drama as a series of emotional confrontations between various pairs and triads of characters. Like the scenes in *Aureng-Zebe*, these often take the form of quarrels leading to reconciliations; the internal drama of Antony's character interests Dryden far more than the external drama of his military engagement. Even Sir Charles Sedley, whom Dryden had cast as an advocate of French conventions in the *Essay of Dramatick Poesie*, did not move so far in that direction in his own *Antony and Cleopatra*, a rhymed tragedy staged less than a year before Dryden's.[24] Sedley also reduces the cast, but his frequent short scenes move back and forth between the tents of Caesar and the Egyptian palace, and his Antony charges Agrippa's army on stage in order to rescue his captured mistress.

The speech Sedley's Antony delivers on that occasion will illustrate the stylistic difference between the plays; like Dryden's Serapion, he speaks of auguries, but the similarity ends there:

> Augures and Entrails, Boys and Quails you ly!
> And I henceforth your Omens will defy.
> Call'd by his Name, may such still prosp'rous be,
> While thus the Gods give Victory to me.
>
> [IV, iii, 5–8]

These stiff couplets, supposedly delivered at a moment of passionate intensity, are quite unlike the vigorous, sinewy blank verse of Dryden's play. Nor is poetic form the only difference: here and elsewhere, Sedley is extremely cautious about metaphorical language, as if he were trying to satisfy the cavils of those "Illiterate, Censorious, and Detracting People" who raised questions about the "lively Images and Elocution" in Dryden's work. The couplet Sedley's Cleopatra addresses to the snake that will kill her is a sufficient example of the resulting flatness:

> Good Asp bite deep and deadly in my Brest,
> And give me sudden and Eternal Rest.
>
> [V, ii, 132–33]

Shakespeare's Cleopatra, by contrast, expresses her emotion at the same moment with a telling metaphor:

> —Come, thou mortal wretch,
> With thy sharp teeth this knot intrinsicate
> Of life at once untie.
>
> [V, ii, 302–04]

In Dryden's version, the knife and the knot become a key and a lock; in developing that image, Dryden deliberately exceeds even Shakespeare's metaphorical density:

> Welcom, thou kind Deceiver!
> Thou best of Thieves; who, with an easie key,
> Dost open life, and unperceiv'd by us,
> Ev'n steal us from our selves: discharging so
> Death's dreadful office, better than himself,
> Touching our limbs so gently into slumber,
> That Death stands by, deceiv'd by his own Image,
> And thinks himself but Sleep.
>
> [V, i, 473–80]

This is but one of many passages in which Dryden revises Shakespeare in the direction of more, not less figurative language.[25] In the "Heads of an Answer to Rymer," which he probably jotted down a few months after finishing *All for Love*, he quotes Rapin's assertion that style is more important than plot in the making of tragedy: "'Tis not the admirable Intrigue, the surprizing Events, and extraordinary Incidents that make the Beauty of a Tragedy, but the Discourses, when they are Natural and Passionate." "So," he continues, "are *Shakespear*'s" (XVII, 193). In imitating Shakespeare, Dryden moved toward a more "Natural" idiom, blank verse, but he recognized that he could render that verse "Passionate" only by resorting to the intricacies of sound and metaphor he had developed in his years as a maker of rhymed plays. In the preface, probably thinking most particularly of Sedley, he makes that point by means of a potent allusion. Referring to "The death of *Antony* and *Cleopatra*" as "a Subject which has been treated by the greatest Wits of our Nation, after *Shakespeare*," Dryden claims that "their example has given me the confidence to try my self in this Bowe of *Ulysses* amongst the Crowd of Sutors; and, withal, to take my own measure, in aiming at the Mark" (XIII, 10). Though introduced casually enough, the Homeric parallel makes a significant claim. After putting off her importunate suitors for twenty years, Penelope announces that she will marry the one who can string the bow of Odysseus and shoot it accurately. The best of the suitors try and fail; Odysseus's son Telemachus, who demands a turn, comes closest. Finally Odysseus himself, disguised as a beggar, effortlessly bends the bow and uses it to slaughter his rivals. Homer even suggests a literary parallel by comparing his hero to a harper stringing his instrument. If we take this allusion seriously, Dryden is claiming to be at least a Telemachus to Shakespeare's Odysseus, a son more than able to "try [him]self . . . amongst the Crowd of Sutors"; indeed, he may even be casting himself as the reincarnated Shakespeare, come home in disguise to claim the palace of poetry and cast out such effete pretenders as Sedley.

"The Vocation of Poverty"

Dryden finished his new tragedy by the summer of 1677, interrupting his efforts only long enough to write a vigorous prologue for *Circe*, an opera by Davenant's son Charles, performed at Dorset Garden on 12 May. Like the epilogue for Etherege a year earlier, this contribution was probably a way of reminding the Duke's players that he might soon be available for more substantial work; such a financial motive would help explain Dryden's willingness to contribute to a play whose epilogue was by Rochester. In a more direct attempt to improve his income, Dryden successfully forced the King's players to agree to give him the third day's proceeds from *All for Love*, his old contract notwithstanding, and the negotiations that led to this decision may have delayed the premiere. In a letter probably written during the last week of June, he speaks of "my Tragedy, which will be acted at Michaelmasse, & is already written" (*Letters*, p. 12). A Michaelmas premiere would have come on 29 September, at the beginning of the theatrical season, but *All for Love* was probably not performed until December.[26]

The same letter, addressed to Edward Osborne, Viscount Latimer, the young son of the powerful Lord Treasurer, reflects Dryden's skill at approaching the great through intermediaries. He has three requests. First he asks Latimer to remind his father of "that hunderd pounds, which is due on My Sallary from Christmasse to Midsummer, last," explaining that he has been too modest and lazy to solicit this payment from "Your Uncle," probably Charles Bertie, who was Secretary of the Treasury.[27] He then alludes more obscurely to another financial matter: "the other part of my businesse depends upon the Kings memory, & your fathers kindnesse, who has promisd My Lord Mulgrave, that I shall not fare the worse for Mr Mayes persecuting me." This "businesse" was evidently Dryden's long-standing request for an addition to the Laureate's salary, probably connected to his proposed epic poem on the Stuarts and certainly opposed by Baptist May, the Keeper of the King's Privy Purse. Finally, Dryden asks Latimer to join his patron Mulgrave in requesting permission from Danby to have *All for Love* dedicated to him. Although only twenty-two years old, Latimer was successful in lobbying for Dryden; all three requests were granted. On 27 July, the Treasury issued a money warrant for £100 to the Laureate; a memorandum notes that "my Lord Treasurer desires this may be one of the first after the weekly payments." Even earlier, on 2 July, Danby had decided that Dryden would have £100 added to his salary of £200 a year; that action was confirmed by a warrant on 21 July and a letter of Privy Seal on 24 July.[28] The Lord Treasurer was also willing to be the dedicatee of *All for Love*, which was published the following March with a substantial dedicatory epistle.

Dryden bestirred himself to write this letter because he had heard that Danby was planning to leave London for a summer holiday; the poet needed the money for his own holiday, during which he intended to work on the sex comedy eventually called *The Kind Keeper, or Mr. Limberham*. Charles II had again suggested part of the plot; in the letter, Dryden calls the King his "parcell poet" or collaborator, and tells Lord Latimer that the play will be similar to *The Fond Husband*, a titillating comedy by Thomas Durfey that had been a huge success for the Duke's Company in May and June. Angling for the time and money needed to perfect the new play, he explains that "The Kings Comedy lies in the Sudds till you please to send me into Northamptonshyre" (p. 11), and he departed for his native county as soon as he had received his salary: in a letter of 20 August, Wycherley told Mulgrave that Dryden was in Northamptonshire, and a letter from Dryden to his old friend Buckhurst, who became Earl of Dorset in October, cannot be much later.[29] Dryden describes himself as "settled in the Country" and declares his intention "to drudge for the winter"; since *The Kind Keeper* can hardly have taken months of effort, we may suppose that he had several other projects in mind. He had finally succeeded in gaining an increment to his salary, and some of his "drudg[ing]" was probably aimed at his long-standing goal of writing an epic poem. Two plays on classical subjects—the version of *Oedipus* that he wrote in collaboration with Lee and the revision of Shakespeare's *Troilus and Cressida*—were probably in their early stages. Yet the only literary text Dryden specifically mentions in his letter to Dorset is a work of criticism, Thomas Rymer's *Tragedies of the Last Age*, sent to the Laureate by the author, who had praised Dryden in his earlier translation of Rapin.

In his letter, Dryden calls Rymer's new book "very learned, & the best piece of Criticism in the English tongue" (*Letters*, pp. 13–14). Impressed with Rymer's skill at "finding out a poets blind sides," he jovially expresses his relief that Rymer has confined his criticism to Shakespeare and Fletcher. But while giving Rymer credit for the learning and penetration of his analytical work, Dryden indicates his low opinion of Rymer's poetry, recommending that he stick to criticism and avoid "exposeing his Edgar to be censured by his Enemyes." *Edgar*, a rhyming "tragedy," appears not to have been acted, but Rymer did expose it in print during this very autumn.[30] His critical opinions proved more stimulating: in the "Heads of an Answer to Rymer," which he jotted down on the flyleaf of the book, Dryden explores the possibility of defending the English dramatic tradition against the preference for the ancient Greek dramatists expressed by Rymer, and his version of the Oedipus story probably had its origins in the comparison between ancient and modern tragedy that was clearly on his mind during this working holiday. In the preface to *All for Love*, also written during this period, Dryden acknowledges that "the Ancients, . . . as Mr. *Rymer* has judiciously observ'd, are and ought to be our Masters," but immediately qualifies Rymer's principle by pointing out that the ancient models, though "regular," are "too little for *English* Tragedy" (XIII, 18). He notes in passing that this distinction might be more fully developed with respect to the *Oedipus* of Sophocles, and his adaptation of *Oedipus* does expand the Greek plot by adding a subplot of secondary characters, some borrowed from Seneca and Corneille, some freshly invented; Dryden's brief preface to the published version defends this "under-plot of second Persons" as a necessary gesture toward English "Custom" (XIII, 116).

By the time he wrote "The Grounds of Criticism in Tragedy," which he published with *Troilus and Cressida* in 1679, Dryden had moved closer to the opinions of the critic he now called "my friend Mr. *Rymer*" (XIII, 228). As usual, he was candid about this change: "I doubt not but I have contradicted some of my former opinions, in my loose Essays" (XIII, 224). In those earlier essays, Dryden had been more interested in defending his own work than in maintaining theoretical consistency, and that practical concern remained important; he now claimed, for example, that the subplot of *Oedipus* had "a necessary dependance on the principal design, into which it is woven" (XIII, 230). But he was also responding to a formidable theoretical challenge, and responding in a revealing way. Although Dryden could be a fierce antagonist in literary, political, or religious controversy, he was always aware of the arguments on the other side. In the writing of criticism as in the writing of plays, one of his characteristic skills was his ability to incorporate the strengths of the competition into his own work: *The Kind Keeper*, with its farcical stage business, bawdy dialogue, and broadly sketched humours characters, shows how fully he understood the comic gifts of Durfey and Shadwell; the mature serious plays, even those explicitly criticizing Racine in their prefaces, betray a considerable debt to French conceptions of character and dialogue; and the late criticism manages to contain the threat posed by Rymer by incorporating those parts of Rymer's argument that Dryden finally felt himself unable to answer, arguments he therefore characteristically made his own.[31]

While Dryden drudged in the country, he presumably kept up with theatrical and political events in London. When the fall season began, Charles Killigrew attempted to take full control of the King's Company, working out yet another agreement with some of the younger actors on 28 September 1677; again, Dryden's name does not appear.[32]

The Parliament, which the King had kept in session in order to keep Shaftesbury in the Tower, was meeting at regular intervals, but usually being quickly adjourned; the major political event of the autumn was the marriage of William of Orange to Princess Mary, his first cousin. This union, which was to have fatal consequences for the Stuart line, had the immediate result of encouraging those who hoped that Charles would now ally himself with the Dutch against the French, though the King, who was secretly negotiating with Louis for further financial subsidies, had no intention of going to war. Dryden shows his awareness of the continuing mutability of English foreign policy in his verses prefixed to Lee's *Rival Queens*, published late this fall, where he notes that "States, and Kings themselves are not secure" (l. 10). Shortly after he returned to London, as he surely did in time for the premiere of *All for Love* in December, he heard the drums of recruiters in the streets; on 18 February 1678, the Parliament voted a supply of a million pounds to support a war. A week later, after making elaborate gestures of humility, Shaftesbury was released from the Tower. His supporters—opponents of France, popery, and the Duke of York—now felt that their position was stronger; Marvell's popular pamphlet, *The Growth of Popery and Arbitrary Government*, appeared anonymously during the winter months.[33]

Dryden's dedication of *All for Love* to Danby, written at this juncture, is more explicitly political than any piece of prose he had yet written: at the level of public debate and propaganda, it answers Marvell and attacks Shaftesbury and Buckingham, but at the level of private communication, it warns Danby of the dangers inherent in his policies. The Laureate begins his address to the Lord High Treasurer by discussing the "tye in Nature betwixt those who are born for Worthy Actions, and those who can transmit them to Posterity" (XIII, 3); true heroes, he argues, will naturally favor writers, but those "who endeavour the Subversion of Governments" will "discourage Poets and Historians." Dryden had been thinking about this issue at least since reading the preface to *Gondibert* as an undergraduate, but in the politically charged atmosphere of early 1678, his dedication was neither intended nor read as an abstract discussion of the ideal relations between politics and aesthetics: it was a defense of the government and a pointed attack on the Opposition. We may measure the intensity of Dryden's feelings on this subject by considering the potent religious metaphors he employs. In praising Danby's management of the Treasury, he draws on the image of divine Creation as an ordering of chaos, a metaphor we have noticed him using several times in discussing literary creation. When Danby took over the Treasury, "All things were in the confusion of a *Chaos*, without Form or Method, if not reduc'd beyond it, even to Annihilation: so that you had not only to separate the Jarring Elements, but (if that boldness of expression might be allow'd me) to Create them" (XIII, 4). In discussing those "Malecontents amongst us, who . . . wou'd perswade the People that they might be happier by a change," Dryden equates Shaftesbury with Satan, explaining that it was "the policy of their old Forefather, when himself was fallen from the station of Glory, to seduce Mankind into the same Rebellion with him, by telling him he might yet be freer than he was" (XIII, 7).[34] An ideal "Minister of State," by contrast, "may stand like an *Isthmus* betwixt the two encroaching Seas of Arbitrary Power, and Lawless Anarchy" (XIII, 5), an image related to Dryden's habitual description of the Civil War as a deluge.

These are powerful metaphors, and Dryden surely intended to please Danby by using them: he effectively emphasizes the real accomplishments of Danby's ministry, declares his own support for "the undoubted Prerogative of the Crown" (XIII, 5), and equates those opposing the government to the rebels and regicides of the Civil War. But panegyric as practiced by Dryden usually involves an unspoken contract: by praising, the poet earns the right to give advice, and this dedication is no exception. Although Danby had tried to push a stringent Test Act aimed at unreconstructed Puritans through the Parliament in 1675, Dryden, mindful of the nonconformity of his own relatives, praises the latitude of the Church of England: "The Moderation of our Church is such, that its practice extends not to the severity of Persecution, and its Discipline is withal so easie, that it allows more freedom to Dissenters than any of the Sects wou'd allow to it" (XIII, 7). Although Danby was among those who had urged the King to threaten Louis by allying himself with William and making warlike noises, Dryden, mindful of the horrifying losses in the last war, explicitly recommends a policy of peace: "Since . . . we cannot win by an Offensive War, at least a Land-War, the Model of our Government seems naturally contriv'd for the Defensive part" (XIII, 6). In the very act of praising a chief minister on whom he was dependent for his livelihood, Dryden thus bravely recommends policies unlike those publicly advocated by that minister.

By the time this dedication was published, Danby was backing away from the idea of going to war with France. The war fever had originated with the Opposition, and the Treasurer had only embraced it for tactical reasons, hoping to use the threat of war as a way to gain a large supply of money for the crown and win concessions from Louis. Within days of the Parliament's voting money for the war, however, Louis captured the important city of Ghent, and that victory made an English intervention much less attractive. In the Parliamentary debates of 16–17 March, Danby joined the Duke of York in opposing Buckingham and Shaftesbury, who wanted an immediate declaration of war; arguing that the Exchequer was deeply in debt and unable to support immediate military action, he persuaded the Lords not to "jump preposterously into a war."[35] Since *All for Love* was in print by 21 March, Dryden had probably written his dedication before this first overt gesture of hesitancy on Danby's part, but if he did not know the secrets of Danby's convoluted machinations, he surely knew that peace and toleration, the policies he recommends in his dedication, were basic instincts of Charles II. Indeed, Dryden's praising Danby for expressing the virtues of the monarch may be another instance of "exhorting to virtue under the pretext of praise." By calling the minister "not so much a Copy, as an Emanation" of the King, Dryden was probably urging him to bring his policies more closely in line with the wishes of the monarch, as Danby did, at least on the war issue. When the Treasurer was impeached a year later, one of the charges was that he had engaged in secret negotiations with France while ostensibly advocating war, and Danby was not alone in playing that double game: in April, the Duke of York was simultaneously writing to his new son-in-law William to urge vigorous prosecution of the war and encouraging his brother Charles to enter into another secret agreement with Louis.[36]

In making his political recommendations to Danby, Dryden was somewhat protected by Charles, but in the preface that follows this dedication, he took an even greater risk by mounting a sharp literary and personal attack on Rochester. Politics may have played a part: when Buckingham was released from the Tower in June of 1677, he moved into Rochester's lodgings in Whitehall,[37] and Dryden may have hoped that Danby, who had opposed the release of Buckingham, would approve of an attack on Buckingham's friend Rochester. But the attack on Rochester, unlike the essentially political attack on Shaftesbury in the dedication, raises issues of morality, professionalism, and class. Referring in general to aristocrats who affect the role of poets, Dryden pretends to use the image of public nudity as a metaphor, knowing full well that his readers will recognize it as a reference to Rochester's drunken escapades with Sedley and others:

> Men of pleasant Conversation, (at least esteem'd so) and indu'd with a triffling kind of Fancy, perhaps help'd out with some smattering of *Latine*, are ambitious to distinguish themselves from the Herd of Gentlemen, by their Poetry; . . . And is not this a wretched affectation, not to be contented with what Fortune has done for them, and sit down quietly with their Estates, but they must call their Wits in question, and needlessly expose their nakedness to publick view? [XIII, 14]

As had been the case years earlier in the controversy with Howard, Dryden's irritation with an aristocratic rival spurs him on to a ringing defense of his own professionalism:

> We who write, if we want the Talent, yet have the excuse that we do it for a poor subsistence; but what can be urg'd in their defence, who not having the Vocation of Poverty to scribble, out of meer wantonness take pains to make themselves ridiculous? [XIII, 14–15]

Dryden argues that aristocrats should leave the task of writing to professionals, who need the meager proceeds of their work, and who have the requisite training and skill. Aristocrats "should be our Patrons," but instead they prove competitors and satiric adversaries, "persecuting *Horace* and *Virgil*, in the persons of their Successors, (for such is every man, who has any part of their Soul and Fire, though in a lesse degree)" (XIII, 16). The modest parenthesis does not alter the fact that Dryden is claiming to be a successor to the classical poets, while denying Rochester "any part of their Soul and Fire."

As in the essay on poetic license of the previous year, Dryden frequently quotes Horace against Rochester as an implicit rebuttal of Rochester's "Allusion to Horace," but this time he goes on to criticize Rochester explicitly for meddling with Horace: "Some of their little *Zanies* go yet farther; for they are Persecutors even of *Horace* himself, as far as they are able, by their ignorant and vile imitations of him" (XIII, 16). By blaming "ignorant and vile imitations" on "their little *Zanies*," Dryden implies that some lesser writer in Rochester's circle, perhaps Shadwell, is the author of the "Allusion," but this is merely a piece of self-defensive rhetoric. Dryden surely realized that the "Allusion" was a better and more stinging poem than Shadwell could write, and the insults he proceeds to heap upon its author are intended for Rochester. Extending his argument by means of another classical allusion, Dryden quotes a passage from the

Aeneid in which Turnus tries to throw a rock at Aeneas but proves too weak to hurl it far enough. Casting Rochester as Turnus, he concludes that "other Arms than theirs, and other Sinews are requir'd, to raise the weight of such an Author" as Horace. Once again, Dryden takes pride in his own poetic "Sinews"; he is also remembering Horace's *Ars Poetica*, in which the Roman poet advises writers to take subjects equal to their strength, and to consider what their shoulders can bear.[38] His mind connected that Horatian passage with the Homeric episode used earlier in the same preface, in which Odysseus proves his identity by his ability to handle the great bow. Later in the same year, in the epilogue to *Oedipus*, Dryden coupled those images, referring to the story of Oedipus as

> A weight that bent ev'n *Seneca*'s strong Muse,
> And which *Corneille*'s Shoulders did refuse.
> So hard it is th' *Athenian* Harp to string!
>
> [ll. 5–7]

Here the bow has become the harp to which Homer compared it, and an even more subtle metamorphosis takes place when Dryden says that Rochester is unable "to raise the weight of such an Author" as Horace. If we think not only of Turnus staggering under the rock, but of Aeneas leaving Troy bearing the human weight of his father Anchises, then the implication is that Dryden is not only a stronger writer than Rochester, but a more legitimate "Successor" to Horace and Virgil. His shoulders can "raise the weight" of a poetic father like Horace, while for Rochester, Horace is not a father, but an inanimate rock that proves too heavy to throw effectively at his stronger rival. Far from being a son of Horace, Rochester is "a Legitimate Son of Sternhold" (XIII, 17), the author of the metrical translation of the Psalms much beloved by Dryden's Puritan ancestors.

At one level, this preface is an astonishing instance of middle-class pride; Dryden boldly claims that aristocrats like Sedley and Rochester are effete, lacking the muscles of those real writers who work for a living. Yet a few pages later, still pretending not to know the identity of the author of the "Allusion to Horace," he calls his antagonist a "Rhyming Judge of the Twelve-penny Gallery," vigorously denying him aristocratic status by lumping him with apprentices and footmen. In the apparent contradictions of Dryden's preface we may detect the breakdown of the feudal assumptions about class that were also being strained by the debates in the Parliament. Officially, a man of Dryden's class was supposed to be deferential toward aristocrats and contemptuous of the inhabitants of the "Twelve-penny Gallery." Dryden's flattering dedications, including the ones to Rochester and Sedley, are sufficient instances of the former convention; his scathing attacks on Settle and Shadwell, whom he considered his social inferiors, may illustrate the latter. But when angered, as he had been by Howard a decade earlier and as he was now by Rochester, Dryden could criticize noblemen for encroaching on his own prerogatives as a professional writer; one of his ways of doing so was to abuse those who outranked him by pretending that he outranked them. In the prologue to *Albumazar*, he had made Howard into a highwayman, and in this preface, he makes Rochester an impoverished and ignorant denizen of the cheap seats in the theatre. If the claims of aristocrats rested upon their glorious lineage, Dryden could attack them by denying that lineage: Sternhold, whom he now called Rochester's father, was not only a notoriously bad poet but a man without claims to a noble family; although he served as Groom of the Robes under Edward VI and Henry VIII, his ancestry is so obscure that the county of his birth remains uncertain.

By giving Rochester that revised genealogy, Dryden was using the same tactic he had employed in anointing Shadwell the son of Flecknoe, and by the time he wrote this preface, he had another reason to couple Rochester and Shadwell: *Timon of Athens*, an adaptation of Shakespeare first performed in January of 1678, in which Shadwell brought a fawning poet on stage in the very first scene. Although another character, Demetrius, insults him as a "gross flatterer" and an author of "damn'd Panegyricks" (III, 200), the poet eagerly provides ludicrous excerpts from his own works; since these include distortions of phrases from *The Tempest* and "The Author's Apology for Hero-ique Poetry," this scene was surely recognized as another in the series of Shadwell's attacks on Dryden.[39] Moreover, the play as a whole makes Shadwell's support for Buckingham and the Opposition clear, and ends with a speech celebrating "Govern-ment . . . in the Body of the People" (III, 272); if the names were not yet current, the political battle lines between Dryden the Tory and Shadwell the Whig were already being drawn.[40]

Dryden's reference to the "Vocation of Poverty" in the preface to *All for Love* probably reflects his conviction that Shadwell and Rochester were in league against him, since it is not only a pointed defense of professional writing but a direct refutation of Shadwell's earlier jibe about his pension. Considered in the particular context of late March 1678, when it first appeared in print, this phrase is also an urgent and sober admission of truth: the docket for the second half of 1677, which should have brought the Laureate £100 pounds on his old salary and £50 on his new addition, is extant, with the date 6 March 1678, but it is blank, and we may infer from later references to arrears that Dryden did not then receive the money due him.[41] The promise of an increased salary that might provide the poet with the necessary leisure for epic composition was thus nullified at the moment when the first larger payment fell due.

Dryden's distress at the interruption of his salary was compounded a few days later by the suppression of *The Kind Keeper*, staged on 11 March by the Duke's Company. The change of company is puzzling. Perhaps the King's players allowed Dryden to market this comedy to the rival house because they were unwilling to give him a third day for it, as they had for his most recent tragedy. There is no record of a protest on their part to the Lord Chamberlain, although they complained loudly when Dryden offered his next serious play, *Oedipus*, to the Duke's players.[42] The King's Company may also have been concerned lest the new play prove offensive, and for cause: it was closed down after three performances. In his prologue, obviously aware that this knockabout farce was an inferior product, Dryden summarizes the changing taste of the audience. Flippantly referring to the time "When Sense in Dogrel Rhimes and Clouds was lost," he acknowledges that playgoers no longer flock to elaborate rhymed tragedies or op-eras, complains that "Comedy is sunk to Trick and Pun," and describes himself as a careful shopkeeper:

He, like the prudent Citizen takes care,
To keep for better Marts his Staple Ware,
His Toys are good enough for *Sturbridge* Fair.

[ll. 15–17]

We do not know exactly who objected to this play or why. Robert Gould, writing in 1685, says that *The Kind Keeper* was "So bawdy it not only sham'd the Age, / But worse, was ev'n too nauseous for the *Stage*."[43] The play as we have it, however, is no more salacious than plenty of comedies that were allowed to have full runs. In his dedication to the published version, Dryden says he has "taken a becoming care, that those things which offended on the Stage, might be either alter'd or omitted in the Press" (sig. A3v), but we have no way of knowing how extensive his revisions were.[44] He also defends himself against a charge of "particular *Satyre*": "whatsoever may have been pretended by some Criticks in the Town, I may safely and solemnly affirm, that no one Character has been drawn from any single man" (sig. A4r). Whether imagined or real, an attack on a prominent keeper of mistresses might have been sufficient cause for closing down the play; Lauderdale, Shaftesbury, and Rochester have been proposed as possible targets, but the evidence is confusing.[45] Although he called the play's closing a "hindrance . . . to me, in point of profit" (sig. A3v), Dryden should have been paid something for *The Kind Keeper*, since there were three performances, but any financial gain he realized was hardly worth the losses he incurred from the controversy. As the dedication makes clear, he had managed to offend friends as well as enemies; the Duke of York was probably among those who objected to the Laureate's attempt to play along with the current fashions in sex comedy, even though the idea for the play had come from the King himself.[46] Like the original text, the exact circumstances of the play's closing are lost to us, but we may be certain that the entire episode was embarrassing for Dryden.

Some time after the banning of *The Kind Keeper*, possibly as early as 21 March, the Duke's Company performed a comedy by Shadwell, *A True Widow*, for which Dryden provided a prologue. His relations with Shadwell can hardly have been cordial at this time. Shadwell probably knew about *Mac Flecknoe* and certainly had no reason to be pleased at Dryden's defection to the company that had presented most of his own plays. Dryden obviously knew that Shadwell had attacked him in *Timon* and a host of earlier plays, and this new play shows no evidence of a truce: a character named Young Maggott gives a speech that closely parodies a speech in *The Indian Emperour*.[47] Shadwell had dedicated *Timon* to Buckingham and would dedicate *A True Widow* to Sedley; the political differences between the rival playwrights were already clear. Friendship for Shadwell thus makes no sense at all as a motive for Dryden's prologue, which has nothing to do with the play to which it is prefixed and never mentions the author. The Duke's Company, with whom Dryden was now allied, probably asked him to write this prologue for the usual fee of four guineas, and as the text makes clear, Dryden took the opportunity to answer those who had thought *The Kind Keeper* a satire on particular keepers of mistresses, and to comment obliquely on the political situation.

In the prologue to *A True Widow*, Dryden repeats the commercial metaphors he had used in the prologue to *The Kind Keeper*, complaining that

> Vice (the Manufacture of the Nation)
> O're stocks the Town so much, and thrives so well,
> That Fopps and Knaves grow Druggs and will not sell.
> In vain our Wares on Theaters are shown,
> When each has a Plantation of his own.
>
> [ll. 4–8]

The Kind Keeper, a play about vice featuring a fop and several knaves, had failed to sell, and Dryden now makes his economic metaphor politically current. He speaks of raising "a Poll . . . from Fools" and laments the fate of "poor Wit," "prohibited . . . As if 'twere made some *French* Commodity" (ll. 11–13), following the exact wording of the Parliamentary action of 18 February, "an act for raising money by a poll and otherwise, to enable his Majesty to enter into an actual war against the French King, and for prohibiting several French commodities."[48] Referring to the reasons for the banning of his own play, Dryden complains about the tendency of playgoers to imagine they are being attacked:

> Fools you will have, and rais'd at vast expence,
> And yet, as soon as seen, they give offence.
>
> [ll. 15–16]

But since neither *The Kind Keeper* nor *A True Widow* entailed unusual theatrical expense, we may suspect that this couplet was also meant to refer to the way the Opposition was now reacting to the army, raised at their own urging, and "at vast expence," but offensive because the King's failure to deploy or disband them raised the spectre of a standing army, which might be used to stifle domestic dissent.[49] Taking aim at the issue of personal satire, which had helped bring down *The Kind Keeper*, Dryden laughs at his detractors:

> Time was, when none would cry, that Oaf was mee,
> But now you strive about your Pedigree.
>
> [ll. 17–18]

As he had insulted Shadwell and Rochester by assigning them new fathers, Dryden now insults those who had objected to his play by picturing them as eager to be thought the blood kin of Limberham, Brainsick, and the other fools who inhabit Mrs. Saintly's bawdy boardinghouse.

In *Oedipus*, the collaboration with Lee to which Dryden now turned his efforts, the main character's "Pedigree" is also a central issue. In the very first scene, the characters discuss Oedipus's physical resemblance to Laius, just as contemporary gossips made much of the close physical resemblance between Charles and his handsome bastard Monmouth, whose military victory at Mons on 17 August 1678 is alluded to in the prologue.[50] Although Dryden and Lee may have completed this play before the Popish Plot scare began in earnest, they were evidently aware of its potential political resonances. *Oedipus* is not a sustained political allegory (few plays of this period are), but it does turn on the question of legitimate succession, and Creon, who proves willing to accuse his fiancée of murder in order to gain the throne, is a recognizable caricature of

Shaftesbury.[51] In his political scheming, Creon plans to take advantage of the common people, who are portrayed as credulous simpletons. As early as the dedication to *Aureng-Zebe*, Dryden had accused Shaftesbury of being "a Prostitute to common Fame, and to the People" (sig. A2v). Creon is also characterized by his physical deformity, doubtless exaggerated by the acting of Samuel Sandford, who specialized in ugly villains. Shaftesbury, who never attained normal height, had been operated on by Locke for a tumor in 1668; that disease left him with a silver tube implanted in his abdomen, and his recent imprisonment had so weakened him that he now walked hunched over, and with the aid of a cane.[52] In Act I, written by Dryden, Eurydice taunts Creon with his "Mountain back" and "distorted legs," and Creon answers by acknowledging his deformity:

> Am I to blame if Nature threw my body
> In so perverse a mould? yet when she cast
> Her envious hand upon my supple joints,
> Unable to resist, and rumpled 'em
> On heaps in their dark lodging, to revenge
> Her bungled work she stampt my mind more fair:
> And as from Chaos, huddled and deform'd,
> The God strook fire, and lighted up the Lamps
> That beautify the sky, so he inform'd
> This ill-shap'd body with a daring soul:
> And making less than man, he made me more.
>
> [I, i, 145–55]

The references to "heaps" and primal "Chaos" will remind us of such imagery in Dryden's attack on Settle, but the speech is even closer to Dryden's famous descriptions of Shaftesbury in *Absalom and Achitophel* and *The Medall*.[53] As in those later poems, Dryden acknowledges Shaftesbury's "daring soul" and formidable mind, which were very much in evidence during the next several years.

Taken as a whole, *Oedipus* is an uneven performance, and Dryden's later efforts to defend it suggest some embarrassment on his part. Building upon the rant, horror, and perverse sexuality that had made his *Rival Queens* the big hit of the previous season, Lee wrote most of the melodramatic dialogue between Oedipus and Jocasta, but Dryden is responsible for the elaborately operatic third act, possibly set by Grabu, which features the appearance of the ghost of Laius in his chariot. This "conjuring" scene builds upon and exceeds those in the "Indian" plays and *Tyrannick Love*: it includes a lilting anapestic song to Apollo, which suggests Dryden's familiarity with the lyric meters of the original Greek choruses; a solemn incantation in trochaic tetrameter for Tiresias, obviously based upon the witches' chant in *Macbeth*; and an irregular song ("Musick for a while") that revealed its true lyric potential when Purcell set it for a revival in the 1690s.[54] Since Dryden later admitted planning the whole plot, he must also share responsibility for the suicidal leap from the tower by Oedipus at the play's conclusion. His cynical epilogue admits that *Oedipus* provides "what your Pallats rellish most, / Charm! Song! and Show! a Murder and a Ghost!" (ll. 31–32), and if this odd mixture

Portrait of Nathaniel Lee, the "Mad Poet." Engraving by Watts after a painting by Dobson.

now seems palpably inferior to *All for Love*, it was more successful: the prompter Downes remembered a run of ten days.[55]

The King's Company, doubtless anticipating such a success from the combined talents of Dryden and Lee, protested to the Lord Chamberlain:

Mr. Dryden has now jointly with Mr. Lee (who was in Pension with us to the last day of our Playing, & shall continue) Written a play call'd AEdipus, and given it to the Dukes Company, contrary to his said agreemt [the contract of 1668], his promise [allegedly made after they granted him a third day for *All for Love*], and all gratitude[,] to the great prejudice and almost undoing of the Company, They being the only Poets remaining to us.[56]

But this complaint, which may not even have been formally submitted, went unheeded, and the scenic complexity of the play shows that Dryden and Lee always intended it for Dorset Garden. Dryden's divorce from the King's players was now complete. During the remaining pathetic years of the company, which finally merged with the Duke's men in 1682, he wrote a number of prologues for his old associates, but he was probably paid a set fee for those; for the rest of his plays, he was now paid like other playwrights, with the profits of the third day.

Dryden's share of the third day's proceeds from *Oedipus*, which he had to divide with Lee, probably amounted to no more than £50, but any payment was welcome under the circumstances. The £150 the Laureate received from the Treasury on 8 June 1678 had been owed him since the second half of 1677, and the next docket, dated 2 December 1678, was another blank.[57] By this time Danby, who had been a reliable paymaster, was fighting for his political life; he was formally impeached on 21 December and sent to the Tower in April 1679, where he remained until early 1684. From the time of Danby's impeachment until the death of Charles II, the payments Dryden received from the Treasury, though always properly labeled as payments of arrears, fell further and further behind; he ultimately received only about half the money due him. Financial considerations were also probably the motivation for Dryden's decision to change publishers at this time, ending his long association with Herringman, which dated back to the days before the Restoration. *Oedipus* was published by Bentley and Magnes, who were already Lee's publishers; they also printed *The Kind Keeper*, though Dryden complained that they had done so in his absence and without his supervision. With his next play, *Troilus and Cressida*, he began an association with Jacob Tonson that would last the rest of his life.

"The Distracted Age"

Outstanding performances by Thomas and Mary Betterton as Oedipus and Jocasta were among the reasons for the popularity of *Oedipus*,[58] and the parts Dryden and Lee constructed for that talented pair are splendid vehicles. Still, some of the play's success may have been due to the good luck or prophetic skill or last-minute revisions by which Dryden and Lee matched their plot to the fantastic Plot now gripping the nation. *Oedipus* features dark prophecies, hidden murders, conspiracies for assassination, and the bullying of terrified witnesses. All these were features of the Popish Plot, that extraordinary national exercise in paranoia that dominated public attention for the next two years.

The informers who invented the Plot and kept it going were an absurd lot: Titus Oates, a homosexual perjurer and sometime Jesuit; Israel Tonge, a crackbrained apocalyptic preacher fixated on the Fire of London; William Bedloe, a self-styled "Captain" and con-man; John Sargeaunt, a priest consumed by his hatred of the

Jesuits; "Colonel" John Scott, a murderer and bigamist who specialized in selling nonexistent tracts of land in America. Yet the nation, terrified by comets, disturbed by the presence of an army, and always susceptible to lurid tales of Catholic conspiracy, was prepared to believe such men. Tonge had tried to interest Parliament in his fantasies as early as June of 1678, but his partnership with Oates proved more successful. Together, they approached the King on 13 August 1678, warning him that his life was in danger. With the aid of some obviously forged correspondence, Oates then succeeded in convincing the government that something was afoot, and he had the good luck or prescience to implicate a man who had indeed engaged in damaging correspondence with Rome: Edward Coleman, formerly secretary to the Duke of York and now secretary to the Duchess. In October, Sir Edmund Berry Godfrey, a magistrate to whom Oates and Tonge had delivered a sworn statement about the Plot, was found strangled and stabbed on Primrose Hill. The forces set in motion by that mysterious death led quickly to the execution of Coleman in December; over the next two years, numerous innocent Catholic priests and laymen followed him to the scaffold. The immediate political consequences included the removal of Catholic peers from the House of Lords (November 1678), the impeachment of Danby (December), the election of the first new Parliament in eighteen years (February 1679), and the exiling of James to Brussels (March).

The Plot came close to Dryden in numerous ways. As early as 1673, his enemies had called one of his plays a "Catholick *Intrigue*," and in this period of guilt by association and innuendo, that phrase had an ominous ring indeed. In 1676, a document listing places where mass was said illegally had mentioned a mountebank's shop "in King Street, by Long Acre," a few steps from Dryden's own home.[59] The rector of Dryden's parish church, William Lloyd, who was already famous for his tracts against the Papists, preached an inflammatory sermon at the burial of Godfrey; Lloyd was also involved in the interrogation of Miles Prance, a Catholic silversmith whose perjured testimony sent three innocent men to the gallows as Godfrey's murderers.[60] Dryden's theatrical associates were not immune: old Michael Mohun of the King's Company, now hobbled by gout, had to request an exemption from the edict of 1 November 1678 forcing all Catholics to move ten miles from London; Matthew Medbourne of the Duke's Company, implicated by Oates, died in Newgate prison in March of 1679.[61] There were even family connections. One of the Jesuits executed for plotting the King's assassination was a Pickering, though his Yorkshire branch of the family was distant from Dryden's, and Elizabeth Dryden's family was closely involved. The name of her cousin Philip, Cardinal Howard, surfaced again and again in the various accounts of conspiracy; William Howard, Viscount Stafford, the aged peer who became a martyr in 1680, was also her cousin. Worst of all, Elizabeth's brother Charles, second Earl of Berkshire, had written compromising letters to Coleman. Fearing for his life, he fled to France in November of 1678; broken in mind and body, he died there in March of 1679, and "Colonel" Scott was soon ready to report an "authentic" deathbed confession in which Berkshire admitted a plot to advance the interests of the Duke of York.[62]

Like most of his countrymen, Dryden initially believed there was some truth to the Plot, though he was sensible enough to doubt the extravagant claims of Oates. He probably knew his brother-in-law well enough to realize that most Catholics hoped for better conditions under James, but to doubt that many would embrace violence to realize those hopes. Discussing the Plot in *Absalom and Achitophel* (1681), he concluded that "Believing nothing, or believing all" were positions of "equal folly" (ll. 116–17), but as the Plot unfolded in 1678 and 1679, he had to be concerned about the possible complicity of his wife's relatives, and about his own close association with the Duke of York. There could be no denying that he had praised the Duke and both his Duchesses in extravagant terms, and he obviously stood to lose if those advocating Exclusion were successful. Although Dryden maintained his loyalty to James during this period of difficulty and exile, he was circumspect about expressing it. The publication of *Oedipus* without a dedication in January 1679 is early evidence of his caution, since neither Dryden nor Lee had previously missed an opportunity to dedicate his work to some prominent person.[63] In this case, however, they were probably afraid to choose a patron, lest he fall from power, as Danby had done; they may also have worried that naming a dedicatee would encourage specific political "applications" of their play.

Appearing as it did during the early stages of the Plot scare, *Oedipus* may have profited from its relevance to current events, but the Plot in general was disastrous for the theatre. For the King's Company, already damaged by internal financial strife, the aging of its original stars, and the defection of its two best playwrights, the preoccupation of London with trials and political maneuvers proved fatal. Drury Lane closed its doors in March of 1679, at least temporarily, and several of the younger actors went off to Edinburgh to join a company playing there. In a prologue written for the ragtag remains of the King's players to use at a summer performance in an Oxford tennis court, Dryden acknowledged that "Discord, and Plots, which have undone our Age / With the same ruine, have o'erwhelm'd the Stage" (ll. 1–2). The actor speaking the prologue refers to the "*Scotch* Rebels," equating the young actors and old scene-keepers now attempting such plays as *The Indian Emperour* in Edinburgh with the rebellious Covenanters cut to pieces by Monmouth's cannon at Bothwell Bridge on 22 June 1679. As these verses honestly admit, the King's Company was now a "broken Troop" (l. 34); not until February of 1680 did they manage a new London production.[64]

Troilus and Cressida, performed by the Duke's Company no later than April 1679, thus came on stage at a time when Betterton's men had no rival theatre to contend with. Even without competition, however, the Duke's players found audiences and profits meager: Aphra Behn, the one woman to compete successfully as a playwright during these years, described their plight in an epilogue for her comedy *The Feign'd Curtizans*, staged shortly after the closing of the King's theatre:

> So hard the times are, and so thin the Town,
> Though but one Playhouse, that too must lie down.[65]

The new Parliament convened on 6 March, two days after James went into exile, but the town was nonetheless "thin," presumably because of the unrest stirred up by the Plot. Although it contains some explicit references to the current troubles, *Troilus and Cressida* is understandably cautious. By bringing on the ghost of Shakespeare to speak the prologue, Dryden effectively claims to be merely the reviser of an older drama, thus discouraging those who might have sought for political allegory, and if some of his additions to Shakespeare's play allude to recent events, most of those passages are local jokes, without much larger resonance. The critical references to priests he adds to speeches by Pandarus and Thersites are no more particular than the anticlerical jibes in his earlier plays; the appeals to monarchial prerogative with which Ulysses begins and ends the play, while certainly intended as gestures of loyalty to the court, are not strongly partisan; and if some early passages about Patroclus's skill at imitating Nestor and Ulysses glance at Buckingham's talents as an impersonator, there is no sustained political allegory against the Opposition of the kind Dryden would soon construct in *Absalom and Achitophel*—indeed, nothing as definite as the impersonation of Shaftesbury as Creon in *Oedipus*.[66]

When the cowardly Thersites worries that he may be "mistaken for some valiant Asse, and dye a Martyr, in a wrong Religion" (V, ii, 74–75), Dryden is alluding to the stubborn refusal of any of those already hanged to confess complicity in the Plot, but he is not making a statement about their guilt or innocence. When Thersites steps in front of the curtain to speak the epilogue, however, the same issue becomes a bit more complicated:

> I cou'd rayl on, but 'twere a task as vain
> As Preaching truth at *Rome*, or wit in *Spain*:
> Yet to huff out our Play was worth my trying,
> *John Lilburn* scap'd his Judges by defying:
> If guilty, yet I'm sure o'th' Churches blessing,
> By suffering for the Plot without confessing.
>
> [ll. 23–28]

At first this looks like standard anti-Catholic propaganda, but the out-of-place reference to John Lilburne, the radical Leveller who successfully defended himself in trials in 1649 and 1653, suggests a strategic equation between religious extremists at both ends of the spectrum. If Dryden was willing to make a joke at the expense of Coleman and the others involved in the Plot, he also wished to remind the Dissenters, now riding high on the crest of Protestant frenzy, that they too had once been thought subversive.

Looked at with hindsight, Dryden's major change in Shakespeare's plot might also seem to have some relevance to the Popish Plot. His Cressida is actually faithful to Troilus, though all the evidence available to her hot-tempered lover makes her look perjured and false; only when she commits suicide does Troilus recognize her innocence, hence the subtitle, *Truth Found Too Late*.[67] When the inevitable Tory backlash came in the 1680s, public opinion swung toward many of those executed during the Popish Plot; like Dryden's Cressida, they were finally considered innocent, slandered victims. Writing about the plot in the summer of 1681, Dryden claimed to have seen through it from the start: "I have often said, even from the beginning of the Discovery, that the Presbyterians would never let it go out of their hands, . . . and that if ever they had tryed one Lord, they would value themselves upon that Conquest, as long as ever it would last with the Populace" (XVII, 209). But when he was composing his play in early 1679, he can hardly have wished to be thought an apologist for those recently executed for treason, whatever his private opinion of their complicity. The story of Cressida's belated vindication is morally relevant to the tendency of Dryden's contemporaries to believe too readily in treacherous conspiracies, but its unfolding as drama is more personal than political; though they have a more tragic outcome, Troilus's suspicions of his mistress are parallel to Aureng-Zebe's jealous rages at Indamora, and thus ultimately rooted in Dryden's own emotional and sexual life.

As a crucial scene makes clear, however, Dryden knew that the loves and jealousies of kings could have serious political consequences. The idea for this confrontation, which has no parallel in Shakespeare, came from that consummate man of the theatre Betterton,[68] and Dryden rose to the challenge, writing the one scene in this play that can stand comparison to his best work, a scene in which we may recognize his subtle response to the political crisis. In this dialogue, Hector urges his brother Troilus to give up Cressida for the good of Troy; one of his arguments is a pointed conditional clause:

Portrait of Thomas Betterton from the studio of Godfrey Kneller, ca. 1690–1700.

> If parting from a Mistriss can procure
> A Nations happiness, show me that Prince
> Who dares to trust his future fame so farr
> To stand the shock of Annals, blotted thus,
> *He sold his Country for a womans love!*
>
> [III, ii, 295–99]

Taken out of context, this speech might be interpreted as a rebuke to the King for maintaining his French Catholic mistress, Louise de Kéroualle, now Duchess of Portsmouth, who was particularly unpopular during the height of the Plot scare. But in the theatre, the sympathies of the audience at this moment are with Troilus, played by Betterton, who has finally won his Cressida, only to be told that she must be sent to the Greek camp in exchange for a Trojan prisoner. To Hector's contention that he ought to give up his mistress for "the publick," Troilus delivers an arrogant reply:

> And what are they that I shou'd give up her
> To make them happy? let me tell you Brother,
> The publick, is the Lees of vulgar slaves:
> Slaves, with the minds of slaves.
>
> [III, ii, 303–06]

This ringing assertion of princely prerogative leads to a heated exchange between the brothers, but they ultimately achieve a reconciliation: Hector, understanding Troilus's strong feelings, offers to break off the treaty and champion the cause of Cressida; Troilus, outdoing him in self-sacrifice, agrees to let Cressida go forth. Though quick to show resentment, both royal brothers finish the scene as magnanimous heroes, making their noble gestures in the name of honor and brotherly affection.

Dryden may well have disliked the vindictive Duchess of Portsmouth, and he may have hoped that Charles would decide to abandon her, but he recognized that if Charles gave up his Catholic mistress as a direct result of public or Parliamentary pressure, he might next be asked to abandon his Catholic brother, Dryden's patron, who was already in exile. During the very spring that saw the premiere of Dryden's play, Charles was scrambling for his own survival. Danby went to the Tower on 16 April, and five days later, the King appointed a new Privy Council including such prominent members of the Opposition as Shaftesbury. Despite these gestures, however, the Opposition proposed a bill excluding James from the succession, so Charles first prorogued, then dissolved his short-lived Parliament. He was now principally dependent on the advice of Robert Spencer, Earl of Sunderland, a self-styled moderate with connections in virtually all factions, to whom Dryden later dedicated the published *Troilus and Cressida*. If Dryden's scene between the royal brothers of Troy is not a political allegory comparable to *Absalom and Achitophel*, since Hector and Troilus cannot be neatly identified with Charles and James, it is a riveting piece of theatre, in which the personal resentments of two well-developed characters also engage the issues of royal privilege, including sexual privilege, that would prove so volatile in the English politics of the next several years.[69]

Stylistically, *Troilus and Cressida* is a somewhat uneasy combination of elements from *All for Love* and *The Kind Keeper*. At its best, the blank verse has the speed and strength we noticed in the earlier tragedy; in the scene between Hector and Troilus, the verse is particularly effective. The bawdy prose jesting of Pandarus, however, is of a piece with the dialogue in *The Kind Keeper*; knowing his audience well, Dryden substitutes current sexual terms for the outdated language of Shakespeare. In juxtaposing these quite different styles, Dryden moves closer to Shakespeare's own practice, and in general, he follows Shakespeare's words more closely in this play than in *All for Love*. Although he devoted considerable effort to cleaning up the somewhat chaotic organization of Shakespeare's play and made one major change in the plot, he was nonetheless impressed with the language of the original, as he acknowledges in the prologue, spoken by Shakespeare's ghost:

> In this my rough-drawn Play, you shall behold
> Some Master-strokes, so manly and so bold,
> That he, who meant to alter, found 'em such,
> He shook; and thought it sacrilege to touch.
>
> [ll. 13–16]

The image of Dryden quaking in the face of Shakespeare's "Master-strokes" is quite different from his confident willingness, a year or so earlier, to try stringing the "Bowe of *Ulysses*," or his attendant claim to be a worthy successor to Horace and Virgil. As the prologue continues, the ghost denies that any contemporary dramatist can qualify as his successor, and delivers a stinging criticism of modern plays:

> Now where are the Successours to my name?
> What bring they to fill out a Poets fame?
> Weak, short-liv'd issues of a feeble Age;
> Scarce living to be Christen'd on the Stage!
> For Humour farce, for love they rhyme dispence,
> That tolls the knell for their departed sence.
>
> [ll. 17–22]

Dryden may have been thinking of his competitors, but his most recent comedy, *The Kind Keeper*, was certainly a farce, and he had abandoned rhyme a scant three years earlier; it is hard to avoid the conclusion that this prologue involves self-criticism at some level of consciousness.

"Shakespeare" then launches into a discussion of "Dulness," which he describes as acceptable in such other arenas as the pulpit and the courtroom, but "insipid" in the theatre. "Dulness," he concludes, "is decent in the Church and State" (l. 32), and in the troubled state of those institutions in the spring of 1679, a little dullness might have been welcome. Yet the most striking stylistic feature of this play is the relative dullness of its figurative language, as if Dryden had lost his literary nerve. In *All for Love*, he had added metaphors to Shakespeare's already luxuriant verse, and if the wildest metaphors in *Oedipus* are the work of the hot-blooded Lee, Dryden had followed suit sufficiently in his own acts. In *Troilus and Cressida*, by contrast, he was concerned to refine, restrict, or "improve" Shakespeare's language. Rymer's theories may have pushed him in this direction, as may his desire to please the Earl of Sunderland, who was known to admire

French plays,[70] but I should also think that Dryden's observation of the damage done to the nation by passionate accusations and denials contributed to his temporary loss of nerve about his own figurative language. Exposed as he was to the ranting summations of Chief Justice Scroggs, who presided over the trials of the alleged Popish conspirators, and the virulent anti-Catholic sermons of William Lloyd, whom he heard each Sunday at St. Martin's in the Fields, Dryden naturally began to question the usefulness of high-pitched language in any arena. Lee's theatrical rant was another cautionary example. But *Troilus and Cressida* is surely an example of overcorrection; the political caution for which Dryden had the excellent motive of survival spawned a literary caution that makes this play less impressive than his work of two years earlier or two years later.

Dryden's prologue to Lee's *Caesar Borgia*, which was probably on stage in May of 1679, provides some evidence about his concerns at this moment. Like contemporary cartoons and broadsides, these verses comically couple the Devil and the Pope, but Dryden also takes the opportunity to grouse again about the reception of *The Kind Keeper* and the hard lot of poets, whose poorly rewarded drudgery is now made worse by the endless appetite of the audience for news. These complaints reflect urgent financial difficulties. The Laureate had now received no salary for a full year, and when payment finally arrived in July 1679, it was only £75. The profits of his last three plays had been meager: he later called the closing of *The Kind Keeper* a financial "hindrance"; the money from *Oedipus* was divided with Lee; and Downes remembered *Troilus and Cressida* as a failure.[71] Although Dryden was now receiving the entire rent from the Blakesley property, that small addition to his income, perhaps £30 a year, was inadequate to support his additional expenses as his sons grew older. The eldest, Charles, was elected a King's Scholar at Westminster in the summer of 1680; in keeping with the school rules, he must therefore have been studying there as a day student in 1679, if not earlier. When Charles became a King's Scholar, he moved into the school as a boarder, and the cost of living in the school was larger than the scholarship. Moreover, the whole process was soon to be repeated by John, Jr., who became a King's Scholar in the summer of 1682.[72] The death in Paris of Charles's namesake, the second Earl of Berkshire, whose flight to France and alleged confession were among Dryden's strong motives for political caution at this time, did not bring Elizabeth a penny.[73]

The lapsing of the Printing Act on 10 June 1679 made it much harder for the government to control the printing of political pamphlets of all persuasions, including one sometimes attributed to Dryden, who I believe was maintaining a careful silence.[74] In July, however, Titus Oates, whose testimony had now sent a number of men to their deaths, suffered his first setback: Sir George Wakeman, the Queen's physician, accused of plotting to poison the King, was acquitted. Among those tried with Wakeman was one of the chaplains attendant on Queen Catharine, James Maurus Corker; remanded to jail, Corker narrowly escaped execution again in 1680, and his survival is important to our story, for it was he who eventually received Dryden into the Roman Catholic Church.[75] In August, the King fell seriously ill, and James had to be recalled from exile. When Charles recovered, he attempted to defuse the situation by sending both his brother and his son away: he ordered York to Scotland as High Commissioner and sent the dangerously popular Monmouth into exile, stripping him of most of his offices; on 14 October, he dropped Shaftesbury from the Privy Council. The Parliament freshly elected to meet that autumn was then successively prorogued for a full year, during which the executions, trials, and hysteria associated with the Plot continued. The main event of the autumn months was the so-called Meal Tub Plot, in which a Catholic midwife named Elizabeth Cellier and a forger named Thomas Dangerfield cooked up some documents designed to suggest that what had been thought a Popish Plot against the King was in fact a "Presbyterian Plot" organized by Shaftesbury and Monmouth.

Undamaged by these obviously fraudulent claims, Shaftesbury and his increasingly efficient organization used their own pamphlets to argue the case for Exclusion, and to insist that the Parliament elected in August and September of 1679, which had an overwhelming majority in favor of excluding James from the succession, should be allowed to convene.[76] At this point, the future Whigs must have missed their best pamphleteer, Andrew Marvell, who had died on 16 August 1678, but the party writers who remained made up in vehemence what they lacked in eloquence. One particularly notorious tract was *An Appeal from the Country to the City*, published in October 1679 as the work of one "Junius Brutus," later revealed as Charles Blount, who had defended Dryden against the censures of the Oxford "Rota" as a teenager. If Dryden had been grateful to Blount in 1673, he can hardly have approved of this shrill pamphlet, in which citizens were asked to "fancy . . . the whole Town in a Flame . . . Troops of Papists, ravishing your Wives and your Daughters, dashing your little Childrens brains out against the walls, plundering your Houses, and cutting your own Throats" (p. 2).

Dryden spent part of this troubled summer and autumn in Northamptonshire,[77] where he probably worked on his contributions to the translation of *Ovid's Epistles* that appeared early in 1680; he may also have been polishing "The Grounds of Criticism in Tragedy," which was entered on the Stationers' Register on 18 June and published with the printed *Troilus* in November. In this essay, expertly juggling the opinions of Longinus, Horace, Rapin, Bossu, and Rymer, Dryden argues more strongly than ever before for the importance of balance and judgment. In criticizing Settle in 1674, he had indicated his distaste for empty noise and bombast, for wild metaphorical invention without judgment and control, but in "The Author's Apology" of 1677, he had emphasized the expressive power of figurative language, maintaining that "lively Images and Elocution" gave poetry its "sinews." Now, without denying the importance of genius and fancy, he swung back toward judgment, illustrating his modified position with revealing revisions of metaphors he had used before:

> Nothing is more frequent in a Fanciful Writer, than to foil himself by not managing his strength: therefore, as in a Wrestler, there is first requir'd some measure of force, a well-knit body, and active Limbs, without which all instruction would be vain; yet, these being granted, if he wants the skill which is necessary to a Wrestler, he shall make but small advantage of his natural robustness. So in a Poet, his inborn vehemence and force of spirit, will only run him out of breath the sooner, if it be not supported by the help of Art. The roar of passion indeed may please an Audience, three parts of which

are ignorant enough to think all is moving which is noise, . . . but it will move no
other passion than indignation and contempt from judicious men. [XIII, 241]

In criticizing Rochester less than two years earlier, Dryden had laid claim to broad
shoulders and powerful sinews; distressed by the musclebound rhetoric of contemporary pamphleteers, he now emphasizes "the help of Art." The image of the wrestler,
which also appears in the preface to this play, comes from Longinus, who described
imitating the giant authors of the past as "enter[ing] into the lists like a new wrestler, to
dispute the prize with the former Champion." As recently as the preface to *All for Love*,
Dryden had seemed confident in his ability to match his muscles with Shakespeare's;
now he says that modern poets, "when we combat for Victory with a Hero, . . . are not
without glory even in our overthrow" (XIII, 228), a more modest position like that
implied by the ghostly prologue.

Thirteen years earlier, defending rhymed drama in the *Essay of Dramatick Poesie*,
Dryden had argued that "a serious Play" was "Nature wrought up to an higher pitch"
(XVII, 74). Now he revises that musical image, arguing that "The Passions . . . suffer
violence when they are perpetually maintain'd at the same height" and asking "what
melody can be made on that Instrument, all whose strings are screw'd up at first to their
utmost stretch and to the same sound?" (XIII, 242). Again, Dryden is modifying rather
than reversing his earlier position; he is not advocating slack strings on the poetic harp,
merely recognizing that high notes are expressive only by virtue of their contrast with
low notes. Thanks to Homer's simile comparing Odysseus stringing his bow to a
harper, which Dryden had already adapted by referring to the "Athenian harp" in the
epilogue to *Oedipus*, these doubts about the expressiveness of "strings . . . screw'd up
. . . to their utmost stretch" also suggest some reconsideration of the Laureate's earlier
claims about his status as a "Successor" to the great poets of the past, with poetic sinews
strong enough to string their bows or lift their weights.

The literary caution Dryden manifests in this essay may have been related in his
mind to the political caution necessary at a time of national unrest; "The Grounds of
Criticism in Tragedy," fundamentally concerned with literary issues, avoids direct
political references, which are common in Dryden's other critical essays. Still, we may
detect Dryden's continuing loyalty to James in the dramatic examples he chooses.
When he criticizes Fletcher for failing to give his Valentinian "those Royal marks,
which ought to appear in a lawfull Successor of the Throne" (XIII, 239), we may hear a
distant echo of the passages in praise of James in the dedications to *Aureng-Zebe* and *The
State of Innocence*, published in happier times. When he refers to Creon in the *Antigone* of
Sophocles as "not a lawful King, but an Usurper," he is misrepresenting the Greek
play, but remembering his own *Oedipus*, in which Creon was a version of Shaftesbury.
When he cites the speech describing the disgraced Richard II after the usurpation of his
throne by Bolingbroke as an example of Shakespeare at his most moving, asking us to
"consider the wretchedness of [Richard's] condition, and his carriage in it; and refrain
from pitty if you can" (XIII, 246), we may suppose that his choice of that particular
passage had something to do with the emotions he felt when James was threatened with
Exclusion.[78]

In dedicating the published version of *The Kind Keeper* to John Lord Vaughan in November, Dryden declared that "Their Authority is, and shall be ever sacred to me, as much absent as present, and in all alterations of their Fortune, who . . . have stopp'd its further appearance on the *Theatre*" (sig. A3v). The reference is pretty clearly to James, who was now "absent" again in Scotland. Still, the third person plural and the vague grammar deliberately make the passage obscure; Vaughan probably knew what Dryden meant, but other readers were less likely to read between the lines.[79] A similar caution is apparent in the dedication of *Troilus and Cressida* to Sunderland, written at about the same time. Dryden takes pride in having "the honour to be known" by Sunderland, and praises the Earl in general terms for his moderation, but avoids any explicit political praise or advice, perhaps because of genuine uncertainty about Sunderland's alliances. At this point, Sunderland appeared to be working on behalf of the exiled James, though he supported Exclusion a year later, lost his post, and had to work his way back into the favor of the court. He also had family connections to Shaftesbury, whose wife was his aunt, and had long been engaged in correspondence with William of Orange. Sunderland's most important partners in the new administration were Lawrence Hyde, son of Dryden's original patron Clarendon, and Sidney Godolphin, who later addressed a poem to Dryden; they too were now speaking the language of compromise and moderation.[80]

If we contrast this dedication as a whole with the dedication of *All for Love* to Danby, written just two years earlier, or the bitterly partisan "Epistle to the Whigs," published with *The Medall* just two years later, the differences are striking: the sharp attacks on Shaftesbury, potent religious metaphors, and opinionated political advice offered in those pieces are replaced here by a cautious rhetoric of moderation, expressed in an elaborate conditional construction:

> If therefore there were one to whom I had the honour to be known; and to know him so perfectly, that I could say without flattery, he had all the depth of understanding that was requisite in any able Statesman, and all that honesty which commonly is wanting; that he was brave without vanity, and knowing without positiveness; that he was loyall to his Prince, and a lover of his Country; that his principles were full of moderation, and all his Councils such as tended to heal and not to widen the breaches of the Nation; that in all his conversation there appear'd a native candour, and a desire of doing good in all his actions; if such an one whom I have describ'd were at the helm, if he had risen by his merits, and were chosen out in the necessity and pressure of affairs, to remedy our confusions by the seasonableness of his advice, and to put a stop to our ruine, when we were just rowling downward to the precipice, I shou'd then congratulate the Age in which I liv'd, for the common safety. [XIII, 220–21]

Reminding Sunderland of a favorite project, Dryden then suggests that he may someday "mak[e] room for" this coyly unnamed man "under a borrow'd name, amongst the Heroes of an Epique Poem." Although he praises Sunderland for his ability "to remedy our confusions," Dryden does not speak about the particular confusions in the body politic at all; he moves on to a discussion of another long-cherished project, an academy to remedy the confusions of the English language—a patriotic, but entirely safe topic.

I have suggested that there was some link in Dryden's mind between the political caution manifested in this dedication and the literary caution manifested in "The Grounds of Criticism." Yet the prologue he wrote for Nahum Tate's *The Loyall General*, probably produced in December 1679, is less cautious, explicitly linking political and theatrical excess:

> The Plays that take on our Corrupted Stage,
> Methinks resemble the distracted Age;
> Noise, Madness, all unreasonable Things,
> That strike at Sense, as Rebels do at Kings!
> The stile of Forty One our Poets write,
> And you are grown to judge like Forty Eight.
> Such Censures our mistaking Audience make,
> That 'tis almost grown Scandalous to Take!
>
> . . . .
>
> A Meal of Tragedy wou'd make ye Sick,
> Unless it were a very tender Chick.
>
> [ll. 12–19; 26–27]

The notion that dramatic success has become "Scandalous" is probably Dryden's way of obliquely criticizing such vulgar exploitations of anti-Catholic feeling as Lee's *Caesar Borgia*; the reference to the inability of the audience to digest "A Meal of Tragedy" is surely his way of complaining about the failure of his own more subtle *Troilus and Cressida*. But this prologue is also much more explicit about Dryden's political position than anything he had written in the previous year. He evidently felt that Monmouth's illegal return to London from exile on 27 November, a defiant act encouraged by Shaftesbury, was tantamount to rebellion against the King. Perhaps he was prompted by the demonstration that occurred in his own parish church, St. Martin's in the Fields, when Monmouth attended the service there on 14 December, or by the shrill tone of Blount and other Whig pamphleteers.[81] Despite ample reasons for discretion, he now dared to compare the Opposition explicitly to the "Rebels" of the 1640s; like those earlier "Rebels," Shaftesbury's men were besieging the crown with petitions requesting a meeting of the Parliament.

Any renewed confidence Dryden might have had, however, was rudely shaken on the evening of 18 December 1679, when he was walking through a narrow passageway called Rose Alley, not far from his home. Suddenly three thugs with cudgels appeared in the darkness. Surrounding the diminutive poet, they beat him senseless; an account published in the *Gazette* two days later suggested that his life was in danger, and the painful crippling of his limbs to which Dryden refers in his later writings may have been the result of fractures suffered in this brutal beating. A manuscript satire on "the Gentlemen-Authors of our own Age," written about 1688, reports that "They wore most of them (especially their Laureat ever since the Rose-Alley Ambuscade) a huge Cane in their hands."[82] Bad as it was, the beating might have been even worse; one contemporary report says that Dryden's attackers ran away when other people arrived on the scene.[83]

The first newspaper account of the episode says that "it is thought to have been the effect of private grudge, rather than upon the too common design of unlawful gain."

Perhaps the men did not take Dryden's money; perhaps one of them said something indicating that he was to consider this beating a punishment for abusing his betters. In the violent world of seventeenth-century London, having someone cudgelled by hired bullies was not uncommon; it provided a way for powerful people to deal with their social inferiors, men not sufficiently "honorable" to be challenged to a duel. An example that might have sprung to Dryden's mind on this occasion was Sir Charles Sedley's hiring of two or three men to assault the actor Kynaston, who had impersonated him on stage in 1669. Whoever had Dryden beaten was thus not only taking physical revenge upon him, but denying him his status as a landed gentleman.

The identity of his enemy was as unclear to Dryden as it remains to us. On 24 December, he placed an advertisement in the *Gazette*, offering a reward of £50 for information about his assailants; the King promised to pardon any "accessary" who would name his partners and employers, but this advertisement, which was repeated in the *Domestick Intelligence* for 2 January 1680, went unanswered. Three different contemporary reports of the incident, all written in late December or early January, blame the Duchess of Portsmouth; a letter from "the pious Mr Nelson" to Dr. John Mapletoft, written on 2 January, is typical:

> Your friend and schoolfellow, Mr Dryden, has been severely beaten for being the supposed author of a late abusive lampoon. There has been a good sum of money offered, to find who set them on work: 'tis said they received their orders from the Duchess of Portsmouth, who is concerned in the lampoon.[84]

The lampoon to which Nelson refers is undoubtedly "An Essay on Satire," a poem then circulating in manuscript, which had already occasioned a quarrel between the Earl of Mulgrave and the Duchess of Portsmouth.[85] Contemporary reports imply that Dryden either wrote the satire or helped Mulgrave write it; since Mulgrave had long been Dryden's patron, and since the two of them had already collaborated on a translation of Ovid's epistle from Helen to Paris, just now being printed by Tonson, that inference was not unreasonable. Some phrases in the poem resemble similar passages in Dryden's work,[86] and some of those criticized, notably Rochester, were people he had recently satirized, though others, such as the King and the fallen Danby, were people he would never have attacked.

Although Dryden had never written a word against any of the royal mistresses, roughly dismissed in the lampoon as "False, foolish, old, ill-natured and ill-bred" (l. 73), the Duchess of Portsmouth might easily have found him a more convenient target for her resentment than an aristocrat like Mulgrave. If she was looking for someone to communicate that resentment to Dryden, her violent brother-in-law, Philip, Earl of Pembroke, was just the man. In March of 1678, Pembroke had kicked a man to death in a tavern; he is a plausible suspect in the murder of Godfrey in October of that year; and he physically attacked Dryden's patron Dorset in November. After committing another murder in 1680, he left the country. He was an ardent Whig, and was reported to maintain "52 mastives and 30 grey-hounds, some beares, and a lyon, and a matter of 60 fellowes more bestiall than they"; three of those bestial fellows may have been Dryden's assailants.[87]

Portrait of Louise Kéroualle, Duchess of Portsmouth, by Pierre Mignard, 1682.

No legal action was ever taken, and the blame for the Rose Alley ambush remains uncertain. From Dryden's point of view, it was a brutal reminder of the class hostility he had already encountered in his dealings with Rochester, and a bitter proof that "the distracted Age" of the Popish Plot was indeed a time for literary and political caution. Despite the fact that contemporary gossip pointed to the Duchess of Portsmouth, who was certainly capable of ordering such an attack, other possibilities surely crossed Dryden's mind. He probably did not know that Rochester had once threatened to have him cudgelled, but he knew he had given the Earl good cause for resentment in the preface to *All for Love*, and he knew that Rochester had been involved in a number of violent incidents.[88] A political motive was also possible: the leaders of the Opposition, to whom the Laureate's court and Catholic connections were no secret, can hardly have enjoyed being compared to the "Rebels" of "Forty Eight" in his last prologue; having him beaten and blaming that attack on the King's unpopular Catholic mistress would have been an effective and ironic way of killing two birds with one stone, though the Duchess, who was primarily interested in her own survival, proved to be as slippery as her friend Sunderland: less than a year later, irritated with York, she was making friendly overtures to Monmouth and allowing Opposition figures to meet in her lodgings.[89]

Dryden's later career gives no indication that he fixed the blame on any of the candidates offered by contemporary gossip or modern scholarship. Rochester died on 26 July 1680; several late references to him by Dryden are simply fond recollections of his wit.[90] Inciting the people to rebellion, Dryden's Absalom says that his father has "grown in *Bathsheba*'s Embraces old" (*Absalom and Achitophel*, l. 710), but that phrase hardly constitutes criticism of the Duchess of Portsmouth on the part of the poet. A Whig attack on Dryden published in the spring of 1682, when the Duchess was briefly in France, calls her "*your late departed friend* / And Patroness, the *French-Miss*," and she did act as his patroness in allowing rehearsals of *Albion and Albanius* at her apartments during the winter of 1684–85.[91] If Dryden suspected the Whigs of being behind the beating, as I have speculated, he never said so directly, and he had plenty of other reasons for the hostility with which he attacked Shaftesbury and his allies during the next several years. In the dedication to *The Duke of Guise* (1683), he says that the Whig pamphleteers attacking that play have "assault[ed] us like Foot-padders in the dark" and boasts that "their Blows have done us little harm" (sig. A3r), turning the earlier episode into a metaphor for later printed attacks. A private letter requesting payment of his salary, probably written in 1684, lists "some hazards of my life from the Common Enemyes" among the reasons why "I merit not to sterve" (*Letters*, p. 21), perhaps another veiled reference to Rose Alley, but hardly explicit. His most direct public reference to the beating comes in the prologue to *The Spanish Fryar*, first performed in November 1680, where he playfully suggests that the hiring of "Night-murth'rers" is an example of the English fondness for changing fashions: whoring is now out of style, replaced by drinking; "Scowring the Watch" has been replaced by "Tilting in the Pit"; and when murder by proxy falls out of fashion, it will be replaced by poisoning, imported from France.

The Rose Alley ambush was no joke; it left Dryden with painful physical injuries. Yet if those responsible hoped to silence him, they failed. Indeed, the literary and political caution we have noticed in Dryden's work of 1679 vanished in his inventive and partisan work of the early 1680s, in which he responded to the most serious political crisis since the Civil War with an outburst of creative vigor. From Dryden's point of view, there were bitter ironies in the incident: the poem for which he was beaten, markedly inferior to his own work in organization, meter, and language, is pretty clearly the unassisted work of Mulgrave, who stated in 1682 that Dryden had been "prais'd and punish'd for another's Rimes," declaring his friend "intirely innocent of the whole matter."[92] If this belated admission of authorship did nothing to salve Dryden's physical wounds, being "punish'd for another's Rimes" ultimately made him braver; perhaps he reasoned that there was no point in being cautious if he could be beaten for a poem he did not write. The final irony thus returned upon those behind the beating: whoever they were, they evidently intended to discourage Dryden's satiric pen by breaking his bones; instead, they unleashed the true powers of the century's greatest satirist.

→ CHAPTER TEN ←

The Tory Satirist
1680–1683

Sons and Successors

While Dryden lay recuperating from the Rose Alley ambush, Tonson published an edition of *Ovid's Epistles, Translated by Several Hands*; contributors included Rymer, Settle, Otway, Tate, and Richard Duke, who had written a poem in praise of *Troilus and Cressida*. Dryden provided three smooth translations, one of them made in collaboration with Mulgrave, and an important preface, probably written before the Rose Alley affair. Coming as it does from a poet who would later support himself by translating thousands of lines of classical verse, this preface is a significant theoretical statement; like "The Grounds of Criticism in Tragedy," published just three months earlier, it celebrates moderation. Dryden distinguishes three kinds of translation:

> First, that of Metaphrase, or turning an Authour word by word, and Line by Line, from one Language into another. Thus, or near this manner, was *Horace* his Art of Poetry translated by *Ben. Johnson*. The second way is that of Paraphrase, or Translation with Latitude, where the Authour is kept in view by the Translator, so as never to be lost, but his words are not so strictly follow'd as his sense, and that too is admitted to be amplyfied, but not alter'd. Such is Mr. *Wallers* Translation of *Virgils* Fourth *Aeneid*. The Third way is that of Imitation, where the Translator (if now he has not lost that Name) assumes the liberty not only to vary from the words and sence, but to forsake them both as he sees occasion: and taking only some general hints from the Original, to run division on the ground-work, as he pleases. Such is Mr. *Cowleys* practice in turning two Odes of *Pindar*, and one of *Horace* into *English*. [I, 114–15]

To "run division on the ground-work," a much-admired musical skill, was to improvise variations over a repeated "ground bass," but Dryden, while conceding the disadvantage of overly literal translation, declares his own preference for the more cautious middle way. He summarizes arguments in favor of "Imitation" by Cowley and

Denham, but respectfully dissents from "the Authority of two great men, . . . I hope
without offence to either of their Memories" (I, 119). Significantly, he does not repeat
his scornful remarks about Rochester's "ignorant and vile imitation" of Horace, which
might certainly have been used here as a cautionary example. The whole tone of this
preface is genial and modest, but by saying that the imitator "assumes the liberty" to
forsake the words and sense of his original, Dryden quietly makes such a translator into
a literary Whig, claiming excessive freedom for himself and failing in his filial duties.

In earlier discussions of the modern poet's relation to his literary fathers, Dryden
had alluded to tests of skill; he had pictured himself stringing the bow of Ulysses (or the
Athenian harp), lifting the weight of Horace, or wrestling with Shakespeare. But in
discussing Ovid, he balances praise for the Roman poet's "Description of the Passions"
with temperate criticism of the "Copiousness of his Wit." This time, he uses a biblical
allusion to make his point, explaining that Ovid "sometimes cloys his Readers instead of
satisfying them: and gives occasion to his Translators, who dare not Cover him, to blush
at the nakedness of their Father" (I, 112). In the story Dryden trusted his readers to
remember, Noah, drunk on his new wine, is found naked in his tent by one of his sons;
two other sons, walking backward to avoid dishonoring their father, cover him, and
when Noah sobers up, he blesses those sons, Shem and Japheth, cursing the disrespectful Ham (Genesis 9:18–29).[1] Again casting modern writers as the sons of the
ancients, Dryden recommends a way of dealing with those fathers that falls between the
extremes represented by the sons of Noah: modern translators should not poke fun at
the weaknesses and obscenities of a father like Ovid, nor should they attempt to cover
up the true character of Ovid's writing with new garments woven out of whole cloth.

Meanwhile the King, who was having his own problems with disrespectful sons,
stripped Monmouth of his one remaining post as Master of the Horse and sent his own
yacht to bring the Duke and Duchess of York back from Edinburgh. London was still
fixated on tales of Catholic conspiracy, as the events of the theatrical season showed. In
early February of 1680, a few weeks before James arrived in the capital, riots against the
Duchess of Portsmouth forced the temporary closing of the Duke's Theatre, and on 31
May, the King's Company gave the premiere of a play by Settle designed to exploit the
continuing interest in the Popish Plot: *The Female Prelate: Being the History of the Life and
Death of Pope Joan*.[2] This virulently anti-Catholic play, later dedicated to Shaftesbury,
was an immediate hit, but the Duchess of Portsmouth, determined to punish Settle
financially as she may have punished Dryden physically, "carryed all the Court with her
to the Dukes house to see Macbeth" on Settle's third day.[3]

With Parliament still prorogued, the political struggle was being acted out in such
arenas as the theatre and the courtroom. Stung by Whig pamphleteering, the government staged a series of trials against printers and publishers of allegedly seditious
pamphlets, while Shaftesbury and his group, not to be outdone, attempted to present
the Duke of York for trial as a Popish recusant, and to have the Duchess of Portsmouth
declared a common prostitute. The King succeeded in stopping both proceedings, but
the City was emerging as a stronghold of Whig sentiment: in September, packed juries
returned verdicts of *ignoramus* in the cases of Francis Smith and Langley Curtis, who

had published tracts irritating to the court.[4] Dryden had already drawn a parallel between current times and the 1640s, when the City had been solidly Puritan, and a similar parallel apparently held good for Oxford: a Royalist center during the Civil War, the university was also now inclined to support the court. When the King's Company performed there in the summer of 1680, Dryden wrote a sharply political prologue reminding the scholars of the damage done to the universities during the Interregnum, damage he remembered well from his own undergraduate days:

> But 'tis the Talent of our *English* Nation,
> Still to be Plotting some New Reformation:
> And few years hence, if Anarchy goes on,
> *Jack Presbyter* shall here Erect his Throne.
> Knock out a Tub with Preaching once a day,
> And every Prayer be longer than a Play.
> Then all you Heathen Wits shall go to Pot,
> For disbelieving of a Popish Plot.
> . . . .
> Religion, Learning, Wit, wou'd be supprest,
> Rags of the Whore, and Trappings of the Beast.
>
> [ll. 9–16; 23–24][5]

    Though tailored as always to a particular audience, this is a strong Tory statement. Dryden refers to the present troubles as "Anarchy" and opposes the figure of "*Jack Presbyter*," with his tiresome sermons and prayers, to that more popular bogeyman the Pope, used as a scapegoat not only in Settle's recent play, but in frequent public Pope-burnings and processions.[6] He reminds his learned audience of the Dissenting suspicion of those who speak Latin, and even implies that the Oxford wits may be justified in "disbelieving of a Popish Plot." Dryden may have been encouraged to make such unguarded assertions by the acquittals of two Catholics tried for high treason in June: evidence presented by the usual dubious informers proved insufficient to convict Roger Palmer, Earl of Castlemaine, and Elizabeth Cellier, the Catholic midwife who had helped concoct the Meal Tub Plot the previous autumn.[7] Whatever his immediate motives for writing it, this witty and combative prologue shows that Dryden was beginning to cast off his earlier caution about expressing his real opinion on the Popish Plot. He had probably now written most of his own next play, *The Spanish Fryar*, which cleverly combines a comic plot exposing a corrupt Catholic clergyman with a serious plot underlining the importance of legitimate succession. By late summer, he was well enough to travel to Staffordshire, where he visited the estate of Sir Charles Wolseley; Wolseley's son Robert, who wrote the epilogue for the new play, may have been present during Dryden's visit to his father.[8]

    In *The Spanish Fryar*, Dryden returned to the mixed-plot tragicomedy, a form he had not used since *The Assignation*. The high plot begins with an ominous set of circumstances resembling those in earlier plays: the royal city is under siege from the Moors, the Queen of Arragon is praying for deliverance, and the old men believe they know the cause of the troubles:

> A Crown Usurp'd; A lawfull King depos'd;
> In bondage held; debarr'd the common light;
> His Children murther'd, and his Friends destroy'd.
>
> [I, p. 2]

Dryden had been using plots involving usurpation ever since *The Indian Queen*, but at the time *The Spanish Fryar* came on stage, its references to an illegitimate succession were particularly urgent. Despite frequent declarations by the King that he had never been married to Lucy Walters, Monmouth's disreputable mother, the Whigs encouraged rumors of a mysterious "black box" containing documents proving that there had been a marriage. During the summer, while Dryden was enjoying his visit to Staffordshire, Shaftesbury sent Monmouth off on a stage-managed "progress" through the West, obviously designed to win support for the notion of declaring him the legitimate successor. On 20 October, just one day before the new Parliament finally convened, York returned to Scotland. Dryden's play was first acted on 1 November, and on 4 November, the second Exclusion Bill was read in the Commons. The Whig strategy was clear: they hoped that the popular outrage against Roman Catholics stirred up by the Popish Plot would spill over onto the Duke of York, leaving the King with no choice but to legitimize Monmouth; their long-range goal, at least in the eyes of conservatives like Dryden, was to establish the principle that Parliament could alter the succession.

Dryden's play, produced as the pressures of the last two years built toward a true crisis, uses its low plot to defuse the issue of Catholicism, venting resentment of Catholic corruption on a nonthreatening figure of fun, Friar Dominic. Remarkably enough, Dryden took the very words in which he describes this figure from a notorious Whig pamphlet. Charles Blount's *Appeal from the Country to the City*, published in the previous autumn, had attempted to stir up the absurd fear that a Catholic successor would return the abbey lands distributed by Henry VIII to the Roman church: "If any men (who have Estates in Abby-Lands) desire to beg their Bread, and relinquish their Habitations and Fortunes to some old greasie bald-pated Abbot, Monk, or Friar, then let him [*sic*] Vote for a Popish Successor" (p. 29). In the opening scene of the play, the soldier Pedro describes the civilians running about the city in fear of the Moorish invasion; they include

> a reverend, fat, old gouty Fryar;
> With a Paunch swoln so high, his double Chin
> Might rest upon't: A true Son of the Church;
> Fresh colour'd, and well thriven on his Trade,
> Come puffing with his greasy bald-pate Quire,
> And fumbling o'er his Beads.
>
> [I, p. 3]

The friar was played by Anthony Leigh, whom the audience would remember as Pandarus in *Troilus and Cressida*; when he comes on stage, he is just as corrupt as this description suggests. But the casual anti-Catholic talk of the comic scenes is of a piece with Dryden's lifelong opposition to avaricious clergymen of all denominations. If plays like Settle's *Female Prelate* were designed to profit from the ugly bigotry stirred up by the Plot, Dryden's jocular scenes between the greedy friar and the lecherous soldier Lorenzo channel such bigotry into harmless humor.[9] The strongest anti-Catholic language in the play comes in the epilogue, but that was written by Wolseley, who is carefully identified in the printed version as "a Friend of the Author's." Dryden's decision to dedicate *The Spanish Fryar* to John Holles, Lord Haughton, the nineteen-year-old son of the Earl of Clare, was part of the same self-protective pretense that this was "a Protestant Play." Unlike earlier dedications, this one is "more like a Preface than a Dedication"; Dryden discusses the difficulties of writing tragicomedy but says virtually nothing about the dedicatee, eschewing "the stale exploded Trick of fulsome Panegyricks" (sig. A4r) lest he betray the differences between his political views and those of Haughton's family.[10]

In the serious plot, Dryden has ample opportunity to deliver his conservative message. Queen Leonora, daughter to a usurper, is betrothed to Bertran but has fallen in love with the victorious soldier Torrismond; her struggles with her passion and her worries about loving someone not of royal blood resemble similar scenes in *Secret Love* and *Marriage A-la-Mode*. Preoccupied with love and hoping to bring disfavor upon Bertran, she does not interfere when he hints that he plans to murder the deposed king, Sancho, who is languishing in prison. No sooner is Sancho reported dead than Torrismond learns that he is actually the son of the old king. When his foster father, Raymond, furnishes him with incontrovertible proof of his identity, Torrismond is trapped between two compelling loyalties:

> *Raymond.* On these old Knees I beg you, e'er I dye,
>   That I may see your Father's Death reveng'd.
> *Torrismond.* Why, 'tis the onely bus'ness of my Life;
>   My Order's issued to recall the Army,
>   And *Bertran*'s Death resolv'd.
> *Ray.* And not the Queen's; ô She's the chief Offender!
>   Shall Justice turn her Edge within your Hand?
>   No, if she scape, you are your self the Tyrant,
>   And Murtherer of your Father.
> *Tor.*   Cruel Fates,
>   To what have you reserv'd me!
> *Ray.*   Why that Sigh?
> *Tor.* Since you must know, but break, ô break, my Heart,
>   Before I tell my Fatal Story out,
>   Th' Usurper of my Throne, my House's Ruin,
>   The Murtherer of my Father, is my Wife!
> *Ray.* O Horrour! Horrour!
>
>   [IV, p. 63]

Torrismond's dilemma is not only a poignant variant of those faced by Orestes and Oedipus, but a more intense version of the dilemma Troilus faces in the most significant scene in Dryden's tragedy, where his brother urges him to give up his true love for the good of his country. A thoughtful viewer could hardly avoid thinking about the

King's problems with his women, including the long-dead Lucy Walters, whose claims to have been his wife were still haunting Charles; the barren Catholic Queen, whose own doctor had been accused of plotting to poison the King; and the Duchess of Portsmouth, who was now confounding all expectations by caballing with the Whigs. Charles's dealings with all these women had far-reaching political consequences, and Torrismond's discovery that he is married to his own family's worst enemy has immediate political consequences in the play. Three different armies, significantly referred to in the stage directions as "Parties," march into the palace courtyard; each claims to represent true loyalty and denigrates the others as "Rebels." Only a miracle, restoring a true succession, can avert disaster, and at the last instant, we learn that old King Sancho is not dead after all. Bertran declares that "Bad men, when 'tis their interest, may doe good" (V, p. 82), and reveals that he has lied about the King's death in order to test Leonora's love for Torrismond; Torrismond, now the lawful successor, embraces his queen, forgives Bertran, and delivers the obvious moral:

> But let the bold Conspirator beware
> For Heaven makes Princes its peculiar Care.
>
> [V, p. 83]

For those still willing to believe the elaborate fictions of Oates and the other informers, the application of this aphorism to contemporary issues would have been obvious: the bold Jesuitical conspirators had been foiled in their plans to murder Charles. But for those like Dryden, who now realized that most of those alleged plans were mere fabrications, and who also considered the Duke of York a prince under the peculiar care of heaven, the real bold conspirators were the Whigs now trying to exclude James from the succession. The specific political references in the play all point in that direction. In his first speech, Torrismond declares his disdain for "popular Applause; the noisie Praise / Of giddy Crowds, as changeable as Winds" (I, p. 7). Unlike Creon in the Dryden-Lee *Oedipus*, who plays upon the ignorance and fear of the common people, Torrismond is motivated by honor and love; Dryden had been developing that contrast between popular politicians like Shaftesbury and loyal aristocrats like Mulgrave since the dedication to *Aureng-Zebe*. Describing the public response to the news of the old king's death, Pedro delivers a speech that clearly communicates Dryden's scorn for Oates and the other inventors of the Plot:

> The Rabble gather round the Man of News,
> And listen with their Mouths;
> Some tell; some hear, some judge of News, some make it;
> And he who lies most loud, is most believ'd.
>
> [IV, p. 54]

Mindful of the strongly Whig character of the City of London, Dryden makes his long-held suspicions of popular mobs quite specific in the crisis of Act IV. When Raymond proposes that the queen choose "some Bold man whose Loyalty you trust, / And let him raise the Train-bands of the City," she scorns the militia as "Gross feeders, Lion talkers, Lamb-like fighters." Raymond's reply is rich with irony, particularly if we remember that the current Lord Mayor and sheriffs of the City were rabid Whigs:

> You do not know the Virtues of your City,
> What pushing force they have; some popular Chief,
> More noisie than the rest, but cries Halloo,
> And in a trice the bellowing Herd come out.
>
> [IV, p. 57]

Having seen "the bellowing Herd" of City Whigs in action at recent Pope-burnings, Dryden tossed them the sop of Friar Dominic, but the message of the serious plot was surely obvious to any thoughtful viewer: altering the succession will rapidly produce confusion and anarchy, with armies clashing in the night, "Where Darkness and Surprise ma[k]e Conquest cheap" (I, p. 8).

Staged by the Duke's Company, with Betterton as Torrismond and the talented Elizabeth Barry as the queen, Dryden's sparkling play was an immediate success, but if he entertained any hope that the sobering message of his serious plot would influence the fractious Commons, he was quickly disappointed. On 11 November, the House passed the second Exclusion Bill, but the Lords decisively rejected the Bill on 15 November, after a heated session in which George Savile, Marquis of Halifax, spoke repeatedly and persuasively against Shaftesbury. The Commons took out their anger by bringing the pathetic old Lord Stafford to trial; like all but one of the Howard peers, Elizabeth Dryden's Protestant brother Thomas, now third Earl of Berkshire, voted to condemn his kinsman, who was beheaded on 29 December.[11] The Benedictine monk James Maurus Corker, who had been condemned to death himself on 17 January 1680, attended Stafford during his last days. Remanded to Newgate prison, where he remained for more than five years, Corker soon published an account of Stafford's trial and death; he is also said to have received more than a thousand converts into the Roman Catholic Church while in prison. Even if we discount this number as a pious exaggeration, Corker was a writer of some power; his description of the way Stafford's dying speech convinced many in the crowd of his innocence is genuinely moving. The example of his wife's martyred kinsman may ultimately have been an important factor in Dryden's own conversion; the persuasive power of Father Corker certainly was.[12]

The proceeds from the third performance of *The Spanish Fryar* were doubtless welcome, but any hopes the Laureate might have had for financial reward from the court were disappointed. On 14 December, frustrated by his own inability to solicit payments from the Treasury, he made out a power of attorney to one George Ward, specifically giving Ward the right "to aske require and receive of the officers and Tellers of his Maj[tyes] Receipt of Exchec[r] all and every such sume and sumes of money as from tyme to tyme or att any tyme hereafter shall be due or payable to mee."[13] Among the reasons why Dryden had received only half his wages since the impeachment of Danby was the refusal of the last several Parliaments to pass bills of supply, and this angry Parliament not only refused to give Charles any money but declared any banker who would advance him money a traitor. On 10 January 1681, faced with this and other rebellious resolutions in the Commons, Charles once again prorogued the Parliament;

before they could reconvene, he dissolved them. For those sharing Dryden's opinions, the crisis was now clearly analogous to the Civil War, which had ended with the shocking execution of a monarch, the disaster miraculously averted in his most recent play. As the play's production in November coincided with the opening of the Parliament in London, its publication in March of 1681 coincided with the opening of the Oxford Parliament, which proved a decisive turning point in English politics, and provided the occasion for Dryden's most famous poem.

"The Publick Theater"

During the brief lull between Parliaments, while both sides were actively promoting their candidates and causes for the new election, Dryden took time to do a favor for Charles Saunders, who was probably a school friend of his own son Charles at Westminster. Saunders was now in his first year at Trinity, Dryden's old college at Cambridge; under Busby, he had written a play, *Tamerlane the Great*, which the struggling King's Company decided to perform. Dryden, who apparently helped Saunders correct and improve his work, contributed an epilogue for the performance, which probably took place in February 1681.[14] Referring to Saunders, who was no older than eighteen, as "the Beardless Author of this Day" (l. 1), and "the first Boy-Poet of our Age" (l. 4), he alludes to another precocious Westminster poet, Cowley, who had indeed "Blossom'd soon," publishing his *Poetical Blossoms* when he was only thirteen. But he also says that Cowley, who died at forty-nine, "Flourish'd long" (l. 7), a curious gesture for a man who was himself now forty-nine, and who still had his great flourishing as a poet ahead of him.

Life expectancy in the seventeenth century was considerably shorter than it is today: not only did thousands die as children, but even those who survived to become adults knew how quickly illness could carry them away. Rochester, weakened by his amorous and alcoholic excesses, died in July of 1680, worn out at thirty-three. The more temperate Lord Ossory, son of Dryden's old patron Ormonde, succumbed to a brief illness a few days later; he was only forty-six. The wrenching Exclusion Crisis through which the country was now passing was based on the possibility that the King, who was only three months older than Dryden, might die at any time. One peer in the last Parliament had even raised the question of Charles's capacity to beget children, should he enter into a new marriage, giving Shaftesbury, who was fifty-nine himself, the opportunity for a comic rejoinder: "Can we doubt when we look at the King that he is capable of getting children? He is only fifty. I know people who are more than sixty and would have no difficulty in getting them!"[15] Dryden's epilogue for Saunders works the other side of the same joke, suggesting that the "sly She-Jockies of the Box and Pit" will prefer "a hot unbroken wit" like Saunders to "an old batter'd Jade" like himself (ll. 20–25).

One result of the precariousness and brevity of life was generational hostility; the young Dryden, for example, had vented his spleen toward "Old three-legg'd graybeards" at eighteen. Younger politicians eagerly plotted the impeachment of older ones in the cases of Clarendon and Danby, in part because they felt they could not afford to wait their turn. In the literary world, such younger men as Ravenscroft (b. 1644) and Settle (b. 1648) had begun to attack Dryden as "old" when he was in his early forties, and that charge would be insistently repeated in the Whig pamphleteering of the next several years. Given these circumstances, Dryden's capacity for friendships with younger writers is striking. Despite his troubles with Ravenscroft, Shadwell, and Settle, who was grinding out his vicious *Character of a Popish Successor* at this very moment, the Laureate had been generously helpful to Crowne (b. 1640?), Lee (b. 1649), Tate (b. 1652), and Duke (b. 1658). In helping Saunders, he was giving his valuable time to a young writer only two years older than his own son.[16]

In the dedication for the published *Spanish Fryar*, first advertised on 9 March, Dryden addresses another teenager, and deftly develops the theme of maturity. Pleased with his success at managing his two plots, he recognizes that "Poets may suspect themselves for the fondness and partiality of Parents to their youngest Children" (sig. A2r), but exempts himself from that charge. He remembers those passages in his own plays that were "bad enough to please" (sig. A2v) and makes fun of his boyish fondness for the "abominable fustian" of Sylvester (sig. A3r). Citing these instances of his own immaturity is Dryden's way of insisting on the better judgment he has gained from experience, and his vigorous self-defense is a necessary answer to "some young Gallants, who pretend to Criticism" (sig. A3r) but lack the maturity to separate substance from mere style. "In a Play-house," explains the experienced poet, "every thing contributes to impose upon the Judgment; the Lights, the Scenes, the Habits, and, above all, the Grace of Action, which is commonly best where there is the most need of it, surprize the Audience, and cast a mist upon their Understandings" (sig. A2v). Not only will theatre audiences be misled by such factors, but "a common Reader" will mistake mere noise for the true sublime, preferring Statius to Virgil, even though "*Virgil* had all the Majesty of a lawfull Prince; and *Statius* onely the blustering of a Tyrant" (sig. A3r).

At this point, the relevance to current politics of what had seemed a merely aesthetic definition of maturity becomes obvious. The Duke of Monmouth, a "young Gallant" blessed with a natural "Grace of Action," was now "pretending" to something a good deal more urgent than mere "Criticism." By organizing his "progresses" through various parts of the country and encouraging him to touch those suffering from scrofula (the "King's Evil"), Shaftesbury and others were trying to give him "the Majesty of a lawfull Prince" by treating him like one. During a hunting visit to Chichester on 13 February, for example, Monmouth's friend Lord Grey arranged to have him greeted by "100 Batchellors all in white, except Black Velvet caps, with white wands in their hands."[17] Dryden evidently regarded such theatrical demonstrations as attempts to "cast a mist upon [the] Understandings" of the public: eight months later, in *Absalom and Achitophel*, he cast Monmouth as King David's rebellious son Absalom, greeted on his progresses by an "Admiring Croud" who "feed their eyes" on his "goodly person," "dazled with surprize" by a prince who "sets himself to show" (ll. 686–88); four years later, in *Albion and Albanius*, he brought a similarly costumed group of young men on stage, calling them the "Property Boys."

The Oxford Parliament, which opened less than two weeks after the printed *Spanish Fryar* was advertised, was a highly theatrical exercise for all parties. Indeed, the very choice of Oxford as a site was symbolic as well as pragmatic. Charles feared the potential for popular violence from the City if the Parliament met in London, and the Whig leaders were sufficiently disgruntled to consider staying in London, complaining that the King was planning a coup against them. But both sides also remembered the history to which Dryden had recently been alluding in his Oxford prologues and epilogues: they knew that Charles I had used Oxford as his headquarters during much of the Civil War, summoning a loyal alternative Parliament there to oppose the Long Parliament in London. Mindful of history and symbolism, the various factions staged their arrivals at Oxford carefully. The King came up in his coach on 14 March (Monday), accompanied by the Queen, the Duchess of Portsmouth, Nell Gwyn, and the brightly costumed Life Guards; drinks were dispensed to the crowds, who drank the monarch's health on their knees. Charles assured the people of his determination to keep both staff and sword in his own hands, received a Bible from the Vice-Chancellor, settled his various women, and went off to the horse-races at Brunton. Shaftesbury arrived on 19 March (Saturday), accompanied by two other Whig earls and two hundred armed men on horseback; in their hats, his followers wore blue ribbons with a combative slogan: "No Popery, No Slavery." Monmouth delayed his entry until the day after Parliament officially opened, arriving with Lord Grey and thirty others on 22 March (Tuesday).[18]

Whether or not Dryden himself was actually present at Oxford, his acute awareness of the theatrical nature of the events now unfolding there shows clearly in the special epilogue he wrote for a performance of *Tamerlane* attended by the King and his mistresses on 19 March. Beginning with the image of a *camera obscura*, which shows "The worlds large Landschape . . . contracted on the Paper," Dryden points out that "Oxford is now the publick *Theater*, / And you both Audience are, and Actors here" (ll. 7–8). Recycling images he had frequently used before, he emphasizes the peace and quiet of the university, arguing that such a setting will calm the wills of the legislators, uniting their "jarring parts . . . like soft Musick." Reaching all the way back to *Astraea Redux*, he combines his favorite image of the storm-tossed ship landing safe on shore with the specific Old Testament story of the Flood:

> Our Ark that has in Tempests long been tost,
> Cou'd never land on so secure a Coast.
> From hence you may look back on Civil Rage,
> And view the ruines of the former Age.
>
> [ll. 17–20]

Dryden evidently had the story of the Flood on his mind, as he had shown by alluding to the sons of Noah in the preface to the Ovid translations a year earlier, but he was surely also aware that the Puritan side had used the Flood as a typological analogue during the days of "Civil Rage": a popular broadside called "England's Miraculous Preservation," for example, had shown the Long Parliament in the ark, while Charles I, Laud, and their supporters drowned in the waves with the other evildoers. Reclaiming this image for the Tory side, Dryden also pictures the ark as the ship of state, but casts Charles II as Noah, steering the ark into the safe harbor of Oxford. As in *Annus Mirabilis*, he was

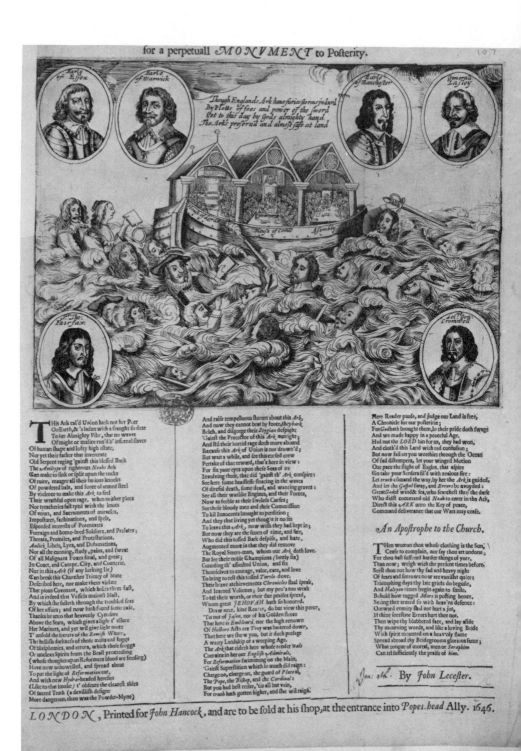

England's Miraculous Preservation Emblematically Described (1646).

appropriating the scriptural imagery of Dissenting propaganda for a Royalist use. He was also reminding the members of Parliament, who still addressed Charles as "Sire," of the King's symbolic status as a patriarch. Here the allusion to the Old Testament is only one of a number of pregnant metaphors, but in *Absalom and Achitophel*, Dryden would base his entire structure upon a similar parallelism, retelling the story of Absalom's rebellion against King David in II Samuel as a cautionary version of Monmouth's threatened rebellion against Charles.

Dryden's epilogue was immediately printed as a single-sheet broadside, and must therefore have been intended as court propaganda, but he obviously knew that neither his poem nor a pleasant evening in the theatre was likely to alter the votes of the Parliament. He could playfully refer to "Mirth" as "the pleasing buisness of the Night, / The Kings Prerogative, the Peoples right" (ll. 26–27), pretending to reconcile the political concepts essentially at issue in the coming Parliamentary showdown, but this was more a joke acknowledging the presence of two royal mistresses than a serious ideological argument.[19] The actual business of Saturday night was not entirely pleasant: a chimney fire in Shaftesbury's chamber led to renewed fears of violence. The next day, the two parties refused to sit together at church, and on Monday, in a "subtle crafty" opening speech, the King insisted on his "Prerogative," refusing to alter the succession; his answer to demands for "the Peoples right" was a vague promise "to remove all reasonable fears that may arise from the possibility of a Popish successor."[20]

Dryden presumably did not know that the King was now in a stronger financial position than during previous Parliaments proposing Exclusion, from which he had hoped for bills of supply. Before going up to Oxford, Charles had concluded a secret verbal agreement with Barillon, the French ambassador, in which Louis promised to pay him £375,000 over the next three years—enough to allow him to dispense with his troublesome Parliament. Consequently he was able to act his part in Oxford with great theatrical verve. On 24 March, when Shaftesbury contrived to pass him a paper advocating that Monmouth be declared the successor, the King replied by alluding to the issues of age and legitimacy that had been at the heart of Dryden's recent plays and poems:

> The *K.* surpriz'd, told the Earl that his Majesty was none of those that grew more timorous with age, but that rather he grew the more resolute the nearer he was to his grave. . . . ["]I would much sooner lose this Life, of which you pretend to be so watchful Preservers, than ever part with any of my Prerogative, or betray this Place, the Laws, or the Religion, or alter the true Succession of the Crown. . . . And in fine, assure your selves that as I love my Life so well, as to take all the care in the world to keep it with Honor, so I don't think it of so great Value neither, after Fifty, as to be preserv'd with the forfeiture of my Honor, Conscience, and the Laws of the Land.["][21]

Like Dryden's epilogue, this exchange was immediately printed; the almost instantaneous reporting of events at this Parliament indicates the urgency of the crisis. The King's stubborn resolve struck a resonant note for Dryden, who had written somewhat timorously himself in the early months of the Popish Plot. Like his royal master, the Laureate had gained confidence from adversity, in his case the Rose Alley episode, and his ensuing literary campaign in defense of the King shows his admiration for Charles's political toughness and style.

Four days after the exchange with Shaftesbury, having created the expectation of a longer sitting by agreeing to have the Sheldonian Theatre refurbished as a meeting place for the House of Commons, Charles came into the House of Lords, apparently ready to hear the day's proceedings. Then, like an actor making a lightning change of costume, he ducked outside, donned his formal robes and crown, which had been hidden in a sedan chair, and dissolved the Parliament. It was not the military coup some had feared, but it was a decisive coup de théâtre. Charles was never to meet another Parliament.

"To Vindicate Himself in Print"

Back in London, the King made effective use of his power over the Church: on 8 April, he published a *Declaration to all His Loving Subjects, Touching the Causes & Reasons That moved Him to Dissolve the Two last Parliaments* and ordered it read from every pulpit in the nation. This brief statement connects Exclusion with past troubles:

> We cannot, after the sad Experience We have had of the late Civil Wars, that Murder'd Our Father of Blessed Memory, and ruin'd the Monarchy, consent to a Law, that shall establish another most Unnatural War, or at least make it necessary to maintain a Standing Force for the Preserving the Government and the Peace of the Kingdom.[22]

In a prologue spoken before the King and Queen at a performance of *The Unhappy Favourite*, a play by John Banks produced in early May, Dryden immediately put that argument into verse. Again alluding to the story of the Flood, he complimented the Queen by calling her "the Royal Dove," reminding his audience of the dove Noah sent out after landing on Mount Ararat, who "first brought back to Man the Pledge of Peace" (l. 6).[23] Deftly expanding that theme, Dryden combines the ideal of international peace, which he had used in dedicating *All for Love* to Danby, with the currently urgent need for civil peace, suggested by the King's *Declaration*:

> Must *England* still the Scene of Changes be,
> Tost and Tempestuous like our Ambient Sea?
> Must still our Weather and our Wills agree?
> Without our Blood our Liberties we have,
> Who that is Free would Fight to be a Slave?
> Or what can Wars to after Times Assure,
> Of which our Present Age is not secure?
> All that our Monarch would for us Ordain,
> Is but t'Injoy the Blessings of his Reign.
> Our Land's an *Eden*, and the Main's our Fence,
> While we Preserve our State of Innocence;
> That lost, then Beasts their Brutal Force employ,
> And first their Lord, and then themselves destroy:
> What Civil Broils have cost we know too well,
> Oh let it be enough that once we fell,

> And every Heart conspire with every Tongue,
> Still to have such a King, and this King long.
>
> [ll. 18–34]

This prologue is recognizably Tory in its sentiments; the reference to "Civil Broils," for example, repeats the King's insistent linking of 1641 and 1681. But the lofty, masquelike language also recalls the Oxford epilogue of two months earlier. The allusion to Eden, with its echo of the title of Dryden's Miltonic opera, complements the opening allusion to the Flood: the Civil War was not only a deluge but a fall from innocence, yet the English, unlike Adam and Eve, have been miraculously restored to their island Eden, which they should now treasure in peace. If we may recognize the Whigs as the "Beasts" who employ "their Brutal Force," they do not seem much more threatening than the fantastic animals in the antimasques of the Jones-Jonson spectaculars, and Dryden's answer to the conspiracies imagined by Oates and pursued by the Whigs is a "Metaphysical" quibble, a proposed "conspiracy" between the hearts and tongues of the King's grateful subjects.

Not many weeks later, however, Dryden apparently descended from these lofty heights onto the dirtier battlefield of prose journalism. The Whigs, recognizing the monarch's resolve and their own weakening position, published numerous answers to the *Declaration*, including *A Letter from a Person of Quality*, an undistinguished pamphlet rehearsing the usual fears of Popery and arguments for Exclusion. The Tories were determined to keep up their side in the war of words; their anonymous answer, *His Majesties Declaration Defended*, looks like the work of the best professional writer in England, and while the evidence remains inconclusive, I shall treat it as Dryden's.[24] We know nothing about the origins of this pamphlet, but there were at least three prominent Tories who might have asked Dryden to write it. Roger L'Estrange, who was linked with Dryden throughout this period, enraged the Whigs by seizing their pamphlets in his role as surveyor of the press and answering them in his role as the government's chief propagandist; in return, they called him "Towser the bulldog" and burned him in effigy at several of their Pope-burnings. L'Estrange briefly attacked the *Letter from a Person of Quality* in his newspaper *The Observator*, and might well have urged Dryden to answer it at length; he promptly praised the Tory pamphlet when it appeared. Lawrence Hyde, who was created Earl of Rochester in 1682, is another possibility; as the son of Clarendon and the brother-in-law of York, he shared Dryden's passion for order and loyalty. A shrewd financier, he was also responsible for the austerity program in the Treasury that was helping Charles live within his means. Dryden, whose salary was effectively cut in half by that fiscal austerity, nonetheless praised Hyde in *Absalom and Achitophel* as "*Hushai* the friend of *David* in distress" (l. 888); a couplet on Hushai's financial management suggests that Hyde may even have aided Dryden financially from his own resources:

> His frugal care supply'd the wanting Throne,
> Frugal for that, but bounteous of his own.
>
> [ll. 892–93][25]

Edward Seymour, whose portrait as Amiel follows that of Hushai, is yet another candidate. Formerly Speaker of the House of Commons, he was now an important advisor to the King, and probably knew Dryden because of his own connection with the Duke of Ormonde and the late Earl of Ossory. In a letter written in November 1681, Ossory's steward, Richard Mulys, says that Seymour asked Dryden to write *Absalom and Achitophel*, then newly published.[26] If the request Mulys had heard about was a general call for help in the current controversy, it might well have produced both the pamphlet, an immediate answer to a particular Whig tract, and the poem, a far more thoughtful and complex response to the upheaval the nation was experiencing.

Whoever wanted the pamphlet written had reason to be pleased with the result. Dryden moves somewhat mechanically through the opposing pamphlet, printing excerpts and demolishing them, as he had done in attacking Howard and Settle, and as he would do in *The Vindication of the Duke of Guise* (1683). His writing, evidently produced without the care that marks his best prose, is always scornful, occasionally clever, and thoroughly unfair. If the biblical and literary allusions in his Oxford epilogue and his most recent London prologue had been genial and conciliatory, advocating loyalty to the crown in a style like that of his Restoration panegyrics, the allusions here are combative and nasty. Probably unaware of the identity of his antagonist, which remains uncertain, Dryden invents a demeaning identity for him—a technique that may remind us of the preface to *All for Love*, where he pretended not to know that it was Rochester who had attacked him. He surmises that the "Phanatique Party," missing the skills of Marvell, have organized a contest to find a writer to answer the *Declaration*; the "person of Quality," winner of that contest, has been "chosen like a new *Matthias*, to succeed in the place of their deceas'd *Judas*" (XVII, 195). This allusion cuts in all directions: since the biblical Matthias was actually chosen by lot, Dryden implies that the Whig pamphleteer has no special claim to argumentative skill, and if Marvell did possess such skill, calling him Judas is hardly a compliment. In a later passage, drawing on the power of English xenophobia, Dryden implies that his antagonist is a Scot: "the barrenness of his Country" accounts for his "two false Grammars, and three Barbarisms, in every Period of his Pamphlet" (XVII, 212–13). Even though the main issues here are political, the man who had mercilessly exposed the solecisms of Howard and Settle could not resist exposing the literary incompetence of the "person of Quality." At the very end, impugning the sincerity of "my suppos'd author," he hopes his adversary will "be made a Bishop, and renounce the Covenant" (XVII, 225); here his lifelong contempt for greedy clerics of all denominations is as important as the particular fictional scenario in which the other author, now pilloried as a Scottish Presbyterian, renounces his beliefs when rewarded with Anglican preferment.

Dryden evidently wrote this pamphlet during the trial of Edward Fitzharris, an Irish Catholic informant who claimed to have explosive information about the murder of Godfrey.[27] The Whigs, anxious to keep the Plot scare active, had impeached Fitzharris in the Parliament of the previous autumn and pressed their right to question him at the Oxford Parliament, but the King, who called that action "an Impeachment made use of to delay a trial" (*Declaration*, XVII, 515), was determined to silence the dangerous Fitzharris; indeed, preventing testimony by Fitzharris was one of his major motives for dissolving the Oxford Parliament. Charles arranged to have Fitzharris tried for treason in a common court of law, where he was convicted on 9 June, but not before Shaftesbury had contrived to have him called to testify before the Middlesex Grand Jury, where he publicly declared that the Duke of York, the Earl of Danby, and the Queen had plotted Godfrey's murder. The King's irritation showed when he refused the petition of Mrs. Fitzharris begging that her husband be merely hanged, not drawn and quartered; Fitzharris suffered the full penalties for treason on 1 July. Although Dryden speaks glowingly of the "many examples of Moderation" in Charles's reign and emphasizes the "temperate and wholsom . . . Constitution" of the English monarchy (XVII, 198, 207), the monarch's actions in the summer of 1681 were bitterly vindictive.[28]

In *Absalom and Achitophel*, which may already have been in progress, Dryden found a way to make lasting art out of this apparent contradiction between the Christian ideal of moderation and the political necessity for vengeance. The assumptions of that great poem are nearly as partisan as those of this shrill pamphlet; comparing the two may help us appreciate how much more subtle Dryden could be when treating political issues in an imaginative and poetic mode. Different as they are, both pamphlet and poem also draw upon Dryden's personal identification with the King, which we first noticed in his poems written around the time of the Restoration. Like his royal master, Dryden was now fifty years old, less wealthy than he wished to be, a firstborn son, a fond father, and the husband of a wife with recusant connections; at some psychological level, his defense of the monarch was thus a kind of self-defense. As he explained in the dedication to *The Spanish Fryar*, published in March of 1681, "a man who is charg'd with a crime of which he thinks himself innocent, is apt to be too eager in his own defence, so perhaps I have vindicated my Play with more partiality than I ought" (sig. A3r–v). Similar language, now applied to the King, recurs in *His Majesties Declaration Defended*: "'tis not deny'd the meanest *Englishman*, to vindicate himself in Print, when he has any aspersion cast upon him" (XVII, 198). At a point in his argument where he might have appealed to Charles's royal prerogative, Dryden stresses a right to self-defense common to the King and "the meanest *Englishman*," a phrase echoing the *Declaration*, where the King had said that the Commons, by failing to vote him an adequate supply, were "endeavoring . . . to reduce Us to a more helpless Condition then the meanest of Our Subjects" (XVII, 514). Since Dryden had often exercised the right to defend himself, and even referred to himself late in life as "naturally vindicative," he was probably thinking of the parallel between his many defenses of his literary actions and the King's recent defense of his political actions.

Dryden's troubles with younger writers, for example, may have contributed to his conceiving the attempt by the Commons to restrict the King's funds as a generational issue. In the dedication to *The Spanish Fryar*, he had expressed his resentment of those "young Gallants" who told him that *The Spanish Fryar*, a subtle play by an experienced professional writer, "wanted the dignity of style." Reversing their proper roles, such young wits were acting like elder statesmen, treating Dryden as if he were a neophyte. The pamphlet complains of similar improprieties in the political arena: "What has his present Majesty deserv'd from his Subjects, that he should be made a Minor at no less than fifty years of age?" (XVII, 204). In a gesture linking the King with other men of his generation (including his Laureate), Dryden speaks of "his Majesties natural love to

Peace and Quiet, which increases in every man with his years" (XVII, 197), but he doubtless also remembered the confrontation between Shaftesbury and Charles at the Oxford Parliament, where the King had insisted that he would not grow "timorous with age." Again, the full development of these tensions comes in *Absalom and Achitophel*, which certainly draws on the reality of generational politics and probably draws on Dryden's own feelings of generational solidarity with the King, but transmutes those realities and feelings into a subtle and complex fiction. When Achitophel interprets David's mercy as lethargic decline and overvalues the youthful vigor of Absalom, Dryden trusts his reader to recognize the appeal of the argument but reject it as specious.

By treating the King as a minor, the Commons were denying him money rightfully his, and Dryden could easily identify with the King's resentment of that treatment. The Laureate's hiring an agent to collect his salary at the end of 1680 coincided with the attempt by the Commons to limit the King's access to loans, and the pamphlet, written some six months later, accuses the House of Commons of a plot to force the King "to take Money upon their Terms, which will sure be as easie, as those of an Usurer to an Heir in want" (XVII, 200)—terms with which the penurious Dryden was all too familiar. A prologue written for an Oxford performance in July of 1681 compares the failure of the King's players to profit from their brief Oxford stint of the previous spring with the failure of the King to secure a supply:

> We look'd what Representatives wou'd bring,
> But they helped us, just as they did the King.
>
> [ll. 19–20]

By identifying with his old associates from the King's Company, who had come away from Oxford with empty pockets, Dryden was again identifying with the King, whose money from Louis did not permit lavish expenditures. If we may believe the story Pope told Spence about the origins of *The Medall*, the vituperative satire on Shaftesbury that Dryden published in early 1682, Charles himself wryly spoke of poverty as a similarity linking him with his Laureate: "One day as the King was walking in the Mall and talking with Dryden, he said: 'If I were a poet (and I think I'm poor enough to be one) I would write a poem on such a subject.'"[29]

Like many Tories, Dryden believed that the whole system by which property was passed down from generation to generation was under attack in the Exclusion Crisis. As a firstborn son, though often "an Heir in want," he had excellent reasons to want that system preserved.[30] His younger brothers were all now in London: Erasmus was a grocer in King Street; Henry, a goldsmith in the City; James, a successful tobacconist. Although they may well have had more money than Dryden, they were essentially of a different class: all had obviously been apprentices, while Dryden had enjoyed a gentleman's education at Westminster and Cambridge and married the daughter of an Earl. He correctly perceived that the continuation of primogeniture, to which he owed those privileges, depended on the preservation of the laws of monarchial succession.

The characterization of Monmouth as Absalom must also owe some of its power to Dryden's identification with Charles in his role as father. Though recognizing his favorite's dangerous weaknesses, Charles was always eager to forgive him, and to suppose that others, like Shaftesbury, were actually to blame for his son's indiscretions. Something of the same mixture comes across in a letter Dryden wrote to Busby in 1682, when his own Charles had been temporarily dismissed from Westminster; admitting his son's faults, Dryden nonetheless suggests that "other boyes combind to discredit him with false witnesseing, and to save them selves" (*Letters*, p. 18). In the pamphlet, Dryden pictures the Duke as a similarly unfortunate victim of a "design" by unscrupulous men devoted to revolutionary ideas and lacking in personal loyalty:

> I am not ashamed to say, that I particularly honour the Duke of *Monmouth:* but whether his nomination to succeed, would, at the bottom be pleasing to the Heads of his Cabal, I somewhat doubt. . . . To have him in readiness to head an Army, in case it should please God the King should die before the Duke, is the design. [XVII, 211]

The same judgment recurs in the preface to *Absalom and Achitophel*, but in that later passage, Dryden's identification with the King is made explicit:

> Besides the respect which I owe his Birth, I have a greater for his Heroique Vertues; and, *David* himself, coud not be more tender of the Young-man's Life, than I woud be of his Reputation. But, since the most excellent Natures are always the most easy; and, as being such, are the soonest perverted by ill Counsels, especially when baited with Fame and Glory; 'tis no more a wonder that he withstood not the temptations of *Achitophel*, than it was for *Adam*, not to have resisted the two Devils; the Serpent, and the Woman. [II, 4]

This account of Monmouth's "easy" nature draws on Dryden's personal experience as well as the myth of the Fall. Four years earlier, in the dedication to *All for Love*, he had applied Satanic imagery to Shaftesbury, comparing him to the "old Forefather" who would "seduce Mankind into the same Rebellion with him, by telling him he might yet be freer than he was" (XIII, 7). But eleven years earlier, when he first cast Monmouth as a tempted Adam, Dryden comically called himself "the Serpent, who first presented the fruit of Poetry to the Wife, and so gain'd the opportunity to seduce the Husband" (X, 107). If Achitophel, that silver-tongued orator, is intended as a complex and devastating version of Shaftesbury, his skill in seduction draws more distantly on Dryden's memories of his own success in securing the patronage of the young and pliable Monmouth.

There is little reason to doubt Queen Catharine's later testimony that Charles wore a crucifix hidden under his shirt beginning in 1679 and used to kiss the portraits of the priests martyred during the Popish Plot when he entered her apartment.[31] Like the King, Dryden had a wife whose friends had been victims of the Plot scare: her exiled cousin the Cardinal, her beheaded cousin Lord Stafford, and her late brother Charles, whose correspondence with the executed Coleman was actually published during 1681 in a collection of *Letters Relating to the Horrid Popish Plott*.[32] But Dryden's earlier caution about those connections had now disappeared, replaced by the firm conviction that the Protestant "Phanatiques" among whom he had been reared were at least as dangerous to the body politic as the Roman Catholics. In the pamphlet, he makes that comparison quite explicit: "Whether Democracy will agree with Jesuitical principles in *England* I am not certain; but I can easily prove to him, that no Government but a Commonwealth is accommodated to the Systeme of Church-worship invented by *John Calvin*" (XVII, 225). He would repeat that opinion in at least three signed works.[33]

In an even more remarkable passage, the pamphlet openly acknowledges England's Catholic past, a fact often forgotten or ignored by Whig propagandists advocating a Protestant succession. Rejecting his adversary's claim that England was "naturally" Protestant, Dryden wonders what "the Law of Nature . . . has to do with Protestants or Papists, except he can prove that the *English* Nation is naturally Protestant; and then I would enquire of him what Countrymen our Forefathers were?" (XVII, 210). Protected by anonymity, Dryden could publish such a passage in June, despite his claim, as recent as March, that *The Spanish Fryar* was "a Protestant Play," appropriately dedicated to "a Protestant Patron." But the lines on the Roman Catholic "Jebusites" in *Absalom and Achitophel* depend on the same historical facts, and that poem, though also published anonymously, was recognized as Dryden's work within days of its publication, as he surely knew it would be. Risky and moving, the poetic version moves beyond historical fact to imaginative sympathy and moral complexity:

> Th' inhabitants of old *Jerusalem*
> Were *Jebusites:* the Town so call'd from them;
> And their's the Native right———
> But when the chosen people grew more strong,
> The rightfull cause at length became the wrong:
> And every loss the men of *Jebus* bore,
> They still were thought God's enemies the more.
> Thus, worn and weaken'd, well or ill content,
> Submit they must to *David*'s Government:
> Impoverisht, and depriv'd of all Command,
> Their Taxes doubled as they lost their Land,
> And, what was harder yet to flesh and blood,
> Their Gods disgrac'd, and burnt like common wood.
>
> [ll. 85–97]

The talk of double taxation and lost land reflects Dryden's awareness of the deprivations suffered by his wife's recusant relatives. In the poem as in the pamphlet, he insists on the weakness of the Roman Catholics, who constituted a tiny percentage of the population and were therefore hardly likely to succeed in an armed revolution, despite the fantasies of Oates: "By force they could not Introduce these Gods; / For Ten to One, in former days was odds" (ll. 122–23). But he was obviously concerned lest he appear overly tolerant of the Papists, and attempted to balance the sympathy implicit in these lines with a nasty passage poking fun at transubstantiation as an "*Egyptian* Rite . . . Where Gods were recommended by their Tast" (ll. 118–19). Nonetheless, many of the Whig pamphleteers who answered his poem thought they detected a Roman Catholic bias; the first of these answers, available on 10 December, links Dryden with L'Estrange by calling him "Towser the Second" and addresses him as a dog in need of worming:

> hold out thy Venom'd Tongue,
> What a huge Worm is here? 'Tis an inch Long,
> And of the Jebusite smells very strong.
> If this won't do thou shalt be fairly hung.[34]

Although Dryden probably expected such counterattacks, his own partisan confidence was based upon the increasing disarray of the Whig cause. On 2 July, the day after the execution of Fitzharris, Shaftesbury was arrested and sent back to the Tower; when his papers were seized, the authorities found a draft of a "Protestant Association" binding its members to resist the succession of James by force of arms, but this potentially damning document proved to be unsigned, undated, and not in Shaftesbury's handwriting. Before Shaftesbury could be tried, a Grand Jury would have to find a true bill, and the events of his first week of incarceration gave him reasons for hope: a London jury, handpicked by the Whig sheriffs, brought in a verdict of *ignoramus* in the case of Stephen College, who was charged with providing the blue ribbons worn by Shaftesbury's men at the Oxford Parliament and writing an obscure broadside that may glance at Dryden.[35] Nothing daunted, the King contrived to have College indicted by a more cooperative jury at Oxford, where the "Protestant joiner" was hanged, drawn, and quartered on 31 August.[36] Titus Oates, who made the mistake of testifying on behalf of College, also felt the King's wrath: he was thrown out of his comfortable lodgings in Whitehall and deprived of his financial allowance.[37] Shortly after moving into new quarters in the City, Oates found two infants on his doorstep, a comic episode mentioned in Dryden's next prologue, spoken at a revival of Lee's *Mithridates* in October:

> some Pious Whore
> Has cast her Mite, and fairly at his Dore
> Laid two small squalling Evidences more;
> Which well instructed, if we take their words,
> In time may come to hang two Popish Lords.
>
> [ll. 28–32]

Dryden's prediction that the children, well instructed in the art of telling lies by their father Oates, will grow up to cause "two Popish Lords" to be hanged may especially indicate his resentment of Oates's testimony against his wife's kinsman Stafford, executed the previous winter.

By the time Dryden wrote these lines, which were immediately printed in Tory newspapers and as single-sheet broadsides, the nation was awaiting the trial of Shaftesbury, who was sufficiently worried to have Arlington propose to Charles that he be exiled to his plantation in South Carolina. During the autumn months, when hardly a week passed without some new publication for or against Shaftesbury, Dryden was polishing *Absalom and Achitophel*, but by the time his poem appeared, on or about 17 November, Shaftesbury's release was inevitable. There was not enough evidence to hope to indict him at Oxford, a ploy Charles had hoped to use again, and the new London Grand Jury declared a verdict of *ignoramus* in the case of a Whig named Rouse on 18 October, a likely sign of how Shaftesbury's case would be settled. Dryden's preface says that Whig pamphleteers "have the advantage of a Jury to secure them" (II, 4), a phrase suggesting that he expected another *ignoramus* verdict in Shaftesbury's case, which came on 24 November. Therefore the notion that he actually expected his poem to influence the trial, which began a scant week after its publication, seems unlikely, though the more general notion of influencing public opinion was surely the reason why someone close to the King, probably Edward Seymour, requested the poem.[38]

Dryden's own account of his motives, in a preface addressed "To the Reader," is slippery. He admits that "he who draws his Pen for one Party, must expect to make Enemies of the other," but goes on to argue that "if a *Poem* have a *Genius*, it will force its own reception in the World." He claims to be writing "to please the more Moderate sort . . . by rebating the *Satyre*," but quickly goes on to threaten his enemies with harsher treatment: "They, who can Criticize so weakly, as to imagine I have done my Worst, may be Convinc'd, at their own Cost, that I can write Severely" (II, 3)—a boast made good in *The Medall*. The claims to moderation are of course conventional, while the threatening language reinforces the parallel we have been noticing between poet and monarch. Charles, who had temporized and compromised for years, was now convincing his enemies, at their own cost, that he could act severely; Dryden, whose writings during the Exclusion Crisis include high-minded pleas for moderation and shrill, combative attacks, was describing *Absalom and Achitophel* as one last attempt at moderate argument.

"Fatall Mercy" or "Good Natur'd Errour"?

Absalom and Achitophel is built upon a typological parallel of the kind Dryden first encountered in the Puritan sermons and illustrations of his youth, which often equated current political heroes with the kings and prophets of the Old Testament. He had used such typology himself in his poems at the time of the Restoration, though more as a matter of passing allusion than as a sustained structure, and a comparison of the exiled Charles to the "banish'd *David*" (*Astraea Redux*, l. 79) was one of those allusions. The story of Absalom's rebellion, as Dryden surely knew, had already been applied to the Duke of Monmouth,[39] but on first examination, the dangers of this story would seem to outweigh its advantages, particularly for a writer concerned to support the court. II Samuel tells a tragic story of sexual sin and retribution. David commits adultery with Bathsheba and arranges for her husband's death; for these sins, he is punished by the rebellion of his favorite son Absalom, who forces his father to abandon the capital city and copulates with the royal concubines "in the sight of all Israel" (II Samuel 16.22). Dryden naturally omits all mention of Absalom's ritual taking of David's women; the only woman his Absalom loves is "the Charming *Annabel* his Bride" (l. 34), obviously Dryden's early patroness the Duchess. But shrewd readers might have remembered some incidents that came close to the shocking parallel that Dryden so carefully suppressed. I have no unequivocal evidence that Monmouth shared a mistress with his father, but he certainly shared Moll Kirke with his uncle, the Duke of York, as they both discovered in 1674, when Monmouth had her third lover, Dryden's patron Mulgrave, arrested by the guards.[40] Moreover, Monmouth was at least socially intimate with three of his father's most prominent mistresses. When he first came to court as "Mr. Crofts" in 1662, Pepys noticed him "hang[ing] much upon my Lady Castlemayne" and heard that "the Queenes, both of them, are mighty kind to him." In 1679, when Monmouth was in deep disgrace with Charles, he asked Nell Gwyn to intercede for him, and in the autumn of 1680, he met several times with the Duchess of Portsmouth in an attempt to secure her influence.[41]

Dryden succeeds in focusing our attention on Absalom as political rebel rather than sexual rival to his father, but his choice of this story would still seem to concede the charges of those who saw the King as an adulterer who would suffer for his sexual excesses. Dryden's old schoolmate Creighton, after all, had blamed the naval disasters of 1667 on the King's adultery, preaching from these very chapters of II Samuel (see above, p. 185). Yet by opening his poem with a passage in which David's polygamy, lawful in his time, serves as proof of his vigorous manhood and even his piety, Dryden brilliantly turns that apparent disadvantage into a rhetorical advantage:

> In pious times, e'r Priest-craft did begin,
> Before *Polygamy* was made a sin;
> When man, on many, multiply'd his kind,
> E'r one to one was, cursedly, confind:
> When Nature prompted, and no law deny'd
> Promiscuous use of Concubine and Bride;
> Then, *Israel's* Monarch, after Heaven's own heart,
> His vigorous warmth did, variously, impart
> To Wives and Slaves: And, wide as his Command,
> Scatter'd his Maker's Image through the Land.
>
> [ll. 1–10]

The opening irony, in which "pious times" turn out to be those *before* the advent of "Priest-craft," immediately signals one target: the clergy, to whom Charles's undisguised fondness for women had always been anathema. By emphasizing Charles's sexual vigor, Dryden also answers the political arguments of those concerned to separate the King as man from the King as King, including the "person of Quality," who had argued that the King was "a publick Person: in his private capacity, . . . he can only eat and drink; and perform some other acts of nature which shall be nameless" (XVII, 217). By naming those acts and associating them with the "pious times" of a monarch who governed "after Heaven's own heart," Dryden insists that Charles's scattering of "his Maker's Image" is an essential and defining part of his kingship.

The brilliant style of this justly famous passage helps make the argument: the emphatic placement of the wonderful verb "Scatter'd" suggests the force of Charles's orgasm, and the teeming alliteration ("pious—Priest-craft—*Polygamy*—Promiscuous"; "man—many—multiply'd—Monarch—Maker's"; "cursedly—confin'd—Concubine—Command") displays an equivalent poetic fecundity. The opening also establishes the voice of the narrator, who shares some opinions with the monarch. When the narrator mutters "cursedly" while describing the confinement of monogamy, he endorses the king's polygamous behavior and implies that he wishes to emulate it, as Dryden himself had done in poetry by writing his poem to Lady Castlemaine and in practice by taking his own actress-mistress. He also enlists the sympathy of all those readers secretly wishing to be sexually "vigorous"; as Pepys's *Diary* shows, even those who worried that the King's sexual behavior reflected upon the court could have active fantasies about his mistresses.

If the opening lines help to defuse the sexual issue that was alive in the politics of the time and dangerously central in the biblical story, the tragic conclusion of his source left Dryden with an even more complex problem. In II Samuel, the loyal Israelites rally to David, and Absalom, fleeing a lost battle, is finally caught in the branches of an oak by his long hair and killed there by Joab, despite David's express orders against harming his son. When the news of this military success comes to David, he is wracked with grief for the loss of Absalom. Movingly set as a verse anthem by Thomas Weelkes, David's lament for his son was frequently sung in English cathedrals; it was surely the part of the narrative that came to the minds of the poem's first readers when they saw the title. Although Dryden is silent about his suppression of the scene of ritual copulation, his preface pointedly discusses his omission of the tragic ending and expresses his hope that the modern Absalom may avoid carrying through the parallel: "The conclusion of the Story, I purposely forbore to prosecute; because, I coud not obtain from my self, to shew *Absalom* Unfortunate. The Frame of it, was cut out, but for a Picture to the Wast; and, if the Draught be so far true, 'tis as much as I design'd" (II, 4).

Dryden evidently wants our awareness of the potential for tragedy to affect our reading of his comic masterpiece, and the language in which he couches these instructions to the reader is revealing. Like a merciful lawyer, the poet has "forbor[ne] to prosecute" the conclusion, a phrase that could hardly have escaped notice in a preface published just after the relentless and successful prosecution of Stephen College, and just before the unsuccessful attempt to prosecute Shaftesbury. Like a kind father, the author "coud not obtain from [him] self to show *Absalom* Unfortunate," and that display of personal reluctance to criticize Monmouth again forces an analogy between poet and monarch, anticipating the poem's complex internal debate about the wisdom of a policy of mercy. A literary version of that debate was still going on in Dryden's own mind as the poem went to press: in the third edition, published by the end of December, David's final speech gains four lines expressing his willingness to pardon Absalom—a surprising addition since the real King had another reason to be angry at his son by the time this revised edition appeared: Monmouth had offered to stand bail for Shaftesbury after the jury's verdict of *ignoramus*.[42] Aware that he was inclined to be less vindictive than Charles, Dryden claims to have "rebat[ed] the Satyre," even though this strategy will not please "the Violent, on both sides," but he also refers to his own descriptive mercy as a fault, albeit a deliberate one: "The fault, on the right hand, is to Extenuate, Palliate, and Indulge; and, to confess freely, I have endeavour'd to commit it" (II, 4).

Such ambiguity about mercy runs right through Dryden's career.[43] At the time of the Restoration, personally thankful that Charles II had forborne to prosecute most of those who had served Cromwell, he praised the Act of Oblivion, describing it as an act of Christian mercy, but even then, he acknowledged the popular belief that Charles I had been destroyed by his own willingness to forgive his enemies:

> But you, whose goodness your discent doth show,
> Your Heav'nly Parentage and earthly too;
> By that same mildness which your Fathers Crown
> Before did ravish, shall secure your own.
>
> [*Astraea Redux*, ll. 256–59]

This paradox occurs in a less convincing form in the Coronation poem; the early verses to Clarendon praise the Chancellor's "soft mercy" as pleasing to the personified Justice; and the King's prayer in *Annus Mirabilis* invokes his own mercy toward his people as a reason why God should be merciful to him (see above, pp. 115, 182, 174). Moreover, many of Dryden's dramatic characters enact similar struggles between the urge to take revenge and the noble impulse to forgive. In a nominally Christian society, forgiveness toward one's enemies was supposedly a shared value; in a violent and retributive society, as Dryden well knew, it was also folly. That was the point of the Italian proverb he quoted in dedicating *Aureng-Zebe* to Mulgrave in 1676: "To forgive the first time shows me a good Catholic, the second time a Fool" (sig. A3r). By 1681, however, Dryden had come to realize the inadequacy of such simple dualities as vengeance and mercy, Papist and Protestant, panegyric and satire, tragedy and comedy. Many of his recent works had exploited tensions between generic, political, and critical extremes: in *Mac Flecknoe*, he inserted satiric language into panegyric and epic structures, separating Shadwell's head from his body with the fine strokes of high art and eschewing the "slovenly Butchering" typical of lesser poems of vituperation; in *The Spanish Fryar*, he used the comic and tragic plots to comment upon each other, slyly advocating loyalty to the Catholic successor in a play containing broad strokes of anti-Catholic humor; in the preface to *Ovid's Epistles*, he laid out three options for translators, recommending the middle path for avoiding the extremes of excessive literalism and excessive freedom. *Absalom and Achitophel* applies a similar three-part scheme to political policy, offering the monarch a third option in dealing with his enemies. Since sweeping amnesty would lead to weakness, and absolutist revenge would risk renewed civil war, Dryden advocates a policy of firm punishment for those who threaten such fundamentals as the succession, but a general stance of toleration and mildness, and a propaganda campaign designed to calm fears of absolutism and win broad support for the King.

In the final paragraph of the preface to *Absalom and Achitophel*, a key document in that propaganda campaign, Dryden uses medical imagery to express this more complex view of the problem of justice and mercy:

> The true end of *Satyre*, is the amendment of Vices by correction. And he who writes Honestly, is no more an Enemy to the Offendour, than the Physician to the Patient, when he prescribes harsh Remedies to an inveterate Disease: for those, are only in order to prevent the Chyrurgeon's work of an *Ense rescindendum*, which I wish not to my very Enemies. To conclude all, If the Body Politique have any Analogy to the Natural,

in my weak judgment, an Act of *Oblivion* were as necessary in a Hot, Distemper'd State, as an *Opiate* would be in a raging Fever. [II, 5]

The analogy between the human body and the body politic was an old convention; Dryden had used it in his first poem, comparing the smallpox on Hastings's body to rebels raising an "Insurrection." Nor was this commonplace restricted to poetry; the King's recent *Declaration* had referred to Parliaments as "the best Method for healing the Distempers of the Kingdom" (XVII, 516). In *Absalom and Achitophel*, however, Dryden puts this stock idea to a precise and complex use. At first, he appears to be drawing an analogy between satirists and physicians, proffering "*Satyre*," which achieves "the amendment of Vices by correction," as an example of a successful remedy. In the talk of "amendment" and "correction," we may also detect his memory of Busby's birch, of which he was now freshly reminded by his own sons; as he professed himself grateful for the correction he had undergone at Westminster, he argued that the nation would be grateful for the correction of his own satire. But the ensuing discussion of medical remedies turns the discussion explicitly toward politics, where "correction" is necessarily more serious. In a medical crisis, Dryden argues, nothing is more useless than "an Opiate," which he specifically compares to "an Act of *Oblivion*." Only "harsh Remedies," doubtless including bleeding and purging, can prevent the doctor from having to call in a surgeon to cut away the disease with a knife. Read in this way, the medical analogy recommends to Charles a policy surprisingly like the selective bleeding Dryden had once praised in his poem on Cromwell, who "fought to end our fighting and assaid / To stanch the blood by breathing of the vein" (*Heroique Stanza's*, ll. 47–48). Harsh though they may be, however, the recommended remedies fall short of surgery; Dryden is not endorsing a policy of wholesale vengeance.[44] In the political context, however, the "harsh Remedies" endorsed here had to include the executions of Fitzharris and College, if not the current attempt to do the same to Shaftesbury.

The same issues and the same metaphors are central to the poem itself. In the midst of a catalogue of Whig conspirators, Dryden tells us that he has ordered these men from bad to worse (l. 583), and his portraits, especially if we include those of Absalom and Achitophel at the beginning, do move by careful gradations from a tone of regret to a tone of outrage. This ordering, a structural principle for the first half of the poem, provides a poetic version of the central political problem now facing the King: how to adjust his policies between the poles of mercy and vengeance. The handsome but pliable Absalom receives sympathetic treatment, typified by the couplet on his failings:

> What faults he had (for who from faults is free?)
> His Father coud not, or he woud not see.
>
> [ll. 35–36]

As his questioning rhetoric reveals, the narrator is not much more willing to see Absalom's faults than is David, who construes his son's "warm excesses" as "Youth that purg'd by boyling o'r" (ll. 37–38). Nonetheless, such "boyling," presumably hotter than the King's own "vigorous warmth," is dangerous, both in the human body and in

the body politic. Before the Opposition takes advantage of the Popish Plot, the King's
policy of mercy helps make his government stable: "*David*'s mildness manag'd it so
well, / The Bad found no occasion to Rebell" (ll. 76–77). But the Plot has "a deep and
dangerous Consequence," again described with the imagery of boiling:

> For, as when raging Fevers boyl the Blood,
> The standing Lake soon floats into a Flood;
> And every hostile Humour, which before
> Slept quiet in its Channels, bubbles o'r:
> So, several Factions from this first Ferment,
> Work up to Foam, and threat the Government.
>
> [ll. 136–41]

In the medical practice of Dryden's time, bleeding was the "harsh Remed[y]" thought
most likely to cure "raging Fevers." In the microcosm of the body, the foaming factions
are also threatening the government with a primal Flood, the image Dryden habitually
used for the Civil War.

Dryden now introduces the enemies of the crown; these "Feinds," especially
Achitophel, are "harden'd in Impenitence" as a result of "their Monarch's fatall mercy" (ll. 145–46), and the specific instance of that mercy Dryden wants us to remember
must be the Act of Oblivion of 1660, by which Charles forgave such offenses as
Shaftesbury's service on Cromwell's Privy Council. By repeating the imagery and some
of the language of his preface, Dryden would seem to be pointing in the direction of
vengeance, but the lengthy and memorable portrait of Achitophel that follows, with
which he was still tinkering while the poem was in press, is not an exercise in unadulter-
ated vituperation. Like Milton's Satan, to whom he bears a deliberate resemblance,
Dryden's Achitophel has fallen from greatness: he is "Sagacious, Bold, and Turbulent
of wit" (l. 153), a formidable man with "A fiery Soul" (l. 156). In lines added to the third
edition, Dryden even explicitly praises Shaftesbury's clean hands and discerning eyes
when he was a judge, perhaps remembering that the young Lord Ashley had helped the
young poet Dryden collect his wife's dowry from the Treasury.[45] In lines that appear in
all versions, he raises the possibility that Shaftesbury's talents might have been better
used:

> Oh, had he been content to serve the Crown,
> With vertues only proper to the Gown;
> Or, had the rankness of the Soyl been freed
> From Cockle, that opprest the Noble seed:
> *David*, for him, his tunefull Harp had strung,
> And Heaven had wanted one Immortal song.
>
> [ll. 192–97]

In Old Testament terms, Dryden probably means that Psalm 109, in which David
curses his enemies, would not have been written had Achitophel remained faithful.[46]
The Psalmist's complaint that "they have rewarded me evil for good, and hatred for my
love" (v. 5) fits particularly well with Dryden's picture of a king whose mercy goes
unrewarded. In modern terms, the notion that the King might have strung "his tunefull

Portrait of Anthony Ashley Cooper, first Earl of Shaftesbury after John Greenhill, ca. 1672–73.

Harp" to praise a more temperate Shaftesbury is more problematic: although Charles could play a bit on the guitar, he was no Psalmist, and these lines may actually point toward Dryden, who might have strung his poetic harp for Shaftesbury in a dedication or panegyric if the brilliant, fiery Earl had remained "content to serve the Crown." If the portrait of Achitophel lacks the element of sympathy that we sense in the portrait of Absalom, there remains, even in the original version, a sense of loss or regret, of great talents misdirected.

When Achitophel tempts Absalom, the loyal youth cites his father's mercy as a reason not to rebel:

> What Millions has he Pardon'd of his Foes,
> Whom Just Revenge did to his Wrath expose?
> Mild, Easy, Humble, Studious of our Good;

> Enclin'd to Mercy, and averse from Blood.
> If Mildness Ill with Stubborn *Israel* Suite,
> His Crime is God's beloved Attribute.
>
> [ll. 323–28]

The last couplet here repeats the paradox Dryden had been developing since his Restoration panegyrics, and he was still making similar claims for Charles a year and a half later: in *The Vindication of the Duke of Guise*, speaking in his own voice, he praises the King by pointing to "that eminent vertue of his *Clemency*; even his enemies must acknowledge it to be *Superlative*, because they live by it" (p. 9). When Absalom considers David's cunningly unnamed brother, the legitimate successor, who "stands possest . . . Of every Royal Vertue" (l. 355), he has to concede that those virtues include mercy; Dryden thus even predicts that James will be merciful to the Exclusionists:

> His Mercy even th' Offending Crowd will find,
> For sure he comes of a Forgiving Kind.
>
> [ll. 359–60]

But Achitophel, sensing an opening, attacks David's mildness:

> 'Tis true, he grants the People all they crave;
> And more perhaps than Subjects ought to have:
> For lavish grants suppose a Monarch tame,
> And more his Goodness than his Wit proclaim.
>
> [ll. 383–86]

In a poem concerned with finding the appropriate combination of justice and mercy, Dryden puts this argument against mercy into the mouth of a Satanic figure, and tells us that Absalom is convinced because Achitophel's specious argument appeals to his own "Mild nature" (l. 478), proof of his royal descent. Such ironic complexity is Dryden's way of suggesting that royal mercy, while often fatal from a political point of view, remains a God-like attribute.[47]

Absalom now gathers the malcontents about him and prepares a rebellion. The catalogue of those involved in the conspiracy includes three more extensive portraits, which continue the motion from sympathy toward vengeance. We have already glanced at the picture of Buckingham as the "various" and ineffective Zimri (see above, p. 182), where Dryden again acknowledges the energy and talent of his victim, but treats him with broad, oxymoronic irony, calling him a "Blest Madman" (l. 553). In the description of the Whig sheriff Slingsby Bethel as the niggardly and hypocritical Shimei, he turns the Dissenting habit of quoting Scripture against a prominent Dissenter, distorting familiar verses to make them into sharp insults:

> For *Shimei*, though not prodigal of pelf,
> Yet lov'd his wicked Neighbour as himself:
> When two or three were gather'd to declaim
> Against the Monarch of *Jerusalem*,
> *Shimei* was always in the midst of them.
>
> [ll. 599–603]

With the portrait of Titus Oates as the serpentine and perverse Corah, we reach an ethical and satirical extreme far removed from the gentle treatment of Absalom. Dryden marks out this portrait as special by abandoning the third person, in which he has described all the other Whigs, to address Corah in the second person:

> Yet, *Corah*, thou shalt from Oblivion pass;
> Erect thy self, thou Monumental Brass.
>
> [ll. 632–33]

As the portrait develops, Dryden scores points by pointing to Oates's obscure birth, strange appearance, and dubious "*Rabinical* degree," but he makes those insults funnier by pretending to be defending and praising his victim—a deadly variant of his technique in *Mac Flecknoe*. The lines on Corah's ancestry and class are typical:

> What tho his Birth were base, yet Comets rise
> From Earthy Vapours ere they shine in Skies.
> Prodigious Actions may as well be done
> By Weavers issue, as by Princes Son.
> This Arch-Attestor for the Publick Good,
> By that one Deed Enobles all his Bloud.
> Who ever ask'd the Witnesses high race,
> Whose Oath with Martyrdom did *Stephen* grace?
>
> [ll. 636–43]

The allusions invalidate the rhetoric: comets were dire apparitions; the "Princes Son" whose cause was furthered by Oates was himself baseborn; and St. Stephen, like Viscount Stafford and many of Oates's other victims, was an innocent martyr. Corah's testimony is thus more likely to ennoble the blood of his victims than the blood of his relatives. Similar ironies attend Dryden's mocking praise of Corah's "Memory, miraculously great," his "Visionary flights," and his "Judgment," chiefly demonstrated by his ability to suit his "wondrous Evidence . . . to the temper of the times." It is no accident that memory, imagination, and a sense of audience are skills central to the making of poetic fictions, including this one. The neatest rhetorical turn in the portrait takes advantage of that important similarity between Dryden's art and Oates's testimony. The narrator pretends to warn others against expressing any doubt about the prophetic accuracy of Oates's claims:

> Let *Israels* foes suspect his heav'nly call,
> And rashly judge his writ Apocryphal;
> Our Laws for such affronts have forfeits made
> He takes his life, who takes away his trade.
> Were I my self in witness *Corahs* place,
> The wretch who did me such a dire disgrace,
> Should whet my memory, though once forgot,
> To make him an Appendix of my Plot.
>
> [ll. 664–71]

In one sense, Dryden was "in witness *Corahs* place" as he composed this poem. Like Oates, whose fictions were sufficiently plausible to hang some thirty-five people, the poet was inventing a pointed version of history, and if those who opposed Oates had learned how quickly he could remember their own involvement in treason, those who had disgraced Dryden now found themselves pilloried in his poem. There is no historical record of a particular injury done to Dryden by Oates, but since Oates rarely lost an opportunity to insult the Duke of York, he may well have said something unpleasant about Dryden, whose loyalty to York was vigorous and unashamed. Dryden had already glanced at Oates in *The Spanish Fryar* and insulted him directly in the prologue to *Mithridates*; he had excellent general motives for disliking a man who had lived, until quite recently, in spacious apartments in Whitehall, enjoying a substantial pension while levelling accusations at several of Dryden's patrons and kinsmen by marriage.[48] Dryden's personal resentment of Oates doubtless helped to motivate these lines, but the portrait, despite its second-person opening and first-person conclusion, is not simply a piece of personal abuse. Corah's success in selling his absurd testimony is an affront to the community, and Dryden's mocking ironies warn Englishmen against proving gullible to such dubious witnesses.

Surrounded by his friends, Absalom now delivers an appealing speech and begins his western "Progress," a conspiracy "colour'd with a smooth pretence / Of specious love, and duty" (ll. 745–46). At this point, in a surprising departure from the narrative mode, Dryden addresses the nation in a prophetic voice as "foolish *Israel*!" (l. 753). He insists that tampering with the succession will leave the people "Defenseless, to the Sword / Of each unbounded Arbitrary Lord" (ll. 761–62), offering a spirited and particular refutation of the ideas of contractual monarchy now being developed by his old schoolfellow, Shaftesbury's secretary Locke.[49] A formidable contribution to the ongoing political argument, this speech draws its rhetorical power from imagery Dryden had long been developing. Here are the concluding lines:

> All other Errors but disturb a State;
> But Innovation is the Blow of Fate.
> If ancient Fabricks nod, and threat to fall,
> To Patch the Flaws, and Buttress up the Wall,
> Thus far 'tis Duty; but here fix the Mark:
> For all beyond it is to touch our Ark.
> To change Foundations, cast the Frame anew,
> Is work for Rebels who base Ends pursue:
> At once Divine and Humane Laws controul;
> And mend the Parts by ruine of the Whole.
> The Tampering World is subject to this Curse,
> To Physick their Disease into a worse.

[ll. 799–810]

Though here expressed with an architectural metaphor, not a musical one, the distinction between patching the flaws of the constitution and changing its foundations again resembles the advice to translators in the preface to *Ovid's Epistles*: as an imitator loses the name of translator by departing from the substance of the original, the political innovator becomes a rebel by attempting to change the foundations.

The ark the rebels are daring to touch is the Holy of Holies, the Ark of the

Covenant symbolizing God's merciful promises to his people. When the Ark was restored to Israel by a dancing David, a man trying to steady it in its wobbly oxcart was struck dead on the spot for touching it; that story, which Dryden evidently expects us to remember, provides a precise commentary on Whig ideas about government. Uzzah, the man struck dead, intended no harm or sacrilege, yet "God smote him for his error" (II Samuel 6.7); Dryden thus argues that even those Whigs without ulterior motives become rebels when they advocate altering the succession. The Whig attempt to "mend the Parts by ruine of the Whole" reverses a phrase in the Oxford epilogue for *Tamerlane*, where Dryden had hoped that the "Arts" of the university would "calm your Wills, unite the jarring parts, / And with a kind Contagion seize your hearts" (ll. 13–14). In Dryden's view, the contagion that had seized England in the ensuing months was not kind, and the quack medicines proposed by "The Tampering World," unlike the harsh but effective remedies prescribed by the King and his poet, were threatening to "Physick their Disease into a worse."

Although this speech comes toward the end, it proves the fulcrum on which the poem's weight turns. A brief catalogue of loyal counselors follows, balancing the earlier catalogue of rebels in intensity if not in length; Dryden knew most if not all of the men he praises here, and his personal loyalty to them informs his praise of their loyalty to Charles.[50] By including the dead Ossory among the Tory heroes, Dryden also achieves a Virgilian and elegiac tone that balances his harsh Juvenalian portrait of Oates as Corah: as he had hoped for the death of Oates in the earlier passage, he regrets the death of Ossory in this one. The loyal bishops and peers give the King their advice in the same medical metaphor Dryden had used in his own preface: "That no Concessions from the Throne woud please, / But Lenitives fomented the Disease" (ll. 925–26). "His patience tir'd" (l. 935), David now delivers his final speech, which is meant to stand as an answer to the specious public arguments Absalom makes in his address to his followers and the even more dangerous private arguments by which Achitophel has seduced Absalom.[51] Still, David speaks of his "native mercy" (l. 939) and criticizes "Th' Offenders" for "question[ing] my Forgiving Right" (l. 944). Even as he announces that the law will now "teach Rebels to Obey" (l. 992), the King regrets the necessity for stern measures:

> Oh that my Power to Saving were confin'd:
> Why am I forc'd, like Heaven, against my mind,
> To make Examples of another Kind?

> [ll. 999–1001]

This portrait of Charles as a merciful monarch reluctant to punish his enemies contains some elements of truth: he was disgusted by the executions of the regicides after the Restoration, for example, and always inclined to such policies as religious toleration (referred to, in a significant phrase, as a Declaration of Indulgence). In 1681, however, a new toughness had taken over. Over the objections of the Parliament, Charles had seen to it that Fitzharris was executed, and he had successfully moved the trial of College to Oxford in order to secure another hanging. The ugly lines in which

Dryden's David predicts the death of his foes reflect the King's new spirit of vindictiveness:

> By their own arts 'tis Righteously decreed,
> Those dire Artificers of Death shall bleed.
> Against themselves their Witnesses will Swear,
> Till Viper-like their Mother Plot they tear:
> And suck for Nutriment that bloody gore
> Which was their Principle of Life before.
>
> [ll. 1010–15]

The prediction that the Plot witnesses would turn against one another had already come true: several of those testifying against Stephen College in August had joined with him in testifying against Stafford the previous December. Painfully aware that his own wife's kinsman had been a victim of these changeable witnesses, Dryden probably approved of the brutal executions of Fitzharris and College, and evidently hoped to see Oates suffer the same treatment.[52] The specific imagery of these lines is more appropriate to Fitzharris and Oates than to Shaftesbury, who had not himself been a witness in the Plot trials, but Shaftesbury had used and manipulated many of those notorious witnesses, most recently College. Charles clearly regarded him as dangerous; as Dryden's poem was being printed, he was refusing the advice of Lord Halifax, who had recommended releasing Shaftesbury as a show of mercy since no conviction could be obtained from a Whig jury. Instead, the King insisted on going through with a trial; he wanted the "paper of association" shown in open court, so that Shaftesbury, even if acquitted, would "go off with a bottle at his tail."[53] His request that Dryden write *The Medall* was a way of continuing the attack on Shaftesbury and indicating his intense dissatisfaction with the outcome of the trial.

With that particular background in mind, we may turn to the question of how to read Dryden's preface, in which he expresses hope for "Reconcilement" and "Composure" between David and Absalom and claims to have no hostility toward Achitophel. Violence was not Dryden's personal style. Not only had he always eschewed the "gentlemanly" mayhem of duelling, but his early and thoughtless praise of military glory had now been replaced by the hope that the protection afforded by the sea might make England a peaceful Eden, secure from foreign enemies and able to avoid costly military adventures. In the literary battles he had fought with Howard, Buckingham, Settle, and Shadwell, he had never initiated hostilities, and had frequently attempted to make peace. That fundamental hope for peace and harmony informs the final passage on Monmouth in the preface:

> Were I the Inventour, who am only the Historian, I shoud certainly conclude the Piece, with the Reconcilement of *Absalom* to *David*. And, who knows but this may come to pass? Things were not brought to an Extremity where I left the Story: There seems, yet, to be room left for a Composure; hereafter, there may only be for pity. [II, 4]

Dryden says that he would have concluded with a scene of "Reconcilement" if he were "the Inventour," the term Ben Jonson and Inigo Jones had used to describe themselves on the title pages of their masques, including one called *Pleasure Reconciled to Virtue*. Although he was too young to have seen those masques performed, Dryden knew their texts well; indeed, the Oxford epilogue for *Tamerlane* and the London prologue for *The Unhappy Favorite*, written earlier in this very year, breathe the spirit of those masques, expressing the hope that an urgent political crisis may be resolved in harmony and Edenic innocence. But Dryden was also aware of the wide gap between the Platonic visions of feudal happiness offered in the Caroline masques and the revolutionary realities of the surrounding world. Even in 1660, he had acknowledged the dangers of living in the dreamworld of the masque, admitting that Charles I's crown had been "ravish[ed]" by his "mildness." Now he knew that Charles II, aware of the lessons taught by history, must be firm, even with his own beloved son. That is surely why the language of mercy, in the preface and in David's final speech, is shadowed by the prophetic possibility that there may someday be room only for "pity." By denying that he is an "Inventour" and laying claim to being "only the Historian," Dryden insists on realities: the typology in the Caroline masques tended to come from classical mythology, but his typology is drawn from a factual account in the Old Testament, an account that ends with a desolate David weeping for his son, but a David who is nonetheless still king.

In the case of Achitophel, the tone of Dryden's preface assumes a broader irony:

> I have not, so much as an uncharitable Wish against *Achitophel*; but am content to be Accus'd of a good natur'd Errour; and, to hope with *Origen*, that the Devil himself may, at last, be sav'd. For which reason, he is neither brought to set his House in order, nor to dispose of his Person afterwards, as he in Wisedom shall think fit. God is infinitely merciful; and his Vicegerent is only not so, because he is not Infinite. [II, 5]

Here Dryden refers to his allegedly charitable feelings toward Shaftesbury as "a good natur'd Errour," comparable to the generosity of the early Christian theologian Origen, who was supposed to have believed that even Satan might someday be saved. Like the Platonic dreams of the Caroline masque, such a belief might be "good natur'd," idealistic, and poetic, but in the present historical moment, a responsible king would have to consider charity toward the chief of those attempting to tear down the foundations of his government an "Errour." When Dryden qualifies the King's status as God's "Vicegerent" by pointing out that Charles's reality, his human finitude, necessarily limits his capacity to achieve the infinite mercy of his Maker, he is also acknowledging that kings need such limits on their mercy in order to survive. The implicit distinction is like the one he had drawn while praising General Monck in *Astraea Redux*, where he contrasted the "fond *Chymaera's*" of poets with the true coin of action (see above, p. 112).

Moreover, if Dryden had personal reasons for praising Shaftesbury's honesty on the judicial bench, he also had personal reasons for his vindictive feelings toward Shaftesbury. In the Bible story the evil counselor Achitophel sets his house in order and hangs himself when things go badly for his side. Such a suicide was hardly a likely outcome in the case of Shaftesbury, who had clung to life against all medical odds for decades, but Dryden can hardly have contemplated it without remembering his friend and patron Clifford, who had hanged himself not long after leaving office as a result of a Test Act favored by Shaftesbury; nor would Dryden have forgotten the £500 he received as a result of Clifford's setting the Treasury in order before leaving office. That memory would not have endeared Shaftesbury to Dryden, and in *The Medall*, published a scant three months later, he utters a number of distinctly uncharitable wishes about his Achitophel: in the "Epistle to the Whigs" prefaced to that poem he even says that Shaftesbury's "Head wou'd be seen to more advantage, if it were plac'd on a Spike of the Tower" (II, 38).

"The Vehicle Call'd Faction"

Among the motives for the shrillness of *The Medall* was the public response to *Absalom and Achitophel*. Private letters and frequent editions attest to the popularity and impact of Dryden's brilliant fable, but the months between the two poems also saw four separate poetic answers to Dryden and a malicious reprint of his elegy on Cromwell. Defending Monmouth and Shaftesbury, the anonymous Whig authors of these answers took issue with Dryden's typological parallels, attacked the Tory lords and bishops he had praised, accused him of writing for money, dredged up the history of his employment by Cromwell's government, insinuated that he was a Papist, called his wife a whore, and proposed hanging him in terms at least as violent as those he flung back at their chief.[54] Contemptible as verse, these poems steal rhymes and lines from Dryden's powerful original; they also borrow freely from each other.[55] Still, their insults can hardly have been pleasant to read, and Dryden took an early opportunity to reply. Another theatrical neophyte, Thomas Southerne, commissioned him to write a prologue and epilogue for his first play, *The Loyal Brother*, produced on 4 February 1682, and Dryden responded with a prologue comparing theatrical critics to "Damn'd Whiggs" (l. 2) and poking fun at a central piece of Whig propaganda, the annual Pope-burning; the epilogue takes particular aim at the incompetence of Whig versifying:

> Whiggs, at their Poets never take offence;
> They save dull Culpritts who have Murther'd Sense:
> Tho Nonsense is a nauseous heavy Mass,
> The Vehicle call'd Faction makes it pass.
>
> [ll. 16–19]

By metaphorically making the Whig poets into malefactors saved by packed juries, Dryden was equating the writers who had attacked him with such "dull Culpritts" as Stephen College. By arguing that Whig audiences were willing to allow "Nonsense" to "pass" as long as it came from the proper "Faction," he was acknowledging a truth that soon came to apply to his own work: a concentration on narrowly partisan argument was unlikely to lead to poetry or drama at a high aesthetic level.

Eager though Dryden may have been to reply to his enemies, he was also conscious that the success of *Absalom and Achitophel* had added to his own fame, making it possible for him to increase his fee for writing prologues. As Pope, whose source was Southerne himself, explains, Dryden's "usual price till then had been four guineas: But when

Southern came to him for the Prologue he had bespoke, Dryden told him he must have six guineas for it; 'which (said he) young man, is out of no disrespect to you, but the Players have had my goods too cheap.'"[56] Dryden's renewed sense of the value of his goods may also have been the result of substantial payments for his poetry: one early letter reports that he received £100 for *Absalom and Achitophel*, presumably from court sources, and Spence's anecdote about *The Medall* has the King rewarding the Laureate for that work with "a present of a hundred broad pieces," coins worth slightly more than a guinea each.[57]

Southerne's play was only one of a long list of new dramas designed to capitalize on the political crisis. Although exact dating for many of these plays is problematic, Shadwell's *The Lancashire Witches*, an operatic spectacle staged by the Duke's Company, was certainly in production during the fall of 1681, if not late in the previous spring; its strongly Whig text was heavily cut by government censors, and both companies evidently got the message that Tory fables were less likely to cause trouble. The results included three King's Company plays of a decidedly Tory complexion: Durfey's *Sir Barnaby Whigg*, a broad farce whose title character is a version of Shadwell; Tate's *The Ingratitude of a Common-Wealth*, a pointedly antidemocratic adaptation of *Coriolanus*; and Southerne's *The Loyal Brother*, in which the title character is a thinly allegorized version of the Duke of York. Not long after the *ignoramus* verdict, the Duke's Company produced Behn's *The Roundheads* and Durfey's *The Royalist*; the titles give a sufficient idea of the plays, both concerned to point parallels between the 1640s and the 1680s.[58] On 9 February, five days after the premiere of Southerne's play at Drury Lane, Dorset Garden presented the most substantial drama written in response to the crisis, Otway's *Venice Preserv'd*, memorable for its complex portrayal of the emotional forces tugging at conspirators of all kinds, its devastating sexual satire against Shaftesbury, and its particular relevance to the most urgent political issues now facing the court: the danger posed by Shaftesbury's "Protestant Association," which Tories imagined as an armed conspiracy, and the intransigent independence of the City of London, which continued to resist attempts by the court to influence the elections of Lord Mayors and sheriffs.[59]

In the months following *Absalom and Achitophel*, Dryden was also considering a dramatic response to current events, thanks to his old partner Lee. As he explains in the *Vindication of the Duke of Guise*, he promised Lee to collaborate with him again after the successful *Oedipus*, and Lee "happen'd to claim the performance of that Promise, just upon the finishing of a Poem, when I would have been glad of a little respite before the undertaking of a second Task" (p. 2). Lee had also placed Dryden in his debt by writing a poem commending *Absalom and Achitophel*; printed in the second edition, his verses "To the Unknown Author of this Excellent Poem" are offered as "Earnest of a Faith renew'd," by which Lee apparently indicates the renewal of his faith in the court. His *Lucius Junius Brutus*, staged just after *The Spanish Fryar* in December of 1680, had been quickly banned for its republican ideology; his *Massacre of Paris*, which was designed to stir up sympathy for the plight of the Huguenots, was abandoned without being produced in 1681, perhaps in light of the censorship of *The Lancashire Witches*. Lee's decision to praise Dryden and rejoin him in composing a Tory play was thus a kind of conversion, practical enough given the climate in the theatre, but also quite possibly brought about by the persuasive force of his partner's poem.[60] By the time he wrote *The Medall*, Dryden had pretty clearly begun work on *The Duke of Guise*; in the "Epistle to the Whigs" prefaced to the new poem, he links the "first Covenant" of 1643 and the "new Association" that had come to light at Shaftesbury's trial with "the holy League of the *French Guisards*" (II, 40). He had made the first of those comparisons twenty-two years earlier, in *Astraea Redux*, and he later claimed that some of the material he contributed to the *Duke of Guise* had also been written in 1660.[61] Whatever the truth of that claim, Dryden was clearly now reading (or rereading) the main source for the new play, the historian Davila, whom he specifically cites in the "Epistle," where he also lays out briefly the parallel between sixteenth-century French politics and the Exclusion Crisis, and reiterates his argument about the republican consequences of Calvinism.[62]

Recapitulating the many issues that were on Dryden's mind during the winter of 1681–82 may help us understand the shrillness of *The Medall*. Like the King, the Laureate was amazed at the continued effrontery of the Whigs, who actually had a medal struck to commemorate the *ignoramus* verdict of the Grand Jury in Shaftesbury's case, even though the tide had clearly turned against them. A month before the verdict, the court had succeeded in promoting the election of a moderate Tory, Sir John Moore, as Lord Mayor; ten members of Shaftesbury's jury were defeated in the December elections for the Common Council of London; and the King now felt strong enough to begin an action of *quo warranto* that would allow him to alter the City's charter. As loyal "addresses" to the crown "abhorring" the "Protestant Association" continued to pour into the capital, the Duke of York was recalled from Scotland; he arrived at Yarmouth a week before the publication of *The Medall*.[63] Yet the Whigs who attacked Dryden during these same months refused to back away from their support for Shaftesbury and their fervent opposition to York's succession.

As a poet, Dryden was obviously irritated by the attacks on *Absalom and Achitophel*, which treated a subtle and complex poem as if it were a simple party tract; he uses some of his space in the "Epistle" to poke fun at those attacks for their false erudition and halting verse, pointing out that his enemies were often reduced to stealing his rhymes. The personal abuse must have also bothered him; his wife can hardly have been pleased at the accusations directed at her in those poems. At a time when he wanted leisure, Dryden's days were being taken up by the collaboration with Lee, which required some historical research. Such minor theatrical tasks as the prologue and epilogue for Southerne also remained necessary for the income they provided, though opportunities for such theatrical income were now shrinking. Hart and Kynaston had signed a secret agreement with the Duke's Company in October 1681, promising not to act with the King's Company, and five days after the publication of *The Medall*, a quarrel between the older actors and the younger actors led to drawn swords and another closing of Drury Lane; in May of 1682, the Company's remaining actors were absorbed by Betterton's troupe.[64] For the next twelve years, writers seeking income from the theatre had only one United Company to approach. Although Dryden had wisely begun giving his plays to the Duke's Company before the last bitter days of the King's Company, the four (now six) guineas from the occasional prologue for his old troupe had surely been welcome (and easy) money. Even if he did receive the rumored payment for *Absalom and*

Achitophel, Dryden remained in urgent need of money to support the expensive education he was giving his sons. The eldest, Charles, was now boarding at Westminster; the second, John, still a day student, was often ill; the third, Erasmus-Henry, was chosen by the King in February 1682 for the next available opening at the Charterhouse.[65]

In the midst of all this came the King's direct request for another poem against Shaftesbury, this one on the occasion of the striking of the audacious Whig medal.[66] By urging Dryden to write a poem on that subject, Charles was asking for a poem in the "advice to a painter" genre, of which there had been scores since the Restoration, most of them coarsely vituperative. Although Dryden had threatened his enemies with his capacity to write "more severely" in the preface to *Absalom and Achitophel*, his experience in vituperation was thus far limited to prose; even *Mac Flecknoe*, still unpublished, had a largeness of gesture that transcended its immediate target and occasion. Moreover, if the "plan" the King sketched out during his walk in the Mall with his poet was at all detailed, it called for a merciless attack on Shaftesbury, an attack unlike the more nuanced portrait in *Absalom and Achitophel*. Although Dryden was willing and able to oblige, he evidently sensed the danger that such an attack, obviously coming from the court and certain to be identified as his, would make a mockery of his earlier claims about Charles's merciful nature and his own. His reference in the poem to Charles as "a forgiving King" (l. 190), which comes in the midst of a chain of curses directed at the City sheriffs, rings like a hollow, distant echo of those earlier lines.[67] To be sure, one of his purposes in *The Medall* was to outdo the Whig writers at their own game of straight vituperation, teaching them a lesson in writing "severely," but by competing in that genre, he was inevitably writing a lesser poem than *Absalom and Achitophel*, a poem more dependent on "the Vehicle call'd Faction," and certain to spawn a new group of counterattacks.

Probably written in some haste,[68] *The Medall* appeared on 16 March, with unsigned prefatory poems by Nahum Tate and Dryden's old schoolfellow Thomas Adams. If it will not bear comparison with Dryden's finest work, it easily surpasses the best of Marvell's "painter" poems. In his opening description of the medal itself, Dryden satisfies the King's desire for a no-holds-barred attack on Shaftesbury:

> Never did Art so well with Nature strive;
> Nor ever Idol seem'd so much alive:
> So like the Man; so golden to the sight,
> So base within, so counterfeit and light.

> [ll. 6–9]

Even these insults, however, are more complex than they may initially seem. Dryden presents the medal as a triumph of art over nature, sounding a theme he will later develop in his brief history of Shaftesbury's ministerial career, where he blames the Earl's "precipitous" advice for the breaking of the triple alliance in the early 1670s and the subsequent costly naval war:

> What wonder if the Waves prevail so far
> When he cut down the Banks that made the bar?

> Seas follow but their Nature to invade;
> But he by Art our native Strength betray'd.
>
> [ll. 69–72][69]

Insisting on the limits of art, Dryden explains that the engraver could never capture Shaftesbury's shifting, mercurial nature:

> Oh, cou'd the Style that copy'd every grace,
> And plough'd such furrows for an Eunuch face,
> Cou'd it have form'd his ever-changing Will,
> The various Piece had tir'd the Graver's Skill!
>
> [ll. 22–25]

Here the combination of the old male image of plowing with the insulting claim that Shaftesbury is a eunuch provides in compact form the kind of sexual insult Otway had dramatized a few weeks earlier in the notorious "Nicky-Nacky" scenes in *Venice Preserv'd*. The climactic direct address to Shaftesbury combines all these themes:

> But thou, the Pander of the Peoples hearts,
> (O Crooked Soul, and Serpentine in Arts,)
> Whose blandishments a Loyal Land have whor'd
> And broke the Bonds she plighted to her Lord;
> What Curses on thy blasted Name will fall!
> Which Age to Age their Legacy shall call;
> For all must curse the Woes that must descend on all.
> Religion thou hast none: thy *Mercury*
> Has pass'd through every Sect, or theirs through Thee.
> But what thou giv'st, that Venom still remains;
> And the pox'd Nation feels Thee in their Brains.
>
> [ll. 256–66]

Now Shaftesbury's "Serpentine . . . Arts" are revealed as those of a "Pander," and the counterfeit gold of his medal is exposed as mercury: the emblem of instability, a potent poison, and a desperate cure for venereal disease.

The Whig response to this poem was even more rapid and intense than the response to *Absalom and Achitophel*. Edmund Hickeringill, congratulating himself on his ability to grow a poem overnight, produced a lengthy counterattack called *The Mushroom* on 17 March, one day after Dryden's poem appeared; five more poems against Dryden, including Settle's belated *Absalom Senior* and Shadwell's abusive *Medal of John Bayes*, were in print by May.[70] All of these poems lampoon Dryden as a mercenary and immoral poet and make gestures in defense of Shaftesbury, but several of them concentrate on two more current issues raised in Dryden's poem. Supporting the King's attempt to gain control of the City of London, Dryden had written a pointed address to "*London*, thou great *Emporium* of our Isle" (l. 167), complaining of "disinchanted Burgers" and grasping merchants who consider it "their Charter to defraud their King" (l. 196); he was answered by several passages praising London as the bulwark of liberty.[71] One of the Whig poets devoted his entire poem to bemoaning the renewed persecution of the Dissenters, who were blamed by the Tories for the *ignoramus* verdict and pilloried in *The Medall* as "Sacrilegious Sects" prepared to murder "Kings and Kingly Pow'r" (ll. 203–04).[72] Indeed, the only passages in Dryden's poem that soften his criticism of Shaftesbury are those describing the Earl's past cooperation with the Puritans, when "His nimble Wit outran the heavy Pack" (l. 45), and predicting his future falling-out with his current Dissenting supporters:

> Yet, should thy Crimes succeed, shou'd lawless Pow'r
> Compass those Ends thy greedy Hopes devour,
> Thy Canting Friends thy Mortal Foes wou'd be;
> Thy God and Theirs will never long agree.
> . . . .
> A Tyrant theirs; the Heav'n their Priesthood paints
> A Conventicle of gloomy sullen Saints;
> A Heav'n, like *Bedlam*, slovenly and sad;
> Fore-doom'd for Souls, with false Religion, mad.
>
> [ll. 273–76; 283–86]

If Dryden was supporting the current offensives of the court in such passages, he was also speaking from his own experiences with hard-nosed London merchants and "gloomy sullen" Puritans.

Yet when presented with public opportunities to counter this new wave of Whig attacks, Dryden retreated into a loftier mode. The Duke of York was back in London by early April; his first appearance at a theatrical presentation came at a performance of *Venice Preserv'd* on 20 April, the day of a splendid banquet in his honor. Here was certainly an occasion for a partisan prologue, but Dryden's verses, while full of loyal Tory sentiments, recover the theme of forgiveness. Referring to the many former Whigs now trimming toward the Duke, he allows that

> late Repentance may, perhaps, be true;
> Kings can forgive if Rebels can but sue:
> A Tyrant's Pow'r in rigour is exprest:
> The Father yearns in the true Prince's Breast.
> We grant an Ore'grown Whig no grace can mend;
> But most are Babes, that know not they offend.
> The Crowd, to restless motion still enclin'd,
> Are Clouds, that rack according to the Wind.
> Driv'n by their Chiefs they storms of Hail-stones pour:
> Then mourn, and soften to a silent showre.
> O welcome to this much offending Land
> The Prince that brings forgiveness in his hand!
>
> [ll. 26–37]

In *The Medall*, published just one month earlier, Dryden had described the crowd as a combination of Milton's Satan leaping over the bounds of Eden and Pindar exceeding the measures of poetry:

> Almighty Crowd, thou shorten'st all dispute;
> Pow'r is thy Essence; Wit thy Attribute!
> Nor Faith nor Reason make thee at a stay,
> Thou leapst o'r all eternal truths, in thy *Pindarique* way!
>
> [ll. 91–94]

If the inappropriate allusions and the comic lengthening of the last line slightly distance the criticism, the lines from the April prologue, in which the same foolish citizens become "Babes" in need of the forgiveness of a fatherly prince, strike a notably softer note. A later prologue to the Duchess, whose pregnancy delayed her return until May, is even more masquelike, deflecting partisan strife into the imagery of the restoration of beauty and art and the resolution of discord into harmony.

Perhaps Dryden felt that *The Medall* had given him a sufficient outlet for his anger. Perhaps he recognized that continuing to counterattack would drag him deeper and deeper into the mud. Perhaps he also took comfort in the knowledge that Tate's *Second Part of Absalom and Achitophel*, to which he was making anonymous contributions, and the collaborative *Duke of Guise*, now ready for rehearsal, were bound to discomfit his literary and political enemies, though neither work approaches the level of Dryden at his best.

The bookseller Tonson's later testimony about the origin of Tate's continuation is plausible enough: "several Persons pressing [Dryden] to write a Second Part, he upon declining it himself, spoke to Mr. Tate to write one, and gave him his Advice in the Direction of it."[73] Although Tate recycles a number of Dryden's phrases, lines, and ideas, his satiric portraits are lifeless, the speeches of his characters are dull, and his poem as a whole lacks a convincing structure. In this undistinguished context, the muscular portraits of Settle and Shadwell as Doeg and Og, identified by Tonson as Dryden's contributions, shine all the more brightly. Settle is presented as an unconscious poet:

> *Doeg*, though without knowing how or why,
> Made still a blund'ring kind of Melody;
> Spurd boldly on, and Dash'd through Thick and Thin,
> Through Sense and Non-sense, never out nor in;
> Free from all meaning, whether good or bad,
> And in one word, Heroically mad.
>
> [ll. 412–17]

In expressing an ironic mercy for Settle, Dryden insults him even more deeply, and works in another passing shot at Shaftesbury:

> Let him [Settle] be Gallows-free by my consent,
> And nothing suffer since he nothing meant;
> Hanging Supposes humane Soul and reason,
> This Animal's below committing Treason:
> Shall he be hang'd who never cou'd Rebell?
> That's a preferment for *Achitophel*.
>
> [ll. 431–36]

Shadwell, by contrast, is "A Monstrous mass of foul corrupted matter" (l. 464); with his bulk and his "Thick Skull," he can survive anything but writing:

> Thou art of lasting Make like thoughtless men,
> A strong Nativity————but for the Pen;
> Eat Opium, mingle Arsenick in thy Drink,
> Still thou mayst live avoiding Pen and Ink.
> I see, I see 'tis Counsell given in vain,
> For Treason botcht in Rhime will be thy bane.
> . . . .
> A Double Noose thou on thy Neck dost pull,
> For Writing Treason, and for Writing dull.
>
> [ll. 480–85; 496–97]

Even in the heat of controversy, Dryden's discrimination did not desert him. The nastier edge of the portrait of Og is an appropriate response to *The Medal of John Bayes*, which is far more abusive than *Absalom Senior*. For all his confusion, Settle occasionally achieved "a blund'ring kind of Melody"; he evidently had a better ear for poetry than Shadwell, whose most recent effort had numerous botched rhymes and many instances of confused grammar.[74] Dryden's assertion that Og deserves hanging as much for the poor quality of his poetry as for its treasonous content may remind us of how much moral value he placed on the task of writing well.

These portraits certainly sound as if they were written in the first flush of anger at the attacks of April and May, and there is good reason to suppose that the *Second Part* was substantially complete by early summer. Its climax comes in lines celebrating the Duke of York's narrow escape from a shipwreck that occurred when he sailed back to Scotland to retrieve his pregnant wife; that near-disaster took place on 6 May. Only in a tacked-on conclusion does Tate refer to the riotous shrieval elections of the summer, in which Charles forced his will on the City in the face of repeated majorities for the Whig candidates.[75] The prologue and epilogue Dryden wrote for the planned summer premiere of *The Duke of Guise* refer explicitly to "hot-brain'd Sheriffs," but these pugnacious poems were not heard because the King, probably acting upon a complaint by the Duke of Monmouth, banned the presentation of the play. As one contemporary newsletter put it, "though his Ma[ties] pleasure is to be dissatisfyed and angry with the Duke of Monmouth, yet hee is not willing that others should abuse him."[76] Given Dryden's careful portrayal of Charles's affection for his wayward son in *Absalom and Achitophel*, and his studied omission of Monmouth from *The Medall*, we might suppose that he would have been more cautious about participating in a play so obviously designed to denigrate Monmouth, and the banning of this play probably made Dryden and Tate cautious about publishing their poem. According to his later testimony, Dryden immediately submitted the script of the play to his old friend Arlington, the Lord Chamberlain, along with a copy of Davila, the main source, "humbly desir[ing] him to compare the *Play* with the *History*." He directed Arlington's attention to the page in Davila from which he had constructed the opening of Act IV, in which the King rebukes the Duke for returning to Paris without his permission, just as Charles had rebuked Monmouth for returning to London without his permission in 1679. This was surely one of the scenes about which Monmouth had successfully complained to his father, but it was also taken quite literally from Davila, as Dryden later pointed out in the *Vindication*.[77]

Arlington, playing for time, returned the manuscript without comment in September, and anonymous Whig attacks on Dryden continued to appear: both *Satyr to his Muse*, available in July, and *The Tory-Poets*, available in early September, repeated the charge that his wife was a prostitute.[78] Nonetheless, Dryden remained silent until the political circumstances that had led to the banning of *The Duke of Guise* changed. Some of the Whigs, recognizing that Charles was succeeding in forcing his will on the City, now began to consider armed rebellion, ironically fulfilling Dryden's prophecies. In September, Monmouth incurred his father's wrath by making another riotous progress to Cheshire, where he caused disturbances that led to his arrest on his return to London. Although later accounts differ, Shaftesbury may have thought this a propitious moment to explore support for an armed "rising"; in any case, he was bound to be implicated. Within days of Monmouth's arrest, the old Earl went into hiding, with some rumors even reporting him out of the country.[79] Just at this point, on 4 October, the mysterious "D. Green" published *Mac Flecknoe*, though I doubt Dryden did anything to encourage this botched and piratical printing, which tries to make an essentially literary satire seem politically current by calling it "A Satyr upon the *True-Blew Protestant* Poet, T. S."[80] At the end of the month, however, the court sent a clear signal of a change in its attitude: the Lord Chamberlain ordered the banned *Duke of Guise* acted, and a week later the trained bands suppressed an attempt to celebrate Guy Fawkes Day.[81] Sensing that the coast was clear, Dryden and Tate published *The Second Part of Absalom and Achitophel* on 10 November; a prologue to the King and Queen, written by Dryden for a performance on 16 November, is also sharply partisan; and the new epilogue spoken at the delayed premiere of *The Duke of Guise* on 30 November is the most vindictive of all Dryden's partisan writings, attacking the moderate "Trimmers" as "Damn'd Neuters":

> Not Birds, nor Beasts; but just a kind of Bat:
> A Twilight Animal; true to neither Cause,
> With Tory Wings, but Whiggish Teeth and Claws.
>
> [ll. 42–44]

Coming as they do from a poet who had appealed so carefully to "the more Moderate sort" just one year earlier, and who had seemed willing to forgive the "Trimmers" as recently as April, these lines attest to the vigor of the Tory revenge, now in full stride; a few days before they were spoken, a broken Shaftesbury fled to Holland, where he died on 21 January 1683.

"What *I* Believe"

The acting of the previously banned play, the publication of the cautiously delayed *Second Part*, and the sharp new prologues and epilogues were all signs of the Tory victory; in dedicating the published *Duke of Guise* to Lawrence Hyde in February 1683, Dryden crowed about the weakening of the Whigs: "Their Tyde of Popularity is spent,

and the natural Current of Obedience is in spight of them, at last prevalent" (sig. A2v).
Yet despite the intensity of his political opinions and the extent of his political labors
during the Exclusion Crisis, he had also been thinking about less temporal issues: late
in November 1682, a few days before *The Duke of Guise* was acted, he issued *Religio Laici
or a Layman's Faith*, a signed poem describing his own religious beliefs. The contrast
between this poem and the work surrounding it is as much a matter of style as substance. *Absalom and Achitophel*, published just one year earlier, had also dealt with
religious questions, past and present, but the confident, sly, wickedly satiric speaker of
that poem is quite unlike the speaker of this one, whose opening lines, justly famous for
their development of the imagery of light, establish a tone of reverent humility:

> Dim, as the borrow'd beams of Moon and Stars
> To *lonely, weary, wandring* Travellers,
> Is *Reason* to the *Soul:* And as on high,
> Those rowling Fires *discover* but the Sky
> Not light us *here;* So *Reason*'s glimmering Ray
> Was lent, not to *assure* our *doubtfull* way,
> But *guide* us upward to a *better Day*.
> And as those nightly Tapers disappear
> When Day's bright Lord ascends our Hemisphere;
> So pale grows *Reason* at *Religions* sight;
> So *dyes*, and so *dissolves* in *Supernatural Light*.

[ll. 1–11]

The announced occasion for this striking departure from the Laureate's earlier
styles was the controversy surrounding the publication of a translation of Father
Richard Simon's *Critical History of the Old Testament* by Henry Dickinson, a young
graduate of Trinity College associated with Dryden's protégé Richard Duke.[82] Despite
a flippant reference to "Some *Jew* . . . chang[ing] the Text" in a prologue written about
this time, Dryden recognized the scholarly importance of Simon's revolutionary
treatise, which discusses the many problems in the transmission of the text of Scripture.[83] He correctly anticipated that Simon's research, which the author employed to
argue that the Catholic church must interpret the Bible in light of its own oral traditions,
might be used in the service of a deistic or "freethinking" disregard for the Bible.
Seizing the opportunity to attack both deism and Catholic authoritarianism, and taking
a passing swipe at Dissenting enthusiasm (by now a familiar target), Dryden described
himself as a moderate Anglican, basing his faith on the Bible:

> More Safe, and much more modest 'tis, to say
> *God wou'd not leave Mankind without a way:*
> And that the *Scriptures*, though not *every where*
> Free from Corruption, or intire, or clear,
> Are uncorrupt, sufficient, clear, intire,
> In *all* things which our needfull *Faith* require.

[ll. 295–300]

Concerned though it was with the authority and interpretation of Scripture, the
new poem was by no means detached from the political concerns that had occupied so

much of Dryden's attention during the Exclusion Crisis, which was, after all, a crisis concerning the religious faith of the future monarch.[84] The preface includes Dryden's most explicit discussion of the Popish Plot: acknowledging the logic of the general fear that the Catholic orders, "outed from their fat possessions" by Henry VIII, might "endeavour a reentrance against those whom they account Hereticks," he refers to "Mr. *Colemans* Letters," the very correspondence that had sent his wife's late brother scurrying into exile, as "the best Evidence" for the Plot (II, 103). Of course, he goes on to argue that Protestant "Fanaticks" are even more dangerous to the state, just as he had in his political pamphlets and poems: "The Doctrines of King-killing and Deposing, which have been taken up onely by the worst Party of the Papists, the most frontless Flatterers of the Pope's Authority [i.e., the Jesuits], have been espous'd, defended and are still maintain'd by the whole Body of Nonconformists and Republicans" (II, 108). The guilt by association in the last phrase resembles the rhetoric Dryden had used in his propaganda; he obviously knew that there were plenty of "Nonconformists" who were not "Republicans." In the same preface, however, he alludes more playfully to the recent political crisis while spinning a learned argument against the damnation of the virtuous heathen:

> Among the Sons of *Noah* we read of one onely who was accurs'd; and if a blessing in the ripeness of time was reserv'd for *Japhet*, (of whose Progeny we are,) it seems unaccountable to me, why so many Generations of the same Offspring, as preceeded our Saviour in the Flesh, shou'd be all involv'd in one common condemnation, and yet that their Posterity shou'd be Intitled to the hopes of Salvation: As if a Bill of Exclusion had passed only on the Fathers, which debar'd not the Sons from their Succession. [II, 99]

Here the reference to "a Bill of Exclusion" is a passing joke; the main issue at hand is Dryden's conviction that "Heathens, who never did, nor without Miracle cou'd hear of the name of Christ were yet in a possibility of Salvation," a belief natural enough to a writer whose vision of heaven surely included Socrates and Homer. So, too, in the poem itself: if we consider the personal resonance of some of Dryden's imagery, we may observe him grappling with the larger questions of belief that had clearly come to occupy much of his reading and thinking, and grappling in a way that came closer to confession than any work he had yet written. Publishing such a poem with "a Name prefix'd, from which the handling of so serious a Subject wou'd not be expected" (II, 98) was an act of considerable personal courage.

As his decision to sign it shows, Dryden cared about this poem, perhaps because he had been thinking about the issues addressed in it all his life. His childhood and education had involved massive exposure to Puritan dogma from Hill and Arminian dogma from Busby, and his marriage into a recusant family had exposed him to some aspects of Roman Catholic thought. *The Indian Emperour, Tyrannick Love, The State of Innocence*, and *The Spanish Fryar*, to take only the most obvious plays, are clearly the work of a man interested in religious matters, whose poems from the Hastings elegy to *Absalom and Achitophel* make frequent, precise allusions to Scripture. Despite the disarming gestures of humility in the preface, where he refers to "my own weakness and want of Learning" (II, 98), Dryden evidently numbered himself among "Those few, by

Nature form'd, with Learning fraught, / Born to instruct, as others to be taught, / [who] Must Study well the Sacred Page" (ll. 326–28). His account of how such men should proceed in studying Scripture and commentary describes a process of essentially literary analysis: they must see "*Which* Exposition flows from *genuine Sense; /* And which is *forc'd* by *Wit* and *Eloquence*" (ll. 332–33). He even repeats particular language he had used of his own writing: when he assures us that "Truth by its own Sinews will prevail" (l. 349), we remember the pride he had taken in the "Sinews" that allowed him to "raise the weight" of his poetic fathers; when he describes the style of the Bible as "*Majestick* and *Divine*" (l. 152), we remember the final paragraph of the preface, which says that "The Expressions of a Poem, design'd purely for Instruction, ought to be Plain and Natural, and yet Majestick" (II, 109). The whole poem reflects careful study of Scripture and controversy, and a casual remark in the preface reveals Dryden's pride in that study: referring to the opinion of St. Athanasius that even the virtuous heathen are damned, the opinion he was daring to contest, he remarks that "Every man who is read in Church History, knows *that* belief was drawn up after a long contestation with *Arrius*" (II, 101). The implication is that the poet, whatever he may say about his own "weak understanding" (II, 102), has strengthened that understanding with a steady diet of reading in Christian history and theology.

Moreover, we have detailed evidence that Dryden was reading widely about religion in the years leading up to this poem. When the widow of George Digby, Earl of Bristol, sold off his library in April of 1680, "John Dryden" purchased ninety-two books, most of them works of theological controversy, as were most of the fifty-four books he bought from the library of an antiquary named Richard Smith in May of 1682. Some of Dryden's purchases at the Digby sale reflect other interests and ailments: he bought a book of Spanish comedies, hardly a surprising choice for a playwright; a French translation of Ovid's *Epistles*, several of which he had published in English versions just four months earlier; and a Latin treatise on cures for kidney stones, perhaps hoping to find some relief from his own "gravel."[85] But most of the works he acquired were Catholic treatises in Latin or French concerning the issues that would loom large in his poetry and life during the later 1680s: reason, revelation, faith, authority. Dryden's purchasing the works of Catholic controversialists so long before his own conversion may seem strange, but he was evidently buying and reading Anglican apologetics as well. In the preface to *Religio Laici*, he acknowledges using "the Works of our own Reverend Divines of the Church of *England* (II, 98); he names "our venerable *Hooker*" and alludes without names to another "Prelate of our Church," possibly William Lloyd, and a "judicious and learned Friend," probably John Tillotson, whose work he had already drawn upon in *Tyrannick Love*.[86] Close parallels of argument and language also make it virtually certain that he used two treatises by Anglican laymen: *The Reasonableness of Scripture-Belief* (1672) by Sir Charles Wolseley, whose country estate he had visited in 1680, and *Considerations . . . relating to the Churches Power in deciding Controversies* (1651), by Hamon L'Estrange, the dead elder brother of his current Tory ally in party controversy.[87] His references to Beza and Buchanan in the prefatory epistle to *The Medall* also indicate some familiarity with Calvinist writings, though he probably collected most of what he knew about these Dissenting authorities from secondary sources.[88]

Dryden may well have felt that deeper knowledge of the arguments of theological controversialists of all kinds was necessary background for the partisan works he was writing in the early 1680s, which necessarily mingle religious and political issues, but even in those poems, his interest in theological issues for their own sake is apparent. I have already argued that the tension between the Christian imperative to forgive one's enemies and the political necessity for vengeance lies at the center of *Absalom and Achitophel*; in claiming, however ironically, to have charity toward Shaftesbury in the preface to that poem, Dryden alludes explicitly to Origen, another Church father. In *The Medall*, that passionately partisan poem, he argues that the political views of the Dissenters lead them to misinterpret the Scriptures:

> They rack ev'n Scripture to confess their Cause;
> And plead a Call to preach, in spight of Laws.
> But that's no news to the poor injur'd Page;
> It has been us'd as ill in every Age:
> And is constrain'd, with patience, all to take;
> For what defence can Greek and Hebrew make?
> . . . .
> But, since our Sects in prophecy grow higher,
> The Text inspires not them; but they the Text inspire.
>
> [ll. 156–61; 165–66]

Attacking the Dissenters, several of whom sat on Shaftesbury's jury, was naturally a central part of Dryden's partisan purpose in *The Medall*, but the argument linking Calvinism with rebellion and political levelling, which predictably appears in the "Epistle to the Whigs," actually receives less development in the poem than this much less political complaint about scriptural interpretation, which anticipates the powerful attack on Dissenting distortions of Scripture in *Religio Laici* (ll. 404–20, quoted in full above, pp. 65–66). Both passages may reflect Dryden's sympathetic identification with the ancient authors of Scripture. Like them, he knew what it was to have his efforts unappreciated: "*Unask'd* their *Pains*, *ungrateful* their *Advice*, / *Starving* their *Gain*, and *Martyrdom* their *Price* (ll. 144–45); like them, he knew what it was to see the "poor injur'd Page[s]" of his work misinterpreted. The arguments he flings at those who profane the "tender Page" with their "horney Fists" (l. 404) reflect the class prejudice and personal anger with which he had long regarded the Dissenters, but some of them may also be borrowed from such Catholic publications as the *Refutation of Perverse Applications of the Scripture* (1579), a French treatise by two Huguenot ministers who decided to return to Catholicism, and another of his purchases at the Digby sale.[89]

If the propaganda of Dryden's Puritan boyhood and the recent Plot scare had presented Roman Catholicism as a monolithic threat, Dryden's reading of such works surely reminded him of the great range of opinion within the Catholic Church. When he cites another Catholic work, Louis Maimbourg's *History of Calvinism*, as a source for some bitter remarks against the Dissenters in the preface to *Religio Laici*, he explains that "A man may be suffer'd to quote an Adversary to our Religion, when he speaks Truth" (II, 107). He also advises "the more moderate and well-meaning Papists, (of which I doubt not there are many)" to "satisfy . . . all reasonable Men, of their sincerity and good meaning to the Government" by "disowning and detesting . . . Jesuitick Principles; and subscrib[ing] to all Doctrines which deny the Popes Authority of Deposing Kings" (II, 104–05). This was precisely what the Earl of Bristol had been trying to do in a famous speech in favor of the Test Act in 1673, when he declared himself "a Catholic of the Church of Rome, not a Catholic of the Court of Rome." Although the Test Act was designed to force his coreligionists out of all official posts, Bristol called it "A bill, in my opinion, as full of moderation towards Catholicks, as of prudence, and security towards the religion of the state"; he was apparently content that the bill made "no mention of barring [Catholics] from private, and modest exercise of their religion."[90] Bristol was evidently concerned to deny involvement in Jesuit political schemes, and another of the books Dryden bought from his collection was an attack on Jesuit activities and the doctrine of Papal infallibility by the English Benedictine John Barnes.[91] Dryden may also have been aware of a more recent tract by another Benedictine, James Maurus Corker's *Roman Catholick Principles* (1680), which devotes considerable space to arguing that neither infallibility nor the Pope's alleged authority to depose kings is a truly Catholic principle, and insists that the Benedictines have no intention of reclaiming their lost lands.

Bristol's bizarre praise for the "moderation" of the House of Commons in 1673 may remind us of the pressure placed on the word "moderation" during these years. Like Dryden, who claimed to be appealing to "the more Moderate sort" of political observer in the preface to *Absalom and Achitophel*, Bristol recognized the importance of claiming the center. One of his daughters married the Protestant Earl of Sunderland, whom Dryden praised for his "moderation" late in 1679, but who lost his power by supporting Exclusion in 1680 and had to abandon his connections with William of Orange in order to regain his place on the Privy Council in July of 1682.[92] In denominational debates, "moderation" was an essential touchstone in the traditional Anglican argument that the English church represented a "middle way" between Papist authoritarianism and Calvinist radicalism; Dryden draws heavily on that tradition in *Religio Laici*, and in dedicating *All for Love* to Danby in 1678, he had even used "Moderation" as a synonym for toleration: "the Moderation of our Church is such, that . . . it allows more freedom to Dissenters than any of the Sects wou'd allow to it" (XIII, 7). Even now, in the midst of renewed persecution of Dissenters by the crown, Dryden essentially repeats Bristol's distinction between the "private, and modest" practice of one's faith and the taking of political action based on that faith. Not only does he advise "the more moderate" Catholics to disassociate themselves from Jesuit principles, but he writes a slippery paragraph in the preface giving the same advice to the Dissenters:

> They may think themselves to be too roughly handled in this Paper; but I who know best how far I could have gone on this Subject, must be bold to tell them they are spar'd: though at the same time I am not ignorant that they interpret the mildness of a Writer to them, as they do the mercy of the Government; in the one they think it Fear,

and conclude it Weakness in the other. The best way for them to confute me, is, as I before advis'd the Papists, to disclaim their Principles, and renounce their Practices. We shall all be glad to think them true *Englishmen* when they obey the King, and true Protestants when they conform to the Church Discipline. [II, 108]

The rhetoric here is precisely parallel to that in the preface to *Absalom and Achitophel*, where Dryden threatens his enemies with his ability to write "more severely" and worries about the consequences of "mildness" for poets and monarchs. The advice to submit and conform is acted out in the poem itself, where Dryden allows himself to make some unorthodox arguments, especially the one against the damnation of the virtuous heathen, but concludes by advising submission to the Church:

> And, after hearing what our Church can say,
> If still our Reason runs another way,
> That private Reason 'tis more Just to curb,
> Than by Disputes the publick Peace disturb.
> For points obscure are of small use to learn:
> But *Common quiet* is *Mankind's concern.*
>
> [ll. 445–50]

Here personal faith is subordinated to political stability, and if we wonder how Dryden could move from the awed invocation of divine revelation in the opening lines to this prosaic and pragmatic conclusion, we might consider the annual fireworks on Guy Fawkes Day and the annual fast in memory of Charles I—public reminders of what had happened when men felt compelled by their faith to engage in revolutionary activity.

If *Religio Laici* were a more typical argument for the Anglican "middle way," dividing its space between an attack on Catholicism and an attack on Dissent, we might fit it more neatly into its political context and discount Dryden's claim to be confessing his own faith as a merely rhetorical stance. In fact, however, the attack on Dissent is confined to a single verse-paragraph, the first half of the poem is devoted to a careful refutation of a proponent of "natural religion," and the arguments against "The partial *Papists*" in the second half of the poem are restricted to the issue of the Church's right to interpret the scriptures. If the preface reflects Dryden's continuing awareness of the political consequences of religious belief, the poem as a whole dramatizes a more abstract and personal struggle to define a sustaining faith. Since he frequented the coffeehouses in which intellectual and political dialogue took place, Dryden had obviously been exposed to the skeptical or "freethinking" approach to religious questions that would ultimately lead to deism, the characteristic heterodoxy of the eighteenth century. Although the word itself was still new, and very few tracts advocating or deploring deism had been published,[93] his summary of the theory of "natural religion" in the poem demonstrates the considerable appeal that theory had for well-educated men, and his refutation of deism as a system too dependent on the dim light of human reason reflects a hard-won humility. So, too, with the passages on Catholicism. If Dryden read the Catholic treatises he purchased at the Digby and Smith sales, he necessarily thought about the comforts of a Church claiming an unbroken and infallible tradition. His sarcastic couplet rejecting those claims—"Such an *Omniscient* Church

we wish indeed; / 'Twere worth *Both Testaments*, and cast in the *Creed*" (ll. 282–83)—
may nonetheless record, at some level of consciousness, the appeal of Catholic certainty. Dryden's resistance to that appeal would ultimately prove temporary; since we know
that he changed his religion within three years of the publication of this Anglican poem,
embracing Catholicism, our reading of *Religio Laici* is inevitably affected by a kind of
hindsight, but we need not read his later Catholicism back into this poem in order to
insist on the urgency and authenticity of the search for religious truth in which *Religio
Laici* was one stage.[94]

The tension between a political conception of religion and a philosophical one,
apparent in the inconsistencies of the poem, is also a part of its metaphorical drama.
The deists, who claimed to be more "rational," indeed more "moderate," than believ-
ers in orthodox religion, did not immediately look like a political threat comparable to
that posed by Catholic or Dissenting extremists, but Dryden's argument against the
rational pride of "the Deist" draws on political imagery, ultimately complicating the
relationship between politics and theology in the poem as a whole. In *The Medall*, both
Shaftesbury and his "Canting Friends" worship false gods. The god of the Dissenters
is "a Tyrant," but Shaftesbury's (if he has any)

> must be one
> That lets the World and Humane-kind alone:
> A jolly God, that passes hours too well
> To promise Heav'n, or threaten us with Hell.
> That unconcern'd can at Rebellion sit;
> And Wink at Crimes he did himself commit.
>
> [ll. 277–82]

The political resonance of these lines is obvious enough, but Dryden was surely also
expressing his religious disagreement with those who would posit such a detached,
Lucretian God. One of the most passionate passages in *Religio Laici* picks up the
political themes of the earlier poem, accusing the deist of imagining himself too strong
and God too weak:

> Dar'st thou, poor Worm, offend *Infinity?*
> And must the Terms of Peace be given by *Thee?*
> Then *Thou* art *Justice* in the *last Appeal;*
> *Thy easie God* instructs Thee to *rebell:*
> And, like a King remote, and weak, must take
> What Satisfaction *Thou* art pleas'd to make.
>
> [ll. 93–98]

The deist, a rebel against God, is the allegorical equivalent of the Puritan political
rebels of the 1640s, who had made their king "remote, and weak" as a prelude to
beheading him; by means of this allegory, Dryden rhetorically ignores class lines and
collapses history, equating the fashionable freethinkers among his contemporaries with
the levelling Calvinist radicals of his boyhood. But this later passage also means to
humble the deist by placing his pride within a more purely theological frame. Like other
men, the deist is a "poor Worm," whose exaggerated faith in his own limited reason is

absurd. If he will "Look humbly upward," he will see his position refuted by the
overwhelming facts of the incarnation and the atonement:

> See God descending in thy Humane Frame;
> Th' *offended*, suff'ring in th' *Offenders* Name:
> All thy Misdeeds to him imputed see,
> And all his Righteousness devolv'd on thee.
>
> [ll. 107–10]

In lines like these, the temporal political concerns apparent in Dryden's other
poems of the period (and elsewhere in this poem) drop away. The daily drama of
Exclusion and party is overwhelmed by the eternal drama of salvation, just as the "dim"
and "borrow'd beams of Moon and Stars" are overwhelmed by the "*Supernatural
Light*" of revelation in the poem's opening lines. For anyone, such concentration on the
eternal will inevitably prove temporary; both in the poem and in his life, Dryden was
unable to shut out the pressing concerns of politics, money, and self-vindication. But
we may glimpse his awareness of the tension between such concerns and the more
lasting issues he sought to address here in his remarks on Athanasius: seeking to explain
why the old bishop had taken such a tough stance on the damnation of the virtuous
heathen, Dryden suggests that he was carried away by the force of controversy:

> *Arius* to confute,
> The good old Man, too eager in dispute,
> Flew high; and as his *Christian* Fury rose
> Damn'd all for *Hereticks* who durst *oppose.*
>
> [ll. 220–23]

Published a day or two before the speaking of an epilogue advocating hanging as "a fine
dry kind of Death" for the Trimmers, these lines betray Dryden's awareness that he
himself was often "too eager in dispute"; in the dedication to *The Spanish Fryar*, he had
actually described himself as "too eager in his own defence" (sig. A3r). Although
Dryden had sought indifference to his literary critics since the earliest days of his
writing career, his success in attaining aloofness had been sporadic, and he was about to
break his resolution again by writing *The Vindication of the Duke of Guise*. In political
controversy, he alternated a rhetoric of forgiveness and unity with a rhetoric of vengeance and scorn; only in *Absalom and Achitophel*, where he dramatized the tension
between these possible stances, was he able to make lasting art out of such controversy.
Religio Laici itself displays the difficulty of transcending the world: the poem occasionally achieves a focus on "*Sacred Truth*," but the preface is almost entirely concerned
with self-defense and partisan dispute, and those impulses frequently come to the fore
in the poem as well.

When he published *Religio Laici*, Dryden obviously did not anticipate his own later
conversion, but he did recognize that any poem about religious doctrine from the
author of *The Kind Keeper* might easily be misunderstood, as he indicated in the preface.
Explaining that his errors were "only those of Charity to Mankind," he invoked the
principle of the Golden Rule, hoping that "such [errors] as my *own* Charity has caus'd

me to commit, that of *others* may more easily excuse" (II, 98). But the immediate response was indifference, and the ultimate response was hardly charitable. Despite modest sales, there was no published reference to *Religio Laici* for a full year, a striking contrast to the immediate mushrooming of answers to his political poems; and when Charles Blount finally did publish his *Religio Laici, Written in a Letter to John Dryden* (November 1683), he completely misrepresented Dryden's position, either from stupidity or malice. Dryden had taken half his space to dismantle deistic arguments; Blount offered an essentially deistic tract as "a Continuance" of Dryden's poem.[95] As late as the summer of 1684, Dryden's regret that the poem had not made a larger impact was still showing; agreeing reluctantly to Tonson's request that he refrain from reprinting it in *Sylvae* (1685), he says he "will for once lay by the Religio Laici, till another time" (*Letters*, p. 23).

By the time "another time" came, however, the restless search for religious truth that makes *Religio Laici* such a dramatic poem had led its author into the church he had once thought greedy and "partial." When he announced his conversion in a long and daring poem, *The Hind and the Panther*, his enemies suddenly remembered *Religio Laici*, and gleefully quoted the Anglican Dryden against the Catholic Dryden.[96] Intent on describing Dryden as a cowardly turncoat, they failed to recognize that he had been brave in describing his own faith in 1682, and was braver still in acknowledging his change of faith in 1687. In both cases, he drew his courage from a conviction vigorously expressed in *Religio Laici*: "*MY* Salvation must its Doom receive / Not from what *OTHERS*, but what *I* believe" (ll. 303–04).

CHAPTER ELEVEN

"Shame of Change"
1683–1687

"Two Scurrilous Libels"—and a Dubious Vindication

At the conclusion of *Religio Laici*, striking a pose of flippant unconcern, Dryden congratulates himself on making his religious opinions clear and declares that he neither expects praise nor fears censure. Yet even censure would probably have been more welcome than the indifference with which the public greeted his confession of faith—especially since the response to *The Duke of Guise*, in which Dryden and Lee had made their political opinions all too clear, was so immediate and noisy. "Our Play's a Parallel," begins the prologue to that "tragedy," and the plot was obviously intended to emphasize resemblances between the French League of the late sixteenth century and the "Protestant Association" of recent years in England; since the play also features an urban mob, its relevance to the current politics of the City was similarly undeniable. The issue, as in any play offering a historical parallel, was how far the parallel extended. Although Dryden solemnly denied that he aimed at "Exposing" particular individuals, anyone attending the play who failed to identify the Duke of Guise with the Duke of Monmouth would have been obtuse.[1] The conclusion, in which Guise is stabbed by eight assassins, had to be painful for any Whig, and the counterattack was swift: Whig partisans in the audience hissed the performances, and two printed attacks appeared before the play was even published.

In *A Defence of the Charter . . . of the City of London*, published in early January of 1683, the Whig lawyer and controversialist Thomas Hunt described the new play as part of the court's campaign "toward making the Charter forfeitable." The King's action of *quo warranto*, begun more than a year earlier, was still in progress, but there was now little reason to expect any other result than the surrender of the City's charter, which duly followed the next summer. Taking out his resentment on the Laureate, Hunt contended that the parallel between Monmouth and Guise logically required identifying the murderous Henri III with Charles II and the devious King of Navarre with the Duke of York, "to whom [Dryden] gives the worst strokes of his unlucky fancy" (p. 25). From Dryden's point of view, this was a dangerous charge of personal disloyalty, literary incompetence, or both. *Some Reflections upon the Pretended Parallel in . . . The Duke of Guise* appeared about the same time. Without a printed text to work with, the author had to go "several times to see the so long expected, and so much talk'd of Play, . . . thoroughly observ[ing] it, even to every Line" (p. 1), but his literary criticism consists of a general charge of "dulness." His personal abuse of "the *old Serpent Bays*," who is portrayed as an ungrateful and self-serving liar, resembles that offered in *The Medal of John Bayes* some six months earlier; Dryden, who was in a position to know, concluded that Shadwell had a hand in this pamphlet.[2]

In both attacks, we may read the frustration of men fighting for a lost cause. Hunt's *Defence*, the bulk of which concerns the controversy over the charter, was declared a libel in January 1683, prompting its author to flee to Holland;[3] Shaftesbury, who was already there, died in Amsterdam later that month. In early February, Monmouth made another attempt at a "progress" to Chichester; rebuffed by the sheriff and scolded publicly in church, he went off to amuse himself in France, riding a dark horse to victory in a race sponsored by Louis XIV.[4] Even in the theatre world, the Whigs were in eclipse: Shadwell's *Lancashire Witches* (1681) was his last new play until *The Squire of Alsatia* (1688); he later blamed Dryden for his frustrations during this period, but it was probably Betterton who decided that the political climate made producing plays by such an unregenerate Whig unwise.[5] Still, as Dryden pointed out in the dedication of the published *Duke of Guise*, the "glorious Work" of the Tory revenge was "yet unfinish'd" (sig. A2v). If the Whigs could no longer mount the kind of public political attack on the court they had mustered two years earlier, they could still inflict real damage on lesser targets. John Crowne's *City Politiques*, a Tory comedy banned the previous summer, was finally acted on 19 January; a few days later, its author was cudgelled in St. Martin's Lane by a man claiming to be acting on behalf of the late Earl of Rochester, now some thirty months dead.[6] Although Crowne's play does indeed make fun of Rochester's deathbed conversion, its essential subject is the shrieval elections; the anonymous cudgeller was more likely paid by the City Whigs than by the ghost of Rochester.

Dryden was probably thinking of this incident as well as his own beating in Rose Alley when he wrote the conclusion of the dedication, addressed to the new Earl of Rochester, Lawrence Hyde. Speaking for himself and Lee, he acknowledged that it was no delight to be "pasquin'd and affronted" by the "inveterate Scriblers" of the Whig party, but correctly pointed out that those pamphleteers were attacking Tory playwrights as substitutes for the King and the Duke, whom they no longer dared to attack directly: "The greatest and the best of men are above their reach, and for our meanness, though they assault us like Foot-padders in the dark, their Blows have done us little harm; we yet live, to justifie our selves in open day, [and] to vindicate our Loyalty to the Government" (sig. A3r). Dryden might have been able to sustain this pose of unconcern if the attacks on *The Duke of Guise* had been merely political, but he could not let the affronts to his character and competence go unanswered, even though he knew he should. In an advertisement attached to the printed edition, which appeared at the end of February, he mentioned "two scurrilous Libels lately printed" and promised an answer: "they shall have a day or two thrown away upon them, though I break an old Custom for their sakes, which was to scorn them" (p. 76). As we have seen, Dryden had broken that "old Custom" several times before, with mixed results. This time another poet, in an anonymous "Epode To his worthy Friend Mr. John Dryden," "Advise[d] him not to Answer Two malicious Pamphlets against his Tragedy called, *The Duke of Guise*,"[7] but Dryden ignored that friendly advice and evidently threw away more than "a day or two" on *The Vindication of the Duke of Guise*, a pamphlet of no less than sixty pages published early in April.

In writing this overlong and unwise self-defense, Dryden moved methodically through the attacks, refuting them paragraph by paragraph as he had done in "The Defence of the Essay" (1668) and *His Majesties Declaration Defended* (1681). As writers, Hunt and Shadwell were no more formidable opponents than Sir Robert Howard and the "Person of Quality," so Dryden gleefully exploited their inconsistencies. Hunt, for example, had emphasized the danger of the new play by referring to it as "frequently acted and applauded" (p. 24); Shadwell, more intent on his personal and literary feud with Dryden, said the play had "not met with the expected Applause" (pp. 1–2). Dryden was unlikely to miss such an opening:

> For shame, Gentlemen, pack your Evidence a little better against another time: You see, *My Lord Chief Baron* [an ironic reference to Hunt, who had failed to secure an appointment to that office], has delivered his Opinion, that *the Play was frequently acted and applauded*; but you of the *Jury*, have found *Ignoramus*, on the *Wit* and the *Success* of it. *Oates, Dugdale* and *Turbevile*, never disagreed *more* than you do. [pp. 13–14]

Cleverly packing his own evidence, Dryden takes only one sentence to move from an inconsistency in the way his attackers chose to denigrate him to a metaphoric parallel between the Whig pamphleteers and the discredited Plot witnesses.

Vulnerable as they were to this kind of answer, Hunt and Shadwell had the truth at least partly on their side, and the rhetoric of Dryden's denials is wonderfully slippery: "As to the Exposing of any Person living," he assures us, "our innocency is so clear, that it is almost unnecessary to say, *It was not in my Thought*; and as far as any one Man can vouch for another, I do believe it was as little in Mr. *Lee*'s" (p. 3). Dryden avoids actually denying that he meant to "Expose" Monmouth, claiming instead that his innocence makes such a denial "almost unnecessary"; he calls Lee's intentions "as little" as his own, a formula allowing those intentions to be quite large for both men. For those of us who remember the way Richard Nixon's spokesmen refused to "dignify a third-rate burglary attempt" by denying responsibility, such phrases have a familiar odor.

Even when attempting to weaken the alleged comparison between Monmouth and Guise, Dryden cannot entirely conceal his reasons for pursuing that parallel: "If we consider their *Actions* or their *Persons*, a much less proportion will be yet found betwixt them: and if we bate the *Popularity*, perhaps none at all" (p. 6). But for a poet who had frequently described the people who rallied around Monmouth as "rabble," "*Popularity*" was precisely the issue. Early in the play, when the beautiful Marmoutier tells Guise that she has seen him "Court the Crowd," he protests that he cannot help his popularity; "But Sir," she replies, "you seek it with your Smiles and Bows, / This Side and that Side congeing to the Crowd" (I, i, pp. 8–9)—a close parallel to Dryden's description of Monmouth in *Absalom and Achitophel*, "On each side bowing popularly low" (l. 689). In a speech evidently recycled from David's closing speech in the same poem, the King in the play moralizes over the bleeding corpse of Guise:

> Beware my Sword, which if I once unsheath,
> By all the Reverence due to Thrones and Crowns,
> Nought shall atone the Vows of speedy Justice,
> Till Fate to Ruine every Traytor brings,
> That dares the Vengeance of indulgent Kings.

[V, p. 76][8]

The language is strikingly similar, but the situation is significantly different: the bloody vengeance threatened in the poem has actually taken place in the play.

The rules of polemic, panegyric, and satire in Dryden's world did not enforce a strict regard for the truth, and we have already had many occasions to observe his skill in manipulating, selecting, and dramatizing facts, but *The Vindication of the Duke of Guise* is the clearest instance of lying in his career, and we may well wonder why he undertook it at all. In writing *The Duke of Guise*, Dryden and Lee used a number of standard self-protective devices: joint authorship, a specific historical source, an ambiguous "paral-lel." Although such devices gave the authors some legal protection, they were meant to be seen through: "Where I make it my business to draw *Likeness*," says Dryden in the *Vindication*, "It will be no hard matter to judg who sate for the *Picture*" (p. 6). Despite his repetition of his hope that the "natural candour and probity of [Monmouth's] temper" would lead to "a perfect submission and reconcilement" (p. 6), he meant this tragedy as an even sharper cautionary fable than the incomplete "Picture to the Wast" he had drawn a year earlier in *Absalom and Achitophel*, and he cannot really have been distressed to find that the theatre audience understood the play. What stung him into replying, in my view, were the aspersions cast on his competence and integrity, particularly since those charges came just after he had published a poem he evidently considered one of his best, in which he had forthrightly revealed some of his most firmly held beliefs.

Hoping for a serious response to *Religio Laici*, Dryden encountered instead the abuse of Hunt, who moves from personal slander—"his understanding is clapt, and his brains are vitiated, and he is to rot the Age"—to the claim that Dryden is "befooling Religion by impious and inept Rhimes." As "a tast of [Dryden's] Atheism and Impiety," Hunt quotes a "blasphemous" couplet he claims to have heard in the play, and hopes that "some honest Judge or Justice may direct a process against this bold impious man" (p. 30). Dryden's reply denies authorship of the couplet, which does not appear in the printed text,[9] and answers Hunt's hope for a court proceeding by twitting the lawyer on his poor performance when assigned to the task of defending the late Viscount Stafford:

> I find 'tis happy for me, that he was not made a *Judge*, and yet I had as lieve have him my *Judge* as my Council, if my Life were at stake. My poor Lord *Stafford* was well helpt up with this Gentleman for his Solicitor; no doubt, he gave that unfortunate Nobleman, most admirable advice toward the *Saving* of his life; and would have rejoyc'd exceed-

ingly, to have seen him clear'd. I think I have disprov'd his instance of my *Atheism*. [p. 18]

The last sentence surely refers not only to Dryden's immediate self-defense, but to *Religio Laici*, which Hunt entirely ignores. Angry at being called an atheist within weeks of the publication of that pious poem, Dryden makes an astonishingly revealing and indiscreet reference to the recent execution of his wife's Papist kinsman—"my poor Lord *Stafford*"—all the more surprising when we realize that Shadwell, in the other attack, had attempted to tar him with the brush of Popery:

> That some *Papists* should think the Assassination of the Duke of *Monmouth* a good thing, I do not so much wonder, but that any who call themselves *Protestants* should herd with such Monsters, and join in the Cry, as it is said they do, and even some who he rais'd, who owe it to him that they eat now, who would, in the height of his Power, have out-fawned his Dogs, this is most monstrous. [p. 22]

In answering these charges, Dryden ignored the insinuation of Papist sympathies, which he might have answered by pointing to *Religio Laici*, and concentrated on the charge of ingratitude, which was actually far more difficult to refute. Since he could hardly deny that Monmouth had been his early patron, he had to settle for contesting the implication that he had received money from the Duke:

> The Obligations I have had to him, were those, of his Countenance, his Favour, his good Word, and his Esteem; all which I have likewise had in a greater measure from his excellent Dutchess, the Patroness of my poor unworthy Poetry. If I had not greater, the fault was never in their want of goodness to me, but in my own backwardness to ask, which has allways, and I believe will ever keep me from rising in the World. Let this be enough, with reasonable men, to clear me from the imputation of an ungrateful man, with which my enemies have most unjustly tax'd me. If I am a mercenary Scribler, the Lords Commissioners of the Treasury best know: I am sure, they have found me no importunate Solicitor: for I know my self, I deserv'd little, and have therefore never desir'd much. [p. 20]

The pose of humility ("my poor unworthy Poetry") is more than a little strained, though Dryden was more "backward to ask" for monetary favors from his patrons than some of his contemporaries. Yet the reference to the Treasury, like the description of Stafford as an "unfortunate Nobleman," seems oddly indiscreet: the Laureate had been limping by on half his salary for over four years, but he had been sufficiently "importunate" to hire an agent to help him collect it (see above, p. 336). Dryden's willingness to point to his embarrassing poverty is an indication of how deeply wounded he was by the charge of ingratitude, which he was quick to hurl back at his own enemies. In the dedication of *Plutarchs Lives* to Ormonde, published a month later, he discussed the reasons behind the disloyalty of the Whigs, making a distinction between those whose earlier loyalty to the crown had not been rewarded, to whom he allowed "some pretence for discontent," and those "whose service ha[d] been, not only fully but lavishly recompens'd, with Honours and preferment," whom he accused of "an ingratitude without parallel" (XVII, 233). But Shadwell had already pointed to a parallel in the behavior of a Tory poet whose first important patroness had been the Duchess of Monmouth, but who had nonetheless now staged the murder of a dramatic version of the Duke.

In the pained squirming of the *Vindication*, we may sense the difficulties caused Dryden and his contemporaries by changing definitions of loyalty. In the feudal past, loyalties had been personal, and a poet, like any other retainer, had been expected to celebrate his patron through all changes of alliance and ideology. The old-fashioned Duke of York embodied and inspired that kind of loyalty; Dryden praises him in the *Vindication* "because he never yet forsook any man, whom he has had the goodness to own for his" (p. 30). In the new, imperfectly understood world of party politics, however, loyalty to a principle would eventually be thought more important than loyalty to a person. Dryden, who had once seen fit to praise the young Monmouth, had been constrained to abandon and attack his former patron when that patron proved a dangerous opponent of the principle of hereditary succession; in the dedication to this very play, he speaks proudly of his "Loyalty to the Government," substituting an abstraction for a person. At the same time, he believed too strongly in the idea of personal loyalty to be able to admit what he had done, and he was perfectly willing to accuse the Whigs, some of whom were acting on principles they held with equal passion, of personal ingratitude toward the King. His equivocation about the parallel in *The Duke of Guise* reflects his historical position at the crossroads between personal and ideological definitions of loyalty.

The old charge of "mercenary scribbling" also carried with it the implication of insincerity, by which Dryden was similarly stung. Claiming particular knowledge of private conversations, Shadwell tells us that when meeting with "some of his old Acquaintance (whom he knows to be of an Opinion which he once profess'd to be of, and much different from what he now pretends)," Dryden says *"that he thinks as they do still, but he must write as he does, he is put upon it,* &c" (p. 3). Dryden normally avoided tavern controversies, preferring to be civil whenever possible; Shadwell's calculated exaggeration of that truth was the kind of charge he had made before and would make again.[10] As with the accusation of ingratitude, Dryden does not so much deny as soften what Shadwell had said:

> I know but four men in their whole Party to whom I have spoken for above this year last past; and with them neither but casually and cursorily. We have been acquaintance of a long standing, many years before this accursed Plot divided men into several Parties: I dare call them to witness, whether the most I have at any time said, will amount to more than this, that *I hop'd the time would come when these names of* Whig *and* Tory *would cease among us; and that we might live together, as we had done formerly.* [p. 21][11]

Dryden acknowledges making conciliatory remarks to his Whig friends, but offers a more general and moderate version of those remarks to replace Shadwell's nasty account of a prevaricating poet's admission that he writes for hire. Nonetheless, the Laureate probably had been *"put upon"* writing *The Medall* by the King, and the distance between the vindictive stance taken in that poem and the more "moderate" stance claimed here is enormous.

"Songs & Rhimes" in "Hard Iron Times"

Dryden's experiences during the last three years had illustrated the limitations and dangers of partisan writing, and he may sometimes have felt tired of party controversy, as he suggests. Not only had he devoted considerable time and effort to the study of religious issues that produced *Religio Laici*, but he had also been involved in discussions of linguistic and literary matters with men opposed to partisan strife. During these years Wentworth Dillon, Earl of Roscommon, was gathering about him a group of men interested in "refining, and fixing the standard of our language"; Dryden, who had long been interested in such a project, was his "principal assistant."[12] As Master of the Horse to the Duchess of York, Roscommon was associated with James, but the "Academy" he assembled was nonpartisan. In a manuscript life of Roscommon, Knightley Chetwood points out that Cardinal Richelieu, who founded a similar academy in France, hoped "to amuse busy & turbulent wits & divert them from speculating into matters of State,"[13] and Roscommon's purpose may have been similar: the busy wits in his "Academy" included Dorset and Halifax, both of whom had taken strong positions against parties. In a poem circulating by 1682, Dorset offered these cynical conclusions:

> After thinking this Fortnight of *Whig* and of *Tory*,
> (This to me is the long and the short of the Story)
> They're all Fools and Knaves; and they keep up this pother
> On both sides, designing to cheat one another.

In his patronage, the witty Earl acted consistently with these nonpartisan sentiments: long a friend of the Tory Dryden, he was now actively subsidizing the Whig Shadwell, his old drinking crony, who had fallen on hard times.[14] Halifax, praised in *Absalom and Achitophel* for choosing "the better side" (l. 885), had now happily accepted the name of "Trimmer," which his enemies meant as an insult; his famous "Character of a Trimmer," arguing the case for nonpartisan moderation, was not printed until 1688, but appears to have been in circulation much earlier—certainly well before the King's death in 1685.[15] Dryden would have been wise to soft-pedal his partisan sentiments in such company, and may have been thinking of such occasions in writing the passage where he claims to wish that party labels would cease.

Despite the announced purpose to reform English, the strongest evidence of the group's activity and influence is a spate of translations of classical texts. Roscommon published a translation of Horace's *Ars Poetica* in 1680, and the young poet John Oldham, perhaps already Dryden's friend, published his own version in 1681.[16] Thomas Creech, who had written a poem in praise of *Religio Laici*, published a translation of most of Lucretius in 1682, perhaps rekindling Dryden's own interest in the Epicurean poet. In an undated letter, Dryden comments on a couplet from an early draft of this translation; the unspecified "company" of literary men who appealed to his judgment may well have been members of Roscommon's "Academy." Although Dryden's letter correctly indicts Creech for "notoriously bungl[ing]" this particular passage, he developed a good relationship with the younger poet: Creech's translations of Horace and Theocritus, both published in 1684, parallel Dryden's work on those two poets, and the

Horace is dedicated to Dryden.[17] The aristocrats were also busy. Chetwood says that the Catholic nobleman Richard Maitland, later Earl of Lauderdale, began to translate Virgil at this time, and Dryden's longtime patron Mulgrave published *An Essay upon Poetry* (1682) in couplets—not a translation, but nonetheless another Horatian exercise; Roscommon's poetic *Essay on Translated Verse* (1684), which Dryden praised in a splendid poem of his own, began as a response to Mulgrave.

Sometime after 1680, Dryden found time to revise a translation of Boileau's Horatian *Art of Poetry* by his friend Sir William Soames, which finally appeared in print during 1683,[18] and the days he "threw away" on the *Vindication* were borrowed from time devoted to a new edition of *Plutarchs Lives*, one of a number of collaborative projects that came to occupy his attention over the next several years. Like *Ovid's Epistles* of 1680, the Plutarch was a translation by a number of hands; Tonson intended to replace North's outdated Elizabethan version, which had been translated at second hand from the French, with a fresh version taken straight from the Greek. The preponderance of Old Westminsters and Trinity men among the translators suggests that Dryden took a leading role in organizing this project, which ultimately occupied five volumes, published over the next three years; his own contributions, the dedication and the "Life of Plutarch," appear in the first volume, advertised early in May of 1683. Many of the same men also contributed to Tonson's *Miscellany Poems* (February 1684), a fat volume of original poems and translations in which Dryden printed twenty-six poems, including new translations from Virgil, Theocritus, and Ovid.[19]

Yet neither his contact with Roscommon's "Academy" nor his immersion in classical studies immediately blunted Dryden's partisan edge. He may have underplayed his partisanship in "casual" private conversations, as the *Vindication* claims, but he did not yet alter his public rhetoric. The dedication of *Plutarchs Lives* moves quickly from praise of the moral and literary accomplishments of the ancients to explicitly political criticism of modern times: "Tis an Age indeed, which is only fit for Satyr; and the sharpest I have shall never be wanting to launce its Villanies, and its ingratitude to the Government" (XVII, 229). Defining gratitude to the government along strictly Tory lines, Dryden devotes most of his space in this dedication to repeating standard imprecations against "Schismaticks" and "Republicans," whom he calls "the Canting party" and "the debauch'd party" (XVII, 232). The new epilogue he wrote for Lee's *Constantine the Great*, spoken in November 1683, is just as sharp in its attack on the "Trimmers" as the epilogue to *The Duke of Guise*, spoken a year earlier. Comically pretending to describe the court of Constantine, Dryden repeats the charge of ingratitude he had levelled at the Whigs in his dedication to the Plutarch translation:

> The Court of *Constantine* was full of Glory,
> And every *Trimmer* turn'd Addressing *Tory*;
> . . . .
> *Whigs* kept the Places they possest before,
> And most were in a Way of getting more;
> Which was as much as saying, Gentlemen,
> Here's Power and Money to be Rogues again.

>   [ll. 7–8; 11–14]

By the time he wrote this epilogue, Dryden had a new reason for his bitterness: the revelation of another "accursed Plot," this one from the Whig side. On 12 June 1683, a poor Anabaptist named Josiah Keeling approached the court with a story at least as wild as the one Oates and Tonge had told in 1678; by the time this new story had been retold, expanded, and embroidered, particularly in the testimony of William Howard of Escrick, who turned state's evidence, it had taken on a colorful shape indeed. A one-eyed Cromwellian soldier named Rumbold, also an Anabaptist, owned a property called Rye House, past which the King usually rode on his way to and from the races at Newmarket; Keeling and subsequent witnesses now claimed that a group of radical Whigs had planned to block the road with a cart, then fire upon the royal coaches with blunderbusses, killing the King and the Duke of York as a prelude to a revolution in London, which would have established either a democracy or a greatly weakened monarchy headed by Monmouth. They had been foiled, so the story ran, because a fire in Newmarket on 22 March had prompted the royal party to return to London a week sooner than planned, catching the Rye House plotters unprepared. There were only two indisputable facts, Rumbold's ownership of the property and the Newmarket fire, but these were soon embedded in accounts of conspiratorial meetings involving high Whig lords; rewards were posted for information leading to the arrest of the alleged plotters. Monmouth's friend Lord Grey, who was captured in July, got his guard drunk and managed a daring escape; Monmouth himself, searched for throughout London, lay low in Bedfordshire at the home of his mistress, Henrietta Wentworth. Considerably less fortunate were Arthur Capel, Earl of Essex, who slit his own throat in the Tower on 13 July; William Lord Russell, executed on 21 July; Algernon Sidney, executed on 7 December; and a number of less prominent Whigs, whose heads stared grimly down from various City gates during the next several months.[20]

The Rye House Plot, as it soon came to be called, neatly confirmed the Tory view of the Whigs as unreconstructed rumpers and regicides, and completed the destruction of the already weakened Whig party. The controversy over *The Duke of Guise*, which might otherwise have continued through the usual series of answers and rebuttals, was probably abandoned because the excitement over the new plot dissuaded Shadwell from replying to the *Vindication*; his sometime ally Settle abandoned the Whig cause a few days before Keeling's revelations, publishing *A Narrative* apologizing for his notorious *Character of a Popish Successor*. On 17 June, when Dryden and the diarist Evelyn attended a dinner at Windsor given by the Earl of Sunderland, the newly revealed plot was doubtless among the topics of conversation,[21] and the search for the alleged plotters came close to the poet's professional world on 13 July, when an anonymous tipster offered his opinion that "the Duke of Monmouth may throu Dorset's Davenant's or Betterton's means be Lodged in one of the two Play houses."[22] By autumn, the fallout from the new plot had reached Dryden's family. On 15 October, one James Dryden, almost certainly the poet's brother, told the Privy Council about the dangerous conversation of a gardener named Scarret. As a tobacconist, James was interested in some "ffruits and rarityes" that Scarret "pretended to have"; he was amazed when Scarret suddenly "began to speake of State affaires," saying "that there was Lads enough, (meaning Apprentices) in London, since his Majesty had taken away their

Charter, to drive his Majesty out of his Dominions." Although James Dryden told him that he "deserved to be Hangd," Scarret persisted, referring to Lord Grey's recent escape and hoping that God would bless the concealed Whig conspirators.[23] We may imagine James Dryden coming to Longacre to consult with his famous brother and being advised to take his story to the Privy Council; the whole episode provides a fascinating glimpse into the London underworld of Dissenting merchants and apprentices, in which the Rye House Plot, whatever it really was, had its origins. Aware of the revolutionary sentiments still prevalent in that world, Dryden doubted the sincerity of the pious "addresses" in which various cities and corporations now deplored the Plot and thanked God for the King's deliverance. His prologue for Lee, written just after this episode, cynically tells us that "every *Trimmer*" in the transparently fictional "Court of *Constantine* . . . turn'd Addressing *Tory.*"

By the time the *Miscellany Poems* were published, Monmouth had negotiated an approach to his father through Halifax and confessed what he knew of the conspiracy, firmly denying any knowledge of assassination plots. But when the Duke of York contrived to have his rival's confession printed in the government *Gazette*, Monmouth denied making the statements attributed to him. Charles angrily told his son to go to hell, allegedly in just those words, and by midwinter Monmouth had sailed for Brussels.[24] The continued urgency of such affairs was surely among the reasons why Dryden chose to begin the *Miscellany Poems*, a volume largely devoted to translations of Virgil, Ovid, and Horace, by reprinting his three major satires: *Absalom and Achitophel*, *The Medall*, and *Mac Flecknoe*. He also included eighteen prologues and epilogues, many of them partisan in tone. The entire volume of *Miscellany Poems*, which Dryden probably helped solicit, select, and arrange, reflects a tension between involvement and retirement, satire and pastoral, contemporary politics and classical scholarship, but this was no simple dichotomy, as Dryden obviously knew.[25] He was experiencing in his social relations the tension played out in the generic clashes between the poems in the miscellany, and if he wished to maintain personal relationships of long standing with men who had chosen the other party, particularly when he shared literary interests with those men, he also needed to argue vigorously for his own principles, to "launce [the] Villanies" of "an Age . . . only fit for Satyr."

The classical poems Dryden chose to translate himself show the range of his political, professional, and personal concerns at this moment. The most obvious was Virgil's fourth eclogue, on whose imagery of rebirth, renewal, and peace he had been drawing since *Astraea Redux*:

> The last great Age foretold by sacred Rhymes,
> Renews its finish'd Course, *Saturnian* times
> Rowl round again, and mighty years, begun
> From their first Orb, in radiant Circles run.
> The base degenerate iron-off-spring ends;
> A golden Progeny from Heav'n descends.

[ll. 5–10]

To publish such a translation in 1684 was to endorse a widely held hope for civil peace.

Chetwood's account of Roscommon's "Academy," for example, describes this period as a "happy, but short Interval, [when] good Men began to know one another better, . . . [and] english good-nature flourish'd."[26] As Chetwood knew when he wrote these words, the happy interval proved short, but when Dryden sat down to translate the fourth eclogue, he had reason to hope for a long period of calm. In a later comment about the last years of Charles II's reign, he explicitly linked the period of personal government after the Rye House Plot with the Restoration: "he had overcome all those Difficulties which for some Years had perplex'd his Peaceful Reign, . . . restor'd His People to their Senses, and made the latter End of his Government, of a piece with the Happy Beginning of it" ("Epistle Dedicatory" to *King Arthur*, sig. A2r). By translating Virgil's eclogue, Dryden was recovering from one of its most important sources the imagery of peace and concord he had last invoked in the prologues and epilogues of early 1681, and contrasting the golden age for which some now hoped again with the "base degenerate iron" years of plots and crises.[27]

If this sonorous translation springs in part from Dryden's participation in the hope for "english good-nature" that was widely shared in 1684, his translation of Ovid's nineteenth love elegy shows his continued need to engage in satire. In Ovid's poem, a lover hoping to sharpen his sexual enjoyment by the thrill of outwitting a jealous husband encourages the husband to guard his wife closely. In Dryden's version, the husband is a "sneaking City Cuckold" (l. 45), and the speaker is a sexually jaded courtier like those attacked in *The Kind Keeper*; contemporary considerations of class and party thus color the sexual politics of the original. But the coloring is slight, and some of the satire may be self-directed; Dryden can hardly have written the following lines without thinking of Anne Reeves:

> The Jilting Harlot strikes the surest blow,
> A truth which I by sad Experience know.
> The kind poor constant Creature we despise,
> Man but pursues the Quarry while it flies.
>
> [ll. 33–36]

Even the selection from Theocritus, at first blush the most purely pastoral of these poems, reveals Dryden's ongoing worry about his finances; here is his version of the race of Atalanta:

> *Hippomenes*, who ran with Noble strife
> To win his Lady, or to loose his Life,
> (What shift some men will make to get a Wife!)
> Threw down a Golden Apple in her way,
> For all her haste she could not chuse but stay:
> Renown said run, the glitt'ring Bribe cry'd hold,
> The Man might have been hang'd but for his Gold.
>
> [ll. 91–97]

We have just seen how quick Dryden was to answer the charge that he was a "mercenary Scribler," and in light of his later confessions about how much worldly fame meant to him, the tension between a personified "Renown" and a "glitt'ring Bribe" is striking.

In a letter to Lawrence Hyde, Earl of Rochester, probably written just after the publication of these translations, Dryden begs for "half a yeare of my salary," citing "extreame wants" and "ill health."[28] Taking the humble stance he had claimed for himself in the *Vindication*, he pretends to be reluctant to list the reasons why he deserves a payment now more than four years overdue: "If I durst I wou'd plead a little merit, & some hazards of my life from the Common Enemyes, my refuseing advantages offerd by them, & neglecting my beneficiall studyes for the King's service" (*Letters*, pp. 20–21). By claiming to have refused "advantages offerd" by "the Common Enemyes," Dryden can only mean that he had spurned the "glitt'ring Bribe[s]" of the Whigs, and it is not difficult to believe that someone in that party had once offered him a financial reward to write for their cause.

Despite the pose of humility ("I onely thinke I merite not to sterve"), the Laureate's frustration about the poor rewards of poetry comes through quite clearly in this letter: "Tis enough for one Age to have neglected Mr Cowley, and sterv'd Mr Buttler." He may have been attracted to Virgil's ninth eclogue, which he also translated for *Miscellany Poems*, because it records the Roman poet's similar frustration with his similarly slender rewards for his service to the state. As Dryden informs his readers in a headnote, the poem is "fill'd with complaints of [the poet's] hard Usage," and the vigorous language of his translation bespeaks Dryden's emotional identification with Virgil. One speaker, Virgil's steward Moeris, complains that

> Songs & Rhimes
> Prevail as much in these hard iron times,
> As would a plump of trembling Fowl, that rise
> Against an Eagle sousing from the Skies.
>
> [ll. 14–17]

Dryden's recent experiences had showed just how hard it was for "Songs & Rhimes" to "Prevail" in the "hard iron times" of political turmoil. He hoped the ensuing golden age of Charles's personal rule would prove kinder to poets, and when Charles died, just one year later, he remembered the image of poets as birds:

> Tho little was their Hire, and light their Gain,
> Yet somewhat to their share he threw;
> Fed from his Hand, they sung and flew,
> Like Birds of Paradise, that liv'd on Morning dew.
> Oh never let their Lays his Name forget!
> The Pension of a Prince's Praise is great.
>
> [*Threnodia Augustalis*, ll. 377–82]

In 1684, however, the penurious Laureate hoped for a more substantial pension than mere praise. In the letter to Rochester, he refers to his expenses in educating his "hopefull" sons, the eldest of whom was now completing his first full year at Trinity College, and makes a specific request for "Some small Employment . . . Either in the Customes, or the Appeales of the Excise" (p. 21). He probably got the idea of asking for a place in the customs from his first cousin John Dryden, a wealthy linen-draper who was appointed to a lucrative sinecure in the customs late in 1683.[29]

Moeris also breaks off singing a pastoral song, explaining that strife and age have weakened his poetic voice:

> The rest I have forgot, for Cares and Time
> Change all things, and untune my soul to rhime:
> I cou'd have once sung down a Summers Sun,
> But now the Chime of Poetry is done.
>
> [ll. 69–72]

As early as *The Conquest of Granada*, Dryden had made self-deprecating remarks about the waning of his poetic powers with age, referring to "forty" as "That wretched, fumbling age of poetry." For a man of fifty-two, suffering "extreame wants" and "ill health," such language was no longer an exercise in bravado, and he did not lack for reminders of his mortality: his old associate Thomas Killigrew, original patentee of the King's Company, died in March of 1683; Charles Hart, who had starred in most of his plays, died in August; and the promising young poet Oldham, barely thirty, died in December. In his elegy for Oldham, published late in 1684, Dryden actually describes himself as a kind of Moeris, complaining that time has mellowed his own work to "the dull sweets of Rime" (l. 21).

Writing words for tuneful singing, however, was among the Laureate's tasks at this time. Late in the summer of 1683, the King dispatched Betterton to France to "fetch yᵉ designe" for an opera, and Betterton managed to persuade the composer Louis Grabu, who had served Charles before, "to go over with him to endeavour to represent something at least like an Opera in England for his Majesty's diversion."[30] Dryden seems to have been involved in the operatic plans from the start, but the story of the collaboration is sketchy at best because both resulting operas were delayed in production. Someone may have considered having Grabu set *The State of Innocence*, if such an inference may be permitted from the odd fact that three separate editions of that opera were printed in 1684, but the idea Dryden settled upon was the story of King Arthur. Charles was now building a new palace at Winchester, home of the Round Table,[31] and the unimpeachably patriotic "matter of Britain" offered excellent opportunities for music and allegory. Such Spenserian episodes as the temptation of Arthur by two singing maidens bathing in a fountain lent themselves readily to musical treatment, and Dryden invented new episodes as well: the unusually cold winter of 1683–84, during which carnival booths, printing presses, and brothels were set up on the frozen Thames, probably suggested the striking frost scene, in which a Cold Genius proves powerless to resist the warmth of love.[32] Since this version of the text is lost, we cannot know whether Dryden invited political interpretations in the main plot, but we may guess that there was some kind of parallel between the Saxon enemies of Arthur and the recently vanquished Whig enemies of Charles.[33] In a letter to Tonson written in August of 1684, Dryden said he had finished all but one act of this new work, which he later described as

> a Play, Of the Nature of the *Tempest;* which is, a Tragedy mix'd with *Opera;* or a *Drama* Written in blank Verse, adorn'd with Scenes, Machines, Songs and Dances: So that the Fable of it is all spoken and acted by the best of the Comedians; the other part of the entertainment to be perform'd by the . . . Singers and Dancers. [XV, 10]

In deference to Grabu's talents and the King's interest in French-style opera, however, Dryden also wrote a fully-sung prologue designed as an allegory of the Restoration, in which Archon (obviously General Monck) miraculously defeats Democracy and Zeal and restores the banished Albion to his kingdom. Perhaps because both Grabu and Charles were more interested in this part than in the Arthurian semi-opera, the prologue grew into a three-act allegory including recent political events, with recitatives, ensembles, and choruses—a "singing opera," as Dryden called it in the same letter, where he described it as finished and ready for performance the next fall. The descent of this text from the Caroline masque by way of Crowne's *Calisto* is apparent,[34] but it seems to have been planned from the start as an expensive Dorset Garden production with scenery and machines of unprecedented splendor, obviously supported by the court but not physically performed at Whitehall. Like *Calisto*, which was practiced at court for months before its official performances, *Albion and Albanius* was rehearsed before the King. There is a clear record of such rehearsals in the apartments of the Duchess of Portsmouth during the winter of 1684–85, and a mysterious report dated 24 May 1684, which states that the King, at Windsor, was "Entertained with Mr Drydens new play the subject of which is the last new Plott," may well refer to some fragmentary read-through of part of *Albion and Albanius*. In 1684, "the last new Plott" could only mean the Rye House Plot, which is fancifully enacted in Act III of the opera: a *"one-Ey'd Archer,"* obviously a version of Rumbold, advances to shoot at Albion, but is thwarted when *"A fire arises betwixt them"* (III, i, s.d.). This "entertainment" can hardly have been a full-scale performance; three months later, Dryden was inquiring about the preparation of costumes, and the elaborate machines required were not yet built and could not possibly have been transported to Windsor. Perhaps Grabu had set some parts of the text and prepared the court singers to perform them in concert; perhaps Dryden, who often read his plays aloud to interested courtiers, simply read the text.[35]

If Dryden did read his libretto before the King, he placed his royal master in a position like that of most modern readers, who must make what sense they can of this opera without access to its music. Though scoffing at Grabu's music has been a commonplace in accounts of this collaboration, the last musicologist to give careful study to the score, which appeared in a sumptuously printed folio in 1687, gives Grabu credit for "respond[ing] instantly to the changing moods of the verse, while retaining an elegant homogeneity."[36] Charles, who was no mean judge, took Grabu quite seriously as a composer, and the score is the work of a meticulous craftsman, highly trained in part-writing and orchestration, if not always as alert to the rhythms of English verse as a native speaker might have been. Despite Dryden's later grumpy comments about the "drudgery" of writing in the various lyric meters used in *Albion and Albanius*, which entail very short lines and force an uncomfortable simplification and compression, the freedom and flexibility of the Pindaric measures in which he wrote some of his most impressive poetry from 1685 on may owe something to this exercise. He groused that his work with Grabu was like being "bound 'Prentice to some doggrel Rhymer, who makes Songs to Tunes" (XV, 10), but the increased musicality of his later poetry bears witness to the usefulness of that resented apprenticeship. As the reclamation of forgotten baroque music continues, perhaps we may even hope for a performance and recording of this work, for without the opportunity to see and hear the composite product, we remain unable to judge it fairly.

"The Disease of Translation"

Dryden may be referring to one or both of these operatic projects in his letter to Rochester, where he says he is "goeing to write somewhat by his Majestyes command," but he seems more likely to be thinking of his translation of Maimbourg's *History of the League*. This new recounting of the events dramatized in *The Duke of Guise* appeared in Paris in October 1683; a pirated Dutch edition was available in England by March of 1684, and Charles, alert to its possible value as propaganda, quickly asked his Historiographer Royal to translate it. Tonson was advertising the book as "in the press" by 16 April 1684, but it did not actually appear until late July; the evidence suggests that Dryden worked steadily on it from March until midsummer, when he went to Northamptonshire to take up the more pleasant exercises in poetic translation that he published in *Sylvae* (January 1685).[37] In dedicating the finished *History* to the King, Dryden speaks of "the Honour of Your Majesty's Commands" and "my utmost diligence to Obey them" (XVIII, 3), but a later reference in the preface to *Sylvae* is a better indication of his true attitude. "For this last half Year," he candidly tells us, "I have been troubled with the disease (as I may call it) of Translation; the cold Prose fits of it, (which are always the most tedious with me) were spent in the History of the League; the hot, (which succeeded them) in this Volume of Verse Miscellanies" (III, 3). The metaphor of disease is not fanciful: in his letter to Hyde, Dryden refers to "my ill health, which cannot be repaird without immediate retireing into the Country," (*Letters*, p. 20), and in his letter to Tonson, written from the country, he says he has just recovered from "a kind of Hectique feavour" and reports that his son John and one of the servants have "fallen ill . . . of the same distemper" (p. 24).[38]

His "cold Prose fits" cost Dryden months of drudgery and yielded little profit. He did what he could to make Maimbourg's history seem urgent in the dedication and postscript, describing the current calm as "a gusty kind of Weather [with] a kind of Sickness in the Air" (III, 4–5), and the Whigs as "Lyons" whose "claws," though now "par'd," "may grow again to be more sharp" (III, 405).[39] But he must have recognized that with Charles firmly in control, historical parallels to recent plots had become less interesting to the public. In his letter to Rochester, he spoke of "neglecting my beneficiall studies for the King's service," and the *History*, "Translated into English According to His Majesty's Command," did not prove financially "beneficiall": shortly after its publication, Tonson told Dryden that his translation was being "commended," but he was still advertising the first edition a year later.[40]

Dryden's framing essays remain important as a victorious summing-up of the Tory arguments he had pursued throughout the Exclusion Crisis and an indication of the direction in which his political and religious opinions were moving in 1684. In the dedication, he uses the conventional hope that his royal master will forgive his failings as a translator to set up an impassioned discussion of the paradox of royal mercy, which had been his central theme in *Absalom and Achitophel*:

> You have not urg'd the Law against them, but have been press'd and constrain'd by it to inflict punishments in Your own defence, and in the mean time to watch every Opportunity of shewing Mercy, when there was the least probability of Repentance: so that they who have suffer'd may be truly said to have forc'd the Sword of Justice out of Your hand, and to have done Execution on themselves. [XVIII, 6]

This grossly overstated argument may have gained a little plausibility from the fact that the imprisoned Earl of Essex had indeed "done Execution on himself" with his razor one year earlier. The postscript, one of Dryden's most severe attacks on the "Sectaries," may remind us that his hatred of Protestant excesses was among the forces that ultimately drove him into the Roman Church. Less than two years earlier, he had prepared his readers for a quotation from Maimbourg by arguing that "A man may be suffer'd to quote an Adversary to our Religion, when he speaks Truth" (II, 107), but in the postscript to *The History of the League*, not even the candid admission that Maimbourg "was formerly a Jesuit" seems to require the least apology. Dryden's account of Maimbourg even suggests that he was identifying at some level with the Catholic cleric whose work he had just finished translating. His description of Maimbourg applies perfectly to his own case: "He is esteemed in the *French* Court equal to their best Writers, which has procur'd him the Envy of some who set up for Criticks. Being a profess'd Enemy of the *Calvinists*, he is particularly hated by them; so that their testimonies against him stand suspected of prejudice." The author of *The Vindication of the Duke of Guise* could hardly have written those phrases without thinking of his own Calvinist enemies, nor could he have written about Maimbourg's "large Salary," "provided plentifully for him" by "The Great King his patron" without thinking of his own financial situation; perhaps his insistence that Maimbourg "has deserv'd it from him" was meant to remind Charles of his own Laureate's urgent requests for support. When Dryden does make a critical comment, declaring that Maimbourg's "particular Commendations of Men and Families [are] superfluous," he quickly remembers his own flattering dedications, and explains that such passages are "pardonable in a man, who having created himself many Enemies, has need of the support of Friends" (XVIII, 415).

In *An Essay on Translated Verse*, which probably appeared while Dryden was working on the *History*,[41] the Earl of Roscommon argues that poetic translators ought to choose their texts on the basis of just such a psychological identification with the original author:

> Examine how your *Humour* is inclin'd,
> And which the *Ruling Passion* of your Mind;
> Then, seek a *Poet* who *your* way do's bend,
> And chuse an *Author* as you chuse a *Friend*.
> United by this *Sympathetick Bond*,

> You grow *Familiar, Intimate* and *Fond*;
> Your *Thoughts*, your *Words*, your *Stiles*, your *Souls* agree,
> No Longer his *Interpreter*, but *He*.
>
> [pp. 6–7]

Dryden, whose poem commending Roscommon appeared with the published *Essay*, declares himself a follower of the Earl's new theory in his preface to *Sylvae*, where he offers his translations as "Examples to [Roscommon's] Rules" and defends his additions on psychological grounds:

> I desire the false Criticks wou'd not always think that those thoughts are wholly mine, but that either they are secretly in the Poet, or may be fairly deduc'd from him: or at least, if both those considerations should fail, that my own is of a piece with his, and that if he were living, and an *Englishman*, they are such, as he woul'd probably have written. [III, 4]

While Dryden's motives for praising Roscommon doubtless included the need for support he had so shrewdly recognized in Maimbourg, he continued to discuss his translations in psychological terms for the rest of his career: as late as the preface to the *Fables* (1700), he speaks of being "embolden'd" to make additions to his translation of Chaucer "because . . . I found I had a Soul congenial to his" (*Poems*, IV, 1457), and his decision to translate no fewer than eight selections from Ovid in the *Fables* doubtless reflects the kinship he then felt with Ovid, who also ended his career out of favor with those in power. If his identification with Maimbourg in the *History of the League*, however fleeting or unconscious, shows us Dryden trying on the mask of a Catholic opponent of sectarian strife, his more complicated poetic identifications with Horace, Theocritus, Lucretius, and Virgil, made in the first flush of his keen interest in Roscommon's theory, are even more important sources for inferences about his thoughts and feelings during the period leading up to his conversion.[42]

The selections from Horace, probably the first of the translations in *Sylvae* to be completed,[43] are poems on friendship, country life, retirement, and simplicity; entering into the spirit of such poems was easy among rural scenes and friendly relatives in Northamptonshire. In addressing two of these translations to his own patrons, Dryden paid them handsome compliments. An ode originally written by Horace on the occasion of a sea voyage by Virgil, "The best of Poets and of Friends" (l. 8), is "inscrib'd to the Earl of Roscomon, on his intended voyage to Ireland," a trip about which Dryden also inquired in his letter to Tonson, but which the Earl, probably suffering from the illness that killed him in January, never made. Another ode, "paraphras'd in Pindarique verse," is "inscrib'd to Lawrence Earl of Rochester," who would surely have known that it was originally addressed to the famous patron Maecenas. Dryden's preface leaves little doubt that Hyde had acted as his financial Maecenas: he speaks of "particular Obligations, which this small Testimony of Gratitude can never pay," describes the original poem as Hyde's "Darling in the *Latine*," and claims to have "taken some pains to make it my Master-Piece in *English*" (III, 16–17). Some of Dryden's enthusiasm about his performance in translating this particular ode has to do with his success in the

Portrait of Lawrence Hyde, Earl of Rochester, by Sir Godfrey Kneller, 1685.

dangerous poetic mode called Pindaric. His preface praises Cowley for "happily restor[ing] this "noble sort of Poetry" (III, 18) to English and criticizes Cowley's many
imitators, but it does not take much reading between the lines to recognize that Dryden
knew he had already outdone Cowley. The musical practice he had undergone in
writing *Albion and Albanius* helped produce the beautifully modulated motion of such
stanzas as these:

> Leave for a while thy costly Country Seat;
>   And, to be Great indeed, forget
> The nauseous pleasures of the Great:
>   Make haste and come:
> Come and forsake thy cloying store;
>   Thy Turret that surveys, from high,

> The smoke, and wealth, and noise of *Rome;*
>> And all the busie pageantry
> That wise men scorn, and fools adore:
> Come, give thy Soul a loose, and taste the pleasures of the poor.
>
> Sometimes, 'tis grateful to the Rich, to try
> A short vicissitude, and fit of Poverty:
>> A savoury Dish, a homely Treat,
>>> Where all is plain, where all is neat,
>>> Without the stately spacious Room,
>> The *Persian* Carpet, or the *Tyrian* Loom,
> Clear up the cloudy foreheads of the Great.

[ll. 12–28]

But there is more at work in this poetry than the controlled freedom of its metrical movement. In his translations from Horace and Lucretius, Dryden was examining the Epicurean ideal of a simple country life, testing whether it might provide an answer to the financial and political problems with which he had been wrestling in recent years.[44] In the dedication of *Amboyna* to the fallen Clifford (1673), he had praised retirement as an ideal for politicians, and Rochester, who lost his powerful position in the Treasury during the summer of 1684, was now in a situation partly analogous to Clifford's.[45] In the dedication of *Aureng-Zebe* to Mulgrave (1676), he had developed the retirement theme again, explicitly citing Epicurus, Lucretius, and Cowley; on that occasion, he had spoken of his own desire to retire from the stage, a wish reiterated in his Oxford prologues and epilogues, with their talk of "peaceful shades." The temporary political calm after the Rye House Plot probably made Dryden freshly aware of the "natural love to Peace and Quiet, which increases in every man with his years" (XVII, 204), and his years were increasing; he celebrated his fifty-third birthday during the very month when he was translating these Horatian poems. Horace's praise of the wholesome air and food of the country corresponded with his own feelings about Northamptonshire; his account of his son's illness in the letter to Tonson concludes with a comforting observation: "though many in this Country fall sick of feavours, few or none dye." But the same letter eagerly inquires about "whether the Dukes house are making cloaths & putting things in a readiness for the singing opera, to be played immediately after Michaelmasse" and discusses the planned casts for revivals of *All for Love* and *The Conquest of Granada* (*Letters*, pp. 23–24).[46] Dryden was obviously looking forward to returning to London in time to see his old and new plays performed, and his continuing interest in "the busie pageantry" of the city meant that summer rambles to Northamptonshire would continue to be his only respite from the "smoke, and wealth, and noise" of London.

The educational expenses of his sons, at least two of whom accompanied him on his trip to the country in the summer of 1684, were among the reasons why Dryden could not consider a more permanent retirement. Writing under the poetic spell of Horace, he could praise "the pleasures of the poor," even arguing that a "fit of poverty" might "Clear up the cloudy foreheads of the Great," but his letter begging for his salary, written to the same Lord Rochester a few months earlier, shows just how urgent the

issue of poverty was for him, and the reference to a "costly country seat," which has no
basis in Horace, comes from a poet who probably knew how much Hyde had paid when
he purchased the manor house at Wooton Bassett from Sir Robert Howard in 1676.[47]
Horace himself had recognized the irony implicit in the tendency of avaricious city-
dwellers to praise the wholesome poverty of the country. His most famous poem on
country life, the second epode, looks like an enthusiastic endorsement of the ideal of
retirement, and the opening lines of Dryden's translation, also published in *Sylvae*,
perfectly capture its tone:

> How happy in his low degree
> How rich in humble Poverty, is he,
> Who leads a quiet country life!
> Discharg'd of business, void of strife,
> And from the gripeing Scrivener free.
>
> [ll. 1–5]

But the tricky ending of this poem reveals that the whole celebration of pastoral
pleasures—"clustring Grapes," "gentle slumber," the "harmless easie joys" of hunting, the "wholesome Food and Country Mirth" of "happy Swains" and "jolly Shep-
heard[s]"—has been a speech "said within himself" by a Roman usurer, who can no
more abandon his financial dealings than Dryden could abandon the city world of
politics, prologues, and profits:

> Resolv'd to leave the wicked Town,
> And live retir'd upon his own;
> He call'd his Mony in:
> But the prevailing love of pelf,
> Soon split him on the former shelf,
> And put it out again.
>
> [ll. 97–102]

Some earlier translators, more simply enamored of the celebration of country pleasures, had downplayed or omitted this ironic conclusion,[48] but Dryden makes it even
more pointed by giving his usurer the name of Morecraft, a London merchant in a play
recently revived by the United Company,[49] and by adding the potent image of a ship
splitting on a hidden shelf.

   That image, long a favorite with Dryden, occurs earlier in Horace's poem, where
the happy man who leads a country life is said to avoid the merchant's fear of the
"dangers of the deep" (l. 13). The conclusion of the ode to Maecenas gives an even
fuller version; celebrating Epicurean detachment, Horace pictures himself as Dryden
may have sometimes hoped he could be:

> secure from Fortunes blows,
> (Secure of what I cannot lose,)
> In my small Pinnace I can sail,
> Contemning all the blustring roar;
> And running with a merry gale,

> With friendly Stars my safety seek
> Within some little winding Creek;
> And see the storm a shore.
>
> [ll. 97–104]

Safe in his little boat, the speaker escapes the fears of "the greedy Merchant" when "the debating winds and billows bear / His Wealth into the Main" (ll. 92, 95–96). Nonetheless, the metaphorical description of those natural forces as "debating" betrays the translator as a man who had often ventured into the stormy seas of political debate.

Horace's sentiments and imagery are anticipated in one of the passages Dryden chose to translate from Lucretius, the opening of Book II of *De Rerum Natura*:

> Tis pleasant, safely to behold from shore
> The rowling Ship; and hear the Tempest roar:
> . . . .
> To see vain fools ambitiously contend
> For Wit and Pow'r; their lost endeavours bend
> T' outshine each other, waste their time and health,
> In search of honour, and pursuit of wealth.
>
> [ll. 1–2, 12–15]

Dryden had quoted this passage in Latin in the dedication to *Aureng-Zebe*, but he had been applying the image of shipwreck to himself since the early poem to Castlemaine, and he knew that he could not really watch the political or literary storms from shore. Like Morecraft, he may have "Resolv'd . . . to live retir'd upon his own," but that resolution, like his "old Custom" of scorning attacks in silence, was sure to be broken. When silence would have served him well, he had been unable to resist answering the attacks on *The Duke of Guise*, and when he made his daring and dangerous conversion to Roman Catholicism, which was to shipwreck his career, he could not resist defending himself in verse. He remained determined to "outshine" his literary rivals, as the letter to Tonson illustrates: "I care not who translates [Virgil] beside me, for let him be friend or foe, I will please my self, & not give off in consideration of any man" (*Letters*, p. 23). "In search of honour, and pursuit of wealth," Dryden was finally more likely to "split upon [his] former shelf" than to achieve the resignation celebrated by the Epicurean speakers of Horace and Lucretius.

As his translation from Ovid in the *Miscellany Poems* of the previous year had shown, Dryden's view of sexuality was now similarly complex: he could look upon those caught in the grip of sexual passion with a bemused and satiric eye, but he could not do so from a posture of ascetic detachment, since he remained aware of the power of *eros* in his own mind. In this new collection, he printed a delightfully bawdy "New Song" about the sexual awakening of "Sylvia the fair, in the bloom of fifteen" and gleefully translated the explicit discussion of human reproduction in Lucretius, which Creech had modestly omitted. In the preface, answering "the Objection [that] arises from the Obscenity of the Subject," he acknowledged his own susceptibility to sexual feeling: "I am not yet so secure from that passion, but that I want my Authors Antidotes against it" (III, 12). These and other selections in *Sylvae* display the eroticism that marks the lyrics in

Dryden's plays, but he was also now giving some emphasis to the transitory and destructive side of sex, perhaps still mindful of the lessons learned from his affair with
Anne Reeves.

From Theocritus, he chose three poems whose eroticism was already darkened by
irony, and translated them in ways that increased the darkness. In the hymn sung by
"twelve *Spartan* Virgins" at the wedding of Helen and Menelaus, the irony is obvious in
the situation. The virgins naively offer a conventional prayer—"Let *Venus* furnish you
with full desires" (l. 82)—but we know that Venus will soon contrive to give Helen to
Paris, and that the result will be the devastation of the Trojan War. Dryden ends his
version by pointing sharply to that irony. In Theocritus, the maidens simply ask Hymen
to rejoice in the marriage; but in Dryden, they sing the "Triumphs" of Hymen, urging
him to "view the mighty spoils thou hast in Battle won" (ll. 95–96)—a reminder of the
real battles and real deaths that will soon spring from this broken marriage. A similar
connection between sex and death is entirely explicit in another idyll. A cruel nymph
(originally a pretty youth) drives her lover to hang himself, but her punishment is swift:
she is crushed in her bath by a falling statue of Cupid. Expiring, she warns future lovers
to "be wise, and love for love return" (l. 111), but the grotesquerie of the deaths is hardly
likely to leave the reader in an erotic mood: the hanged youth "beat[s] his quivering feet
in Air" (l. 97); the "gushing Blood" of the scornful maiden "besmear[s] the Pavement"
(l. 108). The pastoral seduction dialogue between Daphnis and Chloris, in which the
pair do return "love for love," is less violent but not much more optimistic. The nymph
intends to "keep [her] Maidenhead till death, / And die as pure as Queen *Elizabeth*" (ll.
34–35), but yields after some vague promises of marriage and considerable pawing. No
sooner has Daphnis done the "noble deed" than Chloris begins to sound like Milton's
Eve:

> A Maid I came, in an unlucky hour,
> But hence return, without my Virgin flour.
>
> [ll. 116–17]

In a moment of wonderful acuity, Dryden adds a physical detail that dramatizes the
psychological loss Chloris has sustained:

> First rose the Maid and with a glowing Face,
> Her down cast eyes beheld her print upon the grass.
>
> [ll. 129–30]

In Theocritus, the downcast eyes are simply a gesture of modesty on the part of a
woman whose heart is glad; but in Dryden, those eyes see the all-too-temporary "print"
her body has left "upon the grass," itself a traditional symbol for the shortness of human
life. The deflowering, which had seemed so important to both lovers a few minutes
earlier, now seems transitory and empty.

In the published collection, Dryden made his transition from Virgil to Lucretius by
juxtaposing two brief passages on Venus in bed, both turned into "luscious *English*" (III,
12). In the allegorical passage that begins *De Rerum Natura*, Lucretius begs Venus to
"lull the listning world in universal peace" by seducing Mars. "Plung'd in [the] pleasing

death" of orgasm, "Involv'd and fetter'd in the links of Love" (ll. 52, 54), the god of war ought to be unable to deny a request for peace, but Dryden knew how often such hopes had failed in the real world of foreign and domestic politics.[50] In the contrasting passage from *Aeneid* VIII, Venus uses "her conqu'ring Beauty" to persuade her husband Vulcan to make new weapons for her son Aeneas. "Sooth'd with her charms, / Panting, and half dissolving in her arms," (ll. 37–38), Vulcan promises to use the full force of his artistry at the forge, but Dryden has cunningly re-ordered his passages, and we have just read a story from Book X in which the resulting weapons are put to deadly use against the young and admirable Lausus. Once again, sex is linked to death, and if the paired passage from Lucretius provides a more hopeful view, both Lucretius and Dryden knew that the powerful forces symbolized by Venus were at least as likely to spur men on to war as to restrain them.

In Lucretius, the detached resignation that Dryden admired but could not achieve extends to contempt for death, and if we pay attention to Dryden's contention that he has chosen from Virgil and Lucretius "some parts of them which had most affected me in the reading" (III, 3), we can hardly escape the conclusion that death was much on his mind in 1684. From Virgil, he chose the footrace involving Nisus and Euryalus in *Aeneid* V, an ominous episode darkened by our knowledge that the beautiful young runners will die in the night-raid of Book IX, which follows immediately in *Sylvae*. In the other battle scene, the pious Aeneas slays the atheistical Mezentius, whose confident impiety gives him a certain Satanic grandeur.[51] Unfortunately, fighting Mezentius necessitates killing his loyal son Lausus, in whom a grieving Aeneas sees "an image . . . Of his own filial love" (ll. 97–98). The poet who was "affected" by this passage may possibly have been thinking at some level of the difficulties faced by Charles II, whose struggles against the grandly impious Shaftesbury had necessitated punishing his beloved Monmouth.[52] He was more certainly thinking of the death of the promising satirist Oldham, for whom he had a kind of "filial love." In his deeply felt poem "To the Memory of Mr. Oldham," published in November of 1684, Dryden compares his relationship with the younger poet to the friendship of Nisus and Euryalus,[53] and draws upon the speech of Aeneas over the body of Lausus. In the translation, the hero addresses his victim:

> Poor hapless youth, what praises can be paid
> To love so great; to such transcendent store
> Of early worth, and sure presage of more?
>
> [ll. 100–02]

In the elegy for Oldham, Dryden adopts the same questioning mode of address and uses the same rhyme:

> O early ripe! to thy abundant store
> What could advancing Age have added more?
>
> [ll. 11–12]

This question looks rhetorical, but Dryden answers it, pointing out that age might have taught Oldham to write in smoother "numbers." He then denigrates his own metrical skills, attained by years of patient study and practice, as "the dull sweets of Rime" (l. 21).

Part of the power this poem has long had for readers of all kinds comes from its Virgilian resonance; another part comes from the way Dryden's response to Oldham's early death leads him to question the value of his own longer life. In the longest of his selections from Lucretius, the vigorous passage against the fear of death, he wrestles again with that problem, using the rhyme of "store" and more" once again in a climactic triplet:

> And last, suppose Great Natures Voice shou'd call
> To thee, or me, or any of us all,
> What dost thou mean, ungrateful wretch, thou vain,
> Thou mortal thing, thus idly to complain,
> And sigh and sob, that thou shalt be no more?
> For if thy life were pleasant heretofore,
> If all the bounteous blessings I cou'd give
> Thou hast enjoy'd, if thou hast known to live,
> And pleasure not leak'd thro' thee like a Seive,
> Why dost thou not give thanks as at a plenteous feast
> Cram'd to the throat with life, and rise and take thy rest?
> But if my blessings thou hast thrown away,
> If undigested joys pass'd thro' and wou'd not stay,
> Why dost thou wish for more to squander still?
> If Life be grown a load, a real ill,
> And I wou'd all thy cares and labours end,
> Lay down thy burden fool, and know thy friend.
> To please thee I have empti'd all my store,
> I can invent, and can supply no more;
> But run the round again, the round I ran before.

[ll. 121–40]

In his preface, Dryden expresses particular admiration for this "*Prosopopeia* of Nature, who is brought in speaking to her Children, with so much authority and vigour" (III, 12); we may detect in the "authority and vigour" of his translation the urgency of his own search for an answer to the fear of death. In discussing his work on these philosophical selections from Lucretius, he takes pains to separate his own "natural Diffidence and Scepticism" from the "Dogmatical way" of the Roman author, who was "so much an Atheist, that he forgot sometimes to be a Poet." Alert as always to the possibility of attack, he gives a standard Christian refutation of Lucretius's heretical contention that the soul dies with the body, but there is something curious in the way the rejection is phrased: "As for his Opinions concerning the mortality of the Soul, they are so absurd, that I cannot *if I wou'd* believe them" (III, 11, emphasis mine). When he claims to have translated Lucretius "more happily" (III, 9) than Virgil, Dryden means that he has had better luck in catching the tone of the original; according to Roscommon's theory, such a happy confluence of styles had to be grounded on some similarities in personality. When Dryden speaks of "the distinguishing Character of *Lucretius*" as "a certain kind of noble pride, and positive assertion of his Opinions," we may remember that he had once declared himself "too eager" in dispute; when he says that

Lucretius assumes "a Magisterial authority," we may remember that he had himself assumed the role of "a kind of Law-giver" (II, 109) in *Religio Laici*; and when he praises Lucretius for his "sublime and daring Genius," his "fiery temper," "the loftiness of his Expressions, and the perpetual torrent of his Verse" (III, 10), we may remember similar claims by the author of *The Conquest of Granada*. More than that: the poem for Oldham, which has struck many readers as one of Dryden's most personal creations, contains no Christian imagery of any kind. All of its allusions are classical, and its despairing conclusion gives no hint of Christian hope:

> Once more, hail and farewel; farewel thou young,
> But ah too short, *Marcellus* of our Tongue;
> Thy Brows with Ivy, and with Laurels bound;
> But Fate and gloomy Night encompass thee around.
>
> [ll. 22–25]

In the preface to *Sylvae*, Dryden declares that his arguments against the atheism of Lucretius are "my own thoughts abstractedly, and without entring into the Notions of our Christian Faith, which is the proper business of Divines" (III, 11). Despite this disclaimer, he was now reexamining his faith, and the reexamination necessarily included some imaginative consideration of what it would be like to combat the fear of death without recourse to the Christian doctrine of immortality. He was always fascinated by the arguments on the other side, and the ultimate resolution he found in Catholicism was earned by a careful consideration of all the rival systems of belief, including a proud unbelief grounded on reason. As a writer, he might also hope for literary immortality, and at least one contemporary had recently declared that he was "Doubly secur'd of never dying Fame." In a poem called *The Laurel*, published a few weeks after *Sylvae*, an anonymous poet contrasted "that Lectur'd Life of Grave Divines" with the "Immortality" of Dryden's poetic "Lines."[54] Basking in such praise, or contrasting his own fruitful career with the tragically truncated life of the promising Oldham, Dryden may well have felt the power of Nature's scolding of those to whom she has allowed "bounteous blessings." On other days, racked with poor health and depressed by shaky finances, he may have felt the power of her call to lay down his burden. But his ultimate response to the process of self-analysis recorded in the translations in *Sylvae*, at least in poetic terms, was a desire for "more to squander still." Far from content to "run the round again," he was rethinking his most fundamental religious beliefs, seeking new stimulation in a fresh rereading of the classics, and experimenting with new kinds of metrical freedom: triplets and alexandrines are far more frequent in *Sylvae* than in Dryden's earlier verse, and the experiment with Pindaric in the Horatian ode led to an important series of original Pindaric poems.

"A Warlike Prince Ascends the Regal State"

The first of those poems was *Threnodia Augustalis: A Funeral-Pindarique Poem Sacred to the Happy Memory of King Charles II*. Delighted with his triumph over his once formidable enemies, the King had been living a court life increasingly resembling that of his autocratic cousin Louis. On Easter Day of 1684, Evelyn saw him take communion with "3 of his natural Sonns, . . . base sonns of *Portsmouth, Cleaveland, Nelly*, prostitute Creatures . . . after which, he retir'd to a Canopied seate." Such baroque ostentation also marked the Queen's birthday the following November, celebrated by "pageants of Castles, Forts, & other devices . . . all represented in fire," and the winter rehearsals of *Albion and Albanius* in the Duchess of Portsmouth's elaborately decorated chambers must have been similarly lavish. The preparation of costumes and machines delayed the public production well past the autumn date for which Dryden had hoped, and an attack of the gout, which hobbled the King for much of December and January, was doubtless another reason why Charles saw the opera rehearsed at Whitehall rather than produced at Dorset Garden. By the end of January, however, he was much better; on a Sunday night, Evelyn was scandalized by the scene in Portsmouth's "glorious Gallery," where the King was "sitting & toying with his Concubines," with "A french boy singing love songs" and his "greate Courtiers" gambling for high stakes.[55]

The convulsions with which Charles awakened on the morning of 2 February 1685 were thus entirely unexpected, though their ultimate cause, kidney disease, was surely a consequence of his habitual excesses of food and drink. During the next four days, while contradictory rumors flew about and constant prayers were offered up, the King's physicians hastened his end by a series of horrifying treatments: they administered purges, emetics, and enemas, bled him frequently, forced him to sneeze, shaved his head to put blistering chemicals on his scalp, and even made him swallow a magical "Goa stone" taken from the stomach of a rare goat. In the midst of his funeral elegy, Dryden cannot resist poking fun at the incompetence of the doctors. He speaks of "The malice of their Art" and the "pious rigour" of their cures (ll. 177–78), metaphorically describing the disease as a fortress and the doctors as soldiers: "They min'd it near, they batter'd from a far / With all the Cannon of Med'cinal War" (ll. 169–70). Courteous and self-controlled to the end, the King bore his pain patiently and set his affairs in order. He begged his Queen's pardon for his many failures as a husband, asked his brother to look after his mistresses, and blessed his bastard sons (quietly omitting Monmouth, who was plotting in Holland). At the urging of the Duchess of Portsmouth and the Duke of York, he secretly took the last rites of the Roman Catholic Church from a Benedictine monk named Huddleston; despite the pleas of the Anglican bishops attending him, he then declined to take their sacrament.[56] At about noon on 6 February, the struggle was over. For Dryden, who had been brooding on mortality in recent months, and who had suffered another loss in the death of Roscommon in early January, the death of Charles was a powerful instance of the "frail Estate of Humane things, / And slippery hopes below" (ll. 399–400). In practical terms, it meant that the long-feared succession of the Catholic James, whom he had counted as his patron since the middle 1660s, would have to be praised and defended.

On the title page of his poem, Dryden stresses the continuity between the reigns, calling himself "Servant to his late Majesty, and to the Present King," and printing as his Latin epigraph the concluding lines of Virgil's story of Nisus and Euryalus, which he had translated a few months earlier:

Portrait of Charles II attributed to Thomas Hawker, ca. 1680.

> Oh happy pair! for if my verse can give
> Eternity; your fame shall ever live.
>
> [ll. 383–84]

When those stirring lines occur in the *Aeneid*, both heroes are dead, an ominous implication Dryden evidently trusts his readers to ignore, along with the homosexual attachment between Nisus and Euryalus. What he does want his readers to remember is the part of the story he had also used in the elegy for Oldham, the footrace in which the fallen Nisus helps his friend win by tripping Salius. By handing his keys and breeches to James, and by signing a document of dubious legality assigning his brother the profits of the Excise, Charles was tripping up Monmouth and William of Orange, the other racers pursuing the crown, and insuring the succession for which he had fought so vigorously. Since the story of Nisus and Euryalus emphasizes the fallen man's selfless concern for his successor, Dryden conflates it with the myth of Hercules taking the weight of the globe from Atlas, which emphasizes the strength of the man to whom power and burdens are passed:

> As if great *Atlas* from his Height
> Shou'd sink beneath his heavenly Weight,
> And, with a mighty Flaw, the flaming Wall
>   (As once it shall)
> Shou'd gape immense and rushing down, o'erwhelm this neather Ball;
> So swift and so surprizing was our Fear:
> Our *Atlas* fell indeed; But *Hercules* was near.
>
> [ll. 29–35][57]

A later reference to James as the infant Hercules connects the two classical allusions: "*Alcides* thus his race began, / O're Infancy he swiftly ran" (ll. 447–48).

The double emphasis on Charles and James, who were actually too different to accommodate the same metaphors, frequently forces Dryden into such conflation of images, including some less successful attempts to combine Christian and classical ideas. *Threnodia Augustalis* mourns for Charles, praises James, and betrays some of Dryden's own confusions at this time; his inability to maintain a consistent tone is a symptom of the strain. At the moment of his death, Charles is fervently praised for keeping the peace:

> That Peace which made thy Prosperous Reign to shine,
> That Peace thou leav'st to thy Imperial Line,
> That Peace, oh happy Shade, be ever Thine!
>
> [ll. 289–91]

But the successor must soon be praised for his military might, and all of Dryden's skill in modulation cannot suppress the contradiction. With this poem, he begins to use "Warlike" as a standard epithet for James,[58] but his lines in praise of the new King as military leader actually express the personal skepticism about arms we have noticed in his work from *The State of Innocence* on. Using imagery borrowed from the frost scene of his unperformed *King Arthur*, he pictures James thawing out his frozen kingdom:

> So *James* the drowsy *Genius* wakes
> Of *Britain* long entranc'd in Charms,
> Restiff and slumbring on its Arms:
> 'Tis rows'd, & with a new strung Nerve, the Spear already shakes.
> No Neighing of the Warriour Steeds,
> No Drum, or louder Trumpet needs
> T' inspire the Coward, warm the Cold,
> His Voice, his sole Appearance makes 'em bold.
>
> [ll. 470–77]

Portrait of James II by Sir Godfrey Kneller, 1684–85.

In the opera, however, the cold people insist that Love, not War, has both "warm'd" and "arm'd" them; at some level of Dryden's consciousness, the reuse of that imagery involved the same dark connection between sex and death that marks so many of the passages he chose to translate in *Sylvae*. In *Astraea Redux*, he had naively predicted that the British "Lyon" would "assail [his] forraign Foes" (l. 118), but the two disastrous Dutch wars had taught Charles the cost of such adventures. James was a much more appropriate monarch for the "Lyon" epithet, which Dryden uses for him throughout *The Hind and the Panther*, but at the moment of his succession, Dryden expresses the hope that the well-known "Vigour" of James's military "Arm" will make France and Holland afraid to "Provoke his lingring Sword" (ll. 479–82) and thus insure continued peace: "With broken Oaths his Fame he will not stain; / With Conquest basely bought, and with Inglorious gain" (ll. 489–90).

Here and elsewhere, Dryden praises James for scrupulously keeping his word, but that praise might in turn be construed as a covert criticism of Charles, whose promises were far from reliable. So, too, with the paradox of royal clemency. At the poem's mathematical center, Charles is called "That all forgiving King, / The type of him above" (ll. 257–58), but the climactic passage praising him for maintaining the succession draws on *Absalom and Achitophel* and *The Duke of Guise* to emphasize his toughness one more time:

> So much thy Foes thy manly Mind mistook,
> Who judg'd it by the Mildness of thy look:
> Like a well-temper'd Sword, it bent at will;
> But kept the Native toughness of the Steel.
>
> [ll. 323–26]

Not long after these lines were published, James told the French ambassador, Barillon, that he was eager to be crowned before his Parliament met, because after the coronation, "everything done or said against the King [would be] high treason."[59] He had more than enough "Native toughness," but his complete inability to bend was to prove his undoing. If the charming and flexible Charles was "a well-temper'd Sword" who "bent at will," the stolid and intolerant James was an "impenetrable Shield."

That last phrase comes from one of the most puzzling stanzas in this poem, in which Dryden, who had so often identified himself with Charles, attempts to transfer that identification to James:

> A Warlike Prince ascends the Regal State,
>   A Prince, long exercised by Fate:
> Long may he keep, tho he obtains it late.
> Heroes, in Heaven's peculiar Mold are cast,
> They and their Poets are not form'd in hast;
> Man was the first in God's design, and Man was made the last.
>   False Heroes, made by Flattery so,
> Heav'n can strike out, like Sparkles, at a blow;
> But e're a Prince is to Perfection brought,
> He costs Omnipotence a second thought.
>   With Toyl and Sweat,
>   With hardning Cold, and forming Heat,
>   The *Cyclops* did their strokes repeat,
> Before th' impenetrable Shield was wrought.
> It looks as if the Maker wou'd not own
>   The Noble work for his,
> Before 'twas try'd and found a Masterpiece.
>
> [ll. 429–45]

As he had in many other works, including the unperformed *Albion and Albanius*, Dryden emphasizes James's patience in the face of exile and adversity, but his imagery comes from his own poetic labors, and sounds a number of discordant notes. He had employed the metaphor of molding a few months earlier in his elegy for Oldham: "sure our Souls were near ally'd; and thine / Cast in the same Poetic mould with mine" (ll. 3–4). In the case of Oldham, the similarity was satiric talent; in the case of James, it seems to be slow development, an idea more applicable to Dryden than to the new King. If Dryden had died at thirty, he would have left behind three poems, whereas Oldham left behind a substantial book of *Remains in Verse and Prose*; but Dryden had used his years to good advantage, working his way through a number of genres and styles. The new King, by contrast, was indeed obtaining his throne late, but his stern military character had in fact been "form'd in hast": the Civil Wars had forced him to make adult decisions while a teenager, as Dryden notices a few lines later by comparing him to the infant Hercules. The inflexible James and his restless, changeable Laureate were actually cast in very different molds, as the last line of the triplet tacitly confesses: by alluding to Adam, Dryden falls back on the more obvious notion that both "Heroes" and "Poets" are men.

When he refers to "False Heroes, made by Flattery so . . . str[uck] out, like Sparkles at a blow," Dryden wants his readers to think of that much flattered "Sparkle" Monmouth, but Monmouth's supporters during the Exclusion Crisis had already accused the Laureate of making the Duke of York a false hero by flattery. In the second half of this stanza, Dryden is evidently thinking of himself as a poetic maker of heroes, like the Virgil of his epigraph, who hopes that his verses can give immortality. The colorful Virgilian scene to which these lines allude, in which the Cyclopes help Vulcan forge the shield of Aeneas, is a consequence of Vulcan's promise to Venus in the bedroom scene, which Dryden had translated for *Sylvae*; the climactic word "Masterpiece," here applied to the shield and thus to James, was one he had recently used for the first time to describe his own Horatian translation. The passive metaphor, in which both poet and king are slowly formed in a "peculiar Mold," thus blurs into a more active metaphor, in which the poet works hard to bring a "Noble work" to perfection. Dryden identifies himself with the "Toyl and Sweat" of the artisan Cyclopes, and thus ultimately with the heavenly "Maker," but as the contradictions and loose ends of this unsuccessful stanza show, he found it difficult to forge an attractive public image for the new ruler.

Among the most awkward passages are the lines on the grief of James, which insist that Charles's "Pious Brother" was "Guiltless of Greatness" (ll. 36, 45) when attending the dying King. Like the official medical report issued by Dr. Charles Scarbrugh, which also endorses the sincerity of York's distress, these lines were designed to counteract rumors that Charles had been poisoned,[60] but emphasizing the frequency and fervor of James's prayers meant reminding his subjects that the new King was a Roman Catholic, and several passages in this poem come closer to Catholicism than anything Dryden had written before. His account of the prayers for Charles, though abstracted by personification, depends upon the Catholic idea of intercession:

> Mercy above did hourly plead
> For her Resemblance here below;
> And mild Forgiveness intercede
> To stop the coming Blow.

[ll. 86–89]

A later address to Charles in Heaven treats him as a saint who may be invoked:

> Live blest Above, almost invok'd Below;
>   Live and receive this Pious Vow,
> Our Patron once, our Guardian Angel now.

[ll. 385–87]

The quibbling word "almost" reflects some caution on Dryden's part, but he was almost ready to embrace Catholicism himself, and his ambiguous prayer at the poem's end is certainly open to a Catholic reading:

> For once, O Heav'n, unfold thy Adamantine Book;
>   And let his wondring Senate see,
> If not thy firm Immutable Decree,
> At least the second Page, of strong contingency;
> Such as consists with wills, Originally free:
>   Let them, with glad amazement, look
>   On what their happiness may be:
> Let them not still be obstinately blind,
> Still to divert the Good thou hast design'd,
>   Or with Malignant penury,
> To sterve the Royal Vertues of his Mind.
> Faith is a Christian's, and a Subject's Test,
> Oh give them to believe, and they are surely blest!
> They do; and with a distant view I see
> Th' amended Vows of *English* Loyalty.

[ll. 491–505]

The reference to a "Test" and the hope for "amended Vows" reflect James's plan to ask the Parliament to cancel the Test Act barring Catholics from government employment,[61] but Dryden's new master could also read into these lines the more fantastic hope that England would revert to Rome, a hope he cherished despite his declaration that he had no intention of interfering with the Established Church.[62] The renewal of Dryden's warrant as Poet Laureate and Historiographer Royal on 27 April 1685, four days after the Coronation, mentions "the many good and acceptable services performed by him to our royal brother and our self," and one possible inference is that James had read and approved Dryden's latest poem. Still, there is no way of knowing whether James had a hand in this language, which may have been drawn up by the royal scriveners, and the actual grant of Privy Seal requested by this warrant was not issued until 9 March 1686; only then did Dryden begin to collect his salary.[63] Moreover, the poet did not receive a reward comparable to that given his longtime partner in Tory propaganda, the journalist Roger L'Estrange, whom James knighted in his bedchamber on 30 April 1685, remarking on the "particular satisfaction he had in his loyalty."[64]

Although the Treasury documents do not prove that the King took a personal interest in such details as the payment of the Laureate's salary, cynical readers have used them to argue that Dryden's conversion was motivated by money.[65] They might have found stronger evidence for such a view in *Threnodia Augustalis*, which betrays

Dryden's continuing worry about his debts. Even the solemn litany thanking Charles for his many virtues veers off into financial imagery:

> For all those Joys thy Restauration brought,
>   For all the Miracles it wrought,
> For all the healing Balm thy Mercy pour'd
>   Into the Nations bleeding Wound,
>   And Care that after kept it sound,
>
> . . . .
>
> For these and more, accept our Pious Praise;
>   'Tis all the Subsidy
>   The present Age can raise,
> The rest is charg'd on late Posterity.
>
> [ll. 292–96; 304–07]

When "Pious Praise" suddenly turns into a "Subsidy . . . charg'd on late Posterity," we are unavoidably reminded of Charles's financial struggles with his Parliaments, especially since the notion of "Praise" as a kind of "Pension" recurs in the oddly comic passage on the poets as birds (quoted above, p. 392), in which Dryden breaks the decorum of the elegy to complain about his "little Hire" and "light Gain" as Charles's Laureate. At the conclusion, the prayer that the new Parliament will eschew "Malignant penury" evidently reflects Dryden's knowledge that James planned to call a new Parliament and demand a substantial subsidy, as he successfully did in May; Dryden surely also hoped that a better subsidy for the King would produce more regular payment of his own salary, a hope partially fulfilled during the next several years.[66]

Financial considerations were unquestionably urgent for Dryden, who wrote these lines while his old friend Wycherley lay languishing in prison for debt, but before we label him a mercenary turncoat, we should consider how much he stood to lose by converting. Within days of his accession, James appointed Dryden's patron Rochester as Lord Treasurer; Rochester's return to power meant that real control of the Laureate's salary was in the hands of a rigorous Anglican, who sought permission to spend Easter of 1685 at his country estate rather than be seen in the procession accompanying the new King to Mass.[67] Devoted as he was to his sons, Dryden obviously realized that taking them with him into the Roman communion would have a disastrous effect on their educational careers by making them ineligible to take university degrees. He had also seen too many violent changes of power in his lifetime to imagine that the current ascendancy of Catholics would prove permanent. In May of 1685, his longtime enemy Titus Oates was convicted of perjury and whipped through the streets of London;[68] the prologue to *Albion and Albanius*, finally produced in June, takes notice of Oates's punishment, comparing satirical poets to the hangman Jack Ketch, who had the task of lashing Oates. But if Dryden took satisfaction in the punishment of the man he had verbally flagellated as Corah, the reversal of Oates's fortunes was also a reminder of how quickly saviors could turn into scapegoats. As a veteran of pamphlet warfare with plenty of enemies, Dryden knew that the least he could expect as a convert was a new wave of vitriolic attacks; in *The Hind and the Panther*, which was immediately subjected to such attacks, he listed "picque of honour to maintain a cause, / And shame of change, and fear of future ill" (III, 401–02) among the reasons why few Anglicans were willing to convert. Since he had eloquently maintained the cause of the Church of England in *Religio Laici*, he had particular reason to feel the "shame of change."

Yet despite these excellent reasons to keep silence about religious issues, Dryden allowed the imagery of Catholic devotion to seep through into *Threnodia Augustalis*, and the most logical way to account for this incaution is to conclude that he was already thinking seriously about "amending" his own religious "Vows." Enemies of Dryden, beginning in his own time, have delighted in describing his conversion as sheer opportunism, as if courage consisted only in clinging to the verities of one's childhood and schooling, not in bravely examining and rethinking one's beliefs, habits, styles, and critical principles. Readers of this biography, who have already watched Dryden moving restlessly from one point of view to another on so many of the central issues of his century, will recognize this view of his conversion as incomplete and bigoted. Ten years earlier, when he decided to abandon rhymed drama, he had before him the negative example of Settle, whose imitations of his own plays exposed the absurdity of couplet dialogue; the positive example of Milton, whose greatness he acknowledged despite political differences; and the personal conviction that rhyming was hampering the kind of psychological characterization and metaphorical complexity he wanted to achieve. In the case of this vastly more important decision, he was again motivated by negative examples: with writers like Shadwell claiming to represent Protestantism, Dryden was unlikely to write another "Protestant play," and such activities as translating *The History of the League* gave him an increasingly negative view of the Protestant ideology in which he had been reared. There were also powerful positive examples, not least the late King, with whom he had so often identified: rumors of Charles's deathbed conversion had begun to circulate by the time Dryden wrote his poem, and his later defence of the royal papers explaining that conversion suggests that he was in on the secret well before the publication of those papers early in 1686.[69] More important than either positive or negative examples, however, was Dryden's hard-earned personal conviction that Catholicism was the truth, reached at the end of a process of soul-searching stretching over at least four years. In praying that the Parliament would not "be obstinately blind," he was treating "Faith" as light, as he would do in the most memorable passages of *The Hind and the Panther*, and (more humbly) in a touching letter to his kinsman Mrs. Steward, written in 1699: "May God be pleasd to open your Eyes, as he has opend mine: Truth is but one; & they who have once heard of it, can plead no Excuse, if they do not embrace it" (*Letters*, p. 123).

No one will ever know just what combination of events opened Dryden's eyes or exactly when he embraced Catholicism as truth. His circle of acquaintances since the Restoration had included prominent Catholics, and works of Catholic controversy had frequently been on his desk during the last several years.[70] The accession of James probably increased his direct contact with apologists for Rome, including James Corker, newly released from prison, who eventually received him into the Roman Catholic Church. Like Charles II's final confessor Huddleston, Corker was a Benedictine; that order now took charge of the new Queen's chapel in St. James's palace, where the King sometimes attended Mass.[71] Dryden may already have been aware that Corker was the author of the *Memoirs* of his wife's beheaded cousin Lord Stafford, to whom I believe he alludes in *The Hind and the Panther*. On the first page of that poem, Dryden calls the English Catholic martyrs "a slaughtered army"

> whose vocal bloud arose,
> And cry'd for pardon on their perjur'd foes;
> Their fate was fruitfull, and the sanguin seed
> Endu'd with souls, encreas'd the sacred breed.
>
> [I, 15–18]

Stafford was a victim of the perjury of Titus Oates, and Dryden's conversion, which "encreas'd" the "sacred breed" of English Catholics, may have been among the fruits of his kinsman's fate. Later in 1687, when the poet wrote an ode for the marriage of Stafford's daughter Anastasia, he treated Stafford's martyrdom as a source of revelation:

> Now let the reasonable beast, call'd man;
>   Let those, who never truly scan
>   The effects of sacred Providence,
> But measure all by the grosse rules of sence;
> Let those look up and steer their sight,
>   By the great Stafford's light.
> The God that suffered him to suffer here,
> Rewards his race, and blesses them below,
> Their father's innocence and truth to show;
> To show he holds the blood of martyrs dear.
>
> [ll. 31–40]

In these lines, "great Stafford" takes the place of the light of revelation for which Dryden had been seeking in the opening lines of *Religio Laici*.

Dryden's immediate family may also have played a part. I have already reviewed the evidence suggesting that his wife was a "church-Papist," and one of the earliest satiric attacks on Dryden's conversion makes him say that one of his sons persuaded him to convert.[72] Charles, whose "vertuous & pious inclinations" Dryden had praised to Busby (*Letters*, p. 17), left Cambridge without taking a degree sometime during 1685, though there is no evidence to fix the exact date of his departure. John, Jr., was elected to Christ Church from Westminster in the spring of 1685, and would normally have matriculated in June; his failure to do so may be a sign that he had already become a Catholic, and some slender evidence suggests that he was placed under the private tutelage of the Catholic scholar Obadiah Walker in Oxford. Erasmus-Henry, who later became a Roman Catholic priest, left the Charterhouse on 2 November 1685; the Register describes him as "Elected to the University," but he did not attend either Oxford or Cambridge, going instead to the Catholic college at Douai in France.[73] The influence of one of his sons, whose ages in 1685 ranged from seventeen to nineteen, seems unlikely to have been an overwhelming factor in Dryden's conversion, but it need not be entirely discounted. He was a fond father, and a son's conversion might have proved at least a catalyst in his own decision.

Although he was surely turning these issues over in his mind, Dryden was publicly reticent: *Threnodia Augustalis* gives more evidence of his drift toward Catholicism than any of his later public utterances during 1685. The immediate problem he faced, along with Betterton and Grabu, was how to recoup the enormous investment already made in *Albion and Albanius*; reports circulating during the rehearsals had the United Company advancing £4,000 on the opera.[74] The elaborate machines on which this money had been spent, which must have been nearly ready when Charles died, included a version of a "celestial phenomenon" seen by a sea-captain at Calais in March of 1684, a "Poetical Hell" with "a great Arch of Fire," and a "Pedestal [on which] is drawn a Man with a long, lean, pale Face, . . . incompast by several Phanatical Rebellious Heads, who suck poyson from him which runs out of a Tap in his Side" (III, ii, s.d.). This grotesque caricature, an insult to the dead Shaftesbury, was obviously outdated when the opera finally came on stage,[75] but the allegorical style of the text as a whole made it a fairly simple matter to deal with the death of Charles by inserting some "twenty or thirty lines" dramatizing "the Apotheosis of *Albion*" (XV, 13). The show had to go on. Although the theatres reopened within six weeks of the King's death, the United Company delayed *Albion and Albanius* once again, waiting until the town was full for the meeting of the new Parliament (19 May–2 July). Dryden's epilogue, entirely devoted to praising James for his "Plain Dealing," is aimed at the legislators, who had been asked to award the King large revenues for life, with only his word as assurance that they might ever meet again.[76] The King was not alone in asking for money: Betterton doubled his prices for the opera, charging a guinea for the box seats, and Dryden had an edition of the libretto ready for sale at the time of the premiere, complete with a preface answering xenophobic criticism of fully sung operas by French composers; together with Grabu, Dryden also advertised an elegant second edition, with a full printed score, to be sold by subscription at the high price of one guinea.[77] Despite all this careful planning, the timing actually proved disastrous. The opera opened on 3 June; ten days and six performances later, news reached London that the Duke of Monmouth had landed in the West with an army.

When it began, Monmouth's invasion did not look much more real than Dryden's allegorical opera, whose run it spoiled. He had only eighty followers and four cannon when he landed at Lyme Regis, and had hired the three ships in which they came by pawning Henrietta Wentworth's jewels. The men he was able to collect from the western counties, perhaps 7,000 at the moment of greatest enthusiasm, were barely armed; at most one in three had a firearm. The King had been attentive to the state of the army and the militia in the months since his accession, and now received a grant of £400,000 from his Parliament for the purpose of putting down the rebellion. He marched the trained bands through the streets to terrify Monmouth's supporters in London, activated the militia in the West, and dispatched two crack regiments from his well-armed regular forces to head off the rebels. On the night of 5 July, Monmouth led his followers across Sedgemoor in the fog, hoping to surprise the encampment of regular troops at Weston Zoyland, but confusion, poor cavalry leadership by Lord Grey, and the superior discipline of the outnumbered regulars led to a disastrous rout, followed by a disorganized flight. Early on 8 July, a bearded, dirty, and exhausted Monmouth was found asleep in a ditch; a week later, he was beheaded on Tower Hill. Two years earlier, Jack Ketch had bungled the execution of Monmouth's friend Lord Russell, taking three or four blows to sever the head; he did even worse this time, taking no fewer than five. Nor was Monmouth the lone scapegoat: the "Bloody Assizes" held by Chief Justice Jeffries during the next several months sent hundreds of his followers to the gallows and the plantations.[78]

"Truth Has a Language To It Self"

Almost two years later, Dryden mentioned "*James* his late nocturnal Victory" in *The Hind and the Panther* (II, 655), but he published no immediate poetic celebration of Sedgemoor, no final comment on the career of his Absalom.[79] We may detect faint traces of his response to the rebellion in his next published poem, the Pindaric ode "To the Pious Memory Of . . . Anne Killigrew": Anne's "cruel *Destiny*" is personified as a celestial Jack Ketch, unwilling or unable "To finish all the Murder at a Blow" (ll. 154–55); the Last Judgment, in which she will appear as a "Sweet Saint," is called "the last Assizes" (ll. 182). But when the Killigrew ode moves beyond its immediate occasion, Dryden's attention is not primarily fixed on political issues; instead, the poem reflects his urgent interest in the morality of art, an interest rekindled by the example of Anne Killigrew herself.

"The Accomplisht Young LADY Mrs Anne Killigrew, Excellent in the two Sister-Arts of Poësie, and Painting," fell victim to smallpox on 16 June 1685.[80] Her father Henry, an old Royalist and sometime playwright, held the thankless post of Anglican chaplain to the Duke of York, and Anne was Maid of Honor to Maria Beatrice; her late uncle Thomas had been Dryden's theatrical associate, and the famous poet may thus have met the accomplished young lady, whose grieving relatives now decided to print her poems as a memorial. By the time he wrote his own poem, which adorns that slender volume, Dryden had certainly read through Anne's works, either in manuscript or in proof.[81] His poem asks the newly sainted Anne to hear "a Mortal Muse thy Praise rehearse, / In no Ignoble Verse; / But such as thy own voice did practise here" (ll. 16–18); the preface to *Sylvae* had called Pindarics a "noble sort of Poetry" (III, 18), and several of Anne's poems are in Pindarics. Dryden's professional opinion about the quality of her competent but conventional work comes through in his sly manipulation of the poem's shifting tone: his praise of her poetry and painting includes an undertone of patronising irony.[82] Still, something about the directness and innocence of Anne's work evidently moved him. I like to think the lines that brought him up short came from an ode called "The Discontent," in which Anne raises questions about the worth of fame, that false grail Dryden had pursued so long:

But, O, the Laurel'd Fool! that doats on Fame,
Whose Hope's Applause, whose Fear's to want a Name;
    Who can accept for Pay
    Of what he does, what others say;
Exposes now to hostile Arms his Breast,
To toylsome Study then betrays his Rest;
Now to his Soul denies a just Content,
Then forces on it what it does resent;
And all for the Praise of Fools: for such are those,
Which most of the Admiring Crowd compose.
O famisht Soul, which such Thin Food can feed!
O Wretched Labour crown'd with such a Meed![83]

The Laureate could hardly avoid applying these lines on "the Laurel'd Fool" to himself. For twenty-five years, he had been doting on fame, seeking applause by satisfying theatrical fashion, exposing himself in controversial pamphlets, and engaging in such "toylsome Study" as the translation of *The History of the League*. As the translations in *Sylvae* show, he had been unable to embrace the "just Content" of retirement, and his concern for "what others say" was among the reasons dissuading him from publicly acknowledging the religious conversion through which he was now passing. He might well have responded to this passage with anger, perhaps even by refusing to write a prefatory poem for a book containing lines many might read as criticism of his career, but instead, he took the criticism seriously. When he finally announced his conversion, he gave the Hind a speech urging those overly concerned with fame to sacrifice it to a higher cause:

If joyes hereafter must be purchas'd here
With loss of all that mortals hold so dear,
Then welcome infamy and publick shame,
And, last, a long farwell to worldly fame.
'Tis said with ease, but oh, how hardly try'd
By haughty souls to humane honour ty'd!
O sharp convulsive pangs of agonizing pride!
Down then thou rebell, never more to rise,
And what thou didst, and do'st so dearly prize,
That fame, that darling fame, make that thy sacrifice.

                  [*The Hind and the Panther*, III, 281–90]

These self-accusing lines are among the most powerful Dryden ever wrote. Although he indicts himself among the "haughty souls to humane honour ty'd," I believe his willingness to accept criticism from an amateur lady poet of only twenty-five helped lead him to the moment of hard-won humility recorded here. The only precedent for the tone of this passage comes in the Killigrew ode itself, where Dryden's contemplation of Anne's innocence leads him to accuse himself of profaning his art with fashionable obscenity:

O Gracious God! How far have we
Prophan'd thy Heav'nly Gift of Poesy?

> Made prostitute and profligate the Muse,
> Debas'd to each obscene and impious use,
> Whose Harmony was first ordain'd Above
> For Tongues of Angels, and for Hymns of Love?
>
> [ll. 56–61]

Coming as it does from a man who had defended the "alluring delicacy" of Lucretius and the "luscious *English*" of his own translations in a preface published less than a year earlier, this passage is surprisingly strenuous self-criticism. The notion that the blameless "*Vestal*" Anne can somehow "attone" for all the sins of the "lubrique and adult'rate age" is an extravagant conceit, but when Dryden concludes that "Her Wit was more than Man, her Innocence a Child!" (l. 70), he values childish innocence above the supposedly manly wit he had spent a lifetime acquiring. His response to Anne's "natural" poetry fits into a series of experiences in which he allowed himself to be instructed by much younger people. Her explicit discounting of "Art or Labour" at the opening of "The Discontent" would have reminded him of his own poem on the death of the young Oldham: "The ruggeder my Measures run when read," wrote Anne, "They'l livelier paint th' unequal Paths fond Mortals tread" (p. 51); in the elegy for Oldham, published one year earlier, Dryden had argued that "Wit will shine / Through the harsh cadence of a rugged line" (ll. 15–16). During the summer of 1685, he began a friendship with Francis Lockier, aged seventeen, who boldly corrected a literary pronouncement he made at Will's,[84] and he may have been engaged in religious discussions with one of his own teenaged sons. The Christian paradox of wisdom out of the mouths of babes had fascinated him ever since the elegy for Hastings, written in his own youth, in which he had praised the linguistic attainments of his classmate in a complex chiastic couplet:

> Nature gave him, a Childe, what Men in vain
> Oft strive, by Art though further'd, to obtain.
>
> [ll. 25–26]

In the Killigrew ode, another poem for a promising young victim of smallpox, the paradoxical assertion that childish innocence can surpass and atone for manly wit leads immediately to Dryden's finest passage on Nature and Art:

> Art she had none, yet wanted none:
> For Nature did that Want supply,
> So rich in Treasures of her Own,
> She might our boasted Stores defy:
> Such Noble vigour did her Verse adorn,
> That it seem'd borrow'd, where 'twas only born.
>
> [ll. 71–76]

His encounter with Anne's artless but morally impressive poems required Dryden to reconsider the premises of his literary career. The poet who had once scorned the inexperience of "some young Gallants, who pretend to Criticism" had to abandon the pride he naturally took in his age and experience; the man who had often used misogyny as a satiric weapon had to acknowledge that a woman's verses could have "Noble vigour."

Dryden's next task as an official propagandist, another chivalric defence of a dead woman's writings, involved a similar valuing of innocence and directness. Early in 1686, James published two brief statements written by his late brother Charles, giving arguments for his deathbed conversion; in the same pamphlet, he printed a similar statement by his first Duchess, Anne Hyde, who had died in 1671, not long after embracing Catholicism. The Anglican Establishment, already irritated by James's appointments of Catholic officers to the army and his attempts to abrogate the Test Act, could not let such a propaganda offensive pass in silence, and the able controversialist Edward Stillingfleet quickly published *An Answer to Some Papers Lately Printed*, attacking the substance and logic of the arguments made in the "Royal Papers." Dryden, who had been seen attending Mass in January of 1686, clearly had a hand in the court's anonymous counterattack, *A Defence of the Papers Written by the Late King of Blessed Memory, and Duchess of York*.[85] In the very first paragraph of his defense of the Duchess's paper, he praises Anne Hyde for her "Meekness, Devotion, and Sincerity," describing his personal response to reading her letter:

> I am sure I can say, for my own particular, that when I read it first in Manuscript, I could not but consider it as a Discourse extremely moving, plain, without Artifice, and discovering the Piety of the Soul from which it flow'd. Truth has a Language to it self, which 'tis impossible for Hypocrisie to imitate: Dissimulation could never write so warmly, nor with so much life. What less than the Spirit of Primitive Christianity could have dictated her Words? The loss of Friends, of worldly Honours, and Esteem, the Defamation of ill Tongues, and the Reproach of the Cross, all these, though not without the struglings of Flesh and Blood, were surmounted by her; as if the Saying of our Saviour were always sounding in her Ears, *What will it profit a man to gain the whole world, and lose his Soul!* [XVII, 291]

If we take this passage seriously, we may begin to understand how Dryden gathered the strength to bear the "Defamation of ill Tongues" that he knew would follow the news of his conversion. He was himself a master of "Artifice" and "Dissimulation"—indeed, as *The Vindication of the Duke of Guise* shows, he was not above "Hypocrisie." But the strenuous spiritual crisis through which he passed in the middle 1680s made him newly alert to the idea that plain discourse might be "extremely moving," that "Truth" might have "a Language to it self." The innocent prose of Anne Hyde, which he probably first read during the autumn of 1685, was thus a factor in his decision to make his conversion public, even at the cost of losing "Friends, . . . worldly Honours, and Esteem," just as the innocent poetry of Anne Killigrew, which he was studying during the same autumn, pointed him toward a severe examination of the uses to which he had put his own poetic talents. On the first page of *The Hind and the Panther*, he pictures the Catholic Hind as an artless female like the two Annes, "Without unspotted, innocent within, / She fear'd no danger, for she knew no sin" (I, 3–4). The beasts representing the other denominations glare at the Hind because they have not seen her properly:

> They had not time to take a steady sight.
> For truth has such a face and such a meen
> As to be lov'd needs only to be seen.

[I, 32–34]

Again, truth is represented as simple, immediate, intuitive, yet this long, complex, and uneven poem is a tissue of artifice, a baroque beast fable in which animals engage in sophisticated theological debate. Dryden could admire the artlessness of an Anne Killigrew or an Anne Hyde, but he had more than a trick of the old rage, and could not undertake a self-defense entirely expressed in russet yeas and honest kersey noes. Nonetheless, the confessional passages in this poem, most of them cast in the first-person singular, eschew even the thin protection offered by the habitual "we" of Dryden's earlier poetry.

"A Glorious Weight"

The title page of the *Defence* of the Royal Papers includes the phrase "By Command," and Dryden probably also spent some time during 1686 on another task mandated by the King, a translation of a history of religious revolutions by the Frenchman Antoine Varillas. That work never appeared in print, however, probably because a pamphlet by the Anglican clergyman Gilbert Burnet, who had read Varillas in French, exposed a number of factual errors in the original.[86] Once he got free of his official work on these prose tasks, the Laureate apparently went into a kind of hibernation, absenting himself from court and spending some months in the country: in a letter to Etherege of February 1687 he claimed to be "great in idleness—I have made my Court to the King once in seaven moneths, have seen my Lord Chamberlain [Mulgrave] full as often" (*Letters*, p. 26); and two different noble estates cherish traditions alleging that he wrote *The Hind and the Panther* in their gardens.[87] Like earlier trips to the country, this period of retirement was made possible by the Laureate's receiving money owed him by the Treasury: in July, some eight months before the letter to Etherege, he received a partial payment of his arrears from the reign of Charles and a warrant bringing his salary under the new reign nearly up to date—a total of over £575.[88] This long-awaited relief from financial worries was surely a factor in Dryden's decision to avoid the court, and the letter also mentions the place Charles Dryden had secured with Lord Middleton, one of the Secretaries of State; employment for his eldest son relieved the poet of another worry.

Under these circumstances, Dryden might have been expected to lie low, especially since his preface mentions periods of "ill health." At most, he might have continued his successful series of classical translations. His decision to write *The Hind and the Panther*, which made him vulnerable on all sides, is astonishing. The preface insists that the poem "was neither impos'd on me, nor so much as the Subject given me by any man" (III, 121), and since it includes considerable criticism of James's advisors and policies, I see no reason to doubt Dryden's claim. The increasingly aggressive policies of the King had evidently given the new convert cause for concern. Ignoring the advice of the cautious elderly Catholics on his Privy Council, men who had been imprisoned with Stafford during the Popish Plot, James was now attempting to implement the fantastic plans of the Jesuit Edward Petre, a self-important and ill-educated cleric who apparently believed the monarch could forcibly impose his religion upon the country. The Earl of Sunderland, whom Dryden had once praised for his moderation, was another supporter of these immoderate new policies, which forced such sober heads as Rochester out of the government. In his letter to Etherege, Dryden refers obliquely to the removal of Rochester, who left the Treasury in January of 1687 after James failed in an all-out attempt to convert him to Catholicism.[89] He also notices the King's cashiering of two prominent Protestants as part of his continuing campaign to appoint Catholic officers to the army, but does not mention the rumors that he might benefit from the King's policies himself by being appointed Master of an Oxford college.[90] If Dryden had been an opportunistic convert, we might expect to find him actively lobbying for such an appointment and supporting the King's dangerous posture. Instead, he avoided the court and took the side of the moderates. In the letter to Etherege, building on the imagery of idleness, he invokes the memory of Charles: "Oh that our Monarch wou'd encourage noble idleness by his own example, as he of blessed memory did before him for my minde misgives me, that he will not much advance his affaires by Stirring" (*Letters*, p. 27). He soon made those misgivings public: in Part III of *The Hind and the Panther*, the Hind tells the Panther that Anglican military officers ("Your Warrier Offspring") are "the most pleasing objects I can find," and says that if her prayers were heard, "*Caesar* should still have such, and such should still reward" (III, 93–94, 98–99); the Fable of the Swallows satirizes Father Petre and warns the poet's fellow-Catholics against overestimating their power and safety.

We have had frequent occasion to notice Dryden's skill in minimizing or papering over contradictions in his poetry; the many tasks he set himself in *The Hind and the Panther* placed a maximum demand on those skills. By characterizing the various denominations as animals—the Baptist Boar, the Presbyterian Wolf, the Anglican Panther, the Catholic Hind, and so forth—he gained the slight ironic distance characteristic of the beast fable tradition from Aesop on, but risked seeming to trivialize conflicts that mattered deeply to his contemporaries and himself. The baroque splendor to which the poem rises in its most elevated passages is almost always brought back to earth by reminders that the speakers have four feet. In the formal theological debate between the Hind and the Panther in Part II, Dryden had to mount arguments against the very positions he had established a few years earlier in *Religio Laici*; although he does so quite directly, at times nearly quoting his earlier lines, the force of the debate was surely undercut for readers aware that he had once made the opposite argument. In the more "occasional" and satiric Part III, he could not resist replying to personal attacks made on him by two Anglican clergymen: Edward Stillingfleet, his antagonist in the controversy over the Royal Papers, and Gilbert Burnet, who had irritated him by attacking the work of Varillas. Again, the problem is that of accommodating conflicting tones. Dryden attempts to dramatize that problem by having the Hind "discipline a son / Whose uncheck'd fury to revenge wou'd run" (III, 298), but the later lines caricaturing Burnet as an amorous Buzzard—"Broad back'd, and Brawny built for Loves delight, / A Prophet form'd, to make a female Proselyte" (III, 1145–46)—are evidence that the Hind's new son could not really check his satiric "fury." At the end of Part II, the Hind invites the Panther to her country cottage, promising "content of mind, the poor man's Wealth" (II, 659), but her poetic convert Dryden does not consistently embrace the Horatian ideal of "Contempt of wealth, and wilfull poverty" (II, 715). In Part III, he offers an angry reply to those who had already begun to accuse him of converting for monetary gain, and one passage may even glance at his failure to secure the Oxford post.[91] In tone and content, these sniping reflections of Dryden's personal concerns conflict with the intensely lyrical passages of personal confession in which he declares his doubts over and embraces "Good life" as his new "task" (I, 78).

Worse yet, political circumstances changed when the poem was nearly complete. As he explains in his preface, Dryden had designed the poem in part as an argument to persuade the Established Church to agree to a cancellation of the Test Act, but on 4 April 1687, James seized the initiative on that question as well, issuing a Declaration of Indulgence. If the Test Act had been cancelled with the approval of the Establishment, Anglicans and Catholics would have clubbed together to keep the Protestant Dissenters, Dryden's longtime enemies, suppressed. But by issuing the Declaration, James made a bid to ally Catholics and Dissenters against the Establishment, and the Dissenting sects were quick to thank him. Dryden evidently made some adjustments in his poem to reflect this change of policy, but *The Hind and the Panther*, unlike *Albion and Albanius*, could not easily be altered to accommodate new events, and many sections obviously pursue the original argument. One impressive passage on religious toleration describes persecution of "the mind" as "The worst . . . Of all the tyrannies of humane kind" (I, 240–41), but this modern-sounding idealism is quickly followed by a description of radical Dissenters as "A slimy-born and sun-begotten Tribe [of] gross, half-animated lumps" (I, 311, 314). Dryden may have hoped his royal master would be sufficiently pleased with a poem defending the doctrines of the Roman Catholic Church to ignore those inconsistencies, but he did not shrink from attempting to give the King advice: the cautionary Fable of the Swallows is a daring instance of his lifelong practice of mixing veiled criticism with panegyric. His decision to file a petition for the nearly £800 still owed him by the Treasury some three days before the publication of this poem may reflect the Laureate's hope that the King would be pleased; the failure of that petition may reflect James's displeasure at having his confessor Father Petre caricatured as a "Round belly'd . . . Dunce" (III, 464–65).[92]

For all these reasons, *The Hind and the Panther* as a whole is a fascinating, risk-taking failure; so, in my view, are *The Prelude, In Memoriam, Leaves of Grass*, and *Four Quartets*. If *The Hind and the Panther* is unlikely to attain the canonical status enjoyed by these later poems, it is nonetheless Dryden's longest and most complex original poem, and its best passages owe some of their power to the way they pick up and extend kinds of imagery he had been using for years. The poem begins as a catalogue of beasts, but hardly sixty lines have passed before a description of the heretical Fox launches Dryden on the first of his many digressions. Dependent upon his senses, the Fox is a type of the "rational" opponent of revelation; Dryden's highly personal answer, which will ultimately lead to a spirited defense of transubstantiation, combines two of his characteristic metaphorical patterns, the imagery of balance and the imagery of light:

> What weight of antient witness can prevail
> If private reason hold the publick scale?
> But gratious God, how well dost thou provide
> For erring judgments an unerring Guide?
> Thy throne is darkness in th' abyss of light,
> A blaze of glory that forbids the sight.
> O teach me to believe Thee thus conceal'd
> And search no farther than thy self reveal'd.
>
> [I, 62–69]

As far back as *The Conquest of Granada*, Dryden had complained that the "frail reason" of man was inevitably "over-pois'd and kick'd up in the Air, / While sence weighs down the Scale" (Pt. I; III, i, 59–61). Now the contest is between "private reason," itself seen as dependent on sense impressions, and the "antient witness" of an unerring Church. But the odd juxtaposition of the scale image with the imagery of light is a revealing instance of the method of the entire poem. Dryden does not offer a rational argument, a weight to tip the scales in favor of "antient witness"; instead, he appeals to a blazing, glorious revelation, praying that he may learn to believe in a concealed God whose brightness so confounds the senses that it appears as darkness.

Even in Part II, the formal debate on theological issues, a similar appeal to sublimity ultimately replaces argument. Dryden's plays had given him ample experience in writing taut dialogue, and the arguments he gives the Hind to use against the Panther's claims to authority are probably those he had used, in part, to convince himself.[93] But when the Panther challenges the Hind to produce a "living guide" for the "faithfull flock," her reply transcends the ordinary dialogue of debate:

> The Dame, who saw her fainting foe retir'd,
> With force renew'd, to victory aspir'd;
> (And looking upward to her kindred sky,
> As once our Saviour own'd his Deity,
> Pronounc'd his words—*she whom ye seek am I*.)
>
> [II, 394–98]

Argument now yields to the more literary techniques of allusion and metaphor: Dryden wants us to remember Christ's identifying himself to the mob seeking him in the Garden of Gethsemane, and his earlier revelation to the disciples that he was indeed the Messiah, and Aeneas's miraculous appearance out of a cloud in Carthage, which he later translated identically.[94] He wants us to be sufficiently moved to accept the application of all that Christian and classical typology to the Catholic Church without raising the obvious objection that some other church might also claim such authority.[95] Our pleasure in the complexity of Dryden's allusion, which is meant to make us accept his claim on faith, is thus the literary analogue to the blinding light of God's revelation.

The same pattern is repeated and expanded a few pages later, when the Hind chastizes the Panther for her unwillingness to lift the burden of infallibility:

> It then remains that church can onely be
> The guide, which owns unfailing certainty;
> Or else you slip your hold, and change your side,
> Relapsing for a necessary guide.
> But this annex'd condition of the crown,
> Immunity from errours, you disown,
> Here then you shrink, and lay your weak pretensions down.
> For petty royalties you raise debate;
> But this unfailing universal state
> You shun; nor dare succeed to such a glorious weight.
>
> [II, 483–92]

The notion of authority as a heavy "condition of the crown" will remind us of *Threnodia Augustalis*, where James as Hercules stands ready to lift the globe from Charles as Atlas. In this poem, however, the myth of weightlifting is Christian, not classical, and the symbolic burden lifted transcends mere politics. In a highly dramatic scene, the Hind compares the Church's willingness to bear the weighty responsibility of infallibility with Christ's willingness to bear the sins of the world:

> So when of old th' Almighty father sate
> In Council, to redeem our ruin'd state,
> Millions of millions at a distance round,
> Silent the sacred Consistory crown'd,
> To hear what mercy mixt with justice could propound.
> All prompt with eager pity, to fulfill
> The full extent of their Creatour's will:
> But when the stern conditions were declar'd,
> A mournfull whisper through the host was heard,
> And the whole hierarchy with heads hung down
> Submissively declin'd the pondrous proffer'd crown.
> Then, not till then, th' eternal Son from high
> Rose in the strength of all the Deity;
> Stood forth t' accept the terms, and underwent
> A weight which all the frame of heav'n had bent,
> Nor he Himself cou'd bear, but as omnipotent.
>
> [II, 499–514]

Again, the power of the poetry is meant to make us willing to accept the analogy between Christ and the Catholic Church, but the language is of course a pastiche of phrases from Milton, a poet inveterately opposed to Catholicism. As several other passages suggest, Dryden probably took a sly pleasure in using materials drawn from Protestant poetry and polemic for his own Catholic purposes.[96] The confidence and ease with which he appropriates the Miltonic sublime to rhymed couplets may remind us that he had also used the imagery of weightlifting in literary controversy, mocking aristocratic amateurs for their inability to "raise the weight of such an Author" as Horace and taking pride in his own professional "Sinews." In the epilogue to *Oedipus*, he had called that tragic story "A weight that bent ev'n *Seneca*'s strong Muse" (l. 5), and this Miltonic passage ends with an echo of that witty epilogue. The success of the analogy between a Church that lifts the burden of infallibility and a Saviour who lifts the burden of the world's sin thus depends upon a Catholic poet's ability to lift the "glorious weight" of a great Protestant predecessor.

In Milton's version, the angels greet the Son's acceptance of the task of redeeming mankind with a shout of joy and a hymn to God as the "Fountain of Light, thyself invisible / Amidst the glorious brightness where thou sit'st" (*Paradise Lost*, III, 375–76)—language that brings us back to Dryden's description of God's throne as "darkness in the abyss of light." Dryden had used the imagery of light with telling effect in numerous previous works, perhaps most memorably in the opening of *Religio Laici*, where reason, "Dim as the borrow'd beams of Moon and Stars," "*dissolves* in [the] *Supernatural Light*" of religious revelation (ll. 1, 11). In *The Hind and the Panther*, he applies that metaphor to the Anglican Church, which shines by virtue of borrowed beams:

> Then, as the Moon who first receives the light
> By which she makes our nether regions bright,
> So might she shine, reflecting from afar
> The rays she borrow'd from a better star:
> Big with the beams which from her mother flow
> And reigning o'er the rising tides below.
>
> [II, 501–06]

The faint hint of sexuality in "nether regions" and "rising tides below" is explicit when the Panther is described as "the mistress of a monarch's bed" (II, 393). The Hind, by contrast, is the legitimate Bride of Christ, adorned with "heav'nly rays"; she is "one solid shining Diamond, / Not sparkles shatter'd into sects like you" (II, 517, 527–28). These images of light come immediately after the description of the Son's lifting up the weight of the world's sin, and precede the Hind's gloating triumph, which returns to the scale image. Until the Panther can "prove [her] faith Apostolick," argues the Hind, her "weights will in the balance fail: / A church unprincipl'd kicks up the scale" (II, 623–24). Yet the proof of this claim to unique legitimacy is not a weighty factual argument, but a spiritual sign, again expressed as light:

> Thus, while with heav'nly charity she spoke,
> A streaming blaze the silent shadows broke:
> Shot from the skyes a chearfull azure light;
> The birds obscene to forests wing'd their flight
> And gaping graves receiv'd the wandring guilty spright.
>
> [II, 649–53]

If the Panther fails to accept this heavenly sign as proof of the Hind's authority, the reader is meant to be so dazzled by the beauty of the poetry that he will accept not only the claims of the symbolic Hind but the poet's immediately ensuing claims for an earthly King:

> Such were the pleasing triumphs of the sky
> For *James* his late nocturnal victory;
> The pledge of his Almighty patron's love,
> The fire-works which his angel made above.
> I saw my self the lambent easie light
> Guild the brown horrour and dispell the night.
>
> [II, 654–59]

Although Dryden's contemporaries were attentive to comets and other celestial omens, no other witness reports any such phenomenon on the night of Sedgemoor. The "lambent easie light" the poet claims to have seen himself is as much an invention as the "streaming blaze" within the beast fable.[97]

The complexity of all of Dryden's inventions in this poem should stand as a powerful counterargument to those critics who still describe his work as a "poetry of statement," posited upon the "neoclassical" principle of holding a mirror up to nature. The light that illuminates this poem is the light of Dryden's creative imagination, but when he applied the imagery of light to himself, early in the poem, he recognized the ease with which he could be blinded by brilliance, including his own poetic brilliance:

> My thoughtless youth was wing'd with vain desires,
> My manhood, long misled by wandring fires,
> Follow'd false lights; and when their glimps was gone,
> My pride struck out new sparkles of her own.
> Such was I, such by nature still I am,
> Be thine the glory, and be mine the shame.
>
> [I, 72–77]

Again, we may trace particular memories in these lines. Two years earlier, thinking of Monmouth, Dryden had described the "False Heroes made by Flattery so, / [whom] Heav'n can strike out, like Sparkles, at a blow" (*Threnodia Augustalis*, ll. 435–36). Now he applied the same imagery of casual creation to his own considerable pride as a poet, pride he retained "by nature" and revealed in this very poem, but for which he now sometimes felt "shame." Stimulated by the spiritual turmoil of his own conversion and challenged by the daunting task of defending that conversion while criticizing the policies of his Catholic King, Dryden responded by cramming his poem with fables within fables, metaphors within metaphors. Consequently, the poem is not "one solid shining Diamond," but a series of "sparkles," and readers beginning in Dryden's own time have been so confused by the various angles of light that they have ultimately found the poem obscure.[98] Dryden must bear some of the blame for the long history of misreadings this difficult poem has endured, but his failure to control and unify his poem was an inevitable consequence of trying to do too many things at once. Noticing an analogous failure of metrical control in his friend Oldham's "rugged line[s]," he called it "A noble Error, and but seldom made, / When Poets are by too much force betray'd" (ll. 17–18). In *The Hind and the Panther*, he was betrayed by too many inventions, too many styles, too many conflicting purposes.

CHAPTER TWELVE

"The Lab'ring Bee, When his Sharp Sting is Gone" 1687–1694

"This Crumbling Pageant"

If *The Hind and the Panther* itself does not display the calm resolution Dryden now associated with religious certitude, his disciplined refusal to respond to the many attacks on the poem is impressive. Matthew Prior and Charles Montagu, two young wits from Westminster and Cambridge, struck the most telling blow in July of 1687, with *The Hind and the Panther Transvers'd to the Story of the Country-Mouse and the City-Mouse*, an intermittently funny burlesque drawing on *The Rehearsal* and the well-known Horatian beast fable of the two mice. Dryden's friend Francis Lockier remembered him weeping over that pamphlet, exclaiming at the cruelty of "two young fellows that I have always been very civil to" and calling himself "an old man in misfortunes."[1] Nonetheless, Dryden refrained from replying to this squib, or to any of the six printed attacks on him that appeared in the summer and autumn of 1687, which repeated many old charges and invented a few unpleasant new ones.[2] Even Gerard Langbaine's *New Catalogue of English Plays*, which ignores Dryden's religion and politics, but accuses him of whole-sale plagiarism, went unanswered, though Langbaine later blamed Dryden for con-cocting the spurious title page under which his book first appeared.[3] Dryden's restraint in the face of all this abuse may indicate how seriously he took the ideas he had expressed by having the Hind pray for her vengeful son:

> Instruct him better, gracious God, to know,
> As thine is vengeance, so forgiveness too.
> That suff'ring from ill tongues he bears no more
> Than what his Sovereign bears, and what his Saviour bore.
>
> [III, 302–05]

In the cases of Prior and Montagu, Dryden's willingness to forgive led to partial reconciliations, though both men served in the governments of William III: Prior wrote a prologue for a performance of Dryden's *Cleomenes* at Westminster School in 1695, and Montagu was among the old poet's most important patrons in the later 1690s.[4]

Dryden's next public utterance was "A Song for St. Cecilia's Day, 1687," first performed on 22 November to an elaborate setting by Giovanni Baptista Draghi, the Queen's favorite composer. Beginning in 1683, a musical society had commissioned a poet and a composer to collaborate on an ode for this feast: Henry Purcell set a text by Christopher Fishbourne for 1683; John Blow set a text by Oldham for 1684; and William Turner, more famous as a countertenor than as a composer, set a text by Tate for 1685. There was no festival in 1686, but the piece produced by Dryden and Draghi for 1687 was elaborate and expensive. The poem, with its references to the "TRUM-PETS loud Clangor" and the "soft complaining FLUTE," virtually forced the composer to use wind instruments, and the writing for voices and orchestra is dense and complex: Draghi wrote particularly difficult solos for the countertenor Turner and a prodigious bass named Gostling.[5] Not to be outdone, Dryden focused his attention on a display of virtuosity in the poetry, packing an astonishing number of cunning meta-phorical and mathematical symmetries into a lyric so musical in itself that any setting seems almost unnecessary.[6]

With the attacks on his conversion swirling about him, political and religious concerns may have been in Dryden's mind when he wrote this song, but if they were, he sublimated them into the universal and abstract tension between harmony and discord. The poem opens with the ordering of the "jarring Atomes" of chaos by a "tuneful Voice"; this vision of creation as harmony and order, ultimately drawn from the *Timaeus* of Plato, contrasts strongly with the picture of a creator-blacksmith striking out his creatures as "sparkles," which Dryden had used in both *Threnodia Augustalis* and *The Hind and the Panther*. But the vision of harmonious creation is temporary: the passions that music can "raise and quell," which occupy the central stanzas, include "Shrill Notes of Anger," "the Woes of hopeless Lovers," "jealous Pangs, and Despera-tion, / Fury, frantick Indignation." Dryden connects these stylized passions with spe-cific instruments, but the recent attacks on his faith and integrity had certainly re-minded him that people could express "frantick Indignation" in shrill prose and verse. The closing chorus describing the apocalypse, when "the last and dreadful hour / This crumbling Pageant shall devour," returns to a scene Dryden had imagined in both *Threnodia Augustalis* and the Killigrew ode; this particular vision of the end, when "MUSICK shall untune the Sky," may also owe something to his observation of the political disharmony that was untuning the reign of James, a pageant that would crum-ble within the next year.

The private ode Dryden wrote for the marriage of Anastasia Stafford in December of 1687, addressed to his wife's Catholic cousins, might again have provided him an opportunity for some specific riposte to his opponents or some gentle allusion to public policies, but its tone is also elevated and mystical.[7] Like the St. Cecilia ode, this poem celebrates a saint's day, in this case the festival of the martyred St. Anastasia, namesake of the bride. The description of "a spring, in midst of winter" (l. 9) reaches all the way back to the imagery of the Jonsonian masque (see above, p. 51); the next line, in which "the cold seasons leap into a youthfull dance," repeats a crucial verb from the St. Cecilia ode, where "cold, and hot, and moist, and dry, / In order to their stations leap" (ll. 8–9). In one case, the Aristotelian elements leap into proper hierarchical order; in the other, a miracle allows the seasons to leap over their ordinary order, with blissful results.

Such visions of order and miracle, as Dryden surely knew, were far removed from the ongoing events of James's troubled reign. On 11 November 1687, just eleven days before the performance of the St. Cecilia ode, Father Petre was sworn to the Privy Council, an action that enraged not only the Church of England men remaining in the government, but the moderate Catholics with whom Dryden had allied himself.[8] During the same month, James began a well-organized campaign to insure that the Parliament he intended to call in October of 1688 would consist of men willing to repeal the Test Acts,[9] and by the beginning of December, the Queen's pregnancy was common knowledge. Maria had miscarried in 1683 and 1684, and all five of her previous children had died in infancy, but any pregnancy opened the possibility that she might bear a son, a prince who would take precedence over James's Protestant daughters and assure a continued Catholic monarchy. This possibility naturally terrified the leaders of the Established Church, who were already distressed by James's aggressive program to replace placeholders in the military and the judiciary with Catholics whenever he could. The King, however, began the New Year by proclaiming a day of thanksgiving for his consort's pregnancy and prayers for a Prince of Wales, prayers few Anglicans could make sincerely. He also forced Magdalen College at Oxford to accept a new group of Catholic Fellows, including John Dryden, Jr.[10]

If we attempt to reconstruct Dryden's feelings about this appointment, we may sense the conflict in which he found himself: he was surely pleased that his son had gained a comfortable place at Oxford, particularly if he had hoped to become Master of All Souls or Magdalen himself the previous year; but his satisfaction was just as surely tempered by his fear that the King's tactics were antagonizing his Tory supporters, as his praise of Charles II's "noble idleness" in the letter to Etherege suggests. Dryden probably had similar emotions at the end of January 1688, when his friend Father Corker had an audience with the King dressed in his Benedictine habit.[11] Although this symbolic act was a less serious threat to the power of the Anglican Church than the attempt to redesign the Fellowship of Magdalen, which struck at an important training ground for clergymen, the Anglican leaders had to be distressed by the appearance at court of a Catholic cleric in his robes. They also deplored the continued spate of Catholic publications, including the large project on which Dryden was now working, a translation of a life of the Jesuit St. Francis Xavier by the Jesuit Dominique Bouhours. As a convert who had prayed for the faith and humility to accept miracles, Dryden may have found the life of St. Francis a moving document, but as an enemy of Father Petre and the Jesuit faction, he probably realized that he was being asked to serve propaganda purposes with which he was not entirely in sympathy. The royal command to translate this massive life evidently had something to do with the Queen's pregnancy; Dryden's dedication to Maria, published shortly after the birth of her son on 10 June 1688, comments on the efficacy of prayers to St. Francis by the barren Anne of Austria, mother of Louis XIV.[12]

Even before the birth of the Prince, the Anglican bishops were ready to fight back. In April of 1688, James ordered his Second Declaration of Indulgence read in every church in the nation; he was genuinely surprised when William Sancroft, Archbishop of Canterbury, and six other bishops refused to read it. On 18 May, the seven bishops submitted a petition asking that they be excused from reading the Declaration, igniting a contest of wills that gave the growing opposition to James a unifying cause. Alert to the value of public drama, the bishops refused to give recognizances, leaving James with no choice but to send them to the Tower;[13] their trial in late June was the most important test of royal authority since the trial of Shaftesbury in 1681. Both the release of the bishops on bail (15 June) and their acquittal by the jury (29 June) set off "mighty rejoyceing, in ringing of bells, discharging of gunns, lighting of candles, and bonefires in several places."[14] These celebrations of the King's defeat by the defiant bishops, as Evelyn remarks, were "taken very ill at Court," as was "the appearance of neere 60 Earles & Lords &c upon the bench [at the trial] in honor of the Bishops."[15] Both the City Protestants who lit fires in the streets and the "Earles & Lords" who publicly lent their support to the bishops were dramatizing their resistance to James's attempt to impose his will; the accidental but potent juxtaposition of the birth of the Prince and the trial of the bishops gave special intensity to both kinds of demonstration, especially since the court had organized similar bonfires on the birthday of the Prince (10 June) and the official day of thanksgiving for his birth (17 June).

In the midst of this month of unrest, on 23 June, Dryden dutifully issued his poem on the birth of the Prince, *Britannia Rediviva*. Like *Astraea Redux*, which it resembles in its old-fashioned "Metaphysical" imagery and its Virgilian epigraph, this poem makes ambiguous use of the first person plural, beginning with the claim that "we" have been fervently praying for a successor:

> Our Vows are heard betimes! and Heaven takes care
> To grant, before we can conclude the Pray'r:
> Preventing Angels met it half the way,
> And sent us back to Praise, who came to Pray.
>
> [ll. 1–4]

Although the "we" refers most obviously to the English Catholics, it is another gesture of inclusion, expressing the hope that the nation might be united by the settling of the succession, but despite official orders mandating prayers for a Prince, and official fireworks in celebration, many people considered the birth a cause for criticism, not praise. The immediate and persistent rumors claiming that the baby had been smuggled into the palace in a warming pan were a way of expressing Protestant frustration at the prospect of a Catholic succession; when Dryden takes notice of those rumors, he attributes them to "Fiends" and answers them by appealing to the Christian typology of the Incarnation and the Virgilian revelation of Aeneas to Dido, a potent combination he had already employed at the climax of *The Hind and the Panther* (see above, p. 424):

> Fain would the Fiends have made a dubious birth,
> Loth to confess the Godhead cloath'd in Earth.
> But sickned after all their baffled lyes,
> To find an Heir apparent of the Skyes:
> Abandoned to despair, still may they grudge,
> And owning not the Saviour, prove the Judge.
>   Not Great *Aeneas* stood in plainer Day,
> When, the dark mantling Mist dissolv'd away,
> He to the *Tyrians* shew'd his sudden face,
> Shining with all his Goddess Mother's Grace:
> For she her self had made his Count'nance bright,
> Breath'd honour on his eyes, and her own Purple Light.
>
> [ll. 122–33]

At this point the presumably loyal "we" who prayed for the Prince's birth and the presumably Whiggish "Fiends" who cast doubt on its authenticity are in contrast, but in the compressed history of seventeenth-century England that follows, the "we" is the nation as a whole, including all factions:

> Enough of Ills our dire Rebellion wrought,
> When, to the Dregs, we drank the bitter draught;
> Then airy Atoms did in Plagues conspire,
> Nor did th' Avenging Angel yet retire,
> But purg'd our still encreasing Crimes with Fire.
> The perjur'd Plots, the still impending Test,
> And worse; but Charity conceals the Rest.
>
> [ll. 152–58]

As any reader in 1688 would have realized, the rhetorical claim to be concealing "the Rest" out of "Charity" is Dryden's way of glancing at the long opposition to James's succession, and the continuing opposition to his rule. The collective gesture ("*our* still encreasing Crimes") is another of his characteristic first person plurals; as usual, it includes the first-person singular. Not only had Dryden served the Cromwellian government resulting from the "dire Rebellion," as his enemies never tired of reminding him, but the moral failings he attributes to the nation at large were ones to which he had recently confessed himself susceptible:

> Our Manners, as Religion were a Dream,
> Were such as teach the Nations to *Blaspheme*.
> In Lusts we wallow, and with Pride we swell,
> And Injuries, with Injuries repell;
> Prompt to Revenge, not daring to forgive,
> Our Lives unteach the Doctrine we believe.
>
> [ll. 279–84]

There speaks the man who had admitted knowing about "the Jilting Harlot . . . by sad Experience," who had spoken of his "vain desires" and his "pride" as causes for "shame," and who was now struggling to overcome his instinctive need to repel injuries with injuries.

By including himself among the "we" who fail to achieve the Christian ideal of forgiveness, Dryden gains a moral perspective from which to criticize the attacks aimed at the court by the Anglican clergy; he also bravely glances at the vindictive nature of the King. After applying all the appropriate kinds of typology to the Prince, he addresses a gallant stanza to the "Propitious Queen" and concludes with a prophetic warning to the "Great Monarch." As usual, he gives advice under the pretext of praise, informing James that "Justice, is your Darling Attribute" (l. 334). The many Protestants purged from their offices during the last year would not have agreed, and as Dryden develops this idea, he warns the King against "boundless pow'r, and arbitrary Lust" (l. 341). This passage is not only excellent political advice, but an echo of the earlier inclusive confession: "In Lusts we wallow, and with Pride we swell." Like his people and his poet, the King is a Christian who will inevitably fail to achieve the ideals of his faith. On a political level, Dryden advises moderation, ending the poem with the conventional image of "Ballance"; on a moral level, he reminds a king who was all too fond of his status as a sacred monarch that "Resistless Force and Immortality / Make but a Lame, imperfect Deity" (ll. 349–50).

"This Farce of Government"

In fact, James's gestures toward acts of force were far from "Resistless"; he was no Elizabeth. But his enemies were ready to interpret his attempts to give his fellow Catholics even a small share of power and privilege as arbitrary and outrageous, and within a few months, he had become a lame monarch indeed. A few days after the publication of Dryden's poem, the slippery Sunderland, now the King's principal advisor, declared himself a Roman Catholic. Within a week, the Bishop of London, the Earl of Danby, and members of the powerful Russell and Sidney families wrote to William of Orange, inviting him to come to England with an army. James obtusely refused to recognize that his son-in-law was preparing for an invasion until late September, and finally responded by adding Irish Catholic troops to his army, a policy that irritated many officers who had previously supported him. He then made a belated and unconvincing attempt to conciliate his people, abandoning his plan for a new Parliament, dismissing the hated Sunderland, and restoring many excluded officeholders to their places, including the old Anglican Fellows of Magdalen College.[16] John Dryden, Jr., removed from his Fellowship there on 25 October 1688, surfaced on 12 November as a second lieutenant in a Catholic army regiment commanded by his cousin Henry Howard, Earl of Stafford, brother to the Anastasia whose marriage his father had celebrated a year earlier.[17] But this regiment, organized a week after William landed at Torbay, never saw action, as wholesale desertions and uncertain leadership soon rendered James's army incapable of putting up a serious military resistance. London was already in a state of anarchy: on 11 November, for example, "the rabble assembled in a tumultuous manner at St. John's Clerkenwell, the popish monastery" headed by Dryden's friend Father Corker, "on a report of gridirons, spits, great cauldrons, &c. to destroy protestants."[18] This riot was but one of many attacks on Catholic chapels over the next six weeks, during which James fled the capital and William arrived there. On 23

December, King James left England for the last time; the Stuart dynasty Dryden had praised and defended for twenty-eight years was over.

Acting on motives like those of the mobs in the streets, Dryden's literary enemies took the occasion to treat him as a vulnerable target. Sometime during the troubled autumn of 1688, Tom Brown published his effective pamphlet, *The Reasons of Mr. Bays Changing his Religion*, which scores a number of palpable hits on Dryden's various inconsistencies; Brown had a sequel ready for publication before the Revolution.[19] On 5 November, an anonymous poet writing from Exeter taunted Dryden with his failure to rally to the cause of William, whose march toward London had reached that city; this obscure poem begins by contrasting Dryden's wit, which the poet says "has catterwauld too long," with "Lilliburlero," the catchy ballad against the Irish soldiers that was now "the only song."[20] By the end of January, the Commons had voted a resolution to the effect that James's departure was an abdication, leaving the throne vacant; this subterfuge was designed to give the color of legality to the much desired but obviously illegal succession of William and Mary. Before that succession had actually taken place, another anonymous poet had supplied a bogus *Address of John Dryden, Laureat to . . . the Prince of Orange.*[21]

The fictional Dryden of this ephemeral squib is ready to change his faith once more to keep his job, but the real Dryden did not seriously consider taking such an action. In a cancelled passage from the dedication to *King Arthur* (1691), he describes William's administration as "A Government which has hitherto protected me (and by a particular Favour wou'd have continued me what I was, if I could have comply'd with the Termes which were offered me)."[22] His old friend and patron Dorset became William's Lord Chamberlain on 13 February 1689, and we may easily imagine Dorset offering to keep Dryden in office if the poet would relinquish his new faith. We may just as easily understand why Dryden had to refuse those terms. He had warned James against the advisors and policies that cost him his crown, but he had also served James loyally, most recently in celebrating the birth of the Prince of Wales and translating the voluminous *Life of St. Francis Xavier*. His enemies were more alert to his role as apologist for the regime than to the way he used official occasions to offer unheeded advice, and the satiric attacks of the last several months had all snickered at his previous inconsistencies; one more change of faith would have rendered him ridiculous. Moreover, as Dryden's life and writings during his last decade would show, his conversion to Rome was not the mere convenience his antagonists made it out to be, but the end of a long and serious spiritual journey. He had now spent roughly three years living the life of an urban Catholic, joining with his wife and sons in following the yearly cycle of feast days, each prepared for by a period of fasting and marked by confession and communion.[23] Dryden's fondness for the rhythms of that old calendar shows in his poems on the marriage of Anastasia Stafford and the birth of the Prince, both of which conflate seasonal imagery with the specifically Catholic imagery of Church festivals. In *Britannia Rediviva*, the transition from the "bloomy beauties" of "Departing Spring" to the "timely Fruit" of "manly summer" is the feast of Pentecost, a "solemn Sabbath" that "saw the Church attend; / The Paraclete in fiery Pomp descend" (ll. 12–20).

The Revolution spelled an end to such "Pomp" for Catholics, as illegal Masses in private dwellings replaced the colorful services at St. James's and elsewhere available under a Catholic King. Several other prominent converts did reconvert,[24] but Dryden was unwilling to abandon the faith he had embraced at so much cost and could not therefore comply with Dorset's terms. On 9 March 1689, a warrant was issued for the appointment of his old antagonist Shadwell to the post of Poet Laureate. The nonpartisan patron Dorset, who had given Shadwell financial support when Dryden was in office, evidently softened the blow by giving Dryden a "most bountiful Present." In the "Discourse concerning the Original and Progress of Satire" (1692), Dryden says that Dorset's gift arrived "at that time, when I was most in want of it" (IV, 23), and he was certainly short of money by the time he was replaced as Laureate: the last quarterly payment of his salary had come in July of 1688.[25]

Portrait of Charles Sackville, Earl of Dorset, from the studio of Sir Godfrey Kneller, 1694.

In these frightening early months of 1689, the loss of his salary was by no means Dryden's worst fear. The Catholic scholar Obadiah Walker, who may have been John Jr.'s tutor at Oxford, was sent to the Tower in early January; all Catholics had reason to feel endangered. "An order to banish papists 10 miles from London" was among the actions taken when the Prince of Orange convened "a great meeting of the lords spiritual and temporal at Westminster" on 22 December 1688, the day before the old King's departure.[26] Dryden was technically safe from the immediate effects of this order, which excepted "such as have been housekeepers within 10 miles for 3 years past," but the authorities soon began making lists of those Papists who had been in their present parishes for less than three years. Surveying the parish of St. Anne, Soho in March of 1689, they recorded the presence of one "Wm Dayton Housekeeper, a Poet in Gerrard Street, having two sons, both of his own religion, and his wife."[27] This man was almost certainly Dryden, who moved from the house in Longacre where he had lived for nineteen years to a new house in Gerrard Street sometime after Easter of 1687, quite possibly during this troubled winter. If he did move as late as the winter of 1688–89, Dryden may have been motivated by the prospect that the taxes of Catholics would be doubled: under those circumstances, a smaller house with a lower assessment was a desirable economy.[28]

The "two sons" now at home were probably Charles and John. As a Papist, Charles quickly lost his government post with the Earl of Middleton, who remained loyal to James and joined his exiled monarch in France in 1692; John Jr.'s short-lived army commission had evaporated even more quickly than his Oxford fellowship. Dryden's loss of income was thus compounded by the fact that two previously self-supporting sons were now newly unemployed. The youngest son, Erasmus-Henry, was probably now at Douai studying for the Catholic priesthood: under the protection of his mother's kinsman Cardinal Howard, he entered the English College at Rome on [15]/25 October 1690; early in 1691, he moved on to the Dominican monastery at Florence, where he spent two years passing through the normal stages of preparation for ordination. Charles and John were also in Italy by 1692; an attack on their father published in 1690 places Charles in Rome as early as 1687, but this is probably a fiction.[29]

In the volatile atmosphere of the Revolution, the Drydens' decision to move might even have been based on the fear of physical attack; Soho at this time was a new suburb, where a poet hoping to lie low might temporarily avoid his enemies, and I wonder whether the bungling of Dryden's name by the constables resulted from deliberate misinformation given by the poet or his family. But if Dryden was trying to hide in the early months of 1689, his fears were quieted by the end of the year: the prologue to his tragedy *Don Sebastian*, spoken publicly in December of 1689, makes open references to the playwright's losing his pension and paying the double taxes imposed on Papists; Dryden would hardly have called these matters to public attention if he feared further reprisals from the government. The printed play appeared in January of 1690, published by Joseph Hindmarsh, who was later harassed for publishing Jacobite propaganda; Tonson, who had been Dryden's regular publisher for ten years, and who published most of his work during the 1690s, may have been unwilling to issue this play for political reasons, or Hindmarsh may simply have outbid him.[30] Dryden's own caution shows in his decision to dedicate the play to Philip Sidney, Earl of Leicester, whose politics were more acceptable to the new regime than his own, but he felt sufficiently protected to reveal his new address in that very dedication: "Neither has he [Leicester] forgotten a poor Inhabitant of his Suburbs, whose best prospect is on the Garden of *Leicester-House*; but that more than once he has been offering him his Patronage, to reconcile him to a World, of which his Misfortunes have made him weary" (XV, 62–63). Significantly, Dryden claims that Leicester has approached *him* with an offer of patronage; with men like Leicester and Dorset ready to protect him, he was evidently now confident that he would remain unmolested, despite the proclamation of 13 May "requireing all papists forthwith to depart the cities of London and Westminster, and ten miles adjacent."[31]

Nonetheless, Dryden chose to remain rather quiet during 1689; there is no extant record of his activities between the March census of Soho Papists and the speaking of his prologue and epilogue for the November premiere of *The Widdow-Ranter, or The History of Bacon in Virginia*, Aphra Behn's last play. He evidently spent considerable time in writing *Don Sebastian*, which he later described as a "Poem" to which he had "given . . . much application . . . not a Play that was huddled up in hast" (XV, 71); the comedy *Amphitryon*, which he finished early in 1690, was also on his desk. As the self-mocking prologue and dignified preface to *Don Sebastian* show, Dryden was aware of the attacks on him that coincided with the Revolution, as well as several others that appeared during 1689, but he made no direct reply to any of his enemies.[32] We may imagine him following with interest and some hope the news of King James's rapid conquest of most of Ireland in March and April, to which William responded in early May by declaring war on the French, who were supporting James.[33] We may also imagine him taking private pleasure in the unintended results of a revival of one of his plays: on 28 May, Queen Mary, who knew that *The Spanish Fryar* had been banned for its jibes at priests during her father's reign, ordered Dryden's "Protestant play" acted, but the joke was on her, for the Tory message of the play's serious plot, with its strong support for the legitimate succession, made her afternoon in the theatre a long and embarrassing one. According to Daniel Finch, Earl of Nottingham, "some unhappy expressions [in the play] put [the Queen] in some disorder, and forc'd her to hold up her fan."[34]

Dryden may have been glancing at this episode in the prologue for *The Widdow-Ranter*, spoken six months later, in which an actress warns us that the rough Virginians speak plainly about sex: "ev'ry part has there its proper Name." She concedes that "talk[ing] so savour'ly of what they do" shows that the colonists have "good Stomachs," but as a London lady, she would have to behave differently:

> But were I Bound to that broad speaking land,
> What e're they said, I would not understand,
> But innocently, with a Ladies Grace,
> Wou'd learn to whisk my Fan about my Face.

[ll. 26–29]

The fan with which the actress proposes to feign innocence of sexual matters that she evidently comprehends is the same prop the Queen had used to hide her comprehension of the embarrassing political message of *The Spanish Fryar*.[35] The last lines of the same prologue are a more obvious allusion to recent events:

> The Story's true; the Fact not long a-go;
> The Hero of our Stage was *English* too:
> And bate him one small frailty of Rebelling,
> As brave as e're was born at *Iniskelling*.

[ll. 38–41]

As everyone in the theatre would have known, "*Iniskelling*" or Enniskillen was a town in Ireland, whose Protestant men, though greatly outnumbered, had bravely and successfully attacked James's forces in August, during the retreat from Derry.[36] Dryden concedes their bravery (and Bacon's), but as a victim of the allegedly Glorious Revolution, he hardly considered "Rebelling" a "small frailty."

In this prologue, Dryden's first public utterance after the Revolution, we may see the pattern of his work for the rest of his life: to a casual listener, the concluding couplet sounds like a compliment to the brave men of Enniskillen, but for a listener tuned in to Dryden's habitual irony, there is an undertone of cynical wit beneath the compliment, for Dryden believed that those men, however brave, were rebels attacking a sacred monarch—rebels like the men now running the government in London. The joke about the fan is even more private, even more easily deniable, but there are many such private jokes in the work of Dryden's final decade. In Williamite England as in modern military dictatorships, those opposed to the government had to sustain themselves by humor, and particularly prized the rhetorical device that secretly mocked what it seemed to praise. Sometimes the mockery was quite open: the actress speaking the epilogue informs the audience that "he who sent me here, is positive, / This Farce of Government is sure to thrive" (ll. 5–6); while the play itself is a farce about the government of colonial Virginia, the man who sent the actress out to speak these lines considered the government of William's England a farce, though he recognized that it would probably last.[37]

"A Patient Sufferer, and No Disturber of the Government"

Don Sebastian, Dryden's longest, most complex, most mature tragedy, contains some similarly ironic political material, but ultimately moves from the particular to the general, focusing on the moral and psychological issues implicit in the recent political struggle. In his artful preface, Dryden lists the many "discouragements [that] had not only wean'd [him] from the Stage, but had also given [him] a loathing of it." In a tone much like that he had used fourteen years earlier, when he complained of being "the *Sisyphus* of the stage," he explains that his "bad circumstances" have "condemn'd [him] to dig in [the] exhausted Mines" (XV, 65–66) of the theatre, but he actually found rich ore in his own earlier plays, expertly refining material from *An Evening's Love, Tyrannick Love, The Conquest of Granada, Marriage A-la-Mode*, and *Oedipus*, among others.[38] In all those plays, Dryden had presented characters who changed their minds, and Dorax in *Don*

Sebastian is his finest study in the psychology of inconsistency, a part worthy of the skills of Betterton. Before the play begins, this rough Portuguese soldier has become a Moslem out of anger at Don Sebastian; he protects Don Sebastian from the Moors in hope of slaying his king himself in a duel, but his better nature wins out in a supremely dramatic scene of reconciliation (IV, iii, 381–669). The dilemma of Dorax is not a simple allegory of the Revolution, which would have been a dangerous and futile gesture, yet by creating Dorax, Dryden channeled the tension between loyalty and self-interest that many Englishmen felt during and after the Revolution into a richly human drama. Defending the inconsistency of Dorax in his preface, he pointed to Montaigne's famous chapter on human inconsistency, which he had often applied to himself.

Although it includes a rebellion against a Moorish tyrant and a comic mob scene, *Don Sebastian* is not a crude "parallel play" like *The Duke of Guise*, in part because of its complexity: the moral turmoil of Dorax and the political plotting of the scheming courtier Benducar share space with the high tragic story of Don Sebastian and Almeyda, lovers caught in unwitting incest, and the low comic plot of the slave Antonio and his Moorish mistress Morayma. In the dedication, however, Dryden speaks of the "leading men" of "all Parties," who "rise and fall in the variety of Revolutions," but who are actually "whirl'd about by the motion of a greater Planet":

> Ambitious Meteors! how willing they are to set themselves upon the Wing; and taking every occasion of drawing upward to the Sun: Not considering that they have no more time allow'd them for their mounting, than the short revolution of a day: and that when the light goes from them, they are of necessity to fall. How much happier is he . . . who centring on himself, remains immovable, and smiles at the madness of the dance about him. [XV, 59–60]

This poetic prose serves to compliment the Earl of Leicester on his detachment from public affairs, and thus fits into the long sequence of passages in which Dryden praises the ideal of retirement. But he can hardly have written these words without recognizing that his own enforced retirement from his official posts had given him a new opportunity for political detachment, a chance to smile at the "madness of the dance."

Despite these gestures of detachment, and despite the prologue's pointed claim that "a play's of no Religion" (l. 16), *Don Sebastian* contains many passages open to a Jacobite reading.[39] Most of the political aphorisms are capable of more than one application; Dorax's glancing reference to "Mankind that always judge of Kings with malice" (V, 495) is a simple example. Dryden was probably thinking of how ready James's opponents had been to consider the birth of the Prince a fraud, but there had been plenty of other kings in recent memory whose acts and declarations had been treated with similarly malicious suspicions. So, too, with Benducar's warning to the newly victorious Emperor:

> A secret Party still remains, that lurks
> Like Embers rak'd in ashes———wanting but
> A breath to blow aside th' involving dust,
> And then they blaze abroad.
> [II, i, 75–78]

Whigs might have thought with satisfaction of the way the bishops' defiance of James had unified the latent opposition to the King, but Jacobites, currently the "secret Party," might have dreamed of their own hopes for resurgence. Speaking of a comic Moslem cleric called the Mufti, Benducar declares that "Church-men, though they itch to govern all, / Are silly, woful, awkard Politicians" (II, i, 131–32). As Tom Brown's response to these lines shows, the Whigs immediately thought of the political folly of Father Petre, but Dryden (who was no friend to Father Petre and the Jesuits) might also have been thinking of such Anglican clergymen as the Archbishop of Canterbury, who had opposed James vigorously in the battle over the Declaration of Indulgence, but whose scruples about oaths to monarchs now made him incapable of swearing allegiance to William.[40] However admirable as a moral stance, the position in which such "non-jurors" found themselves was politically "awkard."

Other passages are so clearly aimed at the new regime that I wonder how Dryden got away with them. The unscrupulous Mustapha, inciting the mob to riot, reminds them of "the glorious Rapines and Robberies you have committed . . . Your breaking open and gutting of Houses, your rummaging of Cellars, your demolishing of Christian Temples, and bearing off in triumph the superstitious Plate and Pictures, the Ornaments of their wicked Altars" (IV, iii, 125–28). Writing less than a year after mobs inspired by Revolutionary fervor had pillaged the chapels of the foreign ambassadors and the monastery headed by his friend Father Corker, Dryden surely had that episode in mind, and it is difficult to imagine the audience thinking of anything else. The people who attended the theatre were unlikely to have been participants in such mobs themselves, and Dryden could therefore count on appealing to their class snobbery by having Mustapha complain that the "vile Ragga-muffins" he is haranguing have an "offensive . . . savour" (IV, iii, 20–21). But the theatre audience did include military men and politicians who had deserted the cause of James to embrace the cause of William, men who ought to have been distressed by some of the more serious passages in the play. When Benducar tries to tempt Dorax to take part in a conspiracy against the Emperor, for example, the old soldier's reply appeals to the feudal values of honor and loyalty that Dryden associated with the Stuarts:

> He trusts us both; mark that, shall we betray him?
> A Master who reposes Life and Empire
> On our fidelity: I grant he is a Tyrant,
> That hated name my nature most abhors;
> . . . .
> But, while he trusts me, 'twere so base a part
> To fawn and yet betray, I shou'd be hiss'd
> And whoop'd in Hell for that Ingratitude.
>
> [II, i, 288–91; 296–98]

This passage is a rhetorical trap: if an offended member of the audience chose to hiss these lines, he would be acknowledging that he himself deserved to be "hiss'd . . . in Hell" for betraying the lawful monarch. Dorax goes on to extend his argument in a pure Tory vein completely in keeping with the arguments Dryden had made during the Exclusion Crisis:

>   Is not the bread thou eat'st, the Robe thou wear'st,
>   Thy Wealth, and Honours, all the pure indulgence
>   Of him thou wou'dst destroy?
>   And wou'd his Creature, nay his Friend betray him?
>   Why then, no Bond is left on human kind:
>   Distrusts, debates, immortal strifes ensue;
>   Children may murder Parents, Wives their Husbands;
>   All must be Rapine, Wars, and Desolation,
>   When trust and gratitude no longer bind.
>
>   [II, i, 303–11]

This passage may stand as Dryden's stubborn defense of his own loyalty to James, and such distaste for those who betrayed their masters was by no means confined to Jacobites. The old diarist Evelyn considered the new regime a miraculous deliverance, but when John Churchill, Duke of Marlborough was dismissed from his places in 1692, Evelyn reported that he was "disgraced; & by none pittied, being also the first who betrayed and forsooke his Master K: James, who advanced him."[41]

An earlier scene between Dorax and Benducar even glances at the secret vice of the new King:

>   *Bend.* Now *Dorax!*
>   *Dorax.*   Well, *Benducar!*
>   *Bend.*   Bare *Benducar!*
>   *Dor.* Thou woudst have Titles, take 'em then, Chief Minister,
>   First Hangman of the State.
>   *Bend.*   Some call me Favourite.
>   *Dorax.* What's that, his Minion?
>   Thou art too old to be a Catamite!
>
>   [I, i, 65–69]

William III was probably a homosexual, and by the time Dryden's play was acted, his handsome Dutch favorite Hans Willem Bentinck had already been created Earl of Portland, but the Whigs, for whom William was officially the virtuous champion of the Protestant religion, the brave military scourge of the French, and the faithful husband of Mary, could hardly object to this sly passage, for to do so would be to acknowledge that their new monarch was himself a "Catamite." If anyone had objected, Dryden could have defended this passage in purely dramatic terms; it later develops that Dorax's rival in the court of Don Sebastian has been one Enriquez, who has gloriously overcome his "soft effeminate life . . . to struggle to the field, / And meet his glorious fate" at Sebastian's side (IV, iii, 595, 600–01).[42]

Some of the more obviously political passages may have been suppressed in most of the performances. Dryden's preface informs us that the play proved "insupportably too long" in its first performance, and explains that "Above twelve hunder'd lines [were] cut off from this Tragedy, since it was first deliver'd to the Actors." After giving credit to Betterton for "judiciously lop[ping]" the excess lines, Dryden describes them as "the most poetical parts, which are Descriptions, Images, Similitudes, and Moral Sentences" (XV, 65–66), but since Betterton's "judicious" understanding of theatre audiences included a shrewd sense of their politics, we may suspect that some of the "Moral Sentences" he suppressed were those open to dangerous political interpretations. Roger Morrice, a contemporary witness, reports the attendance of the Queen at the play and says it was "well liked, but very much Curtled before it was suffered to be Acted,"[43] implying that the curtailment was not a matter of mere length. In any case, Dryden claims to have restored all the cuts in the printed version, where he makes a point of stating that "the Earl of *Dorset*," who was the official censor by virtue of his appointment as Lord Chamberlain, "was pleas'd to read the Tragedy twice over before it was Acted; and did me the favour to send me word, that I had written beyond any of my former Plays; and that he was displeas'd any thing shou'd be cut away" (XV, 70–71). Dorset might well have sent such a message, but he might nonetheless have gone on to recommend political caution, however reluctantly, and Dryden's citing him here is an act of self-protection.

Don Sebastian was a success; Morrice reports a rumor that Dryden "sold" his third day for 120 guineas, and the dedication and preface, written after the first round of performances, reveal his cautious satisfaction. The preface, largely given over to defending the structure of the play, concludes with a blanket explanation for what could only be construed as self-praise: "Certainly, if a Man can ever have reason to set a value on himself, 'tis when his ungenerous Enemies are taking the advantage of the Times upon him to ruin him in his reputation" (XV, 72). Only one of those "ungenerous Enemies" took the opportunity to renew his attack: within days of the publication of *Don Sebastian*, Tom Brown issued *The Late Converts Exposed*, folding a few last-minute references to the new play into a pamphlet he had largely composed before the Revolution. Rising to Dryden's bait, Brown argued that the old poet had "no reputation to lose," and described his treatment by the new government as merciful: "You have indeed forefaulted your Lawrel, and Historians place; that's all the advantage the times have taken on you, and you may well admire the mercifulness of the Government, that it has not punished your *Panther* ribbaldry, and desertion, (for I will not call it Apostasie in a Poet) with a severer mortification" (sig. A1r). But Brown, who mainly wanted Dryden to answer him, was in no position to press for "a severer mortification." Dryden could afford to ignore both this pamphlet and a third one coupling him with the re-converted actor Joseph Haines, especially since there had been no official response to his recent political gestures.[44] There was even a plan to have *Amphitryon*, which was already finished and delivered to the actors, performed at court on 30 April; the substitution of Crowne's *Sir Courtly Nice* appears to have been a matter of theatrical expediency, based on insufficient rehearsal of Dryden's comedy, which was probably delayed until the fall.[45]

The resources of the United Company during this spring were mainly devoted to *The Prophetess, or Dioclesian*, the first opera since *Albion and Albanius*, staged in late May or early June. The text was an old play by Fletcher and Massinger, adapted by Betterton; the ambitious and elaborate music was by the young English composer Henry Purcell. Dryden, who had long been friendly with Betterton, had probably now met Purcell, who set the songs for *Amphitryon*. He helped with the drafting of Purcell's preface to the published score (advertised shortly after the premiere, though not actually published until February of 1691),[46] and he may have had a hand in the lyrics for some of the songs; he certainly wrote the prologue, which soon proved notorious. After the first wave of operas in the 1670s, which cost both theatres dearly, Dryden had commented that the playhouses were "Like Monarchs, ruin'd with expensive War" (prologue to *Aureng-Zebe*, l. 38). Even without another troupe to compete against, the United Company had lost thousands on *Albion and Albanius*; they were now spending hugely again on *The Prophetess*. Real "Monarchs" had also continued to pursue "expensive War." Evelyn believed that William's first Parliament, dissolved in early February, had "produc'd as universal a discontent, against K. William & themselves, as was before against K: James." A chief cause of that discontent was the "prodigal & careless

Drawing of Henry Purcell by John Closterman, 1695.

menaging [of] the monys raised for the reduction of Ireland."[47] But the main public drama of the spring of 1690 was William's preparation to travel to Ireland to take charge of that campaign, and his departure on 4 June came just after the premiere of this opera.

Perhaps encouraged by hearing such criticism of the regime, and by the fact that no one had called him to task for the political barbs in the prologue and epilogue to *The Widdow-Ranter*, Dryden now ventured to repeat his old comparison between expensive operas and expensive wars: his prologue brought Betterton himself on stage to speak of "vast Expenses close to sight," contrasting with "distant gains; and those uncertain too." When Betterton described the investment in scenery for the opera as "A sweeping Tax, which on our selves we raise," the implied comparison with national affairs was surely obvious; "sweeping" may even be a quibble on the notorious Hearth Tax, removed by William but replaced by the much-hated Poll Tax. A few lines later, complaining about the depletion of the audience by the departure of the military, the prologue refers to "the horrid pomp of War," a Virgilian phrase reminding us of Dryden's mature distaste for all warfare. As political satire, this prologue is not much more daring than the verses surrounding Behn's play or the strongest lines in *Don Sebastian*, but the political atmosphere at the time of the King's departure for Ireland was more highly charged than during the previous winter, and Shadwell, realizing that Dryden intended a "double meaning reflect[ing] on the Revolution," saw to it that the prologue was banned.[48] Any hope Dryden might have had that the discontent with William would lead to another Restoration was dashed by the Battle of the Boyne in July, an unequivocal victory for William's forces that drove James out of Ireland.

We may detect Dryden's response to the suppression of his prologue and the disappointment of his Jacobite hopes in the dedication and prologue for *Amphitryon*, which was probably first acted a month or so before its publication at the end of October. Again choosing a Whig patron, he dedicated the play to Sir William Levenson-Gower, explaining that he intended

> to pitch on such only, as have been pleas'd to own me in this Ruin of my small Fortune; who, though they are of a contrary Opinion themselves, yet blame not me for adhering to a lost Cause; and judging for my self, what I cannot chuse but judge; so long as I am a patient Sufferer, and no disturber of the Government. [XV, 224]

Dryden's cause was indeed lost, but he was willing to be "a patient Sufferer," supporting himself by his pen, and he did not regard the occasional political jibes in his plays and prologues as threatening any real disturbance to the government. He had personal connections with Levenson-Gower, whom he had once visited in Staffordshire,[49] and whose daughter Jane, gallantly complimented in this very dedication, was now being courted by two young men he knew—the poet and critic William Walsh, with whom he had an active correspondence, and the courtier Henry Hyde, son of his Tory patron the Earl of Rochester.[50] Dryden valued his acceptance by such men; he also took the occasion to thank the actors, whom he invited to "share the Praise amongst themselves," and the composer Purcell, whom he complimented as "an *English-man*, equal with the best abroad" (XV, 225). Like his patrons, Dryden's fellow professionals in the theatre evidently regarded his decision to remain a Catholic as his own business, but

Charles Montagu, now Secretary to the Privy Council, had recently written a flattering poem to Dorset alleging that Dryden had been "Enjoyn'd a Penance (which is too severe / For playing once the Fool) to Persevere."[51] Without naming Montagu, Dryden answers him in the preface: "if it be a severe Penance, as a great Wit has told the World, 'tis at least enjoyed me by my self" (XV, 224). He may have felt moved to reply to these lines because he recognized an element of sympathy in Montagu's implied recommendation that he re-convert, sympathy he felt more strongly in the quiet support of men like Dorset, Leicester, and Levenson-Gower.

The opening lines of the prologue tell us even more about Dryden's feelings at this low point in his fortunes:

> The lab'ring Bee, when his sharp Sting is gone,
> Forgets his Golden Work, and turns a Drone:
> Such is a Satyr, when you take away
> That Rage, in which his Noble Vigour lay.
> What gain you, by not suffering him to teize ye?
> He neither can offend you, now, nor please ye.
> The Honey-bag, and Venome, lay so near,
> That both, together, you resolv'd to tear;
> And lost your Pleasure, to secure your Fear.
> How can he show his Manhood, if you bind him
> To box, like Boys, with one Hand ty'd behind him?
> This is plain levelling of Wit; in which
> The Poor has all th'advantage, not the Rich.
> The Blockhead stands excus'd, for wanting Sense;
> And Wits turn Blockheads in their own defence.
>
> [ll. 1–15]

The immediate occasion for Dryden's comparing himself to a stingless bee was probably the banning of the prologue to *The Prophetess*. Recognizing satire as the "Golden Work" of his career, he asks the audience how he can please them without the teasing of his habitual irony. Dryden's criticism had always made room for the "Rage" that produced vivid imagery or Pindaric freedom, and he had recently praised Anne Killigrew's work for its "Noble Vigour." Contemplating an old age in which the political irony that had so often been a source of energy for his verse would be denied him, he naturally feared becoming a "Drone."

"Satyr," thanks to a false etymology, was a spelling Dryden and his contemporaries often used for "satire," and in this case his primary meaning is "satirist," but the notion of the poet as an old and emasculated satyr, whose "Honey-bag, and Venome" have been barbarously torn away, lurks just below the surface. As he would soon show in his vigorous translations of Juvenal and Persius, Dryden knew that comedy and satire originated in phallic ritual, hence his frustration at not being allowed to "show his Manhood" by making political jokes. Nor can he resist applying the political term "levelling" to the implied censorship under which he is now suffering: rich in the wit accumulated over a long career, he must now write like a poor writer, a "Blockhead." But his complaint that "Wits turn Blockheads in their own defence" is a deformation of a line from *The Medall* describing Shaftesbury's political change at the time of the Restoration: "The wretch turn'd loyal in his own defence" (l. 51). As the echo of that vigorous Tory satire suggests, there was no chance that Dryden would actually write like a blockhead, no matter what circumstances might conspire to limit his expression of his satiric rage.

The play itself is one of Dryden's funniest comedies, full of sexual humor and physical farce, but its "lab'ring Bee" of an author did not entirely omit political stings. Jupiter descends from the clouds complaining that "All subjects will be censuring their Kings" (I, i, 59). Mercury describes "Arbitrary Power" as "a knock-down argument" and accuses his "Brother *Phoebus*" of being "a meer Country Gentleman, that never comes to Court . . . drinking all Night, and in your Cups . . . still rayling at the Government" (I, i, 133–42). The servant Sosia complains that great Lords refuse to pay wages, invoking the "Priviledge of their Honour," yet "stand up for Liberty and Property of the Subject," a speech immediately glossed by Mercury as having "something of the Republican Spirit" (II, i, 20–26). The subplot involving the corrupt judge Gripus leads Mercury to the conclusion that "Our Iron Age is grown an Age of Gold: / 'Tis who bids most; for all Men wou'd be sold" (IV, 556–57), an ironic reversal of the Virgilian myth of the Iron Age and the Golden Age, prominent in the eclogues Dryden had translated in 1684 (see above, pp. 390, 392).

These are passing shots, designed to please by teasing, but there were probably some Jacobites who thought they heard a more serious political message in Jupiter's final speech, predicting the birth of his son Hercules:

> From this auspicious Night, shall rise an Heir,
> Great, like his Sire, and like his Mother, fair:
> Wrongs to redress, and Tyrants to disseize;
> Born for a World, that wants a *Hercules.*
> Monsters, and Monster-men he shall ingage,
> And toil, and struggle, through an Impious Age.
> Peace to his Labours, shall at length succeed;
> And murm'ring Men, unwilling to be freed,
> Shall be compell'd to Happiness, by need.
>
> [V, i, 413–21]

Dryden had compared James II to Hercules in *Threnodia Augustalis*, and in *Britannia Rediviva*, he had compared the birth of the Prince, surrounded by rumors and unrest, to the birth of Hercules:

> Thus, when *Alcides* rais'd his Infant Cry,
> The Snakes besieg'd his Young Divinity:
> But vainly with their forked Tongues they threat;
> For Opposition makes a Heroe Great.
>
> [ll. 55–58]

For anyone who remembered this passage, the ending of the new comedy had a special resonance, but like so much that Dryden would write in the 1690s, Jupiter's speech does not insist upon being applied to the contemporary scene; it will work nicely within the context of the myth.[52] To use Dryden's own terms, part of what makes this play great is the way its author had learned to adjust to the role of being in the Opposition.

Safety and Wit

For men in high places suspected of sharing Dryden's opinions, these were difficult times. A "dangerous conspiracy" discovered in June of 1690 resulted in the imprisonment of several men well known to Dryden, including the diarist Samuel Pepys, one of the younger sons of the martyred Lord Stafford, and the Queen's own uncle Henry Hyde, Earl of Clarendon and brother to Dryden's patron Rochester.[53] As William was winning his land victory in Ireland, the French fleet was defeating the Dutch off the coast of England, while the outnumbered English Navy avoided engagement; the English admiral Torrington soon joined Clarendon and Pepys in the Tower. The French missed the resulting opportunity; had Louis chosen to invade England while his ships controlled the Channel and William's troops were in Ireland, he might well have succeeded.[54] Small wonder, then, that imprisonments of "Papists and disaffected persons" continued. Clarendon won his release on 23 October 1690, but on 3 January 1691, he was arrested again; the participants in this new conspiracy allegedly included Richard Grahame, Viscount Preston, who had been Charles II's ambassador to France, and his brother James Grahame, an Army colonel who had been Keeper of the Privy Purse to James II. Both Grahames were married to Howards; the colonel was married to Elizabeth Dryden's niece.[55] In April, the Archbishop of Canterbury and the other non-juring bishops were replaced with clerics who had taken the oaths to William and Mary. Several of the pamphlets on the dilemma of the clergy took passing shots at Dryden, and his old partner Sir Roger L'Estrange spent much of this spring in prison.[56]

Under these circumstances, Dryden had good reasons for caution. In his prologue to Joseph Harris's comedy *The Mistakes* (December 1690), he assured the audience that the author was not a "high Flyer" (l. 27), a term now used for the non-juring bishops, and that the play was "Innocent of all things—ev'n of wit" (l. 26). For a poet hoping to avoid offense, but not willing to give up wit, translation might offer a degree of protection, and Jacob Tonson had been trying to organize a translation of Juvenal and Persius by several hands for some years.[57] On 9 February 1691, Tonson entered three "Satyrs of Juvenal Translated from the Lattin into English verse, by Mr. John Dryden" on the Stationers' Register; the completed collection appeared late in 1692. As the finished translations show, Dryden found many parallels between Juvenal's scathing indictments of a corrupt Rome and his own feelings about contemporary London, but he also continued to comment directly on his own times. In the preface he wrote for Walsh's *Dialogue Concerning Women*, advertised in April 1691, he made a gallant gesture toward the ladies: "For my own part, who have always been their servant, and have never drawn my Pen against them, I had rather see some of them prais'd extraordinarily, than any of them suffer by detraction: And that in this Age, and at this time particularly, wherein I find more Heroines than Heroes" (sig. A4v). The last phrase might be read as a tiny sparkle of Jacobitism by someone aware that the cause of James had many supporters among the aristocratic ladies; at the very least, it repeats the general condemnation of the venal times that Dryden had developed in the subplot of *Amphitryon*.

Remembering the many misogynistic passages in Dryden's earlier and later work, we may also suspect that his newfound concern lest the ladies "suffer by detraction" had something to do with the "numerous Quire of Fair Ladies" who swelled the house "on the Third Day" of *Amphitryon*, giving their "just Applause" to the music of Purcell and their money to the needy poet (XV, 225). Purcell continued much in the public eye. He contributed music to Settle's *Distress'd Innocence* (late October 1690) and to Walsh's *Gordian Knot Unty'd* (November 1690); *The Prophetess*, which had proved a success in the previous summer, was revived over the winter. Hoping to capitalize on Purcell's popularity, Dryden now set about revising the old *King Arthur*, written for Charles II in 1684, so that Purcell could set it as a full-scale semi-opera in time for a late spring opening. As he points out in the dedication, this revision was mainly a process of removing or toning down political references: "not to offend the present Times, . . . I have been oblig'd . . . to alter the first Design, and take away . . . many Beauties from the Writing" (sig. A3r). His decision to dedicate the printed opera to Halifax was another calculated piece of self-protection. In the passion of his high Tory orthodoxy, Dryden had sharply attacked the Trimmers (see above, pp. 371, 388), but this dedication to the chief Trimmer of them all is a shrewd piece of literary trimming by a poet seeking to make a nonpartisan appeal for support. Dryden praises Halifax for retiring from public affairs and blithely claims that the nation, actually at war with France and worried about the state of its Navy, is "secur'd from Foreign Attempts, by so powerful a Fleet, and . . . enjoy[ing], not only the Happiness, but even the Ornaments of Peace" (sig. A3r). He compliments his collaborator Purcell and notes with pride that the manuscript has pleased his "first and best Patroness the Dutchess of *Monmouth*," widow of a martyr to Whiggery, and that "Her Majesty has Graciously been pleas'd to peruse the Manuscript of this *opera*, and given it Her Royal Approbation" (sig. A3v). Since Queen Mary had been badly embarrassed by *The Spanish Fryar* just two years earlier, we may suspect that her perusal of Dryden's manuscript was no idle exercise in literary amusement, and we may be certain that his citing her approval in a dedication printed as the opera came on stage (early June 1691) was a way of declaring his libretto innocent of Jacobite innuendo.

Like *Don Sebastian* and *Amphitryon*, however, *King Arthur* lies open to a Jacobite reading. The only lines clearly referring to William come in the final tableau, where a figure named Honour asks St. George to "smile . . . on that auspicious order":

> Our Natives not alone appear
> To Court this Martial Prize;
> But Foreign Kings, Adopted here,
> Their Crowns at Home despise.

[V, i, p. 51]

Since no king could be more English than Arthur, this reminder that William was a "Foreign King" works against the allegorical reading that would have pleased Queen

Mary and the establishment, a reading in which Arthur represents William and the Saxon Oswald, described as a "bold Invader" in the opening scene, represents James. On that reading, the single combat between Arthur and Oswald at the end would represent the Battle of the Boyne. But since Dryden considered William an "Invader," those who shared the poet's views might privately consider a reading reversing those roles, and see in the final combat a realization of their hopes that James would be restored.[58] The old duke Conon, father of the beautiful, blind Emmeline, describes Oswald as "Revengeful, rugged, violently brave," adjectives applicable to both kings. He goes on to claim that "*Arthur* is all that's Excellent in *Oswald*, / And void of all his Faults" (I, i, pp. 2–3); again, readers of either political persuasion could interpret these lines as they pleased. Neither hero dies, and Dryden takes care to make both Britons and Saxons honorable men, treating the Saxon wizard Osmond as the villain; this strategy is another instance of the time-honored technique of displacing anger toward a king onto his "evil counselors." Dryden was doubtless correct in describing the lines he had been forced to excise from the original opera as "Beauties," but his skill in recasting the opera to make it open to either a Williamite or a Jacobite reading has a beauty all its own.

The clearest instance of Dryden's self-consciousness about his skill in rhetorical manipulation comes in a scene between the "Earthy Spirit" Grimbald and the "Airy Spirit" Philidel. When the play begins, both of these spirits serve the wicked Osmond, rival to the wise Merlin, but Philidel, who "trembles at the yawning gulf of hell" (I, p. 6), cannot bring himself to aid the pagan cause and deserts to the Christians, describing himself to Merlin as "The last seduc'd, and least deform'd, of Hell" (II, p. 10). After Oswald abducts Emmeline, Merlin sends Philidel to find her, but Grimbald binds Philidel in a chain and exults in his capture:

> *Grim.* O Rebel, have I caught thee!
> *Phil.* Ah me! what hard mishap!
> *Grim.* What just Revenge!
> Thou miscreant Elf, thou Renegado Scout,
> So clean, so furbish'd, so renew'd in White,
> The Livery of our Foes; I see thee through:
> What mak'st thou here? Thou trim Apostate, speak.
> Thou shak'st for Fear, I feel thy false Heart Pant.
>
> [III, p. 23]

The terms of abuse—"Rebel, miscreant, Renegado, Apostate"—are precisely those Dryden's enemies had hurled at him when he converted to Catholicism,[59] and the captured Philidel immediately starts to speak the language of Dryden's dedications:

> *Phil.* Ah, mighty *Grimbald*,
> Who wou'd not fear, when seiz'd in thy strong Gripe!
> But hear me, O renown'd, O worthy Fiend,
> The Favourite of our Chief!

Grimbald accurately dismisses this speech as "fulsome Flattery" and refuses to believe Philidel's desperate claim that he has "fled from *Merlin*, free as Air that bore me, / To unfold to *Osmond* all his deep Designs." He does, however, accept Philidel's assurances that he will come along without force, and walks in the direction Philidel points out, where he is immediately ensnared with birdlime. Merlin appears and endorses Philidel's trickery: "Well hast thou wrought thy Safety with thy Wit, / My *Philidel*; go Meritorious on" (III, p. 24). In revising *King Arthur* as in many other projects during this period, Dryden acted like his Philidel, ensuring his safety by using his wit. Philidel's rhetoric to Grimbald blinds his victim with flattery and lies, but it is also Philidel who frees Emmeline from her blindness, infusing drops from Merlin's vial into her sightless eyes. The implication is that flattering one's enemies may ultimately allow one to reveal the truth to one's friends, and I believe the role of Philidel was Dryden's way of dealing with his own feelings about having to cooperate with the Williamite establishment. If his concern for the safety of his family made it necessary for him to avoid brazenly partisan writing, to have his plays vetted by the Lord Chamberlain and the Queen, and to choose such patrons as Leicester, Levenson-Gower, and Halifax, he could still satisfy his need to express his own opinions by using wit and irony.

Throughout *King Arthur*, appearances are unreliable. In a brilliant musical sequence in the second act, Grimbald disguises himself as a shepherd and tries to lead Arthur and his troops into a bog. Beckoned in opposite directions by the canonic singing of choruses led by Grimbald and Philidel, both urging "Hither, this way, this way bend" (II, p. 12), the British troops hesitate until Grimbald "sinks with a Flash," revealing himself as a Satanic agent. To rescue Emmeline, Arthur must destroy an enchanted grove, where "all is but Illusion," as Merlin warns him (IV, i, p. 36). He manfully resists the temptations of two naked sirens in a stream, but when he hacks at a tree with his sword, a bleeding Emmeline appears, begging Arthur not to murder her. Caught between Merlin's injunction and his love for Emmeline, Arthur realizes that "all may be Illusion" and begs the "thick'ning Fogs . . . that belie my sight" to break up. Only the intervention of Philidel, who strikes the false Emmeline with a wand, revealing her as the ugly Grimbald, saves him from falling victim to illusion. Arthur must gain moral vision as his Emmeline gains physical vision, and in both cases Philidel is the agent of truth.

When Emmeline cannot see, she has difficulty imagining battle; her only empirical source is the sound of the trumpet:

> How does so many Men ee'r come to meet?
> The Devil Trumpet vexes 'em, and then
> They feel about for one anothers Faces;
> And so they meet, and kill.

> [I, i, p. 5]

These lines reflect not only the contemporary fascination with epistemology, recently sparked by the publication of Locke's *Essay Concerning Human Understanding* (1690), but Dryden's own distaste for warfare, which may also find expression in one of the conventional pastoral interludes:

> How blest are Shepherds, how happy their Lasses,
> While Drums & Trumpets are sounding Alarms!

> Over our Lowly Sheds all the Storm passes;
> And when we die, 'tis in each other's Arms.

[II, p. 16]

Dryden was once again contrasting the force of arms and the force of love; Charlotte Butler, who sang Philidel's part, also sang Cupid in the famous Frost Scene, where the fair maidens warmed by the beams of Love "Sound a Parley . . . and surrender" to their lovers (III, p. 33). These passages draw their poignance not only from the traditional opposition between pastoral idylls and military horrors, but from the particular situation in 1691. As Dryden's opera opened, the Irish campaign was still dragging on, and the war against France, which would last nine years, was revealing itself as a struggle of sieges and epidemics. One reason for the growing "country" opposition was the conscription for these wars, which took agricultural laborers away from the hayfields celebrated in the last act of *King Arthur* and onto the faraway battlefields of Limerick and Flanders. In the dedication, Dryden praises Halifax for "preventing a Civil War" in 1683, but his terms surely reflect his fear, widely shared, that King William's War would ruin the English: "So many Wives, who have yet their Husbands in their Arms; so many Parents, who have not the Number of their Children lessen'd; so many Villages, Towns, and Cities, whose Inhabitants are not decreas'd, their Property violated, or their Wealth diminish'd, are yet owing to the sober Conduct and happy Results of your Advice" (sig. A1v). This passage, ostensibly praising the policies of the past, proved all too accurate as a prophecy of the future: William, who was reluctant to take the advice of anyone advocating peace, and who spent at least part of every subsequent year of his reign fighting on the Continent, soon diminished the wealth of the nation. Dryden's parallel between expensive wars and expensive operas also proved prophetic. Both *The Prophetess* (1690) and *King Arthur* (1691) were popular successes, but neither made enough money to offset the costs of scenery, costumes and music; *The Fairy Queen* (May 1692), an anonymous adaptation of *A Midsummer Night's Dream* with music by Purcell, cost over £3,000, but "the Company got very little by it."[60]

Needing money himself, Dryden continued to write for the theatre. Even before the premiere of *King Arthur* in late May or early June, he had probably begun work on *Cleomenes, The Spartan Hero*, based on a story from Plutarch. In a letter of 13 August 1691, Walsh asked Dryden whether the play was finished, but Dryden fell ill not long after receiving that letter, and had to ask his friend Southerne to help him complete the last act. The hurry suggests hopes of a fall or winter premiere, and by 6 October, the play was sufficiently finished to be sold to Tonson for 30 guineas.[61] The next day, Dryden wrote to Dorset, reporting a "long indisposition of six weeks" and reminding the Lord Chamberlain of "a favour which your Lordship formerly gave me some hopes of from the Queen" (*Letters*, pp. 48–49). We cannot know what that favor was, but since Queen Mary had approved of *King Arthur* in manuscript, I should think it likely that Dryden hoped she might award him a small pension despite his religion. Such foreign Catholic artists as the ceiling painter Antonio Verrio continued to flourish under the new regime, and Dryden might fondly have hoped that the respect Dorset and others had for his literary talents would have some influence upon the Queen. If he had such hopes, however, he acted imprudently in choosing to dramatize the story of Cleomenes, a brave king ousted from Sparta who languishes in exile in an effeminate Egypt. Since the biblical allegory in *Absalom and Achitophel* had already used Egypt as an allegorical equivalent for France, it was possible to see Cleomenes as an idealized James, though other aspects of the story, such as the heroism of Cleomenes' teenaged son Cleonidas, do not fit such a "parallel" reading.

The play was evidently complete in October, and required nothing unusual in the way of scenery, but it was delayed by a number of factors, including a swordfight in the playhouse that forced a temporary suspension of acting in December.[62] The crowded theatrical schedule for this winter included a revival of *The Indian Emperour* with new music by Purcell, and some repeated performances of *King Arthur*, but any satisfaction Dryden derived from those productions was offset by the fact that neither could offer him any profit. There were new plays as well: Southerne's *The Wives Excuse* (December 1691), for which Dryden wrote a commendatory poem, did not last long, but Durfey's *The Marriage-Hater Matched* (January 1692) was a smash. By now, Dryden's financial situation was desperate: the copyright money from Tonson was long spent, and there could be no third day's profits from *Cleomenes* until the play was produced. A grim little record suggests the plight of the Drydens in midwinter: on 16 January 1692, Sir Robert Howard's son Thomas gave his aunt Elizabeth £5 "in charitye"; the money was probably needed most immediately for the eleven shillings of quarterly tax on the house in Gerrard Street, recorded as paid on that very day.[63]

The wait for *Cleomenes* was to prove yet longer. Shadwell, who was now determined to obstruct Dryden's dramatic efforts, wrote to Dorset on 19 January complaining of the priority given to Durfey and Dryden, and successfully urged that a play by his friend Nicholas Brady be acted next.[64] In February, while Brady's *The Rape* was on stage, *The Gentleman's Journal*, a new literary magazine edited by a French refugee named Peter Motteux, was building up advance publicity for Dryden's tragedy. Motteux, who had evidently read the manuscript, praised Dryden for "mak[ing] his Spartans . . . speak as manly heroic Lacedaemonians," and there was much in *Cleomenes* to please a reader familiar with Corneille and Racine. The play is uncompromising, old-fashioned, self-consciously "literary." Unmixed with comedy, it is a pure tragedy celebrating loyalty, courage, and honor, virtues Dryden thought rare in an England he now considered mercenary and corrupt. The heroic virtues of the Spartan king Cleomenes and his loyal wife contrast starkly with the obvious flaws of the weak Egyptian king Ptolemy and his sensuous mistress Cassandra, who attempts to seduce Cleomenes in a lengthy scene in heroic couplets, a lingering glance backward at Dryden's earlier theatrical style. The most complex character is Cleanthes, captain of the Egyptian guards, who finds it impossible to maintain his loyalty to the Spartan king and his duty to his father, the scheming minister Sosibius, another "evil counselor" like Benducar and Osmond. Dryden's handling of the intense relationship between Cleomenes and the young Cleanthes even suggests a personal identification with Cleomenes. Like the exiled Spartan king, the old poet was grateful for the support of younger men who befriended him despite the possible political cost: Purcell, Southerne, Walsh, and Motteux are examples. The heroic portrait of young Cleonidas may also owe something to Dryden's feelings about the way his own sons had suffered with him. Disabled from employment by their Catholicism, Charles and John left London for Rome sometime during this spring; Cardinal Howard, their mother's kinsman, found Charles a place in the papal guards and employed John in his own house.[65]

Although *Cleomenes* has considerable moral intensity, it actually has fewer explicitly political messages than the other three plays Dryden had staged under the new regime. But with William again away fighting in Flanders, and with rumors of a French invasion flying about, Mary had to be cautious about any play whose hero attempted a coup, and the last act of *Cleomenes* features a failed revolution: Cleomenes and Cleanthes lovingly stab each other when the weak-willed Egyptian populace fails to rally behind their attempt to replace Ptolemy with his brother. On 9 April 1692, when the play was finally ready to come on stage, the Queen instructed the Lord Chamberlain to prohibit the performance.[66] Shadwell may have been the moving force behind this prohibition, but Dryden had friends as well as enemies, and two recently appointed members of the Queen's Privy Council came to his defense. Anthony Carey, Viscount Falkland, produced a French book Dryden had given him "seven or eight years" earlier, in which the poet had listed the story as a possible subject for a play; the claim that Dryden had planned such a play while Charles II was still alive, like Dryden's less well-documented claim that he had written a version of *The Duke of Guise* in 1660, was designed to exonerate him from accusations of deliberately concocting parallels with contemporary events. The Earl of Rochester, uncle to the Queen, who had heard the play in a private reading, also insisted on its innocence, and within a week of the banning, the play appeared, though Luttrell reported that the passages reflecting on the government had been omitted.[67]

When he published *Cleomenes* in May, Dryden said that Dorset had returned the manuscript "without the least alteration," but explained that the play had been "garbled before by the Superiours of the Play-house," whose "Zeal for the Government" had led them "to geld it so clearly in some places, that they took away the very Manhood of it" (sig. A4v–A5r).[68] This imagery makes even more explicit the notion of censorship as castration he had already used in the prologue to *Amphitryon*. Nonetheless, Dryden had learned from his past mistakes, and avoided the elaborate excuses he had made in *The Vindication of the Duke of Guise*: in a gracious dedication to Rochester, he thanked his longtime patron for "having perform'd a just and honourable Action, in Redeeming this Play from the Persecution of my Enemies" (sig. A2r), and in a preface addressed to readers at large, he claimed to be almost indifferent:

> I know it will be here expected, that I should write somewhat concerning the forbidding of my play; but the less I say of it, the better. And besides, I was so little concern'd at it, that had it not been on consideration of the Actors, who were to suffer on my account, I should not have been at all sollicitous whether it were play'd, or no. No body can imagine, that in my declining Age I write willingly, or that I am desirous of exposing, at this time of day, the small Reputation which I have gotten on the *Theatre*. The Subsistence which I had from the former Government is lost; and the Reward I have from the Stage is so little, that it is not worth my Labour. [sig. A4v]

"My Long Laborious Work"

This claim of indifference is evidently exaggerated, but by the time *Cleomenes* came on stage, Dryden had at least one reason to sneer at the small rewards of theatrical writing. During the winter months, while waiting for the long-delayed premiere of his play, he completed a task he had agreed to undertake during the previous summer: a memorial poem for the Countess of Abingdon, who died on 31 May 1691. *Eleonora* was finally published in early March of 1692, and James Bertie, Earl of Abingdon, rewarded Dryden handsomely for his labor: one tradition claims that the present was as large as 500 guineas.[69] I believe that figure is wildly exaggerated, but *Eleonora* may still have been more profitable than any of the four plays Dryden had staged since losing his government posts, and his large output in prose and poetry during 1692 and 1693 suggests a decision to support himself by nondramatic work. For a translation of essays by the French philosopher and critic St. Evremond, published in April 1692, he completed a "Character" of the author begun by his friend Knightley Chetwood. Later in the same year, he wrote a "Character of Polybius" for a translation of the Roman historian by his friend Sir Henry Sheeres, which appeared in November. About the time *Eleonora* was published, he agreed to take on a larger share of the long-promised translation of Juvenal and Persius than originally planned: in February 1692, the *Gentleman's Journal* announced that this translation "by several hands" would be "printed in a short time, Mr. Dryden having done *four* Satyrs of [Juvenal] and *two* of [Persius]." Those six poems already represented twice as much work as the three satires of Juvenal entered on the Stationers' Register a year earlier, and in April, Motteux explained that "the bookseller having thought, with reason, that it would conduce most to his advantage to have the Persius wholly done by Mr. Dryden, hath occasioned a delay in the publication of that and the Juvenal, which, however, will both appear speedily."

Dryden probably devoted much of the spring to finishing his versions of Persius. He selected and supervised the other translators of Juvenal, who included his two elder sons and his old collaborators Duke, Tate, and Creech; a new protégé, William Congreve, translated one satire and contributed a laudatory poem on Dryden's Persius. The long prefatory "Discourse concerning the Original and Progress of Satire," based on a close study of Isaac Casaubon and other scholars, evidently cost Dryden several more months of labor; he dated it 18 August 1692.[70] A substantial borrowing from the Roman historian Tacitus in this essay suggests that Dryden had already begun his part of the group translation of Tacitus announced in 1693 and published in 1698.[71] After completing the "Discourse," Dryden went off for a holiday in Essex, but he did not rest: when he returned to London in mid-October, just before the publication of the Juvenal and Persius volume, he had already translated large selections from Ovid and Homer for Tonson's next miscellany, *Examen Poeticum*, which finally appeared in the summer of 1693. His version of the invocation to Book I of the *Metamorphoses*, in which Ovid asks the gods for inspiration, speaks of "my long laborious Work" (l. 4), a telling interpolation, yet Dryden later referred to that translation as one of his best.[72]

Dryden's capacity to produce work he could be proud of during years of intermittent sickness, painful poverty, and rapid labor is impressive. In his prefatory letter to

Eleonora, he describes his recent "ill health" with one of his favorite metaphors: "I cannot say that I have escap'd from a Shipwreck; but have only gain'd a Rock by hard swimming; where I may pant a while and gather breath: For the Doctors give me a sad assurance, that my Disease [possibly gout] never took its leave of any man, but with a purpose to return." Later in the same paragraph, however, pleased with his performance in the poem, he claims that "the weight of thirty Years was taken off me, while I was writing. I swom with the Tyde, and the Water under me was buoyant" (III, 231–32). Taken literally, "thirty years" would bring us back to the time of the Restoration, and *Eleonora* is a deliberately old-fashioned poem, closely following the organization and rhetorical strategy of Donne's *Anniversaries*;[73] some of the astrological and geometric metaphors recall similar passages in Dryden's earliest poems, the elegies for Hastings and Cromwell.[74] The echoes are not so close as to establish beyond doubt that the old poet was consciously reworking his early elegies, but he was certainly conscious of experiencing a youthful burst of creativity:

> The Reader will easily observe, that I was transported, by the multitude and variety of my Similitudes; which are generally the product of a luxuriant Fancy; and the wantonness of Wit. Had I call'd in my Judgment to my assistance, I had certainly retrench'd many of them. But I defend them not; let them pass for beautiful faults amongst the better sort of Critiques. [III, 232]

The first of these multiple and various "Similitudes" may serve to illustrate the complexity and beauty of this noble poem:

> As, when some Great and Gracious Monarch dies,
> Soft whispers, first, and mournful Murmurs rise
> Among the sad Attendants; then, the sound
> Soon gathers voice, and spreads the news around,
> Through Town and Country, till the dreadful blast
> Is blown to distant Colonies at last;
> Who, then perhaps, were off'ring Vows in vain,
> For his long life, and for his happy Reign:
> So slowly, by degrees, unwilling *Fame*
> Did Matchless *Eleonora*'s fate proclaim,
> Till publick as the loss, the news became.
>
> [ll. 1–11]

Thanks to her charity, humility, and piety, all duly celebrated later in the poem, Eleonora is like a monarch: her death diminishes the nation. Dryden's delicate verses grow more forceful as "mournful Murmurs" build toward a "dreadful blast," but his metaphor derives additional power from public and private memory: readers would surely have remembered the recent death of that "Great and Gracious Monarch" Charles II; Dryden himself may have remembered kneeling in fruitless prayer for Charles I at Westminster on the fateful morning of the execution.

In the Hastings poem, Dryden's immature response to that first wrenching royal death, elegiac nostalgia shares space with satiric bitterness: the youthful poet longs for past virtues as a way of excoriating the failings of the present age. In a vastly more subtle and mature way, Dryden's writings during his last decade recapitulate that combination, as the dedication to this poem shows:

> They say my Talent is Satyre; if it be so, 'tis a Fruitful Age; and there is an extraordinary Crop to gather. They have sown the Dragons Teeth themselves; and 'tis but just they shou'd reap each other in Lampoons. You, my Lord, who have the Character of Honour, though 'tis not my Happiness to know You, may stand aside, with the small Remainder of the *English* Nobility, truly such, and unhurt yourselves, behold the mad Combat. [III, 234]

This passage parallels the remarks about "smil[ing] at the madness of the dance" in the dedication to *Don Sebastian,* but if Dryden was pleased to represent his noble patrons as a "small Remainder," detached from the partisan fray, he could not himself resist opportunities for specific satire, literary and political. The phrase reporting that "They say my Talent is Satyre" looks like a generalized summary of coffeehouse chat, but actually points at Gerard Langbaine, whose *Account of the English Dramatick Poets* (1691), a book quite hostile to Dryden, is also dedicated to Abingdon. Of Dryden, whom he again accused of plagiarism, Langbaine had written: "His Genius seems to me to incline to Tragedy and Satyr, rather than Comedy; and methinks he writes much better in *Heroicks* [rhymed couplets], than in *blank verse*" (p. 131). Dryden's claim that *Eleonora,* "though written in that which they call Heroique Verse, is of the Pindarique nature" may also be a claim to the originality and creativity Langbaine had denied him.

If he looked into the copy of Langbaine's book that was doubtless presented to him as the dedicatee, Abingdon may have realized that Dryden was answering Langbaine, and we may even imagine him being amused, but it is much more difficult to imagine what response Dryden expected the Earl to make to the political language in the elegy itself. In describing the relationship between Abingdon and his wife, the poet naturally has recourse to the traditional hierarchical comparisons between husband and wife, God and humankind, king and subject; unlike Milton, however, he qualifies the traditional view, emphasizing love rather than duty:

> Love and Obedience to her Lord she bore,
> She much obey'd him but she lov'd him more.
> Not aw'd to Duty by superior sway;
> But taught by his Indulgence to obey.
> Thus we love God as Author of our good;
> So Subjects love just Kings, or so they shou'd.

[ll. 177–82]

That wry last phrase acknowledges the failure of Englishmen to love James II, despite his issuing a Declaration of "Indulgence." As the poem draws to a close, Dryden suggests that the Countess was too good to live in an age so bad, and that his praise of her is in effect the satire that he dares not write:

> Let this suffice: Nor thou, great Saint, refuse
> This humble Tribute of no vulgar Muse:
> Who, not by Cares, or Wants, or Age deprest,
> Stems a wild Deluge with a dauntless brest:

And dares to sing thy Praises, in a Clime
Where Vice triumphs, and Vertue is a Crime:
Where ev'n to draw the Picture of thy Mind,
Is Satyr on the most of Humane Kind:
Take it, while yet 'tis Praise; before my rage
Unsafely just, break loose on this bad Age;
So bad, that thou thy self had'st no defence,
From Vice, but barely by departing hence.

[ll. 359–70]

In the winter of 1691–92, when he wrote these lines, Dryden was suffering the "Cares" of bodily sickness and the "Wants" of a doubly-taxed Catholic; his sixty years more than qualified him to speak of "Age." The "rage" he felt at such indignities as the delaying of *Cleomenes* was, in his own phrase, "Unsafely just," yet despite his concern for safety and survival, a concern I believe he was dramatizing in the wittily prevaricating Philidel, Dryden rarely published a work without finding some place to express his distaste for the times. In this case, the political risk taken seems considerable. There is no evidence to suggest that the Earl of Abingdon was a Jacobite; his sister Bridget was married to the Earl of Danby, now called the Marquis of Carmarthen, who was the new King's principal advisor. Like his brother-in-law, Abingdon had signed the letter inviting William to invade; although he had opposed crowning William, preferring a somewhat more legal "regency" scheme, he was now sufficiently trusted to have been reappointed Lord Lieutenant of Oxfordshire.[75] Dryden's moral condemnation of the "bad Age" might be read as a generalized Juvenalian complaint; it closely resembles Juvenal's criticisms of Rome, which he was translating at the same time. But it is hard to imagine anyone, even a grieving husband, reading the line about subjects loving just kings without some inkling of a contemporary political message. Here as elsewhere, Dryden apparently believed that the sheer quality of his poetry would carry him through. At the end of the dedication, he praises Abingdon for "endeavouring to raise for [his wife], the most durable Monument, which is that of Verse" (III, 233), and he clearly expected such noblemen to support the arts, especially poetry.

We may trace the same nostalgia and the same moral fervor in the "Discourse of the Original and Progress of Satire," addressed to Dryden's chief protector in the government, the Earl of Dorset. Dryden's stated task is describing the development of satire from the Greeks to the Romans to the modern poets, but he is at least as interested in a nostalgic recounting of his own career. He reminds Dorset of their friendship at the time of the *Essay of Dramatick Poesie*, "When I was . . . in the Rudiments of my Poetry" (IV, 4), recalls his boyish fondness for Cowley, describes his careful study of Milton and Spenser "about Twenty Years ago" (IV, 84–85; quoted above, p. 257), and gives a sad account of his plan to write an epic poem, which had been much on his mind in the 1670s. Aware that his epic dream will never be fulfilled, he makes an explanation of his failure that deftly skips over the reign of James II: "But being encourag'd only with fair Words, by King *Charles* II, my little Sallary ill paid, and no prospect of a future Subsistance, I was then Discourag'd in the beginning of my Attempt; and now Age has overtaken me; and Want, a more insufferable Evil, through the Change of the Times, has wholly disenabl'd me" (IV, 23). "The Change of the Times" seems a particularly bland formula, coming as it does from a poet who had recently threatened to let his "rage / Unsafely just, break loose on this bad Age." In that same passage in *Eleonora*, striking the pose of the dauntless satirist, Dryden had claimed that he was "not by Cares, or Wants, or Age deprest." The self-pitying talk of being "wholly disenabl'd" here, which contradicts that bravado, is doubtless designed to garner sympathy; it leads quickly to praise of Dorset for his "bountiful Present" to Dryden at the time of the Revolution, "an Action of pure disinteress'd Charity" by a man willing to "lay aside all the Considerations of Factions and Parties."

In expressing his gratitude, Dryden appears to promise not to attack the government: "I must not presume to defend the Cause for which I now suffer, because your Lordship is engag'd against it" (IV, 23), but if Dorset moved on past the "Discourse" to the translations themselves, he surely saw that Dryden was using these translations to defend himself and his principles on almost every page. The third satire of Juvenal, for example, is largely devoted to the parting speech of a man named Umbricius, who has made up his mind to leave the degenerate and corrupt Rome for a simpler life in the country. In Juvenal, the speech begins with three general complaints: there is no place for honest arts in the city, no reward for labor, and Umbricius gets less money each day. The details added in Dryden's rendering make his identification with Umbricius unmistakable:

> Since Noble Arts in *Rome* have no support,
> And ragged Virtue not a Friend at Court,
> No Profit rises from th' ungrateful Stage,
> My Poverty encreasing with my Age,
> 'Tis time to give my just Disdain a vent,
> And, Cursing, leave so base a Government.
>
> [ll. 39–44]

"Friend at Court," "ungrateful Stage," and "so base a Government" have no basis at all in the Latin, but an obvious basis in Dryden's life since the Revolution. Dorset had used his position as Lord Chamberlain to act as Dryden's most important friend at court, effectively defending him from those who wanted to keep his plays off the stage altogether, yet this passage risks insulting him—especially when Dryden refers to the government he served as "base." As in some passages of *Eleonora*, Dryden the poet seems carried away by satirical rage, despite the more cautious stance taken by Dryden the prose dedicator.

Even Dryden's praise of Dorset for exemplifying the ideal of a learned aristocrat who supports the arts ultimately leads to political satire. In the headnote to the third satire of Persius, Dryden recalls having translated the poem at Westminster "for a *Thursday* Nights *Exercise*" (IV, 293), and the fifth satire, a dialogue between Persius and his tutor, is "inscrib'd"

> to my Learned Master Doctor *Busby*; to whom I am not only oblig'd my self, for the best part of my own Education, and that of my two Sons; but have also receiv'd from him the first and truest Taste of *Persius*. May he be pleas'd to find in this Translation,

the Gratitude, or at least some small Acknowledgment of his unworthy Scholar, at the distance of 42 Years, from the time when I departed from under his Tuition. [IV, 323]

His fresh encounter with the Roman satirists naturally reminded the old poet of his first exercises in translation under Busby's careful eye; this touching tribute may also have been motivated by a serious illness Busby suffered at about the time Dryden was working on these translations.[76] But there is more than nostalgia at work here: both the satire Dryden remembered translating as a boy and the one he dedicated to his old schoolmaster celebrate the life of learning, heaping scorn on "Young Noblemen, [who] by reason of their High Birth, and the Great Possessions of their Fathers, . . . are careless of adorning their Minds with Precepts of Moral Philosophy" (IV, 293). The teenaged Dryden had made a similar point in the Hastings elegy, complaining that the death of that promising aristocratic scholar gave "Our *Noble Youth* . . . pretence to be / Dunces securely, Ign'rant healthfully" (ll. 13–14). The old Dryden had before him the extreme example of King William, who was fixated on military adventures and entirely uninterested in intellectual or artistic pursuits. In a passage in the "Discourse" praising Boileau, he goes out of his way to refer to Louis XIV as "the Patron of all Arts," comparing him to Augustus Caesar and extolling "the Bounty of that King to Men of Learning and Merit: A Praise so just, that even we who are his Enemies, cannot refuse it to him" (IV, 12–13). The qualification does not diminish the implicit criticism of William, and the poems themselves make that criticism explicit, especially in Dryden's free and daring rendering of Persius's lines asking Jupiter to punish "savage tyrants," which reflects his opposition to a government he later called "a stupid Military State" ("To Kneller," l. 51):

> Great Father of the Gods, when, for our Crimes,
> Thou send'st some heavy Judgment on the Times;
> Some Tyrant-King, the Terrour of his Age,
> The Type, and true Vicegerent of thy Rage;
> Thus punish him: Set Virtue in his Sight,
> With all her Charms adorn'd; with all her Graces bright:
> But set her distant; make him pale to see
> His Gains out-weigh'd by lost Felicity!
>
> ["Satyr III," ll. 65–72]

As the response to such earlier public events as the plague and the Great Fire had shown, Dryden's contemporaries of all religious and political persuasions were quick to interpret public disasters as punishments for national crimes. When the Navy defeated the French fleet in the battle of La Hogue (19 May 1692), Evelyn wrote a pious diary entry praising "the Providence of God," but when the Army suffered "the deplorable Losse of many brave men" at Steinkirk (24 July/3 August 1692), he blamed "an indiscreete endeavor of K. William." The next summer brought disaster on land and sea: the English merchant fleet carrying spices home from Turkey was shattered in the Mediterranean by the French, and the major battles in the campaign for Flanders were defeats. Evelyn responded to the news of "the taking of our Turkey Marchant[s] & Convoy" by calling it the "forerunner of destruction for our folly & precipitous Change

&c."[77] His second thoughts about the Revolution, shared at this time by many English-men, had brought him quite close to Dryden's idea of William as a "Tyrant-King," imposed on England as a "heavy Judgment on the Times." But Evelyn's misgivings, secretly confided to his diary, were private, while Dryden's Jacobitical interpolations into Persius and Juvenal, however subtle, were public. In an era when the printers of Jacobite propaganda were regularly arrested and sometimes hanged,[78] Dryden's con-tinued insistence on the right of poetry to express dissenting opinions was courageous indeed.

Friends and Enemies

In its discussion of personal and literary satire, the "Discourse" explores another old conflict between Dryden's principles and his practice. While comparing Horace and Juvenal, Dryden notices that Horace's odes and epodes mention "his private Enemies," while his "Discourses, which are more properly call'd the *Roman* Satire . . . correct the Vices and the Follies of his Time, and . . . give the Rules of a Happy and Virtuous Life." Considering the vexed question of specific satire in general, he goes on to declare personal lampoons "a dangerous sort of Weapon, and for the most part Unlawful. We have no Moral right on the Reputation of other Men. 'Tis taking from them, what we cannot restore to them." Among possible "Reasons, for which we may be permitted to write Lampoons," he allows "Revenge, when we have been affronted in the same Nature," and readers of this book will remember some spectacular instances of such revenge in Dryden's own career. The qualification with which he continues, however, reflects his continued respect for the ideal of Christian forgiveness:

> we know, that in Christian Charity, all Offences are to be forgiven; as we expect the like Pardon for those which we daily commit against Almighty God. And this Considera-tion has often made me tremble when I was saying our Saviour's Prayer; . . . For which Reason I have many times avoided the Commission of that Fault; ev'n when I have been notoriously provok'd. [IV, 58–59]

Dryden had in fact written nothing resembling a lampoon for years; his last involvement in pamphlet warfare had been *The Vindication of the Duke of Guise* (1683). He had let Tom Brown's three dialogues go unanswered, and had replied to Langbaine and Charles Montagu by rejecting their charges without mentioning their names. But the "Discourse" itself contains a subtle act of revenge against another enemy. Shadwell was using the office of the Laureate, to which Dorset had appointed him, to hurt the old and impoverished Dryden whenever he could; his machinations had led to the banning of the prologue to *The Prophetess* and the delay of *Cleomenes*. So Dryden, who had never officially claimed *MacFlecknoe*, took this occasion to acknowledge his authorship. At the end of a list of Varronian satires, he included "(if it be not too vain, to mention any thing of my own) the Poems of *Absalom*, and *Mac Fleckno*" (IV, 48). Everyone had long considered Dryden the author of *Mac Flecknoe*, but responsibility for that poem was not a dead issue; as recently as 1687, in the dedication to his own translation of a satire by Juvenal, Shadwell had alleged that Dryden denied writing it to his face. Dryden's quiet acknowledgment here might thus have given Shadwell an opportunity for crowing, but he had no chance to reply: he died of an opium overdose on 20 November 1692, less than a month after the publication of this essay.[79]

Like Dryden, Shadwell had held the two offices of Poet Laureate and Historiographer Royal; on his death, Dorset appointed Nahum Tate Laureate and Thomas Rymer Historiographer.[80] Tate had long been involved with Dryden, most recently as a contributor to the Juvenal translation, but Dryden evidently considered his work second-rate; by translating Ovid, he was deliberately competing with Tate, who had announced plans for a translation of the complete *Metamorphoses* "by several hands."[81] Dryden had also scoffed at Rymer's poetry in private letters, though he treated Rymer's criticism with respect in print. Emboldened by his new appointment, Rymer now published *A Short View of Tragedy* (December 1692), a book dedicated to Dorset and calculated to displease Dryden. Although he did not attack Dryden's plays as specifically as Langbaine had done, Rymer celebrated ancient Greek tragedy at the expense of modern tragedy, criticizing Dryden's hero Shakespeare and even advocating a return to the use of a chorus.

Dryden's irritation at Rymer's pedantic opinions and Tate's pedestrian poetry contrasts strongly with his active support of Congreve, whom he recognized as an authentic talent. According to Southerne, Dryden read the manuscript of *The Old Batchelor*, Congreve's first play, and "sayd he never saw such a first play in his life, but the Author not being acquainted with the stage or the town, it woud be pity to have it miscarry for want of a little Assistance." He then "putt it in the order it was playd," adopting it to "the fashionable cutt of the town," and the comedy had a successful run in the spring of 1693.[82] In a commendatory poem printed with the published play, Southerne made a point that Dryden would make more memorably later in the year: though "holding now from none / But great Apollo his undoubted crown," Dryden was still the leading writer of the nation, and Congreve, "The darling and last comfort of his years," was "The natural successor of his mind."[83] Dryden's generation of dramatists was now nearly extinct; like his enemy Shadwell, his friends Etherege, Otway, and Lee were dead. Only Wycherley, who was well past playwriting, remained; later in this spring, Dryden asked Walsh to contribute a prefatory poem to a proposed edition of Wycherley's poems, explaining that Congreve and Southerne had already agreed to do so (*Letters*, p. 54). Several other young men published defenses of Dryden at about this time. John Dennis answered Rymer in *The Impartial Critick*, advertised in February 1693; he was exchanging friendly letters with Dryden by the next winter. Charles Gildon paid the old poet visits and wrote him a flattering letter dated 10 May 1693; he, too, published an answer to Rymer in the summer of 1694. Joseph Addison contributed a poem in praise of Dryden's translation of Ovid to *Examen Poeticum*; it is dated from Magdalen College on 2 June 1693, but Addison was soon spending time in London with Dryden; if Dennis's later testimony may be believed, Addison tempted the old poet to drink beyond his customary habits.[84]

His friendships with these younger writers were a comfort to the aged Dryden, but his financial troubles continued. In the autumn of 1692, Tonson offered him £50 in advance for some unspecified translations. Dryden successfully insisted on 50 guineas, but according to Tonson's later letter on this subject, our only source, there was no specific contract stipulating what authors or how many lines Dryden would translate. He wrote to Tonson from the country on 3 October 1692, reporting his progress on the first book of the *Metamorphoses* and mentioning a price of 20 guineas for part of that book. After trying unsuccessfully to get that price from Motteux, he sent the manuscript to Tonson, only to receive a carping letter complaining of unfair dealings. Basing his calculations on Dryden's willingness to sell 759 lines of translated verse to "a strange Bookseller" for 20 guineas, Tonson laboriously worked out a formula according to which Dryden was honor-bound to make further contributions to the *Examen Poeticum*, and Dryden eventually gave Tonson the whole first book of the *Metamorphoses*, two episodes from later books, the parting of Hector and Andromache from the *Iliad*, a pair of erotic songs, and a translation of the Latin hymn "Veni Creator Spiritus." Not only did Dryden have to provide a great deal of poetry for little pay, but Francis, Lord Radcliffe, a Catholic gentleman amateur who had made contributions to the miscellany, proved unable to reward him for the dedication. In a letter of 30 August 1693, a month or so after the book appeared, Dryden discusses this matter with Tonson: "I am sure you thought My Lord Radclyffe wou'd have done something: I ghessd more truly, that he cou'd not; but I was too farr ingagd to desist; though I was tempted to it, by the melancholique prospect I had of it" (*Letters*, p. 58). I should think it possible that Tonson, struck by how poor Dryden's return for his efforts had been, made an additional payment to him at this point, despite his hard dealing of the previous winter. In his next letter (13 September; p. 60), Dryden expresses heartfelt gratitude for Tonson's "last kindnesses."[85] A more private financial arrangement also went sour during the spring of 1693: on 9 May, Dryden wrote to Walsh, explaining a long silence:

> I am up to the Eares in law; & have been for six weekes together. I have been cousend of fifty pounds, & more, by one whom I thought my Friend: & am affrayd that at the long run, I will rather loose it, & let him go, whom I have arrested, than prosecute him in the tedious court of Chancery; to do which I must pass through a tedious course of Common Law. [*Letters*, p. 52]

The cheating friend has never been identified, and there was no lawsuit; Dryden evidently lost both his money and his time.

The same letter reports some progress on "a Tragicomedy of the nature of the Spanish Fryar" and urges Walsh to write a preface for it: "I shall be very proud, of your entring into the lists, though not against Rymer; yet as a champion for our cause, who defy the Chorus of the Ancients." The procedure Dryden recommends to Walsh, refuting Rymer without using his name, is the strategy he follows himself in dedicating *Examen Poeticum* to Lord Radcliffe. He treats Rymer with deadly contempt, omitting his name but answering his argument in a way no attentive reader could miss:

> For if we or our greater Fathers [Shakespeare and Jonson], have not yet brought the Drama to an absolute Perfection, yet at least we have carried it much farther than those Ancient *Greeks;* who beginning from a Chorus, cou'd never totally exclude it, as we have done, who find it an unprofitable encumbrance, without any necessity of Entertaining it amongst us; and without the possibility of establishing it here, unless it were

supported by a Publick Charge. Neither can we accept of those Lay-Bishops, as some call them, who under pretence of reforming the Stage, wou'd intrude themselves upon us, as our Superiours, being indeed incompetent Judges of what is Manners, what Religion, and most of all, what is Poetry and Good Sense. I can tell them in behalf of all my Fellows [presumably Congreve, Southerne, and Walsh], that when they come to Exercise a Jurisdiction over us, they shall have the Stage to themselves, as they have the Lawrel. [IV, 367–68]

Dryden's understandable irritation at seeing "Wits of the Second Order" (IV, 364) elevated to his old places fuels this passage, and the dedication as a whole is the least cautious piece of prose he had published since the Revolution. On the opening page, he grouses about the "barren . . . Reward [of] Fame," contrasting his own "unprofitable . . . Study" as a poet with the "Honours of the Gown . . . given to Men of as little Learning and less Honesty than my self." Here Dryden's lifelong jealousy of clergymen and lawyers focuses particularly on the elevation of Rymer and Tate, appointees of a government he proceeds to attack in a fervent Juvenalian criticism of political corruption: "No Government has ever been, or ever can be, wherein Time-servers and Blockheads will not be uppermost. The Persons are only chang'd, but the same juglings in State, the same Hypocrisie in Religion, the same Self-Interest, and Mis-mannagement, will remain for ever" (IV, 363). Even a comparison between Homer and Virgil, which begins as a literary exercise, reveals Dryden's opposition to the costly military adventures of William. "*Homer*, says Dryden, "forms and equips those ungodly Man-killers, whom we Poets, when we flatter them, call Heroes; a race of Men who can never enjoy quiet in themselves, 'till they have taken it from all the World. This is *Homer*'s Commendation, and such as it is, the Lovers of Peace, or at least of more moderate Heroism, will never Envy him" (IV, 374). This preface appeared in print as the summer campaigns of 1693 turned into disaster on land and sea.[86] Its implicit criticism of the government can hardly have escaped notice, and Dryden may also have been thinking about episodes of private violence. The previous winter had furnished gruesome proof of the ability of noblemen to get away with murder: on 9 December 1692, Lord Mohun and his friend Captain Hill attempted to abduct the beautiful actress Anne Bracegirdle from the theatre; when the actor William Mountfort interfered, they followed him home and "ran him through the belly." Mohun was arrested, but Dryden's former antagonist Charles Montagu quickly bailed him out; worse yet, when Mohun was rearrested, he pleaded his privilege and was tried by the House of Lords. Despite unimpeachable evidence proving that Mohun and Hill had lain in wait for Mountford and killed him before he could draw his own sword, the Lords acquitted Mohun by a vote of sixty-nine to fourteen on 3 February 1693.[87] As a landowner, a university man, and a prominent writer with friends among the great, Dryden outranked a mere actor like Mountfort, but he had been beaten up in Rose Alley while holding the position of Laureate, and he now lacked even the flimsy protection of an official post; his fellow Catholics and Jacobites were being constantly harassed and arrested.

Under these circumstances, Dryden's characterizing those in power as "Time-servers and Blockheads" was surely foolhardy, and something in this dedication evidently provoked a reaction. In the letter discussing Radcliffe's inability to remunerate him, Dryden told Tonson that Rymer was at work on a counterattack:

> About a fortnight ago I had an intimation from a friend [Dorset?] by letter, That one of the Secretaryes, I suppose Trenchard had informd the Queen, that I had abusd her Government (those were the words) in my Epistle to my Lord Radclyffe; & that thereupon, she had commanded her Historiographer Rymer, to fall upon my Playes; wch he [the friend] assures me is now doeing. I doubt not his [Rymer's] malice, from a former hint you gave me: & if he be employd, I am confident tis of his own seeking; who you know has spoken slightly of me in his last Critique [*A Short View of Tragedy*]: & that gave me occasion to snarl again. [*Letters*, p. 59]

But if Rymer was working on a specific criticism of Dryden, whether on his own initiative or on orders from above, it never saw print. Dryden's characterization of his own dedication as "snarl[ing] again" suggests his awareness that he had gone too far; his apprehensiveness suggests his vulnerability. As always, he was conscious of his need for friends. In the same letter, he thanks Tonson warmly for keeping him company on his journey to Northamptonshire a few weeks earlier and promises a new Ovidian translation, this one evidently the first book of the *Ars Amatoria*.[88] He also sends a message to his wife, asking her to buy him some plums, and declares himself "Mr Congreve's true Lover." His next letter reports a case of Dryden's habitual "civility to strangers": a party of travellers including "foure Ladyes and two Gentlemen" found themselves "benighted" near the home of Sir Matthew Dudley, with whom the poet was staying; a fish Dryden had caught served them for supper, and he also felt "obligd . . . to resign [his] bed to them" (p. 60). Sleepy from sitting up most of the night, he rejoices in the kindness of Southerne and Congreve, who have promised to meet the coach from Oundle and accompany him on the last four miles of his journey home.

When he returned to London on 20 September 1693, Dryden had a number of projects under way. He had probably finished writing his new tragicomedy, *Love Triumphant*, designed from the start as his farewell play, but he could look forward to the usual time-consuming work necessary to get the play produced; it finally came on stage sometime in January. Translation continued to occupy him: he had been working on Ovid in the country, though his version of the *Ars Amatoria* did not appear in print during his lifetime, and he had probably now promised to participate in a group translation of Lucian.[89] By December, he had "undertaken to translate all Virgil: & as an Essay, ha[d] already paraphrasd, the third Georgique [a poem of over eight hundred lines], as an Example" (*Letters*, p. 64). In time borrowed from these projects, he wrote two fine poems to friends: "To My Dear Friend Mr. Congreve," printed with *The Double Dealer* in December 1693, and "To Sir Godfrey Kneller," printed in Tonson's *Annual Miscellany* for 1694 the following July. In both poems, Dryden draws upon the emotions we have been tracing in his letters and prefaces: he expresses his contempt for critics, his irritation at the appointments of Rymer and Tate, his frustration at the poor monetary rewards of poetry, his distaste for the current regime, his disappointment at being unable to write an epic poem, his pride in his own accomplishments, his belief in the power of poetry (especially satire), and his devotion to his friends. In the dedication of *Examen Poeticum*, these feelings had caused him to "snarl," and in his private letters, he sometimes sounds querulous; but in the poems to Congreve and Kneller, he finds a way to transform his feelings into art.

The master trope of the poem to Congreve is the idea of succession, which had fascinated Dryden throughout his career. Not only had he devoted himself to defending the Stuart succession and based many of his plays on disputed successions to regal thrones, but he conceived of literary history as a succession of paternal and fraternal relationships. His first theatrical prologue refers to Fletcher and Jonson as "Elder Brothers . . . that vastly spent," and his devastating attack on Shadwell in *Mac Flecknoe* offers a comic succession of bad writers as a contrast to the legitimate succession of true poets. When he sat down to praise *The Double Dealer*, Dryden was able to draw on a lifetime of experience in developing the idea of succession; he was also attentive to the recent false succession of Rymer and Tate, and aware that Southerne had already identified Congreve as his true successor. In a witty capsule history of the English theatre, he speaks of the Elizabethan dramatists as "the Gyant Race, before the Flood," credits Charles II with "Tam[ing] us to manners, when the Stage was rude," and complains that "what we gain'd in skill we lost in strength," characterizing his own generation of dramatists as "cultivated," but "curst . . . with want of Genius" (ll. 4, 9, 11–13). Congreve, of course, combines skill and strength, a point Dryden makes by means of an analogy between drama and architecture:

> Firm *Dorique* Pillars found Your solid Base:
> The Fair *Corinthian* Crowns the higher Space;
> Thus all below is Strength, and all above is Grace.
>
> [ll. 17–19]

In a London now transformed by the work of Sir Christopher Wren, such analogies came easily, and Dryden calls attention to his own architectural skill by making this point in a triplet with a closing alexandrine; a few lines later, praising Congreve's mastery of all dramatic styles at a literal level, he repeats that formal structure:

> In Him all Beauties of this Age we see;
> *Etherege* his Courtship, *Southern*'s Purity;
> The Satire, Wit, and Strength of Manly *Witcherly*.
>
> [ll. 28–30]

In Dryden's earlier poems in praise of other writers, the compliments often carry an undertone of irony, which serves to express Dryden's own pride as a writer: he treats Sir Robert Howard as a talented noble amateur but reserves the role of professional for himself; he praises John Oldham's satiric vigor but wryly notes that he had not mastered "the numbers of [his] native Tongue" (l. 14); he credits Anne Killigrew with morality and innocence but treats her poetic and artistic inventions with paternalistic condescension ("What next she had design'd, Heav'n only knows," l. 146). Dryden certainly had not lost his pride, and we may legitimately wonder whether he really believed that Congreve's two comedies heralded a "promis'd hour," a "present Age of Wit" that "obscures the past" (ll. 1–2). A few years later, in a letter remarking upon an innovation in theatrical advertising, "the printing [of] an Authours name, in a Play bill," he reported the revival of a "Comedy of Mr Congreve's calld the Double Dealer, which was never very takeing" (*Letters*, p. 113). But in this unusually gracious poem, he explicitly eschews competition and envy, preferring to celebrate friendship:

> All this in blooming Youth you have Atchiev'd;
> Nor are your foil'd Contemporaries griev'd;
> So much the sweetness of your manners move,
> We cannot envy you because we Love.
>
> [ll. 31–34]

As usual, the first-person plural is an inclusive gesture, but Dryden did not really consider himself Congreve's "Contemporary" or rival, preferring to think of himself as Congreve's poetic father. His praise of Congreve thus includes a proud assertion of his own legitimacy as the rightful monarch of poetry:

> Oh that your Brows my Lawrel had sustain'd
> Well had I been Depos'd, if You had reign'd!
> The Father had descended for the Son;
> For only you are lineal to the Throne.
>
> [ll. 41–44]

The most obvious of many precedents for this imagery in Dryden's work is *Mac Flecknoe*, where the incompetent Flecknoe anoints the incompetent Shadwell as his son and successor. Dryden reclaims that language here for a serious use, but not without glancing at the continuing false succession that has elevated Rymer to the position of Historiographer Royal:

> But now, not I, but Poetry is curs'd;
> For *Tom* the Second reigns like *Tom* the first.
> But let 'em not mistake my Patron's part;
> Nor call his Charity their just desert.
>
> [ll. 47–50]

At the end of *Religio Laici*, Dryden had linked Shadwell with Sternhold on the basis of their common first name; by the same device, he now makes Rymer ("*Tom* the Second") the natural successor to Shadwell ("*Tom* the first"). Since Rymer prided himself on his learning, equating him with the relatively ignorant Shadwell was an effective insult. By claiming Dorset, who had appointed both Toms, as "my Patron," Dryden insists that such noblemen belong by right to the true poets, and warns Rymer against supposing that his new office is the result of "just desert." He predicts that Congreve will "be seen . . . High on the Throne of Wit" (ll. 51, 53), compares his inborn genius to Shakespeare's, and enlists the younger man as a defender of his own reputation:

> Already I am worn with Cares and Age;
> And just abandoning th' Ungrateful Stage:
> Unprofitably kept at Heav'ns expence,
> I live a Rent-charge on his Providence:
> But You, whom ev'ry Muse and Grace adorn,

> Whom I foresee to better Fortune born,
> Be kind to my Remains; and oh defend,
> Against Your Judgment, Your departed Friend!
> Let not the Insulting Foe my Fame pursue;
> But shade those Lawrels which descend to You.
>
> [ll. 66–76]

The rhyme between "Age" and "Ungrateful Stage" repeats Dryden's personal interpolation in the translation of Juvenal's third satire (quoted above, p. 458), but despite the common phrases, the picture Dryden draws of himself here is different from the defiant Juvenalian pose he had struck in that translation and in *Eleonora*, where he had claimed that he was "not by Cares, or Wants, or Age deprest." He acknowledges that he is indeed "worn with Cares and Age," but he does not descend to the maudlin self-pity of the parallel passage in the "Discourse": "Age has overtaken me; and Want, a more insufferable Evil, through the Change of the Times, has wholly disenabl'd me." In this new context, Dryden refers to his own age and fatigue in order to compliment Congreve. His concern about his finances, prominent in his other writings of this period, turns into a joke about living as a "Rent-charge" at "Heav'ns expence." As we have seen in his letter asking Walsh to enter the lists as a champion in opposition to Rymer's opinions, Dryden often asked his younger friends to take his part in literary controversies, but making such a request in a public poem transforms a simple gesture into something larger. By asking Congreve to defend his reputation after his death, Dryden declares the younger man able to take on that task. The epic resonance of a phrase like "the Insulting Foe" even points in the direction of an allegory in which a heroic Congreve, blessed with Shakespeare's genius and adorned by "ev'ry Muse and Grace," defends the corpse of Dryden from the barbaric warriors seeking to despoil it.

In his poem to the court painter Sir Godfrey Kneller, probably written just after the poem to Congreve, Dryden makes that heroic allegory explicit and complex, ultimately claiming the role of heroic defender of the arts for himself. In addition to painting Dryden's portrait, Kneller had given the poet a copy of the Chandos portrait of Shakespeare, and Dryden's expression of thanks for that gift leads into the imagery of heroic warfare:

> *Shakespear* thy Gift, I place before my sight;
> With awe, I ask his Blessing e're I write;
> With Reverence look on his Majestick Face;
> Proud to be less; but of his Godlike Race.
> His Soul Inspires me, while thy Praise I write,
> And I like *Teucer*, under *Ajax* Fight.
> Bids thee through me, be bold; with dauntless breast
> Contemn the bad, and Emulate the best.
> Like his, thy Criticks in th'attempt are lost;
> When most they rail, know then, they envy most.
> In vain they snarl a-loof; a noisy Crow'd,
> Like Womens Anger, impotent and loud.
>
> [ll. 73–84]

Portrait of Dryden by Sir Godfrey Kneller, 1693.

In the *Iliad*, Teucer is a diminutive warrior who seeks protection under the huge shield of Ajax. Dryden plays Teucer to Shakespeare's Ajax, but he nonetheless claims to be "of [Shakespeare's] Godlike Race," a poet in the true succession of English poets. His praise of Kneller's painting, though gracefully and wittily expressed, leaves little doubt that he considers the race of painters inferior to the race of poets; the turning point in this passage comes when Shakespeare's soul, speaking through Dryden, encourages Kneller to be bold. If Dryden needs Shakespeare's protection, Kneller needs Dryden's, and the poet goes on to picture himself fending off Kneller's windy critics:

> Old as she is, my Muse shall march behind;
> Bear off the blast, and intercept the wind.

[ll. 87–88]

Like the poem to Congreve, the poem to Kneller is finally a poem about Dryden.[90] By comparing Kneller's unspecified critics with Shakespeare's, Dryden points directly at Rymer, who had slighted Shakespeare (and Dryden) in *A Short View of Tragedy*; he repeats this criticism of Rymer in the prologue to *Love Triumphant* (January 1694) and in a letter to Dennis (March 1694). When Dryden says that such impotent critics "snarl," he applies to Rymer a verb he had used privately to describe his own ill-tempered response to Rymer in the dedication to *Examen Poeticum* (see above, p. 464). The posture Shakespeare's soul recommends to Kneller, "Contemn[ing] the bad . . . with dauntless breast," is not Shakespearean at all; it is the satiric posture Dryden had claimed for himself in *Eleonora*, where he pictured himself "Stem[ming] a wild Deluge with a dauntless brest," singing the praises of the virtuous Eleonora

> in a Clime
> Where Vice triumphs, and Vertue is a Crime:
> Where ev'n to draw the Picture of [her] Mind,
> Is Satyr on the most of Humane Kind.

But Kneller was no Hogarth, and Dryden was surely aware of the difficulty of producing satire by drawing a picture. Like his other works of this period, the poem to Kneller aims satiric barbs at the court: a progress-piece tracing the development of painting from the cave men to the Renaissance pauses significantly in the Dark Ages, described in language designed to suggest William's England:

> *Goths* and *Vandals*, a rude *Northern* Race,
> Did all the matchless Monuments deface.
> Then all the Muses in one ruine lye;
> And Rhyme began t'enervate Poetry.
> Thus in a stupid Military State,
> The Pen and Pencil find an equal fate.
>
> [ll. 47–52]

Kneller's failure to produce monumental history paintings is like Dryden's failure to write an epic; both are consequences of the corrupt taste of "this Age":

> Thy Genius bounded by the Times like mine,
> Drudges on petty Draughts, nor dare design
> A more Exalted Work, and more Divine.
> For what a Song, or senceless Opera
> Is to the Living Labour of a Play;
> Or, what a Play to *Virgil*'s Work wou'd be,
> Such is a single Piece [a portrait] to History.
>
> [ll. 147–53]

These passages link Dryden and Kneller as skilled artists limited by the lack of "just Incouragement" (l. 164). But the other satiric thrust of this poem is based on the fact that the pen of the writer and the pencil of the artist were not finding an equal fate in England. Dryden had lost his official positions in the Revolution, while Kneller had swerved with the times and maintained his. Dryden was barely scraping by, translating for a bookseller who negotiated payment by the line, while Kneller's studio was filled with fashionable people eager to have their portraits made. Since Dryden believed that

poetry was an older and more significant art than painting, he could not avoid expressing his resentment at Kneller's financial success, even though he recognized that he
might offend Kneller. He argued for poetry's primacy with a witty allusion to Eden, and
described the profitability of painting with an allusion to Jacob's stealing the birthright
of Esau:

> Our Arts are Sisters; though not Twins in Birth:
> For Hymns were sung in *Edens* happy Earth,
> By the first Pair; while *Eve* was yet a Saint;
> Before she fell with Pride, and learn'd to paint.
> Forgive th'allusion; 'twas not meant to bite;
> But Satire will have room, where e're I write.
> For oh, the Painter Muse; though last in place,
> Has seiz'd the Blessing first, like *Jacob*'s Race.

[ll. 89–96]

The apology sandwiched between the two Old Testament stories failed; Kneller was
too vain to tolerate even a gentle joke at his own expense, and in an edition printed after
Dryden's death, he arranged to have these and some other less than complimentary
lines excised.

Dryden's confession that "Satire will have room" may stand as a fitting conclusion
to this account of his struggle for survival in the hostile environment of William's
England. A lesser man might have reconverted, or at least acted the part of "a patient
Sufferer, and no Disturber of the Government." But Dryden knew that satire was his
"Golden Work," his fundamental instinct, his way of being. He could not praise a
painter, even a painter who had made him a handsome present, without slyly indicating
his belief in the primacy of poetry; he could not praise Congreve without indicating his
contempt for Rymer; he could not translate Juvenal and Persius without foisting in
descriptions of his own times; he could not even praise a virtuous dead lady without
taking the occasion to chide his countrymen for their failure to remain loyal to "just
Kings." Looked at in the harsh light of the repressive measures often taken by the
government, such satiric gestures were folly, but Dryden, despite financial exigency
and ill health, was sustained by his pride as a poet. His lines celebrating "*Virgil*'s Work"
as a nobler task than a mere play may indicate his humility in the face of original epic, a
form he had been unable to produce; they probably also function as an announcement
of his intention to abandon the stage for good in order to devote his energies to a new
heroic task: his translation of *The Works of Virgil*.

CHAPTER THIRTEEN

"'Tis Well An Old Age Is Out"
1694–1700

"No Reason to be Asham'd"

On 11 January 1694, John Evelyn "Sup'd at Mr Ed Sheldons where was Mr. Dryden the Poet, who now intending to write no more Plays (intent upon the Translation of Virgil) read to us his Prologue & Epilogue to his last Valedictory Play, now shortly to be Acted."[1] The prologue to *Love Triumphant*, with which Dryden amused his dinner partners on this occasion, is the comic last will and testament of Dryden the playwright:

> He Dies, at least to us, and to the Stage,
> And what he has, he leaves this Noble Age.
>
> [ll. 34–35]

The last words here are of course ironic: although *Love Triumphant* invites no particular political reading, its author evidently considered the age ignoble. Early in the writing, he had described the play to Walsh as "a Tragicomedy of the nature of the Spanish Fryar," and the comic plot, in which two rival soldiers court a woman of reputed fortune and dubious virtue, bears some resemblance to the comic plot of *The Spanish Fryar*. But the high plot, written in blank verse with several long patches of rhyming couplets, celebrates a precious devotion to the niceties of honor that recalls some of Dryden's earliest plays; the stylized posturing of jealous kings and supposedly incestuous lovers takes us all the way back to the world of *Secret Love* or even *The Rival Ladies*.

Self-consciously out of style, the play was "damn'd by the universal cry of the town,"[2] when it came on stage, probably a few days after the dinner party. Since Dryden's letters of this period show his usual keen observation of the shifting tastes of the theatre audience, we cannot suppose that his failure to satisfy those tastes was based on ignorance.[3] He was being deliberately old-fashioned: the thought of writing a valedictory play stirred memories of his theatrical apprenticeship, just as the writing of *Eleonora* stirred memories of his early elegy for Hastings. In the play as in the poem, the nostalgia for a bygone era of high heroic virtue implies satiric contempt for current corruption.

The mock-will in the prologue is explicitly satiric:

> He leaves you first, all Plays of his Inditing,
> The whole Estate, which he has got by Writing.
>
> [ll. 36–37]

To its first auditors at the dinner party and in the theatre, the "whole Estate" was a wry joke about the small profits Dryden had realized from a life of writing plays, but he did not fundamentally mean to make that joke at his own expense: as his frequent remarks about patronage suggest, he believed the nobility were obliged to support the arts, and therefore considered his inability to amass an estate by writing an indictment of the times. At another level, he could take comfort in the fact that his life's work in the theatre, now available from Tonson in a collected edition, was a printed estate to be bequeathed to future readers. Maintaining his bantering tone, he points to a group of readers who have already made practical use of his fine language: "The Beaux . . . For half their Love, is made from scraps of Plays" (ll. 38, 40). Although he makes fun of the "Beaux," Dryden is not really hostile toward them, or toward the "Roaring Boys, / Who come in Drunk, and fill the House with noise," to whom "He leaves his Manners" (ll. 43–44). His bitterness is reserved for Rymer:

> He leaves to the dire Critiques of his Wit,
> His Silence and Contempt of all they Writ.
> To *Shakespear*'s Critique, he bequeaths the Curse,
> To find his faults, and yet himself make worse:
> A precious Reader in Poetique Schools,
> Who by his own Examples damns his Rules.
>
> [ll. 45–50]

Dryden recovers his equilibrium with a gallant compliment to "the Fair": "he wishes you may be, / From your dull Critiques, the Lampooners free" (ll. 51–52). But even this conventional couplet, by its juxtaposition to the curses directed at Rymer, suggests that those who have attacked Dryden, like those who publish nasty rumors about the ladies, are less than gentlemen.[4]

The opening lines of the epilogue, again emphasizing "Good Manners," warn the critics that "nothing shou'd be sed / Against this Play, because the Poet's dead" (ll. 1–2). The prologue has prepared us for this metaphor, but there is still some emotional distance between making one's will and declaring oneself dead, and the bald declaration remains surprising. At some level, Dryden was tired of the rough-and-tumble world of theatrical competition and criticism, and wished for the kind of respect accorded his dead contemporaries. In a letter to Dennis, written in March of 1694, he quotes a witty remark made by "Poor Nat. Lee," who had died in 1692, then remarks that "Otway and He are safe by death from all Attacks, but we poor Poets Militant (to use Mr. Cowley's Expression) are at the Mercy of Wretched Scribblers: And when they cannot fasten upon our Verses, they fall upon our Morals, our Principles of State and Religion" (*Letters*, p. 72). Dryden knew whereof he spoke. In a letter of 22 March 1694 describing the new plays of the season, an anonymous critic calls his new tragicomedy "one of the worst he ever writt, if not the very worst." Although willing to concede that "the generality of our audience . . . relish nothing but variety, and think any thing dull and heavy which does not border upon farce," the critic dismisses Dryden's "comical part," evidently an attempt to satisfy that taste for farce, as "beneath the style and shew of a Bartholemew-fair droll." Not content with thus fastening upon Dryden's work, the writer also falls upon his morals: in his account of *The Double Dealer*, he describes Congreve's "Epistle Dedicatory," written "in so defying and hectoring a style, that it was counted rude even by his best friends" as "a thing he owes to Mr Dryden's treacherous friendship, who being jealous of the applause he had gott by his *Old Batchelour*, deluded him into a foolish imitation of his own way of writing angry prefaces." The anonymous critic's attempt to blame Congreve's supposed failings on his "foolish imitation" of Dryden is all too typical of the kind of attack the old poet had suffered for many years.[5] His preposterous suggestion that a "jealous" Dryden hoped Congreve would discredit himself is belied by Dryden's generous poem to Congreve, printed with *The Double Dealer*.

Weary of such attacks, Dryden now attempted to recover the posture of "Silence and Contempt" toward his detractors that he had long recognized as an ideal. For the four other plays he had published since the Revolution, he had chosen Protestant patrons, praising their tolerance of his views, but he had recently dedicated *Examen Poeticum* to the Catholic Lord Radcliffe, and the printed *Love Triumphant*, published in mid-March of 1694, bears a dedication to James Cecil, fourth Earl of Salisbury, a prominent Catholic and Jacobite whose very name was likely to raise the hackles of Dryden's enemies. Like Dryden, Salisbury had converted to Catholicism during the reign of James II. Received into the Church by Cardinal Howard in Rome in 1687, he stubbornly clung to his new faith, and was sent to the Tower for Jacobite plotting in 1689 and 1692.[6] Dryden had obviously written his dedicatory epistle before Salisbury's death on 25 October 1693 and may even have received a financial reward; he presumably felt honor-bound to print the dedication despite the death of his patron. To dedicate the play to Salisbury was to declare his friendship for a man despised as a plotter, and the text of the epistle sends some strong political signals. A reference to "the Honour of my Wife's Relation to your Noble House, to which my Sons may plead some Title, though I cannot" (sig. A3r), is Dryden's first direct allusion to his wife in all his works; it points to the fact that Elizabeth's maternal grandfather, William Cecil, Earl of Exeter, had also been a Catholic.[7] Dryden had reason to be particularly conscious of the Catholic heritage of his sons at this time. The youngest of those sons, Erasmus-Henry, was now completing his training for the priesthood: he was ordained a deacon on [9]/19 September 1693, and a priest on [9]/19 December 1693.[8]

By pretending to be unable to discuss his patron's religious and political beliefs, Dryden rhetorically emphasizes those beliefs: "I am oblig'd, in common Prudence, to . . . cast under a Veil some other of your Praises, as the Chymists use to shadow the Secret of their great Elixir; lest if it were made publick, the World shou'd make a bad use of it" (sig. A4v). By praising Salisbury for "tak[ing] a particular notice of me, even in this lowness of my Fortunes, to which I have voluntarily reduc'd my self; and of which I have no reason to be asham'd" (sig. A3r), he turns a compliment into a proud assertion of his own integrity. In his private letter to Dennis, he makes a similar gesture, insisting on his sincerity by refusing to make arguments for his religious or political principles:

> For my Principles of Religion, I will not justifie them to you. I know yours are far different. For the same Reason I shall say nothing of my Principles of State. I believe you in yours follow the Dictates of your Reason, as I in mine do those of my Conscience. If I thought my self in an Error, I would retract it; I am sure that I suffer for them; and Milton makes even the Devil say, That no Creature is in love with Pain. [*Letters*, p. 73]

By pointing out that his suffering for his beliefs validates his claim to be following the dictates of his conscience, Dryden refutes the old charge that his conversion was a mere convenience, most recently reiterated by Thomas Rogers, who had addressed him in print a few months earlier as "You, whom Religion *sits so loose about.*"[9]

The letters Dennis was writing to Dryden pose no questions about the older man's faith or morals, praising him as "a Person of Exalted Genius" who "can bestow or confirm Reputation . . . with a breath" (*Letters*, pp. 67, 69). Even in the face of such flattery, Dryden felt a need to justify himself; his letter continues with a general refutation of such moral charges as the anonymous critic's slander about his misleading Congreve: "For my Morals, betwixt Man and Man, I am not to be my own Judge. I appeal to the World if I have Deceiv'd or Defrauded any Man: And for my private Conversation, they who see me every day can be the best Witnesses, whether or no it be Blameless and Inoffensive" (p. 73). Dryden also insists, as he had been doing since the Revolution, that artistic excellence is a nonpartisan matter:

> Hitherto I have no reason to complain that Men of either Party shun my Company. I have never been an Impudent Beggar at the Doors of Noblemen: My Visits have indeed been too rare to be unacceptable; and but just enough to testifie my Gratitude for their Bounty, which I have frequently received, but always unask'd as themselves will Witness. [p. 73]

The major project on which Dryden was now embarking was dependent upon such "Bounty" from prominent men and women of all parties. As he had already explained to Walsh in a letter of the previous December, the translation of Virgil was to be published "by subscription; having an hunderd & two Brass Cutts, with the Coats of Armes of the Subscriber to each Cutt: & every Subscriber to pay five guinneys: half in hande besides another inferiour Subscription of two Guinneys, for the rest whose names are onely written in a Catalogue, printed with the Book" (*Letters*, p. 64). Publication by subscription was not a new idea, and both Dryden and Tonson had experience with it: in 1685, the bookseller William Nott attempted to collect some of the cost of printing Grabu's elaborate score for *Albion and Albanius* in advance by encouraging subscribers to pay at least half a guinea to reserve a copy; in 1688, Tonson published a fine edition of *Paradise Lost* by subscription, printing an epigram by Dryden under the portrait of the poet. For the Virgil project, Dryden and Tonson correctly anticipated persuading one hundred aristocrats to pay the substantial sum of five guineas for an expensive edition on fine paper, adorned with engravings, by promising that each subscriber would have one of the engravings dedicated to him, with his name and coat of arms. They also expected to sell several hundred copies of the same edition at two guineas to subscribers who would simply have their names listed.

The five-guinea subscribers doubtless took pride in seeing their coats of arms displayed beneath the engravings; some may have enjoyed the idea that they were acting as Dryden's patrons, giving him money on which to live while translating the Roman poet. Dryden was not being an "Impudent Beggar" by seeking such support, but he was counting on the continued patronage of "Men of either Party," and the final list of 101 five-guinea subscribers is by no means restricted to people sharing his beliefs. Some of his fellow Catholics appear: Hugh, Lord Clifford, son of his earlier patron the Lord Treasurer, and James Cecil, fifth Earl of Salisbury, the six-year-old son of the dedicatee of *Love Triumphant*, are examples. But the list also includes such pillars of Protestantism as Princess Anne and her husband, Prince George of Denmark. Dryden's old patrons Dorset and Sunderland, both now active in the government he opposed, are on the list; so are at least two government officials who had attacked him in print: Sir Robert Howard, still Auditor of the Receipt, and Charles Montagu, who had risen rapidly under William, reaching the post of Chancellor of the Exchequer in April of 1694. The long list of two-guinea subscribers includes such theatrical and literary associates as Betterton, Anne Bracegirdle, Elizabeth Barry, Congreve, Southerne, and Pepys; it also includes military officers, postmasters, architects, doctors, clergymen, and cabinet ministers. Even the relatives who appear represent a wide range of beliefs. The list includes Elizabeth Dryden's notorious Catholic and Jacobite cousins Bernard and Craven Howard, but three children of the rabid Cromwellian Gilbert Pickering also paid two guineas for the work of their Catholic cousin: Sir John Pickering, the current baronet at Titchmarsh; his brother Theophilus, now a prebendary of Durham Cathedral; and their sister Elizabeth Creed, who remained close to the poet. Tonson, whose main profits would come from a trade version on ordinary paper, would never have begun this expensive and time-consuming project if he had thought that Dryden's Catholicism or Jacobitism would significantly injure subscriptions or sales, though he did later try to persuade Dryden to dedicate the *Virgil* to King William. Dryden refused that request for the same reasons that led him to declare that he had "no reason to be asham'd" in the dedication to *Love Triumphant*. Both men evidently believed that national pride in having a fine English Virgil would weigh more heavily with readers of all classes than the faith and politics of the translator.

"Intent Upon the Translation of Virgil"

On 15 June 1694, mindful of the problems that had followed less formal arrangements in the past, Dryden signed a contract with Tonson specifying terms. Tonson was naturally interested in completing the project expeditiously, so that the subscribers would not have an inordinate wait between making their down payments and receiving their books; he may also have been concerned about Dryden's age and poor health. The contract therefore committed Dryden to devote full time to the translation, undertaking "no Poem or Book in Prose . . . above 1 s[hilling] price" until he completed it. There were two specified exceptions: Dryden had already "engaged to perform" a translation of "a little French Booke of Painting," Du Fresnoy's *De Arte Graphica*, "for some Gentlemen Vertuosoes and Painters," probably including his friend Sir Godfrey Kneller, the portrait painter John Closterman, and the "Vertuoso" Richard Graham, who contributed a "Short Account of the Most Eminent Painters" to the finished work; he also stipulated his intention to write a prologue, epilogue, and songs for a comedy written by his son John, who had sent him the script from Rome. In order to keep Dryden writing at a steady pace, Tonson promised to pay him £200 of "copy money" in four installments: £50 for the *Georgics* and *Pastorals*, several of which Dryden had already translated, and £50 for each four books of the *Aeneid*. Although he promised to help Dryden sign up subscribers for the five-guinea list, Tonson also shrewdly stipulated that the collecting of money for the second list of two-guinea subscribers could not begin until Dryden had finished *Aeneid* VI, at which point the project would be three-quarters done.[10]

Although the financial record is incomplete, careful scholarship has now established that the money for the five-guinea subscriptions, three guineas down and two more on receipt of the book, went entirely to Dryden, while the profits from the trade edition went entirely to Tonson. The problems that later led Dryden to label Tonson a "Sharper" arose from the tangled language in the contract dealing with the "second subscription," the books to be sold for two guineas. The contract stipulates that Dryden will purchase these books from Tonson for "Soe much above the Selling price of the Said Books printed upon Comon paper as the charge of printing them upon the Said best paper Shall amount to or Stand him over and above the price of the books printed upon Comon paper." When the poet and the bookseller quarreled, Dryden may have argued that he expected to pay only a small sum, probably 6s. 4d. per book, representing the difference in cost between printing on expensive paper and common paper, while Tonson argued that Dryden had to pay him not only that differential cost but the "Selling price of the Said Books," at least an additional pound per volume. They may also have disagreed about who should cover the cost of binding the books.[11]

Dryden's profits from the second subscription therefore proved smaller than he had expected, and his dealings with Tonson were also complicated by the shifting value of the currency. The European war represented a steady drain on the English economy, and the activities of counterfeiters and "clippers" had reduced confidence in the value of half-crowns, shillings, and sixpences. Modern economic historians believe that those silver coins were basically "undervalued in relation to gold,"[12] and the value of the golden guinea rose precipitously during the early 1690s. At first, that development looked favorable to Dryden, who was receiving subscription payments in guineas, but in practice, tradesmen were reluctant to change so large a coin; for the ordinary purchases necessary for the household, Elizabeth needed valid shillings, and these soon became hard to find. In the Exchequer, Charles Montagu was wrestling with these problems; his bold solution, successfully imposed on a grumpy Parliament and a suspicious public, was to withdraw all the circulating silver money and undertake a recoinage. This recoinage, which began in February 1696, drove down the value of the guinea; the years immediately before, during, and after its imposition saw economic unrest and uncertainty, frequently reflected in Dryden's complaints that Tonson is paying him in money that will not pass at its full value.

Despite all these problems, the poet's financial situation during the years of work on the *Virgil* was better than it had been since the Revolution. He had probably received most of the 300 guineas due him from down payments for the first subscription by the end of 1695, and Tonson's payments of the four £50 installments of copy money were fairly prompt. Within a year of signing the contract, Dryden had completed over half the translation and received two of those payments.[13] As his speed suggests, he was initially "intent" on the translation. One anecdote alleges that he wrote the first lines with his diamond ring on the window of his cousin John Driden's country house at Chesterton in Huntingtonshire; another alleges that he finished the *Pastorals* at Ugbrooke in Devonshire, home of Lord Clifford; Dryden himself testifies to translating the first *Georgic* at Denham Court in Buckinghamshire, the home of Sir William Bowyer, whom he had known since Cambridge.[14] We may imagine the poet arriving at the country homes of his patrons laden with books and papers; he consulted several Latin editions and most of the earlier English translations of Virgil, and he borrowed extensively from a complete manuscript translation by Richard Maitland, Earl of Lauderdale, a Catholic and Jacobite in exile in France.[15]

Although he probably spent much of this time "drudging" in the country, there is no specific primary evidence to establish Dryden's whereabouts during the summer and autumn of 1694—not even a letter, and this gap in the record may well be another indication of his single-minded devotion to the task at hand. The death of Queen Mary on 28 December 1694 produced a predictable flood of elegies, including poems by Dryden's friends Motteux, Stepney, Congreve, Dennis, and Walsh, but there was no poem by Dryden. One anonymous writer offered the friendly suggestion that Dryden's willingness to correct the work of "an absent Muse" (probably Stepney) was evidence of his good will:

> Ev'n *Dryden* mourns; tho yet he does refuse
> To mourn in public, and exert his Muse;
> Nor can we well his Want of Love suspect,
> Who kindly could an absent Muse correct.[16]

Several others, however, did suspect Dryden of "Want of Love" toward the dead Queen: one referred to his "strange bigotted Muse"; another pointed out the striking contrast between his praise of Louis XIV as a patron of the arts (quoted above, p. 459) and his silence on the death of Mary.[17] I should think Dryden's silence was primarily motivated by his unwillingness to praise a queen he regarded as an undutiful daughter, but the steady pressure of his work on the translation may have reinforced his decision. He made no immediate response to the attacks on his silence, and also ignored the publication in February 1695 of *Prince Arthur*, an allegedly "heroick" poem by the physician Richard Blackmore, who not only stole the plan for an epic on Arthur that Dryden had described in the "Discourse on Satire," but included "An old, revolted, unbelieving Bard" called "*Laurus*" in his poem (p. 167). The death of Dr. Busby on 5

April was more likely to prompt a poem from his old pupil than the death of the Queen, but Dryden, who had complimented Busby hàndsomely a few years earlier in the Persius translation, did not now pause to eulogize the man at whose feet he had first studied Virgil.

Even though he had promised to translate Du Fresnoy before making his contract with Tonson for the Virgil, Dryden delayed that project as well: he certainly did not start working on Du Fresnoy until he had finished the *Georgics* and *Pastorals*, and may well have waited until he finished the first four books of the *Aeneid*. Pressed for time, he was nonetheless unwilling to issue his version of Du Fresnoy without reiterating some of the points he had made in his poem to Sir Godfrey Kneller, published the previous summer, and added "A Parallel of Poetry and Painting" to his prose translation of Du Fresnoy's Latin poem. "An *Essay* begun and ended in twelve Mornings," this rambling and uneven piece bears every sign of haste,[18] but gives us fascinating glimpses into the poet's mind at the halfway point of his great labor on the Virgil. As we might expect, he makes explicit references to his other project: "When I undertook this Work, I was already engag'd in the Translation of *Virgil*, from whom I have borrow'd only two months," he explains at the outset; later he apologizes for writing "with more brevity than I intended," explaining that "*Virgil* calls me." When searching for examples of poetic techniques that parallel painterly techniques, he turns frequently to Virgil, and cannot resist digressions on purely literary questions, such as the relative merits of Homer and Virgil; many of the ideas he tries out in these passages reappear in expanded form in the *Dedication of the Aeneis*. But the "Parallel" also reveals a Dryden who remained keenly interested in other aesthetic, literary, and political issues, despite his arduous labor on the *Virgil*.

On the evidence of this essay, Dryden's declared retirement from playwriting had not diminished his interest in practical and theoretical problems of the theatre. His interest in the capacity of painters to depict the passions of those they portray leads him quickly to a wide-ranging discussion of "the Characters of *Comedy* and *Tragedy*." When comparing history painting to epic poetry, he makes the obvious point that a painter must depict a particular moment, while an epic may stretch over a considerable period of time, and that distinction quickly leads to a digression on the unities in the drama. In the course of illustrating these and other points, he alludes to plays by Shakespeare, Otway, Fletcher, and Stapylton; he also makes specific references, often self-critical, to *The Indian Emperour*, *Tyrannick Love*, *Oedipus*, *The Spanish Fryar*, and *All for Love*.

Discussing his own plays as examples, successful or not, of the imitation of nature or the maintaining of dramatic unity was not merely an exercise in nostalgia; most of the plays Dryden cites had been revived during the 1690s, and were thus familiar to his readers. But the impulse toward recapitulating his career that we have noticed in his other works since the Revolution operates powerfully here, with its usual accompanying sneer at the present. One of his longest digressions answers Rymer's stated preference for a chorus with the eminently pragmatic argument that "it is impracticable on our *Stage*. A new *Theatre* much more ample and much deeper must be made for that purpose, besides the cost of sometimes forty or fifty Habits, which is an expence too large, to be supplied by a *Company of Actors*" (p. xliii). Dryden had made this point more

briefly in his dedication to *Examen Poeticum* (quoted above, pp. 462–63), but when he
wrote the "Parallel," he had another reason besides hostility to Rymer to be thinking
about the expenses sustained by "a *Company of Actors*." During the autumn of 1694,
Betterton and many of the other actors had quarreled over money with Christopher
Rich, who was now managing the United Company. By the time the theatres reopened
after the period of mourning for the death of the Queen, Betterton and his allies had
seceded to form a new company acting at Lincoln's Inn Fields; their first play, produced
in April of 1695, was Congreve's *Love for Love*.[19] Dryden could hardly ignore that series
of events, and he later took sides, predictably endorsing Betterton's company, many of
whom were his old friends.

The conclusion of his remarks on choruses even betrays an interest in returning to
dramatic writing, especially if political circumstances should change:

> I shou'd not be sorry to see a *Chorus* on a *Theatre*, more than as large and as deep again
> as ours, built and adorn'd at a *King*'s Charges, and on that condition, and another,
> which is, That my Hands were not bound behind me, as now they are; I shou'd not
> despair of making such a *Tragedy* as might be both instructive and delightfull, accord-
> ing to the manner of the *Grecians*. [p. xliii]

As Dryden's complaint about having his hands bound suggests, he remained a political
animal. William had done nothing to bear the "charges" of either theatre, but Louis
XIV had supported the elaborate theatres and machines necessary to produce the
operas of Lully. Dryden, who had irritated his enemies by praising Louis as a patron of
the arts in the "Discourse Concerning the Original and Progress of Satire," stubbornly
reiterates that praise in this essay:

> To what height the Magnificence and Encouragement of the present *King* of *France*
> may carry *Painting* and *Sculpture* is uncertain, but by what he has done, before the War
> in which he is ingag'd, we may expect what he will do after the happy Conclusion of a
> Peace, which is the Prayer and Wish of all those who have not an interest to prolong the
> miseries of *Europe*. [p. xxx]

Dryden implies that the King and his merchant supporters would rather "prolong
the miseries of *Europe*" than support the arts in England. As he wrote these words,
William was gathering his forces for another assault on Namur, finally recaptured at
excessive cost in September of 1695. Many sober men in Parliament, including Dryden's cousin from Chesterton, took a similar view; the expenses incurred by six years of
warfare had brought a vocal "country" opposition into existence. Concerned by the
damage done to agriculture by the conscription of farm laborers, such men believed
that the nation was wasting its resources defending the interests of the city merchants,
who stood to profit from the land war in Europe. They were also appalled by the many
recent military failures, at which Dryden also glances in the "Parallel." His transition
from a page lifted from Philostratus to a section developing his own ideas is a sly
metaphor: "as *Convoy Ships* either accompany, or shou'd accompany their *Merchants* till
they may prosecute the rest of their Voyage without danger, so *Philostratus* has brought
me thus far on my way, and I can now sail on without him" (p. xiv). Dryden's readers

would instantly have recognized his allusion to such disasters as the taking of a rich merchant vessel called the Berkeley Castle by the French in early April of 1694,[20] and the rhetorical turn ("either accompany, or shou'd accompany") is the same one employed in the most Jacobitical line in *Eleonora*: "So Subjects love just Kings, or so they shou'd."

The translation of Virgil's *Pastorals* and *Georgics*, which Dryden completed before undertaking Du Fresnoy, also reflects his sympathy with the principles of the "country" party. He recognized that Virgil was a political poet, even when writing about beekeeping or herding flocks, and he translated the political passages with particular relish. One clear example comes near the end of the first *Georgic*; Virgil laments the war then raging throughout his world,

> Where Fraud and Rapine, Right and Wrong confound;
> Where impious Arms from ev'ry part resound,
> And monstrous Crimes in ev'ry Shape are crown'd.
> The peaceful Peasant to the Wars is prest;
> The Fields lye fallow in inglorious Rest.
> The Plain no Pasture to the Flock affords,
> The crooked Scythes are streightned into Swords.
>
> [ll. 678–84]

Most of the material in this passage is Virgilian, but the line about the conscription of the "peaceful Peasant" is entirely Dryden's invention, and the verb "crown'd," which can turn the impersonal "monstrous Crimes" into a version of King William, is his addition as well. His satirical edge had not been blunted by his desire to secure subscribers for the *Virgil*.

After Dryden's initial burst, his progress became slower. A letter to Tonson announcing the completion of *Aeneid* IV, written in the early months of 1695, indicates a plan to move more slowly: "I intend not so much to overtoil my self, after the Sixth Book is ended, if the Second Subscriptions rise, I will take so much the more time, because the profit will incourage me the more" (*Letters*, p. 75). At this point Dryden clearly expected the announcement of the second subscription to bring him another substantial payment, so that his need for the installments of copy money would be less urgent. By 8 June, however, he had realized that "the bargain between us . . . is so much to my loss" (*Letters*, p. 76), and was seeking a meeting with Tonson to clarify matters; he asks the bookseller to "be ready with the price of paper, & of the Books," a clear reference to the dispute about how much he would have to pay for the books ordered by the two-guinea subscribers. Unhappy with the results of that meeting, Dryden went off to the country, staying this time at Burleigh House in Northamptonshire, seat of his wife's kinsman John Cecil, fifth Earl of Exeter.[21]

Dryden's anger with Tonson probably slowed his progress, as did periods of physical illness. His later preface to his son's play mentions an illness at about this time, and in his letter of 29 October [1695], which reports the completion of Book VII, he wearily promises Tonson, "you shall have your bargain if I live, and have my health"

(*Letters*, p. 78). That icy letter reveals Dryden's continued anger with Tonson for his sharp dealing:

> Some kind of intercourse must be carryed on betwixt us, while I am translateing Virgil. Therefore I give you notice, that I have done the seaventh Eneid in the Country: and intend some few days hence, to go upon the Eigth: when that is finishd, I expect fifty pounds, in good silver; not such as I have had formerly. I am not obligd to take gold, neither will I; no[r] stay for it beyond four & twenty houres after it is due. I thank you for the civility of your last letter in the Country: but the thirty shillings upon every book remains with me. You always intended I shoud get nothing by the Second Subscriptions, as I found from first to last. [p. 77]

In the autumn of 1695, before Montagu's proposals for recoinage, the value of the guinea against the pound had risen to 30*s*., so the "thirty shillings upon every book" that Dryden insists on keeping is probably the one-guinea down payment for each two-guinea subscriber. According to the proposals for that subscription, "The Price of the Book is two Guinneys: one of which is to be payd Mr. [Francis] Atterbury [Dryden's friend] at the time of Subscription: the other to my Stationer Mr. Tonson, at the receipt of the Book."[22] Tonson had evidently offered to receive those down payments, but Dryden no longer trusted him. His irritation shows in the "Life of Lucian" (published in 1711, but probably written in 1696 in violation of his contract with Tonson), where he undertakes to explain why "Translation in England come[s] so far short of the *French*; there may indeed, be a Reason assign'd, which bears a very great probability; and that is, that here the *Booksellers* are the Undertakers of Works of this nature, and they are Persons more devoted to their own Gain, than the publick honour" (pp. 55–56).

When Dryden returned to London, he had to devote some time to helping to prepare his son's comedy for the stage. In his preface to *The Husband His Own Cuckold*, finally published in July of 1696, he explains that the play

> was sent me from *Italy* some years since, [probably before the contract with Tonson of 15 June 1694, which mentions "my son's play,"] to try its fortune on the Stage: And being the Essay of a young unexperienc'd Author; to confess the truth, I thought it not worthy of that honour. 'Tis true, I was not willing to discourage him so far, as to tell him plainly my Opinion, but it seems he guess'd somewhat of my Mind, by my long delays of his expectation. [IV, 471]

The "long delays" probably had as much to do with Dryden's work on Virgil and Du Fresnoy as with his diffidence about the play's quality. Young John, however, had urgent reasons to want his play produced. His kinsman, patron, and employer, Cardinal Howard, died on [7]/17 June 1694, leaving "Mr. John & Mr. Charles Dryden fifty Roman Crownes a-piece."[23] By the summer of 1695, that money was long spent, and I should think young John was eager for the income from a theatrical production and printing.[24] He decided to move things along by appealing for help from another quarter, "And therefore in my absence from the Town last Summer, [i.e., in August of 1695, when Dryden made his trip to the country,] took the boldness to Dedicate his Play to that Person of Honour, whose Name you will find before his Epistle."

The "Person of Honour" was Sir Robert Howard, to whom John, Jr. wrote his dedication in a letter dated from Rome on [10]/20 August 1695. The dedication leaves little doubt that the old animosity between Dryden and Howard was still alive; young John appeals to his uncle to put aside old grievances:

> I am confident I cou'd not chuse a more indulgent Foster-Father; and tho' my very Name bears an accusation against me, yet I have the honour also to be related to the Muses by the Mothers side; for you your self have been guilty of Poetry, and a Family Vice is therefore the more excusable in me, who am unluckily a Poet by descent. [sig. A2r]

Howard had mellowed. He was nearly seventy and frequently hobbled with gout, but he was rich and greatly honored by the government, and had married for the fourth time in 1693, to a beautiful maid of honor named Annabella Dives, who was a talented singer and a patroness of Purcell.[25] He received the play, as Dryden tells us,

> with so much Candor and Generosity, as neither my Son nor I cou'd deserve from him. Then the Play was no longer in my power, the Patron demanding it in his own right, it was deliver'd to him. And he was farther pleas'd, during my Sickness [in September?], to put it into that Method in which you find it; the loose Scenes digested into order, and knit into a Tale.

Howard's "Candor and Generosity" led to a reconciliation with Dryden, whose next letter to Tonson mentions "Meeting Sir Ro[bert] Howard at the play-house this morning, and asking him how he likd my Seaventh Eneid" (*Letters*, p. 79). Tonson had not yet delivered the manuscript to Howard, and Dryden asks him to do so; the implication is that Howard was now among those few friends to whom Dryden was circulating his work in progress. The premiere of *The Husband His Own Cuckold* seems impossible to date precisely, but I should think that Howard and Dryden met at Lincoln's Inn Fields to watch a rehearsal of young John's play; in a postscript to the same letter, Dryden informs Tonson that he intends to return to his work on the translation "When my Sonns play is acted, . . . if my health continue." A less likely possibility is that the two old men were attending a rehearsal of their first collaboration, *The Indian Queen*, which was revived at Dorset Garden about this time with new music by Purcell, whose death on 21 November 1695 doubtless came as a blow to both Dryden and the new Mrs. Howard.[26]

If young John's play was indeed in rehearsal during the winter of 1695–96, its premiere may have been delayed because of political circumstances. On 25 February 1696, a conspirator revealed a failed plot to assassinate King William when he went hunting in Richmond Park. Informants claimed that King James was in Calais, ready to descend upon England with an army of fifteen thousand, and that his Catholic and Jacobite supporters in England were preparing to take arms as soon as the deed was done. Among those arrested in the wake of this plot were Dryden's friends Henry Sheeres, Sir Roger L'Estrange, and Col. James Grahame. A Catholic priest named Robert Charnock, executed for his part in the plot on 18 March, was well known to John Dryden, Jr., since he had been the Vice-Master of Magdalen College during James II's attempt to make that college a Catholic enclave in 1687.[27] Aware of such connections, the ever-cautious Betterton may have decided to let the hysteria blow over before producing a play sent over from Rome.

Dryden finished the third installment of the *Virgil*, ending with *Aeneid* VIII, sometime during this troubled winter, and his letter to Tonson on that occasion reflects his exhaustion. Some experience with another bookseller had evidently persuaded him that Tonson was no worse than his competitors: "Upon trial," he declares, "I find all of your trade are Sharpers & you not more than others; therefore I have not wholly left you." He concludes by asking Tonson "to oblige me who am not your Enemy, & may be your friend." The uneasy reconciliation the two men had reached included an agreement that Dryden would furnish fewer notes than had originally been planned; he says he is "not sorry" about that decision, "for to make them good, wou'd have cost me half a yeares time at least . . . It wou'd require seaven yeares to translate Virgil exactly" (pp. 80–81). Dryden's inexact version, still easily the best Virgil in English, took him only three years, but he spent about a year finishing the last four books, despite the fact that he was able to reuse the substantial episodes from Books IX and X that he had published in *Sylvae* (1685). He suffered again from illness, and he needed to steal time for several other projects: the "Life of Lucian" probably cost him at least a month; his beautiful Pindaric ode on the death of Purcell, published in July of 1696, displays a care and polish worthy of its subject; preparing his son's play for publication took time as well.

A letter of 26 May [1696] gives us a glimpse of the old poet negotiating with Tonson for the publication of that play: "Send word if you please, Sir, what is the most you will give for my Sonns play; that I may take the fairest Chapman, as I am bound to do, for his benefit" (*Letters*, p. 82). To this veiled threat to use another publisher, Dryden adds a complaint about the silver in which Tonson made his "last payment of fifty pounds," presumably the copy money for *Aeneid* V-VIII. The coinage crisis was at its height; in his diary entry for 11 June 1696, Evelyn reports "Want of current money to carry on not onely the smalest concernes, but for daily provisions in the Common Markets: Ginnys lowered to 22s: . . . nothing considerable coined of the new & now onely current stamp, . . . no body either paying or receiving any mony."[28] Under these circumstances, we may easily understand Dryden's request to Tonson—"if you have any silver which will go, my wife will be glad of it"—and his postscript noting that "Sir Ro[bert] Howard writt me word, that if I cou'd make any advantage by being payd in clippd money; He woud change it in the Exchequer." Howard, who retained his powerful position in the Treasury, was offering to help Dryden by illegally changing clipped money for newly minted coins, further evidence of their reconciliation.[29] We may recognize Dryden's gratitude in the line from the *Aeneid* (III, 343) that he chose for the title page of his son's play, Andromache's prayer that the young Ascanius will be inspired by his father Aeneas and his uncle Hector.[30]

The prospect of a more reliable silver currency had now reduced the inflated value of the guinea; during the previous winter, Dryden had received guineas valued at 29s. (*Letters*, p. 80), and if he was still holding those coins, he had taken a substantial loss, since Evelyn reports their value in June as 22s. Early in the summer, when Dryden tried to use guineas to pay the famous watchmaker Thomas Tompion for two watches he had ordered for his sons, he "cou'd not perswade him to take gold at any rate." He had to ask Tonson to pay Tompion with "a Goldsmiths bill for two and twenty pounds" in silver, charging that money against "the next fifty pounds which you are to pay me, when Virgil is finishd" (*Letters*, pp. 82–83). In the same letter, perhaps by way of reassuring Tonson, Dryden points out that ten books of the *Aeneid* are done. The eleventh was circulating in manuscript by 3 September 1696, at which time Dryden was in the country at Denham Court, home of his patron Bowyer.[31] By 25 November, he was back in London and nearly finished: in a hurried note asking Tonson to collect the rent for his Blakesley land from "the Carrier of Tocester," he promises that his "studyes," in which he is "deeply ingag'd," will be "finishd in a day or two" (*Letters*, pp. 83–84). Dryden's trusting Tonson to collect that small sum suggests better relations between poet and bookseller, but there was at least one more tiff before the end: in the letter announcing the completion of the translation, Dryden apologizes for an angry letter of the day before, now lost: "What I wrote yesterday was too sharp; but I doubt it is all true" (*Letters*, p. 85).

"Words Are Not So Easily Coyn'd as Money"

Finishing the actual translation must have been a relief, but it did not end Dryden's labors by any means. He had to write his dedications, proofread the text as it emerged from Tonson's shop, and transcribe his marginal notes, which eventually became the "Notes and Observations." Looking to save time, he farmed out the "Life of Virgil," the "Preface to the Pastorals," the "Essay on the Georgics," and the prose arguments for each book to his younger friends Chetwood and Addison, but he spent over two months on the long dedication for the *Aeneis*, which develops the literary-critical ideas about Virgil he had begun to spin in the "Parallel of Poetry and Painting."[32] The translator was also probably involved in the process of selecting which of the engravings would be dedicated to which of the five-guinea subscribers. The brass plates were those used for the folio edition of Ogilby's translation (1654), but Tonson, who had purchased the plates in 1690, had many of them retouched to give Aeneas a hooked nose, so that he would resemble King William. Circumstantial evidence suggests that Dryden undermined this crude attempt at Williamite iconography by expressing his own Jacobite sentiments in significant pairings of patrons and pictures.[33] He also ignored Tonson's request that he dedicate the finished translation to the King, an idea that may even have been seconded by his Catholic sons in Rome.[34] Dryden's actual choice of dedicatees for the three main parts of the translation reflects his stubborn adherence to the political and religious beliefs for which he had suffered. The *Pastorals* are dedicated to Hugh, Lord Clifford, who had often been imprisoned on suspicion of Catholic plotting,[35] and if the other two dedicatees were Anglicans, both had recently refused the loyalty oaths required of officeholders in the wake of the assassination plot, which contained a clause declaring William to be a "rightful and lawful king."[36]

Dryden's letter of 17 February 1697, requesting the Earl of Chesterfield's permission to dedicate the *Georgics* to him, is a forthright Jacobite document:

My Translation of Virgil is already in the Press and I can not possibly deferr the publication of it any Longer than Midsummer Term at farthes[t]. I have hinder'd it thus long in hopes of his return, for whom, and for my Conscience I have sufferd, that I might have layd my Authour at his feet: But now finding that Gods time for ending our miseries is not yet, I have been advis'd to make three severall Dedications, of the Eclogues, the Georgics, and the Eneis. [*Letters*, pp. 85–86]

A year earlier, at the time of the assassination plot, the "return" of James II might have seemed likely to a hopeful Jacobite like Dryden, but with peace in Europe now talked of on all sides,[37] such a second Restoration was again fading into myth. In his witty note of 18 February, accepting the honor of Dryden's dedication, Chesterfield describes himself as "a country Gentleman, who being in no post whereby he may merit such a favour, must value it the more" (*Letters*, p. 87). The word "country" was a political label, and Chesterfield, who had held no government position since the reign of Charles II, had ceased to attend the House of Lords after refusing the oaths. In the same note, he responds to Dryden's passionate Jacobitism with a marvelous understatement: "It looks as if you were tired with the Court."

Dryden naturally returns to the theme of retirement in his published dedication: "You have chosen for your self a private Greatness," he tells Chesterfield, "and will not be polluted with Ambition" (*Poems*, II, 915). The contrast, predictably enough, is between Chesterfield's retirement, praised by allusions to Epicurus and Scipio and connected to the country scenes of the *Georgics*, and "the Court: a place of forgetfulness, at the best, for well-deservers" (p. 916). But that contrast is not sketched in black and white, and politics is only one strand among many in this dedication. If Dryden and Chesterfield were both unhappy with the current regime, they both had fond memories of the court of Charles II, and Dryden's description of the dangers of court life is more subtle, personal, and nostalgic than partisan or polemical:

'Tis necessary for the polishing of Manners, to have breath'd that Air; but 'tis infectious even to the best Morals to live always in it. 'Tis a dangerous Commerce, where an honest Man is sure at the first of being Cheated; and he recovers not his Losses, but by learning to Cheat others. The undermining Smile becomes at length habitual; and the drift of his plausible Conversation, is only to flatter one, that he may betray another.

There speaks a man who had concluded from his earlier experiences with Rochester and Sedley that he was ill fit for court life, but who had considerable experience in the dangerous commerce of undermining smiles and plausible conversations, and who was engaged, at this very moment, in a complex artistic act of flattery. He cannot therefore recommend a Puritanical or ascetic stance toward courts:

Yet 'tis good to have been a looker on, without venturing to play; that a Man may know false Dice another time, though he never means to use them. I commend not him who never knew a Court, but him who forsakes it because he knows it. A young Man deserves no praise, who out of melancholy Zeal leaves the world before he has well try'd it, and runs headlong into Religion. He who carries a Maidenhead into a Cloyster, is sometimes apt to lose it there, and to repent of his Repentance. He only is like to endure Austerities, who has already found the inconvenience of Pleasures. For almost every Man will be making Experiments in one part or another of his Life: And the danger is less when we are young: For having try'd it early, we shall not be apt to repeat it afterwards. [*Poems*, II, 916]

The imagery of gambling and loaded dice picks up a favorite metaphor from Dryden's prologues and epilogues; and if the playful sexual imagery is appropriate to Chesterfield, who had long ago been linked with Barbara Villiers, Anne Hamilton, and even Elizabeth Howard (see above, pp. 124–25), it is also appropriate to Dryden, who had kept a mistress and written a play subtitled *Love in a Nunnery*. In this paragraph, we may see Dryden using personal candor as a form of flattery, offering Chesterfield the mature conclusions of a career spent as a "looker on," and occasional player, in the dangerous dice game of court life. Chesterfield, who had also been an expert player in that game, knew how to act the part of the noble patron. When he received his copy of the splendid folio on 10 August, he wrote Dryden a brief note essaying a few conventional compliments, but he did "not pretend to offer the incence of prase, to him who is the best teacher of others how to give it" (*Letters*, p. 89); instead, he sent along a gift of money that the poet called a "noble present" (p. 90).

Dryden's old friend Mulgrave, dedicatee of the *Aeneis*, had been Lord Chamberlain under King James, attending the King to Mass and supporting his policies, but by 1694, he had made his peace with William's government, becoming a Privy Counselor and Marquis of Normanby. After the assassination plot, however, he too refused to take the oaths. For this scrupulous behavior, Normanby lost his position on the Privy Council, worth some £3,000 annually, but gained the renewed praises of Dryden, who honored him with the *Dedication of the Aeneis*, which is simultaneously an extended piece of literary criticism, a passionate personal apology, and a guide to the political meanings of the original poem and the new translation.[38] Dryden begins by declaring that "An Heroick Poem, truly such, is undoubtedly the greatest Work which the Soul of Man is capable to perform" (*Poems*, III, 1003). In this ringing sentence, we may detect his longtime belief in the superiority of epic as a genre, his disappointment in his own failure to write an original epic, and his pride in having translated one. Yet even this literary declaration may involve some political implications: many in England, not least the King, would have considered such feats of arms as the recent victory at Namur a greater work than any poem, but Dryden could be confident that Normanby, a disgruntled politician and amateur poet, would agree with his stubborn valuing of arts over arms. A little later, expressing his respect for the difficulty of writing heroic poetry, he asks, "what Soul, tho' sent into the World with great advantages of Nature, cultivated with the liberal Arts and Sciences, conversant with Histories of the Dead, and enrich'd with Observations on the Living, can be sufficient to inform the whole Body of so great a Work?" (p. 1004). This pointed rhetorical question is fine praise of Virgil, but it also resembles Dryden's earlier descriptions of the talents and training necessary for modern poets, in which he had insisted on "learn[ing] in severall Sciences" and "experience in all sorts of humours and manners of men" (XVII, 182). Proud of his own talents, education, and experience, Dryden did not consider his "Soul" comparable to Virgil's, but he knew well that there was no one in England who could come close to his success in translating Virgil.

In his interpretation of Virgil, laid out at some length in this essay, Dryden is as interested in the poet's political relations with his patron Augustus as he is in such literary problems as unity, heroic character, and versification. He gives us a Virgil who "maturely weigh'd the Condition of the Times in which he liv'd," and who decided to praise Augustus because "he held his Paternal Estate from the Bounty of the Conqueror, by whom he was likewise enrich'd, esteem'd, and cherish'd" (p. 1014). The resemblance to Dryden, who had defended his loyalty to Charles and James on similar grounds, suggests how strongly the translator identified with the Roman poet. Dryden imagines a Virgil who "dext'rously . . . mannag'd both the Prince and People, so as to displease neither, and to do good to both; which is the part of a Wise and an Honest Man" (p. 1016). He had applied quite similar language to himself in the "Discourse on Satire," alleging that the Zimri portrait in *Absalom and Achitophel* had been so "ridiculous" that "he for whom it was intended, was too witty to resent it as an injury. If I had rail'd, I might have suffer'd for it justly: But I manag'd my own Work more happily, perhaps more dextrously" (IV, 71). Remembering his own success at exhorting the Stuarts to virtue under the pretext of praise, Dryden portrays Virgil doing the same thing: "Oblig'd he was to his Master for his Bounty, and he repays him with good Counsel, how to behave himself in his new Monarchy, so as to gain the Affections of his Subjects, and deserve to be called the Father of his Country" (p. 1016). The particular interpretations of Virgil's work Dryden offers in his notes are compatible with that general view: in a note to the first *Georgic*, for example, he claims to have "discover'd a secret Compliment to the Emperour, which none of the Commentators have observ'd," and argues that the "trembling Charioteer," "force[d] along by "four fierce Coursers" (ll. 693, 690), is an allegory of Augustus's behavior during the triumvirate, when he was "constrain'd against his own temper, to those violent proceedings, by the necessity of the Times in general, but more particularly by his two Partners, *Antony* and *Lepidus*."[39] That kind of determined over-reading makes the tendency of Dryden's contemporaries to see allegory in such works as *The Duke of Guise* seem tame indeed.

The translation itself is also an act of interpretation; Dryden's frequent additions to the Latin are rarely neutral padding. In the dedication, he claims that "the Additions . . . are easily deduc'd from *Virgil's* sense. They will seem (at least I have the Vanity to think so,) not stuck into him, but growing out of him" (p. 1054). A friend like Normanby, sharing many of Dryden's beliefs, might have found his additions natural, but I wonder what a convinced Williamite like Sir Robert Howard thought when he first read the opening lines of Dryden's *Aeneis*:

> Arms, and the Man I sing, who, forc'd by Fate,
> And haughty *Juno*'s unrelenting Hate;
> Expell'd and exil'd, left the *Trojan* Shoar:
> Long Labours, both by Sea and Land, he bore;
> And in the doubtful War, before he won
> The *Latian* Realm, and built the destin'd Town:

His banish'd gods restor'd to Rites Divine,
And setl'd sure Succession in his Line:
From whence the Race of *Alban* Fathers come,
And the long Glories of majestick *Rome*.

[I, 1–10]

Virgil's hero is forced to fly from Troy by fate ("fato profugus"); Dryden's, by a tripling of the participle, is "forc'd," "Expell'd," and "exil'd," and the added words surely point toward James II, a veteran of battles on land and sea, now in exile in St. Germain. Virgil's Aeneas simply brings his household gods into Latium ("inferretque deos Latio"); Dryden's *restores* "His banish'd Gods . . . to Rites Divine," a phrase in which some readers surely read the hopes of the persecuted Catholics. The second line of that couplet—"And setl'd sure Succession in his Line"—is pure invention; it has no real basis in the Latin, but it points to the issue of legitimacy, the central question in the political struggles of Dryden's lifetime. Normanby, whose unwillingness to tell the official lie legitimizing William had just cost him so dearly, was unlikely to miss Dryden's meaning; Howard, pragmatically committed to that lie, was equally unlikely to miss his brother-in-law's stubborn reiteration of his unpopular beliefs. Nor are such political additions an isolated phenomenon; they constitute a continuous strand in the poem's meaning. In the twelfth book, for example, the old king Latinus tries to dissuade Turnus from another battle with the Trojans. In the Latin, he points out to the hotheaded young man that he already possesses the kingdoms of his father Daunus (XII, 22); Dryden's rendering of the line—"You want not Wealth, or a successive Throne" (XII, 34)—might well have reminded some readers that the usurping William III of England was already William III of Orange, heir to a "successive Throne" in Holland.

I do not mean to argue that Dryden's *Virgil* is merely a partisan work of propaganda. He poured into it the literary learning and skill he had spent a lifetime acquiring, and its best passages are vigorous and noble. But I believe we must recognize that this translation, like all translations, is a product of a particular time and a particular maker. When Dryden thought of Virgil composing a poem to please and instruct Augustus, he remembered his own attempts to please and instruct the Stuart monarchs, and the distortions he introduced in pursuing that identification are no greater than the distortions introduced by modern translators, who have also inevitably recast Virgil in their own images. In the most striking passage in the dedication, discussing the inherent difficulty of the translation, Dryden obliquely addresses this problem:

> I am also bound to tell your Lordship, in my own defence: That from the beginning of the First *Georgick* to the end of the last *Aeneid*; I found the difficulty of Translation growing on me in every succeeding Book, for *Virgil*, above all Poets, had a stock, which I may call almost inexhaustible, of figurative, Elegant, and sounding Words. I, who inherit but a small portion of his Genius, and write in a Language so much inferiour to the Latin, have found it very painful to vary Phrases, when the same sense returns upon me. . . . Words are not so easily Coyn'd as Money: And yet we see that the Credit, not only of Banks, but of Exchequers cracks, when little comes in, and much goes out.

Virgil call'd upon me in every line for some new word: And I paid so long, that I was almost Bankrupt. So that the latter end must needs be more burdensom than the beginning or the middle. And consequently, the Twelfth *Aeneid* cost me double the time of the first and second. What had become of me, if *Virgil* had tax'd me with another Book? I had certainly been reduc'd to pay the Publick in hammer'd Money, for want of Mill'd; that is in the same old words which I had us'd before: And the Receivers must have been forc'd to have taken any thing, where there was so little to be had. [pp. 1057–58]

Relentlessly developing the imagery of coining, Dryden brings together the public struggle over the national economy, his own private difficulties with Tonson's payments, his long-held belief that English was "a barbarous Modern tongue" (*Letters*, pp. 70–71), and his struggle to complete what must often have seemed an impossibly large task. If we read the imagery in the context of Dryden's times, we may grasp an even larger meaning. In the recoinage through which England had just passed, an old currency, "clipped" and devalued, had been melted down and reissued. In its fundamental metallic material, the new currency was the old currency, just as Dryden's *Virgil* was fundamentally Virgilian. In its appearance, however, the new currency was freshly "milled" and therefore able to pass in exchange, just as Dryden's translation, freshly processed by a great poet, was able to reach readers who would have been bewildered by the Latin. As its shifting relation to gold showed, the value of the silver currency was ultimately dependent on public trust, on what the local butcher or brewer believed the coins were worth; so, too, with Dryden's *Virgil*, which was to be sold at three different prices, and which would be valued by various readers for various reasons. Subscribers might treat it as a "coffee table book," casually leaving the handsome volume open to the page displaying their names and arms. Classicists might marvel at Dryden's sensitivity to the range of meaning in Latin words.[40] Lovers of English poetry might admire the speed, smoothness, and energy of his couplets. Theatregoers with fond memories of his heroic dramas might enjoy the fine couplet dialogue between Aeneas and Dido in Book IV. Jacobites and Catholics, out of power and out of money, might take comfort in the layer of political suggestiveness.

This passage itself has such a layer: as Normanby and the public reading over his shoulder would have recognized, Dryden's allusions to the credit of banks and exchequers reflect the disillusionment of the "country" party with the government's schemes for raising money to support the European war, including the borrowing of massive sums from the Bank of England. On 9 August 1696, for example, Evelyn complained to his diary about "the Bank lending the King 200[,]000 pounds for the Army in Flanders, that having don nothing against the Enemy, had so exhausted the Treasury of the Nation that one could not have borrowed mony under 14 or 15 per Cent . . . so miserably had we lost our best credit."[41] But politics is not Dryden's only interest, and this dedication, like the one to Chesterfield, means to compliment its recipient by its candor. Dryden's talk of verbal bankruptcy is an important and accurate piece of literary self-criticism: his struggle to avoid repeating himself is often evident in the later books of the *Aeneis*.[42] Strategically placed a few pages before an expression of gratitude for

Normanby's "Bounty" to Dryden "since the Revolution" (p. 1063), the image of the bankrupt poet may also be meant as a subliminal reminder that noble lords should reward poets who honor them with dedications.

The imagery of coins returns once more when Dryden seeks to defend himself from a charge he blames on "false critics, . . . that I latinize too much":

> I carry not out the Treasure of the Nation, which is never to return; but what I bring from *Italy*, I spend in *England*: Here it remains, and here it circulates; for if the Coyn be good, it will pass from one hand to another. I Trade both with the Living and the Dead, for the enrichment of our Native Language. We have enough in *England* to supply our necessity; but if we will have things of Magnificence and Splendour, we must get them by Commerce. Poetry requires Ornament; and that is not to be had from our old *Teuton* Monosyllables. [p. 1059]

In defending the "Ornament" he had imported by anglicizing some of Virgil's Latin vocabulary, Dryden was probably thinking of such passages as the revelation of Venus to her son:

> Thus having said, she turn'd, and made appear
> Her Neck refulgent, and dishevel'd Hair;
> Which flowing from her Shoulders, reach'd the Ground.
> And widely spread Ambrosial Scents around:
> In length of Train descends her sweeping Gown,
> And by her graceful Walk, the Queen of Love is known.
>
> [I, 556–61]

Beautiful in themselves, such Latinisms as "refulgent" and "Ambrosial" help Dryden give these lines an elevated lyricism. Yet the wonderful muscularity of other parts of the *Virgil* comes from his fondness for "*Teuton* Monosyllables," especially in his verbs. Here is the sinking of a ship in the first great storm:

> The trembling Pilot, from his Rudder torn,
> Was headlong hurl'd; thrice round, the Ship was tost,
> Then bulg'd at once, and in the deep was lost.
> And here and there above the Waves were seen
> Arms, Pictures, precious Goods, and floating Men.
> The stoutest Vessel to the Storm gave way,
> And suck'd through loosen'd Planks the rushing Sea.
>
> [I, 165–71]

Other passages brilliantly combine Latin and Saxon vocabulary. Here is Dido's horse, awaiting his rider on the morning of the hunt:

> Her lofty Courser, in the Court below,
> (Who his Majestick Rider seems to know,)
> Proud of his Purple Trappings, paws the Ground,
> And champs the Golden Bitt; and spreads the Foam around.
>
> [IV, 190–93]

Clothed in Latin adjectives ("Majestick," "Purple"), the horse nonetheless "paws" and "champs." Here is Charon, the tough old boatman of the underworld:

> A sordid God; down from his hoary Chin
> A length of Beard descends; uncomb'd, unclean:
> His Eyes, like hollow Furnaces on Fire:
> A Girdle, foul with grease, binds his obscene Attire.
> He spreads his Canvas, with his Pole he steers;
> The Freights of flitting Ghosts in his thin Bottom bears.
> He look'd in Years; yet in his Years were seen
> A youthful Vigour, and Autumnal green.
>
> [VI, 414–21]

In passages like these, Dryden makes good his claim to "Trade both with the Living and the Dead": from Latin, he imports "sordid" and "obscene," adjectives rich in sound and meaning; from Teutonic roots, he takes "foul with grease" and "Freights of flitting Ghosts." When he returned once more to the metaphor of language as precious metal, in his poem "To my Friend, Peter Motteux" (1698), he contrasted English with French by praising his native tongue for being an alloy composed of various metals:

> Their Tongue infeebled, is refin'd so much,
> That, like pure Gold, it bends at ev'ry touch:
> Our sturdy *Teuton*, yet will Art obey,
> More fit for manly thought, and strengthen'd with Allay.
>
> [ll. 44–47]

As much as any other work by Dryden, the *Virgil* demonstrated to future poets how the "sturdy *Teuton*" vocabulary of English might be made to obey the rules of "Art," and how the language might be "strengthen'd" by judicious admixture of imported words.

Dryden had probably finished all three dedications by March of 1697; proofreading and notes continued to occupy him, as did negotiations with the subscribers about the engravings. Late in the day, sometime after 19 June,[43] he finished writing a "Postscript to the Reader," in which he thanked the noblemen at whose homes he had stayed while translating the *Virgil*, and the physicians (William Gibbons and Thomas Hobbs) who had helped him "recover in some measure the health which I had lost by too much application to this Work" (*Poems*, III, 1426). A letter of 6 July shows that the list of two-guinea subscribers was not yet in final form, but the books were finally available by early August, and on 18 August, the poet, who had suffered another bout of illness, was "just ready to take Coach for the Country" (*Letters*, p. 91). His summarizing account of the great effort of the past three years may speak for itself:

> What *Virgil* wrote in the vigour of his Age, in Plenty and at Ease, I have undertaken to *Translate* in my Declining Years: struling with Wants, oppress'd with Sickness, curb'd in my Genius, lyable to be miconstrued in all I write; and my Judges, if they are not very equitable, already prejudic'd against me, by the *Lying Character* which has been given them of my Morals. Yet steady to my Principles, and not dispirited with my Afflictions, I have, by the Blessing of God on my Endeavours, overcome all difficulties; and, in

some measure, acquitted my self of the Debt which I ow'd the Publick, when I undertook this Work. In the first place therefore, I thankfully acknowledge to the Almighty Power, the Assistance he has given me in the beginning, the Prosecution, and *Conclusion* of my present Studies, which are more happily perform'd than I could have promis'd to my self, when I labour'd under such Discouragements. For, what I have done, Imperfect as it is, for want of Health and leisure to Correct it, will be judg'd in after Ages, and possibly in the present, to be no dishonour to my Native Country. ["Postscript to the Reader," *Poems*, III, 1424]

"The Vanquish'd Victor"

By 3 September, when he wrote at some length to his sons in Rome (*Letters*, pp. 92–94), Dryden was able to tell them that "My Virgil succeeds in the World beyond its desert or my Expectations," and a second edition was soon needed. Presumably alluding to his success in soliciting subscriptions from those opposed to his beliefs, he reports that "It has pleasd God to raise up many friends to me amongst my Enemyes; though they who ought to have been my friends, are negligent of me." Generously sharing the profits, he promises to send his sons "thirty guineas, betwixt Michaelmass & Christmass," a project we can observe him pursuing in later letters to Tonson. He also reports having cast a hopeful horoscope for Charles, who had apparently suffered some kind of head injury. Elizabeth, who added her own letter, was anxious for "a true account how my deare Sonn Charlles [h]is head dus" (pp. 95–96), and when Dryden returned to London, he consulted with his surgeon, soliciting a letter to Charles with advice about how "to prevent a Rupture wch He fears" (p. 99).[44] Erasmus-Henry, now Father Thomas Dryden, was back in Rome after spending eighteen months in a monastery in Naples;[45] both his parents ask to be remembered in the prayers of "poor Harry." What Dryden was perhaps too proud to say in the letter, he had evidently said to his wife, who quickly passed it on: "he expresses a great desire to see my deare Charlles: and trully I see noe reason why you should not both come together, to be a comfort to woon another[,] and to us both: if the king of france includ Ingland in the peace" (p. 95). Peace was indeed imminent; the Treaty of Ryswick, ending the Nine Years War, was signed on [10]/20 September. As Elizabeth hoped, the end of the war made travel in Europe easier, but her "deare Jacke" never returned to England, and Charles delayed for almost another year; on [6]/16 November, Erasmus-Henry left Rome for the Dominican monastery at Bornheim in Belgium, where he stayed until after his father's death.[46]

Although "indisposed with a cold" and "thick of heareing," Dryden was already planning another theatrical venture, undertaken at the urging of one of those friends who had recently reappeared from the ranks of his enemies: "After my return to Town, I intend to alter a play of Sir Robert Howards, written long since, & lately put by him into my hands: tis calld The Conquest of China by the Tartars. It will cost me six weeks study, with the probable benefit of an hunderd pounds." A later letter shows that Dryden did pursue this project; sometime in December he wrote to Tonson: "I have broken off my Studies from The Conquest of China, to review Virgil, and bestowd nine entire days upon him" (*Letters*, p. 97). The "review" was necessary for the second edition, carefully corrected and available early the next spring,[47] but the play was never performed.

The other project to which Dryden refers in the September letter is "a Song for St. Cecilia's feast, [which] is troublesome, & no way beneficiall." He pictures himself undertaking the task unwillingly as a favor to "the Stewards of the feast . . . one of them being Mr [Orlando] Bridgman, whose parents are your mothers friends"; he probably also considered the fact that Bridgman had been among the two-guinea subscribers to the *Virgil*. Despite his complaints, he evidently warmed to the task, and *Alexander's Feast, or The Power of Musique* remains the standard by which English poems about music are judged. It was to be Dryden's last exercise in the Pindaric form he had so often employed, and its rhythmic variety and intensity may betray his exhilaration at being free of the task of stringing together the ten thousand couplets that make up the *Virgil*. The original setting by Jeremiah Clarke has vanished, leaving scholars to guess about which parts of Dryden's text were set as recitatives, arias, and ensembles, but the marking of the text makes it clear that each of the seven stanzas concluded with a chorus. Like the first ode of 1687, this one is a virtuoso performance. Dryden celebrates the power of music but demonstrates the power of poetry. Even Handel, in his justly famous setting of 1736, is sometimes overwhelmed by Dryden's rhythmic complexity.[48] First performed on 22 November, the piece was repeated on 9 and 16 December, but no contemporary account of Clarke's setting survives; we may glimpse the reception of Dryden's poem in a letter he wrote to Tonson in December: "I am glad to heare from all Hands, that my Ode is esteemd the best of all my poetry, by all the Town: I thought so my self when I writ it but being old, I mistrusted my own Judgment" (*Letters*, p. 98).

Departing from the conventions of earlier St. Cecilia odes, including his own, Dryden makes this ode a narrative, retelling the myth of Timotheus, royal musician to Alexander the Great, who was reputedly able to arouse his master to various passions by playing and singing in various musical modes. Despite the subtitle (*The Power of Musique*), Dryden's Timotheus is not a mere instrumentalist; the songs he sings evidently have texts, and the poem celebrates and demonstrates how such songs can manipulate emotion by musical and poetic means. For Dryden, the relations between poets and heroes were a central, problematic instance of that capacity for manipulation. In the dedication to *Examen Poeticum* (1693), he had blamed Homer for describing "those ungodly Man-killers, whom we Poets, when we flatter, call Heroes" (IV, 374), and in this poem, Timotheus begins by flattering the man-killer Alexander, singing a lying account of the hero's conception that would make him the son of the fair Olympia, violently begotten by Jove in the guise of a dragon. Dryden recognized the power of poetry to flatter monarchs; a few years later, in his version of Chaucer's tale of a flattering fox and a gullible cock, he would warn "Princes rais'd by Poets to the Gods, / And *Alexander'd* up in lying Odes" against believing "ev'ry flatt'ring Knave's report" ("The Cock and the Fox," ll. 659–61).[49] But if Dryden had often demonstrated his skill at such flattery, he had almost always used the power thus gained to give moral and political advice to his monarchs, some of it quite pointed. Timotheus, a more selfish artist, simply uses his power to demonstrate his skill at manipulating his monarch.

When he sings "The Praise of *Bacchus*," for example, he sends Alexander into a drunken dream of military glory:

> Sooth'd with the Sound the King grew vain;
>   Fought all his Battails o'er again;
> And thrice He routed all his Foes; and thrice He slew the slain.

[ll. 66–68]

The oxymoronic phrase "slew the slain" neatly demonstrates how quickly Timotheus can reduce Alexander to folly, and the same gesture recurs when Timotheus sings of love, causing Alexander to think of "War" as "Toil and Trouble; / Honour but an empty Bubble" (ll. 99–100). Overcome by the beauty of the prostitute Thais, Alexander

> Sigh'd and look'd, and sigh'd again:
> At length, with Love and Wine at once oppress'd,
> The vanquish'd Victor sunk upon her Breast.

[ll. 113–15]

Initially a "God-like Heroe," Alexander has now been reduced to a "vanquish'd Victor," but Timotheus is not done with him. When the musician "strike[s] the Golden Lyre again," he chooses "A lowder yet, and yet a lowder Strain" (ll. 123–24). Roused from his sleep by a nightmare of Furies and unburied corpses,

> the King seyz'd a Flambeau, with Zeal to destroy;
>   *Thais* led the Way,
>   To light him to his Prey,
> And, like another *Hellen*, fir'd another *Troy*.

[ll. 147–50]

Timotheus can make Alexander feel divine, lustful, enervated, or vengeful, but his art has no moral dimension. Perhaps that is part of the meaning of the poem's conclusion, in which Dryden shows how Timotheus is inferior to St. Cecilia:

> Thus, long ago
> 'Ere heaving Bellows learn'd to blow,
>   While Organs yet were mute;
> *Timotheus*, to his breathing Flute,
>   And sounding Lyre,
> Cou'd swell the Soul to rage, or kindle soft Desire.
>   At last Divine *Cecilia* came,
>   Inventress of the Vocal Frame;
> The sweet Enthusiast, from her Sacred Store,
>   Enlarg'd the former narrow Bounds,
>   And added Length to solemn Sounds,
> With Nature's Mother-Wit, and Arts unknown before.
>   Let old *Timotheus* yield the Prize,
>   Or both divide the Crown;
>   He rais'd a Mortal to the Skies;
>   She drew an Angel down.

[ll. 155–70]

At one level, Cecilia is superior because her instrument, the organ, is a "Vocal Frame," sounding like the human voice and accompanying the singing of prayers and praises. Dryden's habitual ranking of poetry above music finds subtle expression in that distinction. At another level, she is superior because of her Christianity. A pagan poet might muster the rhetorical skill to raise a mortal to the skies, at least in the mind of the deluded mortal, but only a "sweet Enthusiast" like Cecilia, whom Dryden imagines as an innocent artist like that "sweet Saint" Anne Killigrew, could draw an angel down. *Alexander's Feast*, which the old poet thought the best of all his poems, thus includes among its many dimensions a self-conscious questioning of the relationship between the artistic power to manipulate one's hearers and the moral imperative to instruct them.

Another possible dimension, as so often with Dryden, is political. The story of a general manipulated by music was not in itself complimentary to Alexander, or to ideals of military heroism generally, and Dryden's reordering of materials gleaned from Plutarch and other ancient sources places Alexander in the worst possible moral light.[50] First heard some six days after William's triumphal entry into London after signing the Peace of Ryswick, *Alexander's Feast* may reflect not only Dryden's general valuing of the arts of peace but his specific opinions about the just concluded war. The court celebrated the treaty with a performance of *Europe's Revels for the Peace*, a conventional masque by Peter Motteux performed by members of both theatrical companies, but the first performance of Dryden's ode at Stationers' Hall may have taken place before the court masque could be mounted,[51] and a politically astute listener might well have heard a quite different perspective on the Peace in some of the language of Dryden's ode.

The thousands of men sacrificed in such meaningless operations as the siege of Namur were grim evidence of the King's "Zeal to destroy," and if William was publicly playing the role of the victorious conqueror, he had won very little in the Nine Years War: the German and Flemish Protestants for whose cause he had supposedly been fighting were worse off than before the war, and the "country party," surveying the damage done to the English economy, might well think of the King as a "vanquish'd Victor." Jacobites might even hear the notes of their own sorrow in Timotheus's song of mourning for Alexander's victim Darius:

> He sung *Darius* Great and Good,
>   By too severe a Fate,
> Fallen, fallen, fallen, fallen,
>   Fallen from his high Estate
>   And weltring in his Blood:
> Deserted at his utmost Need,
> By those his former Bounty fed:
> On the bare Earth expos'd He lyes,
> With not a Friend to close his Eyes.
>
> [ll. 75–83]

James II was not dead (he outlived Dryden by more than a year), but he had certainly been deserted in his need by many whom he had fed, and the new treaty rendered him politically dead, since his remaining supporters in England had been counting on the hope that Louis would be unwilling to make peace until James was restored. Although recent scholarship has stressed such possible political implications in the poem, there is no hard primary evidence to prove that Dryden's contemporaries heard his ode as this kind of "allusive soured statement on the militarism of King William."[52] Curiously enough, however, the repeat performance at the York Buildings on 16 December featured "an Addition of a new Pastoral on the Peace, Composed by Mr Jeremiah Clarke."[53] Did someone decide to balance the program with a piece whose text was less open to a subversive interpretation?

"The Sland'ring Trade"

Everyone knew that Louis, not William, was responsible for the peace: Elizabeth Dryden's letter to her sons, hoping that "the king of france [might] includ Ingland in the peace," reflects the usual understanding, and Evelyn wondered "why France who had such advantage should yield to part with such Conquests. . . . But 'tis imputed to the decay of [Louis's] own health, his apprehension of the Dolphin, the importunitye of Mad: Maintenoon &c."[54] Dryden's next work, a commendatory poem for George Granville on a tragedy called *Heroick Love* (acted in January 1698, printed in February), has a passage contrasting the motives of the two kings:

> Young Princes Obstinate to win the Prize,
> Thô Yearly beaten, Yearly yet they rise:
> Old Monarchs, though Successful, still in Doubt,
> Catch at a Peace; and wisely turn Devout.

[ll. 11–14]

Influenced by the piety of Madame de Maintenon, Louis had been willing to "Catch at a Peace"; like still another "Old Monarch," James II, he was "turn[ing] Devout." But in the larger context of the poem, which discusses the theatre, this couplet refers to Dryden himself, the old monarch of the stage, who had turned devout at considerable cost, and who was now making a gesture similar to the one in the poem to Congreve, resigning his laurels happily to Granville:

> Thine be the Lawrel then; thy blooming Age
> Can best, if any can, support the Stage:
> Which so declines, that shortly we may see,
> Players and Plays reduc'd to second Infancy.

[ll. 15–18]

The ensuing account of the declining stage gives the lie to Dryden's comic picture of himself as an old king willing to "Catch at a Peace"; it is his contribution to the renewed warfare between the two theatrical troupes. His criticisms of "Foreign Monster[s]" and "Mangled Tragedy" (ll. 22, 28) are directed at Christopher Rich's company at Drury Lane; Betterton's old actors at Lincoln's Inn Fields, who produced Granville's play, are "Like Ancient *Rome*, Majestick in decay" (l. 36). As Dryden surely expected, his poem quickly drew an answer from a representative of the younger players: in the preface to a play called *The Fatal Discovery* (acted in March, printed in May), George Powell, an actor in Rich's company, complains that "this great Wit, with his Treacherous Memory, forgets, that he had given away his Lawrels upon Record, no less then twice before, *viz.* once to Mr. *Congreve*, and another time to Mr. *Southern.*" Missing the witty self-reference of the lines on the kings, he reports that Dryden "treats all Crownd Heads much alike . . . he gives one Prince a Kick on the B[um], another a Box on the Ear, and spits in the face of a third." Dryden, whose plays were frequently revived by both houses, had complained that the young players were "Murd'ring Plays, which they miscal Reviving" (l. 24), and Powell rises to the bait. Poking fun at Dryden's age and infirmity, he doubts whether the old poet's "Reverend Crutches have ever brought him within our doors since the division of the Companies." Applying the same imagery to *The Conquest of Granada*, a revival that had evidently raised Dryden's "particular pique," Powell says "'twas very hard crutching up what *Hart* and *Mohun* before us could not prop."[55]

Dryden's poem and Powell's answer are typical of the free-swinging abuse that accompanied renewed theatrical competition, but the internecine warfare between the companies was tame compared to the challenge both theatres now faced from hostile forces in the government and the church. Sunderland, who replaced Dorset as Lord Chamberlain on 20 April 1697, demanded that all new scripts be brought to his secretary for censorship, complaining that "many of the new Plays Acted by both Companies of his Majesty's Comedians are scandalously lew'd and Prophane, and contain Reflections against his Majesty's Government."[56] This official drive to purify the theatre was followed the next spring by a publication that struck directly at Dryden: *A Short View of the Immorality and Profaneness of the English Stage*, by a clergyman named Jeremy Collier. Collier was a bundle of contradictions. He was a learned man, as his frequent citation of classical and patristic texts in this very volume shows, but he had become fixated on the notion that stage plays were sapping the morality of the nation. This old idea had generally been the property of Puritans and Dissenters, but Collier was a strong non-juror: he had recently been in trouble with the authorities for granting absolution to Sir William Perkins and Sir John Friend, Jacobites who were hanged, drawn, and quartered for their part in the assassination plot of 1696.[57] Despite his politics, however, Collier on the theatre is as ascetic as William Prynne. Dryden is not his only target; Durfey and Congreve come in for sustained criticism as well. But Collier evidently sifted the works of Dryden carefully in search of "Cursing and Swearing," "Profaneness," and instances of "the Clergy abused." Not content with quoting and disapproving lines from many of Dryden's plays, he also makes "Remarks upon a Passage or two in the *Dedications* of *Aureng Zebe*, and the *Translation of Juvenal*." In the latter case, he blames Dryden for translating Juvenal correctly: "Why was not the Thought Blanched, the Expression made remote, and the ill Features cast into Shadows?" (p. 71). I cannot imagine Dryden being greatly disturbed by this kind of criticism, but Collier's comments on the dedication to *Aureng-Zebe*, which accuse him of "Blasphemy" and "Atheism," were surely distressing to a man who took his faith seriously.

Typical of the kind of distortion about which Dryden later complained is Collier's reading of Dryden's fine passage on changeability:

> *Our Minds* (says he) *are perpetually wrought on by the Temperament of our Bodies, which makes me suspect they are nearer Allied than either our Philosophers, or School-Divines will allow them to be.* The meaning is, he suspects our Souls are nothing but Organiz'd Matter: Or, in plain English, our *Souls* are nothing but our Bodies; and then when the Body dies, you may guess what becomes of them! Thus the Authorities of Religion are weaken'd, and the prospect of the other World almost shut up. [p. 68]

The key to Collier's passion, as Dryden evidently recognized, may be found in his chapter on abuse of the clergy, which cites instances from *The Spanish Fryar*, *Don Sebastian*, *Cleomenes*, and *Oedipus*. In only one case, the laughable Friar Dominick, is Dryden's alleged abuse even directed at a Christian cleric; the other plays deal with Moslems, Egyptians, and pagans. The passage cited from *Oedipus* is not even by Dryden, but Collier can still blame him for "let[ting] these crude Fancies pass uncorrected in his Friend [Lee]" (p. 108). Convinced that the clergy had a special right to respect, Collier had become a fanatic about anything resembling abuse of his profession, and the political and social atmosphere was receptive to his hand-wringing about the theatre. On 13 May 1698, Dryden's theatrical friends felt the consequences: "The justices of Middlesex did not only present the playhouses, but also Mr. Congreve, for writing the Double Dealer; Durfey, for Don Quixot; and Tonson and Brisco, booksellers, for printing them: and that women frequenting the playhouses in masks tended much to debauchery and immorality."[58]

Both Congreve and the young Whig playwright Sir John Vanbrugh published full-scale refutations of Collier, but Dryden did not immediately reply to Collier by name, contenting himself with a dignified passage in the poem to Motteux, also published in June:

> The Muses Foes
> Wou'd sink their Maker's Praises into Prose.
> Were they content to prune the lavish Vine
> Of straggling Branches, and improve the Wine,
> Who but a mad Man wou'd his Faults defend?
> All wou'd submit, for all but Fools will mend.
> But, when to common sense they give the Lie,
> And turn distorted Words to Blasphemy,
> *They* give the Scandal; and the Wise discern,
> Their Glosses teach an Age too apt to learn.
>
> [ll. 5–14]

The gesture of submission makes possible the crushing claim that Collier and his ilk are defeating their own cause by finding blasphemy where none was intended and retailing it to the public. Dryden continues by repeating the same rhetorical technique at a more personal level, claiming that he is ready to have his genuinely profane writings burnt, but defending his attacks on the clergy as arraignments of "Their Faults and not their Function" (l. 18). Conveniently ignoring Collier's non-juring politics, he connects his enemy with the Puritan clergy of the 1640s, well-known foes of the theatre, who preached "Rebellion, worse than Witchcraft" (l. 19).

In his writings supporting the Stuart monarchy, Dryden had frequently associated the clergy with rebellion, and in the *Dedication of the Aeneis*, he had interrupted his account of Roman history to remark that "the Cause of Religion is but a Modern Motive to Rebellion, invented by the Christian Priesthood, refining on the Heathen" (p. 1012). Collier missed that passage, but another clergyman, Luke Milbourn, quotes it near the beginning of his *Notes on Dryden's Virgil*, a 232-page attack published in 1698. Milbourn says that Dryden's remark

> is malicious enough, and would have been an Invention becoming Mr. *Dryden*'s Wit, had *he* been unhappily *admitted into Holy Orders*; tho for ought I know, *his very Christianity* may be questionable. . . . I'll shew him some Instances of *Rebellions under the pretence of Religion* before *Christianity* was heard of; and since then, I have never heard of any sort of *Christians*, who have *turn'd Religion into Rebellion, and Faith into Faction*, but those of the *Church of Rome*, and their *spawn of the Separation*. [p. 9]

Like Collier, Milbourn rankled at the lack of respect accorded the clergy, and the success of Dryden's *Virgil* was particularly irksome to him because his own translation, published in 1688, had been ignored. Dredging up the ancient charge that Dryden had been refused ordination, he complains that "Mr *Bays* has a spite to a *Country Parson*, because refus'd to be *one*" (p. 19). Displaying a pedantry all too typical of country parsons, he then moves through Dryden's translations of the *Pastorals* and *Georgics*, complaining ad nauseam about every tiny departure from literalism and occasionally offering his own pathetic translations as examples. He has filled his book before he even reaches the *Aeneis*.

Although he was eventually irritated enough to reply to both Milbourne and Collier, Dryden had no fear of financial damage from Milbourne's nit-picking about a successful translation now in its second edition. Since he had declared himself retired from the theatre, apparently abandoning even his plan to revise *The Conquest of China*, his livelihood was not seriously threatened by Collier either, though the public prudishness encouraged and represented by Collier may explain why Tonson never printed Dryden's lively translation of Ovid's *Ars Amatoria*, which he had completed before undertaking the Virgil, and which he inquired about in a letter to Tonson of December 1697 (*Letters*, pp. 98–99). The many-handed translation of Tacitus in which he had participated was published in June 1698,[59] by which time he had probably started work on the series of verse translations that became *Fables Ancient and Modern* (1700). "I will write on," he told Tonson, "since I find I can" (p. 99). If his later account may be trusted, he began with the first book of the *Iliad* and continued with parts of books XII and XIII of Ovid's *Metamorphoses*, which recount the causes of the Trojan War and the quarrel between Ajax and Odysseus over the armor of Achilles. By choosing classical excerpts concerned with war and peace, honor and heroism, Dryden was continuing to explore the issues he had dealt with in compressed, suggestive, and ironic ways in *Alexander's Feast*. I also imagine him taking particular pleasure in translating the outburst with which Agamemnon greets an unwanted rebuke from the prophet Calchas:

> Augur of Ill, whose Tongue was never found
> Without a Priestly Curse or boding Sound;
> For not one bless'd Event foretold to me
> Pass'd through that Mouth, or pass'd unwillingly.
> And now thou dost with Lies the Throne invade,
> By Practice harden'd in thy sland'ring Trade.
>   ["The First Book of Homer's Ilias," ll. 155–60]

"Always a Poet"

We catch a few glimpses of Dryden in the summer of 1698. An anecdote in a letter to Prior of 14 July shows him pencilling a few satiric lines under Kneller's portrait of Tonson; perhaps he was in Kneller's studio in order to sit for the great portrait now at Trinity College, Cambridge.[60] A letter written one week later to John Caryll, later Pope's friend, expresses thanks for a gift of venison and doubts about living another year (*Letters*, p. 100). Dryden's estimate of his chances for survival was not sentimental self-pity. He had been ailing, and his contemporaries continued to die: Sir Robert Howard succumbed on 3 September, and if Dryden had not yet departed for the country, he probably attended Howard's burial in Westminster Abbey on 8 September. A happier event was the return of Charles Dryden from Rome; like his father, Charles was often unwell, but he nonetheless proved a comfort to the old man, as frequent references in the letters attest. They were at Titchmarsh together on 1 October, as we know from the first of a number of letters Dryden wrote to Elizabeth Steward, the daughter of his cousin Elizabeth Creed. These letters, the largest surviving sequence of letters from Dryden to any correspondent, give us invaluable information about his daily life in London and his relations with his Northamptonshire relatives on both sides.

Mrs. Steward, who lived at Cotterstock, a few miles from Titchmarsh, was only twenty-six, and the old poet treats her with a mixture of outmoded gallantry and paternalistic affection. Accepting an often-repeated invitation, he asks, "How can you be so good, to an old decrepid Man who can entertain you with no discourse which is worthy of your good sense & who can onely be a trouble to you in all the time he stays at Cotterstock?" (*Letters*, p. 101). Still, he is confident enough to ask her to lend him her coach for a visit to "My Cousin Dryden of Chesterton some time next week." Subsequent letters written during the same fall express solicitude for Mrs. Steward's health, gratitude to her husband Elmes Steward for a gift of plover, and a desire to repeat the visit the next year. But traveling was an ordeal, and Dryden's letter of 23 November, comically describing his unpleasant coach journey with a flatulent old woman, ends with a sobering account of the consequences: "When I was ridd of her, I came sick home: & kept my House, for three weeks together; but by advice of my Doctour, takeing twice the bitter draught, with Sena in it, & looseing at least twelve Ounces of blood, by Cupping on my Neck, I am just well enough, to go abroad in the Afternoon" (p. 104). Charles was also ill; Dryden's letter of 12 December thanks Mrs. Steward for sending a basket of marrow puddings, which the younger man has been enjoying "for his Suppers" (p. 106).

Portrait of Dryden by Sir Godfrey Kneller, ca. 1698.

Neither the father nor the son was well by Candlemas-Day (2 February 1699), when Dryden wrote again to Mrs. Steward. Their doctors had proposed a trip to Bath for the waters, but Dryden was afraid that "the ayr may do us more harm than the waters can do us good" (*Letters*, p. 109). To her offer of food from the country, he replies by admitting that "a chine of honest bacon wou'd please my appetite more than all the marrow puddings; for I like them better plain; having a very vulgar stomach" (p. 110). Aware that she is "a Poetess" (p. 113), he also reports on his ongoing literary labors:

> In the mean time, betwixt my intervalls of physique and other remedies which I am useing for my gravell, I am still drudging on: always a Poet, and never a good one. I pass my time sometimes with Ovid, and sometimes with our old English poet, Chaucer;

translating such stories as best please my fancy; and intend besides them to add
somewhat of my own: so that it is not impossible, but ere the summer be pass'd, I may
come down to you with a volume in my hand, like a dog out of the water, with a duck in
his mouth. [p. 109]

As Dryden later admits in the preface to the *Fables*, he had long been interested in
modernizing Chaucer, but his patron Leicester, who was a great lover of Chaucer in the
original, had dissuaded him from undertaking that project. Leicester was now dead (6
March 1698), and Dryden, newly struck by the similarities between Ovid and Chaucer,
was adding versions of the *Knight's Tale* ("Palamon and Arcite"), the *Nun's Priest's Tale*
("The Cock and the Fox"), the *Wife of Bath's Tale*, and the pseudo-Chaucerian *Flower
and the Leaf* to the steadily growing pile of Homeric and Ovidian translations on his
desk. Like his selections from Ovid, these were tales that pleased his fancy; both
authors provided ample opportunities for sparkling irony and Jacobite innuendo.[61] His
old friend Pepys recommended that he also include a version of the portrait of the
parson from the General Prologue to the *Canterbury Tales*, a suggestion Dryden embraced because it gave him a chance to strike back at Milbourne and Collier.[62]

There would be original poems ("somewhat of my own") as well. Mindful of the
connections between *Alexander's Feast* and the poems he had chosen to translate,
Dryden was planning to reprint his ode in the *Fables*, and he may already have written
the short epitaph for "A Fair Maiden Lady, Who dy'd at *Bath*,"which he also included.[63] In late December of 1698, he sent an extravagantly complimentary letter to
Mary Somerset, wife of James Butler, second Duke of Ormonde, who was now Lord
Lieutenant of Ireland; similar language in the complex, heavily perfumed poem dedicating "Palamon and Arcite" to the Duchess suggests a similar date of composition.[64]
Printed at the conclusion of the preface, the poem to the Duchess will remind us of such
earlier efforts as the lines to the first Duchess of York, similarly printed in the front
matter to *Annus Mirabilis* some thirty-three years earlier. The poem to Anne Hyde
portrays her social "progress" to the North of England as a "Conquest" analogous to
her husband's recent naval victory at Lowestoft; the poem to Mary Somerset celebrates
her recent visit to Ireland, when "*Hibernia*, prostrate at Your Feet, ador'd / In you, the
Pledge of her expected Lord" (ll. 53–54). A similar airy fantasy informs both texts: the
closing lines of the poem to the Duchess of York make her a phoenix attended by the
"Poet[s] of the air"; the analogous lines in this poem make the Duchess of Ormonde a
dove of peace, an image Dryden had also used for Catharine of Braganza and Maria
Beatrice, but this time the rainbow of the Flood story is "an Omen from your Eyes" (l.
76), so that typology merges into gallant compliment. Celebrating "inviolable Peace,"
Dryden predicts that when Mary returns to Ireland, "The sharpen'd Share shall vex the
Soil no more, / But Earth unbidden shall produce her Store" (ll. 82–83). This image
of magical fertility reverses the bleak picture of fallow fields deserted by conscripted
peasants in the translation of the first *Georgic* (quoted above, p. 480), where "crooked
Scythes are streightned into Swords." The closing lines urge the Duchess, already
mother of three daughters, to produce a son to carry on the Ormonde line; that gentle

injunction to human fertility stands in marked contrast to the violent myth by which Timotheus claims divine lineage for Alexander.

The poem to the Duchess uses its compliments to establish ethical ideals, as does the longest and most important original poem in the *Fables*, the Horatian verse epistle to John Driden of Chesterton, about whose welfare the poet was particularly concerned at this time. In a letter of 18 February 1699, recently rediscovered, he thanks Mrs. Steward for the chine of bacon and tells her that he has recently written twice to "my good Cousin Driden of Chesterton . . . but not hearing from him, am affrayd he is so oppressd with grief, for the late death, of my Cousin Benjamin his Brother, & my great friend, that he is fallen Sick." He hopes that she will "send one of [her] Servants on purpose to Chesterton, to enquire of his Welfare,"[65] and she evidently did so, for in his next letter (4 March), Dryden happily reports that "my Cousin Driden of Chesterton" has sent

> a turkey hen with Eggs, & a good young Goose; besides a very kind letter, & the News of his own good health, which I vallue more than all the rest; He being so noble a Benefactour to a poor, & so undeserving a Kinsman, & one of another persuasion, in matters of Religion. Your Enquiry of his welfare, & sending also mine, have at once obligd both him and me. I hope my good Cousin Stewart [Elmes Steward, his corre-spondent's husband] will often visite him, especially before hunting goes out. . . . Exercise I know is my Cousin Driden's life; & the oftner he goes out, will be the better for his health. [p. 112]

Dryden probably began writing his poem "To my Honour'd Kinsman, John Driden, of Chesterton in the County of Huntingdon, Esquire" during this spring; it brings together the homely personal concerns of these letters—hunting, food, physical health, concern for one's kin—and the political issues with which John Driden had to wrestle as a Member of Parliament. Borrowing heavily from his own translation of the second epode of Horace, Dryden describes his kinsman as an exemplar of the ideal of retirement:

> How Bless'd is He, who leads a Country Life,
> Unvex'd with anxious Cares, and void of Strife!
> Who studying Peace, and shunning Civil Rage,
> Enjoy'd his Youth, and now enjoys his Age:
> All who deserve his Love, he makes his own;
> And to be lov'd himself, needs only to be known.
>
> [ll. 1–6]

In the Horatian translation of 1685, the happy man had also been "void of strife," but strife in that poem was personified as "the gripeing Scrivener," and the fortunate man in the country was "rich in humble Poverty." In this poem, "humble Poverty" disap-pears, replaced by a passage specifying the source of John Driden's wealth and praising his generosity:

> Heav'n, who foresaw the Will, the Means has wrought,
> And to the Second Son, a Blessing brought:

> The First-begotten had his Father's Share;
> But you, like *Jacob*, are *Rebecca*'s Heir.
> . . . .
> So free to Many, to Relations most,
> You feed with Manna your own *Israel*-Host.
>
> [ll. 40–43; 48–49]

Robert Dryden of Canons Ashby, firstborn son of Sir John Dryden the Parliamentarian, had inherited the baronetcy and family seat, but John, the second son, had inherited his estate at Chesterton from Honor Beville, his mother. The analogy with Jacob, who stole the birthright of Esau with his mother Rebecca's connivance, is far from perfect, but may express the poet's hostility toward his cousin Robert, attested to by family tradition.[66] If that analogy is awkward, the ensuing description of John Driden as an Old Testament God granting "Manna" to his wandering people is overblown, though the rhetorical excess suggests how grateful Dryden was for his cousin's generosity toward his "Relations."

Such personal and familial concerns frequently color this rich poem, but national and international politics are also important, and Dryden moves easily from the private to the public. In the opening lines, the "Civil Rage" that both cousins remembered from the 1640s replaces "the gripeing Scrivener" as the leading example of the "Strife" avoided by the blessed country dweller, who now studies "Peace," an ideal recently realized in Europe. John Driden was a Justice of the Peace; the ensuing lines on his skill in arbitrating disputes in his neighborhood apply the language of international affairs to local squabbles. His "contending Neighbours," who have been "Foes before, return in Friendship home" (ll. 7–9) from Driden's informal court:

> Without their Cost, you terminate the Cause;
> And save th' Expence of long Litigious Laws:
> Where Suits are travers'd; and so little won,
> That he who conquers, is but last undone.
>
> [ll. 10–13]

Dryden knew about the expense of lawsuits from bitter personal experience (see above, p. 462), but his description of the victor in such a lawsuit as a conqueror undone by his expenses may remind us of the description of Alexander as a "vanquish'd Victor" in the St. Cecilia ode. Both passages may originate in the belief that William's occasional victories in the Nine Years War had been bought at a terrible price, a conviction shared by Dryden and his cousin. The poet's praise for his cousin's "Decrees," which leave "a lasting Peace behind" (ll. 14–15) reflects a widespread but vain hope that the peace in Europe would last.

A later passage makes the political position implicit in these opening lines entirely explicit:

> Enough for *Europe* has our *Albion* fought:
> Let us enjoy the Peace our Blood has bought.
> When once the *Persian* King was put to Flight,
> The weary *Macedons* refus'd to fight:

> Themselves their own Mortality confess'd;
> And left the Son of *Jove*, to quarrel for the rest.
> Ev'n Victors are by Victories undone.
>
> [ll. 158–64]

In the episode to which Dryden alludes, the army of Alexander, having conquered Darius, refused to push on into India. The analogy between William and Alexander, quite explicit in this poem, strengthens the political innuendo of *Alexander's Feast*, reprinted in the same volume. In a letter to Mrs. Steward, written later in the same year, Dryden reports his suspicion that "the King will endeavour to keep up a standing Army," but takes comfort in the hope that "My Cousin Driden, & the Country Party, . . . will be against it" (*Letters*, p. 124).

In another passage dependent upon the Horatian model, Dryden endorses the pleasure his cousin takes in hunting, but describes the killing of foxes as another act of justice: they are "made to bleed, / Like Felons, where they did the murd'rous Deed" (ll. 56–57). He contrasts the "Chace," by which "our long-liv'd Fathers earn'd their Food" and "purifi'd the Blood" (ll. 88–89) with the uncertain results of modern medicine, taking the occasion to praise his physician friend William Gibbons and strike back at the physician-poet Blackmore, who had called him "*Laurus*" (see above, p. 477). Tossing back the taunt with a rhyme, Dryden calls Blackmore "*Maurus*."

> What Help from Arts Endeavours can we have!
> *Guibbons* but guesses, nor is sure to save:
> But *Maurus* sweeps whole Parishes, and Peoples ev'ry Grave.
>
> [ll. 81–83]

Even physical health, about which both cousins were naturally concerned in their old age, can ultimately be connected to economic and political issues. In his popular satiric poem *The Dispensary* (1699), Dryden's friend Dr. Samuel Garth records Blackmore's opposition to an attempt to set up a free dispensary for the poor. Drawing on that poem, Dryden contrasts the greed of "The Shop-Man," who sells prescriptions at random and lives by destruction, with the generosity of his cousin, who leaves the fields from which he draws his own health in order to serve the public in Parliament:

> You hoard not Health, for your own private Use;
> But on the Publick spend the rich Produce.
>
> [ll. 117–18]

John Driden, who demonstrates his noble generosity by private gifts of food and money to his poet kinsman, thus applies the same generosity to the public by his willingness to serve the nation. In the debates about the standing army, generosity tempered by stewardship is a political principle:

> Patriots, in Peace, assert the Peoples Right;
> With noble Stubbornness resisting Might:
> No Lawless Mandates from the Court receive,
> Nor lend by Force; but in a Body give.
> Such was your gen'rous Grandsire; free to grant

> In Parliaments, that weigh'd their Prince's Want:
> But so tenacious of the Common Cause,
> As not to lend the King against his Laws.
> And, in a lothsome Dungeon doom'd to lie,
> In Bonds retain'd his Birthright Liberty,
> And sham'd Oppression, till it set him free.

[ll. 184–94]

Deliberately ignoring the very different circumstances, Dryden forces an analogy between the current Parliamentary opposition to William's military budget and his grandfather's refusal of the Forced Loan of 1626. At some level, the principle of Parliamentary control of the budget was the same, but the religious beliefs that had inspired old Erasmus to his act of civil disobedience were quite unlike those now embraced by his poetic grandson, many of whose Catholic friends and patrons had recently experienced the "lothsome Dungeon."

Dryden's letter of 4 March 1699 expresses his concern about such persecution: "We poor Catholiques daily expect a most Severe Proclamation to come out against us." The proclamations issued and laws passed during the last years of the century were severe indeed, culminating in a statute making it illegal for Catholics to hold or inherit property, which ultimately had an effect on the Dryden family.[67] Sir Robert at Canons Ashby was unmarried, as were most of his brothers; not one of them had children.[68] When Sir Robert died in 1708, the baronetcy passed to his first cousin John, the wealthy linen-draper of London, and when he died in 1710, it passed to the poet's son Erasmus-Henry, who was then the only surviving son, thanks to the early deaths of his brothers.[69] Aware of the risk that his land might also pass to a Catholic, who could not legally hold it, Robert made a will leaving his property to Edward Dryden, son of the poet's brother Erasmus, the Protestant greengrocer; the title of baronet thus became an empty honor for the poet's Dominican son. But John Driden of Chesterton, though a Protestant and a loyal supporter of the government, felt family loyalty toward his Catholic relatives; ignoring the statutes, which he evidently regarded as "Lawless Mandates," he left £500 to Charles and 100 guineas to Erasmus-Henry.[70] None of these legal actions had taken place by the time Dryden wrote this poem, but the attitudes that inspired them were already in place. The absence of any record of a visit to Canons Ashby by the poet during his adult life confirms the hostility between Sir Robert and his famous kinsman, and Dryden's description of his Chesterton cousin as "so noble a Benefactour to a poor . . . Kinsman, & one of another persuasion" (*Letters*, p. 112) surely reflects gifts of money as well as the occasional turkey hen. In his last letter (11 April 1700), Dryden reports receiving a "noble present" from his "Cousin Driden," who had been in town for the meeting of Parliament.[71] The conclusion of the poem identifies the second son as the "true Descendent of a Patriot Line," a man who does not "think the Kindred-Muses [his] Disgrace," as Sir Robert evidently did, but who takes pride in his cousin's talent, since "A Poet is not born in ev'ry Race" (ll. 195, 201–02).

The conclusion also picks up the theme of mortality, developed before in the discussion of health and the hunting sequence. If the fox is a felon, another small animal is an emblem of the cyclical nature of life:

> The Hare, in Pastures or in Plains is found,
> Emblem of Humane Life, who runs the Round;
> And, after all his wand'ring Ways are done,
> His Circle fills, and ends where he begun,
> Just as the Setting meets the Rising Sun.

[ll. 62–66]

The view of death taken in these lines is classical and resigned, but the concluding lines of the poem add Christian hope and literary pride to the idea of finding one's beginning in one's ending:

> Praise-worthy Actions are by thee embrac'd;
> And 'tis my Praise, to make thy Praises last.
> For ev'n when Death dissolves our Humane Frame,
> The Soul returns to Heav'n from whence it came;
> Earth keeps the Body, Verse preserves the Fame.

[ll. 205–09][72]

"All, All of a Piece Throughout"

As his similarly forthright statement in the "Postscript" to the *Virgil* suggests, Dryden believed his poetry would preserve his fame as well as that of his cousin. While this poem was on his desk, he took steps to ensure the publication of the volume in which it would appear. On 20 March 1699, he signed a contract with Tonson in which the bookseller agreed to pay him "two hundred and fifty guineas, in consideration of ten thousand verses, . . . whereof seaven thousand five hundred verses, more or lesse, are allready in the said Jacob Tonson's possession," and on 24 March, he signed a receipt for the money.[73] I should suppose the verses delivered by March included the first book of the *Iliad* and the longer selections from Chaucer and Ovid; since Dryden treats Boccaccio last in the preface to the *Fables*, I suspect he turned to the Italian fabulist to fill out the collection, which ultimately had many more than ten thousand verses. By mid-July, when he wrote to Mrs. Steward asking her to have some small beer brewed for him in preparation for his summer visit, Dryden thought his collection complete: in a letter to Pepys of 14 July, he says he has "translated as many Fables from Ovid, and as many Novills from Boccace and Tales from Chaucer, as will make an indifferent large volume in folio," to be published "in Michaelmass term next" (*Letters*, p. 115). But the projected autumn publication did not occur, and Dryden continued to revise his own poems. Sometime during his last visit to the country, which lasted from 10 August until 28 September,[74] he showed the verses on John Driden to their addressee, who recommended that he omit "a Satire against the Dutch valour, in the late Warr." With some fear that he had "purgd [those verses] out of their Spirit," he then submitted them to Charles Montagu for further political vetting; his shrewd covering letter refers to the poem's "description . . . of a Parliament Man" as "a Memorial of my own Principles to all Posterity," and informs Montagu that "my Unbyassed friends, who have some of them the honour to be known to you, . . . think that there is nothing which can justly give offence in that part of the Poem" (*Letters*, p. 120).

The letter to Montagu, probably written in October, also shows Dryden trying out some ideas he would develop at greater length in the preface to the *Fables*, and suggesting that he may undertake a complete translation of Homer, whom he now describes as "a Poet more according to my Genius than Virgil." He closes with a tactful request for some kind of pension to support this new project: "Since 'tis for my Country's honour as well as for my own, that I am willing to undertake this task; I despair not of being encouragd in it, by your favour" (p. 121). By 7 November, Dryden was able to tell Mrs. Steward that "the Earl of Dorsett, & your Cousin Montague have both seen the two Poems, to the Duchess of Ormond, & my worthy Cousin Driden: And are of the opinion that I never writt better." Despite the support of these powerful men, "the Court rather speaks kindly of me, than does any thing for me, though they promise largely." Dryden expresses his willingness to "forbear satire" on "the present Government," but reiterates his unwillingness to compromise his religious principles: "I can neither take the Oaths, nor forsake my Religion, because I know not what Church to go to, if I leave the Catholique" (p. 123). By the end of the month, his hopes of official support had evaporated: in a letter of 26 November, he reports that he is "in no Condition of haveing a kindness done me; Haveing the Chancellour [John Lord Somers] my Enemy. And not being capable of renounceing the Cause, for which I have so long Sufferd" (p. 129).

This predictable disappointment was not the only vexation of Dryden's last winter, as he tells Mrs. Steward in a letter of 14 December: "my head is full of cares; and my body ill at ease. My Book is printing, & my Bookseller makes no hast. I had last night at bed time, an unwelcome fit of vomiting; & my Sonn Charles lyes sick upon his bed with the Colique" (*Letters*, p. 130). Yet despite his inability to gain a pension, his continuing irritation with Tonson, and his recurring illnesses, Dryden's spirit remained strong. Fifteen days later, in a letter to the amateur poet Elizabeth Thomas, he complains of "St. Anthony's Fire in one of my legs," with swelling bad enough that he was "too weak to stand upon it," but reiterates his hope of translating Homer, and makes sure that the "Fair Corinna" knows he has a book in press, even mentioning the price: "If I recover, it is possible I may attempt Homer's Iliads: A Specimen of it (the first Book) is now in the Press, among other Poems of mine, which will make a Volume in Folio, of twelve Shillings Price; and will be published within this Month" (p. 132). In the marvelous preface to the *Fables*, probably written during this same December, he puts up an even braver public front, telling the story of an "old Gentleman" who excused his awkwardness in mounting on horseback by asking the "Fair Spectators" to "count Fourscore and eight before they judg'd him."

> By the Mercy of God, I am already come within Twenty Years of his Number, a Cripple in my Limbs, but what Decays are in my Mind, the Reader must determine. I think my self as vigorous as ever in the Faculties of my Soul, excepting only my Memory, which is not impair'd to any great degree; and if I lose not more of it, I have no great reason to complain. What Judgment I had, increases rather than diminishes; and Thoughts, such as they are, come crowding in so fast upon me, that my only Difficulty is to chuse or to reject; to run them into Verse, or give them the other Harmony of Prose. I have so long studied and practis'd both, that they are grown into a

Habit, and become familiar to me. In short, though I may lawfully plead some part of the old Gentleman's Excuse; yet I will reserve it till I think I have greater need, and ask no Grains of Allowance for the Faults of this present Work, but those which are given of course to Humane Frailty. [*Poems*, IV, 1446–47]

The pride Dryden expresses in this passage is also apparent in the concluding pages of the preface, a spirited refutation of the criticisms of Milbourne, Collier, and Blackmore, the last of whom had attacked him again in his *Satyr against Wit* (November 1699), a poem largely aimed at Dr. Garth.[75] Dryden ironically praises Milbourne for achieving the difficult task of writing "even below *Ogilby*" (p. 1461); he pretends to treat Blackmore's poems "more civilly . . . because nothing ill is to be spoken of the dead" (p. 1462). In answering Collier, he piously repeats the gesture of apology for "all Thoughts and Expressions of mine, which can be truly argu'd of Obscenity, Profaneness, or Immorality," and the charge that his clerical adversary "has perverted my Meaning by his Glosses." Looking back over a long career in the theatre, he points out that the plays of "the former Age," notably Fletcher's *The Custom of the Country*, were often filled with "Baudry," and wonders whether "the Times [are] so much more reform'd now, than they were Five and twenty Years ago"—a figure referring to the vogue for sex comedies during the 1670s (pp. 1462–63). Not content with this prose refutation, Dryden also adds a personal proem to his translation of Boccaccio's tale of "Cymon and Iphigenia," gallantly acknowledging his memories of "The Pow'r of Beauty . . . , Which once inflam'd my Soul, and still inspires my Wit" (ll. 2–3), and accusing Collier of "mak[ing] me speak the Things I never thought" (l. 12).

Despite his frequent resolutions to remain aloof, Dryden evidently retained his interest and skill in controversy. His letter to Mrs. Steward of 23 February 1700 encloses "two lampoons lately made," reporting rumors about their authorship and identifying some of the people insulted in them. His letter of 12 March, enclosing the newly published *Fables*, reports the "moderate success" of "Congreves New Play," *The Way of the World*. With his usual sharp judgment, Dryden notes that his protégé's masterpiece "deserves much better" (*Letters*, pp. 133, 134), and his disappointment with the performance given Congreve's play by Betterton and the actors at Lincoln's Inn Fields may have been a factor in his agreeing to do a last piece of theatrical writing for Drury Lane. In his last letter, written to Mrs. Steward on 11 April, he explains this project: "Within this moneth there will be playd for my profit, an old play of Fletchers, calld the Pilgrim, corrected by my good friend Mr Vanbrook [John Vanbrugh]; to which I have added A New Masque, & am to write a New Prologue & Epilogue" (*Letters*, p. 136). The prologue and epilogue, presumably written during the next two weeks, continue the counterattacks begun in the preface to the *Fables*. The shrill prologue relentlessly attacks "*Maurus*" as "A Pedant, Canting Preacher, and a Quack," capable only of writing "Fustian stuff" and "Dead-born Doggrel" (ll. 16, 49, 22–23). The more nostalgic and thoughtful epilogue refutes Collier's assertion that the stage was to blame for the immorality of the times. Accurately recalling the style of Charles II, Dryden explains how "a banisht Court, with Lewdness fraught / The seeds of open Vice returning brought" (ll. 5–6). Remembering Lely's nude paintings of the royal mistresses, he contrasts the former courts, in which "*Misses*" had been "modestly conceal'd," with the times when "*White-hall* the naked *Venus* first reveal'd" (ll. 21–22). But the lines that follow, ostensibly contrasting the courts of Charles and Cromwell, express Dryden's contempt for the hypocrisy of the "Saints" and his conviction that those now calling for censorship were the lineal descendants of the regicides:

> E're this, if Saints had any Secret Motion,
> 'Twas Chamber Practice all, and Close Devotion.
> I pass the Peccadillo's of their time;
> Nothing but open Lewdness was a Crime.
> A *Monarch*'s Blood was venial to the Nation,
> Compar'd with one foul Act of Fornication.
> Now they wou'd Silence us.
>
> [ll. 25–31]

Unwilling to be silenced, Dryden used the "Secular Masque" he added to the Fletcher-Vanbrugh *Pilgrim* to express his views on issues far larger than the alleged immorality and profaneness of the stage. His choice of a deliberately antiquated masque form featuring the pagan deities Janus and Chronos is a nostalgic gesture appropriate for summarizing a century now passing away, and the dominance of Momus, the god of laughter and criticism, turns this brief symbolic scene into an antimasque, an expression of unofficial and sardonic truths. Dryden's own fatigue at the end of his life also finds expression: Chronos enters carrying a scythe and a globe, and declares himself exhausted:

> Weary, weary of my weight,
> Let me, let me drop my Freight,
>   And leave the World behind.
> I could not bear
> Another Year
> The Load of Human-Kind.
>
> [ll. 7–12]

Momus endorses Chronos's plan to lighten his load and declares it "better to Laugh than to Cry" (l. 20). Three more deities—Diana, Mars, and Venus—then enact a masque describing "What Changes in this Age have been" (l. 25). Although the main lines of historical allegory in this masque are clear, it has undertones of irony expressing Dryden's current political and personal beliefs.[76]

Diana's account of the "shouting and hooting" of the hunt leads to an initially enthusiastic but ultimately ironic account of the first part of the century, the age of Elizabeth and James I:

> *Janus.* Then our Age was in it's Prime,
> *Chronos.* Free from Rage.
> *Diana.* ———And free from Crime.
> *Momus.* A very Merry, Dancing, Drinking,
>   Laughing, Quaffing, and unthinking Time.
>
> [ll. 37–40]

Since James I was an inveterate hunter and Elizabeth the "virgin Queen," the virgin huntress Diana may stand for both monarchs. Dryden's Momus, acknowledging the mythic power of the nostalgic notion of a "Merry" Elizabethan and Jacobean England, sardonically points out that those reigns were also an "unthinking Time." Yet this supposedly "unthinking" period before the Civil Wars had spawned that "Gyant Race, before the Flood," the playwrights Dryden thought of as "Strong . . . Syres" ("To Congreve," ll. 5, 3), literary equivalents of those "long-liv'd Fathers" who "earn'd their Food and "purifi'd the Blood" by hunting in the poem to his "Honour'd Kinsman." Dryden's sense of having been born too late, which we noticed as early as the Hastings elegy, recurs here in the notion of the age presided over by Diana as "Prime"; his belief that his own period represented an advance in learning and cultivation, already strong in the *Essay of Dramatick Poesie*, may find expression here in the implications of the word "unthinking." Mars now enters, representing the Civil Wars, and blusters on about trumpets, drums, arms, and honor; Momus responds with a cynicism we have often heard from Dryden's own voice:

> Thy Sword within the Scabbard keep,
>   And let Mankind agree;
> Better the World were fast asleep,
>   Than kept awake by Thee.
> The Fools are only thinner,
>   With all our Cost and Care;
> But neither side a winner,
>   For things are as they were.
>
> [ll. 63–70]

As so often in his career, Dryden offers an allegory with several possible readings. Many of those who heard these lines sung in the theatre, probably to music by Daniel Purcell, would have shared Dryden's view that the bloodshed of the English Civil War had left "neither side a winner," but some would also have thought of the Nine Years War more recently concluded, and of the debates about a standing army in the Parliament of this very spring.

Venus, evidently the presiding deity of the courts of Charles II and James II, receives gentler treatment than Mars. "Nature is my kindly Care," she declares, "*Mars destroys, and I repair*" (ll. 74–75). This was the old contrast between a Lucretian Venus and a brazen Mars that Dryden had emphasized in the translations he published in *Sylvae* (1685), and if his main political intent was to contrast the amorous Stuarts with the martial William, he also meant to express his lifelong preference for beauty over arms, to take one more swipe at Collier and other enemies of sexual language, and to acknowledge his own susceptibility to the ladies. When Chronos complains of his fatigue in the years "since the Queen of Pleasure left the Ground," we may hear a combination of Dryden's political regret at the exile of his beautiful patroness Maria Beatrice and his more personal regret that he was now "Old" and "for Ladies Love unfit," as he laments in the proem to "Cymon and Iphigenia" and in some of his letters to the beautiful Mrs. Steward.[77] But even the fair ladies did not always escape the

wicked wit of Dryden, whose poem to his "Honour'd Kinsman" contains a sharply
misogynistic passage (ll. 17–35), and Venus does not escape the wit of Momus, who
describes her lovers as "all untrue." In that complaint we may hear Dryden's accurate
assessment of court amours under Charles II and his own memory of an actress named
Anne Reeves. Dismissing each of the deities, Momus sings Dryden's farewell to his
century:

> *Momus.* All, all, of a piece throughout;
> Pointing
> to *Diana.*   Thy Chase had a Beast in View;
> to *Mars.*   Thy Wars brought nothing about;
> to *Venus.*   Thy Lovers were all untrue.
> *Janus.* 'Tis well an Old Age is out,
> *Chronos.* And time to begin a New.

[ll. 86–91]

Dryden's own old age was out. Although one tradition reports that he died on the
third night, we are not even certain that he saw the "Secular Masque" performed. The
leg that had been swollen in December flared up again, and gangrene set in; a strong
tradition holds that the old man, tired and sick, refused an amputation offered by one of
his surgeons. On 30 April, the newspapers reported that the famous poet lay dying.[78]
There is of course no record of his receiving the last rites, but a family who had given a
son to the priesthood probably had no difficulty finding a priest to perform extreme
unction, and a man who had suffered so much for his religion was unlikely to omit a last
act of defiant piety. According to his cousin Elizabeth Creed, who was at his bedside,
"he received the notice of his approaching dissolution with sweet submission and entire
resignation to the Divine Will; and he took so tender and obliging a farewell of his
friends, as none but he himself could have expressed."[79] At 3 a.m. on 1 May 1700, with
his son Charles, his wife, and his cousin Elizabeth among those at his side, John Dryden expired.

Dryden attached no special importance to the flesh. In some lines he added to the
Ovidian account of "The Pythagorean Philosophy," an important part of the *Fables*, he
argued that

> Death, so call'd, can but the Form deface,
> Th' immortal Soul flies out in empty space;
> To seek her Fortune in some other Place.

[ll. 251–53]

Still, he would have been both amused and proud at the fuss made over his earthly
remains. The body was quickly buried on 2 May in St. Anne's, Soho; Charles Montagu,
who had once lampooned *The Hind and the Panther*, but who had more recently been
acting as a patron, helped defray the expenses of this first burial. But a few days later,
probably at the intervention of Dorset, the corpse was exhumed and embalmed, lay in
state at the College of Physicians, and was finally buried in Chaucer's grave in Westminster Abbey on 13 May. The undertaker's bill, with its charges for velvet hearse
coverings and plumes for the six white horses, gives some sense of the pomp involved.

Dr. Garth made a funeral oration in Latin, and two collections of generally dreadful poems on the death of the poet were published the next fall.[80]

In the poem to his cousin of Chesterton, Dryden comments on the afterlife of poets: "Earth keeps the Body, Verse preserves the Fame." His poems, plays, and essays have now preserved his fame for nearly three centuries, but his reputation, frequently sullied in his own life by lampooners and rivals, has not yet recovered from the damage it suffered at the hands of Victorian scholars whose own politics compelled them to label him a turncoat and timeserver. Drawing on his confidence in his own talent and his capacity for detachment, Dryden might have tried to treat this gross distortion of his principles and skills with silence and contempt, but in life, he could never sustain that attitude of detachment for long: his need to defend himself and his keen eye for satiric opportunities made replying to attacks too tempting. My attempt to gain him a fairer hearing by assembling a fuller account of his actual circumstances is a scholar's defense; his way of answering the slanders of a Macaulay would have been a wickedly funny poem. With his professional eye for sales, however, I like to think Dryden would share my fondest hope for this book: that it will send readers back to his works with an improved relish for the subtlety, nuance, and power of one of our finest English writers.

APPENDIX A

The Cope, Pickering, and Dryden Families

In the charts that follow p. 12, I offer fuller genealogies of these families than any now available, tracing each family from its earliest known ancestors to Dryden's own generation. I have been able to correct a number of errors in previous accounts, though some questions remain. My major printed sources are the genealogies in Walter C. Metcalfe, *The Visitations of North-amptonshire made in 1564 and 1618–19* (Mitchell and Hughes, 1887), and in the histories of Northamptonshire by Bridges and Baker (see below, ch. 1, n. 5). Whenever possible, I have verified that information by checking original wills.

The Pickering genealogy printed here supersedes that printed in *N&Q* 227 (1982):506–10. Thanks to helpful correspondence received after that publication, I have corrected a few errors and added several other people to the chart.

NOTES TO COPE GENEALOGY

1. William was Cofferer to Henry VII; he also received "a great gilte standynge cuppe with brannches" from "the King of Scottes Jamy," presumably James IV. His will is in the P.R.O., P.C.C. 12 Fetiplace. The cup is mentioned in the will of his son John; see n. 6 below.

2. According to *Visitations*, Appendix, p. 175, Jane remarried after William's death, to William Saunders of Banbury. Her will is in the P.R.O., P.C.C. 7 Porch.

3. Sir Anthony's will is in the P.R.O., P.C.C. 30 Bucke. He was the author of *The historie of . . . Annibal and Scipio* (1544) and *A godly meditacion vpon .xx. select and chosen Psalmes* (1547).

4. Jane's will is in the P.R.O., P.C.C. 23 Lyon.

5. Edwyn and his family, not shown in any printed Cope genealogy, are mentioned in his parents' wills; he was dead by the time his mother made hers.

6. John was sheriff of Northamptonshire and a Member of Parliament. In his will (P.R.O., P.C.C. 25 Noodes), he leaves the "great gilte cuppe" to his grandson Edward, a silver basin to his son George, noting that he has already given George houses and land, and ". . . unto Elizabeth Dryden my Daughter my Manodleyn [mandolin?] boxe of sylver and gilte standynge on three Lyons backes. All the rest better then fyve hundred markes is put into her husbandes hands already wherefore I trust they be contented." On the eventual acquisition of the Cope manor house by the Drydens, see ch. 1, n. 5. On John Cope's desecration of the priory church, see above, ch. 1, p. 22.

515

7. John Aubrey claimed to have learned from Dryden that the name Erasmus was given to his grandfather in honor of the Dutch theologian. Either Dryden or Aubrey was mistaken, however, since the name clearly passed into the Dryden family from this Erasmus Cope. Sir John Cope might possibly have known or at least admired the famous Erasmus, who was in England during his lifetime, but there is no evidence.

8. Like his grandfather, George took a bride from the Spencer family, with whom the Drydens and Pickerings were also politically allied. I have been unable to locate his will.

9. Anthony's will is in the P.R.O., P.C.C. 18 Welles.

10. Eleanor was the daughter of Margaret Tame, third wife of Anthony's father Sir John, by her previous marriage to Humphrey Stafford; see Baker's Cope genealogy (II, 13). Such marriages between step-siblings were not uncommon.

11. Anthony was imprisoned for his Puritan activities. His will (P.R.O., P.C.C. 22 Cope) mentions John Dod.

12. See above, ch.1, p. 4. Sir Edward's will (P.R.O., P.C.C. 84 Soame) also mentions "John Doddes, Preacher of Ashbie," a circumstance suggesting that Dod was still at Canons Ashby as late as 1620. Like his grandfather, Edward married a Raleigh.

13. The *Visitation of 1564*, p. 15, calls this first son George, but Baker (II, 13), who supplies exact dates for his christening and burial, calls him John. The practice of giving a Christian name again to a subsequent son was common.

14. The *Visitation of 1618–19*, p. 79, records the marriage of one of Sir Anthony's daughters to Richard, second son of Thomas Cecil, Lord Burghley. Richard was the uncle of Elizabeth Cecil Howard, mother of Dryden's wife Elizabeth Howard; see above, ch. 5, p. 126.

15. See above, ch. 1, p. 6 and n. 21.

16. Except for Erasmus, who was the son of Elizabeth Yelverton, I have been unable to discover which of Edward's wives was the mother of which of his sons. The Spanish names Paulo and Ferdinando seem odd choices for a man who was a vigorous Puritan, but Edward's third wife, Catherine Aston, came from a recusant family. Dryden's poem "On the Marriage of Mrs. Anastasia Stafford," written after his conversion to Rome, was found in a trunk at Tixall, the Aston family seat in Staffordshire.

17. Edward's will mentions "my sonne William Pemberton" and "my grandchilde John Pemberton." Pemberton was either a son-in-law, though the will does not link him to a daughter, or a stepson.

NOTES TO PICKERING GENEALOGY

1. I have not traced the descendants of Sir James on this chart, but they may be found in the *Minutes of Evidence Given before the Committee of Privileges, to whom the Petition of Thomas Stonor . . . Claiming to be Senior Co-Heir to the Barony of Camoys* [1839], p. 256. Dryden's wife Elizabeth Howard was descended from this Pickering line. See above, ch. 5, p. 126 and n. 17.

2. In the *Visitation of 1564*, p. 43, and in the Pickering pedigree printed by E. R. Pickering (cited above, ch. 1, n. 13), this man is called William of Gretton, but in his will, in the N.R.O. (Peterborough Wills, Book I, f. 297), dated 1547, he is "William Pykering of Titchmarsh." James Pickering of Titchmarsh, presumably William's nephew the son of Gilbert (I), was among the witnesses; "brother Hary," presumably Henry, was to help the widow in her task as executor and be paid for his pains. See the shortened version of the will conveniently printed in Belgion, *Titchmarsh*, p. 37. I have adopted Belgion's method of distinguishing the various Johns and Gilberts in the main line by Roman numerals.

3. See above, ch. 1, p. 2 and n. 4; ch. 1, n. 61.

4. See above, ch. 1, p. 2 and n. 4.

5. His will (P.R.O., P.C.C. 69 Noodes) mentions most of his nieces and nephews; it does not mention children.

6. His father's will (see n. 2 above) leaves him some wagons and harnesses, to be his when

he becomes sixteen, from which I infer an approximate date of birth. The *Visitation of 1564*, p. 43, calls this man "Richard," not Gilbert, and calls the sister married to George Quynten "Alis," not Catharine. The *Visitation of 1618–19*, p. 126, traces the descendants of "Richard." I have preferred the names given in William's will, and have not traced this line further.

7. William died young and unmarried. His will (P.R.O., P.C.C. 13 Spert) leaves horses and farm equipment to his brother Boniface, a horse to his uncle Henry, and five pounds each to his brothers James and John "toward [their] exhibition at the University." There is no evidence that either brother went to the university. For an accurate summary of the will, see H. Warner Allen, *Number Three Saint James's Street: A History of Berry's the Wine Merchants* (Chatto and Windus, 1950), p. 33.

8. Like the later alliance with the Drydens, the Pickering alliance with the Keye or Kaye family seems to have produced two marriages. According to H. H. Spink, *The Gunpowder Plot* (Simpkin, 1902), p. 28, Robert Keyes, who married into the next generation of Pickerings with unfortunate results, was "the son of a Protestant clergyman and probably grandson of one of the Key or Kay family of Woodsome, Almondbury, near Huddersfield, in the West Riding of Yorkshire." Perhaps the "Woodham" of Bridges (and subsequent genealogists) is identical with "Woodsome," where a Tudor hall still stands. Lucy had a brother Robert, but he died in 1596 and was thus not the Gunpowder conspirator; see *N&Q* 15 (1857):149–50.

9. For the Dryden connection to the Oxenbridge family, see n. 3 to the Dryden genealogy.

10. The fragmentary and apparently incorrect list of rectors of Aldwincle All Saints in Bridges (II, 210) shows Boniface as the holder of the advowson; he apparently inherited it from his father Gilbert (I), who acquired the advowsons of Aldwincle All Saints and Titchmarsh St. Mary when he purchased the Titchmarsh manor. Boniface was quite wealthy; his will (P.R.O., P.C.C. 10 Windsor) disposes of substantial holdings of land in a number of villages to his various sons. There seems, however, to have been some coolness between Boniface and his eldest son Gilbert. The third son, Michael, is given elaborate instructions about maintaining his mother Catherine, and large amounts of money and land; Boniface leaves £100 to pay debts incurred by Gilbert.

11. The will of Gilbert (I) is even more illegible than most sixteenth-century documents. A daughter whose married name may be Agnes Abury is mentioned, as is a son-in-law whose name I cannot decipher. The wife of this man is not mentioned; perhaps she was already dead.

12. See above, ch. 1, pp. 4, 12 and nn. 11, 12, 61.

13. For Elizabeth's will, see ch. 1, n. 22, and ch. 1, p. 12. She also mentions her "cousin Mrs. Jane Pickering" (presumably the wife of James son of Boniface) and her "cousin and servant Robert Pickering" (either the son or brother of the same James).

14. Robert was presented to the living of St. Mary Virgin, Titchmarsh in 1568, before his twelfth birthday. Of course, a curate performed his duties; church records list him as "*Scolar dispensat.*" He died at the age of twenty-four, apparently still pursuing his university studies. See Longden, *Northamptonshire and Rutland Clergy*. The eagerness of the family to place a son in the living may be explained by the wealth of the Titchmarsh church; see above, ch. 1, n. 26. One wonders why Dryden's grandfather Henry, who was seventeen when his older brother died, did not succeed him. Perhaps the Church authorities discouraged the appointment of another absentee rector. In any case, Henry went off to Cambridge and Robert Williamson was installed as rector.

15. See above, ch. 1, p. 24 and n. 61.

16. See above, ch. 1, pp. 7, 17 and n. 23.

17. A notable Puritan, as we might expect from his parentage, Lewis entered Gray's Inn in 1592, rode off to meet James in Edinburgh on the death of Elizabeth (as a lobbyist for the Puritans), and was involved in the so-called "Bywater Plot" of 1605. He was also associated with the Montagu family, from whom Gilbert (III) would later take a wife. See W. J. Sheils, *The Puritans in the Diocese of Peterborough*, pp. 111, 115, 117.

18. According to Anstruther, *Vaux of Harrowden*, p. 273, Margaret was governess to the children of Lord Mordant at Drayton, a recusant stronghold. See above, ch. 1, p. 2.

19. See above, ch.1, p. 4 and n. 13.

20. Elizabeth and Michael sued Elizabeth's mother in 1579 about her share of property. See Mark Eccles, "George Whetstone in Star Chamber," *RES* 33 (1982): 385–95.

21. Helen D. Irvine, in *The Victoria County History of the County of Northampton* (III, 167), citing Chancery Inquisition post mortem 209 (33), states that Boniface, who died seized of the advowson of Aldwincle All Saints in 1586, "left it to his younger son John . . . who in 1597 presented his kinsman Henry Pickering." Boniface's will does not mention the advowson specifically, but it does leave his lands in Aldwincle to John. Longden, working from ecclesiastical documents, has Henry taking office five years earlier. P. D. Mundy, in "The Pickerings of Aldwincle All Saints, Northamptonshire," *N&Q* 197 (1952), p. 490, says that the owner of the advowson was "probably" Gilbert (II). Ward refers to the owner as Henry's "father" (p. 324). But Henry's real father, John (I), was dead in 1591, and Bridges's partial transcript (see n. 10 above) shows Boniface as the owner of the advowson in his generation.

22. See above, ch. 1, pp. 4, 5–7 and nn. 21, 22.

23. See Dryden genealogy, n. 8.

24. Horsman appears in the will of Elizabeth, widow of Gilbert (II) and in the will of John (II).

25. An unmarried woman, also mentioned in the wills of both her mother and her brother; the latter provides several rooms to be kept for her use in the manor house.

26. See above, ch. 1, pp. 17, 33 and nn. 42, 82; ch. 5, p. 129.

27. See above, ch. 4, pp. 117–18 and n. 70.

28. See above, ch. 1, pp. 7, 10; ch. 4, p. 117; ch. 7, p. 234; ch. 8, p. 290 and notes to those pages. Her undated will, proved in 1677, is in the P.R.O., P.C.C. 60 Hale.

29. Four younger sons and four daughters, listed in the *Visitation of 1618–19*, p. 127.

30. Four other sons and five daughters, listed in the *Visitation of 1618–19*, p. 128.

31. See above, ch. 1, pp. 6, 11–12, 22; ch. 2, pp. 36, 47; ch. 3, pp. 57, 68; ch. 4, pp. 79–80, 83–85, 90–93, 104, 107–08, 117–18; ch. 7, p. 200 and notes. His brief will, proved 4 December 1672, is in the P.R.O., P.C.C. 153 Eure.

32. See above, ch. 1, p. 7 and n. 22; ch. 2, pp. 46, 56 and n. 28. John's will was not proved until 1647, a fact indicative of the disruption caused by the Civil Wars.

33. See above, ch. 1, p. 7; ch. 4, p. 107; ch. 5, p. 144 and notes. Edward was the "Ned Pickering" often mentioned by Pepys.

34. See ch. 1, n. 22.

35. According to Mundy, "The Pickerings," p. 491, this Henry went to Barbados, married twice, and died there in 1705.

36. Christopher was only eight years old in 1630, when his grandfather James died, but he became the heir, since his father Robert was already dead. In his only serious error, E. R. Pickering makes Christopher a younger brother of Sir John (II), but Bridges and the *Visitation* place him here. On his portrait by Janssens, see above, ch. 1, n. 58. Perhaps the portrait was painted on the occasion of his inheriting the family land.

37. Jane's epitaph in Titchmarsh St. Mary, still extant and given in full by Bridges (II, 386), states that "She died in childbed of her fifth child, in . . . 1657." She must thus have been married before 1652. The epitaph also describes Jane as the daughter of "Sir Charles Mordant, Baronet." If her father was the Sir Charles Mordant of Massingham who succeeded to the Baronetcy in 1638, the estimated dates for his birth and marriage in *The Complete Baronetage* (1615 and 1638) must both be pushed back by at least five years.

NOTES TO DRYDEN GENEALOGY

1. See above, ch. 1, pp. 2–4. John's will is in the P.R.O., P.C.C. 24 Watson. It has a strongly Puritan preamble, and includes a bequest to "Jane Dearron and her children, being of my kyn." Was Jane a poor relative, perhaps a cousin on the Nicholson side, or was this ambiguous phrase a way of acknowledging illegitimate children? John also left money to help his nephews "Davy" and Christopher at Oxford.

2. See above, ch. 1, pp. 4–8. No will exists for Erasmus, though there is a Chancery Inquisition post mortem, in the P.R.O. (vol. 487, fol. 31).

3. As Percy Dryden Mundy has shown, in "Dryden, Throckmorton, Oxenbridge, and Allied Puritan Families," *N&Q* 180 (1941):182–83, George Dryden's third wife, born Catharine Throckmorton, was the widow of Thomas Harby, who owned a manor at Adston. Catharine's daughter by Harby, also named Catharine, married Daniel Oxenbridge, M.D.; their son John, a Puritan divine, went to Boston, Massachusetts, in 1669. As the Pickering genealogy shows, the Pickerings were also allied by marriage to the Throckmortons and the Oxenbridges. George's will is in the P.R.O., P.C.C. 9 Bolein.

4. I have been unable to determine whether this William Bury is the same man who married Edith Pickering. If he was the same man or a relative, there was a link between the Dryden and Pickering families even before the marriage of John Pickering (II) and Susannah Dryden.

5. See above, ch. 1, pp. 2, 8; ch. 2, pp. 36–37.

6. See above, ch. 1, pp. 5–8, 17; ch. 3, p. 67; ch. 4, p. 79.

7. The Salwey or Salway family had long been closely associated with Westminster School; Humphrey Salwey was on the Parliamentary committee supervising the school while Dryden was a student there. On Edward, son of this marriage, see above, pp. 81, 127–28.

8. See above, ch. 1, pp. 5–8; ch. 4, pp. 81, 117.

9. This Thomas Swift was the grandfather of the writer Jonathan Swift; see P. D. Mundy, "The Dryden-Swift Relationship," *N&Q* 193 (1948):470–74.

10. See above, ch. 13, pp. 504, 506 and nn. 66, 69.

11. See above, ch. 13, pp. 500, 503–07, and nn. 70, 71, 72.

12. See above, ch. 13, p. 503 and n. 68.

13. See above, ch. 3, pp. 63, 70–72.

14. This John Dryden, first cousin to the poet, also married a woman named Elizabeth in 1663. He was an official in the Customs, and records concerning payments to him have sometimes been confused with records of payments to the Poet Laureate. See above, ch. 11, p. 392 and n. 29. This John Dryden and his wife Elizabeth Lucke were certainly the parents of Honour Dryden, christened 6 December 1670, Anne Dryden, christened 14 December 1671, and John Dryden, christened 8 November 1678; all those baptisms took place at St. Bride, Fleet Street. They may also have been the parents of the mysterious "Joannes Driden fil: Joannis et Elizabethae," born 21 February 1668/9, and christened at St. Martin's in the Fields on 22 February. This child cannot be the poet's second son John, whose birthdate remains unknown, since the third son, Erasmus-Henry, was born just a few months later, on 2 May 1669; moreover, this John Dryden was presumably the "Joannes Dryden, Puer" who was buried at St. Martin's on 24 February 1668/9, just two days after his christening.

15. See above, ch. 10, p. 346; ch. 13, p. 506 and n. 69. Erasmus, a grocer in King Street, Westminster, succeeded in 1708 to the Dryden baronetcy; his son Edward inherited the land from his cousin Robert, who died unmarried. See P. D. Mundy, "The Brothers and Sisters of John Dryden, the Poet," *N&Q* 193 (1948), p. 122.

16. See above, ch. 10, p. 346. Henry became a goldsmith, perhaps because of his uncle Henry Pickering's marital connection to the Vyners. According to his sister Frances, he died in Jamaica. See Mundy, pp. 122–23.

17. See above, ch. 10, p. 346, ch. 11, pp. 389–90. James owned land in the colony of Maryland but lived and died in London; he seems to have been a tobacconist. See Mundy, p. 123. His will is in the P.R.O., P.C.C. 37 Vere.

18. See above, ch. 4, p. 118.

19. Dryden wrote an epitaph for Erasmus Lawton, Rose's only son; see Mundy, p. 121.

20. Mary's marriage to "Skermardine," queried by Baker (I, 7), may be an error; Thomas Shermerdine married Agnes Emelyn, daughter of Agnes Dryden and Sylvester Emelyn, in 1690. As Mundy points out, "possibly an aunt and a niece both married into the family—or the aunt may have been confused with the niece" (p. 121).

21. See above, ch. 4, p. 118.

22. Abigail, Hester, and Hannah may have all had husbands. According to Malone's handwritten additions to his biography, one of Dryden's sisters married a man named England; another, a man named Blunne; the latter name appears in Mary Dryden's will as "Blunk." The will also mentions "my deare Granddaughter Mary Dryden Josephas"; Mundy supposes that this was a grandchild with the surname Josephas, but Malone read the phrase as the bequest of a book by the historian Josephus to a grandchild named Mary Dryden. See Osborn, p. 136; Mundy, p. 122; Malone, p. 447n.

23. The marriage license for Frances gives her age in 1680 as twenty-four, which is probably off by a decade; see Mundy, pp. 121–22.

24. See Mundy, p. 121.

25. Records relating to Jonathan's college career have sometimes been confused with those of the poet. All information about this branch of the family comes from P. D. Mundy, "The Dryden-Swift Relationship," p. 473.

APPENDIX B

Three Documents on the Westminster School Curriculum

1. THE LAUD DOCUMENT. This manuscript is in the P.R.O. (S.P. 16/181/37). It has been printed in full, with many inaccuracies of transcription, by Sargeaunt in *Annals of Westminster School*, pp. 279–82. Here is a new transcription from the document itself.

This course was in my time taken by the Schoolem^r of Westm:/ spec. for those of the 6. & 7. formes, wherein I spent my time there.

About a q^r of an houre aft^r 5. in the morn. we were called up, by one of the Monitors of the chamber [wth a *surgite*] & after Lat: *pray^{rs}* we went into the cloyst^{rs} *to wash*, & thence in order (2. by 2.) to the schoole. where we were to be by 6 of the clock, at furthest.

Betwene 6. and 8. we repeated o^{ur} *Gramm^r-pts* (out of Lilie for lat: out of Cambden for the gr:) 14. or. 15 being select^{ed} & called out to stand in a semicircle before the M^r and other scholers & there repeate 4 or 5 leaves in either. the M^r appointing who should beginne, & who should goe on wth such & such rules.

After this we had 2. exercises that varied everie other morn: *the first morn:* we made *verses ex tempore* lat: and gr: upon 2 or 3 sev: theames. & they that made the best (2. or 3. of them) had some monie given them by the schoolm^r, for the *most pte. The 2.^{d} morn*: one of the 7.th forme was call^d out *to expound some pte of a latin or gr: authour* (Cicero. Livie. Isocr. Hom^r. Apollinaris^s. Xenoph: &c) & they of the 2. next formes were call^d to give an account of it, some other pte of the day. or else they were all of them (or such as were picked out, of whom the M^r made choice by the feare or confidence discovered in th^r lookes) to *repeat and pronounce distinctlie wthout booke some piece of an Authour* that had been learned the day before.

From 8. to 9. we had time for *Beav^r* & recollect: of o^{ur}selves, & preparation for fut: exercises.

Betwixt 9. & 11. Those *exercises* were reade, wch had bene enjoynd us over night. (one day *in prose*. the next day *in v*) wch were select^d by the M^r. some to be examined & punish^d: other to be comended & propos^d to Imitation.

wch being done, we had the practise of *Dictamina*. one of the 5.th forme being call^d out to translate some sentences of an unexpect^d Author (ex tempore) *into good Latin*. / & then one of the 6. or 7. forme to translate the same (ex tempore also) *into good greeke*.

Then the *M.^{r} himself expound^{ed}* some *parte of a Lat: or Gr: Auth^{or}* (one day in prose. an other in v) *wherein we were to be practicd in the aft^{r}noone*.

At dinner & supper times we reade some portion of the *Lat: Bible* in a *manuscript* (to facilitate the reading of such hands) And, the prebendaries then having th^r Table comonlie in the Hall,

521

some of them had often times good remembrances sent unto them frō thence & wthall a theame to make, or speake some ex-tempore-verses upon.

Betwixt one & 3. That *Lesson w*ch *out of some Author appointed for that day, had bene by the M*r *expounded unto them* (out of Cicero. Virgil. Hom.r Eurip: Isocr. Livie. Saluste. &c.) *was to be exactlie gone thorough,* by *construing* & other grammatical waies, *examining all the Rhetoricall figures,* & *translating* it out of verse into prose, or out of prose into verse. out of gr: in lat: or out of lat: into gr:/ Then were they enjoyned to committe that to memorie against the next morning.

Betwixt 3. & 4. they had a litle respite, the Mr walking out, & they (in beaver-times) going in order to the Hall. & then fitting themselves for theyr next taske.

Betwene 4 or. 5. they repeated a leafe or 2. out of some booke of *Rhetoricall figures,* or choise *Proverbs* & *Sentences* collected by the Mr for that use.

after wch they were practised in translating some *Dictamina* out of lat: or gr: & Sometimes turning lat: and gr: verses into *Engl: verse.*

Then a *Theame* was given them, whereupon to make prose or verses lat: & gr: against the next morning.

After supper (in summer-time) they were 3. or 4 times in a weeke calld to the M.rs chamber (spec: they of the 7. forme) and there instructed out of *Hunter's Cosmographie*[1] & practised to describe & finde out Cities & Countries in the Mappes.

*Upon Sundayes before morn. pray*rs (in summr) they came comonlie into the Schoole (such as were King's-Scholers) & there construed some parte of the *gospell* in gr: or repeated part of the gr: *Catechisme.* For the after-noone they made *verses upon the Preach*rs *sermon.* or epist: & gosp: The best *Scholers in the 7.*th forme were appointed *as Tutors* to reade & expound places of Hom.r Virg. Hor. Eurip: or other gr. & lat: Authors, *at those times* (in the fore-noone, or aft-rnoone or after beaver-times) *wherein the Scholers were in the Schoole in expectation of the M*r.

The Scholers were governed by sev: *Monitores* (2. for the Hall, as manie for the Church, the Schoole, the Feildes, the Cloister (whch last attended them to washing, & were called Monitores immundorū) The Captaine of the Schoole was over all these, & therefore called *Monitor Moni-torū.*

These Monitors kept them strictlie to *speaking of latine,* in thr severall commands. & withall they presented theyr complaints or *Accusations* (as we called them) everie Friday-morn: where the punishments were often redeemed by Exercises, or favours showd to Boyes of extraord: merite. who had the honor (by the Monitor Monitorū) manie times to begge, & prevaile for such remissions. And so, at other times, other *faultes were often punish*d *by Scholasticall taskes* as repeating *whole orat:*s out of Tullie. Isocr: Demosth: or *speaches* out of Virgil. Thucyd. Xenoph: Eurip: &c.

Upon play-dayes (wthin an houre aftr leave granted, & the oppidales dismissed) the scholrs of the house were often *call*d *in againe* for an houre or more, till they had breiflie dispatched the taske of that day.

There was a *writing in capitall lett*rs, wthin the schoole, toward the upp pte of the wall, wch the Mr was wonte to show strangers as a testim: *how he was restrain*d *for leave to play.*

When *Plumpe-Walk*rs came in (.i. such as strived to hold the Mr in long Discourse) the Mr would call out some of his Scholers, to show what verses they could make on a sodaine, upon a theame to be given by them, if they were Scholers.

Everie Friday they had *Repetitions* of what was learned the *form*r pt of ye weeke.

Upon *Saturdayes* they pronounced their *Declamat:* in gr: and lat. & the Preb: did often come in, to give incouragement unto them.

All that were *chosen away by Elect:* tooke thr leave in a pub: Orat: to the Deane Preb. M.r Ush.r Sch.rs / made in the Schoole.

2. THE SHAFTESBURY DOCUMENT.   This manuscript is in the P.R.O. (30/24/ 7/580). It has never been printed.

The Institution of the 2:d forme att Westminster Schoole.—

The Schollers learne the Rudim:ts of Grammer & Syntaxis in English compos'd by m.r Busby or m.r King.

> Esops Fables
> Ovid de Tristibus
> Martialls Epigrams
> Terence

The Gramm.er is divided into 12 or more parts & s.d every morning.

On monday morning after a part is sayd.

They Conster a Fable in Esope, & afterward transcribe the English of it.—

To enable them hereunto they search in their Dictionarys all the words whereof they know not the English and write them down in pap.er

Some of the upp.er boy'es of the forme consters first and the rest conster's after him.—

After this construction of Esope, they repeate the Latine exercises they made the week before all corrected—and shew the exercise given them on the Satterday before to make ag.st monday.

In the afternoone on monday.

They peirce the lesson they construed out of Esope And after yt is performed the mast.er dictates to them 10: or 15 lines in English or sometimes less of some Story of the Roman History or the like w.ch they are to make into Latine ag.st ye next morning, or sometimes to vary the Fable in other words of English and Latine

On Tuesday morning after the part and after they have shown the exercise of the night before

They conster 8 or 10 lines in Ovid de tristibus he tells them some tyme before the lines he would have construed that they may have some tyme to look in the Dictionary the words they know not which they are to write downe in a paper.—

Then one of the foremost boyes conster first and the rest are thereby instructed to conster after him.

After the construction the English is transcribed w.ch they call the making a translation.

In the afternoone they peirce the lines in Ovid w.ch they construed in the morning.—

Then an English is given as the day before to be made into Latine viz. a continuation of the Story of what was in the last dictation.—

On Wednesday morning after the part

They conster 8 or 10: lines of Terence being prepard for it, as in the preceeding dayes institution.—

And they allsoe write a Translation of it and shew the exercise of Latine given them the night before to be made ag.st yt morning.—

In the afternoone of the same day

they peirce what they construed of Terence

And the master dictates an English to be made into Latine agst ye next morning.—

Thirsday in the morning after the part and the shewing the exercise they conster an Epigram in Martiall with the like preparation as in the other dayes constructions and they allsoe write all a translation of it.

And then the master dictates an English to be made into Latine agst. Fryday.

They doe not goe to schoole on Thirsday in the afternoone—Fryeday in the morning after the part

The master dictates corrections of all their exercises w.ch they shew'd every morning of the week before, and they transcribe it from him in pap.er books, and by the correction he makes of the writeing of any one of the boyes the rest correct their writings.

In the afternoone they repeate all they learn'd in Esope, Ovid, Terence & Martiall & ag.st Satterday they transcribe in a fayre book all the corrections, w:ch they writ the day before; and all the Latine words w:ch they look'd in their dictionaryes that week and all the phrases yt were observed to them, in any of their Lessons or makeing their Latines.

On Saterday morning they conster the corrections of all the Latine they made the week before—

And then the mast.ᵉʳ dictates to them some English to be made into Latine ag:ˢᵗ monday and they have it allsoe in charge to gett by heart all the corrections they had that way construed and all the phrases they had corrected

When the master gives them an English to make into Latine; if any phrase occurr to him he gives it to them, and allsoe some prop.ᵉʳ & significant words for some part of the English.—

3. THE FROWICK DOCUMENT. This manuscript is in the library of Dulwich College, 2nd Series, vol. XXIX. *Register of Accounts 1680–1714/5, The Third Book*. It is printed here for the first time by permission of the Governors of Dulwich College.

The fform of Westminster school

In yᵉ first forme is learned yᵉ lattin testament. On Munday. Tuesday. Ovid: de tristibus. Wednesday Æsop's ffables. Thursday. Ovid: de tristibus. ffryday repetition. In yᵉ second form on Mundays Corderius. Tuesdays Ovid: de tristibus. Wednesdays Terence. Thursdays Martiall's distichs. In ye third form. On munday Justin. Tuesday Ovid: Metamorphosis. Wednesday Terence. Thursday Martiall.

/ / /

Above contind:

In yᵉ 4ᵗʰ form D.ʳ Busby's greek grammar. On mundays and Wednesdays yᵉ greek liturgy by Dʳ Duport. Tuesdays and Thursdays yᵉ Anthologia made for the use of Westminster school. These are the morning Authours. The Afternoon as above in yᵉ third form. In the fith form on mundays the greek testament. Tuesdays Homer, Wednesdays Isocrates his Orations, or the Hebrew Psalter. Thursdays Homer. On frydays are repeated 6 or 7 psalms in the Hebrew Psalter. In the Afternoons Juvenall. Terence. Plautus and Justin. In this form are read Aratus his Astronomy. And Dionysius Afer.[2] Sometimes att the Master's pleasure are used Aristophanes. Sophocles. Pindar and Theocritus.

In the sixth form are learned the same bookes.

/ / /

The forme of Exercises

In yᵉ first form Translating out of the Bible into Latin.

In yᵉ second out of Galtruchius concerning yᵉ Heathenish Gods.

Or a dictamen, which is a translation of some English Authour into Lattin.

In the third form a sacred exercise: that is, a chapter of the Bible to be translated into Lattin verse: or any verse or sentence therein to be so translated. All this on Mundays. Against Tuesday mornings a dictamen. against Wednesdays a Theam for verses. Against Thursdays a subject for Prose. against fryday morning a verse exercise.

In the fourth form the same exercise.

In the fith form yᵉ same exercise except that sometimes they turn Horace his Odes into different sort of verses from the Authour. In the third, fourth, and fith form sometimes any oration or description in any Historian is turnd into verse, as yᵉ Master think's fitt. Sometimes an Ode of Horace into Greek Verse.

In yᵉ sixth form yᵉ same exercise in performed.

/ / /

This same was declared att this Colledge in the presence of the Master, Warden, and seniour ffellow, on Thursday the 29ᵗʰ of May, 1684, by Mr ffrowick,[3] that had been Usher under Dʳ Busby for severall yeares, and putt into writing by me William Symes of Ballyoll Colledge in Oxford.

    Ita Testor: John Alleyn: Master.

APPENDIX C

Official Payments to Dryden and His Family

I offer here an attempt to sort out the incomplete and contradictory records of the grant promised to Dryden's wife by the crown in 1662 and the salary promised to Dryden as Poet Laureate and Historiographer Royal. I have examined the most relevant documents in the P.R.O., cited below by their call numbers; less important documents are cited from *C.S.P. Dom.* and *C.T.B.* In the interest of clarity, I have silently expanded abbreviations.

1 January 1662. Dryden addresses a poem to Clarendon.

Later in January 1662. Clarendon reminds Charles "that you have not yett giuen your warrant to my Lord Barkeshyre" (see above, ch. 5, n. 19). Charles replies, indicating that he knows the grant is to be for £11,000 and to be paid at £1,000 a year.

27 February 1662. Warrant for a grant to "Dame Elizabeth Howard" of £3,000 "out of the duty of our growing excise," to be paid at £250 quarterly, beginning "March 25 next" (P.R.O., S.P. 44/5/pp. 179–80). Warrant for a grant to Thomas Earl of Berkshire (her father) for £8,000, to be paid at £250 quarterly, but beginning on 25 March 1665 (P.R.O., S.P. 44/5/pp. 180–81). Elizabeth's grant was meant to begin in 1662, and would ideally have been paid off by 1665, at which point the grant to her father would begin.

28 March 1662. Dockets confirming both grants (*C.S.P. Dom.*, p. 322.)

12 April 1662. Apparent date of letters patent to the Earl of Berkshire for £8,000, according to several later references. No surviving official record with this date.

7 May 1662. Another docket confirming the grant of £3,000 to Elizabeth Howard (*C.S.P. Dom.*, p. 363).

9 May 1662. Letters patent for Elizabeth's grant; no longer extant but referred to in the following warrant.

20 or 21 May 1662. Warrant from Treasurer Southampton for tallies of assignation upon the Excise for Elizabeth's £3,000, "by quarterly payments of £250, each as by the letters patent of the 9th instant" (*C.T.B.. 1660–67*, I, 395). Evidently no real money yet received.

24 July 1662. The Earl assigns his letters patent of April 12, 1662, for £8,000, "charged upon ye Receiver of Yorkshire at £1,000 per annum" to Dame Mary Greaves or Graves, in return for £5,000 cash (P.R.O., S.P. 29/61/47). He also gives her a letter of attorney.

21 Oct 1662.   Berkshire signs a bond to Mary Greaves for £7,400 to secure another loan of £3,700 (P.R.O., S.P. 29/61/47).

9 May 1663.   According to a letter from the King to the Lord Treasurer, dated 25 June 1666 (P.R.O., S.P. 29/159/f. 118 recto and verso), "the said Earle [Berkshire] together with one Sir Thomas Greaves, and the Lady Greaves his Wife, to whome the said Earle had assigned and passed over the said Letters pattents, & the eight thousand poundes payable thereupon as aforesaid, Did by Indenture under their hands and seales dated the nynth day of May in the fifteenth yeare of our Reigne, and in the yeare of our Lord God one thousand, six hundred sixty three (in consideration of the summe of Three thousand poundes and for diverse other good causes and considerations) grant, bargaine, sell, assigne, and sett over unto the Lady Elizabeth Howard (now the Lady Elizabeth Driden) Daughter of the said Earle, her executors and Assignes the said Letters patents of Eight thousand poundes granted as aforesaid, and all and every summe and Summes of money thereby granted by us unto the said Earle, To the sole use and behoofe of the said Lady Elizabeth Howard her executors, administrators and assignes, Which grant and Assignment was notwithstanding intended but as a Security for the payment of Three thousand poundes, at the dayes and times in the said Indenture mentioned and appointed, As may by the same more fully appeare." The phrase "(in consideration of the summe of Three thousand poundes and for diverse other good causes and considerations)" is distressingly vague. The claim that the Earl and the Greaves couple "sold" the letters to "Elizabeth" suggests that "the summe of Three thousand poundes" was paid to Thomas Greaves by Elizabeth on this date in 1663, *before* her marriage, and the editors of *C.S.P. Dom.* (p. 459) summarize the document with that understanding.   If so, perhaps the payment was not cash, but Elizabeth's own letters patent, which were due to be paid more quickly than her father's, and therefore provided better security for a loan to the Earl than his own letters.

1 December 1663.   Dryden marries Elizabeth.

? 1665.   The Earl "is very anxious to pay his creditors." His grant of £8,000 "has brought in nothing," and the King has offered him £8,000 for Berkshire House. He asks for £16,000 cash in lieu of the house and the grant (*C.S.P. Dom.*, p. 138).

Summer 1665.   The Drydens leave London for Charlton, Wilts., to escape the plague.

28 March 1666.   Thomas Earl of Berkshire is assaulted outside his house [presumably Berkshire house, which he did not sell to the King until 1668] by Ralph Marshall and John and James Tisser (*H.M.C.* VIII, ap. I, 118b, 147). When he petitioned the House of Lords that they be sent for a year later, nothing was done. Were these thugs sent to collect a debt? If they had been ordinary criminals, would they not have been punished for assaulting an Earl?

? June 1666.   Petition of Thomas Earl of Berkshire for payment of his pension; he is "in danger of losing his house, the only retreat for himself and family" (*C.S.P. Dom.*, p. 459.) The phrasing suggests that this petition was related to the assault.

25 June 1666.   The King writes a letter to the Treasurer and Under Treasurer of the Exchequer, reviewing the history of the grants and explaining that they have not been paid because the Receiver General of Rents of Yorkshire has insufficient funds; he authorizes the Treasurers to draw the necessary funds from "our Counties of Somersett and Dorsett, or upon such other of our Receivers Generall in any other County or Counties as you shall think may most conveniently bear the same." He stipulates that "the said summe of Three thousand poundes shall be first paid to the said Elizabeth Driden . . . And that the five thousand poundes remayning shall be after paid to the said Earle" (P.R.O., S.P. 29/159/f. 118). From this point on, presumably because of Berkshire's dealings with Mary Greaves, his grant is always referred to as totalling only £5,000.

25 July 1666.   The King dines in public, and Pepys sees Berkshire in a "dirty pickle" (*Diary*, VII, 218).

14 August 1666.   Dryden, from Charleton, writes to Sir Robert Long, Auditor of the Receipt in the Exchequer, thanking him for his help "when you wrought my Lord [presumably Ashley, who was Chancellor of the Exchequer] to Assign the patent." He asks Long to "keep what money you receive for us in your hands till we come up." He also refers to "the unreasonable proposition my Lord Berkshyre made," surely some attempt by the old Earl to get his hands on Elizabeth's money, and encloses a letter by Sir Robert Howard, describing "an enclos'd acquittance signed by Mr Driden and his wife my sister; for seaven hundred sixty eight pounds fifteen shillings." (See McFadden, *Dryden the Public Writer*, pp. 67–70.) This was evidently the first time Elizabeth had received any money on her grant.

22 August 1666.   The King writes a letter to Sir George Carteret (P.R.O., S.P. 44/23/pp. 118–20), reviewing again the history of the grants. He repeats much of his letter of 25 June, adding an explanation for the failure of the assignment to Yorkshire, the fact that those monies had been made part of the jointure of Queen Catherine. "Taking into Our Gracious consideracion the great extremity of the said Earles affaires, & of his present necessity & Wants," the King urges the Treasurers to find some money for the Earl from any source whatsoever. He carefully stipulates that Elizabeth is still to be paid according to the plan outlined in the letter of 25 June.

29 August 1666.   Docket for the payment of £5,000 to Thomas, Earl of Berkshire. The debt to Elizabeth is again mentioned (*C.S.P. Dom.*, p. 76).

31 August 1666.   Privy Seal order for the same £5,000 (*C.T.B., 1667–68*, II, 160).

21 August 1667.   Sir Robert Howard "moves ye Confirmation of a Warrant of the late Lord Treasurer on behalfe of his sister the Lady Draydon, being £3,000 of which part [is] paid" (P.R.O. Kew T29/1/pp. 124–25). The Board of Treasury Commissioners orders "That the remainder of this mony unpaid is put into the £8,000 the Lord Berkshire is to have sett upon the 11 month tax: and what already payed, soe much to be saved to the King of the £8,000. That the Lady have an Order for proportion [i.e., her portion?] by it selfe, in our Order. And that the Order be putt into Sir George Downing's hands to be assigned by the Lord Berkshire to her." There is no record of Berkshire's receiving any money, but payments to Elizabeth follow immediately.

16 September 1667.   "Lady Dreyden to have the £500 from the Receiver of Somersetshire & Dorset, part of the money she was to have had from Sir Steven Fox his assignment and soe much lesse to be assigned her from Sir Steven Fox" (P.R.O. Kew T29/1/p. 152). Fox, at this date Treasurer of the Guards, figures frequently in Treasury records and had frequent dealings with Sir Robert Howard.

19 September 1667.   Payment of £500 to Lady Elizabeth (*C.T.B.*, II, 186).

16 October 1667.   Dryden lends £500 [presumably the same money] to the King. The only extant document recording this loan is P.R.O., E. 403/2772/p. 109, which deals with its repayment nearly six years later. That document, dated 29 November 1671, refers to letters of the Privy Seal dated 16 October 1667 and 30 April 1668. It is not clear what interest was agreed upon. Given the speed of Dryden's appointment as Poet Laureate six months later, I might offer the speculation that these lost letters promised him the reversion of the post.

7 November 1667.   "Lord Berkshire [and] Lady Dryden to be heer about the £8,000 on Sir Steven Fox's £68,000 on Munday" (P.R.O. Kew T29/1/p. 208).

11 November 1667.   Treasury warrant to pay the Earl £6 13s. 4d. for "half-a-year's creation money to the dignity of a Viscount to Sept. 29 last" (*C.T.B.*, II, 201).

13 April 1668.   Dryden appointed Poet Laureate.

30 April 1668.   According to P.R.O., E. 403/2772/p. 109, letters of Privy Seal concerning Dryden's loan were issued on this date. The letters themselves have vanished, but I should infer that Dryden seized the occasion of his appointment to an official post to arrange for some confirmation of his loan and some plan for its eventual repayment.

18 May 1668.   Pepys learns that the King is purchasing Berkshire House (*Diary* IX, 190).

2 June 1668.   Petition from Lady Dryden to the Treasury. "No money now to be had, but she is to be considered when there is money" (*C.T.B.*, II, 340).

15 July 1668.   Petition from Lady Dryden for £657 14s. 4d. Sir Robert Long "to certify the case and whether this be no part of the money fixed for the Earl of Berkshire on the Eleven Months' Tax" (*C.T.B.*, II, 385). Evidently the Treasurers were still attempting to carry out their intentions of 21 August 1667. The exact amount requested was paid a year later.

24 July 1668.   "Report from Sir Robert Long for ye Lady Dryden read. Sir G[eorge] D[owning] to see whether only £5,000 assigned the Earl of Berkshire on the King's £200,000" (P.R.O. Kew T29/2/p. 268).

12 August 1668.   A petition from Lady Dryden results in a warrant for £500 for her on the Receiver of Dorset (the source stipulated in the King's letter of 25 June 1666) (*C.T.B.*, II, 410).

13 August 1668.   A money warrant to Lady Dryden for £523. 10s. 1d. (*C.T.B*, II, 607).

14 October 1668.   Discussion of money owed to Mary Greaves, including memoranda of her dealings with Lord Berkshire (*C.S.P. Dom.*, p. 20).

16 July 1669.   Thomas, Earl of Berkshire dies, apparently intestate. Neither the P.R.O. nor the Wiltshire Record Office has any record of a will or an administration.

After 16 July 1669.   Petition of Elizabeth, Countess Dowager of Berkshire, for a grant of £3,000 promised to her late husband for the benefit of her younger children (*C.S.P. Dom.*, p. 640).

11 August 1669.   £657. 14s. 4 1/2d. paid to Elizabeth (*C.T.B.*, *1669–72,*, III, i, 265). This payment is said to have "discharged in full the grant of £3,000," but as Ward noticed, the record as we have it leaves £450 unaccounted for; presumably one warrant is missing.

18 August 1670.   Dryden appointed Historiographer Royal and confirmed as Poet Laureate at a combined salary of £200 a year (Pat. 22 Car. II, p. 6, n. 6).

11 January 1671.   A warrant for the delivery of a butt of wine, "in kind or in money," together with arrears due on the Laureate's salary (*H.M.C.*, X, iv, 151).

27 January 1671.   Money warrant for £500 owed Dryden as salary (*C.T.B.*, III, ii, 772).

[17] February 1671.   Order to repay Dryden for his loan to the King of £500. A marginal notation on the order for payment of Dryden's salary, dated 18 February 1670 [i.e., 1671], P.R.O., E. 403/1777/p. 232, reads, "Loane on Customes after Michaelmas 1671," and later documents refer to an order to repay the loan dated 17 February.

18 February 1671.   Dryden receives £500 in salary.

29 November 1671.   "By Order dated the xvii[th] day of ffebruary 1670 [i.e., 1671]: To John Dryden Esq. or his Assignes the summe of ffive hundred pounds in repayment of soe much money by him lent unto his Majesty upon the Creditt of the repayment of the same by the Revenue of his Majesty's Customes commencing at the ffeast of St. Michaell the Archangell in the yeare of our Lord God 1671 as by a Talley of Loane levyed at the Receipt of his Majesty's Exchequer Dated with this Order appeareth Together also with the Interest thereof at the rate of vi £ per Cent [i.e., per one hundred pounds] per Annum at the end of every six months untill the repayment of the principall money aforesaid" (P.R.O., E. 403/2772/p. 109). Latin notations refer to the letters of Privy Seal dated 16 October 1667 and 30 April 1668 (see entries under those dates above). Thanks to the Third Dutch Naval War and the Stop of the Exchequer, however, this plan was not carried out.

20 April 1672.   Dryden receives a money warrant for £200 "for one year to Xmas last" (*C.T.B.*, III, ii, 1227).

10 March 1673.   Dryden receives a similar money warrant for £200 (*C.T.B., 1672–75*, IV, 231).

17 June 1673.   Clifford writes to Sir Robert Long from Wallingford House: "Let this Order and the Interest due upon it be paid forthwith out of any money that comes to your hands of His Majesty's Customes" (P.R.O., E. 403/2772/p. 109). According to marginal Latin notations on the same document, Dryden received £15 interest on this day, owed for the period between the original loan and 18 August 1671. This amount seems much too small; perhaps it was the remainder of interest owed him, some of which had been paid earlier.

19 June 1673.   According to the same marginal Latin notations, the principal, £500, was repaid in full by Downing, together with another £45 interest, owed for the period from 18 August 1671 until 18 February 1672 [i.e., 1673]. This latter payment would represent eighteen months' interest at the 6 per cent rate agreed upon in the document of 29 November 1671.

31 December 1673.   Money warrant for £200 (*C.T.B.*, IV, 453).

4 December 1674.   Money warrant for £200 (IV, 626).

28 February 1676.   Money warrant for £100 (*C.T.B., 1676–79*, V, i, 139).

24 March 1676.   Money warrant for £100 (V, i, 33–4, 173).

20 February 1677.   Money warrant for £200 (V, i, 552).

2 July 1677.   Decision to add an additional pension of £100 to Dryden's salary of £200. Warrant 21 July; grant of Privy Seal 24 July (V, i, 462, 698; Appendix v, 1429). The Treasury divided the year into four quarters, beginning on Lady Day (25 March), Midsummer (24 June), Michaelmas (29 September), and Christmas (25 December). On or about each of those dates, Dryden should have now received £50 toward his regular salary of £200 and £25 toward his additional pension of £100. While the record-keeping reflects this promise, the actual payments quickly fell into arrears.

27 July 1677.   Money warrant for £100 for half a year on the old salary (V, i, 704; Appendix v, 1432).

6 March 1678   Blank docket for £150, half a year on old and new salaries; not paid (Appendix v, 1448).

8 June 1678.   Payment of £150 (*C.T.B.*, V, ii, 1017). Counted toward the salary for 1677.

4 July 1679.   Two money warrants: one for £50 on his salary for Lady Day quarter, 1678, one for £25 on his additional pension for Christmas quarter, 1677; money order for the latter dated 5 July 1679; no record of payment but presumably received (*C.T.B., 1679–80*, VI, 121).

22 December 1679.   Two money warrants: one for £50 on his salary for June 24 quarter, 1678, one for £25 on his additional pension for Lady Day quarter, 1678; money order for the latter dated 7 January 1680; payment of £75 on 5 January 1680 (VI, 318, 390).

17 June 1680.   Two money warrants: one for £50 on his salary for Sept. 29 quarter, 1678, one for £25 on his additional pension for June 24 quarter, 1678; money order for the latter dated 30 June 1680; payment of £75 on 28 June 1680 (VI, 576, 593).

16 December 1680.   Money warrant for £50 on his salary for Christmas quarter, 1678; command to issue £50 to "Jno. Dryden" (VI, 768, 767). Probably collected by George Ward; see above, ch. 10, n. 13.

28 June 1681.   Two money warrants: one for £50 on his salary for Lady Day quarter, 1679, one for £50 on his additional pension for half a year to Christmas, 1678; money orders for the latter dated 2 July 1681; payment of £100 on 12 July 1681 (*C.T.B., 1681–1685*, VII, i, 197, 222).

12 January 1682.   Two money warrants: one for £50 on his salary for June 24 quarter, 1679, one for £25 on his additional pension for Lady Day quarter, 1679; money order for the latter dated 16 January 1682; payment of £75 on 23 February (VII, i, 364, 409).

28 August 1682.   Two money warrants: one for £50 on his salary for Sept. 29 quarter, 1679, one for £25 on his additional pension for June 24 quarter, 1679; money order for the latter dated 29 August 1682; payment of £75 on 29 August 1682 (VII, i, 588, 591).

10 March 1683.   Two money warrants: one for £50 on his salary for Christmas quarter, 1679, one for £25 on his additional pension for Sept. 29 quarter, 1679; money order for the latter dated 14 March 1683; payment of £75 on 10 March 1683 (VII, ii, 736, 735).

22 August 1683.   Two money warrants: one for £50 on his salary for Lady Day quarter, 1680, one for £25 on his additional pension for Christmas quarter, 1679; money order for the latter dated 23 August 1683; payment of £75 on 25 September 1683 (VII, ii, 897, 915).

6 May 1684.   Two money warrants: one for £50 on his salary for June 24 quarter, 1680, one for £25 on his additional pension for Lady Day quarter, 1680; money order for the latter dated 12 May ; payment of £75 on 14 May 1684 (VII, ii, 1117, 1128).

15 December 1684.   Two money warrants: one for £100 on his salary for half a year to Christmas, 1680, one for £50 on his additional pension to Sept. 29, 1680; money order for the latter dated 17 December 1684; payment of £150 on 16 December 1684 (VII, ii, 1450, 1456).

6 February 1685.   Charles II dies. Dryden's regular salary of £200 is paid up through Christmas, 1680, and is thus four full years in arrears for a total of £800; his additional pension of £100 is paid up through Michaelmas, 1680, and is thus four years and one quarter in arrears for a total of £425.

27 April 1685.   Renewal of Dryden's warrant as Poet Laureate and Historiographer Royal (*C.T.B., 1685–88*, VIII, 139–40).

18 August 1685.   Payment of £150, bringing his regular salary up to Michaelmas, 1681, and reducing the total arrears owed him from £1,225 to £1,075 (VIII, 309).

9 March 1686.   Dryden receives his first payment for the reign of James II, now more than a year old, £150 for the half year from Lady Day until Michaelmas, 1685 (VIII, 604).

7 July 1686.   Rochester, now Lord Treasurer, realizing that there are insufficient funds to pay Charles's many debts, establishes a policy of paying off those owed at the rate of one-third of their arrears; Dryden accordingly receives £358 6s. 8d. (P.R.O., E. 403/3035/pp. 146–47). On the same day, he receives a money warrant for £225, bringing payments from James up to Midsummer, 1686, but he does not receive the money until 30 September (*C.T.B.*, VIII, 812, 914).

12 March 1687.   Payment of £150, bringing payments up to Christmas, 1686 (VIII, 1248, 1256).

24 May 1687.   Just prior to the publication of *The Hind and the Panther* on 27 May, Dryden petitions for the £716 13s. 9d. still owed him from the reign of Charles II, as well as the £75 owed him for Christmas quarter, 1684–85, which he had missed because James dated his new appointment from Lady Day (P.R.O., S.P. 44/71/*Petitions*, p. 341). He never received the money.

28 June 1687.   Payment of £150, bringing payments up to date (*C.T.B.*, VIII, 1430, 1432).

25 October 1687. A quarter's payment of £75, a mere month late (VIII, 1562, 1564). This may have been received by Elizabeth. A paper signed by Dryden authorizing his wife to receive "the Sum of Seaventy five Pounds due to me as Poet Laureat for One Quarter of a yeare ended at Michas. 1687" was sold at Sotheby's in 1937; see Macdonald, *Bibliography*, p. 51*n*.

17 January 1688. Another payment of £75 (VIII, 1714, 1717).

4 April 1688. Another £75 (VIII, 1845, 1847).

6 July 1688. Another payment of £75 (VIII, 1985), his last from James.

Facts and Questions about Anne Reeves

Anne Reeves, a minor actress in the King's Company, was almost certainly Dryden's mistress, but beyond that, little is known about her. I offer here a chronology of references to her career and her relationship with Dryden; my starting point was a typescript draft prepared by Edward A. Langhans for the entry under her name in the *Biographical Dictionary*.[1] There were evidently several women named Anne Reeves in London after the Restoration, and it is now virtually impossible to determine whether some of the records bearing that name refer to the actress. Further difficulties arise because much of the information we have about Reeves comes from Dryden's opponents in theatrical and political controversy, who were not deeply committed to the truth.

This chronology supersedes the version printed in *Restoration* 10 (1986):1–13. Thanks to helpful correspondence received since that publication, I have made a few additions and corrections.

16 June 1639. Thomas Reeve presents his daughter Anne to be christened at St. Giles, Cripplegate. No contemporary account establishes that the Anne Reeves who was Dryden's mistress was born in London, nor is it certain that Reeves was her maiden name. Of the many women with this name christened in London during these years, however, this one seems the most likely candidate, since the same father presented his son Thomas Reeve to be christened at the same church on 18 April 1641, and since contemporary records do link Anne Reeves with an actor in the King's Company named Thomas Reeves.

18 December 1668. Thomas Reeves appears in a performance of Ben Jonson's *Catiline's Conspiracy*. His name is in the edition printed in that year; this particular performance appears on the Lord Chamberlain's list, and is attested to by many witnesses.[2] According to John Payne Collier's manuscript "History of the British Stage"[3] at Harvard, Thomas was Anne's husband; Montague Summers guesses that he was her brother.[4] Though I know of no hard evidence, I should think it more likely that Thomas and Anne were brother and sister, not merely because of the shaky evidence of the christenings, but because the later attacks on Dryden that mention his affair with Anne never allude to a cuckolded husband.[5]

Season of 1668–69. Thomas Reeves appears as Rangino in Shirley's *The Sisters*, according to prompt notes in a copy now at the Folger Library.[6]

23 July 1669.   Thomas Reeves is listed as "new admitted" to the King's Company in the Lord Chamberlain's records.[7] It was quite normal for actors and actresses to play minor roles before being formally admitted to the company. Although we have no record of his playing any specific roles after this date, Thomas was still legally a member of the company as late as 1673, when his creditors petitioned the Lord Chamberlain for permission to sue him.[8]

December 1670.   Anne Reeves appears as Esperanza in Dryden's *Conquest of Granada*, according to the cast printed in the first edition (1672). The part has very few spoken lines, but may have involved singing. In Part II (probably first performed in early January 1671), Esperanza comes on stage with Almanzor in Act IV, scene iii; he asks her to sing for Almahide; she exits and we hear a voice from offstage, singing the "Song in Two Parts" beginning "How unhappy a lover am I." The song is a dialogue, with alternate verses marked "He" and "She," and might therefore have been performed as a duet, but when Esperanza returns to the stage, Almanzor gives her a diamond to pay for her singing, as if she had sung the entire song. Esperanza's exit may be contrived in order to allow someone else to do the singing,[9] but characters played by Anne Reeves are frequently onstage for the singing of such erotic lyrics. It is possible, for example, that Esperanza sings the song to which the "Zambra Dance" is performed in Part I, Act III, scene i, although the text for this song, beginning "Beneath a myrtle shade," has a male speaker and features explicitly sexual imagery.

Scholars have usually inferred that Dryden was involved with Reeves by the time of the premiere of the *Conquest*. In light of the later claims by his enemies that he had difficulty keeping Reeves to himself, the comparison of Fame to a "little Mistriss of the town" in the epilogue to Part I is curious; see above, ch. 7, p. 219.

15 September 1671.   Anne Reeves is listed as "new admitted" to the King's Company, on the recommendation of "Mr. Killigrew."[10] As in the case of Thomas, she had already played at least one role, and probably a number of smaller ones.

? Late November 1671.   Anne Reeves appears as Philotis in Dryden's *Marriage A-la-Mode*, according to the cast printed in the first edition (1673).[11] This part has a few more spoken lines than that of Esperanza, and may again have involved singing. The song at the opening of the play ("Why should a foolish marriage vow") is unquestionably sung by Doralice and Beliza (Mrs. Marshall and Mrs. Slade, according to the printed cast), but the more sensual song in IV, ii ("While Alexis lay prest") could be sung by Philotis, if she is included among the party who enter a few lines earlier ("Enter the Princess in Masquerade, with Ladies").

Early December 1671.   Buckingham's *The Rehearsal*. In this first version, Bayes simply says that "Amarillis" is his mistress; the long passage (I, i, 180–228) in which Bayes discusses "talking Bawdy" to her and boasts that he is "kept by another woman, in the City" was evidently added later; it first appears in the edition of 1675. The decision to expand the references to Bayes's affair, whether taken by the actors or by Buckingham himself, suggests that Dryden's involvement with Reeves had continued and was more widely known. According to Sam Briscoe's generally reliable *Key to the Rehearsal* (1704), Anne Reeves actually played Amarillis.

In Act V, scene i in all versions of the text, Amarillis comes on stage with the court party, and Bayes promises Smith and Johnson that he will "make her speak very well by and by." She speaks two words ("Invincible Soveraigns") before being interrupted by the "Soft Music" that "invades [the] ears" of the King Usher and signals the return of the rightful kings, to whom she attempts to give the same speech, this time speaking eleven words before being interrupted by a battle. Perhaps Buckingham meant to poke fun at the perfunctory parts Dryden had written for Reeves, or at her limited ability to remember her lines.

In the 1675 version of Act III, scene i, Bayes explains that his new song, which the players have exited without singing, "was made by *Tom Thimble's* first wife after she was dead." The song turns out to be a parody of "Farewell Fair *Armida*," which was widely believed to be by Dryden and was printed several times in 1672.[12] According to Briscoe's *Key*, the original song was "made by Mr. *Bayes* on the Death of Captain *Digby*, Son of *George* Earl of *Bristol*, who was a passionate Admirer of the Dutchess Dowager of *Richmond*, call'd by the Author, *Armida*; he lost his Life in a Sea-Fight against the *Dutch*, the 28*th* of *May*, 1672" (pp. 6–7). Digby's noble father had written at least two plays, and might well have known Dryden, but if the imprint date of the first edition of *Westminster-Drollery* is correct, the song was in print before young Digby's death. The Duchess of Richmond was the celebrated beauty Frances Stuart, whom Huysmans painted in armor as Minerva; Pepys saw that painting in 1664.[13] Does this connection have anything to do with the bad joke in I,i about "Armarillis," or with the frontispiece to the second volume of Buckingham's *Works* (1715), which shows Amarillis in armor, in a pose derived from the Huysmans painting?[14]

All three editions of *Covent-Garden Drollery* (1672) also print another parody of "Farewell Fair *Armida*," this one entitled "Farewell, dear *Revechia*" and evidently designed to twit Dryden on his affair with Reeves. In his reprint of the second edition, Montague Summers unaccountably attributes this song to Dryden himself.[15] In its text, the speaker, presumably meant to be Dryden, says he will go to the country, live with fools, and carve Revechia's name on every tree. Summers took this to be a reference to Dryden's sojourn at the Howard estate in Wiltshire, where he went to avoid the plague in 1665–66; that seems preposterously early, since Anne's first recorded theatrical appearance was in late 1670. Later in his career, however, Dryden often went to the country during the summer, as we know from his correspondence, and it is not impossible that he did so in the early 1670s, prompting some not particularly witty poet to write this song.

9 January 1672.   Elizabeth Bracy seeks permission to sue Anne Reeves for £4 10*s*. owed for clothes.[16] As a "sworn" member of the theatrical company, Anne was protected from ordinary prosecution. Those seeking to recover moneys from such people had to procure permission from the Lord Chamberlain to "take their course at law." The record states that Reeves is to appear "on Tuesday morning," but there are no further references to this suit in the Lord Chamberlain's papers, so we may only guess about the outcome: the Lord Chamberlain may have decided that the claim was spurious, the debt may have been paid, or Bracy may have decided against pursuing a lawsuit.

10 April 1672–18 November 1673.   During this period, seven different people sought permission to sue the actor Thomas Reeves, possibly Anne's brother, for various debts. They include a grocer from Bloomsbury market, a bricklayer named Allen, and a widow named Frances Davies who kept a brewhouse at Paul's Wharfe. The addresses and occupations of these creditors lend some weight to the speculation that Thomas may have been the "Mr Reeves" who owned a parcel of land in Russell Street, very close to the Bridges Street theatre, according to Lacy's map of the parish of St. Paul's Covent Garden.[17] The amounts sought range from £8 to £60; taken together, they might have been enough to ruin a man whose annual income from the theatre was probably less than £50. Although six of the seven seeking permission to sue Reeves were told to take their course at law, a thorough search of Chancery records has failed to turn up any lawsuits. Either Thomas managed to settle these claims before his creditors went to court or the creditors concluded that he was not worth suing.

?July 1672.   (Possibly earlier, depending on the uncertain date of the premiere of Ravenscroft's *The Citizen Turned Gentleman*.) Anne speaks the epilogue to a special performance of Dryden's *Secret Love* acted by women only. Such performances were a desperate attempt on the part of the King's Company to attract an audience to Lincoln's Inn Fields, where they were acting after the fire that destroyed their theatre at Bridges Street in January. Anne presumably had a role in the play; both the text of this epilogue and her definite later appearance in a "breeches" role make it virtually certain that she took one of the male parts in this performance, though there is no evidence to tell us which. The epilogue was first printed in *Covent-Garden Drollery* (1672).

? After July 1672.   (Dating again dependent on Ravenscroft.) Anne Reeves plays the page

Ascanio in Dryden's *The Assignation, or Love in a Nunnery*, according to the cast printed in the edition of 1673. Again, this may have been a singing role; Ascanio is on stage for the song and dance in III, ii. Did Anne's participation in this play have anything to do with the later allegations that she had "turned Nun"?

? Before March 1674. Anne plays the servant Orilla in Suckling's *Brennoralt*, according to a manuscript cast in the Bodleian copy. L. A. Beaurline, who prints this cast in his edition of Suckling,[18] dates this revival between 1673 and 1675; Arthur H. Scouten believes it took place before the King's Company moved into their new playhouse at Drury Lane on 26 March 1674. Scouten bases his date on evidence suggesting that some of the other actors would not have been available in earlier or later seasons; his suggestion is the most plausible we are likely to have, but records of all the actors are patchy, and the date cannot be considered firm.[19]

23 April 1674. A revival of *Marriage A-la-Mode*. If available, Anne presumably played Philotis.

17/27 July 1674. Giovanni Salvetti, the Florentine resident in London, writes a letter reporting a rumor about Anne Reeves and the Spanish ambassador, the Marquis of Fresno: "The Spanish ambassador has returned from the Baths still with a sore indisposition, having profited not at all from the waters, and it is rumoured that his Excellency owes his sickness to a beautiful actress from the Theatre Royal called Madam Reeves. She, under the pretext of turning nun, went overseas to be treated, but it is thought that she died while seeking the cure."[20]

As subsequent entries show, Anne clearly did not die, and the rest of this report may also be unreliable. It is nonetheless significant as the first of many references to Anne's going abroad to turn nun, and the first of many references to her spreading venereal disease.

21 December 1674. A revival of *The Rehearsal*, presumably including the expanded references to the Dryden-Reeves affair that were printed in the edition of 1675. Did Anne play Amarillis, or was she abroad?

14 June 1675. An undated roster of the King's Company gives this date next to Anne's name, as if she had been resworn at that time. A similar list on an unpaginated roll has an identical entry.[21] Why did Anne leave the stage, and for how long? Her appearance in the manuscript cast for *Brennoralt*, which remains difficult to date, is the only record placing her in London between the failure of *The Assignation* in 1672 and this date about three years later. If she left because of a pregnancy (as was frequent with actresses), Dryden's enemies failed to take advantage of that fact. The revived *Rehearsal*, for example, while adding a great deal of dialogue on Amarillis, says nothing about her leaving the stage at this time; the jokes about Amarillis would surely have lost much of their bite if Anne were no longer on the stage. Nor do the later attacks on Dryden in the 1680s refer to a pregnancy, though several of them allege that Dryden caught venereal disease from Anne. The date on the Lord Chamberlain's document only makes sense as a date for a reswearing, so Anne must have been off the stage at some point. I should suppose her absence was brief.

19 June 1675. Another performance of *Marriage A-la-Mode*. Note that Anne had been resworn just five days earlier. Did she return to the company in order to play Philotis?

July 1675. The famous comedian Joseph Haines speaks a prologue to Jonson's *Ev'ry Man out of his Humor*.

> So fast from Plays approv'd and Actors known,
> To drolling, stroling Royal Troop you run,
> That *Hayns* despairing is Religious grown.
> So Crack enjoy'd, the queazy Gallants slight,
> And she, though still her beauty's height
> In rage turns Nun and goes to Heav'n in spight.
> O Novelty, who can thy pow'r oppose!

> Polony Bear or strainge Grimace out-goes
> Our finest language and our greatest shows.
> . . . .
> I will reform—
> But what Religion's best in this lewd Town,
> My friends I'm yet like most of you, of none.

This was first printed in Duffett's *New Songs and Poems* (1676). In his reprint of the third edition of *Covent-Garden Drollery*,[22] G. Thorn-Drury gives an account of Anne Reeves on which later scholarship has depended without sufficient reexamination. He quotes this passage and the epilogue to Otway's *Don Carlos* (see below), claiming that both refer to Anne's leaving the stage to become a nun. But the point of Haines's prologue is that audiences are forsaking the regular theatres for a visiting French troupe, driving him to such despair that he is considering becoming religious, just as gallants forsake a "Crack" they have already enjoyed, who responds by turning nun. There is no specific reference to Anne or to actresses. Note also that the epilogue was spoken shortly after Anne's return to the stage. If, as seems highly unlikely, her absence was an attempt to "turn Nun," it was over. Even in the face of the rumor reported by Salvetti, I wonder whether this epilogue was meant to have any reference to Anne Reeves at all.

21 December 1675. A revival of *The Conquest of Granada*. Did Anne again play Esperanza?

8 June 1676. Otway's *Don Carlos*. The epilogue, spoken by a very young girl (possibly Anne Bracegirdle), is a conventional plea for applause, ending with these lines:

> But now, if by my Suit you'l not be won,
> You know what your unkindness oft has done;
> I'l e'en forsake the Play-House, and turn Nun.

Thorn-Drury and later scholars have also connected these lines to Anne Reeves; again, there is nothing sufficiently specific to justify that reading.

?Late 1676. Possible date of "A Session of the Poets," later printed in the "Antwerp" edition of Rochester's poems (1680) and in Buckingham's *Works* (1704), but attributed to Settle in one contemporary manuscript. The authorship of this poem remains undetermined. The passage on Dryden is as follows:

> In the head of the gang John Dryden appear'd
> That ancient grave wit so long lov'd and fear'd
> But Apollo had heard a story i'the town
> Of his quitting the Muses to wear the black gown,
> And so gave him leave, now his poetry's done,
> To let him turn priest, when Reeve is turned nun.

The remarks about Dryden's "quitting the Muses" and being done with poetry presumably reflect his abandoning rhymed drama, a decision he had announced in the prologue to *Aureng-Zebe* (1675): "Our Author . . . Grows weary of his long-lov'd Mistris, Rhyme." The rumor that he planned to take orders probably reflects his interest in a post at Oxford, though his enemies in literary controversy had been hinting at his supposed desire to take the cloth since 1668 (see above, ch. 8, p. 270 and n. 43). Perhaps the author of this poem also remembered the preface to *Tyrannick Love*, printed in 1670, in which Dryden had pointed out that "Religion was first taught in Verse (which the laziness or dulness of succeeding Priesthood, turned afterwards into Prose)" (X, 109). With that passage in mind, the author of the "Session" poem could take pleasure in having Apollo propose that Dryden might become a priest when Reeves became a nun, meaning both these ideas as preposterous. On that reading, the lines might simply mean that it was about as plausible that Dryden the well-known opponent of clerics might become one himself as that his mistress the sexy actress might become a nun, though both notions had been rumored before, as we have seen. Summers, in his edition of *Roscius Anglicanus*, prints "since Reeves is turned

Nun," silently and significantly emending the text to support his claim that Anne left the stage in the spring of 1675 "to take the veil" (pp. 100–01). He has been frequently followed in both the emendation and the conclusion. Given the fairly continuous record of Anne's career as an actress, particularly her official reswearing in 1675, it seems at least as likely that the anonymous satirist intended a joke, which was misinterpreted as an allegation of fact by later antagonists of Dryden.

11 March 1678.   Premiere of *The Kind Keeper*, Dryden's play satirizing keepers of mistresses, which was banned after three performances (see above, ch. 9, pp. 309–10 and notes). In Act II, scene i, Tricksy, Mr. Limberham's mistress, threatens to go to a nunnery as a way of extracting a promise from her keeper to settle £200 a year on her. Would Dryden have written such a scene if his own mistress had gone to a nunnery? Would he have written such a play if he was himself still keeping a mistress?

Late Spring 1678.   A manuscript lampoon on Dryden entitled "Upon a late fall'n Poet. Suppos'd to be Written by Mr Shadwell." According to this abusive poem, both Anne Reeves and a prostitute named Sue Willis had broken off with Dryden:

> For his Whores, Reeves, & Willis, as most Men doe say,
> Who both Cashier'd him for want of pay.
> There's noe fucking *on Tick*, till a Poets Third Day.
>
> . . . .
> For Reeves, (tho' a Bawd she ever had beene)
> Yet held it a much lesse shame & lesse Sin,
> To live a Bawd still, than remaine Whore to him.[23]

Whoever wrote these stanzas knew that Dryden's affair with Anne Reeves was over, and was trying to put the worst possible construction on the end of their liaison. He also accuses Anne of having given venereal disease to the "Wild-House Spaniards," a recurrence of the rumor reported four years earlier by Salvetti.[24]

1679.   A "Mis Reeves" arrives at the convent of the Blue Nuns in Paris, apparently as a servant to Mary Elizabeth Savile, who came there with her mother, Lady Mary Savile.[25] This convent can be connected to Dryden's recusant relatives by marriage in several ways. Philip Howard, second cousin to Dryden's wife and Grand Almoner to Queen Catharine from 1665 until 1672, was named a Cardinal on 27 May 1675. He went to Rome for the ceremony, taking along his nephew Thomas, son of Henry Howard, sixth Duke of Norfolk.[26] In the same year, Henry's daughter Frances, niece to the new Cardinal, entered the convent of Blue Nuns as a boarder. Lady Mary Savile made a profession in 1690, after the death of her husband, but her daughter, to whom "Mis Reeves" was a servant, did not become a nun; she married Thomas Howard, nephew to the Cardinal, a staunch Roman Catholic and supporter of James II who was drowned in 1689. Thomas's sister, Lady Frances Howard, eventually left the convent to marry the Marquis of Valpareisa, a Spanish grandee. Staying at a convent was not an unusual thing for an Englishwoman on the continent to do. Charles II's mistress Barbara Villiers Palmer, now the Duchess of Cleveland, also stayed at the convent of the Blue Nuns with her daughter during 1675,[27] and the actress Elizabeth Bowtell frequently stayed in various convents in France and Belgium in the later 1680s.[28]

If the "Mis Reeves" recorded here was Anne, she went, however briefly, to a convent connected in several ways with Dryden's recusant relatives by marriage. On the face of it, there would be nothing preposterous about Anne's becoming a servant to a wealthy woman. Her affair with Dryden was almost certainly over by this date; the reswearing of 1675 is the last solid theatrical mention of her, and even if she took part in some revivals during 1675 and 1676, as I have speculated, there is no later performance with which we may even conjecturally connect her. Still, the absence of a first name for this servant renders this record even more inconclusive than the others. If the rumors about Anne's turning nun came *after* this date, one might trace them to this visit to a convent, but the "Session" poem antedates this record by two years.[29]

1682.   In the wake of *Absalom and Achitophel*, Dryden was the subject of a series of vituperative pamphlets and poems, many of which glance at the Reeves affair.[30] The most important references are as follows:

The Medal of John Bayes, probably by Shadwell, takes up the affair in its prose preface and in its verse:

> His prostituted *Muse* will become as common for hire, as his Mistress *Revesia* was, upon whom he spent so many hundred pounds; and of whom (to shew his constancy in Love) he got three Claps, and she was a Bawd. Let all his own *Romantick* Playes shew so true and so Heroic a Lover.
>
> [sig A1v]

> He boasts of Vice (which he did ne'r commit)
> Calls himself *Whoremaster* and *Sodomite*;
> Commends *Reeve*'s Arse, and says she Buggers well,
> And silly Lyes of vitious pranks does tell.
>
> [p. 4]

The past tense of the prose passage establishes that even his enemies knew Dryden's affair with Reeves was long over. Shadwell does not blame Dryden for having a mistress, but for failing to keep her to himself and for telling false tales of sexual exploits. Obviously none of his charges can be verified.

Directions to Fame, a poem in praise of the murdered Thomas Thynne, has a digression on Dryden:

> He, who can bring Eclipses of the Stage,
> His Muse can suit to this, and the last Age,
> Can his Play's Epilogues so dext'rous make,
> As for his Prologues some may them Mistake:
> And with more readiness his Prologues turn
> To Epilogues, than for's Religion burn.
> How easily these *Hero*'s of his Pen,
> Of Mushrooms may he fancy into Men?
> The sooner, if by Sonnets he did more,
> Than Pious Priests could ever do before,
> And to Religion turn'd his own dear Whore.
>
> [pp. 9–10]

Here the poet seems to concede Dryden's skill in order to attack his inconsistency. The charge that he "turn'd his own dear Whore . . . to Religion" might reflect actual rumors about Anne's entering a nunnery, but might also simply be based on the earlier "Session" poem.

Absalom Senior, probably by Settle, makes much of the claim that Dryden sought the Provostship of Eton. Settle includes Dryden's sexual immorality among reasons why he failed to secure the post:

> Besides, lewd Fame had told his plighted Vow,
> To *Laura's* cooing Love percht on a dropping Bough[,]
> *Laura* in faithful Constancy confin'd
> To *Ethiops* Envoy, and to all Mankind.
> *Laura* though Rotten, yet of Mold Divine;
> He had all her Cl[aps], and She had all his Coine.
> Her Wit so far his Purse and Sense could drain,
> Till every P[o]x was sweetn'd to a Strain.
> And if at last his Nature can reform,
> A weary grown of Loves tumultuous storm,

'Tis Ages Fault, not His; of pow'r bereft,
He left not Whoring, but of that was left.

[pp. 33–34]

If "*Laura*," an obvious coinage for the mistress of the Laureate, is meant to be Reeves, this passage presents new problems. The charge that she has been involved with "*Ethiops* Envoy" must refer to Mohammed Ohadu, the Moroccan ambassador, who was in London only during the first half of 1682, and who was rumored to be a ladies' man.[31] If we could believe that charge, it would place Anne Reeves in London in 1682; by that date, Mary Elizabeth Savile was also back in England and married, so Anne's presence in London at this date does not preclude her being the "Mis Reeves" who went to Paris with the Savile ladies. The rest of the passage, evidently dependent on *The Medal of John Bayes*, repeats the same old charges about expense and venereal disease.

22 November 1686.   One "Ann Reeues of g^{rt} Russ: str" was buried at St. Giles in the Fields. The address corresponds to that of the piece of property assigned to "Mr Reeves" on Lacy's map.

2 November 1689.   Another "Anne Reeues" was buried at St. Bride, Fleet Street.

24 December 1690.   Another "Ann Reeves, a woman" was buried at St. Clement Danes. Any or none of these three might have been the actress.

Notes

Place of publication is London if not otherwise noted.

ABBREVIATIONS

AFP	*Archivum Fratrum Praedicatorum*
B.L.	British Library
BNYPL	*Bulletin of the New York Public Library*
C.S.P. Dom.	*Calendar of State Papers, Domestic Series*
C.T.B.	*Calendar of Treasury Books*
DNB	*Dictionary of National Biography*
EA	*Études Anglaises*
ECTI	*The Eighteenth Century: Theory and Interpretation*
EHR	*English Historical Review*
EIC	*Essays in Criticism*
ELH	*ELH, A Journal of English Literary History*
ELN	*English Language Notes*
ES	*English Studies*
HLB	*Harvard Library Bulletin*
HLQ	*Huntington Library Quarterly*
H.M.C.	*Reports of the Historical Manuscripts Commission*
JEGP	*Journal of English and Germanic Philology*
JWCI	*Journal of the Warburg and Courtauld Institutes*
MLN	*Modern Language Notes*
MLQ	*Modern Language Quarterly*
MLR	*Modern Language Review*
MP	*Modern Philology*
N&Q	*Notes & Queries*
N.R.O.	Northamptonshire Record Office
PBA	*Proceedings of the British Academy*
PBSA	*Publications of the Bibliographical Society of America*
P.C.C.	Prebendary Court of Canterbury
PCRS	*Publications of the Catholic Record Society*

PLL	*Papers on Language and Literature*
PLPLS	*Proceedings of the Leeds Philosophical and Literary Society*
PMLA	*Publications of the Modern Language Association*
POAS	*Poems on Affairs of State*, ed. George deForest Lord, 7 vols. (New Haven: Yale University Press, 1963–1975).
PQ	*Philological Quarterly*
P.R.O.	Public Record Office
RECTR	*Restoration and Eighteenth-Century Theatre Research*
RES	*Review of English Studies*
SB	*Studies in Bibliography*
SECC	*Studies in Eighteenth-Century Culture*
SEL	*Studies in English Literature*
SP	*Studies in Philology*
SVEC	*Studies in Voltaire and the Eighteenth Century*
TCBS	*Transactions of the Cambridge Bibliographical Society*
TLS	*Times Literary Supplement*
TN	*Theatre Notebook*
TRI	*Theatre Research International*
TS	*Theatre Survey*
YES	*Yearbook of English Studies*

PREFACE

1. "Dryden," in *Lives of the English Poets*, ed. G. B. Hill, 3 vols. (Oxford, Clarendon, 1905), I, 411.

2. Their works, frequently cited hereafter by their last names, are: Charles E. Ward, *The Life of John Dryden* (Chapel Hill: University of North Carolina Press, 1961); James M. Osborn, *John Dryden: Some Biographical Facts and Problems* (rev. ed., Gainesville: University of Florida Press, 1965); Walter Scott, *The Works of John Dryden*, 18 vols. (William Miller, 1808), vol. I; and Edmond Malone, *The Critical and Miscellaneous Prose Works of John Dryden*, 4 vols. (Cadell and Davis, 1800), vol. I.

3. For a full discussion, to which I owe the Bernini example, see Robert Ashton, *The English Civil War: Conservatism and Revolution 1603–1649* (Weidenfeld and Nicolson, 1978), p. 22.

4. For a summary and critique of this position, see Nicholas Tyacke, "Puritanism, Arminianism, and Counter-Revolution," in *Origins of the English Civil War*, ed. Conrad Russell (Macmillan, 1973), pp. 119–43.

5. George McFadden, *Dryden the Public Writer, 1660–1685* (Princeton: Princeton University Press, 1978), p. 3.

CHAPTER 1. THE MILK OF THE WORD

1. In his "Dedication" to Dryden's *Dramatick Works*, 6 vols. (1717), I, sig. 8. Compare Dryden's account of his own personality, in the "Defence of an Essay of Dramatique Poetry" (1667): "My Conversation is slow and dull, my humour Saturnine and reserv'd," in *The Works of John Dryden*, ed. Edward Niles Hooker, H. T. Swedenberg, et al. (Berkeley: University of California Press, 1955-), IX, 8. Quotations from Dryden's works follow this edition whenever possible; when necessary, I refer to the California edition as *Works*. Quotations from the *Virgil* (1697) and the *Fables* (1700) follow *The Poems of John Dryden*, ed. James Kinsley, 4 vols. (Oxford: Clarendon, 1958); I refer to Kinsley's edition as *Poems*. Quotations from other works not yet printed in the California edition normally follow the first printed editions. All poems, including prologues and epilogues, are cited by line number; prose, by volume and page from *Works*, or by page or signature from the original editions; plays, by act, scene, and line from *Works*, or by act and page from the original editions. When quoting front matter, I have silently reversed italics.

2. Even Pope, whom we normally think of as Dryden's immediate literary successor, mentions his childhood efforts in his poems; in the *Epistle to Dr. Arbuthnot*, l. 128, he tells us that he "lisp'd in numbers, for the Numbers came." All citations of Pope's works follow *The Twickenham Edition of the Works of Alexander Pope*, ed. John Butt et al. (Methuen, 1950–67). Pope also provides considerable raw material for biograph-

ical speculation in his remarks to Spence, which include an account of a play he wrote as a boy, based on incidents from the *Iliad*; see Joseph Spence, *Observations, Anecdotes, and Characters of Books and Men*, ed. James M. Osborn, 2 vols. (Oxford: Clarendon, 1966), I, 15.

3. Alan Everitt singles out Northamptonshire as a textbook case of this process in "The Local Community and the Great Rebellion," in *The Historical Association Book of the Stuarts*, ed. K. H. D. Haley (New York: St. Martin's, 1973), p. 93.

4. The Lay Subsidy of 1525 is in the P.R.O. (E. 179/155/154); it is conveniently reprinted in Helen Belgion, *Titchmarsh Past and Present* (Titchmarsh: by the author, 1979), pp. 34–35. I accept Belgion's suggestion that the man called "James Stanvens" in the Subsidy is the "James Staynbancke of Titchmarsh, yeoman," whose will, returning his estate at Pilton to his daughter "Elizabeth Pykering," and leaving presents of sheep to her children, is in the N.R.O. (Peterborough Wills, Book E, f. 30).

5. Northamptonshire had two great county histories before the Victoria series: *The History and Antiquities of Northamptonshire Compiled from the Manuscript Collections of John Bridges*, 2 vols. (Oxford, 1791), and George Baker's incomplete but monumental *History and Antiquities of the County of Northampton*, 2 vols. (Nichols, 1822–41). Both Bridges (I, 224) and Baker (II, 13), citing royal patents, explain that the monastery lands at Canons Ashby were granted in 1537 to the courtier Francis Bryan; one year later, there was a license of alienation to John Cope, who was knighted later in the same year. Cope built a house, sometimes called Cope's Ashby, from the materials of the priory; his will, proved in 1558 (P.R.O., P.C.C. 25 Noodes), stipulates that his third wife, Margaret Tame, is to retain occupancy of the house. An indenture of 1573 in the N.R.O., D (CA) 598, records John Dryden's acquisition of "the site of the late Monastery of Canons Ashby," though the Cope heirs retained the glass, ceilings, furniture, and windows of the house. The old Cope house did not actually become the property of the Dryden family until 1665, when Sir Robert Dryden purchased it from one Gerrard Usher, who had purchased it from the descendants of Edward Cope, John Cope's grandson and heir; Sir Robert had pulled down what was left of the Elizabethan house by 1669. Later scholars have confused the story by assuming that there was only one house; Ward's account, for example, (pp. 4, 321) is incorrect. For accurate details, see the National Trust publication on the recently restored Dryden house: Gervase Jackson-Stopps, *Canons Ashby* (Hatfield: National Trust, 1984), especially pp. 41, 44. For genealogies of the Copes, Pickerings, and Drydens, see the charts following p. 12 and Appendix A.

6. According to Belgion, "Wool probably paid for the beautification of the Titchmarsh church as it did for the churches of Cavendish, Lavenham, and Long Melford in East Anglia" (p. 25). *The Agrarian History of England and Wales* (Cambridge University Press, 1967–), vol. IV, *1500–1640*, ed. Joan Thirsk, explains that "parts of Northamptonshire . . . had fallen readily into the grasp of the enclosing farmer, for its soils were nowhere specially fertile for corn whereas it grew good grass, and was eminently suited to cattle and sheep grazing" (p. 233). When Titchmarsh was enclosed in the eighteenth century, traces of earlier enclosures were found; perhaps they were of Tudor origin.

7. Percival Wiburn, quoted in W. J. Sheils, *The Puritans in the Diocese of Peterborough 1558–1610* (Northampton: Northamptonshire Record Society, vol. 30, 1979), p. 2.

8. John Walker, *The Sufferings of the Clergy* (1714), p. 91.

9. "Even that indefatigable collector of evidence the martyrologist John Foxe recorded only one instance of martyrdom in the county" (Sheils, pp. 14–15).

10. See Belgion, p. 42.

11. *Church History of Britain* (1655), Book X, p. 35.

12. "The truth of this," says the first man to retail the story about the horse in print, "was attested to by Mr William Perkins, who had it from Mr Clement Cotton, to whom Mr Pickering gave the above relation." James Caulfield, *History of the Gunpowder Plot* (Vernor and Hood, 1804), pp. 67–68. On the later raid, see Godfrey Anstruther, *Vaux of Harrowden: A Recusant Family* (Oxford: Oxford University Press, 1953), p. 392. The raid was an attempt to capture the Jesuit Gerard, who had escaped from the Tower in 1597 and was thought to be an uncaptured conspirator from the Gunpowder Plot; he was actually in Liège.

13. According to Walter C. Metcalfe, *The Visitations of Northamptonshire in 1564 and 1618–19* (Mitchell and Hughes, 1887), p. 127, the Browne woman who married a Pickering was named Ellen, a name she also has in the Pickering pedigree printed by E. R. Pickering in *The Umfrevilles: Their Ancestors and Descendants* (Clapham: Batten's Office, c. 1860), p. 43. F. I. Cater, in "Robert Browne's Ancestors and Descendants," *Transactions of the Congregational History Society* 2 (1905), p. 154, calls her "Dorothy," and mistakenly states that her husband was Sir Gilbert (II), the squire, an error repeated by Sheils, p. 24.

14. Sheils, pp. 1, 13.

15. Quoted in Sheils, p. 107.

16. For an excellent modern account of Dod's long career, see William Haller, *The Rise of Puritanism* (New York: Columbia University Press, 1938), pp. 54–69. On Cope's invitation to Dod, for which he was presented to the Church courts, see Sheils, p. 86. After the death of King James, Dod recovered his preaching license; Richard Knightley, a friend and ally of Sir Erasmus Dryden, presented him to the living at Fawsley.

17. *A Plaine and Familiar Exposition of the Fifteenth, Sixteenth, and Seventeenth Chapters of the Prouerbs of Salomon* (1609), sig. A2r.

18. I accept Ward's conjecture about his birthdate (p. 5), based on his documented matriculation at Emmanuel College, Cambridge, in 1618. Malone (p. 20n) reckons his birthdate as 1588, but this must be incorrect, since it would make Erasmus thirty at the time of his going up to Cambridge; sixteen was a much more normal age. Ward's guess would also make Erasmus twenty-eight, not forty-two, at the time of his marriage, and would have him fathering his last child at fifty-two, not sixty-six.

19. For stunning color photographs of both the Winter Parlor and the biblical mural, see John Cornforth, "Canons Ashby Revisited—II, *Country Life* 176 (5 July 1984), pp. 22–23. The room containing the mural is still called the Spenser room, as it was during Dryden's life. Dryden told John Aubrey that the poet Edmund Spenser, first cousin by marriage to Sir Erasmus Dryden, was a frequent visitor to Canons Ashby. See *Brief Lives*, ed. Andrew Clark, 2 vols. (Oxford: Clarendon, 1898), II, 232. Douglas Hamer, in "Some Spenser Problems," *N&Q* 180 (1941):206–09, has cast some doubt on the accuracy of this tradition.

20. The B.L. has editions dated 1598, 1600, 1603, 1612, and 1630. The first three are by one "R. C."; only the last two are edited by Dod and Cleaver. The B.L. catalogue identifies R. C. as Roger Carr; Lawrence Stone, in *The Family, Sex and Marriage in England 1500–1800* (New York: Harper and Row, 1977), p. 27, identifies him as Robert Cawdrey and implies that an edition was published as early as 1562. I have been unable to locate one earlier than 1598; my citations follow the edition of 1630.

21. For the meeting in Northampton, see *C.S.P. Dom., 1626–27*, p. 15. For the meeting of the Privy Council, see *Acts of the Privy Council, 1627*, p. 25. The petition is in the P.R.O. (S.P. 16/526/18) but is undated; the date proposed for it in *C.S.P. Addenda, 1625–49*, p. 198, [Feb.] 1627, seems logical, given the claim to have been imprisoned for seventeen days and the known date of incarceration, 19 January. Edmund Hampden, who joined in the petition, sent another petition of his own on 2 June 1627, alleging that he was "dangerously sick" (S.P. 16/66/17). For Pickering's transfer to Middlesex, on 13 June, see *Acts of the Privy Council, 1627*, p. 342. There appears to be no record of Dryden's transfer to Oxfordshire; Sir Cope Doyley wrote to the Privy Council on 24 August to complain that he had no appropriate place in which to house his prisoner (S.P. 16/74/95); they answered suggesting Henly upon Thames on 28 August (*Acts*, p. 507). Both men appear on a list of prisoners released on 2 January 1628 (*Acts, 1628*, p. 217). Misled by an old-style date, Ward incorrectly reports that they were released in February 1627 (p. 323); he also misses John's death. My earlier guesses at the dating of this episode, published in "John Dryden's Pickering Ancestors," *N&Q* 227 (1982), p. 509, n. 20, were incorrect. My thanks to Richard Cust of the University of Birmingham, who directed me toward the documents that establish the correct sequence of events. For other documents related to the Forced Loan, see *C.S.P. Dom., 1625–26*, p. 435, and John Rushworth, *Historical Collections*, 4 parts (1659–1701), I, 418. Dryden's reference comes in the poem "To my Honour'd Kinsman," ll. 184–94.

22. The will of Lady Elizabeth Pickering, widow of Gilbert (II), proved in 1620 (P.R.O., P.C.C. 76 Soame), refers to John (II) as her "deere and onlie sonne." Besides Erasmus Dryden, the other trustees of the estate of John (II) were Robert Horsman (his brother-in-law), Francis Nicolls, and Edward Bagshawe, Counsellor-at-Law, whose son attended Westminster School with Dryden. The will was proved in 1628 (P.R.O., P.C.C. 19 Barrington). The Titchmarsh Parish Register records the christening of Gilbert (III) on 10 March 1610 / [1611]; the *DNB*, which misdates his birth, also omits his schooling at Emmanuel College, Cambridge from 1625 until 1629. Records of the Oundle School begin in 1626; the first list of students includes "Joannes Pickering son of John Pickering of Titchmarsh" and "Edward Pickering son of John Pickering of Titchmarsh." See Belgion, *Titchmarsh*, p. 69. According to the Pickering family monument, printed in full by Bridges (II, 366–68), three younger children—James, Elizabeth, and Frances—"died young," but Frances, the eldest daughter, mentioned as a "sweete grandchilde" in her grandmother's will (1620), was still alive at the time of her father's will (1627), in which she receives a portion of £1,000.

23. Ward's account of the marriage (p. 3) erroneously implies that Sir John Pickering (II) was alive at

the time and incorrectly refers to him as "the uncle of Mary Dryden." He was in fact her first cousin. The house called Brookside Farm bears the date 1628 in iron numbers above its attic window, and has five hearths, the number on which Mary Dryden was taxed in later years. For a detailed description, see Helen Belgion, "John Dryden's Titchmarsh Home," *Northamptonshire Past and Present* 5 (1975):278–79. Dryden's baptism is recorded among Bridges's papers in the Bodleian, on what looks like a copy of the lost parish register; see Osborn, pp. 285–86. Accounts of Henry Pickering's life have been plagued by error. According to the accurate research of Henry Isham Longden, *Northamptonshire and Rutland Clergy* (Northampton: Archer and Goodman, 1938–52), he was the seventh son of John Pickering (I), a fact confirmed by the will of John (II), which mentions "my uncle Henrie." He matriculated at Christ's College, Cambridge, in March 1583, took his B.A. in 1587 and his M.A. in 1590, and was presented to the living of Aldwincle All Saints in 1592. Edmond Malone, misled by an inaccurate transcription of Henry's gravestone in Bridges, reported that he had become rector of All Saints in 1647 and died ten years later in 1657, both errors frequently repeated. In fact, Henry died in 1637, after more than forty years in his pastorate. He may have retired from active service in 1632; the *Institution Books*, in the P.R.O., series A, vol. III, p. 6, record the appointment of one John Webster as rector in April of 1632.

24. The sale of the next presentation is recorded in *Chancery Inquisitiones post mortem*, vol. 446, no. 84, a document largely concerned with the wardship of Gilbert (III). Perhaps John (II) was trying to prevent the king from making the next appointment during the minority of his son, a tactic frequently used by the Laudians. Despite the sale, however, that is exactly what happened: when Robert Williamson, mentioned in numerous Pickering wills, died in 1631, the king, according to the *Institution Books*, appointed Robert Williamson, Jr. "rationi minoris etatis Gilberti Pickeringe." Two years later, young Williamson resigned, and the sale was finally honored, with predictably Puritan results.

25. Perhaps Dryden's father left Cambridge without a degree because of scruples: "Oxford after 1581 required all students of 16 years of age and over to subscribe to the Thirty-Nine Articles on matriculation, [but] Cambridge made no such demand until 1616 and even then subscription was made a condition for taking degrees, not for matriculation." Vivian H. H. Green, *Religion at Oxford and Cambridge* (SCM Press, 1964), p. 112. This difference in regulations would explain why young Erasmus went to Cambridge, although his father and older brothers had all gone to Oxford.

26. The fullest contemporary source on Hill's career is the funeral sermon preached for him by Anthony Tuckney, ΘΑΝΑΤΟΚΤΑΣΙΑ, *or, Death Disarmed* (1654); the phrase about his preaching occurs on p. 58; the account of his call to Titchmarsh is as follows: "He come's to be more taken notice of by many both great and good men, and so by some of eminent worth and honour, he was called to the Pastoral charge of *Titchmersh*, in *Northamptonshire*, where he laboured faithfully in Gods Harvest about eight or nine years, and partly by preaching and conversing up and down with others; but especially (otherwise then our *Erratick Itineraries* use is) with his own Parochial charge, he proved a great blessing, not onely to that Town, but also to the Whole Countrey" (p. 51). The living was a rich one: the *Institution Books* give its annual value as £45; Aldwincle All Saints, by comparison, was worth a mere £12 4s. 2d.

27. See Belgion, p. 79.

28. *A Plaine and Familiar Exposition of the Ten Commaundements* (1606), p. 197. The B.L. copy bears the signature of "Jacobus Rex," an intriguing circumstance since James "silenced" Dod a few years later. Although this treatise was so frequently attributed to Dod that he acquired the name "Decalogue Dod," he and Cleaver deny authorship in the front matter (sig A2v). This edition is dedicated to Anthony Cope, the famous Sheriff of Oxfordshire and M.P. for Banbury, who was sent to the Tower in 1586 for his Puritan agitation; he was second cousin to Edward Cope of Canons Ashby, who evidently shared his sentiments, and who may have written the prefatory verses signed E. C. On wet-nursing generally, see Stone, pp. 64, 66, 159.

29. As Conrad Russell explains in his Introduction to *The Origins of the English Civil War*, "The Parliamentary gentry were the conservatives, standing for the outdated values of the Elizabethan world in which many of them had grown up" (pp. 5–6).

30. From a letter by Deane describing his troubles, in the N.R.O. (part of Baker MSS. 12069). For a lively account, see Helen Belgion, "Village violence at Titchmarsh in 1660," *Northamptonshire Past and Present* 4 (1971–72):155–57. Both the *DNB* and *The Complete Baronetage* erroneously give Sir Gilbert (III) a second wife from the Pepys family, whereas his wife Elizabeth Montagu, mother of his twelve children, survived him. On her attempt to bribe Pepys, see *The Diary of Samuel Pepys*, ed. Robert Latham and William Matthews, 11 vols. (Berkeley: University of California Press, 1970–83), I, 178; all citations of Pepys follow

this edition. Elizabeth was never reconciled to the Anglican Establishment. When Nathaniel Whiting, who was ejected from Aldwincle All Saints for nonconformity in 1662, was licensed to conduct Dissenting services in 1672, one of the locations was Lady Pickering's house. For all the documents on Sir Gilbert's pardon, see below, ch. 4, n. 63.

31. The quoted phrase is from the will of Lady Elizabeth (cited above, n. 22). According to Walker, *Sufferings of the Clergy*, p. 91, Sir Gilbert (III) "was first a *Presbyterian*, then an *Independent*, then a *Brownist*, and afterwards an *Anabaptist*. He was a most furious, fiery, implacable Man; was the principal Agent in casting out most of the Learned Clergy; a great oppressor of the County." This description, quoted in virtually every account of Pickering, comes from the papers of one "*Jer. Stephens* of Wooton," who was among Pickering's victims; the claim that Pickering's changes of denomination ended in his becoming an Anabaptist is highly unlikely, given the records of the christenings of his twelve children in the Titchmarsh Parish Register, though the description of his behavior as "furious, fiery, implacable" tallies well with his conduct in 1660.

32. In *The Vindication of the Duke of Guise* (1683), he argues that the Whigs should renounce the notion "that the *King* is but an *Officer in Trust* . . . because both Scripture and Acts of Parliament oblige them to it, and we will then thank their *Obedience* for our quiet" (p. 8). In *His Majesties Declaration Defended* (1681), there is a similar passage: "We read of a divine Command to obey Superior Powers; and the Duke will lawfully be such. . . . Besides this, we have the Examples of Primitive Christians, even under Heathen Emperors, always suffering, yet never taking up Arms, during ten Persecutions" (XVII, 210). On the attribution to Dryden of this anonymous treatise, see below, ch. 10, n. 24. A more immediate source for the reference to the early Church is *A Sermon Preached before the House of Lords* (1678), by Thomas Lamplugh, who was the vicar of St. Martin's in the Fields, Dryden's parish church in London, from 1670 until 1673: "The Emperors, for the first Three hundred years after Christ, for the generality, were very bad; but especially to the Christians, they were bloody and cruel: And yet we never read of any Insurrection of the Christians against them" (p. 40).

33. I have discussed this aspect of Augustine's thought, with particular reference to music and rhetoric, in *Unsuspected Eloquence: A History of the Relations between Poetry and Music* (New Haven: Yale University Press, 1981), pp. 43–55. In Calvin, the locus classicus is Book I, ch. xi of the *Institutes*, which begins as an analysis of the second commandment, against graven images. Predictably, Dod and Cleaver's exposition of that commandment borrows copiously from Calvin, citing many of the same scriptural passages; see *Ten Commaundements*, pp. 56–63.

34. There were pamphlets and chapbooks claiming to record Dod's sayings as early as 1671, with regular publications under such titles throughout the eighteenth century. I quote from a reprinted collection, *Memorials of the Reverend John Dod*, ed. John Taylor (Northampton: Taylor and Son, 1875), p. 13. "Holmby-House" is Holdenby House, an enormous showplace built in the vain hope that the Queen would visit it; the expense ruined Hatton. See Mark Girouard, *Life in the English Country House: A Social and Architectural History* (New Haven: Yale University Press, 1978), p. 112.

35. Quoted in Oliver Millar, *The Age of Charles I: Painting in England 1620–1649* (Tate Gallery, 1972), p. 60.

36. See Barbara K. Lewalski, *Protestant Poetics and the Seventeenth-Century Religious Lyric* (Princeton: Princeton University Press, 1979).

37. Donald Davie, *A Gathered Church: The Literature of the English Dissenting Interest, 1700–1930* (Routledge & Kegan Paul, 1978), pp. 25–26.

38. *Ten Commaundements*, p. 197; *A Plaine and Familiar Exposition of the Eleuenth and Twelfth Chapters of the Prouerbes of Salomon* (1607), p. 113.

39. Letter to Mrs. Steward, dated Nov. 7 [1699], in *The Letters of John Dryden*, ed. Charles E. Ward (Durham: Duke University Press, 1942), p. 124. All subsequent citations of Dryden's letters follow this edition.

40. See Stone, *The Family, Sex and Marriage*, pp. 162–63, 170, etc. Stone claims that such "severe repression of the will of the child . . . tend[ed] to produce adults who were cold, suspicious, distrustful, and cruel, unable to form close emotional relationships with others, and liable to sudden outbursts of aggressive hostility towards each other" (pp. 193–95). I see little evidence of such pathology in the adult Dryden.

41. Stone finds "the roots of affective individualism in seventeenth-century Puritan sectarianism" (p. 138).

42. All fourteen of Mary's children were alive when their father made his will in 1654; the youngest, Elizabeth, had been born that very year. Of the ten daughters, at least nine lived to be married, as the genealogy in Appendix A shows. Nowhere is there a record, as there would have been in most families, of a child's dying in infancy. P. D. Mundy, in "The Pickerings of Aldwincle All Saints," *N&Q* 197 (1952):490–92, gives Dr. John Pickering's date of birth as 1596, an impossible date given his father Henry's marriage license to Isabella Smith, dated 1600. Mundy was misled by a dismal rhyming epitaph in Aldwincle All Saints, which states that "The deceased I. P. wrote this epitaph 1652." The next line reads "Aged LVI," so Mundy took fifty-six to be John Pickering's age when he wrote the poem, but I rather suspect it was his age at death, which would give us the more plausible birthdate of 1603, since we know he died in 1659. His will forgives Mary for any outstanding debts owed him for "physicke" for her family, and mentions his "beloved nephew Mr. John Dryden."

43. For accurate information on Ford and Hill, see Longden, *Northamptonshire and Rutland Clergy*. On their sermons delivered before the Long Parliament, see John F. Wilson, *Pulpit in Parliament: Puritanism during the English Civil Wars 1640–1648* (Princeton: Princeton University Press, 1969).

44. When Nathaniel Whiting, who succeeded Ford at Aldwincle in 1653, was deprived for nonconformity in 1662, he was also deprived of his post as a schoolmaster. Ward consequently speculates that "Henry Pickering had earlier served the same school" (p. 8). In fact, the available evidence confirms the existence of a school during Henry's tenure, but shows that he himself was not its master. On 19 May 1663, one Richard Thorpe made his will, settling land on the Aldwincle School "in thankfulness to God who at that towne did by means of my honest and first schoolmaster Mr. Smith move mee to take up a fix'd resolution to the ministry." See A. J. Shirren, "The Whitings of Etton and Aldwincle," *N&Q* 198 (1953), p. 197. Thorpe took his B.A. at Queens' College, Cambridge in 1624; he would thus have been a schoolboy in Aldwincle about 1615. Perhaps the mysterious "Mr. Smith" was related to Henry Pickering's wife Isabella Smith, Dryden's grandmother.

45. *The Trade of Truth Advanced* (1642), pp. 5–6.

46. [Clement Walker], *Anarchia Anglicana: Or The History of Independency* (1649), Part II, p. 153.

47. A danger noted by Dod and Cleaver: "let us beware of the company of Idolatrous persons, and reading their bookes. For as an honest and chaste Woman cannot bee long in the company of Adulterers, but she shal be stained with their impurity, and get some blot by their filthinesse: So it is impossible, that one should conuerse with Idolaters, and not receiue some taint of their superstition" (*Ten Commaundements*, p. 58).

48. *Truth and Love Happily Married in the Saints*, delivered 3 April 1648, published in *Six Sermons* (1649), pp. 29, 33.

49. "A Letter to the Seniors of Trinitie-Colledge in Cambridge," printed as front matter to *The Best and Worst of Paul*, preached in Trinity chapel on 27 February 1648, in *Six Sermons*, sig. A5r.

50. See Russell Fraser, *The War Against Poetry* (Princeton: Princeton University Press, 1970), especially pp. 67–68, 142–43. On political opposition to the stage, see Margot Heineman, *Puritanism and Theatre: Thomas Middleton and Opposition Drama under the Early Stuarts* (Cambridge: Cambridge University Press, 1980), ch. 2. For a full philosophical and psychological discussion, running from Plato to Sartre, see Jonas Barish, *The Antitheatrical Prejudice* (Berkeley: University of California Press, 1981).

51. See "The Rhetorical Renaissance," ch. 4 of *Unsuspected Eloquence*.

52. *The Works of Archbishop Laud*, ed. W. Scott and J. Bliss, 7 vols. (Oxford: John Henry Parker, 1847–60), VI, 57.

53. *Institutes of the Christian Religion*, Book I, ch. xi, par. 2, following the text edited by John T. McNeill and translated by Ford Lewis Battles, vols. XX–XXI of *The Library of Christian Classics* (Philadelphia: Westminister Press, 1960), XX, 101.

54. *The Correspondence of John Cosin, D.D.*, 2 vols. (Durham: Surtees Society, 1869), I, 163–67; the source is Rawlinson MSS A, 441, f. 28. In his translation of Virgil (1697), Dryden describes how Apollo

> Ordains the Dances, and renews the Sports:
> Where painted *Scythians*, mix'd with *Cretan* Bands,
> Before the joyful Altars join their Hands.

[IV, 207–09]

55. *Institutes*, I, xi, 7; in *The Library of Christian Classics*, XX, 107.

56. This picture, reproduced in "Canons Ashby Revisited—II," "shows three sides of a room with Tudor windows . . . with a wall clock and a bird cage to the left and right of the central window. Above the clock an angel is holding up one end of a drapery from whose centre appears a sunburst with the Sacred Monogram in Hebrew letters, which hovers over a cloth-covered table with the arms of Dryden and Cope standing on it. To the left and right of it an uncertain number of figures stretch out—apparently all men on the left and women on the right." As Cornforth suggests, "it appears to show the male and female members of the Dryden family at prayer"(p. 21).

57. See Roy Sherwood, *The Court of Oliver Cromwell* (Croom Helm, 1977), pp. 25, 27.

58. Millar, *The Age of Charles I*, pp. 29–30. The portraits of Dryden's cousin Christopher Pickering as a child, inscribed "Cornelius Janssens pinxit," and of Elizabeth, wife of Sir Gilbert Pickering (III), appear facing pp. 50 and 284 of A. M. W. Stirling, *Life's Little Day* (Thomas Butterworth, 1924), along with some wildly inaccurate family legends about Drydens and Pickerings. Stirling identifies Christopher as the son of Gilbert (III), but none of Gilbert's sons bore that name; for Christopher's actual ancestry, see the Pickering genealogy, Appendix A. I have been unable to discover who now owns the paintings.

59. Roger Ascham, *The Scholemaster* (1570), Book I, p. 26v.

60. Francis Peck, ed., *Desiderata Curiosa* (1771), I, 48.

61. According to Bridges, Gilbert (I) "possessed employments of trust and credit under the Lord Treasurer *Burleigh*, by which he considerably improved his fortune" (II, 383). But Gilbert (I) died in 1556, and Cecil did not become Lord Treasurer until 1572; John (I), Gilbert (II), and John (II), however, all served the Cecils; see Belgion, p. 42. The John Pickering who was in Italy in 1581 was arrested as a spy in Rome and later stayed with Arthur Throckmorton in Florence; see A. L. Rowse, *Ralegh and the Throckmortons* (Macmillan, 1962), pp. 92–93. Rowse describes him as the John Pickering who matriculated at St. John's College, Cambridge, in 1572, "the son of Sir William Pickering of Titchmarsh." But J. and J. A. Venn, in *Alumni Cantabrigiensis*, which Rowse cites, describe that same matriculant as "perhaps 4th son of John [(I)] of Titchmarsh." Since that John Pickering's sister Elizabeth married Throckmorton's brother Robert, he is a likely candidate.

62. See the passage on his reading Sylvester, cited below, n. 77.

63. See D. J. Gordon, "Poet and Architect: The Intellectual Setting of the Quarrel between Ben Jonson and Inigo Jones," *JWCI* 12 (1949):152–78.

64. *Ben Jonson*, ed. C. H. Herford and Percy and Evelyn Simpson, 11 vols. (Oxford: Oxford University Press, 1925–52), I, 146. All subsequent citations of Jonson's works follow this edition.

65. *Mercurius Britannicus* 101 (13–20 October 1645), p. 903.

66. Stephen Orgel and Roy Strong, *Inigo Jones: The Theatre of the Stuart Court* (Berkeley: University of California Press, 1973), p. 51.

67. In *The Poems of Thomas Carew*, ed. Rhodes Dunlap (Oxford: Clarendon, 1949), p. 170.

68. In *Cultural Materialism: The Struggle for a Science of Culture* (New York: Random House, 1979), Marvin Harris argues that such early states as Egypt "invested . . . heavily in the construction of monumental statues, altars, temples, pyramids, and other religious structures . . . to convince the peasants that the elites were benevolently trying to control the supernatural and natural forces upon which human health and well-being were said to be dependent. It is always cheaper to produce obedience through mystification than through police-military coercion" (p. 102). Charles I, by contrast, was eventually forced to resort to military coercion because the art that embodied his mystification, unlike the pyramids, was hidden from most of his subjects.

69. "Late Mannerist artists were pre-occupied by the effects of the hours, seasons, climate, sunrise, moonlight, fire or candlelight, sunshine and shade." Orgel and Strong, *Inigo Jones*, p. 47.

70. See James W. McKinnon, "The Meaning of the Patristic Polemic against Musical Instruments," *Current Musicology* 1 (1965):69–82; Augustine, *Confessions*, X, 33; Erasmus, Commentary on 1 Corinthians 14.19, which includes a harsh condemnation of the English fondness for "gurgling" polyphony; and Calvin, *Theological Treatises*, trs. J. K. S. Reid, vol. XXIII of *The Library of Christian Classics* (Philadelphia: Westminster Press, 1954), pp. 53–54, which complains that "the pope . . . has reduced the psalms . . . to a murmuring among themselves without understanding."

71. Ironically, a secular version of this idea was gaining adherents in the most sophisticated court circles during Charles's reign: the Lawes brothers were beginning to set poetic texts in a recitative style derived from the *seconda practica* of Monteverdi. The aesthetic theory behind this new style, which in England appealed only to a coterie, was that a simple texture and a flexible form would allow the composer to

express the text and make the words more audible than they had been in such contrapuntal forms as the madrigal. Neither Peter Smart nor William Lawes would have acknowledged that they had anything in common; a metrical Psalm text by Sternhold or Hopkins, sung to a foursquare chorale melody, hardly resembles a lyric monody by Carew, set to an extended recitative by Lawes—except that both styles assume the primacy of the text. See Murray Lefkowitz, *William Lawes* (Routledge & Kegan Paul, 1960), ch. vii.

72. "Epistle Dedicatory" to *The Strength of the Saints*, preached 19 April 1648, in *Six Sermons*, sig. A2v. Note that the odd word "taking," meaning impressive or seductive, also occurs in the passage from Jonson's *Hymenai*, quoted above, p. 24.

73. See W. S. Reid, "The Battle Hymns of the Lord," *Sixteenth Century Essays and Studies* 2 (1971):36–54.

74. See Belgion, *Titchmarsh*, p. 49; cf. Hill, *The Season for Self-Reflection* (1644), p. 36: "Away with *Ceremonies, Altars*, and *Crucifixes*." On iconoclasm generally, see John Phillips, *The Reformation of Images: Destruction of Art in England, 1553–1660* (Berkeley: University of California Press, 1973).

75. A fuller sample will illustrate Ford's predictably Puritan opinions on this issue: "Certainly (as one saies) *grace in the heart* is the best tune to any Psalme; and without this, the best tun'd voyce is but howling and bawling in the eares of the Almighty. . . . Nor do we exclude all modulation or tuning of the voyce according to the Lawes of Musick, provided there be no affectation of it so as our hearts be wholly taken up with it. Provided also there be no empty tautologies or chaunting over and over the same things, tossing of the word of God from one to the other, like that Cathedral Musick intended onely to please the eare." *Singing of Psalms the Duty Of Christians* (1653), p. 67.

76. There were editions of 1605, 1621, 1633, and 1641. My citations follow the text of The *Complete Works of Joshua Sylvester*, ed. Alexander B. Grosart, 2 vols. (Edinburgh: Edinburgh University Press, 1880). Grosart's copy-text is the folio of 1641.

77. Apparently quoting from memory, Dryden alters three words in the passage, arguably bringing about some minor metrical improvement. Sylvester's text reads:

> But, when the Winter's keener breath began
> To crystallize the *Baltike* Ocean,
> To glaze the Lakes, and bridle-up the Flouds,
> And perriwig with wool the bald-pate Woods.

[II, iv, 184–87]

78. David Daiches, *A Critical History of English Literature*, 2 vols. (Secker and Warburg, 1960), I, 356.

79. Peter Skrine, *The Baroque: Literature and Culture in Seventeenth-Century Europe* (Methuen, 1978), p. 14. On the different definitions and chronology of the baroque in various arts, see *Unsuspected Eloquence*, p. 207*n*.

80. I, i, 23; 49–52; 169; 179; 183.

81. In *Dryden's Poetic Kingdoms* (Routledge & Kegan Paul, 1965), p. 26, Alan Roper suggests that Dryden's reference to Venus is meant as an anagram for *naevus*. But if Dryden meant to be using the Latin word, he formed its plural incorrectly; the proper form would be "naevi," a word used by Thomas Hill in *The good old way, God's Way, to soule-refreshing rest* (1644): "*Jerome*, though learned to admiration, doted on the merit of *virginity*. It were easie to shew the *naevi*, the blemishes of others"(p. 13). The meter of Dryden's line suggests that he meant to treat "naeve" as a monosyllabic coinage, as Whiting had done. This is the strongest of many verbal resemblances between *Albino and Bellama* and Dryden's early verse. Some later poetry may still show Whiting's influence; consider this parallel:

> The soule mounts heaven, when earths aged womb
> The Skeleton (her issue) does entombe.

[Whiting, p. 70]

> When Sinews o're the Skeletons are spread,
> . . . .
> The Sacred Poets first shall hear the Sound,
>   And formost from the Tomb, shall bound:
> . . . .
> Like mounting Larkes.

["Killigrew" ode, ll. 186, 188–89, 192]

82. In "The Whitings," p. 145, Shirren attributes the prefatory verses to Col. John Pickering, brother of Sir Gilbert (III), a possible candidate chronologically, but a man who was such a fierce Independent in religion that he seems unlikely to have approved of Whiting's poetry. Since Dr. John Pickering's epitaph in Aldwincle church (see above, n. 42) is equally wretched verse, it seems simplest to conclude that we are dealing with only one bad poet signing himself "I. Pickering."

83. In his "Character of Polybius" (1693), written for the translation of Henry Sheeres, Dryden claimed that he had read Polybius in English at ten; presumably he used the translation of Edward Grimeston (1634).

CHAPTER 2. WESTMINSTER SCHOOL

1. There is no hard evidence establishing the date of Dryden's arrival at Westminster. Malone first guessed 1642 (p. 13); later, without giving a reason, he pushed his estimate forward to 1644, in the notes in his own copy of the biography in the Bodleian, which he had corrected toward a second edition (see Osborn, p. 137). Perhaps Malone had calculated that since Dryden went up to Cambridge in 1650 and there were seven forms, 1643 was the earliest possible date; the revised phrase—"about the end of 1644, at which time he was above 13 years old"—sounds as if someone had provided him with fuller information. More recent scholars have followed Ward's guess, 1646; David Wykes, in *A Preface to Dryden* (Longmans, 1977), pp. 11–12, not only accepts this date, but speculates that Dryden was still at home at the time of the battle of Naseby (June 1645), and recounts a skirmish of 1644 at Canons Ashby as if it might have directly affected Dryden, who was either well across the county at Titchmarsh or (as I believe) already at school.

2. Tuckney, ΘΑΝΑΤΟΚΤΑΣΙΑ, p. 52.

3. *God's Eternal Preparations for his Dying Saints*, sig. B1r, in *Six Sermons*. This information invalidates Wykes's claim that "we may reasonably suppose that life in Titchmarsh was fairly peaceful in those years" (p. 12).

4. On the "challenge" system and the method of selection for King's Scholars, see John Sargeaunt, *Annals of Westminster School* (Methuen, 1898), pp. 24–28; on Dryden's coming first in his major election, p. 90. On Locke's Westminster career, see Maurice Cranston, *John Locke: A Biography* (New York: Macmillan, 1957), pp. 18–28. In an anonymous letter in the Bodleian (Rawlinson D. 327/328b.), dated 10 October 1656, an Oxford undergraduate reports to his father on his efforts to have a younger brother admitted to Westminster; he describes an interview with Busby, who "tould me by the order of ye schole none could be admitted as King's schollers but such as were trained up in ye schole one twelve moneth."

5. See Rushworth, *Historical Collections*, II, 803–17.

6. See G. F. Russell Barker, *Memoir of Richard Busby* (Lawrence and Bullen, 1895), p. 3.

7. See Bagshawe's ill-tempered pamphlet, *A True and Perfect Narrative of the Differences between Mr. Busby and Mr. Bagshawe* (1659). Bagshawe continued in his argumentative ways: he sought the abolition of hoods and caps at Oxford, was ejected from a vicarage for nonconformity, and was finally imprisoned for attacking the government; see Barker, pp. 75–76. His lawyer father, who had been associated with the Drydens and Pickerings in the 1620s and 1630s, surprised everyone by becoming a Royalist in 1644. See Mary Frear Keeler, *The Long Parliament* (Philadelphia: American Philosophical Society, 1954), pp. 94–95.

8. "The Virtuous Education of Youth," in *Sermons Preached on Several Occasions*, 2 vols. (Bohn, 1865), I, 426, 431. This sermon was not actually preached; the death of Charles II canceled the service.

9. *Of Gifts and Offices in the Public Worship of God* (Dublin, 1679), cancel page after separate title for *The Gift of Prayer*.

10. From the letter cited above, n. 4.

11. For the letters to Busby, see *Letters*, ed. Ward, pp. 17–20. Hooke designed the "*Musaeum*" now called the Busby Library and the parish church at Willen, where Busby had land. For references to both projects, see *The Diary of Robert Hooke*, ed. Henry W. Robinson and Walter Adams (Taylor and Francis, 1935), pp. 403–09. For photographs of the church, see A. E. Richardson, "An Unknown Wren Church in Buckinghamshire," *English Life* 7 (1926):6–10, a useful article despite its mistaken attribution of the church. In *Diaries and Letters of Philip Henry*, ed. M. H. Lee (Kegan Paul, 1882), there are interesting reminiscences of life in the school during the 1640s. Henry remembers hearing Thomas Hill preach (p. 9); he also claims to have told Busby that the principles he learned from his Laudian Master made him a nonconformist (pp. 211–12).

12. "To M[r]. L. Maidwell on his new method," ll. 7–14. This poem, probably composed in 1684, was first printed by John Barnard and Paul Hammond in "Dryden and a poem for Lewis Maidwell," *TLS* (25 May 1984), p. 586. Alan Roper, in a letter to the *TLS* (22 June 1984), p. 696, has questioned the authenticity of the poem, but see the reply by Barnard and Hammond, also in the *TLS* (29 June 1984), p. 727, and G. J. Clingham, "Dryden's New Poem," *EIC* 35 (1985):281–83. To the evidence in favor of Dryden's authorship of this admittedly mediocre poem, I might add two small rhetorical parallels. "What I am / From his examples and his precepts came" (ll. 9–10) makes the same gesture as Dryden's praise of Henry Dickinson in *Religio Laici*: "Yet what they are, ev'n these crude thoughts were bred / By reading that, which better thou hast read" (ll. 226–27). The double negative of line 15, "Nor thou the least," is like those used in Dryden's poem "To Dr. Charleton," ll. 22, 27, 33, 43.

13. *The Lover*, no. 27 (17 April 1714).

14. See Ward, pp. 10–11; Wykes, p. 12. Sargeaunt, who prints the Laud document (pp. 279–82), identifies it as describing the school "in the time of Wilson or Osbaldeston"; the P.R.O. dates the document itself as "probably 1630." My own suspicion is that the document describes the routine under Wilson, and that Laud copied it as part of his campaign against Osbaldeston.

15. Complete transcriptions of all three documents appear in Appendix B.

16. The Gregory notebooks (Trinity College Library, Add. MSS c. 227–30) have been briefly described by Paul Hammond in "Dryden and Trinity," *RES* n.s. 36 (1985), pp. 36–37. The "title" pages, which bear the signatures of Gregory, as well as those of Adam and David Whitford, who went from Westminster to Christ Church, Oxford, feature the word "Westmonast." The phrases and vocabulary from Ovid's *Metamorphoses* are extremely simple, as we might expect from the Frowick document, which lists the *Metamorphoses* as a text for the third form. The last of the notebooks ends with several pages from a printed text of Book XV of the *Metamorphoses*. The book at Harvard has been described by Osborn, pp. 245–46. Paul Hammond, the current expert on early Dryden signatures, regards those in this book as "probably the poet's." The marginalia and Latin interlineations are in at least four hands; the book was evidently passed down from schoolboy to schoolboy.

17. "Dedication" to Dryden's *Dramatick Works*, sig. A7r.

18. All citations of *The Rehearsal* follow the edition of D. E. L. Crane (Durham: University of Durham Publications, 1976); see I, i, 80–140 (pp. 5–7).

19. His headnote to his translation of the third satire of Persius (1692) records his memory of having translated the same poem "when I was a *Kings-Scholar* at *Westminster* School, for a *Thursday* Nights *Exercise*" (*Works*, IV, 293); the Frowick summary lists "a verse exercise" as a normal assignment "against fryday morning." The old Dryden believed that his schoolboy translations were still in the hands of Busby, but no such exercises are now in the Westminster archives.

20. Among loose papers kept in the front of Busby's remarkable "Catalogue of all my best Bookes," a handwritten list of over two thousand titles, is an additional list of books written on the back of what appears to be just such an exercise, a rendering of Horace, Book 2, Ode 16 into epic hexameters.

21. "Dedication," sig. A9v.

22. Especially in the essay on translation prefixed to *Ovid's Epistles* (1680), with its famous division of types of translation: "metaphrase," "paraphrase," and "imitation," quoted below, ch. 10, p. 330.

23. See Oliver Farrar Emerson, "John Dryden and a British Academy," *PBA* 10 (1921):45–58.

24. See Sargeaunt, *Annals of Westminster School*, p. 69. According to Foster Watson, *The English Grammar Schools to 1660: Their Curriculum and Practice* (Cambridge: Cambridge University Press, 1908), sixteenth-century schools were different: "No English composition was taught and . . . no well-instructed man . . . was particularly concerned to show that he could use his mother-tongue" (p. 139). For an account of some early attempts to instruct students in English, see Kenneth Charlton, *Education in Renaissance England* (Routledge and Kegan Paul, 1965), pp. 119–23. For an intriguing argument about the literary consequences of educations like Dryden's, see John R. Mulder, *The Temple of the Mind: Education and Literary Taste in Seventeenth-Century England* (New York: Pegasus, 1969).

25. Cartwright's *Poems* were not printed until 1651, though many of them circulated in manuscript and some appeared in collections before then. *The Royal Slave*, however, was separately published in 1636, and Busby's library includes a copy of this first edition; I strongly suspect Dryden had read at least the play while still at school.

26. Sargeaunt, *Annals*, p. 69.

27. See Sargeaunt, pp. 13, 101; Locke's account book is in the Bodleian Library, MSS. Locke F. 11.

28. According to S. R. Gardiner, *History of the Great Civil War*, 3 vols. (New York: AMS Press, 1965), II, 192–93: "On April 20 [1645] Colonel Pickering, a zealous Independent, arrived at Abingdon to command one of the newly-formed regiments. The men had no objection to take military orders from him, but when their new Colonel proceeded to preach a sermon to them they broke into mutiny." For further information on Colonel John Pickering, see Mark A. Kishlansky, *The Rise of the New Model Army* (Cambridge: Cambridge University Press, 1979), pp. 42, 63, 71–72; apparently this incident led to an edict against lay preaching.

29. See Hyder E. Rollins, "A Contribution to the History of the English Commonwealth Drama," *SP* 18 (1921):267–333, especially pp. 277–96.

30. For an excellent account, see P. W. Thomas, *Sir John Berkenhead (1617–1679): A Royalist Career in Politics and Polemics* (Oxford: Clarendon, 1969).

31. Five of the authors of additional elegies added to the volume in a "Postscript" are identified as Westminster scholars, and literary historians have traditionally assumed that Hastings was their schoolmate. Ward doubts this explanation, and suggests that *Lachrymae Musarum* was "merely a 'project'" (p. 335). Michael Gearin-Tosh, in his recent account of Marvell's contribution to the same volume, "Marvell's 'Upon the death of the Lord Hastings'," *Essays and Studies* 34 (1981), p. 110, notes that "a broadside in the Thomason collection [669 f. 13(6)] states that Lord Hastings was actually present at the siege of Colchester." If true, this unconfirmed report would also cast doubt upon the traditional assumption that Hastings was at Westminster with Dryden. Still, there is external and internal evidence to support that assumption: although school records do not begin until after the Restoration, the *Record of Old Westminsters* of G. F. Russell Barker (Chiswick Press, 1928), shows a number of later scholars from the Hastings family; the absence of any explicit reference to military prowess in any poem in the volume and the emphasis on Hastings's intellectual and linguistic attainments in many poems, not least Dryden's, would be most easily explained if Hastings did attend Westminster.

There has also been some confusion about Richard Busby's relationship to the memorial volume, described on its title page as "Collected and set forth by R. B." Hugh Macdonald, in *John Dryden: A Bibliography of Early Editions and Drydeniana* (Oxford: Oxford University Press, 1939), identifies "R. B." as Richard Brome, one of the contributing poets, but notes in his addenda (p. 323) that Busby is another possibility, a conjecture supported, without further evidence, by Arthur W. Hoffman, *John Dryden's Imagery* (Gainesville: University of Florida Press, 1962), p. 3. Brome's own poem, however, which appears last of the original group of elegies, strongly suggests that he was the editor, for example in these lines:

> Sad *World*, I tell thee *Who* he was, not *What*;
> *That* would o'er-swell the Volume, Read thou that
> In the precedent Elegies, here writ,
> By Masters of best Eloquence and Wit.

[p. 75]

A later note makes much better sense as an apology by Brome than as one by Busby: "Of all those the Noble, Reverend and worthy Writers nominated in the Catalogue without their due Additions of Title, or listed contrary to their Degree or Quality, a Pardon is most humbly desired for the Collector, whose Crime of Ignorance grew out of want of timely Instruction" (p. 77). Busby, who is hardly likely to have wanted instruction about the titles of the contributors, may have looked over the poems by his own students; Brome was surely the "Collector."

32. For samples of critical responses by Dr. Johnson, Sir Walter Scott, and Mark Van Doren, see Hoffman, pp. 4–5; on the versification, see *Works*, I, 173–74.

33. As Paul Hammond has pointed out to me, there may be some emphasis on "*Noble*" as well as "*Youth*" here; in a time when many noblemen did not bother to educate their sons, the example of Hastings, well-schooled but dead, might not have been an encouraging one.

34. The Frowick document lists Aratus as a text; since Busby's library contains no edition earlier than that edited by John Fell in 1672, this particular study probably postdated Dryden's schooldays. Busby's edition of Tycho Brahe is dated 1572, however, and there was certainly some serious study of astronomy in the 1640s. One of Dryden's sources for these lines is Claudian, perhaps by way of Wilkins's *Mathematical Magick*; see Richard N. Ringler, "Two Dryden Notes," *ELN* 1 (1964):256–61. Busby continued to purchase

the most advanced works in the sciences; at his death, his library contained books by Gassendi, Descartes, Barrow, and many other mathematical and medical authorities.

35. See, for example, Irvin Ehrenpreis, "Continuity and Coruscation: Dryden's Poetic Instincts," in *John Dryden II* (Los Angeles: Clark Library, 1978), pp. 3–26.

36. As Gearin-Tosh has pointed out (pp. 108–09), *Eikon Basilike* was circulated in "tiny, concealable copies." The concealment in the case of *Lachrymae Musarum* was the use of Hastings as a surrogate for Charles. Yet the fullest modern account of Dryden's poem, in Ruth Wallerstein, *Studies in Seventeenth-Century Poetic* (Madison: University of Wisconsin Press, 1950), pp. 115–42, while quite valuable for placing the poem in the context of other funeral elegies of its period, misses the Royalist implications of the central lines. Accounts correctly stressing those implications include James D. Garrison, *Dryden and the Tradition of Panegyric* (Berkeley: University of California Press, 1975), pp. 147–49, and George McFadden, *Dryden the Public Writer*, pp. 23–24.

There was ample precedent for the clouding of the sun as a negative version of the standard royal image, for example in these lines from Thomas Carew's poem "Upon the Kings sicknesse," probably written during the final illness of James I in 1625:

> That ruddie morning beame of Majestie [Charles],
> Which should the Suns ecclipsed light supply,
> Is overcast with mists and in the liew
> Of cherefull rayes, sends us downe drops of dew.
> [ll. 29–32; *Poems*, ed. Dunlap, pp. 35–36]

This poem first appeared in 1640, and was probably known by Dryden, but I am not arguing so much for a specific influence as for the pervasiveness of this kind of language in the poetry of the first half of the century. Jonson's masques repeatedly invoke such images, and at the climax of Cartwright's *The Royal Slave*, Cratander (the character played by Busby) is saved from execution by an eclipse: "The glorious Sun hath veyl'd his face in clouds." *The Poems and Plays of William Cartwright*, ed. G. Blakemore Evans (Madison: University of Wisconsin Press, 1951), p. 250.

37. When James II was born in 1633, for example, Osbaldeston had his students write poems to celebrate the event; four lines from Cowley's contribution will suffice as an example of the resulting flood of conceits:

> Him safely kill (If any such you meete)
> Whose heart's less fil'd with bonfire then the streete.
> Let every oake sweat rich falernian wine,
> And grow incorporate with his wife the vine.
> [B. L. Royal MSS. 12 A. XII, f. 2b., printed by Sargeaunt, p. 282]

38. *The Medall*, ll. 263–66; for the other metaphors, see ll. 8–10, 34–35.

39. D. Brunton and D. H. Pennington, *Members of the Long Parliament* (Allen and Unwin, 1954), pp. 15–16, 188.

40. Orgel and Strong, *Inigo Jones*, p. 59.

41. *Complete Poems and Major Prose*, ed. Merritt Y. Hughes (Indianapolis: Bobbs-Merrill, 1957), p. 784. All subsequent citations of Milton from this edition.

42. "To *P. Rupert*," ll. 7–8; *The Poems of John Cleveland*, ed. Brian Morris and Eleanor Worthington (Oxford: Clarendon, 1967), p. 33. This poem first appeared in 1647, and Dryden might thus have read it before composing his poem on Hastings, but again I am not arguing so much for a specific influence as for a general one.

43. For Dryden's literary heirs in the next century, who were also fond of Hamlet, "elegiac action is seldom undertaken at any great distance from satiric or mock-heroic manoeuvres, for to regret the past is by implication to condemn the present." Paul Fussell, *The Rhetorical World of Augustan Humanism* (Oxford: Clarendon, 1965), p. 283.

44. *Verses by the University of Oxford on the Death of . . . Sir Bevill Grenville* (1643; repr. 1684), pp. 10-11.

45. P. W. Thomas, *Sir John Berkenhead*, p. 97.

46. "Upon the Death of the Lord Hastings," ll. 25–26, in *Andrew Marvell: The Complete Poems*, ed.

Elizabeth Story Donno (Harmondsworth: Penguin, 1972), p. 48. On Marvell's politics in this period, see chs. 1–2 of Annabel M. Patterson, *Marvell and the Civic Crown* (Princeton: Princeton University Press, 1978), and John Dixon Hunt, *Andrew Marvell: His Life and Writings* (Ithaca: Cornell University Press, 1978), especially pp. 67–69.

CHAPTER 3. TRINITY COLLEGE

1. Of fifteen chests of arms, Cromwell seized ten. See James Bass Mullinger, *The University of Cambridge from the Election of Buckingham to . . . the Decline of the Platonist Movement* (Cambridge: Cambridge University Press, 1911), pp. 231–37.

2. *The good old way . . . to soule-refreshing rest*, p. 45. Puritans had no patent on this idea. The funeral sermon preached for Hill's Laudian predecessor, Thomas Comber, ejected in 1644, praised his attention to poor scholars: "the flower of Learning, which grew in poverties Garden, was most watered by his encouragement." Robert Boreman, *The Triumph of Faith over Death* (1654), p. 10.

3. On the visitations and ejections at Cambridge, see G. B. Tatham, *The Puritans in Power* (Cambridge: Cambridge University Press, 1913), pp. 93–151; Hugh Kearney, *Scholars and Gentlemen: Universities and Society in Pre-Industrial Britain, 1500–1700* (Faber and Faber, 1970), pp. 102–03; and especially J. W. Twigg, "The Parliamentary Visitations of the University of Cambridge, 1644–45," *EHR* 98 (1983):513–28.

4. Mullinger, pp. 264–66; for a complete text of the Parliamentary declaration in answer to the petition, see *Cambridge University Transactions during the Puritan Controversies*, ed. James Heywood and Thomas Wright, 2 vols. (Bohn, 1854), II, 458–60.

5. Mullinger, p. 311.

6. J. H. Monk, *Memoir of Dr James Duport* (Cambridge: Cambridge University Press, 1826), p. 11.

7. A[braham] H[ill], "The Life of Dr. Barrow," in *The Works of Isaac Barrow*, 8 vols. (Oxford: Oxford University Press, 1830), I, x. For a complete Latin text of the oration that gave offense, see *The Theological Works of Isaac Barrow*, ed. Alexander Napier, 9 vols. (Cambridge: Cambridge University Press, 1859), IX, 48–78.

8. The simple division of the Long Parliament and later groups into "Presbyterians" and "Independents" has of course been superseded by the more careful research of Jack Hexter and later historians. For recent developments in the ongoing scholarship, see David Underdown, *Pride's Purge: Politics in the Puritan Revolution* (Oxford: Clarendon, 1971).

9. Most notably in *A Testimony from the World against Divinity Degrees in the University* (1654), best known for its remarkable appendix, *The Right Reformation of Learning*, in which Dell advocates having universities "in every great town or city in the nation," a reform not attempted until the nineteenth and twentieth centuries. On Dell's career and opinions, see Eric C. Walker, *William Dell: Master Puritan* (Cambridge: Heffer, 1970).

10. See Mullinger, pp. 245–46; 367–68.

11. *Rump: Or An Exact Collection of the Choycest Poems and Songs Relating to the Late Times* (1662), Part I, p. 15.

12. "Ad Academicos in Comitiis," in *Theological works*, IX, 35–47.

13. According to Trinity statutes, the library was not normally open to undergraduates. Either those rules were ignored, or Dryden had some kind of special permission. His memory of this particular experience apparently failed him, since the specific footnote to which he refers in the *Life of Plutarch* does not occur in the Trinity copy; see Hammond, "Dryden and Trinity," p. 52. But neither of these problems invalidates Dryden's praise of his old college. As will be apparent, I am greatly indebted to Hammond's essay, and to his personal assistance during my own visit to Trinity.

14. As Hammond has shown, payments to Hill and Rowles for their expenses are recorded in the Trinity Muniments ("Dryden and Trinity," p. 36n). On the preference for Christ Church, see Sargeaunt, *Annals of Westminster School*, p. 31.

15. Hammond has reproduced Dryden's signature as plate III in "Dryden's Employment by Cromwell's Government," *TCBS* 8 (1981):130–36. Dryden officially matriculated on 6 July 1650 and was admitted as a scholar of Trinity on 2 October 1650. His stipend was paid to him from the first quarter of 1651 until the third quarter of 1655, despite the fact that a scholar had been elected in his place on 23 April 1655. Residence in Cambridge colleges during this period, however, was often erratic, with some students

remaining in residence throughout vacations and others remaining away during term-time. See W. J. Harrison, *Life in Clare Hall Cambridge, 1658–1713* (Cambridge: Heffer, 1958), pp. 68–74.

16. Duport's *Rules* exist in two similar manuscripts: Cambridge University Library MS Add. 6986 and Trinity College Library MS O.10A.33; they have been printed (incompletely and inaccurately) by G. M. Trevelyan in "Undergraduate Life under the Protectorate," *Cambridge Review* 64 (22 May 1943):328–30. Holdsworth's *Directions for a Student* exist in two quite different manuscripts: Emmanuel College MS 48 (E) and Bodleian MS Rawlinson D 200 (B); they have been printed by Harris Fletcher in *The Intellectual Development of John Milton*, 2 vols. (Urbana: University of Illinois Press, 1961), II, Appendix II. For the debate about the date and authorship of this treatise, see Mark H. Curtis, *Oxford and Cambridge in Transition, 1558–1642* (Oxford: Clarendon, 1959), pp. 289–90; Hugh Kearney, *Scholars and Gentlemen*, p. 103; and especially John A. Trentman, "The Authorship of *Directions for a Student in the Universities*," *TCBS* 7 (1978):170–83.

17. Monk, *Memoir*, p. 11.

18. See Hammond, "Dryden and Trinity," p. 38. Dryden's degree of academic distinction has been underestimated in the past because the *Ordo Senioritatis* prints the names of graduates of King's College before those of Trinity; their precedence, as Hammond correctly indicates, "is historical not intellectual" (p. 37*n*).

19. Creighton's reminiscences, set down when he was eighty-eight years old, are in the Trinity College Muniments, "Great Volume of Miscellany Papers III," no. 42. As Hammond explains (p. 41), Creighton did not come up to Trinity from Westminster until 1655, so his memory may have been based on Westminster as much as Trinity; on the other hand, this piece of evidence might suggest that Dryden *did* return to college after his father's death in June of 1654. Certainly Ward's flat statement that he "left Cambridge with his B.A. degree in March 1653/4" (p. 16) is more definite than the evidence will bear.

20. On Hill and the mathematics chair, see above, ch. 5, p. 129. On science at Trinity, see Phillip Harth, *Contexts of Dryden's Thought* (Chicago: University of Chicago Press, 1968), pp. 15–19, and Hammond's careful reexamination of the evidence ("Dryden and Trinity," pp. 53–56). For the scientific metaphors in Templer's works, see Hammond, pp. 46–47.

21. See, for example, Ward, pp. 14–16, a speculative account called into question by both Harth and Hammond.

22. Though Dryden proudly signs his verses to Hoddesdon, "J. Dryden of Trin. C.," the book received its imprimatur on 7 June 1650, when Dryden had been at Trinity less than a month. The year date for the letter to Honor is now illegible; Malone thought it was 1655, but the California editors argue for 1653 (I, 185–86). If Malone was correct, the letter is further evidence that Dryden returned to college after his father's death.

23. ΘΑΝΑΤΟΚΤΑΣΙΑ, p. 43 marg.

24. The title page describes him as "John Templer, B.D., late Fellow of *Trinity* Colledge in *Cambridge*, and now Minister of the Gospel at *Balsham* in *Cambridge-shire*."

25. See, for example, *An Olive Branch of Peace and Accommodation*, preached in 1645 (1648).

26. On the disputed authorship of the *Notes and Observations*, from which this passage comes, see below, ch. 8, n. 19.

27. *The Reason of Episcopal Inspection* (Cambridge, 1676), p. 16.

28. H. Hasselwood, *Dr. Hill's Funeral-Sermon* (1654); Robert Boreman, *The Triumph of Faith over Death* (1654), including a Latin epitaph by Duport praising Comber as "Atlas *Religionis* Orthodoxae."

29. Trinity College Muniments, "Conclusions and Admonitions 1607–73," p. 221.

30. The elegies for Metcalfe by the Royalists James Duport and Nicholas Hookes (in *Musae Subsecivae* and *Miscellanea Poetica*) describe him as innocuous, and he does not seem to have been particularly partisan; he left five pounds to Thomas Hill. As Hammond has pointed out (p. 39*n*), the document alleging that Akehurst was Vice-Master (B.L. Add. MS 5846, p. 226) is a University list; according to College records, Akehurst seems to have acted as Vice-Master only between October 1653 and October 1654; he was never formally elected to the post. Hookes, in the Latin dedication to *Miscellanea Poetica* (1653) calls him "*Vice-Praesuli*."

31. Joseph Hunter, *The Rise of the Old Dissent Exemplified in the Life of Oliver Heywood* (Longmans, 1842), p. 445.

32. For a letter defending Akehurst from this accusation, see Charles Henry Cooper, *Annals of Cambridge*, 6 vols. (Cambridge: Warwick, 1842–1908), III, 457–58.

33. "Conclusions and Admonitions," p. 237.

34. See above, n. 19.

35. See Hammond, p. 39.

36. One of Elizabeth Creed's inscriptions in Titchmarsh church celebrates the bravery of this servant, who recovered from his wounds only to be drowned in the Nene while attempting to learn to swim.

37. "Upon a late fall'n Poet," stanza [15], following the text given by James Osborn in "Dryden, Shadwell, and 'a late fall'n Poet'," in *John Dryden II*, p. 35.

38. *A Panegyrick to My Lord Protector* (1655), p. 7.

39. "To the Author upon his Amanda," in *Amanda, a Sacrifice To an Unknowne Goddesse*, bound and paginated continuously with *Miscellanea Poetica* (1653), p. xix.

40. The original has a picture of three tiny crowns, a transparent rebus.

41. In the case of Lovelace's *Lucasta*, this censorship had been severe enough to provoke an attack from Marvell; see Patterson, *Marvell and the Civic Crown*, pp. 17–19.

42. These include an appreciative Latin poem to Busby, whom Hookes calls "father" in all the languages he knows; a poem on the death of Alexander Rokeby, who came up from Westminster with Dryden, and like Hookes had Akehurst for his tutor; elegies for Metcalfe, the old Vice-Master, and Thomas Comber, the ejected Master, but not for Hill; and poems written for public occasions at Trinity, including a Guy Fawkes party.

43. After a brief stay at Oxford, Montagu migrated to Sidney Sussex College, Cambridge. His Puritan grandfather opposed some of the actions of the Long Parliament and died a prisoner; his father was a Royalist. His father's first cousin, another Edward Montagu, was the second Earl of Manchester, Presbyterian patron of Thomas Hill and Chancellor of Cambridge University, who supervised the wholesale ejections of 1645 but was himself ejected for refusing the Engagement in November 1651. For Hill's elaborate thanks to Manchester for his long patronage, see the "Epistle Dedicatory" to *The Best and Worst of Paul*, in *Six Sermons*. Another cousin, also an Edward Montagu, was Pepys's employer, later the Earl of Sandwich, whose sister Elizabeth was the wife of Gilbert Pickering (III); see above, ch. 1, p. 12 and n. 30. A simplified Montagu genealogy, based on information in the *DNB* and in Esther S. Cope, *The Life of a Public Man: Edward, First Baron Montagu of Boughton, 1562–1644* (Philadelphia: American Philosophical Society, 1981), pp. 217–18, may help sort out the confusion caused by the large number of men named Edward Montagu:

Sir Edward Montagu ⨯ Elizabeth Harrington
(1532–1602)   (d. 1618)

Edward, first Baron Montagu of Boughton (1562–1644) [allied with Sir Erasmus Dryden in petition for Northamptonshire Puritan clergy, 1604; died a prisoner of Parliament]

James, Bishop of Winchester (1568–1618)

Sir Henry, first Earl of Manchester (1566–1642)

Sir Sidney (1571–1644) [expelled from Parliament as a Royalist, 1642] = Paulina Pepys

Edward, second Baron Montagu of Boughton (1616–1684)

Edward, second Earl of Manchester (1602–1671) [patron of Thomas Hill; Parliamentary General; Chancellor of Cambridge University]

Edward (1625–1672) [fought for Parliament at Marston Moor; on the Protector's Privy Council; defected to Charles II with the fleet, 1660; made Earl of Sandwich]

Elizabeth = Gilbert Pickering (III) Dryden's first cousin; see Pickering genealogy (Appendix A)

Edward (1635–1665) [Westminster and Cambridge; dedicatee of *Amanda*; said to have influenced his cousin to embrace the cause of Charles II; killed at Bergen]

44. See Thomas, *Berkenhead*, pp. 133–38.

45. *Gondibert*, ed. David F. Gladish (Oxford: Clarendon, 1971), II, vii, 12.

46. Dryden retained his respect for Davenant even when he came to disagree with his theories: in the essay "Of Heroick Plays" (1672), he notes that he is "dissenting much, from his [opinion], whose memory I love and honour. But I will do it with the same respect of him, as if he were now alive, and overlooking my Paper while I write" (XI, 10–11).

47. For details, see chs. 5 and 6 of Alfred Harbage, *Sir William Davenant, Poet Venturer, 1606–1668* (Oxford University Press, 1935).

48. *Lives of the Poets*, I, 417.

CHAPTER 4. FROM PROTECTORATE TO RESTORATION

1. See G. E. Aylmer, *The State's Servants: The Civil Service of the English Republic, 1649–1660* (Routledge & Kegan Paul, 1973), pp. 214–16. The document appointing Erasmus is in the P.R.O. (S.P. 25/75/p. 67), dated 25 January 1654. Ward (p. 16) considers it "by no means certain" that the Erasmus Dryden appointed was the poet's father, but the presence on the Privy Council of his kinsmen Pickering and Montagu argues strongly for that identification, as does the fact that the Christian name Erasmus, which came into the Dryden family from Erasmus Cope, brother of Elizabeth Cope Dryden, was most likely to be found in the branch of the family shown in Appendix A. The only other men bearing that name at this time were Dryden's brother (b. 1638), his cousin the son of Sir John (b. 1643), and his cousin the son of William (b. 1649); all were much too young to hold a government post.

2. As Malone notes with some horror (p. 22), Erasmus Dryden's will (P.R.O., P.C.C. 28 Aylett) is remarkable for having no religious preamble. The evidence for his service as Justice of the Peace is in one of the Vestry-books of Aldwincle St. Peter's, dated 1653.

3. Malone (pp. 440–41) calculates the annual rent at £60; Ward (p. 336), working from different evidence, calculates it at £82 10s.

4. This document, in the P.R.O. (S.P. 18/180/95), is accurately reproduced and transcribed by Paul Hammond in "Dryden's Employment by Cromwell's Government," p. 130 and Plate I; Hammond's comparison of the signature with other early Dryden signatures disposes of Ward's doubts about the identity of the John Dryden who accepted the fifty pounds. On Thurloe's career, see Aylmer, pp. 258–60, and D. L. Hobman, *Cromwell's Master Spy: A Study of John Thurloe* (Chapman and Hall, 1961).

5. These documents, also transcribed by Hammond, are S.P. 18/182/f. 229 and B.L. MS Lansdowne 95 f. 41ᵛ. The first of them gives numbers next to the names—9.6 in the cases of Milton, Marvell, and Sterry; 9.0 in the case of Dryden. Pierre Legouis, Marvell's biographer, took these numbers to be yards of mourning requested and allowed; his resulting assertion that Dryden was not given mourning has been frequently repeated, but seems highly unlikely, given Dryden's close connection to the Lord Chamberlain, who was issuing the mourning. J. M. French, Milton's biographer, took the numbers to be figures in shillings and pence, a reading accepted by Hammond, but 9 shillings in 1658 would have bought enough mourning for several men, and many of the other documents having to do with the issuing of mourning specify "yards." One of those documents, S.P. 18/182/f. 295, provides a clue that may unravel the mystery. Its entries include:

	yards		yᵈˢ
To Garter principall King of armes	9.	for his men	9
. . . .			
To Lancaster Herald	9.	for his men	6

If we apply this pattern to the document on the secretaries, Milton, Marvell, and Sterry were issued 9 yards of mourning for themselves and 6 yards for a servant; Dryden, who had no servant, got 9 yards for himself.

6. The date of Pickering's appointment as Lord Chamberlain is uncertain. He may have been named to the post as early as 10 August 1655, though he does not seem to have performed official functions before 1657 or 1658. See Sherwood, *The Court of Oliver Cromwell*, pp. 64–67.

7. *A Second Narrative of the Late Parliament* (1658), p. 13.

8. Bodleian Library MS Rawlinson A 62 f. 49.

9. *The English Parnassus* of Josua [*sic*] Poole (1657) has a fourteen-page preface signed "J.D." The B.L. copy has a manuscript signature that has been thought to be Dryden's, but Paul Hammond, in

"Dryden's Library," *N&Q* 229 (1984):344–45, has conclusively demonstrated that the signature is not the poet's; the preface, which makes statements about the English language and classical tongues in direct contradiction to everything Dryden would later write on these subjects, seems unlikely to be his. Each of the three volumes of the English translation of *Astrea* (1657–58), has a brief epistle "*To the Reader*" signed "J.D." These seem much more likely candidates to be by Dryden; Osborn prints them (pp. 193–96). The preface to Dr. Charleton's treatise on *The Immortality of the Human Soul*, which dates from early 1657, is perhaps the most likely of all to be Dryden's. On its dating, see below, ch. 5, n. 27.

10. *The Wild Gallant*, I, ii, 99–100; 108–09; *The Reasons of Mr. Bayes's Changing his Religion* (1688), Part I, p. 114.

11. Susannah Dryden Pickering, sister of Dryden's father and mother of Sir Gilbert Pickering, was almost certainly the "Lady Pickering" who is recorded as having paid her annual rates of 12 shillings on a house in what is now Pickering Place, adjacent to Berry's the wine merchants, in 1652. See H. Warner Allen, *Number Three Saint James's Street: A History of Berry's the Wine Merchants* (Chatto and Windus, 1950), pp. 23–24, 34–35. This house was across the street from Berkshire House, where Dryden's future wife Elizabeth Howard resided when in London, an intriguing circumstance. Lady Pickering did not pay her rates in 1653 and was marked down as "gon," but she evidently remained in London, since she described herself in her will (P.R.O., P.C.C. 78 May), made on 26 June 1658, as "of Whitehall in the Citty of Westminster," a plausible address for the mother of the Lord Chamberlain. She was then "in good and perfect health"; the Titchmarsh Parish Register records her burial on 16 April 1661.

12. Shadwell, *The Medal of John Bayes*, sig. A1r. Osborn makes a strong argument for the authenticity of this story (p. 178); Ward (p. 183) disagrees.

13. David Masson, *The Life of John Milton*, 6 vols. (Macmillan, 1877), V, 376–98.

14. MS note by Jonathan Richardson, Sr., p. cxix of his annotated copy of *Remarks on Milton's Paradise Lost by Jonathan Richardson Father and Son* (1734), now in the London Library. Printed by V. de Sola Pinto in *Sir Charles Sedley, 1639–1701* (Constable, 1927), p. 94n. For some doubts about the authenticity of this anecdote, see Malone, pp. 112–15, and Morris Freedman, "Dryden's Reported Reaction to *Paradise Lost*," *N&Q* 203 (1958):14–16.

15. On Marvell's ancestors, see John Dixon Hunt, *Andrew Marvell*, p. 19.

16. If the "Mr. Sterry" who also marched with Dryden was Nathaniel, the younger brother of Cromwell's chaplain Peter Sterry, he was more nearly Dryden's contemporary, and might have brought him into contact with his older brother, who was a most unusual Puritan in his devotion to music and art, and in the extravagant metaphors of his sermons and prayers; for samples, see Sherwood, pp. 108–10. The *DNB* speculates that it was Peter Sterry who was appointed Latin Secretary on 3 September 1657, at the same time as Marvell, but since Peter is recorded as marching in the funeral with the other chaplains, the Mr. Sterry who walked with Dryden was probably Nathaniel. William Riley Parker, in *Milton: A Biography*, 2 vols. (Oxford: Clarendon, 1968), II, 1062, identifies Nathaniel as the secretary. I should think the "Mr. Sterry" whom Pepys met on 8 March 1660, who had just returned from a mission as secretary to the Ambassador to Sweden, was also Nathaniel (*Diary*, I, 83).

17. William Dugdale to John Langley, printed by Percy Scholes in *The Puritans and Music in England and New England* (Oxford University Press, 1934), p. 144.

18. H. J. Oliver, *Sir Robert Howard (1626–1698): A Critical Biography* (Durham: Duke University Press, 1963), p. 9.

19. Sherwood, p. 67.

20. For the proclamation, see Sherwood, p. 95. My thanks to my student Grant Gilezan, who pointed out this parallel to me.

21. These examples are offered by Christopher Hill in *God's Englishman: Oliver Cromwell and the English Revolution* (New York: Dial, 1970), pp. 150–51.

22. See Rollins, "A Contribution to the History of the English Commonwealth Drama," cited above, ch. 2, n. 29.

23. See John Freehafer, "The Formation of the London Patent Companies in 1660," *TN* 19 (1965):6–30, and Gunnar Sorelius, "The Early History of the Restoration Theatre: Some Problems Reconsidered," *TN* 33 (1979):52–61.

24. On Lawes and his publications, see Willa McClung Evans, *Henry Lawes: Musician and Friend of Poets* (New York: Modern Language Association, 1941); for a partial list of Playford's publications, see Percy

Scholes, *The Puritans and Music,* pp. 130–31. On Katharine Philips, see Evans, pp. 202–07; on secular music in Puritan households, see Scholes, ch. XII.

25. P.R.O., S.P. 18/153/123, f. 254, printed in full in Scholes, pp. 282–83.

26. On 19 December 1666, Pepys met Hingston and learned from him that "many of the Musique are ready to starve, they being five years behindhand for their wages" (*Diary,* VII, 414).

27. Evans, p. 227. Pepys provides an example of the King's taste in music on 20 November 1660: "after supper, a play—where the King did put a great affront upon Singleton's Musique [John Singleton was a member of the royal orchestra], he bidding them stop and bade the French Musique play—which my Lord [Edward Montagu] says doth much out-do all ours"(*Diary,* I, 297–98).

28. Denis Stevens, *Thomas Tomkins, 1572–1656* (New York: Dover, 1967), pp. 58, 154–55.

29. The petition, by Peter Lely, George Geldorp, and Balthazar Gerbier, is in B.L. MS Stowe 184, f. 283, printed in H. C. Collins Baker, *Lely and Kneller* (Philip Allan, 1922), p. 4.

30. "To Sir Godfrey Kneller," especially ll. 145–65.

31. Garrison, *Dryden and the Tradition of Panegyric,* pp. 149–55.

32. In a helpful note on these lines, the California editors cite a parallel passage from John Bate, probably based on Nicholas Hilliard's *Treatise concerning the Art of Limning* (*Works,* I, 199–200). Vertue, who first told the story of Cromwell's request, thought Lely was the painter, but Oliver Millar, in *Sir Peter Lely* (National Portrait Gallery, 1978), p. 47, points out that Lely's Cromwell is evidently a copy of Cooper's; the two painters were neighbors.

33. Marvell's poem was to have appeared in the same volume with those by Dryden and Sprat, *Three Poems upon the Death of his late Highnesse Oliver Lord Protector* (1659), but at the last moment Herringman, who had entered that title in the Stationers' Register, decided against publishing the book, which was then issued by one William Wilson; at the same time, Marvell's poem was deleted and a poem by Waller, already published separately, was substituted. Marvell's poem was also deleted from the posthumous Folio edition of his works (1681); the B.L. has a copy in which about half the poem remains. See *Works,* I, 187, and Donno's edition of Marvell, p. 276.

34. B.L. M.S. Lansdowne 1045. This manuscript, the *only* holograph of any Dryden poem, was discovered by Anna Maria Crinò. See *TLS* (Sept. 22, 1966), p. 879. Vinton A. Dearing printed "A New Critical Text" based on that manuscript in *PBSA* 69 (1975):502–26; Paul Hammond has discussed "The Autograph Manuscript of Dryden's *Heroique Stanza's* and Its Implications for Editors" in *PBSA* 76 (1982):457–70. The accidentals of the manuscript are quite different from those of any version printed in the poet's lifetime.

35. See above, ch. 1, n. 67.

36. See above, ch. 1, n. 37.

37. The source for the story of how the corpse "purged and wrought through all" its coverings and coffins is the account of George Bate, one of Cromwell's physicians, *Elenchus Motuum Nuperorum in Anglia* (1685), Part II, p. 236.

38. "A Poem upon the Death of His Late Highness the Lord Protector," ll. 299–304; in Donno, p. 156.

39. Steven N. Zwicker's discussion of this poem in *Politics and Language in Dryden's Poetry* (Princeton: Princeton University Press, 1984), ch. 3, which came to my attention after I had written my own account, develops the idea of Dryden's uncertainty in some detail.

40. H. J. Oliver, in *Sir Robert Howard,* p. 12, prints a letter from Howard to the Royalist John Mordaunt written in June 1659; Howard's imprisonment, which Oliver tentatively dates to 1658, doubtless had to do with Royalist activities. There are no records but Howard's own remark that he wrote some of his poems in prison.

41. Robert Gould's poem *The Laureat* (1687) is typical:

> Had *Dick* still kept the Regal Diadem,
> Thou had'st been Poet Laureat to him,
> And, long e're now, in Lofty Verse proclaim'd
> His high Extraction among princes fam'd;
>
> . . . .
>
> Nay, had our *Charles* by Heavens severe Decree,
> Been found, and Murther'd in the Royal Tree,

> Even thou hadst prais'd the Fact; his Father Slain,
> Thou call'st but gently breathing of a Vein.

[p. 1]

42. *The militant Church triumphant*, sig. A3r. Hill used the same image again in *The good old way . . . to soule–refreshing rest* (1644), p. 52: "The Lord . . . hath *opened* many *veines*."

43. Osborn prints the most likely candidates, pp. 193–99.

44. On the Post Fines document, now in the Clark Library, see *Works*, I, 270. For Henley's letter, see B.L. MS Sloane 813, f. 71, and Oliver, p. 65 and note.

45. See above, p. 82 and n. 18.

46. For details, see Oliver, pp. 5–8.

47. See Michael Foss, *The Age of Patronage: The Arts in Society 1660–1750* (Hamish Hamilton, 1971), p. 33.

48. Although Oliver doubts the certainty of this identification, Osborn and the California editors support it; there is no other obvious candidate, as Dryden wrote the only prefatory poem.

49. See J. W. Johnson, "Dryden's Epistle to Robert Howard," *Ball State Teachers College Forum* 2 (1961):20–24, and David M. Vieth, "Irony in Dryden's Verses to Sir Robert Howard," *EIC* 22 (1972):239–43.

50. Did Dryden enjoy alluding to a poem early enough that its Puritan author could still praise the stage at the very moment when the theatre was returning to legitimacy?

51. Notably by the California editors, who regard this passage as "deplorably reminiscent of Milton's praise of Shakespeare" (I, 208).

52. As Oliver notes (p. 18), Howard's song, "Ah, mighty Love, what power unknown" appears, in a setting by Henry Lawes, in *Select Ayres and Dialogues* (1669); since Lawes died in 1661, he had probably set the song before the printing of Howard's book.

53. See *Unsuspected Eloquence*, pp. 217–28, 241–44.

54. On 5 March 1660, for example, Pepys visited a "Mr. Pinkny . . . [who] showed me how he hath alway kept the Lion and Unicorne in the back of his chimney bright, in expectation of the King's coming again" (*Diary*, I, 77).

55. Oliver, p. 16.

56. Among many precedents, we may cite two. Sylvester, in *The Divine Weeks*, writes of

> A confus'd heap, a *Chaos* most deform
> . . . .
> Where th' Elements lay jumbled all together,
> Where hot and cold were jarring each with either.

[I, i, 258, 261–62]

Cartwright, in his poem on the marriage of Princess Mary to William of Orange (1641), is even closer to Dryden's later formulations:

> Thus while Cold things with Hott did jarre,
> And Dry with Moyst made Mutuall Warre,
>   Love from the Masse did leap;
>   And what was but an Heap
> Rude and Ungatherd, swift as thought, was hurld
> Into the Beauty of an Ordred World.

[*Poems and Plays*, ed. Evans, p. 540]

57. McFadden argues that "this couplet wittily suggests Sir Robert's remarkable skill as a fortune hunter" (p. 66), but Howard did not make his disastrous second marriage until 10 August 1665, and he could not have been wooing the lady in question in 1660, since she was widowed only months before he married her. See Oliver, pp. 124–25.

58. French (and Spanish and Italian) influences on Dryden have not been sufficiently studied; surely some student of comparative literature should produce a book on this topic, perhaps using Emile Audra's study of French influences on Pope as a model. One chapter of such a book should concern Malherbe. Here it will be sufficient to cite just two stanzas whose imagery closely resembles that of *Astraea Redux*; many

others are equally suggestive. In his ode "Au Roy Henry le Grand, sur l'heureux Succez du Voyage du Sedan," Malherbe begins:

> Enfin apres les tempestes
> Nous voicy rendus au port;
> Enfin nous voyons nos testes
> Hors de l'injure du sort.
> Nous n'avons rien qui menace
> De troubler nostre bonace;
> Et ces matieres de pleurs,
> Massacres, feux, et rapines,
> De leurs funestes espines
> Ne gasteront plus nos fleurs.

The second stanza of the ode "Sur l'attenta commis en la personne de Henry le Grand, le 19 de Décembre 1605," sounds a similar note:

> O que nos fortunes prosperes
> Ont un change bien apparent!
> O que du siecle de nos peres
> Le Nostre s'est faict different!
> La France devant ces orages,
> Pleine de meurs et de courages
> Qu'on ne pouvoit assez loüer,
> S'est faict aujourd'huy si tragique,
> Qu'elle produit ce que l'Affrique
> Auroit vergongne d'avoüer.

[*Les Poésies de M. de Malherbe*, ed. Jacques Lavaud, 2 vols. (Paris: Droz, 1936), I, 33, 43]

59. See ll. 1030–31. The beginning of the same sentence, "Henceforth a Series of new time began" (l. 1028), echoes the beginning of the peroration in *Astraea Redux*, "And now times whiter Series is begun" (l. 292).

60. "Ode Upon His Majesties Restoration and Return," in Cowley's *Complete Works in Verse and Prose*, ed. A. B. Grosart, 2 vols. (1881; repr. Hildesheim: Georg Olms, 1969), I, 161.

61. *To the King, upon his Majesties Happy Return* (1660), p. 4.

62. From a letter by Erasmus to the orator of the University of Louvain, as translated by Francis Morgan Nichols in *The Epistles of Erasmus*, 3 vols. (Longmans, 1901), I, 366; see Garrison's analysis, pp. 20–22.

63. *The Journals of the House of Commons* (1803), VIII, 67, record the reading of "the humble petition of *Gilbert Pickering* Baronet" on 9 June, followed by the following resolution: "That Sir *Gilbert Pickering* Baronet shall be excepted out of the Act of general Pardon and Oblivion, for and in respect only of such Pains, Penalties and Forfeitures (not extending to Life) as shall be thought fit to be inflicted on him by another Act, intended to be hereafter passed for that Purpose." Stern as this edict sounds, its effect was to save Pickering from the death penalty. Identical resolutions were passed for many other offenders, including Milton. Pickering's "humble petition" doubtless argued that he had never approved of the execution of the King, and there is one piece of evidence to support that view. On 3 December 1656, Walter Gostelowe wrote a letter to Cromwell urging him to accept Charles II, in which the following passage occurs: "Sir Gilbert Pickering was pleased in his garden pryvately (when he disowned to me at all his consent to the kinge's death) to give me to understand, with how much unwillignes you weare at last drawne to head that violent and rashe zealous part of the army at Tryploheath." *Thurloe State Papers*, 7 vols. (1742), V, 674. Pickering was pardoned thanks to a motion introduced in the House of Lords on 11 August 1660 by his brother-in-law Edward Montagu, now Earl of Sandwich. On 13 August, he was included in an act preventing former associates of Cromwell, including John Ireton, from holding public office. See *Journals*, VIII, 117–18; *H.M.C.*, V, 55.

64. 16 May 1660; *Diary*, I, 142.

65. I quote Dryden's translation, I, 213–20; the original passage is as follows:

> Ac, veluti magno in populo cum saepe coorta est
> seditio, saevitque animis ignobile vulgus;
> jamque faces et saxa volant; furor arma ministrat:
> tum, pietate gravem ac meritis si forte virum quem
> conspexere, silent, arrectisque auribus adstant.

[I, 148–52]

As Herbert Tucker has pointed out to me, Virgil was himself reversing a simile in the *Iliad* (II, 144–49), in which a speech by Agamemnon shakes an assembly of Greeks as the winds raise waves on the sea.

66. Dryden's translation, VI, 1168–77; here is the Latin:

> Excudent alii spirantia mollius aera,
> credo equidem: vivos ducent de marmore vultus;
> orabunt causas melius; coelique meatus
> describunt radio, et surgentia sidera dicent:
> tu regere imperio populos, Romane, memento:
> hae tibi erunt artes; pacisque imponere morem,
> parcere subjectis, et debellare superbos.

[VI, 847–53]

67. As McFadden argues, "It is evident . . . that the best is being made of a rather disappointing case" (p. 30). My account of the Coronation poem owes much to McFadden's.

68. For arguments defending and attacking Dryden's claim, see Charles H. Hinnant, "The Background of the Early Version of Dryden's *The Duke of Guise*," *ELN* 6 (1968):102–06, and Lawrence L. Bachorik, "*The Duke of Guise* and Dryden's *Vindication*: A New Consideration," *ELN* 11 (1973):208–12. Neither mentions the lines in *Astraea Redux*.

69. See above, ch. 1, p. 12 and n. 30.

70. For information on Henry Pickering, see P. D. Mundy, "The Pickerings of Aldwincle All Saints, Northamptonshire," *N&Q* 197 (1952):490–92. *The Complete Baronetage*, III, 151, errs in calling him the "only son" of the Rev. Henry, and in giving his father's death date (1637) as 1657. The evidence for Mary Dryden's removal to Whaddon is the marriage license of her daughter Lucy, which records the consent of "the widow Dryden, of Whaddon, co. Cambridge." See P. D. Mundy, "The Brothers and Sisters of John Dryden, the Poet," *N&Q* 193 (1948), p. 121. On Susannah Dryden Pickering, see above, n. 11.

71. Pierre de Cardonnel, *Complementum Fortunatarum Insularum* (1662).

72. See Malone, p. 432*n*. Modern art historians I have consulted agree that the style of cravat is post-Restoration.

CHAPTER 5. "DRAYDON THE POET"

1. On the Coronation cavalcade and ceremony, see *A Circumstantial Account of the Preparations for the Coronation of His Majesty King Charles the Second . . . From an Original Manuscript by Sir Edward Walker* (Baker, 1820), especially pp. 70–75. Less reliable accounts are Pepys, *Diary*, II, 81–88 (22–23 April 1661), and *The Diary of John Evelyn*, ed. E. S. de Beer, 6 vols. (Oxford: Clarendon, 1955), III, 276–84; all subsequent citations of Evelyn follow this edition. I am inferring Sir Robert's place in the parade; the others are specifically recorded. On the Duke of Buckingham's suit, see Winifred, Lady Burghclere, *George Villiers, Second Duke of Buckingham* (John Murray, 1903), p. 122.

2. See *H.M.C.*, IV, 309.

3. For biographical facts on the first Earl of Berkshire, see G[eorge] E[dward] C[okayne], *The Complete Peerage* (St. Catherine's Press, 1912) and F. E. Paget, *Some Records of the Ashtead Estate and of its Howard Possessors* (Lichfield: Lomas, 1873); both these accounts allege that Berkshire opposed the plan of withdrawing the Prince and did not accompany him to the Continent, but a letter cited in *H.M.C.*, VI, 102b, reports that the Prince has set to sea "with Lord Berkshire," and Elizabeth's petition (V, 131b) clearly states that her husband is in Holland. See also *H.M.C.*, IV, 308–09; V, 48, 149; VI, 129a, 132b, 134a; X, iv, 65; XIV, ii, 72.

4. On the Catholicism of the Earl of Exeter, see *The Complete Peerage*. For an excellent general account of Catholic practice at this time, see John Bossy, *The English Catholic Community, 1570–1850*

(Darton, Longman, & Todd, 1975), especially chs. 6 and 7. On 21 April 1637, Viscount Conway informed a correspondent that "Lord Andover hath lately married Mrs. Dorothy Savage, contrary to his father's liking and protestations to him, but *si violandum est jus* it was to be done for her." *H.M.C.* XIV, ii, 42. In *The Jacobean Age* (Longmans, 1938) p. 129*n*, David Mathew states that Andover became a Catholic upon his marriage, evidently inferring that the first Earl's disapproval of his son's marriage had to do with the recusancy of the Savage family, but the letter gives no basis for such an inference. Dorothy was the aunt of the third Earl Rivers, with whom the Earl of Berkshire was paired in the Coronation procession; we may infer that the in-laws were eventually reconciled. On Philip, Cardinal Howard, see G. Anstruther, "Cardinal Howard and the English Court," *AFP* 28 (1958):315–61.

    5. Parker, *Milton*, I, 36.

    6. William Harris, *Some Memoirs of the Life and Character of the Reverend and Learned Thomas Manton* (1725), p. 35. By calling Berkshire "a Jansenist Papist," Harris presumably meant to indicate that the Earl was not sympathetic to the Jesuits; compare Sir Simonds D'Ewes's defense of his friend the Count of Egmont in 1641: "'Tis true hee is a papist, but a presbiterial one, and one that hates the Jesuits." *The Journal of Sir Simonds D'Ewes*, ed. Willson Havelock Coates (New Haven: Yale University Press, 1942), p. 174. Harris is not precise about dates, but the account of Manton in the *DNB* makes it possible to date this incident between 1666 and 1670, when Manton was arrested. These are plausible years for Berkshire to have had a house in St. Giles's adjoining Lord Wharton's. At the time of Elizabeth's wedding to Dryden, he was presumably still in Berkshire House, since the license records her as a resident of St. Martin's in the Fields, the parish in which Berkshire House was located. After the Fire, however, he seems to have rented it out: Clarendon lived there in late 1666, and the King bought the house in 1668 as a residence for the Duchess of Cleveland; see Pepys, *Diary*, VII, 375 (19 November 1666); IX, 190 (8 May 1668). Still, the absence of any other reference to the first Earl as a recusant and the long gap before the publication of Harris's work make it equally possible that the "Jansenist Papist" whose kindnesses were remembered was the second Earl, Charles, who succeeded his father in late 1669, and who was unquestionably a recusant. For other documents linking Manton and Wharton, see *H.M.C. Ormonde*, n.s. IV, 349; *C.S.P. Dom. 1663–64*, p. 484.

    7. *Critical Works of John Dennis*, ed. Edward Niles Hooker, 2 vols. (Baltimore: Johns Hopkins University Press, 1939–43), I, 289. Dennis says that the play was a failure and the visit for the purpose of consolation, but John Downes, the prompter of the Duke's Company, remembered Cowley's play as a hit, "perform'd a whole Week with a full audience." See his *Roscius Anglicanus* (1708), ed. Judith Milhous and Robert D. Hume (Society for Theatre Research, 1987), p. 25 (following the original pagination supplied in brackets). Subsequent citations of Downes follow this text, using original pagination.

    8. According to Gerald Brenan and E. P. Stratham, *The House of Howard*, 2 vols. (Hutchinson, 1907), Henry Howard "took a leading part in the various efforts which were being made, from 1661 onwards, to procure a relaxation of the severe penal laws against Catholics" (II, 577). He was the effective leader of the family well before 1677, since the brother from whom he inherited the title was an imbecile confined in Italy. Charles Howard was visited as early as 1655 by Evelyn, who remarked on his "rare plants" and his "Elaboratory" (*Diary*, III, 154). According to Thomas Birch, *The History of the Royal Society*, 4 vols. (1756–57), I, 163, "Mr. CHARLES HOWARD was proposed candidate by Col. TUKE [on 24 December 1662], and was presently chosen; his desire being to be rather admitted by scrutiny, than by the privilege of his birth." This "desire" presumably constituted a claim by Howard to be a serious scientist, which he was. On Tuke's leadership in the group of Catholics exerting "pressure for toleration," see John Miller, *Popery and Politics in England 1660–1688* (Cambridge: Cambridge University Press, 1973), pp. 96–97.

    9. The letter, dated [20]/30 June 1693, is in the Bodleian (Carte 209f74); Osborne prints the relevant passage, p. 290. John R. Sweney calls attention to the importance of Howard's testimony in "The Religion of Lady Elizabeth Howard Dryden," *N&Q* 217 (1972):365.

    10. According to J. Anthony Williams, *Catholic Recusancy in Wiltshire, 1660–1791* (Catholic Record Society monograph series, no. 1, 1968), pp. 238–39, there were seven "popish recusants" reported at Charlton in 1676, when Charles Howard was Earl of Berkshire. Malone, characteristically following up on the information recorded upon Charles Dryden's admission to Trinity College, Cambridge, in June 1683, when he was listed as "born at Charleton," reports his efforts to find a baptismal record (p. 46*n*). Later, in discussing Dryden's conversion, he speculates that Lady Elizabeth "had long been a papist" (p. 189). Paget, who examined the register himself, found no entry connected with the Howards before 1709 (p. 201), and a

recent search of the registers of Charlton and of Malmesbury Abbey by Mr. K. H. Rogers of the Wiltshire Record Office failed to discover any record of young Charles's christening. The Drydens might have waited to have the child christened until their return to London, but in that case one would expect to discover a record in one of the London parish registers, which are unusually complete; the register of St. Martin's in the Fields records the christening of the youngest Dryden son, Erasmus-Henry; see below, ch. 7, n. 17. Of course, the parish registers of the churches near Charlton may simply be defective; according to E. A. Wrigley and R. S. Schofield, *The Population History of England 1541–1871* (Cambridge: Harvard University Press, 1981), under-registration averages at least 4 percent. Still, I should think it at least possible that young Charles was baptized by a family priest. As John Bossy points out, "baptism was a field where practically no one was really prepared to question paternal authority; . . . missionaries conceded that, if a Catholic couple gave birth while living in the household and under the guardianship of a Protestant relative, it would be proper for the child, if so demanded, to be baptised in church" (*The English Catholic Community*, pp. 134–35). Applying the same principle, we may imagine the Protestant Dryden consenting to a Catholic christening of his son because he was staying in a Catholic household, and Elizabeth's Catholic brother may have been wielding "paternal authority" at Charlton when Charles Dryden was born on 27 August 1666; Pepys saw the first Earl, Elizabeth's father, in London on 25 July. Among reasons why Elizabeth might have chosen her eldest brother as his godfather was his recent loss of his own small son; on 10 August 1663, the Countess of Devonshire informed Lord Bruce that "My Lord and Lady Andover are in great affliction for the loss of their son" *H.M.C.* XI, vii, 170). That child was the third of Andover's sons to die young; Waller had provided an epitaph for one of the earlier ones.

11. B.L. Add. MS 19253, "Number 20," f. 25.

12. Maurice Cranston's biography of Locke contains a modern instance of this dubious inference: a note on Chesterfield (p. 378) reads "He was the patron of Dryden, whose wife had been his mistress." Dryden's dedicating a section of his Virgil to the aged Chesterfield in 1695 surely had nothing to do with Chesterfield's flirtation with Elizabeth in 1658!

13. "Number 12," f. 12.

14. The poem is probably by Samuel Pordage. The author of *Satyr to his Muse* (1682), possibly Shadwell, amplifies the same dubious charge, making Dryden say:

> Against my Will I Marry'd a rank W——,
> After two Children and a Third Miscarriage,
> By Brawny Brothers hector'd into Marriage.

[p. 4]

15. *Diary* IX, 24 (14 Jan 1668); Pepys's editors note that there is no evidence to confirm or deny the rumor, but Pepys seems unlikely to have called an earl a colonel. See the entry for Moll Davis by Edward A. Langhans, Philip H. Highfill, and Kalman P. Burnim in their *Biographical Dictionary of Actors . . . 1660–1800*, (Carbondale: Southern Illinois University Press, 1973-). The authors allege that Charles Howard, second Earl of Berkshire is meant, but he was never a colonel. Thomas, the second son, who became third Earl of Berkshire in 1679, was a colonel of cavalry on the Royalist side in the Civil War; since he had the same name as his father, he may have been the father of the actress. Sir Robert was also a colonel, but Pepys always calls him "Sir Robert." Philip, who was a Colonel in the Guards, is also a plausible candidate. But since the duties of the Gentlemen of the Bedchamber included providing companions for the King's bed, the old Earl might conceivably have been responsible for procuring his illegitimate granddaughter. For an account of those duties, see John Harold Wilson, *A Rake and his Times* (New York: Farrar, Straus, and Young, 1954), pp. 56–57.

16. See the Cope genealogy, Appendix A.

17. Anne Pickering's ancestry is traced in *Minutes of Evidence Given before the Committee of Privileges, to whom the Petition of Thomas Stonor . . . Claiming to be Senior Co-Heir to the Barony of Camoys* ([1839]), p. 256. For genealogies of the Howards, see the charts in Brenan and Stratham, *The House of Howard*. Paget provides more detailed information about Elizabeth's branch of the family, not all of it correct. On her brothers Robert, Philip, James, and Edward, see E. S. de Beer, "The Dramatist Sons of Thomas, Earl of Berkshire," *N&Q* 187 (1944):19, 214–15, and the identically titled article by H. S. Howard in the same issue, pp. 281–83.

18. For more information about the King's literary tastes, see Godfrey Davies, "Charles II in 1660," *HLQ* 19 (1956):245–75.

19. *Notes which Passed at Meetings of the Privy Council between Charles II, and the Earl of Clarendon, 1660–67*, ed. W. D. Macray (Nichols, 1896), p. 54; *C.S.P. Dom., 1661–62*, p. 288. McFadden (pp. 43–44) was the first to suggest the relevance of this note to Dryden's marriage, shrewdly pointing out that the assignment of a dowry to Elizabeth by Charles invalidates the speculation that the Earl awarded her a dowry in order to dispose of her, as if she were damaged goods. The notion that Clarendon was prompted by Dryden's poem is mine. For the confusing record of what happened to the money, see Appendix C.

20. Macray, p. 70. On the petitions, see Oliver, pp. 41–42.

21. Further evidence of the connection between Dryden and Clarendon comes in a letter of February 1663 from Dryden's patron the Earl of Orrery, which thanks Clarendon's son Henry Hyde, Lord Cornbury for his "favour" to Dryden and promises to have Dryden wait upon Cornbury. Bod. MS Clarendon 79 f. 84.

22. Quoted by Sir Charles Firth in his posthumous essay, "The Royalists under the Protectorate," *EHR* 52 (1937), p. 641; the entire essay is highly relevant to the plight of the Howards.

23. For an excellent account, with a facsimile of the letter, see Osborn, pp. 271–74. Ward claims that "a close examination of this letter suggests that it is in a hand quite dissimilar to the poet's" (p. 341). My own comparison with the early signatures reproduced by Hammond and the holograph of the Cromwell poem satisfies me that the letter is indeed a holograph.

24. For the sale, see *C.S.P. Dom., 1663–64*, p. 677. On Henry Pickering, see above, ch. 4, n. 70.

25. See P. H. Hardacre, "Clarendon, Sir Robert Howard, and Chancery Office-Holding at the Restoration," *HLQ* 38 (1975):207–14.

26. See Oliver, pp. 38–39; the Serjeant Painter was responsible for "all the King's works, palaces, barges, coaches, etc."

27. The treatises are *The Immortality of the Human Soul* and *The Natural History of Nutrition*; Osborn prints both, pp. 196–97, dating both 1659. The Yale copy of *Immortality*, from which he presumably worked, has had its printed date of 1657 altered to 1659 in old ink; Herringman actually entered that treatise on the Stationers' Register on 16 February 1657. So if Dryden did in fact write the preface, he probably knew Charleton while he was still in the employ of the Protectorate.

28. See Birch, *History of the Royal Society*, I, 25, 166, 272, etc.

29. Birch, I, 125, 127.

30. See above, p. 123 and n. 8. On the whole subject of who joined the Royal Society and why, see Michael Hunter, "The Social Basis and Changing Fortunes of an Early Scientific Institution: An Analysis of the Membership of the Royal Society, 1660–1685," *Notes and Records of the Royal Society* 31 (1976): 9–114; on the Howards, see pp. 15, 88, 103.

31. For a full account, see Emerson, "John Dryden and a British Academy," cited above, ch. 2, n. 23.

32. Hunter, in his "Analysis of the Membership," makes the suggestion that "the selection of such eminent figures as . . . Denham . . . and Dryden [both on the first list of six to be considered for expulsion] may have been intended to caution others" (p. 55).

33. For an engaging discussion of what Dryden may have meant by the word "Sceptical" at various times, see Harth, *Contexts of Dryden's Thought*, pp. 1–35.

34. Hunter, "Analysis of the Membership," p. 34.

35. *An Olive Branch of Peace*, sig. A3v, in *Six Sermons*. The "Epistle" is dated 29 May 1648.

36. For the elections of Denham, Waller, and Cowley, see Birch, I, 4, 12, 16, 17. For Denham's expulsion, see above, n. 32. Waller, who had been somewhat active during the 1660s, replied to an attempt to dun him for his dues in 1682 that "he, being perpetually in parliament, had never been able to attend the Society, either to serve them or receive any advantage thereby" (Birch, IV, 130). Cowley does not appear on the list of Fellows drawn up in 1663, since he had already retired to the country (see Emerson, p. 51).

37. For a summary of attacks on the Royal Society, see Michael Hunter, *Science and Society in Restoration England* (Cambridge: Cambridge University Press, 1981), pp. 136–38. On "Latitudinarianism and Science in Seventeenth-Century England," see the article thus titled by Barbara J. Shapiro, *Past and Present* 40 (1968):16–41.

38. Hunter, *Science and Society*, pp. 115–16.

39. See Hugh Ormsby-Lennon, "Radical Physicians and Conservative Poets in Restoration England: Dryden among the Doctors," *SECC* 7 (1978):389–410.

40. *Diary*, V, 37.

41. For an ingenious argument to this effect, see Emerson, p. 52.

42. 3d edition (1722), pp. 111–13.

43. Hunter, "Analysis of the Membership," p. 35.

44. Hunter, *Science and Society*, pp. 4–5, 111–12.

45. Quoted by Ormsby-Lennon, pp. 406–07, brackets his, italics mine. Ormsby-Lennon found this remarkable advertisement on the last page of Sir Kenelm Digby, *A Late Discourse*, 2nd edition (1660). Digby was among the Roman Catholic Fellows of the Royal Society.

46. *Leviathan*, ed. C. B. Macpherson (Harmondsworth: Penguin, 1968), Part I, ch. iv, p. 102. Subsequent citations follow this edition.

47. I owe this suggestion to Maynard Mack.

48. On the disputed authorship of the *Notes and Observations*, see below, ch. 8, n. 19. I have no doubt that these words are Dryden's.

49. He had already used a similar metaphor in a political context in *Astraea Redux*:

> We thought our Sires, not with their own content,
> Had ere we came to age our Portion spent.
>
> [ll. 27–28]

For some acute comments on these lines as the "first appearance of one of Dryden's obsessive images," see McFadden, pp. 38–39.

50. See above, ch. 2, n. 25 and n. 36. The adult Dryden certainly borrowed a scene from Cartwright: *Don Sebastian* I,i closely follows *The Royal Slave* I,ii.

51. See above, ch. 4, p. 116 and n. 68.

52. See Robert D. Hume, "Securing A Repertory: Plays on the London Stage 1660–5," in *Poetry and Drama 1570–1700: Essays in Honour of Harold F. Brooks*, ed. Antony Coleman and Antony Hammond (Methuen, 1981), pp. 158–72.

53. The Prologue requests an astrological reading for 5 February, and Evelyn reports seeing the play on that date. Pepys saw a performance at court on 23 February. Ward, following Eleanor Boswell, *The Restoration Court Stage* (Cambridge: Harvard University Press, 1932), p. 281, supposes that the premiere might have been at court (p. 33 and note), but a court premiere would have been an unusual occurrence. *The London Stage, 1660–1800*, 5 parts in 11 vols. (Carbondale: Southern Illinois University Press, 1960–68), Part 1, ed. William Van Lennep, Emmett L. Avery, and Arthur H. Scouten (1965), p. 62, places the premiere at Vere Street, which seems the only plausible venue, especially given the allusions in the prologue to the success of *The Adventures of Five Hours* at the rival theatre at Lincoln's Inn Fields. Unless otherwise noted, all dates of play premieres follow those given or suggested in *The London Stage*.

54. For detailed information about all these matters, see the articles by Freehafer and Sorelius cited above, ch. 4, n. 23, and Judith Milhous, *Thomas Betterton and the Management of Lincoln's Inn Fields, 1695–1708* (Carbondale: Southern Illinois University Press, 1979), ch. 1.

55. On 4 July 1661, shortly after the opening of Lincoln's Inn Fields, Pepys went to Vere Street, where he saw *Claracilla*, but found it "strange to see this house, that used to be so thronged, now empty since the opera begun" (*Diary* II, 132).

56. "You'll wonder much, if it should prove his [the author's] Lot, / To take all *England* with a *Spanish* plot," following the text edited by B. Van Thal (Holden, [1927]), p. xxxviii. On the King's proposing the Spanish source to Tuke, and on Tuke's composing the play on a visit to Henry Howard of Norfolk, cousin to Sir Robert and Lady Elizabeth, see the interesting introduction to this edition by Montague Summers.

57. See Oliver, p. 43, who concludes that this episode "almost certainly had something to do with the theater."

58. See Oliver, pp. 43–44; *The London Stage*, I, 50, 58.

59. "Shadwell had his first play mounted in 1668; Behn in 1670; Crown and Settle in 1671; Ravenscroft in 1672." Hume, "Securing a Repertory," p. 165.

60. Waller helped several courtiers translate Corneille's *Pompey* and wrote an alternative ending to *The Maid's Tragedy*, but no complete plays. *The London Stage* dates the premiere of *Pompey the Great* sometime during January 1664 (I, 73), and the alternative final act of *The Maid's Tragedy*, though not published until

1690, was probably also on stage sometime in 1664; see Robert D. Hume, "*The Maid's Tragedy* and Censorship in the Restoration Theatre," *PQ* 61 (1982):484–90. Denham contributed one act to a translation of Corneille's *Horace* by Katharine Philips, acted at court on 4 February 1668. Cowley revised *The Guardian*, a play he had written before the Restoration, as *Cutter of Coleman Street*, but wrote no new material for the theatre. Denham's *The Sophy* was also revived; see *The London Stage*, I, 44, 168.

61. In Van Thal's edition, p. xxxvii.

62. The theory that Dryden worked from a lost play by Brome was developed by Alfred Harbage in his important article, "Elizabethan-Restoration Palimpsest," *MLR* 35 (1940):287–319. In the same article, Harbage makes a strong argument that Howard's *The Great Favourite* or *The Duke of Lerma* (1668) is based on a play by John Ford; Howard's preface, like Dryden's, acknowledges the existence of an earlier source without naming it. These circumstances suggest one way of accounting for the curious assertion that Dryden "stole" *The Wild Gallant* from Howard, as alleged in "The Session of the Poets, to the Tune of Cock Lawrel":

> Sir Robert Howard, called for over and over,
>   At length sent in Teague with a packet of news,
> Wherein the sad knight, to his grief did discover
>   How Dryden had lately robbed him of his Muse.
> Each man in the court was pleased with the theft,
>   Which made the whole family swear and rant,
> Desiring, their Robin in the lurch being left,
>   The thief might be punished for his 'Wild Gallant.'

> [*POAS*, I, 330]

The poem was not printed until 1697 the MS followed by *POAS* is dated 1666. George Lord guessed that the actual date was 1668, but Gillian Fansler Brown, in *RECTR* 13, i (1974):19–26, has shown that the poem dates from 1664. All the evidence may be reconciled if we suppose that Hart delivered several of Mosely's old manuscripts to Howard, and that Dryden appropriated the one that became *The Wild Gallant*.

63. For a fine discussion of Jonsonian elements in this play, see Ned Bliss Allen, *The Sources of Dryden's Comedies* (Ann Arbor: University of Michigan Press, 1935), pp. 10–21. Allen's theory that Dryden wrote some of the play before coming to London in the late 1650s seems unlikely to me. The eminently practical Dryden would hardly have written a play when there was no legal theatre to produce it.

64. Compare Isabelle's similar description of Burr: "look you where he stands in ambush, like a Jesuite behind a Quaker, to see how his design will take" (III, i, 226–27).

65. J. A. Van Der Welle, in *Dryden and Holland* (Groningen: Wolters, 1962), p. 13, points to this line but silently assumes it was in the version of 1663.

66. See Kathleen Lynch, "D'Urfé's *L'Astrée* and the 'Proviso' Scenes in Dryden's Comedy," *PQ* 4 (1925):302–08.

67. *Diary*, IV, 8 (8 January 1663).

68. *Diary*, IV, 56 (23 February 1663).

69. See Judith Milhous and Robert D. Hume, "Dating Play Premières from Publication Data, 1660–1700," *HLB* 22 (1974), p. 380. This important article, often cited below as "Dating," suggests earlier dates than those in *The London Stage* for a number of plays. As Milhous and Hume are engaged in revising the first volume of *The London Stage* for a new edition, these findings will eventually be incorporated into its calendars.

70. See McFadden, p. 52. There is no real evidence, though Dryden's assertion that Castlemaine's "applause and favour did infuse / New life to my condemn'd and dying Muse" ("To Castlemaine," ll. 53–54) would fit neatly with the circumstance that the court performance took place after those at Vere Street.

71. "Our Poet" chooses English gentlemen and ladies as his judges,

> But if their Censures should condemn his Play,
> Far from Disputing, he does only pray
> He may *Leanders* Destiny obtain:
> Now spare him, drown him when he comes again.

> [ll. 21–24]

72. "I have already quitted the character of a modest Man, by presenting you this Poem as an acknowledgment, which stands in need of your protection; and which ought no more to be esteem'd a Present, then it is accounted bounty in the Poor, when they bestow a Child on some wealthy Friend, who can give it better Education. Offsprings of this Nature are like to be so numerous with me, that I must be forc'd to send some of them abroad; only this is like to be more fortunate then his Brothers, because I have landed him on a Hospitable shore" (IX, 25).

73. In *Complete Poems of George Etherege*, ed. James Thorpe (Princeton: Princeton University Press, 1963), p. 36.

74. *Diary*, VI, 191 (15 August 1665).

75. Pickering's complaints to Pepys begin as early as 17 August 1661 (*Diary*, II, 156); for Pepys's own worries, see 31 December 1662 (III, 302–03).

76. The poem, not published until it appeared in an unauthorized collection in 1674, must have achieved some circulation, since the author of the "Session of the Poets" (quoted above, n. 62) continues as follows:

> Dryden, who one would have thought had more wit,
> The censure of every man did disdain,
> Pleading some pitiful rhymes he had writ
> In praise of the Countess of Castlemaine.

Paul Hammond, in "Dryden's Revision of *To the Lady Castlemain*," *PBSA* 78 (1984): 81–90, discusses the various manuscripts in which Dryden's poem circulated.

77. McFadden (pp. 52–53) quotes an interesting passage from Castlemaine's enemy Clarendon, which suggests the accuracy of Dryden's praise; he also argues that Dryden could have avoided such "dynamic moral issues," and that his taking such a risk "shows his inveterate will to teach."

78. Not only is this line paradoxical, but its very diction suggests Donne's Holy Sonnet ("Batter my Heart"), especially these lines:

> Reason your viceroy in mee, mee should defend,
> But is captiv'd, . . .
>   . . . for I
> Except you'enthrall mee, never shall be free.

[*Complete Poetry*, ed. John T. Shawcross (New York: New York University Press, 1968), p. 344]

79. B.L. Add. MS 37206, f. 74, as printed in *The Dramatic Works of Roger Boyle*, ed. William Smith Clark, 2 vols. (Cambridge: Harvard University Press, 1937), I, 26.

80. F. 54, printed in Clark, I, 25.

81. As Robert D. Hume remarks, in *The Development of English Drama in the late Seventeenth Century* (Oxford: Clarendon, 1976), "*The Generall* is basically an inflated Caroline *précieuse* tragi-comedy" (p. 195).

82. Printed by Osborn, p. 194.

83. See *Works*, VIII, 289–92.

84. Sir John Harington's translation, reprinted in 1634 and well known by Dryden's contemporaries, rendered these opening lines as follows:

> Of Dames, of Knights, of armes, of loves delight,
> Of courtesies and high attempts I speake.

85. For an excellent short account of romance and its relations with epic, see Henry Knight Miller, *Tom Jones and the Romance Tradition* (Victoria, B.C.: ELS Monograph Series, no. 6, 1976), especially ch. 1.

86. On [15]/25 May 1663, Giovanni Salvetti, an agent of the Florentine government, wrote a letter reporting that "the King passes his time twice or thrice a week at his Theatre Royal, newly built with artistic scenes and machines all designed by Sir Robert Howard, judged here to be the greatest master of perspective in Europe." This unique testimony may be a result of Howard's habitual claim to expertise in all fields of endeavor, but John Orrell, who published it, correctly notes that it sheds new light on Howard's qualifications as "Serjeant Painter to the King," which office he had sold some three months earlier. See "A New Witness of the Restoration Stage, 1660–69," *TRI* 2 (1975), p. 22.

87. The California editors (I, 283, 298n) give Dryden credit for "virtually all" the play. Harold Oliver, in *Sir Robert Howard*, pp. 63–67, puts up an argument in favor of Howard's claim; he demonstrates that the

one attempt to sort out the collaboration by textual analysis, John Harrington Smith, "The Dryden-Howard Collaboration," *SP* 51 (1954):55–74, is based on false premises. George McFadden, in *Dryden the Public Writer*, bases an entire chapter on the supposition that Dryden wrote the play and was enraged when Howard published it as his own; his claims that various prologues refer to this supposed slight have not convinced all reviewers; see, for example, Phillip Harth in *JEGP* 78 (1979):128–30. The one contemporary reference I have found comes in Tom Brown's *The Late Converts Exposed* (1690), where "Bays" is made to confess to various subterfuges: "Sometimes for an extraordinary consideration, I give leave to some noble Baronet to father one of my Plays, and afterwards when I have serv'd my turn, and got all I can out of him, I make bold to take the Brat home again, as I did my *Indian* Queen" (p. 51). The implication, that Howard paid Dryden for the right to claim authorship, seems dubious indeed.

88. *Diary*, V, 33 (1 February 1664).

89. See Milhous and Hume, "Dating," p. 381.

90. For a more explicit instance of this ancient coupling of money and feces, compare Dryden's poem to his friend the dramatist Thomas Southerne, "On His Comedy, Called *The Wives Excuse*" (1692). Contrasting Southerne's failed comedy with more successful farces, Dryden says that "Farce, in it self, is of a nasty scent; / But the gain smells not of the Excrement" (ll. 7–8).

91. The direct influence of this play on Voltaire's *Alzire* (1736) has been overstated; see Theodore E. D. Braun, "*Alzire* and *The Indian Emperour*: Voltaire's Debt to Dryden," *SVEC* 205 (1982):57–63.

92. See the entry under "Dutch Wars" in the *Companion* to Pepys's *Diary*, vol. 10 of the Latham and Matthews edition.

CHAPTER 6. "TO DELIGHT THE AGE"

1. See Osborn, pp. 209–10. Their residence at this time has not been located, but was most likely in the parish of St. Clement Danes.

2. For a discussion of pamphlets making this argument, see Michael McKeon, *Politics and Poetry in Restoration England: The Case of Dryden's Annus Mirabilis* (Cambridge: Harvard University Press, 1975), p. 48n.

3. See Oliver, *Howard*, p. 124. Howard would later claim that he won the lady on his own, not needing the letter of recommendation from Charles; see p. 129. The Drydens' departure for the country cannot be precisely dated. Samuel Holt Monk, in his headnote to the *Essay of Dramatick Poesie* (*Works*, XVII, 331), attempts to place their departure between 3 June and 25 June, but the order for payment on Lady Elizabeth's dowry which he dates as 25 June 1665 is in fact dated 25 June 1666. See Appendix C.

4. In *Examen Poeticum* (1693), Dryden translated the passage in Ovid he partially follows here, a simile for the pursuit of Daphne by Apollo, in which a greyhound "licks / His Chaps in vain, and blows upon the Flix" ("The First Book of Ovid's Metamorphoses, ll. 722–23). One somewhat tarnished piece of anecdotal evidence supposedly records a later hunt at Charlton. In the *Memoirs of the Life, Writings, and Amours of William Congreve*, compiled by Charles Wilson, 2 vols. (1730), II, 22–32, Elizabeth Thomas ("Curll's Corinna") tells a wild story about Dryden's predicting a series of accidents that then supposedly befell his son Charles. Malone reprints most of her story and systematically discredits it (pp. 404–21). Nonetheless, some truths probably lurk behind this fanciful account: given his lifelong interest in astrology, I do not doubt that Dryden was concerned to know the exact minute of Charles's birth, and the account of the accident that supposedly occurred at Charlton in 1674, in which Charles is left behind to study his Latin while Dryden participates in a hunt organized by Elizabeth's brother Charles, then second Earl of Berkshire, is not entirely implausible.

5. On Dryden's fondness for fishing, see Malone, pp. 520–21. Other details of Baskerville's account may also be interesting to those envisioning Dryden's environment: "Five miles forward on this road which leads through Brayden forest, lies Gazing; here Mr. Washington hath a fair house and a walled park. Mr. Milborne and Mr. Essex have likewise fair houses in the same parish; at Charlton, hard by lies the Earl of Berkshire's house. Masberry or Malmsbury a market town two miles forward in this road was heretofore more famous for a great abbey in it and yet 'tis not decayed as it is in many other places, for the town makes use of the abbey church and keeps it up, and Sir Thomas Ivie now owns a house in the abbey and makes it his dwelling place, who is so curious in his gardens that it's worth a traveller's pains to go to see it, for on the walls of the abbey which are high and broad he shall find curious borders set with various flowers suitable to

every season, which affords a delicate scent, and sight to the eye, as you go from his dwelling-house to a fine banquetting house, a furlong from it on the wall" (*H.M.C.*, XIII, ii, 298).

6. In the letter to Robert Howard prefixed to *Annus Mirabilis*, in which the verses to the Duchess were first printed (*Works*, I, 56).

7. On the attribution of this poem, see George deForest Lord, "Two New Poems by Marvell?," *BNYPL* 62 (1958): 551–70.

8. See *Works*, I, 277.

9. Much of the language of this passage recurs in *Threnodia Augustalis* (1685), Dryden's poem on the death of Charles II, where the restored King is fondly remembered as a "New-born Phoenix" surrounded by a "gay Harmonious Quire" of "officious Muses" (ll. 364–80); Dryden explicitly identifies himself as one of the "airy Choristers" (l. 372).

10. Malone (pp. 62–68) established these identifications; Frank L. Huntley, in a monograph *On Dryden's "Essay of Dramatic Poesy"* (Ann Arbor: University of Michigan Press, 1951), cast some doubt on the identification of Eugenius as Buckhurst, alleging that Buckhurst was in action with the fleet that day. But Stanley Archer, in "The Persons in *An Essay of Dramatic Poetry*," *PLL* 2 (1966): 305–14, has shown that Buckhurst's song, "To all you ladies now at Land," which Matthew Prior described as written on the eve of Lowestoft, was actually published in January 1665. He also shrewdly points out that "if Dorset [Buckhurst's later title] had participated in the battle, Dryden would hardly have missed the opportunity of alluding to the action in his Dedication of the Essay" (pp. 306–07).

11. Dorothy Savage, wife to Charles Howard, Lord Andover, eldest brother of Sir Robert Howard and Elizabeth Howard Dryden, was the sister of John Savage, Earl Rivers, who died in 1654; Katherine was his daughter.

12. See Sorbière's *Relation d'un voyage en Angleterre* (Paris, 1664) and Sprat's *Observations on Monsieur Sorbier's Voyage into England* (1665). For an account of this quarrel and its relevance to Dryden, see George Williamson, "The Occasion of *An Essay of Dramatic Poesy*," *MP* 44 (1946): 1–9. For a larger discussion of the "public" implications of the *Essay*, ranging over Dryden's entire career, see Cedric D. Reverand, "Dryden's 'Essay of Dramatic Poesie': The Poet and the World of Affairs," *SEL* 22 (1982): 375–93.

13. See Archer, p. 314.

14. See Archer, pp. 307–13, an excellent discussion.

15. See Monk's headnote (*Works*, XVII, 358).

16. For a full discussion, see Robert D. Hume, *Dryden's Criticism* (Ithaca: Cornell University Press, 1970), pp. 190–203.

17. Consider this passage from the dedication, which anticipates many of the conclusions of the *Essay*: "All the *Spanish* and *Italian* Tragedies I have yet seen, are writ in Rhyme: For the *French*, I do not name them, because it is the Fate of our Country-men to admit little of theirs among us, but the Basest of their Men, the Extravagances of their Fashions, and the Frippery of their Merchandise. *Shakespear* (who with some Errors not to be avoided in that Age, had undoubtedly a larger Soul of Poesie than ever any of our Nation) was the first, who to shun the pains of continual Rhyming, invented that kind of Writing which we call Blanck Verse" (VIII, 99).

18. For a useful summary of Howard's argument, see Oliver, pp. 88–94.

19. See "Of Heroique Plays," prefaced to *The Conquest of Granada* (1672), the preface to *Ovid's Epistles* (1680), the preface to *Sylvae* (1685), the "Discourse concerning the Original and Progress of Satire" (1693), and references to the unpublished essay on versification in the preface to *Albion and Albanius* (1685) and the preface to the *Aeneis* (1697).

20. The scanty evidence consists of a letter by Henry Savile, dated 4 May 1665, in which he describes a play he calls *The Widow* by Orrery. Orrery wrote no such play, and the incident Savile describes, the comic plight of the man who needs to find the nearest close stool, corresponds to *All Mistaken*. See Robert D. Hume, "Dryden, James Howard, and the Date of *All Mistaken*," *PQ* 51 (1972):422–29.

21. When Pepys saw the play on 2 March 1667, he was enthusiastic in his praise for Nell Gwyn: "but so great performance of a comical part was never, I believe, in the world before as Nell doth this, both as a mad girle and then, most and best of all, when she comes in like a young gallant; and hath the motions and carriage of a spark the most that ever I saw any man have. It makes me, I confess, admire her" (*Diary*, VIII, 91).

22. For details, see the excellent headnote to the play by John Loftis (*Works* IX, 338–39).

23. This assault is recorded in Berkshire's petition requesting that his assailants—Ralph Marshall, John Tisser, and James Tisser—be arrested by the House of Lords (*H.M.C.* VIII, ap. I, 118b, 147). Because the assault took place while Parliament was prorogued, nothing was done.

24. According to a petition tentatively dated 1665 (*C.S.P. Dom.*, p. 138), the Earl was "very anxious to pay his creditors," and willing to sell Berkshire House to the King. A later petition (? June 1666, *C.S.P. Dom.*, p. 459) complains that he is "in danger of losing his house, the only retreat for himself and his family."

25. In the letter to Howard prefixed to *Annus Mirabilis*, Dryden says, "I should do you that justice to the Readers, to let them know that if there be any thing tolerable in this Poem, they owe the Argument to your choice, the writing to your encouragement, the correction to your judgment, and the care of it to your friendship" (I, 59). Earlier in the same letter, he mentions having sent Howard a play for his perusal, presumably *Secret Love*. The dating of the letters Howard and the Drydens sent to Sir Robert Long about Elizabeth's money suggests that a letter from Wooton Bassett could reach Charlton in a day's time.

26. The relevant passage is quoted in full in Appendix C, under 9 May 1663, the date of the mortgage.

27. P.R.O., S.P. 29/159/f. 118.

28. Richard Sheppard, who signed S.P. 29/159/f. 118 verifying that it was a true copy, was the "Mr Sheppeard" who sent the Drydens their acquittance to be signed upon receipt of the first payment in August 1666. See the letter of 13 August 1666 from Sir Robert Howard to Sir Robert Long, which the Drydens enclosed with their letter of 14 August (*Letters*, p. 145). As McFadden points out (pp. 67–69), the person whom Sir Robert Long "wrought . . . to Assign the patent" was Anthony Ashley Cooper, Baron Ashley, Chancellor of the Exchequer, referred to in Sir Robert Howard's letter as "my Lord Ushley." As the Earl of Shaftesbury, Ashley was later Dryden's bitter foe, but at this point, he had no reason to oppose the grant; his wife, Margaret Spencer, was sister to the widow of Henry Howard, Elizabeth's brother, who had died in 1663. Henry's will, chiefly concerned with disposing of his guns and hounds, is in the P.R.O., P.C.C. 56 Bruce; he left each of his siblings £40.

29. *Diary* VII, 218 (25 July 1666).

30. P.R.O., S.P. 44/23/ff. 118–20.

31. For an exhaustive study of the various uses to which prophecies and portents were put by various political and religious groups, see McKeon, *Politics and Poetry*.

32. In his forthcoming edition of Dryden's poems, Paul Hammond gives a detailed account of Dryden's sources, which I follow; the most surprising of his discoveries is Dryden's apparent knowledge of a thanksgiving sermon for Lowestoft, preached in Northampton by one Simon Ford, *The Lord's Wonders in the Deep* (Oxford, 1665).

33. Although dated 1 October 1666, the "Third Advice" was not printed until 1667; *POAS*, I, 68. For many examples of pamphlet literature on the Great Fire, see the publications listed in McKeon's very full bibliography.

34. See *Works*, I, 264–65.

35. *Complete Works*, ed. Grosart, II, 298–99. In the late poem "To my Honour'd Kinsman," Dryden returns to this idea, though his political purposes there are quite different:

> Some Overpoise of Sway, by Turns they share;
> In Peace the People, and the Prince in War.
>
> [ll. 180–81; cf. 171–94]

36. See McKeon, ch. 3.

37. Compare also the "silver shower" the Spaniards expect from Mexico in *The Indian Emperour*, I, i, 30, quoted above, ch. 5, p. 155.

38. See McKeon, pp. 53–54.

39. I owe this point to George Lord.

40. Sternhold and Hopkins, *The Whole Booke of Psalmes, Collected into English Meeter* (1601), p. 59.

41. Readers of McKeon's learned and penetrating study will recognize both my general indebtedness to his work and my slightly different perspective on the "generality theory of value."

42. *Diary*, VII, 401; VIII, 14.

43. Ward (p. 47) points out that there is no hard evidence on which to date their return, speculating that Dryden could have traveled back and forth to Charlton. But since such a journey would have taken a week over terrible roads, and since playwrights normally instructed the actors in their parts, I think it more

likely that the Drydens returned to London on a permanent basis. For the date of the premiere of *Secret Love*, see n. 52 below.

44. The first printed account of this lost "ur-*Rehearsal*" comes in the *Key to the Rehearsal* printed by Sam Briscoe in 1704, but the "Session of the Poets to the Tune of Cock Lawrel," now dated as 1664, claims that

> a Play Tripartite was very near made
> Where malicious *Matt Clifford* and Spiritual *Spratt*
> Were Joyn'd with their Duke, a Peer of the Trade.

See above, ch. 5, n. 62. Clifford, later Master of the Charterhouse School and the author of attacks on Dryden, was Buckingham's secretary; Sprat was his chaplain. For a full account, see the Introduction to Robert D. Hume's edition of *The Rehearsal* (in press). On the scuffle over *The United Kingdoms*, see the Introduction to *The Country Gentleman*, by Howard and Buckingham, ed. Arthur H. Scouten and Robert D. Hume (Philadelphia: University of Pennsylvania Press, 1976), p. 17. The ultimate source is Sam Briscoe's *Key to The Rehearsal* (1704), pp. xi-xii, 17. On Henry Howard's death, see above, n. 28.

45. See Oliver, *Howard*, pp. 131–32.

46. Not printed with the play, Howard's song survives in a musical manuscript at the Clark Library, and was printed in the 1690s; see Oliver, *Howard*, p. 137.

47. See Burghclere, *Buckingham*, pp. 57–60, 142–46, 157–62.

48. In *The Medal of John Bayes*, pp. 9–10, Shadwell records Anne's patronage of Dryden, as does the poet himself in the dedication of the printed *Indian Emperour*. Neither source is specific about whether Anne helped promote Dryden's play before or after the plague.

49. Here and generally, I follow the persuasive arguments of McFadden, especially ch. 2. Although it will be apparent that we differ on many details, McFadden's essential insight, his contention that politics was a central motivation for the Dryden-Howard feud, is a genuine breakthrough.

50. Oliver prints most of the letter, p. 127.

51. See Clarendon's remarkably detailed letter on his dealings with Howard, printed in the article by Hardacre cited above, ch. 5, n. 25, especially pp. 212–14.

52. See John Harrington Smith, "Dryden and Buckingham: The Beginnings of the Feud," *MLN* 69 (1954): 242–45. Pepys saw Buckingham's play on 5 February 1667; if the prologue refers to Nell Gwyn's dancing in *Secret Love*, which seems likely, Dryden's play must have been produced in late January or very early February. Putting these plays in correct order is complicated by the discovery of a very early cast list for *The Chances*, including both Nell Gwyn and Walter Clun, who was murdered on 2 August 1664. I should suppose this pre-plague production was Fletcher's text, not Buckingham's revision. See K. Robinson, "Two Cast Lists for Buckingham's 'The Chances'," *N&Q* 224 (1979): 436–37. For further evidence pointing to a premiere of Dryden's play on 28, 29, or 31 January 1667, see Arthur H. Scouten, "The Premiere of Dryden's *Secret Love*," *Restoration* 9 (1985):9–11. Buckingham might have taken offense at the second prologue to *Secret Love*, which refers to critics as "Butchers" and claims that only those who have written plays themselves have a right to criticize, a point Dryden makes with the first of his many metaphors drawn from gambling:

> Those who write not, and yet all Writers nick
> Are Bankrupt Gamesters, for they damn on Tick.

[ll. 57–58]

Buckingham, who was well known for criticizing loudly from the pit, had not yet produced an original play; he had lost so much money gambling in France in 1661 that he resolved to give up "deep play." See Burghclere, *Buckingham*, pp. 118–19.

53. See Burghclere, *Buckingham*, pp. 168–78.

54. *Diary*, VIII, 40.

55. The phrase is from Shadwell's *Medal of John Bayes*; see above, ch. 4, p. 81.

56. See Pepys's account of the duel, *Diary* IX, 26–27 (17 January 1668).

57. Pepys attended a prizefight at Vere Street on 1 June 1663 (*Diary*, IV, 167).

58. Pepys, *Diary*, VIII, 167–73 (15, 16, 20 April 1667).

59. See John Harold Wilson, *A Rake and his Times*, p. 130.

60. Pepys, *Diary*, VIII, 362 (29 July 1667).

61. See Burghclere, *Buckingham*, pp. 179–82.

62. For an excellent account of the sources, see John Loftis's headnote to the play (*Works*, IX, 355–69). On the collaboration, see F. H. Moore, "The Composition of *Sir Martin Mar-All*," *SP* extra series 4 (1967):27–38.

63. See *Works*, IX, 353–54.

64. Pepys, *Diary*, VIII, 363–64 (29 July 1667).

65. McFadden argues that "Howard let his brother-in-law and sister in for a very bad investment, and no doubt gained credit for himself by doing so" (p. 70); he implies that Dryden had reason to resent Howard's action. But the investment was ultimately repaid with some interest, and without Howard's intervention at this point, the Drydens might never have received the rest of Elizabeth's dowry. Overt hostilities began later. For more details, see Appendix C.

66. See Wilson, *A Rake*, pp. 96–97. In 1663, Buckingham bought the farm at Chertsey where Cowley spent his final years; see p. 19.

67. John's exact date of birth is not known; the dates of birth we have for Charles and Erasmus-Henry stem from school records, confirmed in the case of Erasmus-Henry by the Parish Register of St. Martin's in the Fields, and in the case of Charles by his horoscope, preserved, along with his father's, in the Bodleian (MS Ashmole 243). See Paul Hammond and Simon Bentley, "The Nativities of John and Charles Dryden," *Restoration* 9 (1985):56–60.

68. See Oliver, *Howard*, p. 134, and Clayton Roberts, *The Growth of Responsible Government in Stuart England* (Cambridge: Cambridge University Press, 1966), pp. 155–69, especially p. 160, on Andover's surprising position.

69. See Burghclere, *Buckingham*, pp. 185–87.

70. According to McFadden, "Sir William Coventry, Sir Thomas Clifford, and Andrew Marvell, opponents of Clarendon on almost every matter of policy, [were] incapable of the cynicism that would make him out a traitor" (p. 62), but John Dixon Hunt, in *Andrew Marvell*, pp. 162–65, cites conflicting contemporary documents that make Marvell's position seem a little less certain.

71. Clarendon's petition is quoted in Burghclere, *Buckingham*, p. 187.

72. See George R. Guffey, "Politics, Weather, and the Contemporary Reception of the Dryden-Davenant *Tempest*," *Restoration* 8 (1984), pp. 6–7.

73. Dryden's preface gives Davenant credit for inventing Hippolito and Dorinda, and explains that Dryden then wrote the dialogue; Dryden also gives the older man the scenes with the sailors. For some acute commentary on these claims, see Maximillian Novak's headnote (*Works*, X, 321–22).

74. On 14 January, Pepys visited Mrs. Pierce and his wife, "and there they fell to discourse of the last night's work at Court, where the ladies and Duke of Monmouth and others acted *The Indian Emperour*—wherein they told me these things most remarkable: that not any woman but Duchesse of Monmouth and Mrs. Cornwallis did anything like, but like fools and sticks; but that these two did do most extraordinary well—that not any man did anything well but Captain Obryan, who spoke and did well; but above all things, did dance most incomparably" (*Diary*, IX, 23–24).

75. Katharine Eisaman Maus, "Arcadia Lost: Politics and Revision in the Restoration *Tempest*," *Renaissance Drama* 13 (1982), p. 201.

76. See Shakespeare's *The Tempest*, III, ii, 54–82. This and all subsequent citations of Shakespeare follow the text and lineation of the Arden edition, Harold F. Brooks and Harold Jenkins, gen. eds., (Methuen, 1946–).

77. See Guffey, pp. 2–4.

78. *Diary*, VIII, 522 (7 November 1667).

79. In the original edition, "To the Reader," sig. A2r–v. On the likelihood that the original was by Ford, see Harbage, "Elizabethan–Restoration Palimpsest," pp. 297–304; Oliver, in *Sir Robert Howard*, pp. 140–41, points to parallels with the work of Shirley and suggests that the original may have been written in collaboration.

80. For Howard's political innuendo, see McFadden, pp. 74–76. For evidence that Clarendon was friendly to the order of Benedictines, see William Maziere Brady, *Annals of the Catholic Hierarchy* (Rome: Tip de la Pace, 1877), p. 111.

81. Howard and Dryden were living together at the time Hart purchased these manuscripts and were collaborating on *The Indian Queen*. "The Session of the Poets to the Tune of Cock Lawrel," now dated to 1664, has a puzzling stanza in which the Howards accuse Dryden of having stolen *The Wild Gallant* (see above, ch. 5, n. 62). I should suppose that there were several old plays in varying states of revision in Howard's lodgings in 1663, and that Dryden did some work on the one that eventually became *The Duke of Lerma*.

82. McFadden claims that "it is beyond reasonable doubt . . . that . . . the rift in the lute was Howard's printing of *The Indian Queen*, without any mention of a collaborator, in his *Four New Plays* (1665)" (p. 72), but Howard and Dryden, as we have seen, were on quite cordial terms throughout 1666, and on the issue of *The Indian Queen*, Dryden had contented himself with the bare statement that "part of [that] Poem was writ by me." John Harrington Smith, in "Dryden and Buckingham: The Beginnings of the Feud," argues that the prologue to *Albumazar* was aimed at Buckingham's appropriation of *The Chances*, a revision Dryden later praised. Moreover, Dryden would in that case have waited nearly a year to comment on Buckingham's work. The fact that this prologue was first spoken *the day after* the premiere of *The Duke of Lerma* convinces me that Dryden was offended by Howard's new play and was immediately striking back. McFadden (p. 78) makes the shrewd suggestion that *Albumazar*, a play featuring an astrologer, was revived in order to attack Buckingham, who had been imprisoned for casting the King's horoscope.

83. We know the details of this contract because of a document the other sharers in the King's Company planned to submit to the Lord Chamberlain when Dryden broke his agreement with them in 1678; Osborn prints a transcript (pp. 204–05). We do not have a precise date; the contract with the players might have been signed before or after Dryden's appointment as Poet Laureate. In their complaint, the other sharers allege that this contract has been worth £300 or £400 a year to Dryden; Leslie Hotson, in *The Commonwealth and Restoration Stage* (Cambridge: Harvard University Press, 1928), declares this estimate "considerably inflated" (p. 245). Even allowing for exaggeration, it was probably a better and more steady source of income than Dryden's irregularly paid salary as Poet Laureate—at least until the disastrous fire of January 1672, which destroyed the Bridges Street theatre.

84. *C.S.P. Dom.*, *1667–68*, p. 341; P.R.O., L.C. 3/25/p. 156; 3/26/p. 206. The Earl of Manchester's first cousin Elizabeth was the wife of Dryden's first cousin Sir Gilbert Pickering, who died in 1668, but Dryden's reputation was sufficient to secure him the post. In all the attacks made against him in the ensuing years, no rival ever alleged that his appointment was "fixed." McFadden (p. 77) supposes that a reference to "Lawreats" in the prologue to *Albumazar* refers to "an effort by Sir Robert Howard to snatch the laureateship for himself." But if Howard had made such an attempt, such attacks on him as Shadwell's *The Sullen Lovers* would surely have taken advantage of the fact.

85. Malone (pp. 553–56n) prints the Latin document, which refers to Dryden's "vitae probitas, bonarum literarum scientia, morumque integritas, vel ipsius domini Regis testimonio perspectae sunt." While these are doubtless conventional phrases, the bishop was nonetheless put into the position of praising Dryden's morality a week or so after the premiere of *An Evening's Love*, which featured a particularly scabrous prologue. Another relevant document has recently come to light; see John R. Sweney, "An Unnoticed Dryden Document at Lambeth Palace," *N&Q* 224 (1979):11–12.

86. For details, see Appendix C.

87. See Osborn, pp. 210–11. Since the rate books for 1668–69 are missing, the Drydens may have moved in as much as a year earlier. See Ward, p. 345.

88. For a full account of Dryden's sources, see *Works*, X, 433–43.

89. Pepys, *Diary*, IX, 248 (22 June 1668), quoting the bookseller Herringman.

90. See Hume, *Development*, pp. 89–90, 296–97.

91. *The Friendly Vindication of Mr. Dryden* (Cambridge, 1673), which is in fact an attack on Dryden, alleges that he "had been so frankly obliging as (where he could not use a Character, or apprehended the License) to assign it to some other Poet of his Cabal. . . . That this was a *Sir Positive Truth* Mr. *Dryden* had not fore-head enough to denie" (p. 8). I should suppose, however, that Shadwell had had ample opportunity to observe the Howard brothers and needed no hints from Dryden to draw his caricatures.

92. For a text of this second petition and a summary of Howard's remarks on his own behalf, see Oliver, *Howard*, pp. 127–29. The quarreling couple finally made a financial settlement in 1670.

93. Lost for centuries, this play has recently come to light; see the edition of Arthur H. Scouten and Robert D. Hume (cited above, n. 44.)

94. See McFadden, pp. 79–80. Acknowledging the incompleteness of this explanation, McFadden goes on to point out that Dryden was also asserting "the right of a professional . . . writer to argue and defend himself with his pen, even against a member of the nobility" (pp. 82–83). We shall probably never know all the reasons for the bitterness of the quarrel in 1668.

95. This and all citations of Shadwell's plays follow *The Complete Works of Thomas Shadwell*, ed. Montague Summers, 5 vols. (Fortune, 1927); this passage occurs at I, 11. Assessing the relation this preface bears to Dryden's "Defence" is problematic because of uncertain dating. Shadwell's dedication is dated 1 September 1668; the preface may be earlier; the edition was entered into the Stationers' Register on 9 September and the Term Catalogue in November. Pepys had seen the "Defence" and the reply to it by "R. F." on 20 September. It is just possible that Shadwell is echoing Dryden, rather than the other way around, which makes more sense to me; in any case, he picked up the same phrases again when caricaturing Dryden as Drybob in *The Humorists*.

96. According to Macdonald, *Bibliography*, p. 94, copies of the edition containing the "Defence" are "very rare."

97. In *A Letter from a Gentleman To the Honourable Ed. Howard Esq.* (1668), the charge is as follows: "I have heard from a very brave Gentleman, who was lately engaged to waite upon the Squire [Dryden], that his cold Answer has discouraged the Honourable Person [Howard] from such an Expectation" (p. 12). Richard Flecknoe has been thought to be the author, but for strong arguments against this inference, see Maximillian E. Novak, "Dryden's 'Ape of the French Eloquence' and Richard Flecknoe," *BNYPL* 72 (1968), pp. 503–04. In *The Medal of John Bayes*, Shadwell is more specific:

> 'Gainst him a scandalous Preface didst thou write,
> Which thou didst soon expunge rather than fight.
>
> [p. 9]

98. *Diary*, IX, 311 (20 September 1668).

CHAPTER 7. "SUCCESS, WHICH CAN NO MORE THAN BEAUTY LAST"

1. See *Works*, X, 475.

2. *Diary*, II, 188 (30 September 1661).

3. *Diary*, VII, 39 (11 February 1666); VI, 320–23 (6–8 December 1665). Sandwich was appointed to this post as a way of protecting him from his enemies in Parliament, who would otherwise have impeached him for embezzling naval spoils when he was an Admiral of the fleet, but he made a considerable success of it, negotiating an important treaty with the Spaniards before returning to England in 1668.

4. For the dinner party, see *Diary*, VIII, 451–53 (27 September 1667). For Elizabeth Pickering's marriage, see IX, 332 (20 October 1668).

5. Pepys, *Diary*, IX, 190–91 (18 May 1668)

6. *London Stage*, I, 153–55. The text of *The Heiress* is lost. The thin and garbled evidence for Dryden's involvement comes in a letter by Mrs. Evelyn, dated 10 February 1669, describing the play as "one of my Lord of Newcastle's, for which printed apologies are scattered in the assembly by Briden's [sic] order, either for himself who had some hand in it, or for the author." *The Diary and Correspondence of John Evelyn*, ed. William Bray, 4 vols. (Colburn, 1857), IV, 14. Dryden had helped Newcastle with *Sir Martin Mar-All*, and had probably used the device of distributing a printed sheet to the audience for *The Indian Emperour*, so that Mrs. Evelyn's testimony is not entirely implausible. See Judith Milhous and Robert D. Hume, "Lost English Plays, 1660–1700, *HLB* 25 (1977), pp. 16–17.

7. See the edition of Hume and Scouten, cited above, ch. 6, n. 44, and Annabel Patterson, "*The Country Gentleman*: Howard, Marvell, and Dryden in the Theatre of Politics," *SEL* 25 (1985):491–510. On the dismissal of Coventry, an episode in which Charles "allowed his hatred to sway his judgement," see J. R. Jones, *Country and Court* (Cambridge: Harvard University Press, 1978), p. 167.

8. No one seems to have noticed that Shadwell's prologue to this play, acknowledging his having adapted it from Fountain, strongly echoes Dryden's prologue to *Albumazar*, in which Dryden had complained about Howard's stealing *The Duke of Lerma*. Shadwell's prologue begins with the image of theft ("One of the Poets (as they safely may / When th' Authour's dead) has stollen a whole Play") and refers to

"the bold Purloiner of the Play." Dryden had complained, a year earlier, about "Authors [who] make whole Playes, and yet scarce write one word," "bold Padders" who rob living and dead playwrights. See Summers's edition, I, 101.

9. See Bruce King, *Dryden's Major Plays* (Edinburgh: Oliver and Boyd, 1966), pp. 50–58.

10. See Cyril Hughes Hartmann, *Clifford of the Cabal* (Heinemann, 1937), pp. 20–21.

11. Jones, *Country and Court*, p. 169.

12. See Evelyn, *Diary*, III, 528–29.

13. Hartmann describes Sir Robert as "one of [Clifford's] best friends" (p. 290), but McFadden describes their exchange of letters about the dangerous political allegory in Howard's poem "The Duel of the Stags" (1668) as "pro forma, intended mainly to keep lines of communication open" (p. 85). It would have been increasingly difficult for Howard and Clifford to maintain a close friendship in light of their political differences.

14. At this time, Clifford and Monmouth were also on good terms. Clifford had helped Monmouth straighten out his tangled financial affairs a year earlier; portraits by Lely of the Duke and his Duchess, Dryden's early patroness, hung in Clifford's country house at Ugbrooke Park. See Hartmann, pp. 43–45.

15. According to the preface to the published play, "This poem . . . was contrived and written in seven weeks, though afterwards hindred by many accidents from a speedy representation, which would have been its best excuse" (X, 111).

16. See K. H. D. Haley, *The First Earl of Shaftesbury* (Oxford: Clarendon, 1968), p. 276. According to a letter of 17 June 1669, quoted in *C.S.P. Dom.*, "A great fit of melancholy has possessed the gentry and good subjects, by the news of her Majesty's miscarriage"(p. 369).

17. The Parish Register of St. Martin's in the Fields records the christening on 20 May of "Erasmus Henricus Dryden, fil: Joannis et Elizabethae, nat. 2 Maii 1669." In light of my speculation that Charles was named for his recusant uncle, the choice of two names with highly Protestant connotations may be significant. Years later, when he became a Dominican priest, Erasmus-Henry changed his name to Thomas. Did he do so in honor of his Howard grandfather? Ward discovered the purchases of silver in the registers of Blanchard and Child, printed in F. G. Hilton, *The Marygold by Temple Bar* (1902), pp. 28 ff.

18. The complaint of the players, dated 6 June 1670, and Fuller's answer, dated 16 June (P.R.O., C. 7/486/74/1–2), are printed in the appendix to *Works*, X. An important passage, however, is omitted from Fuller's reply. It follows the sentence that now ends in the tenth line of p. 547, ". . . himselfe and family," and reads: "And beeing in truth also deterred by their or Some of theire great words and threats; One of them by name Mr. Wintersell, plainly telling this Defendant that they could spend more att Law than this defendant could. And that they would keepe him out of his moneye till he should be glad to take what they would please to give him."

19. On the "seminal" importance of *Tyrannick Love* for the sub-genre of "horror tragedy," see Hume, *Development*, pp. 279, 284–85.

20. Apparently, Dryden was not particularly adept at reading his plays aloud to the actors; see the anecdotes collected in *The London Stage*, I, cli.

21. For a list of Mohun's roles, see *The London Stage*, I, ccl.

22. This scene has been particularly important for those concerned to argue that Dryden's heroic plays are satiric or self-parodic. D. W. Jefferson was the first to make this suggestion, in "The Significance of Dryden's Heroic Plays," *PLPLS* 5 (1940):125–39; his student Bruce King has greatly extended his argument in *Dryden's Major Plays*. Much subsequent criticism has been concerned to answer King, and to quarrel with his emphasis on farcical elements in the serious plays, but the more subtle understanding of Dryden's many purposes in these plays that is now emerging owes a debt to Jefferson and King. Derek Hughes, for example, in a paragraph including some strenuous disagreement with King, puts the problem neatly: "More than any writer since Chaucer, Dryden knew the narrowness of the division between tragic flaw and comic deficiency, and the ease with which one could suddenly modulate into the other. . . . The heroic plays can seem to invert all traditional dramatic order, for tragedy in its usual sense is acted out in a subsidiary level of the play and a counterpoint of unwitting comedy is provided not by the low characters of a subordinate plot but (on a few occasions) by the heroes and heroines in the full flight of their idealism." *Dryden's Heroic Plays* (Macmillan, 1981), p. 2.

23. A note in the *Letters of Philip, Second Earl of Chesterfield* (Lloyd, 1829), p. 95, claims that the Earl of

Berkshire "died of an accidental fall, in the ninetieth year of his age." According to Paget's genealogy in *Ashtead and its Howard Possessors*, however, the Earl was christened in 1587, and was thus only eighty-two at the time of his death, though Paget contradicts himself in his text (p. 60*n*), claiming that Berkshire was eighty-nine at the time of the Restoration. The *Complete Peerage* gives his birthdate as "about 1590."

24. For details, see Appendix C.

25. Osborn (pp. 270–71) prints an excerpt from a Dutch newspaper published in 1670, alleging that Thomas Sprat had been appointed Historiographer Royal in June 1669, and wonders whether Sprat's disappointment at failing to gain the post was a motive for his participation in *The Rehearsal*. But Sprat is recorded as having participated in the "ur-*Rehearsal*" before the plague (see above, ch. 6, n. 44), and his position as Buckingham's chaplain gave him sufficient reason to oppose Dryden, with whom he had once been associated (see above, ch. 5, n. 7).

26. The complete patent is printed by Malone (pp. 553–59).

27. Jones, *Country and Court*, p. 172. On Milton's possible involvement, see Parker, *Milton*, I, 613.

28. In her Ph.D. dissertation, "Milton's Immediate Influence on Dryden" (University of Arizona, 1978), Donna Elliott Swaim argues that Dryden first read *Paradise Lost* in the winter of 1668–69. Given its rough correspondence with the putative anecdote about Buckhurst, the date seems a plausible one, though I do not concur with Swaim's notion that Dryden was influenced to "return to religion" (p. 27) by Milton, nor with her description of *Tyrannick Love* as a "thoroughly serious Christian play" (p. 38).

29. For the sources of this anecdote and the scholarly controversy about it, see above, ch. 4, n. 14.

30. For detailed information about Anne Reeves, see Appendix D.

31. Evelyn saw Streeter's sets at a court performance on 10 and 11 February 1671; they were presumably the same ones used at Bridges Street (*Diary*, III, 569–70).

32. *Diary and Correspondence*, ed. Bray, IV, 56–57.

33. See, for example, his complaints about *An Evening's Love*, which he calls "a foolish plot, & very prophane, so as it afflicted me to see how the stage was degenerated & poluted by the licentious times" (*Diary*, III, 510–11).

34. For some details supporting this speculation, see above, Appendix D, p. 533.

35. See *Aeneid*, V, 477–81; IX, 433–37; *Iliad* X, 455–57. Reuben Arthur Brower, in "Dryden's Epic Manner and Virgil," *PMLA* 55 (1940), pp. 124–26, points out the parallel between the image of the poppy and the death of Euryalus. Dryden probably had the Homeric source of Virgil's lines in mind, however, since the parallel passage in the *Iliad* (VIII, 306–08) specifically mentions a poppy. Dryden's trumpets may have been suggested by the "tuba terribilem sonitum" after the deaths of Nisus and Euryalus (*Aeneid* IX, 503).

36. The original and persuasive reading of this play by Derek Hughes (*Dryden's Heroic Plays*, pp. 79–117) makes much of the disparity between what Almahide and Almanzor say and what they do, but the audience's awareness of that disparity would depend on how the actors played their parts.

37. See *The Censure of the Rota on Mr Driden's Conquest of Granada* (Oxford, 1673), attributed to Richard Leigh, in which "Another *Virtuoso* said he could not but take notice how ignorantly some charged *Almanzor* with transgressing the Rules of the *Drama*." This speaker mockingly defends the irregularities of the hero on the grounds that "*Almanzor* was neither Mr *Drydens* Subject, nor *Boabdelins*, but equally exempt from the Poets Rules, and the Princes Laws, and in short, if his revolting from the *Abencerrages* to the *Zegrys*, and from the *Zegrys* to the *Abencerrages* again, had not equally satisfi'd both parties, it might admit of the same defence, Mr *Drydens* Out-cries, and his Tumults did, that the Poet represented Men in a *Hobbian* State of War" (pp. 2–3).

38. Dryden had used the scale metaphor before in *Annus Mirabilis*; see above, pp. 172–73. He may, however, have been freshly reminded of the passage in Cowley applying such imagery to Cromwell while considering the Hobbesian ideas he employed in this play. Thomas Tenison, later the vicar of St. Martin's in the Fields while Dryden was a parishioner there, quotes Cowley's stanza (without supplying the poet's name) in his interesting tract *The Creed of Mr. Hobbes Examin'd* (1670), p. 160. This pamphlet is cast in the form of a dialogue between Hobbes and a student, and dedicated to the Earl of Manchester, who was Tenison's patron, had been the patron of Thomas Hill, and was connected by marriage to Dryden.

39. Ormonde, who had been dismissed as Lord Lieutenant of Ireland at Buckingham's insistence, retained his place as Steward of the Household, and was writing in that capacity. For details, see Appendix C.

40. See Milhous and Hume, "Dating," p. 388.

41. See above, ch. 6, p. 197 and n. 95. The brief preface to *The Royal Shepherdesse*, with its praise of Jonson and criticism of those who bring "debauched persons" on the stage, reiterates Shadwell's position.

42. *Epigrams of All Sorts*, pp. 51–52. The following lines seem particularly designed to answer Dryden's epilogue:

> Yet know, who e'r thou art, dost lest esteem
> Of *Johnson* for the faults oth' Times, not him,
> Had he writ now, h'ad better writ than thee,
> Hadst thou writ then, th'adst writ far worse than he.

Flecknoe hedged his bets by pretending not to know who was the author of the epilogue ("who e'r thou art"), and by reprinting his epigram in praise of Dryden, which had first appeared in 1670.

43. This attack on Dryden has been little noticed in the scholarship. Richard L. Oden, who reprints in facsimile most of the prefaces and prologues in which Dryden and Shadwell conducted their controversy in *Dryden and Shadwell* (Delmar, N. Y.: Scholars' Facsimiles, 1977), mentions Drybob briefly (p. xx); Michael W. Alssid, in "Shadwell's *Mac Flecknoe*," *SEL* 7 (1967): 387–402, has a brief discussion (pp. 396–97). Summers, in his edition of Shadwell, misses all the references, including the direct quotations from Dryden.

44. Phrases about breaking jests or making repartees occur at I, 213, 215, 224, etc.

45. In a letter to his kinswoman Mrs. Steward, written in 1699, Dryden mentions "physique and other remedies which I am useing for my gravell" (*Letters*, ed. Ward, p. 109). In 1680, he purchased several medical treatises on cures for kidney stones; see below, ch. 10, n. 85.

46. The phrase is from Shadwell's preface (I, 183); the original version of *The Humorists* was preserved in manuscript and has now been published in an edition by Richard Perkin (Dublin: Laurel House, 1975). The major parts are considerably different, but Drybob's part is virtually unaltered.

47. For the evidence for dating the publication, see David Vieth, "The Discovery of the Date of *Mac Flecknoe*," in *Evidence in Literary Scholarship*, ed. René Wellek and Alvaro Ribeiro (Oxford: Clarendon, 1979), p. 71*n*.

48. In dedicating *Marriage A-la-Mode* to Rochester, Dryden says the play has "receiv'd amendment" from Rochester, and thanks him for calling it to the King's attention: "You may please likewise to remember, with how much favour to the Authour, and indulgence to the Play, you commended it to the view of His Majesty, then at *Windsor*, and by His Approbation of it in Writing, made way for its kind reception on the Theatre" (XI, 221). The King was at Windsor between 27 May and 13 July; see *Works*, XI, 487.

49. See Vivian de Sola Pinto, "Rochester and Dryden," in *Renaissance and Modern Studies* 5 (1961), pp. 31–32.

50. "An Allusion to Horace," probably written in early 1676, in *Complete Poems of John Wilmot, Earl of Rochester*, ed. David Vieth (New Haven: Yale University Press, 1968), pp. 123–24.

51. For the poems lampooning Howard, see *POAS*, I, 338–41; on their authorship, see David Vieth, *Attribution in Restoration Poetry* (New Haven: Yale University Press, 1963), pp. 250–54. On Buckingham as leader of the wits, see Wilson, *A Rake and his Times*, pp. 152–53; on the court wits generally, see Wilson's *The Court Wits of the Restoration: An Introduction* (Princeton: Princeton University Press, 1948). Another "courtly" song, "Fare well Fair Armida," printed in several collections in 1672, was popularly attributed to Dryden. For details, see above, Appendix D, pp. 533–34.

52. *C.S.P. Dom., 1671–72*, p. 58. I have been unable to discover what Captain Bowen's request was.

53. See Robert D. Hume, "The Date of Dryden's *Marriage A-la-Mode*," *HLB* 21 (1973):161–66.

54. An elaborate recent article by Michael McKeon, "Marxist Criticism and *Marriage A-la-Mode*," *ECTI* 24 (1983):141–62, singles out these issues as central, but without reference to the particular biographical reasons why Dryden (and Buckingham) were concerned about class and "keeping" at this time.

55. *The Mall, or The Modish Lovers* was not published until 1674, but Dryden refers to its very title here, and the incidents he describes closely resemble its plot. *The Mall* is similar to *Marriage A-la-Mode* in several respects. Courtwell arrives from Spain to discover that his uncle wants him to marry the widow Mrs. Woodbee, the secret wife of his friend Lovechange, just as Palamede arrives from abroad to discover that his father wants him to marry Melantha, the secret mistress of his friend Rhodophil. An opening scene, in which Lovechange gives the servant Peg money in order to gain access to Mrs. Easy, is generally similar to the longer and funnier scene between Palamede and Philotis in *Marriage A-la-Mode* (V, i, 30–76). In an episode

derived from Dryden's *The Rival Ladies*, Courtwell is pursued by his Spanish lady, Camilla, who disguises herself as a man, Perigreen; before discovering her identity, Courtwell wounds her in a duel. Disguises multiply when old Mr. Easy beds Peg, who is wearing Mrs. Easy's masquerade costume while the real Mrs. Easy is committing adultery with Lovechange in the park. Mrs. Woodbee thinks she has foiled that tryst by keeping the assignation herself; if her plans had worked, the play would indeed "of Husbands tell, / for Wenches, taking up their Wives i' th' *Mell*." But she unwittingly makes love in the dark with Courtwell, who is disguised as Lovechange. A witty servant, Amorous, wins his love, Grace, with a series of tricks and disguises like those in *Sir Martin Mar-All*. Dryden's reference to a "brisk bout" picks up a word frequently used in *The Mall*; Courtwell, for example, is called "a brisk Gallant" in the *Dramatis Personae*.

Published in 1674 as the work of one "J. D.," *The Mall* was printed by Scott and Saintsbury, but cannot possibly be Dryden's; John Dover has been proposed as the author, but there is no hard evidence. See Judith Milhous and Robert D. Hume, "Attribution Problems in English Drama, 1660–1700," *HLB* 31 (1983), pp. 23–24, and "Dating," p. 387*n*. Either the play was on stage much earlier than has been thought or Dryden had seen a manuscript; the former seems more likely to me, since a reference to an unstaged play could hardly hope to pass as a successful joke. The mysterious "J. D." might have simply vulgarized aspects of *Marriage A-la-Mode*, since he pretty clearly borrowed from Dryden's other comedies, but the epilogue makes more sense if *The Mall* was the earlier play, and if Dryden drew upon it, making its devices much more subtle and refraining from the explicit, staged adultery. There is no topical reference in *The Mall* that would force us to date it as late as 1674; a reference to "each Ninny of the Town" in the prologue picks up the name Shadwell had given Edward Howard in 1668. Theatre records for the King's Company for the fall of 1671 are almost entirely absent; the only certain performance we know of is *The Rehearsal* on 14 December, attended by Evelyn. As Robert D. Hume points out in a private communication, the plot incidents here summarized also fit fairly well with Shadwell's *Epsom-Wells*, first produced in December of 1672, but if Dryden was aiming at Shadwell, we should again have to suppose that he had read a manuscript, and that he was willing to write a joke that few in the audience would understand. In the absence of better evidence, I offer the hypothesis that *The Mall* had been staged before *Marriage A-la-Mode*, and that Dryden, conscious of some plot similarities, wished to separate his high comedy from its low farce.

56. Wilson, *A Rake*, 195–96; Hume, "The Date of Dryden's *Marriage A-la-Mode*," p. 166.

57. Here and elsewhere, I follow the argument of George McFadden, "Political Satire in *The Rehearsal*," *YES* 4 (1974):120–28. For some thoughtful qualifications of McFadden's argument, see John H. O'Neill, *George Villiers, Second Duke of Buckingham* (Boston: Twayne, 1984), pp. 102–110.

58. For details about the new playhouse, see Robert D. Hume, "The Nature of the Dorset Garden Theatre," *TN* 36 (1982):99–109.

59. The earliest printed source for this often-repeated tradition is Thomas Davies, *Dramatic Miscellanies*, 3 vols. (Dublin, 1784), III, 171–72.

60. On snuff-taking, see Malone, pp. 518–19; Osborn, pp. 70–71. Elkanah Settle, in his *Notes and Observations on the Empress of Morocco . . . Revised* (1674), accuses Dryden of deliberately distorting the text of his play: "But why his *Eyes* should be so dimm or his *Spectacles* so *dull*, as to let such [errors] as these slip without the lest mentioning them amongst their fellows I cannot guess, unless he design'd them" (p. 54).

61. *Letters*, p. 58. Dryden's epistolary complaints about his health begin as early as 1684; see *Letters*, p. 20. The eighteenth-century commentators are Charles Lamotte and the anonymous annotator of the Van Pelt Fourth Quarto of *The Rehearsal* at the University of Pennsylvania; see the article by Hugh Ormsby-Lennon cited above, ch. 5, n. 39, pp. 389–90 and notes.

62. These four letters did not see print until 1687, when Clifford was dead; the first three are undated. Clifford, who may have had a hand in *The Rehearsal*, refers in the first letter to "the gross scurrility of your last Prologue," which I take to be a reference to the prologue to *An Evening's Love*, first published on 13 January 1671. In the last of his letters, dated 1 July 1672, Clifford complains of his failure to draw a reply.

63. This document, P.R.O., E. 403/2772/p. 109, gives details of the agreement to repay Dryden and refers to an "order dated the xvii^th day of February 1670 [i.e., 1671]. It details a plan for payments with interest "every six months untill the repayment of the principall money aforesaid." For a full transcription, see Appendix C.

64. On 20 April 1672, he received £200 "for one year to Xmas last"; *C.T.B., 1669–72*, III, ii, 1227. Despite this unambiguous record, McFadden claims that "Dryden received nothing" (p. 124), and blames this imaginary nonpayment on the actions of Sir Robert Howard, who became Secretary to the Treasury in

October 1671. But the record shows no disturbance of Dryden's salary. The money warrant issued on 20 April 1672 was followed by a virtually identical one on 10 March 1673; *C.T.B., 1672–75*, IV, 231.

65. See below, ch. 8, n. 28.

66. The prose description of the staging of this prologue comes from Sloane MS 4455 f. 26v., quoted in *The London Stage*, I, 193.

67. Dorset Garden cost £9,000; Drury Lane, only £4,000; see Hume, "The Nature of the Dorset Garden Theatre," p. 101.

68. See David Ogg, *England in the Reign of Charles II*, 2 vols. (Oxford: Clarendon, 1934; rev. ed. 1955), I, 351.

69. *Diary*, III, 576–77.

70. On Whiting, see above, ch. 1, n. 30. Mary Dryden paid her Hearth Tax in 1670 (P.R.O., E. 179/157/446, printed in Belgion, *Titchmarsh*, p. 62). Her will, proved in 1677 (P.R.O., P.C.C. 60 Hale), leaves her body "to Rest till the time of my Changing shall come in that great appearing of my Lord and Saviour with all his Saints."

71. See Anstruther's essay on Cardinal Howard (cited above, ch. 5, n. 4), p. 321, and Brady, *Annals*, pp. 128–29.

72. *Diary*, III, 605–06 (12 March 1672).

73. Wilson, *A Rake*, pp. 205–06.

74. Ogg, I, 359–61.

75. *Roscius Anglicanus*, p. 32.

76. Downes, p. 32; but see n. 205 of the Milhous-Hume edition on the difficulty of dating this episode.

77. Dating the plays of this period is difficult. *The Citizen Turn'd Gentleman* was certainly on stage on 4 July 1672, but may well be earlier. The all-female revival of *Secret Love* and the premiere of *The Assignation*, both of which refer to the Mamamouchi, must be later than *The Citizen*, though we have no exact evidence on which to say how much later. See Milhous and Hume, "Dating," pp. 385–86. My best guess is that Ravenscroft's play was on stage by April or May, that the revived *Secret Love* followed soon after, and that *The Assignation* was on stage by early fall. The dating of *Amboyna* is also problematic; see n. 86 below.

78. *The Careless Lovers* (1673), sig. A4r. Ravenscroft's "Epistle to the Reader" in the published version admits that he wrote the prologue "in Requital to the *Prologue*, before the *Assignation*" and tells a story about an argument between two prostitutes, one of whom points out that "two of a Trade can seldome agree" (sig. A2v).

79. *The Reformation* (1673), IV, i, p. 48. Again, the date of performance is uncertain, but if I am correct in interpreting the Tutor's line about a father and son in love with the same woman as a swipe at *The Assignation*, we can at least place *The Reformation* after that play.

80. These four pamphlets, usually now called the "Rota" pamphlets, are *The Censure of the Rota* (Oxford, 1673), attributed to Richard Leigh by Anthony à Wood; *The Friendly Vindication of Mr. Dryden* (Cambridge, 1673), variously attributed to Robert Howard, Settle, Ravenscroft, and Martin Clifford; *Mr. Dreyden Vindicated* (1673), a genuinely friendly defense attributed to Charles Blount by family tradition; and *A Description of the Academy of the Athenian Virtuosi* (1673), also friendly to Dryden. For a detailed discussion, see McFadden, pp. 145–56.

81. Ogg, I, 362–64.

82. Wilson, *A Rake*, p. 208.

83. The reprinted version of *The Emblem of Ingratitude, A True Relation of the Unjust Cruell and Barbarous Proceedings against the English at Amboyna In the East-Indies, by the Neatherlandish Governor and Councel there* was advertised in the Term Catalogue for 24 June 1672.

84. For a detailed argument to this effect, see Colin Visser, "John Dryden's *Amboyna* at Lincoln's Inn Fields, 1673," *RECTR* 15 (1976):1–11.

85. A printed advertisement for *The Dutch Cruelties at Amboyna: With the Humours of the Valiant Welch-Man* "Acted by Men and Women," i.e., not by puppets, is in the P.R.O. (S.P. 29/317/187); the announced performance was on 11 November 1672. Two days later, the Lord Chamberlain forbade di Voto to use actors from the patent companies or to "Act any Play usually acted at any of ye said Theatres Nor take peeces or Sceenes out of ye Playes Acted at ye said Theatres" (P.R.O., L.C. 5/140/p. 129).

86. For a summary of Shaftesbury's speech, see Haley, *Shaftesbury*, pp. 316–17. The dating of *Amboyna* is problematic. Ward argued that it belonged in the spring of 1672, supposing that Dutch War

propaganda would more naturally come at the beginning of the war and that di Voto was pirating scenes from an already performed play the following November; see "The Dates of Two Dryden Plays," *PMLA* 51 (1936):786–92. But in the *Advertisement* printed with *King Arthur*, which listed his plays "in the Order I wrote them," Dryden placed *Amboyna* after *The Assignation*, which cannot possibly be earlier than the summer of 1672 (see n. 77 above). Moreover, the reprint of the source pamphlet for *Amboyna* was not available until late June of 1672 (see n. 83 above), and propaganda was even more urgent during the meeting of Parliament than at the outset of the war. Although the reference to Carthage is a commonplace, I should also think it more likely that Dryden was echoing Shaftesbury's speech than vice versa. All this evidence points to the spring of 1673, but that leaves the problem of di Voto, whose play would then antedate Dryden's. The order forbidding di Voto to "take peeces or Sceenes out of yᵉ Playes Acted at yᵉ said Theatres" certainly sounds as if he was stealing from an already performed play. Still, di Voto might possibly have put together a crude play from the same pamphlet independently; Dryden's play has no "Valiant Welch-Man." The quick closing down of di Voto's version may have been an attempt by the King's Company to protect a play they were planning but had not yet produced.

87. See Evelyn, *Diary*, IV, 5 (15 March 1673).

88. See Oliver, *Howard*, pp. 183–88.

89. Jones, *Country and Court*, pp. 177–79; Haley, *Shaftesbury*, pp. 323–25.

90. For details, see Appendix C.

91. Hartmann, in *Clifford of the Cabal*, pp. 298–300, casts some doubt on Evelyn's circumstantial account of Clifford's suicide, pointing out that Clifford had made his will some weeks in advance. Most historians, however, have accepted Evelyn's account; see *Diary*, IV, 18–23.

CHAPTER 8. "ANOTHER TASTE OF WIT"

1. See the passage about *The Assignation* as a "Catholick *Intrigue*," quoted and discussed above, ch. 7, p. 238. One of Dryden's anonymous defenders tried the same tactic in reverse, identifying the "Athenian Virtuosi" of the "Rota" with Dissenting religion by accusing them of admiring the dismal poetry of Sternhold, Hopkins, and Robert Wild: "The Author of the Censure of the *Rota*, you must know, is very intimate with Dr. *Wild*, and was with him eating of Herrings, when his Spouse run out with a herrings tail bobbing in her mouth, to receive the Letter from the Post which brought the joyful newes of his Majesties toleration" (*A Description of the Academy*, p. 11).

2. The two plays were entered on the Stationers' Register on 18 March, advertised in *The London Gazette* for 29 May–2 June, and appeared in the Term Catalogue for 16 June. By the time he wrote the dedication of *The Assignation*, Dryden had seen all of the "Rota" pamphlets, which evidently appeared in the early months of 1673. The author of the *Description of the Academy* says that *The Censure of the Rota* appeared "in cold winter weather" (p. 5); the two real defenses of Dryden, advertised in the Term Catalogue for 6 May, were probably available sooner. I should suppose that Dryden wrote his dedications in April.

3. Settle describes himself on the title page of *The Empress of Morocco* as a "Servant to his Majesty," a phrase that appears on Dryden's title pages as well. Settle had once had a right to claim that distinction; he had been appointed "Sewer in ordinary" to Charles on 27 February 1672; the document (P.R.O., L.C. 3/27/p. 94) identifies him as "one of the poettes in His Maᵗˢ Theatre Royall." The authors of *Notes and Observations*, however, point out that an announcement in the *London Gazette* for 11–15 December 1673 had stripped all such unpaid royal servants of their immunity from prosecution; they sneer at Settle's losing "his priviledge of poet in extraordinary to his Majesty." In the preface to *The Libertine* (1676), Shadwell alludes to the fact that "Protections are taken off" and wonders how Settle can "presume to write himself . . . Servant to his Majesty." See *Works*, XVII, 390, 409–10, 388n.

4. On the musical climax, see Curtis A. Price, *Henry Purcell and the London Stage* (Cambridge: Cambridge University Press, 1984), pp. 9–11.

5. On Sedley's two acts of public nudity, which occurred in 1663 and 1668, see Vivian de Sola Pinto, *Sir Charles Sedley* (Constable, 1927), pp. 61, 110–11. Burnet's report of Rochester's remark comes in *Some Passages of the Life and Death of John, Earl of Rochester* (1680), p. 12.

6. Although he does not point to this verbal echo, McFadden was the first to link these remarks with Dryden's later complaints about May; see pp. 127, 136–37. Ward (p. 97), had suggested Buckingham as the target, but the Duke was hardly a "middling sort of courtier." McFadden argues (pp. 127–28, 158–60) that

NOTES TO CHAPTER 8

Dryden was aiming at Sir Robert Howard as well as Baptist May, but that argument is based on the dubious premise that Dryden was still angry about *The Indian Queen* and the false premise that Howard had interrupted payment of Dryden's salary in 1672. For discussions of these issues, see above, ch. 6, n. 82; ch. 7, n. 64. Still, McFadden is surely correct in pointing out that Howard, in a later letter to Rochester, ironically picked up phrases from this dedication; see pp. 174–75. Throughout this discussion, my thinking has been greatly stimulated by McFadden's account of Dryden's wary approach to Rochester. I have a number of particular disagreements, as will be apparent in the notes, but McFadden's account has made mine possible.

7. McFadden suggests that Rochester helped Dryden secure the £500 paid him in February 1671 (p. 159). But Ormonde and Clifford were active in Dryden's interest at that time, and there is no evidence that Dryden had met Rochester until several months later. Perhaps Rochester helped to expedite the payment of Dryden's salary for 1672, £200, which he received on 10 March 1673; *C.T.B., 1672–75*, IV, 231.

8. He received £200 on 31 December 1673, £200 on 4 December 1674, £100 on 28 February 1676, another £100 on 24 March 1676, £200 on 20 February 1677, and £100 on 27 July 1677. See Appendix C.

9. *Diary*, IV, 117 (19 April 1663).

10. McFadden points to the relevance of these remarks, pp. 162–63.

11. *The Letters of John Wilmot Earl of Rochester*, ed. Jeremy Treglown (Oxford: Basil Blackwell, 1980), p. 120. As John Harold Wilson showed in his earlier edition of *The Rochester-Savile Letters*, (Columbus: Ohio State University Press, 1941), p. 41, this letter, in which Rochester responds to a report of Dryden's displeasure at the "Allusion to Horace," may be dated with reasonable certainty to the spring of 1676.

12. See McFadden's convincing development of this idea, especially p. 164.

13. For a fuller discussion, see Pinto, "Rochester and Dryden," pp. 39–47.

14. Ward, recognizing that Buckingham had achieved his appointment in May, dated this letter too early on that basis in his edition, an error repeated by Treglown, p. 86. In the biography, realizing that the inclusion of the already spoken prologue and epilogue demanded a date as late as July, Ward guessed that Dryden did not have up-to-date information (p. 348, n. 5). But Dryden is clearly referring to the irony of Buckingham's angry resignation from a post he had recently been eager to secure. See Wilson, *A Rake*, p. 220.

15. See Anstruther, "Cardinal Howard and the English Court," pp. 322–40.

16. See Ogg, I, 372–88; Jones, *Country and Court*, 181–85; Wilson, *A Rake*, pp. 224–49.

17. J. S. Clarke, *The Life of James the Second*, 2 vols. (1816), I, 487–88. Berkshire was possibly referring to this episode when he alluded to James's "former displeasure with me" in a letter written to Edward Coleman, York's secretary, on 10 September 1674; this is one of a group of letters in code, signed "William Rice," but attributed to Berkshire in George Treby's *Collection of Letters . . . Relating to the Horrid Popish Plott* (1681); the passage occurs on p. 98.

Clarke's *Life* is based on a mysterious manuscript in James's own hand, now lost; two different sources claim that manuscript was revised and corrected by Dryden himself, and prevented from its intended publication by the Glorious Revolution. See Roswell G. Ham, "Dryden as Historiographer-Royal: The Authorship of *His Majesties Declaration Defended*, 1681," *RES* 11 (1935), pp. 287–88.

18. In discussing this passage, McFadden (pp. 166–67) corrects Scott, who had not realized that the "prince" being praised was James, not Charles.

19. In his *Notes and Observations . . . Revised* (imprint date 1674, but not advertised until early 1675), Settle identified his antagonists as Dryden, Crowne, and Shadwell, but wrote as if Dryden had been the ringleader. John Crowne, years later, admitted having written "three parts in four" of the pamphlet; see the "Epistle to the Reader" prefaced to his *Caligula* (1698). Shadwell, who often attacked Settle, never admitted having taken part. Although Ward devotes an appendix to his doubts about Dryden's share in the *Notes and Observations*, the California editors have reprinted it, following Malone and Scott, who believed that Dryden wrote the preface, the parody of the opening of Act II, and the postscript. In quoting from the *Notes and Observations*, I shall assume that Dryden wrote only the preface and postscript. In an article on "Elkanah Settle and the Genesis of *Mac Flecknoe*," *PQ* 43 (1964), p. 62, McFadden shrewdly points out that "the so-called 'Postscript' follows the thought of the 'Preface' without a break in continuity. Both appear parts of a single composition, split in half." Anne Doyle, in "Dryden's Authorship of *Notes and Observations on the Empress of Morocco* (1674)," *SEL* 6 (1966):421–45, is inclined to give him a larger share, and argues that he "must have been the instigator of the attack" (p. 424). It seems more likely to me that Crowne was the principal author, and that he persuaded Dryden to frame his nit-picking textual criticism of Settle's play with

582

the more general criticism of the preface and postscript. The California editors, like Doyle, are inclined to believe that Dryden wrote the poetic parody of the opening of Act II; the lines are so clumsy metrically that I find it difficult to believe they are Dryden's. Maximillian Novak, in his excellent introduction to *The Empress of Morocco and its Critics*, a facsimile reprint of all the documents in the controversy (Los Angeles: Clark Library, 1968), takes a position like mine.

20. The author of *Raillerie a la Mode Consider'd* (1673) praises Dryden for thus refusing to defend himself against those tracts; see p. 27.

21. See Robert D. Hume, "Dryden on Creation: 'Imagination' in the Later Criticism," *RES* n.s. 21 (1970):295–314.

22. See George McFadden, "Dryden's 'Most Barren Period'—and Milton," *HLQ* 24 (1960):283–96.

23. *Reflections on Aristotle's Treatise of Poesie . . . By R. Rapin* was licensed on 26 June 1674. Rymer's preface suggests that he had seen the postscript to *Notes and Observations*. "Although a Poet is oblig'd to know all Arts and Sciences," he writes, "yet he ought discreetly to manage this knowledge" (sig. A8v). This sounds like a response to Dryden's insistence that "A man should be learn'd in severall Sciences, and should have a reasonable *Philosophicall*, and in some measure a *Mathematicall* head; to be a compleat and excellent Poet" (XVII, 182). For Rymer's praise of the night passage, see sig. b1r.

24. Dryden also owned the 1611 folio of Spenser, a book later owned by Pope, but made few marginalia in it; see Osborn, pp. 241–45.

25. According to *A Character of the True Blue Protestant Poet*, an attack on Settle published in April 1682, "the better half of his Generation are *Barbers*."

26. The unpaginated "Epistle Dedicatory" of *A Narrative Written by E. Settle* (1683) gives Settle's account.

27. See Novak's introduction to the facsimile reprint, especially pp. xiv-xvii.

28. There were two separate agreements between the sharers of the company in the wake of the fire. According to articles dated 17 December 1673 (BL Add. MS 20,726, ff. 8–9v), the ten leading players and the poet agreed to pay six men who were putting up the actual money for the new building a daily rent of £3 10s. after beginning to act in the Drury Lane theatre; this agreement provided for a higher rent if the building cost more than the initial estimate, as it did. This entire set of papers has now been printed; see Judith Milhous and Robert D. Hume, "Charles Killigrew's 'Abstract of Title to the Playhouse'," *Theatre History Studies* 6 (1986):57–71. In a separate indenture signed by the same eleven sharers on 20 March 1674, recited in a later lawsuit (P.R.O., C. 6/221/48), the sharers agreed to contribute money in proportion to their shares toward the building of a new scenehouse. Since "single sharers" were assessed £160 each, Dryden probably had to pay £200. In a copy of the part of this indenture dealing with Nicholas Burt, one of the "single sharers," printed by John Payne Collier in *Shakespeare Studies* IV (1849):147–55, "John Dryden" appears on the list of those who "have disbursed and laid out amongst them several great sumes . . . for the building of a scene house" (p. 149). Hotson's account of these agreements (pp. 254–56) is overly compressed and somewhat misleading; he omits Dryden from the list of those signing the scenehouse indenture.

29. "This Play was left in Mr. Dryden's hands many years since: The Author of it was unknown to him, and return'd not to claim it; After Twelve Years expectation, Mr. Dryden gave it to the Players. . . . I have heard him say that finding a Scene wanting he supplyd it" ("The Bookseller to the Reader," signed by R. Bentley, sig. A2r-v). Swinburne thought he had identified the scene; see his *Complete Works*, ed. Edmund Gross and Thomas James Wise, 14 vols. (Heinemann, 1926), XIV, 411–21. Since twelve years would bring us back to 1662, this comedy may have been another of the old plays in the bundle bought by Hart from Moseley, which had already yielded *The Wild Gallant* and *The Duke of Lerma*; Alfred Harbage, in "Elizabethan-Restoration Palimpsest," pp. 305–07, argues thus, attributing the original to Brome; see also Milhous and Hume, "Attribution Problems," pp. 24–25.

30. On the early preparations, see the letter from James Vernon, dated 22 August 1673, in *Letters to Sir Joseph Williamson*, ed. W. D. Christie, 2 vols. (Camden Society, 1874), I, 180–81. On the importance of the "innovative and daring" *Psyche*, in which "the synthesis of music and drama . . . is remarkably good, certainly unmatched in any later semi-opera," see Price, *Henry Purcell and the London Stage*, pp. 296–97.

31. The *London Stage* gives 30 April as a conjectural date for a performance of the operatic *Tempest*. Dryden may have been referring to a not-yet-produced extravaganza, as he would certainly have been aware of the preparations by the rival house, but I should think it more likely that the new *Tempest* had already had

its premiere by 26 March, the date of this prologue. The authorship of the operatic *Tempest*, long attributed to Shadwell, is now in doubt. See Charles E. Ward, "*The Tempest*: A Restoration Opera Problem," *ELH* 13 (1946):119–30, and Maximillian Novak, "Elkanah Settle's Attacks on Thomas Shadwell and the Authorship of the 'Operatic *Tempest*'," *N&Q* 113 (1968): 263–65.

32. Hart and Mohun were making such decisions because Killigrew had pawned his shares in the company and no longer took much interest in its day-to-day operations. See Hotson, *Commonwealth and Restoration Stage*, pp. 256–57. For a full account of the French musicians, who staged a number of operas, see Pierre Danchin, "The Foundation of the Royal Academy of Music in 1674 and Pierre Perrin's *Ariane*," *Theatre Survey* 25 (1984):55–67. Since these musicians presented an opera for the marriage of the Duke of York and Maria Beatrice, the often-repeated notion that *The State of Innocence* was intended for that occasion is dubious.

33. It is difficult to imagine how the King's Company might have staged land and sea battles on stage. Yet in the operatic *Tempest*, the Duke's Company staged a shipwreck, and on 21 August 1674, Evelyn saw a mock-battle at Windsor: "There was approches, & a formal seige, against a Work with *Bastions*, Bullwarks, Ramparts, Palizads, hornworks, Conterscarps &c: in imitation of the Citty of *Maestrict*, newly taken by the *French*: & this being artificialy design'd & cast up in one of the Meadows at the foote of the long *Terrace* below the Castle, was defended against the *Duke of Monmouth* (newly come from that real seige) who [with the Duke of York] attaqu'd it with a little army, to shew their skill in *Tactics . . .* to the greate satisfaction of a thousand spectators" (*Diary*, IV, 42).

34. Parker, *Milton*, I, 578–79. I owe the reading of *Samson Agonistes* as an attack on the theatre to Professor George Lord.

35. Aubrey's account of this visit, *Brief Lives*, II, 72, is the earliest of many versions. See Morris Freedman, "Dryden's 'Memorable Visit' to Milton," *HLQ* 18 (1955):99–108; Parker, *Milton*, I, 634–35.

36. I follow the text printed in Milton's *Complete Poetry and Major Prose*, ed. Hughes, p. 209.

37. See Morris Freedman, "Milton and Dryden on Rhyme," *HLQ* 24 (1961):337–44.

38. For a list of these borrowings, see Edward Le Comte, "*Samson Agonistes* and *Aureng-Zebe*," *EA* 11 (1958):18–22; most of them were listed in an anonymous article in the *Gentleman's Magazine* for October 1762, which Le Comte cites. In Dryden's own lifetime, Gerard Langbaine, a fanatical detector of plagiarism, noticed the borrowings; see his *Account of the English Dramatick Poets* (1691), p. 157.

39. I owe these figures to Morris Freedman, "The 'Tagging' of Paradise Lost: Rhyme in Dryden's *The State of Innocence*," *Milton Quarterly* 5 (1971):18–22. Freedman's examples point in the direction of a larger study of this work that might prove fruitful, though I do not agree with his conclusion, in which he argues that Dryden's "self-confidence and self-possession may have caused him to overreach himself, to overestimate his own art and seemingly underestimate Milton's. The uncertainty with which he finally carried out his work testifies perhaps to a growing awareness of how brash he had been in his original ambition" (p. 21). In my view, Dryden was neither "brash" in undertaking the opera nor "uncertain" in carrying out the task.

40. I have discussed some of these passages in "Milton on Heroic Warfare," *Yale Review* 66 (1976):70–86.

41. *Marriage A-la-Mode* was revived on 23 April; *The Indian Emperour* on 12 May; Lee's *Nero* was on stage on 16 May, possibly earlier; *The London Stage* gives 19 November for Duffett's *Mock-Tempest*, but Milhous and Hume, in "Dating," p. 386, argue that "performance in the late spring of 1674 must be considered entirely possible."

42. Dryden visited Evelyn on 27 June 1674, just before the players went to Oxford; since Evelyn was well acquainted with Bathurst, "who had formerly taken particular care of [his] Sonn," perhaps Dryden wished to know how he might frame an approach to Bathurst. See *Diary*, IV, 37, 68.

43. I quote the "Session of the Poets" later printed in the "Antwerp" edition of Rochester's poems (1680) and in Buckingham's *Works* (1704). On the authorship of this poem, which has also been attributed to Settle, see Vieth, *Attribution in Restoration Poetry*, pp. 296–321; Vieth sees no compelling reason to assign the poem to any of the three candidates. In an article on "Dryden's Anti-Clericalism," *N&Q* 179 (1940):254–57, E. S. de Beer argued from this poem that it was "probable that about 1676 Dryden was contemplating applying for a post for which holy orders were essential" (p. 256); this plausible inference has been rejected by later editors of Dryden's poetry. The passage on Dryden also refers to Anne Reeves; see above, Appendix D, pp. 532–39. Rumors about Dryden's having been refused ordination, which recur again and again in attacks on him, begin as early as 1668, in *A Letter from a Gentleman to the Honourable Ed. Howard Esq.*, by "R.

F." That tract speaks scornfully of the "admirable Dispute between a Christian and a Heathen Priest" in *The Indian Emperour*, "which . . . shows how great a loss the Church had of him, when he was diverted from entering into Orders" (p. 7).

44. On the financial record, see Judith Milhous, "The Duke's Company's Profits, 1675–1677," *TN* 32 (1978), p. 82; on the quarrel of the King's Company, see her *Thomas Betterton and the Management of Lincoln's Inn Fields*, p. 32.

45. For a full account of *Calisto*, see Boswell, *Restoration Court Stage*, pp. 177–227.

46. The source is "Some Passages of the Life of Mr. John Crown," which first appeared in Dennis's *Original Letters* (1721), nine years after Crowne's death. See *Critical Works of John Dennis*, ed. Hooker, II, 404–06. Rochester's attack on Crowne's *Charles the Eighth* in his *Timon*, which was circulating in late spring of 1674, is further reason to doubt Dennis's story; see *Poems*, ed. Vieth, pp. 90–91.

47. Printed in *Miscellany Poems* in 1684, this epilogue was first attributed to Dryden in the edition of 1702, after his death, but before Crowne's. James Kinsley argues in favor of that attribution; see his edition of Dryden's *Poems*, IV, 1952–53. In his edition of *The Prologues and Epilogues of John Dryden* (New York: Columbia University Press, 1951), pp. 341–45, William Bradford Gardner argues against Dryden's authorship, offering the theory that Crowne wrote this epilogue, then "toned it down," producing the epilogue actually used; following Gardner, the California editors have silently omitted the poem. Another hypothesis is that Dryden and Crowne collaborated on this prologue, as they had earlier done in the *Notes and Observations*, in which case I should suppose that the lines I have quoted, which Kinsley also praises as the best in the poem, are Dryden's. One possible reason why the poem appeared anonymously in 1684 is that Henrietta was by then notoriously the mistress of Monmouth, whom Dryden had attacked.

48. See Ogg, II, 527–28; 533.

49. Anstruther, "Cardinal Howard," p. 340; John Kenyon, *The Popish Plot* (Heinemann, 1972), pp. 22–3.

50. Treby, *A Collection of Letters*, p. 103–04; on the authorship of these letters, see above, n. 17. Uncertain support for an ongoing relationship between Dryden and the second Earl of Berkshire comes from Elizabeth Thomas's anecdote about Charles Dryden's horoscope (see above, ch. 6, n. 4), in which Dryden and Charles are supposed to have visited Berkshire during August of 1674.

51. Louis, who was still at war with the Dutch, was concerned to prevent the English Opposition from forcing an anti-French policy on the court. See Ogg, II, 534–36.

52. McFadden speculates "that Dryden offered the King the option of a happy or an unhappy ending to his 'tragedy,' and that the King opted for the present denouement" (p. 192). But some at least in Dryden's audience would have known that the real Aureng-Zebe was alive, so a genuinely tragic ending was probably not a real option. McFadden's chapter on this play (pp. 183–202) makes out a reasonable case for the loyal Aureng-Zebe as a general analogue for the loyal James.

53. The profits from *Aureng-Zebe* were probably offset by the ongoing debts incurred by the King's Company since the fire of 1672. Such acts of anarchy as the actors' seizing the cash box after performances (see n. 44 above) were unlikely to result in income for Dryden, who said in the dedication that he "subsist[ed] wholly by [Charles's] Bounty" (sig. A2r). Taken literally, that remark would mean that Dryden was now receiving no income from his shares in the King's Company.

54. McFadden has pointed in the direction of such an argument in his essay on "Dryden's 'Most Barren Period'—and Milton." See especially the examples on pp. 289–94.

55. The passages are I, pp. 8, 13; II, pp. 20, 26; III, p. 31; IV, p. 50.

56. See William Frost, "*Aureng-Zebe* in Context: Dryden, Shakespeare, Milton, and Racine," *JEGP* 74 (1975), especially pp. 28–32.

57. See Frost, pp. 35–39, a discussion of parallels with Racine's *Mithridates*. In his notes to *Aureng-Zebe*, Montague Summers notes a close parallel between Aureng-Zebe's outraged speech on finally understanding Nourmahal's incestuous longing and Seneca's *Hippolytus*, II, 671ff. See *Dryden: The Dramatic Works*, 6 vols. (Nonesuch, 1931–32), IV, 496. Racine's *Phèdre*, based on Seneca, did not appear until 1677.

58. See Jean Hagstrum, *Sex and Sensibility from Milton to Mozart* (Chicago: University of Chicago Press, 1980), which includes a brilliant chapter on Dryden's treatment of love (pp. 50–71) and a discussion of Pope's *Eloisa* alert to its considerable debt to *Aureng-Zebe* (pp. 121–32).

59. There may have been some coolness between Dryden's Northamptonshire relatives and his wife. A letter written to Malone on 18 May 1799 by Lady Dryden of Canons Ashby alleges that Elizabeth "resided

in Lodgings in London when my grandmother visited her; but having, to bad conduct before marriage, united bad conduct afterwards, & having used Mr Dryden very indifferently, the family confined their attentions to formal tea visits, as I have heard" (printed in Osborn, pp. 261–62). This century-old piece of gossip seems to concern Elizabeth's declining years, after John's death. I wonder whether the reluctance of the Drydens to deal with the poet's widow did not in fact have more to do with her Catholicism than with any alleged "bad conduct."

60. From the *Memoirs of . . . Congreve*, cited above, ch. 6, n. 4.

61. Samson calls Dalila a "Traitress" at line 725; the bulk of the speech, however, is drawn from the chorus after her departure:

> Is it for that such outward ornament
> Was lavish't on thir Sex, that inward gifts
> Were left for haste unfinish't, judgment scant,
> Capacity not rais'd to apprehend
> Or value what is best
> In choice, but oftest to affect the wrong?
> Or was too much of self-love mixt,
> Or constancy no root infixt,
> That either they love nothing, or not long?

[ll. 1025–33]

CHAPTER 9. "THE BOWE OF ULYSSES"

1. P.R.O., L.C. 7/1/p. 5.

2. Downes, *Roscius Anglicanus*, p. 36.

3. The players mention Dryden's complaints about money and insist on his being under contract in their petition to the Lord Chamberlain of 1678, possibly never submitted, printed in Osborn, pp. 204–05. For the agreement with Charles Killigrew, see Hotson, *Commonwealth and Restoration Stage*, pp. 258–61.

4. See Rochester's reply to Savile, in *Letters*, ed. Treglown, p. 119; on the dating of this letter, see above, ch. 8, n. 11.

5. See Appendix C. Ward, who missed the second payment, incorrectly states that Dryden's salary was now in arrears (p. 115).

6. Osborn, p. 204.

7. See Ward, p. 336, n. 30.

8. P.R.O., P.C.C. 60 Hale. The omission of Dryden's second son John is puzzling.

9. I add these arguments for an early date for the composition of *Mac Flecknoe* to those meticulously laid out by David Vieth in "The Discovery of the Date of *Mac Flecknoe*," in *Evidence in Literary Scholarship*, pp. 63–87. Vieth's central point is that the poem abounds in particular references to plays staged and published up until July of 1676, and has no such references to later works. I am particularly impressed by the multitude of references to *Psyche* and *The Virtuoso*, including a number of borrowings from the dedication to the latter play.

10. "My Picture left in Scotland," in Herford and Simpson, VIII, 149–50. See *Works*, II, 326.

11. Maximillian Novak, in "Dryden's 'Ape of the French Eloquence' and Richard Flecknoe," *BNYPL* 72 (1968):499–506, suggests that Dryden resented an attack Flecknoe made on Davenant. The fullest discussion of Dryden's reasons for choosing Flecknoe is Paul Hammond, "Flecknoe and *Mac Flecknoe*," *EIC* 35 (1985):315–29.

12. Most of these are noted in *Works*, II, 311–27.

13. In the portrait of Shadwell as Og, which he contributed to *The Second Part of Absalom and Achitophel*, largely by Nahum Tate, Dryden advises Shadwell to "Eat Opium, mingle Arsenick in thy Drink" (l. 482). For a sample of the abuse that prompted this response, see Shadwell's claim that Dryden contracted venereal disease from Anne Reeves, in *The Medal of John Bayes*, sig. A1v, quoted above, Appendix D, p. 538.

14. Fifteen manuscripts are now known to survive: see David Vieth, "Dryden's *Mac Flecknoe*, The Case Against Editorial Confusion," *HLB* 24 (1976):204–45, and Paul Hammond, "The Robinson Manuscript Miscellany of Restoration Verse in the Brotherton Collection, Leeds," *PLPLS* 18 (1982):275–324. The

young poet John Oldham dated his handwritten transcript "Aº 1678," and the wits of the Rochester circle may be referring to *Mac Flecknoe* when they urge Dryden to abandon satire and return to the stage in "Advice to Apollo 1678," a poem probably written in 1677; see *POAS* I, 392–95. One anecdote published in early 1682 has Dryden sending Shadwell "a *Mac-Flecknoe* and a brace of lobsters for his Breakfast; All which he knew he had a singular aversion for." See Vieth, "Discovery," pp. 67–68.

15. According to Otway, Dryden, "being ask't his opinion of this Play, very gravely Cock't and cry'd, *Igad he knew not a line in it he would be Author of.*" See Macdonald, *Bibliography*, pp. 211–12.

16. See Hotson, *Commonwealth and Restoration Stage*, pp. 260–61.

17. On 6 April 1676, John Verney reported this rumor to Ralph Verney: "Some say the Lady Ambassador Berkeley hath declared herself a papist in France, as the Lords Mulgrave and Peterborough have done here" (*H.M.C.* VII, app. 467).

18. Montague Summers cites the parallel passages in his edition of Dryden's *Dramatic Works*, III, 580.

19. Quoted in Haley, *Shaftesbury*, p. 417.

20. *C.T.B. 1676–79*, V, i, 552.

21. In *Mac Flecknoe*, Dryden describes the Barbican area, "Where their vast Courts the Mother-Strumpets keep" (l. 72). Vieth describes this passage in "The Author's Apology" as an "inside joke"; see "Discovery," p. 83.

22. Dryden may have been publicly repaying a private compliment from Wycherley, whose "Epistle to Mr. Dryden, occasion'd by his desiring the Author to joyn with him in Writing a Comedy" probably dates from around this time. B. Eugene McCarthy, in *William Wycherley: A Biography* (Athens: Ohio University Press, 1979), p. 101, suggests that the poem, not published until the eighteenth century, was written "before 1677." An interesting fair copy of the poem in the handwriting of Alexander Pope is in the Berkshire Record Office (Trumbull Add. MSS 18). Dryden's reference to *The Plain Dealer* may also help us date the composition of this essay. R. D. Hume, pointing to the long gap between the composition and publication of *The State of Innocence*, argues that "we cannot be sure just when ['The Author's Apology'] was written" (*Dryden's Criticism*, p. 210n). But the definite reference to Wycherley's new play is evidence that Dryden was at least polishing the essay not long before its publication, and I believe the entire "Apology" was written at the last minute.

23. "I never writ anything for myself but Antony and Cleopatra," "A Parallel of Poetry and Painting" (1695), p. liv.

24. Sedley's play had its premiere in February 1677. In his headnote to *Antony and Cleopatra* in *The Poetical and Dramatic Works of Sir Charles Sedley*, 2 vols. (Constable, 1928), I, 190, Vivian de Sola Pinto argues that Dryden wrote his play to compete with Sedley, but the reference to "godlike Romans" in the prologue to *Aureng-Zebe* suggests that the project was in his mind well before Sedley's play. Citations of Sedley follow Pinto's edition.

25. Here and elsewhere, I follow Maximillian Novak's excellent headnote to this play (*Works*, XIII, 363–89). As Novak points out, "Dryden's method of revising Shakespeare's lines in *The Tempest* and in *Troilus and Cressida* involved a toning down of hyperboles and metaphors"; *All for Love*, in which metaphorical language is expanded, "presents a completely different approach" (XIII, 370).

26. The evidence for a December premiere for *All for Love* is the "pay-sheet" for 12 December printed in *Works*, XIII, 627. Milhous and Hume, who raise the possibility that this may be a forgery, nonetheless consider a December premiere "quite likely" ("Dating," p. 386). Ward dated Dryden's letter to Lord Latimer in July of 1677, but one of Dryden's requests in that letter, an increase in his salary, was granted on 2 July, and Midsummer, a "quarter-day" on which payments were due, was 24 June. Unless Dryden was unaware of the action granting him an increase, the letter would fall somewhere between those dates.

27. Ward and McFadden both assume that the "Uncle" of Latimer to whom Dryden referred was Robert Bertie, third Earl of Lindsey. But Charles Bertie, Lindsey's brother, Danby's brother-in-law, and Latimer's uncle, was now Secretary to the Treasury, a post once held by Sir Robert Howard, who was now Auditor of the Receipt. Documents concerning Dryden's salary frequently bear his name. On 24 March 1676, for example, Bertie ordered Howard to pay Dryden £100 (*C.T.B., 1676–79*, V, i, 173). J. R. Jones describes Bertie as "Danby's confidential agent" (*Country and Court*, p. 204). Dryden was far more likely to have been a petitioner at Charles Bertie's door than at the door of his brother the Earl.

28. For details, see Appendix C.

29. For Wycherley's letter to Mulgrave, see Robert J. Allen, "Two Wycherley Letters," *TLS* (18 April

1935):257. Allen prints the letter from a copy in the Orrery papers at Harvard. Wycherley's comments on Rymer are more hostile than Dryden's; he tells Mulgrave, "your favourite Plays, The King and no King, The Maid's Tragedy, and Rollo, are all torn in Pieces by a New Critique lately publish'd by Rymer, which we intend Jack Markham shall answer. The book is duller than his Play of Edgar, which he promises to publish as a Pattern for exact Tragedies." I have been unable to identify Jack Markham. For Dryden's letter to Dorset, see *Letters*, pp. 13–14. The letter was posted from the home of Sir Thomas Elmes at Lilford, who was presumably the "Cousin" of whose tiresome "Discourse" Dryden complains in his letter: "he talkes nothing all day long to me in french & Italian to show his breeding." Elmes's mother, Grace Bevill Elmes, was the sister of Honor Bevill Dryden, wife to Dryden's uncle Sir John Dryden of Canons Ashby; see Baker, *Northamptonshire*, I, 433–34. Elmes was thus not actually Dryden's second cousin, as Ward claims (p. 121); seventeenth-century speakers used the term "cousin" loosely to indicate some connection, even a remote one by marriage.

   30. Licensed 13 September 1677. Although *The London Stage* speculates about a possible performance, basing that speculation entirely on the fact of the play's publication, Robert D. Hume crisply refers to the play as "unacted" (*Development*, p. 166).

   31. For a full discussion of the relationship between the "Heads of an Answer" and "The Grounds of Criticism in Tragedy," see Robert D. Hume, *Dryden's Criticism*, pp. 102–23.

   32. Hotson, *Commonwealth and Restoration Stage*, pp. 261–62.

   33. See Haley, *Shaftesbury*, pp. 434–41.

   34. In "Dryden in 1678–1681: The Literary and Historical Perspectives," in *The Golden and the Brazen World*, ed. John M. Wallace (Berkeley: University of California Press, 1985), p. 60, Phillip Harth argues that a passage from this dedication about changing one's party, often thought to apply to Shaftesbury, is more likely to be an attack on Buckingham. Dryden had excellent reasons to attack both men in a dedication to Danby, but the satanic imagery in the passage I am quoting here is surely aimed at the twisted Shaftesbury. While the idea that Dryden was attacking Shaftesbury in *The Kind Keeper* remains problematic (see below, n. 45), the portrait of Creon in *Oedipus*, with its emphasis on physical deformity, is surely aimed at Shaftesbury, whatever the date of the play (see above, pp. 311–12 and n. 52).

   Harth wishes to discount these early instances of Dryden's hostility to Shaftesbury in the interest of a larger argument. His article raises a number of objections to modern accounts of Dryden's political opinions in the years in question, essentially arguing that *Absalom and Achitophel* (November 1681) was his first unequivocally Tory statement. Harth notes that *A Modest Vindication of the Earl of S[haftesbur]y* (early fall 1681), an attack on Shaftesbury, links Dryden to the Whig leader, accusing him of writing "Panegyricks upon *Oliver Cromwel*, and Libels against his present Master." The notion that Dryden had attacked the King was grounded on the mistaken attribution to him of Mulgrave's "Essay on Satire"; see below, nn. 85, 86, 92. Two later attacks expand the notion that Dryden once flirted with the Whigs. In the anonymous *Heroic Scene* (early 1686?), a supposed dialogue between Dryden ("Johnny") and Roger L'Estrange ("Hodge"), "Johnny" confesses to such trimming:

> When the exalted Whigs were in their pride
> I spent my oil and labor on their side,
> Wrote a Whig play and Shaftesbury outran,
> For all my maxims were Republican;
> For the Excluding Bill I did declare,
> Libell'd and rail'd and did not Monarch spare.
> . . . .
> But a reserve I kept for Monmouth still
> Should he prevail, I with such equal skill
> With satire mingled praise he could not take it ill.
> And had that prince victorious been at Lyme,
> I the Black-box had justifi'd in rhyme.
>
> [ll. 59–64; 81–85; *POAS* IV, 83–84]

In *The Laureat* (1687), Robert Gould makes similar charges, arguing that Dryden wrote *The Spanish Fryar* because he had lost his pension, and that he attacked "Kingly Power" as "Arbitrary Lust" until gaining a "Pension," which "chang'd both thy Morals, and thy strain" (p. 3). These charges can be easily disproved.

The addition to Dryden's pension was granted in the summer of 1677, three years before *The Spanish Fryar*; payments on both salary and pension fell into arrears when Danby was impeached in December 1678 and never recovered. There is no evidence that Dryden ever endorsed Exclusion or argued for "Republican maxims"; on the contrary, respect for kingly authority runs steadily through his works, including *The Spanish Fryar*. If the treatment of Monmouth in *Absalom and Achitophel* mingles praise and satire, or at least sympathy and satire, *The Duke of Guise* is hardly the work of a man keeping "a reserve" for Monmouth.

My own explanations of the motives behind the works Dryden wrote in these years, laid out in some detail in this chapter and the next, thus differ substantially from Harth's. Not only do I believe Dryden was hostile to Shaftesbury as early as the dedication to *Aureng-Zebe* (1676), but I accept his authorship of *His Majesties Declaration Defended*, which Harth doubts (see below, ch. 10, n. 24). If Dryden was initially cautious in the face of the Popish Plot, I believe he had begun to take a recognizably Tory position by the end of 1679. His writings during these years vary considerably from each other in the intensity of their Tory politics, as I have tried to show, but there is no basis for thinking that he was ever a Whig.

35. See Andrew Browning, *Thomas Osborne Earl of Danby*, 3 vols. (Glasgow: Jackson, 1951), I, 268–69.

36. See F. C. Turner, *James II* (Eyre and Spottiswoode, 1948), p. 140.

37. Browning, *Danby*, I, 240.

38. *Ars Poetica*, ll. 38–40.

39. In his essay on "Elkanah Settle and the Genesis of *Mac Flecknoe*," pp. 69–71, and in *Dryden the Public Writer*, pp. 177–79, George McFadden explains and analyzes the echoes of Dryden in *Timon*. In both cases, he argues that Shadwell was attacking Dryden because his own comedy, *A True Widow*, "was being withdrawn in favor of his new rival's *Limberham*," and that Dryden then retaliated with *Mac Flecknoe*. I accept neither argument. I have already given my reasons for believing, with David Vieth, that *Mac Flecknoe* was composed in late 1676, and there is no evidence that Shadwell's play was "withdrawn" to make room for Dryden's. There is internal evidence for a March premiere for *A True Widow*, a reference to 21 March in the text itself, which would put it on stage immediately after the closing of *The Kind Keeper*. The evidence for a later performance is Shadwell's statement in the dedication that his play failed because of the troubled times, which has been taken to be a reference to the Popish Plot; the spring months, however, were troubled by the expectation that war with France was imminent; see, for example, Savile's letter to Rochester of 25 June 1678 (*Letters*, ed. Treglown, pp. 194–97). Another argument for a later performance is the long delay before the publication of the play, easily explained by the Popish Plot and Shadwell's decision to change publishers at just this juncture. John Harrington Smith accepts the date offered by Summers, December 1678 (*Works*, I, 361); Gardner accepts the textual evidence for a premiere on 21 March 1678 (*Prologues and Epilogues*, pp. 243–44), as does *The London Stage*; Maximillian Novak assumes that Shadwell's play was "first performed in March 1678" (*Works* XIII, 448); Milhous and Hume, surveying the evidence, conclude that "no final answer is possible" ("Dating," p. 387). I offer the close connection between Dryden's prologue to his own *Kind Keeper* and his prologue to *A True Widow* as a further argument for an early date; whenever *A True Widow* was actually performed, I should think Dryden wrote his prologue for Shadwell's play immediately after the banning of *The Kind Keeper*. Oden takes that position in *Dryden and Shadwell*, p. 182.

40. See Gunnar Sorelius, "Shadwell Deviating into Sense: *Timon of Athens* and the Duke of Buckingham," *Studia Neophilologica* 36 (1964):232–44.

41. I was once tempted to believe that this interruption of the Laureate's salary reflected Danby's irritation at Dryden's having presumed to recommend alternate policies to him in a publication just now coming from the press, but I now think that explanation unlikely. The blank docket probably reflects the sorry state of the Treasury at a time when efforts were being made to raise money for a war against France; for an account of Treasury difficulties at that time, see Browning, *Danby*, I, 270–71. Since Dryden received £150 on 8 June, he cannot have been in any permanent trouble with Danby. See Appendix C.

42. A contemporary manuscript satire, "Upon a late fall'n Poet," however, says that Dryden "pretended in kindnesse (yᵉ Dukes House to chouse) / He had throwne up his Share, at yᵉ other House." If, as Osborn suggests, the author was "an actor, associated with the King's Company," this may be evidence of resentment on their part. The same poem also indicates some irritation on the part of "Those Writers, who supported yᵉ [Duke's] House before," and it may be this line that led the copyist to attribute the poem to Shadwell. See *John Dryden II*, pp. 36, 48.

43. From Robert Gould's "A Satire against the Play-House," published in his *Poems* (1689), p. 176, but "Writ in the year 1685," according to the author. Neither Gould nor John Tutchin, who refers to the

play's obscenity in his *Poems on Several Occasions* (1685), p. 66, alleges that any particular person was attacked. The first printed attempt to identify a target appeared in 1760. See Susan Staves, "Why Was Dryden's *Mr. Limberham* Banned? A Problem in Restoration Theatre History," *RECTR* 13 (1974):1–12.

44. Montague Summers, in *Dryden: The Dramatic Works*, 6 vols. (Nonesuch, 1931–32), laments the fact that "we possess but an emasculated script of this sparkling comedy," but informs us that Woodall's "name in the original script was Stains" (IV, 535), and annotates a line about "A Punk of two Descents" by telling us that "This was originally 'Very punk of very punk,' but great exception having been taken to the phrase Dryden altered it to the present form" (IV, 540). Infuriatingly, Summers does not reveal his source. Had he actually seen the original script, which Malone described as "found by Lord Bolingbroke among the sweepings of Pope's study" (p. 118)? If so, where is that script today?

45. The two main candidates are Lauderdale and Shaftesbury, both prominent keepers of mistresses, though Staves doubts that either of them was aimed at. The manuscript satire "Upon a late fall'n Poet" suggests that the actor playing Father Aldo was dressed in a costume resembling that of some prominent figure who had helped to fill the house on Dryden's third nights. Osborn tentatively interprets that evidence as pointing to Lauderdale, and suggests that the satire directed at old, fumbling lechers may have been the King's idea; see *John Dryden II*, pp. 45–46. Many scholars have claimed that the King stopped the play, but the only contemporary evidence, Dryden's later preface, points to James, Duke of York, whom Lauderdale had faithfully supported; see n. 46 below. York might well have stopped the play if he thought it an attack on Lauderdale, whose savage repression of Dissent in Scotland had incurred the wrath of the Opposition. Still, as a supporter of the government, Dryden had no obvious reason to attack Lauderdale.

He did, however, have reasons to attack Shaftesbury, and had done so without question in the dedication to *All for Love*, published in the same month as the first performance of *The Kind Keeper*. Yet Staves argues against Shaftesbury as a target on the grounds that he was probably too weak to have the play stopped; *Sir Popular Wisdom*, a lost play described by Marvell as an attack on Shaftesbury, appeared in November, while he was still incarcerated, and he was obviously unable to stop it. Although I believe York stopped *The Kind Keeper* for reasons having nothing to do with Shaftesbury (see n. 46 below), I should think it possible that Dryden aimed some glancing blows at Shaftesbury. Limberham is physically frail, as was Shaftesbury, and some of his sexual foibles resemble those of Antonio in Otway's *Venice Preserved*, who is certainly a caricature of Shaftesbury. A possible source for Dryden's reference to himself as a "prudent Citizen" marketing his "Staple Ware" in the prologue to *The Kind Keeper*, an image he repeated in his prologue to Shadwell's *A True Widow*, is a pamphlet attacking Shaftesbury, published a week or so before Dryden's play and probably written by Marchamont Needham. This squib alleges that Shaftesbury, upon his dismissal as Lord Chancellor, "hied as fast as he could into the City, with Resolution to become a Citizen, and . . . drive a great Trade in the small Wares of Popularity" (*Honesty's Best Policy*, p. 13, quoted in *Works*, XIII, 462). I also wonder whether Dryden's reference to plantations in his prologue to Shadwell's play is a passing reference to Shaftesbury, who had a profitable plantation in South Carolina.

In an essay on the authorship of *Sodom*, J. W. Johnson raises the possibility that the character of Woodall owes something to Rochester, who had actually impersonated tradesmen and quacks while hiding from the wrath of the King in the City; the word "Sodom" occurs in Act IV, scene 1. But since Woodall engages our sympathies, these glancing resemblances to Rochester's career do not constitute an attack comparable to that in the preface to *All for Love*. See "Did Lord Rochester Write *Sodom?*," in press.

46. McFadden thus interprets Dryden's dedication, in which the poet says that he has altered his play because "their Authority is, and shall be ever sacred to me, as much absent as present, and in all alterations of their Fortune, who for those Reasons have stopp'd its farther appearance on the *Theatre*" (sig. A3v). As McFadden shrewdly points out, James was in exile in Scotland ("absent") when Dryden wrote this dedication late in 1679; his "Fortune," thanks to the Popish Plot, had undergone considerable "alterations." The story of James's intervention in the controversy about which theatre company would have Settle's *Empress of Morocco* is evidence that he sometimes interested himself in the affairs of the company bearing his name; see above, ch. 8, p. 258 and n. 26. Still, McFadden's assertion that the play "had met with some disapproval in the Duke of York's household" (p. 207) must remain, like so much else about this play, a speculation. The religious satire in the play is not directed against Catholics, but against hypocritical Dissenters like Mrs. Saintly; though the Duke had mistresses, none of the characters resembles him in the least.

When the California editors reach *The Kind Keeper*, they will face not only these puzzles, but significant problems in annotation, since the dialogue has more slang and cant terms than appear in any other play by

Dryden, as well as references to current jokes now difficult to recover. When Woodall is first caught with Tricksy by Limberham, for example, she pretends he is "the *Italian* Seignior, who is come to sell me Essences." Limberham responds by guessing that "'tis he the *Lampoon* was made on"; according to the stage direction, he then "Sings the Tune of *Seignior*, and ends with Ho, ho." I should suppose the lampoon here alluded to is Rochester's "Signior Dildo," which informs the ladies that they may buy dildoes at shops selling essences:

> At the Sign of the Cross in St. James's Street,
> When next you go thither to make yourselves sweet,
> By buying of powder, gloves, essence, or so,
> You may chance t' get a sight of Signior Dildo.

[ll. 9–12]

As another reason why York might have closed the play, I offer the notion that the Duchess might have been offended by this song, which links her Italian court ladies with dildoes, or by Woodall's broad impersonation of an Italian merchant.

47. See Shadwell's *Complete Works*, ed. Summers, III, 409.

48. See *Works*, I, 362. The image of shopkeepers selling their wares was much in Dryden's mind during this period; in the epilogue to Lee's *Mithridates*, staged in February, he had contrasted the "Pair of faithful Lovers" in that play with modern "Cullies," who "purchase but sophisticated Ware" (ll. 1, 20–21).

49. In a private communication, Cedric Reverand has pointed out to me that Dryden used the same words in the *Fables*, interpolating a complaint about William's standing army into one of his versions of Boccaccio: he refers to "the rude Militia" as "Mouths without Hands; maintain'd at vast Expence, / In Peace a Charge, in War a weak Defence" ("Cymon and Iphigenia," ll. 400–02).

50. As Maximillian Novak points out, Sophocles does not introduce the idea of physical resemblance between Oedipus and Laius until nearly the end of the play (*Works*, XIII, 475). For visual evidence of the resemblance between Monmouth and Charles, compare the miniature of Monmouth as a boy by Samuel Cooper with William Dobson's portrait of Charles II at the same age; these are reproduced facing p. 17 of Bryan Bevan, *James Duke of Monmouth* (Robert Hale, 1973). Only York, who had obvious reasons, ever alleged that Monmouth was not the son of Charles; see Bevan, p. 13.

51. The date of the first performance is unclear; it may have come at the very beginning of the 1678–79 theatrical season, in September, but some uncertain evidence, mainly a reference to Pope-burnings in the epilogue, points to a premiere in November. Our uncertainty on this point is distressing, since a later premiere would have given Dryden and Lee an opportunity to make explicit references to the Popish Plot, as McFadden argues they did (pp. 209–211). If we accept an early date, as references to the victory at Mons and the Woolen Act may suggest, we must conclude instead that the playwrights were simply lucky in choosing a plot that turned out to be relevant to current events. For a full survey of the problem, see Maximillian Novak's headnote to the play, *Works*, XIII, 443–44.

52. On Sandford's roles, see *Works*, XIII, 445. On Shaftesbury's ailments, see Haley, *Shaftesbury*, pp. 27, 202–05, 451.

53. See *Absalom and Achitophel*, ll. 150–75; *The Medall*, ll. 18–25, 256–57, etc.

54. On the musical history of the play, see Price, *Henry Purcell and the London Stage*, pp. 105–11. Dryden gave the details of the collaboration in the *Vindication of the Duke of Guise* (1683): "I writ the first and third acts of *Oedipus*, and drew the *Scenary* of the *whole play*" (p. 42).

55. *Roscius Anglicanus*, p. 37.

56. Osborn, p. 204. The dating of this document is also problematic. Osborn thought that it was drawn up in January or February 1678, before the production of *The Kind Keeper*, which is not mentioned. Novak raises the possibility that the King's players were not interested in *The Kind Keeper*, as I have also suggested, and posits "spring or early summer" for the petition. John Harold Wilson, in *Mr. Goodman the Player* (Pittsburgh: University of Pittsburgh Press, 1964), p. 61, dates it in "the summer of 1678." Milhous and Hume, in their forthcoming *Document Register*, will date the petition [?August 1678].

57. See Appendix C.

58. *Roscius Anglicanus*, p. 37.

59. Quoted in Kenyon, *The Popish Plot*, p. 29.

60. See Kenyon, pp. 77, 84, 134–35, and A. Tindal Hart, *William Lloyd* (Church Historical Society, 1952), especially pp. 17–39. This William Lloyd (1627–1717) was vicar of St. Martin's in the Fields from 31

January 1677 until 3 October 1680, when he became Bishop of St. Asaph; although he was initially suspected of being "the supposed creature of the king and the Duke of York" (Hart, p. 25), his sermons and tracts following the Popish Plot are violent against Roman Catholics. He is not to be confused with either William Lloyd the Jesuit, a victim of the Plot, or William Lloyd (1637–1710), the nonjuring Bishop of Norwich.

61. See Wilson, *Mr. Goodman the Player*, p. 63.

62. See Kenyon, pp. 39–40. Kenyon believes that the account of Scott's many crimes and aliases offered by Arthur Bryant in *Samuel Pepys: The Years of Peril* (Collins, 1935), pp. 203–09, sufficiently discredits his claims; Bryant also cites a repudiation of Scott's story by Colonel Roper (p. 275*n*). The supposed confession, printed by John Pollock in *The Popish Plot* (Duckworth, 1903), pp. 376–77, is not implausible on internal evidence alone. The Berkshire of this document claims to be loyal: "I would have run any hazard rather than have suffered any injury to have been done to his Majesty's person: 'tis true I would have been glad to have seen all England Catholic, but not by the way of some ill men." Despite its tainted source, this attitude tallies with the other evidence we have about Berkshire's opinions.

63. The only previous play by Dryden to appear without a dedication was *Secret Love*, which Charles II had declared to be "his play." Lee had dedicated *Nero* to Rochester, *Sophonisba* and *Gloriana* to the Duchess of Portsmouth, *The Rival Queens* to Mulgrave, and *Mithridates* to Dorset.

64. Smith (*Works*, I, 367) and Gardner (*Prologues and Epilogues of John Dryden*, p. 257) both date this prologue to the summer of 1680. Pierre Danchin, *Prologues and Epilogues of the Restoration, 1660–1700* (Nancy: Presses Universitaires, 1981–), Part II, vol. iii, p. 284, gives "July 1680 (?)." The King's Company is recorded as having acted at Oxford in 1680, but this prologue only makes sense if spoken in the summer of 1679. By 1680, most of the "*Scotch* Rebels," who went to Edinburgh about April 1679, had returned to the Company, and the political part of that joke would have been much more current in 1679 than in 1680, when there were other problems, as Dryden's prologue for 1680 shows. The speaker's comparison of his own "broken Troop" to an even worse group of Irish players probably refers to an Irish company that appeared in Oxford in the summer of 1677. Oxford theatrical records are patchy, and the absence of a specific reference to a visit by the King's players in the summer of 1679 is therefore insignificant. With their London theatre closed and their company split by the Scottish rebellion, the remaining actors must have decided that Oxford would be a good place to pick up a little money.

65. Quoted in Wilson, *Mr. Goodman the Player*, p. 65. Wilson's account of the "Decline and Fall" of the King's Company, ch. v, is exemplary.

66. McFadden (pp. 212–15) attempts to match the characters in the play with contemporary figures, even arguing that Thersites is meant to represent Titus Oates, but as Maximillian Novak points out (*Works*, XIII, 551), he presents little evidence.

67. Novak makes the intriguing suggestion that "Dryden may have decided to reduce his original main title, *Truth Found too Late*, to the status of subtitle in order to avoid controversy" (*Works*, XIII, 498).

68. See Dryden's preface (XIII, 227).

69. I am dependent here on Novak's fine account of the way this scene comments on public affairs (*Works*, XIII, 518–19), but must point out that the riots against the Duchess of Portsmouth at the theatre, described there as occurring in 1679, in fact occurred in February of 1680 and are thus irrelevant to Dryden's play.

70. Novak offers these theories (*Works*, XIII, 501–02).

71. *Roscius Anglicanus*, p. 41.

72. See Sargeaunt, *Annals of Westminster School*, pp. 110–11.

73. His will, dated 5 September 1673 and signed on 24 October 1678, just before he left England, was proved on 4 June 1679. It mentions a conveyance of his property, doubtless designed to escape the added taxation of recusants, and leaves any proceeds to his wife.

74. Ward (pp. 154–55) attempts to attribute to Dryden a pamphlet defending York published during the summer of 1679. As Thomas C. Faulkner has shown, this is certainly not Dryden's work; see "Dryden and *Great and Weighty Considerations*: An Incorrect Attribution," *SEL* 11 (1971):417–25. To Faulkner's excellent arguments might be added Dryden's political caution at this time, which is also a reason for doubting John Harrington Smith's back-dating of the "Prologue to Oxford, 1680" to 1679 (*Works*, I, 362–63). See below, ch. 10, n. 5.

75. For an account of Corker's career, see T. A. Birrell, "James Maurus Corker and Dryden's Conversion," *ES* 54 (1973):461–68.

76. See Jones, *Country and Court*, p. 210. For fuller information on the Printing Act, see Timothy Crist, "Government Control of the Press after the Expiration of the Printing Act in 1679," *Publishing History* 5 (1979):49–77.

77. See the dedication to *The Kind Keeper*, sig. A4r.

78. McFadden (p. 222) argues that the compassion Dryden thought Shakespeare elicited in this scene was the emotion he himself wished to elicit in the serious plot of *The Spanish Fryar*. Dryden may also have known that Nahum Tate was planning a version of *Richard the Second*; when that play came on stage in December of 1680, its parallel to Exclusion was so obvious that it was banned, though the King's players tried to sneak it back on stage as *The Sicilian Usurper*.

79. McFadden was the first to explain this reference; see above, n. 46.

80. Kenyon, p. 184, describes Sunderland as devoted to the interests of James, but he lost his post early in 1681 for having supported the Exclusion Bill; see Ogg, II, 593–94, 606. For a reference to Godolphin's poem, now lost, see *H.M.C.*, VIII, i, 15. Macdonald (p. 120*n*) states that Sunderland's sister was the wife of Dryden's brother-in-law Thomas Howard, now third Earl of Berkshire, an error repeated by Ward (p. 138) and in *Works*, XIII, 524. Thomas had two wives, first Frances Harrison, then Margaret Parker. It was another of Elizabeth Dryden's brothers, Henry, who was married to Elizabeth Spencer, widow of James, Lord Craven, and she was Sunderland's aunt, not his sister. Since Henry died in 1663, this distant familial connection seems unlikely to be the reason why Dryden and Sunderland had met.

81. On this incident, see Bevan, *Monmouth*, p. 115. Dryden might have picked up his references to "Forty One" and "Forty Eight" from a Tory *Answer to An Appeal from the Country to the City*, available late in the autumn and eventually acknowledged by Roger L'Estrange; see especially p. 14. Since the date of *The Loyall General* is uncertain, we cannot know exactly what prompted Dryden's prologue, but his reference to the idling of water-men by cold winter weather may support the conjectural dating of the play to December 1679.

82. *A Journal From Parnassus*, ed. Hugh Macdonald (Dobell, 1937), p. 6.

83. This is the testimony of the diarist Narcissus Luttrell, in *A Brief Historical Relation of State Affairs*, 6 vols. (Oxford: Oxford University Press, 1857), I, 30.

84. This letter was among the documents about the Rose Alley affair collected by Malone for use in a second edition; they are printed in Osborn, pp. 144–45. Like Nelson, both Luttrell and the Italian diplomat Francesco Terriesi blamed the Duchess of Portsmouth for the attack; for their testimony, see Pinto, "Rochester and Dryden," p. 37.

85. Rochester sent his friend Henry Savile a copy on 21 November 1679; both Rochester and Colonel Edward Cooke, who wrote his account in a letter to Ormonde dated 22 November, report the quarrel between Mulgrave and the Duchess. For Rochester's letter, see *Letters*, ed. Treglown, p. 232–33; the relevant excerpt from Cooke's letter to Ormonde appears in the notes. Despite Mulgrave's later claim that he wrote this poem in 1675, the version we have must be later than 12 September 1679, the date of the death of Dorset's wife, to which it refers. My citations follow the text given in *POAS* I, 401–13.

86. The assertion that "bringing wit and friendship to Whitehall" is impossible (l. 32) resembles Dryden's remark about courts in the dedication of *Marriage A-la-Mode* to Rochester (XI, 221–22). The phrase about "the forced scenes of our declining stage" (l. 38) is close to the opening of Dryden's prologue to Shadwell's *A True Widow*: "Y'are welcome to the downfal of the Stage" (l. 2). Viscount Dunbar, attacked at line 55, had also been attacked in Dryden's letter to Rochester (quoted above, p. 252). The contrast between Shaftesbury's crippled limbs and his "hard mind" and "vig'rous thoughts" (ll. 102–16) is like that made in the courtship scene between Creon and Eurydice in *Oedipus* (quoted above, p. 312). Someone noticing any or all of these resemblances might plausibly have concluded that Dryden had a hand in the poem.

87. Aubrey, *Brief Lives*, I, 317. Mulgrave's poem actually has a passing reference to "Pembroke's mastiff" (l. 183). For details of Pembroke's notorious career, see Kenyon, *The Popish Plot*, pp. 267–69.

88. In a letter to Savile, the Earl says that if Dryden "falls upon me at the blunt, which is his very good weapon in wit, I will forgive him, if you please, and leave the repartee to Black Will, with a cudgel." For years, scholars cited this passage as "proof" of Rochester's responsibility for the attack on Dryden, though Malone (pp. 134–35) hedged his bets by blaming both Rochester and the Duchess of Portsmouth. The letter has been shown to date from 1676, a circumstance that may weaken the case against Rochester, though it does not entirely eliminate him as a suspect; see John Harold Wilson's edition of *The Rochester-Savile Letters*, pp.

41, 87–88, 115. Articles by Wilson and Vivian de Sola Pinto in *RES* 15 (1939):294–301; 16 (1940):177–78 argue against blaming Rochester for the attack, a position further developed by Wilson in *The Court Wits of the Restoration*, p. 118. In his later article on "Dryden and Rochester," Pinto speculates that "Black Will" is a misreading for "Black Phill" (p. 35) and cites a contemporary poem that may connect Pembroke with the Rose Alley affair (p. 38). Treglown, in his edition of Rochester's letters, casts new doubt on the exoneration of Rochester, pointing out that "the quarrel between the two poets continued throughout the period, gaining in intensity" (p. 120*n*). In my view, the strongest argument against Rochester's having been responsible is the mild tone of his references to the satire at the time; neither his letter to Savile describing the satire (*Letters*, ed. Treglown, pp. 232–34) nor his "Epistolary Essay from M. G. to O. B. upon Their Mutual Poems" (in *Poems*, ed. Vieth, pp. 144–47) sounds like the work of a man preparing to have his adversary beaten.

89. Several years later, a poem friendly to Dryden blamed the Whigs for their "base *Rose-Alley* Drubs." See *Juvenalis Redivivus* (1683), p. 30, attributed to Thomas Wood on Luttrell's copy. On the meetings between the Whigs and the Duchess of Portsmouth, which spawned a rumor reported by Locke to the effect that the Duchess was urging the King to appoint Shaftesbury as Lord Treasurer, see Haley, *Shaftesbury*, pp. 585–95.

90. For samples, see Pinto, "Dryden and Rochester," p. 38.

91. Edmund Hickeringill, *The Mushroom* (1682), p. 13. For contemporary reports of Portsmouth's departure and return, see Luttrell, I, 161, 169. In an anonymous political pamphlet published in June of 1681, Dryden had gone out of his way to point out that Louise was "a *French* Woman, [but] an *English* Dutchess," and to remind the Whigs, who were once again accusing her of protecting "the Popish interest," of their own "politick assignations at her Lodgings" (XVII, 202). On the rehearsals of the opera, see above, ch. 11, p. 394 and n. 35.

92. For details, see Macdonald, *Bibliography*, pp. 217–18.

CHAPTER 10. THE TORY SATIRIST

1. In his rhyming opera *Noah's Flood* (November 1679), intended as a sequel to Dryden's own *State of Innocence*, Edward Ecclestone devotes most of Act V to the story of Noah's sons.

2. Ironically, the King's players were available to produce this anti-York play because York's return from Scotland had precipitated the return of their deserters, who had been performing for the Duke's entourage in Edinburgh; Crowne's *Thyestes*, a horror tragedy staged in March, was the company's first new London play in nearly a year. The authors of *The London Stage* tentatively assign a known performance of Etherege's *She Would if She Could* on 27 January 1680 to the King's Company, on the incorrect grounds that "it first produced the play." The Duke's Company, who actually gave the first performance in 1668 (*London Stage*, I, 129), and who are recorded as presenting the play at court on 27 February 1680, were obviously the performers on this occasion. Wilson, in *Mr. Goodman the Player*, pp. 64–69, argues that *Thyestes*, with its prologue referring to the return of the actors from Scotland, was the play with which the company reopened Drury Lane, but Robert D. Hume, in a private communication, considers it unlikely that the theatre was entirely dark for a year.

3. See Wilson, "Theatre Notes from the Newdigate Newsletters," *TN* 16 (1961), p. 80.

4. See Crist, "Government Control of the Press," pp. 61–66.

5. This prologue appears in two versions, one in an edition of Lee's *Sophonisba* printed in 1681, the other in Dryden's *Miscellany Poems* of 1684, where it is dated 1680. John Harrington Smith's argument for back-dating this prologue to 1679 (*Works*, I, 362–63) is based on an incorrect date for the opening of Settle's *The Female Prelate* and on the very dubious notion that the company would have tried in Oxford a play they had not yet performed in London. Gardner, moving the other way, dates the prologue to 1681 (p. 259). Danchin prints both versions (II, iii, 270, 286), dating one "July 1679 (?) or perhaps 1680," the other "1680–1681 (?)." I have argued that the Oxford prologue beginning "Discord and Plots" belongs in the summer of 1679; see above, ch. 9, n. 64. This one fits best in the summer of 1680, when the King's Company unquestionably visited Oxford; see Sybil Rosenfeld, "Some Notes on the Players in Oxford, 1661–1713," *RES* 19 (1943), pp. 369–70. Dryden's speaker says that "if Anarchy goes on, . . . No Zealous Brother there wou'd want a Stone, / To Maul Us Cardinals, and pelt Pope *Joan*" (ll. 11, 21–22). Kinsley (IV, 1873–74) infers from these lines that a version of this prologue was spoken for a performance of Settle's *Female Prelate* by an actor playing a cardinal, and that it was then clumsily adapted for later use with Lee's play. A simpler

theory would be that the King's players went to Oxford and presented their latest hit, and that Settle's crude play, with its vicious anti-Catholic slant, displeased the Oxford audience; the actors then decided to do Lee's play instead, and Dryden wrote a prologue alluding to the failure of *The Female Prelate*. The final four lines, which appear only in the version printed with Lee's play, would make perfect sense if this were the case:

> Your wiser Judgments farther penetrate
> Who late found out one Tare amongst the Wheat.
> This is our comfort, none e're cry'd us down,
> But who dislik'd both *Bishop* and a *Crown*.

On this reading, the "Tare amongst the Wheat" would be *The Female Prelate*, the one play disliked by the Oxford audiences; the actor assures them that only Puritan "fanatics," "who dislik'd both *Bishop* and a *Crown*,"have ever "cry'd down"the theatre.

6. Pope-burnings, traditionally held on Guy Fawkes Day (5 November), were now also held on the anniversary of the accession of Queen Elizabeth (17 November). Shaftesbury's Green Ribbon Club had held a spectacular one on 17 November 1679, and there were similar performances on 17 November 1680 and 17 November 1681, the date of publication of *Absalom and Achitophel*. On 5 November 1681, however, the loyal Busby had his Westminster boys burn Jack Presbyter; see Luttrell, I, 142.

7. See Haley, *Shaftesbury*, p. 578.

8. See Osborn, pp. 216–17. For another connection between Dryden and Wolseley, see above, p. 374 and n. 87.

9. McFadden makes this point in his fine discussion of this play (pp. 218–26); for a spirited account of the play's political implications, see Judith Milhous and Robert D. Hume, *Producible Interpretation: Eight English Plays, 1675–1707* (Carbondale: Southern Illinois University Press, 1985), pp. 146–49.

10. Harth, in "Dryden in 1678–1681," pp. 68–71, gives details of the political activities of the Holles family, and points out that Tonson advertised the published play in a Whig journal, *The True Protestant Mercury*. This helped to produce "the mistaken impression that Dryden was leaning toward the Whigs" (p. 71).

11. Evelyn, *Diary*, IV, 234.

12. See Birrell, "James Maurus Corker and Dryden's Conversion," p. 462, and Corker's own *Stafford's Memoires* (1681). By 1683, Dryden was referring in print to "My poor Lord *Stafford*"; he may have been specifically thinking of Stafford in a passage on Catholic martyrs in *The Hind and the Panther* (1687); and in his poem celebrating the marriage of Stafford's daughter (1687), he referred to "the great Stafford" as "crowned . . . with a deathless diadem." See above, ch. 11, p. 415.

13. Coleman O. Parsons, "Dryden's Letter of Attorney," *MLN* 50 (1935):364–65, prints the entire document, which is in the Watson Autograph Collection in Scotland. Parsons speculates that Dryden may have made this arrangement because he planned to leave town, an odd thing to do in midwinter. Osborn (p. 217) offers two more plausible hypotheses: that Dryden simply hired Ward to look after his interests with the Treasury, or that Dryden had borrowed money from Ward. Whatever the reason, Ward presumably rented the right to collect Dryden's salary, with a percentage as an incentive; he went right to work, extracting a £50 payment two days later; see Appendix C, p. 530.

14. *The London Stage* guesses at a premiere in March; Macdonald, *Bibliography*, p. 158, guesses February, a more plausible date since the King's players were ready to give the play at Oxford in March.

15. Quoted in Haley, *Shaftesbury*, p. 604.

16. Like Dryden and Saunders, Lee and Duke were Old Westminsters and Trinity men; Duke retained his connection with Trinity, where he read an English poem before the King and Queen in 1681; see Luttrell, I, 130. If Dryden enjoyed the teaching relationships he had with these younger writers, his renewed contact with Westminster would also have reminded him that such prominent teachers as Busby enjoyed far more affluence than he could hope for as a poet, and he may possibly have angled for a similar post for himself at just this time. On 28 January, Richard Allestree, Provost of Eton, died; the old poet Waller was among those who sought his position, and several later attacks on Dryden claim that he too was a candidate. See Pierre Legouis, "Dryden and Eton," *MLN* 52 (1937): 111–15. During Allestree's final illness, Evelyn met him at the home of John Dolben, the Bishop of Rochester, whom Dryden praises in *Absalom and Achitophel* and refers to as someone he knows well in a letter to Busby (*Diary*, IV, 211; *Letters*, p. 19). But there is no firm evidence, and one poet might easily have been mistaken for the other as the rumor

spread; like the less well-defined sinecure Dryden had earlier sought at Oxford, the position normally required its holder to be in holy orders, and the King appointed a clergyman named Zachary Cradock on 24 February.

17. See *An Historical Account of the Heroick Life and Magnanimous Actions of the Most Illustrious Protestant Prince, James Duke of Monmouth* (1683), p. 107. Scott misread this passage, thinking that it described Monmouth's arrival at the Oxford Parliament in March, an error repeated in *Works*, XV, 376.

18. For details, see Ogg, II, 616; Haley, pp. 631–32; Bevan, 136–37.

19. On the publication, see Macdonald, *Bibliography*, p. 140. In his headnote to this epilogue (*Works*, II, 388), H. T. Swedenberg says that "Dryden expended his eloquence in the hope that the King and Parliament might reach accord." Swedenberg incorrectly refers to the end of the session as "a prorogation" and patronizingly concludes that "only a poet could have thought any other result possible." Like almost everyone, Dryden surely expected a short and acrimonious session; his gestures in the direction of harmony and peace in the epilogue are merely conventional.

20. Both the speech and the Opposition characterization of it are quoted in Haley, pp. 632–33.

21. *The Earl of Shaftesbury's Expedient for Settling the Nation, discoursed with His Majesty in the House of Peers at Oxford, March the 24th, 1680–1*, pp. 5–7.

22. I quote the text conveniently printed in Appendix A of *Works*, II, 514.

23. Dryden may again have remembered Ecclestone's opera on Noah's flood; the passage on the dove in that work bears a general resemblance to these lines:

> But see the *Dove* with an indulgent care,
> Hasts to the Ark, through the mild peaceful Air,
> And in his [sic] beak an *Olive* Branch doth bear:
> Emblem of Peace, white Parlee Flag, which he,
> The Ensign waves, to set the Monarch free;
> Pen'd up in th'Ark, which on the Mount doth stand,
> In safety now upon the stable Land.
>
> [p. 33]

24. Roswell G. Ham first attributed this work to Dryden; see "Dryden as Historiographer-Royal: The Authorship of *His Majesties Declaration Defended*, 1681," *RES* 11 (1935):284–98. Ham's external evidence includes a contemporary manuscript attribution on a copy of the pamphlet and a reference to the pamphlet as Dryden's in the *History of England* (1718) by Laurence Eachard, who probably knew Dryden. Although the California editors have printed the text, Edward Saslow has argued against Ham's attribution in "Dryden as Historiographer Royal and the Authorship of *His Majesties Declaration Defended*," *MP* 75 (1978): 261–72, and Phillip Harth, in "Dryden in 1678–1681," p. 59, has accepted his arguments. While Saslow is correct in pointing out that the Historiographer Royal was under no compunction to write political propaganda, his dismissal of the many verbal parallels between this pamphlet and other works by Dryden as mere "commonplaces" is unconvincing to me. I am particularly impressed by the virtually exact repetition of the reference to "the Childrens play of, This Mill grinds Pepper and Spice; that Mill grinds Ratts and Mice" (XVII, 196) in *The Vindication of the Duke of Guise* (p. 40). Let me add three more verbal parallels to those adduced by Ham: the political differences between London and Southwark (XVII, 196) are also mentioned in Dryden's Oxford prologue of the same summer (II, 184, l. 11); the homely allusion to the "Interest of the Nation abroad . . . left in the Suds" (XVII, 204), repeats an expression Dryden had used about the incomplete *Kind Keeper* (*Letters*, p. 11); the suggestion that the "Person of Quality," having "been in pain about laying his Egg," must therefore "cackle" (XVII, 215), uses a word repeated in Dryden's epilogue to Southerne's *The Loyal Brother* (II, 192, l. 2). I have little doubt that Dryden had a hand in this tract. Those reluctant to accept the attribution should compare other controversial works known to be Dryden's, especially *The Vindication of the Duke of Guise*.

25. In praising Hyde's financial management, even though he suffered under it, Dryden was following the principles laid down in a letter from Ormonde to the Duke of York, written on 27 May 1681: "no man that means well to the King, will repine [at the] retrenchments and frugality now made and practised." For generous quotations and an illuminating analysis, see McFadden, pp. 230–33. Mindful of their long friendship and fundamental agreement on political issues, Dryden also dedicated three later works to Hyde: *The Duke of Guise* (1683), a sparkling translation of the twenty-ninth ode of Horace's First Book (1685), and

Cleomenes (1692). For evidence suggesting that Hyde gave Dryden financial support, see above, ch. 11, p. 397 and n. 47.

26. *H.M.C. Ormonde*, VI, 233; see also Wallace Maurer, "Who Prompted Dryden to Write *Absalom and Achitophel?*" *PQ* 40 (1961):130–38.

27. For Dryden's specific references to Fitzharris, see XVII, 221. For details of the controversial trial, see Haley, *Shaftesbury*, pp. 642–51.

28. For a reading of *Absalom and Achitophel* emphasizing its similarly conventional claims to moderation, see Zwicker, *Politics and Language in Dryden's Poetry*, especially pp. 47–50, 85–103.

29. *Anecdotes*, ed. Osborn, I, 28.

30. For a full-scale exposition of this idea, see McFadden, pp. 239–43.

31. See Kenyon, *The Popish Plot*, p. 166.

32. See above, ch. 8, n. 17.

33. See the passage on "the Doctrines of King-killing and Deposing" in the preface to *Religio Laici* (November 1681), quoted above, p. 373. In the dedication to *Plutarchs Lives* (May 1683), Dryden argued that "the pretended Reformation of our Schismaticks, is to set up themselves in the Papal Chair; and to make their Princes only their Trustees: So that whether they or the Pope were uppermost in *England*, the Royal Authority were equally depress'd" (XVII, 231–32). In the postscript to *The History of the League* (July 1684), he noted that "some of the *Jesuites* are the shame of the *Roman* Church, as the Sectaries are of ours. Their Tenets in Politicks are the same; both of them hate Monarchy, and love Democracy" (XVIII, 403).

34. *Towser the Second a Bull-Dog* (1681); the Yale copy, like Luttrell's, is dated 10 December 1681; the usual attribution to Henry Care stems from Malone. The other Whig writers who attacked Dryden make similar charges: Christopher Nesse refers to his "Romanizing mind" in *A Key (with the Whip) to open the Mystery and Iniquity of the Poem Called Absalom and Achitophel* (1682), p. 27; the author of *Poetical Reflections on a Late Poem Entituled Absalom and Achitophel* (1682) says that Dryden's "Soul's Religion's Prop, and Native Grace" is "*Rome*" (p. 3).

35. Stephen Dugdale and Roger L'Estrange accused College of having written the broadside entitled *A Raree Show*; College denied the charge. The poem is a dialogue between "Leviathan," evidently Charles II, and "Topham," the sergeant-at-arms of the House of Commons. Many of its references are exceedingly obscure, not least those in the following exchange:

> *Topham*
> But child of heathen Hobbes, with a hey, with a hey,
> Remember old Dry Bobs, with a ho,
> For fleecing England's flocks
> Long fed with bits and knocks,
> With a hey, trany nony nony no.
> *Leviathan*
> What's past is not to come, with a hey, with a hey,
> Now safe is David's bum, with a ho;
> Then hey for Oxford ho,
> Strong government, raree show,
> With a hey, trany nony nony no.
>
> [*POAS*, II, pp. 429–30, ll. 51–60]

E. F. Mengel, whose edition I follow, assumes that "old Dry Bobs" is Charles I, but since Charles had many children, that seems an odd reading. Could College be referring to Dryden, who had been called "Drybob" by Shadwell? Is the "David" whose "bum" is now safe the King? Did College (or whoever wrote this drivel) know that Dryden was at work on *Absalom and Achitophel?*

Since the Harvard copy of *A Raree Show* is dated 9 April 1681, such an inference might lend weak support to Tonson's (or Tate's) assertion that Dryden "undertook the poem of *Absalom and Achitophel* . . . In the year 1680," first printed in a headnote to *The Second Part of Absalom and Achitophel* in an edition of *The Second Part of Miscellany Poems* published in 1716. Malone (pp. 141–42) suggests that this testimony may be reconciled with the occasion if we suppose that Dryden began his poem at the very end of 1680 on the old calendar, i.e., before 25 March, just after the dissolution of the Parliament. H. H. Schless, in *POAS*, III, 279, argues that "Dryden had been working on an *Absalom* since before Nov. 1680," but his argument is highly conjectural: the portrait of William Waller as Arod in *The Second Part*, which has sometimes been claimed for Dryden, "would certainly seem to have been written prior to 15 Nov. 1680," so Schless supposes that Dryden omitted it from the original poem, on which he had been working for a long time, and made it available to Tate. Since the lines simply refer to Waller's *activities* before the posited date, and since they are not necessarily Dryden's, this is hardly an overwhelming argument. Yet Ward, without citing anything like evidence, claims that "there can be little doubt that these months [autumn 1680] marked the actual beginning of *Absalom and Achitophel*" (p. 156). Harth, in "Dryden in 1678–1681," p. 64, correctly points out that "if [Dryden] began work on *Absalom and Achitophel* at this time, it must have been a very different poem from the one he published in November 1681, which is closely tied to the events and attitudes of the latter year." Mengel, in *POAS*, II, 453, accepts the more normal idea that Dryden began the poem after the dissolution of the Oxford Parliament.

36. Haley, *Shaftesbury*, pp. 663–64; Luttrell, I, 117–18, 120–21.

37. Luttrell, I, 119, 125.

38. On the acquittal of Rouse, see J. R. Jones, *The First Whigs* (Oxford University Press, 1961), pp. 191–92. That acquittal and Dryden's remark about juries are additional evidence in support of Phillip Harth's vigorous argument against the long-repeated notion that the poem was meant to influence the trial; see "Legends No Histories: The Case of *Absalom and Achitophel*," *SECC* 4 (1975):13–29. One of the Whig pamphleteers attacking the poem implies that Dryden hoped to influence the trial, but his main point is that Dryden was overconfident in expecting Shaftesbury to be condemned: "And if the season be well observ'd, when this Adulterate Poem was spread, it will be found purposely divulg'd near the time when this Lord [Shaftesbury], with his other Noble Partner [Lord Howard of Escrick], were to be brought to their Tryals. And I suppose this Poet thought himself enough assur'd of their condemnation; at least, that his *Genius* had not otherwise ventur'd to have trampled on persons of such eminent Abilities, and Interest in the Nation" (*Poetical Reflections*; preface, sig. B1r). Christopher Nesse, in *A Key (with the Whip)*, repeats that second charge:

> Thou wast Cock-sure he would be damn'd for Ay,
> Without thy presence, thou was then employ'd,
> To Brand him, 'gainst he came to be Destroy'd:
> 'Fore hand preparing him for th' Hangmans Ax,
> Had not the Witnesses been found so Lax.
>
> [p. 24]

Nonetheless, Dryden's reference to Whig juries in the preface is evidence that he was far from "Cock-sure."

Perhaps the publication on 17 November was timed to coincide with the anniversary of Elizabeth's accession to the throne, once again celebrated by a spectacular Pope-burning including the incineration of an "effigie of the observator" L'Estrange as a "towser"; see Luttrell, I, 144; Haley, 673. The notion that the King himself directly requested the poem, first printed by Tonson in 1716, seems less likely to me than the testimony of Mulys, who points to Seymour as the instigator of the poem in a letter written two days after it was published.

39. For an account of the many prose tracts using the Absalom story at this time, including one entitled *Absalom's Conspiracy, Or, the Tragedy of Treason* (1680), see Richard F. Jones, "The Originality of *Absalom and Achitophel*," *MLN* 46 (1931):211–18. For other sources and analogues, see Howard Schless, "Dryden's *Absalom and Achitophel* and *A Dialogue between Nathan and Absolome*," *PQ* 40 (1961):139–43; Barbara K. Lewalski, "*David's Troubles Remembered*: An Analogue to *Absalom and Achitophel*," *N&Q* 11 (1964):340–43.

40. On Mulgrave's arrest, see Bevan, *Monmouth*, pp. 45–46. In his introduction to the *Anthology of Poems on Affairs of State* (New Haven: Yale University Press, 1975), p. xix, George Lord lists Moll Kirke among Charles's mistresses, but I have been unable to discover any firm contemporary evidence. *The Memoirs of the Court of Charles the Second by Count Grammont*, written by the Catholic courtier Anthony Hamilton, has frequent references to a Miss Warmenstré or Warminster; in the edition of Sir Walter Scott (Bohn, 1846), a note (p. 355) cites some thirdhand gossip claiming that this lady was actually Mary Kirk, but it is impossible to reconcile the account given there with other reports of the career of Mary (or Moll) Kirk, who was a Maid of Honor to the second Duchess of York. The edition of Allan Fea (Bickers, 1906) corrects this error (p. 118*n*). In the *Memoirs of the Court of England in 1675* by Marie Catherine, Baronne D'Aulnoy,

trans. Mrs. William Henry Arthur, ed. George David Gilbert (Routledge, 1913), Monmouth's mistress is described under the fictitious name "Emilie"; in their introduction, the translator and editor identify her as "Moll Kirke" (p. xviii). "Emilie" is not linked with the King.

41. See Pepys, *Diary*, III, 191 (7 September 1662). "The Queenes" were the newly married Catharine and the Queen Mother, Henrietta Maria. On the approaches to Nell Gwen and the Duchess of Portsmouth, see Bevan, *Monmouth*, pp. 114–15, 133. The Whig pamphleteers, friendly to Monmouth, naturally do not mention these possible parallels, but one of them points to the sexual part of the biblical story at some length: Christopher Nesse, in *A Key (with the Whip)*, devotes considerable space to retelling the part of II Samuel in which Achitophel "gave . . . *Absalom* those damn'd Designs, / *First* to act Incest on th' *Kings Concubines*" (p. 23) then complains that Shaftesbury never gave Monmouth such advice! Tate, in *The Second Part of Absalom and Achitophel*, represents Achitophel considering whether Absalom should "Attempt his [David's] Bed, / Or Threat with open Arms the Royal Head"(ll. 861–62).

42. As in the case of the more extensive revisions of the character of Achitophel, one possible theory is that these lines were in Dryden's manuscript but were cancelled for some reason in the first edition and restored in the second; on Monmouth's offer to bail Shaftesbury and subsequent disgrace, see Luttrell, I, 147, 150.

43. Some of these passages are quoted and discussed by Phillip Harth in "Dryden's Public Voices," in *New Homage to John Dryden* (Los Angeles: Clark Library, 1983), pp. 3–27.

44. Zwicker takes a harder line: "The poem advocates that a surgery be performed on the body politic, that a diseased limb be sacrificed in order to save the state. . . . The harsh remedy that this poem prescribes is the block for Whig leaders" (pp. 49, 93). The imagery of Dryden's own preface, however, suggests that the harsh remedies (whatever they are) will help *avoid* surgery.

45. See McFadden, p. 258. Nesse, in *A Key (with the Whip)*, p. 25, accuses Dryden of adding this passage for money, though he does not say who paid him; this senseless accusation may lie behind the later story that Dryden added the lines in gratitude for a favor supposedly done his son Erasmus-Henry by Shaftesbury—a fiction systematically discredited by Malone (pp. 144–50). For two completely different bibliographical theories about how this passage came to be altered, see Vinton Dearing's textual notes (*Works*, II, 411–12) and Edward Saslow, "Shaftesbury Cursed: Dryden's Revision of the *Achitophel* Lines," *SB* 28 (1974):276–83. Though both necessarily involve guesswork, Saslow's is more persuasive to me.

46. See H. Hammond, "'One Immortal Song,'" *RES* 5 (1954):60–62.

47. Zwicker hears a "suggestion of incredulity" in Absalom's lines on his father's mercy (p. 98), but Dryden himself continued to praise Charles for his clemency.

48. See McFadden, p. 261.

49. I refer of course to Locke's *Two Treatises of Government*, written partly in refutation of Sir Robert Filmer's *Patriarcha*, which was newly printed in 1680. Some of Dryden's argument in this speech on government, especially the appeal to Adam (l. 771), superficially resembles Filmer, but James Daly points out that Dryden's denial of absolutism and emphasis on moderation and balance make his political thought quite unlike Filmer's. See *Sir Robert Filmer and English Political Thought* (Toronto: University of Toronto Press, 1979), pp. 182–83.

50. The catalogue begins with Ormonde (Barzillai), mourns for Ossory ("His Eldest Hope"), and includes three loyal clergymen—William Sancroft, Archbishop of Canterbury, Henry Compton, the "Sagan of Jerusalem," and John Dolben, Dean of Westminster and Bishop of Rochester. On Dryden's relations with Dolben, see above, n. 16. A list of loyal peers includes Adriel (Mulgrave), Jotham (Halifax), Hushai (Hyde), and Amiel (Seymour).

51. A Catholic priest whom Spence "often met at Mr. Pope's . . . [said] that King Charles obliged Dryden to put his Oxford speech into verse, and to insert it toward the close of *Absalom and Achitophel*" (*Anecdotes*, I, 28–29). As Osborn points out (II, 614), the close parallels are actually between David's speech in that poem and the royal *Declaration* printed in April, which Dryden had already defended.

52. I consider the much-debated reference to Corah calling "for *Agag*'s murther" (l. 676) most likely to allude to the execution of the aged and feeble Stafford a year earlier. Nesse (p. 34) thought Agag was James, Duke of York, who appears earlier in the poem as David's unnamed brother; Sir Edmund Berry Godfrey and Charles I have also been proposed.

53. See Haley, p. 673. Given these remarks by Charles, I must disagree with McFadden, who claims that Dryden's motive for writing the poem was "to bring home to Charles himself the depth of contempt and

powerlessness he would sink to if he should fail to be steady" (p. 242). Charles was remarkably "steady" throughout the crisis; unlike his brother James, he also recognized the dangers of appearing to be overly autocratic or absolutist.

54. For complaints about the typology, see the passages from Nesse cited above, n. 41. For attacks on Dryden's friends, see Nesse, pp. 36–40, *Poetical Reflections*, pp. 8–11, *Azaria and Hushai*, pp. 26–30. All the attacks call Dryden a "pecuniary poet" or some such name. *A Panegyrick on the Author of Absolom and Achitophel* is entirely concerned with his writing the elegy of Cromwell. For insinuations that Dryden was a Papist, see n. 34 above. The lines from *Azaria and Hushai* attacking Elizabeth are quoted above, ch. 5, p. 125. For proposals that Dryden be hanged see above, p. 349, and below, n. 55.

55. One example will suffice. *Towser the Second a Bulldog*, available on 10 December 1681, suggests that one effective medicine for Dryden would be "Oil of Crab-tree," a reference to the Rose Alley episode. Nesse, a month or so later, picks up both that phrase and the language of the conclusion (quoted above, p. 349):

> Or was't the *Oil* of Crab-Tree, which Anoints,
> (As in *Rose-Ally* once) thy nasty Joints?
> No better Antidote is found to fetch
> That plaguy poison out of th' Whiffling Wretch;
> If this Beasts Tongue be not cut out and *dri'd*,
> Or th' Head hang'd up, in Tyburn Tippit ti'd.

[p. 26]

56. Quoted in *Works*, II, 397.

57. See *H.M.C.*, X, iv, 175; Spence, I, 28.

58. On these and other political dramas, see Hume, *Development*, pp. 341–60; Ward, arguing entirely from internal evidence, sought to date *The Loyal Brother* in the autumn, before Shaftesbury's trial (p. 355), but a February reference to Southerne's drama as "a new play" in the Newdigate newsletters renders that speculation unlikely. For the latest scholarship on the dates of the other plays, see Milhous and Hume, "Dating," pp. 390–93.

59. See Haley, *Shaftesbury*, pp. 684–704, and Jones, *The First Whigs*, pp. 201–06. Recent scholarship by David Bywaters and John Wallace has helped us understand Otway's specific political intent in *Venice Preserv'd*; for a summary, see Milhous and Hume, *Producible Interpretation*, pp. 173–76.

60. For a full text of Lee's commendatory poem, see *Works*, II, 469; on his politics, see Robert D. Hume, "The Satiric Design of Nat. Lee's *The Princess of Cleve*," *JEGP* 75 (1976), pp. 121–22, and Richard E. Brown, "Nathaniel Lee's Political Dramas, 1679–1683," *Restoration* 10 (1986):41–52.

61. See above, ch. 4, p. 116 and n. 68. Another possible influence is John Northleigh's *The Parallel: or The New Specious Association*, listed in the Term Catalogue for February 1682. Northleigh's main purpose is to show close links between the Association found in Shaftesbury's closet and the Scottish Solemn League and Covenant of 1643, but he also lists a series of parallels between the Association and the French Holy League; see pp. 26–27.

62. "Any one who reads *Davila*, may trace your Practices all along. There were the same pretences for Reformation, and Loyalty, the same Aspersions of the King, and the same grounds of a Rebellion. I know not whether you will take the Historian's word, who says it was reported, that *Poltrot* a *Hugonot*, murther'd *Francis* Duke of *Guise* by the instigations of *Theodore Beza*: or that it was a *Hugonot* Minister, otherwise call'd a *Presbyterian*, (for our Church abhors so devilish a Tenent) who first writ a Treatise of the lawfulness of deposing and murthering Kings, of a different Perswasion in Religion: But I am able to prove from the Doctrine of *Calvin*, and Principles of *Buchanan*, that they set the People above the Magistrate; which if I mistake not is your own Fundamental" (II, 40). Cf. the passage on Calvin in *His Majesties Declaration Defended*, quoted above, p. 348, and the postscript to *The History of the League* (XVIII, 400–01).

Many scholars have supposed that the poem Dryden had just finished when Lee asked him to honor his old promise was *The Medall*; see, for example, Harth, *Contexts of Dryden's Thought*, p. 189, where Dryden is said to have been working on *The Duke of Guise* "from about the beginning of April until the end of June."

The publication in March of a reference to Davila, however, suggests that he was thinking and reading about the French League earlier, and that Lee actually approached him after the completion of *Absalom and Achitophel*, a poem that surely took more effort than *The Medall*, and one after which he might reasonably have hoped for some leisure.

63. For more details about these events, see H. H. Schless's excellent pages on the shrieval elections, *POAS*, III, 297–16, and Haley, *Shaftesbury*, pp. 687–89.

64. The secret agreement was printed by Charles Gildon in his *Life of Betterton* (1710), pp. 8–9. On the fight, see Wilson, "Theatre Notes from the Newdigate Newsletters," p. 80, and Hotson, *Commonwealth and Restoration Stage*, pp. 268–71. The agreement to merge the companies, substantially complete in May, took effect the following November. For a summary of sources describing the merger, see *The London Stage*, I, 309.

65. The three letters to Busby by the Drydens present some problems in dating. The first of them, in which Dryden speaks of John's "chine-cough" and says that "his constitution is very tender" (*Letters*, p. 17), could easily be as early as this winter. Dryden takes the occasion to "wish the Eldest may also deserve some part of your good opinion," a phrase that may indicate that Charles had already incurred Busby's displeasure. Elizabeth's letter (p. 150), dated "Ascension Day," may be confidently dated 25 May 1682; she promises "to take care that [John] shall duely goe to church heare [presumably at St. Martin's in the Fields] . . . till he comes to be more nearly under your care in the college," a clear reference to the upcoming summer election, in which John became a King's Scholar and a boarder. The long letter on the occasion of Charles's dismissal (pp. 18–20) mentions John's election, and therefore cannot be earlier than the late summer of 1682 or later than the early spring of 1683, when Charles, restored to Busby's favor, was duly elected to Trinity; I should consider the autumn months of 1682 the most likely date. Dryden may have decided to send his third son to the Charterhouse School because of the problems the two older boys had with Busby; if so, he was aware of those problems before they reached a crisis; a letter from the King to the governors of the Charterhouse, dated 28 September 1682, refers to "letters of 28 Feb. last [i.e., 1682, in which] we recommended Erasmus Henry Dryden to be elected and admitted . . . on the first vacancy." Erasmus-Henry was in fact elected on 12 September 1682, at which point he probably became a day student, and admitted on 5 February 1683, at which point he became a boarder. See *C.S.P. Dom., 1682*, pp. 436, 446, 452; *1683*, p. 33; and Malone, p. 149*n*.

66. The medal, handsomely reproduced in *Works*, II, 43, bears the date of Shaftesbury's acquittal (24 NOV 1681), but the date of its issue is not certain. The California editors were unable to find a reference earlier than 16 March 1682, the date of publication of Dryden's poem (see II, 286), but Christopher Nesse, in *A Key (with the Whip)*, says that Dryden has added his new lines to the Achitophel portrait after "Seeing his [Shaftesbury's] Sun break forth from th' Cloud of Shame" (p. 27), surely referring to the scene on the obverse of the medal. Luttrell dated his copy of Nesse's poem 13 January, and the third edition of *Absalom and Achitophel*, with the added lines, was available in late December, so I should think the medal was in circulation by the middle of December. This would also fit the evidence of Edmund Hickeringill's *The Mushroom*, which says that Dryden's poem is of "*three months Birth*" (p. 16).

67. A similar claim in the "Epistle" also sounds tired and perfunctory: "no sober man can fear [Arbitrary Power], either from the King's Disposition, or his Practice" (II, 39).

68. Hickeringill seeks to contrast the three months he claims Dryden has spent on *The Medall* with his own overnight composition, but I should think it unlikely that Dryden spent a great deal of time composing his poem.

69. Hickeringill was presumably seeking to answer these lines in the "Post-Script" to *The Mushroom*, where he pictured Shaftesbury preventing a flood: "*What a blemish is it* to a man of *so great wit* [i.e., Dryden], . . . to rake up *dirt to asperse* the glory of most *renowned Patriots?* that hazzard their lives (*Hard fate!*) to stand *in the Gap*, and in the *fury of a Rageing Tide*, with great peril, and *hazzard of themselves*, their estates, families, and *Posterities*, to prevent (*if possible*) a *threatening deluge* and inundation" (p. 20). Both authors were probably aware of recent floods in Holland, where the dikes had burst; see Luttrell, I, 160–61.

70. *The Medal Revers'd*, probably by Samuel Pordage, appeared by the end of March, followed in April by *The Loyal Medal Vindicated* and *Absalom Senior*, and in May by *The Medal of John Bayes*. Another Whig pamphleteer, mourning the death of Monmouth's friend Thomas Thynne, devoted several pages of his *Directions to Fame* to attacking Dryden. Thynne was murdered in February by three thugs hired by his wife's

Swedish lover, Count Koningsmark, and his Whig eulogist may have believed that Dryden had written some verses in praise of Koningsmark, for which there is only one manuscript attribution as evidence; see Osborn, pp. 269–70.

71. See the passage in *The Medal Revers'd* beginning "*London*, the happy Bulwork of our Isle" (p. 13), and the passage on "our glorious City" in *The Medal of John Bayes* (pp. 16–19), with its references to "*ancient Charters*" and "*stronger Liberties*."

72. Shaftesbury's jury included at least two French Huguenots, Thomas Papillon and John Dubois, and a number of English Dissenters. Shadwell, in his "Epistle to the Tories" prefixed to *The Medal of John Bayes*, nonetheless claimed that "the City has not seen a Jury better qualified; nor was there one Dissenter amongst them" (sig. A3r). *The Medal Revers'd*, clearly the work of a Dissenter, is subtitled *A Satyre against Persecution* and complains at length of the sufferings of the nonconformists; for contemporary references to that persecution, see Luttrell, I, 156, 162, etc. Papillon and Dubois were the Whig candidates in the hotly contested shrieval elections of the summer of 1682.

73. In the preface of 1716, cited above, n. 35.

74. For one example, consider the passage on Dryden's early employment by Herringman, quoted above, ch. 4, p. 95, where Shadwell rhymes "prefer" with "Bookseller," and slides clumsily back and forth between addressing Dryden in the second person and describing him in the third.

75. I follow here the argument laid out by H. H. Schless in *POAS*, III, 278. Schless argues that the poets delayed publication because they feared a Whig victory in the battle over the shrieval elections; I should think it more likely that they were frightened by the banning of *The Duke of Guise* in July. For contemporary testimony about the shrieval elections, see Luttrell, I, 155, 196–227.

76. See Wilson, "Theatre Notes from the Newdigate Newsletters," p. 81. This item first appeared on 29 July; the banning took place on 18 July, and the official record is still in the P.R.O., L.C. 5/16/p. 101. Despite the quoted claim that the King was motivated by his personal affection for Monmouth, there seems to have been political concern as well: Crowne's *City Politiques*, a comedy on the shrieval elections, was licensed on 15 June, but banned on 26 June (L.C. 5/144/pp. 247, 260).

77. Here is the relevant dialogue between the King and the Duke of Guise:

> *King.* I sent you word you should not come.
> *Guise.* Sir, that I came——
> *King.* Why, that you came, I see.
>   Once more, I sent you word, you should not come.
> *Guise.* Not come to throw my self, with all submission,
>   Beneath your Royal Feet: to put my Cause
>   And Person in the Hands of Soveraign Justice!
> *King.* Now 'tis with all submission, that's the Preface,
>   Yet still you came against my strict Command,
>   You disobey'd me, *Duke*, with all submission.
> *Guise.* Sir, it was the last necessity that drove me
>   To clear my self of Calumnies, and Slanders,
>   Much urg'd, but never prov'd, against my Innocence;
>   Yet had I known it was your express Command,
>   I should not have approach'd.

[IV, i, p. 37]

Cf. H. C. Davila, *The Historie of the Civill Warres of France*, trans. Charles Cotterell and William Aylesbury, 2 vols. (1647); Dryden's own copy remains in the Clark Library:

> They entered into the King's chamber; who (while the Duke of Guise bowed himself with a lowe reverence) said to him with an angry look, *I sent you word that you should not come.* To these words the Duke with the same submission he had used to the Queen, but with more moderate words, answered, *That he was come to put himself into the arms of his Majesties justice, to clear himself of those calumnies that were cast upon him by his enemies; and that neverthelesse he would not have come, if he had been plainly told that his Majesty had commanded him to stay.* [II, 682]

Dryden's account of his dealings with Arlington comes in *The Vindication of the Duke of Guise*, p. 2.

78. For the lines from *Satyr to his Muse*, see above, ch. 5, n. 14; the passage from *The Tory-Poets* is similar:

> His *Muse* was prostitute upon the Stage,
> And's *Wife* was Prostitute to all the age:
> The Wife is Rich although the Husband Poor,
> And he not honest, and she is a Whore.
>
> [p. 2]

The claim that Elizabeth was "Rich" contradicts all the available evidence; once her grant from the crown was paid off in 1669, she had no recorded income.

79. See Haley, *Shaftesbury*, pp. 711–15.

80. See Macdonald, *Bibliography*, p. 30.

81. The order for the acting of the play is in the P.R.O., L.C. 5/144/p. 291. Not much later, on 18 December, Crowne's *City Politiques* was similarly released from its prohibition of the previous summer (L.C. 5/144/p. 325). On the Guy Fawkes episode and the similar attacks on Trimmers made during this month by L'Estrange's *Observator*, see Haley, *Shaftesbury*, p. 724.

82. For a complete account of the controversy and a plausible series of inferences about Dryden's involvement, see Harth, *Contexts of Dryden's Thought*, pp. 174–97. Harth believes that Dickinson's translation came to Dryden's attention through Tonson, who had agreed to publish it, but then got cold feet when he heard that the French original had been burned in Paris; though printed at Tonson's direction, the book therefore appeared with the imprint of Walter Davis on 14 January 1682. When Tonson published an expanded edition in May, Duke, Lee, and Tate contributed commendatory poems, as they had for *Absalom and Achitophel*, and Harth believes that the "Digression to the Translatour of Father *Simon*'s Critical History of the Old Testament," which now occupies ll. 224–51 of Dryden's poem, was originally another commendatory poem for this edition, but that Dryden "changed his mind . . . as he began to see the possibility of a much more ambitious undertaking" (p. 194).

83. The quoted phrase is from the prologue to Nathaniel Lee's *Princess of Cleve*, l. 12. Since it may well reflect Dryden's reading of Father Simon, this phrase is further evidence in support of Robert D. Hume's contention that this play, sometimes thought to have been performed as early as 1680, was in fact first staged in December 1682 or slightly later; see "The Satiric Design of Nat. Lee's *The Princess of Cleve*," p. 119. A later reference to "*Achitophel*" (l. 25) might have lost some of its urgency after the death of Shaftesbury, news of which reached England late in January.

84. For the most political reading the poem has had, see Zwicker, *Politics and Language in Dryden's Poetry*, pp. 103–22. Arguing that Dryden "was moved to personal confession in 1682 in order to articulate the king's position at a time when the king's own expression of that position would have been difficult" (p. 106), Zwicker portrays Charles II, who had always favored "liberty to tender consciences," as reluctant to go along with the campaign of repression against the Dissenters that came in the wake of the Exclusion Crisis, but forced into it by his allies the bishops. But the "breaking up of conventicles" after the *ignoramus* verdict at Shaftesbury's trial was surely undertaken with the King's full consent; all the evidence suggests that Charles was genuinely enraged. Moreover, both the preface and the text of Dryden's poem contain savage criticism directed at the Dissenters. Reading the poem as a political act desired by the King also requires dismissing Dryden's confessional gestures as merely rhetorical. I am more inclined than Zwicker to take those gestures seriously, not least because Dryden bravely signed the poem, claiming it as his own personal confession of faith. Political purposes would have been adequately served by an anonymous poem, as they were in the cases of *Absalom and Achitophel* and *The Medall*.

85. The works to which I refer here are numbers 87, 54, and 20 on a complete annotated list of the books bought at both sales, published by T. A. Birrell in "John Dryden's Purchases at Two Book Auctions, 1680 and 1682," *ES* 42 (1961):193–217. Both Osborn and Ward took occasion to doubt whether the John Dryden who is listed as purchasing these books was the poet, pointing out that there were other men named John Dryden in London at the time. The only other John Dryden with enough money to buy books, however, was the poet's first cousin, a wealthy linen-draper; he is unlikely to have been able to read Latin, French, and Spanish. Moreover, the purchase of medical books on cures for kidney stones, pointed out to me by Mrs. Marjory Clifford, is further evidence in favor of the poet as purchaser. For other possible connections between the poet and the Digby family, see above, ch. 5, n. 45, and Appendix D, p. 534.

Further evidence that Dryden was reading Catholic apologetics comes in the preface to *Religio Laici* itself: Richard H. Perkinson, in "A Note on Dryden's *Religio Laici*," *PQ* 28 (1949):517–18, identifies the "learned Priest" mentioned in the preface (II, 104) as one Peter Walsh, a Franciscan who was friendly with Dryden's patron Ormonde. The same page also alludes to Cardinal Robert Bellarmine and Father Hugh Cressy.

86. The reference to "a Reverend Prelate of our Church" (II, 104–05) has been thought applicable to Bishop Edward Stillingfleet, with whom Dryden later engaged in controversy, but I should think it more likely to be a reference to William Lloyd, vicar of St. Martin's in the Fields, Dryden's own parish church, from 1677 until 1680. Lloyd's lengthy anonymous treatise of 1677, *Considerations touching the True Way to Suppress Popery in this Kingdom; by Making a Distinction between Men of Loyal and Disloyal Principles in that Communion*, gives Catholics precisely the same "Charitable advice" Dryden describes here, suggesting that they prove their loyalty by disavowing the Pope's alleged authority over kings. By 1680, Lloyd had become Bishop of St. Asaph and was thus a "Prelate." On Tillotson, see David Brown, "Dryden's 'Religio Laici' and the 'Judicious and Learned Friend'," *MLR* 56 (1961):66–69.

87. For parallels with Wolseley, see Harth, *Contexts*, pp. 108–15, 293–97; for parallels with L'Estrange, see Sanford Budick, *Dryden and the Abyss of Light* (New Haven: Yale University Press, 1970), pp. 243–53. L'Estrange's treatise was among the few English books purchased by Dryden at the Smith sale (Birrell, no. 131).

88. For examples of Dryden's habits in doing "research," see John Harrington Smith, "Some Sources of Dryden's Toryism, 1682–84," *HLQ* 20 (1957):233–43.

89. Birrell, no. 44. This treatise, *La déclaration et refutation des fausses suppositions et perverses applications d'aucunes sentences des sainctes Escritures*, by Matthieu de Launoy and Henry Pettier (Paris, 1578), has several suggestive parallels with Dryden's work. Like Dryden, the authors describe their style as "bas & simple" (sig. ††ii). They also argue that "Iesu-Christ a voulu, que la doctrine de l'Euangile fût confirmee par miracles" (p. 22; cf. *Religio Laici*, ll. 148–50). In an instance of class snobbery like that Dryden directs against the Dissenters in ll. 400–20, they describe "Caluin & autres de même farine" as "hommes pauures, nuds, miserables, pecheurs, & de nature menteurs & ignorans"(p. 193).

90. The speech is summarized in *Cobbett's Parliamentary History*, 36 vols. (Bagshaw, 1808), IV, 564–66.

91. Birrell, no. 17.

92. For Sunderland's return to office in July 1682, see J. P. Kenyon, *Robert Spencer, Earl of Sunderland* (Longmans, 1958), pp. 80–83.

93. For a learned discussion of deist tracts and manuscripts that may have been available to Dryden, see Harth, *Contexts*, pp. 58–88. The preposterous notion that Dryden himself was a deist has continued to rear its head from time to time; see William Empson's attempt to revive it in "Dryden's Apparent Skepticism," *EIC* 20 (1970): 172–81, and answers by Phillip Harth and Robert D. Hume in the same volume, pp. 446–50, 492–95; see also Harth's incisive review of Budick, *PQ* 50 (1971):424–26.

94. Modern scholarship has inevitably been affected by such hindsight. Louis Bredvold's influential study, *The Intellectual Milieu of John Dryden* (Ann Arbor: University of Michigan Press, 1934), which described Dryden as a "Pyrrhonist," sought evidence of Dryden's incipient conversion in *Religio Laici*. This view was systematically and powerfully attacked by Elias Chiasson, "Dryden's Apparent Scepticism in *Religio Laici*," *Harvard Theological Review* 54 (1961):207–21, and by Thomas Fujimura, "Dryden's *Religio Laici*: An Anglican Poem," *PMLA* 76 (1961):205–17; both these articles show that the arguments Dryden makes may be frequently encountered in Anglican writings of his century. Phillip Harth's careful and learned study, *Contexts of Dryden's Thought*, is our fullest and best account of the intellectual background to his religious poetry.

95. Blount's relations with Dryden are maddeningly difficult to sort out. He defended the Laureate from the censures of the Rota at the age of nineteen (see above, ch. 8, p. 247), but wrote an inflammatory Whig pamphlet during the Popish Plot scare, from which Dryden lifted some descriptive phrases for his *Spanish Fryar* (see above, p. 333). By 1683, Blount should have realized that Dryden's "Protestant play" was written from a point of view quite unlike that of his pamphlet, and may have decided to pay him back in kind with his own *Religio Laici*. Harth argues for such a reading: "Unless we are willing to suppose that Blount was obtuse . . . , we cannot assume that his motives were innocent. . . . In reality, Blount's book is an answer to Dryden's poem, disguised as a sequel" (*Contexts*, pp. 91–92). Even Blount's effusive "Epistle Dedicatory" may have an ironic edge; consider what a Whig and deist like Blount might have meant by this sentence:

"'Tis a Question not easily to be decided, Whether you have been more serviceable to the Peace of the *State* in your *Absolom and Achitophel*, or to the *Church* in your *Religio Laici*?" (sig. A7r). Yet Sanford Budick, whose reading of Dryden's poem resembles Blount's, "can see no compelling reason to discard Scott's view" that Blount regarded Dryden with real respect; see *Dryden and the Abyss of Light*, p. 16n. Such a view makes sense only if we take Blount to have been a fool.

Dryden's last comment on Blount may have looked like praise to an uninformed reader, but it was actually quite nasty; it comes in his discussion of the contributors to a translation of Lucian published in 1711: "The wit of Mr. Blount, and his other performances, need no recommendation from me; they have made too much noise in the world to need a herald" (p. 50). Blount's passion for his dead wife's sister made a considerable "noise in the world" when he shot himself in July of 1693 (see Luttrell, III, 149, 174). When the translation of Lucian was finally published in 1711, Sam Briscoe explained that "The Life by Mr Dryden, and some of the Dialogues, were done before and in the year 1696," but the translation had been announced in the *Gentleman's Journal* for June of 1693, and Blount had obviously done his part by that summer. Dryden's contributions, however, must have been written at about the time Briscoe indicates: he compliments Walter Moyle, another contributor, on his election to Parliament, which took place late in 1695. Moreover, our timing of Dryden's progress in his translation of Virgil points to 1696 as a likely year for him to have stolen time to work on Lucian.

96. See especially *The Revolter* (1687), a "tragi-comedy" juxtaposing quotations from the two poems.

CHAPTER 11. "SHAME OF CHANGE"

1. See Hume, *Development*, p. 224. For a stimulating general discussion of the difficulties that obtain in reading "parallel" plays, see John M. Wallace, "Dryden and History: A Problem in Allegorical Reading," *ELH* 36 (1969):265–90.

2. He refers to the authors of the *Reflections* as "my *Templar* and *Poet* in *association* for a *Libel*" (p. 40), and claims to be able to separate those accusations originating with the unnamed attorney, whom he accuses of casting an illegal ballot in the shrieval elections, from those originating with "the *Northern Dedicator*" (p. 25), a slur at Shadwell for his frequent dedications to the Duke of Newcastle.

3. See Luttrell, I, 247.

4. On Monmouth's visit to Chichester, where he was insulted by a sermon against rebellion in the cathedral, see Bevan, *Monmouth*, p. 157; on his victory in the horserace, see J. N. P. Watson, *Captain-General and Rebel Chief* (Allen & Unwin, 1979), pp. 157–58.

5. In dedicating *Bury-Fair* to Dorset in 1689, Shadwell complained that "for near Ten years I was kept from the exercise of that Profession which had afforded me a competent Subsistence" (sig. A3r), and implied that Dryden was to blame. But in *A Journal from Parnassus* (c. 1688), "Flecknoe" (clearly Shadwell) is described as one "whom long ago sly Betterton, / Of his dull Scenes asham'd & weary grown, / Cashier'd from Pay" (p. 8).

6. The primary record is in the *Entring Book* of Roger Morrice, quoted in *The London Stage*, I, 318.

7. This poem has sometimes been attributed to Lee, though there is no contemporary external evidence; for purely stylistic reasons, not least the ode form, I should think Oldham might be a candidate.

8. Dryden's account of who wrote what parts of the play in the *Vindication* claims "only the *First Scene* of the Play; the whole *Fourth Act*, and the *first half*, or somewhat *more* of the *Fifth*" (p. 3). Still, these lines at the very end bear his stamp; compare particularly *Absalom and Achitophel*, l. 1005: "Beware the Fury of a Patient Man."

9. Hunt's version of the couplet is as follows:

> For Conscience, and Heavens fear, Religious rules
> They are all State bells to toll in pious fools.

The *Vindication*, which says that the couplet occurs "in the second or third Act" (i.e., in a passage not claimed by Dryden) gives a smoother version:

> *For Conscience or Heavens fear, religious Rules*
> *Are all State-bells to toll in pious Fools.*

Dryden goes on to explain that "the Verses are not *mine*, but Mr. *Lees*: I ask'd him concerning them, and have this account, that they were spoken by the *Devil*" (p. 18). Late in the first act, a devil gives a speech in couplets into which these lines might indeed fit, but they do not appear there, or indeed anywhere in the play. Did Dryden or Lee purposely excise them?

10. Shadwell later claimed that he had "taxed" Dryden with writing *Mac Flecknoe*, and that Dryden had "denied it with all the Execrations he could think of"; see the dedication of *The Tenth Satyr of Juvenal* (1687) to Sedley, sig. A3r. If this allegation was true, and if the incident occurred before the controversy over *The Duke of Guise*, Shadwell had good reason to portray Dryden as unwilling to acknowledge in person what he had said in print. The incident might have taken place while *Mac Flecknoe* was circulating in manuscript, or after the first printing by "D. Green," in which case it would antedate the *Reflections*, but confronting Dryden might have seemed even more urgent after *Mac Flecknoe* was reprinted in *Miscellany Poems* (1684), where it appears, though unsigned, in immediate juxtaposition with *Absalom and Achitophel* and *The Medall*.

11. We may only guess at the identities of the "four men" in the Whig party. Five possible candidates are Sir Charles Wolseley, on whose work Dryden had just drawn for *Religio Laici*; his son Robert, who had written the epilogue to *The Spanish Fryar*; the young John Holles, Lord Haughton, to whom that "Protestant Play" had been dedicated; Charles Blount, the early defender of Dryden and Whig pamphleteer, who would soon publish his misreading of *Religio Laici*; and Sir Robert Howard, with whom Dryden had once "live[d] together," and whom he probably saw when dealing with "the Lords Commissioners of the Treasury." In the case of Robert Wolseley, there is evidence of continued good relations. His preface to *Valentinian*, a tragedy "Alter'd by the Late Earl of Rochester" and finally published in 1684 (imprint date 1685), is friendly to Rochester and hostile to Dryden's patron Mulgrave, but the references to Dryden are uniformly respectful.

12. The quoted phrases are from Elijah Fenton's introduction to *The Works of Edmund Waller* (1730), p. lxxvii. For a modern account, see Carl Niemeyer, "The Earl of Roscommon's Academy," *MLN* 49 (1934):432–37.

13. Quoted by Niemeyer, p. 434. Chetwood contributed to several of Dryden's collaborative translations and anthologies.

14. The stanza from the poem follows the text printed by Brice Harris in *Charles Sackville, Sixth Earl of Dorset* (Urbana: University of Illinois Press, 1940), p. 81; see also pp. 75, 124.

15. See the introduction to *The Complete Works of George Saville, First Marquess of Halifax*, ed. Walter Raleigh (Oxford: Clarendon, 1912).

16. Our evidence about who participated in Roscommon's "Academy" is fragmentary. There is anecdotal evidence connecting Oldham with Dorset, and his publications praise Roscommon; the California editors suppose that he may have "wished to enter Roscommon's circle of noblemen and writers," but conclude that his hope "seems not to have been realized" (II, 384). Oldham's name does not appear in the obviously incomplete lists of participants set down years later by Chetwood and Fenton; no real conclusions can be drawn.

17. See *Letters*, pp. 14–16, and Paul Hammond, "The Integrity of Dryden's Lucretius," *MLR* 78 (1983), p. 1, n. 4. The story that Dryden maliciously encouraged Creech to translate Horace in the hope that he would fail, first developed by Tom Brown in *The Late Converts Exposed* (1690), pp. 53–54, is a slander. The truth, as related by Southerne, is that Dryden attempted to dissuade Creech; see Malone, pp. 509–11.

18. The absence of an entry in the Stationers' Register or the Term Catalogues makes it impossible to date this publication more precisely. Tonson, writing in 1708, says that Soames made his translation in 1680 and requested Dryden's help in revising it: "I saw the Manuscript lye in Mr. Dryden's Hands for above Six Months, who made very considerable Alterations in it." See Macdonald, *Bibliography*, p. 36.

19. Arthur Sherbo has greatly extended our knowledge of the contributors to these projects. See "The Dryden-Cambridge Translation of Plutarch's *Lives*," *EA* 32 (1979):177–84, and "Dryden as a Cambridge Editor," *SB* 38 (1985):251–61.

20. See Luttrell, I, 262–94; Ogg, II, 647–50; Bevan, *Monmouth*, pp. 158–63; Watson, *Captain-General and Rebel Chief*, pp. 146–67.

21. *Diary*, III, 317–18.

22. P.R.O., S.P. 29/428, no. 108. "Davenant" is of course Charles, the son of Dryden's collaborator, now "proprietor" of the Duke's Company.

23. P.R.O., S.P. 29/433/ff. 258–59, a report of the testimony of James Dryden and Nathaniel Gwynne. After the Privy Council meeting of 26 October, "Henry Scarrot being examined by Mr. Blathwayt

sayes he is a gardner at Hampstead. That he knows James Dryden, but not Nathaniel Dryden [obviously someone's error for Nathaniel Gwynne]. He denies the words laid to his charge or any words to that effect. That he was in Dryden's Company Sunday sennight where there was another man whom he knows not & believes himself to have been then a little in Drink but that he did not say those Words" (S.P. 29/433/ff. 20ff., "no. 8"). The endorsement of James Dryden's "Information against Scarrot" (S.P. 29/433/f. 260) gives his address as "St. Bartholemew Lane," and the poet's brother was a resident of that parish: his children Erasmus, Edward, and Mary were all baptized at St. Bartholemew in the Exchange (10 November 1681, 25 April 1685, and 23 September 1686), and his will, dated 30 June 1691 (P.R.O., P.C.C. 37 Vere) requests that he be buried in St. Bartholemew Church.

24. See Bevan, *Monmouth*, pp. 164–71.

25. See Judith Sloman, *Dryden: The Poetics of Translation* (Toronto: University of Toronto Press, 1985), especially pp. 63–76. In *Miscellany Poems*, argues the late Professor Sloman, "the world of satiric controversy is contrasted with, perhaps even supplanted by, the world of pastoral or scholarly retreat, which is ultimately symbolized by translation itself" (p. 63). I am in closer agreement with the idea of "contrast" than with the idea of "supplanting."

26. Quoted by Niemeyer, pp. 433–34.

27. Virgil's poem celebrates the birth of a consul's son, and was often read as an unconsciously Christian prophecy. Princess Anne, who married George of Denmark on 28 July 1683, was pregnant when the poem was published; Dryden may have been glancing at that pregnancy in choosing this poem, but the baby was stillborn on 30 April 1684. Earl Miner argues for this hypothesis in "Dryden's Messianic Eclogue," *RES* 11 (1960):299–302, but confuses the dating, apparently supposing that Dryden included the translation in the miscellany because his opportunity to use it as a panegyric had already come to naught. When the poem appeared in February, there was every reason to think Anne's pregnancy would produce a live birth. In any case, Dryden recycled much of the messianic imagery in *Britannia Rediviva* four years later.

28. Malone and subsequent scholars have placed this letter in the late summer of 1683, citing the June dinner party with Sunderland, who is mentioned, and the payment of a quarter's allowance to Dryden in August of that year. In his important article, "Dryden in 1684," *MP* 72 (1975), pp. 252–53, Edward Saslow presents powerful arguments for redating it to 17 March 1684, not least an annotation reading "17 March 1673/4" on the holograph; that is clearly an error, but correcting one digit gives us an excellent date. To his formidable arguments, I would add the fact that Dryden's salary was more than usually overdue at this moment. In 1682, he had received quarterly allowances in January and August; in 1683, those payments had come in March and August; when no payment arrived in March of 1684, Dryden might logically have requested one. A payment finally arrived in May, but it was again only a quarter's salary, despite Dryden's plea for half a year's salary. There was no summer payment, and on 15 December 1684, he received half a year's salary; see Appendix C.

29. This John Dryden, son of the poet's uncle William, was nominated Collector of Customs by Henry Guy on 12 November 1683; letters patent were ordered prepared on 3 December; Great Seal papers were apparently dated 17 December. See *C.T.B.*, VII, ii, 949, 972, 1275.

30. On 14 August 1683, the Newdigate newsletters reported Betterton's plans to mount an opera in the French style, and his journey to the Continent. Writing from Paris on [15]/25 August, Richard Grahame, Viscount Preston, the Ambassador to France, acknowledged a royal request for assistance in this project, sent to him from Sunderland and delivered by Betterton; on [12]/22 September, he sent word to the Duke of York that Betterton was bringing Grabu back with him. See Wilson, "Theatre Notes from the Newdigate Newsletters," p. 82; *H.M.C.*, VII, iii, 288, 290. Already known to Dryden for his theatre music, Grabu had held a court post in England from 1665 until 1679, but his salary, like Dryden's, had been irregularly paid; when he gave up and returned to France at the height of the Popish Plot scare, he was owed well over £500; see *Works*, XV, 340. We do not know what financial inducements or hopes Sunderland authorized Betterton to offer to Grabu, but they were sufficient to secure his return.

31. See McFadden, pp. 265–66.

32. Although the only version of *King Arthur* that remains is the heavily revised one mounted in 1691, Curtis Price bravely attempts to sketch some possible political meanings of the original; see *Henry Purcell and the London Stage*, pp. 290–93. Much of what he offers is suggestive, though the claim that Dryden admired Trimmers flies in the face of the two passages explicitly attacking Trimmers quoted above, ch. 10, p. 371; ch. 11, p. 388.

33. For an account of the "Carnoval on the Water," see Evelyn's diary entry for 24 January 1684; *Diary*, IV, 362–63. I am inferring that some version of the frost scene was in the original *King Arthur*.

34. See Paul Hammond, "Dryden's *Albion and Albanius*: The Apotheosis of Charles II," in *The Court Masque*, ed. David Lindley (Manchester: Manchester University Press, 1984), pp. 169–83.

35. For the record of the "repetition that has been made before his Majesty at the Duchess of Portsmouth's," see the letter from Edward Bedingfield to the Countess of Rutland, dated 1 January 1685, *H.M.C.*, XII, v, ii, 85. For the fragmentary record of 24 May 1684, see Wilson, "More Theatre Notes from the Newdigate Newsletters," p. 59. *The London Stage* glosses this record as a performance of *The Duke of Guise*, which was not a new play and not about the new plot; Saslow ("Dryden in 1684," pp. 251–52) was the first to see that the description fits *Albion and Albanius* more closely; his argument that this newsletter note records a "performance" will not fit with the other evidence about the much-delayed premiere of June 1685, but some kind of rehearsal or read-through is certainly a possible explanation.

36. See Price, *Henry Purcell and the London Stage*, pp. 268–69, and the dramatically impressive excerpt there transcribed into modern clefs. As Price correctly notes, the "daunting use of French clef-groupings" in the original printed score has discouraged serious study and analysis of Grabu's music.

37. See Alan Roper, "Dryden's 'The History of the League' and the Early Editions of Maimbourg's 'Histoire de la Ligue'," *PBSA* 66 (1972):263–74, and Saslow, "Dryden in 1684," pp. 248–50.

38. There was marked scientific interest in the chills and fever associated with malaria at this time. On 11 July 1683, for example, Evelyn witnessed an experiment at the Royal Society by "*Dr. Slaer* attempting to demonstrate the several fermentations in our bodies, viz that of our bloud in *Paroxysmes* of Agues & Feavors." By introducing chemicals into a test tube full of human blood, Slare attempted to demonstrate "the hot fit, succeeding the rigor of the Cold." He was then asked to repeat the experiment using "*Jesuits Powder*" or quinine. *Diary*, IV, 324–25. Cf. Dryden's letter to Hyde on his salary: "A quarters allowance is but the Jesuites powder to my disease; the fitt will return a fortnight hence" (*Letters*, pp. 20–21).

39. McFadden (pp. 269–76) argues that the weather imagery is a direct refutation of Halifax's *Character of a Trimmer*, and it may well be, but the imagery is obviously commonplace, and there is no absolute proof that Dryden had read that unpublished essay.

40. See Alan Roper's entertaining headnote; *Works*, XVIII, 423.

41. There is no firm evidence for the date of the first edition beyond its imprint of 1684, but since Dryden's letter to Tonson, evidently written in August of 1684, recommends a second edition and notes a printer's error in his own commendatory poem, Roscommon's *Essay* had probably appeared in the late spring or early summer.

42. This is the conclusion reached by Paul Hammond at the conclusion of "The Integrity of Dryden's Lucretius," p. 23. Hammond's important and persuasive essay contradicts many of the assertions in Norman Austin's influential earlier account of these poems, "Translation as Baptism," *Arion* 7 (1968):576–602.

43. According to the preface to *Sylvae*, Dryden began with the short poems by Horace and Theocritus, expecting that his "humour would have wasted it self" in these lyrical exercises, but "finding something that was more pleasing in them, than my ordinary productions" (III, 3), he went on to choose and translate the weightier selections from Virgil and Lucretius with which the published collection begins. The letter to Tonson promises "four Odes of Horace, which I have already translated" (p. 23), but does not mention Theocritus at all.

44. Dryden's preface provides evidence that he thought of Horace as an Epicurean: "let his *Dutch* Commentatours say what they will, his Philosophy was Epicurean; and he made use of Gods and providence, only to serve a turn in Poetry" (III, 16). Dryden obviously understood the difference between the actual Epicurean philosophy of the ancient world and the popular notion of "epicures" as debased hedonists. For an excellent brief summary of Epicurean ideas, see Martin Ferguson Smith's introduction to *Lucretius: De Rerum Natura* (Heinemann, 1975), pp. xxviii–lxiii.

45. Rochester did not leave the government; he was "kicked upstairs" to the less important position of President of the Privy Council; see Ogg, II, 655.

46. The sparse theatrical records for the 1684–85 season give no indication of a performance of either of the plays Betterton discussed reviving with Dryden in the conversation recorded in this letter. *All for Love*

was performed at court on 20 February 1686, and a reprint of *The Conquest of Granada* in 1687 may be evidence of a revival.

47. The dedication to *Cleomenes* (1692) contains a puzzling reference to some piece of generosity from Hyde to Dryden, who says, "I shall be proud to hold my Dependance on you in Chief, as I do part of my small Fortune in *Wiltshire*" (sig. A3v). On this phrase Malone based the conjecture that Elizabeth's father had granted Dryden a piece of property near Charlton at the time of their marriage (pp. 442–44), but no record of any such transaction survives, nor would Dryden's holding such property depend upon Hyde. Sir Robert Howard, however, who acquired the manor of Wooton Bassett in Wiltshire when he married Honoria O'Brien in 1665, sold it to Hyde in 1676. Although the sales agreement (Bod. MS Don. c. 68 f. 11) makes no mention of Dryden, one possible theory is that Hyde allowed Dryden to retain some small piece of that estate, originally given to him by his brother-in-law.

48. For an extended account, see H. A. Mason, "Dryden's Dream of Happiness," *Cambridge Quarterly* 8 (1978–79):11–55; 9 (1979–80):218–71, especially pp. 22–36.

49. *The Scornful Lady* of Beaumont and Fletcher; a performance on 23 February 1684 is recorded in P.R.O., L.C. 5/145/p. 120.

50. Rubens had drawn on this myth in his *Peace and War* of 1629, painted for Charles I; his *Horrors of War*, painted in 1638, shows an armed Mars leaving a pleading Venus. For an acute discussion of the relevance of these paintings to contemporary European feelings about warfare, see Theodore S. Rabb, *The Struggle for Stability in Early Modern Europe* (New York: Oxford University Press, 1975), pp. 129–34.

51. I cannot pass by this episode without noting some unfortunate errors in modern accounts of Dryden's translation. It is Mezentius, not Aeneas, whom Dryden describes as "Collected in himself," and Dryden therefore had excellent reason to borrow that phrase from Milton's description of Satan as "in himself collected." Sloman's discussion of the Satanic elements in Aeneas's character (*The Poetics of Translation*, p. 92) is thus grounded on a fundamental misreading. Nor does Mezentius "commit suicide," as Sloman claims (p. 93); trapped under his fallen horse, he can offer no resistance to Aeneas. Dryden's account of his death in the 1685 version reads clearly: "He said; and to the Sword his throat apply'd" (l. 239). The reversal of the nouns in the *Virgil* of 1697, a reading adopted in the California edition, is surely a printer's error.

52. Dryden probably never knew about Monmouth's last visit to his father, on 10 November 1684. Despite his banishment, Monmouth slipped back into England in disguise; according to the one primary account, by the Presbyterian minister William Veitch, the King gave his bastard jewels valued at £10,000. See Bevan, *Monmouth*, pp. 177–79; Watson, *Captain-General and Rebel Chief*, pp. 185–86.

53. For a suggestive discussion of the complexity of this allusion, see Dustin Griffin, "Dryden's 'Oldham' and the Perils of Writing," *MLQ* 37 (1976):133–50, especially pp. 138–42.

54. In addition to the publication of *Sylvae*, the author of *The Laurel* appears to have been stimulated by seeing Riley's fine portrait of Dryden, painted about this time. For a reproduction and illuminating commentary, see James M. Osborn, "A Lost Portrait of John Dryden," *HLQ* 36 (1973):341–45.

55. *Diary*, IV, 374–75, 395, 413. The date of the Sunday on which Evelyn saw and deplored the King's "unexpressable luxury" is uncertain; his entries, added much later, imply that it was 25 January, but his conclusion, "six days after was all in the dust," suggests that it may have been 1 February, the evening before Charles suffered his first attack. Luttrell reports that "his majestie, the night before he was taken ill, was to visit the dutchesse of Portsmouth" (I, 327).

56. Huddleston had been instrumental in saving Charles from pursuit after the battle of Worcester, and was exempted by name from the acts banishing priests during the Popish Plot scare. All the details in this paragraph depend upon the carefully documented account given by Raymond Crawfurd in *The Last Days of Charles II* (Oxford: Clarendon, 1909).

57. The reference to "the flaming Wall" at the end of the world comes from a passage in Lucretius (I, 73) a few lines further on from one Dryden had translated in *Sylvae*.

58. For recurrences of the word, see *Albion and Albanius*, III, i, 196; "To my Friend Mr. J. North-leigh," l. 10; "To the Pious Memory of . . . Anne Killigrew," l. 131.

59. See Turner, *James II*, p. 256.

60. Crawfurd prints the entire report in Latin and provides a translation, pp. 66–80; for the passage on James's grief, see pp. 67, 79. After a careful survey of all the primary sources and the medical evidence they

provide, Crawfurd concludes that the story of poisoning retailed by James Welwood, later physician to Queen Mary, is "grotesque" (p. 12). Nonetheless, scholars partial to Monmouth continue to take seriously the notion that Charles was poisoned because he was planning to send James to Scotland and recall Monmouth; see, for example, Watson, *Captain-General and Rebel Chief*, pp. 186–89.

61. See McFadden, p. 297.

62. For that declaration, made to the Privy Council on the day of Charles's death, and printed at their insistence, see Turner, *James II*, p. 240.

63. *C.T.B., 1685–88*, VIII, 139–40, 604.

64. Luttrell, I, 340.

65. Dryden's detractors in his own lifetime often called him "mercenary," a charge predictably repeated in many of the pamphlets attacking his change of religion. But the real damage to his modern reputation comes from Macaulay's hostile account (1865). When Macaulay found the Privy Seal order renewing Dryden's patent, he inferred that the second annual pension of £100, which had actually been awarded Dryden by Charles in 1677, was a bribe from James designed to persuade him to convert; see his *History of England*, 6 vols. (Macmillan, 1914), II, 850–52. As Ward points out (p. 216), Macaulay's malicious inference from incomplete evidence was repeated by W. D. Christie in his influential Globe edition of Dryden's poems (1871), and by the *Encyclopedia Britannica*. The factual error was exposed over fifty years ago; see Louis I. Bredvold, "Notes on John Dryden's Pension," *MP* 30 (1933):267–74. Unhappily, the notion that Dryden's conversion was insincere has proved stubborn and persistent, not only in the popular imagination, but in the writings of historical and literary scholars who should know better.

66. The facts about payments to Dryden under James may be found in Appendix C.

67. See Turner, *James II*, p. 247.

68. See Evelyn, *Diary*, IV, 445.

69. Luttrell reports rumors of the King's conversion before 25 February 1685 (I, 332); Dryden's poem, one of the last to appear, was advertised on 14 March. Earl Miner suggests that Dryden's reference to Charles "Providing for events to come" (l. 216) may glance at the conversion (*Works*, III, 309), but the stanza in which that phrase occurs is concerned with the way Charles "bequeath'd supream command" to James. Evelyn saw the Royal Papers in Pepys's possession on 2 October 1685; see *Diary*, IV, 475–79. Dryden's *Defence* of the paper by the first Duchess of York, which was published along with the two papers by Charles II, mentions reading her confession "in Manuscript" (XVII, 291); one might reasonably infer that he had also seen the holographs of the King's papers, though fixing a date is impossible.

70. For his purchases of books of Catholic divinity, see above, ch. 10, p. 374 and n. 85. Victor M. Hamm has made some further suggestions about works of this kind that Dryden may have read; see "Dryden's *Religio Laici* and Roman Catholic Apologetics," *PMLA* 80 (1965):190–98, and "Dryden's *The Hind and the Panther* and Roman Catholic Apologetics," *PMLA* 83 (1968):400–15. While some of Hamm's arguments about specific tracts are less convincing than others, Dryden was obviously quite familiar with the issues addressed in controversial literature on both sides. Macaulay's claim that "he knew little and cared little about religion" (*History*, II, 850) is false.

71. See Birrell, "James Maurus Corker and Dryden's Conversion," p. 462.

72. "One son turn'd me, I turn'd the other two," says "Johnny" in the *Heroic Scene*, l. 102; *POAS* IV, 84.

73. The Latin poem Charles Dryden contributed to the Cambridge volume on the death of Charles II (March 1685) is the last piece of evidence placing him at Trinity. Obadiah Walker was apparently a secret Catholic long before his public acknowledgment of his faith; see Evelyn, *Diary*, IV, 509–10. Luttrell reported a rumor that Walker had professed himself a Catholic in late February of 1686, but did not report his appearing in public as a Catholic until late December of that year (I, 373, 391). The contemporary evidence connecting John Dryden, Jr., with Walker is an attack in the form of a supposed *Address of John Dryden, Laureat to His Highness the Prince of Orange* (1689), which refers to

> That *Oxford* Nursling, that sweet hopeful Boy,
> His Father's, and that once *Ignatian* Joy;
> Design'd for a new *Bellarmin Goliah*,
> Under the great *Gamaliel Obadiah*.

[pp. 3–4]

James II placed John, Jr. on the list of proposed new fellows of Magdalen College in a letter to Samuel

Parker, Bishop of Oxford and new Master of Magdalen, dated 31 December 1687. Fellows were ordinarily required to hold at least a B.A., and a letter of 8 January 1688 notes that "it would be very necessary for [those being intruded] to have mandates for their degrees." Although there is no record of young Dryden's being awarded a degree, he was admitted to the Fellowship on 11 January 1688. His education under Walker, if it ever took place, may have been regarded as sufficient. He was crossed off the Buttery Book, along with the other intruders, on 25 October 1688. See J. R. Bloxam, *Magdalen College and King James II, 1686–88*, Oxford Historical Society vol. VI (Oxford: Clarendon, 1886), pp. 225–33, 265. On Erasmus-Henry's departure from the Charterhouse, see Malone, p. 426. The entry in the *Liber Ruber* of the English College at Rome recording Erasmus-Henry's enrollment there on [15]/25 October 1690 notes that he studied philosophy at Douai, but gives no dates for that study; see *PCRS* 40, p. 111. My conclusions about the relevance of this information to the date of Dryden's conversion are in agreement with those offered by Edward Saslow in "Angelic 'Fire-Works': The Background and Significance of *The Hind and the Panther*, II, 649–62," *SEL* 20 (1980), pp. 375–76.

74. See the letter cited above, n. 35.

75. Dryden's preface credits Betterton with the descriptions of the sets, but I do not agree with McFadden's generous idea that this claim will "absolve Dryden of responsibility" for this last attack on his dead adversary (see pp. 288–89).

76. See Turner, *James II*, pp. 267–74.

77. See Macdonald, *Bibliography*, pp. 128–29.

78. See Bevan, *Monmouth*, pp. 195–235; Watson, *Captain-General and Rebel Chief*, pp. 192–266. Of Monmouth's followers, Turner estimates that about three hundred were hanged and nearly a thousand transported. See *James II*, p. 283.

79. The young poet Matthew Prior, a Westminster and Cambridge man whom Dryden probably knew, did publish an "Advice to a Painter" poem on Monmouth's rebellion and death, which draws liberally on *Absalom and Achitophel*. Prior uses Dryden's biblical names for some of his characters and adopts a tone that mixes satire with regret. See *POAS*, IV, 44–49.

80. Smallpox was especially virulent in 1685; Evelyn, who lost two daughters during that year, on 14 March and 29 August, calls the disease "universaly very contagious" (*Diary*, IV, 463; cf. 420–31, 464).

81. As Earl Miner argues (*Works*, III, 318), echoes of Anne's poems in Dryden's establish his knowledge of her work. The volume was entered on the Stationers' Register on 30 September 1685 and advertised on 2 November. The pagination begins with Anne's poems; the front matter, including Dryden's poem, has empty brackets in which page numbers have not been printed. I should suppose Dryden wrote his poem during October.

82. Two excellent articles on this aspect of the poem are A. D. Hope, "Anne Killigrew, or the Art of Modulating," *Southern Review* 1 (1963):4–14; and David Vieth, "Irony in Dryden's Ode to Anne Killigrew," *SP* 63 (1965):91–100.

83. *Poems by Mrs Anne Killigrew* (imprint date 1686), p. 54.

84. According to Lockier, Dryden was holding forth on the excellence of his own *Mac Flecknoe*, declaring that it was "the first piece of ridicule written in heroics," when Lockier courageously disagreed, instancing Boileau's *Le Lutrin* and Tassoni's *Secchia Rapita*. Dryden, far from resenting this correction, invited him for a visit. See Spence, *Anecdotes*, ed. Osborn, I, 274–75.

85. Evelyn's famous diary entry of 19 January 1686 records hearsay, but is nonetheless significant as the first reference to Dryden as a Catholic: "*Dryden* the famous play-poet & his two sonns, & Mrs. *Nelle* (Misse to the late . . .) were said to go to Masse; & such purchases were no greate losse to the Church" (*Diary*, IV, 497). Nell Gwyn ("the Protestant whore") did not become a Catholic; Thomas Tenison, vicar of St. Martin's in the Fields, is known to have attended her on her deathbed in 1687 and preached her funeral sermon. But she did leave £50 to the Catholic poor of St. James's parish, and as Saslow shrewdly points out, she might have attended Mass without converting; see "Angelic 'Fire-Works'," p. 375*n*. Luttrell's entry for 14 January, noting that "Several persons have appear'd publickly to be papists, which have been only suspected before" (I, 369), may reflect the same rumors about Dryden. One manuscript copy of "To Mr. Bays," a poem attacking Dryden for his conversion, is a letter dated 20 April 1686; see *POAS* IV, 74.

Dryden's comic verse-epistle to Etherege in Hudibrastics, probably written in May or June of 1686, may contain some sly hints of his conversion. He refers to "worldly pomp . . . (Which Poet has at Font defy'd)" (ll. 64–65); editors have noted the allusion to the service of baptism, but have missed the possibility that Dryden is speaking of his new baptism as a Catholic. He also jokingly describes Etherege as a missionary "Ad partes Infidelium" (l. 14), the phrase used to describe such Catholic missionaries as St. Francis Xavier, whose life he translated in 1688. This letter, not published until 1691 but evidently much circulated in manuscript, answers one written by Etherege to Lord Middleton on [19]/29 April 1686; see *The Letterbook of Sir George Etherege*, ed. Sybil Rosenfeld (Humphrey Milford, 1928), pp. 79–82.

The extent of Dryden's contribution to the *Defence* of the royal papers has been a crux in Dryden studies. Malone believed that he wrote only the third part, the defense of the Duchess's paper, and Earl Miner has supported that position; see "Dryden as Prose Controversialist: His Role in *A Defence of the Royal Papers*," *PQ* 43 (1964):412–19. Some of Miner's "external evidence," however, is dubious. He argues that the printer left a blank page between part 2 and part 3, recognizing that part 3 was by a different author, but part 2 simply ends on a recto, and beginning part 3 on a recto, normal printing practice, requires that the verso of p. 85 be blank; moreover, p. 85 ends with a catchword for the opening of part 3. Charles Ward believed that Dryden wrote all three parts (see pp. 219, 359), a position supported by Edward L. Saslow in "Dryden's Authorship of the *Defence* of the Royal Papers," *SEL* 17 (1977):387–95. While the first two parts are indeed less vigorous than the last, where Dryden warms to the task of defending a wronged lady, I believe he had a hand in all three, though he need not have been the only author.

Let me add the following internal evidence to the ongoing argument. In the Preface, the author writes: "I hope I shall discover the foul Dealing of this Author [Stillingfleet], who has obscur'd, as much as he is able, the Native Lustre of those Papers, and recommended by a false Light his own sophisticated Ware; part of which may certainly deserve the clearest Light which can be given it by the Hands of the Under-Sheriff, or of somebody whom I will not name" [i.e., the hangman] (sig. A4r). For "sophisticated Ware," cf. Dryden's epilogue to *Mithridates*, l. 21, and his *Religio Laici*, l. 237. For the rhetorical trick of refusing to name something, cf. *His Majesties Declaration Defended*: "there is a certain story of the Dog in the Manger, which out of good manners I will not apply" (XVII, 219). Two other passages employing theatrical metaphors have the ring of Dryden: "And who can tell . . . what it serves for, but to do the Church of *England* the same good Office which they do themselves, who, when Vice is ridicul'd on the Stage, fall out with the Actors or Poet, and will needs be the fools of the play" (p. 20). This comes very close to Dryden's complaints about the audiences for comedies, especially his prologue to Shadwell's *A True Widow* (quoted above, ch. 9, p. 311). Later, referring to Stillingfleet's repeating one of his weaker arguments, he says, "This Actor went off the Stage but now, and needed not return so soon, with no wiser a Part" (pp. 66–67); cf. a similar remark in *An Essay of Dramatick Poesie* (quoted above, ch. 6, p. 163).

86. On 29 April, Tonson entered "*The history of the revolucons wch have hapned in Europe in the matter of religion* written by Monsieur Varillas, and translated into English according to his Majties command, by Mr. Dryden" on the Stationers' Register. Burnet published his *Reflections on Mr. Varilla's History* in Amsterdam later in 1686; Varillas quickly wrote an *Answer*, and Burnet published his *Defence of the Reflections* in August or September of 1687, also in Amsterdam, with a sneering comment to the effect that Dryden's caricature in *The Hind and the Panther* was "wreak[ing] his Malice on me for spoiling his three moneths labour." See Macdonald, *Bibliography*, p. 257, and Roper's long note, *Works*, XIX, 452–54.

87. The houses are Ugbrooke in Devonshire, home of Dryden's patron Clifford, later possessed by his son Baron Chudleigh, and Rushton Hall, Northamptonshire, then owned by Viscount Cullen. See Osborn, pp. 219–20. Precisely dating a visit by Dryden to either of these estates is impossible, but I should think he was in the country during the autumn of 1686. His preface says that the poem "was written during the last Winter and the beginning of this Spring; though with long interruptions of ill health, and other hindrances" (III, 121). By 12 January 1687, Dryden was far enough along for Tonson to enter a caveat forbidding anyone else to enter the poem on the Stationers' Register, and if an anecdote placing him in a coffeehouse in January may be believed, he had returned to London (see n. 90 below); his letter to Etherege of 16 February is dated from London.

88. For details, see Appendix C.

89. "I cannot help hearing, that white Sticks change their Masters," writes Dryden, alluding to the badge of office of the Lord Treasurer. On Rochester's dismissal, see Luttrell, I, 391. James actually organized "a dispute between" two Catholic clerics and two Anglican ones "for the satisfaction of the earl of Rochester"—a debate that must have resembled the one in Part II of *The Hind and the Panther*. Miner's note quoting this letter (*Works*, III, 414) contradicts his incorrect earlier assertion that Rochester and his brother Clarendon were "turned out of office . . . by New Year's of 1685/6" (III, 328).

90. Dryden's remark that "officers of yᵉ Army are not immortall in their places because the King finds they will not vote for him in the next Sessions" refers specifically to Richard Lumley, Earl of Scarborough, and Charles Talbot, Earl of Shrewsbury; another letter to Etherege from Thomas Maule, dated 25 January, explains that "the King has taken away my Lord Shrewsbury's and my Lord Lumley's regiments for reasons best known to himself, though the town will have it because of their refusal to comply with the King's desires in taking off the Test" (*Letterbook*, ed. Rosenfeld, p. 355). Ironically, Lumley was a recent convert from Catholicism to Protestantism.

Dr. Thomas James, Warden of All Souls, died on 5 January 1687, and there were rumors that Dryden would succeed him, but the appointment went to Leopold Finch, son of the Earl of Winchilsea, who was a Fellow of All Souls. According to a letter in the Bodleian (MS Eng. hist. c. 6, f. 122), dated 19 January 1686[7], "The contest lay between Mʳ Dryden and him, which yᵉ King decided in his Favor on Monday last." Another anecdote alleges that Finch insulted Dryden in a coffeehouse during the same month; see *H.M.C.*, XII, viii, 202. On 30 June 1687, a month after the publication of *The Hind and the Panther*, a newsletter to Marseilles reported a similar rumor about the presidency of Magdalen: "A mandate is said to be gone down [to] Oxford for Mr. Dryden to go out Doctor of Divinity, and also that he will be made President of Magdalen College"; see *H.M.C. Downshire*, I, i, 251. At this point, the presidency of Magdalen was the subject of a power struggle between the King, who had mandated the election of the manifestly unqualified Anthony Farmer, and the Fellows, who had defied him by electing Dr. John Hough; eventually James forced the college to accept Samuel Parker, Bishop of Oxford, who presided over the intrusions of a number of Catholic Fellows, including Dryden's son; see Turner, *James II*, pp. 335–44. Undatable rumors also held that Dryden would be sent to Ireland to become Master of Trinity College, Dublin. For a thorough sifting of the evidence, see Roswell G. Ham, "Dryden and the Colleges," *MLN* 49 (1934):324–32.

91. Two of the attacks on Dryden for his conversion—"To Mr. Bays" and the *Heroic Scene*—were circulating in manuscript before the publication of *The Hind and the Panther*. "To Mr. Bays" has traditionally been attributed to Dorset—quite wrongly, I think, in light of Dorset's continued support of Dryden. It opens by calling him a "mercenary renegade." In the *Heroic Scene*, "Johnny" says, "I felt my purse insensibly consume / Till I had openly declar'd for Rome" (ll. 104–05); for both poems, see *POAS*, IV, 79–90. Dryden deals with such attacks by letting the Panther claim that the Hind's converts are men "of no religion . . . who unfed / Have follow'd you for miracles of bread" (III, 195–97); he then has the Hind ask the Panther to "Judge not by hear-say, but observe at least, / If since their change, their loaves have been increast" (III, 223–24). Dryden's salary had not been increased, though it was being paid more promptly; in the Hind's Fable of the Pigeons, the "Plain good Man" (James II) is praised for the way he treats his servants: "their Pay was just, / And ready, for he scorn'd to go on trust" (III, 919–20). In the same fable, the Anglican Pigeons are described as greedy claimers of official places:

> But when some Lay-preferment fell by chance
> The Gourmands made it their Inheritance.
> When once possess'd, they never quit their Claim,
> For then 'tis sanctify'd to Heavn's high Name;
> And Hallow'd thus they cannot give Consent,
> The Gift should be prophan'd by Worldly management.
>
> [III, 968–73]

I believe these lines refer either to Dryden's failure to secure the mastership of All Souls, or to his rumored earlier failure to become Provost of Eton; see above, ch. 10, n. 16. In both cases, the posts continued in the hands of Anglican clergymen. Echoing this passage, Thomas Heyrick, author of *The New Atlantis* (summer 1687), has his "Bavius" curse the clergy, explaining that he had once sought such a post:

> 'Tis true I once, ('tis an unwelcome thought,
> But what their odious Race hath dearly bought,)
> Such is the fate of Poets, press'd with want,
> Did seek among their Train my Seat to plant,
> And would you think the *Gourmands* the request would grant?
>
> [p. 60]

"Bavius" goes on to complain that his clerical foes called his life into question and "Rip[ped] up [his]

Morals." Yet Heyrick need not have had firsthand information; he could easily have been drawing on Settle's passage about Eton in *Absalom Senior*.

92. For details, see Appendix C. Perhaps sensing the danger, Etherege was curious to know "how this poem is approved by the court" (*Letterbook*, ed. Rosenfeld, p. 221).

93. For a useful schematic diagram of this debate, see Harth, *Contexts*, pp. 36–37; see also his analysis of Part II, pp. 268–88. Thomas H. Fujimura has advocated a "biographical approach," arguing that "the Panther stands not only for the Anglican Church but for Dryden's former views." See "The Personal Drama of Dryden's *The Hind and the Panther*," *PMLA* 87 (1972):406–16.

94. In his note (*Works*, III, 395), Earl Miner lists the parallels with John 18.3–9 and Dryden's *Aeneis*, I, 834; the earlier scene in which Christ acknowledges his identity (Matthew 11.2–6, Mark 8.27–30, Luke 9.18–35) is not verbally so close, but fits Dryden's gloss: "Nor less amaz'd this voice the *Panther* heard, / Than were those *Jews* to hear a god declar'd" (II, 400–01). The Jewish officials in the Garden were not hearing "a god declar'd"; the Jewish disciples were.

95. In the *Reflections upon The Hind and the Panther* added to Martin Clifford's *Notes upon Mr. Dryden's Poems*, now finally printed in 1687, the anonymous author makes precisely that objection: "*She whom ye seek am I*, is not a sufficient Warrant for the Church of *Rome*'s claiming an Infallibility in all her Decrees; no more than a *Mountebank* is to be credited, who after a deal of Scaffold-Pageantry to draw Audience, entertains them by decrying all others with a Panegyrick of his own *Orvietan Balsom*" (p. 24). Anthony à Wood attributed this essay to Tom Brown, and his testimony has generally been accepted, but as Brown's biographer points out, two other tracts attributed to Brown in the same place are certainly not his; see Benjamin Boyce, *Tom Brown of Facetious Memory* (Cambridge: Harvard University Press, 1939), p. 21*n*.

96. When the Hind complains that the Panther has "learn'd this language from the blatant beast" (II, 230), the context requires that the "blatant beast" be identified as the Presbyterian Wolf, though Dryden obviously knew that Spenser had used that term for Rome. When the Hind refers to the Test Act as "your censing Test," used to "fume the room" (III, 753), the Catholic practice of using incense in the liturgy is ironically misapplied to the Anglican Establishment.

97. For a full discussion, see Saslow's essay on "Angelic 'Fire-Works'," cited above, n. 73.

98. Miner's notes to the poem in *Works* III correct numerous influential misreadings by Scott and others, and recent scholarship has begun to explain the poem more carefully and take it more seriously. See especially William Myers, "Politics in *The Hind and the Panther*," *EIC* 19 (1969):19–34, and D. W. Jefferson, "The Poetry of *The Hind and the Panther*," *MLR* 79 (1984):33–44.

CHAPTER 12. "THE LAB'RING BEE"

1. Spence, *Anecdotes*, ed. Osborn, I, 278–79.

2. These included Gilbert Burnet's *Defence of the Reflections*, Robert Gould's *The Laureat*, Martin Clifford's *Notes upon Mr. Dryden's Poems* (with the added *Reflections upon the Hind and the Panther*), and Thomas Heyrick's *The New Atlantis*. For samples of their contents, see above, ch. 9, n. 34, ch. 11, nn. 86, 91, 95. Dryden may have been out of London in the late summer and early autumn; his authorizing his wife to receive the salary due him at Michaelmas suggests as much (see Appendix C).

3. The dating of Langbaine's book remains a puzzle. Both the spurious title page (*Momus Triumphans*) and the legitimate title page bear the date 1688, and the book was entered in the Term Catalogue for December 1688, where Macdonald's *Bibliography* therefore places it. But Anthony à Wood's manuscript note in the Bodleian copy claims that the book was published in December 1687, in which case a printed date of 1688 would not be unusual, since booksellers tended to give the next year's date to books published late in the year. Moreover, the absence of any reference to the political turmoil of the Revolution seems odd indeed for a book published in the troubled month of December 1688. I have therefore tentatively followed Osborn (p. 235) in supposing that Langbaine's book appeared late in 1687. By 1691, when he published his *Account of the English Dramatick Poets*, Langbaine was certain that Dryden was responsible for the spurious title page, and attacked him at length, though without any indication of personal knowledge. An anonymous writer in *The Moderator* for June 1693 answered him and defended Dryden. See Macdonald, *Bibliography*, pp. 269–70.

4. On Prior's prologue, see Stanley Archer, "A Performance of Dryden's *Cleomenes*," *N&Q* 216 (1971):460–61. Further evidence of Prior's later attitude toward Dryden comes in a letter he wrote to

William Aglionby on 17/27 August 1697, in which he wished Dryden were "enough of our side to write a panegyric upon the King" (*H.M.C. Bath*, III, 154). There is one surviving friendly letter from Dryden to Montagu; two other letters to Mrs. Steward refer to "your Cousin Montague," though the relationship between Charles Montagu and the Pickerings was fairly remote: Mrs. Steward's grandmother Elizabeth Montagu, sister to the Earl of Sandwich and wife of Gilbert Pickering (III), was Charles Montagu's first cousin once removed. See *Letters*, pp. 120–21, 123, 129.

5. Malone's long account of the St. Cecilia Festival (pp. 254–307) is filled with valuable lore, though his assertion that Draghi came to England with Maria of Modena is incorrect. For even fuller information, see William Henry Husk, *An Account of the Musical Celebrations on St. Cecilia's Day* (Bell and Daldy, 1857). For excerpts from Draghi's setting, see Ernest Brennecke, "Dryden's Odes and Draghi's Music," *PMLA* 49 (1934):1–34.

6. See *Unsuspected Eloquence*, pp. 218–20, 224–28, and the scholarship cited there. For a suggestive account of Dryden's assimilation of his many poetic sources, see Richard Luckett, "The Fabric of Dryden's Verse," *PBA* 67 (1981):289–305.

7. I accept Earl Miner's careful argument for December 1687 as the date of this beautiful and little-known poem; see "Dryden's Ode on Mrs. Anastasia Stafford," *HLQ* 30 (1967):103–11.

8. Luttrell, I, 419.

9. See Jones, *Country and Court*, p. 242.

10. See above, ch. 11, n. 73.

11. Luttrell, I, 430; late in April, "Father Corker [was] made provincial of the Benedictines colledge at St. John's Clerkenwell"(I, 438).

12. For an excellent summary of the evidence, see Alan Roper's headnote, *Works*, XIX, 449–90.

13. See Jones, *Country and Court*, p. 239.

14. Luttrell, I, 448; the celebrations for the birth of the prince on 10 June are similarly described: "the cannon at the Tower were discharged, and at night bonefires and ringing of the bells were in several places"(I, 442).

15. *Diary*, IV, 588.

16. Evelyn, *Diary*, IV, 599; Luttrell, I, 468.

17. Stanley Archer discovered this fascinating fact; see "A Dryden Record," *N&Q* 211 (1966):264–65. An unfortunate misprint in Archer's article identifies the colonel of the regiment as "Lord Strafford," but the source, *English Army Lists and Commission Registers, 1661–1714*, ed. Charles Dalton (1960), II, 199, correctly identifies him as H[enr]y, Earl of Stafford, who succeeded to his martyred father's titles in June of 1685 and was created Earl of Stafford on 5 October 1688, shortly before he took command of the regiment. One Edward Ravenscroft, possibly the dramatist, was a first lieutenant, as was another Stafford whose first name is not given, presumably one of Henry's young brothers, John or Francis. John Stafford had contributed translations of Virgil to *Miscellany Poems* (1684) and *Sylvae* (1685); see Margaret Boddy, "The Manuscripts and Printed Editions of the Translation of Virgil made by Richard Maitland, Fourth Earl of Lauderdale, and the Connexion with Dryden," *N&Q* 211 (1965), p. 149.

18. Luttrell, I, 474.

19. As Boyce points out in *Tom Brown of Facetious Memory*, p. 19*n.*, Brown's allusion to the memory of John Bunyan in his preface insures that the first pamphlet is later than 31 August; the second pamphlet, apparently written immediately, was licensed in December 1688, but Brown waited until 1690 to publish it, adding a few references to *Don Sebastian* to the material on *The Hind and the Panther* and the translation of Bouhours that he had already written.

20. When reprinted in 1707, this poem was attributed to Rymer, but Dryden does not seem to have blamed Rymer for it; in the preface to *Don Sebastian* (1690), he was still referring to "the Learned Mr. Rymer" (XV, 68–69).

21. Later attributed to Shadwell, this poem connects Dryden's son John with Obadiah Walker, a timely insult in a month when Walker was imprisoned; see Luttrell, I, 493.

22. This canceled passage survives only in the Bodleian copy; see Fredson Bowers, "Dryden as Laureate: The Cancel Leaf in 'King Arthur'," *TLS* (10 April 1953), p. 244.

23. See Bossy, *The English Catholic Community*, pp. 110–21.

24. Joseph Haines the actor, who had become a Roman Catholic, spoke a special "Recantation-Prologue" before playing Bayes at a revival of *The Rehearsal* in April of 1689. On 5 May 1689, Luttrell

reported that "Mr. Slater, late minister of Putney, made his publick recantation at the Savoy church of his being a papist, and is since turned protestant" (I, 530).

25. For some stories about Dorset's charity to Dryden, see Stanley Archer, "Two Dryden Anecdotes," *N&Q* 218 (1973):177–78. In 1709, Prior claimed that Dorset had replaced Dryden's lost salary with "an Equivalent out of his own Estate," but as Ward points out (p. 362), there is no other evidence supporting that claim. Dryden was frequently in financial difficulty during the last decade of his life; his own passage thanking Dorset for "laying aside all the Considerations of Factions and Parties, to do an Action of pure disinteress'd Charity" speaks of only one "Present," made "since this Revolution." While the dating is vague, I should think that the gift came at the time of Dryden's removal from office.

26. Luttrell, I, 490.

27. *H.M.C.*, *House of Lords*, XII, App., vi, p. 8.

28. Ward, who recognized that the "Dayton" of the St. Anne's census was probably Dryden, says that Dryden moved to Gerrard Street "early in 1688" (p. 235). He also claims that the new house was "no doubt a considerable improvement over the place in Longacre." The evidence casts doubt upon both statements. Dryden paid his rates on the house in Longacre until Easter of 1687, the last hard evidence of his presence there, but two casual references to Longacre in Brown's *Reasons of Mr. Bays Changing his Religion*, published late in 1688 (pp. 10, 12), suggest that Brown at least thought he was still there a few months before the Revolution. In his "Fable of the Bat and the Birds," which concerns Dryden's loss of his government posts, and which was finally published early in 1690, as part of *The Late Converts Exposed*, Brown again places Dryden in Longacre (p. 59); the setting for that fable is the period of the Revolution. Osborn points out that the rate books of St. Anne, Soho, are missing from 1687 to 1690, so that Dryden's arrival there is difficult to date, but guesses that he moved there about the time of the Revolution (p. 212). Ward's claim that the Gerrard Street house was an improvement is doubtful, since the rates Dryden paid in Longacre were higher, usually 18s. as opposed to 11s. in Gerrard Street, with the possibility that the 11s. was the double rate chargeable to Catholics. For an excellent map showing the expansion of London during these years, see Evelyn, *Diary*, V, opposite p. 62.

29. In the third of Tom Brown's attacks, *The Reasons of Mr. Joseph Hains the Player's Conversion & Reconversion* (1690), Haines tells "Bays" a story about a sexual encounter with a bookseller's wife in Rome: "I stept into the Shop, sending my company away before me, amongst whom was a certain young Gentleman that I suppose you may know, for he has written a very pretty Latin Copy of Verses upon *Arlington* Gardens" (p. 21). Charles Dryden's Latin verses on Lord Arlington's gardens had appeared in *Sylvae* (1685). Although Brown's pamphlet mentions Cardinal Howard several times, he never mentions the cardinal's relation to Dryden's wife.

Brown links Haines with "a certain *English* Peer, who is now in durance" (p. 18). This man was undoubtedly James Cecil, fourth Earl of Salisbury, who was received into the Roman Catholic Church by Cardinal Howard in Rome during 1687; see Godfrey Anstruther, "English Dominicans in Rome," *AFP* 29 (1959), p. 195. Salisbury was imprisoned for treason several times after the Revolution; he was the dedicatee of Dryden's last play, *Love Triumphant*. Haines returned from Rome no later than 1688. Brown's pamphlet refers to Lee's *Massacre of Paris*, acted in the spring of 1689, and to the raising of regiments for Ireland, but does not mention *The Prophetess* or the Battle of the Boyne; I should therefore suppose it was completed by April 1689 and appeared not long after *The Late Converts Exposed*, which was available in January 1690. Although it proved prophetic, I should think that Brown's placing Charles in Rome in 1687 was a fantasy; for evidence that Brown knew that two of Dryden's sons were at home, see n. 44 below.

Ward pictures Erasmus-Henry as "preparing for a religious life and soon to go to Rome," but since the record of his entry into the English College mentions his having studied philosophy at Douai, and since there is no record placing him in England after he left the Charterhouse in 1685, I should imagine he was in France by 1687 at the latest. In a letter to Walsh that Ward places early in 1691, Dryden says that he is "encumberd with some necessary business, relating to one of my Sonns" (*Letters*, p. 33), but there is no evidence to suggest which son or what business. Erasmus-Henry left the English College at Rome on [18 February]/1 March 1691 to enter the Dominican monastery at Florence (*PCRS* 40, p. 111). The records of that convent, the *Liber Consiliorum Coenobii Fesulari 1595–1728* (Laurentian library S. Marco 874) show that he was sent there by his kinsman Cardinal Howard. He passed the Council for clothing on [13]/23 March 1691, impressing the examiners with his skill in Latin and philosophy; he passed the Council for profession on [16]/26 February 1692, and took his "minors" on [8]/18 September 1692. For transcriptions of these documents, I am indebted to Father Godfrey Anstruther, who forwarded his notes on Erasmus-Henry to Mrs. Marjory Clifford, who in turn shared them with me.

John Dryden, Jr., witnessed his father's signature on a receipt from Tonson on 6 October 1691, a fact that places him in London at least that late. Charles's "Song to a Lady who discovered a new star in Cassiopeia," for which he wrote both words and music, appeared in *The Gentleman's Journal* for February 1692; Charles may have still been in London at that time, though his father, who gave Motteux a song of his own at the same time, might easily have submitted his son's work. Both sons were contributors to the translation of Juvenal and Persius that appeared in October of 1692; in a note appended to the translation of the second satire of Persius, Dryden says "the first half of this Satyr was translated by one of my Sons, now in *Italy*" (IV, 291). Given the difficulties of winter travel, I should think that Charles and John went to Rome in the spring of 1692. Ward, who missed the reference in the Persius translation, places their departure a year later (pp. 262–63).

30. Hindmarsh was fined for publishing seditious pamphlets in April of 1691; see Luttrell, II, 214. Macdonald guesses that Tonson's failure to publish the play "may conceivably have been due to the political situation" (*Bibliography*, p. 120n). Kathleen Lynch supposes that he was outbid; see *Jacob Tonson: Kit-Cat Publisher* (Knoxville: University of Tennessee Press, 1971), p. 26. There is no hard evidence.

31. Luttrell, I, 533. Brown's dialogue between Haines and Bays alludes to the groundlessness of Dryden's fears: Haines tells a story about finding it impossible to persuade the constable to search his house, despite his many proofs that he was a papist; Bays replies that "the Rabble wou'd not do me that Christian favour as to break my Windows" (p. 30).

32. The attacks in 1689 include an anonymous poem called *The Deliverance* (February), the dedication to Shadwell's *Bury-Fair* (June), the prologue to James Carlile's *The Fortune-Hunters* (acted in March, published in June), and another anonymous poem called *The Murmurers* (July), unique among attacks on Dryden in referring to his wife's Catholicism. See the passage on "Balaam" and his "Midianitish wives" [sic] (p. 14). Dryden's prologue to *Don Sebastian* refutes the essential argument of most of these attacks by pointing out that "there's no Pretension, / To argue loss of Wit from loss of Pension" (ll. 3–4). Discussing his sources in the preface, he points out that "the Ancients . . . were never accus'd of being Plagiaries, for building their Tragedies on known Fables" (XV, 69), an equally general refutation of the shrill charges of Langbaine, who recognized these remarks as aimed at him, and attempted to answer them in his *Account of the English Dramatick Poets*, p. 162.

33. Luttrell, I, 517, 531–32.

34. See *The London Stage*, I, 371.

35. For two recurrences of this image, see Dryden's epilogue to *Henry the Second*, l. 27, and his prologue to his own *Love Triumphant*, ll. 23–26.

36. Luttrell, I, 570.

37. In the preface to *Don Sebastian*, published two months later, Dryden says that he "see[s] very little probability of coming out" of his "bad circumstances" (XV, 65). In their annotations of the prologue and epilogue to Behn's play (III, 504–07), the California editors unaccountably fail to discuss the political implications of the lines I have cited.

38. For a number of parallels with these earlier plays, see D. W. Jefferson, "'All, all of a piece throughout': Thoughts on Dryden's Dramatic Poetry," in *Restoration Theatre*, ed. John Russell Brown and Bernard Harris (New York: St. Martin's, 1965), pp. 159–76. For a learned study of Dryden's debt to epic and romance, see Derek Hughes, "Dryden's *Don Sebastian* and the Literature of Heroism,"*YES* 12 (1982):72–90.

39. In his headnote to the play, published in 1976, Earl Miner instructs readers to "resist" comparisons between the world of the play and the world of England in 1689; see especially XV, 404. But John Robert Moore, in "Political Allusions in Dryden's Later Plays," *PMLA* 73 (1958):36–42, an article ignored by Miner, had already argued persuasively for the political application of much of the play. Moore's article, which I follow in part, is a pioneering account of the play's political meaning, though I do not entirely agree that Benducar is to be identified as Sunderland, who was in Holland when the play opened. In April of 1691, Sunderland returned, kissed William's hand, and declared himself a Protestant (Luttrell, II, 216); he played an important part in the government after 1693. Benducar is a composite portrait of the sleazy courtier, drawn from many men of Dryden's acquaintance, perhaps most recently Sunderland. In an article published since I wrote my own account, David Bywaters has given an even more particular account

than Moore's; see "Dryden and the Revolution of 1688: Political Parallel in *Don Sebastian*," *JEGP* 85 (1986):346–65. Bywaters argues that the Mufti represents Dryden's old antagonist Gilbert Burnet.

40. Brown quotes these lines in *The Late Converts Exposed* and comments as follows: "Whether you had an eye upon your own Church-men, when you wrote these lines, does not signify a farthing, but for your comfort, Mr. *Bays*, the Character suits them as exactly, as if they had sate for their Pictures" (sig. A3r). A reference to "the Five Bishops . . . not swearing to the present Government" (p. 38) suggests that Brown was aware of another possible application. For references to the difficulties Sancroft incurred by refusing to take the oaths, see Evelyn, *Diary*, 614, 620, 626, 631, 637, etc.

41. *Diary*, V, 86.

42. As Miner points out, the actual Don Sebastian "is thought to have been homosexual" (*Works*, XV, 388). In his "Life of Lucian" (published 1711; written c. 1696), Dryden notes that Lucian was "more accus'd for his Love of Boys than of Women," and goes on to speak of homosexuality as a "detestable Passion" and an "abominable Subject, which strikes me with Horrour when I name it" (pp. 29–30). Such opinions were common enough among Dryden's contemporaries, but I suspect he went out of his way to express disgust for homosexuality in the 1690s because of his opposition to the King.

43. Roger Morrice, in his *Entring Book*, quoted in *Works*, XV, 382n.

44. In the absence of a written reply from Dryden, Brown attempted to concoct a spoken one: "I hear you threatned to send one of your Sons to give me a little bodily chastisement, if it were not below 'em. Truly, Sir, I am heartily sorry for their sakes, that I am no Livery-man as yet, or one of the City Common-Council; next Spring it may be you'll find me advanced to that Honourable preferment, for I have above forty of the best hands in the Parish in order to it already. But why, Mr. *Bays*, do you talk only of one Son, send them both a Gods name, and rather than fail, appear at the head of them your self" (sig. A2v). Though Brown was no politician (see Boyce, p. 29), his claim that he will soon be elected to the "City Common-Council" sounds like a threat. The whole passage suggests his frustration at failing to engage Dryden in a pamphlet war.

45. The cancelled entry for *Amphitryon* on the Lord Chamberlain's list is a puzzle. Ward argues that "all the evidence points to an early acting, in the spring, on the public stage" (p. 246), but there is actually no evidence of a performance before 21 October. Milhous and Hume point out that virtually every play published during the 1690s appeared in print within about a month of its premiere, probably because there was now little legal protection from piracies; they therefore accept, with Macdonald and the California editors, the likelihood of an October premiere ("Dating," pp. 395–96). That leaves the problem of the April cancellation. Had the decision not to perform Dryden's play been political in motivation, someone (Tom Brown, surely) would have crowed about it in print; the absence of any such comment leads me to believe the players were simply too busy with the new opera to rehearse the comedy properly. If Dryden's characterization of himself as a bee without a sting in the prologue to *Amphitryon* was prompted by the banning of his prologue to *The Prophetess*, that would be further evidence for an autumn premiere.

46. The preface, printed in *Works*, XVII, 324–26, has long been regarded as a piece of ghostwriting by Dryden, since it exists in his handwriting (B.L. MS Stowe 755, fols. 34–35v). Curtis Price raises the interesting possibility of a collaboration; see *Henry Purcell and the London Stage*, pp. 264–65. This was probably the second time Dryden had helped a composer draft a preface. Grabu's preface to the folio score of *Albion and Albanius* begins with Dryden's favorite image of the shipwreck, and is in an English style well beyond what Grabu could have written on his own. The California editors raise the possibility that Dryden gave Grabu "some English assistance" (XV, 324); I should think he wrote the whole preface.

47. *Diary*, V, 4, 22.

48. This story first appeared in print in John Oldmixon's *Muses Mercury* in 1707, when both Dryden and Shadwell were dead; it gains plausibility because the prologue is missing from most printed copies of the play. According to Oldmixon, Shadwell was determined to "put a stop to" the prologue "Because while Mr. Dryden was Poet Laureat, he wou'd never let any Play of his be Acted." The California editors consider the story "incorrect as a whole" on the grounds that Shadwell's plays were acted while Dryden was Laureat (III, 508), but it is true that no new play by Shadwell appeared between 1681 and 1688, and that he blamed his lack of success in those years on Dryden (see above, ch. 11, p. 382 and n. 5).

49. Dryden's dedication to Levenson-Gower includes a "warm Remembrance of your noble Hospitality to me at *Trentham*, when some years ago I visited my Friends and Relations in your Country" (XV, 224). Two possible occasions are his known visit to Sir Charles Wolseley in Staffordshire in the summer of

1680 (see Osborn, pp. 216–17, 220), and the wedding of Anastasia Stafford in 1687, which he might well have attended.

50. On Walsh's flirtation with Jane Levenson-Gower, see Phyllis Freeman, "William Walsh and Dryden: Recently Recovered Letters," *RES* 24 (1948):195–202, especially pp. 196–98. Jane married Henry Hyde on 2 March 1692.

51. *An Epistle to . . . Charles Earl of Dorset* (1690), p. 3. Following Malone, the California editors guess that Dryden's phrase about "a great Wit" refers to Brown, but the close verbal resemblance between these lines and Dryden's answer makes it obvious that he was replying to Montagu.

52. For a fine analysis, on which I depend, see James D. Garrison, "Dryden and the Birth of Hercules," *SP* 77 (1980):180–201. Like Milhous and Hume, who have written usefully on this comedy in *Producible Interpretations*, pp. 201–27, I am not entirely convinced by Garrison's attempt to describe the love triangle as an allegory, "an allusion to the political struggle between William (false Amphitryon) and James (true Amphitryon), vying to occupy the bed of England (Alcmena)" (p. 194; cf. Milhous and Hume, p. 220). But Garrison's essay is of great importance to me, not only in my reading of this play, but in my reading of Dryden's development in the 1690s in general.

53. On the imprisonment of Pepys, Clarendon, and Stafford in June 1690, see Luttrell, II, 63. I take it that "Mr. Stafford (son to the late Lord Stafford)" is not Henry, whom James had made Earl of Stafford, and who was colonel of the short-lived regiment in which John Dryden, Jr. held a commission; Luttrell would presumably have called him the Earl of Stafford, not "Mr. Stafford." There were two younger brothers, John and Francis; see above, n. 17.

54. On the naval debacle, see Luttrell, II, 67–68, 73, and Evelyn, *Diary*, V, 27–29, where the commanders of the fleet are described as "debauched young men." On the French failure to capitalize, see Jones, *Country and Court*, pp. 263–65.

55. On the alleged conspiracy of January 1691, see Luttrell, II, 152–53; Evelyn, *Diary*, V, 41. As ambassador to France, Richard Grahame had been involved in the operatic schemes that led to *Albion and Albanius*; see above, ch. 11, p. 393 and n. 30. He was told to prepare for death in April of 1691, but was pardoned in May (Luttrell, II, 212, 214, 237). His wife was Lady Anne Howard, daughter of the Earl of Carlisle and cousin to Dryden's wife. Colonel James Grahame escaped to France after his brother's arrest and was pardoned in February of 1692 (Luttrell, II, 162, 356). He was in trouble again a few months later (II, 434, 448). His wife was Dorothy, daughter of William Howard, fourth Earl of Berkshire, Elizabeth Dryden's brother.

56. On the deprivation of the nonjurors, see Evelyn, *Diary*, V, 48–49. Anthony à Wood thought that *The Tribe of Levi*, a satirical poem attacking the clergy, was Dryden's work; an anonymous reply, *Rabshakeh Vapulans*, contains a passage against Dryden. Tom Brown's attack on Bishop William Sherlock, *The Reasons of the New Convert's Taking the Oaths*, also glances at Dryden. All were published in 1691. On L'Estrange's imprisonment, see Luttrell, II, 217, 234.

57. See *Works*, IV, 513. Some evidence supporting the idea that the translation had been long planned comes in Dryden's headnote to the sixth satire of Juvenal, against women, which says that "Sir C[harles] S[edley] . . . , after a long delay, at length absolutely refus'd so ungrateful an employment" (IV, 145–46). Even more certain evidence comes in the preface to *The Tenth Satyr of Juvenal Done into English Verse* (1693) by J[ohn] H[arvey]; see Harold F. Brooks, "Dryden's Juvenal and the Harveys," *PQ* 48 (1969), pp. 12–13.

58. The most serious attempt to sort out the possible political meanings of *King Arthur* is that of Curtis Price; see *Henry Purcell and the London Stage*, ch. 7. I follow Price in believing that two readings were possible; I am not convinced that Merlin represents Halifax (see especially pp. 294–95).

59. See, for example, the anonymous poem "To Mr. Bays," which calls Dryden a "mercenary rene-gade" (l. 1) and a "Rebel to God" (l. 71). The anonymous "Heroic Scene" even uses the Spanish spelling adopted here, "renegado" (l. 71). See *POAS*, IV, 79, 83. For a typical reference to Dryden as an "apostate," see the passage from Tom Brown quoted above, p. 442.

60. See the passage from Cibber quoted in *The London Stage*, I, 397, and Downes, *Roscius Anglicanus*, pp. 42–43.

61. Since Southerne acknowledged writing half of the last act of *Cleomenes* in his dedication to *The Wives Excuse*, which was published before *Cleomenes* was acted and included a commendatory poem by Dryden, there can be little doubt that he did so. Malone prints Dryden's receipt, which he found in Tonson's papers (p. 455n).

62. See Luttrell, II, 313, 315.

63. See Oliver, *Howard*, p. 279, and Osborn, pp. 212–13.

64. *H.M.C.*, IV, Appendix, pp. 280–81.

65. The letter from Cardinal Howard to Lord Medford at St. Germain cited above, ch. 5, n. 9, dated [20]/30 June 1693, refers to "two Brothers Catholique gentleman [*sic*] caled M[r]. Charles and John Draytons (sonnes to the famous Poet Laureat Drayton in London) one wheareof I hav[e]. in the interim, gotta place of Cameriero d'Honore with our ould man [the Pope!], and th'other liveth with me." In 1697, Elizabeth Dryden addressed a letter to her sons "Al Illustrissimo Sig[re] Carlo Dryden, Camariere d'Honore A S.S.," i.e., Servus Servorum, or the Pope; see *Letters*, p. 96. We may thus infer that Charles had the place in the Papal guards, while John, Jr. lived with Cardinal Howard.

66. Luttrell, II, 413.

67. Luttrell, II, 422; for the appointments of Rochester and Falkland to the Privy Council, see II, 372, 387.

68. Since he had praised Betterton for his care and skill in cutting *Don Sebastian*, Dryden's phrase about "the Superiours of the Play-house" probably indicates Thomas Davenant, the much-disliked patentee.

69. W. D. Christie, in the "Memoir" of Dryden prefixed to the Globe edition of the poems (1870), gives this figure (p. lxvi). Infuriatingly, he gives no source; the kindest possible assumption is that some descendant of Abingdon had mentioned this figure to him. Abingdon had plenty of money; he contributed £30,000 to the war chest for William's invasion in 1688. Still, 500 guineas would have been a handsome present indeed, and Dryden's continuing references to his poverty make it very unlikely that he received such a sum.

70. We know that Dryden chose his colleagues on this project because of a letter from George Stepney to Leibnitz, dated 8/18 March 1693, printed in *State Papers . . . From the Revolution to the Accession of the House of Hanover*, ed. John M. Kemble (Parker and Son, 1857), pp. 120–22. He probably also revised their work; see *Works* IV, 513–14. Congreve's commendatory poem is printed in the Appendix to *Works* IV. No one seems to have noticed that Dryden got the title and the idea of his famous "Discourse" from Oldham. The "Advertisement" to Oldham's *Satyrs upon the Jesuits* (1682) rejects the idea of writing such an introduction: "The Author might here (according to the laudible custom of Prefaces) entertain the Reader with a Discourse of the Original, Progress, and Rules of *Satyr*, and let him understand, that he has lately Read *Casaubon*, and several other Criticks upon the Point; but at present he is minded to wave it, as a vanity he is in no wise fond of" (sig. A2r). Dryden's translation of the third satire of Juvenal is indebted to an earlier version by Oldham; see K. Robinson, "Juvenal, Oldham, and Dryden," *N&Q* 224 (1979):518–20.

71. In a private communication, Steven Zwicker has pointed out to me that Dryden's virtually verbatim quotation of a passage from Tacitus on Roman censorship in the "Discourse" may reflect his efforts on the Tacitus project. Zwicker also believes that this project "may have been a Jacobite enterprise." Dryden, John Dennis, and Sir Roger L'Estrange are among those translators whose full names are given. "Mr. J. S.," another contributor, may well be John Stafford, son of the martyred Viscount. The *Gentleman's Journal* reported that "three Persons of Quality" were translating Tacitus in July 1693; the book finally appeared in 1698.

72. In a letter to Tonson of 3 October 1692, quoted by Tonson in a subsequent letter, Dryden called his translation "one of the best I have ever made" (*Letters*, p. 50); in the dedication to *Examen Poeticum*, he called his "Translations of *Ovid* . . . the best of all my Endeavours in this kind" (IV, 369).

73. See Donald R. Benson, "Platonism and Neoclassic Metaphor: Dryden's *Eleonora* and Donne's *Anniversaries*," *SP* 68 (1971):340–56.

74. Consider these parallels:

> This is th'imperfect draught; but short as far
> As the true height and bigness of a Star
> Exceeds the Measures of th' Astronomer.
>
> [*Eleonora*, ll. 263–65]

> Come, learned *Ptolomy*, and trial make,
> If thou this Hero's Altitude canst take;

> But that transcends thy skill; thrice happie all,
> Could we but prove thus Astronomical.
>
> ["Hastings," ll. 38–41]

> But 'twas her Saviour's time; and, cou'd there be
> A Copy near th' Original, 'twas she.
>
> [*Eleonora*, ll. 299–300]

> Transcribe th' Original in new Copies . . .
>
> ["Hastings," l. 101]

> The Figure was with full Perfection crown'd;
> Though not so large an Orb, as truly round.
>
> [*Eleonora*, ll. 272–73]

> For in a round what order can be shew'd,
> Where all the parts so *equall perfect* are?
>
> ["Heroique Stanza's," ll. 19–20].

75. These facts about Abingdon's career follow the account in *The Complete Peerage*.

76. In December of 1691, Busby was "given over," and there was discussion of his successor (Luttrell, II, 324), but he recovered and lived until 1695.

77. *Diary*, V, 101, 111, 148.

78. On 19 January 1693, "Mrs. Ann Merryweather was condemned to be burnt for printing king James declaration and other treasonable pamphlets last summer" (Luttrell, III, 16); she was pardoned on 23 February (III, 42). Another printer named Anderson was not so fortunate; he was hanged on 16 June 1693 (III, 118).

79. For Shadwell's complaint, see above, ch. 11, n. 10. For evidence that Dryden acknowledged writing *Mac Flecknoe* in conversation with others, see above, ch. 11, n. 84. For Shadwell's death, see Luttrell, II, 621. The translation of Juvenal and Persius was advertised as published in the *London Gazette* for 24–27 October, but since Tonson sometimes failed to publish books when he advertised them, it is just possible that the acknowledgment of *Mac Flecknoe* was a last-minute alteration after Shadwell's death.

80. Luttrell, II, 623.

81. In his letter to Tonson of 3 October 1692, written before Shadwell's death, Dryden says that his translation of Book I of the *Metamorphoses*, "coming out before the whole translation will spoyl Tate's undertakings" (*Letters*, p. 50). One volume of the group translation organized by Tate appeared in 1697. Dryden's willingness to "spoyl [his] undertakings" does not suggest deep respect or strong friendship for Tate.

82. B.L. Add. Ms. 4221 (341), printed in Macdonald, *Bibliography*, p. 54n.

83. Malone prints this poem, p. 228n.

84. The first extant letter from Dennis to Dryden is dated "Jan. 1693–4" (*Letters*, pp. 65–67); Gildon's letter is printed out of chronological order in Ward's edition (pp. 138–39); Addison's poem appears in *Examen Poeticum*, pp. 247–49); for Dennis's remarks about Dryden drinking with Addison, see Spence, *Anecdotes*, ed. Osborn, I, 319.

85. Another possibility is that Dryden is thanking Tonson for giving him an unusually good price for *Love Triumphant*, which was probably finished during this stay in the country. Dryden's dedication for that play, presumably written after he completed it, must antedate the death of the dedicatee, James Cecil, fourth Earl of Salisbury, on 25 October 1693.

86. The elusive date of publication of *Examen Poeticum* depends in part on the dates of those disasters. In a letter to Walsh written during the summer of 1693, Dryden says that "Tonson has . . . fayld me in the publishing his Miscellanyes" (*Letters*, p. 56). The book had been advertised as published in the *Gentleman's Journal* in both June and July, but was evidently still in the final stages of preparation. In the same letter, Dryden reports the loss of the merchant fleet and the taking of the town of Huy, both of which took place in mid-July. He also reports that "our Fleet yesterday was in Torbay." In his edition of the letters (p. 165),

Ward dates the letter 17 August on the grounds that the fleet arrived in Torbay on 16 August, but in the notes to his biography (p. 365), he accepts the redating to 20 July proposed by H. H. Adams in "A Note on the Date of a Dryden Letter," *MLN* 44 (1949):528–31. Dryden was reporting rumor, and ships of various kinds were straggling into port throughout late July. A slightly earlier date would also account for Dryden's informing Tonson on 30 August of a rumor that had reached him "About a fortnight ago . . . by letter" (p. 58). Since Tonson had traveled to Northamptonshire with Dryden sometime *after* the letter to Walsh, Dryden had a long coach journey during which he could have passed along that news.

87. See Luttrell, II, 637, 638; III, 27, 29–30. Dryden's friend and patron Rochester was one of the few lords who voted to convict.

88. Ward (pp. 264, 365) argues that "Ovid" is a slip for "Virgil," but as William Frost points out (*Works*, IV, 759), the first book of the *Ars Amatoria* has 772 lines, the number Dryden says he is translating.

89. On the dating of the translation of Lucian, see above, ch. 10, n. 95.

90. On this point especially, my reading of the Kneller poem owes much to Cedric D. Reverand II, "Dryden on Dryden in 'To Sir Godfrey Kneller'," *PLL* 17 (1981):164–80.

CHAPTER 13. "'TIS WELL AN OLD AGE IS OUT"

1. *Diary*, V, 164.

2. An anonymous letter of 22 March 1693/4, quoted in *The London Stage*, I, 433–34. First printed by Malone in his edition of Shakespeare (1821), this manuscript has apparently disappeared.

3. See, for example, his letter to Walsh of 9 or 10 May 1693, in which he gives a detailed report of a new farce by Durfey (*Letters*, p. 53).

4. A few years later, in the *Dedication of the Aeneis*, Dryden again links critics and lampooners: "We are naturally displeas'd with an unknown Critick, as the Ladies are with a Lampooner, because we are bitten in the dark, and know not where to fasten our Revenge." As noted above (ch. 1, n. 1), my citations of the *Virgil* and the *Fables* follow James Kinsley's edition of *The Poems of John Dryden*, which I shall cite as *Poems*; this passage appears at III, 1008–09.

5. From the letter cited above, n. 2. Note the similarity to Tom Brown's charge that Dryden had maliciously encouraged Creech to translate poets for whom his talents were ill-suited.

6. See Anstruther, "English Dominicans in Rome," p. 195; Luttrell I, 493; II, 123, 444, 629.

7. Scott and other scholars have supposed that Dryden was alluding to the fact that Salisbury's great-grandfather, the second Earl, had married Katherine Howard, who was Elizabeth Dryden's aunt. Dryden was doubtless aware of that link, but his reference to "your Noble House" surely indicates the Cecil family, of whom Elizabeth's mother was one.

8. See Anstruther, "English Dominicans in Rome," p. 187.

9. *The Loyal and Impartial Satyrist* (November 1693), quoted in Macdonald, *Bibliography*, p. 276.

10. The contract survives as B.L. Add. MS. 36,933 and Add. Charter 8,429. It is described by H. B. Wheatley in "Dryden's Publishers," *Transactions of the Bibliographical Society* 11 (1909–11), pp. 36–38, and will be printed in full as an appendix in the California volumes devoted to the *Virgil*.

11. The tangled history of Dryden's financial dealings with Tonson, somewhat misconstrued by Ward, has been laid out with admirable care and clarity by John Barnard in "Dryden, Tonson, and Subscriptions for the 1697 *Virgil*," *PBSA* 57 (1963):129–51. I have some minor corrections to offer, which will appear in due course, but in general I follow Barnard's scrupulous work. I am also grateful to Alan Roper for letting me see an advance draft of the headnote to the forthcoming California edition of the *Virgil*, which contains much useful information.

12. See Jones, *Country and Court*, pp. 270–71.

13. In his letter to Tonson of 8 June [1695], Dryden says it is "high time for me to think of my second Subscriptions"; since the soliciting of those names could not begin until Book VI of the *Aeneid* was done, we may infer that Dryden had reached that point. Barnard and the California editors follow Ward in estimating that the *Georgics* and *Eclogues* were finished by October 1694, and *Aeneid* I–IV by April 1695. This dating is ultimately dependent on Malone's guess that the letter from Dryden to Tonson announcing completion of *Aeneid* IV falls in April of 1695. Dryden's two months of work on the translation of Du Fresnoy must also fit somewhere into this timetable: that book was licensed on 27 October 1694, entered on the Stationers'

Register on 10 April 1695 and advertised as published late in June. The California editors guess that he had finished Du Fresnoy by the time the publisher, William Rogers, entered it on the Stationers' Register, but that guess depends on the uncertain April date for the letter about finishing *Aeneid* IV. Whatever the ordering of Dryden's tasks was, he did a prodigious amount of work between June of 1694 and June of 1695.

14. See Malone, p. 233; Arthur Clifford, *Collectanea Cliffordiana* (Paris, 1817), p. 91; and Dryden's "Postscript to the Reader," *Poems*, III, 1425–26.

15. William Frost believes that Dryden even consulted the translation of Gavin Douglas, in Middle Scots; see "Dryden and the Classics: With a look at His 'Aeneis'," in *Writers and their Background: John Dryden*, ed. Earl Miner (Bell & Sons, 1972), pp. 267–96. Lauderdale's translation was published in 1709, and its relation to Dryden's work has been much studied. In "Dryden-Lauderdale Relationships, Some Bibliographical Notes and a Suggestion," *PQ* 42 (1963):267–72, Margaret Boddy muddied the waters considerably by attempting to redate most of Dryden's correspondence with Tonson during this period in support of a complicated theory about Lauderdale's influence on Dryden. Most of her assertions are refuted by John Barnard in "The Dates of Six Dryden Letters," *PQ* 42 (1963):396–403. The most thorough study of Dryden's indebtedness to Lauderdale is Arthur Sherbo, "Dryden and the Fourth Earl of Lauderdale," *SB* 39 (1986):199–210.

16. *The Mourning Poets* (1695), p. 4. In a letter to Tonson of 14/24 February 1694, Stepney hoped that Dryden would correct and improve his poem; see Macdonald, *Bibliography*, p. 281.

17. *Urania's Temple: or, A Satyr upon the Silent Poets* (1695), p. 6; *An Ode Occasion'd by the Death of the Queen, with a Letter from the Author to Mr. Dryden* (1695), sig. A2r.

18. At one point, Dryden thanks "Mr. *Walter Moyle*, a most ingenious young Gentleman, [for] furnish[ing] me (according to my request) with all the particular passages in *Aristotle* and *Horace*, which are us'd by them to explain the *Art of Poetry* by that of *Painting*: which if ever I have time to retouch this *Essay*, shall be inserted in their places" (pp. xxxiii–iv). We may infer that Dryden, working in haste, asked his friend Moyle to undertake this bit of research, but that the results arrived too late for him to make use of them.

19. For a detailed account, see Judith Milhous, *Thomas Betterton and the Management of Lincoln's Inn Fields*, chs. 3–4.

20. Luttrell, III, 291, 294, 298. Dryden may also have been thinking of the taking of the entire Smyrna fleet by the French in June of 1692; see above, ch. 12, p. 459 and n. 77.

21. See Dryden's "Postscript to the Reader," *Poems*, III, 1426.

22. The proposals survive in the Cambridge University Library, Add. MS. 4429 (10); Ward prints them in *Letters*, p. 172. Contemporary newspapers furnish no evidence that Tonson ever printed these proposals; in a letter that must be at least as late as November 1695, Dryden was still asking "to see how Mr Congreve & you have worded my propositions for Virgil" (*Letters*, p. 79). His next letter points out that "you might have spard almost all your trouble, if you had thought fit to publish the proposalls for the first Subscriptions: for I have guineas offerd me every day" (pp. 80–81). The "trouble" to which Dryden alludes must be Tonson's effort to solicit five-guinea subscribers, but that list was already so full by October 1695 that Dryden had to ask Tonson to make room for some important aristocrats who would otherwise be omitted by persuading "some of your friends . . . to take back their three guineas" (p. 78). The size of the five-guinea subscription was limited by the fact that there were only 102 engravings, one of which (the title page) had no sponsor. The size of the two-guinea subscription, however, was theoretically open. If Tonson had really failed to publish the proposals for that second subscription, Dryden would surely have complained; perhaps they were printed as a one-page flyer, with the result that no copy has survived.

23. *PCRS*, vol. 25, p. 90.

24. In a letter to her sons written on 3 September [1697], Elizabeth urged them to return to England on the grounds that "you doe but just make shift to Live wheare you are" (*Letters*, p. 95).

25. See Oliver, *Howard*, pp. 274–82; 297–301.

26. A manuscript cast for the operatic *Indian Queen* makes a date after the secession of Betterton's troupe in April 1695 necessary; the publication of the music in late autumn of 1695 provides a *terminus ad quem*; see *The London Stage*, I, 433. In previous years, fancy operas had often been produced in May or June, but the confusion caused by the secession makes it very unlikely that Rich's company could have mounted the opera in the spring. George Powell's preface to *The Fatal Discovery* (1698) says that Dryden never came to Drury Lane "since the division of the Companies."

Milhous and Hume acknowledge the difficulty of dating the premiere of young John's play; if the usual publication lapse of only a month or so is applied, the play might have been acted as late as June of 1696, as they suggest ("Dating," pp. 399–400). As I suggest below, such a delay might have been caused by political caution. Still, I should think the winter of 1695–96 possible, given the evidence of Dryden's letter about meeting Howard at the playhouse, especially if the production took place before the discovery of the assassination plot late in February. The long publication delay would then be accounted for by Dryden's preoccupation with the *Virgil*, or by caution about publication in the wake of the assassination plot. Rapid publication had to do with the danger of piracy, and John Jr.'s undistinguished play was unlikely to be pirated.

27. See Luttrell, IV, 21–25; Evelyn, *Diary*, V, 234.

28. *Diary*, V, 245–46.

29. See Oliver, *Howard*, p. 299. A correct understanding of this proposition disposes of Boddy's attempt to redate this letter to 26 May 1695, a suggestion accepted by Barnard. Howard and Dryden were not yet reconciled at that point, nor could Dryden have been ready to sell his son's play to Tonson, since that play had not yet been revised. Barnard was misled by Dryden's complaint that he "lost thirty shillings or more by the last payment of fifty pounds, wch you made at Mr Knights." He assumed that this complaint must have followed the payment closely, and correctly reckoned that the only one of the £50 payments to fall in the spring was the one for *Aeneid* I-IV, probably made sometime between February and April of 1695. But a letter from Dryden to Tonson written in the winter of 1695–96, in which he speaks of "the four remaining Books," complains that "I shall loose enough by your bill upon Mr Knight," clearly the £50 payment for *Aeneid* V-VIII; "haveing taken it all in silver, & not in half Crowns neither, but shillings and sixpences, none of the money will go; for which reason I have sent it all back again, & as the less loss will receive it in guinneys at 29 shillings each" (*Letters*, p. 80). Given the firm evidence pointing to 1696 as the year of Dryden's letter of "May 26th," I suppose he was reminding Tonson once again of this episode, hoping that his bookseller would find a way to make payment for young John's play in reliable silver.

30. See Frost, "Dryden and the Classics," pp. 272–73.

31. A letter bearing this date from Daniel Bret to Theophilus Hastings, seventh Earl of Huntingdon, reports that "Mr. Dryden is upon the 12th Book of his Virgil, the 11th is said by good judges to outdo the original" (*H.M.C. Hastings*, II, 280). In the "Postscript to the Reader," Dryden says that he translated the last book at Bowyer's country house (*Poems*, III, 1426)

32. A mysterious "MS. of Mr Drydens in w^h he directs his Freind Mr Graham to settl' Acc^{ts} w^h Mr J. Tonson his Bookseller," first reported by Thomas Birch in 1736, but long lost, says that the "Preface to Marq. of Normanby cost Mr D. above two months." See Osborn, p. 13*n*. In their forthcoming headnote to the *Virgil*, the California editors persuasively establish a timetable for Dryden's work during this period. They conclude that he worked on the *Dedication to the Aeneis* from early December 1696 until early February of 1697, then wrote the shorter dedications for the *Pastorals* and *Georgics*, both finished by the end of March. He then worked on his notes, proofreading the sheets of the text as they came from Tonson, drew up a list of errata, and finally decided to add a postscript, which he finished sometime after 19 June. Changes in the inscriptions and assignments of the engravings were still being made in July.

33. In his letter to his sons of 3 September [1697], Dryden says that Tonson "has missd of his design in the Dedication: though He had prepard the Book for it: for in every figure of Eneas, he has causd him to be drawn like K. William, with a hookd Nose" (*Letters*, p. 93). Steven Zwicker spins an ingenious argument about the political iconography of the plates in *Politics and Language in Dryden's Poetry*, pp. 190–96. The forthcoming California edition will also devote considerable attention to this problem. Let me add one small point to the ongoing discussion: the plate dedicated to Sir Robert Howard, which Zwicker calls "the most personally insulting of the assignments" (p. 194), shows Aeneas being prevented from killing Cydon by Cydon's seven brothers. In the passage being illustrated, Virgil mentions Cydon's homosexuality, and Dryden's translation, as Zwicker points out, "makes specific and harsh a condemnation which in Virgil is certainly oblique" (p. 195). Logically enough, Zwicker concludes that Dryden still had hard feelings toward Howard, who was on the other side politically. As we have seen, however, the production of young John's play brought about a reconciliation, and the *Dedication of the Aeneis* refers to "that Excellent Person Sir *Robert Howard*: who is better conversant than any Man that I know, in the Doctrine of the Stoicks" (*Poems*, III, 1025). In the autumn of 1697, after the publication of the *Virgil*, Dryden was at work revising an old play by Howard. I should think it just possible that no insult was intended. Someone had to be the dedicatee of this plate, and there was a presentable reason why Howard should be the man: he had seven brothers, as his

brother-in-law Dryden obviously knew, and there had been at least two incidents in which some of those brothers had backed Howard in swordfights (see above, ch. 5, p. 138; ch. 6, p. 178).

34. In the letter of 3 September [1697], Dryden tells his sons, "I remember the Counsell you give me in your letter: but dissembling, though lawfull in some Cases, is not my talent" (*Letters*, p. 93). A later letter refers to "two letters which I sent My Sonns, about my Dedicating to the King, of which they receivd neither"(pp. 99–100).

35. See Luttrell, II, 447, 454–56, *C.S.P. Dom., 1692*, p. 325, and the full account of Clifford in the notes to the forthcoming California *Virgil*.

36. On Normanby's refusal to take the oaths, see the *DNB*, s.v. Sheffield; on Chesterfield's refusal, see Luttrell, IV, 22.

37. See, for example, Evelyn's entry for 31 January 1697: "the Parliament are in greate distresse to furnish another Summers Campagne: . . . peace much talked of, but nothing don" (*Diary*, V, 263).

38. The following discussion is generally indebted to Steven Zwicker's challenging reading of the *Dedication of the Aeneis* in *Politics and Language in Dryden's Poetry*, pp. 178–90. Zwicker's emphasis, as his title announces, falls upon the political innuendo in the dedication; I am trying to show how those ideas operate in concert with Dryden's literary and personal concerns.

39. Kinsley does not print all of Dryden's notes; I cite this one from the first edition, pp. 626–27. For a similar argument based on somewhat different evidence, see Thomas H. Fujimura, "Dryden's Virgil: Translation as Autobiography," *SP* 80 (1983):67–83.

40. William Frost, *Dryden and the Art of Translation* (New Haven: Yale University Press, 1955; repr. Hamden: Archon, 1969) remains the best full-length study. See also T. W. Harrison, "Dryden's *Aeneid*," in *Dryden's Mind and Art*, ed. Bruce King (Oliver and Boyd, 1969), pp. 143–67, and Robert Fitzgerald, "Dryden's *Aeneid*," *Arion* 2 (1963):17–31.

41. *Diary*, V, 255.

42. One example will suffice: the last line of Book XII is an exact repetition of the last line of Book X, even though Virgil's Latin in the two instances is different.

43. As the California editors show, a reference in the "Postscript" to the new Earl of Peterborough, Charles Mordaunt, who succeeded to that title on the death of his Jacobite uncle Henry on 19 June 1697, determines the date.

44. According to Elizabeth Thomas's fanciful account (see above, ch. 6, n. 4), Charles fell five stories from an old tower in the Vatican; Malone's scorn for this story (pp. 417–18) is certainly justified. The surgeon was probably Dr. Thomas Hobbs, a subscriber to the *Virgil*. For a full account, see Alan Roper's entertaining note on the career of Hobbs in the forthcoming California *Virgil*.

45. He was assigned to the "convent of St. Thomas in Naples" in a Latin document dated [14]/24 August 1694; see Anstruther, "English Dominicans in Rome," p. 188. An Italian document dated [1]/11 February 1696, citing the need for priests in England, "dispenses" him from Naples. The need was severe: the provincial, Edward Bing, had been imprisoned. But Father Dryden seems to have returned to Rome. He was one of the three priests in residence in the Dominican monastery of Saints John and Paul when the Pope visited there on [26 August] / 5 September 1697 to inspect the building before handing it over to another order. See Anstruther, pp. 188, 171, 175–76.

46. Anstruther, p. 177. Father Dryden was accompanied on this journey by Father Worthington, who visited him on his deathbed in 1710.

47. The printer, a man named Everingham, gave Tonson an account for paper on 28 March 1698; the book must have been available about that time. Dryden, who complains bitterly that "the Printer is a beast, and understands nothing I can say to him of correcting the press," took unusual care with his corrections and revisions; see *Letters*, pp. 97, 99, 180.

48. For a clear discussion, with examples, see D. T. Mace, "Musical Humanism, The Doctrine of Rhythmus, and the St. Cecilia Odes of Dryden," *JWCI* 27 (1964):251–92, especially p. 278.

49. Cedric Reverand II assigns considerable importance to these humorously self-conscious lines in his forthcoming book on the *Fables*.

50. "Dryden has altered the chronology of Alexander's campaign. In the historical accounts the burning of Persepolis happened while Darius was still alive to avenge it; Dryden gives a particularly unpleasant twist to Alexander's character by making him feast in Persepolis as it were over Darius' body." Thus Ruth Smith, in a learned account of "The Argument and Contexts of Dryden's *Alexander's Feast*,"

SEL 18 (1978), p. 474. The poem has been much studied, and Smith's voluminous footnotes will indicate the range and disagreement of the scholarship.

51. The conjectural date given for Motteux's masque in *The London Stage*, I, 488 (4 November 1697) is unlikely, since William did not return to London until 16 November. The other evidence cited in the *London Stage* entry points to a performance on 29 November, a week after the first performance of *Alexander's Feast*.

52. The phrase is Robert P. Maccubbin's; see "The Ironies of Dryden's 'Alexander's Feast; or the Power of Musique': Text and Contexts," *Mosaic* 18 (1985), p. 37.

53. For the advertisements from the *London Gazette* giving details of the December performances in the York Buildings, see *The London Stage*, I, 489.

54. *Diary*, V, 269–70.

55. I quote the unpaginated "Preface to the Reader," a document that does not seem to have been much consulted by theatre historians. Among useful facts in Powell's account is a list of plays by Dryden revived by Rich's troupe after the splitting up of the companies: *Don Sebastian, Secret Love, Marriage A-la-Mode*, and *King Arthur*. Betterton's troupe revived *Oedipus* and *Troilus and Cressida* during the same period. Powell was a hothead in life as well as in print; a document dated 1 May 1698 orders his arrest for drawing his sword in a coffeehouse quarrel; see P.R.O., SP 44/349, p. 70.

56. I quote Sunderland's order of 4 June 1697, P.R.O., LC 5/152, p. 19; for his appointment, see LC 5/166, p. 1.

57. See Evelyn, *Diary*, V, 236 and n. 1.

58. Luttrell, IV, 379.

59. See Macdonald, *Bibliography*, p. 177.

60. For the letter, see *H.M.C. Bath*, III, 239; Malone believed Kneller's last and best-known portrait of Dryden had been painted in 1698 (p. 434*n*).

61. For tantalizing brief discussions of the *Fables*, see Zwicker, *Politics and Language in Dryden's Poetry*, pp. 158–76, and Sloman, *Dryden: The Poetics of Translation*, pp. 138–73. For a fuller study particularly interested in the vexed issue of whether or not the *Fables* are a unified whole, see Reverand's forthcoming book.

62. See *Letters*, pp. 115–16.

63. According to her monument, the lady died on 6 September 1698; see *Poems*, IV, 2081.

64. One of the great comic errors in Dryden scholarship is the acceptance of this letter as one written to the Duke of Ormonde from 1858, when it was first printed, right through the publication of Ward's edition of the letters in 1942. Pierre Legouis finally set things straight; see "Dryden's Letter to 'Ormond'," *MLN* 66 (1951):88–92. Both the letter and the poem make much of the Duchess's descent from the Plantagenets and her recent journey to Ireland. For a reading of the poem sensitive to its political and moral complexity, see Cedric D. Reverand II, "Dryden's Final Poetic Mode: 'To the Dutchess of Ormond' and *Fables*," *ECTI* 26 (1985):3–21.

65. For a complete text of the letter, with illuminating commentary, see Alan Roper, "Bringing Home the Bacon in a New Dryden Letter," *Clark Library Newsletter* 5 (1983):1–3.

66. See the letter from Lady Dryden to Malone of 20 April 1799, quoted in full in Osborn, pp. 254–57: "From family differences, Mr. John Dryden and Sir Robert were not on good terms."

67. The statute was 11 and 12 William III; Dryden comments bitterly on its passage by the House of Commons; see *Letters*, 134, 188.

68. Richard, the fifth son, died unmarried in 1668. All sources describe Robert, John, Erasmus, and Bevill as unmarried. A manuscript genealogy of the Drydens dated 1684, at present in the Clark Library, lists Benjamin, the seventh son, as "now living unmarried at cir: 30 ann:" Baker's genealogy gives Benjamin's birthdate as 25 July 1649 and refers to him as married, leaving a blank for his wife's name, but shows him dying without offspring. We may deduce from the recently rediscovered letter that Benjamin died in the winter of 1698–99.

69. John, Jr. died of a fever in Rome on [6]/16 April 1703; Malone and others mistakenly gave his date of death as 1701. Charles drowned while attempting to swim across the Thames, and was buried at Windsor on 20 August 1704. See Osborn, pp. 281–82. Erasmus-Henry, now Father Thomas Dryden, returned to England sometime before 1706, when he tried to claim the estate of Sir Henry Pickering in a Chancery suit; see *Letters*, pp. 178–79. The complicated process by which the baronetcy passed from Sir Robert to John son of William, to Erasmus-Henry son of the poet, to Erasmus brother of the poet is correctly laid out in Lady

Dryden's letter to Malone (Osborn, p. 255) and in Baker's Dryden genealogy. Ward's assertion that Erasmus-Henry "succeeded to the Dryden baronetcy upon the death of his uncle Erasmus" (p. 319) is doubly wrong: Erasmus succeeded Erasmus-Henry, not the other way round. Father Worthington's touching account of his visit to his dying colleague makes a point of noting that the Protestant relatives of Father Thomas Dryden received his priestly colleague graciously; see *PCRS*, vol. 25, pp. 108–10, 146. The Dominican Obituary Roll in the priory at Woodchester, Gloucestershire, after noting his succession to the baronetcy, says that Erasmus-Henry's relatives "stole away" his land. This is technically untrue, as Sir Robert was perfectly within his rights in making a will devising his lands to young Edward.

70. John Driden's will is not in the P.C.C. records, but is recited in a Chancery suit (P.R.O., C 9/445/77). I should guess from the absence of a legacy to John, Jr., that the will was made between the death of young John in 1703 and the death of Charles in 1704 and for some reason unaltered. There is no evidence that Erasmus-Henry collected his legacy. See Malone, pp. 325–27; Ward, p. 370.

71. Malone's skepticism about a family tradition that the present was as large as £500 is surely justified; see pp. 326–27.

72. For a thoughtful reading of this entire poem, see Jay Arnold Levine, "John Dryden's Epistle to John Driden," *JEGP* 63 (1964):450–74.

73. Malone prints the entire text, pp. 560–62.

74. See *Letters*, pp. 117–19.

75. On the publication date of this poem, which bears an imprint date of 1700, see Osborn, p. 77*n*.

76. See Alan Roper, "Dryden's 'Secular Masque'," *MLQ* 23 (1962):29–40.

77. See, for example, the opening of the letter of 2 February 1699: "Old Men are not so insensible of beauty, as it may be, you young ladies think" (*Letters*, p. 108).

78. See Malone, pp. 335–42.

79. I quote her inscription in St. Mary Virgin Titchmarsh, printed in full by Malone, pp. 564–66.

80. Malone's careful account (pp. 367–78) discredits the wild myths later retailed by Elizabeth Thomas; he prints Russell's bill (pp. 562–63). He did not know, however, that the body was actually buried in St. Anne's; see Ramsay W. Couper, "John Dryden's First Funeral," *The Athenaeum* 4005 (30 July 1904):145–46.

APPENDIX B

1. "Hunter's Cosmographie" is presumably the *Rudimenta Cosmographica* of Joannes Honterus (Tiguri, 1546).

2. As Professor Moti Feingold of Boston University has pointed out to me, this Dionysius was the Periegetus (Afrus), whose *Orbis habitabilis descriptio* was often bound with the *Astronomicon* of Aratus.

3. "Mr ffrowick" does not appear in the *Record of Old Westminsters* or the matriculation lists of either university. His "severall yeares" as Usher under Busby cannot be precisely dated.

APPENDIX D

1. Cited above, ch. 5, n. 15. My thanks to Professor Langhans, to Robert D. Hume, who was his courier, to Judith Milhous, who provided advice about chancery matters, and to Julie Stone Peters, who pursued some Reeves leads in London.

2. *The London Stage*, I, 149–50. All subsequent dates of performances, unless otherwise annotated, follow this calendar.

3. Cited by Langhans in the typescript draft.

4. John Downes, *Roscius Anglicanus*, ed. Montague Summers (Fortune, 1928), p. 87. Thomas Reeves is among those mentioned by Downes as "Bred up from Boys" to be actors (p. 2); for the possibility that Anne may have been a member of the company from the start, see the notes to Downes's original pp. 2–3 in the Milhous-Hume edition.

5. If my inference that Thomas and Anne were brother and sister is correct, then some interesting documents must be eliminated from the record. These include a legal document dated 3 June 1678, in which one Anne Reeve, widow of Thomas Reeve in the parish of St. Botolph's without Aldgate, was ordered to provide an inventory of his goods (Guildhall MS 9050/12/f. 7r). That inventory (Guildhall MS 9053/7),

filed by Anne Reeve and one Robert Edmonds of Stepney in Middlesex, a weaver, describes the contents of a small house—table and chairs, fire irons, linen, and so forth—for a total of £6 15s. 8 d. Guessing from the address of Robert Edmonds, I should suppose that these were the Thomas and Anne Reeve who christened their daughter Sara at St. Dunstan's Stepney on 23 September 1642. This Anne Reeve signs the bond promising to make the inventory with a neat monogram; the possible inference that she could not write her name in full would seem to weigh heavily against her being the actress, though Nell Gwyn, who took far larger parts than Anne Reeves, also had minimal skill in writing.

6. This copy, once at Sion College, is reprinted by Edward A. Langhans in *Restoration Promptbooks* (Carbondale: Southern Illinois University Press, 1981).

7. P.R.O., L.C. 3/26/p. 207.

8. The last such record, dated 18 November 1673, is P.R.O., L.C. 5/190/p. 59.

9. Curtis A. Price, in *Music in the Restoration Theatre* (Ann Arbor: UMI Research Press, 1979), p. 42, cites this song as an example of "songs from behind the scenes," and guesses that "Esperanza probably does not sing the song." There is no evidence other than the text.

10. L.C. 3/27/p. 95.

11. For the date of this premiere, see Robert D. Hume, "The Date of Dryden's *Marriage A-la-Mode*," cited above, ch. 7, n. 53.

12. It appears in the first edition of *Westminster-Drollery* (imprint date 1671, but possibly later); in *New Court-Songs and Poems by R. V., Gent* (1672); and in three different editions of *Covent-Garden Drollery* (all 1672; the second advertised on 21 November). For bibliographical details, see Macdonald, *Bibliography*, pp. 78–81. For the tune to which this song and its many answers and parodies were sung, see C. L. Day, *The Songs of John Dryden* (Cambridge: Harvard University Press, 1932), pp. 36–38.

13. *Diary*, V, 254.

14. This amusing illustration is reproduced as the frontispiece to *Works* XI.

15. *Covent-Garden Drollery*, ed. Montague Summers (Fortune, 1927), p. 114.

16. L.C. 5/14/p. 132.

17. The records of the attempts to sue are in the P.R.O., L.C. 5/189 and 190; for information about *A Mapp or Description of the parish of St Paul Covent Garden* (1673), by John Lacy (probably not the actor of that name), see Edward A. Langhans, "Pictorial Material on the Bridges Street and Drury Lane Theatres," *TS* 7 (1966), p. 86.

18. *The Works of Sir John Suckling: The Plays* (Oxford: Clarendon, 1971), pp. 293–94.

19. In a private communication cited in the previous version of this chronology, R. D. Hume pointed out that such a cast could conceivably have been assembled as early as 1670 or as late as 1677. A letter from A. H. Scouten in response to the published chronology argues that Hancock, Ivory, and Byrd, all of whom appear in the manuscript cast, were probably inactive by 1676 or earlier, and that Venner and Rutter were probably unavailable between 1670 and 1672.

20. See John Orrell, "A New Witness of the Restoration Stage, 1670–1680," *TRI* 2 (1976), p. 92. My thanks to Professor Scouten for directing my attention to this record.

21. P.R.O., L.C. 3/28/p. 203, and L.C. 3/24/n.p.

22. *Covent-Garden Drollery*, ed. G. Thorn-Drury (Dobell, 1928), pp. 135–37.

23. Stanzas [6] and [8] of the poem as printed by James Osborn in "Dryden, Shadwell, and 'a late fall'n Poet'," in *John Dryden II* (Los Angeles: Clark Library, 1978), p. 34. Osborn identified the "Wild-House Spaniards" as "the staff of Ronquillo, the Spanish Ambassador, at Weld House, Lincoln's Inn Fields." Although Ronquillo was indeed the ambassador at the time of this lampoon, the reference is presumably to the Marquis de Fresno, whom rumor had connected with Reeves in 1674.

24. Stanza [10] and p. 40.

25. "Diary of the Blue Nuns," *PCRS*, vol. 8, p. 29. George McFadden was the first to point out the possible relevance of this record; see his excellent article on "Political Satire in *The Rehearsal*," *YES* 4 (1974), p. 120n.

26. C. F. R. Palmer, *The Life of Philip Thomas Howard* (Richardson, 1867), p. 162. See also the letters of Cardinal Howard, in *PCRS*, vol. 25.

27. "The Diary of the Blue Nuns," p. 25.

28. See Judith Milhous, "Elizabeth Bowtell and Elizabeth Davenport: Some Puzzles Solved," *TN* 39 (1985), p. 126.

29. The name Anne Reeve also appears in the records of the Franciscan Nuns at Bruge, but these references can surely be discounted. They concern one Mary Barnes, "Daughter to John Barnes & Ann Reeues," born in London in 1673, who took orders in 1698; the account of her death in 1727 notes that "her Father was a Queaker & her mother a Anabaptista." See *PCRS*, vol. 24, pp, 55, 207.

30. All these attacks are conveniently available in facsimile in *Drydeniana VI* (New York: Garland, 1975).

31. See *POAS*, III, 165–66, where H. H. Schless proposes this identification. This was the second time Anne had been connected with exotic diplomats; cf. the references to her poxing the Spaniards in 1674 and 1678. Schless also suggests that some of the references to Anne and "nunneries" may reflect the slang use of "nunnery" as a term for a brothel, but the pairing of such references with words like "Priest" and "Religion" in some of the attacks makes this gloss seem unlikely to me.

Index

The main text and footnotes are fully indexed here, but the appendices are not. Main entries for aristocrats come under family names; married women are indexed by their married names; characters in plays are not indexed.